THE ENCYCLOPEDIA OF
ORSON WELLES

THE ENCYCLOPEDIA OF
ORSON WELLES

CHUCK BERG   TOM ERSKINE

with
John C. Tibbetts
James M. Welsh
Series Editors

Checkmark Books®
An imprint of Facts On File, Inc.

The Encyclopedia of Orson Welles

Checkmark Books
An imprint of Facts On File, Inc.
132 West 31st Street
New York NY 10001

Library of Congress Cataloging-in-Publication Data

Berg, Chuck.
The encyclopedia of Orson Welles / Chuck Berg with Tom Erskine, John C. Tibbetts, James M. Welsh.
p.   cm. — (Great filmmakers series)
Includes bibliographical references and index.
ISBN 0-8160-4390-6 (hc) — ISBN 0-8160-4391-4 (pb)
1. Welles, Orson, 1915—Encyclopedias. I. Erskine, Thomas L.
II. Tibbetts, John C. III. Title. IV. Series.
PN1998.3.W45 B47 2002
791.43'0233'092—dc21
2002004375

Text design by Erika K. Arroyo
Cover design by Nora Wertz
Illustrations by John C. Tibbetts

Printed in the United States of America

VB JT 10 9 8 7 6 5 4 3 2 1

This book is printed on acid-free paper.

CONTENTS

FOREWORD: REMEMBERING ORSON WELLES

vii

PREFACE: ORSON WELLES AND THE GRAND ILLUSION

xi

ACKNOWLEDGMENTS

xiv

INTRODUCTION

xv

HOW TO USE THIS BOOK

xvii

ENTRIES A–Z

1

CONTRIBUTORS

439

BIBLIOGRAPHY

441

INDEX

443

To my family—my wife, Beth, our son, Nathan, our daughter-in-law, Yuki, and our grandsons, Calvin and En—for their love, laughter, and support. And to my parents, Richard and Frederica Berg, who took me to the movies (and showed me life).

—C.B.

▣ ▣ ▣

To my wife, Edna Quinn

—T.L.E

FOREWORD

◻ ◻ ◻

REMEMBERING ORSON WELLES

Note: Ruth Warrick began her film career as the first wife of Charles Foster Kane in Welles's Citizen Kane. *After appearing in another Welles film,* Journey into Fear, *she went on to other feature roles in* The Corsican Brothers *(1941),* The Iron Major *(1943),* China Sky *(1945), and* Song of the South *(1946). Beginning in the 1950s she turned to television for the roles for which she is most famous today—Ellie Banks on the sitcom* Father of the Bride, *Hannah Cord on the nighttime soap* Peyton Place, *and Phoebe Tyler on* All My Children. *In 1980 she published her autobiography,* The Confessions of Phoebe Tyler. *This remembrance comes from an interview recorded in Kansas City in 1986.*

—John C. Tibbetts

I was just 21 when I first met Orson Welles. I had been acting since I was 16 in high school in my native St. Joseph, Missouri. I got my first critical notices in *The Royal Family.* After coming to Kansas City and graduating from Southwest High, I went to the University of Kansas City and played the Resident Theatre many times. Then along came the "Miss Jubilesta" [a word coined from "jubilee" and "fiesta"] festival, sponsored by the Kansas City Chamber of Commerce to promote the new Philharmonic Hall. Headliners like Jack Benny and the Wayne King Orchestra were scheduled to perform. I was delegated to travel all over Kansas and Missouri promoting the festival and participating in the selection of the Jubilesta Queen. Part of my duties were to accompany her to New York for more promotions. When she returned home, I stayed on, hoping to pursue a career as a model or an actress. The year was 1938. I started getting jobs on radio soap operas. I

even took on a job appearing in a demonstration of early television. (How little I knew that I would spend the second half of my career in that medium!) I met a man and got married. And somewhere in that time, perhaps on a radio show where we appeared together, I first met Orson Welles. I think I knew then that my life would change. "There is a tide . . ." as Shakespeare wrote. Orson was already a god to me. He was doing historic things at the Mercury Theatre. Nobody has ever done in such a short period of time as many brilliant productions as he had done—and on a shoestring. He was very busy then, taking on any kind of job to support the Mercury, even commuting to Hollywood to do radio shows. But somehow he remembered me from our radio show. I was dumbfounded when my agent called me and said Orson was in New York and wanted to see me at the Waldorf Towers. I got there late; but Orson got there later. He told me that *Citizen Kane* was ready to go,

Ruth Warrick

that the only part not yet cast was for a very key role, Emily Norton Kane, the niece of the president of the United States, who becomes Kane's first wife. "She must be a lady," he said, explaining his wanting to test me for the role; "and there are no ladies in Hollywood!" I had already turned down several offers to go to Hollywood because I didn't want to leave New York. But this seemed right, so I went and was tested and within 36 hours I was on the plane bound for Hollywood. So here I was, just 21, married, and going to have a baby (nobody knew it yet) and about to make my first film. But don't think I wasn't criticized for my decision. I was accused of possessing too much vanity, for forsaking being a wife and mother for a career in acting.

Orson had a plum contract with RKO, the envy of everyone. The reason he got it was that the studio had been taken over and George Schaefer, head of RKO, had heard Orson in "The War of the Worlds" and pushed the deal through to get him to come make movies. And of course Orson paid for that. A lot of people in Hollywood resented his privileged position, and they were determined that he was not going to succeed. When he took so long to finally get started on *Kane*—he discarded several projects during more than a year's time—they were ready to pounce.

But, of course, Orson was brilliant. How vividly I recall how happy he was working with Gregg Toland on the set. They were so thrilled about it. I remember them taking an ax to chop a hole in the floor to place the camera below floor level. Together they choreographed that whole film. Just in their positioning of the characters you could tell so much about their roles. You could see the film without ever hearing a word and still know everything about the characters' interactions. And he worked on the cutting, too. Robert Wise has told me that although he was credited as the editor, much of the time he spent just looking over Orson's shoulder. Many directors like to talk down to actors and treat them like puppets. Not Orson. He encouraged our own interpretations in our lines, but he never budged from his own ideas about our blocking. And he instilled in all of us the joy of creation, that we were communicators doing something important. He gave me courage and strength and pride in what I was doing.

Although I remember times during the shooting when he seemed to be eating all the time—and consuming 30 cups of coffee in a day—he was quite trim then and probably in the best shape of his life. He was very slim and beautiful (enhanced by his wearing a corset). In my presence I never saw him in those legendary temper tantrums, and I never saw him drink too much. Sure, he would occasionally have two steaks at one sitting. And he would get angry at Joe Cotten and me if we didn't join him in a big breakfast after working all night. He would work 36 hours at a time, sleeping only for a few hours at a time. He was hyperactive. People don't realize now what a horrible time he had with the makeup, too, especially with the contact lenses. He'd have to be in makeup at 4:30 in the morning.

Orson and I had a very, very special relationship. It was not physical, except for a very short period of time (and that was not the most important part of it). I wonder if I might not have reminded him of his mother, who was an elegant, lovely lady. I knew there was something special between us from the very first, the day he tested me on the set on RKO Sound Stage II. I didn't learn until later that it was unusual for the star to be present at the tests. Somebody else usually feeds the lines. The room was huge, the same set that Rogers and Astaire had used for their musicals. It was cold and damp, and there was a kind of a putrid odor in the air. And there we sat, in just one little pool of light in the middle of the room. And we were just ready to shoot when there appeared suddenly six men in long overcoats and felt hats. I thought, my goodness, these are gangsters who have come to stop the film. And when they came closer, we realized they were RKO brass from New York. After congratulating Orson on beginning the film, they called in a dump truck, which deposited a ton of rank flowers on the floor. They explained these were flowers pilfered from Forest Lawn graves. They were sorry about the condition of the flowers, but they had been fresh months ago when Kane had first been announced. Everybody laughed at the joke and shook hands. But they didn't leave. Instead, they just folded their hands and said, "OK. Genius, show us. Start filming. Be a genius."

Orson, who was usually unflappable in any situation, broke out in a cold sweat. I didn't know at the time that this was actually the very first time that Orson was to work before a camera (actually none of us had ever worked before the camera). He was using our test not only to test me but to test himself. I saw he was in trouble. Really upset. I put my arm through his and drew him to the back of the set. I mopped his brow and made some small talk, trying to give him some time to settle down and recover himself. That moment a special bond grew between us. And I realized then that I was already playing the role of Emily Kane, as a lady. And, of course, a lady always puts a gentleman at his ease. From that time on, whenever we would be together, he would just quietly stare into my eyes, and I would touch his face. Well, eventually the RKO brass left. After that we worked on a closed set. There literally was nobody allowed on that set, no top brass, no publicity people, no visitors. Just the crew and the actors.

So many people ask me about the famous "Breakfast Table" sequence. It lasts barely two minutes, but it spans the whole sad history of Kane's first marriage. It was the last thing I shot with Orson. I was aware that this was a key scene, and I was a little worried and unsure about it. It was shot fairly quickly, with pauses only to change his makeup. Instinctively, I played the character as if she were my mother and reacting to him the way my mother would have. But during that whole scene, he hardly directed me at all. It was only many years later that I had the chance to ask him why. He said, "First of all, you didn't need any direction; secondly, I was the one who was changing. You were being true to your own character while I was changing into a monster."

Did I know *Citizen Kane* was going to be the classic it has become? Of course I didn't. Orson says he did, and maybe he did know. At least I knew it was going to be totally different from other films of the time.

He didn't have much respect for people who just made money, which, of course, came back to haunt him later. He would say that anybody who just made money should get down on his knees before creative people and beg them to do something with it. Good luck. It gave me a sense of the importance of being an artist. But Orson had to pay a price for his talent. When you frustrate a great talent like him, when you don't allow him to perform as well as he was able, to do the things he can do, when you have some advertising ninny to criticize him, that's when he would get livid. And rightfully so. Here was a major talent being badgered by a little mind. So he would drink and eat excessively, even to the point of endangering his life. And after his problems with the release of *Kane,* all the trouble with Louella Parsons and with the RKO brass, he was hounded. They do things like that in Hollywood.

I worked with Orson again on *Journey into Fear.* I played the part of Joe Cotten's wife. The name "Norman Foster" appears as director on the credits, but I can tell you that Orson directed a lot of that picture. That was at the time that Orson had been asked to go to Brazil to work on behalf of the Good Neighbor Policy. Norman was brought in to finish things while Orson was gone. But Orson really did that picture. He really did set it all up. Unfortunately, he got seduced by all that was going on down there and failed to finish either it or *The Magnificent Ambersons.* I saw little of him after that.

Because of Orson, I was able to withstand criticism much later for forsaking my movie career to go into television soap operas. Remembering his advice about always honoring your profession, I could say every easily, "I need the job, it is good work, it's regular work, and I'll always play it as though it is the most important work I'll ever do." I'm proud of my work over the years on *The Guiding Light* and *All My Children.* And I continue to take time off to work in "live" theater.

The last time I saw Orson was on a special edition of *Good Morning, America,* the year before he died, when three of us surviving cast members in *Citizen Kane* had a sort of reunion. He was there at six o'clock in the morning, sharp. I realized then that he probably was a more lonely man than many of us had thought. He would hide himself behind his enormous body and his caustic wit. At the end he was hardly drinking at all, and he had lost a lot of weight. He was getting ready to do a film version of *Cradle Will Rock.* But he died before he could get started on it. He was careless about losing weight, gaining it again, then losing it again. That's what killed Mario Lanza and Zero Mostel. Orson needed to make up his mind whether he would be a large man or a man that should control his weight consistently. One or the other. But there he was, that day, ready for the television cameras; and that special magic between us was still there. I loved him so.

—Ruth Warrick

PREFACE

口口口

ORSON WELLES AND THE GRAND ILLUSION

"It appears you are predestined everywhere to find a theater and actors. We have here commenced a play which is not altogether pleasant."

—Goethe, *Wilhelm Meister's Apprenticeship*

Ever the magician at heart and in design, Orson Welles played out his illusions in full view of his audience. "He was, literally, a magician," wrote friend and associate Gore Vidal, "fascinated by legerdemain, tricks of the eye, forgeries, labyrinths, mirrors reflecting mirrors. . . . He was a master of finding new ways of seeing things that others saw not at all."

Like those postmodernist prestidigitators Penn and Teller (and, before them, the French conjuror-cum-filmmaker Georges Méliès), his miracles and frauds were simultaneously on display, provoking our credulity and incredulity at the same time. He transformed the aperture of the camera and the frame of the film into arenas of magic, shrouding his gothic mysteries in cloaking shadows, pricking the faces of his characters with dramatic lighting accents, exaggerating the perspectives of his deep-focus frame with distorting wide-angle lenses, and counterpointing his complex narratives with multilayered soundtracks. He was the man behind the curtain, both charlatan and wizard. His favorite image of himself was that of a saturnine, costumed stage magician (see his roles in the eponymous *Cagliostro,* 1949, and *F for Fake,* 1975)—whether he was entertaining school chums during his boyhood with the cheap tricks he learned from traveling vaudevillians, delighting the troops in wartime with sawed-off ladies in his traveling *Mercury Wonder Show* (documented in the film *Follow the Boys,* 1944), or, finally, on television trotting out parlor tricks and feats of clairvoyance in various programs like *I Love Lucy* and *The Tonight Show* with Johnny Carson. The long black cloaks he affected to the end of his days grew ever more capacious with his 400-pound girth—all the better to hide the rabbits, cards, and other appliances of his craft that might be needed at any moment.

The real mystery was that Orson Welles in plain sight was just as mysterious as the Orson Welles who hid behind numerous false noses, slouch hats, and flapping capes. The personae were so interchangeable we could scarcely distinguish one from the other. Indeed, his biographers claim that Orson Welles reinvented himself time and again. More accurately, like all conjurors he was a master of misdirection. We were complicit in his enigmas. He led us up his various garden paths, and we followed, willingly. Putting it another way, we knew there was *always* something up his sleeve; we counted on it. Doubtless, he could echo wryly the words of Medardus the Friar in E.T.A. Hoffman's *The Devil's Elixirs* (1817): "I am what I seem to be, yet do not seem to be what I am; even to myself I am an insoluble riddle, for my personality has been torn apart."

As enormous as his waistline grew in life—he was more *sleight* of hand than *slight* of hand—his shadow has loomed even larger in death. He always loved to play games with eternity. He wore the mask of Death in his first film, *Hearts of Age* (1934); spoke in a disembodied voice in the *Shadow* radio series; turned the destruction of New Jersey into a Halloween charade in *The War of the Worlds* (1938); died within the first few minutes of screen time in *Citizen Kane;* came back from the dead in *The Third Man;* suffered a fatal plunge from a clock tower in *The Stranger;* obliterated all traces of his past life in *Mr. Arkadin;* drowned in a garbage canal in *Touch of Evil;* trundled away in a preposterously large coffin at the end of *Chimes at Midnight;* and mysteriously appeared and disappeared at the snap of a finger in *A Safe Place.* After his death in 1985, he left behind an empty coffin and an unmarked grave—an escape artist to the end. Perhaps, like Harry Lime in *The Third Man,* he never died at all, but remains forever shadowed somewhere in the half-light of a doorway. Or, like Charles Foster Kane, he lives on in the fractured portrait assembled from the shards and fragments of his unfinished projects, newly restored and released (see the recent restoration of *It's All True*). He's like the trickster described in Ingmar Bergman's *The Seventh Seal* (1957), who achieves the ultimate feat—keeping the juggled balls suspended in midair.

Thus, Orson Welles was the first American film director whose celebrity outpaced the success and/or notoriety of his movies. His only rival in that regard was Alfred Hitchcock (a British émigré at that). Before the days of these two masters of image-building, how many American directors were as widely known for their public personae as their onscreen achievements? D.W. Griffith outlived his megaphone and boater hat and faded away into the drab wallpaper of an only dimly remembered Hollywood past. Cecil B. DeMille, the builder of bathtub extravaganzas of biblical proportions, shriveled before our eyes into an antique caricature of rock-ribbed conservatism (we always suspected that under those silly puttees were feet of clay). The whole world certainly knew who Charlie Chaplin was, but long before his death in 1977, the exiled artist had been absent from the public eye so long that only his films remained to testify that he had actually lived at all.

Not so Orson Welles. His fame and his girth expanded as his film career progressed—or, sadly, *regressed*. It hardly matters that his best work had been done by the age of 26, when he had successfully made the transition from wunderkind on Broadway and in radio to film director at RKO with *Citizen Kane* (1941) and *The Magnificent Ambersons* (1942). As commentator James Naremore has noted in his estimable *The Magic World of Orson Welles,* "The familiar story of how he conquered Hollywood with an energetic, youthful, iconoclastic film, and then became an outcast, has been more important to subsequent generations of directors than almost anything in his work...." Just 10 years after the premiere of *Citizen Kane* he was being described by critic Walter Kerr as "an international joke, and possibly the youngest living has-been." But Welles seems to have suffered the brickbats of critics and the reversals of fortune with amazing fortitude and amiability. In his last two decades, he forged on, cannily, if shamelessly, using television to promote himself and maintain his reputation. Thanks to his skills as a raconteur, multiple appearances on the NBC *Tonight Show* established Welles as the Grand Old Man of the cinema for younger viewers who had probably not seen much of his earlier and greatest work. When Welles later became the sophisticated spokesman for Paul Masson vineyards, his image saturated the airways. With epicurean elegance, Welles declaimed his final mantra, "We'll sell no wine before its time." Regarding a commercial he made for dog food, he confided to a friend with characteristic aplomb, "No, I do not eat from the can on camera, but I *celebrate* the contents." His articulateness and his distinctive voice conveyed an authority and prestige far beyond the merits of the situation. Ironically, even though no one was willing or eager to fund his later motion picture projects, by that time his image, charisma, and voice had taken on a life of their own.

There is a sort of tragedy here, to be sure, at least a serio-comic one suffered only by overreachers like Welles. In the words of biographer Joseph

McBride, his was "the nightmarish dilemma faced by a legendary man being swallowed up in his self-created image and ultimately being destroyed by it." It was not all his fault, of course. He never was patient with mediocrity. Novelist Charles Maturin put it succinctly more than 170 years ago in that greatest of all gothic novels, *Melmoth the Wanderer* (just one more of Welles's unrealized projects): "How dreadful is the conflict of superior intellect and a burning heart, with the perfect mediocrity of the characters and circumstances they are generally doomed to live with. . . . The greater strength we exhibit, we feel we are more paralyzed by the weakness of our enemies—our very energy becomes our bitterest enemy."

In his last finished film, *F for Fake,* Welles assured us one last time that his life, like his work and the film medium he manipulated so extravagantly, was merely an unstable compound of art and illusion. Behind the mystery there was only fraud. "I am a charlatan," he declares at the beginning of the film. But when his mysteries are revealed, they are still mysterious. As G.K. Chesterton once wrote, "The writer is there to explain the mystery; but he ought not to be needed to explain the explanation."

—James M. Welsh
Salisbury, Maryland
—John C. Tibbetts
Mission, Kansas
July 2001

ACKNOWLEDGMENTS

The book before you was ultimately a group effort, since Orson Welles was too large a talent for two or three writers, and the body of scholarship surrounding his work is enormous. Most of the entries in the encyclopedia were written by Chuck Berg at the University of Kansas, who started the project, or by Tom Erskine and series editor Jim Welsh at Salisbury University, who helped him complete it. Richard Vela of the University of North Carolina at Pembroke covered the Welles Shakespeare films, a topic unto itself. John Tibbetts contributed the Ruth Warrick interview that serves as our foreword and many drawings and entries as well. The Rev. Gene D. Phillips of Loyola University, Chicago, wrote 20 entries after having completed his own work on the *Encyclopedia of Stanley Kubrick* (Facts On File, 2002); other entries were written by Richard C. Keenan of the University of Maryland, Eastern Shore, and University of Kansas graduate Ron Wilson. In Salisbury, Maryland, Jessica Blewitt assisted with the research, as did Kathryn C. Kalmanson, head of reference at Salisbury University's Blackwell Library, and her helpful staff, especially Gaylord Robb and Terry Daenzer.

At the University of Kansas in Lawrence, Chuck Berg also had research assistance from colleagues and students, notably series editor John C. Tibbetts and Matt Messbarger, who served as his research assistant during the summer of 2001; Kansas kudos are also in order for Therese Dugan, Aaron Hauser, and Jim Williams. We are all of us grateful, of course, to Facts On File's arts and humanities editor in chief, James Chambers, who demonstrated extraordinary patience and tact while waiting for us to assemble the manuscript.

—C.B. and T.L.E.

INTRODUCTION

To try to take the measure of a larger-than-life figure such as Orson Welles is perhaps folly. Inevitably, Welles's biographers have analogized their task as being comparable to the search for the "real" Charles Foster Kane undertaken by the reporters of "News on the March," the newsreel introducing the plot of *Citizen Kane.* Still, the quest to survey the public life of Welles as it boomed forth in theater, radio, movies, television, and print, is a "who done it" at once compelling and instructive.

Welles, by physical stature as well as by intellect, artistry, and audacity, was a giant. Indeed, if anyone qualifies for the "great man" treatment, it is Welles. At the same time, we know about Welles's foibles, his gargantuan appetites, and the seemingly self-destructive behavior that so often put him at odds with those he needed to successfully realize his visions. Nonetheless, with *Citizen Kane,* still widely regarded as the greatest of all American movies, and *War of the Worlds,* the most sensational program in the history of radio, Welles stands today as a colossus whose huge portfolio and memory are embedded in the contemporary world's cultural consciousness.

In tracing Welles's career—standing backstage in 1936 at Harlem's Lafayette Theatre on the opening night of the exotic "voodoo" *Macbeth,* sitting in a CBS control room in 1938 as the switchboard lit up with anxious calls about an invasion from Mars, or eavesdropping on Welles and cinematographer Gregg Toland

setting up a deep-focus shot for *Citizen Kane* in 1940—one is amazed at his curiosity, his quick mind, his boldness, his artistry, and, as much as anything else, his energy. Indeed, the charismatic supernova was a whirlwind whose range seemed to encompass everything and everyone. In 1944, after campaigning vigorously for the reelection of President Franklin Roosevelt, he even flirted with an offer to run for the U.S. Senate from Wisconsin. A decade earlier, while still a teenager, he co-authored a prompt-book called *Everybody's Shakespeare* that many credit with having made the Bard accessible to several generations of schoolchildren. The long list of accomplishments, outlined in the pages that follow, continues on.

After living with Welles for the past several years, like the reporter Thompson in *Citizen Kane,* the subject of my own detective work remains elusive. Still, what is apparent is that Welles loved life, people, and, perhaps most of all, his work. Who else would repeatedly "invest" his own funds in highly personal noncommercial projects? Welles also loved magic, and pondering the illusory nature of truth and the surfaces as well as vital essences of things. In his own way he was a philosopher-artist whose meditations on the nature and vicissitudes of the human experience still cause us to pause, look, listen, and reflect—and, not incidentally, be moved.

Welles, who made his own biography a dynamic artwork by varying its details according to whim or exigency, was at heart a trickster. Cutting with and against the grain, he was, in his own idiosyncratic way, a kind of utilitarian, an "actor" with the soul of an artist whose quest involved doing whatever was necessary to get the next show up and running. There were, of course, the crushing disappointments of projects jettisoned. And yet, regardless of outcome, there was joy in the process of filmmaking itself. Even at the end of his life, the prospect of grabbing a camera and dashing off with a group of friends to improvise a scene was something that stirred his blood and animated his soul.

Along with everything else in a Welles film—the story, the characters, the mise-en-scène—there is passion. That joie de vivre is among the reasons explaining why Welles's work continues to live.

—Chuck Berg
Lawrence, Kansas
March 2002

HOW TO USE THIS BOOK

Undertaking a book on Orson Welles, probably America's foremost director, is daunting, not because there were so many films that he personally directed, but because his scattered talents ran in so many directions, because he appeared in so many films directed by others, because he had so many dealings with so many creative people in radio, theater, film, and television on both sides of the Atlantic, and beyond, and because so many gifted critics, academic and journalistic, at home and abroad, have obsessed over his work, an obsession we have come to appreciate. Readers will find entries on all of those major critics whose research, we hope, has been intelligently digested throughout the *Encyclopedia*. Because the work of Peter Bogdanovich, Jonathan Rosenbaum, Pauline Kael, Robert Carringer, James Naremore, Frank Brady, Peter Cowie, Charles Higham, Simon Callow, and others is so well known and also cited in our "Selective Bibliography," we have not referenced their books entry-by-entry where cited when noted and quoted in the entries. They will appear as old friends, both to us and to many readers. But when we have gone beyond the standard body of Welles scholarship to cite particular books on individual talents such as John Huston, Robert Wise, Richard Fleischer, Carol Reed, and others, we have attempted to reference them at the end of the entries.

So what was our giddy intent in this mad and presumptive enterprise? *The Encyclopedia of Orson Welles,* like all of the books we have collectively done for Facts On File, is intended to be a convenient reference tool for those seeking basic information about the director, an A-to-Z Who's Who and a reader's companion to a troubled and vexing legendary career and to the hundreds of people who helped or impeded it. The book provides extended coverage of the films Welles directed, early and late, at home and abroad, and the cast, crews, and producers who facilitated them. One particular challenge was to make the *Encyclopedia* comprehensive and yet not repetitious and to provide balanced and readable coverage. Though we do not expect many readers to read the book cover to cover, we have sought a consistency of style, not easily achieved since so many hands were involved in writing the book, though not so many as some of the other encyclopedias in the series: Please see our list of contributors to sort out who was who. As Vincent Canby once described Darryl F. Zanuck's opinion of writers in the *New York Times* (January 6, 1980), "Writing is like football, something to be done in teams," and, for good or ill, this *Encyclopedia* was of necessity a collaborative effort, "done in teams," though we hope that does not show. Although our target audience may be general readers interested in Welles, we hope that the book may also stimulate some interest among specialists, such as those interested primarily in the Welles Shakespeare. The Shakespeare entries therefore may be pitched to a different level of knowledge and expertise; but we have also attempted to eschew the jargon of the specialists so as not to baffle the general reader. We can only hope that these goals have been achieved and that the book may be read with some degree of pleasure and instruction.

—C.B. and T.L.E. and J.M.W.

"Admiral of the Sea" (radio, 1942) In 1942, WELLES, one of the top-paid entertainers of the day, was making more money for radio appearances than for directing films. One of the most lavishly produced programs of the period was *Cavalcade of America* which was sponsored by Dupont and broadcast by NBC. In a script for *Cavalcade* loosely adapted by Welles, Robert Meltzer, and Norris Houghton from the biography of Christopher Columbus by noted historian Samuel Eliot Morison, Welles celebrated the spirit of exploration in general and Columbus in particular. The 1942 Columbus Day broadcast was at once informative and entertaining, even comedic in spots, and inspirational. For example, a stuffy professor rattled off lists of facts only to be cut short by Welles, who then interviewed a member of Columbus's crew. On a more serious note, Welles offered stirring readings of Walt Whitman's *Passage to India* and Joaquin Miller's *Columbus.*

The show was also important for introducing elements that would be incorporated into later Welles broadcasts. There was his opening greeting, "Hello Americans," and, perhaps with a tip of the hat to W.C. Fields, a precocious little girl who corrects Welles's narration, much to the great man's annoyance. The inclusion of historical figures, here, the hypothetical crewman, was also new and something that would reappear in future broadcasts. In addition to being aired across the United States, the program was beamed throughout the Western Hemisphere, largely because of Welles's celebrity in Latin America due to his filming of *IT'S ALL TRUE.*

—C.B.

Adventures of Harry Lime, The (radio, 1951–1952) This British radio series starred WELLES as Harry Lime, the indelible character first essayed by Welles for CAROL REED's classic film, *THE THIRD MAN* (1949). After a five-year hiatus away from radio, Welles, seeking funds for his own projects, returned to the airwaves in August 1951 with *The Adventures of Harry Lime.* Produced in London, the project was the brainchild of a young British Broadcasting Company (BBC) producer, Harry Alan Towers. Welles, initially skeptical about giving life to a character left for dead at the conclusion of Reed's film, changed his mind when Towers explained: "We start off with ANTON KARAS on the zither playing *The Third Man* theme, which everybody knows, and then we interrupt it with a shot. And you say, 'That was the shot that killed Harry Lime. He died in the sewers beneath Vienna, but before he died he lived many lives. How do I know? I know because my name is Harry Lime.' And then we lash into anything we can cook up."

Although the title *The Third Man* belonged to British movie mogul ALEXANDER KORDA, the film's screenwriter, GRAHAM GREENE, owned the dramatic and literary rights to the character "Harry Lime." Korda and Greene, both Welles admirers, gave their approval to the BBC project. Greene, however, negotiated veto power over the scripts although it was a right he rarely used. The writing chores fell mainly to Ernest Borneman, a Canadian anthropologist who had collaborated with Welles on an aborted screen adaptation of Homer's *Ulysses*. In addition to writing 12 of the episodes himself, Welles narrated each show and starred as Harry Lime. Recalling his glory days in radio in New York in the late 1930s, Welles also produced and directed each of the 52 weekly episodes aired by the BBC's Light Programme service. In addition to the cachet of Welles's name and the reputation of the motion picture, the radio spin-off received an additional boost when the *Empire News* adapted the scripts into short stories that it published each Sunday during the program's first two months on the air.

FRANK BRADY points out that the series represented a substantial leap in radio production technique because it was recorded on tape, rather than direct-to-disc, which gave Welles greater flexibility in producing, planning, and timing, since the recorded materials could be easily edited. Indeed, the new audio tape medium enabled Welles to build each program in the manner of his work as a film director. Rather than record a program "live" in real time, now Welles could construct each show scene by scene, just as he had done in shooting and editing his films. The show also benefited from the atmospheric underscoring provided by the zither of Anton Karas, who had been instrumental in the success of *The Third Man*.

The character of Harry Lime had to be substantially revised in its adaptation from the screen to the airwaves. In the film, Greene's character was amoral, ruthless, and cold, indifferent to the suffering he caused. For the BBC, instead of being despicable, Lime became a lovable rogue, a philosophizing confidence man with a taste for the good life, one of the many attributes given the character patterned on Welles himself. In yet another instance of Welles's art imitating Welles's life, Lime's cosmopolitan insouciance, his love of food and drink, and his romantic intrigues all reflected the persona of Lime's author.

Thematically, the plots involving espionage, spying, and smuggling intersected with a host of post–World War II concerns. At the same time, and in a manner comparable to that of Ian Fleming's James Bond, Lime functioned as a surrogate for audiences wanting to transcend the bounds of their everyday lives to participate vicariously in fantasies of adventure, intrigue, and romance.

For devotees of Welles, one of the most interesting episodes in *The Adventures of Harry Lime* involved a character called Gregory Arkadian, one of the world's richest men, who hires Harry to help him pass a U.S. security check in order to gain a lucrative construction contract to build a U.S. air base in Portugal. Specifically, Arkadian wants Harry to find out what happened to him during a period in which he claims to have had amnesia. Harry uncovers a convoluted story identifying Arkadian as a former Polish gangster, his betrayal of accomplices, and his absconding with the gang's fortune, the bankroll upon which Arkadian's "legitimate" empire was built. Harry relates the story to Arkadian's daughter, and then tells Arkadian that his daughter now knows the truth. Fearing his daughter's rejection, Arkadian commits suicide in a singularly spectacular way by jumping from his private plane.

Significantly, the program became the basis for Welles's script for MR. ARKADIN (also titled *Confidential Report*), his film of 1955. According to Brady, during the show's taping, Welles told the actor playing the part of Arkadian: "I'll do a film with this story one day." The actor, Frederick O'Brady, excited about the prospect of starring in a Welles film, soon had his hopes dashed when Welles added: "Of course, *I'll* play Arkadian." For the film, in which Welles does in fact play the arch-villain, Welles changed the character's name from "Arkadian" to the less Armenian-sounding "Arkadin."

The Adventures of Harry Lime was a hit that captured the British imagination perhaps to an even greater extent than *The Third Man* had. It successfully aired in Canada, Australia, South Africa, and Hong Kong; with other actors taking the role of Lime, it was translated into Spanish, French, Hebrew, Dutch, German, and Italian. In the United States, because of the hubbub stirred by the introduction of national network television, *The Third Man: The Lives of Harry Lime,* as it was called in the United States, was largely ignored and even deprecated. Jack Gould, the distinguished television critic of the *New York Times,* called it "a hackneyed trifle that primarily serves as a means for Orson to brush up on his guttural flourishes." Welles, however, was heartened by the show's overwhelming success throughout Britain. Following a performance of OTHELLO in Northumberland, a backstage visitor, queried by the great man about what he thought of the play, responded: "Mister Welles, for us, you'll never be nothing but 'Arry Lime."

DAVID THOMSON recalls hearing the show as a boy: "They were cheerful melodramas, rich in atmosphere and a sign of how much Orson Welles remained attached to the ethos of THE SHADOW. The Harry Lime shows invoked a world of evil geniuses, the European demimonde, Lime's insouciance, skulduggery, the bitter laughter of fading women of the world and the nocturnal hum of smart cities." For Welles, the show was also a means of paying bills involved in the editing of *Othello.*

—C.B.

Alland, William (1916–)

A frequent collaborator of Welles best known for his role as Jerry Thompson, the inquiring lead reporter in CITIZEN KANE, Alland also emulated the voice of Westbrook Van Voorhies, the famous narrator of THE MARCH OF TIME, for the voice-over commentary of *Kane's* parodistic NEWS ON THE MARCH sequence. Born in Delmar, Delaware, Alland became an actor and stage manager with Welles's MERCURY THEATRE and assistant director of the company's CBS radio series. In addition to the roles he played in *Citizen Kane* mentioned above, Alland also served as the film's dialogue director. He also appeared in small roles in Welles's THE LADY FROM SHANGHAI (1948) as a reporter, and MACBETH as the second murderer (1948). In 1952, he became a producer in low-budget films, including many in the science-fiction genre such as *It Came from Outer Space* (1952), *The Creature from the Black Lagoon* (1954), *This Island Earth* (1955), *The Mole People* (1956), *The Deadly Mantis* (1957), and *The Space Children* (1958).

During the heyday of the various incarnations of the Mercury Theatre, Alland played many different roles including the assassin in Welles's stage production of Shakespeare's JULIUS CAESAR (1937), and the agent in Welles's radio version of Joseph Conrad's HEART OF DARKNESS. On the set of *Citizen Kane,* as Welles was coping with learning how to direct himself as an actor, he used Alland as a "double" to rehearse Kane's movements so that Welles the director could make adjustments before playing the scene himself. As a trusted Mercury colleague, Welles relied on Alland as well as JOSEPH COTTEN and cinematographer GREGG TOLAND to approve or reject the takes in which he acted. As *Kane's* dialogue director, Alland's main job was to help Welles prepare his lines which, as was usual with Welles, he had difficulty remembering. Welles also had difficulty with memorizing Kane's various movements and actions, whose precise execution were critical to the film's carefully controlled mise-en-scène or visual design. SIMON CALLOW reports that Alland maintained that these shortcomings were in part due to Welles's fear of letting go. "If he ever let himself go in a part he'd lose control," Alland said.

Alland has famously and repeatedly told a story about Welles "letting go" in the scene in which Kane destroys SUSAN ALEXANDER's bedroom apartment in XANADU. Coming off the set bloodied from the damage caused by the release of his character's pent-up rage, a trembling Welles, Alland recalls, repeatedly intoned, "I really felt it. I really felt it!" Welles, when queried by PETER BOGDANOVICH about Alland's recollection, said: "Naw. I'm sure that's one of those memories after the event that are more creative than accurate. I came off with a bleeding wrist—that's what I came off with."

—C.B.

Ambler, Eric (1909–)

Eric Ambler's espionage novel JOURNEY INTO FEAR (1940) was adapted to film in 1943 by ORSON WELLES, who claimed that he and JOSEPH COTTEN wrote the script; NORMAN FOSTER was the nominal director; and Welles produced the film. Welles described the novel and his film adaptation to PETER BOGDANOVICH: "It was the opposite of an action picture, since it was based on the kind of thing Ambler does so well, which is anti-action, antiheroics, and all that. And they took out [in the editing] everything that made it interesting except the action."

Eric Ambler was born in London in 1909, the son of Alfred and Amy Ambler, who were semi-professional stage performers. A talented student, Ambler won a scholarship that enabled him to attend Colfe's Grammar School and then, after winning another scholarship, studied engineering in London. Like his parents, Ambler was interested in the theater and decided to become a playwright. Because of the General Strike of 1926, Ambler abandoned his literary studies and went to work at the Edison Swann Electric Company, but he maintained his interest in the theater. In 1935, he switched gears and wrote a thriller, *The Dark Frontier* (1936), which was followed by five other novels, all written before 1940. In addition to *Journey into Fear*, other early Ambler novels have been adapted to the screen: *Background to Danger* (a.k.a. *Uncommon Danger*, 1943), *A Coffin for Dimitrios* (1944), and *Epitaph for a Spy* (a.k.a. *Hotel Reserve*, 1944). After serving in World War II in a film unit, he became a screenwriter and by 1958 had written 12 scripts that were produced by British film companies. In 1957, he moved to Hollywood, but he made his mark in television with the *Checkmate* series (1959–62). The only feature film made from an Ambler script was *The Wreck of the Mary Deare* (1959), but his novel *The Light of Day* (1962) was adapted to film as the well-known *Topkapi* (1964). Though he continued to write, his film career was effectively over in the 1960s, and he moved to Switzerland. He moved back to London because of ill health. His last novel, *The Care of Time,* was published in 1981. *Here Lies,* his autobiography, was published in 1985.

References Ambler, Eric. *Here Lies: An Autobiography* (London: Weidenfeld & Nicolson, 1985); Ambrosetti, Ronald J. *Eric Ambler* (New York: Twayne, 1994); Wolf, Peter. *Alarms and Epitaphs: The Art of Eric Ambler* (Bowling Green, Ohio: Bowling Green State University Press, 1993).

—T.L.E.

Anderegg, Michael A. (1942–)

Michael Anderegg, a professor of English at the University of North Dakota, had written books on directors *William Wyler* (1979) and *David Lean* (1984) and edited the collection *Inventing Vietnam: The War in Film and Television* (1991) by the time he wrote *Orson Welles, Shakespeare, and Popular Culture,* published by Columbia University Press in 1999. Anderegg was born in Paris, France, in 1942, raised in Los Angeles, and educated at UCLA (B.A., 1968) and Yale University (Ph.D., 1972). In his WELLES book he chose to focus on Welles as a popularizer of Shakespeare (see SHAKESPEARE BY WELLES) and as an unparalleled mediator between high and low culture. The strength of this book resides not so much in its speculations concerning popular culture, which tend toward the obvious, as in its treatment of the director's experiments in popularizing Shakespeare's plays on stage and, especially, on screen—his "theatrical" MACBETH, his "realistic" CHIMES AT MIDNIGHT, and his "filmic" OTHELLO. Jonathan Rosenbaum praised the book as an important contribution "that throws light not only on certain neglected aspects of Welles's work—particularly EVERYBODY'S SHAKESPEARE and the Mercury Text Records—but also on a fresh new approach toward understanding his career as a whole." In his book *Movie Wars* (2000), Rosenbaum cites Anderegg's discussion of the so-called 1992 "restoration" of Welles's *Othello,* which had been long out of distribution since its original release in 1952: "To term the project authorized by BEATRICE WELLES-SMITH as a 'restoration' is to make nonsense of the word. One cannot restore something by altering it in such a way that its final state is something new. To restore means, if it means anything, to bring back to some originary point—itself, of course, an extremely dubious concept." Anderegg considers the 1992 *Othello* "not an act of restoration," but as "something new," that, as Rosenbaum explains, "alters not only Welles's original sound design and Francesco Lavignino's score, but also reloops some of the dialogue with new actors, eliminates some words 'so that a lip-synch could be achieved,' and reedits one sequence entirely." The book's final chapter deals with "Welles as Performer."

—J.M.W.

Armstrong, Louis (c.1898–1971)

If WELLES had succeeded in bringing his 1941 vision of the omnibus film IT'S ALL TRUE to the screen, it would have included *JAZZ STORY,* an episode chronicling the history of American jazz as told through the life of Louis Armstrong, the venerable African-American jazz trumpeter-singer. Along with Armstrong, *Jazz Story* was to also have featured pianist-composer DUKE ELLINGTON and pianist-singer Hazel Scott. FRANK BRADY suggests that of the four segments planned for *It's All True,* it was the jazz story that most interested Welles since it would allow him to work with personal musical heroes such as Armstrong.

Armstrong, one of the most influential performers in the annals of jazz, was noted for his virtuoso trumpeting and inimitably gravelly voice both of which radiated warmth and good cheer. Crossing over to the general public in the postwar years with mainstream pop hits such as "Hello Dolly," Armstrong traveled throughout the world, often on behalf of the U.S. government, thus earning the sobriquet "America's Ambassador of Goodwill." A beloved entertainer-musician, Armstrong appeared in a number of films usually "playing" himself, singing, trumpeting, and mopping his forehead with his signature white handkerchief. He was the subject of a "CBS Reports" television documentary, *Satchmo the Great,* which was released theatrically as a feature film.

Among Armstrong's Hollywood films are *Ex-Flame* (1930); *Pennies from Heaven* (1936); *Artists and Models* (1937); *Every Day's a Holiday* (1938); *Dr. Rhythm* (1938); *Going Places* (1938); *Cabin in the Sky* (1943); *Jam Session* (1944); *Atlantic City* (1944); *Hollywood Canteen* (1944); *New Orleans* (1947); *Carnegie Hall* (1947); *A Song Is Born* (1948); *The Strip* (1951); *Here Comes the Groom* (1951); *Glory Alley* (1952); *The Glenn Miller Story* (1954); *High Society* (1956); *The Beat Generation* (1959); *The Five Pennies* (1959); *Paris Blues* (1961); *When the Boys Meet the Girls* (1965); *A Man Called Adam* (1966); and *Hello Dolly!* (1969); he also appears in the award-winning documentary, *Jazz on a Summer's Day* (1960).

References Bergreen, Laurence. *Louis Armstrong: An Extravagant Life* (New York: Broadway Books, 1997); Bigard, Barney. *With Louis and the Duke: The Autobiography of a Jazz Clarinetist* (New York: Oxford University Press, 1985); Pinfold, Mike. *Louis Armstrong: His Life and Times* (New York: Universe Books, 1987).

—C.B.

Around the World in 80 Days (play, 1946)

WELLES had been enamored of Jules Verne's 1873 novel, *Around the World in 80 Days,* since the late 1920s, when he had seen a ragtag yet no less memorable stage adaptation as a child. In 1938, he selected Verne's story as one of his first shows for the MERCURY THEATRE ON THE AIR. A year later, he presented another radio version for THE CAMPBELL PLAYHOUSE to commemorate Howard Hughes's three-day, around-the-world flight in a twin engine monoplane. In 1945, there was a third radio adaptation of Verne's tale for Welles's series, THIS IS MY BEST.

Welles had also envisioned *Around the World in 80 Days* as a film, and after writing a screenplay, pitched the idea to RKO boss GEORGE SCHAEFER during Welles's early days with the studio. Schaefer, however, wasn't interested. As 1945 gave way to 1946, Welles, casting about for a vehicle that would return him to the New York theater scene in a burst of glory, dug out the old scenario, wrote a quick adaptation of it as a musical spectacular, engaged the legendary COLE PORTER to write the songs, and began searching for backers. Flamboyant showman MIKE TODD, a Broadway hitmaker who had been looking for an opportunity to work with Welles, jumped on the bandwagon, agreeing that *Around the World in 80 Days* would be a sensation.

Verne's plot was in the picaresque tradition. Phineas Fogg, a taciturn and fastidious Englishman, wagers that he can circumnavigate the globe in 80 days and return to his club at a specific, predetermined time. Accompanied by Passepartout, his valet, and Detective Fix, hired by Fogg's club to verify his progress, Fogg begins his adventure. Along the way are various obstacles that he confronts with stiff-upper-lip aplomb. Traveling by boat, train, balloon, bicycle, elephant and any other means of conveyance handy, he eventually winds up back in London, where he saunters nonchalantly into his club, 10 minutes before his deadline, to calmly declaim: "Gentlemen, I am here."

Welles's conception for his musical spectacle was big, brassy and bold, a noisy melange of disparate elements which in hindsight might be interpreted as Wagnerian in its *Gesamtkunstwerk* layerings of music, drama, dance, film, and even elements from the circus. Alternatively, one might regard *Around the World* as a forerunner to postmodern intertextuality with its jarring juxtapositions of clashing elements, a quality alluded to by the *New York Times*'s Lewis Nichols, whose review notes, "There are too many styles fighting among themselves. Mr. Welles, as Knark Fix, plays the part with vast burlesque and is, himself, very funny at it. He has given Arthur Margetson some amusing lines as Fogg, which that actor plays suavely. The rest of the show wanders off from the comedy, however." Was Welles behind or ahead of his time? Or, were there other problems?

One shortcoming that everyone agreed upon was the tepid Cole Porter score. Before Porter had signed on, Broadway insiders told Welles that the legendary tunesmith was played out. Todd, however, insisted that Porter be included in the deal since he had been a key part of Todd's 1943 Broadway musical smash, *Something for the Boys*. Later, when *Around the World* was beginning to list out of control, Porter proved a friend and gentleman, waiving his lucrative royalty agreement with Welles until such time the show started turning profits. Alas, that never happened.

Todd was a different story. Sensing disaster as the show rehearsed for its Boston opening, Todd pulled up stakes after a run-through of a scene set in an Oklahoma oil field in which Welles explained that at the climax, one of the wells would begin to gush and everyone and everything, including the costumes, would be drenched in black gold. An incredulous Todd approached the stage, asking Welles, "An oil well on stage? Are you crazy? How will we clean the costumes after the show?" Shrugging his shoulders, Todd resigned as the show's producer and chief backer, saying: "I'm sorry, Orson, but I've decided I simply can't afford you. The show is yours from this moment on."

Although the show lumbered on through previews in Philadelphia and a New York run of 75 performances at the Adelphi Theater, Welles was never able to cope with its financial demands. With a huge payroll that included 55 stagehands for the show's complex effects and an orchestra of 36, Welles dug deep into his own pockets to such an extent that when the curtain mercifully closed on August 3, 1946, *Around the World in 80 Days* had cost him vir-tually all his savings. Also lost were large sums that had been invested by ALEXANDER KORDA, whatever money Mike Todd had put in, and the rights to his beloved and now mortgaged IT'S ALL TRUE. At one point, with his back against the wall, Welles talked HARRY COHN of Columbia Pictures out of $25,000, in exchange for agreeing to direct RITA HAYWORTH in a project that eventually would become THE LADY FROM SHANGHAI (1947). For years to come, Welles was hounded by the Internal Revenue Service because of bad tax advice on structuring the write-off of the overall $325,000 bill that he had acquired in trying to make a go of the show.

Although saddled by personal debts and tax woes, Welles was still in demand, although he would be forced to take virtually any money-making opportunity that presented itself. While he could exercise his craft in radio and in the films of others, the exercise of his own art would be largely confined to his own mostly independent and spartan projects.

In retrospect, especially in terms of his career in film, one of *Around the World*'s most fascinating aspects was the inclusion of filmed episodes, a strategy that he had used twice before. In 1938, Welles shot a film for the production of TOO MUCH JOHNSON; unfortunately, the cramped conditions of the theater didn't allow for an adequate throw for the projector, thus making it impossible to screen the film. Welles had better luck with GREEN GODDESS, a brief theatrical turn that Welles starred in during the summer of 1939 for the RKO vaudeville circuit; in that production, a filmed prologue helped streamline and focus the exposition. For *Around the World in 80 Days,* just days before the play's opening in Boston, Welles hastily filmed five brief episodes, again, to center the exposition and provide segues to bridge narrative gaps. The filmed episodes also provided time to change scenery and set up the show's more complex theatrical effects. For the vignettes, which included scenes of the interior of the Bank of England and a storm-tossed ship at sea, the idea was to simulate the herky-jerky stylistics of the "silent" cinema while Welles provided narration from a backstage microphone hooked up to the theater's sound system. In a sense, it was a harbinger of the kind of mixed- and multimedia events that became a vogue in the 1960s under the rubrics of "happenings" and "performance art."

—C.B.

Around the World with Orson Welles (television, 1955)   Based on the success of his six-week TV series for the British Broadcasting Company, THE ORSON WELLES SKETCHBOOK (1955), the BBC offered WELLES a second TV series, *Around the World with Orson Welles.* Recalling the informality of the radio series ORSON WELLES'S ALMANAC (1941–42), the *Around the World* programs for the BBC consisted of filmed, on-location "essays" on topics ranging from bullfighting, Viennese coffee, old-age pensioners in London, and the joie de vivre of bohemian life along the Left Bank of Paris. As with *The Orson Welles Sketchbook,* British viewers embraced the *Around the World* shows, praising the host's compelling personality and his ability to draw out interviewees. In spite of a modest salary, Welles enjoyed the travel necessitated by the program's on-location format and his role as interviewer.

The episodes of *Around the World with Orson Welles* were produced for the BBC by Huw Wheldon, and broadcast in 1955.

—C.B.

Astor, Mary (Lucille Vasconcellos Langhanke) (1906–1987)   Actress Mary Astor was one of many stars who appeared on ORSON WELLES's THE CAMPBELL PLAYHOUSE during its run from 1938 through 1939. She starred in "Royal Regiment." Astor (whose original name was Lucille Langhanke) was born in Quincy, Illinois, on May 3, 1906. She was educated at the Highland School and later at the Kenwood-Loring School for Girls, a private school where her mother taught. At an early age she decided, with her parents' support, that she wanted a career in the movies; and after she graduated from the Kenwood-Loring elementary school (she worked for a while on her high school diploma through home schooling, via the Horace Mann curriculum), she and her parents moved to New York City in 1919. Astor met Lillian Gish, who promised her an audition with D.W. Griffith; but Griffith was put off by Astor's father's pushiness and meddling.

Mary Astor *(National Film Society Archive)*

She finally secured a six-month contract with Famous Players–Lasky, but when the contract expired she had not appeared in a film (she wrote, "A scene cut from a picture and a shelved one-reeler are not much of a recommendation"). The picture that started her career was *The Beggar Maid* (she wrote that she was typecast as a "simple farm girl") a two-reeler that was followed by five more two-reelers. Her first feature film was *John Smith* (1922). During the 1920s she made 39 feature films, playing opposite Douglas Fairbanks, Jr. (*Don Q, Son of Zorro,* 1925) and John Barrymore (*Don Juan,* 1926), with whom she had an affair. After making another 43 films during the 1930s, she finally made the two pictures for which she is most remembered. Playing opposite Bette Davis in *The Great Lie* (1941), she won an Academy Award for best supporting actress in 1942. Also released in 1941 was *The Maltese Falcon* with Humphrey Bogart; Astor, who played Brigid, said of her performance, "And if I'd had my druthers, I would have preferred getting my Oscar for Brigid rather than for Sandra [her role in *The Great Lie*]." Following her success, she was signed to a seven-year contract with MGM; her best pictures for MGM were *Meet Me in St. Louis* (1944) and *Little Women* (1949). Astor was also active in the early days of live television and appeared on *Studio One, Philco Playhouse, Producers Showcase, Playhouse 90,* and *U.S. Steel Hour.* In the late 1940s, however, her film career was in decline; she made only nine films after *Little Women.* Her last film, however, was the memorable *Hush, Hush, Sweet Charlotte* (1964), in which she played opposite Bette Davis and for which she received excellent reviews. Although in demand for television work, Astor turned her attention to writing, published some novels, and also wrote *My Story: An Autobiography* (1959), a spiritual account of her survival from problems with alcoholism, and *A Life on Film* (1967). A heart condition caused her to become less active, and she died of emphysema in 1987.

References Astor, Mary. *A Life on Film* (New York: Dell, 1972); ———. *My Story: An Autobiography* (New York: Doubleday, 1959).

—T.L.E.

Atkinson, [J.] Brooks (1894–1984) J.

Brooks Atkinson succeeded STARK YOUNG as drama critic of the *New York Times* in 1926, a post he held until 1960, except for the period from 1941 to 1946, when he served abroad as a war correspondent. In 1934, Atkinson praised WELLES's portrayal of Tybalt in the Cornell company's production of *Romeo and Juliet* at the Martin Beck Theatre. When Welles opened NATIVE SON at the St. James Theatre on March 17, 1941, Atkinson hailed the production as "the biggest American drama of the season." He was less kind to the Welles production of BRECHT's *Galileo* in 1947, however, and he lambasted the 1956 production of KING LEAR, concluding that "Orson Welles has more genius than talent."

Atkinson was born on November 28, 1894, the son of Johnathan H. Atkinson, in Melrose, Massachusetts. Educated at Harvard University, he was appointed instructor of English at Dartmouth College in 1917, then worked as a reporter for the Springfield, Massachusetts, *Daily News.* In 1918, he became the assistant to the drama critic of the *Boston Transcript* and by 1922 he was literary editor of the *New York Times.* After 34 years of experience on the drama desk of the *Times,* he was appointed critic-at-large from 1960 to 1971. He also reported on American theater for the London *Daily Telegraph.*

Atkinson was the author of many books. He edited *New Voices in the American Theatre,* published by Modern Library in 1955, for example, but is perhaps best remembered as a theater historian for his affectionate account *Broadway,* published by Proscenium in 1970. As a gifted newsman, he won a Pulitzer Prize in 1947 for his reporting on the Soviet Union and as a respected critic an Antoinette Perry ("Tony") Award in 1960 for distinguished achievement in the theater. That same year the Mansfield Theater in New York was renamed the Brooks Atkinson Theater in his honor. Atkinson died on January 13, 1984.

Reference Herbert, Ian, ed. *Who's Who in the Theatre,* 16th ed. (London: Pitman, 1977).

—J.M.W.

Auer, Mischa (1905–1967) WELLES loved

character actors. One of his favorites was Mischa Auer. In the late 1940s, Auer, like Welles, departed from Hollywood for the Continent. Settling in Rome in 1949, Auer spent the rest of his career playing character roles in European-made features. Auer's wonderfully eccentric Flea Trainer in Welles's MR. ARKADIN (1955) was one of his most memorable roles. Welles, impressed with his work in *Mr. Arkadin,* cast him as the Don for the ill-fated DON QUIXOTE. When that production dragged on for years, after several scenes had been shot in Spain in 1955, Auer was forced to drop out in favor of Francisco Reiguera.

Auer was born in St. Petersburg, Russia, and brought to the United States by his grandfather, concert violinist Leopold Auer. Though born Mischa Ounshowski, the young boy, upon adoption by his grandfather, took his surname. Educated at the Ethical Culture School in New York City, Auer made his stage debut in a 1925 production of Ibsen's *The Wild Duck.* His first film appearance was in *Something*

Always Happens (1928). He soon became typecast as a typically sinister figure with exotic, foreign eccentricities. In 1936, he was nominated for a best supporting actor Oscar for his portrayal of the free-loading Carlo in *My Man Godfrey*. With a long-term contract at Universal, he played both heavy and comedic roles.

Among the more than 100 films he appeared in are *Mata Hari* (1932), *Tarzan the Fearless* (1933), *Viva Villa!* (1934), *Bulldog Drummond Strikes Back* (1934), *The Lives of a Bengal Lancer* (1934), *The Crusades* (1934), *100 Men and a Girl* (1937), *You Can't Take It with You* (1938), *Destry Rides Again* (1939), *Hellzapoppin* (1941), *Lady in the Dark* (1943), *Sentimental Journey* (1946), *Bachelor in Paris* (1952), *The Monte Carlo Story* (1957), *A Dog, a Mouse and a Sputnik* (1958), and *Arrivederci Baby* (1966), his last film. Auer also played the lead in *Cracked Nuts* (1941).

References Lamparski, Richard. *Whatever Became of . . .?* (New York: Crown, 1966); Stuart, Ray. *Immortals of the Screen* (New York: Bonanza, 1967).

—C.B.

Austerlitz (aka *The Battle of Austerlitz*)

CFPI/Dubrava/Galatea Film/Jadran/Lyre Films/Michael Arthur Films/SCLF, 166 minutes (France), 122 minutes (U.S.A.), 1960. **Director:** Abel Gance; **Producer:** Alexander Salkind and Michael Salkind; **Screenplay:** Gance, Nelly Kaplan and Roger Richebe; **Cinematographer:** Henri Alekan; **Music:** Jon Ledrut; **Editor:** Leonide Azar and Yvonne Martin; **Cast:** Pierre Mondy (Napoléon Bonaparte), Jean Mercure (Talleyrand), Jack Palance (General Weirother), Michael Simon (Alboise), Jean-Louis Trintignant (Ségur fils), Martine Carol (Joséphine de Beauharnais), Leslie Caron (Mlle de Vaudey), Claudia Cardinale (Pauline Bonaparte), Rossano Brazzi (Lucien Bonaparte), Ettore Manni (Lucien Bonaparte), Jean Marais (Carnot), Vittorio de Sica (Pope Pius VII), and Orson Welles (Robert Fulton)

French film director Abel Gance is an icon of the international film. His *Napoleon* (1927) stands as one of the crowning achievements of silent film. In *Austerlitz,* Gance attempted to bring the basic techniques of the cinema—essentially, sound, color, and widescreen cinematography—to a modern retelling of Napoleon's story. Sadly, to cite FRANK BRADY, *Austerlitz* proved "a feeble imitation" of *Napoleon*. For his part, WELLES, as inventor Robert Fulton, pops up in France to offer Napoleon an opportunity to be the first to use the steamboat, an offer turned down. Symptomatic of the period's international co-productions, the 1959 mounting of *Austerlitz* employed to minimal effect a cast of European and American stars. Critic Peter John Dyer advised that *Austerlitz* was "strictly for connoisseurs of Gance's brand of hyperbolic history." The history was not only hyperbolic but often just plain wrong. For example, in a scene that takes place near Parliament between the English leaders Nelson and Pitt, one can glimpse the profile of Big Ben, a feature of the London skyline that did not rise until 50 years later. At the end of the elaborate pageant with its parade of guest stars, Napoleon finally prevails and defeats the Austro-Russian army.

—C.B.

Balanchine, George (1904–1983) In 1938, at the age of 22, WELLES's manic career with its often overlapping commitments to various theater and radio projects was complicated by the prospect of becoming a father. During the same period, his life became even more convoluted, due, unwittingly, to Balanchine, the great Russian dancer-choreographer. In January 1938, Balanchine took his 21-year-old protégée, Vera Zorina, to see the Welles production of *The Shoemaker's Holiday.* At a post-show party, when Zorina and Welles were introduced, she was "totally bedazzled." He was, too. In *Zorina,* her autobiography, the dancer recalled Welles as Byronic, "with one quizzical eyebrow slightly raised, and often laughing in a special throaty way." The pair soon became an "item" covered by the New York gossip columnists, much to the consternation of Zorina, a very jealous Balanchine, and the humiliated Virginia Welles, Orson's pregnant wife. For Welles, in spite of Zorina's later claims that the relationship was platonic, it was a time during which he boasted of having discovered the extraordinary litheness and stamina of ballerinas. Balanchine, regardless of what had actually happened, reconciled and eventually married Zorina. Virginia Welles, distressed by her husband's well-publicized affair with Zorina and other infidelities, divorced Orson in 1940.

George Balanchine was born Georgi Balanchivadze, son of Georgian composer Meliton Balanchivadze. He attended the Imperial Ballet School, St. Petersburg, and performed throughout Russia. In 1924, he joined Diaghilev's Ballets Russes as a principal dancer and choreographer. After moving to the United States in 1933, he became director of ballet for the Metropolitan Opera House, and helped found the School of American Ballet. A pioneer of modern ballet, Balanchine developed a choreographic style emphasizing pattern and design, rather than narrative. In 1948, Balanchine was appointed artistic director and principal choreographer for the New York City Ballet. Among his more than 90 dances are *Serenade, Concerto Barocco, Bourree Fantastique, Seven Deadly Sins, Agon,* and *Don Quixote.* He created the choreography for *Slaughter on Tenth Avenue,* which appeared in the Broadway musical *On Your Toes* (1936). His film credits include *The Goldwyn Follies* (1938), *On Your Toes* (1939), *I Was an Adventuress* (1940), and *Star Spangled Rhythm* (1942), which featured Zorina.

References Buckle, Richard. *George Balanchine, Ballet Master: A Biography* (New York: Random House, 1988); Taper, Bernard. *Balanchine: A Biography* (Berkeley: University of California, 1996).

—C.B.

Barrymore, John (1882–1942) As a child, WELLES had watched from the wings as John Barrymore, who was a friend of his father's, performed as

Hamlet on the New York stage. Barrymore was Welles's idol, and although the two did not work together extensively, Welles maintained close ties to the veteran actor. Welles also saw Barrymore perform in Vitaphone's first "talkie," *Don Juan* (1926), a film that Welles's father thought would kill the movies. Welles has described Barrymore as "a golden boy, a tragic clown grimacing in the darkness," and he has stated that "in his time (and mine), nobody in our language was ever as good as Barrymore . . . or as bad." When Welles went to Woodstock, Illinois, in 1934 to participate in fund-raising for the Todd School, he cast *TRILBY*, one of the three plays scheduled for production, and assumed the role of Svengali. According to biographer FRANK BRADY, Welles "attempted to capture the ambience and appearance of Barrymore's Svengali" (Barrymore's film version had appeared in 1931). *BRIGHT LUCIFER*, a play that Welles wrote in 1934, also contains oblique references both to Welles and to Barrymore, who have characters closely modeled after them. CHARLES HIGHAM has written, "The play becomes paroxysmal in its final pages, perhaps more purely reflecting Welles's disordered subconscious than anything he ever wrote or would have dared to stage." In 1937, CBS engaged Welles to adapt some Shakespearean plays for radio; not to be outdone, rival NBC hired Barrymore, and their series premiered three weeks before Welles's. While filming *CITIZEN KANE,* this "rivalry" between Welles and Barrymore was utilized on the *Rudy Vallee Show,* which billed the two actors as "The Two Greatest Shakespearean Actors in the World Today." In the course of the shows the two even sang "By the Light of the Silvery Moon" and exchanged quips. Barrymore, jokingly deprecating Welles, states ironically, "Why, he's another John Barrymore." The pair's most memorable performance on the Vallee show was in *JULIUS CAESAR;* Welles played Brutus and Barrymore played Cassius in the tent scene before the battle of Philippi. At one point Barrymore's line, "Has it come to this?" reverberates about the aging star's decline. In 1939, Welles appeared in *GREEN GODDESS,* a short vaudeville version of a play that blended high comedy with melodrama; and Barrymore, who was appearing in another show in Chicago, occasionally joined the

John Barrymore *(National Film Society Archive)*

cast and improvised lines for his character. Welles remained a supporter of Barrymore through his idol's decline.

Barrymore, the youngest of the celebrated Barrymore acting family, was born on February 15, 1882, in Philadelphia. After a brief career as a cartoonist for a New York daily, he followed family tradition and turned to acting, making his stage debut in 1903 in *Magda*. He soon became a stage idol and worked extensively in Shakespearean roles. His most acclaimed performances were as Richard III in 1920 and Hamlet in 1922. He made his first film appearance in 1913 and enjoyed enormous popularity. With the advent of sound, his voice, coupled with his striking profile, made him a box-office hit. In order to exploit his stage reputation, Hollywood frequently had him recite speeches from Shakespeare's plays. Unfortunately, by the time talkies appeared Barrymore was past his prime. His excessive drinking, begun at an early age, began to interfere with his memory, and he frequently had to read his lines from cue cards. As the years passed, his roles began to mirror his life as he played aging actors in their declining years. He died in 1942.

References Brady, Frank. *Citizen Welles* (New York: Scribner's, 1989); Higham, Charles. *Orson Welles: The Rise and Fall of an American Genius* (New York: St. Martin's Press, 1985); Kobler, John. *Damned in Paradise: The Life of John Barrymore* (New York: Atheneum, 1977); Leaming, Barbara. *Orson Welles: A Biography* (New York: Viking, 1985).

—T.L.E.

Battle of Neretva, The   Commonwealth United Entertainment/Echberg/Film Production Organisation/ Igor Film/United Yugoslavia Producers/Vereinigte/ Yugoslavia Film, 175 minutes (Bosnia), 134 minutes (Italy), 102 minutes (U.S.A.), 1969. **Director:** Veljko Bulajic; **Producer:** Steve Previn; **Executive Producers:** Anthony B. Unger and Henry T. Weinstein; **Screenplay:** Steven Bulajic, Ratko Djurovic, Ugo Pirro and Bulajic; **Cinematographer:** Tomislav Pinter; **Music:** Bernard Herrmann and Vladimir Klaus-Rajteric; **Editor:** Vojislav Bjenjas and Robert Perpignani; **Cast:** Yul Brynner (Vlado), Curt Jurgens (General Lohring), Silva Koscina (Danica), Hardy Krüger (Colonel Kranzer), Franco Nero (Captain Michael Riva), and Orson Welles (Chetnik Senator)

This internationally co-produced war film was situated in 1943 Yugoslavia, where a group of Yugoslav partisans ward off German and Italian incursions. Along with WELLES, the heroic tale of resistance during World War II featured Yul Brynner, Curt Jurgens, Sylva Koscina, Hardy Krüger, and Franco Nero. Although *The Battle of Neretva* did not travel well in terms of attracting a broad international audience, the CinemaScope feature did garner an Oscar nomination in the category of Best Foreign Film. It was filmed on location in Yugoslavia.

For Welles, *The Battle of Neretva* was a means of angling an opportunity to produce his long-planned adaptation of *Dead Calm*. "I only did *Neretva* so I could make THE DEEP in Yugoslavia," Welles told PETER BOGDANOVICH. "[The Yugoslavians] gave me their services in exchange for mine." It should be remembered that in 1968, Yugoslavia was a commu-

nist state under the tight reins of Marshal Josip Broz Tito, and that all of the nation's filmmaking activities were controlled by the state.

—C.B.

Battle Over Citizen Kane, The (television, 1996)   The first hour of this "American Experience" television documentary produced by Thomas Lennon and Michael Epstein sets up parallel biographies of ORSON WELLES and newspaper tycoon WILLIAM RANDOLPH HEARST (1863–1951), "both of them arrogant and egomaniacal and ruthless," according to *Washington Post* television critic Tom Shales, "but where Hearst was vindictive and mad for power, Welles was creative and a slave to his own imagination." Elements of both were factored into the character of Charles Foster Kane.

The film summarizes Welles's career in radio and theater and incorporates clips from the "voodoo" MACBETH Welles staged in Harlem and set in Haiti. The first hour climaxes with the MERCURY THEATRE radio broadcast of THE WAR OF THE WORLDS and the subsequent charges of panic and disorder caused by the dramatization. When a CBS radio executive urged Welles to insert a disclaimer 15 minutes into the broadcast, Welles is reported to have replied: "They're scared? Good. They're supposed to be scared. Now, let me finish."

Welles underestimated the controlling power of his subject, according to WILLIAM ALLAND, who played the reporter in *CITIZEN KANE* assigned to discover the meaning of "ROSEBUD," Kane's dying word: "I think they thought they could get away with it," Alland speculated. "I don't think they realized how touchy the old man was." The irony was that, as the film explains, "For the first time ever, the methods Hearst had used to lay bare the lives of others had been used on him." Hearst had once claimed, according to Douglas Fairbanks, Jr., "You can crush a man with journalism, but not with motion pictures." Little did he know. Hearst could malign Welles as a communist and as a homosexual and forbid his papers to advertise the film, but ultimately he could not destroy *Citizen Kane*. The film was programmed to self-destruct, however, because of its experimental techniques and challenging narrative approach. It was arguably the greatest American film ever made, but it was also a commercial failure.

Hearst was especially upset by the way the film portrayed his mistress, the actress MARION DAVIES. As Tom Shales wrote in his review, "The Tycoon Who Tried to Raze 'Kane,'" Davies was "a very charismatic comic actress" who had demonstrated her talent in such films as *Show People* (1928), for King Vidor, and *Going Hollywood* (1933), for Raoul Walsh. Douglas Fairbank, Jr., remembers her as being a "glorious gal" in real life, "full of wit [and] humor." Welles presented Davies as an untalented, would-be opera singer (played by DOROTHY COMINGORE), and a miserably unhappy alcoholic. Even Welles himself later admitted in a 1982 British television interview, "I thought we were very unfair to Marion Davies." Hearst wanted "to buy the negative of the film and burn it so that it would never be released," as Shales described the conflict.

The documentary worked as oral history, including such Welles colleagues as editor ROBERT WISE, FRANK MANKIEWICZ, whose father, HERMAN MANKIEWICZ, wrote the screenplay, RUTH WARRICK, who played the first Mrs. Kane, journalist Jimmy Breslin, and Welles advocate writer-director PETER BOGDANOVICH, as well as William Alland and Douglas Fairbanks, Jr. The film was narrated by Richard Ben. Its main flaw was to suggest that Welles was a one-shot talent whose career was essentially over after *Citizen Kane,* though, in fact, other remarkable features were to follow. Orson Welles was neither doomed nor an artistic failure. After first being screened at the Sundance Film Festival in Park City, Utah, *The Battle Over Citizen Kane* first aired on "The American Experience" on January 29, 1996, and was later nominated for an Academy Award. In September of 2000 the documentary was released on video by WGBH Boston Video. The documentary was later included in the *Citizen Kane* DVD released by Warner Home Video in 2001.

References Burr, Ty. "Ego Brainiac," *Entertainment Weekly,* 55; Todd, McCarthy. "*Citizen Kane* DVD," *Variety,* October 8–14, 2001): 61; Tom Shales. "The Tycoon Who Tried to Raze 'Kane,'" *Washington Post,* January 29, 1996: D1, D5.

—J.M.W.

Baxter, Anne (1923–1985) When Anne Baxter played Lucy Morgan in WELLES's *The Magnificent Ambersons* (1942), it was her first major film role. The granddaughter of noted architect Frank Lloyd Wright, she was born May 7, 1923, in Michigan City, Indiana, but she was raised in Bronxville, New York, in wealthy Westchester County. After studying drama with Maria Ouspenskaya, she debuted on Broadway at the age 13 in *Seen But Not Heard.* Other Broadway roles led to her screen debut in 1940 with *Twenty-Mule Team.* Three movies later she was cast as Lucy Morgan. When the film was subjected to radical cutting, over Welles's objections, her role in the film, PETER COWIE believes, was substantially reduced. As ROBERT WISE and MARK ROBSON, his assistant, worked on cutting the film, Welles cabled them on April 2, 1942, and requested that they provide the film with a happy ending. One of the scenes that he suggested be added to go with the end titles was one with TOM HOLT, who played George Amberson Minafer, and Baxter sitting happily in an open car. In her memoir, *Intermission* (1976), Baxter recounts an incident in which an intoxicated Welles gets her to drive him home from a party given by JOSEPH COTTEN: "six feet four and 250 pounds, and what seemed like six hands on my shirt." Despite her anger at his advances, she did say, when the filming was completed, that he was the best director she had ever worked with. Later, when Republic Pictures was casting *MACBETH,* she was one of three actresses (the others were MERCEDES MCCAMBRIDGE and AGNES MOOREHEAD) that Welles recommended for the part of Lady Macbeth. After *The Magnificent Ambersons,* Baxter made 45 more films, most of them undistinguished, but she did have excellent roles in two outstanding pictures. She won a best supporting actress Oscar for *The Razor's Edge* (1946) and was nominated for another Oscar for her role as an ambitious, unscrupulous young actress in *All About Eve* (1950). In 1961 she left Hollywood to accompany her second husband, Randolph Galt, to the Australian outback. She later returned to the United States and recounted her experiences in *Intermission: A True Story* (1976). In 1971, she replaced Lauren Bacall in *Applause,* a musical adapted from *All About Eve.* Instead of playing the younger actress (Eve), she now played the role of the older actress (Margo Channing) who is supplanted by Eve. She died of a stroke in 1985.

References Baxter, Anne. *Intermission: A True Story* (New York: Putnam, 1976); Cowie, Peter. *A Ribbon of Dreams: The Cinema of Orson Welles* (So. Brunswick, N.J.: A.S. Barnes, 1973).

—T.L.E.

Baxter, Keith (1933–) Actor Keith Baxter played Prince Hal for ORSON WELLES in both the theatrical and cinematic versions of CHIMES AT MIDNIGHT (1960 and 1966, respectively). He was born April 29, 1933, in Newport, the son of Stanley Baxter Wright and his wife, Emily Marian (Howell). He was educated at Barry Grammar School and Newport High School, after which he entered the Royal Academy of Dramatic Arts, where he was a bronze medallist upon completing his studies in 1956. After touring in repertory theater, he made his London debut in *Tea and Sympathy* in 1957 at the Comedy Theatre. Before he appeared in Welles's theatrical *Chimes,* Baxter had appeared in the Theatre in the Round and the Strand. Despite his limited stage experience, he had, according to FRANK BRADY, "the Shakespearean look Orson was searching for." CHARLES HIGHAM contends that "the best performance in the picture was given to Keith Baxter, a virile and strikingly handsome actor who admirably achieved the character of Prince Hal."

Baxter made his New York stage debut in 1961 as King Henry VIII in *A Man for All Seasons.* Most of Baxter's theatrical roles were in classic theater: *The Rivals, The Country Wife, Antony and Cleopatra, Macbeth, Three Sisters,* and *Much Ado about Nothing.* His films include *The Barretts of Wimpole Street* (1957) and *Ash Wednesday* (1973). He also appeared in television productions, most notably in *Saint Joan.*

Reference Herbert, Ian, ed. *Who's Who in the Theatre.* 16th Ed. (London: Pitman, 1977).

—T.L.E. and J.M.W.

Bazin, André (1918–1958) No doubt the most influential film critic of his generation who nourished the creative talents of the French New Wave, André Bazin also championed the career of ORSON WELLES in France by writing *Orson Welles: A Critical View,* published by Les Editions du Cerf in 1950, subsequently translated into English by Jonathan Rosenbaum and published in the United States by Harper & Row in 1998. As FRANÇOIS TRUFFAUT noted in his "Foreword" to the book, Bazin was 28 years old when he attended the Paris premier of CITIZEN KANE in July of 1946. Bazin and Jean-Claude Tachella interviewed Welles in 1948 for *L'Écran français,* published on September 21 of that year. Bazin sides with Jacques Doniol-Valcroze in grouping Welles with the cinema's greatest directors—Griffith, CHAPLIN, Stroheim, Eisenstein, and Renoir. As Bazin wrote, "France had *La Règle du Jeu;* Hollywood, *Citizen Kane.*" Truffaut's long, 27-page "Foreword" to the book is a tribute to Bazin as well as to Welles. This is followed by a "Profile of Orson Welles" written by the poet-filmmaker JEAN COCTEAU, who met Orson Welles in 1936 in Harlem, when Cocteau saw "his *Black Macbeth,*" because, Cocteau explains, "I wanted to sketch the profile of a friend whom I like and whom I admire."

Born in Angers in 1918, Bazin developed into a journalist and theoretician who taught at the Institut des Hautes Études Cinématographiques. Dudley Andrew credits Bazin with having charted the major areas of what later became cinema studies. He pioneered the notion of authorship in cinema through his writings on Welles, Chaplin, Jean Renoir, Jean-Pierre Melville, and Jacques Tati, which led his disciples at *Cahiers du Cinéma* (which Bazin edited) to create the *politique des auteurs,* later popularized in America by Andrew Sarris as the "auteur theory." Bazin became the surrogate father and mentor of the young critic and enthusiast François Truffaut and died while Truffaut was engaged in making his first feature film, the groundbreaking *Les Quatre Cents Coups,* known in America as *The 400 Blows* (1959), which Truffaut subsequently dedicated to Bazin.

—J.M.W.

Bennett, Richard (1873–1944) Richard Bennett was featured in two WELLES film productions: JOURNEY INTO FEAR and THE MAGNIFICENT AMBERSONS, though in the latter he was in failing health while attempting to realize his role as Major

Amberson. Born in Deacon's Mills, Indiana, on May 21, 1873, he made his stage debut in Chicago in 1891 and soon became a matinee idol. His first film appearance was in the silent *Damaged Goods* (1914). He fathered a progeny of actresses—Barbara, Constance, and Joan Bennett, all of them children by his second wife, Adrienne Morrison. Among his better-known films: *Arrowsmith* (1931), *Song of Songs* (1933), and *Nana* (1934).

Welles was eager to cast Richard Bennett in his TARKINGTON adaptation because he was a fan of Bennett's in the theater. Welles told PETER BOG-DANOVICH, "He had the greatest lyric power of any actor I ever saw on the English-speaking stage." Moreover, he was the perfect choice, chronologically to play the elder Major Amberson, since his own career paralleled the period of Tarkington's story. The problem, however, was that by the time he appeared in *Ambersons,* he was, according to Welles, "incapable of remembering even a single word of dialogue, so I spoke every line, and he repeated it after me, and then we cut my voice from the sound track." According to Welles, he found Bennett in Catalina in a small boardinghouse, "which was, I guess, the inspiration for the boardinghouse at the end of my original version of *Ambersons.*" The Bogdanovich book contains a letter dated February 11, 1942, from Richard Bennett to "Orson Boy": "I feel sure you understand my gratitude—lifting as you did 'an old scow' from the mud banks and permitting it to see the sunshine once more." Welles also cast Bennett as the ship's captain in *Journey into Fear* in 1943, despite the problems just noted with *Ambersons.*

—T.L.E. and J.M.W.

Bernstein, Dr. Maurice (1886–1965)

Maurice Bernstein (Dadda) was a physician who had an affair with ORSON WELLES's mother and who became Orson's surrogate father and then his legal guardian. He was born in 1886 in Russia and immigrated with his parents, Jacob and Tuba Bernstein, to Chicago in the late 1880s. After graduating from the Northwestern University Medical School, he began practicing medicine, specializing in orthopedics, in Chicago in 1908. Three years later, after physically attacking his clinical supervisor, he moved his prac-

tice to Kenosha, Wisconsin, although he continued to work with the Michael Reese Hospital in Chicago. According to CHARLES HIGHAM, he was also a specialist in hormone therapy, helped raise $400,000 for a foot hospital in Chicago, and "worked on the discovery of mucin as a treatment for stomach ulcers, vitamin D deficiency as a cause for decayed teeth in children, methods of discovering a child's sex before it was born, and the infantile paralysis virus." In 1915, he visited New York, where he met Minna Elman, older sister of renowned and wealthy violinist Mischa Elman, who considered Bernstein a fortune hunter. Minna Elman overcame her brother's objections to Bernstein, and prevailed upon her brother to give her the dowry of $15,000 that Bernstein had made a condition for the marriage. The marriage lasted only four months. Bernstein then met BEATRICE WELLES, Orson's mother, but his visits to her house were covered by his being the physician of Lucy Ives, Beatrice's mother, who lived with Beatrice. When Lucy Ives died in 1918, Orson, his brother, Dickie, his parents, and Dr. Bernstein moved to Chicago.

In Chicago, Bernstein opened the doors to Chicago musical society to Beatrice, who was an accomplished pianist with social ambitions. He also became quite fond of Orson, who called him "Dadda" (Bernstein called Orson "Pookles"), and he gave Orson two presents that were to shape his future: a toy theater and a magic set. The precocious Orson, who quickly learned how to use his gifts, then gave performances to appreciative adult audiences. Bernstein also encouraged, with Beatrice's assistance, Orson to play the piano, and he and Beatrice, who were subscribers, took Orson with them when they attended the summer opera festival at nearby Ravinia. When they all traveled to Grand Detour, Illinois, a town about 100 miles from Chicago, they went in two cars: Orson's father and older brother in one, and Orson, Beatrice, and Bernstein in the other. After Beatrice's death, Bernstein and Orson's father shared a home in Chicago and traveled together in Europe in 1924. After Orson's father bought a hotel in Grand Detour, Orson divided his time between his father, with whom he also traveled, and Bernstein, who lived in Chicago. In 1929, Bernstein married Edith Mason, a star with the

Chicago Opera Company. To marry Bernstein, she had to get a divorce from Giorgio Polacco, who was her former coach and a conductor. Higham describes the bizarre conditions Polacco imposed upon the lovers: "Miss Mason must give up eating pie and agree in writing to abandon her addiction to it; Dr. Bernstein must force her to give up smoking; and he and she must pay Polacco one hundred thousand dollars for the loss of her sexual favors." The mercenary Bernstein agreed only to the first two conditions; in order to save money, Bernstein had Polacco move in with the Bernsteins at Edith's house, where the two men shared her. This marriage lasted only two years, after which Edith divorced Bernstein and remarried Polacco.

Upon his father's death in 1930, Welles was to inherit six-sevenths of his estate when he reached the age of 25; the remainder would go to his older brother, Dickie, when he became 35. Bernstein was appointed both boys' legal guardian and in that capacity "continually nibbled at the estate," in Higham's words. After the divorce from Mason, Bernstein married for the third time. Hazel Moore had been the wife of Edward Moore, the Chicago music critic, and had earlier, before the Mason marriage, had an affair with Bernstein. After Bernstein's third marriage, Welles saw less of him, but when he did visit the Bernsteins, he addressed, as SIMON CALLOW puts it, "the equally vexed questions of his legacy and his future: intertwined problems, in fact." Callow concludes, "There is no doubt of his love for Orson, but there is a possibility that he tried to cheat him, too." When Welles went to Ireland at the age of 16, he wrote several letters to Bernstein, who typed them up and distributed them to their friends. Most of the letters ended with a request for money. Callow sees in Bright Lucifer, a play Welles wrote, a parallel between the relationship between Jack, the protagonist, and his guardian and the loathing that Welles felt for the Bernsteins. After his return from Ireland, Welles was committed to a career in the theater, despite the objections of Bernstein, who saw no future for Welles in drama. Although he had misgivings about Welles's theatrical ambitions, Bernstein remained close to Welles and was best man when Welles wed Virginia Nicolson. After Welles moved to

California, he sent for Bernstein and employed him as his own physician until he was accepted by the California Medical Board. After he began his medical practice in California, Bernstein continued to treat Welles and to offer his counsel.

When Bernstein died in 1965, from a fall from a ladder, Welles had mixed emotions. According to BARBARA LEAMING, Welles cared for Bernstein but had questions about his legacy: "I do not think that Dadda Bernstein had any notion that he was stealing from me," but "there is the moment when you wonder how he can possibly have justified keeping all that money. He bought a big house in Los Angeles out of my money, and decorated it entirely with furniture which had belonged to my mother." Welles was unsuccessful in getting the money or the furniture, which Hazel Moore had distributed to her friends before she entered a retirement home.

—T.L.E.

Berry, John (Jack) (1917–1999)

John Berry was a regular member of the radio MERCURY THEATRE COMPANY and also appeared with other Mercury regulars in ORSON WELLES's stage adaptation of RICHARD WRIGHT's NATIVE SON, which had its premiere on March 24, 1941. Berry was born in New York City in 1917 and was a child actor on stage and in vaudeville. He directed and acted with Welles's Mercury Theatre before he moved to Hollywood to assist Billy Wilder on his Double Indemnity (1944). His films are varied in content and quality: he made melodramas (Tension, 1949, and He Ran All the Way, 1951), a soap opera (From This Day Forward, 1946), and a musical remake of Pépé le Moko and Algiers (Casbah, 1948). Because of the communist scare of the 1950s he was blacklisted after being identified as a communist by Edward Dmytryk and other Hollywood witnesses. In order to raise funds for himself and others who were blacklisted after the House Un-American Activities Committee hearings, he directed a 16mm documentary entitled The Hollywood Ten. He then moved to France, where he continued to direct films, and to London, where he directed avant-garde stage productions. In the 1970s he returned to Hollywood and resumed his directing career with Claudine (1974); he also directed The Bad News Bears

Go to Japan (1978), *Angel on My Shoulder* (1980), and *A Captive in the Land* (1991). Jack Berry died on November 30, 1999.

—T.L.E.

Bessy, Maurice (1910–1993) French film critic Maurice Bessy wrote one of the first critical surveys of the cinema of ORSON WELLES in 1963, entitled *Orson Welles: An Investigation into His Films and Philosophy,* published by Editions Seghers in the respected Cinéma d'Aujourd'hui directors' series, edited by Peter Seghers. In 1971, the book was translated into English by Ciba Vaughan and published by Crown Publishers, New York. In addition to Bessy's critical and biographical survey, the book includes a sampling of interviews, articles and film reviews, quotations and documents, such as a previously unpublished screenplay for *SALOME*. The book concludes with a filmography, bibliography, and index. Bessy usefully provides a cross-section of Welles's critical standing in France at the time the French New Wave was gaining currency by quoting several French critics, such as Henri Agel from *Les grandes cinéastes* (1959), Alexandre Astruc and Louis Aragon from *Les lettres français* (1959), ANDRÉ BAZIN from *L'Écran français* (1948).

—J.M.W.

Big Brass Ring, The An unproduced film script by WELLES written in 1979 at the urging of director and close friend HENRY JAGLOM. Jaglom, hoping to persuade one of the avowed Welles-admirers from among Hollywood's new wave of 30-something moguls to bankroll a full-blown production of the script, envisioned *The Big Brass Ring* as Welles's Hollywood comeback as a triple-threat director-actor-screenwriter.

Was Jaglom's optimism justified?

The plot centers on the relationship between a presidential hopeful and his aging adviser. Opening with a youthful Senator Blake Pellarin on the verge of winning the presidency due in part to the mentoring of Kim Menaker, the script informs us that the old man was a former Roosevelt aide who before joining Pellarin's campaign had been advising an African dictator. The mentor, whom Welles envi-

sioned playing, turns out to be a homosexual who develops a crush on the younger man, an infatuation he keeps to himself except for letters to a former lover about his obsession.

Jaglom set Welles up with luncheons with various producers to discuss the project. But while the moguls were delighted to meet and dine with the great man, in the end, none came forth with a deal. Ironically, and sadly, but also understandably, Welles was deemed unbankable by the very Hollywood establishment that had cheered him so lustily in 1975 when Welles received the American Film Institute's Third Life Achievement Award. Jaglom, thinking that a commitment from a major star to play Pellarin might give the project a boost, pitched the role to Warren Beatty, Clint Eastwood, PAUL NEWMAN, Jack Nicholson, Robert Redford, and BURT REYNOLDS. All six declined politely.

So, was this final rejection of Welles by Hollywood part of an ongoing and impenetrable conspiracy? That's the view taken by Jaglom. Gore Vidal, another of Welles's social chums, viewed things similarly. Indeed, in his obituary of Welles for *The New York Review of Books,* Vidal wraps up his tribute with a gushing assessment of the script for *The Big Brass Ring,* which he said illustrated "[Welles] at the top of his glittering form."

DAVID THOMSON, as well as the putative Hollywood conspirators who supposedly denied Welles a chance for a final "hurrah," took a different view. Of the actors who turned Welles down, Thomson says that "their decisions not to be Blake Pellarin seem to me evidence that one can be an international icon without losing all reason." Thomson, author of *Rosebud: The Story of Orson Welles* (1996), a balanced yet pull-no-punches biography, concludes that "*The Big Brass Ring* is as bad as anything Welles ever did or attempted." As for Menaker's homosexuality, Thomson says: "Welles was *not* gay. Why? He couldn't conceive of loving any other person in the world [than himself]. So Menaker's love for Pellarin is an odious, smarmy parody of affection. Welles was gay in a way uniquely his: he loved himself."

Readers interested in forming their own conclusions about the script, and Welles, are directed to an edition of *The Big Brass Ring* published in 1987, credited as a work by Orson Welles "with Oja Kodar." OJA KODAR was the Yugoslavian sculptress who served as Welles's muse and companion during the last years of his life.

—C.B.

Black Magic   Edward Small Productions/United Artists, 102 minutes (U.S.), 1949. **Director:** Gregory Ratoff; **Producer:** Ratoff; **Screenplay:** Charles Bennett (based on the 1848 novel *Mémoires d'un médecin* by Alexandre Dumas *père*); **Cinematographers:** Ubaldo Arata and Anchise Brizzi; **Music:** Paul Sawtell; **Editors:** James McKay and Fred Feitshans; **Cast:** Orson Welles (Count Cagliostro/Joseph Balsamo), Nancy Guild (Marie Antoinette/Lorenza), Akim Tamiroff (Gitano), Frank Latimore (Gilbert), Valentina Cortese (Zoraida), Margot Grahame (Mme. Du Barry), Stephen Bekassy (Count DeMontagne), Berry Kroeger (Alexander Dumas, Sr.), Raymond Burr (Dumas, Jr.), Gregory Gay (Chambord/Monk), Charles Goldner (Dr. Franz Anton Mesmer), Lee Kresel (King Louis XV/Innkeeper), Robert Atkins (King Louis XV)

U.S. costume film shot in Italy starring ORSON WELLES. Produced in Rome in late 1947 and early 1948, *Black Magic* was Welles's first European film. Based on the historic figure Cagliostro, the 18th-century hypnotist, magician, and scoundrel who plots to take over an empire, the story had been proposed to Welles several years earlier by director Gregory Ratoff, then working for DARRYL ZANUCK at Fox. Welles rejected Ratoff's offer as well as one from Greta Garbo, who had proposed to play opposite him as Cagliostro's mistress. However, in fall 1947, when a new offer to play Cagliostro was tendered by American producer EDWARD SMALL, Welles was receptive.

Several factors prompted the turnabout. First, since Cagliostro was a magician, the role would permit Welles to exhibit his prestidigitatory talents. Second, there was a promising script by Charles Bennett (whose films included Alfred Hitchcock's notable *Blackmail* of 1929) that seemed to catch the tumult of Cagliostro's stormy career. Third, and much to Welles's delight, producer Small had engaged Ratoff to direct. Fourth, and in contrast to his previously

tempestuous relationships with producers, Welles and Small hit it off. There was also the prospect that Small might produce Welles-directed versions of OTHELLO and *MOBY DICK*. Fifth, and most pressing, Small's generous salary was a means for Welles to help pay off debts for his failed 1946 stage production of *AROUND THE WORLD IN 80 DAYS*. For Welles, acting was once again a matter of economics rather than artistry.

At the production's onset, everyone was happy. The easygoing Ratoff idolized Welles and was happy to accept his uncredited directorial assistance. On one occasion, a visitor to the set reported seeing Welles atop a coach directing a large mob scene. When the guest asked for Ratoff, Welles pointed to the director, fully costumed, in among the mob of extras. Off the set, Welles was regarded by the Italians as an international celebrity. Among the invitations from Rome's elite was one from Pope Pius XII, who granted him a 45-minute audience. As for his personal life, Welles, now estranged from wife RITA HAYWORTH, was in the midst of a torrid affair with 22-year-old Italian actress Lea Padovani, who had had a small part in *Black Magic*. In spite of the production's auspicious beginnings, there were soon problems on the set.

Welles, always concerned about his diminutive nose, was worried about having arrived in Rome without a supply of false noses. More serious was the unraveling of Welles's relationship with Ratoff, who halfway through the production appeared on the verge of a nervous breakdown. Part of Ratoff's discontent was caused by Welles's attempt to juggle a schedule that quickly careened out of control. At one point in the midst of shooting, for example, Welles made a quick and unannounced trip to London to discuss plans for a film version of *Cyrano de Bergerac* with British producer ALEXANDER KORDA.

More serious was the mounting pressure on Welles from Republic Pictures, which had bankrolled his production of *MACBETH*. When Republic's brass learned that Welles had deserted his editing suite to take a role in another director's film, they were furious. To placate Republic's justifiable ire, Welles put himself on an impossible regimen, acting in *Black Magic* during the day, while editing *Macbeth* through the night. *Black Magic* co-star Nancy

Guild recalls that Welles appeared excessively fretful due to his lack of sleep and worries about *Macbeth*.

Given the arduous shooting conditions, it is little wonder that when finally released in 1949, *Black Magic* was met by indifferent reviews that dismissed it as a heavy, hammily acted costume melodrama. For Welles, the fateful decision to take on the role of Cagliostro before finishing *Macbeth* served to confirm Hollywood's view of him as unreliable. This was doubly unfortunate since Welles had intended *Macbeth* as a demonstration of his ability to work within the system. By shooting *Macbeth* on schedule and within budget, Welles had made it halfway in proving his point. Sadly, the point was lost forever when Welles bungled *Macbeth*'s completion by accepting an inconsequential acting job in a film that today has been all but forgotten.

Black Magic was promoted as "The biggest picture in ten years! The greatest cavalcade of intrigue, spectacle, adventure and excitement you'll ever see on the screen." In contrast, were the critics' reactions, typified by C. A. Lejeune, who wrote: "At times a grotesque, and at others a melancholy spectacle; including one scene of humiliating burlesque at the expense of physical disability that is as vile as anything I have witnessed in a cinema. But on the whole, absurdity predominates, and one must grin if one is to bear it. Whether Mr. Welles deliberately enhanced the joke by adding bad acting to bad material is between him and his own soul."

Along with Welles and co-star Nancy Guild, the film featured Akim Tamiroff, Valentina Cortese, Margot Grahame, Charles Goldner, and Frank Latimore.
—C.B.

Black Museum, The (radio, 1952) Following WELLES's success in the British Broadcasting Company's 1951–52 radio series, THE ADVENTURES OF HARRY LIME, BBC producer HARRY ALAN TOWERS invited Welles to return to the airwaves as host and narrator of *The Black Museum*. Based on accounts of actual murder cases from the files of Scotland Yard, each of the 39 episodes opened with Welles rummaging around the Yard's huge homicide warehouse, spying a seemingly innocent everyday item (a teacup or a piece of carbon paper, for instance), picking that

object up, and then beginning a tale in which the object would eventually prove crucial to the unfolding of a grisly crime. The sound design of the opening was atmospherically embellished by the background tolling of Big Ben, the clanging of heavy doors, and the host's footsteps reverberating against the warehouse's cold stone floors. After Welles's introduction, the crime was dramatized by the show's capable and versatile cast, before giving way to a concluding wrap-up delivered by Welles. Like *The Adventures of Harry Lime,* the show quickly became a hit in no small measure because of Welles's commanding presence. Although his primary responsibilities were those of host and narrator, Welles occasionally took a role in the dramatic reenactments. Efficiently directed by Tig Roe (who had also presided over *The Adventures of Harry Lime*), *The Black Museum* was broadcast in the United States by the Mutual Broadcasting Service.

Based on its widespread popularity, Towers, the show's dynamic young producer, invited Welles to consider yet another new radio series, SHERLOCK HOLMES.
—C.B.

Black Rose, The Twentieth Century–Fox, 120 minutes, 1950. **Director:** Henry Hathaway; **Producer:** Louis D. Lighten; **Screenplay:** Talbot Jennings, from the novel by Thomas B. Costain; **Cinematography:** Jack Cardiff; **Art Direction:** Paul Sheriff and W. Andres; **Editor:** Manuel del Campos; **Music:** Richard Addinsell; **Cast:** Orson Welles (Bayan), Tyrone Power (Walter of Gurnie), Cecile Aubry (Maryam, the Black Rose), Jack Hawkins (Tristram, the Bowman), Michael Rennie, Finlay Currie, Henry Oscar, Herbert Lom, Mary Clare, Laurence Harvey, Alfonso Bedoya, Gibb McLaughlin, James Robertson Justice, Bobby Blake

In this lavishly mounted 13th-century dramatic adventure, an adaptation of the best-selling novel of the same title by Thomas Costain, WELLES effectively plays Bayan, a swarthy Mongol chieftain, opposite TYRONE POWER's Walter of Gurnie. Although Welles took delight in the general camaraderie among cast and crew and in donning his elaborate makeup, director HATHAWAY, initially pleased to be working with Welles, grew increasingly impatient with the actor's challenges to his directorial authority, concluding that "He's a great actor and everything—but he's only trouble." Part of the problem, suggests BARBARA LEAMING, was Welles's difficulty in balancing being a player in Hathaway's *Black Rose* company while simultaneously running off to direct scenes in his own ongoing production of OTHELLO. Whatever the case, Hathaway resented Welles's imperious and resistant manner, concluding: "He's such a conniving bastard."

Interestingly, the film was not released in Germany largely because of German antipathy toward Welles, who had earlier suggested in the press that he doubted that there were many genuine anti-Nazis among the German people. Fox's decision to bypass Germany was further rationalized by the poor box office showing of *PRINCE OF FOXES* (1949), which, like *The Black Rose,* had co-starred Powers and Welles. Produced in England and North Africa by Louis D. Lighten, *The Black Rose* also featured Cecile Aubry, Jack Hawkins, Michael Rennie, Finlay Currie, Henry Oscar, and Herbert Lom.

—C.B.

Blessed and the Damned, The (play, 1950)

In 1950, WELLES, mired in the financial morass surrounding the cash-strapped production of his film adaptation of *OTHELLO,* was searching for quick and easy means of generating money. One of the strangest of these artistic cum fund-raising ventures was a hastily assembled evening of theater called *The Blessed and the Damned* (and, later, for the German tour of the show, *AN EVENING WITH ORSON WELLES*). Reuniting with his old friends from Dublin's GATE THEATRE, MICHEÁL MACLIAMMÓIR and HILTON EDWARDS, Welles's plan was to offer two one-act plays. The first of these, *THE UNTHINKING LOBSTER,* was an original comedy by Welles poking fun at Hollywood producers, a target the director knew intimately from his own tempestuous and frustrating relationships with the industry's leading moguls. The second one-acter was *TIME RUNS,* a loose reworking of the legend of Dr. Faustus laced with quotations from Christopher Marlowe, Milton, and Dante, but,

significantly, not Goethe, a reflection of Welles's antipathy toward Germany and its recent Nazi past.

The big problem with the production concerned language. The plays were delivered in English, but the audiences were French (with *An Evening with Orson Welles,* the audiences were German). The language barrier also proved difficult in terms of Welles's working with his French and German stagehands. These conditions were further complicated by Welles's punishing post-performance forays into Paris's exotic night life, a debilitating if effusive pastime that soon took its toll on Welles's ability to maintain rehearsal and performance regimens. Still, the show carried on at the Théâtre Edouard VII in Paris from June 19 to August 4, 1950, to mostly appreciative if somewhat baffled theatergoers whose ability to decode the fast-flying English dialogue was more than a bit daunting.

At the conclusion of its six-week run in Paris, *The Blessed and the Damned* was retitled *An Evening with Orson Welles.* With its new name, the show was revised for the German tour, with a truncated version of OSCAR WILDE's *THE IMPORTANCE OF BEING EARNEST* taking the place of *The Unthinking Lobster.* To spice up the evening, Welles added a grab bag of magic tricks. He also featured EARTHA KITT, his latest discovery and love interest, singing sultry versions of DUKE ELLINGTON ballads. In Germany, Welles and company visited Frankfurt, Munich, Cologne, Dusseldorf, and Berlin. Although artistically and economically disappointing, the ragtag production of *The Blessed and the Damned* (and *An Evening with Orson Welles*) provided Welles an opportunity to freely experiment and improvise.

—C.B.

Blitzstein, Marc (1905–1964)

An American composer with strong leftist leanings, Marcus Samuel Blitzstein was born in Philadelphia on March 2, 1905. In his 20s, Blitzstein traveled to Europe to study with composers Nadia Boulanger and Arnold Schoenberg. He was influenced by the music of Kurt Weill early on and came to believe that music should have social relevance.

ORSON WELLES clearly appreciated Blitzstein's talents and encouraged him to write the musical score for the Orson Welles stage production of SHAKE-SPEARE's *JULIUS CAESAR.* SIMON CALLOW describes Blitzstein's score as "a series of grinding processional interludes scored for a band consisting of trumpet, horn, percussion, and Hammond organ," all of which contributed to the fascist implications of the Welles production by freely quoting Mussolini's anthem, the "Giovinezza." He also wrote the score for Welles's stage production of George Büchner's experimental play, *DANTON'S DEATH.* Working independently of Welles, Blitzstein composed a Piano Sonata, a Piano Concerto, and two operas—*The Condemned* (concerning the Sacco and Vanzetti case) and *The Harpies.*

Blitzstein is probably best remembered, however, both for his 1937 left-wing musical drama, THE CRA-DLE WILL ROCK, produced by Orson Welles, and his English-language adaptation of the Kurt Weill-BERTOLT BRECHT reworking of John Gay's *The Beggar's Opera, The Threepenny Opera* (1952), which had a long and successful run in Manhattan as an Off-Broadway production. At the suggestion of Brecht, Blitzstein expanded a song, "Nickel under Foot," into what Simon Callow describes as "a full-length piece about the varieties of prostitution." The result was *The Cradle Will Rock,* which was originally commissioned by the FEDERAL THEATRE PROJECT of the Works Progress Administration, one of a number of funding agencies established by the Roosevelt administration to support the arts during the Great Depression. Dedicated to Brecht, this "play" is actually a politically radical, pro-labor opera in 10 scenes, set in a mythic locale called Steeltown, U.S.A., during a labor strike. Although the FEDERAL THEATRE PROJECT was highly receptive to plays with themes that were left of the political center, *Cradle's* "agit-prop" message proved too controversial for Washington's political sensitivities. The play, scheduled to open on June 16th at the Maxine Elliott Theater, was cancelled and the theater closed on its opening night by an order from the WPA. Welles, who doubled as actor and producer of *Cradle,* neatly circumvented this unprecedented government censorship by renting the Venice Theater, 21 blocks away, and asking the opening night audience to leave the padlocked Elliott and walk to the new location to see the performance, presented without sets or costumes.

For the premiere performance, Blitzstein sat onstage at an upright piano, playing the score, singing the musical *recitative,* and delivering stage directions and background description. The cast, prevented by union regulations from appearing onstage, stood on cue and delivered their songs and spoken lines from their seats. The show continued its run at the Venice through July 1, 1937. Blitzstein's "play with music" was adapted to cinema, finally, in 1999, by Tim Robbins, who also included the political machinations involved behind the scenes and the sociopolitical context of the 1930s.

When called before the House Un-American Activities Committee in 1958, Blitzstein admitted his former membership in the Communist Party but refused to name names. Thereafter, he became semi-reclusive in New York but was well off financially because of the *Threepenny* royalties, especially his popular ballad "Mack the Knife," which was recorded by LOUIS ARMSTRONG, Bobby Darin, Ella Fitzgerald, and others. He came to a bad end in 1964, when he was beaten to death by three sailors in a back alley in Martinique.

Reference Gordon, Eric A. *Mark the Music: The Life and Work of Marc Blitzstein* (New York: St. Martin's Press, 1989).

—R.C.K. and J.M.W.

Bogdanovich, Peter (1939–) American critic, journalist, writer, and director who became a staunch defender of ORSON WELLES in the aftermath of the controversy PAULINE KAEL instigated in her essay "Raising Kane" over the appropriate credits for the authorship of *CITIZEN KANE,* asserting that much of the credit properly belonged to HERMAN MANKIEWICZ. Born in Kingston, New York, on July 30, 1939, the son of still-life and landscape painter Boris Bogdanovich, young Peter Bogdanovich studied acting at Stella Adler's Theatre Studio and made his stage debut at the American Shakespeare Festival. In 1959, he directed and starred in an Off-Broadway stage production of the Clifford Odets play *The Big Knife,* before turning to film criticism, and, finally, film directing. As a freelance critic he wrote for *Esquire,* the *New York Times,* the *Village Voice, The Saturday Evening Post,* and *Cahiers du Cinéma,* then went on to build a reputation by writing books on some of the greatest film directors: John Ford, Howard Hawks, Alfred Hitchcock, Fritz Lang, and Alan Dwan, the "Last Pioneer," as Bogdanovich called him. He was the author of *The Cinema of Orson Welles,* published by the Museum of Modern Art in 1961.

By 1962 he began easing his way into filmmaking, eventually working as second unit director for Roger Corman on *The Wild Angels* (1966). To his credit, Bogdanovich was able to make the creative transition, though John Baxter has noted, acidly, "Of all trades ancillary to the cinema, few offer worse preparation for a directing career than criticism," an odd assertion if one thinks of Lindsay Anderson, Tony Richardson, FRANÇOIS TRUFFAUT, and Jean-Luc Godard, in the shadow of whom Bogdanovich was attempting to reinvent himself. In 1967, he directed

The Great Professional—Howard Hawks for BBC television, then worked for the following three years on another documentary, *Directed by John Ford* (1971). Meanwhile, however, he directed his first feature film for Roger Corman, *Targets* (1968), a competently made B-movie about an ailing star-actor (Boris Karloff), a young director (Bogdanovich), and a psychotic sniper haunting a drive-in movie theater.

In the early 1970s, Bogdanovich went into partnership with FRANCIS FORD COPPOLA and William Friedkin to form The Directors Company, an independent unit at Paramount, which produced his breakthrough picture, *The Last Picture Show* (1971), nicely adapted from the novel by Larry McMurtry, and starring Timothy Bottoms, Jeff Bridges, Cybill Shepherd, Cloris Leachman, Ellen Burstyn, and John Ford regular Ben Johnson in the film's strongest performance as Sam the Lion. Legend has it that Bog-

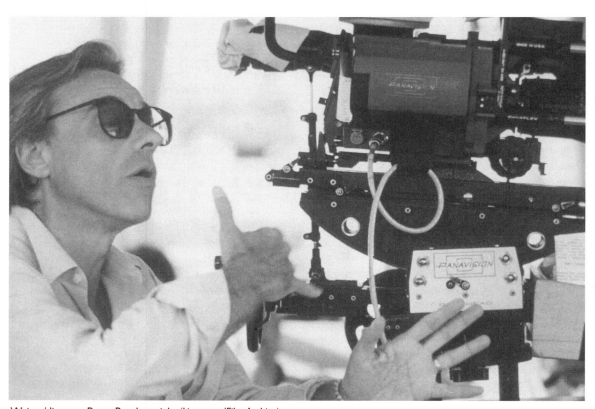

Writer/director Peter Bogdanovich *(Literature/Film Archive)*

danovich's wife, Polly Platt, first introduced him to the novel, which appealed to him because of the misleading title (he thought it was about movies), and scouted the Texas locations that made the story work. Ben Johnson and Cloris Leachman won Academy Awards for best supporting actor and actress, and, suddenly, Bogdanovich was golden.

Polly Platt continued to work with Bogdanovich on his next feature, *Paper Moon* (1973), starring Ryan O'Neal as a depression-era con artist and O'Neal's daughter Tatum as his sidekick, drifting through Kansas. The film won Oscar nominations for best adapted screenplay (Alvin Sargent) and best supporting actress (for both Madeline Kahn and Tatum O'Neal, who won the Academy Award). By that time, however, Bogdanovich was romancing Cybill Shepherd, determined to make her into a star, and divorced Polly Platt, whose talents had helped to define his initial success. He achieved some further attention by reinventing screwball comedy for Barbara Streisand in *What's Up Doc?* (1972). He starred Cybill Shepherd in the Henry James adaptation, *Daisy Miller* (1974), after which his directing career went into a definite decline. He wrote and directed *At Long Last Love* (1975), *Nickelodeon* (1976), *Saint Jack* (1979), and *They All Laughed* (1981). A far better picture was *Mask* (1985), starring Eric Stoltz as Rocky Dennis, a teenage boy suffering from a rare, disfiguring disease, craniodiaphyseal dysplasia, that causes abnormal calcium deposits on the skull, and Cher as his gutsy mother who refuses to give up hope. This unconventional film, based upon a true story, was well received critically.

Bogdanovich continued to pursue his interest in Hollywood and in other established directors beyond Welles. His book *Who the Devil Made It* (Knopf, 1997) features interviews with Hitchcock, Hawks, Lumet, Lang, Preminger, and other auteur talents. In June 2002, he co-hosted the CBS television special celebrating the American Film Institute, "AFI's 100 Years . . . 100 Passions." Bogdanovich also staged a directorial comeback in 2001 with *The Cat's Meow,* a film that revisits a notorious Hollywood scandal from the 1920s, featuring Edward Herrmann as William Randolph Hearst, Kirsten Dunst as Marion Davies, Eddie Izzard as Charlie Chaplin, and Cary Elwes as

the silent movie producer Thomas Ince, who died after a weekend excursion on the Hearst yacht. In a *Variety* review of August 13, 2001, Derek Elley described the film as a "semi-comedic speculation" about Ince's death and speculated that the movie would probably have done better at the box office 30 years ago, but now, with younger audiences barely aware of Hearst or even Chaplin, it would appeal mainly to an older audience of "mature film buffs curious to check out what Bogdanovich is up to after a half-decade spent in the telemovie wilderness."

Bogdanovich nurtured his friendship with Welles after reinventing himself in the shadow of the master. In 1973, he provided the voice-over for F FOR FAKE. He also stood by to help with the ill-fated THE OTHER SIDE OF THE WIND, part of which was filmed in Bogdanovich's Bel Air home, but which ended up being confiscated in Iran after the Ayatollah Khomeini turned Iran into a theocratic dictatorship. The final straw was a dispute over the release of the book *This Is Orson Welles,* which Welles refused to authorize at the last minute. Bogdanovich sent all of the material (which had been stored for years in different places) to Welles, who then turned it over to OJA KODAR, who was supposed to see that it was published. Kadar approached Bogdanovich about helping her to organize the material, but Bogdanovich, who was having his own financial and emotional problems at the time, referred her to JONATHAN ROSENBAUM, who shaped the material and saw the book through publication long after Welles's death. Edited by Rosenbaum, *This Is Orson Welles* was published by HarperCollins in 1992. Partly because the book published the lost section of THE MAGNIFICENT AMBERSONS, partly because of its portrait of "an artist whose colossal creative power was offset by disarming insecurities," Michael Church in his *TLS* review (May 7, 1993) called the book "a work of major film-historical importance." The manuscript was lost for five years, then found by Oja Kodar after Welles died, and after he had rewritten it. Rosenbaum took a "mountain of transcripts" and somehow managed to organize the book. Its publication history was as curious as the oversized talent that was its topic.

References Abramowitz, Rachel. *Is That a Gun in Your Pocket?* (New York: Random House, 2000);

Bogdanovich, Peter. *Who the Devil Made It* (New York: Alfred A. Knopf, 1997).

—J.M.W.

Bourbon, Diana (1900–1978) Program coordinator for THE CAMPBELL PLAYHOUSE, a 1938–40 radio drama series presided over by WELLES.

Riding the publicity set in motion by the October 30, 1938, broadcast of THE WAR OF THE WORLDS, Welles was the talk of the nation. So, too, the MERCURY THEATRE ON THE AIR, which had been a "sustaining" or nonsponsored series supported and aired by CBS. The Campbell Soup Company, believing that Welles and his Mercury troupe could help sell more soup, offered to sponsor the program. On December 9, 1938, the *Mercury Theatre on the Air* officially became *The Campbell Playhouse*. Now Welles and executive producer JOHN HOUSEMAN would have to work closely with the Ward Wheelock Advertising Agency, Campbell's representative. In the 1930s and 1940s, in contrast to contemporary broadcasting, advertising agencies, rather than the networks or independent producers, produced the programs. In the new arrangement, adman Ward Wheelock and his assistant, Diana Bourbon, became integral parts of *The Campbell Playhouse*'s production process. It was Bourbon, installed in the position as "program coordinator," who was most important due to her close daily contact with the production of each weekly show.

Functioning like a network censor, Bourbon had to approve all scripts prior to rehearsal and broadcast. She served as the program's de facto financial officer in that any expenditure for star talent beyond each program's normal budget had to be "green-lighted" by her. Bourbon also had the tricky task of critiquing each program. Finally, as Campbell's in-studio representative, Bourbon had to keep Welles and Houseman thinking about ratings, and therefore what might most effectively appeal to the national network audience. All of these responsibilities put her in direct conflict with Welles and Houseman. Welles, in particular, had difficulty dealing with the constraints that it was her responsibility to implement and enforce.

As Welles's schedule became increasingly harried with his new responsibilities for RKO, he was forced to commute each week by air between Hollywood and New York, where *The Campbell Playhouse* originated. Finally, after Welles's repeated entreaties, Campbell and CBS agreed to transfer the show to Hollywood. Making the move west with Welles were actors AGNES MOOREHEAD, JOSEPH COTTEN, RAY COLLINS, EVERETT SLOAN, GEORGE COULOURIS, and composer BERNARD HERRMANN. Bourbon made the move as well. Her job of keeping the increasingly overcommitted and distracted Welles focused on the sponsor's needs became even more problematic. Tensions with Bourbon continued to escalate. Her weekly critiques grew more pointed. They also fought over casting. For one show, Bourbon wanted Welles to hire Irene Dunne, but he refused, dismissing the popular actress as a second-class talent. Eventually, he was forced to capitulate, and Dunne was hired. The prebroadcast, blue-penciling of scripts continued as well. It was clear that *The Campbell Playhouse*'s days were numbered. Finally, in March 1940, Welles had had enough: "I'm sick of having the heart torn out of a script by radio censorship," he explained.

Still, as SIMON CALLOW points out, Bourbon was one of the few people who treated Welles as an equal. Indeed, she had earned his grudging respect. Wanting to end the series on a positive note, in part because of that respect for Bourbon, Welles suggested a reprise of JANE EYRE. Rochester was a role that Welles felt he owned. For the title character, Welles suggested VIVIEN LEIGH, who had just attained worldwide fame as Scarlett O'Hara in *Gone With the Wind* (1939). Bourbon and the sponsor agreed. *Jane Eyre* was a fitting coda.

In retrospect, the 61 episodes of *The Campbell Playhouse* constitute a watershed for radio drama and for Welles, whose sense of dramatic storytelling was both refined and broadened by the experience. In her own way, the bright and incisive Bourbon helped contribute to that legacy.

Bourbon also enjoyed a brief career as a screenwriter. Her credits include *Atlantic Adventure* (1935), *Roaming Lady* (1936), and *Born That Way* (1937).

—C.B.

Bowles, Paul (1910–1999) Composer, novelist, and hip guru to the Beat Generation, Paul Bowles was born on December 30, 1910, on Long Island, the son of a dentist. He decided to become a composer because, as he recalled, "When I was a child, I preferred my own music to other people's." ORSON WELLES became interested in Bowles because of the director's desire to adapt *The Italian Straw Hat,* a popular comedy written by Eugéne Marin Labiche in 1851, into the stage production HORSE EATS HAT. Playwright Edwin Denby would write the script and Paul Bowles would compose the music, which would then be arranged by VIRGIL THOMSON. DAVID THOMSON describes the working relationship between Bowles and Thomson: "Bowles was the composer but he needed Thomson to assist with the orchestration. And there was so much music—not just the pit orchestra but pianos that played automatically and musicians in one of the boxes closest to the stage." In DOCTOR FAUSTUS, Welles's next play, he had Bowles compose the score, which consisted of woodwinds. According to FRANK BRADY, Bowles created "an eerie, dissonant music, also reminiscent of radio drama . . . and played by an unseen orchestra." The following year when Welles was working on *The Second Hurricane,* an opera for schoolchildren, Bowles was again involved, this time playing AARON COPLAND's music on the piano when Welles was putting the opera on for potential financial backers. In 1938, Welles had Bowles write a score for a small orchestra for the film segment of TOO MUCH JOHNSON, but Bowles's work was eliminated to economize, and MARC BLITZSTEIN played a piano accompaniment instead.

Aaron Copland, later famous for *Appalachian Spring* and *Billy the Kid,* was the mentor of Paul Bowles, who taught him the technique of composition, then traveled with Bowles to Europe in 1931. During a holiday in Tangier with Copland, Bowles completed *Sonata for Oboe and Clarinet,* his first major musical work. Bowles supported himself until the end of World War II by composing ballets, film scores, and incidental music for Broadway plays for GEORGE BALANCHINE, Salvador Dali, ELIA KAZAN, as well as Orson Welles.

Bowles had also dabbled in painting and had published surrealist poems in the Parisian review *Transition.* Gertrude Stein discouraged him from writing poetry, but Bowles later demonstrated that he had a larger talent for writing when he published *The Sheltering Sky* in 1949, a challenging and eccentric, partly autobiographical *roman à clef,* now regarded as a masterpiece, set in Algeria on the Sahara, which Bowles had first explored as early as 1931. In 1938, he married the lesbian novelist Jane Auer, who became the model for Kit Moresby, the central character of his first novel. The marriage lasted until her death in 1973. Described as the "last existentialist" and the "poet of existentialism," Bowles translated Sartre's play *Huis-Clos,* now better known in English as *No Exit,* thanks to Bowles. Bowles chose to live most of the last 50 years of his life in Tangier, where he was often visited by disciples and other writers, such as Tennessee Williams, Truman Capote, William Burroughs, and Allen Ginsberg. Bowles appeared as himself, serving as the bemused "narrator" for the film adaptation of *The Sheltering Sky* directed by Bernardo Bertolucci in 1990. In 1972, Bowles published his autobiography, *Without Stopping.* Before his death at the age of 88 Bowles made his final film appearance in the documentary portrait directed by Jennifer Baichwal, *Let It Come Down: The Life of Paul Bowles* (1999).

References Caponi, Gena Dagel. *Paul Bowles: Romantic Savage* (Carbondale: Southern Illinois University, 1994); Dillon, Millicent. *You Are Not I: A Portrait of Paul Bowles* (Berkeley: University of California, 1998); Green, Michele. *The Dream at the End of the World: Paul Bowles and the Literary Renegades in Tangier* (New York: Harper, 1992); Patteson, Richard F. *A World Outside* (Austin: University of Texas Press, 1987); Sawyer-Laucanno, Christopher. *An Invisible Spectator: A Biography of Paul Bowles* (New York: Ecco Press, 1990).

—J.M.W.

Brady, Frank (1934–) At the time Frank Brady's *Citizen Welles: A Biography of Orson Welles,* an academic biography of the director, was published by Scribner's in April 1989, the author was teaching cinema at St. John's University in New York. Getting it published was an ordeal for Brady, as detailed by Marie S. Marich in *Variety* (June 7–13, 1989), entitled "Brady's Orson Welles bio. in print after 16-year delay." Brady's biography was started before the biographies written by BARBARA LEAMING and CHARLES HIGHAM were completed and was to have been published by Prentice Hall. When Prentice Hall was purchased by Simon & Schuster, the Brady manuscript was dropped because by then other WELLES biographies had been announced. Stein & Day then agreed to publish the book, but went into bankruptcy, and the manuscript, "listed as an asset," according to *Variety,* "was frozen under bankruptcy laws," and Brady had to resort to litigation in order to win back his manuscript. Since the book's publication had been delayed by over a decade, Brady updated, revised, and included an epilogue, which attempts to come to terms with Welles's critical reputation after the director's passing.

In writing the book, Brady had the cooperation of Welles's daughters and also managed to meet with Welles "several times" before the director's death in 1985. "Although film has been the insignia of Welles's contemporary achievement," Brady wrote, "it was in the legitimate theatre that he wielded his greatest influence." It was "as a result of his experience with the theatre" that Welles "brought new life to film," which finally "became and remained his muse." Brady's book was the most "academic" of the first biographies published, one disadvantage being that it sometimes tended to get bogged down in its richness of detail. The scholarly apparatus includes a selected list of stage plays, radio dramas, and films directed by Welles, along with the credits for the films. It also details the roles played by Welles and provides a very helpful bibliography. The title *Citizen Welles* was suggested by the French director JEAN RENOIR, who once said: "Orson Welles is an animal made for the screen and the stage. When he steps before a camera, it is as if the rest of the world ceases to exist. He is a citizen of the screen." Brady's goal was "to capture the man in all his professions."

—J.M.W. and T.L.E.

Brecht, Bertolt (1898–1956) Experimental
German playwright Bertolt Brecht was the author of the play *The Life of Galileo.* Brecht and CHARLES LAUGHTON, who was to play the title role of the scientist, had worked on a production and were interested in having WELLES direct the play, supposing that

MICHAEL TODD would produce it. When Todd withdrew his financing for AROUND THE WORLD IN 80 DAYS, a stage play which Welles was also to direct, Todd and Welles parted company. *Around the World in 80 Days* was finally produced without Todd's financial backing, but the *Galileo* project was never completed by Welles. It was produced by JOHN HOUSEMAN, however, in Hollywood, on June 30, 1947. It opened in New York in December of 1947 to audience acclaim, but by then Brecht had been summoned by the House Un-American Activities Committee and left the country and returned to Germany, because, Orson Welles later claimed, "he believed himself [to be] a perfect Marxist," though, in fact, Welles considered Brecht "more of an anarchist." JOSEPH LOSEY directed the stage production for John Houseman.

Brecht also had encouraged MARC BLITZSTEIN to expand his song "Nickel Under Foot" into a full-length piece about the varieties of prostitution. A grateful Blitzstein dedicated THE CRADLE WILL ROCK "to Bert Brecht: First because I think him the most admirable theatre writer of our time; secondly because an extended conversation with him was partly responsible for writing the piece."

Born in Augsburg, Germany, on February 10, 1898, Brecht is perhaps best known for *Dreigroschenoper* (*The Threepenny Opera,* 1931) and became the most influential German playwright of the 20th century. Like many European artists, he immigrated to America with the coming of the Third Reich and Hitler's rise to power and, like Fritz Lang and Jean Renoir, found work in Hollywood. He collaborated with Fritz Lang on the screenplay of *Hangmen Also Die* (1943), set in Nazi-occupied Czechoslovakia, and strongly critical of German oppression. Having faced political repression in Germany, he found himself, as a committed Marxist, also hounded in cold war America. He finally settled in communist East Germany.

Reference Willett, John. *The Theatre of Bertold Brecht: A Study from Eight Aspects* (New York: New Directions, 1975).

—J.M.W. and T.L.E.

Brook, Peter (1925–) British film and theater director who directed WELLES in a 1953 televi-

sion production of KING LEAR, Welles's American television debut.

Peter Brook first proposed working with Welles on an avant-garde production of SALOME to be costumed by Salvador Dali; Brook sought Welles for the role of Herod. Welles immediately accepted the offer, but never followed through. When they met months later, a determined Brook proposed another project. It, too, evaporated because of Welles's unreliability. Undaunted, Brook invited Welles to join him in the United States for a 1953 television production of *King Lear* for *Omnibus,* the prestigious weekly arts program sponsored by the Ford Foundation's Television-Radio Workshop and broadcast by CBS. Welles leaped at the opportunity.

King Lear, after all, was one of Welles's favorite Shakespeare plays. Welles had also recently proclaimed that in contrast to film, television was an actor's medium rather than a director's medium. He was excited about making his American acting debut in the new medium. For Welles, it was also a means of reducing a debt owed to the IRS, which had refused to allow him to take a business loss from his substantial investment in the disastrous production of AROUND THE WORLD IN 80 DAYS (1946). VIRGIL THOMSON, who scored the Brook production, recalled: "It was arranged that Welles could come in [to New York], work, live in a good hotel [the Plaza], but he could spend no money beyond his actual expenses. He didn't have money to buy cigarettes or anything like that, so he would borrow from friends and pay them back in France." Welles was also pleased that Brook had hired MICHEÁL MACLIAMMÓIR, his old friend from Dublin's GATE THEATRE, for the role of Edgar.

Welles, fresh from scouting locations for MR. ARKADIN in Europe, arrived at the first rehearsal on time, announcing to Brook: "Let's eat, and I'll tell you how I think Lear should be played!" In spite of whatever trepidations Brook might have had about his star showing up in New York on time, the rehearsals and live telecast went smoothly. Of his relationship with Brook, Welles told *The New Yorker:* "It's been terribly exciting working with Peter Brook. I think he's the best Shakespearean director." The 73-minute *King Lear,* which aired on October 18, 1953, was a huge success, earning Welles his best American reviews in years. *Cue* magazine trumpeted: "Like a confidently patient boxer who lets his opponent flail away for eight or nine rounds and then calmly steps in to finish the fight with one blow, Orson Welles burst into television (after several years of watchful waiting) and knocked everything for a loop. The performance he gave as King Lear established a new high for the medium in terms of power, heart and sheer artistry." Although many hoped that Welles would stay in New York and participate in television's rapidly unfolding evolution, the actor, anxious to reassume his mantle as film director, returned to Europe to start shooting *Mr. Arkadin.*

Brook, while still at Oxford University in 1943, made his first film, a student project called *Sentimental Journey.* That same year he went to London to direct his first professional play, *Dr. Faustus.* Rapidly ascending to the top of the British theater scene, Brook took on directing assignments of an often experimental nature in Paris, Moscow, and New York, as well as in London. He also directed a number of edgy British films, including the financially and critical successful *Lord of the Flies* (1963) and *The Persecution and Assassination of Jean-Paul Marat as Performed by the Inmates of the Asylum of Charenton Under the Direction of the Marquis de Sade* (1967). In 1970, Brook founded the experimental International Center of Theater Research in Paris. In 1974, as the Centre for International Creation, the laboratory's experimental improvisational workshops became the prime source of Brook's theatrical productions.

Brook's feature films include *The Beggar's Opera* (1953), *Moderato Cantabile* (1963), *Tell Me Lies* (1968), *King Lear* (1971), *Meetings with Remarkable Men* (1979), *The Tragedy of Carmen* (1983), *Swann in Love* (1984), and *The Hahabharata* (1990).

References Brook, Peter. *Between Two Silences: Talking with Peter Brook,* ed. Dale Moffitt. (Dallas, Tex.: Southern Methodist University, 1999); Hunt, Albert. *Peter Brook* (New York: Cambridge University Press, 1995).

—C.B.

Bugs Bunny Superstar Warner Bros., 94 minutes, 1975. **Director:** Larry Jackson; **Producer:** Richard Waltzner; **Cinematographer:** Gary Craver; **Music:** Carl

W. Stalling and Ian Whitcomb; **Editor:** Brian King; **Cast:** Robert Clampett (Himself), Tex Avery (Himself), Friz Freleng (Himself), Chuck Jones (Himself), Mel Blanc (Himself), Arthur Q. Bryan (Himself), Orson Welles (Narrator)

In the wake of the huge success of *That's Entertainment!,* the 1974 retrospective of spectacular production numbers from classic MGM musicals, Hollywood's other major studios looked to their vaults in efforts to replicate MGM's stunning triumph. Warner Bros. turned to its heralded Looney Tunes catalog. The happy result was *Bugs Bunny Superstar,* directed by Larry Jackson. Included in the documentary compilation are nine complete classic cartoons, among them "I Taw a Putty Tat," "Rhapsody Rabbit," "My Favorite Duck," and "A Wild Hare"; home-movie footage of animation greats Robert Clampett, Text Avery, Friz Freleng, and Chuck Jones cavorting; and a history of "Termite Terrace," the little shack on the Warner Bros. lot that in the 1930s and 1940s housed the animation unit that birthed Bugs and pals Porky Pig, Daffy Duck, and Elmer Fudd. Cementing the elements of the documentary pastiche together is WELLES's properly orotund narration. Among the raves is a summary quip from *The Internet Movie Guide: "Bugs Bunny Superstar* is a treat for children and adults alike—particularly in its narration, which is by none other than Orson Welles."

Original music was created by venerable cartoon composers Carl W. Stalling and Ian Whitcomb. The cinematography was handled by Gary Graver, who also shot Welles's F FOR FAKE (1973) and THE OTHER SIDE OF THE WIND (1970–1976).

—C.B.

Butterfly   Par-Par Films/Analysis, 108 minutes, 1981. **Director:** Matt Cimber; **Producer:** Cimber; **Screenplay:** Cimber and John Goff (based on *The Butterfly* by James M. Cain); **Cinematographer:** Eddy Van Der Enden; **Music:** Ennio Morricone; **Editor:** B.A. Schoenfield and Stan Siegel; **Cast:** Stacy Keach (Jess Tyler), Pia Zadora (Kady); Orson Welles (Judge Rauch), Lois Nettleton (Belle Morgan), Edward Albert (Wash Gillespie), Stuart Whitman (Rev. Ravers), Ed McMahon (Mr. Gillespie), June Lockhart (Mrs. Gillespie), and James Franciscus (Moke Blue)

A 17-year-old sexpot reappears in her father's life and commits incest with him, thus setting off a grotesque series of plot developments. *Halliwell's Film and Video Guide* wrote: "Risible concatenation of murders, repentances, illegitimate sex and various kinds of lust, all revolving around butterfly marks and set in 1937 backwoods Arizona. *Tobacco Road* it ain't, though." FRANK BRADY, a bit more diplomatic, describes *Butterfly* as "a slight effort." Brady adds that "Orson, white-haired and bearded and with steel-rimmed glasses, credibly plays a judge and is the only actor who distinguishes himself in this forgettable movie." Although Welles tried to help promote the film by giving interviews, he mainly hoped that the Pia Zadora vanity project would just go away. It did.

—C.B.

Callow, Simon (1949–) British actor, director, and writer Simon Callow was well prepared to survey the career of a great American actor and director in his book *Orson Welles: The Road to Xanadu* (London: Jonathan Cape, 1995; New York; Viking, 1996). Callow was born in London on June 15, 1949, educated at Cambridge University and the University of Belfast in Northern Ireland, then trained at the London Drama Centre. On the London stage Callow created the role of Mozart in Peter Shaffer's *Amadeus* and later performed in a minor role in Milos Forman's film adaptation in 1984. Subsequent film roles included *A Room with a View* (1985), *Maurice* (1987), *Howards End* (1992), *Four Weddings and a Funeral* (1994), and *Jefferson in Paris* (1995). His film debut as director was *The Ballad of the Sad Café* (1991). Before writing his WELLES biography, Callow had written several books on the craft of acting— *Being an Actor, A Difficult Actor,* and *Shooting the Actor.*

The London *Evening Standard* called Callow's book on Welles a "monumental two-part work," and *Kirkus Reviews* compared Callow's achievement to that of FRANÇOIS TRUFFAUT's excellent interview book on Alfred Hitchcock. To capture a sense of the difficulty of researching his book, Callow begins by quoting what Welles said to Jean Clay in 1962: "If you try to probe, I'll lie to you. Seventy-five percent of what I say in interviews is false." Welles thought the "best service anyone could render to art" would

be to "Destroy all biographies. Only art can explain the life of a man—and not the contrary." Callow warns that "A question mark hovers over practically every aspect of Welle's life and work," all the "more surprising since he is among the most fully documented artists of the twentieth century." Although Callow can claim to have unearthed "missing details," he explains that his main task was "as much to re-evaluate the known facts as to establish new ones." His book takes a middle-of-the-road approach, avoiding the hero worship of BARBARA LEAMING and PETER BOGDANOVICH as well as the iconoclastic treatment of CHARLES HIGHAM and the academic debunking of the Welles legend by FRANK BRADY.

—J.M.W. and T.L.E.

Campbell Playhouse, The (radio, 1938–1940) Riding the wave of publicity set in motion by the tumultuous October 30, 1938, broadcast of THE WAR OF THE WORLDS, WELLES was the talk of the nation. So, too, the MERCURY THEATRE ON THE AIR, which had been a "sustaining" or nonsponsored series supported and aired by CBS. The Campbell Soup Company, believing that Welles and his Mercury troupe could help sell more soup, offered to sponsor the program. On December 9, 1938, the *Mercury Theatre on the Air* officially became *The Campbell Playhouse.* Now, Welles and executive producer JOHN

HOUSEMAN would work most closely with the Ward Wheelock Advertising Agency, Campbell's representative. It should be remembered that in the 1930s and 1940s, in contrast to contemporary broadcasting, it was the advertising agencies, rather than the networks, that actually produced the programs. In the new setup, adman Ward Wheelock and his assistant, DIANA BOURBON, would become integral parts of the production process.

For its debut broadcast, Welles had HOWARD KOCH adapt the Daphne du Maurier best-selling novel, *Rebecca*. With guest star MARGARET SULLAVAN in the title role, and such Mercury regulars as AGNES MOOREHEAD, JOSEPH COTTEN, EVERETT SLOANE, RAY COLLINS, and GEORGE COULOURIS on hand, the 60-minute broadcast was a smash. Listeners, critics, and, most significantly, the sponsor, were pleased. At the drama's conclusion, and before going off the air, Welles and Sullavan stepping out of character bantered flirtatiously. Then a transatlantic phone conversation with Daphne du Maurier, who had been listening in England via shortwave, ensued. With typical British aplomb, du Maurier said: "Good evening, Mr. Welles. It's nearly three o'clock here in London. It's not often that an author has the chance to hear the voices of her own characters speaking to her from across the Atlantic Ocean. I've enjoyed it enormously." Sullavan asked du Maurier two questions about the story: "Is there really a Manderley and what is Mrs. de Winter's first name?" Like any good storyteller, du Maurier provided circuitous responses that preserved the plot's mysteries. That first show also introduced the phrase, "obediently yours," which became a Welles trademark. In his role as host, Welles had brought up the curtain with the words: "So ladies and gentlemen, and Miss du Maurier, the 'Campbell Playhouse' is *obediently yours* [italics mine]."

As the series unfolded, thanks to a sponsor willing to spend for high-profile guests, Welles shared the Campbell microphone with such stars as LAURENCE OLIVIER, Lucille Ball, Noah Beery, Katharine Hepburn, Gertrude Berg, Ida Lupino, and HELEN HAYES. The series also helped catapult Welles to even greater heights of celebrity. In 1938, Welles was selected by a Scripps-Howard poll as the year's favorite broadcast personality and named "Outstanding New Radio Star of 1938."

Along with the recognition came new opportunities and responsibilities. In 1939, Welles signed with RKO, and soon began shuttling between New York, where *The Campbell Playhouse* originated, and Hollywood. Given that a one-way transcontinental flight in 1939 was a grueling 18-hour affair, Wheelock began complaining that Welles was spending too much time in the air and on the West Coast. Welles offered a solution—produce the show in Los Angeles. Wheelock failed to grasp the logic of Welles's commonsense proposal. For months, a flurry of demands, memos, and legal threats circulated among Welles's management, Wheelock, Campbell, and CBS. Diana Bourbon's prickly notes on each script and broadcast added fuel to the debate. Finally, Wheelock (plus Campbell and CBS) relented. *The Campbell Playhouse* moved to Hollywood in November 1939.

Welles arranged to have his best actors transferred to Los Angeles. Agnes Moorehead, Joseph Cotten, Ray Collins, Everett Sloane, and George Coulouris all made the move. So, too, did Diana Bourbon, Wheelock's associate, who had the increasingly difficult job of keeping the ever-harried Welles focused on the sponsor's needs for the show. In addition to battling with RKO's top brass over HEART OF DARKNESS, Welles was in the midst of a torrid affair with actress DOLORES DEL RIO, and the collapse of his first marriage. There were also financial problems. Quite simply, and in spite of his handsome income, Welles was living beyond his means. Tensions with Bourbon continued to escalate. Along with her weekly memos, they fought over Irene Dunne, a Bourbon favorite, whom Welles refused to hire. Finally, he was forced to capitulate. There was also more prebroadcast, blue-penciling of scripts. It was clear that *The Campbell Playhouse*'s days were numbered. Even if by some miracle Campbell had been willing to renew the contract on its expiration date of March 1940, Welles had had enough: "I'm sick of having the heart torn out of a script by radio censorship," he explained. Producing hour-long radio dramas was no small task.

Wanting to end the series on a positive note, Welles suggested a reprise of *JANE EYRE* after several other ideas fell through. Edward Rochester was a role Welles felt he owned. For Jane, Welles suggested VIVIEN LEIGH, who had just attained worldwide fame as Scarlett O'Hara in *Gone With the Wind* (1939). Bourbon and the sponsor agreed. *Jane Eyre* was a fitting coda.

In retrospect, the 61 episodes of *The Campbell Playhouse* constitute a watershed for radio drama and for Welles, whose sense of dramatic storytelling was broadened by the experience.

—C.B.

Cantril, Albert Hadley (1907–1969) American psychologist who wrote *The Invasion from Mars* (1940), a scholarly treatment of the psychological impact of the infamous Welles 1938 broadcast of THE WAR OF THE WORLDS.

In the wake of the controversy surrounding the 1938 broadcast of *The War of the Worlds* by the MERCURY THEATRE ON THE AIR, editorial writers and pundits seized upon the event as a springboard for discussions dealing with the role of the mass media and propaganda in a democratic society. Just as the story was starting to fade, Princeton University announced that it was undertaking a study of the psychology of panic and mass hysteria and linking that to the growing influence of radio. The government-funded study headed by Princeton psychologist Hadley Cantril sought to determine the general extent and nature of the public responses to the *The War of the Worlds* broadcast, and the social-psychological reasons explaining those different reactions among various individuals.

Cantril's study offered some fascinating conclusions. The lower the education of those listening to the broadcast, the more likely they were to believe that the show was real. Individuals from southern states were generally more frightened by the broadcast than those from New England. About 2 million people believed that the broadcast was a true and realistic description of an actual invasion from Mars. In 1940, Cantril's study was published as a book by Princeton University Press under the title *The Invasion from Mars*. In addition to Cantril's research, the book also included a script of the broadcast that referred to HOWARD KOCH as the script's author.

When Welles reviewed the book's galley proofs in preparation for writing a foreword, he became incensed to find Koch named as author. Welles's arrangement with Koch was that for a nominal writing fee of $75, Koch would receive copyright ownership of the scripts upon which he had worked. Welles, however, was adamant that while Koch should receive credit, so, too, should JOHN HOUSEMAN, PAUL STEWART, BERNARD HERRMANN, and engineer John Dietz. Welles was also insistent about his own contribution. "The idea of *The War of the Worlds* broadcast and the major portion of its execution was mine," Welles wrote to Cantril. "Howard Koch was very helpful in the second portion of the script and did some work on the first, most of which it was necessary to revise."

After a heated exchange of letters between Welles, Cantril, the publisher, and even Koch, the book was finally published with a reference on the title page referring to "the complete script of the famous Orson Welles Broadcast." However, as FRANK BRADY indicates, Koch was cited in several places, including a table of contents entry listing Koch as the script's author. Welles, to his credit, let the matter drop. But the incident pointed to the general difficulty of assigning authorship in essentially collaborative media such as radio and film. The contretemps also served as an omen to the much nastier and protracted battle over the screenplay credits for CITIZEN KANE.

Reference Hanson, Jarice, and David J. Maxcy. *Sources. Notable Selections in Mass Media* (Guilford, Conn.: Duskin Publishing Group, 1996).

—C.B.

Captured on Film: The True Story of Marion Davies Timeline Films, 65 minutes, 2001. **Director:** Hugh Munro Neely; **Writers:** Elaina B. Archer, Neely, and John J. Flynn; **Narrator:** Charlize Theron

This documentary intends to set the record straight about MARION DAVIES, an actress who was also for 30 years the mistress and companion of WILLIAM RANDOLPH HEARST and whose memory and reputation were, according to some sources, maligned by the way Susan Alexander Kane was presented in CITIZEN

KANE (1941). Born in Brooklyn on January 3, 1897, Marion Davies began as a showgirl and stereotypical "gold-digger," but she was not without talent and went on to become a noted comedienne, unlike the untalented Susan in WELLES's film; moreover, although Susan leaves Kane and XANADU in the film, Davies never left Hearst, even when his health began to fail and his fortune edged toward bankruptcy. According to Kevin Brownlow, these two myths were unfairly created by Orson Welles in Citizen Kane, as Welles himself admitted in later years.

This documentary traces her career, drawing upon the scholarship of Kevin Brownlow, Jeanine Basinger, Fred Lawrence Guiles, and Cari Beauchamp. By 1927, her skill as a comedienne became apparent in two films, *The Red Mill* and *Quality Street,* and by the time she made *The Patsy* for King Vidor in 1928, "she could be regarded as the first screwball comedienne," Kevin Brownlow claims, "long before CAROLE LOMBARD came along with the talkies." Although she did later develop a drinking problem (as does Susan Alexander Kane in Welles's film), Davies was well known for her kindness and generosity. In 1928, she established the Marion Davies Children's Clinic in California, for example, and when Ingrid Bergman became the object of scandal because of her affair with Roberto Rossellini, Marion Davies defended Bergman as the rest of America was turning against her. As Tennessee Williams once said, according to the documentary, "Marion Davies makes up for the rest of Hollywood."

Welles later regretted that Marion Davies was assumed to be one and the same with Susan Alexander Kane, her allegorical double in *Citizen Kane.* "Marion was never one of Hearst's possessions," Welles remarks in an interview. "She was the precious treasure of his heart for more than thirty years. Love is not the subject of *Citizen Kane.*" William Randolph Hearst was with Davies the night he died, August 13, 1951, but she was not invited to the funeral in San Francisco. She survived Hearst by 10 years and died in 1961 of cancer at the age of 64. *Captured on Film: The True Story of Marion Davies* is available from Milestone Film & Video, P.O. Box 128, Harrington Park, N.J. 07640.

—J.M.W.

Carringer, Robert L. (1941–) Professor Robert Carringer of the Department of English and Cinema Studies at the University of Illinois at Urbana-Champaign wrote two books concerning the first two films of ORSON WELLES, both of them published by the University of California Press. *The Making of Citizen Kane* (1985) was based on extensive research in previously inaccessible studio archives and upon numerous interviews with original participants involved in the making of CITIZEN KANE, not least of which, Welles himself. The book was illustrated with original production documents, art department sketches, and production photographs. In his book *Movie Wars* (2000), JONATHAN ROSENBAUM notes that Carringer "thoroughly demolished [Pauline] Kael's claims about [Herman] Mankiewicz's exclusive authorship of the script." More generally, Carringer stressed the importance of the film as a collaborative effort, giving particular credit to the contributions of cinematographer GREGG TOLAND, writer HERMAN J. MANKIEWICZ, editorial supervisor JOHN HOUSEMAN, and art director Perry Ferguson, all of whom conspired to make "the greatest film ever made," a "towering force in the history of film and the standard by which all other films are to be judged."

Carringer's follow-up book was *The Magnificent Ambersons: A Reconstruction* (1993). Welles said in a BBC interview near the end of his life that the RKO studio executive "destroyed *Ambersons,*" and "the picture itself destroyed me." The studio edited 43 minutes out of the film, footage that was discarded and apparently lost. Carringer's research on *Ambersons,* which began with his final chapter in the *Kane* book, entitled "Collaboration and *Ambersons,*" also resulted in a videodisk album that, in the words of Nina Darnton of the *New York Times* (April 24, 1987) "attempts to indicate, as closely as possible, the film Welles had intended to make." Carringer rejects the legend that *Ambersons* was an absolute masterpiece, ruined by studio butchers, claiming instead that there were "real and serious problems with the original film," not only its "unrelenting bleak vision," but structural problems as well. "What was there is one of the most beautiful films ever to come out of Hollywood," but one with problems that only Welles himself could have addressed, but could not in fact address since he had chosen to travel to South America during the film's post-production Carringer established himself as the foremost authority on the production history of these two extraordinarily important films.

—J.M.W.

Carson, Johnny (1925–) Affable and popular stand-up comedian, born in Corning, Iowa, in 1925, who inherited *The Tonight Show* after successful runs by Steve Allen, who originated the late-show format for NBC television, and Jack Paar, who redefined the program with a temperamental twist that made the show both fascinating and unpredictable. After becoming the regular host, Carson perfected the comic monologue, which opened the program, followed by a talk-show format that brought in celebrity guests such as ORSON WELLES. Welles himself did a turn as guest host on July 5, 1971, then returned for multiple appearances during the mid-1970s when he was quite active on the talk-show circuit. Always at ease on camera, Welles became a frequent *Tonight Show* guest in 1976, appearing on January 26, March 3, March 25, April 9, May 7, July 16, September 23, October 27, December 2, and December 30, returning in 1977 on February 3 and April 13. Carson co-hosted the televised American Film Institute's "Life Award" ceremony for Orson Welles, the third recipient after James Cagney and director John Ford, in February of 1975. After his 30-year hosting stint for NBC, Carson retired from *The Tonight Show* on May 22, 1992.

References Carson, Johnny. *Happiness Is a Dry Martini* (Greenwich, Conn.: Fawcett, 1968); Leamer, Laurence. *King of the Night: The Life of Johnny Carson* (New York: Morrow, 1989); Smith, Ronald L. *Johnny Carson: An Unauthorized Biography* (New York: St Martin's Press, 1987).

—J.M.W.

Carter, Jack African-American actor Jack Carter played the title role in ORSON WELLES'S stage production of Shakespeare's *MACBETH* when it appeared in 1936 as part of the FEDERAL THEATRE PROJECT. Welles believed that Carter "was absolutely superb onstage." In the "voodoo" *Macbeth,* Carter was, according to CHARLES HIGHAM, a natural:

"Carter had the personality, the presence, the dynamic energy needed to play Macbeth; stripped to the waist, he looked like a Greek god cast in black marble; dressed in Napoleonic uniform, he was a surrogate Henri Christophe [King of Haiti]." Carter was a huge, violent, egotistical man with large appetites who also was a part-time gangster skilled with his fists and with a gun. Working with such an actor was extremely difficult, but Welles, himself a temperamental egotist, succeeded because, as Higham put it, he could "flatter him, cajole him, control him with seeming invisibility, making Carter's megalomaniac decisions always seem to be the actor's own." Carter and Welles became friends and often, after the performance ended, went off together drinking and carousing all night.

The play, which opened April 14, 1936, was well received, and Carter's performance was praised. After 10 weeks at the Lafayette Theatre, the play moved to the Adelphi on Broadway, at which point Carter began to deteriorate, possibly because of unfavorable reviews. BROOKS ATKINSON of the *New York Times* wrote, "He [Carter] has no command of poetry or character." He began to drink excessively and then abruptly left one performance at intermission and did not return. Later in 1936, however, when Welles decided to follow *HORSE EATS HAT* with a classical play, he cast Carter again, this time as Mephistopheles in Christopher Marlowe's *DOCTOR FAUSTUS.* BARBARA LEAMING examines this improbable casting and comments, "As far as Carter's drinking was concerned, Orson thought the electric excitement he would inevitably bring to the show well worth the risk." Leaming then quotes Welles himself: "We [he and Virginia] kept him in our little apartment on 14th Street for ten days before the opening to keep him from going on a binge or doing something Barrymoresque." When the play opened January 8, 1937, Carter performed well and continued to do so throughout the play's successful run at Maxine Elliott's Theatre. DAVID THOMSON describes the scenes between Carter and Welles (as Faustus) as "a model for Welles, not just of black and white men together but of a nobleman and a devil who require each other for life to begin." After Welles moved to Hollywood and began production plans for the projected HEART OF DARKNESS film, he wrote into the script a part for Carter, who was to play the steersman; Carter signed a contract with the studio, but Welles never made the film. Carter did, however, appear in four other films: *St. Louis Gal* (1938), *The Devil's Daughter* (1939), *Take My Life* (1941), and *Miracle in Harlem* (1948).

—T.L.E.

Casino Royale
Columbia Pictures/Famous Artists, 130 minutes, 1967. **Directors:** John Huston, Ken Hughes, Val Guest, Robert Parrish, and Joseph McGrath; **Producers:** Charles K. Feldman and Jerry Bresler; **Screenplay:** Wolf Mankowitz and Anthony Squire, adapted from the novel by Ian Fleming, with Michael Sayers, Billy Wilder, Ben Hecht, John Huston, Val Guest, Joseph Heller, and Terry Southern; **Cinematography:** Jack Hildyard; **Editor:** Bill Lenny; **Music:** Burt Bacharach; **Cast:** Orson Welles (Le Chiffre); David Niven (Sir James Bond), Deborah Kerr (Lady Fiona), William Holden (Ransome), Charles Boyer (Le Grand), Kurt Kaznar (Smernov), John Huston (McTarry/M), Peter Sellers, Woody Allen, Ursula Andress, et al.

A comedy-adventure film with WELLES in the featured role of Le Chiffre, an agent of SMERSH, an international crime organization. Based on Ian Fleming's 1953 James Bond novel, producer Charles Feldman's lavish production was a spoof with David Niven as a retired, middle-aged Agent 007, who is talked out of retirement to fight the nefarious powers of SMERSH. Top billing, though, went to Peter Sellers, then at the height of his popularity. Describing Sellers as insecure, Welles told BARBARA LEAMING that Sellers was so anxious about "competing" with him, that he refused to work directly on-camera with the great man. Consequently, their scenes together had to be shot separately. The disjunctive results were further exacerbated because Welles and Sellers were literally not reading from the same page. Indeed, each was working from a different version of the script, a consequence of Sellers having brought in his own scriptwriters to finesse his lines. Thus, as Welles later mused, there was "a marvelous surreal quality to the whole thing because there had been no coordination whatsoever between my lines and his." Sellers was

further irritated when he learned that his acquaintanceship with Princess Margaret had been trumped by Welles, whose friendship with the royal went back to 1951, when Welles had been in London to direct OTHELLO at the St. James Theatre.

Described by the critics as a "mess," *Casino Royale* suffered from more than Sellers's idiosyncracies. It also suffered because of its indeterminate paternity, a result in part of having had five directors, JOHN HUSTON, Ken Hughes, Val Guest, Robert Parrish, and Joseph McGrath. The list of credited and uncredited screenwriters was yet another source of chaos; along with Welles were Wolf Mankowitz, John Law, Michael Sayers, Billy Wilder, Ben Hecht, Joseph Heller, Terry Southern, as well as directors Huston and Guest. Muddled casting was also a factor. In addition to Welles, Sellers, and Niven, *Casino Royale* featured campy cameos by Ursula Andress, Joanna Pettet, Woody Allen, Deborah Kerr, William Holden, Charles Boyer, John Huston, George Raft, Jean-Paul Belmondo, Peter O'Toole, Jacqueline Bisset, and race-car driver Stirling Moss.

For Welles, given the shoestring economies of his post-RKO productions, the spectacle of *Casino Royale's* huge and wasted budget was painful. Even more unsettling was that *Casino Royale* went on to become a box office smash, largely, Welles maintained, because of an effective promotional campaign headed by an eye-grabbing poster displaying "a great naked girl entirely covered with tattoos. Very sexy!," exclaimed Welles. Today, among the few elements of the film worthy of discussion are Welles's villain and Burt Bacharach's catchy Oscar-winning ballad, "The Look of Love." Still, Welles's acting and scripting chores for Feldman's money-making fiasco netted a fresh supply of cash to catch up on arrears.

In spite of its box-office success, the critics panned *Casino Royale*. John Russel Taylor called it "one of those wild wacky extravaganzas in which the audience is expected to have a great time because everybody making the film did. It seldom works out that way, and certainly doesn't here." Judith Crist pointed out: "The dialogue is witless and unhampered by taste, and the interminable finale is a collection of clichés in a brawl involving the cavalry, parachuted Indians, split-second appearances by George Raft and Jean-Paul Belmondo, every variety of mayhem, and Woody Allen burping radiation as a walking atom bomb."

—C.B.

Castle, William (1914–1977) WELLES and Castle met briefly in 1938, when Welles gave Castle the use of the Stony Creek Theatre in Connecticut to stage his *Not for Children.* Their next meeting involved THE LADY FROM SHANGHAI (1948), one of the best examples of film noir filmed in the United States. The exact nature of the collaboration between Welles and Castle, who was officially an associate producer (RICHARD WILSON was the other associate producer), is difficult to determine because they each give contradictory accounts. In his "Almanac" column in the New York *Graphic,* Welles wrote a laudatory review of Castle's recently released *When Strangers Marry* (it was only the third film that Castle directed): "It isn't as slick as *Double Indemnity* or as glossy as *Laura,* but it's better acted and better directed by William Castle than either." As a result of that review, Castle called Welles, who suggested they work together: "Let's do a picture together, Bill. You direct and I'll produce—or I'll direct and you produce." Castle, who had made the highly successful *The Whistler* (1944), was looking for material to use in Whistler sequels; and found Sherwood King's novel *If I Should Die before I Wake* (1939). He bought the rights to the film for $200 with another $400 promised if a film was produced from it. It is unclear as to whether Castle's rights lapsed or whether he sold them to HARRY COHN, head of Columbia Studios, where Castle was under contract. At any rate, Castle wrote a 10-page treatment of the proposed film; in Cohn's absence a Columbia executive rejected the script because he knew that Cohn would not make a picture with the lead actress as a murderer. Welles's account is quite different. According to Welles, he was thinking of making a low-budget thriller like Castle's *When Strangers Marry* and was speaking with Cohn on the telephone when Cohn asked which picture he'd like to make. Welles said he saw a copy of King's novel in paperback (the novel, however, did not appear in paperback until 1962) and mentioned the title to the enthusiastic Cohn. Castle sent his 10-page treatment to Welles, who had already made a deal with Cohn. To appease an understandably (if Castle's story is true) upset Castle, Welles made Castle an associate director on the film. The film's locale was changed from New York to Mexico, and the low-budget film became a high-cost vehicle for star RITA HAYWORTH. The film's title was changed to *Black Irish* and then to *Take This Woman* before it was retitled *The Lady from Shanghai.* According to Welles, he rented the *Zaca,* Errol Flynn's boat, at $1,500 a day for use in the film; Castle writes that Welles asked him to negotiate the lease of the *Zaca.* Welles also claimed to have written the script for the film; JONATHAN ROSENBAUM, who edited the Welles/Bogdanovich interviews, writes that Fletcher Markle told him that he, Castle, and Welles worked on the script in New York and that later Castle and Welles worked on the script in Acapulco. Castle's diary entries about the shooting of the film make interesting reading. Castle writes that he was left to be "reptile director" and do location shooting after Welles left for California. Shortly after Welles left, Castle became very sick and was sent to recover at Cedars of Lebanon Hospital in Hollywood. Castle says he survived to "spite" Welles, who wore a black suit when he visited him in the hospital. Castle not only survived, but went on to fulfill his dream, which was the title of his autobiography: *Step Right Up! I'm Going to Scare the Pants Off America.* Many of the more than 50 films that he directed were westerns, thrillers, and horror films, which fared better at the box office than they did with the critics. Representative titles: *Masterson of Kansas* (1955), *Johnny Stool Pigeon* (1949), and *Macabre* (1958). His "scariest" film as a producer was Roman Polanski's *Rosemary's Baby* (1968). As an actor, he appeared, appropriately, as a producer in Hal Ashby's *Shampoo* and as a director in John Schlesinger's *The Day of the Locust* (both in 1975). He died of a heart attack in 1977 when he was producing the film *2000 Lakeview Drive* for MGM.

Reference Castle, William. *Step Right Up! I'm Going to Scare the Pants Off America* (New York: G. P. Putnam's Sons, 1976).

—T.L.E.

Catch-22 Paramount Pictures, 120 minutes, 1970. **Director:** Mike Nichols; **Producers:** John Calley and Martin Ransohoff; **Screenplay:** Buck Henry (based on *Catch-22* by Joseph Heller); **Music:** Richard Strauss; **Cinematographer:** David Watkin; **Editor:** Sam O'Steen; **Cast:** Alan Arkin (Captain John Yossarian), Martin Balsam (Colonel Cathcart), Richard Benjamin (Major Danby), Art Garfunkel (Captain Nately), Buck Henry (Lt. Colonel Korn), Jack Gilford (Captain "Doc" Daneeka), Bob Newhart (Major Major), Anthony Perkins (Chaplain Captain A.A. Tappman), Paula Prentiss (Nurse Duckett), Martin Sheen (1st Lt. Dobbs), John Voight (1st Lt. Milo Minderbinder), Charles Grodin (Captain Aarfy Aardvark), Orson Welles (Brig. General Dreedle)

Directed by MIKE NICHOLS and adapted by Buck Henry from Joseph Heller's cult antiwar novel about World War II, the film featured ORSON WELLES as Brigadier General Dreedle as part of an impressive ensemble cast. But even that all-star cast could not

Welles as General Dreedle, with Martin Balsam (Colonel Cathcart) and Alan Arkin (Yossarian) in *Catch-22* *(Literature/Film Archive)*

make this antimilitary satire a hit. An emblem of blustering World War II incompetence, General Dreedle (Welles) is seen as the protagonist Yossarian sees him, when, for example, Dreedle presents a medal to a naked Yossarian for a pointless and failed bombing mission against the harmless town of Ferrara. In fact, Yossarian, recognizing the pointlessness of the mission, had dropped the bombs into the ocean. Nothing in Heller's story makes sense because nothing makes sense in the world in which it is set. The film deserved better than it got.

—J.M.W.

Cavett, Dick (1936–) Writer, comedian, and television personality Dick Cavett was born in Gibbon, Nebraska, on November 19, 1936, the son of A.B. and Eva Cavett. After graduating from Yale University in 1958, Cavett became a television comedy writer for Jack Paar on the NBC *Tonight Show,* and later for Paar's successor, JOHNNY CARSON. He also wrote for MERV GRIFFIN and Jerry Lewis. After guest hosting *The Tonight Show,* he had his own series, *The Dick Cavett Show* on PBS in 1970, which included multiple appearances by ORSON WELLES on May 14 (with Jack Lemmon), July 27, and September 14, when Welles was active on the television talk-show circuit. Famous for his wit and sophistication, Cavett also worked as a stand-up comedian in nightclubs, and, later, as host for the Pittsburgh Symphony Orchestra on National Public Radio.

References Cavett, Dick, and Christopher Porterfield. *Cavett* (New York: Harcourt, Brace Jovanovich, 1974); Cavett, Dick, and Christopher Porterfield. *Eye on Cavett* (New York: Arbor House, 1983).

—J.M.W.

Ceiling Unlimited (radio, 1942–1943) In September 1942, with direct U.S. involvement in World War II not yet a year old, Welles was asked by CBS to produce, write, direct, and narrate a weekly war-related series. Reflecting the sponsorship of the Lockheed-Vega Aircraft Corporation, each 15-minute episode of *Ceiling Unlimited* was designed to take the domestic audience up into hostile skies with U.S. fighter pilots and bombardiers. While casting a favorable light on the aircraft industry, the program succeeded in bringing aspects of the war home, thus reminding the audience of "why we fight." To generate story lines, Lockheed-Vega set up a research office in Washington to dig up actual air adventures for dramatization. Assigned to the show's writing team was ARTHUR MILLER, the future Pulitzer Prize–winning playwright, who helped create the show's format. Welles, to prepare himself for the series, visited Lockheed-Vega's California factories and read stories about flying. In the show's uncredited cast and production team were a number of MERCURY THEATRE and *CITIZEN KANE* alumni, including RAY COLLINS, JOSEPH COTTEN, EVERETT SLOAN, PAUL STEWART, and composer BERNARD HERRMANN.

Each show focused on an individual plane, making it a character as "alive" as the crew that manned it. There were stories about Flying Fortresses and their high-altitude bombing runs over enemy industries. Other tales put audiences in cockpits of U.S. fighter planes taking on Messerschmitts over Germany and Zeroes over Guam. In a conversation with Leonardo da Vinci, Welles, with the roar of engines in the background, told the inventor, "We've given your bird a great heart and we've given her claws, too, machine guns and cannons . . . we built this murderous beautiful plane, Mr. da Vinci, because we're fighting for our life. We're at war and we've got to win." Other cast members re-created the heroics of U.S. pilots in the pitch of combat.

Like *HELLO AMERICANS,* a companion war-boosting radio series produced by Welles for CBS during the same period, *Ceiling Unlimited* provided effective wartime propaganda praised by the public and critics alike. *Ceiling Unlimited*'s run extended from November 9, 1942, to February 1, 1943.

—C.B.

Chaplin, Charles (1889–1977)

Charles Chaplin was born in London on April 16, 1889. Both of his parents were moderately successful music hall entertainers. When he was still a youngster, his father died of alcoholism, and his mother retired from the stage because of poor physical health and mental illness. Consequently, Chaplin was forced to earn his living in vaudeville before he reached his teens. Mack Sennett, the creator of the Keystone comedies, saw Chaplin perform while the comedian was touring the United States with Fred Karno's vaudeville company and invited Chaplin to go into pictures in 1913. Chaplin left the stage for a career in movies the following year. Chaplin created the character of Charlie the Tramp shortly after joining Sennett, for whom he made his first short comedies. He explained that the Tramp was his conception of the average man. The Tramp is everyman, with whom we can all identify: the well-meaning but inept little fellow whose reach forever exceeds his grasp, but who is always ready to pick himself up, dust himself off, and continue down the road of life, twirling his cane with disarming bravado. Chaplin portrayed the Tramp as a rambunctious ragamuffin who felt that he had to cheat to survive in a bold and brutal world.

Chaplin left Sennett's Keystone studio in 1915 after a year, and transferred first to Essanay, and then to Mutual in 1916–17. The greatest of his Mutual shorts is *The Immigrant* (1917), which dealt with a subject close to Chaplin's heart, since he had come to America himself as an immigrant in 1913. Moreover, because the immigrant is perhaps the quintessential example of a lonely outsider striving for acceptance in an alien milieu, the role fit the personality of Charlie the Tramp perfectly. When Chaplin left Mutual for First National in 1918, he took yet another step toward total artistic control of his films. Chaplin now became his own producer, as well as writer, director, and star.

Chaplin and ORSON WELLES had crossed paths occasionally in Hollywood; Chaplin had discovered a young actress who he thought had promise, and Welles cast her in *Citizen Kane* as Kane's second wife; she was, of course, DOROTHY COMMINGORE. The following year Welles presided at a rally in New York's Carnegie Hall on October 16, 1942, at which Chaplin was one of the featured speakers. The event, sponsored by the Artists' Front to Win the War, was aimed at championing a second front during World War II to help Russia ward off the Nazi invasion.

Chaplin recalls in his autobiography that Welles spoke first. Welles stated, "The President says we're going to have a second front. . . . We have a right to say we're glad to hear it," since the Russians were

U.S. allies. Although the audience responded favorably to Welles's remarks, Chaplin found them too subdued. "That made me all the more determined to speak my mind," he comments. But it was thought in some quarters that Chaplin had allowed himself to get carried away by his enthusiasm for the Russian cause. Indeed, he began by addressing the audience as comrades: "When one sees the magnificent fight the Russian people are putting up, it is a pleasure and a privilege to use the word *comrade.*" He went so far as to say that he was not concerned by reports "that after the war Communism may spread over the world." Chaplin notes in his autobiography that when the communist paper, the *Daily Worker,* applauded his oration, "I was apprehensive." Well might he have been: Although few observers took exception to Welles's speech afterward, Chaplin's words would come back to haunt him.

Chaplin recalls in his autobiography an earlier encounter with Welles in July 1941. Welles was having dinner at Chaplin's home in Beverly Hills, and he proposed a film project to Chaplin. He explained that he was planning to do a series of documentaries, one of which would be based on the life of Henri Landru, the notorious French wife-murderer known as Bluebeard. It seems that Welles had had a conversation with a French lawyer whose partner had defended Landru; and Welles thought of making a movie about Landru with Chaplin playing the lead. (Actually, the correct term for such a film would be a docudrama, since the film would be a reenactment of Landru's life with Chaplin playing the serial killer.)

Chaplin reports: "I was interested, as it would be a change from comedy, and a change from writing, acting and directing myself as I had done for years. So I asked to see the script.

"'Oh, it isn't written yet,' he said, 'but all that's necessary is to take the records of the Landru trial and you'll have it.' He added: 'I thought you might like to help with the writing of it.'

"I was disappointed. 'If I have to help in writing the script, I'm not interested,' I said, and the matter ended there.

"But a day or so later it struck me that the idea of Landru would make a wonderful comedy. So I telephoned Welles. 'Look, your proposed documentary about Landru has given me an idea for a comedy. It has nothing to do with Landru, but to clear everything I am willing to pay you five thousand dollars, only because your proposition made me think of it.'"

Welles hesitated, since he had wanted to direct the film, with Chaplin as his star, and had himself already begun working on the scenario.

"'Listen, Landru is not an original story with you or anyone else,' I said; 'it is in the public domain.'"

"He thought a moment, then told me to get in touch with his manager. Thus a deal was negotiated: Welles to get $5,000 and I to be clear of all obligations. Welles accepted but asked for one provision: that after seeing the picture he could have the privilege of screen credit, to read: 'Idea suggested by Orson Welles.' I thought little of the request because of my enthusiasm." But the matter did not end there.

Welles remembered the whole matter differently. He told PETER BOGDANOVICH that he composed a complete screenplay, with Chaplin in mind for the role of Landru, and submitted it to him. Chaplin said, "Woonderful—I'm going to act it for you!" But then, at the last minute, Chaplin reversed himself: "No, I can't—I've never had anybody else direct me. Let me buy it." So Welles said that Chaplin made the film as MONSIEUR VERDOUX. "My title was *The Ladykiller.*"

Chaplin, for his part, insisted that Welles had given him the raw idea for a movie about Landru, and flatly denied that Welles had shown him a screenplay; but Welles said to Bogdanovich, "I still have a copy of it." More precisely, Welles maintained that he turned over to Chaplin a preliminary draft of the screenplay, which contained specific incidents, two of which Chaplin eventually used in *Verdoux.* The first one, BARBARA LEAMING points out, was described by Welles in an interview in the *Baltimore Evening Sun* on October 13, 1941. That lends credence to Welles's contention that he had sketched out the story line for the proposed film, even if it was not the complete script that he said it was. He mentioned in the interview that he had sold Chaplin this material because Chaplin was the only living actor who could play the role of Landru. As he told Bogdanovich, the opening scene of Chaplin's film—which he had described in the 1941 interview—"was from my version: the neat little bourgeois in the garden of his little villa briskly, neatly, delicately clipping his edge while in the background thick, black crematory smoke pours up out of the chimney," where Verdoux is disposing of the remains of his latest wife. "At least Charlie didn't change *that*."

According to Welles, Chaplin also retained the scene in which Verdoux tries to kill one redoubtable female played by Martha Raye, but fails. "It was the funniest sequence in *Verdoux,*" said Welles.

Welles was chagrined when the film premiered in April 1947 that his contribution to the picture was not mentioned in the screen credits. When he complained to Chaplin, the latter relented and had an official screen credit for Welles inserted in the opening credits of the film. Welles explained why he thinks Chaplin acquiesced: "Well, he was attacked terribly in New York when it opened; it was the worst lynching by critics you've ever heard. And the next day—after they'd all said, you know, 'Who gave him this *awful* idea?'—up on the screen went my billing: 'Based on an idea suggested by Orson Welles.' It's the only credit I ever got on the picture."

In 1963, in an interview in the *London Times,* Welles said that he wrote the first version of the script for *Verdoux.* Chaplin wrote a scathing letter to the *Times,* denouncing Welles. The *Times* sent a copy of the letter to Welles, informing him that the letter was too virulent to publish. Welles remembered Chaplin stating in the letter that Orson Welles, who had made a "ridiculous" picture like THE TRIAL, could not possibly have had anything to do with *Monsieur Verdoux.*

Joyce Milton writes that Chaplin threatened to sue both Welles and the *Times.* Welles was in financial straits at the time, and so the *Times* settled out of court, paying Chaplin—a millionaire several times over—£500 to call off the dogs.

It is a pity that Welles's relationship with Chaplin turned sour over *Verdoux.* Welles esteemed Chaplin as the first great filmmaker to write, direct, and star in his own films; as such, Welles saw Chaplin as a kindred soul. Although no film director ever again would have the total artistic independence that Chaplin enjoyed during his career, some filmmakers have succeeded in creating personal films, despite studio interference; one of them was Orson Welles.

References   Chaplin, Charles. *My Autobiography* (New York: Penguin, 1992); Douglas, Ann. "Charlie Chaplin, Comedian," *Time,* Special Issue: Artists and Entertainers of the Century (June 8, 1998): 18–24; Leaming, Barbara. *Orson Welles: A Biography* (New York: Viking, 1985); Milton, Joyce. *Tramp: The Life of Charles Chaplin* (New York: Da Capo, 1998); Robinson, David. *Chaplin: His Life and Art* (New York: Da Capo, 1994); Wallach, George. "Charlie Chaplin's *Monsieur Verdoux* Press Conference," *Film Comment* 5, no. 4 (Winter 1969): 34–41.

—G.D.P.

Charles Foster Kane

Who is Charles Foster Kane? That is the puzzle posed by ORSON WELLES's masterpiece of 1941, CITIZEN KANE. At the beginning of the film, we learn through the NEWS ON THE MARCH newsreel that, at the height of his powers, Kane was a larger-than-life public figure who owned 37 newspapers, a chain of radio stations, and a vast portfolio of diverse investments. We also learn that he had sought the governorship of New York State as a stepping-stone to the White House, and that he had married a president's niece, but having been caught up in an affair with Susan Alexander, retired from public life to his palatial mansion, XANADU.

The most ingenious formal aspect of *Citizen Kane* is its flashback structure, which provides an array of insights into the charismatic Kane through the unique viewpoints of five "witnesses": his guardian and financial adviser, Walter Parks Thatcher; his business manager, Bernstein; his best friend, Jedediah Leland; his second wife, Susan Alexander; and Raymond, the butler who presides over Xanadu. Probing each of these characters about various aspects of Kane's life is Thompson, a reporter assigned the task of finding out what made Kane tick and what his dying word, ROSEBUD, might have meant.

At the end of the film Thompson concludes that Rosebud might be the missing piece of the jigsaw puzzle that was Kane, the key to unlocking the mystery of his powerful yet enigmatic persona. The film leaves us without a definite answer about Kane, which helps explain its enduring fascination. It is the haunting ambiguity shrouding the dynamically compelling Kane that pricks our imaginations and keeps us wondering about who he was and what he wanted. In the process those questions double back on our own quests for self-enlightenment about the human enterprise at large and about our own personal stories.

Due to *Citizen Kane*'s iconic status it is not surprising that Charles Foster Kane has become the stuff of popular imagination and, indeed, popular culture. The character's continuing resonance is a tribute to how Kane was delineated in the script by Welles and HERMAN J. MANKIEWICZ. It also reflects the character's resemblance to real-life titans WILLIAM RANDOLPH HEARST, SIR BASIL ZAHAROFF, Harold F. McCormick, and HOWARD HUGHES.

That Kane still lives is a crowning tribute to actor-director Welles, whose embodiment of the mythical tycoon from a young man of 20 to an old man of 70 is startling in the breadth of its emotional and dramatic registers.

—C.B

Chimes at Midnight (play, 1960) *Chimes at Midnight* came into being because of HILTON EDWARDS of Dublin's GATE THEATRE who presented WELLES an opportunity to star in and direct any stage production of Shakespeare on the condition that it open in Ireland. Welles needed little prompting. The prospect of returning to Dublin after almost 30 years and working with colleagues Edwards and MICHEÁL MACLIAMMÓIR was an offer not to be ignored. After mulling over several possibilities, Welles turned to FIVE KINGS, his bold yet failed 1939 production that had attempted to blend together large chunks of Shakespeare's *Henry IV, Part I; Henry IV, Part II; Henry V; Richard II;* and *The Merry Wives of Windsor.* Shortening the 1939 script and simplifying its technical demands, Welles—citing the lines "We have heard the chimes at midnight" uttered by Falstaff in *Henry IV, Part II*—dubbed the new venture *Chimes at Midnight.*

Also significant was Welles's decision to focus the drama on Falstaff, a character that had long fascinated the director. At the same time, Welles began thinking about using the play, as he had done with MACBETH, as the launching pad for a film. In the meantime, Edwards arranged a provincial tryout in Belfast, hoping for a year-long run at Dublin's Gaiety Theatre, and then a move to London's West End. Welles added

the possibility of an intercontinental tour to take in Paris, Athens, Brussels, and Cairo.

Casting the play in London with himself as Falstaff, newcomer KEITH BAXTER as Prince Hal, Reginald Jarman as King Henry IV, and Thelma Ruby as Mistress Quickly, there was a harried week of rehearsals before opening on February 24, 1960, for a five-day preview run at Belfast's Grand Opera House. In spite of a grueling dress rehearsal that had left the cast fatigued on opening night, the reviews, if not raves, were at least approving. Welles's Falstaff, lecherous yet gentlemanly, comic yet thoughtful, was a triumph. Welles, underscoring his personal involvement with the character, told biographer MAURICE BESSY that Falstaff was "an affirmative spirit, courageous in many ways, even when he makes sport of his own cowardice. He is a man who represents a virtue that is disappearing, he is waging a battle lost in advance. I don't believe that he is looking for anything. He represents a value, he is goodness. He is the character in which I most believe, the most entirely good man of all dramatic literature. His faults are minimal, and he derives the most enormous pleasure from them. His goodness is like bread, like wine."

Since the building housing the Gate Theatre had been closed because of financial difficulties, Edwards next installed *Chimes at Midnight* at Dublin's Gaiety Theatre. Again, reviews were good, but hardly raves. As audiences started to dwindle after the first week, so, too, did the hope of taking the show to London, the ultimate destination that Edwards and Welles had envisioned. With Welles growing increasingly impatient with his cast (except for Keith Baxter), and with talk of Welles directing LAURENCE OLIVIER in the London debut of Eugène Ionesco's RHINOCEROS, plans for filming the play were similarly dashed.

In 1964, with partial funding in place, Welles finally began shooting the film version of *Chimes at Midnight,* which after a protracted, stop-start, two-year production schedule, was finally finished and released in 1966.

—C.B.

Chimes at Midnight International Films Espanola/Alpine Productions, 115 minutes, 1966. **Director:** Orson Welles; **Producers:** Emiliano Piedra and Angel

Escolano; **Executive Producer:** Alessandro Tasca di Cuto; **Screenplay:** Welles (based on *Richard II, Henry IV Parts I and II, Henry V,* and *The Merry Wives of Windsor* by William Shakespeare and material from *The Chronicles of England* by Ralph Holinshed); **Cinematographer:** Edmond Richard; **Editor:** Fritz Mueller; **Cast:** Orson Welles (Sir John Falstaff), Keith Baxter (Prince Hal, Henry V), John Gielgud (King Henry IV), Jeanne Moreau (Doll Tearsheet), Margaret Rutherford (Mistress Quickly), Norman Rodway (Henry Percy, Hotspur), Marina Vlady (Kate Percy), Alan Webb (Justice Shallow), Walter Chairi (Silence), Michael Aldrich (Pistol), Tony Beckley (Poins), Fernando Rey (Worcester), Andrew Faulds (Westmoreland), José Nieto (Northumberland), Jeremy Rowe (Prince John), Beatrice Welles (Falstaff's page), Paddy Bedford (Bardolph), Julio Peña, Fernando Hilbeck, Andrès Mejuto, Keith Pyott, Charles Farrell

With his last completed Shakespeare (see SHAKESPEARE BY WELLES) film, *Chimes at Midnight,* WELLES culminated 35 years of rethinking and reshaping Shakespeare's history plays. In 1930, when he was a 15-year-old graduating senior at the Todd School for Boys, he adapted, staged, and acted in a conflation of the early history plays that he called *Richard III.* BARBARA LEAMING writes that the faculty forced headmaster ROGER "Skipper" HILL to "pull Welles' cork . . . do a little editing on this thing," and cut the three-and-a-half-hour production, which the school program describes as "Beginning with Edward's return from exile and carrying through his reign and that of his deformed and unprincipled brother Richard, to the beginning of the Tudor line by Richmond." Leaming speculates that Welles never got over the forced cuts, and eight years later, after his spectacular

Welles showing the jovial side of Sir John Falstaff in *Chimes at Midnight* (Literature/Film Archive)

successes on the New York stage, he tried again. This time Welles distilled *Richard II, Henry IV, Parts I and II,* and *Henry Fifth,* into the first part of his projected FIVE KINGS, a MERCURY THEATRE Presentation, featuring Welles as FALSTAFF and BURGESS MEREDITH as Prince Hal. It played Boston, Philadelphia, and Washington, D.C., but closed before reaching New York City. According to Robert Hapgood, the play now traced "in a single, very long evening the whole career of Harry Monmouth from Prince Hal cavorting with Falstaff in the tavern to King Henry V wooing Katherine after his victory at Agincourt." Welles focused on the main characters of Falstaff, Hal, and Hotspur, and developed the figure of the Chorus, making him, as SIMON CALLOW says, "in effect, the historian Holinshed from whom Shakespeare had drawn so much of the detail of the play."

In 1960, when Welles was in his 40s, he opened his third attempt, now called *Chimes at Midnight,* in Ireland, where it played briefly in Belfast and Dublin but closed before it reached its intended venue in London. Of the new play, Welles said, "It's the essential idea I had for *Five Kings,* except that *Five Kings* made the dramatic mistake, I think of going and doing *Henry V* in the same evening, which I shouldn't have done. The basic idea to do the two Henrys as a single play and take the main theme and stay with it is what I was trying for." Welles again played Falstaff, with KEITH BAXTER playing Prince Hal, as he would in the film. This time Welles used the narrative line from Shakespeare's *Henry IV, Part I,* with parts of *Henry IV, Part II,* and the death of Falstaff from *Henry V.* The program describes this play as "the adventure of the Fat Knight and the Prince of Wales," a shift in emphasis that, according to MICHAEL ANDEREGG, moved "away from history and toward satire." Welles had hoped to secure funding to film the Irish version inexpensively in Yugoslavia, but it was not until 1964, when he moved to Spain, that he found backers and made the film for, as Leaming says, "a measly $800,000."

Welles applied the lessons learned in filming OTHELLO under adverse circumstances to the problems he encountered with *Chimes.* Anticipating difficulties, he announced he would rely on close-ups because "the number of sets available to me is so restricted that the film must . . . work essentially through the faces." He drew on his own experiences of rushing in to do a few days acting in other people's films, to make the best use of his five days with JEANNE MOREAU and ten days with JOHN GIELGUD, using doubles to economize. According to Leaming, producer Alessandro Tasca claimed that in the scenes with Jeanne Moreau, "Whenever it's not her face, it's a double. *Even* in the love scene. Every reverse shot is a double," since "there were always locals willing to rent their backs to him if he needed to double the real actors later." Welles created the great battle scenes in *Chimes* with no more than 180 people, says DAVID THOMSON, by filming "in one of Madrid's parks . . . with lines of horses. But then, day after day, Welles went back to the park with just a few men, some weapons, and water to obtain the terrible scenes of close slaughter that make the sequence so powerful and such a feat of montage." The problems he could not overcome remain in the film, including the slightly out of sync sound in the first reel, and the sound of a generator humming in the background when MARGARET RUTHERFORD, as Mistress Quickly, delivers her speech on Falstaff's death.

The film opens with a long shot of two men walking through the snow. It is Falstaff (Orson Welles) and Shallow (Alan Webb) who walk into the massive interior of a wooden building with a prominent beamed ceiling. The two old men talk about old times, and Falstaff comments, "We have heard the chimes at midnight," then, at Shallow's, "Jesus, the days that we have seen" (2H4 3.2.214–218), the scene fades to rousing music and to a shot of horsemen approaching large Tudor buildings, different from the snowbound scene that opened the film. As the titles appear, the film has shifted to the heroic past the two men remember. Once again, as in *Othello* and to some extent *MACBETH,* Welles uses a circular framework that here, as in *Othello,* throws the action into a recollected time. A Breugelesque line of people are silhouetted walking across a windy plain, and, at the point when the titles say "Narration Based on Holinshed's Chronicles Spoken by RALPH RICHARDSON," a group of armed men in a long shot, with gallows and hanged men behind them, turn to face the camera, just as Richardson begins reading from

Holinshed the story of how King Richard II was murdered, perhaps at Henry Bolingbroke's orders, and how Mortimer, the presumed heir before Henry's coming to power, is now in the hands of Welsh rebels. The shot fades from the castle exterior to an interior as Mortimer's cousins, Northumberland (José Nieto), Henry Percy, known as Hotspur (Norman Rodway), and Worcester (Fernando Rey) approach Bolingbroke, now King Henry IV (John Gielgud), to ransom Mortimer.

Although for the most part Welles slights the political context of the Henriad, he establishes here the principal oppositions that will lead to the Battle of Shrewsbury. In the scenes following Henry's refusal, "To ransom home revolted Mortimer" (1H4.1.3.92), Welles visually establishes a context for Hotspur, when Northumberland and Worcester tower over the ranting Hotspur. In one shot, for example, Worcester's cloak remains visible in the left side of the frame, making Hotspur look very much like a puppet on a stage as he complains about "this king of smiles, this Bolingbroke" (1H4.13.246). At the end of this rant, Welles uses Hotspur's description of Prince Hal for an interesting transition. Hotspur says of Hal, "I would have him poisoned with a pot of ale" (1H4.1.3.233), and Welles cuts to a shot of a pot of ale, which, when lowered, reveals the face of Prince Hal with the busy tavern behind him.

This shift begins a series of contrasts between court and tavern. Anthony Davies reduces the issue to its most elemental terms when he characterizes the court as stone and the tavern as wood. "The interaction throughout the film of wood and stone as seminal spatial elements sustains the central conflict between the waning world of organic spontaneity on the one hand, and the emerging world which is to be rational, detached, opportunistic and essentially inorganic, on the other." Welles, in an interview with PETER BOGDANOVICH, fleshes out the opposition when he says, "There's this triangle: the prince, his king-father, and Falstaff, who's a kind of foster father." In another interview, Welles calls Falstaff "a man defending a force—the Old England—which is going down." Clearly several critics view Hal as choosing between elements in the contrast between Court/King/stone/new with Tavern/Falstaff/wood/

old, although, as Michael Anderegg points out, the longer list of "binary oppositions" that Shakespeare posed in his Henriad, have become in Welles's film, "unbalanced, diminished, reversed, or exploded."

Welles draws freely from several scenes in *Henry IV, Part I* to sketch out the relationships between Poins, Prince Hal, and Falstaff. Poins picks the sleeping Falstaff's pocket and shows a piece of paper to Hal (1H4 3.2.). Falstaff wakes, brags of his profession as one who takes "purses by the moon" (1H4 1.2.14), then realizes that his own pocket has been picked and raises an uproar. The Hostess (Margaret Rutherford) enters to defend her house against accusations of being a home for thieves (1H4 3.3.55) and bawds (H5 2.1.32–38), though that is clearly what it is. Asked by Hal how much was taken, Falstaff claims to have lost money and jewelry, and, when Hal shows him to be a liar, Falstaff blames the corrupting influence of "villainous company" (3.3.10). When Hal leaves for the castle, Falstaff asks how things will be when Hal is king. Here Welles takes the famously revealing monologue, "I know you all, and will a while uphold / the unyok'd humor of your idleness" (1H4 1.2.195–217), and has Hal say it to Falstaff, although Falstaff turns it into a jest, saying, "Do not thou, when thou art king, hang a thief" (1H4 1.2.62). When Hal leaves, with the castle in the background and the tavern's beams in the foreground as he turns and runs toward the castle, it is as Samuel Crowl discusses, the first of several such departures in the film.

Cutting to Hotspur's castle, Welles shows the firebrand taking a bath in a small tub, surrounded by armaments. Hotspur busily reads a letter that warns him against conspiring to overthrow Henry. Welles contrasts the sounding trumpets and walls of weapons with the agitated, naked man, who jumps out of the tub and, at the line "That roan shall be my throne" (1H4 2.3.70), drops his towel, comically exposing himself while boasting of his conquests. Hotspur is dressing when Worcester arrives outside. Inside, Lady Percy, with comic sweetness, tries to get her husband to tell her about the business he has begun. Having resisted both the letter and his wife, Hotspur rides off with Worcester. Welles cuts to the Gadshill robbery (1H4 2.2), filming in Madrid's Casa de Campo park, where he also shot the Shrewsbury battle scenes. Echoing Hotspur's dressing amid the armor of the last scene, Welles has Hal help Falstaff put on the great white monk's cloaks with which he and the other robbers disguise themselves before attacking the pilgrims. Welles cuts off the tops of the trees in the robbery scene to emphasize the bandits scurrying about when Poins and Hal, disguised in black cloaks, rob the robbers and take back the money.

Welles cuts from this comic action to the grim face of Henry IV, who inquires after his son and receives word that an army is gathering under Hotspur. Welles constructs a scene by drawing from the first act of *Henry IV, Part I* and the last act of *Richard II*. King Henry says he sins "In envy that my Lord Northumberland / Should be the father to so blest a son" (1H4 1.1.78–79) while his own son, just shown engaging in a robbery, "doth frequent, / With unrestrained loose companions" (R2 5.3.1–12). Again, Welles cuts to a scene which fulfills the negative prophecy when it shows Hal and Poins riding up to the tavern after their trick. Inside the tavern, Falstaff delivers a comic story of fighting a multitude of robbers. When Hal catches him in his lies, Falstaff claims that he knew by instinct his attacker was Hal and was thereby prevented from fighting the true prince. Falstaff and Hal then take turns pretending to be the king. The room fills with laughing women, barking dogs, and general confusion as boys push the massive Falstaff, a cooking pot crown on his head, up to the raised chair that serves for a throne. Welles keeps the camera placed well below Falstaff, emphasizing the big man's comic grandeur. When they reverse roles, the massive Falstaff fills the foreground as Hal, with the pot now on his head, names the old man's vices. Falstaff laughingly delivers his defense, "Banish not him," but Welles cuts to show Falstaff's uncertain expression as Hal says that as king "I do, I will" (1H4 2.4.466–481). The Hostess says the king's men are at the door, and people scramble to hide, and Hal, having jumped into bed with one of the women, tells the sheriff that Falstaff is not there. After the sheriff leaves, the Hostess complains that Falstaff owes her money and tells Hal that Falstaff complains about the prince. Hal promises to repay the money owed.

When Falstaff steps into another room, Doll Tearsheet (Jeanne Moreau) rises suddenly from the covers, pronounces "Thou whoreson" so that it sounds like "Orson," and embraces Falstaff because he will be going to war. Falstaff looks out a window and sees Hal again leaving him and going toward the castle.

King Henry's voice provides a transition as the scene fades to the court. Sending the others away, the king wonders aloud whether Hal might simply be a "revengement and a scourge for me / To punish my mistreadings" (1H4 3.2.1–11). Hal, in this first scene with his father, promises to "redeem all this on Percy's head" (1H4 3.2.132). Welles cuts now to the preparations for war, pulling together dialogue between Pistol, Bardolph, and Nym from *Henry V*, conversations between Falstaff and the Lord Chief Justice from *Henry IV, Part II*, and a conversation between Falstaff and Westmoreland from *Henry IV, Part I*, including their comments about the ragtag crew that Falstaff has collected to follow him, which Falstaff himself describes as "the cancers of a calm world and a long peace" (1H4 4.2.29–30), and concluding with the Chief Justice shouting after Falstaff "God send the Prince a better companion," and Falstaff replying, "God send the companion a better prince" (2H4 1.2.199–201). Welles cuts first to the rebel camp where Hotspur calls Hal "The nimblefooted madcap Prince of Wales" (1H4 94–95), and then back to Shallow's house where Shallow, Silence, and Falstaff conscript the likes of Moldy, Wart, Francis Feeble, Shadow, and Bullcalf, releasing only those who can buy their way out.

Welles cuts to the windy battlefield at Shewsbury and shows Worcester and Henry IV meeting on the battlefield. Henry tries to make peace, and Hal offers to fight Hotspur in personal combat. When Worcester returns to the rebel camp, he omits Henry's entreaty for peace, but tells Hotspur about Hal's challenge. As Hotspur looks off into the fog and smoke across the field, Welles cuts to Hal in a reverse shot looking out into the same gray scene. Falstaff delivers his soliloquy on honor (1H4 5.1.127–141), which Welles has him speak directly to Hal. Perhaps as a visual underscoring of Falstaff's deflation of the military and honor, Welles uses low-angle shots of the rebel knights being lowered by ropes from trees and into their saddles as the patient horses are kept in place by foot soldiers. In a parallel scene, the king's knights are lowered from makeshift scaffolds onto their horses, and Pistol, Bardolph, and Nym try to lift Falstaff and lower him to his horse, but the rope breaks, and the huge armored knight falls to the ground.

Many writers have noted parallels between Welles's battle sequence and Sergei Eisenstein's *Alexander Nevsky* (1938), John Ford's westerns, and, for PAULINE KAEL, the Renaissance painter Uccello. JOSEPH MCBRIDE says the battle sequence is "one of the greatest achievements in action direction in the history of the cinema," which though it is "constructed in a highly orchestrated rhetorical pattern," affects the audience, "not as an artistic demonstration but as an overwhelming physical experience." Welles understood the problem of establishing the reality of battle and suggested he wanted to avoid OLIVIER's problem in *Henry V,* where "you see people riding out of the castle and suddenly they are on a golf course somewhere charging each other." According to Anthony Davis, "Instead of shooting short bursts of action and building them into a sustained sequence, Welles reversed the process and shot long, uninterrupted takes of action, from which he selected short lengths. He found that this method gave him the realism he sought." According to Welles, the actors "didn't seem to be really fighting until they had time to warm up. That's why the takes were so long, since there was no way of beginning the camera later and cutting. But I knew I was only going to use very short cuts." To further achieve his effects, he says, "We shot with a big crane very low to the ground, moving as fast as it could be moved against the action." He claims to have "intercut the shots in which action was contrary, so that every cut seemed to be a blow, a counter-blow, a blow received, a blow returned," but both Anthony Davis and JAMES NARE-MORE have demonstrated that the editing was far more complex. Robert Hapgood comments that the chief effect of the sequence is not "a meaningful struggle between two sides" because often "it is impossible to tell who is winning and who is losing," and concludes that "as Welles shows the increasing

brutality and squalor of the fighting . . . his chief point seems to be the political meaninglessness of it all."

Falstaff's comic role acts as a counterbalance throughout the battle scenes. Welles shows the mounted knights from each side beginning the charge, followed by foot soldiers, and in the midst of the action the square figure of the helmeted and armored Falstaff urging his soldiers on with stiff motions of his sword as he lumbers along, marching to a very different beat from the rest of the combatants. As the armies collide, Falstaff manages to find a quiet grove. Welles's battle scenes, with their emphasis on close combat, and scenes of men clubbing bodies and pulling horsemen to the ground, and of bodies fighting and twitching in the mud, find a suitable echo only years later in Kenneth Branagh's "mud and blood" version of *Henry V* (1989).

As the first great onslaught slows, Hal rides up, takes off his helmet, and asks Falstaff, "What stand thou idle here?" (1H4 5.3.39). Falstaff seems isolated, a fat man in huge armor, waving his unused sword and gesturing in false bravado as he recounts his imaginary deeds. Suddenly, Hotspur rides up behind Falstaff. Welles frames Hotspur in the background, Falstaff in the middle, and Prince Hal in the foreground, with Falstaff waving his sword at first one and then the other mounted knight. At Hal's challenge, "Two stars keep not their motion in one sphere" (5.4.65), he and Hotspur close visors and

Welles as Falstaff with Jeanne Moreau as Doll Tearsheet in *Chimes at Midnight* *(Literature/Film Archive)*

fight, while Falstaff finds a convenient tree, venturing out only to cheer Hal on. Welles omits Shakespeare's confrontation between Douglas and Falstaff, so, as Hotspur and Hal fight, Falstaff here simply slips and falls, apparently knocking himself out. Meanwhile, as Hotspur stands over Hal and raises his sword, Hal thrusts up from below and runs him through. Keith Baxter as Hal concludes Hotspur's dying speech with a thoughtful and somber delivery, as the battle briefly almost seems to stop around them. Welles seems to use Hal's line referring to the dead Hotspur, "This earth that bears [thee] dead / Bears not alive so stout a gentleman" (1H4 5.4.92–93), as a transition, playing on the notion of a stout gentleman, to have Hal discover Falstaff, lying massively on the ground. When Hal inspects the body, he notices the steamy breath rising from the visor and delivers his line, "Embowell'd will I see thee by and by" (1H4 5.4.109), with a comic touch. Hal leaves, and Falstaff throws open his visor and goes to claim Hotspur's body.

The trumpets sound surrender, and the victorious King Henry seated on his horse, sends "Ill spirited Worcester" (1H4 5.5.2) to be executed. Walking across the field of dead wounded bodies, Hal and his brother, Prince John, see the body of Hotspur draped across Falstaff's back. Falstaff takes credit for killing the rebel and scoffs at Hal's protests. Departing from Shakespeare's arrangement, Welles includes King Henry as a witness. The silent man looks from his son to the dead Hotspur, and to his son again before walking away. Welles closes the battle sequence with Falstaff's paean to sack to which Falstaff attributes both wit and courage (2H4 4.3.86–125). As he concludes, he sees Hal for the third time walking away into the distance.

Using Ralph Richardson reading from Holinshed as a transition across images of hanged rebels, Welles shifts to an interior, Christmas in London, where the sick King Henry asks about Hal and is told Hal is with his old friends. Filled with sorrow, King Henry worries about "the rotten times that you shall look upon / When I am sleeping with my ancestors" (2H4 4.4.60–61). He falls, knocks over the crown, and is carried to bed, where he asks that the crown be brought and put on the pillow next to him. Rising,

he goes to a window to deliver his speech on sleep, ending with the line, "Uneasy lies the head that wears a crown" (2H4 3.1.4–31). Meanwhile Hal, standing in the country, with Poins beside him, echoes his father's mood, saying "Before God, I am exceeding weary" (2H4 2.2.1). Falstaff's Page, played by young BEATRICE WELLES, approaches with a letter in which Falstaff warns Hal against keeping company with Poins. The same sad mood begins the next shot in this sequence as Welles first cuts to a close-up of Falstaff saying, "'Sblood, I'm as melancholy as a gib-cat or a lugged bear" (1H4 1.273–74), then stitches lines from the two parts of *Henry IV* with some from *The Merry Wives of Windsor* to draw a melancholy picture of the idle Falstaff. While Hal and Poins look on from the rafters, Doll, Pistol, the Hostess, and Falstaff demonstrate that not too much has changed at the tavern. Falstaff chases Pistol off, and Doll rushes up to ask Falstaff, "Are you not hurt i' the groin? Methought 'made a shrewd thrust at your belly" (2H4 2.4.210–211), lines that Shakespeare gave to the Hostess, but that here introduce the affection between Falstaff and Doll, who says, significantly, "I love thee better than I love e'er a scurvy young boy of them all," a line that, according to BRIDGET GELLERT LYONS, Welles added. When Falstaff unflatteringly characterizes Hal and Poins, the two young men drop down from the rafters. Hal accuses Falstaff of speaking ill of him, but Falstaff denies it, and Hal notes the parallels to Falstaff's previous lies. Hal begins to make his way through crowds of dancers, while Falstaff, who gets caught up in the dance, reaches the stable just as Hal rides away for the fourth time, again with the castle in the background as his destination. Falstaff, meanwhile, says he will go to visit Shallow, and Doll bids him farewell.

Welles cuts to the castle interior, where Hal enters to find his father in bed with the crown lying next to him. When the king does not stir, Hal assumes his father is dead and takes the crown to another room and kneels. At this point Welles cuts to a shot of Falstaff and Shallow in the middle of a conversation that echoes the opening of the film. "We have heard the chimes at midnight" (2H4 3.2.214–215) says Falstaff, as he and Shallow talk about dead friends. Welles then cuts back to the bedroom, where the king awakens and finds the crown gone, then paces through the cavernous halls looking for his son and predicting the doom of the state (2H4 4.5.92–137). The king stumbles, and Hal, wearing the crown, kneels to embrace his father and give him back the crown. Hal explains that he wore the crown, "To try with it, as with an enemy / That had before my face murdered my father" (2H4 4.5.165–167). The king embraces his son, and Hal leads him to the raised throne, with sunlight beaming down, where the king repents how he gained the throne, but advises his son on how to keep it, and then dies. Welles here frames the action in the castle's monumental architecture. With his dead father slumped in the throne behind him, Hal stands above the assembled mourners and vows that "The tide of blood in me . . . [will] flow henceforth in formal majesty" (2H4 2.129–133).

From this solemn moment, Welles cuts back to Shallow's house, where Silence and Shallow dance while Falstaff looks on. After Shallow falls and has to be carried out, Pistol rushes in with the news that the old King Henry is dead and Hal is now king. Grasping the news, Falstaff rushes forward, a towering though precarious figure who seems ready to fall out of the frame. Excitedly, the group rushes out, and standing on a hill in the snow, Falstaff utters, "Let us take any man's horses; the laws of England are at my commandment . . . and woe to my Lord Chief Justice" (2H4 5.3.135–137). Welles cuts to Hal, now king, the crown on his head, as he rides through the shouting crowds. When Falstaff and Shallow arrive at the cathedral, it occurs to Falstaff that he might be better dressed, but then, he reasons, "This poor show doth better. This doth infer the zeal I had to see him" (2H4 5.5.13–14). As the solemn procession continues down the nave of the cathedral, Falstaff suddenly calls out, "God save thee, my sweet boy!" (2H4 5.5.41). Without turning, the new king says, "I know thee not, old man. Fall to thy prayers" (2H4 5.5.47), then turns to face the kneeling and amazed Falstaff. The king calls the memory of his former self and friends a dream and says, "being awak'd, I do despise my dream" (2H4 5.5.51). Welles cuts back and forth between the two faces, both apparently in pain, keeping them out of the same frame and shooting the king from below while keeping the camera looking

down at the now banished Falstaff. Outside, afterward, Falstaff tries to tell Shallow that the king "must seem thus to the world," and says, "I shall be sent for in private to him" (2H4 5.5.77–78). Falstaff's image diminishes into a distant doorway.

Welles cuts to Prince John, the Bishop, and Westmoreland commenting on the king's banishing of his old friends until they are reformed. Just then, however, Doll is carried along by a group of soldiers while she cries out for Falstaff, then the sheriff gives the order to send Falstaff to the Fleet, and the Page enters crying that Falstaff is very sick. The brief sequence ends with Bardolph saying, "The King is a good King, but it must be as it may" (H5 2.1.125). Welles here cuts back to the new king and has Westmoreland introduce the foreign wars of *Henry V,* saying, "No King of England if not King of France" (H5 2.2.193). Welles then applies Shakespeare's lines about "the man committed yesterday, / That rail'd against our person" (H5 2.2.40–41) to Falstaff, and shows the king trying to excuse Falstaff by saying that "excess of wine . . . set him on" (H5 2.2.42), lines that perhaps recall Falstaff's rousing speech to sack at the Battle of Shrewsbury. Finally, Welles cuts to the tavern, where Falstaff's friends gather around the huge coffin. The Hostess delivers her eulogy (H5 2.3.9–26), then stands at the gate as Bardolph and Peto pull the coffin and the Page follows behind. Ralph Richardson's voice concludes with the description of King Henry V's reign, including the lines, "So humane withal, he left no offense unpunished nor friendship unrewarded. For conclusion, a majesty was he that both lived and died a pattern in princehood, a lodestar in honor, and famous to the world away."

Perhaps it is not surprising that this film, which resonates with so much of Welles's life and surfaced so many times during it, has been viewed as an analogue to the Welles biography. Jack Jorgens, for example, calls *Chimes* "the most *personal* of Shakespeare films" and suggests that Welles "perhaps . . . saw too much of himself in Falstaff." Jorgens characterizes the film as "the story of a fat, aging jester exiled from his audience and no longer able to triumph over impossible obstacles with wit and torrential imagination." Barbara Leaming comments that "Orson managed to bring into the foreground a dramatic story that had personally obsessed him all along: the story of the father, the mentor, and the young man's quandary about which of them to reject for the other." For her, "Hal's renunciation of drunken Falstaff in favor of the father, the king," is "also the story that as a youth he [Welles] had lived out when he rejected drunken Dick Welles [his father] in favor of Skipper Hill" [headmaster at the Todd School], and she goes on to say, "Significantly, Orson's Falstaff mingles traits of both Dick *and* Skipper."

James Naremore, on the other hand, comments on Welles's statement to ANDRÉ BAZIN that Shakespeare's "humanity came from his links to the Middle Ages, . . . and his pessimism, his bitterness—and it's when he allows them free rein that he touches the sublime—belong to the modern world, the world which had just been created." According to Naremore, "Shakespeare's links to 'the countryside' are very like Welles's own attachment to a vanished Wisconsin, and the bard's 'sublime' is very similar to the director's romantic quarrel with industrialism." Finally David Thomson, who admits to "being tough on the film," says that Falstaff "is someone that Hal has to be rid of . . . Falstaff was the Welles who owed money all over the world, who had abandoned and exploited associates, who had lied, tricked and feasted away the years endeavoring to protect his own quality, his legendary goodness. He was an embarrassment to himself and to others—there is no escape from this, not even in the hay, the daffodils and the excitement of a new film. So *Chimes at Midnight* is often wondrous and nearly always chaotic."

Looking at the film in the context of Welles's oeuvre, rather than his life, Joseph McBride calls *Chimes at Midnight* "Welles's masterpiece, the fullest most completely realized expression of everything he had been working toward since *Citizen Kane,* which itself was more an end than a beginning." According to McBride, "In *Chimes at Midnight,* Welles has fused his own viewpoint and that of his hero into a direct communication of emotion. His style, though every bit as deliberate and controlled as in *Kane,* no longer demands our attention for itself." Michael Anderegg says that *Chimes at Midnight* "has become a text that can be claimed equally by those whose interest in

Welles is primarily an interest in cinema and by those who study the ways Shakespeare's plays have been reconfigured and revivified via various cultural venues," and concludes that "the symbiosis of Shakespeare and Welles fulfills itself in a text that does more than justice to a complex of Shakespearean themes while it effectively summarizes and distills much of what we know as the Wellesian cinema."

References Anderegg, Michael. *Orson Welles, Shakespeare, and Popular Culture* (New York: Columbia University Press, 1999); Callow, Simon. *Orson Welles: The Road to Xanadu* (London: Vintage, 1996); Crowl, Samuel. *Shakespeare Observed: Studies in Performance on Stage and Screen* (Athens: Ohio University Press, 1992); Davies, Anthony. *Filming Shakespeare's Plays: The Adaptations of Laurence Olivier, Orson Welles, Peter Brook, Akira Kurosawa* (Cambridge, U.K.: Cambridge University Press, 1988); Hapgood, Robert. "*Chimes at Midnight* From Stage to Screen: The Art of Adaptation" (*Shakespeare Survey 39*. 39–52); Jorgens, Jack J. *Shakespeare on Film* (Lanham, New York, London: University Press of America, 1991); Leaming, Barbara. *Orson Welles: A Biography* (New York: Penguin Books, 1989); Lyons, Bridget Gellert, ed. *Chimes at Midnight: Orson Welles, Director* (New Brunswick, N.J. and London: Rutgers University Press, 1988); McBride, Joseph. *Orson Welles.* rev. ed. (New York: Da Capo Press, 1996); Naremore, James. *The Magic World of Orson Welles.* rev. ed. (Dallas, Tex.: Southern Methodist University Press, 1989); Rothwell, Kenneth S. *A History of Shakespeare on Screen: A Century of Film and Television* (Cambridge, U.K.: Cambridge University Press, 1999); Thomson, David. *Rosebud: The Story of Orson Welles* (New York: Alfred A. Knopf, 1996); Welles, Orson, with Peter Bogdanovich, edited by Jonathan Rosenbaum. *This Is Orson Welles* (New York: HarperCollins, 1992).

—R.V.

Citizen Kane

Citizen Kane   Mercury Productions/RKO Radio Pictures, Inc., 119 minutes, 1941. **Director:** Orson Welles; **Producer:** Welles; **Executive Producer:** George J. Schaefer; **Associate Producer:** Richard Baer; **Assistant Producers:** William Alland and Richard Wilson; **Assistant Directors:** Eddie Donahoe and Fred A. Fleck; **Screenplay:** Herman J. Mankiewicz and Welles; **Cinematographer:** Gregg Toland; **Music:** Bernard Herrmann and Herman Ruby (lyrics for "Charlie Kane"); **Art Director:** Van Nest Polglase; **Special Effects:** Vernon L. Walker;

Welles on the campaign trail as Charles Foster Kane
(Literature/Film Archive)

Editor: Robert Wise; **Cast:** Orson Welles (Charles Foster Kane), Joseph Cotten (Jedediah Leland/Newsreel Journalist), Dorothy Comingore (Susan Alexander Kane), Agnes Moorehead (Mary Kane), Ruth Warrick (Emily Norton Kane), Ray Collins ("Boss" Jim W. Gettys), Erskine Sanford (Herbert Carter/Newsreel Journalist), Everett Sloane (Mr. Bernstein), William Alland (Jerry Thompson/Narrator), Paul Stewart (Raymond), George Coulouris (Walter Parks Thatcher), Fortunio Bonanova (Matiste), Harry Shannon (James Kane), Gus Schilling (John, Head Waiter/Newsreel Journalist), Philip Van Zandt (Mr. Rawlson), Georgia Backus (Bertha Anderson), Sonny Bupp (Kane III), Buddy Swan (Kane, age eight), Al Eben (Solly), Tom Curran (Teddy Roosevelt)

Citizen Kane continues to be celebrated as the greatest film of all time. "Everything that matters in cinema since 1940," director FRANÇOIS TRUFFAUT famously suggested, "has been influenced by *Citizen Kane.*" Although made and released in the midst of great controversy because of its protagonist's putative resemblance to WILLIAM RANDOLPH HEARST, *Citizen Kane* nonetheless received nine Oscar nominations. It was hailed by the critics for its bold themes and equally bold narrative structure and style. Today, the film and its director are inextricably linked in the annals of film history as well as in the iconography of American popular culture.

Citizen Kane stands as WELLES's crowning achievement. Made in 1941 by his MERCURY THEATRE company at RKO when he was only 26, remarkably, *Citizen Kane* was his first feature film. As its producer, director, co-author, and star, Welles, notwithstanding key contributions by talented collaborators such as cinematographer GREGG TOLAND, co-screenwriter HERMAN J. MANKIEWICZ, and composer BERNARD HERRMANN, deserves to be credited as the film's author. Critics voting in polls such as those conducted by the distinguished film journal *Sight and Sound,* routinely place *Citizen Kane* at the top of their "Best Films" lists. Equally significant are the views of filmmakers ranging from the aforementioned Truffaut to STEVEN SPIELBERG who all point to *Kane* as the greatest film of all time as well as an enduring source of inspiration. When Spielberg bought one of the three ROSEBUD sleds made especially for *Kane* at an auction presided over by Sotheby Parke-Benet for $55,000 in 1982, the most financially successful director in motion picture history explained his seemingly extravagant decision by saying: "This [sled] is a symbolic medallion of quality in movies. When you look at Rosebud, you don't think of fast dollars, fast sequels, and remakes. This to me says that movies of my generation had better be good."

Why has *Citizen Kane* continued to so powerfully impress those who love and care about movies? First, there's the story. In short, *Citizen Kane* is a compellingly told mystery that poses the central question, Who was Charles Foster Kane? Second, there's the script and its unique structuring of the story. Instead of presenting Kane's saga as a typically told chronological tale, the Oscar-winning script by Welles and Mankiewicz allows, perhaps even forces the audience to draw its own conclusions about the protagonist by presenting five interpretations of Kane as told from the contrasting points of view of five different "witnesses." Third, there's the acting. Welles's compelling Oscar-nominated portrayal as Kane, who ages before our eyes from a dynamic young man in his 20s to a doddering senior in his 70s, remains one of film history's great performances. Also significant are the film's supporting players. From JOSEPH COTTEN's principal role as Kane's best friend, Jedediah Leland, to RAY COLLINS's cameo role as Kane's political opponent, Boss James W. Gettys, each of the film's many characters resonate with depth and dimensionality. Fourth, there's the film's bravura technique. From Oscar-nominated cinematographer Gregg Toland's startling deep-focus cinematography to Oscar-nominated editor ROBERT WISE's incisive editing and Oscar-nominated Bernard Herrmann's insinuating musical score, *Citizen Kane* is a virtual textbook of sophisticated techniques exemplifying the artistic best in mise-en-scène, cinematography, lighting, editing, music scoring, and sound design. Fifth, and perhaps most important, is Welles's directorial élan. Given *Citizen Kane*'s riveting story, brilliant script, superb acting, and cutting-edge technique, we should remember that it was producer-director Welles who was responsible for molding the film's various elements into a unified and mesmerizing whole. Sixth, *Citizen Kane* is remembered because of the still smoldering controversy stirred by its putative relationship to reality. In 1941, working from the assumption that the characters of Kane and Susan Alexander were based on the real-life figures of media magnate William Randolph Hearst and his mistress, movie star MARION DAVIES, Hearst unleashed the fury of his influential national chain of newspapers on Welles and his audacious film. Finally, a seventh reason for explaining the esteem for and, in fact, the mythos surrounding Welles and *Citizen Kane* has to do with the fact that the producer-director was but a 25-year-old tyro when he was invited by RKO to make his film debut largely on his own terms. In the Old Hollywood of 1941, where producers and directors had to work their way up through the system, the unprecedented carte blanche given the "Boy Wonder" was something strongly resented by the film colony's establishment. At the same time, the chutzpah and accomplishment of

Welles's once-in-a-lifetime opportunity is the stuff of legends, and, as such, the source of fevered dreams by legions of aspiring young filmmakers who from 1941 down to the present have fantasized about storming the bastions of Hollywood to wrest from the Old Guard another *Citizen Kane*, a film that would live on forever and, not incidentally, put a young director's name at the top of the marquee.

Citizen Kane opens with an ominous visual and musical design that immediately draws attention to a forbidding wrought-iron gate punctuated by the initial "K." In the murky background looms XANADU, the palatial yet haunting estate of one of the world's great titans. As the camera takes in the exotic details of the grounds—monkeys claustrophobically caged in the private zoo, deserted gondolas rocking languorously on a private lake, manicured lawns and shrubbery worthy of Versailles—there is a castle on a distant hill with a solitary light shining from a win-

Welles as the defeated Charles Foster Kane *(Literature/Film Archive)*

dow. As the camera cuts to the interior, we encounter an old and dying man who clutches a crystal ball enclosing a winter tableaux with make-believe snow. He utters a single word—"Rosebud"—and dies, dropping the ball, which fragments into a multitude of shards.

Suddenly, and with no preparatory transition, the film cuts to a slickly produced newsreel, NEWS ON THE MARCH. Adroitly patterned after THE MARCH OF TIME, the nation's most popular newsreel during the 1930s and 1940s, Welles's pseudo-newsreel recounts the colorful career of CHARLES FOSTER KANE (Welles), newspaper baron, shaper of news and public opinion, and presidential hopeful. When the newsreel abruptly stops in the darkened screening room, Rawlston (Philip Van Zandt), *News on the March*'s editor, prods his reporters to go out and dig up the real Kane. "It's not enough to tell us what a man did," Rawlston declares. "You've got to tell us who he was. What were the last words he said on earth? Maybe he told us all about himself on his deathbed. When Charles Foster Kane died he said but just one word—'Rosebud.' Now what does that mean?"

With the film's quest clearly established at the onset thanks to Welles's adept use of the newsreel, *Citizen Kane,* in many respects, becomes a noirish mystery. Who is Charles Foster Kane? In order to answer this central question that so effectively propels the narrative momentum of the film, Welles and co-scriptwriter Mankiewicz came up with an ingenious "solution." Instead of providing a "well-told" story whose denouement gives us a finalizing answer in which the driving question is answered, the script is structured to give contrasting versions of the "truth." At the end, while many of the fascinating details of Kane's life have been filled in, like a jigsaw puzzle missing several key pieces, we still don't have the complete "picture." Rosebud remains a mystery, and so, too, does Kane.

Jerry Thompson (WILLIAM ALLAND), *News on the March*'s ace reporter, functions as the audience's surrogate. Essentially, we tag along with Thompson as he travels around the country to query five of Kane's closest associates pursuant to his quest for the truth. As Thompson's reportorial "portrait" of Kane begins

to take shape, so, too, does ours. The five accounts come from Walter Parks Thatcher (GEORGE COULOURIS), a crusty J. P. Morgan-like Wall Street banker; Bernstein (EVERETT SLOANE), Kane's loyal assistant; Jedidiah Leland (Joseph Cotten), Kane's former best friend and newspaper colleague and also, to an appreciable degree, Kane's conscience; Susan Alexander (DOROTHY COMINGORE), Kane's second wife; and Raymond (PAUL STEWART), the taciturn and shifty-eyed butler at Xanadu. Thanks to Welles's intricate flashback structure, we also get significant "takes" on Kane from Emily Norton Kane (RUTH WARRICK), a president's niece and Kane's first wife, and Kane's mother (AGNES MOOREHEAD).

Thompson's quest begins in the cryptlike library of Thatcher, who though long dead, "speaks" through his memoirs. As Thompson reads, we see Kane as a boy (Buddy Swan), playing with his sled on a desolate, snow-covered Colorado hillock. Thanks to his mother, who years earlier had settled a boarding-house bill with a prospector from Kansas who had "paid" with a bundle of stock certificates, the mother, and soon the boy, are destined to be rich beyond their wildest dreams as sole owners of one of the world's leading silver mines. The stern Mrs. Kane, in order to ensure that her son has all of life's advantages, appoints the firm of Thatcher and Company as trustees of the fortune and guardian of her son. When Thatcher arrives to take the boy east to be educated, young Charles, upset about the impending separation from his family, lashes out and strikes Thatcher with his sled. The seeming coldness of the mother's decision is explained by the clear although implied suggestion that Kane's father (Harry Shannon) is an alcoholic, who though devoted to the boy, nonetheless beats him when under the influence. As alluded to in the words of Thatcher, this pivotal scene in the Kane family's ramshackle Colorado home establishes the central theme of Kane's unhappy childhood. Significantly, sympathy for the boy's plight—as a victim of child abuse, and as a virtual orphan uprooted from his family—remains throughout the film, thus nuancing responses to Kane's often reckless and megalomaniac behavior as an adult. Regardless of how selfish or brutal the adult Kane appears, we "understand" that it's not all his fault, that, indeed, in some way, he's a victim of circumstances beyond his control.

Through one montage sequence of quick cuts, we follow Kane as he grows up, at each stage tormenting Thatcher with his rebellious antics. When he reaches age 21, Charles assumes responsibility for what has become the world's sixth-largest private fortune. Still taking no stock in Thatcher's entreaties to accept his responsibilities as an adult and member of the nation's financial aristocracy, Kane decides in a moment of apparent whimsey to take personal charge of a small New York newspaper, the *Inquirer*. Abetted by Leland and Bernstein, Kane leverages the paper into a powerful empire of 37 newspapers. In the process, he becomes a self-proclaimed champion of the common man. Operating from an idealistically

progressive Declaration of Principals, Kane uses the *Inquirer* to attack Thatcher and other captains of finance and industry, including, ironically, himself, since the broad holdings of his vast stock portfolio make him a major oligarchic capitalist as well. Kane's motivations are complex, a seeming combination of a lingering adolescent rebelliousness, a perverse pleasure in taking down members of his own elite class, and, going back to his childhood, a consuming desire to be connected, to be accepted, and, indeed, to be loved.

From Bernstein, we learn, along with Thompson, about the beginnings of the *Inquirer*'s rejuvenation, Kane's enlistment of college chum Leland as his chief sounding board and drama critic, and Kane's entry into national politics via his propagandizing for U.S.

Welles as Kane at breakfast with Ruth Warrick *(Literature/Film Archive)*

entry into the Spanish-American war, an incident also appearing on Hearst's résumé. Significantly, Bernstein recounts Kane's wooing of Emily, the president's niece. Through another flashback, we come to appreciate the complexities of the marriage, whose gradual dissolution is brilliantly rendered in the famous breakfast room sequence in which quickly cut shots trace the couple's decline from happy newlyweds to estranged antagonists who, at the end of the montage sequence, sit across from each other in stony silence. Thompson, at the end of his interview, asks if Bernstein knows what "Rosebud" might signify. Bernstein suggests that it might have been a girl, but, in fact, he doesn't really know.

Thompson next calls on Leland, now a salty old resident in a Manhattan retirement complex who barters his recollections for the promise of a few good cigars, something his doctors have forbidden. Leland provides information about the early days of the *Inquirer* and, in flashback, we witness the poignant moment when Kane issues his Declaration of Principals. Leland also chronicles the troubled relationship with the star-crossed Susan Alexander, Kane's second wife, whose abortive opera career was obsessively promoted by Kane. Through Leland, we witness their innocent first meeting, where she sings sweetly, a brief but wonderful moment when he seems to have momentarily relaxed to the point of dropping his persona as Charles Foster Kane, man of influence and power. Leland then goes on to comment on the end of their barren relationship at Xanadu, with the aging Kane wandering aimlessly through the great halls while Susan sits working huge jigsaw puzzles. We also learn that it was the devastating review of Susan's opera debut—which an intoxicated Leland had started, but which Kane himself had finished in keeping with his colleague's negative lead—that was responsible for the breakup of the two men's friendship.

Thompson next visits a sad and half-drunk Susan Alexander, now a second-rate singer in a New Jersey nightclub whose major asset is her faded celebrity as Mrs. Charles Foster Kane. Susan's flashback reveals how Kane was initially drawn to her because, unaware of his fabulous wealth and power, she liked him for himself. The ensuing liaison between the sweetly naive Susan and Kane leads to his political undoing, when Kane's overmatched opponent in the New York gubernatorial race, "Big Jim" Gettys (Ray Collins), tells Kane that unless he withdraws, he will expose the affair to Kane's wife, Emily, and the public. Kane, in a remarkable confrontation with Gettys witnessed by both Susan and Emily, refuses to withdraw. Caught in one of film history's most dramatic depictions of unalloyed hubris, Kane is incapable of calculating the consequences of his dire decision on Emily, Susan, and, indeed, himself. When Kane's rival papers get hold of the story, he is politically ruined and loses the election. The prospect of divorce is cruelly twisted with news that his wife and son have been killed in an auto accident.

Susan's impossible opera career is also chronicled. Though not overtly stated, it's clear that Kane, defeated in politics, has made Susan's career his next personal project. Using his wealth and influence, he builds a $3 million opera house for her, and whips up a huge press campaign leading up to her debut. In the process, we witness Susan's agony as the unwitting and fragile vessel of Kane's unbridled ambition. There's the comic-tragic singing lesson with Señor Matiste (Fortunio Bonanova), bullied by Kane (and his money) into seeing things Kane's way, in spite of Matiste's insistence that Susan has "no talent." Alas, at the end, there is no Pygmalion-like transformation, and in a series of brilliantly staged opera scenes, we witness Susan's public humiliation. Aside from the glowing reviews in Kane's papers (save for the Leland-Kane pan), Susan's pathetically strained efforts produce only unintended consequences. Among the "thumbs downs" revealed by Welles's probing camera are shots of a stagehand holding his nose, opera devotees sniffing their nostrils, and, in one of the film's most savage-comic moments, an inebriated Jedidiah Leland responding to the opera by idly converting his program into a chorus line of paper dolls. Once again, Kane's maniacal hubris has pushed things to the brink. Susan, unable to cope with the now ritual degradation of performing, tries to kill herself with an overdose of sleeping powder. Her attempted suicide finally brings Kane's cruel charade to a halt, whereupon the now hopelessly estranged couple retreats from the outside world to

Xanadu. Eventually, the emptiness of their lives drives Susan off. Kane, in another of the film's signature scenes, unleashes his fury in an orgy of destruction that leaves the contents of Susan's abandoned bedroom in broken and utter disarray. Following her departure, Kane is left alone in his vast mausoleum.

Finally, Thompson concludes his quest by going to Xanadu to quiz Raymond. Although he had served as Kane's butler, Raymond is likewise puzzled by "Rosebud." At the film's conclusion, as reporters gather at Xanadu to compare notes and wrap up their stories, they concede that Rosebud, like a missing piece of a picture puzzle, is probably a lost and unretrievable piece of the mystery that is Kane. As the reporters disappear into the dark recesses of Xanadu, the camera begins a majestic pan over a huge storeroom filled with the high-priced baubles of Kane's thoughtless consumption. As rare statues, paintings, and other objets d'arts pass slowly by, the camera continues on to a heap of Kane's possessions that are being incinerated in a blazing furnace. As Herrmann's ominous music chills the spine, one of the workmen picks up a sled. It turns out that it is the very sled we saw Kane playing with when he was a boy in Colorado. As the camera tracks even closer and a workman thrusts the sled into the burning inferno, we can read its now blazing lettering—"Rosebud." The perspective then shifts to Xanadu's exterior, where the camera reverses the trajectory it had taken two hours earlier in the film's very first sequence. As a plume of black smoke curls up from one of Xanadu's chimneys, the camera tracks back from the castle until coming to rest on the wrought-iron fence and its signature "K" that opened the film.

Has the riddle of Kane been answered? Hardly. Indeed, the dramatic revelation of Rosebud as Kane's boyhood sled, while providing a literal association between the word and its real-world referent, hardly satisfies curiosity. Why, many have asked, is Kane thinking about his sled in his last moment of life? Is it possible that Rosebud signifies something other than the sled? Perhaps, it indeed is a reference to Kane's painful childhood separation from his parents? Or the loss of his first wife and son? Or, to Susan Alexander, or the dashing of his political career, or the loss of his best friend, Jedediah Leland? Perhaps

Rosebud points to the optimism inherent in the precepts that guided the writing of his Declaration of Principals? Or is Rosebud, to use Alfred Hitchcock's term, merely a MacGuffin, a clever yet essentially inconsequential plot device designed to trigger the story's action, and therefore a means of giving the characters something to do, something to ponder and chase down? Given the volumes of critical analyses lavished on *Citizen Kane,* no one has yet solved the riddle of Kane to the satisfaction of all parties. Like Hamlet, Kane remains a powerful and dramatically compelling character, whose perfectly and intriguingly constructed ambiguity has kept even his most sophisticated analysts guessing. It is that ambiguity, the refusal of the film to yield up easy answers, and its consequent invitation to viewers to participate in their own constructions of the story, that keeps *Citizen Kane,* like the Sphinx or the Mona Lisa, perpetually fresh and invigorating.

Thematically, Welles was always interested in power and love—and failure. Contrary to the conventions of the Hollywood success story with its happy ending, in approaching *Kane* (as well as his subsequent work), Welles was determined to make a "failure story." With that in mind, Welles noted that at the end, his protagonist "must retreat from a democracy which his money fails to buy and his power fails to control. There are two retreats possible: *death* and the *womb.* The house [Xanadu] was the womb." In elaborating further, Welles said: "Kane, we are told, loved only his mother—only his newspaper—only his second wife—only himself. Maybe he loved all of these, or none. It is for the audience to judge. . . . The point of the picture is not so much the solution of the problem as its presentation."

Citizen Kane is, indeed, justly celebrated for its "presentation." Borrowing on innovations he helped advance in lighting for the theater and sound in radio, as well as from the deep-focus approach of cinematographer Gregg Toland, Welles's visual and sound designs for *Kane* are still arresting, even for those weaned in the digital age. As noted by critic ANDRÉ BAZIN, deep-focus cinematography, by keeping everything in front of the camera in sharp focus, allows for the dynamic interplay of characters and objects both close to and distant from the camera.

Welles and Toland exploited these possibilities in several famous scenes, one of which is the unbroken long shot used to capture Susan's attempted suicide. In the foreground of Susan's darkened bedroom, we see in the lower left-hand corner of the frame, an empty glass glazed with the powdery residue of the sleeping medicine that she has just taken. In the middle of the frame, we observe Susan's near lifeless body draped over her bed. In the background, the door to her bedroom is traced by the light shining in around the jamb from the hallway. The hushed and tragic quiet of the room is disturbed when we hear a knock at the bedroom door. Next we hear Kane calling, "Susan, Susan." Even though we do not see Kane, his presence grows "larger" as his knocking and calls for "Susan" become increasingly insistent. Suddenly, Kane comes crashing through the door to directly witness the sorrowful consequence of his hubris. The emotional voltage of the scene is undeniable. Its power is even more amazing when we realize that its impact has been achieved through mise-en-scène and lighting and sound, rather than through camera movement and editing.

While *Citizen Kane* is uniformly praised for its stylistic and technical innovations, the acting in the film also deserves to be mentioned since it, too, contributes so much to the film's compelling dynamics. Although most members of the cast had extensive dramatic experience with Welles working in New York on various Mercury Theatre and radio projects, they, like Welles, had never appeared in a feature film. Still, one senses in *Kane*'s individual and ensemble scenes, the esprit and craft that were among the Mercury hallmarks. Welles's arresting rendering of Kane, with its demand for playing the character as both a young and old man, remains one of film history's towering turns. Joseph Cotten as the ruminative Jedidiah Leland, Everett Sloane as the avuncular Bernstein, Agnes Moorehead as Kane's stern mother, and Dorothy Comingore as the vulnerable Susan Alexander are equally compelling and convincing.

At the time of its release in 1941, *Citizen Kane* provoked considerable controversy because of Charles Foster Kane's resemblance to newspaper tycoon William Randolph Hearst. As suggested by Timothy W. Johnson, "Time has proven that whether or not

Hearst was the original inspiration for the character has nothing to do with the power and artistry of the film." While there is no question about the influence of Hearst on Mankiewicz, it seems clear that in etching his Kane as both a screenwriter and actor, Welles also had at least partially in mind the powerful billionaire industrialists SIR BASIL ZAHAROFF and HOWARD HUGHES, real-life "successes" who at the ends of their lives could also be deemed "failures."

In the early 1970s, another controversy arose over the film when critic PAULINE KAEL charged in several articles and her 1971 tome, *The Citizen Kane Book,* that Welles's reputation as *Kane*'s auteur had been grossly inflated. Instead of Welles, Kael's revisionist account argued that Herman J. Mankiewicz should be credited as the film's primary author. While her hysterical argument has been largely put to rest, it nonetheless points to the collaborative nature of film at large, and to the hundreds of specific artists and craftsmen who contributed so mightily to *Kane*. Timothy W. Johnson reminds us that "Any attempt to ascertain the exact contribution of any one of these people can only be of very limited success, involving as it must, memories, egos, and controversies. What is important is the film itself." Indeed, it is. *Citizen Kane* lives!

—C.B.

Citizen Welles, Inc. This project centered in Chicago is dedicated to preserving and restoring prints of Welles's films, such as *The Stranger, The Trial, Othello,* and *Chimes at Midnight*. It is sponsored by Intermission Productions and headed by Michael Dawson, who describes his operation as an "official-unofficial" archive. Dawson has been working on a massive Welles documentary (18 hours of film already shot in 35mm) that Dawson would like to see completed in two parts, from "Cradle to *Kane*" and then his career after *Kane*. One early achievement was the restoration of the Welles *Othello* (1992–93), available on VHS and DVD; a major challenge has been the effort to untangle the ownership and copyright for *Chimes at Midnight*. Queries should be sent to Citizen Welles, Inc., P.O. Box 84, Clarendon Hills, Illinois 60514.

—J.M.W.

Clair, René (1898–1981)

When WELLES chose to update *Un Chapeau de Paille d'Italie* as the debut offering by PROJECT 891, only VIRGIL THOMSON, sensing the musical possibilities, was enthusiastic about the 1851 French farce by Eugene Labiche and Marc Michel. Welles, who according to FRANK BRADY had always been fond of the play, became especially excited about the project's prospects after viewing French director René Clair's silent film version of the Labiche-Michel comedy, *The Italian Straw Hat* (1927). Indeed, Welles sought to emulate onstage Clair's briskly paced cinematic action and ever intensifying build-up of comic suspense. Welles also wanted to deal with a more frank approach to sex, which Clair's film with its allusions to adultery had handled exquisitely. However, as the production approached its opening at the Maxine Elliott Theatre on September 26, 1936, Welles decided to change the name of his play to HORSE EATS HAT. Quite simply, he was apprehensive that if he used the title *The Italian Straw Hat,* that people who had seen the René Clair film might stay away or, even worse, be tempted to make invidious comparisons. A new title implied a new conceptualization.

In 1939, when Welles was giving himself a crash course in the basics of filmmaking in preparation for his first RKO directing assignment, he avidly screened the films of Ford, Hitchcock, Lang, Vidor, Capra, and Clair, in an effort to better understand how the great directors achieved their goals.

Clair, one of cinema's most celebrated directors, became interested in storytelling through putting on puppet shows. After military service in World War I, during which he was badly wounded, he wrote for a Paris journal. In 1920, thanks to friends in the film industry, he made his debut as a film actor and appeared in the Feuillades serials *L'Orpheline* and *Parisette* (both 1921). In 1922, when he realized that he hated acting but loved filmmaking, he went to Brussels, where his brother Henri Chomette was working as assistant to director Jacques de Baroncelli, and apprenticed under Baroncelli.

In 1923, he debuted as a film director with *Paris qui dort* (*The Crazy Ray*), which he also wrote, and which included the core elements of his style, an intuitive sense of comic timing, a celebration of movement, and stylish charm. With the satiric *The Italian Straw Hat* (1927), his silent era masterpiece, Clair became an international figure. He also contributed to the impressive French avant-garde with *Entr'acte* (1924). Although initially skeptical about sound, his early talkies, especially as *Le Million* (1931), influenced filmmakers everywhere. A total filmmaker who either wrote or collaborated on his films' scenarios, Clair continually explored the possibilities of visual form, movement, and sound. Many of his published ideas about film were collected together and issued under the titles *Reflection Faite* (1951) and *Cinéma d'Hier, Cinéma d'Aujourd'hui* (1970). Deeply devoted to his French heritage, he nonetheless also made films in England and, during World War II, in the United States.

Among Clair's other films are *Le Fantôme du Moulin Rouge* (1925), *Le Voyage Imaginaire* (1926), *La Proie du Vent* (1927), *Les Deux Timides* (1928), *Sous les Toits de Paris* (*Under the Roofs of Paris,* 1930), *À Nous la Liberté* (1931), *Quatorze Juillet* (*July 14th,* 1933), *Le Dernier Milliardaire* (1934), *The Ghost Goes West* (U.K., 1935), *Break the News* (U.K., 1938), *Un Village dans Paris* (1939), *The Flame of New Orleans* (U.S., 1941), *I Married a Witch* (U.S., 1942), *It Happened Tomorrow* (U.S., 1944), *And Then There Were None* (U.S., 1945), *La Silence est d'Or* (*Man About Town,* 1947), *La Beauté du Diable* (*Beauty and the Devil,* 1950), *Les Belles de Nuit* (*Beauties of the Night,* 1952), *Les Grande Manoeuvres* (*The Grand Maneuver,* 1955), *Porte de Lilas* (*Gates of Paris,* 1957), *La Française et l'Amour* (*Love and the Frenchwoman,* 1960), *Tout l'or du Monde* (1961), *Les Quatre Verités* (*Three Fables of Love*—the "Two Pigeons" episode, 1962), and *Les Fêtes Galantes* (1965).

References Dale, R.C. *The Films of René Clair* (Metuchen, N.J.: Scarecrow, 1986); Greene, Naomi. *René Clair: A Guide to References and Resources* (Boston: G.K. Hall, 1985); McGerr, Celia. *René Clair* (Boston: Twayne, 1980).

—C.B.

Cloutier, Suzanne (1927–)

In 1950, in the midst of the troubled filming of OTHELLO, WELLES had to recast Desdemona when Lea Padovani stormed off the set. First, he persuaded Cecile Aubry, with whom he had worked on THE BLACK ROSE

(1950), to take the part. Two days later, she, too, deserted to appear in another film, *Bluebeard*. Betsy Blair, who had been recommended by director Anatole Litvak, was next. Although a capable young actress, Blair was soon rejected by Welles because she didn't have the proper maturity for the Moor's bride. Finally, Welles tried Suzanne Cloutier, a young French-Canadian actress in her early 20s who had appeared in several films in her native Quebec. Cloutier fit the bill. Welles first met her at the Venice Film Festival in 1949 after seeing her performance in Julien Duvivier's film *Au Royaume des Cieux*.

Welles biographer PETER NOBLE describes Cloutier's initial impact on the *Othello* troupe: "With her wide-eyed innocence, coupled with a will of iron and a determination to get her own way at all costs, she constituted a strange mixture. Orson, who found her a fascinating psychological study and who spent hours trying to get the performance he wanted from her, nicknamed her 'The Iron Butterfly,' and the name stuck until the film was finished." Cloutier's standoffishness extended to her personal relationship with her director. As FRANK BRADY notes, in spite of Welles's months-long seduction, she was adamant. Her interest in Welles was strictly professional, confined to her best efforts at characterizing Desdemona. Because she rejected Welles's advances, he sometimes treated her poorly. Once, at dinner with the other members of the cast, he stung: "You contribute nothing to the conversation unless you talk about yourself."

In 1951, while editing *Othello,* Welles began to grow dissatisfied with Cloutier's voice. Cloutier, though, was not available to do her own dubbing, since she was in England making *Derby Day* and also preparing for her marriage to Peter Ustinov. Welles then hired Scottish actress Gudrun Ure for redubbing some of the lines. Eventually, much to his technicians' chagrin, Welles decided to redub all of Cloutier's lines. Whether his intent was artistic, or personal, or some combination, will probably never be known. Revenge, though, was certainly part of the mix. Indeed, Frank Brady quotes Welles as saying: "We'll have Ure dub the entire Desdemona. I can't wait to see what Cloutier's reaction will be when she attends the premiere and finds out it's not really her,

at least not her voice, and many shots not her body— on the screen." The last phrase refers to Welles's decision to leave shots of Lea Padovani's Desdemona in the final version of the film.

Later in 1950, before Welles had started editing *Othello,* he also hired Cloutier for the role of Miss Pratt in THE UNTHINKING LOBSTER, the director's satiric one-act jibe at Hollywood, a part of the double bill, THE BLESSED AND THE DAMNED, that played in Paris during the summer. Although Cloutier had been scheduled to play Helen of Troy in the double-bill's second one-acter, TIME RUNS, Welles's reworking of the Faust story, at the last minute, he instead gave the part to EARTHA KITT, whom he had just met at a Paris nightspot during the show's rehearsals.

Before acting, Cloutier was a successful New York model. Her films include *Temptation* (1946), *Au Royaume des Cieux* (1949), *Juliette ou la Clef des Songes* (1950), *Doctor in the House* (1954), and *Romanoff and Juliet* (1961), the last with husband, Peter Ustinov. Her 17-year marriage to Ustinov ended in divorce in 1971. After her divorce, she produced documentary films into the 1990s.

—C.B.

Cocteau, Jean (1889–1981)

Jean Cocteau's *The Blood of a Poet* (1930) was a widely influential feature-length experimental film, a personal exploration of the poet's inner life, his fears and obsessions, his relationship to the material world, and his obsession with death. Along with the surrealist masterpiece *L'Age d'Or* (*The Golden Age,* 1930) by Luis Buñuel and Salvador Dali, it helped define an inherently personal and poetic approach to the experimental film. In 1934, the 19-year-old WELLES, assisted by William Vance, a fellow 19-year-old actor in the company of the Woodstock Summer Theatre Festival, used Vance's 16mm camera to shoot a send-up of Cocteau's and Buñuel-Dali's art film landmarks in a four-minute, non-narrative, satirically surreal parody called *Hearts of Age* (1934). The film also contains oblique homages to the expressionist film classics, *The Cabinet of Dr. Caligari* (1919) and *Nosferatu* (1922). *Hearts of Age,* an intentionally aimless series of symbolic images suggesting preoccupations with sex and death, is generally listed as Welles's first film.

Significantly, it also anticipates Welles's lifelong interrogation of what he regarded as overaestheticized symbolism. However, given Welles's own penchant for symbolism (such as his incorporation of the sled and glass-enclosed winter scene in CITIZEN KANE), it could be argued that Cocteau and Buñuel-Dali, while providing an artistic stance against which to resist, also provided inspiration. Welles's referencing of Cocteau's film also points to the fact that the 19-year-old possessed a breadth of cultural knowledge expanding well beyond Shakespeare.

In 1936, Cocteau, in New York for a quick stop amid a tour around the world in 80 days for a Paris newspaper, attended Welles's "voodoo" MACBETH as the guest of VIRGIL THOMSON, who had written the production's music. When the curtain opened, Thomson recalls Cocteau whispering, "Why this Wagnerian lighting?" At the conclusion of the performance, which he judged "exquisite," he answered his initial question himself, noting how the lighting contributed to the aura of violence: "Well, I think for a jungle setting it's a perfectly good idea."

Cocteau, like Welles, was a wunderkind who began writing at 10 and was a published poet, magazine editor, and darling of the international intellectual set by age 16. He became a leading figure in French cultural life between the two world wars. Although participating in the various art and intellectual movements that washed across the Continent during his lifetime, he was first and foremost a poet. In the mid-1920s, in order to gain a better self-understanding, he used opium, acquiring an addiction that was eventually cured.

The themes enumerated in *The Blood of a Poet* mentioned above were elaborated on in Cocteau's two other personal films, *Orpheus* (1950) and *The Testament of Orpheus* (1960). Although these three films have been criticized by some as arty and pretentious, they also are among film history's most inventive and disturbing and personal works. More conventional in terms of their narrative concerns and structures are Cocteau's other landmark films, *Beauty and the Beast* (1945), a poignantly haunting rendering of the children's story, and *Les Parents Terribles* (*The Storm Within*, 1948), an adaptation of his stage play dealing with stressful family relationships. In addition to his own films, Cocteau contributed scenarios and narrations to a number of other dramatic and documentary works. For many years, Cocteau served as the honorary president of the Cannes Film Festival.

References Brown, Frederick. *A Impersonation of Angels: A Biography of Jean Cocteau* (New York: Viking, 1968); Steegmuller, Francis. *Cocteau: A Biography* (Boston: Little, Brown, 1970).

—C.B.

Cohn, Harry (1891–1958)

As president of Columbia Studios, Harry Cohn had under contract RITA HAYWORTH, whom he treated as, in FRANK BRADY's words, "a combination daughter, slave, and financial investment." He was understandably upset when Hayworth spurned VICTOR MATURE and fell in love with ORSON WELLES because he sensed that Welles might interfere with his plans for her career. He even barred Welles from Columbia Studios. According to Welles, Cohn "felt a tremendous *proprietary* sense for Rita," and "had been lusting for her ever since he signed her, and chasing her around the desk." Even if he could not prevent her marriage to Welles, Cohn could keep her from performing as Welles's assistant in the wartime MERCURY WONDER SHOW. He also had her dressing room bugged and assigned people to keep track of her whereabouts. CHARLES HIGHAM describes her feelings about Cohn: "She hated his dourness, his lack of polish or grace, his calling her a 'dumb broad' and attacking Orson as 'a washed-up so-called genius.'" (Welles was not fond of Cohn, who, he said, "looked like a gargoyle off of a spire on Notre Dame.") Cohn was therefore delighted when the Welles-Hayworth marriage started to disintegrate. It was Welles's desperate attempt to raise money for his stage production of AROUND THE WORLD IN 80 DAYS, after producer MIKE TODD left the project, that brought Welles, Hayworth, and Cohn together again. Welles claims that he telephoned Cohn and asked Cohn for $50,000 in exchange for Welles writing and directing a film for him without pay; and Bob Thomas, author of *King Cohn* agrees with the $50,000 figure. Frank Brady and BARBARA LEAMING believe that it was $10,000. The story about which film Welles would do also varies: Welles says that during the phone conversation he saw a paperback titled *THE LADY FROM SHANGHAI;* Welles elsewhere says it was *If I Die Before I Wake,* but the book had not appeared in paperback at the time of the conversation. Welles and William Castle adapted Sherwood King's *If I Die Before I Wake,* and the budget was established at $2,300,000. Welles and Cohn were at odds from the start. Concerned about his star's image, Cohn was upset about Welles making Hayworth a blonde with short hair; and Cohn was outraged about what he regarded as waste and extravagance; Welles was more concerned about the look of the film. According to Welles, Cohn bugged his quarters, so Welles daily addressed the hidden microphones. Over Welles's objections, Cohn insisted on including more close-ups of Hayworth; Welles believed that close-ups were antithetical to the role he was creating for Hayworth. Upset with the complexity of the plot and fearing that the film would be a financial disaster, Cohn had Welles insert a song entitled "Please Don't Kiss Me" for Hayworth to sing. He hoped thereby to get record and sheet music sales. When the film was finally finished in March 1947, Cohn was concerned about its possible adverse effect on Hayworth's image and hoped to have her complete some other films before the release of *The Lady from Shanghai.* The film was released about a year after its completion. After the filming, Hayworth wanted to go to Europe, and Cohn reluctantly acquiesced. She met Aly Khan, and Cohn again tried to break up one of her romances, but he was no more successful than he had been with Welles.

Cohn, who was born on July 23, 1891, in New York City, was the son of an immigrant tailor. He left school at an early age and worked in a wide variety of jobs (shipping clerk, pool hustler, fur salesman, vaudeville performer, trolley conductor) before he became Carl Laemmle's personal secretary. Laemmle, who founded Universal Studios, also employed Harry's brother, Jack, and Joe Brandt. When Harry, Jack, and Joe left Laemmle to form the C. B. C. Film Company in 1920, only Harry went to Hollywood to supervise production; the other two worked on sales and distribution. By 1924, the prosperous film company became Columbia Studios, which he ruled with an iron hand. He was called "Harry the Horror," and screenwriter Ben Hecht dubbed him

"White Fang," a nickname that persisted. A combative person, Cohn fought with his performers and with his own brother, Jack, who in 1932 unsuccessfully attempted a coup. Harry Cohn won the battle and became undisputed president of Columbia. Hated and feared but financially astute, Cohn was an intriguing and effective studio head.

References Dick, Bernard F. *Merchant Prince of Poverty Row: Harry Cohn of Columbia Pictures* (Lexington, Ky.: University Press, 1993); Thomas, Bob. *King Cohn: The Life and Times of Hollywood Mogul Harry Cohn* (Beverly Hills, Calif.: New Millennium Press, 2000).

—T.L.E.

Colbert, Claudette (Claudette Lily Chauchoin)

Colbert, Claudette (Claudette Lily Chauchoin) (1905–1996) Claudette Colbert co-starred with ORSON WELLES in two films, *TOMORROW IS FOREVER* (1946) and *ROYAL AFFAIRS IN VERSAILLES* (1954). She was born on September 23, 1905, in Paris, but came to New York when she was six years old. She made her stage debut in 1923 and appeared on Broadway from 1925 through 1929. Although she made her screen debut in the silent *For the Love of Mike* (1927), she made her reputation in sound films, playing a variety of roles. She was effective playing the femme fatale in *The Sign of the Cross* (1932) and *Cleopatra* (1934), but her role as the irresponsible heiress in Frank Capra's screwball comedy *It Happened One Night* (1934), for which she won the Oscar for best actress, established her as a talented comic performer. In 1946, she played opposite Welles in *Tomorrow Is Forever,* a film about a man, assumed to be dead, who returns to find his wife married to another man. Welles, whose appearance was altered in the course of the film to make it difficult to identify him, played the returning husband, and Colbert played the wife. The film was very successful and made Welles, according to CHARLES HIGHAM, "bankable as an actor." She next appeared with Welles in SACHA GUITRY's *Royal Affairs in Versailles* (Welles played an obese and gouty Ben Franklin), a "woman's film" that did not do well at the box office. Some of her better-known films include *Drums along the Mohawk* (1939), *The Palm Beach Story* (1942), *The Egg and I* (1947), *Thunder on the Hill* (1951), and *Parrish* (1961). Her last film was *The Love Goddesses* (1965), although she continued to make some stage appearances. She died in 1996.

References Everson, William. *Claudette Colbert* (New York: Pyramid, 1976); Quirk, Lawrence J. *Claudette Colbert: An Illustrated Biography* (New York: Crown, 1985).

—T.L.E.

Collins, Ray (1888–1965)

Ray Collins was one of the MERCURY THEATRE players who moved to Hollywood with ORSON WELLES and was especially memorable for his portrayal of Boss Jim Gettys, the shrewd politician who spoiled the political ambitions of CHARLES FOSTER KANE by disclosing the scandal of Kane's "love nest" with Susan Alexander. He later played Uncle Jack in *THE MAGNIFICENT AMBERSONS* (1942) and District Attorney Adair in *TOUCH OF EVIL* (1958). He also was cast in the stage adaptation of RICHARD WRIGHT's *NATIVE SON,* the last stage production mounted by Orson Welles and JOHN HOUSEMAN before *CITIZEN KANE* in 1941.

Welles as Kane threatens Ray Collins as Boss Jim Gettys
(Literature/Film Archive)

Collins was born in 1888 in Sacramento, California, the son of a noted drama critic. He made his stage debut at the age of six, played in stock companies, and appeared on Broadway before moving to Hollywood, where he had his first Hollywood role in John Ford's *The Grapes of Wrath* (1940). He also appeared in William Wyler's *The Best Years of Our Lives* (1946), in King Vidor's adaptation of *The Fountainhead* (1949), and in many less distinguished films, including three in the Ma and Pa Kettle series. Toward the end of his career he was best known as Lieutenant Tragg, a regular on the popular *Perry Mason* television show. He died of emphysema in 1965.

—J.M.W.

Comingore, Dorothy (1913–1971)

Dorothy Comingore, who played in *CITIZEN KANE,* was born in Los Angeles on August 24, 1913. She attended the University of California. As Linda Winters she clowned with the Three Stooges in their comedy shorts of the mid-1930s; and she played in low-budget programmers like *Blondie Meets the Boss* (1939). The only film of consequence in which she appeared was Frank Capra's *Mr. Smith Goes to Washington* (1939), with JAMES STEWART. CHARLES CHAPLIN saw her in summer stock and made her his protégée (and mistress) for a time. Then WELLES cast her as Susan Alexander, the second wife of CHARLES FOSTER KANE, in *Citizen Kane;* he thought she could be convincing as the pathetic waif that Kane picks up. Comingore was chagrined to have Welles tell her that Susan was probably the most important character in the film. When she auditioned for the role, she told PAULINE KAEL, Welles turned to screenwriter HERMAN MANKIEWICZ and asked for his reaction. Mankiewicz responded, "Yes, she looks precisely like the image of a kitten we've been looking for." While she was waiting for principal photography to begin, she subsisted on unemployment checks of $18 a week, since her career was in the doldrums at that point. Welles insisted that she use her real name again.

Welles took a special interest in coaching her for her role, and sometimes he was rough on her while directing her on the set. When RUTH WARRICK, who played Kane's first wife, asked him to ease up on

Dorothy Comingore as Susan Alexander, flanked by Orson Welles as Kane and Ray Collins as Boss Jim Gettys
(Literature/Film Archive)

Comingore, Welles replied that "it was good for the character," according to FRANK BRADY. He wanted Comingore to see him as the overwhelming figure that Susan saw Kane to be.

Since Kane was based in some ways on WILLIAM RANDOLPH HEARST, it has been logically assumed that Susan was modeled to some extent on Hearst's mistress, MARION DAVIES, since Susan is Kane's mistress long before she is his wife. Frank Brady states quite perceptively: "The parallel to Marion Davies was strong in the scenes of Susan's drinking, doing jigsaw puzzles, complaining of having no friends at the castle, and so on; however, for Susan Alexander Kane the singer, it is fairly certain whom Welles had

in mind. He has said that he drew a great deal of the picture from the heir of the farm machinery family—*not* Robert McCormick, the newspaper magnate as is often mentioned—but from Harold McCormick and his days connected with the Chicago Civic Opera House. After his divorce from Edith Rockefeller, Harold McCormick had married a temperamental and rather mediocre soprano, Ganna Walska, whom he attempted to propel into operatic stardom, unsuccessfully as it developed." BERNARD HERRMANN, who composed the film's score, confirms in a memo to Welles that Susan's opera career is modeled on that of "G.W."; i.e., Ganna Walska.

It is true that Hearst did not build an opera house for Marion Davies, as Kane does for Susan; but Hearst did found Cosmopolitan Pictures in 1919 as an independent production company to showcase her. The big difference between Susan and Marion is that, while Susan was a second-rate performer, Marion definitely was not. Marion Davies was at her best as a witty comedienne in lighthearted silent comedies such as *Little Old New York* (1923). Unfortunately, Hearst was committed to making her a big star in dramatic roles for which she was ill-suited, such as Mary Tudor in *When Knighthood Was in Flower* (1922). Moreover, Hearst's papers systematically overpraised her pictures and her performances in them, until the public grew tired of both. The comparison with Kane employing his newspapers to make the opera-going public buy Susan as a diva is unmistakable.

Dorothy Comingore told Kael that she initially shot some tests for *Kane,* and that "all of these tests were incorporated into the film; they were never retaken." Actually, these scenes were not tests at all. Welles did not want the studio administration to know that he and cinematographer GREGG TOLAND were experimenting with unconventional techniques. So he reported that he was shooting some tests before principal photography commenced on July 30, 1940; and this footage was used in the film.

One of Comingore's scenes, which was done under the guise of a test, begins with the camera photographing Susan from above, through a cracked skylight, as she sits at a table in a cheap café, drinking alone. The camera moves downward through a lap dissolve toward Susan. She is then interviewed by Jerry Thompson (WILLIAM ALLAND), a reporter, about Kane, recently deceased. During the scene in which Susan makes her operatic debut, the camera climbs to the rafters of the opera house; a stagehand expresses his disappointment with her singing by pinching his nose.

When Susan attempts suicide in order to put a stop to Kane's futile attempts to foist her on the public as an opera star, she is freed of the opera house he built for her, says LAURA MULVEY. But "he constructs another monumental setting, a mausoleum to preserve her in a living death" for XANADU.

Kane and Susan are dwarfed in the huge rooms in the mansion. At times Welles has their voices echo on the soundtrack, as if they were conversing across a canyon, emphasizing the emptiness and loneliness of their lives. In later years, Welles was at pains to minimize the parallels between Susan and Marion Davies. In his Introduction to the reissue of her autobiography, *The Times We Had,* in 1971, 10 years after her death, he writes: "Xanadu was a lonely fortress and Susan was quite right to escape it. . . . But Marion Davies was never one of Hearst's possessions, and she was the treasure of his heart. Theirs was truly a love story. Love is not the subject of *Citizen Kane.*"

Dorothy Comingore got mixed reviews. Some reviewers admired the intensity of her performance; one critic described her as combining emotional power with a natural beauty—the "most astonishing young actress since Garbo was a pup." By contrast, another critic complained that Kane's second wife was too shrill, adding that the ear of an audience can only endure so much. Leigh Woods comments in an article on the acting in *Kane* that the shrillness Comingore was criticized for comes in the later scenes, when she whines pathetically about the humiliation of her ruined opera career and still later about being cooped up with an aging husband in a museum. These scenes, Woods avers, are an emblem of the passion that Comingore brings to the role, as Susan seeks to come to terms with her wretched life.

The basis for the negative notices which Comingore's performance drew, CHARLES HIGHAM astutely notes, is that Susan is fundamentally a disagreeable character who ultimately fails to enlist our sympathies. "At first a mindless girl, then later a loud-mouthed and vulgar middle-aged woman." But Comingore's fresh, unsophisticated performance is in the right key from beginning to end.

Comingore became pregnant during filming, and Gregg Toland had to adroitly conceal her condition in photographing her as shooting progressed. After she gave birth, she could not consider taking part in Welles's next film, THE MAGNIFICENT AMBERSONS. When Welles, who narrated the trailer for *Kane,* states, "You don't know Dorothy Comingore, but you will soon," he made a prophecy that was never to be fulfilled. He told PETER BOGDANOVICH that she was wonderful in the film, "and she turned down every offer she got for three years. She was waiting for another part like that one. And then there were no more parts."

She played in the film version of Eugene O'Neill's *The Hairy Ape* (1944) and in *Any Number Can Play* (1949), with Clark Gable. Her last picture was *The Big Night* (1951), directed by JOSEPH LOSEY. It was a low-budget revenge melodrama with John Barrymore, Jr. Her performance was as good as her lines in the hack script allowed. After the movie's release, clouds were gathering over the careers of both Comingore and Losey, because they were both suspected of being communists.

With the tense period of uncertainty known as the cold war came the anticommunist witch-hunt, called the Red Scare, encouraged by Senator Joseph McCarthy and carried on by the hearings conducted by the House Un-American Activities Committee (HUAC). Those "friendly witnesses" who were suspected of having communist affiliations were granted immunity from prosecution in exchange for informing on friends in the film industry, most of whom had long since abandoned any interest in politics. One such friendly witness, Comingore was appalled to discover, was her husband, Richard Collins.

One of the things held against Comingore by the committee was that she, along with Orson Welles, had belonged in 1942 to the Sleepy Lagoon Defense Committee, a leftist coalition that helped in the release of 17 young Chicanos who had been framed for murder. Comingore was blacklisted, but not Welles, who did not begin to have the left-wing associations that she and her husband Richard Collins had.

Losey was also blacklisted and continued his film career in England. But blacklisting was the final blow to Comingore's career; she never acted again. She died by her own hand in 1971. Without question, her role as Susan Alexander in *Citizen Kane* was her finest hour.

References   Brady, Frank. *Citizen Welles: A Biography of Orson Welles* (New York: Scribner's, 1989); Higham, Charles. *The Films of Orson Welles* (Los Angeles: University of California Press, 1973); Kael, Pauline. "Raising Kane," in *The Citizen Kane Book* (Boston: Little, Brown, 1971): 1–86; Mulvey, Laura. *Citizen Kane* (London: British Film Institute, 1992); Welles, Orson. "Introduction," to Marion Davies, *The Times We Had* (New York: Bobbs-Merrill, 1975); Welles, Orson, and Peter Bogdanovich. *This is Orson Welles* (New York: Da Capo, 1998); Woods, Leigh. "The Acting in *Citizen Kane*," in *Perspectives on Citizen Kane,* ed. Ronald Gottesman (New York: G. K. Hall, 1996): 213–28.
—G.D.P.

Compulsion

Compulsion   Twentieth Century–Fox, 103 minutes, 1959. **Director:** Richard Fleischer; **Producer:** Richard D. Zanuck; **Screenplay:** Richard Murphy (adapted from the novel by Meyer Levin); **Cinematographer:** William C. Mellor; **Editor:** William Reynolds; **Music:** Lionel Newman; **Cast:** Orson Welles (Jonathan Wilk), Diane Varsi (Ruth Evans), Dean Stockwell (Judd Steiner), Bradford Dillman (Artie Strauss), E.G. Marshall (District Attorney Harold Horn), Martin Milner (Sid Brooks), Richard Anderson (Max Steiner)

ORSON WELLES co-starred in this true-crime tale inspired by the infamous Loeb-Leopold murder case, in which two homosexuals, Artie Strauss (BRADFORD DILLMAN) and Judd Steiner (DEAN STOCKWELL) kill a youngster just for the thrill of it. Welles plays Jonathan Wilk, based on Clarence Darrow, who defended Nathan Leopold and Richard Loeb, the murderers of teenage Bobby Franks.

Welles had recently directed *TOUCH OF EVIL,* which won the grand prize at an international film festival in Brussels and was hailed all over Europe; but it was not a success in the United States. Still, he was disappointed when he was not asked to direct *Compulsion* as well as to star in it. As CHARLTON HESTON has said, Welles had the reputation among Hollywood's moguls of being extravagant. So Twentieth Century–Fox hired him for 10 days to play Wilk, after which he was scheduled to go to Hong Kong for another movie.

RICHARD FLEISCHER, a capable director of film noir movies such as *Narrow Margin* (1952), was chosen to helm the picture. Welles had narrated Fleischer's previous picture, *THE VIKINGS* (1958), an elaborate adventure with Kirk Douglas; and Fleischer had already found him somewhat daunting to work with. "You don't know how to handle him," Fleischer told BARBARA LEAMING. "He's got this overpowering voice and presence. . . . I don't think you can ever understand him." Fleischer continued, "You have to be very careful in directing Orson; you have to gain his confidence. He watches the director to see how the director has prepared," and how he handles other actors and the crew. "If he has no confidence in you, he will steamroller you, flatten you right out. So he has to feel he can trust you."

Welles seemed to be testing Fleischer one day, when the director told him to exit the scene by going through the door on the left. For no discernible reason Welles said that he preferred to exit on the right. Fleischer patiently explained that there was no set to cover that exit. "If you turn right and we pan with you, you will be off the set." "You know what I would say if I were directing this picture?" Welles responded; he would wait until they built another wall for the set. "Orson," Fleischer said, "that's the reason why I am directing this picture and you are not." "You are absolutely right," Welles conceded, and exited on the left.

Compulsion was a pacesetter in its treatment of homosexuality in a way that was relatively forthright for American movies at the time. Geoffrey Shurlock, the industry censor, insisted that the restrictions of the industry's censorship code prohibited Fleischer from depicting homosexuality in any explicit way. Nonetheless, in spite of some censorial interference, the film depicted the homosexual ambience of the story in a satisfactory fashion. Artie is a "textbook case" in homosexuality, given his deep-seated attachment to his domineering mother; likewise, Judd is recognizable as homosexual in his submissive relationship with his strong-willed companion. Indeed, their mutual attachment to each other testifies to the sexual orientation of the pair—although Wilk glosses over his rich client's homosexuality in defending them. His defense takes the form of attacking the wealthy establishment that shaped the pair, spoiled by the affluent families.

In short, *Compulsion* was more frank in treating the two protagonists than *Rope* (1948), Alfred Hitchcock's version of the same murder case. In fact, Welles was pleased with the honesty of Richard Murphy's script, derived from Meyer Levin's novel; and he was happy to be offered a plum role modeled on Clarence Darrow. At the movie's climax, Wilk delivers his final plea to the judge and jury, which is very much tailored to the address that Darrow gave; essentially, it is a denunciation of capital punishment, condemning the philosophy of "an eye for an eye."

Welles wanted to give this speech all in one extended take, without cuts. But Fleischer decided against it; filming Wilk's 10-minute oration in a single shot, uninterrupted by cuts to other angles, would require an immensely complicated setup, involving a number of technical problems necessitated by numerous shifts of the camera and the lights. In brief, shooting the speech in a single take would have taken some days, and Welles's time on the picture was limited.

Consequently, Fleischer opted to film the sequence in a number of short takes. Nevertheless, Welles gave a sustained reading of the lengthy oration and built it up to a dramatic climax. Welles filmed the scene, writes FRANK BRADY, "in a sweltering courthouse, with his collar wilted, his hair disheveled, his shirt sleeves in garters, and his pants hoisted by wide suspenders." Ever attentive to his makeup, he applied large amounts of gum arabic to distort his nose, in an effort to resemble Darrow all the more.

Welles holds his listeners in thrall, as he says in part: "The world has been one long slaughterhouse from the beginning until today—and the killing goes on and on and on. Why not read something? Why not think? Instead of blindly shouting for death? . . . It's taken the world a long, long time to get even where it is today. Your honor, if you hang these boys, you turn back to the past. I'm pleading for the future. Not merely for these boys but for all boys, for all the young. I'm pleading not for these two lives but for . . . life itself, for a time when we can learn to overcome hatred with love, when we can learn that all life is worth living and that mercy is the highest attribute of men. Yes, I'm pleading for the future in this court of law—I'm pleading for love."

Welles's summation to the judge and jury remains one of the longest monologues ever committed to film; he is admirable in his restraint. He told PETER BOGDANOVICH that he employed a teleprompter when he filmed the speech: "I knew the speech, but the fact that the teleprompter was there took that awful nervous strain out of it. They moved it around outside the shot, and I don't think I glanced at it—but knowing it was there, I was at ease."

That Welles did not need to look at the teleprompter is highly unlikely. Martin Ritt, who directed him in THE LONG HOT SUMMER (1959), said later, that he was irritated that Welles did not bother to learn his lines perfectly. And FRED ZINNEMANN, who directed Welles in A MAN FOR ALL SEASONS (1966), recalled that Welles was "only superficially acquainted with his lines." By the late 1950s, it appears that Welles took the trouble to learn his dialogue only if he was directing a picture from his own screenplay.

When principal photography was completed on *Compulsion,* Welles only had to re-record some of his lines, where the live soundtrack was not clear because of camera noises or the rustling of the extras on the huge, crowded courtroom set. By then Welles had learned that the Internal Revenue Service had been able to garnishee his $100,000 fee for the film because of Welles's back taxes. In addition, Welles was still annoyed that he had not gotten to direct this film. As a result, he was grumpy and disagreeable when he watched his scenes being run off, prior to redubbing some lines that evening. Welles was apoplectic at what he considered the incompetence of the filming. He lashed out at Fleischer, producer Richard Zanuck, and cinematographer William Mellors. Mellors, who had won an Academy Award for *A Place in the Sun* (1951), was not prepared to sit still for this onslaught. He was furious at Welles and was ready to deliver a Sunday punch on his jaw when Fleischer restrained him. With that, Welles stormed out of the projection room.

Fleischer and Zanuck sometime later proceeded to the sound studio, ruefully wondering if Welles was going to show up. They found that Welles had begun the re-recording session without them. He behaved with asperity when he was asked to redub a particular passage that was unacceptable because of the camera noise. In a great huff, Welles said that the technical difficulty with the camera was not his fault, and so he refused to re-record the lines. "This is now a matter between you and the Screen Actors Guild. Good night!"

Welles barreled out of the studio and headed for the pier to board a ship for China. Fleischer adds that the sound editor was able to salvage the dialogue Welles refused to redub by reconstructing Welles's lines from snatches of dialogue in other scenes, with a procedure that Fleischer called "handknitting." Having simmered down while at sea, Welles telegraphed Fleischer an apology for his acerbic behavior.

Perhaps Welles was already aware that he would receive widespread plaudits for his performance in a movie that he had quite unfairly said was poorly directed and photographed. Welles shared the best actor award at the Cannes International Film Festival with his co-stars, Bradford Dillman and Dean Stockwell. But the general consensus of reviewers was that Welles had overshadowed their performances. In fact, he simply took over the film as soon as he entered it, which was halfway through the picture. Similarly, his performance dominated THE THIRD MAN, made 10 years earlier, even though he was only in the last half of the movie. *Compulsion* and *The Third Man* represent the peak of Welles's performances in films other than his own.

References Bourne, Stephen. *Brief Encounters: Homosexuality on Film* (London: Cassell, 1996); Brady, Frank. *Citizen Welles: A Biography of Orson Welles* (New York: Scribner's, 1989); Fleischer, Richard. *Just Tell Me When to Cry: A Memoir* (New York: Carroll & Graf, 1993); Leaming, Barbara. *Orson Welles: A Biography* (New York: Viking, 1985); Tyler, Parker. *Screening the Sexes: Homosexuality in the Movies* (New York: Da Capo, 1993); Welles, Orson, and Peter Bogdanovich. *This Is Orson Welles* (New York: Da Capo, 1998).

—G.D.P.

Confidential Report Alternate title for Welles's 1955 film, MR. ARKADIN.

Copland, Aaron (1900–1990) Aaron Copland, arguably the dean of 20th-century American composers, by pointing out the need for an indigenous American operatic theater, served as an indirect yet significant influence on WELLES's 1936 decision to undertake the production of THE CRADLE WILL ROCK.

In 1937, Welles helped mount Copland's *The Second Hurricane,* an operetta for children with a libretto by Edwin Denby, at the Henry Street Settlement. In 1939, Welles and Copland collaborated in the ambitious but ultimately disastrous production of Welles's *FIVE KINGS.*

In his autobiography, *The New Music 1900–1960,* Copland says that he "was born on a street in Brooklyn that can only be described as drab. . . . It probably resembled most one of the outer districts of lower-middle-class London, except that it was peopled largely by Italians, Irish, and Negroes. I mention it because it was there I spent the first twenty years of my life." It is mentioned here because it points to a uniquely American background that would become a defining dynamic in Copland's profoundly American-esque compositions.

Coming late to music at age 12, Copland learned the rudiments of piano by studying informally with his sister. Eventually, his nonmusical parents arranged for a professional piano teacher, Leopold Wolfsohn. Later, he would study with Rubin Goldmark. Exhilarated by his discovery of music, Copland pushed himself to the point of receiving a scholarship to study in Paris. Like many ambitious American musicians of the period, Copland's enthusiasms were given focus by Nadia Boulanger, the celebrated classical music pedagogue. Meeting many of the leading musical personalities of the day and writers such as James Joyce, Ernest Hemingway, and Ezra Pound, Copland found his horizons both in and beyond music extended. Though much of his music was abstract and dissonant, he began to call more frequently on his American heritage. For example, his affinity for jazz, a reflection of his big city background, bubbled up in works such as *Jazz Concerto for Piano and Orchestra* (1926) and *Piano Variations* (1930). Later, there was a turn toward rural America, and the simplicity and charm of its folk songs, hillbilly tunes, and hymns. This direction was most popularly expressed in Copland's three "Wild West" ballets, *Billy the Kid* (1938), *Rodeo* (1942), and *Appalachian Spring* (1944).

Copland's tendency to write increasingly short and often repetitive phrases coupled with his sweeping songlike melodies made his music particularly amenable to the often cut-and-paste and dramatic necessities of film and theater scoring. In 1939, although he found collaborating with Welles difficult because of the director's inaccessibility (a consequence of Welles trying to balance a murderous schedule of radio commitments with an ever-escalating set of logistical nightmares associated with the mounting of the overly ambitious *Five Kings*), Copland had an impressive success with his score for *The City,* a prize-winning documentary directed by Ralph Steiner and Willard Van Dyke for the 1939 New York World's Fair. Hollywood sat up and took notice, and called. Along with his first feature, *Of Mice and Men* (1939), Copland went on to score *Our Town* (1940), *The Red Pony* (1949), *Something Wild* (1961), and *Love and Money* (1982). In 1949, Copland won an Oscar for his score for *The Heiress.*

Copland maintained a busy composing schedule throughout his life. He taught for a number of years at Harvard, and published such notable books as *What to Listen for in Music* (1939; rev. ed. 1957), *Copland on Music* (1960), and *The New Music: 1900–1960* (rev. ed. 1968).

References Copland, Aaron, and Vivian Perlis. *Copland. 1900–1942* (New York: St. Martin's Press, 1987); Pollack, Howard. *Aaron Copland: The Life and Work of an Uncommon Man* (Urbana: University of Illinois Press, 1999).

—C.B.

Coppola, Francis Ford (1939–) Coppola made *Apocalypse Now* (1979), derived from Joseph Conrad's novella HEART OF DARKNESS, which ORSON WELLES had planned to film. Coppola was born in Detroit, Michigan, on April 7, 1939. He grew up in Queens, a borough of New York City, where he made his first films as a youngster with an 8mm camera. He attended Hofstra University on a drama scholarship and directed several plays. He earned his bachelor's degree in 1960 and entered the film school at the University of California at Los Angeles, where he studied on campus for two years.

Francis Ford Coppola became the first major American film director to emerge from a university degree program in filmmaking. He received his Master of Cinema degree from UCLA in 1968, after submitting his first film of consequence, *You're a Big Boy*

Now (1967), a free-wheeling comedy about a young man on the brink of manhood, to the university as his master's thesis.

In the spring of 1975 Coppola announced that he planned to make a film based on Conrad's *Heart of Darkness* (1899), but updated to the Vietnam War. A great fan of Orson Welles, Coppola was well aware that Welles had written a screenplay based on the same novella, which had gone unproduced. As for Conrad's novella, the story is narrated by the seaman, Marlow. He is charged with investigating the life of Kurtz, an ivory trader whom Marlow tracks down in the jungle. Gradually, Marlow unearths the hideous facts about Kurtz by inquiring about him from those who knew him. When Kurtz first went to the Congo, he had wanted to civilize the natives he dealt with in the jungle. But he was not equipped with the kind of deep moral convictions that would sustain him while he faced the challenges of the wilderness all alone. After all, if one lacks strong ethical principles, the superficial restraints that civilized society places on one's behavior are quickly forgotten in the isolated, barbaric atmosphere of the wilderness. In Kurtz's case, once he was on his own in the jungle, he became guilty of the most appalling behavior. In the course of the novella, Kurtz becomes ruler of a tribe of savages whom he allows to worship him as a god, and in this manner he keeps them subservient to him. In fact, he has engaged with the tribesmen in the most barbaric pagan rites, which have been offered in his own honor.

The jungle, then, becomes a metaphor for the heart of darkness that lies within each of us: our inclination to evil. Marlow learns, from the gradual deterioration of Kurtz and others like him, that one can only cope with one's personal capacity for evil by recognizing it for what it is. Hence, he depicts human nature with a potential for greatness, which is coupled with an inclination toward evil that can undermine that capacity for goodness. In short, the story represents a journey into the dark heart of a human being. For Kurtz's sojourn in the jungle is a metaphor for the journey of life, during which each of us must choose between good and evil.

The first attempt to bring *Heart of Darkness* to the screen was made by Orson Welles, who had origi-

nally hoped that his film adaptation of Conrad's story would be the first film he made in Hollywood for RKO, the studio with which he signed a contract in 1939. Welles wanted to begin shooting the film in the fall of 1939. He had planned to be the voice of Marlow, the narrator of the story, voice-over on the sound track as well as to appear onscreen as Kurtz. (The script is dated November 30, 1939. JONATHAN ROSENBAUM's essay on Welles's *Heart of Darkness* contains script extracts from Welles's draft of the screenplay; the prologue to the film proper in the script is printed in full as a companion piece to Rosenbaum's article. Both items are cited below in the bibliography.)

The draft of Welles's screenplay for *Heart of Darkness* was literally taken from the source story. As a

Director Francis Ford Coppola *(Literature/Film Quarterly Archive)*

matter of fact, ROBERT CARRINGER notes in his book on Welles that Welles actually tore pages of the story out of the paperback edition of the novella "and pasted them onto sheets of typing paper; and he worked his way through these, marking the passages that were to be retained and crossing out the rest." Occasionally, however, Welles "changed or added a line or two," and made other alterations in the screenplay. Thus he updated the story to the present and made Marlow, the film's narrator, an American; but Welles maintained that whatever changes he made in the original story Conrad himself would have desired, were he alive at the time the film was being made.

Welles told PETER BOGDANOVICH that he planned to film the story in the first person: "The camera was going to be Marlow." Welles had insisted on the use of the subjective point of view, whereby the film was to be shot from Marlow's point of view; virtually everyone and everything would be seen through Marlow's eyes. Marlow himself would be visible in the course of the movie when his image was reflected in a mirror or in a windowpane. He would also be visible in the early scenes when Marlow is aboard his boat in New York Harbor, prior to his voyage.

Since Conrad employed first-person narration in the novella, Welles wanted to direct the film so that the subjective camera would serve as the eyes of the main character. In essence, the filmgoer is supposedly looking through Marlow's eyes at the action as it transpires. That is why, as Rosenbaum points out, Welles states in the prologue for the film, in which Welles planned to demonstrate the use of the subjective camera in the movie to follow, the following remark, addressed directly to the moviegoer: "You aren't going to see this picture—This picture is going to happen to you."

Rosenbaum comments on the prologue: "It serves the ingenious function of demonstrating the ... gimmicky aspects of the technique *before* the story begins, thus clearing the way for its subsequent use as a serious narrative device."

An excellent example of the subjective camera occurs in the climactic scene when Marlow disembarks from his boat at Kurtz's outpost in the jungle.

As Welles conceived this shot with the "first-person camera" in mind, Marlow walks up the hill from the dock and enters Kurtz's compound, and proceeds to his lair. Kurtz is ensconced in a decaying temple, sitting regally upon a throne, and the camera tracks forward as Marlow walks toward the throne. This shot was to be accomplished in an extended take, employing the subjective camera, with the filmgoer seeing exactly what Marlow sees.

In sum, by employing the subjective camera, Welles thus provided a visual corollary to Conrad's first-person narration in the book. Moreover, Welles in his script evoked the first-person feel of Conrad's novella by accompanying his use of the seeing-eye camera with Marlow's running commentary, voiceover on the sound track, which was to be spoken by Welles himself in the person of Marlow.

The opening scene has Marlow about to set out from New York Harbor on his journey to find Kurtz. He has been employed by an unnamed government to bring Kurtz back from some unspecified country in South America to assume some kind of political leadership role. Carringer points out that "parallels are repeatedly drawn between Kurtz's leadership style and contemporary fascist regimes in Europe." As a matter of fact, while Welles was preparing *Heart of Darkness,* Hitler invaded Poland and World War II got under way. Indeed, in Marlowe's confrontation with Kurtz, the latter's despotism is clearly linked to the tyranny sweeping over Europe at the time. Kurtz symbolizes fascism by lording it over the natives, and he also refers directly to Hitler in the dialogue. In fact, Welles says in SIMON CALLOW's book, "The picture is frankly an attack on the Nazi system."

Thus Kurtz says to Marlow, "There is a man now in Europe trying to do what I've done in the jungle. He will fail. In his madness he thinks he can't fail, but he will." By contrast, Kurtz is confident that, in creating a kingdom in the jungle, he has succeeded. "I'm above morality," he declares. "I've climbed higher than other men and seen farther. I'm the first absolute dictator." He implies that he will not be the last.

As in Conrad's book, Kurtz has fallen seriously ill by the time Marlow reaches him; and he dies before Marlow can bring him back to America. Following the novella, Kurtz's last utterance as he expires is,

"The horror! The horror!" Apparently Kurtz realizes what a ruthless savage he had become at the moment that death overtook him.

When Welles finally turned in his proposed budget for the production, it ran to more than $1 million—much to the dismay of RKO's front office since that was exactly twice the budget for the average RKO film. The studio brass accordingly insisted that Welles cut his budget in half, and he responded that he would do his best to be obliging.

Unfortunately, plans to film *Heart of Darkness* were finally abandoned by the studio when it became obvious that *Heart of Darkness,* with its elaborate jungle sets and "casts of thousands," could never be made for $500,000. In fact, Welles's script called for 3,000 black natives to be seen bowing down to Kurtz in one sequence, which caused RKO executives to point out to the front office that there were only four or five hundred black extras in all of Hollywood. Undaunted, Welles then turned his attention to making CITIZEN KANE; unquestionably, *Heart of Darkness,* as an examination of a powerful, legendary man, prefigures *Kane.* At all events, Welles shelved *Heart of Darkness;* and devoted himself to *Citizen Kane;* and the rest, as they say, is history.

Coppola, who was a great aficionado of Welles's films, was to some degree inspired to make a film adapted from Conrad's novella by Welles's aborted project. Moreover, PETER COWIE points out the many affinities between the films of Welles and Coppola, suggesting that it is not surprising that both filmmakers would be attracted to the same literary source. "The two men are tightly linked by their fascination with the diabolical," he writes; "the notion of man as fallen angel." Their antiheroes "arouse a tantalizing sympathy in the audience." There is a distinct kinship between Welles's ruthless, despotic CHARLES FOSTER KANE and Hank Quinlan, the corrupt cop in TOUCH OF EVIL on the one hand, and Coppola's Mafia bosses Vito Corleone and his son Michael Corleone in the *Godfather* trilogy. Not surprisingly, then, both Welles and Coppola were drawn to Conrad's Kurtz, yet another fallen angel.

The screenplay for Coppola's film *Apocalypse Now* was by John Milius, Michael Herr, and Francis Coppola. The script had updated the story to the Vietnam War and turned Kurtz from an ivory trader into a Green Beret officer who defects from the American army and sets up his own army across the Cambodian border, where he proceeds to conduct his own private war against the Vietcong.

After examining Milius's first-draft script for *Apocalypse Now* (dated December 5, 1969), film scholar Brooks Riley points out in *Film Comment* that Coppola stuck very close to Milius's original scenario when he revised it for production six years later. If the revised script "strayed from the first draft," she writes, *"it was not so much away from Milius's conception"* of the plot *"as toward Milius's source, the Conrad novel."* (Emphasis added.) In brief, *Heart of Darkness* is the spine of *Apocalypse Now.*

Captain Benjamin Willard (Martin Sheen), who is the central character and narrator of the movie, is mandated by his superior officers to penetrate into the interior of the jungle and track down Colonel Walter E. Kurtz (Marlon Brando), a renegade officer who has raised an army composed of deserters like himself and of native tribesmen, in order to fight the war on his own terms. When he locates Kurtz, Willard is to "terminate his command with extreme prejudice," which is military jargon meaning that Willard should assassinate Kurtz. Colonel Kurtz, it seems, has taken to employing brutal tactics to attain his military objectives; indeed, some of his extreme measures have sickened the members of the army intelligence staff who have succeeded in obtaining information about him.

Coppola does have Willard narrate the film (with narration written by Michael Herr), in much the same way that Welles has Marlow narrate the story (although Coppola does not employ the subjective camera in the fashion in which Welles had planned to utilize it in *Heart of Darkness*). Thus Willard's initial reaction to his mission, expressed voice-over on the sound track, is that liquidating someone for killing people in wartime seems like "handing out speeding tickets at the Indianapolis 500." Besides, even though Willard has been ordered to eliminate no less than six other undesirables in the recent past, this is the first time his target has been an American and an officer. He therefore decides to withhold judgment about Kurtz until he meets up with him personally.

By the time that Willard's boat reaches Kurtz's compound in the heart of the dark jungle, the modern weaponry associated with the helicopter attack earlier in the movie has been replaced by the weapons of primitive man, as Kurtz's native followers attack the small vessel with arrows and spears. In entering Kurtz's outpost in the wilderness, Willard has equivalently stepped back into a lawless, prehistoric age, where barbarism holds sway.

In fact, the severed heads that lie scattered about the grounds mutely testify to the depths of pagan savagery to which Kurtz has sunk during his sojourn in the jungle. Furthermore, it is painfully clear to Willard that, despite the fact that Kurtz's native followers revere him as a god, Kurtz is incurably insane.

By now Willard has definitely made up his mind to carry out his orders by killing Kurtz; and Kurtz, who has sensed from the beginning the reason why Willard was sent to find him, makes no effort to stop him. As Willard reflects in his voice-over commentary on the sound track, Kurtz wants to die bravely, like a soldier, at the hands of another soldier and not to be ignominiously butchered as a wretched renegade. Willard accordingly enters Kurtz's murky lair and "executes" him with a scimitar. Afterward, as Willard leaves Kurtz's quarters, Kurtz's worshipful tribesmen submissively lay their weapons on the ground before him as he passes among them. Clearly they believe that the mantle of authority has passed from their deceased leader to the man he allowed to slay him. But Willard, his mission accomplished, walks out of the compound and proceeds to the riverbank, where his patrol boat awaits him.

On the surface, Welles's scenario is very different from Coppola's film. Yet, although the settings and backgrounds of the two adaptations are quite different, there are some notable similarities. For example, both Welles's version and Coppola's version begin with the protagonist's explanation of how he got the appointment that necessitates his excursion upriver. Both Welles's Marlow and Coppola's Willard are despatched to journey up a primeval river to find someone who has disappeared into the interior and never returned.

Moreover, one of the elements of Coppola's film that parallels Welles's script is the employment of Willard as the narrator of the film, just as Marlow is the narrator of Welles's screenplay. Hence both the screenplay of *Apocalypse Now* and that of Welles's *Heart of Darkness* remain most faithful to their common source by depicting the action through flashback, with the narrator's comments on the action heard, voice-over, on the sound track.

In 2001, Coppola released *Apocalypse Now Redux,* the director's cut of *Apocalypse Now,* with 53 minutes of additional footage added to the film as originally released. Coppola thereby brought fresh acclaim to his version of Conrad's *Heart of Darkness.* In his article on *Apocalypse Now Redux,* Howard Hampton mentions the Welles scenario, and that Welles not only planned to play both Kurtz and Marlow in his adaptation, but also "to shoot the entire movie in first-person POV, with the camera showing everything through Marlow's eyes." He adds, "If it had been green-lighted instead of *Kane,*" it would have been interesting to see "Orson Welles playing Citizen Kurtz." In some ways Coppola realized Welles's dream of doing a screen adaptation of Conrad's story set in modern times: updated to World War II in Welles's version and to Vietnam in Coppola's *Apocalypse Now.*

References Boyum, Joy Gould. *Double Exposure: Fiction into Film* (New York: New American Library, 1985); Callow, Simon. *Orson Welles: The Road to Xanadu* (New York: Penguin Books, 1997); Carringer, Robert. *"Heart of Darkness,"* in *The Making of Citizen Kane* (Los Angeles: University of California Press, 1985), 1–15; Cowie, Peter. *The Apocalypse Now Book* (New York: Da Capo, 2001); Cowie, Peter. *Coppola: A Biography,* rev. ed. (New York: Da Capo, 1994); Hampton, Howard. *"Apocalypse Now Redux,"* Film Comment 37, no. 3 (May–June 2001): 36–42; Ondaatje, Michael. "*Apocalypse Now* and Then," *Film Comment* 37, no. 3 (May–June 2001): 43–47; Riley, Brooks. "'Heart' Transplant," *Film Comment* 15, no. 1 (September–October 1979): 26–27; Rosenbaum, Jonathan. "The Voice and the Eye: A Commentary on the *Heart of Darkness* Script," *Film Comment* 8, no. 4 (November–December 1972): 24–26; Welles, Orson. "Introductory Sequence to the Unproduced *Heart of Darkness,*" *Film Comment* 8, no. 4 (November–December 1972): 24–26; Welles, Orson, and Peter Bogdanovich. *This Is Orson Welles* (New York: Da Capo, 1998).

—G.D.P.

Cornell, Katherine (1893–1974) WELLES toured the country as part of Katherine Cornell's stage company in 1933–34. Through THORNTON WILDER, a noted American playwright, Welles met ALEXANDER WOOLLCOTT, the leading Broadway drama critic, who in turn got Welles a meeting with GUTHRIE MCCLINTIC, Cornell's husband and the director of the three plays the company was slated in perform in repertory. McClintic, who had the authority to cast the productions, was so impressed by Welles that he gave him three roles: Mercutio in Shakespeare's *Romeo and Juliet,* Octavius Moulton-Barrett in Rudolf Besier's *The Barretts of Wimpole Street,* and Marchbanks in Shaw's *Candida.* The tour began in Buffalo on November 29, 1933, and lasted eight months, covered 17,000 miles, and played in 77 cities, where some 225 performances were given. Welles received excellent reviews, particularly for his Mercutio (Cornell wrote, "It was obvious from the time that he gave his first performance with us that he was a tremendously talented boy"), though McClintic was not complimentary about his Marchbanks performance. Welles involved himself in every aspect of the plays, but not everyone was pleased with his participation. FRANK BRADY writes, "He made it clear to everyone—sometimes a bit too pompously—that he was interested in both directing and producing, as well as acting, and had every intention of doing either or both as soon as possible." Welles left the troupe in the spring and then rejoined it in the fall in Detroit. Despite his success as Mercutio, Welles found that McClintic had replaced him with Brian Aherne, whom McClintic and Cornell wanted for *The Barretts of Wimpole Street.* Welles reluctantly accepted the roles of Tybalt and Chorus in *Romeo and Juliet.* As Tybalt, Welles attracted the attention of JOHN HOUSEMAN, famous stage director, who, according to Brady, "was mesmerized by the vision of Tybalt, which he believed elevated Welles to almost a reincarnation of Thespis, a modern dramatic deity."

Katherine Cornell, who was born on February 16, 1893, in Berlin, Germany, was the daughter of a theater manager in Buffalo. She made her New York debut with the Washington Square Players on November 13, 1916, in the role of a Samurai mother in *Bushido.* In London in 1919, she starred as Jo in the stage version of Louisa May Alcott's *Little Women* and then came back to New York to play on Broadway in Clemence Dane's *Bill of Divorcement* (1921). In the same year she married Guthrie McClintic, who directed many of the plays she appeared in. The two also formed a production company. Though she regularly performed on Broadway, she also toured the country, appearing in a variety of plays. One of her best roles was as Elizabeth Barrett Browning in *The Brownings of Wimpole Street,* one of the plays Welles appeared in with her. Brooks Atkinson, drama critic for the *New York Times,* wrote of her performance: "By the crescendo of her playing, by the wild sensitivity that lurks behind her ardent gestures and her piercing stares across the footlight she charges the drama with a meaning beyond the facts it records." In 1935, at the age of 43, she was playing Juliet, a role she also played during the 1933–34 tour. John Mason Brown of the *New York Post* wrote, "Her Juliet is deeper, surer and more commanding than it ever was." She appeared in Jerome Kilty's *Dear Liar* in 1959 and retired from the stage in 1961, when her husband died. She wrote two autobiographical books, *I Wanted to Be an Actress* (1939) and *Curtain Going Up* (1943). She died in Vineyard Haven, Massachusetts, June 9, 1974.

Reference Malvern, Gladys. *Curtain Going Up! The Story of Katherine Cornell* (New York: Messner, 1947).

—T.L.E.

Cortez, Stanley (Stanislaus Krantz) (1908–1997) Stanley Cortez, born Stanislaus Krantz on November 4, 1908, in New York City, was the cinematographer for ORSON WELLES for *THE MAGNIFICENT AMBERSONS* (1942). "My people are Middle European," Cortez told CHARLES HIGHAM in an interview published in *Hollywood Cameramen* (1970), "my mother was born in Hungary and my father was born in Austria." After attending New York University, Cortez worked with portrait photographer Edward Steichen. "I started out in New York as a designer of studio settings," Cortez told Higham, "then as an assistant to great photographers who specialized in photographing men in elegant clothes." Cameraman Van Der Beer helped Cortez get employed as a cameraman for Pathe News in

New York, which taught him how to photograph action with newsreel accuracy. The next stage in his career took him to Paramount, where he worked with gifted professionals such as Karl Struss, Charles Rosher, Hal Mohr, and Arthur Miller. In 1932, he directed a short film, *Scherzo,* and by 1936 he had his first assignment as cinematographer, *Four Days' Wonder.* During World War II he served as a photographer with the Signal Corps.

Orson Welles had seen his work and wanted him to shoot *The Magnificent Ambersons.* "He gave me complete freedom," Cortez said of Welles, "but every one of his suggestions was of enormous importance." For the sleigh scene it was his idea to capture the atmosphere of Currier and Ives prints that, along with the singing of "The Man Who Broke the Bank at Monte Carlo," helped to establish the period of Booth Tarkington's novel. Of course, more film was shot than Welles was able to include in the picture, which caused critics to regard the picture as a "flawed masterpiece." GEORGE SCHAEFER, the studio boss who hired Welles, resigned and was replaced by CHARLES KOERNER, whose goal was to shape films for double features. "He came out with the arbitrary edict that no film left the studio longer than 7,500 feet, no matter what the picture was," Cortez remembered: "as a result, an hour of my best work went, magnificent things, shots involving new small arcs I used for the first time."

"Apart from *Ambersons,*" Cortez believed, "the most exciting experience I have had in the cinema was with Charlie Laughton," and, no doubt, besides *The Magnificent Ambersons,* his best work was represented by *The Night of the Hunter* (1955) for CHARLES LAUGHTON, *Shock Corridor* (1963) shot in 16 days for Sam Fuller, and *The Three Faces of Eve* (1957), for writer-director Nunnally Johnson, a psychological film involving a woman (JOANNE WOODWARD) with three personalities. The film was a challenge, but, as with *Ambersons,* the challenge was met.

References Higham, Charles. *Hollywood Cameramen: Sources of Light* (Bloomington: Indiana University, 1970); Leyda, Jay. *Voices of Film Experience, 1894 to the Present* (New York: Macmillan, 1977).

—J.M.W.

Costello, Dolores (1905–1979) Actress Dolores Costello played Isabel Amberson in ORSON WELLES's film adaptation (1942) of BOOTH TARKINGTON's novel *THE MAGNIFICENT AMBERSONS.* Welles was especially anxious to cast her in the film because she not only had the necessary patrician gentility, but she also was the ex-wife of JOHN BARRYMORE, who was Welles's idol as a young man. Welles successfully lured her out of her self-imposed retirement, but his comments to PETER BOGDANOVICH suggest that she was not particularly enthusiastic about being in the film: "You might have thought she'd want to watch what we were up to. In rehearsal, I mean. But she was quite unfocused." JAMES NAREMORE's evaluation of her performance is quite positive: "Dolores Costello, an agelessly beautiful silent actress who had come out of retirement, makes Isabel into a golden-haired Madonna, a woman so abstracted into a complacently sweet and self-sacrificing role that she becomes almost invisible."

Dolores Costello *(National Film Society Archive)*

Dolores Costello, the daughter of Maurice Costello, the first male star of silent films, was born on September 17, 1905, in Pittsburgh. As children she and her sister Helene appeared in some of their father's Vitagraph films. After doing some modeling, she returned to films on the East Coast at age 17, although she and Helene also worked on the stage, where their dance duet in the *George White Scandals of 1924* earned them contracts with Warner Bros. In 1926, she appeared in *The Sea Beast* with John Barrymore, whom she married in 1928. For the next few years she was a box-office draw, but she retired in the 1930s to have children—one of them was John Barrymore, Jr., another actor. After she and Barrymore were divorced in 1935, she returned to making films, but she began playing maternal roles in such pictures as *Little Lord Fauntleroy* (1936). She appeared in six more films in the next three years, went into retirement, and then Welles cast her in *The Magnificent Ambersons.* She again retired, this time to her avocado farm in California. She died in 1979.

Reference Bodeen, De Witt. *From Hollywood: The Careers of Fifteen Great American Stars* (South Brunswick, N.J.: A.S. Barnes, 1976).

—T.L.E.

Cotten, Joseph (1905–1994)

Joseph Cotten joined ORSON WELLES's MERCURY THEATRE in 1937 and later starred in the first three Welles's films: CITIZEN KANE (1941), *THE MAGNIFICENT AMBERSONS,* and *JOURNEY INTO FEAR* (both in 1942). Cotten first met Welles when the two were working on the CBS "School of the Air" series and were convulsed at the line "barrels and barrels of pith," behavior that Cotten, in his autobiographical *Vanity Will Get You Somewhere,* thought established them as "unreliable influences." In 1936, Cotten joined Welles in the first production of the FEDERAL THEATRE PROJECT 891 of the WPA. The play, HORSE EATS HAT, was an adaptation of *The Italian Straw Hat* (1927), a film farce directed by RENÉ CLAIR, which, in turn, was adapted from a play written by Eugene Marin Labiche. Cotten, who played the part of the frantic bridegroom, was the only actor to receive critical praise. The *New York Times* reviewer predicted that he "will be sought after by commercial producers." He next appeared as the only adult in THE SECOND HURRICANE, a children's opera that Welles staged with composer AARON COPLAND in 1937. They did not appear together again professionally until Cotten joined the Mercury Theatre. Cotten described the Mercury Players as a "young, enthusiastic group" which included "a terribly talented, handsome young actor named Joseph Cotten." One of the Mercury productions was Thomas Dekker's *The Shoemaker's Holiday,* in which Cotten played the lead, Rowland Lacy. Cotten recounts how Welles told him, "You'll never make it as an actor," but "as a star, I think you might well hit the jackpot." During the Mercury Theatre years Cotten also participated in the film clip that was made as a part of TOO MUCH JOHNSON, a play that Welles was staging. Cotten also appeared with Welles on THE CAMPBELL PLAYHOUSE in "Mutiny on the Bounty"; Welles was Captain Bligh, and Cotten was Fletcher Christian.

When Cotten moved to Hollywood, Leland Hayward became his agent, and Cotten was reunited with Welles for *Citizen Kane.* According to Cotten, when he met Welles at the home of the Mankiewiczes, Welles asked him, "Why don't you think of yourself as Jedediah Leland?" Cotten described his most difficult scene in the film as the one where he plays Leland as an elderly man in a sanitarium, speaking a monologue about his days with Kane. His favorite scene in the film occurs when he gets drunk and tells Welles off. When the scene was shot, Cotten was exhausted, a state he likened to drunkenness, so the scene, including the unintentional substitution of "dramatic crimitism" for "dramatic criticism," was convincing. During the shooting of *Citizen Kane,* Welles pushed his cast to the limit, and several actors complained. According to CHARLES HIGHAM, AGNES MOOREHEAD and Joseph Cotten "never complained and indeed vibrated to their friend's relentless yet devoted handling."

Cotten next appeared as Eugene Morgan in Welles's *The Magnificent Ambersons* and after Welles left for Brazil became involved with ROBERT WISE in the recutting of the film after it received a negative response from a preview audience in Pomona, California. Cotten sent Welles a letter about the recutting that infuriated Welles, who thought that Wise had used Cotten to legitimize the editing, which took place in Welles's absence. "He had become, with the best will in the world, an active collaborator with Wise. . . ." Welles went on to BARBARA LEAMING about what he saw as Cotten's betrayal, comparing Cotten to Judas. Welles was particularly upset with Cotten, whom he regarded as a friend whom he had asked to "join him in adapting *Journey into Fear* (1943) from ERIC AMBLER's novel into a screenplay," but Cotten, who had the lead role in the film, does not provide any details about his contributions to the script. He does say that Ambler liked the film, but said it was so unlike his novel that he could sell the movie rights again. Cotten was also part of Welles's entourage for the *WONDER SHOW,* a kind of vaudeville entertainment, in which he was JoJo the Great, one of Welles's assistants. Cotten, who had facilitated

Joseph Cotten

Welles's romance with RITA HAYWORTH, was his best man when Welles married Hayworth, September 7, 1943. The following year he appeared with Welles in another show for the war effort, "The Texarkana Program" (June 3). Cotten and Welles next appeared together in CAROL REED's *THE THIRD MAN* (1949), in which Cotten played the lead role of Holley Martins; Welles played Harry Lime. According to DAVID THOMSON, Reed was delighted to have Welles and Cotten in the film: "Reed was happier still: Cotten and Welles were chemistry together, and they would be fun to work with." Cotten was also cast as a senator in Welles's *OTHELLO* (1952), had a cameo role in his *TOUCH OF EVIL* (1958), and appeared in his *F FOR FAKE* (1974). SIMON CALLOW has written of the relationship between Cotten and Welles: "Welles had conceived an enormous affection for Cotten, something very much like love. He was everything that Welles would have liked to have been: soigné, good-looking, graceful, balanced, normal. . . . In *Horse Eats Hat,* Welles gave him his first break; he continued to nurture his career until Cotten no longer needed him."

Joseph Cotten, who was born on May 15, 1905, in Petersburg, Virginia, studied at the Hickman School of Expression in Washington, D.C., before going to New York City in 1924. He worked in a paint warehouse on West Broadway for a while before moving to Miami, where he wrote some theater reviews for the *Miami News.* After he obtained a letter of introduction to Broadway producer David Belasco, he moved back to New York and worked for him. He then was hired by Edward Goodnow as part of the cast that was to put on plays at Boston's Copley Theatre. In his autobiography, Cotten wrote, "This was the early thirties, and my next intent was to crash radio. . . . At one of those auditions I met another actor—a young man named Orson Welles."

In his non–Wellesian roles Cotten starred in several memorable films, including *Portrait of Jennie* (1948), for which he won a best actor award at the Venice Film Festival; *Niagara* (1953) with a young Marilyn Monroe; *Hush Hush . . . Sweet Charlotte* (1965) with an old Bette Davis; *Petulia* (1965) about London's "swinging 60s"; and *A Delicate Balance* (1973).

Orson Welles as Charles Foster Kane, flanked by Joseph Cotten as Jed Leland and Everett Sloane as Bernstein, when Kane becomes owner of the *New York Daily Inquirer* *(Literature/Film Archive)*

Reference Cotten, Joseph. *Vanity Will Get You Somewhere* (San Francisco: Mercury House, 1987).

—T.L.E.

Coulouris, George (1903–1989) The experienced British actor who played Walter Parks Thatcher in CITIZEN KANE (1941), the guardian of young CHARLES FOSTER KANE who managed the boy's fortune until he came of age, was born in Manchester, England, on October 1, 1903, the son of Nicholas and Abigail (Redfern) Coulouris, and educated at the Manchester Grammar School. He left home in 1923 and worked as a waiter on an ocean liner before going to London to study acting at the Central School of Speech Training and Dramatic Art with Elsie Fogerty. His first stage appearance was at the Rushholme Repertory Theatre in Manchester in May of 1926. His first role on the London stage was Sir Thomas Grey in Shakespeare's *Henry V* in October of 1926, one of many Shakespearean roles essayed during his long and active career. By 1929, he was playing the Duke in Shakespeare's *Measure for Measure* in New York. His first film role in Britain was in *The Late Christopher Bean* (1933), after having played Tallant in the stage play.

In 1937, Coulouris became one of the original members of ORSON WELLES'S MERCURY THEATRE, first appearing as Marc Antony in Welles's experimental

Welles as Kane gets bad news from Walter Parks Thatcher (George Coulouris, left), with Everett Sloane, right, as Bernstein *(Literature/Film Archive)*

modern-dress production of *JULIUS CAESAR.* Other Mercury Theatre productions followed, such as *HEARTBREAK HOUSE* in which he played Boss Mangan. SIMON CALLOW has described Coulouris as "a sort of licensed melancholic within the group" adding that the rehearsals for *Heartbreak House* were "dominated by the never-ending feud between Coulouris and Welles." This dour figure was perfectly matched for the role of the prissy Walter Parks Thatcher in *Kane.* His performance in *Citizen Kane* led to many film roles, several in 1943, including *This Land Is Mine, For Whom the Bell Tolls,* and *Watch on the Rhine.* Other character roles followed throughout the 1940s and beyond, but Coulouris remained active onstage as well as continuing to act in films. In 1973, for example, he appeared in *Papillon,* in 1974 in *Murder on the Orient Express* and Ken Russell's *Mahler,* and in 1979 in *The Long Good Friday.* In the mid-1980s George Coulouris became disabled by Parkinson's disease and died of a heart attack in 1989.

—J.M.W. and T.L.E.

Coward, Noël (1899–1973) Leading personality of the London stage who had a famously misunderstood spat with the teenaged WELLES in Dublin in 1931.

During his 1931 stay in Dublin, flush with success from his debut as a professional actor at the GATE THEATRE, the 16-year-old Welles, along with his varied theatrical activities, enjoyed partaking of the spirited pub debates that followed each evening's show. On one such occasion, as Welles and some of his colleagues were comfortably ensconced in a downtown watering hole, Coward, then the toast of the London stage, swept in with a group of friends. Seating themselves at a nearby table, Coward's entourage was regaled by the great man recounting stories about his recent hit, *Cavalcade* (1930). As FRANK BRADY points out, in 1931, Great Britain had just come off the gold standard, a benchmark of British security. The retreat from gold, coupled with other economic woes triggered by the worldwide depression, had caused British patriotism to waver. For Coward, *Cavalcade* was intended to both entertain and rouse flagging British spirits. Indeed, at the play's end, Coward gave a stirring speech in which he concluded: "In spite of the troubled times we are living in, it is pretty exciting to be English." The play, which was supported by King George V and Queen Mary, became a national sensation.

Welles, eavesdropping from the next table, misunderstood Coward. On the incorrect assumption that Coward had been berating the Empire, Welles, with youthful passions perhaps inflamed by alcohol, jumped to his feet and castigated Coward in a fiercely pro-English speech. Coward, not one to be verbally intimidated, stood his ground and fired back. "Neither of us said anything in the least brilliant," Welles later recalled. Brady states that both men periodically recalled the incident with laughter.

Still, Welles never seems to have hesitated in using Coward to his own advantage. When he was auditioning for the part of Lamont Cranston for *THE SHADOW* in 1935, Welles, to attract attention, walked boldly into the broadcast studio and proclaimed: "I am Noël Coward!" Affecting his own idiosyncratic version of Coward's British accent, Welles got the part. SIMON CALLOW elaborates on how Welles developed the role. "Welles played Cranston rather leisurely and mild, with careless charm in the more or less English accent still synonymous with a private income; there is about the interpretation a suggestion of silk dressing gown and cigarette holder: this was his Noël Coward performance." Several years later in

1939, when Welles was presiding over another radio series, *THE CAMPBELL PLAYHOUSE,* the program's announcer, in his introduction of Welles, said at one point: "He [i.e., Welles] had four hits last year on Broadway, which beats Noël Coward's record from here to Kalamazoo." Such references indicate that for Welles, Coward remained a rival, albeit a distant rival, against which to measure himself. At the same time, Coward, given his prissy manner, was an easy mark for the darker side of Welles's sometimes malevolent sense of humor. Coward enjoyed giving as good as he got. In 1960, when Welles directed the London debut of Eugene Ionesco's *RHINOCEROS* with LAURENCE OLIVIER and Joan Plowright, Coward, expanding on a passionate dislike for Ionesco, also took the opportunity to twit Welles, opining that the American had "directed it into the ground."

Welles and Coward also obliquely crossed paths in 1949, during the casting of *THE THIRD MAN.* British director CAROL REED wanted Welles for the key role of Harry Lime. However, American producer DAVID O. SELZNICK, who controlled the film's U.S. distribution rights, argued for Coward, largely on the strength of his wartime films, including *In Which They Serve* (1942), for which Coward had won a special Academy Award for his "Outstanding Production Achievement." Ultimately, Reed prevailed, thus leaving the path clear for Welles's indelible portrait of the seductive yet sinister Harry Lime.

Coward embodied the mid-20th-century concept of sophisticated, leisure-class Englishness. A gifted actor, writer, composer, lyricist, painter, and bon vivant, Coward made his stage debut at the age of 12. His first film appearance was in noted American director D.W. Griffith's *Hearts of the World* (1918). In 1921, on a visit to New York, he discovered Broadway, and, in the process, his metier. Incorporating a Broadway-like pace and pizzazz into his own theatrical ventures and music, Coward scored big with "jazz age" Brits who readily took to his frothy send-ups of life among the idling elite. His flamboyant style of upper-crust dress was widely imitated by young men who donned dressing gowns, smoked cigarettes from ostentatious cigarette holders, and called each other "dahling."

Coward's popularity reached its zenith in 1930 with the fashionable *Private Lives,* which was adapted to film in 1931. When Britain was plunged into World War II, he altered his persona along "stiff upper lip" lines in the morale-boosting movies *This Happy Breed* (1942), *In Which We Serve* (1942), *Blithe Spirit* (1945), and *Brief Encounter* (1945). Eclipsed by younger stars after the war, Coward struck a resonant chord with older fans and the curious in largely nostalgic revues. His *Song at Twilight* (1966), an autobiographical drama about the pain of an aging homosexual writer pressured to write dishonestly about himself throughout his career, revived interest in Coward's works and life. Coward also wrote a novel, *Pomp and Circumstance* (1960), and three autobiographies, *Present Indicative* (1937), *Middle East Diary* (1945), and *Future Indefinite* (1954). He was knighted in 1970. Today, Coward's plays and songs are often revived in productions seeking to re-create a sentimental look at British popular culture of the 1920s through the 1940s.

Noël Coward

References Coward, Noël. *Noël Coward: An Autobiography* (London: Methuen, 1986); Fisher, Clive. *Noël Coward* (New York: St. Martin's Press, 1992); Hoare, Philip. *Noël Coward: A Biography* (New York: Simon & Schuster, 1996); Webbe, Gale D. *Noël Coward: A Bio-Bibliography* (Westport, Conn.: Greenwood, 1993).

—C.B.

Cowie, Peter (1939–)

According to the *Los Angeles Times,* "the swift success of Tantivy [Press] and its creator Peter Cowie parallels the dynamic growth of movies themselves in the last decade." The son of the writer and poet David Cowie, Peter Cowie, educated at Cambridge, because an articulate and well-informed film historian and critic. Cowie founded the annual *International Film Guide* series and was a driving force in film-related publishing. His book, *A Ribbon of Dreams: The Cinema of Orson Welles* (London and New York: Zwemmer and A.S. Barnes, 1965) set an important precedent for WELLES scholarship. The evocative title was drawn from a statement Welles had made: "The camera is much more than a recording apparatus, it is a medium via which messages reach us from another world, a world that is not ours and that brings us to the heart of a great secret. Here magic begins . . . A film is a ribbon of dreams." The book was later reissued as a paperback in a "much revised and enlarged version" under the title *The Cinema of Orson Welles* in 1978 by the Tantivy Press, London, and A.S. Barnes in America. The project began with an interview Cowie was granted by Welles in 1963. In discussing CITIZEN KANE, Cowie moves beyond the Hearst controversy, asserting that the film "is of primary importance in the history of the cinema because of the audacity and virtuosity of Welles's technique, and because of the influence that the style was to exert on films in all parts of the world for the next two decades." In his survey of Welles scholarship written for *Focus on Citizen Kane* (1971), RONALD GOTTESMAN wrote that Cowie's book "is still the best introduction in English to Welles's achievement in cinema, and his chapter on *Citizen Kane* is a model survey and analysis of a film—balanced, shrewd, and original."

—J.M.W.

Crack in the Mirror

Twentieth Century–Fox, 97 minutes, 1960. **Director:** Richard Fleischer; **Producer:** Darryl F. Zanuck; **Screenplay:** Jules Dassin (a.k.a. Mark Canfield), based on the novel by Marcel Haedrich; **Cast:** Orson Welles (Lamoricier), Juliette Greco, Bradford Dillman, Alexander Knox, Catherine Lacy, William Lucas

Following the critical and box office success of COMPULSION in 1959, Twentieth Century–Fox reassembled the team of WELLES, actor BRADFORD DILLMAN, director FLEISCHER, and the father-son producing team of DARRYL and Richard ZANUCK (in the credits, father Darryl is listed for *Crack in the Mirror,* while for *Compulsion,* it is son Richard whose name appears). Mark Canfield's screenplay (actually written by the blacklisted Jules Dassin), based on a novel by Marcel Haedrich, tells two parallel stories involving romantic triangles. The film's most ingenious strategy involved casting the three principal actors in dual roles. Consequently, Welles had the dubious distinction of playing two older men whose lovers (Juliette Greco) throw them over for younger men (Dillman). In the first story, Welles plays a drunken sadist, a construction crew foreman who is murdered by his mistress with the aid of her young lover. In the second story, Welles is Lamoricier, Paris's most famous lawyer, who, in spite of failing health, still is attracted to his mistress (again, Greco). Clearly, the double-casting strategy was intended to draw parallels between characters separated by class. Zanuck was also undoubtedly pleased to be able to "hire" six actors for the price of three. Still, by casting Welles as the tyrannical old laborer and cuckolded lawyer, and Greco as the mistress in each story, and Dillman as the young laborer and young attorney, the film makes its basic point that everyone, whether rich or poor, faces similar moral dilemmas.

In spite of its ambitions, *Crack in the Mirror* proved a critical and box office disappointment, perhaps because of the confusion in following the two stories resulting from the double-casting strategy. Still, as FRANK BRADY points out, Welles has a wonderful scene at the end of the film where his lawyer's soliloquy rings out in a manner recalling his magisterial speech at the conclusion of *Compulsion.* Produced entirely in Paris, the film benefits from its French look and sound. Also featuring Alexander Knox, Catherine Lacy, and William Lucas.

Reference Fleischer, Richard. *Just Tell Me When to Cry: A Memoir* (New York: Carroll & Graf, 1993).

—C.B.

Cradle Will Rock, The (play, 1937)

ORSON WELLES's stage production of MARC BLITZSTEIN's *The Cradle Will Rock* (1938) has a long and tortuous history. Author-composer Marc Blitzstein described *The Cradle Will Rock,* which he wrote in 1936, simply as "a play with music." Producer JOHN HOUSEMAN claimed its "prime inspiration" was *The Threepenny Opera* and bits of Gilbert and Sullivan, with "recitatives, arias, revue patters, tap dances, suites, chorales, silly symphonies, continuous incidental commentary music, [and] lullaby music." He described it, variously, as "an opera, a labor opera, a social cartoon, a marching song, and a propagandistic tour de force." *The Cradle Will Rock* started with a dramatic sketch Blitzstein wrote in 1935 to a song entitled "The Nickel Under the Foot." It was BERTOLT BRECHT who advised Blitzstein to expand the sketch into a full-blown agitprop "play with music," a hymn for the rights of the American labor movement.

The play was to have been produced by the FEDERAL THEATRE PROJECT, headed by HALLIE FLANAGAN, who in turn delegated the production (#871) to Orson Welles and John Houseman. Will Geer was cast to play Mr. Mister, the Lord of Steeltown, against Howard da Silva's proletarian hero, Larry Foreman. Mr. Mister battles the labor-agitating Foreman for the industrial and social salvation of the town. During the play's four-month rehearsal period, labor unrest was building in the country at large. The great sit-down strike in Flint, Michigan, mobilized the United Auto Workers, who demanded union recognition and a 30-hour week. Seven auto plants were closed in the Midwest, and, as Houseman remembers, the very day *The Cradle Will Rock* went into rehearsal, "there were riots in Akron and Pontiac as strikes halted work in the Chrysler and Hudson auto plants," as well as at General Motors. Then John L. Lewis announced his intention "to unionize the steel industry," which led to strikes and riots in Chicago, where both strikers and policemen were injured and killed.

Thus, the stage was set for a pro-union play to run squarely into political fallout. Budgets were cut as news reached Washington about Blitzstein's "dangerous" play. But Houseman was still determined, as he recalls in his memoir *Run-Through,* "to get Marc Blitzstein's play with music onto the stage of Maxine Elliott's Theatre against a variety of odds." To build support in New York, hundreds of guests were invited to the play's final run-through, but the next day armed guards took over the theater. An obvious solution was to move the production to another theater, but Actors' Equity members were then forbidden to perform the piece "on any stage or for any management other than . . . the Federal Theatre of the WPA." At the last minute, a kind of solution was found as the Venice Theatre on 59th Street engaged. "The entire cast and the entire first-night audience marched twenty-one blocks up Broadway to the other theatre," recalls Stanley Kauffmann, "with no scenery and with Blitzstein at the piano." The cast members performed from their seats in the audience in a kind of quasi-impromptu manner. After a number of special matinees, the play had its official premiere at the Windsor Theatre on January 3, 1938, and ran for 108 performances. It has been revived several times, but it has never reached a large audience.

—J.C.T.

Cradle Will Rock

Touchstone Pictures, 133 minutes, 1999. **Director:** Tim Robbins; **Producers:** Jon Kilik, Tim Robbins, and Lydia Dean Pilcher; **Screenplay:** Tim Robbins; **Cinematography:** Jean Yves Escoffier; **Editor:** Geraldine Peroni; **Production Design:** Richard Hoover; **Music:** David Robbins, with songs by Marc Blitzstein; **Cast:** Hank Azaria (Marc Blitzstein), Ruben Blades (Diego Rivera), Joan Cusack (Hazel Huffman), John Cusack (Nelson Rockefeller), Cary Elwes (John Houseman), Philip Baker Hall (Gray Mathers), Cherry Jones (Hallie Flanagan), Angus MacFadyen (Orson Welles), Bill Murray (Tommy Crickshaw), Vanessa Redgrave (Countess La Grange), Susan Sarandon (Margherita Sarfatti), Jamey Sheridan (John Adair), John Turturro (Aldo Silvano), Emily Watson (Olive Stanton), Bob Balaban (Harry Hopkins),

John Carpenter (William Randolph Hearst), Gretchen Mol (Marion Davies), Steven Skybell (Bertolt Brecht), Susan Heimbinder (Eva Blitzstein), Chris McKinney (Canada Lee), Adele Robbins (Augusta Weissberger), et al.

Stanley Kauffmann considers the Tim Robbins film "a mess." Certainly there is no questioning its ambitious agenda, as it attempts to reproduce not only ORSON WELLES's *THE CRADLE WILL ROCK*'s first performance but the backstage shenanigans behind that performance and the complex sociopolitical contexts of the time. Against the backdrop of the Depression and political turmoil in Spain, Italy, and Germany, Robbins assembles a crazy-quilt pastiche to accompany the behind-the-scenes preparations by the players and producers—most notably MARC BLITZSTEIN (Hank Azaria), Orson Welles (Angus Mcfayden), JOHN HOUSEMAN (Carey Elwes), and HALLIE FLANAGAN (Cherry Jones). The screenplay incorporates numerous distracting subplots involving the artist Diego Rivera (Reuben Blades)—a wholly invented incident—NELSON ROCKEFELLER (John Cusack); a poor starving starlet (Emily Watson) who gets the role of the Prostitute; a Russian art collector (Susan Sarandon) who buys up da Vinci paintings for WILLIAM RANDOLPH HEARST (John Carpenter); a daffy socialite (Vanessa Redgrave) who tries to lend a hand to save the show; a talented Italian actor (John Turturro) with a wife and family to support; and a wholly invented mentally unstable lovelorn vaudeville ventriloquist named Tommy Crickshaw (Bill Murray). While one might expect to find BERTOLT BRECHT (Steven Skybell) in the cast, why Rockefeller, Rivera, Hearst, and MARION DAVIES (Gretchen Mol)? Among these impersonations, Kauffmann opined that only Hallie Flanagan, as portrayed by Cherry Jones, "takes on any reasonable life."

So intent is Robbins at establishing a densely textured contextual tapestry of events surrounding the production of *Cradle Will Rock* that the story of the play itself gets lost in the process. Too many cooks have spoiled this broth. Meanwhile, after almost two hours, the film finally lumbers to the finale—the march of the players up Fifth Avenue and into the Venice Theatre for the actual production. What transpires is indeed a compelling re-creation of that miraculous performance as, one by one, the cast members rise from their seats to join in the performance. However, irritating and intrusive crosscutting to digressive subplots again mars the dramatic thrust. One watches in bewilderment the wretched business with Bill Murray, who loses his mind as his dummy crumples to the stage floor. The final scenes of *Cradle Will Rock* are given over to shots of the dummy's funeral procession. What this all means is up for grabs, although one might surmise that the procession symbolizes the death of vaudeville and the birth of guerrilla theater.

Reference Robbins, Tim. *Cradle Will Rock* (New York: Newmarket Press, 1999).

—J.C.T. and J.M.W.

Danton's Death (play, 1938) Although WELLES and JOHN HOUSEMAN had wanted to open the MERCURY THEATRE's second season with a comedy, when *TOO MUCH JOHNSON* failed in its August trial run, their only practical recourse was to lead off with the already planned *Danton's Death.* In adapting the 1835 play by Georg Büchner (1813–37), Welles pared down the story about the French Revolution's Reign of Terror to a crisp, intermissionless 90 minutes. In contrast to Max Reinhardt's epic 1927 version, which focused on the story of the mob, Welles molded his version as a drama of revolutionary motivations, charting the transition from authentic revolutionary fervor to what one critic described as "military dictatorship and the degradation of liberty and equality to battle cries of international carnage." In his 1939 modern dress version of *JULIUS CAESAR,* Welles had clearly implicated Mussolini's fascist Italy. With *Danton's Death,* Welles took aim at both Nazi Germany and the Soviet Union. His concern was with the corruption of people's parties, the slide toward totalitarianism, the installation of dictatorships, and the betrayal of democratic principles.

The reference to the Soviet Union was problematic to members of the American Communist Party, which up to *Danton's Death,* had supported the general left-leaning tendencies of the Mercury Theatre. MARC BLITZSTEIN, a loyal Communist and the show's composer, told Welles that the play was likely to offend Communist sensibilities with its allusions to Stalin and the Soviet Union. As a result, Welles made several small changes. Still, the connection was clear to everyone except the politically obtuse. *Danton's Death*'s political overtones could not have been more appropriate to 1938, especially in the wake of the infamous nonaggression pact that had just been signed by Hitler and Stalin.

The most striking feature of the production was Stephen J. Tichachek's sparse design and a cyclorama made up of skull-like Halloween masks. Combined with Jean Rosenthal's evocative lighting, the masks became the embodiment of the suffering masses, sometimes bloody red, at other times ashen gray. At center stage was an elevated platform, which rose at various points to become the Chamber of Deputies, the Conciergerie, and a tumbrel, the cart that carried the condemned to the guillotine. In the cast were MARTIN GABEL as Danton; Arlene Francis as Marion, Danton's mistress; Vladimir Sokoloff, reprising his role as Robespierre from the 1927 Reinhardt production; Virginia Welles as Anna Stafford; JOSEPH COTTEN as Barrerre; and Welles as Saint-Just, Robespierre's lieutenant and the prosecutor of the tribunal that delivered Danton's death sentence.

Reviews were largely unsympathetic. There were raves from the *New York Times*'s BROOKS ATKINSON and the *Brooklyn Daily Eagle*'s Arthur Pollock. Otherwise the notices were brutal. Sidney B. Whipple of the *New York World-Telegram* whined that "[*Danton's Death*] needs a student of the French Revolution to decipher it." STARK YOUNG of *The New Republic* complained about Moscow Art Theatre veteran Vladimir Sokoloff's Robespierre: "Mr. Sokoloff fought so valiantly with the English language as to be something of a solo drama for himself . . . for the words stuck, clung and spit themselves beyond our normal listening habits." Sokoloff, it might be pointed out, had just acquitted himself well in the diction department in a role in the 1937 Warner Bros. film *The Life of Emile Zola*. Richard Watts, Jr., of the *New York Herald-Tribune,* summarily concluded: "For the Mercury Theatre, the honeymoon is over."

Commentators have pointed out that the brickbats directed at *Danton's Death* perhaps had more to do with the shifting winds of critical taste. It should not be forgotten that just days previous to the opening of *Danton's Death,* Welles had shocked the world with his famous broadcast of THE WAR OF THE WORLDS. Indeed, many of the same critics who had helped build Welles up as "The Boy Wonder," were now looking for chinks in his armor. So while there was genuine excitement among theatergoers anxious to see Welles's latest, among the critics, there were those jealous of his celebrity, looking for an opportunity to help dish out his comeuppance. Two days after penning his positive review, Arthur Pollock of the *Brooklyn Daily Eagle* wrote of Welles's predicament: "If they [i.e., bright young men] begin with work that is superlative where can they go from there? They must either repeat themselves or face the prospect of long years getting better all the time. At 23, a man's future must appall him if he has begun where others, at their peak, left off. Is he good enough to get better throughout two-thirds of a lifetime? . . . If *Danton's Death* does not seem very important it is, after all, simply because Orson Welles did it. He suffers by comparison with himself. Done by anyone else this *Danton's Death* would have looked like an American miracle. Done by anyone else it would not seem quite so precious." Such is the cruel fate too often suffered by the gifted.

Slammed by most of the critics and ultimately boycotted by the American Communist Party, *Danton's Death* ran for a disappointing three weeks, November 5 to November 26, 1938.

References Baruch, Robert. *Georg Büchner and Franz Wedekin: Precursors of German Expressionism* (Ann Arbor: University of Michigan Press, 1971); Hauser, Ronald. *Georg Büchner* (New York: Twayne, 1974); Hilton, Julian. *Georg Büchner* (New York: St. Martin's Press, 1982); Lukács, György. *German Realists in the Nineteeth Century* (Cambridge, Mass.: MIT Press, 1993).

—C.B.

David and Goliath [*David e Golia*]

Allied Artists/Ansa Cinematografica, 95 minutes, 1960. **Director:** Richard Potter and Ferdinando Baldi; **Producer:** Emimmo Salvi; **Screenplay:** Umberto Scarpeli, Gino Mangini, Ambrogio Molteni, Salvi; **Cinematography:** Carlo Fiore and Adalberto Albertini; **Editor:** Franco Fraticelli; **Music:** Carlo Innocenzi; **Cast:** Orson Welles (King Saul), Ivo Payer (David), Kronos (Goliath), Edward Hilton (Prophet Samuel), Massimo Serato (Abner), et al.

A 1960 Italian film directed by Richard Pottier and Ferdinando Baldi starring WELLES as King Saul. In the late 1950s and early 1960s, the vogue for biblical epics was at its peak. Taking advantage of new widescreen formats, color, and stereophonic sound, what these films lacked in subtlety they attempted to make up for in spectacle. Like any successful trend, a bandwagon with a host of imitators soon formed. The universally panned *David and Goliath* was just such a film. Produced cheaply in Italy with a virtual no-star cast, Welles, always strapped for cash, succumbed to financial temptation, thus allowing his great but fading talent and fame to be exploited by the highest of the low bidders.

When the film opened in New York in October 1961, it was consigned to neighborhood theaters. Eugene Archer, in a brief pan for the *New York Times,* wrote: "Peering over the balustrades as King Saul is a malevolent Orson Welles, whose resonant tones provide occasional relief from the rest of the screeching, but have no relationship to the mouthings of his impressively bearded visage. Only a lip-reader could tell what the formidable Mr. Welles was actually saying to the camera, but it looked to us as if he were expressing his opinion of the picture, in no uncertain terms." Even the critics, at least those like Archer, took pity on Welles's plight in such dismal circumstances.

—C.B.

Davies, Marion (Marion Cecilia Douras)

(1897–1961)   Although she has been seen as the model for Susan Alexander, Kane's mistress and eventual second wife in *CITIZEN KANE* (1939), Marion Davies was for more than 15 years a talented film actress with a flair for comedy. In his biography of Davies, Lawrence Guiles's introduction is entitled "She Was a Daisy, But No Susan Alexander." There is no question, however, that WELLES's film did adversely affect Davies's career. Guiles believes that "the damage which Welles knew had been done to Marion's career was a trivial matter to a genius."

Born in Brooklyn on January 3, 1897, Davies (her stage name) debuted in a Broadway chorus line at age 16, did some modeling, appeared in the *Ziegfeld Follies of 1916,* and made her first film appearance in *Runaway Romany* in 1917. She met publishing magnate WILLIAM RANDOLPH HEARST, who determined to make her a Hollywood star. To that end he created Cosmopolitan Pictures to produce her films, which were distributed by Paramount Pictures, and used his vast newspaper empire to publicize the films, which all lost money. In 1924, Cosmopolitan and Davies moved to the Goldwyn Company, which subsequently merged with Metro to form MGM. LOUIS B. MAYER, MGM production chief, went out of his way to please Hearst and Davies. MGM even built a 14-room bungalow on the MGM lot for her use. Indicative of some of the resentment at Davies's superstar treatment is the following "poem" attributed to wit Dorothy Parker:

> Upon my honour
> I saw a Madonna
> Sitting alone in a niche
> Above the door
> Of the glamorous whore
> Of a prominent son-of-a-bitch.

Davies and Hearst entertained a great deal, particularly at the San Simeon castle on the California coast. Since Hearst's wife would not consent to a divorce, Hearst and Davies could not get married. Davies's career, which might have been more successful without Hearst's interference, began to decline, and after several roles that Hearst wanted for Davies went instead to Norma Shearer, Irving Thalberg's wife (Thalberg was in charge of production at MGM), Davies and the bungalow moved to Warner Bros. in 1934. In 1937, the Hearst newspaper empire had severe financial problems, and Davies's film career was at an end. After Hearst died in 1951, she married and spent the 10 years before her death in 1961 as a business executive.

When Welles arrived in Hollywood in July 1939, his marriage to his wife, Virginia, was in trouble. After she divorced Welles in December 1939, she married CHARLES LEDERER at Hearst's castle, San Simeon, and returned to Lederer's home with her daughter Chris, Welles's first child. HERMAN MANKIEWICZ, who knew all the details, met with Welles, who was experiencing some problems in selecting material for his first film for RKO. Although the story about Hearst, an American tycoon, was Mankiewicz's, Welles had sole screen credit until Mankiewicz persuaded the Screen Writer's Guild to give him credit as "co-author." Guiles describes Welles's film as "the Juggernaut that

Comedienne Marion Davies *(National Film Society Archive)*

would careen unfeelingly over Marion Davies, flattening all of her modest triumphs and her three major ones." Although Mankiewicz knew that Davies was a talented actress, he also knew that a similarly talented Susan Alexander would weaken the idea of Kane's malevolent power. The most striking similarities between Davies and Alexander were their loneliness as their men absorb themselves in business, their alcoholic bouts, and their love for jigsaw puzzles. Hearst read the script and apparently did not mind the way he was treated, but he was furious with the portrait of Susan (Davies) as an alcoholic.

References   Davies, Marion. *The Times We Had: Life with William Randolph Hearst* (Indianapolis: Bobbs-Merrill, 1975); Guiles, Fred Lawrence. *Marion Davies: A Biography* (New York: McGraw-Hill, 1972).

—T.L.E.

Dean Martin Comedy Show, The (television, 1965–1974)

When the successful movie and TV comedy team of Dean Martin and Jerry Lewis broke up in 1956, few expected that it would be Martin who would have the more successful solo career. During its enormously popular 1965–74 run on NBC, Martin sang, did comedy, and schmoozed with guests in an easygoing, low-key manner. Welles, who became one of Martin's favorite celebrity personalities, made his debut on the show in September 1967, singing "Brush Up Your Shakespeare" as a duet with the host; he also performed one of Shylock's speeches from Shakespeare's *The Merchant of Venice.*

Welles was persuaded to guest with Martin thanks to Greg Garrison. In 1946, Garrison was a youngster who had worked backstage on Welles's 1946 production of AROUND THE WORLD IN 80 DAYS. By 1967, having risen up through the ranks, Garrison was producing *The Dean Martin Comedy Show.* Remembering the older man as a mentor and father figure, Garrison argued that the exposure of Martin's show might open up new opportunities for Welles in America. Welles said yes. After his successful debut, Welles appeared twice a year, through the 1971 season. Usually, there would be a skit, and then a segment devoted to Martin and Welles trading quips, generally at their own expense, much to the audi-

ence's delight. Although Welles's purists found his self-deprecating hi-jinx offensive, Welles and Martin had a jolly good time of it.

Just as Garrison had predicted, Welles's revived celebrity led to conversations with Hollywood dealmakers about possible directing, producing, and acting assignments. On a more practical level, Welles's handsome appearance fees were used to help defray his still staggering tax bill, ironically, in view of Garrison's involvement, a debt originating over two decades previously with the disastrous *Around the World in 80 Days.*

—C.B.

Deep, The (a.k.a. Dead Reckoning)

Uncompleted, color, 1967–1969. **Producer:** Orson Welles; **Director:** Welles; **Screenplay:** Orson Welles (based on *Dead Calm,* by Charles Williams); **Directors of Photography:** Willy Kurant, Ivica Rajkovic; **Production Data:** Filmed off the Dalmatian coast at Hvar and Primosten, Yugoslavia, 1967–1969. **Cast:** Laurence Harvey (Hughie Warriner); Jeanne Moreau (Ruth Warriner); Orson Welles (Russ Brewer); Oja Kodar (Rae Ingram); Michael Bryant (John Ingram)

This eventually ill-fated project began with welles's enthusiasm for a best-selling thriller by Charles Williams called *Dead Calm* (1963). It's a survival story dealing with a storm-tossed young man hauled aboard a honeymooning couple's yacht navigating the tempestuous seas of the South Pacific, who leads his rescuers into a horrific ordeal. Welles envisioned the project as having great audience appeal, something he now actively sought, especially after a string of recent disappointments.

Indeed, during the mid-1960s, Welles's THE IMMORTAL STORY (1968), given a perfunctory screening on French television and an equally perfunctory theatrical release in France as *Une Histoire Immortelle,* virtually died for want of bookings elsewhere. Likewise, CHIMES AT MIDNIGHT (1966; titled *Falstaff* for its 1967 U.S. release), made little impression either with the critics or at the box office; even Welles had reservations, believing he had erased too much of the humor from his limning of Falstaff. In the meantime, DON QUIXOTE remained unfinished, and plans for a bullfighting film, THE SACRED BEASTS, had to be jettisoned when another film on the topic, Francesco Rosi's *The Moment of Truth,* wound up a box office failure. There had even been talk of adding another two reels to "update" THE MAGNIFICENT AMBERSONS, using the same actors, now 15 years older.

Welles began planning *The Deep* in August 1968, when he hired Willy Kurant, his trusted cinematographer from *The Immortal Story.* Using money he earned from an appearance in THE BATTLE OF NERETVA (1968), Welles proceeded to Yugoslavia in September, hired JEANNE MOREAU and LAURENCE HARVEY as his leads, and rented a yacht. Cast as the victim of the psychopath was sculptor, OJA KODAR, Welles's current lover whom he had first met in Zagreb during the production of THE TRIAL (1962). Significantly, Kodar also invested in the film. Welles took the role of Russ Brewer, the wealthy honeymooner of the novel, while Harvey played the homicidal young villain. According to Kurant, there was tension between Moreau and Kodar both at sea and the port where part of the picture was shot.

Regrettably, Kurant had to leave the production at the halfway mark due to a previous commitment to shoot a Marlon Brando picture, *The Night of the Following Day.* With Kurant's assistant, Ivica Rajkovic, now lensing the film, Welles continued on. However, as CHARLES HIGHAM points out in *Orson Welles: The Rise and Fall of an American Genius,* Welles lost his concentration during the final weeks of production. An ailing Laurence Harvey was an additional difficulty. Most serious, as was so often and sadly the case with a Welles production, the director had simply run out of money. With his and Kodar's personal capital exhausted, he threw in the towel when it came time to dub the dialogue, add the music, and take care of other postproduction chores. Higham suggests that Welles had become impatient with the picture and that "his old unease and fear about completing a film had resurfaced." Whatever the case, and in spite of news items dribbled out during the next several years that the film would be completed sometime "soon," Welles's production of *The Deep* was officially suspended in 1970. It was completely abandoned when leading man Laurence Harvey died of cancer on November 25, 1973. The film remains unseen by the public, except for several excerpts noted below.

The unavailability of a complete print of *The Deep* makes it impossible to assess the film's qualities. However, Willy Kurant and Jeanne Moreau, who were in a position to know, have voiced little enthusiasm for it. In fact, Higham suggests that the best thing to come out of the production was Welles's growing relationship with Kodar. He took special delight when she successfully exhibited her work throughout Europe. He was also captivated by what he described as her half-Hungarian, half-Yugoslav nature, at once tempestuous and composed. Interestingly, Welles' wife, PAOLO MORI, took her husband's new relationship in stride without threatening either scandal or divorce. Kodar and Mori continued as personal and professional touchstones throughout the duration of Welles's life.

BARBARA LEAMING reports that Welles sent his script to ROGER HILL who, having sold the Todd Academy, had retired to Florida with his wife, Hortense, where they ran a charter boat service. Specifically, Welles wanted Hill to check the accuracy of the technical details pertaining to yachting. Leaming, pointing to the patch-quilt nature of Welles's productions at this point, tells how Welles enlisted Hill to shoot some footage in the Bahamas, where Welles showed up with Kodar and a batch of costumes. Together, they shot a scene in which Welles's character topples from a boat Hill had hired. This was to be followed by a second scene, a bloody underwater fight with Welles's and Harvey's characters. For Hill, the only problem was the absence of Welles and Harvey for the second scene. After finally finding someone of Welles's girth and stature who was also willing to dye his hair to match that of the maestro's, Hill filmed the scene with the two stand-ins. All went well except for one detail—the fake blood turned green underwater. If the production had been in black and white, it wouldn't have been a problem. Alas, *The Deep* was a color film.

Footage from Welles's aborted *The Deep* was shown at the American Film Institute's "Working with Welles" seminar at the Directors Guild of American Theater, Hollywood, 1978. Scenes from *The Deep* were also included in Gary Graver's *Working with Orson Welles,* and Oja Kodar's and Vassili Silovic's

1995 compilation film, *Orson Welles: The One-Man Band*.

In 1989, Charles Williams's novel *Dead Calm* was successfully brought to the screen by director Philip Noyce in a tautly told and eponymously titled adaptation featuring Nicole Kidman (Rae Ingram), Sam Neill (John Ingram), and Billy Zane (Hughie Warriner).

References Higham, Charles. *Orson Welles: The Rise and Fall of an American Genius* (New York: St. Martin's Press, 1985); Leaming, Barbara, *Orson Welles: A Biography* (New York: Viking Press, 1985).

—C. B.

Del Río, Dolores (1905–1983) Exotic Mexican actress courted by ORSON WELLES and featured in *JOURNEY INTO FEAR* (1942). Dolores del Río was born Lolita Dolores Martinez Asunsolo Lopez-Negrete in Durango, Mexico, on August 3, 1905, and educated in Mexico City at the Convent of St. Joseph. She married Jaime del Río in 1920. Her first husband died in 1928. She was "discovered" by director Edwin Carewe, who brought her to Hollywood to play a vamp in *Joanna* (1925). In 1926, her role as the French barmaid Charmaine in Raoul Walsh's *What Price Glory?* made her a star. Subsequent roles included *The Loves of Carmen* (1927) and *Ramona* (1928). During the 1930s, del Río starred in the Latin American musicals *Girl of the Rio* (1932) and *Flying Down to Rio* (1933). After divorcing her second husband, MGM art director Cedric Gibbons in 1940, del Río began an affair with Orson Welles at the time he was working on *CITIZEN KANE*. Welles then featured her in *Journey into Fear,* adapted from an ERIC AMBLER novel, before he left her for another Latin trophy, RITA HAYWORTH (born Margarita Carmen Cansino), whom he married in 1943. Thereafter, del Río returned to Mexico, where she continued her movie career in the emerging Mexican national cinema, ultimately starring in *Maria Candelario* (1944), the first Mexican film to be recognized at the Cannes Film Festival. In 1947, she appeared in *The Fugitive,* John Ford's adaptation of GRAHAM GREENE's *The Power and the Glory,* set in Mexico, and later played Indian women in two Westerns—Don Siegel's *Flaming Star* (1960) and John Ford's *Cheyenne Autumn* (1964). Her last film was *The Children of Sanchez* (1978). She died in Newport Beach, California, on April 11, 1983.

Reference Hershfield, Joanne. *The Invention of Dolores del Río* (Minneapolis: University of Minnesota Press, 2000).

—J.M.W.

Dietrich, Marlene (Maria Magdalene Dietrich) (1901–1992) Marlene Dietrich was a close friend of WELLES, who persuaded her to play the role of Tanya, the madam of a brothel in his film *TOUCH OF EVIL* (1958). Dietrich was born on December 27, 1901, in Berlin. She was a budding violinist, but a wrist injury caused her to turn to acting. After studying acting in Max Reinhardt's drama school, she won stage and film roles in Germany. American film director Josef von Sternberg discovered her performing on the stage, cast her as Lola Lola in his *The Blue Angel* (1930), and brought her to America, where Paramount Studios saw her as competition for MGM's Greta Garbo. She appeared in seven films directed by von Sternberg, who created the glamorous, seductive persona that she was associated with in all her films. Her most notable American collaborations with von Sternberg were *Morocco* (1930), *Blonde Venus* (1932), and *The Scarlet Empress* (1934). When Nazi agents offered her a lucrative deal to get her to return to Germany, she refused, and in 1939 she became an American citizen. She was given the Medal of Freedom in 1947 for participating in war bond drives, making anti-Nazi propaganda films, and entertaining American troops. She acted in the Welles's *MERCURY WONDER SHOW,* where she did a mind-reading routine and was sawed in half (this act was originally designed for and performed by RITA HAYWORTH, Welles's then wife) by magician Welles. Some of the *Mercury Wonder Show* skits were later condensed and filmed for inclusion in the patriotic *FOLLOW THE BOYS* (1944). Roles were scarce for Dietrich after the war, but she got good parts in two excellent films: *Witness for the Prosecution* (1958) and *Judgment at Nuremberg* (1961). It was her "cameo" role as Tanya (she has four minutes of screen time) in Welles's *Touch of Evil* (1958), however, that was her most memorable part. She

Marlene Dietrich

appeared in the film as a favor to Welles, who told PETER BOGDANOVICH that he wrote her whole character after filming had begun. Welles added, "It's her last great role." In the film Tanya reads the tarot cards and tells Hank Quinlan (Welles), "Your future is all used up." BARBARA LEAMING applies these words to Welles himself after he left the United States. Dietrich said, "I never said a line as well as the last line of the movie—'What does it *matter* what you say about people?'" Welles was always a Dietrich fan and friend. He offered her the role of the exiled countess in his *MR. ARKADIN,* but she had other commitments. She was originally going to play the part of the hostess in his *THE OTHER SIDE OF THE WIND* but had to withdraw from the film. Dietrich also was an admirer of Welles. She wrote, "When I have seen him and talked with him, I feel like a plant that has been watered."

References Dickens, Homer. *The Films of Marlene Dietrich* (Secaucus, N.J.: Citadel, 1980); Frewin, Leslie. *Diet-* *rich* (New York: Avon, 1969); Higham, Charles. *Marlene* (London: Granada, 1978); Walker, Alexander. *Dietrich* (London: Thames & Hudson, 1984).

—T.L.E.

Dillman, Bradford (1930–) Brad Dillman appeared in RICHARD FLEISCHER's *COMPULSION* (1959), a feature film modeled after the Leopold-Loeb thrill murder of Bobby Franks in 1924. In only his second film, Dillman shared an award at Cannes in 1959 for best actor with co-stars ORSON WELLES and DEAN STOCKWELL. Dillman played a mother-dominated sadist who plots with his submissive friend (played by Dean Stockwell) a cold-blooded murder. Welles played the lawyer who defended the two killers. The following year Fleischer and Welles, along with producer DARRYL ZANUCK, attempted to duplicate the success of *Compulsion* with *CRACK IN THE MIRROR;* Dillman co-starred in the psychological thriller. Before his screen career began in 1958, Dillman, who was a Yale graduate, made his Broadway debut in 1953. His most outstanding stage performance was in *Long Day's Journey into Night* (1956). Between 1960 and 1989, Dillman appeared in about 30 films, but, with the exception of *The Way We Were* (1973), most of them were undistinguished.

Reference Fleischer, Richard. *Just Tell Me When to Cry: A Memoir* (New York: Carroll & Graf, 1993).

—T.L.E.

Dinesen, Isak (Karen Dinesen) (Baroness Karen Blixen-Finecke) (1885–1962) Isak Dinesen's tale "The Immortal Story" from her *Anecdotes of Destiny* (1958) is the source of ORSON WELLES's *THE IMMORTAL STORY* (1968), an hour-long film originally produced for French television. The film was the first part of a two-part project that would star Welles and JEANNE MOREAU. The film was shot in 1956 and released in 1968, when it was shown at the New York and London film festivals. Welles, who had been fascinated by Dinesen, traveled to Denmark to see her, but after a three-day stay in a hotel, an intimidated Welles left without meeting her. DAVID THOMSON writes of the relationship: "What is more far-fetched is that Welles did not even appreciate the astonishing, ravaged, syphilitic beauty of the elderly Dinesen. But he felt kinship with her lofty, lucid prose, as well as her unyielding sense of destiny and commitment." In 1953, Welles had written an adaptation of Dinesen's "The Old Chevalier" as one of the sketches in *Paris by Night,* which he wrote for ALEXANDER KORDA, and he had hoped that *The Immortal Story* would be followed by three other screenplays he derived from Blixen's works. In the 1980s, Welles returned to Dinesen's works once more; his screenplay *Da Capo,* based on Dinesen's "The Dreamers" from *Seven Gothic Tales* (1934) and "Echoes" from *Last Tales* (1957), was meant to star OJA KODAR, his longtime mistress and artistic collaborator. The script was written for North Star Productions, but neither North Star nor any other Hollywood producers were enthusiastic about the screenplay, which they found, according to BARBARA LEAMING, "too poetic, too fanciful, not pragmatic."

Karen Dinesen was born in 1885 in the village of Rungstedlund, which is about 15 miles north of Copenhagen, Denmark. Wilhelm Dinesen, her father, was an adventurous man who had fought in the Prussian-Danish war of 1864 and who had lived among Native Americans for two years. He hanged himself when she was 10 years old. Raised by her mother and a tyrannical aunt, she chafed under restrictions and rules and escaped into her writing, which she began when she was eight years old. Home schooled, she did attend a school of design in Copenhagen before she entered the Danish Royal Academy of Art. In 1910, she traveled to Paris, ostensibly to continue her art studies, and three years later she became engaged to a Swedish cousin, Baron von Blixen-Finecke, whom she married in Mombasa, Kenya, in 1914. Her husband was not her intellectual equal and he was a prodigious woman-izer who was not only unfaithful to her, but also infected her with syphilis, which she had to return to Denmark to treat. Although he had gone to Africa to farm, he was more interested in big-game hunting and had several distinguished clients, including Ernest Hemingway. While she was in Africa, Dinesen began an affair with Denys Finch-Hatton, a relationship that angered Hemingway, who had earlier suggested that his Nobel Prize should have gone to her. Welles told PETER BOG-

DANOVICH that "he hated her. The old Baron Blixen—her husband—was Hemingway's great pal out of Africa, and she's left him for another man." (Dinesen's husband died in an automobile accident in 1946.)

When Dinesen returned to Rungstedlund in 1931, she adopted the pseudonym Karen Blixen and continued to write. Her first book in English was *Seven Gothic Tales* (1934), which was followed by the book that brought her worldwide renown, *Out of Africa* (1937), which was later made into an award-winning film (1985), starring Meryl Streep as Blixen and Robert Redford as Finch-Hatton. She went on to write several other books of fiction that established her as an international author of note.

References Migel, Parmenia. *Titania: The Biography of Isak Dinesen* (New York: Random House, 1967); Thurman, Judith. *Isak Dinesen: The Life of a Storyteller* (New York: St. Martin's Press, 1982).

—T.L.E.

Directed by John Ford
California Arts Commission/AFI, 90 minutes, 1971. **Director:** Peter Bogdanovich; **Producers:** George Stevens, Jr., and James R. Silke; **Narrator:** Orson Welles; **Interviewer:** Peter Bogdanovich

A documentary film PETER BOGDANOVICH made to honor director John Ford's career, with narration by ORSON WELLES. Bogdanovich's interest in Welles was surpassed only by his interest in Ford, whom he interviewed in 1967 for *Movie Magazine* in Britain. In 1968, Bogdanovich's monograph *John Ford* was published by the University of California Press. It began with the director remarking, memorably, "My name's John Ford. I make Westerns." The documentary film followed three years later, giving Bogdanovich the chance to work with two of the directors he most admired. This was one of several projects Welles narrated during 1971–72, followed by his narration for Peter Collinson's *To Kill a Stranger* (1972) and television narration for *The Crucifixion, Salvador Dali par Jean-Christophe Averty,* and *The Last of the Wild Mustangs,* all during 1972.

—J.M.W.

John Ford

As he had done with his adaptations of SHAKE-SPEARE, Welles edited with abandon by stripping Marlowe's five-act tragedy down to a sleek 85-minute, nonstop production suitable for modern audiences. Ruling out a modernizing of the Elizabethan prose, Welles focused instead on keeping everything in motion. By thoughtful excisions, and reorderings of various actions, and dropping minor characters and scenes, Welles exploited the precise timing of effects that had been one of the hallmarks of his radio productions. As for staging, he called on lighting mastermind Abe Feder to create effects that he would later adapt to film. Working with three trapdoors, strategically placed black curtains, and explosive bursts of light, Welles caused his actors to appear and disappear as if by magic. Eerily amplified offstage voices and composer PAUL BOWLES's dissonant score added to the otherworldly atmosphere.

Marlowe's tale of diabolical powers stems from the mythical 16th-century figure of Doctor Faustus, a German scholar who seeks the power of a godlike knowledge far beyond that of mere mortals. Negotiating a pact with the devil brokered by the demon-messenger Mephistopheles, Faustus is granted 24 years to enjoy his superhuman powers before surrendering his soul to the dark side. During that period, he travels about the world with Mephistopheles, rendering himself invisible at will, and conjuring up just about anything he pleases. Alas, when his superhuman powers are about to expire, Faustus is reduced to a quaking wreck, who is led off to his midnight appointment in Hades.

Doctor Faustus, like Welles's other theater works of the period, sought direct engagement with the audience. For *Faustus,* Welles broke the "separating" frame of the proscenium arch by extending a V-like projection from the stage into the orchestra seats, thus allowing some of the action to be staged up close and personal. At another point in the show, Bill Baird's puppets explored the Seven Deadly Sins from the theater's upper left box; all voices were rendered by Baird's wife, Cora. In the midst of the tragedy, there were bits of comic relief by the principals as well as by a group of vaudevillians recruited by Welles. Another comic send-up occurred during the visit by

Documentary on St. Peter's Basilica A short home movie made by a nine-year-old WELLES on a trip to Vatican City in 1924 with his father, this little commented upon and now lost travel film has significance as Welles's first direct experience with filmmaking.

—C.B.

Doctor Faustus (play, 1937) As *HORSE EATS HAT* continued its surprisingly successful run into 1937, WELLES and JOHN HOUSEMAN prepared their next production for PROJECT 891, *Doctor Faustus,* the classic 1589 play by Christopher Marlowe. As FRANK BRADY points out, it was appropriate that the first major starring and directing role of the 21-year-old Welles should be the work of the precocious Elizabethan dramatist who made his reputation with plays written in his 20s.

Faustus and Mephistopheles to the pope, which was played as slapstick.

Welles, donning a heavy beard and grotesque makeup, was an impressive Faustus, at once brooding, imposing, and cocksure. Mephistopheles, played by African-American actor JACK CARTER (who had starred in Welles's infamous "voodoo" MACBETH), with his bald pate and menacing look, was equally impressive. Other members of the first-rate cast included Charles Peyton (the Pope), J. Headley (Cardinal of Lorraine), Bernard Savage (Valdes), and, as one of three scholars, Joseph Wooll, alias JOSEPH COTTEN, Welles's close friend and frequent collaborator. Amazingly, the mélange of disparate theatrical elements worked and Welles's *Doctor Faustus* was pronounced a triumph. BROOKS ATKINSON of the *New York Times,* typifying the response, called it "imaginatively alive," "nimble," and "frank and sensible theater" that while being faithful to the spirit of Marlowe was also "easy to understand."

The dramatic use of lighting, which would become a hallmark of Welles's approach to filmmaking, was also singled out for praise. Atkinson elaborates on this important point: "Modern stagecraft is represented in the wizardry of lighting; the actors are isolated in eerie columns of light, which are particularly well suited to the diabolical theme of *Doctor Faustus.* On the Elizabethan stage the lighting was supplied from heaven; the plays were for the most part played in the afternoon under the open sky. Beguiling as that must have been for pastorals and gentle poetics, electric lighting is more dramatic because it can be controlled. The modern switchboard is so incredibly ingenious that stage lighting has become an art in its own right. The pools and shafts of light and crepuscular effects communicate the unearthly atmosphere of *Doctor Faustus* without diminishing the primary importance of the acting. And when the cupbearers of Beelzebub climb up out of hell, the furnace flares of purgatory flood up through a trapdoor in an awful blaze of light, incidentally giving the actors a sinister majesty."

BRET WOOD observes that the most prominent aspect of *Doctor Faustus* was removing the story from any particular geographic or temporal setting. Since Faustus represents everyman, Welles, short of putting his characters in modern dress, erased any reference points that might have separated Marlowe's world from that of the contemporary audience. "The purpose," says Wood, "was to show that man's struggle to maintain independence and purity is the same in the 20th century as it was in the 16th."

It should also be pointed out that by eliminating the standard theatrical intermission, Welles, consciously or not, was emulating the convention of the continuous, nonstop, hour-and-a-half to two-hour feature film. He obviously appreciated the continuously building narrative arc of the uninterrupted theatrical film, and the strong characters and clearly drawn plots that made it emotionally and dramatically satisfying for audiences.

Doctor Faustus was a box office success playing to standing-room-only audiences several days each week. Instead of an anticipated run of several weeks, the play ran for several months. Nonetheless, it was an expensive production and the 50-cents top ticket price often failed to cover ongoing expenditures. Given that *Doctor Faustus* was a federal project, it would often take weeks for requisitions for such items as replacement props to be processed. As a result, Welles kept things going by dipping into his own pocket when something was needed. At the end of the run, he had spent thousands of dollars from his radio income to keep *Doctor Faustus* afloat. The habit of personally subsidizing his productions was a behavior that later would cost him dearly, especially with the calamitous AROUND THE WORLD IN 80 DAYS (1946). Toward the end of his life, he recalled the situation philosophically: "I was probably the only person in American history who ever personally subsidized a government agency."

—C.B.

Don Quixote 1955–1973. **Director:** Orson Welles; **Producer:** Welles and Oscar Dancigers; **Screenplay:** Welles (based on *Don Quixote de la Mancha* by Miguel Cervantes); **Assistant Director:** Paolo Mori; **Cinematographer:** Jack Draper; **Assistant Cinematographer:** Giorgio Tonti; **Editors:** Renzo Lucidi, Maurizio Bonanni; **Music:** Hans Gunther Stumpf; **Cast:** Francisco Reiguera (Don Quixote), Akim Tamiroff (Sancho Panza), Orson Welles (Narrator), Patty McCormack (Dulcinea)

WELLES had long been fascinated with Miguel de Cervantes's *Don Quixote de la Mancha,* originally published in two parts, *El ingenioso hidalgo Don Quixote* (1605), and *Segunda parte del ingenioso cavallero Don Quixote de la Mancha* (1616). Among the features most attractive to Welles were Cervantes's whimsical yet poignantly telling insights into the foibles and yet also hopes of mankind. There was also the irrepressible character of the errant knight of the title, who like Welles, had tilted against the established order's real and figurative windmills. As was his custom, Welles took great liberties with the original story. The most significant of these was the updating of Cervantes's 15th-century Spanish setting to the postindustrial 20th-century. In one scene, for example, Quixote and Panza ride into a contemporary city on horse- and mule-back to contend with cars, cabs, buses, neon signage, and other accoutrements of modernism. Cheered on by those that they meet, the two time-travelers pass by a large billboard advertising Don Quixote Beer, a bit of reflexive fun masterfully brewed by Welles. In another old-world-meets-new-world confrontation, Quixote and Panza enter a movie theater where the good knight, upon observing an onscreen damsel in distress, leaps to her rescue, and in an act of gallantry, plunges his lance through the screen, thus vanquishing the onscreen villain. This was another "inside" joke, a colorfully cinematic allusion to Welles's own battles against the Hollywood mainstream. The adroit interactions between "real" and "onscreen" characters also anticipate Woody Allen's effective use of the same strategy in *The Purple Rose of Cairo* (1985).

In discussing *Don Quixote* with PETER BOG-DANOVICH, Welles elaborated on his conception of "contemporary": "He [Don Quixote] can't *ever* be contemporary—that's really the idea. He never was. But he's alive somehow, and he's riding through Spain even now. . . . The anachronism of Don Quixote's knightly armor in what was Cervantes's own modern time doesn't show up very sharply now [in the novel]. I've simply translated the anachronism. My film demonstrates that he and Sancho Panza are eternal." Indeed, *Don Quixote,* like *FIVE KINGS* and *CHIMES AT MIDNIGHT,* is another effort at coming to terms with the passing of chivalry. Here, rather than presenting a character victimized by changes in soci-ety, Welles keeps Quixote in a state of blissful ignorance of contemporary affairs, a stance made possible by the protective interventions of Panza. In contrast to the roughed-up-by-life CHARLES FOSTER KANE, George Minafer, FALSTAFF, or Mike Vargas, Quixote remains an innocent.

The story of the shooting and editing of *Don Quixote* is a saga comparable to that of the making of Welles's OTHELLO. Initial funding came in 1955 from CBS, which had commissioned Welles to adapt Cervantes's story into a half-hour teledrama. However, after a dissatisfied CBS executive screened samples of the unedited footage shot in Mexico and Spain, the network pulled out. Since Welles's vision of the project had enlarged to feature film proportions, the rejection was, ironically, good news. In the process, he had added himself as a narrator to help frame the story. In the expanded version, *Don Quixote* opens with Welles reading the Cervantes novel in the lobby of a Mexican hotel. A young American tourist, played by child actress PATTY MCCORMACK, asks Welles what he is reading. Sweeping her up into his lap, he begins the tale. The plan was for Welles's voice to periodically reenter to provide continuity. As the film's structure continued to evolve, Welles later added a documentary subplot exploring Spanish history and culture. In one scene shot in front of a bullring, the subject of bullfighting is introduced when McCormack asks Welles, "Was Mr. Quixote a bullfighter?"

The shooting of *Don Quixote* proceeded in stop-start fashion for over 18 years. Many of the scenes were approached with extraordinary spontaneity. Welles biographer PETER COWIE described the situation: "[Welles] would meet his actors and technical crew in front of his Spanish hotel each morning and then would set about improvising the film in the streets in the style of Mack Sennett." When there weren't funds to hire professional 35mm equipment and crews, Welles used the less expensive but technically inferior 16mm gauge. Such difficulties were dictated by economics and also Welles's desire to stay clear of any meddling that might come from backers. However, without sustained external funding, Welles shot whenever he had a few days and a few dollars earned from one of his acting jobs in other directors' movies. In 1960, for example, he took the role of

King Saul in the biblical epic *DAVID AND GOLIATH* in order to help keep this pet project going. It was a role that should have only taken several days to film. Welles, however, was able to protract the shooting schedule of his segment, thus increasing his paycheck and the sum he consequently could invest in *Don Quixote.*

As a result of the extended 1955–73 shooting schedule, there were lapses of years, even decades, between shots intended to be edited together for specific scenes. It was an impossible situation. Patty McCormack, for example, eventually grew too old to continue her role as the little girl. More daunting was the death of his "star," the marvelously weathered Francisco Reiguera who had been such a visually striking Don Quixote. Some of the footage had been shot in color, some in black and white. As for locations, there was footage from Mexico and Spain, as well as from Italy. Welles, who was generally able to rationalize even the most unorthodox situations, felt for a number of years that the emerging film's inherent disjointedness was an asset, and that, indeed, the disjunctions and dislocations fit in with and subtly underscored Quixote's misalignment with the present. In 1972, he started calling the project *When Are You Going to Finish Don Quixote?,* a playful tilt at the question that had been put to him repeatedly during the past 17 years. That is when he also began to think about integrating the piles of accumulated footage into a documentary essay about contemporary Spain.

In May 1986, a 45-minute assemblage of some of the *Don Quixote* footage that had been compiled by archivists of the Cinematèque Français was shown at the Cannes Film Festival. Although praised for its visual splendors, the narrative was so fragmentary that it was almost impossible to follow. As he often did in the editing process, Welles dubbed the voices of his principal characters—here, Quixote and Panza— himself. Still, the images of Francisco Reiguera's Don Quixote and AKIM TAMIROFF's Sancho Panza were impressive in and of themselves. Also, there were echoes of the Wellesian theme of a strong inner-directed individual wrestling with both his own illusions and a harsh world indifferent to those marching to the beats of their own drummers. The uncom-

pleted *Don Quixote* stands as a testament to Welles's unyielding individuality and vivid imagination.

—C.B.

Drake, Herbert   *New York Herald Tribune* theatre critic Herbert Drake played a Keystone Kop in the footage ORSON WELLES shot that was later included in his stage farce *TOO MUCH JOHNSON.* By the time Welles moved to Hollywood, Drake had become his assistant and press agent. When the *CITIZEN KANE*/*WILLIAM RANDOLPH HEARST* brouhaha began, Drake was accused of leaking to the press the tie between Kane and Hearst, which he subsequently denied. When *Citizen Kane* was screened for influential film critics and a columnist, it was Drake who called them about their responses, which were, with the exception of columnist Hedda Hopper's, quite favorable. Later, Drake sent some stills from *Citizen Kane,* some information about the stars, and a plot summary to several journals, including *Friday.* On the basis of that material Dan Gillmor, *Friday*'s editor, concocted a story that ended with "Wait until she [*Louella Parsons*] finds out that the picture's about her boss [Hearst]." Needless to say, problems ensued. According to SIMON CALLOW, Drake promoted *Citizen Kane* with a vengeance. Drake was also involved in the controversy over who wrote the screenplay for *Citizen Kane.* In a letter to Welles, Drake wrote, "Mankiewicz is threatening to come down on you because you are a juvenile delinquent credit stealer beginning with the Mars broadcast and carrying on with tremendous consistency." A little later, Drake wrote to Welles to assure him that MANKIEWICZ did not want to pursue the matter.

When Welles was casting *JOURNEY INTO FEAR* (1942), he gave Drake a role as a steward. After the film was completed and while Welles was in Brazil, Drake and the Mercury staff were thrown off the RKO lot by CHARLES KOERNER, RKO head, who was determined to get rid of Welles.

—T.L.E.

Dreamers, The   *The Dreamers,* a script by WELLES intended as a starring vehicle for OJA KODAR, his companion and collaborator from 1962 to 1985, reflects the director's long-standing fascination with the work of Danish novelist ISAK DINESEN. In the script's prologue, Welles describes his obsession with the author, whose novella he had previously adapted for *THE IMMORTAL STORY* (1968). He mentions a lengthy fan letter to her that he destroyed. There was also a trip to Copenhagen for a meeting that he backed out of at the last minute because of his anxiety about meeting her. *The Dreamers,* based on a 1978 script by Welles titled *Da Capo,* was adapted from two stories by Dinesen from her first major book, *Seven Gothic Tales* (1934).

Thanks to director HENRY JAGLOM, Welles was able to secure financing to revise *Da Capo* for Northstar Productions, run by Hal Ashby, the director of the Oscar-winning *Coming Home.* However, after reading the new version, now called *The Dreamers,* Northstar opted to bypass its option. Like a host of other would-be producers for *The Dreamers,* Northstar found the story and treatment lacking in commercial appeal.

Still, the script has been praised, even by CHARLES HIGHAM, one of Welles's severest critics, who found it "intensely poetic and filled with heightened prose of a quality seldom heard on the screen" and "one of the most intriguing works of the master." FRANK BRADY, noting Oja Kodar's contributions to the revised script, said that *The Dreamers* had "the elements of a haunting, poetic film: a storyteller's story told in hazily delineated scenes, filled with psychological and romantic excursions into inner fantasies."

The story centers on a 19th-century opera singer, Pellegrina Leoni (to have been played by Oja Kodar), who is gifted with an ethereal bel canto voice and billed as the greatest singer in the world. However, when her voice fails, she abruptly departs in search of new experiences and adventures. In one of her treks, she discovers a young boy in a secluded mountain village whose voice recalls her own transcendent soprano limnings. Tragically, she is destroyed after being denounced as a witch.

Using his own funds, Welles shot a brief part of *The Dreamers* in his Los Angeles home in 1980, hoping that the sample scene might help generate financing. In the scene photographed by Gary Graver, Pellegrina (Kodar) bids adieu to Marcus (Welles), her oldest and most trusted friend, telling

him that she must depart immediately. He pledges his continued support, offering to send money whenever she might need it. JONATHAN ROSENBAUM described the excerpt in an article in *Sight and Sound:* "Admittedly, the scene is no more than an unfinished fragment: Welles never got round to shooting his own close-ups (in the part of Marcus Kleek, the elderly Dutch Jewish merchant who is Pellegrina's only friend), and the dialogue—a lonely duet of two melodious accented voices, accompanied by the whir of crickets and even the faint hum of passing traffic—is recorded in direct sound. But the delicate lighting, lyrical camera movement and rich deployments of blue, black and yellow, combined with the lilt of the two voices, create an astonishing glimpse into the overripe dream world that Welles envisioned for the film."

After Welles's death, Kodar screened the scene for a conference on the director at New York University, confirming that it was shot at night in Welles's Los Angeles home. She also pointed out that the sound of crickets was intended to add atmosphere, while also muting the ambient sounds of nearby freeway traffic. Frank Brady, like Rosenbaum, was fascinated by the segment's "subdued, pastoral quality that one can imagine would have pervaded the entire work. The dialogue is soft, somber, with the camera, and our attention, focused on Kodar. The camera angles and movements are straightforward, in keeping with the hushed quality of the drama. We do not see Welles's face, but view much of the conversation from directly behind him, almost looking over his shoulder. He remains, however, a magisterial presence and voice."

Welles projected that *The Dreamers* could be shot for $6 million, a small sum for a feature film in the early 1980s. Still, backing was not forthcoming, even though Welles argued that it would be his most important film.

—C.B.

Drunkard, The, or, The Fallen Saved (play, 1934) Toward the end of the 1934 summer *WOODSTOCK DRAMA FESTIVAL,* a virtually impromptu production of *The Drunkard, or, The Fallen Saved* was mounted as a tribute to the festival's two guest artists

from Ireland, MICHEÁL MACLIAMMÓIR and HILTON EDWARDS, who had given WELLES his first taste of professional theater at Dublin's GATE THEATRE in 1931. MacLiammóir and Edwards were particularly curious about the 1844 William H. Smith melodrama since CHARLIE CHAPLIN has once called it the funniest play he had ever seen.

The five-act play concerns a villainous lawyer, Cribbs, who holds a grudge against the Middleton family, even though he has served as their attorney. When young Edward Middleton's father dies, Cribbs tries to persuade Edward to dispossess a poor mother and daughter who are Middleton's tenants. Instead, Middleton falls in love with Mary, the daughter, and marries her. However, Middleton has an Achilles' heel—he drinks. Cribbs insidiously abets Middleton's penchant for alcohol in a crass attempt to gain power over the young man's affairs. Down and out on New York City's skid row, Middleton is rehabilitated by his foster brother William and a philanthropist, Arden Rencelaw, who help him reunite with Mary and their young daughter. At last confronted, Cribbs is forced to admit that he has hidden Middleton's grandfather's will and that Middleton is in fact still a wealthy man.

The Drunkard was first presented as part of a temperance crusade in Boston in 1844. In its original form, it was a sobering morality play whose sermonizing intent was clearly indicated by the subtitle, *The Fallen Saved.* In 1850, it was revived by several New York theaters, most notably at Barnum's American Museum, where it set a box office record. Interestingly, *The Drunkard* was not played for laughs until 1933, when a small Los Angeles theater reconfigured the play as a piece of comedic nostalgia owing much more to the slapstick of the silent film period than to Smith's moralizing. The comedically revised play was a hit, running for 20 years, a record run surpassed only by the New York production of *The Fantasticks.* Since then, *The Drunkard* has become a staple of summer and community theaters throughout the United States.

In the 1934 Woodstock production, the play's cast of loafers, bumpkins, maniacs, spinsters, and other ne'er-do-wells were played strictly for laughs, with the audience encouraged to join in with appropriate

hissing, booing, and applause. There were also sing-alongs inserted at the drop of a hat, lustily sung by the combined vocal forces of cast and audience. Among the favorites was the aptly ironic "Little Brown Jug." Along with the fun, there was also the redemptive message of villainy foiled and virtue rewarded. In all, it was an evening of pure, grassroots Americana.

The Woodstock rendition made such a favorable impression on MacLiammóir and Edwards that upon their return to Dublin, *The Drunkard* was immediately added to the Gate Theatre's upcoming season.

Reference Moody, Richard. *Dramas from the American Theatre, 1762–1909* (Cleveland and New York: World Publishing Co., 1966).

—C.B.

Duel in the Sun Vanguard Productions/ Selznick Releasing Organization, 126 minutes, 1946. **Director:** King Vidor (and William Dieterle, Josef von Sternberg, William Cameron Menzies, Hal Kern, and Chester Franklin, all uncredited); **Producer:** David O. Selznick; **Screenplay:** David O. Selznick, from Oliver H.P. Garrett's adaptation of the novel by Niven Busch, published in 1944; **Cinematography:** Lee Garmes, Harold Rosson, and Ray Rennahan, et al.; **Editors:** Hal Kern, William H. Ziegler, and John Faure; **Music:** Dimitri Tiomkin; **Cast:** Orson Welles (narrator, uncredited), Jennifer Jones (Pearl Chavez), Gregory Peck (Lewt McCanles), Joseph Cotten (Jess McCanles), Lionel Barrymore (Senator McCanles), Lillian Gish (Laura Belle McCanles), Charles Bickford (Sam Pierce), Butterfly McQueen (Vashti), Walter Huston (Sin-killer), Herbert Marshall (Scott Chavez), Tilly Losch (Mrs. Chavez), Harry Carey, Otto Kruger, Sidney Blackmer, et al.

A U.S. film directed by King Vidor featuring WELLES as narrator (uncredited). This David O. Selznick big-budget western, based on the best-selling 1944 novel by Niven Busch, featured an all-star cast that included Welles's friend and MERCURY THEATRE colleague JOSEPH COTTEN, along with Jennifer Jones, then producer Selznick's mistress. Welles's mellifluous bass-baritone is heard against the film's opening sequence, an ominous desert landscape draped by bloodred crimson skies, relating the tale of the doomed heroine: "Deep among the lonely, sun-baked hills of Texas, the great and weather-beaten stone still stands. The Comanches call it 'Squaw's Head Rock.' Time cannot change its impassive face, nor dim the legend of the wild young lovers who found heaven, and hell, in the shadows of the rock. For when the sun is low and the cold wind blows across the desert, there are those who still speak of Pearl Chavez, the half-breed girl from down along the border, and of the laughing outlaw with whom she had kept a final rendezvous, never to be seen again. And this is what the legend says: 'A flower, known nowhere else, grows from out of the desperate crags where Pearl vanished. . . . Pearl, who was herself a wild flower, sprung from the hard clay, quick to blossom . . . and early to die."

DAVID THOMSON says that Selznick, worried about the film's racy content, had Welles write and deliver the prologue just prior to *Duel in the Sun*'s release in order that the narrative might "cast the film's trashy story as some kind of prairie legend." Expecting, and needing, a big paycheck, Welles had to wait until Christmas 1946 for Selznick, "an uneasy but fairly intimate friend," to respond. Instead of money, Welles received a pair of antique dueling pistols valued at only $150. Selznick, claiming that the Internal Revenue Service would have grabbed anything more substantive, explained the pistols' value from an antiquarian point of view. Welles accepted the "joke" and thereafter sent the mogul two glass pistols filled with candy each Christmas.

The massive western, which *Time* magazine described as "a knowing blend of oats and aphrodisiac," also featured Gregory Peck, Lionel Barrymore, Herbert Marshall, Lillian Gish, Walter Huston, Otto Kruger, and Sidney Blackmer.

—C.B.

Edwards, Hilton (1903–1982) British actor-director Hilton Edwards, distinguished for his Shakespearean performances, gave ORSON WELLES his first professional acting break at the GATE THEATRE in Dublin in 1931. Edwards was born in London on February 2, 1903, the son of Thomas George Edwards and his wife, Emily, and educated at the East Finchley Grammar School and at St. Aloysius, Highgate. Edwards made his stage debut at the Windsor Theatre Royal in 1920 and his London debut at the Old Vic in 1922. Together with MICHEÁL MACLIAMMÓIR, Edwards had founded the Gate Theatre in 1928. They had met as actors at Anew McMaster's Intimate Shakespeare Company and left in the company of each other, as lovers. In 1934 it was Edwards who accepted Orson Welles's invitation to participate, with MacLiammóir at the Todd School Summer Festival in Woodstock, Illinois. Of the plays Edwards directed at Woodstock, he took the 19th-century thoroughly American melodrama THE DRUNKARD back to the Gate Theatre in Dublin, where it became part of their repertoire.

Edwards and MacLiammóir worked closely together as theatrical partners for over 50 years. In 1960, for example, the same year Edwards directed Orson Welles in the stage production of CHIMES AT MIDNIGHT, he also directed MacLiammóir's adaptation of *The Informer* at the Olympia Theatre in Dublin. Hilton Edwards often compared Welles to America, according to FRANK BRADY: "Because of their immensity, everything you can say about them—negative or positive—*had* to be true."

Edwards and MacLiammóir had invited Welles to direct and act in any Shakespearean play of his choice, so long as it first was staged in Ireland. After a false start with *The Merchant of Venice,* Welles selected his compilation of the so-called Henriad, *Chimes at Midnight.* After five performances in Belfast, Northern Ireland, the play was moved to the Dublin Gaiety Theatre. Originally the play was slated for London's West End, but it closed in Dublin before getting there. Since the 1920s Edwards directed over 300 plays at the Gate Theatre and at the Gaiety Theatre in Dublin. From 1961 to 1963, Edwards served as head of Irish Television.

References Fitz-Simon, Christopher. *The Boys: A Double Biography* (London: Heinemann, 1994); Luke, Peter, *Enter Certain Players: Edwards-MacLiammóir and the Gate* (Dublin: Dolmen Press, 1978)

—T.L.E. and J.M.W.

Ellington, Duke (c. 1899–1974) If WELLES had succeeded in bringing his original 1941 vision of the four-part omnibus film IT'S ALL TRUE to the screen, it would have included a segment devoted to the history of jazz, a topic of consuming passion for Welles. JAZZ STORY was also to have been an opportunity for Welles to collaborate with two of his musical heroes, African-

American jazz legends Duke Ellington (pianist-composer) and LOUIS ARMSTRONG (trumpeter-vocalist). Although Welles had put Ellington on the studio payroll to begin writing the score, the project was abandoned under pressure from RKO when Welles's relationship with the studio started to unravel.

Pianist-composer Ellington is one of jazzdom's most celebrated icons. His big band, which he successfully kept employed for half a century, was his primary "instrument," a multifaceted organization of great versatility that was the sounding board for Ellington's fertile writing and arranging imagination. From the "jungle style" of the Cotton Club revues of the early 1930s to his sacred works of the 1970s, Ellington covered a gamut of styles with an élan that earned him a reputation as the most important composer in jazz.

Gaining national-international recognition during the heyday of the 1930s' Big Band Era, the Duke Ellington Orchestra made numerous appearances in band shorts, jazz documentaries, and Hollywood feature films. Among Ellington's Hollywood films are *Murder at the Vanities* (1934); *Belle of the Nineties* (1934); *The Hit Parade* (1937); *Cabin in the Sky* (1942); *Reveille with Beverly* (1942); and the impressive *Anatomy of a Murder* (1959), for which he wrote the score, and briefly appeared playing piano.

References Berg, Chuck. "Jazz in Film and Video," in *The Oxford Companion to Jazz* (New York: Oxford University Press); Dance, Stanley. *The World of Duke Ellington* (New York: Da Capo, 2000); Laurence, A.H. *Duke Ellington and His World: A Biography* (New York: Routledge, 2001); Rattenberry, Ken. *Duke Ellington, Jazz Composer* (New Haven, Conn.: Yale University Press, 1993).

—C.B.

Evening with Orson Welles, An (play, 1950)
Immediately following the close of THE BLESSED AND THE DAMNED in Paris at the Théâtre Edouard VII, WELLES plotted to take the show on tour to Germany. Retitling the production, *An Evening with Orson Welles,* and dropping THE UNTHINKING LOBSTER in favor of an abbreviated 45-minute version of OSCAR WILDE's THE IMPORTANCE OF BEING EARNEST, Welles further spiked the presentation with displays of his own magic tricks and sultry songs delivered by his newest discovery and love interest, the soon-to-be legendary chanteuse, EARTHA KITT.

Held over from *The Blessed and the Damned,* the Paris incarnation of the anthology, was Welles's one-act play, TIME RUNS, a loose and greatly truncated adaptation of Christopher Marlowe's *Doctor Faustus* (1604). The production also featured Welles's two friends from Dublin's GATE THEATRE, MICHEÁL MACLIAMMÓIR and HILTON EDWARDS. In *Time Runs,* the part of Mephistopheles, which had been played in Paris by Edwards, was taken over by MacLiammóir. The evening's entertainment also included scenes from Shakespearean plays such as OTHELLO and *JULIUS CAESAR* played by Welles and MacLiammóir.

The German tour of *An Evening with Orson Welles* opened in Frankfurt on August 7, 1950, and included stops in Munich, Cologne, Dusseldorf, Hamburg, Berlin, and other cities. Given Welles's unease with most things German, and his passionate antipathy toward the country's recent Nazi past, Welles's tour of Germany became something to be endured rather than savored. His surly press conferences with German journalists—including the quip, "What's wrong with this country? They haven't produced a decent film since the war"—resulted in coverage approaching the enmity shown to him by the Hearst papers in 1941 in the wake of the stormy release of CITIZEN KANE. Not surprisingly, given the controversial press treatment and the hot summer weather, many of the performances were poorly attended. As reported by FRANK BRADY, and in contrast to the outright rosy account of the German tour by BARBARA LEAMING, Welles maintained that the only successful show in Germany was a performance for English soldiers at a camp in Bad Oynhausen, where the jokes and comic setups of *The Importance of Being Earnest* were instantly understood, prompting Welles to conclude, "They laughed from the stomach, not from the head."

After finishing the last performance of *An Evening with Orson Welles* at the Titania Palast in Berlin, the show played for 10 days in Brussels, after which Welles resumed postproduction work on his troubled film adaptation of *Othello.*

—C.B.

Everybody's Shakespeare   A series of three text-books on Shakespeare (see SHAKESPEARE BY WELLES) by Welles and ROGER HILL devoted to, respectively, *TWELFTH NIGHT, The Merchant of Venice,* and *JULIUS CAESAR,* initially published by the Todd Press in Woodstock, Illinois, in 1934, and later, issued in a single volume as *Everybody's Shakespeare* by Harper and Row in 1939. As SIMON CALLOW points out, actors and audiences of the 1920s and 1930s were wary of Shakespeare, fearing that which they didn't know. Roger Hill, headmaster of the Todd School for Boys, and his precocious protégé, sought to challenge this cultural-intellectual inferiority complex by making Shakespeare accessible to young people. Along with pointing to the plays' excitement, they cut and pruned everywhere, getting to the quick of things in truncated versions of the scripts that were "acterly."

Hill, in his introduction, emphasized that Shakespeare's vitality could most fully be appreciated when experienced in the theater (rather than through reading). That theme was echoed in Welles's preface to the annotated plays, "On Staging Shakespeare and on Shakespeare's Stage."

> Shakespeare said everything. Brain to belly; every mood and minute of a man's season. His language is starlight and fireflies and the sun and the moon. He wrote it with tears and blood and beer, and his words march like heartbeats. He speaks to everyone and we all claim him but it's wise to remember, if we would really appreciate him, that he doesn't properly belong to use but to another world that smelled assertively of columbine and gun powder and printer's ink and was vigorously dominated by Elizabeth.

While foreshadowing the dramatic bravura that would mark his future writings, from screenplays to newspaper columns, it also was a declaration of the basic principle that "the play is the thing." Each volume included a breezy biography of Shakespeare, a discussion of Shakespeare's language, and a shortened version of the script spiked with numerous annotations; there were tips on acting, suggestions for staging, copious historical notes, all of which were lavishly illustrated by Welles.

What Welles had created, with Hill serving primarily as cheerleader and foil, was a series of tours through the plays' main plots, with storyboard tracings of the action, spiced with stage directions, commentaries on the language, and historical asides. In *The Merchant of Venice* book, for instance, Welles limned a series of sketches of notable Shylocks throughout theatrical history, including those of actors Sir Henry Irving, Walter Hampden, Williams Charles Macready, James W. Wallack, George Arliss, Edwin Forrest, E.T. Davenport, Richard Mansfield, and David Warfield, all of whom were depicted in a variety of costumes, characteristically posed, and rendered by Welles from contemporary tintypes or photos. Welles also added in small type before the scenes, excerpts from Raphael Holinshed's *Chronicles of England, Scotland, and Ireland* (1581), from which Shakespeare and other Elizabethan playwrights took much of their source material. In effect, this allowed the reader to savor the very lines that had inspired Shakespeare as he took pen to paper.

Welles and Hill, as reflected by their liberal editing, which included rewordings of Shakespeare's more arcane utterances, stressed that their books were intended as catalysts for experimentation. "This is a book of ideas," they said, "and whenever it inspires other ideas it will have value. Your idea is as worth trying as anyone's. Remember that every single way of playing Shakespeare—as long as the way is effective—is right." At the same time, they also included many more stage suggestions beyond those indicated by Shakespeare himself. Still, the injunction to experiment coming so early in Welles's career is significant, especially in view of his highly individualistic approach to the Bard in his Shakespeare films, *MACBETH, OTHELLO,* and *CHIMES AT MIDNIGHT* (a melding of *Richard II; Henry IV, Part I; Henry IV, Part II; Henry V;* and *The Merry Wives of Windsor*), and in stage productions such as his 1936 "voodoo" *Macbeth* for the FEDERAL THEATRE PROJECT.

The blue-covered, gold-labeled books proved highly effective introductions to understanding and producing Shakespeare throughout the United States. In 1934, the first edition of the books was printed and sold by mail and to bookstores by the Todd School. In

1939, they were issued together in one volume called *Everybody's Shakespeare* and distributed by publishing giant, Harper and Row. Later, Harper sold its school text business to McGraw-Hill, which kept *Everybody's Shakespeare* in print until the mid-1970s. The work was praised by educators, drama teachers, students, and the press. In hailing *Everybody's Shakespeare,* the *Chicago American* said that "Orson Welles in endeavoring to unschoolmaster the Bard went a good distance in canceling the curse of compulsory Shakespeare." The *New York Herald Tribune* touted the book by calling it "a lifeline to Shakespeare."

Everybody's Shakespeare is arguably the most influential secondary text in the annals of American theater education. It was a pioneering work that made Shakespeare fun for secondary school students without undermining the plays' integrity. Ultimately, over 100,000 copies were sold. Although it never produced significant royalties, or fanfare, its authors viewed *Everybody's Shakespeare* with justifiable pride. *Everybody's Shakespeare* remains one of Welles's most significant contributions to American culture.

—C.B.

Falstaff, Sir John/Sir John Oldcastle (c. 1377–1417)

A fat old knight and reprobate, perfectly realized by ORSON WELLES in *CHIMES AT MIDNIGHT*, famous for his wenching, gambling, and mischief, who is for a time boon-companion to Prince Hal, the son and heir of King Henry IV, eventually to become after his father's death King Henry V, described by Shakespeare as "the mirror of all Christian kings." Falstaff was Shakespeare's greatest comic creation, and, if Orson Welles was not born to play him, this was a role Welles eventually grew into.

Shakespeare surely based the character of Falstaff, at least in part, upon an actual historical figure, Sir John Oldcastle (c. 1377–1417), a friend of Henry V and a soldier in the Welsh campaigns who later commanded English troops in France. Shakespeare took the concept and, elaborating upon the character of Sir John, factored in components of a stock figure, the *miles gloriosus* or "braggart soldier," and transformed what J. Dover Wilson called a "sawdust theatrical puppet" into a larger-than-life Lord of Misrule who would dominate both parts of *Henry IV,* a king of mirth and mischief who holds court at the Boar's Head Tavern. Shakespeare's Falstaff was also a master rhetorician, far more clever and manipulative than his inferior minions, Pistol, Bardolph, and Nym, who survived him into *Henry V.* As Samuel Johnson wrote in the 18th century, Falstaff was no doubt corrupt, but his vices, "which may be despised but hardly detested," are then offset by "the most pleasing of all qualities, perpetual gaiety."

Fascinated by the character, Welles built his screenplay for *Chimes at Midnight* around his own portrayal of Falstaff, who is so central to the action, development, and concept that the film is also known by its alternate title, *Falstaff.* Dover Wilson has called Falstaff's role in the two parts of *Henry IV* "a masterpiece of construction." If so, then Welles's achievement might be called a masterpiece of reconstruction. In his cycle of history plays known as the "Henriad," Shakespeare dramatized the passage from medieval kingship to modern kingship. Like *THE MAGNIFICENT AMBERSONS, Chimes at Midnight* is an elegy, a lament for a way of life whose time has come and gone. Moving from the high spirits of *1 Henry IV* to the tragic overtones of *2 Henry IV,* Falstaff is the human wreckage left behind as Prince Hal ascends the throne to become King Henry V. Falstaff is all feeling, a palpitating mass of humanity whose "goodness," Welles noted, "is like bread and wine." An ultimately fragile figure, Falstaff is gradually destroyed as his young friend Prince Hal assumes power, as Welles seemingly takes his cue from the 19th-century romantic critics of Shakespeare. As with his other films, *Chimes at Midnight* is yet another Wellesian meditation on the corrupting influence of power and the way the world changes around us. This film, a dream project with a patchy production his-

Poster by John Tibbetts

tory, represents the culmination of Orson Welles's mature career.

Reference Wilson, J. Dover. *The Fortunes of Falstaff* (Cambridge, U.K.: Cambridge University Press, 1964).

—J.M.W. and C.B.

Faulkner, William (1897–1962) Faulkner

wrote *The Hamlet,* which was filmed as THE LONG HOT SUMMER, co-starring ORSON WELLES. Faulkner was born in Albany, Mississippi, on September 25, 1897; he won recognition as a major American novelist, epitomized by his receiving the Nobel Prize for literature in 1949. After serving in World War I, Faulkner decided to pursue a career as a novelist.

The first of his novels to attract attention in literary circles was *The Sound and the Fury* (1929), which recounts the story of the Compson family, a once-proud Southern clan that has fallen on evil days. *Sanctuary* (1931) told the lurid tale of a college co-ed kidnapped by a gangster; she stays on with him

because of her morbid fascination with his decadent world. The novel caused a sensation and was a best-seller. *The Hamlet* (1940), discussed below, was one of several Faulkner works to be filmed. *Intruder in the Dust* (1948), another popular novel by Faulkner, is a mystery story with racial implications. *The Reivers* (1962), Faulkner's last major novel, tells the story of a country boy who learns a great deal about the dark side of life in the course of his first journey to Memphis.

Throughout the 1930s, Faulkner intermittently composed short shories about a crafty, ambitious young Southerner named Flem Snopes. He did so with a view to weaving these tales eventually into the fabric of a novel. Finally, in 1940, Faulkner published *The Hamlet,* which incorporated these earlier episodes with additional material, in order to round out the story, which is set before World War I.

The theme that links the novel's varied incidents, including those of the Texas ponies and the salted silver mine, is the way that greed and self-interest infect human behavior. Even the marriage of Flem and Eula Varner revolves around the theme of greedy self-interest, since Flem agrees to wed Eula and give her unborn child a name in exchange for cash and some of Will Varner's real estate holdings. So in the world of *The Hamlet* even marriage is reduced to a crass business transaction. At the novel's conclusion it is evident that the novel is the story of Flem's upward progress from near-rags to near-riches, from a dirt farmer to the ownership of a substantial bank balance.

Perhaps because *The Hamlet* began its creative life as a series of short stories, some literary critics felt that the novel lacked a strong sense of unity. Indeed, one reviewer termed the book a collection of episodes, strung together like beads on a string.

In 1955, Jerry Wald, a Hollywood producer, optioned the movie rights to *The Hamlet.* Wald paid Faulkner $25,000 for the screen rights; he decided that the film should be shot in color and widescreen. Wald borrowed the title, *The Long Hot Summer,* from part three of the book, "The Long Summer." "We changed the name," director Martin Ritt (*Hud*) explained at the time, "so people wouldn't confuse it with that other *Hamlet.*"

Wald hired Orson Welles to play Will Varner. According to CHARLES HIGHAM, Ritt maintained that Welles was on his best behavior during production. FRANK BRADY, however, tells a different story; he cites Ritt as saying, "Two weeks after we started, you could bet we wouldn't finish the film." Ritt could be every bit as volatile as Welles on the set, and the pair quarreled about everything from camera angles to the interpretation of dialogue. Welles recalled that he hated making the movie and was doing it for the handsome salary ($150,000).

Ritt remembered that Welles brought a considerable reputation, with an ego to match, to the set. Gabriel Miller cites Ritt as recalling that Welles kept saying to him, "You don't know a hell of a lot about making movies"; to which Ritt replied, "I know a hell of a lot about people and what their behavior has to be, in order to make my film work." And so it went.

An index of Welles's view of the picture as less than a significant film was that he did not bother to learn his lines perfectly. Ritt was understandably nettled, and Welles countered that any bit of dialogue that he forgot could be added to the sound track during post-production. Ritt reluctantly agreed to this procedure, although he pointed out somewhat caustically to Welles that the latter had memorized lengthy speeches in Shakespeare's plays and hence should have been willing to master the relatively simple lines in the movie script.

Ritt's relationship with Welles reached the boiling point one day when Ritt was ready to shoot a scene and found Welles sitting around, reading a Spanish newspaper. "He's not prepared for the scene," Ritt states in Miller's book. "I'm pretty mad, so I tell everyone, that's it; we'll shoot something else." That night Welles phoned Ritt and said, "Marty, why'd you do that? You humiliated me in front of everyone." "I humiliated you?" Ritt answered; "what the hell do you think you did to me?" Ritt adds, "then I told him the facts of life. We got along fine after that." The two men gradually developed some respect for each other. Meanwhile, Wald suggested rather sarcastically that Welles's thick Southern drawl might require subtitles—a remark that Welles let pass, since he did not vary his Southern accent throughout the film. Nor

should he have—actually, Welles's mastery of the Southern accent is quite skillful.

Withal, the picture somehow was finished. Welles did have some happy memories of the production experience. He told PETER BOGDANOVICH, "I enjoyed very much working with JOANNE WOODWARD," who played his daughter, Clara, "and with Angela Lansbury," who played his mistress, Mary.

The screenplay was by the husband-wife team of Irving Ravetch and Harriet Frank, Jr. Oddly enough, it was probably the novel's episodic narrative structure, which literary critics had decried when it came out, that made *The Hamlet* easily adapted for film. Several incidents in the novel, some of which had been published separately as short stories before their inclusion in *The Hamlet,* constitute self-contained units. The screenwriters therefore were able simply to pick the episodes they judged screenworthy and drop the rest; in this way they could develop to their fullest dramatic potential those incidents they did retain.

The principal episodes from the novel that found their way into the script were the barn-burning episode and the incidents dealing with the spotted horses and the hidden treasure. Ravetch and Frank placed these items and the others they adapted from the novel within an overall narrative framework of their own devising. Some of the material supplied by the screenwriters to fill out the movie's scenario departed considerably from the plot of the novel. Nonetheless, they combined their own story material with the material from the novel so adroitly that the movie remains essentially what Cleanth Brooks called *The Hamlet:* "a sort of sardonic Horatio Alger story, a tale of commercial success in which the poor but diligent young man marries the boss's daughter and becomes a financial power."

Welles garnered a good press for his portrayal of Will Varner, which was termed an intelligent, shrewd performance. Indeed, Welles enacts the role without compromise, presenting Varner as the blustering, cigar-chomping patriarch of the clan. Yet at times he projects a touching vulnerability; there is, for example, his scene with Mary Littlejohn (Angela Lansbury). Varner, a widower who hopes to dodge marrying his middle-aged mistress, reflects that he is over 60 and not much good for anything anymore.

Mary responds, "Don't tell me you're too old; I happen to be in a position to know better." With that, comments DAVID THOMSON, "Welles lets a little burp of satisfaction escape Varner's lips, and one eyebrow arches like a salute to Varner's own ego."

Although Welles was not happy making the movie, *The Long Hot Summer* was an enormous success. Whatever his artistic differences with Martin Ritt, Welles gives a bravura performance as the rough-hewn, imposing lord of the plantation and ultimately dominates the film.

References   Brady, Frank. *Citizen Welles: A Biography of Orson Welles* (New York: Scribner's, 1989); Brooks, Cleanth. *William Faulkner: The Yoknapatawpha Country* (New Haven, Conn.: Yale University Press, 1966); Hahn, Stephen. "*The Hamlet*," in *A William Faulkner Encyclopedia,* ed. Robert Hamblin and Charles Peek (Westport, Conn.: Greenwood, 1999), 165–68; Higham, Charles. *Orson Welles: The Rise and Fall of an American Genius* (New York: St. Martin's Press, 1985); Knight, Arthur. "Filming Faulknerland: *The Long Hot Summer*," *Saturday Review* (December 7, 1957): 52; McGilligan, Patrick. "Ritt Large: An Interview with Martin Ritt," *Film Comment* 22, no. 1 (January–February, 1986): 38+; Miller, Gabriel. *The Films of Martin Ritt: Fanfare for the Common Man* (Jackson: University Press of Mississippi, 2000); Thomson, David. *Rosebud: The Story of Orson Welles* (New York: Vintage Books, 1997); Welles, Orson, and Peter Bogdanovich. *This Is Orson Welles* (New York: Da Capo, 1998).

—G.D.P.

Federal Theatre Project (1935–1939)   This courageous yet star-crossed experiment in founding a national public theater supported some of WELLES's earliest and most significant theater work. Established under President FRANKLIN DELANO ROOSEVELT's WORKS PROGRESS ADMINISTRATION (WPA) in 1935 by an act of Congress, the Federal Theatre Project, like other New Deal initiatives, was designed to put people idled by the Depression back to work. Harry Hopkins, Roosevelt's senior adviser, also stressed the goal of providing "free, adult, uncensored theater." HALLIE FLANAGAN, director of the Vassar Experimental Theatre, was appointed its national director, and during its early years it succeeded in providing work for theater artists and, in the process, offering lively theater to the public.

At its apex, the Federal Theatre employed 10,000 people, most of whom had been on relief. In New York alone, 5,385 theater people went back to work in productions that during its four-year run attracted over 12 million people to its various venues. Other companies sprang up across the country, providing audiences, many first-time playgoers, with a variety of generally high quality theater. Productions spanned a gamut that included revivals of classics, new works, children's plays, foreign-language plays, marionette shows, and dance concerts. Though officially administered from Washington, the individual units of the Federal Theatre Project were in practice quite autonomous.

The New York branch, for which Welles and collaborator JOHN HOUSEMAN worked, was headed by playwright Elmer Rice. It generated controversy almost immediately with the debut of the *Living Newspaper,* a hard-hitting series of theatrical documentaries that tackled the nation's most pressing economic and social issues. In what was to be its initial production, *Ethiopia* (1936), a probing examination of Mussolini's attack on that African country, excerpts from speeches by Mussolini and Roosevelt were to have been included. However, because of State Department concerns about offending the Italian dictator, *Ethiopia* was pulled from the schedule. This kind of censorship, a violation of Hopkins's pledge for a politically unfettered Federal Theatre, culminated in the resignation of an outraged Rice. It was a dark omen of things to come.

Welles and Houseman had to deal with their own censorship problems. In their attempt to mount the avowedly left-wing musical, THE CRADLE WILL ROCK (1937), they ran afoul of federal bureaucrats and subservient unions afraid of right-wing reactions to the anti-capitalist MARC BLITZSTEIN show. The company carried on in spite of the duress, including a boycott of the production by the Musicians Union, and *The Cradle Will Rock* was successfully staged in an impromptu and stripped-down version.

Flanigan also appointed Houseman to head the NEGRO THEATRE PROJECT, a unit of the Federal Theatre housed at the Lafayette Theatre in Harlem. It was here that Welles staged the "voodoo" MACBETH in 1936, an all-black production in which the setting had been changed to Haiti. There were also, as was customary with Welles's adaptations of Shakespeare, changes in the play itself, including a transformation of the three witches into voodoo doctors. Enjoying a long run at the Lafayette, and a prominent national tour, Welles's *Macbeth* was one of the Federal Theatre's most successful productions.

In 1939, because of the Federal Theatre's overtly liberal orientation and myriad other controversies, conservative legislators in the U.S. Congress initiated an investigation that resulted in a refusal to appropriate further funding. The Federal Theatre Project was dead. Still, its legacy continued to live in the work of the thousands of theater professionals that it had touched. Welles and Houseman were two of its most distinguished alumni.

—C.B.

Feldman, Charles K. (Charles Gould)

(1904–1968) In 1943, agent-producer Charles K. Feldman organized a group of Hollywood performers who appeared in *FOLLOW THE BOYS* (1944), a wartime movie. Among the stars who performed routines was ORSON WELLES, who "sawed" MARLENE DIETRICH in two as part of his magic act. In 1947, Orson Welles stayed for a while at the home of Feldman, who persuaded Republic head, HERBERT J. YATES, to produce a *MACBETH* for $700,000, with $100,000 going to Welles, who would write, direct, and star in the film. When *Macbeth* dragged on and on, there were problems, not the least of which was Welles's presence in Europe. DAVID THOMSON describes the situation Welles left to his associate, RICHARD WILSON: "So Wilson fought the studio battles, with no support from Charlie Feldman, who only wanted the damn thing over." Welles had better luck with *PRINCE OF FOXES* (1949), a film in which Welles played Cesare Borgia, a character FRANK BRADY suggests resembled Welles: "The handsome Borgia was taller than most men of his day, and had broad shoulders. He was also a show-off, dressing himself in insolent magnificence, a study in gaudy conceit." Feldman had convinced HENRY KING, the director, that Welles would be excellent and well behaved. He was, but Brady believes that King did follow some of Welles's suggestions about camera

placement and that, as a result, "the film does contain a richness and depth of image that surpasses *The Black Swan,* which it most closely resembles." Feldman next cast Welles in *CASINO ROYALE* (1967), a spoof of the James Bond pictures: Welles was not only to act in the film, but to help write it. Wolf Mankowitz, another writer assigned to the film, and Welles often got together to discuss the film, despite Feldman's intent to keep the writers apart so they would not, as BARBARA LEAMING puts it, "dilute one another's best ideas." Mankowitz warned Feldman about Peter Sellers, another lead: "I told Charlie that Sellers would fuck everything up: he wanted different directors, he wanted to piss around with the script." In response to a *Casino Royale* question by PETER BOGDANOVICH, Welles said, "That was Feldman [the producer] running scared. How that picture was a success, I can't imagine."

Charles Feldman, who was born in New York City on April 26, 1904, was educated at the University of Michigan and at the University of Southern California. In 1928, he set up a law practice in Los Angeles, only to leave it in 1932 to become head of Famous Artists, a leading Hollywood talent agency. *Pittsburgh,* the first film he produced, appeared in 1942. Some of his most outstanding productions were *Red River* (1948), *The Glass Menagerie* (1950), *A Streetcar Named Desire* (1951), and *The Seven-Year Itch* (1955). His last film, *The Honey Pot,* appeared in 1967.

Reference Feldman, Charles K. *Follow the Boys* (Universal City, Calif.: Universal Pictures, 1944).

—T.L.E.

Ferry to Hong Kong

Rank/Twentieth Century–Fox, 113 minutes, 1959. **Director:** Lewis Gilbert; **Producer:** George Maynard; **Screenplay:** Lewis Gilbert and Vernon Harris; **Cinematography:** Otto Heller; **Editor:** Peter Hunt; **Music:** Ken Jones; **Cast:** Orson Welles (Capt. Hart), Curt Jurgens (Mark Conrad), Sylvia Syms (Liz Ferrers), Jeremy Spenser (Miguel Henriques), Noel Purcell (Joe Skinner), Margaret Withers (Miss Carter), John Wallace (Police Inspector), et al.

A 1958 British film directed by Lewis Gilbert and starring WELLES in the role of Captain Hart. "*Ferry to Hong Kong . . .* is recommended to only the morbidly curious who can see Orson Welles giving his worst performance—and we mean ever," proclaimed Howard Thompson in the *New York Times.* So what happened? The dramatic situation, though simple, was fraught with possibilities—an Austrian rogue is stuck on a ferryboat from which he cannot depart because he is wanted by the police in both Hong Kong and Macao, the ferry's two stops. Welles (the boat's scruffy captain) saw the setup as inherently comic. Co-star Curt Jurgens (the wanted man), on the other hand, saw the film as a dramatic adventure. Director Lewis Gilbert, caught in the middle, essentially let each star go his own way.

Welles told PETER BOGDANOVICH that he played the captain as "a low-low-comedy character. And, there was Curt Jurgens playing it dead straight. So that only made it funnier—his playing it that way. And it only made Curt angrier that it went on like that." Although everyone, with the notable exception of Jurgens, had an apparently rollicking good time on location in Hong Kong and Macao, the fizz generated on set didn't carry over to the screen. The failure of *Ferry to Hong Kong* was a particularly nasty blow to the Rank Organization, which saw the film as a bid to compete in the global market of international epics. Still, as Welles told Peter Bogdanovich, it was "an outstanding failure." Along with Welles and Jurgens, *Ferry to Hong Kong* features Sylvia Syms, Jeremy Spenser, and Noel Purcell.

—C.B.

F for Fake (aka *Fake, Hoax, Vérité et mensonges [Truth and Lies]*)   Films de l'Astrophore/Saci/Janus Film, 85 minutes, 1973. **Director:** Orson Welles; **Producers:** Dominique Antoine and François Reichenbach; **Screenplay:** Welles and Olga Palinkas (Oja Kodar); **Cinematographers:** Gary Graver and Christian Odasso; **Music:** Michel Legrand; **Editors:** Welles, Marie Sophie-Dubus, and Dominique Engerer; **Cast (as themselves):** Welles, Oja Kodar, Elmyr de Hory, Clifford Irving, Edith Irving, François Reichenbach, Joseph Cotten, Rochard Drewett, Laurence Harvey, Jean-Pierre Aumont, Nina Van Pallandt, Richard Wilson, Paul Stewart, Howard Hughes, Sasa Devcic, Gary Graver, Andrew Vincent Gombea, Julio Palnkis, Christian Odasso, François Widoff, Peter Bogdanovich, William Alland

F for Fake occupies a unique nitch in the WELLES directorial oeuvre in that it was motivated largely by an attempt to reduce a huge tax debt owed to the Internal Revenue Service. As BARBARA LEAMING tells the story, Welles hit upon the idea of putting together a television special from footage for a British Broadcasting Company (BBC) documentary shot by noted French documentarist François Reichenbach about art forger Elmyr de Hory, whom author Clifford Irving had written about in the book *Fake.* Welles, like many experienced filmmakers working in the genre of the compilation documentary, proved adept at taking previously existing film materials and reshaping their meanings by juxtaposing them with new visual material. Thus, instead of starting with footage that he himself had conceptualized and photographed, Welles, this time, taking a page from Dadas like Duchamp with their "ready-mades," largely used *found* footage.

Welles set about his task in 1972 by negotiating the rights to all material Reichenbach had shot including out-takes. Flattered by the Great Man's interest in his film, Reichenbach found an editing room in Paris for Welles. In turn, Welles included Reichenbach in several shots for the new film, the additional footage being shot in France, Ibiza, and the United States. Relishing the process of reworking Reichenbach's material on de Hory, with its central theme of artistic deception, the project proceeded smoothly. However, just as Welles was adding final touches to the production, news arrived of the scandal involving Clifford Irving's fake biography of fabled billionaire HOWARD HUGHES, for which Irving had concocted all of Hughes's "quotes." Welles, awed by the magnitude of Irving's deliriously preposterous counterfeit, decided to further expand the project by focusing not just on de Hory, but also on Irving, and, for good measure, on himself.

What common ground did Welles find among de Hory, Irving, and himself? First, there was the animosity that each man had toward the putative experts in their fields. Interwoven with this antipathy for critics were questions about the nature of art. What is real art? Is it, as Welles suggests, "a lie which makes us see the truth?" Does the meaning of a work of art depend on the name of the artist? Is a Picasso

Welles the hoaxer, with Oja Kodar in *F for Fake* (Literature/ Film Archive)

by Picasso inherently superior to a "Picasso" by de Hory, even if we can't distinguish one from the other? Does it really matter whether or not Picasso's name is faked? And, as Welles asks, what about those artisans like the builders of the great cathedral at Chartres whose names will forever be anonymous?

De Hory, for his part, explains how he could not make a living by selling his own paintings. This led him to copy the styles of modernists such as Picasso and Braque. Eventually, his "Picassos" and "Braques" became so convincing that he was able to sell them as "authentic" works. Irving corroborates de Hory's mimetic ability. "I had Elmyr paint me a Picasso and a Braque," Irving notes, "and I took them to the Museum of Modern Art to be authenticated. After two hours, the museum experts assured me they were absolutely genuine." De Hory and Irving take further delight by pointing out that a host of Impressionistic "masterpieces" in the world's greatest museums and collections are, in fact, fakes rendered authentic by de Hory.

Irving, like de Hory, had his own original work rejected by the experts. When his novels failed to attract favorable attention from the critics and didn't sell, Irving turned to telling the stories of others. First, there was *Fake,* the book about de Hory. Looking to score a best-seller, Irving took on the life story of the world's most famous recluse, Howard Hughes. Denied access to his subject, Irving resorted to his

craft as a novelist, and invented responses that Irving claimed had been uttered by Hughes himself. It was one of the great hoaxes of American letters.

Welles, in his own autobiographical comments, talks about his reputation as a perennial fabricator who, at 16, talked his way into a position at Dublin's GATE THEATRE by presenting himself to MICHEÁL MACLIAMMÓIR and HILTON EDWARDS as a veteran of the New York stage. Welles further links the subject of artistic deception to his infamous 1938 radio broadcast of *WAR OF THE WORLDS.* JOSEPH COTTEN and RICHARD WILSON, two of Welles's oldest and most valued friends, talk about Welles's legacy as an artistic imposter and creative conjurer. They also point out that *CITIZEN KANE* was originally to have been based on the life of Howard Hughes, rather than WILLIAM RANDOLPH HEARST, thus inviting comparisons between Welles and Irving.

Welles includes a newsreel biography of Hughes, a self-reflexive parody of the *NEWS ON THE MARCH* sequence that opens *Citizen Kane.* This raises the issue of how much the name of an artist should count in judging art. Specifically, Welles seems to be making a defense against critic PAULINE KAEL's charge that Welles was a fraud who had deceived the world into believing that he had created *Citizen Kane,* when, according to Kael, it was HERMAN J. MANKIEWICZ who should be accorded the honor. For Welles, the question of authorship is largely a smoke screen. What is important is the work of art itself. On this point, Welles refers to the thousands of unknown workers who contributed to building the cathedral at Chartres. It is the material fact of the artwork, not the name of the author, that is central. If there were no experts, Welles says, there would be no fakers. Indeed, for Welles, the reification of the artist's name has more to do with enhancing the market value of the art work than with its intrinsic aesthetic worth.

Suddenly, the film shifts gears. In place of the loosely based documentary approach focused on the three "fakers" and their ruminations about art and illusion, Welles cuts to a story about OJA KODAR, Welles's companion and collaborator from 1962 until his death in 1985. Addressing the camera, Welles tells us that Pablo Picasso once devoted an entire summer to painting a series of 22 portraits of Kodar. In return for her taking time to pose, Picasso gave her the paintings with the proviso that they not be sold. Later, when the portraits were exhibited publicly, Picasso disowns the works, claiming that they are fakes. Kodar, trying to mollify the artist, takes Picasso to the obscure studio of her grandfather, where he explains that, as a world-class art forger, he had burned Picasso's originals in order to create a whole new and fictional phase of the artist's career. With the completion of the allegory, Welles, who had promised at the film's onset to tell the truth for an hour, confesses that the story is a fabrication, pointing out that the hour had elapsed prior to the beginning of the unfolding of Kodar's tale.

F for Fake is a meditation on lies, counterfeits, and forgeries, artful and otherwise. In the film, Welles sums things up: "Every true artist must, in his way, be a magician, a charlatan. Picasso once said he could paint fake Picassos as well as anybody, and only someone like Picasso could say something like that and get away with it. But an Elmyr de Hory? Elmyr is a profound embarrassment to the art world. He is a man of talent making monkeys out of those who have disappointed him. This film doesn't exalt the forger. It denounces the art market, because it is elementary, isn't it, that if you don't have the market, then fakers couldn't exist." As for Hughes's counterfeit biographer, Welles adds: "And Clifford Irving? He couldn't make it with his fiction, but making a fake made him the best-known writer in the world. Who are the experts?"

What about Welles? Is *F for Fake,* perhaps, a demi-forgery, given that Welles, starting with François Reichenbach's documentary on de Hory, could be said to have merely puffed up the piece by adding bits and pieces of his and Irving's stories? The critics were divided following the film's premiere at film festivals in New York and San Sebastian. On one hand, the *Village Voice*'s Andrew Sarris seriously debated adding *F for Fake* to his "ten best" list before dropping it. On the other hand, the *New Republic*'s Stanley Kauffman dismissed the film as "an *ad hoc* pastiche that Welles is trying to pass off as a planned work of charlatanry."

Given its unorthodox subject matter and quasi-documentary approach, it's not surprising that *F for Fake* was a commercial failure when initially released in 1974. Today, however, *F for Fake* is generally regarded as Welles's most personal and revealing film. Here, more than in any other of his works, the great director lays bear his artistic soul. Although there is little of the brilliant mise-en-scène of Welles's early and middle period narrative films, *F for Fake* is an editing tour de force. It also is a lively reminder of the incisive self-questioning that Welles directed to both himself and to the vexing world of commercial film.

—C.B.

F for Fake Trailer (film, 1973)

Although designed to promote the American release of WELLES's feature film, *F FOR FAKE* (1973), the *F for Fake Trailer* stands as an innovation in the genre of promotional "trailers" by not including any footage from the theatrical film it was designed to ballyhoo. Cinematographer Gary Graver, who shot *F for Fake* and *FILMING OTHELLO* (1978) as well as the *F for Fake Trailer,* notes that it was a "totally new film." Its content consisted largely of nude figure studies of the beautiful OJA KODAR, Welles's companion and collaborator from 1962 until his death in 1985. However, given that the idiosyncratic documentarylike approach of *F for Fake* made it a less than promising box office attraction, it is not surprising that the American distributor balked at spending the money necessary to cut the *F for Fake Trailer*'s negative and make prints. The length of the film is given by various Welles biographers as 10, 12, or 19 minutes long.

JOSEPH MCBRIDE makes the interesting observation that on those rare occasions when Welles dealt directly with sexual themes, that it was in a generally oblique, almost puritanical manner. However, under the influence of Oja Kodar, Welles, McBride points out, "burst forth with an increasingly frank exploration of eroticism (both heterosexual and homosexual) in *THE IMMORTAL STORY, The Other Side of the Wind,* and *F for Fake,* as well as in his and Kodar's untitled screenplay, *THE BIG BRASS RING.*" In the *F for Fake Trailer,* the erotic influence of Kodar is at once conceptual and at the center of the frame.

—C.B.

Filming Othello   Independent Images, 90 minutes, 1978. **Director:** Orson Welles; **Producers:** Klaus Hellwig and Jurgen Hellwig; **Screenplay:** Welles; **Cinematographer:** Gary Graver; **Music:** Francesco Lavagnino and Alberto Barbaris; **Editor:** Marty Ross; **Cast (as themselves):** Welles, Micheál MacLiammóir, Hilton Edwards, the cast of *Othello* (1952)

Welles's highly personal *Filming Othello,* as suggested by the title, ostensibly takes as its subject the saga of the making of OTHELLO, Welles's cinematic adaptation of the Shakespearean classic, which was released in 1952 after a protracted and difficult production process that had commenced in 1948. *Filming Othello* is not, however, just history. While incorporating the past, *Filming Othello,* like F FOR FAKE, is essentially a meditation on the amorphous state of reality, especially when considered as the manipulatable raw material of the artistic process.

The impetus for *Filming Othello* came in 1974, when German Television invited Welles to appear in an interview about the making of the 1952 film, which would appear in tandem with an airing of *Othello.* Athough rejecting the German offer, Welles liked the idea. Using his own money, Welles began the new project by shooting an interview in Paris with MICHEÁL MACLIAMMÓIR and HILTON EDWARDS, his acting colleagues from Dublin's GATE THEATRE who had appeared with Welles decades earlier in *Othello.* Like the years' long, stop-start shooting schedule of *Othello,* Welles, because of budgetary exigencies, wasn't able to complete the reverse shots with MacLiammóir and Edwards for the new film until two years later in 1976, during a trip to Dublin. Welles, by seamlessly integrating interview footage shot years and miles apart, demonstrated, as he had in *Othello,* the capacity of film to transcend the barriers of time and space through the magic of editing.

There were also shots of MacLiammóir and Edwards at the Gate Theatre, plus an hour of footage shot in Venice with Welles riding through the canals, ensconced in a gondola, pointing out locations where various scenes from *Othello* had been photographed. In addition to footage from the release print of *Othello,* Welles added long-abandoned outtakes. Just as he had showed little hesitation in severely editing Shakespeare to pick up the pace or sharpen a point for modern audiences, Welles felt few compunctions about editing himself. Thus, scenes from the original film were often trimmed and reordered. An additional trip to Morocco, where Welles had shot other scenes for *Othello,* was planned but abandoned due to a funding shortfall. The original sound track was stripped to make way for Welles's voice-over narration. The shots of Welles commenting while working at his moviola were photographed in the living room of his Beverly Hills home in 1976.

After three years of typical Wellesian stop-start production, *Filming Othello* was finished in 1977. In 1978, *Filming Othello* premiered at the Berlin Film Festival; it was also televised in Germany. It ran for three weeks in New York in 1979, and then virtually disappeared. Like *F for Fake, Filming Othello* was an untenable theatrical release. Brief clips of *Filming Othello* can be seen in Gary Graver's documentary, *Working with Orson Welles* (1992).

While an obviously fascinating footnote for Welles devotees, *Filming Othello* is also instructive to film students as a demonstration of how complex spatial and temporal realities are the playthings of those conjurers who, like Welles, are also called filmmakers. *Filming Othello* was Welles's last finished film.

—C.B.

First Person Singular   (radio, 1938)   Amidst the swell of publicity arising from WELLES's appearance on the cover of the May 9, 1938, issue of *Time* magazine, CBS presented the 23-year-old "Boy Wonder" with an extraordinary offer—to star in, write, direct, and produce an hour-long weekly series of dramatic broadcasts over which he would have complete creative control. In his previous radio work, Welles had been a hired gun. Now, thanks to CBS, he would have a chance to freely test his own ideas as to what radio drama might be.

As alluded to in the show's title, each of the nine programs would be narrated by Welles in the first person. If not the leading part, he would also play a major role. His aspirations soaring, Welles exclaimed to the press: "I think it is time that radio came to realize the fact that, no matter how wonderful a play may be for the stage, it cannot be as wonderful for the air. The Mercury Theatre has no intention of producing its stage repetoire in these broadcasts. Instead, we plan to bring to radio the experimental techniques which have proved so successful in another medium, and to treat radio itself with the intelligence and respect such a beautiful and powerful medium deserves." Welles believed that the first-person strategy was particularly effective in establishing a one-to-one relationship with the listener. It would also call on Welles's own compelling voice to provide the intimate bond linking each week's drama with the audience.

For the show's debut broadcast of July 11, 1938, Welles adapted Bram Stoker's *Dracula*. Already well known as a novel (1897), a Broadway play (1927), and a film (1931), *Dracula* had all the elements necessary for a gripping radio tale. Hiring JOHN HOUSEMAN as his executive producer, and casting many of his MERCURY THEATRE colleagues in key roles, Welles was now looking beyond the Great White Way to all "the Broadways of America." To establish the show's gravity, Welles used Tchaikovsky's Piano Concerto No. 1 in B-flat Minor as the theme. Dan Seymour's sober introduction, with a recitation of the Mercury Theatre's various deeds gave way to Welles, as Welles, who chatted about the novel's unique place in literature. With the sounding of sinister chimes scored by BERNARD HERRMANN, the story began. Welles took the roles of Jonathan Harker and Count Dracula, for which he created a chillingly eerie East European accent. Other Mercury regulars were GEORGE COULOURIS (Dr. Seward), MARTIN GABEL (Van Helsing), RAY COLLINS (the Russian Captain), and AGNES MOOREHEAD (Mina). The show was an unqualified success earning raves from all the big papers including the *New York Times*. Listeners agreed with the critics and flooded CBS with bags of fan mail.

Buoyed by the hearty response, Welles and his Mercury crew plunged into the remaining eight stories with gusto. The other dramatizations under the aegis of *First Person Singular* were:

Treasure Island (July 18, 1938), based on the novel by Robert Louis Stevenson. In contrast to the multiple viewpoints of *DraculaF*, here, *Treasure Island*'s story is told from the perspective of Jim Hawkins as a boy of 14 (Arthur Anderson), and as an adult of 33 (Welles, who also essayed the sinister Long John Silver). Given the experimental nature of the broadcasts, Welles used sound effects to an unprecedented degree, accomplishing what otherwise would have been necessary to describe via narration. The same can be said of Herrmann's innovative music, which evoked powerful images and emotions that even narration could not have expressed. Another innovation, and soon a Wellesian trademark, involved the tone of the narrator's voice. Instead of remaining a detached and neutral observer, Welles's narrator varied the pitch and tempo of his delivery in accordance with the immediate needs of the dramatic moment. Thus, when the action shifted into high gear, so too did the voice of the narrator. On the other hand, when there was a moment of comic relief, the narrator affected a neighborly jocularity. *Treasure Island* featured another prominent member of the Mercury family, WILLIAM ALLAND.

A Tale of Two Cities (July 25, 1938), based on Charles Dickens's novel. Here, the Mercury Theatre re-created Dickens's French Revolution right down to the incessant clicking of Madame de Farge's knitting needles. Welles played both Dr. Alexander Minette and Sydney Carton, who elects martyrdom so that the woman he loves can marry another man who otherwise would have been led to the guillotine. Among the members of the supporting cast was ERSKINE SANFORD as the president.

The Thirty-Nine Steps (August 1, 1938). Although Alfred Hitchcock had made a well-known film out of John Buchan's novel in 1935, Welles opted to follow the novel rather than the film. Again, Welles played two roles, the wrongly suspected American Richard Hanney and the Scotsman Marmaduke Jopley. Welles, who loved tweaking his elders, concluded the broadcast with these words: "Ladies and Gentlemen, if you missed Madeleine Carroll [who starred in Hitchcock's film opposite Robert Donut's Hanney] in our 'stage' version of *The 39 Steps*, the young lady in the movie, in common with almost anything else in that movie, was the child of its director's own unparalleled and unpredictable fancy. If you missed anything you must blame Mr. Alfred Hitchcock."

I'm a Fool; The Open Window; My Little Boy (August 8, 1938). This broadcast was unique in that it anthologized three dramatic miniatures. In the first, *I'm a Fool,* based on a Sherwood Anderson short story about being lovesick, Welles played the part of Joe, a young midwesterner. *The Open Window* was adapted from a story by Saki. The final drama, based on a story by Carl Ewald called *My Little Boy,* was a moral fable that dealt with anti-Semitism, a topic virtually ignored by radio at that time. For the latter, Welles played a loud and opinionated father who suffers growing pains as severe as those experienced by his son.

Abraham Lincoln (August 15, 1938). Just an hour-and-a-half before a scheduled address by President ROOSEVELT, *First Person Singular* offered an adaptation of John Drinkwater's play, *Abraham Lincoln.* In his introduction, Welles stated: "Lincoln's words are still entirely alive and his person preserved in a fine and very famous play." Adding biographical details from Lincoln letters, speeches, and debates, Welles, in the title role, stressed the overarching universality of Lincoln's humanity. Alluding to Roosevelt's upcoming address, Welles, in his role as narrator, stated: "Much of this you will recognize, and much of it is news . . . as if it were happening in the White House tonight."

The Affairs of Anatole (August 22, 1938). Arthur Schnitzler's sophisticated treatment of Vienna's elite social life was wittily adapted by the Mercury group with Welles playing Anatole, who gives voice to the playwright's philosophy: "We all play parts. Happy is he who knows it."

The Count of Monte Cristo (August 29, 1938). Adapted from Alexander Dumas's novel, which was originally serialized by a Parisian newspaper, the popular *Count of Monte Cristo* had appeared in no less than four motion pictures (two in 1912; a John Gilbert version in 1923; and a 1934 "talking" rendition with Robert Donat). Speak-

ing to the difficulties of paring down the sprawling novel, Welles opined that Dumas must have employed a legion of ghostwriters since no one could have written all the books that appeared under Dumas's name. With the perhaps tenuous relationships with his own "ghosts" in mind, FRANK BRADY cites a somewhat imperious Welles: "It is not expected of Pharaoh that he build with his own hands, his own pyramids."

The Man Who Was Thursday (September 5, 1938). The final offering in *First Person Singular's* test run was an adaptation of G. K. Chesterton's best-known novel, a spy story written during the anarchic bomb-lobbing days of 1908. Welles—who took the role of Gabriel Sime, otherwise known as Thursday—had a particular fondness for Chesterton's flowing prose and his overlapping concerns with politics, anarchy, integrity, and religion. Because of his own expanding girth, Frank Brady suggests, Welles might have identified with Chesterton as "one of the world's most famous fat men."

First Person Singular was a sustaining program, i.e., a program without sponsorship, whose production costs a network could justify as part of its "public interest" responsibilities under the Communications Act of 1934. For the still growing networks, the unsold or sustained time slots provided opportunities to present cultural programming and to also test new program formats. *First Person Singular* was a bit of both, an experiment designed to make literary classics "come to life" for the general public, a goal that Welles had first formally enunciated with the publication of EVERYBODY'S SHAKESPEARE just four years earlier.

CBS was elated with *First Person Singular* and at the end of *The Man Who Was Thursday* sent a spokesman to the microphone to officially announce its renewal. It had been a tumultuous nine weeks. However, Welles's vision of radio as being related to but different from theater had been forcefully demonstrated. In the process, Welles and the Mercury Company had produced a host of narrative and technical innovations. When the program went back on the air the following week, the name *First Person Singular* had been dropped in favor of MERCURY THEATRE ON THE AIR.

References Brady, Frank. *Citizen Welles: A Biography of Orson Welles* (New York: Scribners, 1989); Wood, Bret. *Orson Welles: A Bio-Bibliography* (Westport, Conn.: Greenwood Press, 1990).

—C.B.

Fitzgerald, F. Scott (1896–1940) Leading American short story writer and novelist whose 1940 short story "Pat Hobby and Orson Welles" makes fictional use of WELLES.

"Pat Hobby and Orson Welles" was published in the May 1940 edition of *Esquire* magazine. The tale begins with Hobby, a put-upon Hollywood screenwriter, and his difficulties in gaining access to his studio. In a state of quasi-paranoia, Hobby begins to think that actor–director Orson Welles is responsible for forcing him out. Suddenly, people begin to address him as "Orson," although any physical or other resemblances are slight. In an elaborate ruse to gain entry to the studio, Hobby has makeup artist Jeff Boldini give him a make-over as Welles with a beard (a ploy used by Welles to avoid autograph seekers), and drive him to the studio in a car whose window has a sign bearing Welles's name. Hobby, unaware of the sign put in place by Boldini, doesn't understand why there are crowds gathered around the car staring at him. Flummoxed, he retreats to a bar where he buys a drink for every bearded man. That an author of F. Scott Fitzgerald's rank would include Welles in one of his stories is an indication of the status and national reputation enjoyed by Welles in 1939.

Fitzgerald, best known for his depictions of the Jazz Age, attended Princeton University. Although achieving recognition for his literary skills, poor grades forced him to leave. Shortly thereafter, he joined the U.S. Army. In 1918, he met Zelda Sayre (1900–48), the daughter of an Alabama Supreme Court justice. To prove his worth to himself and to Zelda, Fitzgerald rewrote the novel he had started at Princeton. In 1920, *This Side of Paradise* was published and Fitzgerald married Zelda.

The success of *This Side of Paradise* opened doors to top literary magazines such as *Scribner's* and well-paying general circulation weeklies such as *The Saturday Evening Post*. During this period he published stories such as "The Diamond as Big as the Ritz" which were anthologized under the title *Tales of the Jazz Age* (1922). Fame and prosperity, though not unwelcome, proved difficult to handle. In *The Beautiful and Damned* (1922), Fitzgerald probes the life that he and Zelda feared, a descent into ennui and dissipation.

In 1924, the Fitzgeralds moved to the Riviera, where they joined a group of high-spirited American expatriates. Their experiences on the French Mediterranean are described in Fitzgerald's last completed novel, *Tender Is the Night* (1934). Following their arrival on the Riviera, Fitzgerald completed *The Great Gatsby* (1925), the definitive Jazz Age novel, which unflinchingly plumbs the tenor of the 1920s, at once so dazzling and vulgar, and depressing and promising.

Fitzgerald, succumbing to his worst apprehensions, soon began to drink heavily. Complicating matters was Zelda's mental breakdown in 1930. In 1932, she suffered another collapse that left her incapacitated for the duration of her life. Fitzgerald told the story of his downward slide in *The Crack-Up*, published in 1945, five years after his death. In 1937, having relocated to Hollywood, where he became a screenwriter, he met Sheilah Graham, a noted Hollywood gossip columnist with whom he lived for the rest of his life. In 1939, he started work on a novel about Hollywood, *The Last Tycoon* (1941), which was finished by Edmund Wilson after his death.

—C.B.

Fitzgerald, Geraldine (1914–) Geraldine Fitzgerald appeared in two plays with ORSON WELLES, SHAW's *HEARTBREAK HOUSE* and Shakespeare's *KING LEAR,* and was rumored to have had an affair with him. Fitzgerald was born November 24, 1914, in Dublin, the daughter of a prominent attorney. She received her dramatic training at Dublin's GATE THEATRE, where Welles had also appeared before leaving for New York. In 1934, she made her film debut in the United Kingdom and received excellent notices for her part in *Turn of the Tide* (1935) and in *The Mill on the Floss*. In 1936, after having moved to New York, she was cast as Ellie Dunn in the MERCURY THEATRE production of *Heartbreak House*. JOHN HOUSEMAN, Welles's partner at Mercury, had

auditioned her for the part when Welles made his appearance. According to SIMON CALLOW, she was impressed: "In a brilliant phrase, she compared his personality to that of a lighthouse: when you were caught in its beam, you were bathed in its illumination; when it moved on, you were plunged into darkness." CHARLES HIGHAM describes the relationship between Welles and Fitzgerald: "Intensely Irish, she had a tremendous attraction for Welles, and there were widespread rumors of an affair between them. Further gossip surrounded her son, Michael Lindsay-Hogg, today a prominent theatrical director, because of his striking resemblance to Welles." After the Mercury Theatre experience, she moved to Hollywood, where she appeared in several Warner Bros. melodramas including *Dark Victory* (1939). Also in 1939, she was nominated for a best supporting actress Oscar for her role in the classic melodrama, *Wuthering Heights.* Unhappy with subsequent roles, she fought with the studio but lost her battle and did not appear in any American films from the late 1940s until 1958, when she had a role in *Ten North Frederick.* Although she continued to appear in good films (*The Pawnbroker,* 1965; *Rachel Rachel,* 1968; and *Harry and Tonto,* 1974), she played character roles rather than leads. She made her last film in 1988 in *Arthur 2: On the Rocks* (1988); she had appeared in the original *Arthur* in 1981. She continued to appear on stage, and her best performance was in 1971, when she appeared in the Broadway revival of O'Neill's *Long Day's Journey into Night.*

—T.L.E.

Five Kings (play, 1939)

For years, WELLES had dreamed of reducing Shakespeare's history plays to a single evening of theater called *Five Kings.* He also longed to play FALSTAFF. Finally, with substantial backing from the Theatre Guild, Welles embarked on preparations for what he envisioned as his theatrical magnum opus. Adapting the two parts of HENRY IV, and *Henry V,* as well as bits excerpted from *Richard II* and *The Merry Wives of Windsor,* and insisting on an epic production, Welles's project, in the words of BURGESS MEREDITH, who played Prince Hal, was "a brilliant concept of a great man," but one which eventually came crashing down. "None of us came up to the vision," Meredith added, "because of fatigue, logistics and time." What happened?

In 1939, Welles, although still doing often brilliant work in radio, was starting to buckle under the impossible pressures he had created for himself. Increasingly estranged from MERCURY THEATRE co-founder JOHN HOUSEMAN, his administrative right-hand man who had allowed his artistic vision to soar, Welles, from all appearances, seemed to be on the verge of a nervous breakdown. He was drinking heavily. His womanizing and deteriorating marriage were also beginning to take tolls. He was often late for rehearsals. Most telling, he seemed no longer capable of making crisp, clear decisions. Indeed, he was never able to give adequate shape to the sprawling, albeit "brilliant," concept. (When Welles returned to *Five Kings* in 1960 for *CHIMES AT MIDNIGHT,* he found a means of dealing with his material by focusing on what DAVID THOMSON calls "the natural dramatic beauty of the story of Hal and Falstaff.")

There were also the usual money problems, this time exacerbated by Mercury's near insolvent state, a result of the failures of the Mercury-produced *DANTON'S DEATH* and *TOO MUCH JOHNSON,* both in 1938. There was also a skyrocketing budget to take care of the large 42-member cast, the orchestra, an array of costumes, and such special needs as a recalcitrant revolving stage. And then, because of his radio commitments and extracurricular activities and general state of disorganization, there was the problem of Welles's absenteeism. AARON COPLAND, the distinguished American composer hired to score the show, complained that he never had enough time with Welles for the director to explain exactly what he wanted the music to do. Copland's demur was hardly unique. When the chaotic production finally opened at the Colonial Theater in Boston on February 29, 1939, the curtain was an hour late.

As the show began, Meredith whispered to Welles, "How'd we get ourselves into this frigging nightmare?" "Don't worry," Welles said. "There is a thing called magic—theatre magic—it's here—wait and see! Now take this pill. It's potent. It's called Benzedrine." That night, there was little magic, theatrical or otherwise. The turntable failed to function. Actors were injured in the battle scenes. And when the final curtain came down for the few spectators still in the theater, it was 1:30 A.M.! The tired show limped on to Philadelphia with Welles cutting and rearranging at every turn, but to no avail. Alas, smarting from less than sympathetic reviews and drained of money, including that from the Theatre Guild and from Welles's radio earnings, Welles's dream of bringing his epic vision of Shakespeare's history plays to Broadway was dashed. It was a dream that simply wasn't ready for presentation. The show closed in Philadelphia in late March.

Copland wrote to fellow composer VIRGIL THOMSON that "Orson's stock is very low at the moment. Last year's hero arouses very little sympathy." Even Welles's most loyal supporters felt let down. As some commentators have suggested, *Five Kings* was really about the dissolution of a friendship. Indeed, the spectacularly successful Welles-Houseman relationship had come to an end. For Welles, in spite of the bitter disappointment, there was the ongoing success of his radio work. And looming just around the corner was Welles's extraordinary contract with RKO and the making of CITIZEN KANE.

—C.B.

Flaherty, Robert Joseph (1884–1951)

Two stories by Robert Flaherty were optioned by ORSON WELLES for the projected film, *IT'S ALL TRUE*. "The Captain's Chair" was the basis for the North American segment; and "Bonito, the Bull" told the traditional story of how the president of Mexico spared a bull in response to the plea of a small boy.

Frequently described as the "Father of the American Documentary Film," Robert Flaherty was a fiercely independent figure in the documentary movement in the first half of the 20th century. He was born in Iron Mountain, Michigan, on February 16, 1884, and educated at Upper Canada College, Toronto. During the first decade of the new century, he worked as an explorer, surveyor, and prospector for the Canadian Grand Trunk Railway. In the midteens he surveyed for William MacKenzie, an industrial entrepreneur, searching for iron ore deposits along the Hudson Bay. It was at this time that he took a camera with him while traveling through the land of the Inuit. However, his footage was destroyed in a fire. Five years later, a determined Flaherty returned to the Hudson Bay area to shoot more film of Eskimo life. Released as an experiment by Pathé Exchange, the resulting documentary feature was *Nanook of the North* (1922), a popular sensation and a landmark documentary film. Its success encouraged Flaherty to devote the rest of his life to making documentaries about faraway and exotic cultures whose ways of life were threatened by modernization. He traveled to Samoa in 1923–25 and produced *Moana* for Paramount. Again, as in *Nanook,* he captured on film a "primitive" and "natural" way of life that was rapidly disappearing. Two more films about the South Seas followed in the late 1920s, *White Shadows in the South Seas* and *Tabu* (for both of which he received co-production credit).

As the box office cachet of these films began to wane, Flaherty was forced to look elsewhere for financing. In 1931, he went to work for John Grierson of the Empire Marketing Board in Great Britain. *Industrial Britain* was the result, although Grierson himself made the final edit. A year later, Flaherty then moved on to the Aran Islands, off the coast of Ireland, to begin shooting *Man of Aran* (1934). It was a gritty picture of the rugged life of the local fishermen. His next project was *Louisiana Story* (1948), a lyric and poetic tribute to Cajun life in the bayous.

For all the respect, even the veneration, accorded Flaherty in his lifetime—the term *documentary* was coined to describe his film, *Moana*—he remains a controversial figure. In his zeal to document the disappearing traditions of "primitive" ways of life, he frequently staged and even falsified the conditions he found. For example, the Eskimos he photographed in *Nanook* had long abandoned activities like igloo building. Yet, he asked them to relearn the procedure for the camera. Some of the fishing and hunting sequences were also staged. In *Moana* he photographed an initiation ceremony wherein young males were painfully tattooed—even though that particular ritual had not been practiced by the tribe for years. For *Man of Aran* he staged a shark hunt in a lashing storm, against the better judgment of the fishermen. And in *Louisiana Story* he faked a tug-of-war between a young boy and a ferocious alligator.

While Flaherty's visual style was rather pedestrian, he had a canny sense of the medium's technological possibilities. He pioneered the use of long lenses for close-up work, utilized the new panchromatic film (for *Moana*), deployed the new 35mm Arriflex camera (for *Louisiana Story*), initiated the practice of shooting and printing film on site, and encouraged the subjects of his films to assist in the filmmaking process. Other methods were unpredictable, even erratic. He usually worked without a plot or a script in an attitude characterized by his wife and associate, Frances, as "nonpreconception." He camped out with his subjects, and he watched and waited. He shot miles of film, seemingly without any preplanned purpose, and eventually used only a small percentage of the footage. In this way he allowed the film to assume its own shape, as it were. Only later did he begin to impose his own vision and organization onto the product. "What he seeks out among his peoples are their consistent patterns of physical behavior," writes commentator Jack C. Ellis, "—rather than aberrations of human psyches and antisocial actions which are the basis for Western drama from the Greeks on. Flaherty may ultimately have been most concerned with the human spirit, but what he chose to show were its basic material manifestations. . . . What it means to survive, to exist in the culture and in the environment one is born into, are the stuff of which his films are made." Flaherty's example was followed by other American filmmakers, notably by Merian C. Cooper and Ernest B. Schoedsack in *Grass* (1925), which recorded the migration of 50,000 Bakhtiari tribesmen in central Persia (Iran) to find pasturelands for their herds; and in popular travel-expedition pictures by the husband-and-wife team of Martin and Osa Johnson, such as *Wonders of the Congo* (1931) and *Baboona* (1935).

Reference   Barsam, Richard. *The Vision of Robert Flaherty: The Artist as Myth and Filmmaker* (Bloomington: Indiana University Press, 1988).

—J.C.T. and R.W.

Flanagan, Hallie (1890–1969)

Flanagan, as head of the FEDERAL THEATRE PROJECT, helped sponsor and support some of the most innovative and daring theater ventures in American theater history,

including the WELLES-directed productions of *MACBETH* and *HORSE EATS HAT*, both in 1936.

Born in Redfield, South Dakota, Flanagan studied at Grinnell College in Iowa, before serving a tenure as an assistant to Professor George Pierce Baker and his 47 Workshop at Harvard, a laboratory for playwrights whose alumni include some of America's greatest literary names. In 1925, after having returned to her alma mater to teach, Flanagan was appointed professor of drama and director of experimental theater at Vassar College. She took a leave of absence between 1935 and 1939 to head the Federal Theatre Project. Afterward, she returned to Vassar, retiring in 1952. In addition to writing numerous articles for leading journals and magazines, she authored *Shifting Scenes of the Modern European Theatre* (1928) and *Dynamo, the Story of the Vassar Theatre* (1943). Her most important book, *Arena, the Story of the Federal Theatre* (1940), chronicles the tumultuous four years she spent as the director of the Federal Theatre Project.

In his Foreword to Flanagan's *Arena*, JOHN HOUSEMAN writes: " . . . if the Federal Theatre in its brief existence showed the energy and the quality that caused a leading New York critic to describe it as 'the chief producer of works of art in the American theatre,' the credit is mostly Hallie Flanagan's. The choice of personnel was hers; so was the imagination and the nerve. . . . It is for those three frantic and fantastic years that she will be remembered—the years in which she and her collaborators turned a dubious and pathetic relief project into what remains, after forty years, the most creative and dynamic approach that has yet been made to an American national theatre."

References   Bentley, Joanne. *Hallie Flanagan: A Life in the American Theatre* (New York: Knopf, 1988); Flanagan, Hallie. *Arena, the Story of the Federal Theatre* (New York: Duell, Sloane & Pearce, 1940); Sternsher, Bernard, and Judith Sealander. *Women of Valor: The Struggle against the Great Depression as Told in Their Life Stories* (Chicago: Ivan R. Dee, 1990).

—C.B.

Fleischer, Richard (1916–)

Director Richard Fleischer and ORSON WELLES worked together in three films during the late 1950s. Welles provided the narration for *THE VIKINGS* (1958) before he played an attorney in two of Fleischer's films. For his role as Clarence Darrow in *COMPULSION* (1959) Welles shared the best actor award at Cannes with co-stars BRADFORD DILLMAN and DEAN STOCKWELL. Welles had wanted to direct the film, but producer Richard Zanuck, mindful of Welles's reputation for extravagance, selected Fleischer, who was understandably apprehensive about working with Welles: "He's got this overpowering voice and presence. You really have to feel your way for a while to see whether you can direct him or whether he's going to direct you." Welles's performance as Darrow was brilliant. He did his 10-minute summation to the jury in one take, with the aid of teleprompters; the speech was later edited to break up the scene visually. Because of the success of *Compulsion,* Zanuck again enlisted Welles, Dillman, and Fleischer for *CRACK IN THE MIRROR* (1960), which failed miserably. Part of the problem might have been that three actors, including Welles, had to play two parts, which left audiences a bit confused. CHARLES HIGHAM, however, pointed the finger at Fleischer's "claustrophobic direction."

Richard Fleischer, the son of animator Max Fleischer, was born on December 8, 1916, in Brooklyn. He gave up his intended medical career while he was studying at Brown University and enrolled at Yale University, where he studied drama. His film career began in 1942 at RKO, where he directed short wartime documentaries, some of them for the "This Is America" series. He also created "Flicker Flashbacks," which were compilation short films with footage from silent films. Of the films, mostly crime dramas, he made before *Compulsion,* there are only a few (*20,000 Leagues Under the Sea* [1954] and *The Girl in the Red Velvet Swing* [1955]) which are memorable. After *Compulsion,* however, Fleischer directed several popular films: *Dr. Doolittle* (1967), *The Boston Strangler* (1968), and *Tora! Tora! Tora!* (1970). After 1970, he turned from big-budget films to crime dramas (*The New Centurions* [1972], *The Don Is Dead* [1973], and *Mr. Majestyk* [1974]). Since then his films, with the exception of *Conan the Destroyer* (1984) have been forgettable. His last film, *Call from Space* (*Showscan*), was made in 1990.

References Fleischer, Richard. *Just Tell Me When to Cry: A Memoir* (New York: Carroll & Graf, 1993); Smith, Scott. *The Film 100: A Ranking of the Most Influential People in the History of the Movies* (Secaucus, N.J.: Carol, 1998).
—T.L.E.

Follow the Boys Universal Pictures, 122 minutes, 1944. **Director:** Edward Sutherland; **Producer:** Charles K. Feldman; **Screenplay:** Lou Breslow and Gertrude Purcell; **Cast:** Orson Welles, George Raft, Vera Zorina, Marlene Dietrich, Jeanette MacDonald, Sophie Tucker, Donald O'Connon, Peggy Ryan, W.C. Fields, et al.

A U.S. film with WELLES evoking his persona as magician. This 1944 release directed by Eddie Sutherland features Welles as himself in a guest cameo doing a spoof on one of his magic acts in collaboration with friend MARLENE DIETRICH, an illusion that he had done on numerous occasions as part of his MERCURY WONDER SHOW. For Welles, the establishment of the Mercury Wonder Show in 1943 was an opportunity to realize his fondest childhood ambition of becoming a professional magician. It was also an opportunity to create goodwill since the show was performed free for servicemen during World War II.

Welles, in spite of having underwritten the show's costs including all props and personnel, never profited from the Mercury Wonder Show during its 1943 Los Angeles run. It did, however, generate huge publicity including spreads in *Life, Look,* and *Collier's,* the nation's leading photo-magazines. Consequently, when producer CHARLES K. FELDMAN was assembling a group of stars for a film to entertain the troops under the aegis of the Hollywood Victory Committee, Welles was invited to reprise one of his Mercury Wonder Show stunts.

Like many wartime films of the period, *Follow the Boys* is a backstage revue. Here the plot involves George Raft who plays a tap dancer, a Hollywood star who tries to volunteer but flunks his army physical. To make up for not wearing the uniform and going overseas, Raft's character puts together a show similar to those that were being staged at the time by both the Hollywood Victory Committee and the United Service Organizations (USO). As Raft's show tours the front lines, the troops are regaled by the talents of an all-star cast that included Jeanette

MacDonald, Sophie Tucker, Dinah Shore, W. C. Fields, the Andrews Sisters, Donald O'Connor, the Rhythm Boys, Leonard Gautier and his trapeze-swinging dog act, and prizefighter Slapsie Maxie Rosenbloom. For the movie, Welles reprises his trick of sawing a woman in half.

RITA HAYWORTH, whom Welles would marry following the 1943 summer run of the Mercury Wonder Show, was Welles's usual accomplice in the trick. However, because of her contract obligations to Columbia Pictures, Hayworth wasn't able to participate. Marlene Dietrich, a friend of both Welles and Hayworth, consented to step in and substitute for Hayworth. Although lasting only six minutes, Welles's segment was praised by audiences and critics who generally considered it the film's highlight. "Orson, we haven't rehearsed this," exclaims a concerned Dietrich as the scene opens. Welles, garbed in white tie and tails, calls on two soldiers selected from the audience to saw the screen diva in two. "Gentlemen,"

Orson Welles in *Follow the Boys (National Film Society Archive)*

he intones gravely, "I think you ought to know we lose a girl at every performance." "But Orson," rejoins a now concerned Dietrich, "how does this trick work?" With an ironic grin, Welles replies: "Just wait, Marlene. This'll kill you." When the servicemen have completed the grisly task, the lower half of Dietrich's body separates and walks offstage. Dietrich's top half concludes the sequence with a revengeful reprisal at her dilemma. She hypnotizes Welles, who topples over as the scene fades to black.

Follow the Boys also features Vera Zorina, Charley Grapewine, Grace MacDonald, Charles Butterworth, Peggy Ryan, Arthur Rubinstein, Ted Lewis's Band, and others.

Reference Hirschhorn, Clive. *The Universal Story* (New York: Crown, 1983).

—C.B.

Foster, Norman (1900–1976) Actor and director Norman Foster directed JOURNEY INTO FEAR (1943) at RKO, with WELLES and JOSEPH COTTEN in the leading roles. Born in Richmond, Indiana, as Norman Hoeffer, on December 13, 1900, Foster began his professional life as a journalist who later turned to acting. After working in stock companies, he made his Broadway directorial debut in 1926. He broke into Hollywood in 1929, first as an actor and subsequently as a director of "B" productions for Twentieth Century–Fox, where he directed his first film, *I Cover Chinatown,* in 1936, and later directed several films in the Mr. Moto and Charlie Chan series. Foster had also written radio scripts for Welles's MERCURY THEATRE. In 1942, Welles was directing *THE MAGNIFICENT AMBERSONS* and planning the documentary IT'S ALL TRUE, while also developing *Journey into Fear.* One of the four stories in the projected anthology film *It's All True* was "My Friend Bonito" (aka "The Story of Bonito the Bull," based on a story by filmmaker ROBERT FLAHERTY), which was being shot by Norman Foster in Mexico. Welles was so impressed by Foster's work he planned to make Foster his co-director on that (failed) project. However, when Welles needed Foster's help in developing *Journey into Fear,* he recalled him from Mexico and insisted that Foster direct *Journey into Fear* instead. Welles also produced *Journey into Fear,* and with Cotten wrote the screenplay, based on a novel by ERIC AMBLER. This proved an unfortunate mistake for Foster, according to SIMON CALLOW: "*My Friend Bonito* was firmly on its way to being a masterpiece, while *Journey into Fear* was a badly written jumble, devoid of artistic merit." Upon returning to Hollywood in December of 1942, Foster learned that *My Friend Bonito* had been officially cancelled. Although Welles gives full credit to Foster as director and denies that he was ever to be credited as the director, he has acknowledged a "collaborative" effort in the direction, shared with Foster and Cotten. It was the last film with which Welles was directly involved prior to his trip to Brazil for the State Department.

In later years, Foster became a journeyman Hollywood film and television director specializing in genre pictures, primarily westerns, including two Davy Crockett films in 1955 and 1956. Foster's last film was made in 1967. He died in 1976.

—R.C.K. and T.L.E.

Fountain of Youth
Welles Enterprises/Desilu, 25 minutes, 1958. **Director:** Orson Welles; **Executive Producer:** Desi Arnaz; **Screenplay:** Welles (based on the short story "Youth from Vienna" by John Collier); **Cinematographer:** Sidney Hickox, **Editor:** Bud Molin; **Art Direction:** Claudio Guzman; **Makeup:** Maurice Sneiderman; **Cast:** Orson Welles (Host/Narrator), Dan Tobin (Humphrey Baxter), Joi Lansing (Carolyn Coates), Rick Jason (Alan Brody), Billy House (Albert Morgan), Nancy Kulp (Mrs. Morgan), Marjorie Bennet (Journalist)

In 1956, WELLES was given his first chance to direct in the new medium of television. The offer was made by old friend Lucille Ball, who ran the hugely successful Desilu Productions with her husband, Desi Arnaz. The plan was for Welles to produce, direct, write, and host a series of half-hour television films that would essentially update the late-1930s' radio format Welles used for *FIRST PERSON SINGULAR, MERCURY THEATRE ON THE AIR,* and *THE CAMPBELL PLAYHOUSE.* Specifically, the series would combine Welles's first-person radio style with television's inherent sense of intimacy.

To test the viability of the plan, a 25-minute pilot, *The Fountain of Youth,* was shot in 1956. The story was loosely based on the John Collier short story "Youth from Vienna." "How would you like to stay just as young as you are, not to grow a day older . . . for the next two hundred years?" narrator Welles asked. He then went on to guide viewers through a romantic triangle with a twist concerning a scientist (Dan Tobin), the girl he loves (Joi Lansing), and a tennis-playing cad (Rick Jason). After a research trip to Vienna, the scientist returns to find "his" girl and the tennis champ about to be married. His wedding gift is an elixir, "the fountain of youth" of the title. However, there's a catch. There's only one dose, and it can't be divided. Unable to resist temptation, the girl and the cad each consume the youth serum in secret, quickly refilling the phial with an innocuous substitute fluid. Over the next several years, they see signs of aging, not in themselves, but in each other. The couple breaks up, and the girl returns to the scientist. The camera then moves in on Welles, who confides to the audience: "Humphrey [the scientist] knew she would be back because the elixir contained nothing but salt water all along."

Set in the 1920s, period musical pieces such as "Oh, You Beautiful Girl" are heard in the background in variations by banjo and honky-tonk piano. Welles's voice is an almost constant presence, filling in narrative gaps, providing background, and in general setting the stage for each shift in scene. There is rapid cutting to slides that help capture the atmosphere of the 1920s. Sometimes the stills forward the action in almost freeze-frame, *tableau vivant* fashion. Instead of using straight cuts between all scenes, Welles occasionally starts a scene in darkness. He then brings up the light to show a new character or situation, a strategy recalling his theatrical lighting approach for *DOCTOR FAUSTUS.* The technique also recalls the iris-in of the silent film period, a device Welles employed so effectively to establish a sense of the historic past in *THE MAGNIFICENT AMBERSONS.*

The Fountain of Youth is a small marvel. As DAVID THOMSON notes: 'His [i.e., Welles's] narrator is in and out of the picture. The use of fake backdrops, theatrical lighting and flat-out trickiness is exhilarating and witty. The show resonates with the enthusiasms of a kid who has woken up to find a new kind of train set. Welles was young again. One has to wonder if he couldn't have revolutionized television." Alas, Welles would never get that chance because of the pilot's high cost and scheduling overruns, factors intolerable to a highly organized, factorylike organization like Desilu Productions. The final blow came when Desilu couldn't find a sponsor. *The Fountain of Youth* thus languished in Desilu's vault for two years.

Finally, the unsold television pilot was broadcast on *The Colgate Palmolive Theatre,* NBC-TV, September 16, 1958. The reviews were positive. In the *New York World-Telegram and Sun,* Harriet Van Horne wrote: "Should an eager chap from one of those opinion surveys corner you and ask, 'What, in your judgement, does television need right now?', look him straight in his avid eye and say, 'Orson Welles.' . . . Now, why can't we see Mr. Welles every week?" Ironically, the show the networks wouldn't touch in 1956 won a special Peabody Award in 1958 for "Creative Achievement."

Welles, a victim of his not completely undeserved reputation for being unable to stay within budget and schedule, was unfortunately never able to fully test his wings in a weekly television format. The networks were probably also wary of his penchant for experimentation. *The Fountain of Youth,* in spite of the hurrahs, was judged by some as a bit arty and perhaps too sophisticated for the "average" television viewer.

The Fountain of Youth was first shown theatrically in 1969 at the Los Feliz Theater in Hollywood.

—C.B.

Fowler, Roy A. (1929–) In *Focus on Citizen Kane* (1971), RONALD GOTTESMAN praises Roy Fowler's "pioneering little book," *Orson Welles: A First Biography* (London: Pendulum, 1946), written when the author was only 17 years old. Fowler's biographical information about WELLES and production information about CITIZEN KANE is not only important, according to Gottesman, "but essentially accurate" and "presented gracefully." Fowler's account of *"l'affaire Kane"* is of particular interest. As Fowler tells it, HEARST newspaper Hollywood columnist LOUELLA PARSONS, after screening the picture at RKO, telegraphed her boss that the film was, "in part, an unauthorized biography of William Randolph Hearst and such a one that showed him in an unfavorable light." Consequently, Hearst "immediately requested that the film be withheld from circulation." The battle was soon joined by Hedda Hopper, an actress turned columnist, a rival of Louella Parsons, and "a personal friend of Welles." The director claimed that "there was nothing in the film connected in any way with Hearst, save that his name was mentioned as a living person, contemporary to Kane." Speaking before the Author's Club in Los Angeles on January 27, 1941, "with Puckish indignation," Welles announced, "When I get *Citizen Kane* off my mind, I'm going to work on an idea for a great picture based on the life of William Randolph Hearst." The day before, Welles had signed a three-picture contract with RKO, but RKO, intimidated by Hearst, stalled on scheduling press previews that had been set for March 12, and Welles then threatened to sue RKO for breach of contract if the film were not promptly released. The film premiered at the New York Palace on May 1, 1941, with Welles and his then companion, DOLORES DEL RÍO, attending. The Hollywood premiere followed on May 8, but, Fowler reported, reviewers were puzzled. Going into wide release, the film "suffered badly" in rural America. The same pattern, "critical acclaim [and] relative financial failure" was true in England. Although deemed "the best picture of 1941 by both the National Board of Review and the New York Critics' circle," *Citizen Kane* won only a single Oscar, "for the year's best original screenplay." Gottesman contended that Fowler's "analysis covers briefly all aspects of the film and holds its own without apology."

—J.M.W.

France, Richard (1938–) Actor, playwright, and theater historian Richard France teaches at the City University of New York and has written two books on ORSON WELLES: *The Theatre of Orson Welles* (Bucknell University Press, 1977), and *Orson Welles on Shakespeare: The W.P.A. and Mercury Theatre Playscripts,* originally published by Greenwood Press in 1990 and reissued as a Routledge paperback in 2001, with a foreword by SIMON CALLOW. The latter book is an especially useful reference tool that includes annotated editions of the "voodoo" MAC-

BETH (1936), the modern-dress JULIUS CAESAR (1937), and Welles's compilation of Shakespeare's history plays, FIVE KINGS (1939), productions done for the WORKS PROGRESS ADMINISTRATION FEDERAL THEATRE PROJECT and for Welles's own MERCURY THEATRE production company. Background detail is covered by France's 36-page general introduction, and the scripts include production information, as well as Welles's marginalia.

France's earlier book, *The Theatre of Orson Welles*, combined thorough research and many anecdotes to provide a guide to the Mercury Theatre plays ("voodoo" *Macbeth*, DOCTOR FAUSTUS, THE CRADLE WILL ROCK, *Julius Caesar*, *The Shoemaker's Holiday*, DANTON'S DEATH, and *Five Kings*). France carefully describes the sets and lighting, as well as Welles's textual changes and directions for actors. France also provides information about the dramas that Welles staged for radio from 1934 to 1940. The appendices contain cast lists for the stage productions and selected radio credits. The book also contains several production photographs and a helpful bibliography.

—J.M.W. and T.L.E.

Frost, David (1939–) ORSON WELLES was a frequent guest on David Frost's late-night television program. Known for his quick wit and interesting conversation, Welles often made quotable observations about himself. On one occasion, he told Frost, "I played a star part the first time I ever walked onstage and I've been working my way down ever since." Prior to his guest appearances on Frost's talk show, Welles had had a memorable film encounter with Frost in THE V.I.P.'s (1963), which is recounted by both DAVID THOMSON and CHARLES HIGHAM. Higham writes, "David Frost, in a cameo role, plays a reporter who meets Max [Welles as a film director named Buda] at Heathrow Airport. 'Aren't you rather overweight?' he asks Buda. 'Overweight, *Me*?' snaps

Buda and then realizes that the reporter was talking about his luggage."

David Frost, born on April 7, 1939, is the son of Wilfrid, a Methodist minister, and Mona Frost, who lived in Tenterden in the county of Kent in England. He was first educated at the Crescent and Froebel House in Bedford, then, because his father changed churches, the Gillingham Barsole Road Country Primary Junior Boys' School, and then the Wellingborough Grammar School. Frost was an accomplished lay preacher by the time he was 17, but he also enjoyed television and was a talented mimic of television personalities. He entered Cambridge in 1958, where he was active in Footlights, the theater group, and in student publications. As a result of some of the skits he did for Footlights, Anglia Television gave him a five-minute spot. Frost wrote some articles, appeared on television in a series entitled *Let's Twist . . .*, began appearing in cabarets, and finally landed a job with the British Broadcasting Corporation (BBC). His second pilot for the BBC was *That Was the Week That Was* (TW3), which premiered on November 24, 1962. Willi Frischauer, author of *Will You Welcome Now . . . David Frost,* wrote that "the phenomenon of the show was this very young man, this 'nonpersonality,' taking over by the sheer force of nonpersonality." Frost then hosted an American version of TW3, which ran from 1964 through 1965, with regulars Alan Alda, Buck Henry, and Phyllis Newman. In 1966, the first of the *Frost Programme* shows appeared in England.. From 1969 to 1972 Frost hosted the *David Frost Show,* a talk show replacement for the *Merv Griffin Show,* which had moved to CBS. Frost was absent from American television until 1977, when his series of interviews with former president Richard Nixon was shown.

Reference Frischauer, Willi. *Will You Welcome Now . . . David Frost* (New York: Hawthorne Books, 1971).

—T.L.E.

Gabel, Martin (1912–1986) American actor who appeared with WELLES on radio and with the MERCURY THEATRE.

Welles and actor Martin Gabel first worked together on radio in the popular series, THE SHADOW. Welles, the preeminent broadcasting personality of the 1930s, then hired Gabel for a memorable radio production of Victor Hugo's *Les Miserables* in the part of Javert. Gabel was invited to join the Mercury Theatre, and appeared as Cassius in its celebrated modern dress version of *JULIUS CAESAR* (1937) and in *DANTON'S DEATH* (1938). In 1938, Gabel reprised his role as Cassius in a radio adaptation of the updated Shakespeare play for the debut of Welles's new radio series for Mutual, *FIRST PERSON SINGULAR*. In 1956, Gabel, as a Broadway producer, helped sponsor Welles's return to the Great White Way in a stage production of *KING LEAR*.

Born in Philadelphia and educated at Lehigh University, Gabel made his Broadway debut at the age of 21 in 1933. After World War II, with solid Broadway acting and directing credits to his name, Gabel tried his hand at film directing, scoring an impressive critical hit with *The Lost Moment* (1947), starring Susan Hayward and Robert Cummings. On Broadway, he co-produced several successful stage productions including a successful revival of the hit 1939 play, *Life with Father*. He also hosted the early TV quiz show *With This Ring* (1951) and was a frequent panelist on the witty 1950s game show, *What's My Line?*, which also featured his wife, actress Arlene Francis.

Gabel's acting credits in film include *14 Hours* (1951), *M* (1951), *Deadline USA* (1952), *The Thief* (1952), *Tip on a Dead Jockey* (1957), *Marnie* (1964), *Lord Love a Duck* (1966), *Divorce American Style* (1967), *Lady in Cement* (1968), *There Was a Crooked Man* (1970), *The Front Page* (1974), and *The First Deadly Sin* (1980).

—C.B.

Garland, Judy (Frances Gumm) (1922–1969) While WELLES was married to RITA HAYWORTH, his second wife, he had several affairs, one of which was with actress Judy Garland. When the affair was ended, the two remained good friends. In fact, according to BARBARA LEAMING, in later years Garland twice called him when she was contemplating suicide, once in Los Angeles and once in London. Leaming recounts a story about Welles forgetting to give a carload of flowers to Judy when he saw her and then returning home with the flowers. Only the timely intervention of Shifra Haran, who was accustomed to covering for Welles, saved the day; Haran disposed of the incriminating card, and Hayworth assumed the flowers were intended for her.

Judy Garland was born June 10, 1922, in Grand Rapids, Minnesota, to vaudeville performers. She made her stage debut at three and sang with her two older sisters in an act called the "Gumm Sisters Kiddie Act." The sisters changed their last name, at George Jessel's suggestion, to Garland, and Garland later changed her first name from Frances to Judy. At 13 she had a personal audition with MGM production boss LOUIS B. MAYER, who promptly signed her to a contract because of her voice. Her first feature film was *Pigskin Parade* (1936), but she made her reputation with *Broadway Melody of 1938,* when she sang "Dear Mr. Gable" to a photograph of the star. She first appeared with Mickey Rooney, who was to be her co-star in some nine films, in *Thoroughbreds Don't Cry* (1937). Her most memorable role was as Dorothy in *The Wizard of Oz* (1939), which has become a film classic. She won a special Oscar for being "best juvenile performer of the year." Despite her film success, she had severe emotional and mental problems, caused in part by her inability to control her weight, and was seeing a psychiatrist when she was 21. She nevertheless was a successful screen actress: *Meet Me in St. Louis* (1944) provided her with a chance to use her singing, comedic, and dramatic talent. After the film was released, she married Vincente Minnelli, who directed the film, and had a daughter, Liza Minnelli, who later became a superstar in her own right. This marriage, like her first to David Rose, ended in divorce. When her psychological problems intensified, however, she started being late for work, was suspended by the studio, and finally in 1950 was fired by MGM. Sid Luft, her third husband, became her manager and was responsible for her comeback in London and in New York. This was followed in 1954 by her role in *A Star Is Born;* she received an Academy Award nomination for her part as a young actress whose career blossoms as that of her aging actor husband (played by James Mason) declines. Her private life, however, was in shambles. Problems with Luft, lawsuits, nervous breakdowns, and suicide attempts marked her life in the late 1950s. Of the last three films she appeared in, all made in the early 1960s, *Judgment at Nuremberg* (1961) gave her the best opportunity to display her dramatic talent. After her divorce from Luft, she married twice more and attempted more comebacks, but she and her career were exhausted. She died in Lon-

don of an accidental overdose of sleeping pills June 23, 1969. Her story has achieved cult status, partly as a result of the success of her daughter, Liza Minnelli, who resembles her mother in appearance, style, and voice.

References   Clarke, Gerald. *Get Happy: The Life of Judy Garland* (New York: Dell, 2000); Morella, Joe, and Edward Z. Epstein. *Judy: The Complete Films and Career of Judy Garland* (New York: Carol, 1969); Morley, Sheridan. *Judy Garland: Beyond the Rainbow* (London: Pavilion, 1999).
—T.L.E.

Gate Theatre

It was at the GATE THEATRE in Dublin, Ireland, where WELLES made his professional acting debut on October 13, 1931, in the role of Duke Karl Alexander in the Dublin premiere of Lion Feuchtwanger's *JEW SUSS.*

In the first decades of the 20th century, the Abbey Theatre was at the center of Irish theatrical life. However, by the mid-1920s, there was grumbling that in its perhaps too comfortable role as the country's national theater, the Abbey had become too conservative. In 1928, in response to this perception, actors MICHEÁL MACLIAMMÓIR and HILTON EDWARDS established the Gate Theatre. In contrast to the Abbey, which maintained a policy of emphasizing plays exploring Irish themes and experiences, the Gate mounted an ambitious program of works from all periods and countries. MacLiammóir and Edwards also aspired to high production standards comparable to those of the best theaters of Europe. Largely because of its acclaimed tours abroad, the Gate soon came to be regarded as one of the world's leading theaters.

The Gate's division of labors was generally clear. Edwards handled the business end of things, while MacLiammóir functioned as artistic director. Thus, credit for the Gate's artistic success can be largely attributed to the finesse of MacLiammóir's multiple talents as a persuasive leading man, director, and designer. Still, Edward's savvy business instincts as well as his acting skills and general understanding of theater were essential.

In October 1931, a 16-year-old Welles found himself in Dublin. In a twist of fate, he was there because of his guardian, DR. MAURICE BERNSTEIN.

The good doctor, worried that the young man had become too enamored of theater, sent him to Ireland for a bucolic drawing and writing tour in order to distance the young Welles from the stage. Bernstein hoped that upon his return, Welles would see the wisdom of pursuing a conventional liberal arts education at a school like Harvard or Princeton. Traveling the countryside, the young man gave writing and drawing his best shot. He could only muster a half-hearted effort. It was theater that he wanted. He thus plotted a course for Dublin, home of the Abbey and the Gate. In Dublin, he found his way to the Gate and a performance of the Earl of Longford's *The Melians*. Spotting a familiar face in the production, a lad he had met while treading through the heather, Welles pressed for an interview with Hilton Edwards, the Gate's manager. Upon meeting Edwards, as Welles recalled, the 16-year-old boy-giant presented himself as an 18-year-old adventurer, an actor from New York visiting after a season with the Theatre Guild in New York. Edwards, in a slightly different version of the meeting, recollected that although he assumed the story a deception, he was nonetheless taken with the strapping youngster because he desperately needed someone of Welles's stature and booming voice to play Duke Karl Alexander for an already advertised production of *Jew Suss*. Edwards gave Welles an impromptu audition. Although Welles was uncharacteristically nervous, Edwards had seen enough to hire him on the spot. Recovering his self-confidence, Welles attacked the role of the duke with aplomb. MacLiammóir, noting the youngster's élan, recalled with tongue partly in cheek: "[Welles] knew that he was precisely what he himself would have been had God consulted him on the subject at his birth. He fully appreciated and approved of what had been bestowed, and realized that he couldn't have done the job better himself. In fact, he would not have changed a single item."

Welles was a rousing success. He earned raves in the Dublin paper. There were even plaudits from the *New York Times* (see JEW SUSS). For Welles, his triumph as a professional actor at the age of 16 confirmed that his destiny was in theater. His wagon was now firmly hitched to Thespis's star. For Dadda Bernstein, however, Welles's trip to Ireland was a bitter pill to swallow. Instead of "enlarging" the young man's horizons as Bernstein had intended, the trip only sealed the tyro's resolve to make his mark in theater. For Welles, the adventure at the Gate also marked the onset of important lifetime professional and personal relationships with Edwards and MacLiammóir.

—C.B.

Get to Know Your Rabbit
Warner Bros., 91 minutes (U.S.), 1972. **Director:** Brian DePalma; **Producers:** Steven Bernhardt, Paul Gaer, and Peter Nelson; **Screenplay:** Jordan Crittenden; **Cinematographer:** John A. Alonzo; **Editor:** Peter Colbert and Frank J. Urioste; **Music:** Jack Elliott and Allyn Ferguson; **Cast:** Tom Smothers (Donald Beeman), John Astin (Mr. Turnbill), Katharine Ross (Terrific-Looking Girl), Orson Welles (Mr. Delasandro), Susanne Zenor (Paula), Samantha Jones (Susan), Allen Garfield (Vic), Hope Summers (Mrs. Beeman), Charles Lane (Mr. Beeman), Jack Collins (Mr. Reece), Larry D. Mann (Mr. Seager), Jessica Myerson (Mrs. Reese), M. Emmet Walch (Mr. Wendel), Helen Page Camp (Mrs. Wendel), Paul Shear (Flo)

After scoring modest countercultural successes with *The Wedding Party* (1969), which introduced Robert De Niro and Jill Clayburgh to movie audiences, and *Hi, Mom!* (1970), with another De Niro appearance, director Brian DePalma was signed to a "youth market" contract by Warner Bros. to helm the anti-establishment comedy, *Get to Know Your Rabbit*. Written as a vehicle for Tommy Smothers by Jordan Crittenden, the plot centers on businessman Donald Beeman (Smothers) who decides to "drop out" of the mainstream to pursue his dream of becoming a tap-dancing magician. Abetting his quest is master prestidigitator Mr. Delasandro (WELLES). Although intended to capitalize in the mini-cycle of "dropout" films popular with youth audiences of the period, the 1970 production of *Get to Know Your Rabbit* ran into difficulties when DePalma's innovations, including a plan to intercut 16mm footage into the standard feature gauge 35mm footage, ran afoul of studio chiefs John Calley and Ted Ashley. Eerily similar to Welles's tempestuous relationship with RKO in the early 1940s, Warners threw DePalma off the picture, which was recut and released two years later in 1972. For

Welles fans, the film's enduring value lies in the scenes in which the maestro demonstrates his magical prowess. Along with Smothers and Welles, the film featured Katharine Ross as the Terrific-Looking Girl and John Astin as Mr. Turnbill.

—C.B.

Gielgud, Sir John (1904–2000) The great classical actor Sir John Gielgud, often considered the equal of LAURENCE OLIVIER as an interpreter of Shakespeare, worked with ORSON WELLES on *CHIMES AT MIDNIGHT* (1960) as Bolingbroke, the usurper of Richard II who becomes King Henry IV, and the father of Prince Hal. Gielgud was born in London on April 4, 1904, the son of Frank and Kate Gielgud. After attending the Westminster School, he entered the Royal Academy of Dramatic Art and then made his London debut at the Old Vic in 1921 as the Herald in *Henry V.* During his long theatrical career, Gielgud played Hamlet over 500 times. Although his most outstanding achievements have been in the theater, Gielgud began his screen career soon after his stage debut in *Who Is the Man?* (1924). He worked with TONY RICHARDSON in three films, *The Loved One* (1965), *Charge of the Light Brigade* (1968), and *Joseph Andrews* (1976). Like Olivier later in his career, Gielgud took on less taxing film roles rather than dealing with the rigors of the stage. His diplomat Darwin in David Hare's *Plenty* (1985), for example, was brilliant, as was his portrayal of the novelist dying of rectal cancer in Alain Resnais's *Providence* (1977), but his supreme screen performance was as the lead in Peter Greenaway's *Prospero's Books* (1991), an absolutely defining interpretation of the role.

Before appearing in *Chimes at Midnight,* Gielgud had twice met Orson Welles, once with the Oliviers, when Gielgud's incredulous response to Welles's declaration that he intended to play Othello in London wounded Welles's oversized vanity; and, second, when Welles dined with Gielgud and actor RALPH RICHARDSON. On this occasion, Gielgud wrote that Welles "shouted and drew so much attention to us that everyone in the restaurant began staring. Ralph and I felt like two little boys from Eton who had been taken out at half term by a benevolent uncle." He later discussed with Welles the possibility of being

Sir John Gielgud

cast in *THE TRIAL* (1963), but Gielgud feared that he would not be paid for the part and so rejected the offer.

In the production of *Chimes at Midnight,* CHARLES HIGHAM felt that Gielgud "was made to act with unnecessary effeminacy as Henry IV," but Higham also felt that "one of the finest moments in Welles's films is the speech 'uneasy lies the head,' delivered with an exhausted, agonizing pain by John Gielgud." Welles was quite an admirer of Gielgud. Before the shooting of *Chimes* began, Welles told KEITH BAXTER, who played Prince Hal, "I'm in such awe of him [Gielgud]. No actor can touch him in Shakespeare." He also told PETER BOGDANOVICH, "I suppose the two nicest actors I've ever worked with in my life are Gielgud and Heston." Gielgud reciprocated Welles's sentiments by praising Welles's "extremely perceptive appreciation of the Shakespearean text." Gielgud was appointed Chevalier of the Légion d'Honneur after performing in Paris and was knighted in 1953. He also received honorary doctorates from St. Andrews University (1950) and Oxford University (1953). He was nominated for an Oscar for his portrayal of King Louis VII in *Becket* (1964) and won an Academy Award for his role as the droll butler in *Arthur* (1981). Gielgud wrote several autobiographical memoirs: *Early Stages* (1939), *Stage Directions* (1963), *Distinguished Company* (1972), and *Shakespeare—Hit or Miss?* (1991).

Reference Brandreth, Gyles. *John Gielgud: A Celebration* (London: Pavilion, 1994).

—T.L.E. and J.M.W.

Gleason, Jackie (1916–1987)

Gleason, Jackie (1916–1987) In 1955, when WELLES planned to stage KING LEAR and Ben Jonson's *Volpone* in New York, he wanted to cast Jackie Gleason as the parasitic Mosca; Welles himself would play the title role. Of this casting, FRANK BRADY wrote, "The two fat men would in character outwit and outpaunch the other on the stage." Unfortunately, familiar financial problems caused Welles and his backers to jettison *Volpone,* but Welles had a great deal of respect for Gleason, whom Welles dubbed "The Great One," a nickname that Gleason retained. Five years later, Welles again tried to cast Gleason in one of his pictures, THE TRIAL. Gleason would have played the part of the Advocate, but, according to Welles, he "wouldn't fly." In response to PETER BOG-DANOVICH's question about casting Gleason as the Advocate, Welles said, "I wanted Gleason being a legitimate actor." He added that Gleason was a "superb serious actor."

Gleason was, according to Andrew Bergman, "perhaps the greatest actor ever to appear on television." Born on February 26, 1916, in Brooklyn, he was the product of a broken home and was "educated" in pool halls. He worked in vaudeville, nightclubs, roadhouses, and carnivals before receiving a film contract with Warner Bros. in 1940. His early films were undistinguished, and he made his mark on the stage and, particularly, on television in the 1950s with the comedies *The Life of Riley* and *The Honeymooners* and the variety shows *Cavalcade of Stars* and

The Jackie Gleason Show. On his show he created several memorable characters, one of which, Ralph Kramden, became the lead in *The Honeymooners.* In his later films he was a success in comedy (*Smokey and the Bandit, I* and *II* (1977 and 1980), especially because he was paired with BURT REYNOLDS, and in serious roles (*The Hustler,* for which he received an Oscar nomination for his role as the legendary Minnesota Fats, and *Requiem for a Heavyweight,* both 1962). For his performance in the stage musical *Take Me Along* he won a Tony in 1959. He died of cancer on June 24, 1987.

References Bacon, James. *How Sweet It Is: The Jackie Gleason Story* (New York: St. Martin's Press, 1985); Bishop, Jim. *The Golden Ham* (New York: Simon & Schuster, 1956).

—T.L.E.

Goddard, Paulette (Marion Levy)

Goddard, Paulette (Marion Levy) (1911–1990) Paulette Goddard appeared with ORSON WELLES in his CAMPBELL PLAYHOUSE radio presentation of *Algiers* on October 8, 1939. Goddard played the Parisian Gaby in the radio remake of *Algiers,* an adaptation of *Pepe le Moko* by Henri La Barthe; Welles was to play Pepe, who utters the notorious invitation: "Come wiz me to zee Casbah." The production was noted for its use of sound effects to create the right atmosphere. Welles also attempted to cast her in *Carmen,* a picture he planned to make for SIR ALEXANDER KORDA, but the project was abandoned.

Goddard was born on June 3, 1911, in Great Neck, Long Island, New York. At the age of 14 she became a Ziegfeld Girl known as "Peaches." Before she was 20 she had married a rich lumber baron, retired from the stage, and obtained a Reno divorce before moving on to Hollywood. She had some bit parts in films before signing with Hal Roach's stock company. She soon met CHARLIE CHAPLIN, to whom she was secretly married in either 1935 or 1936, the year Chaplin's *Modern Times* was released—she and Chaplin starred in the film. She also appeared in Chaplin's *The Great Dictator* (1940), but she was also busy making other films, most of them undistinguished. Before VIVIEN LEIGH was given the role of Scarlett O'Hara in the film adaptation of Margaret Mitchell's *Gone With the Wind,* Goddard was the favorite to get that choice role. After divorcing Chaplin in 1942, she married actor BURGESS MEREDITH two years later and became one of Paramount's major stars. She specialized in sexy vixens and was adept at comedy. Some of her films were *Diary of a Chambermaid* (1946), *Bride of Vengeance* (1949), *Babes in Bagdad* (1952), and *Sins of Jezebel* (1953, in which she played the title role). She divorced Meredith in 1950, made her last film except for *Time of Indifference* (1964) in 1954, married novelist Erich Maria Remarque in 1958, and lived with him in Europe until 1970, when he died.

References Bachardy, Don. *Stars in My Eyes* (Madison: University of Wisconsin Press, 2000); Gilbert, Julie Goldsmith. *Opposite Attraction: The Lives of Erich Maria Remarque and Paulette Goddard* (New York: Pantheon Books, 1995).

—T.L.E.

Goetz, William (1903–1969)

In 1943, producer Goetz, then at Twentieth Century–Fox, first became involved with WELLES when he and Fox head DAVID O. SELZNICK were asked if they could salvage the footage of Welles's star-crossed *IT'S ALL TRUE*. Like everyone else who had screened Welles's material, Goetz and Selznick simply didn't see how a feature film could be made from the footage. At about the same time, Selznick approached Welles with an offer to play the brooding Rochester in an adaptation of Charlotte Brontë's classic novel, *Jane Eyre,* to be directed by Brontë devotee ROBERT STEVENSON and produced by Goetz. Although there were problems between Welles and leading lady Joan Fontaine and director Stevenson, *JANE EYRE* was reviewed positively and did excellent business. In 1944, Goetz sought Welles for the lead in a film to be produced by a new motion picture company, International Pictures. Welles agreed, and with CLAUDETTE COLBERT, starred in *TOMORROW IS FOREVER,* a successful woman's picture released in 1946. Goetz, now a firm Welles backer, but still wary because of the *It's All True* debacle, hired him to direct and star in *THE STRANGER* (1946) for International Pictures. Although put on a tight leash in terms of closely following the ANTHONY VEILLER script, Welles complied on the basis of a promise

made by Goetz to negotiate a four-picture deal upon *The Stranger*'s successful completion. Although the film came in under budget and ahead of schedule, the reviews, at best, were lukewarm. With an imminent box office failure on his hands, Goetz backed out of the promised four-picture deal. Welles, equally dismayed with Hollywood's conservatism, shortly left town to return to the New York theater scene and a long-dreamed of theatrical adaptation of *AROUND THE WORLD IN 80 DAYS.* Interestingly, when Welles was strapped for cash in the midst of producing his adaptation of the Jules Verne novel, Goetz loaned him $7,500 to help keep the venture afloat.

Goetz, after dropping out from Pennsylvania College in the early 1920s, entered the film business as a production assistant. His upward career path got a boost when he became the son-in-law of MGM boss LOUIS B. MAYER. Joining Fox in 1930 as an associate producer, he became a vice president of Twentieth Century–Fox when the two companies merged in 1933. In 1942, Goetz ascended to the company's board of directors and for two years filled in for DARRYL ZANUCK, then serving in the military, as production chief. In 1945, he formed International Pictures. When International merged with Universal in 1946, he became head of production for Universal International. In 1954, he founded William Goetz Productions and became an independent producer, releasing through Columbia. He later held executive positions with Columbia and Seven Arts. Goetz was also one of the first Hollywood producers to adapt the now standard practice of compensating stars with a percentage of the profits from their pictures instead of a salary.

As an associate producer, Goetz's films include *The Bowery* (1933), *Moulin Rouge* (1934), *The House of Rothschild* (1934), *The Mighty Barnum* (1934), *Clive of India* (1935), *Call of the Wild* (1935), *Les Miserables* (1935), and *Cardinal Richelieu* (1935). His credits as a producer include *Jane Eyre* (1944), *The Man from Laramie* (1955), *Autumn Leaves* (1956), *Sayonara* (1957), *Me and the Colonel* (1958), *They Came to Cordura* (1959), *The Mountain Road* (1960), *Song Without End* (1960), and *Assault on a Queen* (1966).

—C.B.

Gottesman, Ronald (1933–) In 1971 film scholar Ronald Gottesman edited and published *Focus on Citizen Kane,* a critical collection for the Prentice Hall "Film Focus" series. The series intended to "focus" on "the best that has been written about the art of film and the men who created it," and the CITIZEN KANE volume was one of the first titles to appear. At the time Gottesman was an associate professor of English at Livingston College of Rutgers University in New Jersey, and had collaborated on several cinema books with Harry M. Geduld of Indiana University, his co-editor of the "Film Focus" series. He later became editor of the G.K. Hall "Guide to References and Resources" series on major film directors, as his academic career took him from the East Coast to positions at UCLA and the Doheny Library at USC. The anthology offered contextual essays by Gottesman and William Johnson, major reviews by John O'Hara, Bosley Crowther, Otis Ferguson, and others, essays by ORSON WELLES, BERNARD HERRMANN, cinematographer GREGG TOLAND, and others, and commentaries by Jorge Luis Borges, ANDRÉ BAZIN, FRANÇOIS TRUFFAUT, Andrew Sarris, Arthur Knight, and others. The book begins with cast and credit information and ends with a 14-page script extract, a selected bibliography, and a filmography. John O'Hara considered *Citizen Kane* "the best picture he ever saw" and Welles "the best actor in the history of acting." Gottesman takes the film "text" seriously and notes "obvious parallels between Kane and Gatsby," the eponymous hero of F. Scott Fitzgerald's signature novel. Gottesman adroitly surveys the reception of the film, starting with "critical fallacies" following the premiere on May 1, 1941, accusations that "Welles was too young to make a good picture," that "the film was too subjective, the plot too complicated and the story boring, that the techniques and special effects were eclectic and derivative, that they departed too radically from accepted conventions— and so forth." It was not until the 1960s that "anything like genuine analysis and criticism" began to "come to terms with the heft, complexity, and resonance" of the film. The book is indicative of the quality of cinema studies at the time film was coming of age as an academic discipline.

In 1976, Gottesman edited another Welles title, *Focus on Orson Welles,* also published by Prentice Hall. Gottesman declares in his introduction that "homage best describes the motive for this selection." The essays are divided into three sections. The first, "The Man," contains biographical material by PETER BOGDANOVICH and KENNETH TYNAN, and an interview with CHARLTON HESTON, conducted by James Delson. The second, "The Techniques," contains an overview of Welles's films by Richard T. Jameson, who claims that THE LADY FROM SHANGHAI, is "the pivotal film in Welles's career." The second essay, "Orson Welles's Use of Sound," by Phyllis Goldfarb, effectively ties together sound and space in Welles's films. The third part, "The Films," contains individual essays on the major Welles films. Gottesman writes that he regrets that "there was not more first-rate material available on THE MAGNIFICENT AMBERSONS and THE TRIAL," though PETER COWIE's essay on *The Trial* is clearly outstanding. Essays in this section were written by several established film critics, including JOSEPH MCBRIDE, David Bordwell, Jack Jorgens, and JAMES NAREMORE. The book includes a filmography, a selected bibliography, and an index.

—J.M.W. & T.L.E.

Gottfredsen, Mary Blanche Head Wells (1853–1942) Mary Head Wells, ORSON WELLES's paternal grandmother, was born in 1853, though her father, Orson Sherman Head, gave as her birth date 1847, when his first-born child, Mary Maria, died in infancy. Mary Jane Treadwell was her mother. Her father, a former state senator and a district attorney, and mother lived in a luxurious estate in Kenosha, Wisconsin. When she was 14, she left Kenosha and traveled to St. Joseph, Missouri, where she met Richard Jones Wells, a freight clerk. Richard got a five-day leave to travel to Kenosha to meet Mary's parents, and on October 29, 1868, the couple were married, and Mary got a $60,000 dowry. Shortly after their return to St. Joseph, they took a suite of rooms at the Pacific House, which burned down shortly before Christmas. They stayed at two different houses before Richard was transferred to Saxton, where they lived in the depot freight building. Richard then switched to farming, but they quickly ran up debts they could not pay. When their farm was sold, Mary persuaded her exasperated father to buy the land. After the birth of their son, Richard Hodgdon Wells (Orson's father), the couple returned to Kenosha, where her father was in ill health. He died in the winter of 1875, leaving Mary only one-seventh of his estate, payable to her only upon her husband's death. A dispirited Richard left her and went to Chicago, but the Head family lawyers found him and served him with divorce papers; the divorce was final in July 1881. Although Mary had him declared legally dead in 1885 so that she could get her inheritance, Richard was in New York City.

Mary then married Frederick J. Gottfredsen, a wealthy brewer of Danish descent, whom the Heads also disapproved of. Mary left the Head mansion and with her husband's money built another mansion (Rudolphsheim) near that of the Heads. The Gottfredsen brewery business declined, and soon her husband was operating as an agent for the Pabst Brewing Company. Mary's son Jacob Rudolph, whose father was Frederick Gottfredsen, followed his father into the brewing business, but Richard Head Welles (Head was substituted for Hodgdon in order to placate the Heads, and the *e* was added) went to work for the Bain Wagon Works, which was run by his aunt and uncle Harriet and George Yule.

Mary opposed her son Richard's marriage to Beatrice Ives, whom she considered, with some justification, a radical; she also thought that Beatrice was marrying Richard for his money. When Orson was born, it was the formidable Mary who was responsible for George Orson Welles's name. CHARLES HIGHAM states that since Orson's older brother, RICHARD IVES WELLES, had been named for the other side of the family, the Welleses and the Iveses, Mary wanted the second son, Orson, to be named after her own father and uncle, Orson and George Head. Orson was not fond of his grandmother Mary, who became eccentric and strange as she aged. She was a Christian Scientist, but Orson, who visited her occasionally when she was in her 70s, maintained that she also practiced some form of witchcraft, but Orson did not always tell the exact truth, sometimes preferring his own embellished accounts of events. At any rate, she frightened him, and she, in turn, was con-temptuous of him because, Higham believes, he was "artistic, unathletic, and showed no indication that he could follow in the Head tradition of business or the law." Higham describes an encounter between the two in which Welles stabbed himself with a rubber dagger and fell to the floor, thereby hoping to frighten his grandmother. She was not taken in by the ruse and told him to grow up and go into the automobile business like his father. This "automobile talk" is reminiscent of the battles between young George Minafer and his Aunt Fanny in THE MAGNIFICENT AMBERSONS. Welles also claimed that when his father died, the service, which was conducted at Rudolphsheim, was led by a Lutheran minister who added, at his grandmother's urging, "elements of a highly questionable character" into the Lutheran service; but the service was actually conducted by an Episcopal priest. BARBARA LEAMING, who often accepts Welles's historical accounts, writes that Welles accused his grandmother of being "a witch who performed satanic rituals at Dick's [his father's] funeral." Welles told Leaming, "She was a witch, a genuine witch—short, fat, and foul-smelling." Higham believes that the reason Welles never mentioned his grandfather Orson Head, from whom he inherited, according to Higham, his "electricity and demonic intensity," was his loathing for his grandmother Mary, who he thought had put a curse on his parents' marriage. Higham even sees Mary as the inspiration for the old lady in the rocking chair in Welles's early film HEARTS OF AGE. Higham also sees Welles's recurrent fears about insanity as deriving from his grandmother, especially since his brother, Dickie, spent so much time in mental hospitals. Mary died in 1942 at the age of 88.

—T.L.E.

Green Goddess, The (play, 1939) In 1939, vaudeville, beat down by competition from movies and radio, was on its last legs. Vaudeville entrepreneurs, in their final and desperate efforts to stem the tide, attempted to exploit the competition by having popular radio-movie stars like Jack Benny appear live on what was left of the vaudeville circuit. WELLES, "The Man from Mars," as he was often called in the period following the 1938 broadcast of THE WAR OF

THE WORLDS, seemed a likely candidate, in the manner of Benny, to deliver big box-office returns with a well-paced and lively 20 or 30 minutes of diversion.

Welles, offered a huge sum for his efforts, couldn't say no, especially with lingering debts left over from the recently aborted production of *FIVE KINGS* (1939). After mulling over several possibilities for his vaudeville debut, Welles settled on *The Green Goddess,* a 1921 thriller by Scottish critic-playwright William Archer that he had just adapted for radio. Like *TOO MUCH JOHNSON,* he prepared a brief film that would set up the dramatic situation. The four-minute film, after opening on a map of India and then tracking to Nepal and Katmandu, cut to a plane flying at night in a harrowing lightning storm. Suddenly, a mountain range looms, and the inevitable happens—the plane crashes. Accompanying the film was a recording of the plane's motor mixed with sounds of wind, rain, thunder, and the explosion of the crash. As the screen ascended after the film, the playlet about the fate of the three British survivors, a husband and wife and the pilot, and a rajah's attempt to seduce the wife, took center stage.

On June 21, 1939, after a desultory week's run at Chicago's Palace Theatre, Welles, promoted as "the man who scared the world, and then charmed it," took his vaudeville turn to the Stanley Theater in Pittsburgh. Following a typical program of various musical acts, Welles and his small company, the evening's prestige attraction stood ready. "Good evening. This is Orson Welles and the Mercury Theatre in a presentation of *The Green Goddess,*" intoned the great voice from behind the curtain. The applause was polite. The screen then lowered and the film started. Suddenly there was laughter. The unintended uproar was provoked by the reverse unreeling of the film. (The projectionist in Chicago had not rewound the film.) As the plane reassembled itself from the fiery crash and proceeded in an eerie backwards trajectory, the recorded sounds began from the opposite and correct direction, with its effects arranged in a dramatic arc starting at pianissimo and ending with crashing sforzandos. As the play commenced with Welles heavily made up as the Rajah, the sound effects continued at an ear-splitting volume. Exasperated, Welles, stepping out of character, angrily

ordered the record shut off. He also apologized to the audience and offered refunds to those not satisfied. No one departed, and the unintentionally surreal performance continued.

More significant than the mishap with the film was the audience's lukewarm response, a replay of the tepid reaction *The Green Goddess* received in Chicago the week before. Convinced there was little to do to try to save the project, Welles made a gallant effort by doing impersonations of the Rajah as the character might have been played by a fussy CHARLES LAUGHTON, a stentorian JOHN BARRYMORE, a carefully modulated Alfred Lunt, and a suave Herbert Marshall. Alas, the impersonations were not enough. Instead of soldiering on and collecting his big pay-checks, Welles canceled the rest of the scheduled two-month tour. Thus, Welles's first and only vaudeville appearance effort ended, in the words of *Variety,* as "the worst fiasco ever to leaden the heart of an agonized actor."

—C.B.

Greene, Graham   (1904–1991) Novelist-screenwriter Graham Greene was born in Berkhamsted, Hertfordshire, England, on October 2, 1904. He attended Berkhamsted School and Balliol College, Oxford. He married Vivien Dayrell-Browning in 1927, and converted to his wife's religion, Roman Catholicism, in 1926. From 1926 to 1930, he was a staff writer for the *London Times.* He moved on to writing novels, often with psychological and religious overtones, including *The Confidential Agent* (1939), *The Ministry of Fear* (1943), and *Our Man in Havana* (1958). He wrote film criticism for *The Spectator* and other periodicals in the 1930s and served as an espionage agent for the Foreign Officer during World War II. Greene wrote several screenplays, and many of his novels were adapted for the screen. He received the Order of Merit from the queen of England in 1986. He died in Vevey, Switzerland, on April 3, 1991.

More than one commentator on the fiction of novelist-screenwriter Graham Greene has suggested that Greene's work as a screenwriter influenced his writing style. In his book on Greene, Gene Phillips cites Greene scholar Roger Sharock as saying,

"Long before they were made into film scripts, his narratives were crisply cut like cinema montage." Greene, however, disagreed with this view. He told Phillips, "I don't think my style as a writer has been influenced by my work for the cinema. "My style has been influenced by going to the cinema over the years."

Greene was one of the first major literary talents to have shown serious interest in writing *for* the motion pictures. He always approached screenwriting as an exercise of the writer's creative abilities; and he had little time for those writers who looked upon it solely as hack work, whereby they could augment their income.

Nevertheless, he was very much aware that there are certain drawbacks to film writing that aren't applicable to other kinds of writing. He described

Graham Greene

the scriptwriter as the "forgotten man" once the film went into production, since after that point other hands might make alterations to the screenplay. Still, Greene was a realist, and he never expected to exercise a significant amount of influence over the production of a film he had written. "It is impossible for the screenwriter to have the technical knowledge required to control the filming of a script," he explained. "This is a fact, not a complaint."

Green wrote his first screenplay for the 1937 film *21 Days,* based on a John Galsworthy short story. The result turned out to be a pretty mediocre affair, and Greene decided that he would never again adapt another writer's work for the cinema. He broke this rule only once. In 1957, Otto Preminger asked him to adapt George Bernard Shaw's *Saint Joan.* Although the film was a flop, Greene defended his script "for keeping a sense of responsibility to the author while reducing a play of three-and-a-half hours to a film of less than two hours."

All of the other screenplays Greene wrote were based on his own fiction. The first of these was an adaptation of his novel *Brighton Rock* (1947), a stark tale of a tough young gangster. *The Fallen Idol* (1948) was the first of a trio of masterful films that he made in collaboration with director CAROL REED—one of the most significant creative associations between a writer and a director in the history of film.

The Fallen Idol was based on Greene's short story *The Basement Room,* and focuses on a youngster who suspects the family butler of murdering his wife. Greene regarded this script as one of his favorites, because he preferred adapting a short story for the screen to adapting a novel. "Condensation is always dangerous," he observed, "while expansion is a *form* of creation." Following the success of their first venture, Greene and Reed went on to make THE THIRD MAN (1949), for which Greene wrote an original screenplay. The film deals with the black market in postwar Vienna, and won the Grand Prize at the Cannes Film Festival.

As Greene told Phillips, his approach to writing a script was always to write a very detailed treatment, which he would then turn into a script. "I write the treatment like a novel," he said, in order to develop the plot and characterizations to their fullest dramatic potential. He found it almost impossible to capture these elements in "the dull shorthand of a script. One must have the sense of more material than one needs to draw on." Hence, he added, "what today is known as the novel of *The Third Man* was really the treatment which I did before writing the script. That is why I say in the preface of the published version that it is a work not written to be read but only to be seen."

The Third Man, therefore, had to start as a story which could then serve as the raw material for the script that Greene had been asked to write. He conceived the idea of a story set in postwar Vienna. Greene had heard about the penicillin racket operating there and the sewers that ran under the city; and so the various elements of the story took shape around a racketeer named Harry Lime, who would be played by ORSON WELLES, as the villain of the piece. The hero of *The Third Man* is an American author of pulp fiction, Holley Martins (JOSEPH COTTEN) who goes to Vienna to visit his buddy from schooldays, Harry Lime. Martins soon learns that Lime, believed to be dead, was involved in the black market in Vienna, trafficking in pirated penicillin, which was of such a poor quality that it had caused an epidemic in the city. Martins reluctantly agrees to help the police apprehend Lime, who is a fugitive at large.

Greene recalled for Phillips that the American backer of the film, DAVID O. SELZNICK, was not entirely happy with the way that things were progressing. "But Graham, you can't have a film about one guy searching obsessively for another guy," the producer of *Gone With the Wind* and other films objected. "It's not natural. It's the result of your English public schools. And, who's going to go to see a film called *The Third Man?* What we want is something in the nature of *Nights in Vienna*." Despite Mr. Selznick's reservations, Greene went ahead.

Greene revised his preliminary treatment in tandem with director Carol Reed. The first alteration that one notices between Greene's treatment and the finished film is that the protagonist, Holley Martins, is an Englishman in the treatment but becomes an American in the film—simply because Joseph Cotten was chosen for the part. One change dictated

another. Thus, when the hero became an American, the villain had to be American, too, since Holley Martins and Harry Lime were boyhood friends. Accordingly, Orson Welles was chosen to play Harry. This was an extraordinary felicitous bit of casting. Welles appears in only a handful of scenes, but his is the performance that one remembers most.

The film reaches its climax in an exciting chase through the shadowy sewers of Vienna. There is a memorable shot near the end of this sequence taken from street level, showing Lime's fingers desperately reaching through a sewer grating, in a vain attempt to escape to the street through a manhole by dislodging its cover. The pursuit finally ends with Martins obliging the gravely wounded Harry by killing him before the police can find him.

Lime's corrupt charm is perfectly epitomized in a line Greene credits Welles with adding to his dialogue. Harry tells Holley not to think too badly of the decadence of Vienna, since out of the Italy of the Middle Ages, which was just as decadent, came the Renaissance, while a respectable country like Switzerland only managed to produce the cuckoo clock. In summing up Welles's performance in *The Third Man,* film critic Penelope Houston writes, "Harry Lime walked straight into the cinema's mythology on the strength of a line of dialogue about Switzerland and cuckoo clocks and a shot of a hand clutching at a sewer grating."

It has been said that the only thing Orson Welles had to do to dominate a scene was to enter it. Accordingly, Greene felt that Welles simply took over *The Third Man* as soon as he entered the picture, although he did not appear until the film was half over. *The Third Man* undoubtedly represents the pinnacle of Welles's performances in films directed by someone other than himself. *The Third Man* was an enormous critical and popular success, and represents the peak of the cinematic careers of both Greene and Reed. They followed it a decade later with *Our Man in Havana,* an entertaining spy spoof about a British undercover agent working in pre-Castro Cuba, based on Greene's novel of the same name.

Greene wrote an original screenplay for *Loser Takes All* (1956), a light comedy about an accountant who becomes a successful gambler. He termed the film a "frivolity," and it is of slight importance in the canon of his screenplays. He derived his script for *The Comedians* (1967) from his grim novel set in Haiti during the dictatorship of Papa Doc Duvalier, and this film was his last work for the cinema.

It is safe to say that the best films Greene scripted provide a fitting tribute to a writer who showed that the alliance of the novelist and the screenwriter can be a fruitful one, especially when they happen to be the same person.

References Greene, Graham. "*Preface* to *The Third Man,*" in *The Graham Greene Film Reader,* ed. David Parkinson (New York: Applause Books, 1995), 429–34; Gribble, Jim. "The Third Man: Greene and Reed," *Literature/Film Quarterly* 26, no. 3 (Summer 1998): 235–39; Houston, Penelope. *Contemporary Cinema* (Baltimore: Penguin Books, 1969), 38; Kael, Pauline. *Kiss Kiss Bang Bang* (New York: Bantam Books, 1969), 13; Noss, Robert. *The Films of Carol Reed* (New York: Columbia University Press, 1987); Phillips, Gene. *Graham Greene: The Films of His Fiction* (New York: Columbia University Teachers College Press, 1974); ———. "Carol Reed: The Disenchanted," in *Major Film Directors of the American and British Cinema,* rev. ed. (Cranbury, N.J.: Associated University Presses, 1999), 163–76; Schwab, Ulrike. "Authority and Ethics in *The Third Man,*" *Literature/Film Quarterly,* 28, no. 1 (Winter 2000): 2–6; Wapshott, Nicholas. *Carol Reed: A Biography* (New York: Knopf, 1994); Sragow, Michael. "Truer to *the* Main Man of *The Third Man,*" *New York Times,* May 9, 1999, sec. 2: 19, 28.

—G.D.P.

Griffin, Merv (1925–) *The Merv Griffin Show,* a nightly television talk show hosted by Merv Griffin, frequently had ORSON WELLES as a guest or as a guest/host. It was Griffin who encouraged Welles to move from Sidonia, where his home had been flooded and which was somewhat inaccessible, to Las Vegas, which was a short flight from Los Angeles and also the site where Griffin initially produced his show. During the 1970s Welles had appeared frequently on television, his prime source of income, but because Welles was so close to Griffin's studio, he most often appeared on Griffin's show. Welles's imposing physical presence, his wit, and his propensity for making interesting and amusing comments

made him a popular guest. FRANK BRADY reports that in response to Griffin's query about his religious beliefs Welles commented, "I try to be a Christian. I don't pray really, because I don't want to bore God." In fact, Welles did not want to bore anyone. It was on Griffin's show in 1983 that JOHN HOUSEMAN, Welles's MERCURY THEATRE partner in the 1930s, and Welles were reunited after they had split up in 1940. CHARLES HIGHAM describes the meeting: "As he [Houseman] entered the set, Welles embraced him, and these two very large men did a kind of bear waltz around the studio floor." On October 9, 1985, he made his last appearance on Griffin's show. Since BARBARA LEAMING, Welles's "official" biographer, had just published her book on Welles, Griffin anticipated that having her and Welles as guests might produce some interesting disagreements about Welles's life. Griffin was disappointed. Welles and Leaming chatted nostalgically about Welles's life, and Welles performed some magic tricks. Welles died that night after the show.

Merv Griffin was born on July 6, 1925, in San Mateo, California, where he spent his childhood. At an early age he put on shows in his neighborhood, sang, and began to play the piano. He got his professional start as a singer on radio station KFRC in San Francisco in 1945. After singing with the Freddy Martin orchestra from 1948 to 1952, in 1956 he became a singer on the *Robert Q. Lewis Show* on television. He signed a film contract with Warner Bros. in 1953 and appeared in *So This Is Love.* He hosted *Look Up and Live,* a religious show, and *Word for Word,* a game show, but it was not until 1962, when he substituted for Jack Paar on *The Tonight Show,* that his career really began. Such was his success on *The Tonight Show* that he got his own late-night talk show, *The Merv Griffin Show,* on CBS in 1962. Griffin wanted to move the show from New York to the West Coast and had some trouble with CBS, which cancelled the show in 1971. He then signed on with Westinghouse, which produced the show. Perhaps because of his game-show background, he was very successful at creating his own game shows, notably *Jeopardy!,* so popular that it has lasted for years and even become a board game. *Wheel of Fortune,* another of Griffin's creations, has also enjoyed enormous success. Griffin has become a multimillionaire and amassed a show business empire with several hotels, radio stations, production facilities, and even closed-circuit television for horse- and dog-racing venues.

Reference Druxman, Michael B. *Merv* (New York: Nordon, 1980); Griffin, Merv, and Peter Barsocchini. *Merv: An Autobiography* (New York: Simon & Schuster, 1980).

—T.L.E.

Guitry, Sacha (Alexandre-Georges Pierre Guitry) (1885–1957) French actor, author, producer of more than 120 plays, screenwriter, and director Sacha Guitry made two films that featured ORSON WELLES as an actor, *Si Versailles m'était conté* (ROYAL AFFAIRS OF VERSAILLES, 1953, with Welles playing Ben Franklin in an all-star cast) and *NAPOLÉON* (1954, with Welles playing Hudson Lowe). In her book *Sacha Guitry* (1981), Bettina Knapp credits Guitry for having invented the narrated technique known in France as *cinéma commenté* in his film *Le Roman d'un tricheur* (*The Story of a Cheat*, 1936), claiming that Orson Welles "was inspired to avail himself of this same method in *CITIZEN KANE*."

Sacha Guitry was born in St. Petersburg, Russia, on February 21, 1885, the son of the celebrated French actor Lucien Guitry. Educated at the lycée Jeanson-de-Sailly, the younger Guitry wrote his first play, an operetta in verse, in 1901. His father became the director of the Théâtre de la Renaissance the next year, and the son became a member of the company. By 1911, Guitry had established himself as an actor and playwright, and in 1915 he made his first film, *Ceux de chez nous* (*Those from Our Land*), but he continued writing successful plays throughout the 1920s. After a successful American tour in 1927, Guitry again turned to filmmaking, directing six films in 1935 and 1936. Like Orson Welles, Guitry came to filmmaking through a successful career in the theater, and like Welles, he was married and divorced many times. He was greatly honored in France, named Chevalier de la Légion d'Honneur as early as 1923, and awarded the Grande Médaille d'Or de la Société des Auteurs in 1955. Though suffering from a painful illness in 1956, Guitry directed *Assassins et voleurs* (*Assassins and Thieves*), the last of his 32 films, in 1956. He died the next year on July 24, 1957, and was buried at the Montmartre cemetery near his father's grave.

Reference Knapp, Bettina. *Sacha Guitry* (Boston: Twayne, 1981).

—J.M.W.

Hamlet (play, 1934)   A production of *Hamlet* was included in the 1934 summer repertory of the WOODSTOCK DRAMA FESTIVAL as a star vehicle for MICHEÁL MACLIAMMÓIR, who along with HILTON EDWARDS, had journeyed from Dublin's GATE THE-ATRE to the American heartland to work with their young protégé, WELLES. Directed by Edwards, the production featured MacLiammóir as the Prince of Denmark, a role that he had successfully essayed under Edwards's guidance at the Gate in 1932 and 1934. Welles played Claudius. The play was respect-fully received. However, there weren't any out and out raves primarily because of MacLiammóir's lan-guorous limning. Charles Collins of the *Chicago Tri-bune* in his mixed notice said: "MacLiammóir has youth and the romantic qualifications for the great role—a sensitive and poetic face which wears the mask of tragedy nobly . . . slowness of pace is MacLiammóir's handicap."

As for Welles's Claudius, Collins let himself go: "Into this version of the world's most interesting drama, Orson Welles, the bright morning star of Woodstock drama, fits himself with zest. He views the fratricidal king as decadent and monstrous enough to make the situation between uncle and nephew as melodramatically simple as that between Oliver Twist and Fagin. With the courage of his 19 summers and the impact of his vigorous imagination, Mr. Welles plays the king much as CHARLES LAUGHTON played Nero, lasciviously, swinishly. With no beard to hide a sensuously made-up face, and with bangs half-obstructing his sidelong eyes, this king is frankly degenerate. So much of an eye-catcher is this king that he at times hampers the play . . . [during the play within a play] he allows the audience to be conscious of nothing but the king, for during the major part of the scene he is busy making love to his queen. Sitting with Miss Louise Prussing, who obligingly bared one shoulder to make the most seductive Gertrude in my experience, Mr. Welles exchanged caresses, ripe plums, California grapes and lawless looks with her, interjecting so much amorous business as to fairly hog the scene. It is brilliant tech-nical character work, but it flattens the drama, which, as Hamlet remarks, is the thing."

Here, at the onset of his career, is a telling obser-vation on Welles's acting approach. At once brilliant and commanding and even audacious, his roles also verged on a rarefied form of the melodramatic, at once compelling, uniquely eccentric, and over-the-top. In SIMON CALLOW's words: "It is hard to imagine what else, at his age, he could do—other than play safe and dull. He could hardly create a credible mid-dle-aged, adulterous, guilt-haunted, manipulative politician-king. Instead, he did something in broad strokes which made a strong impact, sustained, always sustained, by that mighty organ, his voice." Going for broke, Welles's excesses were those of a singularly gifted young actor possessed of ambition and courage.

Callow also makes the point that working under Edwards's direction was another opportunity to study the Irishman's technique close at hand. "[Welles] learned his grammar of stagecraft directly from Hilton: what he had to say was different, as was his way of saying it, but the swiftness of transition, the economy of action and precision of focus that characterised Hilton's work were all to inform Welles's work as a director."

Reference Callow, Simon. *Orson Welles: The Road to Xanadu* (New York: Viking Press, 1995).

—C.B.

Hardwicke, Sir Cedric (1893–1964) British

character actor Cedric Hardwicke appeared on radio with ORSON WELLES in the CBS Summertime Festival of 1937, playing Malvolio to Welles's Duke Orsino in SHAKESPEARE's *TWELFTH NIGHT.* Hardwicke was born in Lye, Stourbridge, Worcestershire, and educated first at Bridgnorth School and later trained at the Royal Academy of Dramatic Art in London. His stage debut was in 1912 in *The Monk and the Woman.* His film debut was in 1913 in a short entitled *Riches and Rogues.* Military service interrupted his stage career during World War I, when he served as a captain in the British army from 1914 to 1921. Hardwicke performed not only on stage and screen but also starred in the radio series *Bulldog Drummond* from 1961 to 1962. He was knighted in 1934, the same year he played King Charles II in *Nell Gwyn,* and three years before he first met Orson Welles. In 1955, he played King Edward IV in LAURENCE OLIVIER's film adaptation of Shakespeare's *Richard III.* His other well-known films were: *Stanley and Livingstone* (1939, one of the films Welles says he saw as preparation for his *HEART OF DARKNESS* script), *The Moon Is Down* (1943), *I Remember Mama* and *The Winslow Boy* (both 1948), *A Connecticut Yankee in King Arthur's Court* (1949, playing King Arthur), *The Desert Fox* (1951), *Around the World in 80 Days* (1956), and *The Pumpkin Eater* (1964). He also wrote the autobiographical *A Victorian in Orbit* (1961) and a book on the theater, *Let's Pretend* (1932).

References Hardwicke, Cecil. *A Victorian in Orbit: The Irreverent Memoirs of Sir Cedric Hardwicke as Told to James Brough*

(Westport, Conn.: Greenwood Press, 1961); ———. *Let's Pretend: Recollections and Reflections of a Lucky Actor* (London: Grayson & Grayson, 1932).

—T.L.E. and J.M.W.

Harvey, Laurence (Lauruska Mischa

Skikne) (1928–1973) Laurence Harvey, born Lauruska Mischa Skikne, was a British actor who appeared with ORSON WELLES in *THE BLACK ROSE* (1950) and then was cast by Welles as the male lead in *THE DEEP,* the film adaptation of *DEAD CALM.* He played opposite OJA KODAR, Welles's mistress and creative collaborator in the film, which was never completed. Although there were other reasons for the failed film, one of them certainly was the poor health of Harvey, whom CHARLES HIGHAM describes as "miscast as the young, muscular, psychopathic villain."

Laurence Harvey, who was born on October 1, 1928, in Yomishkis, Lithuania, immigrated to South Africa with his Jewish parents when he was a child. He got his start in theater with the Johannesburg Repertory Company when he was 15, at which age

Laurence Harvey *(National Film Society Archive)*

he joined the army and served throughout World War II. After the war he moved to England. and entered the Royal Academy of Dramatic Art. Three months later, he joined a Manchester repertory company and soon was playing leading roles. In 1948, he made his film debut with *House of Darkness* and spent most of the 1950s working in British films, usually in leading roles. During this period he also was active on the stage, and his title role as Henry V in SHAKESPEARE's play received critical acclaim both at the Old Vic in London and in the subsequent American tour, 1958–59. His best-known role in British film was as the callous young executive on the make, sexually, socially, and financially, in *Room at the Top* (1958). During the 1960s he starred in many American films, most notably in *Butterfield Eight* (1960, with Elizabeth Taylor) and *The Manchurian Candidate* and *Walk on the Wild Side* (both in 1962). His outstanding British films included *Of Human Bondage* (1964), *Darling* and *Life at the Top* (both 1965), and *A Dandy in Aspic* (1968). His last film, *Welcome to Arrow Beach/Tender Flesh* (1974) appeared the year after his death of cancer in 1973.

References Hickey, Des, and Gene Smith. *The Prince: Being the Public and Private Life of Laruska Mischa Skika, a Jewish Vagabond Player, Otherwise Known as Laurence Harvey* (London: Frewin, 1975); Perrigrew, Terence. *British Film Character Acrons* (London: David & Charles, 1982).

—T.L.E.

Hathaway, Henry (1898–1985)

Henry Hathaway directed ORSON WELLES in THE BLACK ROSE (1950), in which he portrayed "Bayan the Conqueror." One of Hollywood's most prolific and enduring contract directors, Henry Hathaway excelled at virtually every genre and mode of film-making. He was born on March 13, 1898, in Sacramento, California, the only child of acting parents Rhoady de Fiennes and Jean Hathaway. At age 10 he turned his back on formal education and worked as a child actor for Allan Dwan's American Film Company. "I was doing everything," Hathaway recalled in a 1974 interview. "Whenever they needed a kid, I was it. If the Indians had to steal a child . . . it was me." After serving as a gunnery instructor in World War I, he returned to Hollywood as a prop man for

director Frank Lloyd. Stints as assistant director for Josef von Sternberg and Victor Fleming convinced him that the only security in the picture business lay in directing. His own debut as a director came with an adaptation of Zane Grey's *Heritage of the Desert* in 1932. During the next two years Hathaway did eight more low-budget Grey adaptations, most of them starring a young Randolph Scott.

His "breakthrough" picture, *Lives of a Bengal Lancer* (1935), featured Gary Cooper in a swashbuckling saga of life in India under the Raj. Having gained something of a reputation as an action director, Hathaway immediately switched gears with another Cooper vehicle, *Peter Ibbetson* (1935), a fantasy romance about a convicted murderer who enjoys a dream romance with the woman he loves. *The Trail of the Lonesome Pine* (1936), a Technicolor melodrama about feuding mountain families, revealed yet another Hathaway gift, the ability to craft a piece of rural Americana. These three aspects of Hathaway's talents were to surface repeatedly in his subsequent career. For example, his action pictures included the combat drama, *The Desert Fox* (1951), and more swashbucklers, such as *The Black Rose* (1950), about a disinherited Saxon noble (TYRONE POWER) in Mongolia, and *Prince Valiant* (1954), a stylish Arthurian saga featuring a splendid sword fight between Robert Wagner and James Mason. His distinguished series of westerns included *Rawhide* (1951); and a series of John Wayne vehicles, *North to Alaska* (1960), *The Sons of Katie Elder* (1965), and *True Grit* (1969), for which Wayne's portrayal of the cantankerous, one-eyed Rooster Cogburn won him an Oscar. Affectionate portraits of homespun Americana included *The Shepard of the Hills* (1941) and *Home in Indiana* (1944).

To his reputation for expertise in these three genres Hathaway added another after the war, a skill in making documentary-style thrillers, beginning with *The House on 92nd Street* (1945). This *March of Time*-like story was taken from the case files of the FBI and chronicled the infiltration of a spy ring of fifth columnists. Shot on location, it spawned numerous imitators, including Hathaway's own *13 Rue Madeleine* (1946), a story of the operations of the OSS during the war; *Call Northside 777,* a superior noir about a cynical newspaperman (James Stewart) who endeavors to overturn the wrongful conviction of an accused murderer; and *Fourteen Hours* (1951), a fact-based account of a suicide attempt by a man on a ledge high above New York City. Related to these pictures are several notable crime noirs, especially *Kiss of Death* (1947), whose nominal star, VICTOR MATURE, was overshadowed by Richard Widmark's spectacularly over-the-top performance as a giggling, psychotic killer. The naturalism of these pictures—including the use of location photography, hand-held 16mm cameras, and natural sound recording—was nothing short of a revolution in postwar filmmaking, and placed Hathaway on a par with other practitioners of the noir style such as Jules Dassin and Anthony Mann.

Hathaway was famous for his willingness to take on virtually any kind of project in the offing. On the whole, however, he preferred his noirish documentaries. "Those documentaries are my favorites," he said with characteristic practicality; "it's the genre I like best. Most people seem to prefer my westerns, but I'm not so fond of them. They're so damn difficult. There's no proscenium arch; you're outside and you've got to create your own. You can't have a man backing in from the sidelines and saying 'Stick 'em up' when you could have seen him coming for 12 miles. Just getting people in and out of scenes is hard and frustrating." Critic and historian Andrew Sarris was rather dismissive of him in his book, *The American Cinema* (1968): "Hathaway's charm consists chiefly of minor virtues, particularly a sense of humor, uncorrupted by major pretensions, but this charm is also a limiting factor. The professional detractors of Ford and Hawks almost invariably attempt to palm off Hathaway as a reasonable facsimile, but such a comparison is patently absurd." Historian Scott Eyman is more generous, observing that Hathaway was one of the most dependable, versatile craftsman in Hollywood. He was for Twentieth Century–Fox what Raoul Walsh had been for Warner Bros., "the hardnosed professional who would take on a troublesome story or an obnoxious actor and, one way or another, turn out a watchable, if not always galvanic, film. In return, they would be occasionally favored with a first-rate script and sober actors."

Much of Hathaway's success undoubtedly derived from his solid professional relationship with his boss at Fox, DARRYL F. ZANUCK. "In the 20 years I worked for Darryl, I never turned down one script he handed me," he recalled. "I made pictures. Some dogs, yes, but a lot of good ones too. When I went into the hospital for a cancer operation in 1950, [Zanuck] gave me a script to work on while I recuperated, which not too many people did after cancer operations back then. But Darryl was right about both the script and my recovery; he held up the film [*The Desert Fox*] until I could do it." Hathaway died in Los Angeles on February 11, 1985.

Reference Canham, Kingsley. *The Hollywood Professionals: Michael Curtiz, Raoul Walsh, Henry Hathaway* (New York: A.S. Barnes, 1973).

—J.C.T.

Hayes, Helen (Helen Hayes Brown)

(1900–1993) Helen Hayes was a famous American actress whom WELLES induced to appear on his *CAMPBELL PLAYHOUSE,* a radio show that featured prominent actors performing dramas. Presuming on his friendship with Hayes and her husband, Charles MacArthur, Welles got her to appear in her critically acclaimed role as Victoria in *Victoria Regina;* Welles played Prince Albert. Welles and she also acted together in the Campbell productions of George du Maurier's *Peter Ibbetson* (1939) and in *Arrowsmith* (1939), which Welles adapted from the Sinclair Lewis novel. Hayes, who was born in Washington, D.C., made her first stage appearance at the age of five, played the lead in Frances Hodgson Burnett's *Little Lord Fauntleroy* at seven, and the dual lead in the stage adaptation of Mark Twain's *The Prince and the Pauper* at the age of eight. During her teens she appeared in many plays and in a few silent films. Her career as an adult actress began with a role in Eleanor Porter's *Pollyanna,* and by 1925 she was playing Cleopatra in Shaw's *Caesar and Cleopatra.* She moved to Hollywood with her screenwriter husband, MacArthur, after their marriage in 1928, and for her role in her first film, *The Sin of Madelon Claudet* (1931), she won an Academy Award for best actress. Her other notable films include *A Farewell to Arms* (1931), *Anastasia* (1956, as Dowager Empress), and *Airport* (1970), for which she won an Academy Award for best supporting actress. Other outstanding stage roles include Mary Queen of Scots in Maxwell Anderson's *Mary of Scotland* and Viola in Shakespeare's *Twelfth Night* in 1940. John Mason Brown wrote of her performances as Victoria and Mary, "Miss Hayes succeeds with Victoria, as she succeeded with Mary, in being a queen without even forgetting she is a woman." She also appeared in plays by Tennessee Williams, Eugene O'Neill, and THORNTON WILDER. As a stage actress/manager, she had only two rivals, Katherine Cornell and Judith Anderson. Such was her standing in theatrical circles that the Fulton Theatre in New York was renamed the Helen Hayes to honor her. When the theater was demolished in 1982 in order to provide space for a new hotel in Times Square, theatergoers caused such a row that another Broadway auditorium was named after her in 1983. In 1962, she and Maurice Evans put together some scenes from Shakespeare's plays and staged the result at the American Shakespeare Theatre in Stratford, Connecticut. They subsequently toured the country with the program. In 1964, she established the Helen Hayes Repertory Company to sponsor Shakespeare readings at American colleges and universities. She also made some television appearances and co-starred with Mildred Natwick in *The Snoop Sisters,* a television series that aired in 1972. The U.S. Mint in 1984 struck a commemorative gold coin with her portrait. She also received a Life Achievement Award at the Kennedy Center and was given the National Medal of Arts in 1988. Her writings include *A Gift of Joy* (1965), *On Reflection* (1968), her autobiography, with Anita Loos, *Once Over Lightly* (1971), *Where the Truth Lies* (1988), and, with Katherine Hatch, *My Life in Three Acts* (1990). She is also the mother of actor James MacArthur.

References Barrow, Kenneth. *Helen Hayes: First Lady of the American Theater* (Garden City, N.Y.: Doubleday, 1985); Murphy, Donn B., and Stephen Moore. *Helen Hayes: A Bio-Bibliography* (Westport, Conn.: Greenwood, 1993); Wollstein, Hans J. *Vixens, Floozies, and Molls: Twenty-Eight Actresses of the Late 1920s and 1930s* (Jefferson, N.C.: McFarland, 1999).

—T.L.E.

Hayworth, Rita (Margarita Carmen Cansino) (1918–1987)

Rita Hayworth, ORSON WELLES's second wife, co-starred with him in THE LADY FROM SHANGHAI, which he also directed. Hayworth first met Welles when they appeared together in "There Are Frenchmen and Frenchmen" on *The Orson Welles Show* December 29, 1941. Returning from Brazil by way of Mexico in 1942, Welles saw a back issue of *Life* magazine that featured a pinup photo of Hayworth kneeling on a bed, and that photo rekindled his interest in her. He even publicly stated that he would marry her. In 1943, when Welles met her again at a summer party given by JOSEPH COTTEN, she was in a relationship with actor VICTOR MATURE, who was serving in the Coast Guard 3,000 miles from Hollywood. Welles asked her out to dinner, and she accepted, much to the consternation of HARRY COHN, the jealous head of Columbia Studios, where she was under contract. Despite the opposition of Cohn, who barred Welles from the Columbia lot, and columnist LOUELLA PARSONS, who publicly warned Hayworth about Welles, the couple continued their relationship—she even appeared onstage with Welles in his MERCURY WONDER SHOW until Cohn stopped her—and were married on September 7, 1943, with Cohn's reluctant blessing. According to CHARLES HIGHAM, Welles's "marriage to Rita Hayworth backfired; instead of earning him a further career, it reduced him to being merely her actor husband." In Hollywood they were described as "the Beauty and the Brain." FRANK BRADY characterized them as Professor Higgins and Eliza Doolittle, suggesting that Welles was attempting to provide her with culture, a task he apparently soon tired of. After living for a while at Welles's smallish house on Woodrow Wilson Drive, the couple moved to more spacious quarters in West Hollywood after Hayworth became pregnant. She put most of the money into the house, which was in her name, and she even loaned him $30,000 without interest to help him cope with his heavy debts. Her stardom and box-office appeal led Cohn to cast her in *Tonight and Every Night,* a film that featured wartime dancers performing throughout the Blitz. Because she had weight problems caused by overeating and her pregnancy, choreographer Jack Cole subjected her to lengthy dance rehearsals, which left her exhausted. Welles, in the meantime, was unemployed, restless, aware that he was living in her shadow, and plagued with lawsuits from unpaid Mercury investors and from his first wife, VIRGINIA LEDERER, who charged him with violating the terms of their divorce contract. Hayworth gave birth to a daughter, Rebecca, on December 17, 1944, a year during which Welles was politically active in support of President Roosevelt. Welles and Haywood moved again, this time to Brentwood, where her father lived with them; Hayworth's mother had died a short time after Rebecca's birth. At this point the marriage was in deep trouble. When she was queried, after she and Welles had completed the radio show "Break of Hearts" (September 11, 1944) about how she coped with her husband, Hayworth answered, "He goes his way and I go with him." While the popular Hayworth was preoccupied making *Down to Earth,* Welles continued to have financial and professional problems, which were only somewhat abated when he was cast in THE STRANGER. Meanwhile, a neglected Hayworth began to date singer Tony Martin, which angered Welles, who attempted a reconciliation with her. On December 5, 1945, she announced that she and Welles were separated. In an interview with columnist Florabel Muir of the *Hollywood Citizen News,* Welles commented on the separation: "Now why is it that a girl will marry a guy, knowing what he is, having no illusions whatever, and then never be satisfied until she has made him over entirely on a new plan of her own?" The couple had an explosive battle at Chasen's in Hollywood, and then they met to determine the separation agreement. In 1946, after the failure of his stage version of AROUND THE WORLD and his failure to stage BRECHT's *Galileo,* Welles set out to make *The Lady from Shanghai.* Haywood, apparently willing to try a reconciliation with Welles for the sake of her daughter, Rebecca, agreed to star in the film. Welles, however, told PETER BOGDANOVICH that the script was originally written for BARBARA LAAGE, with whom Welles was having an affair, and that "it was Harry's idea *and* hers that she play that part, thus making it a big, expensive Hayworth 'A' picture—which was the last thing I wanted to be involved in." Welles had Hayworth cut her

trademark long auburn hair and had it dyed blond. DAVID THOMSON believes that Hayworth was photographed with "fascinated loathing." However, according to Joe Morella and Edward Z. Epstein in their *Rita: The Life of Rita Hayworth* (1983), "Rita was delighted with her husband's plans for dramatically changing her image. At last she had an opportunity to be a real actress." There were problems on the set, including Hayworth's illnesses, and the reconciliation effort was hampered by the presence on the set of Barbara Laage. Despite the unpromising situation, Welles and Hayworth continued their relationship during the filming and, sporadically, afterward in France. The divorce was finally granted in 1948. Although the marriage lasted only four years, Morella and Epstein glowingly wrote, "Myths about her [Hayworth] have overwhelmed and supplanted truths: *Her marriage to Orson Welles was a disaster.* This lie has been so magnified and embellished over the years that the truth—that theirs was one of the great love stories—has never been revealed."

Rita Hayworth, who was born on October 17, 1918, in Brooklyn, New York, was the daughter of two dancers, Eduardo Cansino and Volga Haworth. She began dancing professionally when she was 12 years old, and when she was 13, she was appearing in night clubs in Tijuana and Agua Caliente. According to David Thomson, Hayworth told Welles that her sexual exploitation began with her father, with whom she appeared professionally and with whom she traveled as husband and wife. Winfield Sheehan, production head at Fox Studios, signed her to a contract, and she appeared in her first film, *Under the Pampas Moon,* in 1935. She appeared in bit parts, usually as a dancer, for Fox, but when Fox merged with Twentieth Century Pictures, Sheehan lost his power, and her contract was terminated. Her floundering career was rescued by Edward Judson, an older businessman, who married her in 1937 and took control of her career. He changed her name to Rita Hayworth, changed her hair from black to red, raised her hairline, got her a press agent and a contract with Columbia Pictures, and also involved her in the Hollywood social scene. She continued to appear in films, but it was not until she had an important role as an unfaithful wife in Howard Hawks's *Only Angels*

Rita Hayworth *(National Film Society Archive)*

Have Wings (1939) that she began to be seen as a budding star. Her sexual image was enhanced by her role as a seductress in *Blood and Sand* (1941), and she appeared in musicals with both Fred Astaire (*You'll Never Get Rich* [1941] and *You Were Never Lovelier* [1942]) and Gene Kelly (*Cover Girl* [1944]). During World War II she became the quintessential "pinup" girl, due in large part to the *Life* magazine photo that was put on the atomic bomb that was dropped on Bikini. Her image as "sex goddess" was established by her title role in *Gilda* (1946), in which she performed a kind of striptease with long black gloves while she "sang" (her voice was dubbed) "Put the Blame on Mame, Boys." She was at the height of her career and certainly Columbia's greatest star when she met Orson Welles.

After her divorce from Welles, she went to Europe and had a relationship with Prince Aly Khan, a married wealthy playboy whose father was the religious leader of millions of Muslims. When she returned to Hollywood, she told Columbia that she would not be available to appear in films, and the studio cancelled her contract, which was paying her $250,000 a year. She married the prince in 1949, but when the marriage ended in divorce two years later, she returned to Columbia Pictures and resumed her film career but never regained the popularity she enjoyed in her heyday. In her title role in *Salome* and in her role as the prostitute in *Miss Sadie Thompson* (both in 1953) she embodied the image that she had established with her fans. After her marriage to singer Dick Haymes in 1953, she was absent from films, but she returned again, after the Haymes marriage ended in 1955, to making films, but her image was altered. She was an older woman in *Separate Tables* (1958), but that success was not followed by others. In the late 1960s, she began appearing in European films and in 1971 attempted a stage play but could not remember her lines. When her memory continued to decline, her condition was attributed to alcoholism, but she was eventually diagnosed as having Alzheimer's disease, which she died of in 1987. In 1983, Lynda Carter played her in a television film entitled *Rita Hayworth: Love Goddess.*

References Hill, James. *Rita Hayworth: A Memoir* (London: Robson, 1983); Hershfield, Joanne. *Mexican Cinema/Mexican Women* (Tucson: University of Arizona Press, 1996); Kobal, John. *Rita Hayworth: The Time, the Place and the Woman* (London: W.H. Allen, 1977); Leaming, Barbara. *If This Were Happiness: A Biography of Rita Hayworth* (New York: Ballantine, 1989); Ringgold, Gene. *The Complete Films of Rita Hayworth: The Legend and Career of a Screen Goddess* (New York: Carol, 1974).

—T.L.E.

Hearst, William Randolph (1863–1951) ORSON WELLES'S *CITIZEN KANE* (1941) was largely based on the life of newspaper magnate William Randolph Hearst. After learning from Hollywood gossip columnist Hedda Hopper that *Citizen Kane* was about him, Hearst contacted LOUELLA PARSONS, his own Hollywood columnist, who arranged for a screening of the film. When Parsons told him that the film was libelous, Hearst threatened Hollywood studio heads with disclosure about their own private lives. According to FRANK BRADY, Hearst also, the night of January 8, 1941, "issued a directive to all his newspapers throughout the country stating that until further notice, there was to be no publicity, articles, or mention of any kind of *any* RKO film." On January 14, 1941, Hearst changed his mind and attacked Welles in the Hearst newspapers, and he subsequently enlisted the aid of MGM mogul, LOUIS B. MAYER, who offered to buy the film from RKO. Hearst was not through with Welles, whom he attacked in April when Welles broadcast "HIS HONOR, THE MAYOR," which the Hearst newspapers attacked as "communistic." Hearst newspapers also publicized the fact that Welles was one of the "left-wingers" who signed a petition protesting the deportation of Harry Bridges, the leftist union labor leader. As a result of these charges, the Federal Bureau of Investigation (FBI) began reporting on Welles's activities, but the FBI surveillance did not reveal any communist ties to Welles, who had successfully sued a gossip columnist who had called him a "communist." While Hearst did not succeed in blocking the release of *Citizen Kane,* he did hurt it at the box office by threatening some theater owners: the film actually lost $150,000.

William Randolph Hearst was born on April 29, 1863, the son of George Hearst, a U. S. senator whose wealth, like Kane's, came from mines, and Phoebe Apperson. His mother, who took the young Hearst on art tours of Europe, was probably responsible for Hearst's later art collecting, a trait he shared with Kane. Besides being an art connoisseur, he was also a rebel who, again like Kane, was asked to leave private schools and universities, in Hearst's case, St. Paul's and Harvard. After leaving Harvard, where he wrote for the *Harvard Lampoon,* Hearst worked as a journalist for Joseph Pulitzer's *New York World* before he took charge, at the age of 23, of his father's *San Francisco Examiner,* which he developed into a profitable paper. In 1895, he bought the *New York Morning Journal* to compete with Pulitzer's *New York World.* Like Kane, Hearst spent lavishly and even hired the staff of his competition's paper. Soon he had a nationwide chain of newspapers, and, like Kane, he had political ambitions. Although he was twice elected to the U. S. House of Representatives (1903–07), he was unsuccessful in his campaign for mayor of New York City and, like Kane, for governor of New York State. In 1904, he came in second in the voting for the Democratic nomination for the presidency.

With architect Julia Morgan, Hearst worked on the development of his La Casa Grande estate at San Simeon, which was the model for Kane's XANADU. With his mistress, actress MARION DAVIES, with whom he lived for 30 years, Hearst entertained lavishly at San Simeon, where the worlds of entertainment and politics mixed. He also built Davies a 110-room beach house in Santa Monica. (Hearst's wife, dancer Millicent Willson, who bore him five sons, never was divorced from Hearst.) Like Kane, Hearst advanced his mistress's career, even building her a bungalow on her studio's lot; but Davies, unlike Kane's second wife, hardly needed his assistance. Like Kane, Hearst eventually lost some of his business empire, but when he died in 1951, his holdings included 16 daily newspapers, two Sunday-only newspapers, and nine magazines. Davies was with him when he passed away.

William Randolph Hearst

References Nasaw, David. *Chief: A Life of William Randolph Hearst* (Boston: Houghton Mifflin, 2000); Pizzirola, Louis. *Hearst over Hollywood: Power, Passion, and Propaganda in the Movies* (New York: Columbia University Press, 2002); Swanberg, W.A. *Citizen Hearst: A Biography of William Randolph Hearst* (New York: Scribner's, 1961).

—T.L.E.

Heartbreak House (play, 1938) On the heels of its hit productions of JULIUS CAESAR (1937) and *The Shoemaker's Holiday* (1938), the MERCURY THEATRE concluded its debut season with a production of GEORGE BERNARD SHAW's 1921 play, *Heartbreak House*. For the experimentally inclined Mercury Theatre, producing a realistic drama by a living play-wright was a challenge. In fact, Shaw's naturalistic play was selected in part as a means of responding to criticisms alleging that Mercury's productions had relied too heavily on "gimmickry." It was also undertaken because of the play's warnings about upper-middle-class complacency, the threat of war, and the end of civilization. These were issues especially pertinent to the great national debate then going on between isolationists and interventionists about whether or not the United States should prepare to enter the war on the side of the European democracies. Welles also was attracted to Shaw's Fabian ideals, which helped provide the play's philosophical underpinnings, and which had also helped inspire American liberalism.

Negotiations with Shaw were tough. Welles, who was in the habit of cutting even Shakespearean classics down to lean 90-minute productions, could not get Shaw to budge on the matter of editing. Thus, Welles's 1938 *Heartbreak House* ran just as it had in 1921 when it first opened in London, without a single change in either Shaw's dialogue or stage directions. Although some complained that the three-hour production sometimes bordered on the tedious, the Mercury's *Heartbreak House* received good if not great reviews, which Welles and JOHN HOUSEMAN had expected, given their inability to streamline Shaw's work. Still, the production proved that the Mercury could navigate the waters of the theatrical mainstream as well as anyone else in town.

Set in England. in 1915, the plot centers on the young Ellie Dunn's romance with a rich, elderly businessman, Boss Mangan, and her decision as to his proposal of marriage. Mrs. Hesione Hushabye, the daughter of Captain Shotover, a retired naval officer and wealthy inventor of sophisticated arms, advises that the marriage would be a mistake. Mangan is invited to Heartbreak House, Captain Shotover's estate, in order that Mrs. Hushabye might expose his more sinister side. With typical Shavian aplomb, the playwright then introduces an outsider, a burglar who is caught and passes his hat around for tips as he recites the story of his miserable life. At the end, Shaw brings things to a close with a deus ex machina, an explosion that kills the burglar and Mangan, but spares the others. When asked about the play's meaning, Shaw refused to explain, saying, "I am only the author." Still his critique of upper-class amorality and frivolousness was a clear example of "Englishmen fiddling while Europe smoulders."

Welles assembled a first-rate cast. Mady Christians played Captain Shotover's daughter, Hesione Hushabye; Hector, her amorous husband, was essayed by Vincent Price; the beautiful young Irish actress GERALDINE FITZGERALD, recommended to Welles by MICHEÁL MACLIAMMÓIR and HILTON EDWARDS of Dublin's GATE THEATRE, made her American debut as Ellie Dunn; GEORGE COULOURIS played Boss Mangan; ERSKINE SANFORD was Mazzini Dunn; Eustace Wyatt portrayed the burglar; and in the role of Captain Shotover was Welles, heavily but effectively made up as the 88-year-old octogenarian inventor of death machines.

In his preface to the play, Shaw mentions the hopeless indifference of polite people to politics and war, thus exposing the evasive weakness and insensitivity of those too comfortably ensconced in a world of inherited money and property. It was a theme that the spirited Welles-directed project successfully brought home. Given the steep royalty rates demanded by Shaw, and the expense of John Koenig's impressive but expensive naturalistic rendering of the captain's nautically themed manor, *Heartbreak House* failed to meet expenses. Still, it was an effectively contrasting production in the Mercury's first and hugely successful repertory season.

Heartbreak House ran for 48 performances, from April 29 to June 11, 1938, at the Mercury Theatre.

—C.B.

Heart of Darkness

When WELLES signed with RKO in 1939, he was determined to adapt *Heart of Darkness,* Joseph Conrad's 1899 novella, as his first Hollywood film. Asked by PETER BOGDANOVICH about his attraction to Conrad, Welles said: "I think I'm made for Conrad. I think every Conrad story is a movie. There's never been a [good] Conrad movie, for the simple reason that nobody's ever done it as written. My script [for *Heart of Darkness*] was terribly loyal to Conrad." It also was intended by Welles as an allegory on fascism. "Remember the time I was working on that, 1939–1940. War hadn't started [for the United States], and fascism was the big issue of the time. It was a very clear parable."

Conrad's story was based on the cultural shock he experienced in 1890, when he worked in the Belgian Congo. The narrator, Marlow, recounts a journey on an African river. He has been commissioned by an ivory company to take command of a stranded cargo boat upriver. As he cuts his way through the dense jungle, Marlow witnesses the brutalization of natives by white traders. He also hears stories about a Mr. Kurtz, the ivory company's most successful agent. When he finally reaches Kurtz's remote outpost, he sees a line of human heads mounted atop poles. In this alien world without tethers to his own culture, Kurtz has exchanged his soul for a brutal and brutalizing realm. Kurtz, it turns out, is suffering from a fatal illness. His bloody reign is about to end. As Marlow transports him downriver, Kurtz rationalizes his unsavory deeds as a visionary quest. To Marlow, Kurtz's dying words, "The horror! The horror!" stand for the despair resulting in his encounter with human depravity.

Although drawing on his 1938 radio script for *Heart of Darkness,* Welles came up with the radical idea of shooting much of the film from Marlow's point of view. While "subjective camera technique" had often been used in small doses, Welles's plan for such extensive use of the first-person device was unprecedented. "The camera was going to be Marlow, which is ideal for that particular kind of story, because he's in the pilot house and he can see him-

Joseph Conrad

self reflected in the glass through which you see the jungle," Welles told Peter Bogdanovich. "So it isn't that business of a hand-held camera mooching around pretending to walk like a man. It's kind of the perfect setup, because you needed a lot of narration [for Conrad], and you would see the man who was talking reflected in the glass as you went up the river, and so on. It would have worked, I think. I did a very elaborate preparation, such as I've never done again—never could. I shot my bolt on the reproduction on that picture. We designed every camera setup and everything else—did enormous research in aboriginal, Stone Age cultures in order to reproduce what the story called for. I'm sorry not to have got the chance to do it. The reason we didn't was because we couldn't knock $50,000 off the budget."

In Welles's script, the heart of darkness is moved from the Belgian Congo to a mysterious land. The role of Elsa, who appears only at the end of Conrad's novella, was enlarged by Welles. Instead of hearing of Kurtz's fate at the end of the story, she accompanies Marlow upriver to help find him. She is virginal, yet voluptuous and unfulfilled. Marlow loves her, but she loves Kurtz, who in turn has become involved with an exotic native girl. Welles hoped to devise a way of getting around the censors to show the interracial couple in a loving embrace. Thematically, Welles viewed Kurtz as representing dictatorial fascism. "The picture is, frankly, an attack on the Nazi system," Welles told assistant HERBERT DRAKE.

Welles's script was completed and mimeographed on November 30, 1939. Ignoring the political undercurrents, RKO boss GEORGE SCHAEFER gave the project his full support. During the next several months, there was extensive preproduction planning and testing. The cast members, most of whom would be reprising roles they had played for the 1938 MERCURY broadcast of *Heart of Darkness,* included Vladimir Sokoloff (Doctor), Edgar Barrier (Strunz), Norman Lloyd (Adalbert Butz), ERSKINE SANFORD (Ernest Stitzer), Dita Parlo (Elsa Gruner), Robert Coote (Eddie), Gus Shilling (Frank Melchers), GEORGE COULOURIS (Carba de Arriaga), RAY COLLINS (Blauer), John Emery (de Tirpitz), and Frank Readick (Meuss). Welles was slated to essay both Marlow and Kurtz. Welles had African-American actor JACK CARTER (his Macbeth and Mephistopheles) signed to play a ferryman, a modern incarnation of Charon guiding "guests" across the River Styx.

In spite of Schaefer's backing, Welles's *Heart of Darkness* fell prey to circumstances beyond anyone's control. Because of the expanding war in Europe, RKO and the other major Hollywood studios were beginning to suffer serious declines in foreign revenue. As a result, all previously approved projects, including *Heart of Darkness,* were reviewed in order to find ways of paring costs. There were also growing front office concerns about Welles's plan for shooting Marlow from an exclusively first-person, point of view. Finally, RKO threw in the towel. It just couldn't afford to produce *Heart of Darkness* as envisioned by Welles.

—C.B.

Hearts of Age, The   Home Movie, 5 minutes, 1934.
Directors: Orson Welles and William Vance; **Producer:** William Vance; **Screenplay:** Orson Welles; **Cinematographer:** William Vance; **Cast:** Orson Welles (Death), Virginia Nicolson (Old Lady), Edgerton Paul (Man in Blackface), William Vance (Native American)

Made when WELLES was only 19, *The Hearts of Age* is a five-minute 16mm silent film directed by Welles and William Vance, who also acted as producer of the film. It was filmed at the old firehouse at Woodstock, while Welles was there at the Todd School conducting a "Summer Festival of Drama." Virginia Nicolson, Welles's first wife, who also appeared in the film, told RICHARD FRANCE that the film was intended to be a joke: "There was no script. Orson simply amused himself thinking up totally unrelated sequences to be shot à la grand guignol." JOSEPH MCBRIDE finds the film prophetic of Welles's later *CITIZEN KANE* (1941) and also sees the influence of German expressionism. PETER BOGDANOVICH finds the film's obsession with old age a recurrent theme in Welles's films and states that the "signature is so unmistakably his." According to Welles, the film was a "put-on," a "charade" of the surrealism found in avant-garde films like JEAN COCTEAU's *Blood of a Poet* (1930), Robert Weine's *The Cabinet of Dr. Caligari* (1919), and Cocteau and Buñuel's *Un Chien Andalou* (1928).

The film begins with a spinning, *Citizen Kane*-like, Christmas tree ball and a white-garbed Father Time figure holding a globe. Next there is a montage of ringing bells, which is followed by a shot of Nicolson made up to resemble an old lady; she is shown rocking back and forth on one of the ringing bells. Edgerton Paul, in black face, next appears pulling the bell rope; the old woman is on the roof above him. After the initial shot is repeated, there is a tilt shot of a gravestone with three longish shadows moving behind it. Then there is a hand holding a gravestone tipped the opposite way. After a shadow hand rings a shadow bell, the hand bell drops to the ground, and the next shot is of the old lady riding a large bell as Paul continues to pull the rope. The old lady opens up an umbrella, which she puts over her head. A close-up of a spinning globe follows, and then there are two hands (one a white shadow—the shot is in negative—and the other a real hand) on the gravestone. The shadow hand beckons, and then Welles appears as Death at the top of some stairs. Garbed in *Caligari*-like attire, he descends the stairs, an action that is twice repeated. Two unrelated shots follow: Nicolson as a Keystone Kop, and Vance as a blanketed Native American. After Death gestures with his Wellesian cane, a hand pours money onto the floor, and the money is swept away. Death's actions irritate the old woman, and then the Paul character swings from a noose. Next there is a sketch of the hanged Paul, and then a hand is shown drawing a bell as if to sign the drawing.

At the end of the film, Death carries a candelabra into a dark room, puts it on the piano, and plays as the camera tilts expressionistically to the right. As he plays, the camera tracks in to his fingers; and when he hits a wrong note, he stops and tries to determine what has happened. After, à la *Un Chien Andalou,* he finds the old woman dead in the piano, he opens his piano bench and browses through some tombstone-shaped slabs: "Sleeping," "At Rest," "In Peace," "With the Lord," and "The End." He then resumes playing, and then the audience sees a bell, his fingers playing the piano, and "The End" slab.

CHARLES HIGHAM sees autobiographical elements in the film. He believes the old woman resembles Welles's grandmother MARY GOTTFREDSEN, whom Welles feared and detested; and he points out that Welles had a lifelong obsession with "skulls, graves, and grave inscriptions." SIMON CALLOW, perhaps the most generous critic of the film, considers it "a highly distinctive piece of work," which "is full of life and imagination, highly theatrical, but keen to exploit the freedom and the tricks of the cinema." Callow also finds an interesting parallel between *The Hearts of Age* and Sergei Eisenstein's first film, *Even a Wise Man Stumbles,* in that both early films reflect the influence of *Caligari* and blend theatricality with cinematic experimentation.

—T.L.E.

Hecht, Ben (1893–1964) Renowned screenwriter Ben Hecht first met ORSON WELLES in the mid-1930s when both were in New York City, and Hecht tried unsuccessfully to get Welles an acting job with MGM in 1939, just prior to Welles's arrival in Hollywood. In 1940, Welles, despite being barred from Columbia Studios by HARRY COHN, often visited the set of *Angels Over Broadway,* directed by Hecht and starring RITA HAYWORTH, his new love. William MacAdams, author of *Ben Hecht* (1990), asserts that Hecht and Welles had much in common: both had been given almost complete control over their films. Hecht had written, produced, and co-directed four films. MacAdams further claims that Hecht, not Welles (uncredited) and JOSEPH COTTEN, wrote Welles's *JOURNEY INTO FEAR.* According to MacAdams, Hecht signed on July 23, 1941, a contract with RKO to adapt ERIC AMBLER's *Journey into Fear* to the screen. The script was completed by the end of August, after which it was revised by Richard Collins and Ellis St. John. FRANK BRADY states that Welles "coauthored an entirely new script with Joseph Cotten," who is credited with the script. CHARLES HIGHAM agrees with Brady and also claims that Hecht "never quite completed it [the script]." MacAdams suggests that Hecht expected the script squabble: "Hecht had written the script knowing he wouldn't receive screen credit, well aware of Welles's penchant for grabbing everything he touched." Small wonder then that Hecht would side with fellow writer HERMAN MANKIEWICZ in the dispute over the script credit for Welles's *CITIZEN KANE.* In her "Raising Kane" essay in *The New Yorker* (February 20 and 27, 1971), PAULINE KAEL recounts the following: "Nunnally Johnson says that while *Citizen Kane* was being shot, Mankiewicz told him that he had received an offer of a ten-thousand-dollar bonus from Welles (through Welles's 'chums') to hold onto the original understanding and keep his name off the picture." When Mankiewicz went to Hecht for advice, Hecht said, "Take the ten grand and double-cross the son of a bitch." Frank Brady's account is similar, but MacAdams raises the ante to a $50,000 bribe. Hecht, who had earlier used his column in *PM,* a New York left-wing tabloid, to defend Welles and Mankiewicz against WILLIAM RANDOLPH HEARST's minions, who were trying to prevent the release of *Citizen Kane,* promised Mankiewicz that he would write an article for the *Saturday Evening*

Post, exposing Welles's "bogus" claims. The article was never written after Mankiewicz dropped the matter.

Ben Hecht, the son of Russian immigrants, was born on February 28, 1893, in New York City, but he spent his childhood in Racine, Wisconsin. He left home for Chicago when he was 16 and began a career in journalism, though he was also writing short stories and working on a novel. He started the *Chicago Literary Times* in 1923, but when he arrived in New York in 1925, he had very little money. Scriptwriter Herman Mankiewicz, an old friend, got him a job at Paramount Studios in Hollywood, where he began a 40-year career in screenwriting. He wrote quickly, seldom taking more than two or three weeks to complete a script. He was much in demand, and he was paid well, earning more than $260,000 in 1937, for example. He was credited for writing the stories or scripts for more than 70 films, but he also worked on many other scripts, some of which are well known, for which he did not receive credit, among them *Queen Christina* (1933), *Gone With the Wind* (1939), *Gilda* (1946), *Rope* (1948), and *Roman Holiday* (1953). In the first Academy Award ceremony, he received an Oscar for best original story for his work on von Sternberg's *Underworld* (1927) and one later in 1935 for *The Scoundrel,* which he co-directed and co-wrote with Charles MacArthur, with whom he often collaborated on plays and films: Hecht and MacArthur wrote the stage play *The Front Page,* which has several times been adapted to film (once as Hawks's *His Girl Friday,* 1940), and *Twentieth Century,* which he also adapted to film (1934). The major films for which he wrote scripts are *Gunga Din* and *Wuthering Heights* (both 1939), *Notorious* (1946), and *A Farewell to Arms* (1957). Hecht was politically involved, and his criticism of British policies and his support of the Jewish resistance movement in Palestine in the 1940s resulted in the British removing his name from the credits in his films for some five years. He continued to write until his death in 1964, while he was working on the script for *CASINO ROYALE* (1967).

References Macadams, William. *Ben Hecht: The Man Behind the Legend* (New York: Scribner, 1990); Martin, Jeffrey Brown. *Ben Hecht, Hollywood Screenwriter* (Ann Arbor: UMI Research Press, 1985).

—T.L.E.

Hello Americans (radio, 1942–1943) In September 1942, with direct U.S. involvement in World War II not yet a year old, WELLES was asked by CBS to produce, write, direct, and narrate a weekly war-related series to be called *Hello Americans.* A series of dramatizations designed to help build public support and understanding of the country's Latin American neighbors, the 30-minute programs were aired under the aegis of the Office of the U.S. Coordinator of Inter-American Affairs, which though it had dropped its sponsorship of Welles's *IT'S ALL TRUE,* still valued Welles as its on-the-air ambassador.

On the surface, each program appeared to be a variety show featuring the music and culture of the particular nation being visited. In *Brazil,* the series' first broadcast, Welles, drawing on themes developed in *The Story of Samba* episode of the uncompleted *It's All True,* reminded listeners that the chic Latin musical form so popular in movies and swank nightclubs originated in the impoverished backstreets of Rio. In one of the show's most engaging bits of cultural education, one first hears the rhythmic pulse of jungle drums; other instruments are added gradually, paving the way for a full-blown samba, at which point Welles exclaims: "Dig that rhythm you cats, that's the Amazon and the Conga talking." Other Latin tunes were performed on the debut broadcast by the popular Carmen Miranda.

There were also dramatizations with members of the cast portraying American engineers and businessmen commenting on America's vital interests. Given the social-political turmoil of Brazil and other Latin American nations, Welles and the Office of the U.S. Coordinator of Inter-American Affairs were especially concerned with the threat of fascism and its appeal to oppressed populations who might see powerful dictators as forces for positive change. Like Welles's uncompleted *It's All True, Hello Americans* used entertainment as a subtle means for conveying ideas that might help build greater understanding and support of U.S. hemispheric neighbors south of the border. In the show's uncredited cast and production team were a number of MERCURY THEATRE and *CITIZEN KANE* alumni, including RAY COLLINS, JOSEPH COTTEN, EVERETT SLOANE, PAUL STEWART, and composer BERNARD HERRMANN.

Like *Ceiling Unlimited,* a companion war-boosting radio series produced by Welles for CBS during the same period, *Hello Americans* provided effective wartime propaganda praised by the public and critics alike. *Hello Americans'* run extended from November 15, 1942, to January 31, 1943.

Speaking of *Hello Americans,* Welles told PETER BOGDANOVICH: "They were good shows, I thought. All inter-American affairs. I did the A-B-Cs of the Caribbean. And they were very amusing. I didn't really do much of it—the writers were awfully good. And it was a good form. A-B-C: 'A' is for 'Antilles,' 'Antigua,' and so on. We went through like that, and did little things and big things, with music and stories each week. I'm queer for the Caribbean anyway—not as it exists, but as it was in my mind in the eighteenth and nineteenth centuries. The Caribbean is just great stuff. All of it."

—C.B.

Herrmann, Bernard (1911–1975) Born in New York City on June 29, 1911, Herrmann attended De Witt Clinton High School. He won a composition prize at age 13 and later attended New York University. He founded and conducted the New Chamber Orchestra when he was 20. He studied composition with Philip James, Bernard Waginaar, and Albert Stoessel at the Juilliard School.

In 1934, he was appointed composer-conductor by CBS radio, which put a 23-piece orchestra at his disposal. ORSON WELLES invited Herrmann to score and conduct the MERCURY THEATRE radio dramas that he was regularly presenting on CBS. From the beginning, Welles found him an autocratic and uncompromising perfectionist who was difficult to work with. But Welles, who customarily exercised creative control over the dramas in which he appeared, thought Herrmann's skills as composer-conductor were well worth whatever arguments they had while preparing a play for airing. After all, as SIMON CALLOW observes, Herrmann's "peppery personality complemented Welles's in its fanatical perfectionism."

Welles starred in a radio *MACBETH* in the autumn of 1934; Callow reports that he insisted on having a Highland bagpipe to lend Herrmann's score more of a Scottish flavor. Herrmann resented this unwelcome intrusion on his orchestration. Indeed, he broke his baton, threw his script up in the air, and stalked out of the studio minutes before air time. "I dragged him back," Welles says in *This Is Orson Welles.* Welles concludes laconically, "Benny was an emotional-type conductor."

Bret Wood terms Herrmann's score for Welles's radio version of Bram Stoker's *Dracula* (July 11, 1938) "one of Herrmann's best radio scores, which alternates between alarming flourishes and moments of soothing, hypnotic music." Welles liked to dramatize classic novels for radio, and that same year he dramatized H. G. WELLS's *WAR OF THE WORLDS.*

This radio play, broadcast on Halloween (October 30, 1938), caused panic in the streets all over Amer-

Bernard Herrmann

ica when listeners who tuned in late were not aware that the program was a dramatization, and not an on-the-spot newscast of an actual invasion of our planet by hostile aliens. The drama begins with an announcer repeatedly interrupting the broadcast of Ramón Raquello and his orchestra from the Meridian Room of the Park Plaza Hotel with news bulletins about the developing crisis. It was Herrmann who supplied the music.

Welles also presented a radio adaptation of Daphne du Maurier's *Rebecca* (December 9, 1938); Callow praises Herrmann's "waltz-laden score," full of heart-freezing motifs created by tremolo strings. Welles's production was a year before Hitchcock's movie of the same novel. Welles also presented BOOTH TARKINGTON's *THE MAGNIFICENT AMBERSONS* (October 19, 1939); Herrmann's heavily orchestrated music, punctuated by a graceful waltz, was similar to the score he wrote for Welles's film version three years later.

Because of Herrmann's close association with Welles on radio, it was inevitable that Welles would want him to score CITIZEN KANE. Herrmann went on the studio payroll on October 21, 1940, and continued collaborating on the movie for 14 weeks. Herrmann writes in "Score for a Film":

"*Citizen Kane* was the first motion picture on which I had ever worked. I had heard of the many handicaps that exist for a composer in Hollywood. One was the great speed with which scores often had to be written—sometimes in as little as two or three weeks. Another was that the composer seldom had time to do his own orchestration. And again—that once the music was written and conducted, the composer had little to say about the sound levels or dynamics of the score in the finished film.

"Not one of these conditions prevailed during the production of *Citizen Kane.*

"I was given 12 weeks in which to do my job. This not only gave me ample time to think about the film and to work out a general artistic plan for the score, but also enabled me to do my own orchestration and conducting.

"I worked on the film, reel by reel, as it was being shot and cut. In this way I had a sense of the picture being built, and of my own music being a part of that building."

FRANK BRADY states that, as Welles worked on the script, "he could hear in his mind the suggestion of music that should be inserted" in a scene; "pencilled notations began to fill his script, indicating where music was needed." Herrmann composed two principal leitmotivs (themes associated with particular persons or objects). He states in his essay "Score for a Film" that they are meant "to give unity to the score as a whole" by their recurrence. One motif is associated with Kane's power, the other with the mystery of ROSEBUD. Both of these leitmotivs are heard in the film's prologue.

The prologue begins with the camera focusing on the NO TRESPASSING sign attached to the front gate of Kane's castle, XANADU. The camera then climbs over the fence to which the sign is attached and moves forward through a series of lap dissolves toward the fortress at the top of the hill, which is set against a dark sky.

The first motif, "a simple four-note figure in the brass—is that of Kane's power. It is given out in the very first two bars of the film. The second motif is that of Rosebud. Heard as a solo on the vibraphone, it first appears during the death scene at the very beginning of the picture," just as Kane expires on his deathbed. Both leitmotivs are repeated during the film "under various guises." François Thomas cites Herrmann as recalling that the prologue was the first sequence for which he composed music; "both themes sort of automatically presented themselves to me."

The scenes set in the office of *The Inquirer,* at the outset of Kane's career as a newspaper publisher, "take place in the eighteen-nineties, and, to match its mood, I used the various dance forms popular at that time. Thus, the montage showing the increase of circulation of *The Inquirer* is done as a can-can scherzo. *The Inquirer*'s campaign against the traction trust is done in the form of a gallop. Kane and his friend Leland arrive at the office to the rhythm of early ragtime. This whole section, in itself, contains a kind of ballet suite in miniature."

Herrmann even includes the vibrant music of a brass band to accompany Kane's rise to power in the newspaper world. "There's some music in the film Herrmann didn't write," Welles told PETER BOG-DANOVICH: At a party to celebrate the success of *The Inquirer,* a snappy song by the brass is played, then sung by Kane's friends and associates; it is entitled "Oh, Mr. Kane." The tune came from a Mexican march that Welles once heard while south of the border, "A Poco No," by Pepé Guizar. Welles had lyricist Harry Ruby write new English lyrics for its use in the movie. The boisterous melody is played throughout the closing credits, to recall Kane's victories rather than his defeats.

Herrmann notes in "Score for a Film," "Most musical scores in Hollywood are written after the film is entirely finished, and the composer must adapt his music to the scenes on the screen. In many scenes in *Citizen Kane* an entirely different method was used, many of the sequences being tailored to match the music. This was particularly true in the numerous photographic montages, which are used throughout the film to denote the passing of time.

"The most striking illustration of this method may be found in the 'breakfast montage' between Kane and his first wife. Here, in the space of three or four minutes, Welles shows the rise and fall of affection between two married people. The setting is a breakfast table. The young couple enters, gay and very much in love. They talk for a few seconds, then the scene changes. Once more we see them at the breakfast table, but the atmosphere has changed. Discord is beginning to creep into the conversation. Brief scene after brief scene follows, each showing the gradual breakdown of their affection, until finally they read their newspapers, opposite each other, in silence.

"For this montage, I used the old classic form of the theme and variations. A waltz in the style of Waldteufel is the theme. It is heard during the first scene. Then, as discord crops up, the variations begin. Each scene is a separate variation. Finally, the waltz theme is heard bleakly played in the high registers of the violins."

In brief, in the music for this sequence, Herrmann begins with a waltz associated with the early period of Kane's marriage to his first wife, Emily (RUTH WARRICK), and concludes on a sour note, presaging how the deterioration of their marriage will end in divorce.

If Emily is linked to an elegant waltz that recalls the 19th-century composer Emil Waldteufel, Kane's second wife, Susan (DOROTHY COMINGORE), is linked with brash, lowdown jazz. When the reporter Jerry Thompson (WILLIAM ALLAND) pays Susan a visit in the wake of Kane's death, she is singing in a tawdry Atlantic City cabaret, El Rancho. While he interviews her, the 1933 jazz tune, "In a Mizz," by Charles Barnet and Haven Johnson, is playing in the background. Herrmann repeats the number in a flashback in which Kane quarrels bitterly with Susan in the midst of a picnic in the Everglades shortly before their breakup. This time the lyrics are audible on the sound track, and they comment ironically on the angry couple: "There ain't no true love."

In an earlier flashback, Kane futilely attempts to make Susan an opera star; Herrmann was called upon to compose a mini-opera for Susan's debut. Welles dispatched a telegram to Herrmann on July 18, 1940, three months before Herrmann came to Hollywood; it is cited in *This Is Orson Welles:* "Opera sequence is early in shooting, so must have fully orchestrated recorded track before shooting. Susie sings as the curtain goes up in the first act, and I believe there is no opera of importance where soprano leads with her chin like this. Therefore suggest it be original."

Welles wanted elaborate costumes and lavish scenery for the pseudo-opera, so he indicated that Herrmann's opera be modeled on *Salammbo,* by Ernest Reyer, which was derived from a novel by Flaubert; this would allow Susan to appear as a grand opera courtesan in ancient Carthage. Three days later, Herrmann wired Welles: "Think *Salammbo* idea the best. Grand opportunity for magnificent French-Oriental opera aria, . . . with heroine singing wild amorous aria while awaiting her lover." He added that Welles should supply a text for the aria.

During further interchanges Herrmann and Welles concurred that Susan's singing should not be blatantly awful, but rather amateurish and weak, in order to arouse pity, rather than derision, in the filmgoer. JOHN HOUSEMAN, who worked with Welles on his stage and radio productions, wrote the brief

French libretto for the fake opera—with lines borrowed from French playwright Racine's *Phèdre,* and not from Flaubert's novel. Herrmann entitled the opera *Salaambo,* rather than *Salammbo,* to indicate to opera buffs that he was writing in the manner of Reyer's *Salammbo,* but not actually using Reyer's work. He said that his *Salaambo* was composed in the style of the 19th-century French operatic school of Reyer, Massenet, and Saint-Saëns. His deliberately overdone orchestration goes beyond the more bombastic opera scores of the German composer Richard Strauss (*Salome*), whom he had in mind while orchestrating his *Salaambo.*

Herrmann wrote an orchestral prelude, an opening aria for soprano, another aria to follow it, and a final aria to ring down the curtain. Welles ultimately edited out the middle aria, and cut directly from Susan's opening aria to the aria at the finale. Thomas, who has written the best article on Herrmann's score for *Kane,* emphasizes that during the performance Susan is not singing off-key, as some film critics have assumed. "Dorothy Commingore has been dubbed by a light lyric soprano who agreed to sing out of her range and to strain her natural abilities," thereby indicating that Susan simply cannot reach the higher registers that the score calls for. Similarly, Herrmann states in "The Contemporary Use of Music in Film" that he wrote Susan's role in the opera for a voice far exceeding the singer's capabilities, "so that a girl with a modest voice like Susan's" would be completely hopeless in it.

Welles actually hired Jean Forward, a 16-year-old soprano from the San Francisco Opera, to dub Susan's vocal part in the opera. "Using a massive orchestra," larger than he employed for the rest of the film, Herrmann adds a "Straussian dimension" to the Reyer palette, Callow comments: "horns whooping, trumpets braying, flutes skirling, over which the soprano hurls herself, surfing over the cascades of glissandi, finally leaping up to a lurid high D," which she never quite reaches. Forward's voice was "true but tiny," and Welles set her adrift in a sea of heavy orchestral accompaniment; "like Susan Alexander Kane, she sinks," Callow concludes. In summary, Herrmann told Ted Gilling, Susan is portrayed as singing in a key that is too high for her voice; that—

combined with the overpowering orchestration—give the effect that she is struggling "in quicksand." This is just what Jed Leland (JOSEPH COTTEN) means when he says in his review of Susan's performance that she is "an incompetent amateur."

In the film's epilogue, which takes place after Kane's death, the "Power" theme and the "Rosebud" theme from the prologue return. The camera pulls back to show a long shot of the great hall of Kane's castle, Xanadu. Kane's collection of paintings and statues, scattered pell-mell all over the place, are surrounded by large packing cases. The "Power" theme is heard in the muted brass, "as a final comment on Kane's life," Herrmann observes in "Score for a Film." The mood is morbid and brooding. Among the bric-a-brac is the old sled, Rosebud, which Kane had cherished from his childhood; it lies among the discarded items that have been consigned to a blazing furnace, where the flames devour it. The "Rosebud" theme is heard when the burning sled is shown in close-up, this time played by full orchestra.

Then the film's opening shot is reversed, as the camera retreats from Kane's mansion and winds up outside the gate with the NO TRESPASSING sign once more visible, as the "Rosebud" theme and the "Power" theme are heard for the last time. Herrmann pulls out all the stops as the final chords are played, featuring brass, percussion, and high strings.

Herrmann concludes his essay:

"Finally, a word about the dubbing of the music—that is, the recording of the score into the final sound track. Too often, in Hollywood, the composer has little to say about this technical procedure. Two full weeks were spent in the dubbing room," and the music was recorded under the supervision of both Welles and Herrmann. "The result is an exact projection of the original ideas in the score. Technically no composer could ask for more."

After *Citizen Kane,* Herrmann scored William Dieterle's *The Devil and Daniel Webster* (1941, a.k.a. *All That Money Can Buy*), in which a failed farmer sells his soul to the devil (WALTER HUSTON) for seven years of good luck. He is saved from hell by the 19th-century orator Daniel Webster (Edward Arnold), who eloquently pleads his case before Satan and a jury of the damned. Leslie Halliwell says the film displays "the whole cinematic box of tricks which Hollywood had just learned again through *Citizen Kane.*" Inexplicably, Herrmann won an Academy Award for this picture, rather than for *Kane.*

Herrmann's score for *Kane* was passed over by the Motion Picture Academy possibly because he inserted some preexisting music by other composers in the underscore. For example, as noted already, the song that is sung at the *Inquirer* party, "Oh, Mr. Kane," was adapted from a Mexican march; and the jazz tune "In a Mizz" was sung in the background at the Everglades picnic. In addition, Herrmann borrowed music from the studio music library for the fake newsreel about Kane's life—which was precisely the source of the music that was used in newsreels at the time.

When film composer John Addison (*Tom Jones*), chairman of the music branch of the Motion Picture Academy, was asked by a journalist in 1987 about the norms by which the committee judged scores nominated for an Oscar, he replied that they took a dim view of "scores diluted by the use of preexisting music," not written by the composer, unless the amount of original music substantially outweighed the borrowed music. Addision cited a score that had lost out that year (Abigail Mead's music for STANLEY KUBRICK's *Full Metal Jacket*) because 50 percent of the movie's music consisted of pop tunes used throughout the score; and only half of the score therefore was the original work of the composer. In Herrmann's case, *Kane* has, all told, 23 minutes of preexisting music punctuating the dramatic score, while 32 minutes of music is his own original scoring—well over half of the total dramatic score for the picture.

As a matter of fact, Herrmann's "Devil's Violin Concerto" in *The Devil and Daniel Webster,* a demonic *danse macabre,* was built on "Pop Goes the Weasel"; still the entire underscore for the film has a larger percentage of original music than the score for *Kane.* While Herrmann's background music for *Devil* is certainly adequate, it is simply no match for what Joseph Miliciar terms Herrmann's "virtuoso fusion of music and drama" in *Kane.*

Welles commissioned Herrmann to score his next picture, *The Magnificent Ambersons,* from the Booth Tarkington novel, set in the late 19th century. The film opens with a horse-drawn trolley stopping on the street where the Ambersons, one of the first families of Indianapolis, live. A theme from Waldteufel's waltz suite "Toujours ou jamais" is heard, with Herrmann's variations of the theme played throughout the scene. The wistful, fragile waltz (a favorite of Welles) is perfectly suited to a film that portrays a bygone era. Emily's theme in *Kane,* we recall, also evoked Waldteufel. Emil Waldteufel composed light dance music in the vein of Johann Strauss, Jr.; and, like Strauss, he was best known for his waltzes. Later on, the liveliness of a winter scene, in which young George (TIM HOLT), the Amberson heir, takes his girl for a sleigh ride, is captured by Herrmann's airy, tinkling tune, which he entitled "Snow Ride" in the score. Herrmann gave the sequence "a sort of music-box orchestration," JAMES NAREMORE observes, "evoking the sparkle of ice and the jingle of bells."

The fortunes of the Amberson family steadily decline in the course of the picture. Herrmann embellished the elegant Christmas ball in the Amberson family mansion with a lovely waltz. As CHARLES HIGHAM describes the scene, "A fine, gliding camera movement accompanies the guests" as they assemble for the festivities. "The camera retreats before them, taking in richly flowered wallpaper, chandeliers, the shimmer of brasswork," as the couples engage in a formal dance.

Herrmann's bittersweet waltz, Higham comments, is sentimental, yet touched with sadness, prefiguring how the once-proud Amberson clan is facing a bleak future. As Thomas notes, "Waltzes associated with disintegration and decay became one of Herrmann's trademarks," never more apparent than in *Ambersons.*

Herrmann's score for *Kane,* as we know, was recorded under the supervision of both the director and the composer. But Herrmann was not so lucky with *Ambersons.* The studio recut the movie after Welles was sent to South America to make IT'S ALL TRUE. On the basis of some negative reactions by the audience to previews of *Ambersons,* ROBERT WISE, who edited the film, told this writer, the studio replaced the closing sequence that Welles had shot with a substitute ending. It was filmed by another director, as Wise, who later became a director himself (*West Side Story*) stated.

When Herrmann learned that his score had been tampered with in the course of the reediting of the movie, and that a studio composer, Roy Webb, had supplied the music for the substitute scenes, the temperamental Herrmann insisted that his name be removed from the film's credits. Interestingly enough, when Milan Music released a recording entitled *Bernard Herrmann Film Scores* in 1993, with Elmer Bernstein conducting the Royal Philharmonic, the final track, called "Bernard Herrmann on Film Music," gives Herrmann's remarks, which were recorded before his death in 1975. He declares unequivocally that he scored both *Kane* and *Ambersons*.

Herrmann was slated to do the score for JOURNEY INTO FEAR, which Welles was set to direct and star in. This World War II thriller about smuggling munitions into Turkey was taken away from him by the studio in the wake of several artistic differences. Welles was replaced by NORMAN FOSTER as director, although he still played Colonel Haki, head of the Turkish Secret Service; he also unofficially supervised the scenes in which he appeared and helped out Foster with some other scenes as well. Nevertheless, Herrmann left the film after it was taken away from Welles, and his unfinished score was completed by Roy Webb, who received sole screen credit for the music (just as Foster received sole screen credit as director).

Be that as it may, Herrmann was committed to writing film music, given his Oscar for *The Devil and Daniel Webster* and the wide acclaim he received for the *Kane* score. In the course of "Bernard Herrmann on Film Music," he explains why he devoted so much of his creative energy to movie music:

"A composer who writes for the cinema reaches a worldwide audience"; moreover, music makes a significant contribution to the art of cinema, because film depends on music: "A film cannot come to life without the help of music of some kind; a film is not complete without music." He recalls receiving letters from filmgoers asserting that movies need little or no music at all: "This is rubbish. All you have to do is look at a film without music and it would be almost unbearable to look at."

"A film is made up of segments that are put together—artificially linked by dissolves or cuts or montages. It is the function of music to cement these pieces into one design; hence the audience feels that the sequence of scenes is inevitable." In other words, musical bridges lead the filmgoer from one scene to the next.

Herrmann died in his sleep after completing the recording sessions for his underscore for Martin Scorsese's *Taxi Driver* (1976). Robert De Niro starred as the deeply disturbed New York taxi driver of the title, who becomes obsessed with the violence and squalor of the netherworld in which he works; the film climaxes with his final descent into lurid violence, which is harrowing to watch. Some critics found the movie a brilliant evocation of hell on earth; others thought it irredeemably sordid and repelling—but all of them seemed to agree that Herrmann's final film score was among the movie's discernable virtues. As one critic put it, watching the film without Herrmann's music would have made the violence unbearable. This observation recalls Herrmann's own statement in "Bernard Herrmann on Film Music" that, without music, any film would be unbearable to look at.

Herrmann was nominated for an Academy Award for *Taxi Driver* and actually won posthumously the award for best score from the British Academy of Film and Television Arts.

Herrmann composed operas like *Wuthering Heights,* ballets, a symphony, and a cantata, *Moby Dick.* In "Bernard Herrmann on Film Music" he explains why he wrote more for the film medium than for the concert hall: "I feel it as the responsibility of any gifted composer of our time to do a certain amount of creative work in the media. All composers have to do the music of their time. Mozart and Hayden were not above writing dinner music for playing while their patrons ate; Bach thought nothing of writing his weekly cantata for a church service. It's only a question of the time in which one lives. At the present time cinema and television are the great vehicles for contemporary music."

Herrmann was convinced that no director understood the function of music as a narrative device better than Orson Welles. Furthermore, his scores for both Welles and Hitchcock make it plain that he established a powerful, distinctive style that continues to be emulated.

References Brady, Frank. *Citizen Welles: A Biography of Orson Welles* (New York: Scribner's, 1989); Brown, Royal. "Herrmann, Hitchcock, and the Music of the Irrational," *Cinema Journal* (Spring 1982): 25–35; Callow, Simon. *Orson Welles: The Road to Xanadu* (New York: Penguin, 1997); De Palma, Brian. "Remembering Herrmann," *Take One,* Special Hitchcock issue (May 1976): 41; Donnelly, Kevin. ed., *Film Music: Bernard Herrmann and Other Composers* (New York: Continuum, 2001); Gilling, Ted. "The Color of the Music," *Sight and Sound* 41 (new series), no. 1 (Winter 1971): 36–39; Halliwell, Leslie. *Film Guide,* ed. John Walker, rev. ed. (New York: HarperCollins, 2001); Herrmann, Bernard. "The Contemporary Use of Music in Film: *Citizen Kane* and *Psycho,*" *University Film Study Center Newsletter* 7, no. 3 (February 1977): 5–10; ———. "Score for a Film," in *Perspectives on Citizen Kane,* ed. Ronald Gottesman (New York: G. K. Hall, 1996), 573–75; Higham, Charles. *The Films of Orson Welles* (Los Angeles: University of California Press, 1973); LoBrutto, Vincent. *Stanley Kubrick: An Autobiography* (New York: Da Capo, 1999); Naremore, James. *The Magic World of Orson Welles* (Dallas, Tex.: Southern Methodist University Press, 1989); Thomas, François. "Music Keys to *Kane,*" in *Perspectives on Citizen Kane,* ed. Ronald Gottesman (New York: G. K. Hall, 1996), 172–96; Welles, Orson, and Peter Bogdanovich. *This Is Orson Welles* (New York: Da Capo, 1998); Wood, Bret. *Orson Welles: A Bio-Bibliography* (New York: Greenwood Press, 1990).

—G.D.P.

Heston, Charlton (1924–) Charlton Heston was born Charles Carter on October 4, 1924, in Evanston, Illinois; he took the name of his stepfather while still a child. He was educated at New Trier High School in Winnetka, Illinois, and at Northwestern University in Evanston. After his service in the Air Force during World War II, he gained stage experience at the Thomas Wolfe Memorial Theater in Asheville, North Carolina. Heston's Broadway stage debut was in *Antony and Cleopatra,* starring KATHARINE CORNELL. He gained national attention by playing in some classic dramas on the TV series *Studio One.* His first film was William Dieterle's noir, *Dark City* (1950). Heston appeared in such films as Cecil B. DeMille's *Greatest Show on Earth* (1952) and *The Ten Commandments* (1956), before being asked to star in *TOUCH OF EVIL* at Universal. He played Miguel "Mike" Vargas, a Mexican police detective; he was offered the role because Universal wanted a bankable star in the picture. For those who complained about a white actor playing a Hispanic, Heston declared to James Delson that he played Vargas as an intelligent, educated professional; his performance "doesn't contribute to the stereotype of the sombrero Mexican lazing around in the shade."

It was Heston's clout that enabled ORSON WELLES to direct as well as co-star in the film. Welles played Hank Quinlan, a smalltown police inspector who has taken to framing suspects when he fears he does not have enough evidence on them to get a conviction. In Heston's autobiography, he recalls that when the studio called him about the part, they said, "We've got Welles to play the heavy." Heston wondered if they could really not have thought of the obvious: "Why not ask him to direct too? He's a pretty good director, you know." Since the films that Welles had directed earlier in the 1950s had not been hits, the front office hired Welles as director as well as actor on the stipulation that he would be paid only for acting in the picture. So Orson directed what turned out to be a classic film for nothing. Moreover, the parsimonious studio allocated a budget "of less than a million dollars for the whole film," Heston continues; "that left little money for the actors. Nevertheless, they all wanted to work for Orson, in the first film he'd directed in Hollywood in ten years." MARLENE DIETRICH, JOSEPH COTTEN, and other stars appeared in cameos just to be in a Welles film.

One reason the film had a tight budget, Heston explains, was that "Orson came on the picture like the chains clanking behind Marley's ghost. He didn't deserve it. He had his flaws as a filmmaker, but waste and inefficiency were not among them. I know directors who have wasted more money on one picture than Orson spent on the sum total of all the films he made in his career.

"Still, he knew he had to make the studio believe in him. He did this very resourcefully. The Sunday before shooting started, Orson called some of the actors to his house for an undercover rehearsal of the first day's work, a sound-stage interior of a tiny apartment. The next day, Orson began laying out a master shot that covered the whole scene. It was a very complicated setup, with walls pulling out of the way as the camera moved from room to room, and four principal actors, plus three or four bit players, working through the scene."

The scene, which was 12 pages long, "was scheduled for three days of shooting, which is about reasonable," Heston continues; "that would be a little over four pages a day." Welles worked out the technical problems of shooting the complicated scene with director of photography RUSSELL METTY, who had photographed THE STRANGER. The scene depicts how Quinlan surreptitiously places dynamite in the motel room of Manuelo Sanchez as spurious evidence that the suspect caused an explosion that killed two Americans.

On the first day of shooting, Heston recalls, "Lunch came and went and we were still rehearsing the shot; no camera had yet turned. Studio executives began to gather in uneasy little knots in corners, a bit daunted about approaching Orson while he was cuing an extra's move just as the tracking camera picked him up. They were also very worried. With most of the first day gone, not a frame of film had passed through the gate yet.

"About four o'clock, Orson called for a take, the first of a good many. Just after six, he said silkily, 'Cut! Print the last three takes. That's a wrap on this set; we're two days ahead of schedule.' He'd designed his master to include all the coverage he needed in the twelve-page scene, scheduled for three shooting days: close-ups, two shots, over-shoulders, and inserts. All this was planned, of course, to astound Universal, which it surely did. It was also a fine way to shoot the scene.

"The front-office people never came near the set again. They kept hoping for another miraculous twelve-page day. They never got one, but Orson had persuaded them that even if he did get into trouble, he could get out of it. As a matter of fact, they were dead right; he had a remarkably sure foot for tightropes."

Delson commented to Heston that he handled himself well "when the famous Wellsian scene-stealing took place." For example, when Vargas confronts Quinlan with his suspicion that Quinlan planted evidence of Sanchez's motel room, Quinlan raises his cane in anger; its threatening shadow falls across Vargas's face, implying how Quinlan overshadows Vargas at this point—he still has power and influence in the town. In playing the scene Heston did not flinch in the face of Welles's threatening gaze, as Delson pointed out to him. "Well, I am happy to subscribe to the thesis that I can stand on equal ground with Orson in a scene," he answered.

"We finished the film on April 2," Heston records in his autobiography; "we were one night over our thirty-day schedule; and $31,000 over the $900,000 budget—a reasonable overage, considering the meagerness of the budget to begin with. Welles supervised the editing and dubbing of the rough cut throughout the summer. After Welles delivered the rough cut to Universal, Edward Muhl, studio chief, found the film excessively gloomy and dark; he therefore asked Edward Nims, head of post-production, who had edited The Stranger, to reedit certain scenes. Muhl further enlisted a young journeyman contract director named Harry Keller to shoot a few brief additional scenes to clarify the story line. These scenes were shot on November 19, 1957, with Welles barred from the set.

"They did a half day's work without me," Welles told PETER BOGDANOVICH. "Heston kept phoning me to say what he was doing, and to ask if it was all right, because if I didn't approve he would walk off the set." Welles dispatched a letter to Heston, cited in This Is Orson Welles, on November 17, implying that Heston should at the very least "insist on a certain standard of professional capacity and reputation in the choice of an alternate director. UNLESS THE STUDIO IS STOPPED THEY ARE GOING TO WRECK OUR PICTURE." (The caps are Welles's.) He refers to Heston's owning a piece of the film, saying, "You must realize that, if you have a financial interest in the picture, I have a professional one."

After Heston consulted with his lawyer and made one last futile appeal to Muhl, he shot the additional footage with Keller. When Heston reported to Welles that he was satisfied with Keller's work, Welles replied immediately in another letter: "The fact that your director is not, after all, a certifiable incompetent" seemed to be enough to satisfy Heston. He was reserving judgment until he saw Nims's cut of the film, and he did so on August 28. He fired off a 58-page memo to Muhl, suggesting some improvements. Welles later sent a copy to Heston, with a cover letter, in which he stated that Muhl assured him that Nims was honoring many of Welles's suggestions. Welles only hoped that that was true.

As a matter of fact, some of the modifications that Welles suggested were made, but the front office ultimately cut the film from 108 minutes to 93 minutes to run as the bottom half of a double bill, with no press showing. In 1976, the missing footage was discovered and restored to the film. In the 1990s, Welles's memo was unearthed, and the film was released on video and DVD in a version closely approximating Welles's suggestions. If some of Welles's scenes that had been originally jettisoned were restored, so were those that Keller shot. There is one scene of Keller's that is easy to spot.

In it Vargas and his new wife, Susan (JANET LEIGH), are driving down a country road together. The actors converse amorously in front of a process screen, with images of traffic footage projected on it. By contrast, when Welles shot scenes in a moving car, he insisted on filming them on location on a real road, in the interests of realism. So the rear-screen projection in Keller's car scene gives it away as not being Welles's work; at its conclusion Vargas stops the car and kisses his wife—the studio brass insisted on this bit of romance because they felt that the film was lacking in love interest. Suffice it to say that scene is executed in a perfunctory, uninspired fashion that likewise indicates that Welles did not film it.

Asked by Bogdanovich how he liked working with Heston, Welles replied, "He's the nicest man to work with that ever lived in movies. . . . All you have to do is point, and Chuck can go any direction." Stuart Kaminsky observes, "Beginning with his portrayal of the Mexican border detective Vargas in *Touch of Evil,* Heston has been enthusiastically willing to risk supporting the work of a director or writer who appears to be commercially off limits. In each case Heston has chosen to play characters who question the rigid ideals of heroism, the very ideals with which he is often associated" in films like William Wyler's *Ben-Hur* (1959). Such maverick characters were played by Heston in Nicholas Ray's *55 Days at Peking* (1962) and Sam Peckinpah's *Major Dundee* (1965). The versatile actor continued acting throughout the 1990s; he played a cameo role in Tim Burton's *Planet of the Apes* (2001), a remake of Franklin Schaffer's original version, which starred Heston in 1967.

References Delson, James. "Heston on Welles," in *Perspectives on Orson Welles,* ed. Morris Beja (New York: G. K. Hall, 1995), 63–72; Heston, Charlton. *In the Arena: An Autobiography* (New York: Simon & Schuster, 1995); Kaminsky, Stuart. "Charlton Heston," in *International Dictionary of Films and Filmmakers: Actors,* ed. Nicholas Thomas, rev. ed. (Detroit: St. James Press, 1997), vol. 3, 459–61; Murch, Walter. "Restoring the Touch of Genius to *Touch of Evil,*" *New York Times,* September 6, 1998, sec. 2:1, 16; Welles, Orson, and Peter Bogdanovich. *This Is Orson Welles* (New York: Da Capo, 1998).

—G.D.P.

Higham, Charles (1931–) Charles Higham, a prolific journalistic critic and celebrity biographer, is portrayed as a character in WELLES's THE OTHER SIDE OF THE WIND, filmed in 1970 but still unfinished in 1985, when St. Martin's Press published his book, *Orson Welles: The Rise and Fall of an American Genius.* This study of Welles followed best-selling biographies with similarly structured titles, such as *Bette: The Life of Bette Davis, Kate: The Life of Katharine Hepburn, Errol Flynn: The Untold Story, Marlene: The Life of Marlene Dietrich,* and *Charles Laughton: An Intimate Biography.* His St. Martin's Press book on Welles followed *The Films of Orson Welles,* published by the University of California Press in 1970. RONALD GOTTESMAN included a chapter from this book in his critical anthology, *Focus on Citizen Kane* (Prentice Hall, 1971), because Higham's first book on Welles "shows how much can and needs to be done with respect to assembling the facts about a film's conception, production, and release, about the incredibly complicated interdependence of contributors that is at once the bane and glory of film-making." Another Higham title that touched upon the work of Orson Welles was *Hollywood Cameramen,* published by Indiana University Press in 1970 in the "Cinema One" series. This book included a chapter on STANLEY CORTEZ (born Stanley Krantz in 1908), who was the lighting

cameraman for THE MAGNIFICENT AMBERSONS (1942). Ambersons is discussed in detail since Cortez established a "rapport" with Welles and was given "complete freedom" on the project. Higham's second Welles book, *The Rise and Fall of an American Genius,* was extensively researched when Higham had an appointment as Regents Professor at the University of California at Santa Cruz, at which time he interviewed DOLORES DEL RÍO, JOSEPH COTTEN, WILLIAM ALLAND, ROBERT WISE, Stanley Cortez, and others who had known and worked with Welles. "Today in his seventieth year," Higham writes in his Introduction, "Orson Welles is as famous as he has ever been. His Paul Masson wine commercials, glowing with good cheer, recently reestablished him as a public figure with a whole new generation that could barely have known his name." The director's public image was perhaps second only to that of Alfred Hitchcock in America. Higham sorts out deceptions Welles had planted with interviewers, telling KENNETH TYNAN, for example "that he was from unmixed English colonial stock, when in fact his family had both Welsh and French elements; that his father was born in Virginia and moved to Wisconsin because he owned two factories there, when in fact he was the son of an obscure Missouri railroad clerk," that he "inaccurately claimed to be related to Under Secretary of State Sumner Welles and to Adlai Stevenson," and that "he had met Ravel and Stravinsky through his mother, when in fact he had not." Additional fabrications were foisted upon his friend the French critic MAURICE BESSY, "head of the Cannes Film Festival, who wrote a book-length essay in French on Welles's life and philosophy." Intending to sort out these scrambled facts, Higham effectively placed Welles in a historical context in 1985, the year the book was published, and, unfortunately, the year the larger-than-life director died. Higham's book concludes with two appendixes, the first covering radio, television, film, and theater, the second a discography (done in collaboration with Miles Kreuger), followed by a selected bibliography and index. It represents a major contribution to Welles scholarship.

—J.M.W.

Hill, Roger (Skipper) (1895–1991) Roger "Skipper" Hill, who later became the school head-master, taught English, ran the athletic program, specializing in basketball, and directed the theater offerings at the Todd School, which his father, Noble Hill, owned and where he was the headmaster while ORSON WELLES attended Todd. Hill was perhaps his only friend. According to Welles, who spoke on his radio show, "AN EVENING WITH ORSON WELLES," "I fell in love with Roger Hill. I tried to find a way to capture the attention of this fascinating man who fascinates me tonight as much as he did the first I laid eyes on him." BARBARA LEAMING describes Hill as "the father that Welles desperately wanted: strong but not threatening, trustworthy without being predictable, many-layered but not complicated." At Todd, Welles participated in drama and with the cooperation of Hill was responsible for several outstanding productions. Their friendship lasted until Welles's death. According to DAVID THOMSON, it was at Todd that Welles learned "to use the school's limited technical resources to great effect," thereby acquiring the ability to make "a lot out of a little." During his first year at Todd, Welles put on musicals, designed sets, and acted in plays as the leader of the Todd Troupers, a student group Hill assembled to stage productions on campus and on the road, thereby providing his company with more critical audiences. The Todd Troupers even performed at the Goodman Theatre in Chicago. In his last year at Todd, Welles and Hill mounted a production of *JULIUS CAESAR,* which Welles adapted, directed, and acted in as both Cassius and Antony. Welles was so close to Hill that when Welles's father died, and Welles was free to name his guardian, he wanted Hill; but because of his long-standing relationship with DR. MAURICE BERNSTEIN, chose him, with Hill's assent.

When Welles graduated from Todd, Hill urged him to attend Harvard, but Welles headed for Ireland, where he began his professional acting career. During his year abroad, he kept in touch with both Bernstein and Hill, and when he returned to the United States, he went back to Todd, where he (Hill hired him as Todd's drama coach) and Hill put on *TWELFTH NIGHT,* planned an acting edition of Shakespeare's plays, which they hoped to publish (after being published by the Todd Press, the plays were put together by Harper & Row and sold as EVERYBODY'S SHAKE-SPEARE), and worked on *Marching Song,* a play about abolitionist John Brown. After another year in Europe, Welles again returned to Todd and went on tour with the GUTHRIE MCCLINTIC/KATHERINE CORNELL repertory company during 1933 and 1934. In the summer of 1934, Welles again returned to Todd, this time to stage a summer stock drama festival at Woodstock, a nearby town. With Hill's financial backing and the aid of actors HILTON EDWARDS and MICHEÁL MACLIAMMÓIR, with whom he had acted at Dublin's GATE THEATRE, Welles staged three plays. After the summer festival, Welles moved to New York City, where Virginia Nicholson soon joined him. Roger Hill and his wife, Hortense, were among the guests at both the secret and the official weddings of Welles and Nicholson. After the Welles/JOHN HOUSE-MAN *'Tis Pity She's a Whore* production foundered, Welles and his wife returned to Woodstock, where Hill bought them a car and supplied them with a weekly allowance while Welles was to work on an autobiographical play, *Bright Lucifer,* with the understanding that Hill would receive a share of any profits the play made. Hill remained a loyal and reliable Welles supporter. When CITIZEN KANE had its Chicago premiere, Hill wrote a special song for the occasion and had it sung by some of his Todd Troupers. In 1947 when he was preparing to shoot his OTHELLO film, for which he had no American financing, he called on Hill to send him some film stock so that he could begin the film. Barbara Leaming writes, "There was something boyish and impulsive about the enterprise [*Othello*] so that, for Orson, it was only natural to think of, and to appeal to, the Todd School when no one else was about to help." Welles and Hill, who spent a great deal of time working on Todd/Welles memorabilia, maintained their correspondence; and in 1978, Hill appeared at the American Film Institute's *Working with Welles* series. In 1983, at Welles's invitation, Hill visited him in California and was alarmed at Welles's physical and mental condition. He advised Welles to give up filmmaking. Meanwhile, Hill's own physical condition was deteriorating and he had to be hospitalized. After working with Welles, who sought his help in reediting *Rip Van Winkle Renascent,* a Todd School

film, Hill returned home. He came back to Hollywood, however, for the Welles memorial service, at which he gave a moving tribute.

—T.L.E.

His Honor, the Mayor (radio, 1941)

This program is of primary interest for what it reveals about WELLES's political mind-set during the turbulent months prior to U.S. entry into World War II. The broadcast also became entangled in the turmoil surrounding CITIZEN KANE. The origins of the program start with a memorandum from the U.S. Justice Department to historical novelist James Boyd to counter Axis propaganda in the United States through a series of radio broadcasts devoted to dramatizing the essential meaning of the U.S. Constitution's Bill of Rights. Out of this noble yet pragmatic political undertaking was born The Free Company, whose members included noted writers Robert E. Sherwood, William Saroyan, Marc Connelly, Stephen Vincent Benét, Maxwell Anderson, ARCHIBALD MACLEISH, Paul Green, Sherwood Anderson, and Boyd. Welles was invited to join the effort and contributed *His Honor, the Mayor,* a 30-minute drama for which he served as narrator.

Broadcast on CBS on April 5, 1941, the story, which Welles wrote in the midst of editing *Citizen Kane,* concerned a public official who champions the rights of his enemies, the "White Crusaders," to free assembly. Inspired by the ideals of Abraham Lincoln, the freedom-loving mayor defuses a volatile situation driven by racial, political, and class hatred. Embedded within the drama is an olive branch directed to HERMAN J. MANKIEWICZ, Welles's estranged co-author of *Citizen Kane.* In the drama, the one Jewish family in the small Texas border town is named Mankiewicz; although the target of the White Crusaders' anti-Semitism, the Mankiewiczes are good people, loved and respected by everyone else. As for casting, Welles used his principal players from *Citizen Kane,* RAY COLLINS (Mayor Knaggs), AGNES MOOREHEAD (the mayor's wife), PAUL STEWART, ERSKINE SANFORD, RICHARD WILSON, and EVERETT SLOANE.

After the broadcast, and to everyone's surprise, *His Honor, the Mayor* was savagely attacked by the newspapers of WILLIAM RANDOLPH HEARST. Like the

Hearst papers' attack on the as yet unreleased *Citizen Kane* several months earlier, again, Welles, and now The Free Company, were accused of propagandizing on behalf of communism. Significantly, although The Free Company's broadcasts had been running for several months, *His Honor, the Mayor* was the first of its shows to be smeared. The transparency of Hearst's assault was picked up immediately. *Time* magazine, coming to Welles's defense, pointed out that the slurs coincided with the imminent release of *Citizen Kane* and could therefore be discounted. Welles received similar support from the *New York Times,* which editorialized that future historians might be misled by Hearst's yellow journalism if "unaware that the campaign against Mr. Welles was more concerned with a motion picture [i.e., *Citizen Kane*] than with radio."

Welles came to his own defense in a statement carried by many non-Hearst papers: "William Randolph Hearst is conducting a series of brutal attacks on me in his newspapers. It seems he doesn't like my picture *Citizen Kane.* I understand he hasn't seen it. I am sure he hasn't. If he had, I think he would agree with me that those who have advised him that 'Kane' is Hearst have done us both an injustice. I have stood by silently in the hope that this vicious attack against me would be spent in the passing of a few weeks. I had hoped that I would not continue to be the target of patriotic organizations who are accepting false statements and condemning me without knowing the facts. But I can't remain silent any longer. The Hearst papers have repeatedly described me as a Communist. I am not a Communist. I am grateful for our constitutional form of government, and I rejoice in our great American tradition of democracy. Needless to say, it is not necessarily unpatriotic to disagree with Mr. Hearst. On the contrary, it is a privilege guaranteed me as an American citizen by the Bill of Rights."

A further consequence of the fallout from the broadcast of *His Honor, the Mayor* precipitated by Hearst's scurrilous attacks on it and *Citizen Kane,* was the onset of FBI surveillance of Welles that lasted for years. Later, Welles sued a gossip columnist who had called him a communist in print, a case he won in Los Angeles Superior Court. Eventually, and in spite of "evidence" supplied by Hearst sympathizers, FBI director J. Edgar Hoover backed down and closed the file. Welles was a liberal, but never a communist.

—C.B.

History of the World: Part I Brooksfilms/ Twentieth Century–Fox, 92 minutes, 1981. **Director:** Mel Brooks; **Producer:** Brooks; **Screenplay:** Brooks; **Cinematographer:** Woody Omens; **Music:** Brooks and John Morris; **Editor:** John C. Howard; **Cast:** Mel Brooks (Moses/Comicus/Torquemada/Jacques/Louis XVI), Dom DeLuise (Julius Ceasar), Madeline Kahn (Empress Nympho), Harvey Korman (Count De Monet), Cloris Leachman (Madame Lafarge), Ron Carey (Swiftus), Gregory Hines (Josephus), Sid Ceasar (Chief Caveman), Pamela Stephenson (Mademoiselle Rimbaud); Henny Youngman (Chemist), Mary-Margaret Humes (Miriam), and Orson Welles (Narrator)

Mel Brooks's *History of the World: Part I* is a noisy and unfocused send-up of everything sacred. It is divided, in vaudeville-like fashion, into a number of skits: *Dawn of Man; The Stone Age; Old Testament; The Roman Empire; The Spanish Inquisition; The French Revolution;* and *Coming Attractions,* the latter punched up by a "Jews in Space" intergalactic musical extravaganza. To add mock solemnity to the occasion, Brooks hired WELLES and his mellifluous voice-of-authority to provide narration emanating, it seems, from heaven itself.

The film found little support among the critics. *Halliwell's Film and Video Guide,* for example, dismissed it as "a woeful collection of schoolboy scatology." Even Roger Ebert, a Brooks partisan, found little to like. Like *Halliwell's,* the *Chicago Sun-Times* critic found that "It is in unfunny bad taste." Ebert also points to one of the film's problems: "It thumbs its nose at icons that have lost their taboo value for most of us, and between the occasional good laughs, we're a little embarrassed that the movie is so dumb and predictable."

—C.B.

Holt, Tim (Charles John Holt) (1918–1973) Tim Holt played the part of George Minafer in WELLES's *THE MAGNIFICENT AMBERSONS* (1942). Holt was born on February 5, 1918, in Beverly Hills, California. His father, Jack Holt, was an established western star in silent and sound films. His sister, Jennifer, and brother, David, also appeared in several westerns, some with their father. Holt attended Culver Military Academy, but found time for an early start as an actor. At the age of 10 he appeared in *The Vanishing Pioneer* (1928); and within nine years he had adult roles in not only Westerns (he reportedly said that John Ford had attempted to get him killed in some scenes in *Stagecoach* [1939]), but in some quality films, among them *Stella Dallas* (1937). Before Welles cast him in the role of George Minafer, a part Welles himself had taken in his radio adaptation of the BOOTH TARKINGTON novel on October 29, 1938, Welles told PETER BOGDANOVICH that he screened several of Holt's western films. Welles commented on Holt's performance: "One of the most

interesting actors that's ever been in American movies, and he *decided* to be just a cowboy actor. Made two or three important pictures in his career, but was very careful not to follow them up—went straight back to bread-and-butter westerns." CHARLES HIGHAM, who believes that several scenes with Holt and ANNE BAXTER (Lucy Morgan) were cut when the film was radically shortened, suggests that Welles may have cast Holt because he "looked rather like a small-boned, slighter version of Welles." (Higham sees George as Welles's alter ago and suggests that both George and Welles were due a "comeuppance.") Welles's assessment of Holt's career was on target. After *Ambersons,* Holt appeared in more westerns, the best of which were Ford's *My Darling Clementine* (1946) and JOHN HUSTON's *The Treasure of the Sierra Madre* (1948), in which

Tim Holt, Dolores Costello, and Joseph Cotten in *The Magnificent Ambersons* (Literature/Film Archive)

he played Curtin, Humphrey Bogart's conscientious partner—it was the best role of his career. After making *The Monster That Challenged the World* (1957), he apparently decided that it was time to abandon his film career. He went into business, and at the time of his death in 1973 he was the manager of an Oklahoma radio station.

Reference Lahue, Kalton C. *Riders of the Range: The Sagebrush Heroes of the Sound Screen* (South Brunswick, N.J.: A.S. Barnes, 1973).

—T.L.E.

Horne, Lena (1917–) Sultry black singer and actress Lena Horne had an affair with ORSON WELLES during the mid–1940s from the time Welles was acting in *JANE EYRE* (1944) through the time Horne was acting in *Ziegfeld Follies* (1946). The affair began before his marriage to RITA HAYWORTH and continued sporadically after it, even after Horne was married to Lennie Hayton. DAVID THOMSON discusses the relationship in terms of Welles's portrayal of Rochester in *Jane Eyre.* Noting that Welles's makeup for the film made him look quite dark, Thomson writes, "But his Rochester sports a sultry tan—as if we are meant to believe in his time spent in Jamaica, or because Welles had a fancy to look darker than his current girlfriend, Lena Horne." Thomson also speculates about Welles perhaps imagining her "in some movie that told the story of jazz, of song and the whole life America was denying itself in being so wary of things sepia." At any rate, Horne and Welles only once worked together professionally, on a radio show entitled "Something About Joe."

Lena Horne, who was born on June 30, 1917, in Brooklyn, was the daughter of a divorced actress. After she left school at 16, she joined the chorus at Harlem's Cotton Club and became a popular nightclub singer. She signed a contract with MGM soon after she turned 20, and her first film, *The Duke Is Tops,* was released in 1938. She was the first African American to sign a long-term contract with a major Hollywood studio, but her roles, which always included singing, were designed so that they could be cut from the pictures when they were screened in the South. She did have substantial roles in two all-black musicals, *Cabin in the Sky* and *Stormy Weather* (both in

1943). Thomson writes that LOUIS B. MAYER, head of MGM, "looked at her and wondered if he and MGM could let her pass [for white]," and concludes that "There was maybe too much of the lady in her, or too much anger at the white world, for her to be an actress." Horne did have trouble getting roles in the 1950s, when she was blacklisted because of her ties to outspoken activist Paul Robeson. In 1969, she played opposite Richard Widmark in *Death of a Gunfighter* and later appeared in *The Wiz* (1978). On the stage she received a Tony Award for *Lena Horne: The Lady and Her Music,* a one-woman show that she took on an international tour. She also received a Lifetime Achievement Award at the Kennedy Center in 1989. She has written two autobiographical volumes: *In Person* (1951) and *Lena* (1965).

References Haskins, James. *Lena Horne* (New York: Coward-McCann, 1983); Horne, Lena. *In Person* (New York: Greenberg, 1950); Palmer, Leslie. *Lena Horne* (New York: Chelsea House, 1989).

—T.L.E.

Horse Eats Hat (play, 1936) In April 1936, WELLES and producer JOHN HOUSEMAN broke into New York's theatrical big time with the infamous "voodoo" *MACBETH,* an exotic revamping of SHAKESPEARE's classic tragedy produced under the aegis of the NEGRO THEATRE PROJECT, a division of the FEDERAL THEATRE PROJECT. Believing that it was time for blacks to produce and direct, as well as act, Welles and Houseman convinced Federal Theatre chief HALLIE FLANAGAN to let them start a new federal theater group devoted to revivals of great dramas, a theater version of Mortimer Adler's "Great Books" program at the University of Chicago. Dubbed Project 891, the new troupe's official government file number, Welles and Houseman set up shop at the Maxine Elliott Theater in midtown Manhattan. After the *sturm und drang* of the "voodoo" *Macbeth,* Welles wanted to change the pace with something comedic, and spiced with sex. At the suggestion of composer VIRGIL THOMSON, Welles chose *Un Chapeau de Paille d'Italie (The Italian Straw Hat),* a 1851 farce by Eugene Labiche and Marc Michel, as Project 891's first undertaking.

Welles's approach to the show was influenced by French director RENÉ CLAIR's silent film version of the Labiche-Michel comedy, *The Italian Straw Hat* (1927). Specifically, Welles sought to transfer Clair's briskly paced cinematic action and suspenseful comic build-ups to the stage. He also wanted a franker approach to sex, something that Clair's film handled with Gallic charm and finesse. As the project approached its September 26, 1936, opening at the Maxine Elliott Theatre, Welles changed its name from *The Italian Straw Hat* to *Horse Eats Hat*. He had become concerned that using Clair's title might keep away those who had seen the film, and who might therefore have assumed that Welles's production was an adaptation of Clair's film. With the new title came a new approach.

In preparing the script with Edwin Denby, Welles shifted the time to the turn of the century. And by resetting it to the Midwest, the play became Americanized as well. Still, there was a Continental touch owing as much to the spirits of Dada and Surrealism as to Labiche and Michel. Indeed, Denby, who had lived in Paris, brought in elements of the 1920s' avant-garde. For his part, Welles, liberated from the sobering influence of John Houseman then in Canada working to extend his visa to America, gave vent to his passion for the robust knockabout traditions of vaudeville. His penchant for magic was yet another influence. Indeed, there was a complex, seven-door set by Nat Karson for "magical" appearances and disappearances. Bill Baird, the famous puppeteer, was recruited to design "break-up" furniture for the more riotous moments. Welles was also open to serendipity. In rehearsing a scene with JOSEPH COTTEN swinging on a chandelier, an on-stage fountain accidentally got turned on. Everyone laughed. Welles said, "keep it." A new gag had been added to the show. The circuslike atmosphere was further underscored by the exuberant music by PAUL BOWLES and Virgil Thomson. And at intermission, the audience was regaled by a band of musicians blasting away from a box near the stage. A player piano on the balcony added to the jollity.

The story of *Horse Eats Hat* is simple. A groom en route to his wedding loses a gift, an Italian straw hat, intended for his bride. His frantic efforts to find or replace the hat become the mainsprings driving the comic setups and chases. Along the way, the humor ranges from off-color and bawdy to vulgar. Learning of the script's sexual content, a representative of the WORKS PROGRESS ADMINISTRATION, the Federal Theatre's overseer, was sent to a rehearsal to "advise." A list of offensive items was compiled, presented to Welles, and then promptly "lost." Welles was not going to have his production subjected to the "whims" of federal censors.

One of the fascinating aspects of *Horse Eats Hat* was the action taking place on the audience's side of the proscenium arch. The musicians in the box seats playing at intermission provide one example. At some performances, an apparently drunk man, sleeping in the balcony and roused by the raucous sounds of the player piano, got up, reeled to the railing, and fell headlong into the seats below. In a variation of the same gag, at other performances, a piano tuner working on the same player piano in the balcony, gets up, stumbles, and tumbles into the void. Whether Welles was aware of BERTOLT BRECHT at this time is hard to say. What is clear, though, is that Welles, conscious of Brecht or not, was working along similar lines in terms of directly involving his audience in the totality of the theater experience, forcing his spectators to confront the means of making theater as well as the issues raised by the play itself.

Given that performances of *Horse Eats Hat* varied from night to night, a cult following developed with some fans coming back repeatedly to see what genie might jump from the Wellesian bottle. Welles was always inclined toward mischief, and in *Horse Eats Hat,* that impulse popped up everywhere. While the show had its devotees, it also had its detractors, principally among those who conceived of good theater in terms of the "well-made play." For such traditionalists, *Horse Eats Hat* was a puzzlement, a chaotic jumble not worth fussing about. Still, the nightly mayhem was a spectacle to behold. Indeed, each night, much of the set was destroyed. But with government resources at hand, the set could be rebuilt each day, and then smashed to pieces again each evening. Yes, there were budgetary limitations. But with a mandate to put as many actors and technicians to work as possible, the manpower available to Welles was unprecedented for him—and for American theater history. With the collapse of the Federal Theatre

Program in 1939, Welles was never again able to attain a comparable level of support for his always grand theatrical visions.

The large cast included Welles intimates Joseph Cotten as the bridegroom Freddy, Virginia Welles as the bride Myrtle Mugglethorp, and Arlene Francis as Tillie. As for the critics, John Chapman of the *New York Daily News* complained that the stylized lunacy expressed an explosive disintegration of sorts "in which the effort not to make sense is too often a strain upon players and audiences." The *New York Times* seemed to be of two minds: "It was as though Gertrude Stein had dreamed a dream after a late supper of pickles and ice cream, the ensuing revelations being crisply acted by giants and midgets, caricatures, lunatics and a prop nag [i.e., the "horse" of the title]. . . . Probably it is bad, certainly it is not good in the usually accepted sense of the theatre, but it *is* the only one of its kind." Still, audiences came. Part of its appeal might have had to do with the fact that *Horse Eats Hat* ignored the profound yet prosaic issues arising out of the grind of the depression. It also spoke to those attuned to the compelling nonsense first stirred up by the Dadaists and Surrealists. Even JOSEPH LOSEY, the future film director who was then one of Welles's most dogged detractors, was impressed, calling it "imaginative, vigorous and delightful." But then there was Senator Everett Dirksen of Illinois, a politician-turned-critic who blasted *Horse Eats Hat* in the *Congressional Record* as "salacious tripe."

Putting the critics aside, *Horse Eats Hat* was a box office success, running for over three months from September 26 to December 5, 1936.

—C.B.

Houseman, John (Jacques Haussmann)

(1902–1988) John Houseman first saw ORSON WELLES in December 1934, when Welles played Tybalt in the MCCLINTIC/CORNELL production of *Hamlet*. In his memoirs Houseman describes Welles's performance: "What made this figure [Tybalt] so obscene and terrible was the pale, shiny child's face under the unnatural growth of dark beard, from which there issued a voice of such clarity and power that it tore like a high wind through the genteel, modulated voices of the well-trained professionals

around him." SIMON CALLOW comments on the nature of the relationship between the two men: "The emotion is the classic one described by Plato's Diotima: the longing for something in another which one feels oneself to lack, mingled aspiration and abnegation, hope predicated upon hopelessness; the desire for completion by one whom one perceives already to be complete." About three weeks after he saw Welles perform, Houseman approached him about playing the part of McGafferty, a 60-year-old capitalist in ARCHIBALD MACLEISH's *PANIC*. MacLeish, who had reservations about the young Welles playing the part of a considerably older man, was impressed by Welles's reading of the part, and on March 15, 1935, *Panic* began a three-day run at the Phoenix Theatre. Welles got good reviews, and an extract, featuring Welles, from the play was broadcast. Houseman and Welles subsequently planned to stage John Ford's *'Tis Pity She's a Whore,* but due to lack of funding the production came to naught.

Houseman, who headed the NEGRO THEATRE PROJECT under the aegis of the FEDERAL THEATRE PROJECT (FTP), next hired Welles to direct Shakespeare's *MACBETH,* which Virginia, Welles's first wife, had suggested they set in 19th-century Haiti at the court of rebel king Henri Christophe. Welles directed, and Houseman was the producer of the "voodoo" *Macbeth.* Houseman essentially freed Welles to direct, while he handled labor problems with the union. The play, which was the first sponsored by the Federal Theatre Project, was a success, but there was already friction between Houseman and Welles, who was unwilling to have Houseman share any credit for the production. In spite of this, Houseman seems to have decided to cast his lot with Welles, and he left the Negro Theatre Project, though he stayed with the Federal Theatre Project. HALLIE FLANAGAN, who directed the FTP, was receptive to Houseman's idea of forming a Classical Unit under the FTP. The Classical Unit was retitled Project 891, and its first production was *HORSE EATS HAT,* a loose adaptation of *An Italian Straw Hat,* which Welles and Edwin Denby turned into an American farce. The practical Houseman and the creative, innovative Welles were again at odds. Callow writes, "It was Houseman's unhappy lot to point out the realities of

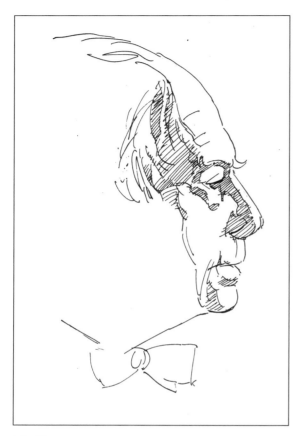

John Houseman

the situation to Welles—any situation," and Welles "was only interested in possibilities, not limitations." After the play had its run, Houseman turned to directing Leslie Howard in *Hamlet,* but the production was a disaster, and he and Welles, who had been acting in TEN MILLION GHOSTS, were reunited for a production of Marlowe's DOCTOR FAUSTUS, which was an unqualified success. Houseman and Welles then began rehearsals on MARC BLITZSTEIN's THE CRADLE WILL ROCK, which, in spite of government intervention and labor problems, was finally produced in altered and diminished circumstances. At the first performance, Houseman stressed that the performance was an artistic protest, rather than a political one. In 1937, after government funding for the Federal Theatre Project was withdrawn, House-

man and Welles formed the MERCURY THEATRE, a repertory company. Their first production was an anti-fascist JULIUS CAESAR, which was a commercial and critical success; and their THE SHOEMAKER'S HOL-IDAY was almost as successful. Because of their success, Welles was approached by the Theatre Guild to mount a theatrical production: Welles was to direct and Houseman to produce FIVE KINGS. That same year, Houseman and Welles staged Shaw's HEART-BREAK HOUSE, which ran for 40 nights. As a result of their successes, CBS offered Welles the opportunity to do a weekly radio show featuring the classics; Houseman was the executive producer of the MER-CURY THEATRE ON THE AIR. Houseman helped Welles select the works to be dramatized and, in Welles's frequent absences, worked on the scripts. Welles described Houseman's Mercury contributions to PETER BOGDANOVICH: "For the radio shows, he acted as super editor over all the writers; he produced all the first drafts. In the theatre, he was the business, and, also, you might say, the political, boss. That last was important, particularly in the WPA. Without his gifts as a bureaucratic finagler, the shows just wouldn't have gone on. I owe him much." In 1939, Welles and Houseman returned to the *Five Kings* project, and after the play opened in Boston to mixed reviews, it died in Philadelphia. Although the radio broadcast of THE WAR OF THE WORLDS brought Welles fame, his stage direction of DANTON'S DEATH, produced by Houseman for Mercury, resulted in a failure that almost bankrupted Mercury. After Welles signed his famous RKO contract and went to Hollywood, Houseman accompanied him and was offered the chance to write a first draft of the film adaptation of Joseph Conrad's HEART OF DARKNESS, which Welles planned to make his first film; but Houseman turned down the offer and returned East, where he went back to work on Mercury business, particularly THE CAMPBELL PLAYHOUSE, which had succeeded the *Mercury Theatre on the Air.* When the Mercury cast moved to Hollywood, Houseman rejoined Welles, who was working on the script for CITIZEN KANE. According to Welles, Houseman also worked with HERMAN MANKIEWICZ on the script, but Houseman refused any writing credit on the film. At a momentous meeting at Chasen's restaurant in Hollywood,

Houseman and Welles broke up their relationship. Houseman claims that when Welles learned that the Mercury bank account was practically dry and that the Mercury regulars, who had been brought to Hollywood to appear in *Kane,* could not be paid and retained, Welles accused Houseman of stealing the money. DAVID THOMSON has Welles telling Houseman, "You're the one who lies! That's why they [the Mercury players] hate you! You're the crook and they know it!" When informed that Welles had played down the seriousness of the incident, Houseman told FRANK BRADY, "Orson is full of *shit.*" Two years later, Houseman, who had purchased the rights to stage RICHARD WRIGHT's *NATIVE SON,* offered Welles the job of directing the play, and Welles not only accepted, but brought his Mercury players with him.

John Houseman, who was born on September 22, 1902, in Bucharest, Romania, moved to Paris with his parents in 1906 and to England in 1909. Educated at Clifton College, he received a Senior Scholarship in Modern Languages at Trinity College, Cambridge, but he never attended the university. After working in Argentina during 1919–20, he returned to England, where he worked for a wheat brokerage firm. After he ignored a conscription notice from the French army, he lost his French citizenship and became a British citizen in 1924. While working in England, he wrote *The Plains,* a volume of short stories, and contributed articles to the *New Statesman.* He spent the rest of the 1920s in the United States, first as a representative for the grain company and then as president of his Oceanic Grain Corporation, which went bankrupt in the 1929 Great Crash.

After changing his name to John Houseman in 1931, he and Lewis Galantière worked on a successful comedy of manners, *Lovers, Happy Lovers;* and he and A. E. Thomas produced *A Very Great Man,* a comedy, which opened in Cleveland. During 1931–32 he also adapted *Her Three Men* from its French source and *Gallery Gods* from its German source. In 1934, he directed *Four Saints,* which had a successful Broadway run, *Lady from the Sea,* and Maxwell Anderson's *Valley Forge.* He also collaborated with African-American poet Countee Cullen on a black *Medea,* so when he met Welles, he was already established as a successful director/producer.

In 1941, after the rift with Welles, Houseman went on to work as vice president for DAVID O. SELZNICK Productions, but left Selznick after Pearl Harbor to work for the government in its overseas radio division. After World War II, he became the producer of several quality films, including *The Blue Dahlia* (1946), *Letter from an Unknown Woman* (1948), *The Bad and the Beautiful* (1952), *Julius Caesar* (1953), *Lust for Life* (1956), and *This Property Is Condemned* (1962). According to Richard Hummler's *Variety* obituary (November 2, 1988), "Houseman's films garnered a total of twenty Academy Award nominations and seven Oscars, five of them for *The Bad and the Beautiful.*" In 1955, while working on *Lust for Life,* Houseman met Welles again, this time in London, where Welles was appearing in the stage version of *MOBY DICK.* According to Thomson, the meeting went well until Welles again turned on the man whom Thomson describes as "the best professional ally he had ever had": "For twenty years, you son of a bitch, you've been trying to humiliate and destroy me!" The two did not meet again for almost 30 years. During this period he occasionally returned to New York to produce and direct Broadway plays and television specials. From 1956 to 1959 he was the artistic director of the American Shakespeare Festival (two of his productions were transferred to Broadway) and from 1959 to 1964 he was the artistic director of the UCLA Professional Theatre Group. During the 1959–60 season he was the executive director for the television show *Playhouse 90.* In 1967, Houseman directed the drama division of the Juilliard School of Performing Arts at Lincoln Center; then in 1972 he launched with Margot Harley the Acting Company, a nonprofit troupe for Juilliard graduates. Houseman, who made his screen acting debut in 1963 in *Seven Days in May* (actually he appeared briefly in Welles's *TOO MUCH JOHNSON,* a film sequence that was included in the play of the same name), made his acting mark in *The Paper Chase* (1973), for which he received an Academy Award for best supporting actor. He later reprised this Oscar role as Professor Kingsfield, the rigid disciplinarian and fussy law professor in a television series, *The Paper Chase.* He also appeared in several other films, including *Rollerball* (1975), *The Cheap*

Detective (1978), *My Bodyguard* (1980), *Ghost Story* (1981), *The Winds of War* (1983), *The Naked Gun: From the Files of Police Squad,* and *Another Woman* (both 1988). He died in his home in Malibu October 31, 1988, of spinal cancer; ironically, that was the 50th anniversary of the *War of the Worlds* broadcast. His three-volume autobiographical memoirs began with *Run-Through* (1972), followed by *Front and Center* (1979), and *Final Dress* (1983). The first two volumes were nominated for National Book Awards. The three autobiographical volumes were followed by two additional books, both published in 1986: *Unfinished Business* and *Entertainers and the Entertained.*

References Houseman, John. *Unfinished Business: A Memoir* (London: Chatto and Windus, 1986); ———. *Final Dress: A Memoir* (New York: Simon & Schuster, 1983); ———. *Front and Center* (New York: Simon & Schuster, 1979); ———. *Run-Through: A Memoir* (New York: Simon & Schuster, 1972).

—T.L.E.

House of Cards Universal Pictures, 105 minutes, 1968. **Director:** John Guillermin; **Producer:** Dick Berg; **Screenplay:** James P. Bonner, adapted from the novel by Stanley Ellin; **Cinematography:** Alberto Pizzi; **Editor:** Terry Williams; **Music:** Francis Lai; **Cast:** Orson Welles (Charles Leschenhaut), George Peppard, Inger Stevens, Keith Mitchell, Ralph Michael, Maxine Audley, William Job

A U.S. film directed by John Guillermin. In this tale of international intrigue, WELLES, as the villainous Charles Leschenhaut, heads a powerful group so intent on gaining political power that it resorts to kidnapping a child. In the final showdown, a cornered and frightened Leschenhaut backs through a railing and plunges to his death, a scene recalling the ending of Welles's THE STRANGER in which Welles's character, Charles Rankin, suffers a similar fate. The engaging mystery drama was based on the 1967 novel *House of Cards,* by Stanley Ellin.

—C.B.

Howard, James (1953–) James Howard compiled *The Complete Films of Orson Welles,* published by Citadel Press in 1991. It follows the usual Citadel format, which balances the text with photographs and stills in equal proportion. The book opens with a section entitled "About Orson Welles," comprised of short quotations from actors and directors who knew, respected, or worked with Welles, such as Jean Cocteau, John Huston, Michael Powell, Charlton Heston, Henry Jaglom, and others. This is followed by a 22-page biographical career survey and illustrated entries for 58 films Welles directed or appeared in, including a catch-all category covering "European Films, 1964–70." The book wraps up with a chapter on radio and television work and another covering "Unrealized and Unreleased Projects," finishing with an odd listing of the director's "Favorite Movies," in fact a list of what Welles considered the "12 Best Movies of All Time," compiled for the Brussels Film Festival of 1952: *City Lights, Greed, Intolerance, Nanook of the North, Shoeshine, The Battleship Potemkin, The Baker's Wife, La Grande Illusion, Stagecoach, Ninotchka, The Best Years of Our Lives,* and *Bicycle Thieves.* Instead of a conclusion, the book offers an anecdote involving Welles with a rabbit in his pocket attending a birthday party given for Louis B. Mayer. As an unappreciated "magician of the cinema," Howard concludes, "Welles was forced to spend far too long waiting for someone to ask him to produce the rabbit from that particular hat."

—J.M.W.

Hughes, Howard (1905–1976) Inventor and industrialist turned movie producer and director, Howard Hughes helped to inspire ORSON WELLES'S *F FOR FAKE* (1973) because of the hoax perpetrated by freelance writer Clifford Irving, who claimed to have compiled through tape recordings an "authorized" autobiography of Hughes, whose personal life and habits had become increasingly secretive, bizarre, and eccentric. Welles had seen François Reichenbacher's documentary footage about the art forger Elmyr de Hory, whose life had been depicted in Clifford Irving's book *Hoax.* Welles saw the Reichenbach footage after Irving's own hoax concerning Hughes has been exposed, and bought Reichenbach's footage, which he interspersed with his own footage about various fakes and forgeries. The Irving-Hughes scandal helped to give currency to the concept Welles was developing for his film, which was finally as much about Irving as it was about the art forger de Hory. "Every true artist must in his own way be a magician, a charlatan," Welles once remarked, according to FRANK BRADY. DAVID THOMSON believes that Howard Hughes was also a source for the young aviation tycoon who became the key figure in Welles's screenplay for *THE SMILER WITH THE KNIFE,* an unrealized project.

Howard Hughes was born in Hodson, Texas, on December 24, 1905. As a young man he inherited the fortune of the Hughes Tool Company, founded by his father. By the time he was 20, Hughes was investing in Hollywood films and romancing stars such as Ava Gardner, Ginger Rogers, and Katharine Hepburn. One of the films he produced was the Hecht-MacArthur classic, *The Front Page* (1931). In 1932, he left Hollywood and worked briefly at American Airlines, where he learned about aviation. In the late 1930s, Hughes broke several flying records before he returned to filmmaking in 1943 with *The Outlaw,* considered so risqué that its release was delayed for several years. The flamboyant Hughes continued to fly, but in 1946 crashed and nearly died. As a result of this accident, he became increasingly reclusive, although he did continue to run his various business enterprises. Possessed of a huge fortune, Hughes gained control of RKO in 1948, and the company lost a great deal of money. After buying the outstanding stock of the company, he made $10 million when he subsequently sold the studio. He had a similar financial coup in 1966, when he sold his TWA stock for more than a half-billion dollars. At that point, Hughes went into seclusion, taking up quarters at the Desert Inn Hotel in Las Vegas, where, cared for by a cadre of male Mormons, he continued to conduct his business affairs. For years, no one outside of this inner circle had seen him. After his death in 1976, there was extensive litigation over his estate. Jonathan Demme's film *Melvin and Howard* (1980) concerns one such fake will.

References Brown, Peter H., and Pat H. Broeske. *Howard Hughes: The Untold Story* (New York: Signet, 1996); Hack, Richard. *Hughes, the Private Diaries, Memos and Letters: The Definitive Biography of the First American Billionaire* (Beverly Hills, Calif.: New Millennium Press, 2001).

—T.L.E. and J.M.W.

Huston, John (1906–1987) John Huston directed ORSON WELLES in *MOBY DICK,* wherein he portrayed the character of Father Mapple. Born on August 5, 1906, in Nevada, Missouri, to Rhea Gore and Walter Huston, John Marcellus Huston began his show business career onstage in Dallas, Texas, as "Yankee Doodle Dandy" at the age of three. Huston attended Lincoln Heights High School in Los Angeles from 1921 to 1922 and dropped out to become an art student at the Smith School of Art and Art Student's League. In 1924, John Huston left Los Angeles for New York, where he began a professional acting career at the Provincetown Playhouse. His debut as a professional actor was in a 1925 production of *The Triumph of the Egg.* In 1926, Huston went to Mexico following a mastoid operation. There he received an honorary commission in the Mexican cavalry. He married Dorothy Jeanne Harvey in 1926 and settled in Malibu, California, to pursue a career as a writer. After a brief publishing career in New York, he received an offer to become a contract writer for Goldwyn Studios in 1930. This began Huston's screenwriting career in the commercial cinema.

After six months at Goldwyn, with no writing assignments, Huston was hired by Universal Studios, where he was a contract writer from 1931 to 1933. Some of the films that Huston helped script include, *A House Divided, Law and Order,* and *Murders in the Rue Morgue.* Following a stay in Great Britain, where he was employed by British-Gaumont, Huston returned to the United States and appeared in the WPA Theatre production of *The Lonely Man* in Chicago. Huston became a contract writer for Warner Bros. from 1938 to 1941. Among the films Huston wrote at Warner's were *Jezebel, The Amazing Dr. Clitterhouse, Juarez, Dr. Ehrlich's Magic Bullet,* and *High Sierra.* His scripts for both *Dr. Ehrlich's Magic Bullet* and *High Sierra* received Oscar nominations and provided Huston with the opportunity to direct a feature film as a result of a clause in his contract. The film Huston chose was Dashiell Hammett's *The Maltese Falcon,* which had been filmed twice before by Warner's. The film featured Humphrey Bogart, the star of *High Sierra* and a Warner's contract actor of long standing. After another screenwriting assignment, *Sergeant York,* Huston directed *Across the Pacific* and *In This Our Life,* both 1942, before entering the military service following Pearl Harbor.

John Huston was commissioned as a lieutenant in the Signal Corps, which enlisted a number of Hollywood directors to record the war's progress. Huston made three outstanding wartime documentaries: *Report from the Aleutians* (1943), *The Battle of San Pietro* (1942–43), and *Let There Be Light* (1946). The latter film concerned psychologically disabled veterans and their attempts to adjust to civilian life. The film was suppressed by the military and not shown publicly until 1980.

Following his military service, Huston contributed to the screen adaptation of Ernest Hemingway's *The Killers* (1946), produced by Mark Hellinger and directed by Robert Siodmak. In November, 1946, Huston directed a stage production of Jean-Paul Sartre's *No Exit,* translated by PAUL BOWLES at the Biltmore Theatre in New York. Huston's next film, *The Treasure of the Sierra Madre* (1948), is considered by many to be one of his finest achievements as a director. The film featured Humphrey Bogart and Huston's father, Walter Huston, who received an Academy Award for best supporting actor. John Huston received Oscars for Best Screenplay and Best Director, thus marking the first time a father and son were nominated, and won for the same film. Huston's screenplay was adapted from the novel by B. Traven. Huston's next film, *Key Largo* (1948), based on the verse drama by Maxwell Anderson, was his last film for Warner Bros.

Huston and producer Sam Spiegel formed their own production company, Horizon Pictures, the first production of which was *We Were Strangers* (1949), with John Garfield and Jennifer Jones. In 1947, Huston with director William Wyler and screenwriter Phillipe Dunne formed the short-lived Committee for the First Amendment in protest of the treatment of the Hollywood Ten by the House Un-American Activities Committee (HUAC). In 1950, Huston directed *The Asphalt Jungle,* the progenitor of the heist film, and the end of his film noir period. Huston received Oscar nominations for both direction and screenplay for the film. Huston's next film, *The Red Badge of Courage* (1951), was based on the story by Stephen Crane and starred Audie Murphy. The film received critical, if not box-office success. The next and final film for the short-lived Horizons Pictures company was *The African Queen* (1951). The film was shot in the Congo under adverse conditions and starred Humphrey Bogart and Katharine Hepburn. The film's screenplay, an adaptation of the novel by C.S. Forester, was written by James Agee and John Huston. The film was both a box-office and critical success and garnished Humphrey Bogart his only Academy Award as best actor. Throughout the 1950s Huston undertook projects that were filmed in various countries and based on literary source material—a staple of his screen work. These films include *Moby Dick* (1956), *The Roots of Heaven* (1958), both featuring Orson Welles, and *The Misfits* (1961). In the 1960s, Huston supplemented his directorial duties by acting in a number of films. Beginning with *The Cardinal* (1963), for which he received an Academy Award nomination for best supporting actor, Huston's subsequent acting career included such films as *Candy* (1968), *Myra Breckenridge* (1970), *Battle for the Planet of the Apes* (1973), and most prominently, *Chinatown* (1974). Among Huston's most critically acclaimed films as a director in the 1960s and 1970s are: *Night of the Iguana* (1964), *Fat City* (1972), *The Man Who Would Be King* (1975), and *Wise Blood* (1979). After a fiasco film version of the Broadway musical *Annie* (1982), which garnered Huston a nomination for Worst Director from the Razzie Awards, the director returned to critical acclaim with *Under the Volcano* (1984) and *Prizzi's Honor* (1985). Huston received an Academy Award nomination for best director for *Prizzi's Honor,* an adaptation of a Richard Condon crime novel. In 1983, Huston was awarded the American Film Institute's Lifetime Achievement award. And in 1985, the Director's Guild of America presented Huston with its most prestigious award, the David Wark Griffith Award for Career Achievement. Thus Huston's career reached a more successful conclusion than Welles's. In 1986, Huston, in ill health, began work on what was to be his final film, an adaptation of James Joyce's short story *The Dead.* The film was written by his son, Tony Huston, and starred Huston's daughter, Anjelica. Huston entered Charlton Memorial Hospital in

Fall River, Massachusetts, on July 28, 1987. Huston died on August 28, 1987, in Middletown, Rhode Island, at the age of 81.

References Cohen, Allen, and Harry Lawron. *John Huston: A Guide to References and Resources* (New York: G.K. Hall, 1997); Huston, John. *An Open Book* (New York: Knopf, 1980).

—R.W.

Huston, Walter (Walter Houghston)

(1884–1950)   Actor Walter Huston appeared in two of ORSON WELLES's *CAMPBELL PLAYHOUSE* radio productions, *Les Miserables* and THE *MAGNIFICENT AMBERSONS.* On April 7, 1939, *Les Miserables* aired with Huston appearing as Jean Valjean and Welles as Inspector Jouvert. (Welles had earlier done a seven-episode radio production of Dumas's novel in 1937; Welles played Valjean.) On October 29th of that year, Huston appeared as Eugene Morgan in Welles's adaptation of BOOTH TARKINGTON's *The Magnificent Ambersons.* FRANK BRADY writes that Huston "played the part of Eugene Morgan with subtlety, gentleness, depth, and a voice that was barely above a whisper." Huston's wife, Nan Sunderland, played the part of Isabel Minafer.

Walter Huston, who was born in Toronto on April 6, 1884, studied to be an engineer but was bitten by the stage bug. However, after some vaudeville appearances and a part in a play, Huston quit the stage in 1906 in order to support his wife and child, JOHN HUSTON, who became a talented actor and director. In 1909, he left his engineering job and returned to vaudeville and the legitimate stage. After having starring roles in *Mr. Pitt* and in *Desire Under the Elms* in the 1920s, he switched to film in 1929, although he occasionally appeared on Broadway. His first film was *Gentleman of the Press* (1929), but his title role in D. W. Griffith's *Abraham Lincoln* (1930) established him as a film star. In 1936, the New York Film Critics named him best actor for his role in the film adaptation of Sinclair Lewis's *Dodsworth,* a role that he had earlier played in the stage version of the novel on Broadway. Other important films in which he appeared were *Gabriel Over the White House* (1933), *Rhodes of Africa* (1936), *The Maltese Falcon* (1941), *The Shanghai Gesture* (1942), and *Duel in the Sun* (1947). His best role was in son John Huston's *Treasure of the Sierra Madre* (1948), for which he won a best supporting actor Oscar.

References Stuart, Ray. *Immortals of the Screen* (New York: Bonanza Books, 1965); Weld, John. *September Song: An Intimate Biography of Walter Huston* (Lanham, Md.: Scarecrow, 1998).

—T.L.E.

I'll Never Forget What's 'is Name   Universal Pictures, 99 minutes, 1967. **Director and Producer:** Michael Winner; **Screenplay:** Peter Draper; **Cinematography:** Otto Heller; **Editor:** Bernard Gribble; **Music:** Francis Lai; **Cast:** Orson Welles (Jonathan Lute), Oliver Reed (Andrew Quint), Carol White, Harry Andrews, Michael Hordern, Wendy Craig, Marianne Faithfull

A British film directed by Michael Winner starring WELLES and set in swinging London of the 1960s. Welles plays advertising mogul Jonathan Lute for whom Andrew Quint (Oliver Reed), a trendily successful but dissatisfied television commercial director, works. Quitting his high-paying yet ethically questionable job, Quint seeks to reestablish his integrity by working on a small literary magazine. Alas, the "little" journal is owned by Lute, who persuades his talented malcontent to return to the big-time advertising game. The dramatic comedy, shot on location in London and Cambridge, also features Carol White, Harry Andrews, Michael Hordern, Wendy Craig, and Marianne Faithfull. The film was distributed in the United States in 1968.

—C.B.

Immortal Story, The   ORTF/Albina Films, 58 minutes, 1968. **Director:** Orson Welles; **Producer:** Micheline Rozan; **Screenplay:** Orson Welles, based on the novella by Isak Dinesen (Karen Blixen); **Cinematog-**raphy: Willy Kurant; **Editors:** Yolande Maurette, Marcel Pleut, Françoise Garnault, and Claude Farny; **Cast:** Orson Welles (Mr. Clay), Jeanne Moreau (Virginie Ducrot), Roger Coggio (Elishama Levinsky), Norman Eshley (Paul), Fernando Rey (Merchant)

ORSON WELLES's *The Immortal Story* is based on ISAK DINESEN's novelette "The Immortal Story," which was written in 1951 and published in her *Anecdotes of Destiny* (1953). According to CHARLES HIGHAM, *The Immortal Story* was to be the first of a two-part film, both of which were to feature Welles and JEANNE MOREAU. The second part, according to Higham, would have been *The Deluge at Nordenay,* also based on a Dinesen story, but the second part was never made. JONATHAN ROSENBAUM, who edited the BOGDANOVICH interviews with Welles, disagrees with Higham, however, claiming that the second part of the projected film was to have been an adaptation of Dinesen's "The Heroine," starring OJA KODAR, but notes that the shooting in Budapest was halted when the film's producer lacked the necessary funds. According to Welles, there were to be three companion pieces to *The Immortal Story*—the third, which was to be based on Dinesen's "A Country Tale," was to star Peter O'Toole. The 58-minute *Immortal Story,* which was made for the Organisation Radio-Télévision Française (ORTF), was shot in color, despite Welles's objections. Welles, whose directing career had included no color films, believed that "color enhances the set, the scenery, the costumes, but mysteriously enough it only detracts from the actors." After the film was shown on French television, an English-language print was released theatrically in Great Britain and the United States.

Welles, who began shooting the film in Paris and in Madrid in 1966 (Higham says 1967), omitted some of Dinesen's material, but kept very close to the dialogue in her story. Dinesen's story is set in 19th-century Canton, but Welles switched the setting to Macao, which is described as the "wickedest city in the world" in Welles's THE LADY FROM SHANGHAI (1948). He also borrows the names of his principal characters, Paul and Virginia, from a romantic novel by Bernardin de St.-Pierre. Welles's first cinematographer was Walter Wottiz, but Welles apparently was not satisfied with his work, perhaps because, as Higham suggests, the cameraman was too awed and intimidated by him. Willy Kurant, whose work Welles had seen and admired, replaced him after two days of shooting. Although the rest of the production crew initially resented Kurant's hiring, he and Welles, according to Higham, "were in rapport from the beginning."

The film begins in darkness, and an iris shot slowly reveals the setting, Macao, where a rich, old, emotionally dead American millionaire, Mr. Clay (Orson Welles), is, like CHARLES FOSTER KANE, isolated and cut off from the world in his gloomy, XANADU-like mansion. Clay sits in his library with his accountant, Levinsky (Roger Coggio), who is reading his account ledgers. Clay asks him if he knows of anything else to read. After a discussion of several books, Levinsky reads one of Elisha's prophecies about how God will finally bring relief and make "the lame man leap as a hart." Clay is understandably not interested in hearing about lame, gouty men like himself, and tells Levinsky an ostensibly true story recounted to him by a sailor. The sailor says that a rich old man once gave him five guineas to impregnate his young wife so that the old man would at last have an heir. When Levinsky, whose life is as miserably isolated as Clay's (both have retreated to their houses), responds that the story is so common that it is seafaring myth, Clay replies, "If this story has never

happened before, I will make it happen now. I do not like pretense. I do not like prophecies. I like facts."

The rest of the film concerns Clay's futile efforts to turn the story into reality, or as JAMES NAREMORE puts it, "art into life—to possess the story by becoming both its author (or, more precisely, its auteur) and one of its characters." The cast that Clay assembles with Livinsky's help, is hardly what he sought: Paul, the savvy sailor (Norman Eshley) is an innocent (Naremore describes him as "virginal"), and Virginie (Jeanne Moreau), the modest young wife, is an older woman finally willing to prostitute herself. She is, moreover, also the daughter of the former owner of Clay's home. Levinsky goes to see Virginie, whose response is influenced by her memories of the house her father lost because of Clay's deviousness. Welles's cinematography is evocative of her nostalgic associations with the past. Meanwhile, Clay picks up Paul, an Adonis–like sailor down on his luck, found in an alley. Paul accompanies Clay back to the mansion, where the two sit across from each other at a table, a visual separation that also suggests differences in age and circumstance.

Paul is as reluctant as Virginie to participate in Clay's perverse scenario. Yet the couple does get together in what James Naremore terms "the most explicitly erotic moment in any of Welles's films." Clay voyeuristically watches them making love. The setting for their liaison is lit by candles that are reflected in mirrors, providing a warm, golden color that bathes the bodies of the two lovers. This romantic effect is further enhanced by the thin mosquito netting, which, as it moves, veils, then reveals the lovers.

Naremore writes that they "are transformed into a Paul and Virginie worthy of St. Pierre's fiction [the novel *Paul and Virginie*]." However, at one point Clay, from his balcony vantage point, comments that the lovers "move" at his bidding and that he is in control. He sees himself as the puppet master. The later scenes involving the isolated Clay are lit in a cold, austere manner that reflects his sterility. Although Clay seems to have achieved his goal of providing the fact of the story, he is thwarted when the sailor, who has fallen in love with the "wife," refuses to take Clay's money and says that he will not tell any of his sea-going colleagues what has happened. If he did tell them, he does not think that they would believe him. Thus, there is no sailor who will tell a true story about being paid to impregnate a rich man's wife. Clay, having only briefly succeeded in his role as puppet master, fails and dies.

In many ways, the film is thematically Wellesian. Like CITIZEN KANE, it features a rich, powerful man who is isolated by his wealth, intent upon control, and desirous of experiencing love, however vicariously. Ultimately, his power proves impotent. In one scene he is photographed against a background of mirrors that reflect his image, a technique reminiscent of the use of mirrors in both *The Lady from Shanghai* and *Citizen Kane,* and one that implies Clay's complex and fragmented personality. Like *Kane,* the film has an object that calls to mind an ideal distant past: *Kane* has a paperweight with a snow scene; *The Immortal Story* has a seashell that Paul gives to Virginie.

Both lovers have pasts that they carry with them like baggage. Paul, who was marooned on an island, had imagined an ideal girl who lived with him in a cave. Virginie, whose first love affair was punctuated by an earthquake (as she trembles and shakes, so does the earth), has had a difficult life. When he nears the nude Virginie, however, Paul confuses her with his "dream girl," and when Virginie nears orgasm, she thinks that there is another earthquake. Their encounter proves to be more than a feat of Clay. Both are renewed by their encounter, but Clay crumbles, and dies. Levinsky comments, "It is very hard on people who want things so badly. If they cannot get these things, it is hard, and when they do get them, surely it is very hard."

The last scene of the film has Levinsky sitting on the porch with the dead Clay in his chair and Virginie watching Paul leave. As he holds the shell to his ear, Levinsky hears the "song" Paul said the shell produced. Naremore reads this as Levinsky's reawakened passions, those that had been repressed over the years: "With this recognition, this memory of an elemental life force, the film ends, the screen fading to a white tinged with pink, like the color of a sea shell."

For Bogdanovich, the story concerns more than a puppet master; it is about a film director. When he points out that "a director basically does what Charlie Clay tries to do in the movie," he means casting actors who will follow a script. Welles responds, "No—he was trying to be God, not a director. I don't see any connection." However, the film does seem to not only reflect Welles's other films, but his own life. Like Clay, he has power, but of a limited sort, and his efforts to produce a show are likewise limited. Welles says of Clay, "he dies of disappointment," a statement that foreshadows the series of disappointments Welles was to experience during his final days.

—T.L.E. and J.M.W.

Importance of Being Earnest, The (play, 1950)

The Importance of Being Earnest: A Trivial Comedy for Serious People, first performed in 1895 and published in 1899, is widely regarded as OSCAR WILDE's greatest theatrical achievement. The three-act play, a witty satire of Victorian social hypocrisy, remains a staple of repertory and community theaters around the world.

In 1950, WELLES condensed Wilde's first act to some 45 minutes in order that it fit into his theatrical potpourri, AN EVENING WITH ORSON WELLES, which toured throughout Germany in August 1950 before ending with a 10-day run in Brussels in September. In the abridged version, Welles was Algernon Moncrieff, while the part of John Worthing was taken by MICHEÁL MACLIAMMÓIR, Welles's old friend from Dublin's GATE THEATRE. Lee Zimmer was Lane, the Butler. Welles, one of theater history's greatest scene stealers and craftiest adapters, adroitly shifted the best lines of Lady Bracknell into his own dialogue as Algernon, thus assuring himself of some of the play's best laughs. The selection of *The Importance of Being Earnest* was in large part motivated by the fact that the play had just fallen into the public domain, thus eliminating any need to pay royalties.

FRANK BRADY, noting the difficulty that German audiences had with the pell-mell pace of the English dialogue, notes that Welles believed that the only successful performance of *An Evening with Orson Welles* was for an audience of English soldiers at Bad Oynhausen, who immediately understood Wilde's humor, prompting Welles to conclude, "They laughed from the stomach, not from the head."

—C.B.

Ionesco, Eugène (1912–1994) Romanian-born avant-garde French playwright Eugène Ionesco wrote the absurdist play RHINOCÉROS (1960), an allegory of totalitarian conformity, which WELLES adapted for the Royal Court Theatre in April of 1960, for a production that would star Joan Plowright and LAURENCE OLIVIER, but the actor and director did not get along, and this was the last play Welles would undertake. Welles was not only well aware of Ionesco's work, but entered into the Ionesco controversy spawned in London by KENNETH TYNAN, the theater critic of *The Observer,* who first argued that Ionesco's work should be known in England, then, after TONY RICHARDSON mounted *The Chairs* at the Royal Court, had doubts and second thoughts, sparking an extended debate in 1958 that involved not only Ionesco, but Orson Welles on July 13, who identified himself "as one of M. Ionesco's enthusiasts," though Welles did not believe that "to enjoy a play is necessarily to approve its 'message.'"

Though Ionesco was born in Romania, his mother was French, and the family soon settled in Paris, where he grew up. In 1925, his family returned to Romania, where Ionesco learned Romanian, was educated at the University of Bucharest, and taught French. In 1938, Ionesco earned a government grant to study literature in France, where he settled permanently with his family, escaping the incipient fascism of the so-called Iron Guard. In Paris, he found employment at a publishing firm but did not turn to writing plays until the age of 36. Frustrated by an attempt to learn English through conventional primers, yet fascinated by the difficulty of human communication, Ionesco pioneered the Theatre of the Absurd with *La Cantatrice chauve* (*The Bald Soprano*) in 1950, an "anti-play" with a circular plot, populated by eccentric caricatures speaking at cross purposes, followed by *Les Chaises* (*The Chairs,* 1952), *Le Roi se meurt* (*Exit the King,* 1962), and other more conventional later plays.

An anarchist at heart, Ionesco dismissed not only John Osborne and ARTHUR MILLER, but even BRECHT and Sartre as merely "the new *auteurs du boulevard,* representatives of a left-wing conformism which is just as lamentable as the right-wing sort." So he turned to the Absurd: "If man is not tragic, he is ridiculous and painful," he wrote, "'comic' in fact, and by revealing his absurdity one can achieve a sort of tragedy." Though initially misunderstood and dismissed by some as a fraud, Ionesco's work was defended by the popular French playwright Jean Anouilh, and eventually Ionesco earned fame and recognition and became highly regarded for his innovations. His dramatic theory was discussed by the playwright in his *Notes et contre-notes* (*Notes and Counter-Notes*), published in 1962. In 1969, Ionesco won Le Prix National du Théâtre, and the following year he was elected to the French Academy. *The Bald Soprano* set records as one of the longest-running shows in theater history, achieving a 30-year run in 1987 at the theater of La Huchette in Paris.

References Gaensbauer, Deborah B. *Eugène Ionesco Revisited* (New York: Twayne, 1996); Lane, Nancy. *Understanding Eugène Ionesco* (Columbia: University of South Carolina Press, 1994).

—J.M.W.

Ishaghpour, Youssef (1940–) Youssef Ishaghpour, a French critic born in Teheran in 1940, spent over 37 years researching his monumental three-volume study entitled *Orson Welles Cinéaste: Une Caméra Visible,* published in Paris by Éditions de la Différence in 2001, and covering "The Odyssey of Orson Welles" in over 2,000 pages. Volume I, concerning "The Works," takes its title from a comment by Welles: "For our dependence on the image is enormous. . . ." Volume II covers "The films of the American Period," and Volume III "The Films of the Nomadic Period," as Welles traveled the world while seeking funds to complete his projects.

Ishaghpour, who has lived in Paris since 1958, studied cinema at l'École Louis Lumière et l'Idhec and the sociology of art and philosophy to become Docteur d'État ès Lettres. Then becoming professor of the Université René Descartes, Paris V, Ishaghpour has published profusely on painting (six books covering modern artists and Persian miniatures), philosophy, literature, and cinema. His eight books on cinema include *D'une image à l'autre: la nouvelle modernité du cinéma* (1982), *Visconti: le sens et l'image* (1984), *Cinéma contemporain: de ce côté du miroir* (1986), *Formes de l'impermanence: le style de Yasujiro Ozu* (1994), *Opéra et théâtre dans le cinéma d'aujourd'hui* (1995), *Le Cinéma* (1996), *Archéologie du cinéma et mèmoire du siècle* (2000).

—J.M.W.

Is Paris Burning? Paramount/Seven Arts, 173 minutes, 1966. **Director:** René Clément; **Producer:** Paul Graetz; **Screenplay:** Gore Vidal, Francis Ford Coppola, and Marcel Moussy, adapted from the book by Larry Collins and Dominique Lapierre; **Cinematography:** Marcel Grignon; **Editor:** Robert Lawrence; **Music:** Maurice Jarré; **Cast:** Orson Welles (Raoul Nordling), Gert Frobe (General Von Choltitz), Jean-Paul Belmondo, Charles Boyer, Leslie Caron, Kirk Douglas, Glenn Ford, Yves Montand, Alain Delon, Jean-Pierre Cassel, Claude Dauphin, Anthony Perkins, Simone Signoret, Robert Stack

In this docudrama staging of the liberation of Paris during the Nazi retreat of 1944, WELLES appears as Swedish consul Raoul Nordling. With an unwieldy cast of 24 stars, and a sprawling script by Gore Vidal and Francis Ford Coppola, Welles's role—like those of Jean-Paul Belmondo, Charles Boyer, Leslie Caron, Kirk Douglas, Glenn Ford, Yves Montand, Alain Delon, Jean-Pierre Cassel, Claude Dauphin, Anthony Perkins, Simone Signoret, Robert Stack, and the others—tended to get lost amidst the *Sturm und Drang* of the convoluted extravaganza. In her review, Judith Crist dismissed the multistoried saga as muddled and confused: "An incoherent, ponderous and shallow tribute to one of the great experiences of our time, an insult to those with intimate knowledge of or experience with the liberation of Paris, an embarrassment for those interested in spectacular moviemaking."

For Welles, as he told BARBARA LEAMING, there was a chilling dimension to the shoot. "I was in a rather poor picture called *Is Paris Burning?* in which we had a scene where they were loading Jews into cattle cars in the station in Paris and sending them away. It was at exactly the same station where it actually happened, probably the same cars, and about 60 percent of the people were real veterans of this experience. They kept opening up their sleeves and showing me their tattoo numbers. And a lot of the Germans were real Germans—if not from that scene,

at least they were from the German army—and it was so unpleasant I really could hardly get through the day. The whole Pirandelloish mystery of reality was morbidly mixed up in it. Intolerable."

By accepting the part of Raoul Nordling in *Is Paris Burning?*, Welles displeased the producers of his own CHIMES AT MIDNIGHT, who had understandably wanted him to finish that film's editing and postproduction in timely fashion so that it could be screened at the 1965 Cannes Film Festival. As things developed, *Chimes at Midnight* was accepted at Cannes the following year as the official Spanish entry for 1966.

The film is based on the 1965 book, *Is Paris Burning?* by Larry Collins and Dominique Lapierre.

—C.B.

It's All True (play, 1998) Jason Sherman's *It's All True,* a play that dramatically re-creates the staging of ORSON WELLES's THE CRADLE WILL ROCK, was first produced in Toronto on December 31, 1998, and was revised and produced again in Toronto in December 1999. The play, which is set in the Maxine Elliott Theatre and other locations in New York City in 1937, includes the following characters: Orson Welles, the director; JOHN HOUSEMAN, the producer; MARC BLITZSTEIN, the composer; Jean Rosenthal, the stage manager; Howard da Silva, an actor who plays "Larry Foreman"; Olive Stanton, an actress who plays the "Moll"; Eva Blitzstein, Marc's wife; Virginia Welles, Welles's first wife; a Waitress, a Chorus of Workers, and a Young Man.

When the play opens, Houseman and Welles, who have received a WORKS PROGRESS ADMINISTRATION (WPA) telegram forbidding them to open *The Cradle Will Rock* as scheduled, are breaking the news to an outraged Marc Blitzstein. He reminds Welles of his promise to "make magic" and declares his readiness to put the show on anywhere, even a living room or a garage. A flashback to Welles, who is in his dressing room after a performance of *Faustus,* which also concerns selling one's soul for promises, follows. Welles promises Blitzstein that he will direct Blitzstein's musical. Next there is an audition in which Olive Stanton reads for the part of the "Moll," a reading that features Welles making snide comments about Houseman: "Though sometimes I don't know if he's decided between riding my coattails or stepping on them." Olive and da Silva, who plays Larry Foreman, leave together for his apartment. The next scene takes place at the legendary nightclub, "21," where Blitzstein and Virginia, who comes across as a jealous wife, get into a tiff. After Welles joins them, there is more bickering, which ends with Welles telling Blitzstein, "Don't tell me how to run my rehearsals." When Virginia tells Welles, "I want you home or out," and leaves, Welles responds to Blitzstein with an ironic, self-pitying, "Poor me. Just another fucked-up artist who doesn't understand women." Welles, however, does know how to get performances from actors. He has da Silva break off his relationship with Olive, which enables Olive to bring added emotional depth and credibility to her performance. Blitzstein, who knows what Welles has done, comments sarcastically, "Well done, Magician."

Union problems, financial shortages, and political strife predominate in the rest of the play. Union musicians protest against amateur musicians playing in the show; theaters are unavailable because of government pressure; the workers' chorus is deleted because of lack of funds; union actors cannot act without being paid; and left-winger da Silva accuses Houseman of being "a true Boss." Da Silva even tells Blitzstein that Welles is more interested in himself than in the show: "All he ever cared about was doing a musical. He don't believe in this show." On the personal level, Eva Blitzstein, Marc's dead wife, reappears to remind him of his homosexuality and his failures. Virginia tells Welles, "You haven't got a single friend in the whole world." Blitzstein is banished from rehearsals, and Houseman is relieved of all responsibilities for the show. Nevertheless, "the show must go on," and does. The play is performed at the Venice Theatre before a packed, nonpaying house, with actors, who know they will incur union wrath, sitting in the audience, singing and acting from their seats; Blitzstein plays the piano. Olive, who had earlier been unwilling to participate in the artistic-political action, appears and performs. As the show unfolds, Welles remarks, "Magic."

Sherman's play, with its title from Welles's abortive *IT'S ALL TRUE* film, examines the truth, so difficult to determine in matters relating to Welles, behind the events surrounding the staging of *The Cradle Will Rock*. Sherman encapsulates the themes, the people, and the times in which Welles and Houseman staged the left-wing, controversial play. The emphasis on Welles as magician and faker (a reference to Welles's *F FOR FAKE*), the animosity between Welles and Houseman, the increasing distance between Virginia and Welles, the philandering of Welles (he is sleeping with a waitress at the "21"), the egotism of Welles, the governmental fears of liberals, the ironic protests of unions against a pro-union play, the insecurity of Blitzstein—all are captured in this play, which in its premiere ran for six weeks.

—T.L.E.

It's All True RKO Radio Pictures, 1941–1942.

"Four Men on a Raft" **Director:** Orson Welles; **Producer:** Welles; **Associate Producer:** Richard Wilson; **Cinematographer:** George Fanto; **Cast:** Manuel Olimpio Meira (Jacare), Jeronimo Andre de Souza, Raimundo Correia Lima (Tata), Manuel Pereira da Silva (the jangadeiros), Francisco Moriera da Silva (the young bride), Jose Sobrinho (the young husband)

"The Story of Samba" **Director:** Orson Welles; **Producer:** Welles; **Associate Producer:** Richard Wilson; **Screenplay:** Robert Meltzer; **Cinematographer:** Harry J. Wild; **Cast:** Grande Othelo (performer), Pery Ribeiro (performer)

"My Friend Bonito" **Director:** Norman Foster; **Producer:** Orson Welles; **Story:** Robert Flaherty; **Cinematographer:** Floyd Crosby; **Cast:** Jesus Vasquez (Chico)

In later years, WELLES came to regard the tangled saga of his 1941–42 production of *It's All True* as "the one key disaster in my story. It cost me many, many other pictures which I never made; and many years in which I couldn't work at all." This sad assessment gains credibility when one looks at the film's convoluted background story.

The tale begins in 1941, just before America's entry into World War II, when the United States was looking to shore up its hemispheric relations with its neighbors south of the border. NELSON ROCKEFELLER, although a Republican and a future governor of New York, was then serving in the Democratic administration of President FRANKLIN DELANO ROOSEVELT as coordinator for inter-American affairs. In late 1941, speaking on behalf of the U.S. State Department and also as a stockholder sitting on the Board of Directors of RKO for whom Welles worked, Rockefeller invited the young director to be a special ambassador for the nation's Good Neighbor Policy, which aimed to help stem Nazi influence in Latin America. Welles's job was to go to Brazil to make a documentary about Rio's *Carnaval,* broadcast upbeat reports on Brazil back to the United States, and socialize with prominent Brazilians, all in the name of fostering hemispheric goodwill.

Accepting the job, Welles initially felt comfortable in leaving the editing of THE MAGNIFICENT AMBERSONS and shooting of JOURNEY INTO FEAR to others. After all, he had been asked to serve his country. What's more, the now expanded, three-story concept for his Good Neighbor film had the joint backing of both RKO and the U. S. government. Significantly, Welles had been promised control of the editing of *Ambersons* and *Journey into Fear* by RKO boss GEORGE J. SCHAEFER, who further pledged to send the footage of both films to Brazil, along with editing equipment and assistant editors. So, it was off to Rio and *Carnaval.*

In spite of logistical problems, Welles was immediately enchanted with the country's people and music. In Brazil, shooting in color for the first time, he captured the revelry of Rio's *Carnaval* for a segment of *It's All True* under the working title, "The Story of Samba." For the reenactment of a voyage by peasants to petition the Brazilian government for welfare to help their impoverished village, Welles switched to black-and-white for what he planned to call "Four Men on a Raft." He sent trusted friend NORMAN FOSTER to Mexico to begin work on a third segment, the story of a boy and his bull, which was titled "My Friend Bonito." Sadly, problems developed for Schaefer, which in turn meant problems for Welles. Because of budgetary woes in part caused by Welles's various MERCURY projects, Schaefer was fired as RKO studio head in June 1942, and replaced by CHARLES KOERNER, a former

theater manager who valued entertainment rather than art.

With Welles off the lot, one of Koerner's first decisions was to take over the editing of *The Magnificent Ambersons,* a change of affairs that resulted in the film's severe mutilation. A similar fate befell the Welles-produced *Journey into Fear.* When Welles finally returned to Hollywood from Brazil in July 1942, Koerner broke Welles's contract and had him fired. That, in turn, left the miles of *It's All True* footage in limbo. Without George Schaefer, Welles's chief backer to intercede on his behalf, Welles found himself a director without a studio.

In spite of these reversals, Welles had fallen in love with his star-crossed project. He was determined to make a success of *It's All True.* Although RKO refused to sell him the footage outright, he leveraged his acting fee for the studio's JANE EYRE to gain temporary control of the film. During the mid-1940s, still dedicated to the project, he periodically announced a number of new and increasingly grander plans for bringing *It's All True* to the screen. Alas, they all came to naught. Finally, in 1946, having failed to find backers, ownership of the footage reverted back to RKO.

For Welles, *It's All True* was a disaster of incalculable proportions. It was the "magnificent obsession" that cost him his credibility as a Hollywood director. Having sunk so much of his own capital into the doomed *It's All True* project, it was also the undoing of the best chance he ever had to establish and stabilize a strong financial base.

For decades, it was assumed that Welles's *It's All True* footage had vanished. Then in 1985, the material was "discovered" in the RKO archive in Salt Lake City. In 1993, IT'S ALL TRUE: BASED ON AN UNFINISHED FILM BY ORSON WELLES, a documentary drawing on Welles's footage, debuted at the New York Film Festival. An earlier 22-minute work-in-progress version, *It's All True: Four Men on a Raft,* was shown at the 1986 Venice Film Festival.

—C.B.

It's All True: Based on an Unfinished Film by Orson Welles

Paramount Pictures/Les Films Balenciaga/French Ministry of Education/French National Center for Cinematography/Canal +/R.

Films/La Fondation GAN pour le Cinéma, 86 minutes, 1993. **Directors:** Richard Wilson, Myron Meisel, Bill Krohn; **Producers:** Regine Konckier, Richard Wilson, Bill Krohn, Myron Meisel, Jean-Luc Ormieres; **Script:** Bill Krohn, Richard Wilson, Myron Meisel; **Senior Research Executive:** Catherine Benamou; **Cinematographer:** Gary Graver, **Music:** Jorge Arriagada; **Editor:** Ed Marx; **Cast:** Miguel Ferrer (Narrator)

IT'S ALL TRUE, ORSON WELLES's ill-fated Latin American project for RKO and the U.S. State Department's early-1940s' "Good Neighbor" program, is a project Welles came to believe was cursed. When he returned to the United States from Brazil in the summer of 1942, CHARLES KOERNER, RKO's new Hollywood production head, fired Welles and confiscated the footage he had shot in Brazil for two of the film's three tales, "The Story of Samba (Carnaval)" and "Four Men on a Raft"; Koerner also took away the footage shot by NORMAN FOSTER in Mexico for the third story, "My Friend Bonito." During the next several years, Welles, in spite of valiant efforts, was unsuccessful in regaining control of the footage. As RKO's assets were eventually sold to HOWARD HUGHES, and then Desilu, and finally Paramount, Welles's footage for *It's All True* was presumed to have been discarded or lost.

Amazingly, the footage was found in a Paramount vault in 1985, just before Welles's death. In 1986, a 22-minute rough-cut of "Four Men on a Raft" was assembled by longtime Welles assistant RICHARD WILSON and shown to acclaim at the 1986 Venice Film Festival. At about the same time, a group of documentarians headed by Bill Krohn and Myron Meisel and joined by Wilson started work on the project that eventually would become *It's All True: Based on an Unfinished Film by Orson Welles.* Film historian Catherine Benamou was brought in to add her expertise on Welles's involvement with the U.S. Inter-America Office during the early 1940s.

Thanks largely to Benamou's research, the 1993 film is a revisionist work that challenges a number of suppositions about Welles during this tumultuous period. Indeed, through interviews with participants in *It's All True,* the documentary makes the point that Welles's Brazilian venture started going awry when he became fascinated with the black villagers who attempt to petition the Brazilian government regarding their impoverished conditions in "Four Men on a Raft," and the mostly black revelers and musicians who animate the footage of "The Story of Samba (Carnaval)." Welles's sin, as far as the white Brazilian ruling class and the U.S. State Department were concerned, was in focusing on black rather than white Brazil. In addition to racism, the documentary outlines how RKO's financial struggles of the period also figured in; RKO, like Hollywood's other major studios, sought escapist fare to distract audiences from the war. For RKO, the third strike against Welles involved the still moldering corpses of *CITIZEN KANE* and *THE MAGNIFICENT AMBERSONS,* both large box-office failures. In short, Koerner and the RKO brass in New York were compelled to cut losses. RKO's corporate downsizing started with Welles and the MERCURY Unit.

The documentary directly contradicts clichés about Welles being a wastrel and also being self-destructive. Indeed, instead of writing off Welles's Brazilian interlude as a failure, the film argues that in shooting *It's All True,* Welles was forced to perfect techniques that allowed him to go it alone. While learning how to shoot on location with small crews and minimal financial support, Welles developed directorial resources that enabled him to produce films such as *CHIMES AT MIDNIGHT* and *F FOR FAKE,* thus making him, arguably, the greatest "independent filmmaker" of all time.

It's All True: Based on an Unfinished Film by Orson Welles, was in production from 1985 to 1993. The documentary was first shown at the New York Film Festival in October 1993.

References Garcia, Marcia. "Re-Inventing Orson Welles," *Films in Review* (May–June 1994); Lane, Anthony. "The Current Cinema: Going South," *The New Yorker* (November 1993); McBride, Joseph. *Orson Welles,* revised and expanded ed. (New York: Da Capo Press, 1996).

—C.B.

Jack Benny Show, The (radio, 1943) When comedian Jack Benny fell ill with pneumonia after a grueling tour of entertaining troops at the height of World War II, WELLES was called on to preside over his top-rated radio show sponsored by Grape-Nuts. In spite of Welles's vast experience in radio drama, comedy in the Benny mode was a new challenge. First, there was a live audience that was encouraged to interrupt and interact with the onstage proceedings. Second, Benny offered himself—as a miser and putative violinist—as the butt of many of the show's gags. There were also mini-dramas during which the actors would step out of the comedic plays-within-plays to poke fun at fellow cast members. For example, Mary Livingston's character might refer to "that guy on the radio . . . the one who saws the violin," thus drawing the audience into the joke of one cast member gibing another. For Welles, it was a productive diversion and an opportunity to study firsthand the inner workings of America's most popular radio program. A year later, Welles would put to use many of the lessons learned hosting *The Jack Benny Show* in his own radio variety show, ORSON WELLES'S ALMANAC.

BARBARA LEAMING points out that much of the ribbing taken by Welles on the Benny show was aimed at his supposed genius and its attendant haughtiness. "I used to play Orson Welles all the time on Jack Benny," he told Leaming in reference to the show's skits in which he made fun of himself as brusque, snobbish, and insolent. "That's the Orson Welles everybody still thinks I am. The secretary used to atomize the microphone before I would speak into it! You know, a lot of people believed it. In other words, the comedy figure rubbed off on me." Still, as Leaming observes: "Surely Orson's early comic version of himself on *The Jack Benny Show* was based on something tangible in his character. Otherwise, it would not have worked effectively as parody."

—C.B.

Jaglom, Henry (1943–) ORSON WELLES appeared as an endearing Jewish musician and chessplayer in *A SAFE PLACE,* directed by his friend and supporter Henry Jaglom in 1971. Jaglom was born in New York (or perhaps London?) on January 26, 1943 (or in 1941 or 1939—sources vary), educated at the University of Pennsylvania, and trained at the Actor's Studio. Jaglom started his show business career as an Off-Broadway actor and eventually found television roles in such series as *The Flying Nun* and *Gidget.* He made his screen acting debut in 1968 in *Psych-Out* and went on to appear in other independent movies, notably *Drive, He Said* and Dennis Hopper's *The Last Movie,* both made in 1971. Welles directed Jaglom in an unrealized film project, *THE OTHER SIDE OF THE WIND* (1970–76). Jaglom tried his hand at filmmaking in Israel in 1967, when he shot a three-hour documentary on the Six-Day War, a film that was never released. *A Safe Place,* which he also wrote and edited, marked his directorial debut.

Jaglom was Welles's chief advocate in the director's later years and endeavored to raise money to back Welles's film projects. After failing to raise money to produce THE DREAMERS, an adaptation of two ISAK DINESEN stories, Jaglom persuaded Welles to write a screenplay. Welles reluctantly complied and finished THE BIG BRASS RING. Arnon Milcham, an Israeli producer, promised to back the film with an $8 million budget, providing that Jaglom and Welles got a leading star for the film. Perhaps because the film dealt with homosexuality (a film producer has an affair with a former teacher-mentor, to be played by Welles), Jaglom was unsuccessful in finding a film star to appear in the picture. Among the actors approached were Jack Nicholson, Warren Beatty, Clint Eastwood, Robert Redford, and BURT REYNOLDS, all of whom had at one time or another expressed admiration for Welles and expressed the desire to be in one of his films. The failure to finance either of the two projects disheartened Welles. Jaglom had been videotaping and audiotaping conversations with Welles for years and remained his staunch supporter. At Welles's memorial service on November 4, 1985, Jaglom was one of the prominent speakers. Jaglom's film, *Someone to Love* (1988), was dedicated "with love to Orson Welles."

References Allon, Yoram. *The Wallflower Guide to Contemporary North American Directors* (London: Wallflower, 2000); Katz, Ephraim. *The Macmillan International Film Encyclopedia* (New York: Macmillan, 1994); Thomson, David. *A Biographical Dictionary of Film* (New York: Knopf, 1994).

—T.L.E. and J.M.W.

Jane Eyre

Jane Eyre Twentieth Century–Fox, 96 minutes, 1944. **Director:** Robert Stevenson; **Producer:** William Goetz; **Screenplay:** Robert Stevenson, Aldous Huxley, and John Houseman, adapted from the novel by Charlotte Brontë; **Cinematography:** George Barnes; **Editor:** Walter Thompson; **Music:** Bernard Herrmann; **Cast:** Orson Welles (Rochester), Joan Fontaine (Jane Eyre), Peggy Ann Garner (young Jane), Margaret O'Brien (Adele), Sara Allgood (Bessie), John Sutton (Dr. Rivers), Agnes Moorehead (Aunt Reed), Henry Daniell (Brocklehurst), Ethel Griffies, Aubrey Mather, Mae Marsh, Hillary Brooke, Barbara Everest, Elizabeth Taylor.

A U.S. film adaptation of Charlotte Brontë's 1847 novel, directed by Robert Stevenson, and featuring welles as Edward Rochester and Joan Fontaine as Jane Eyre. Produced by William Goetz for Twentieth Century–Fox as a lavishly mounted costume drama designed to capitalize on the success of such historical romances as *Gone With the Wind* (1939) and *Rebecca* (1940), *Jane Eyre* proved to be Welles's only opportunity to play a full-blown romantic lead in a genuine Hollywood love story.

Rochester was the first of many acting jobs that Welles took in the films of other directors primarily for financial rather than artistic reasons. Here, the actor's handsome $100,000 fee was based on his still potent celebrity as a star of stage, screen, and radio. In addition to acting, Welles served as the film's uncredited associate producer, a position that gave him considerable clout in reworking the script with Aldous Huxley and making suggestions to director Robert Stevenson. Welles also deserves credit for having given a young, 10-year-old Elizabeth Taylor her first notable role.

To achieve a svelte leading man look, Welles labored hard to shape up by dieting, submitting to steam baths, and wearing corsets. Sensitive to what he perceived as a nose too small relative to his large frame, Welles bulked up his proboscis in emulation of the aquiline profile of his friend, actor JOHN BARRYMORE. Welles's Rochester also sports a swarthy tan that some said had been calculated to make him look darker than his then current paramour, African-American singer-actress LENA HORNE.

Critical opinion on Welles's performance as Rochester varies. While there are striking and characteristic Wellesian moments, the pivotal Welles-Fontaine coupling fails to generate palpable romantic heat. Indeed, Welles's Rochester is essentially an outcast, a great man so self-obsessed with his alienation that we never really believe his need for Jane. Although he had played Rochester in several radio

Welles as Rochester with Joan Fontaine in *Jane Eyre* *(Literature/Film Archive)*

adaptations of the play, Welles did not have a deep attachment to the role in this production. In *Jane Eyre,* Welles was a "gun for hire," gladly exploiting his acting talent in order to help fund his own directorial ambitions.

James Agee, one of the period's most thoughtful critics, found little to like and much to scorn in *Jane Eyre,* including Welles's performance: "A careful and tame production, [it features] a sadly vanilla-flavoured Joan Fontaine, and Orson Welles treating himself to broad operatic sculpturings of body, cloak and diction, his eyes glinting in the Rembrandt gloom, at every chance, like side orders of jelly." Part of the problem, suggests BARBARA LEAMING, is that Welles,

especially in the wake of his overlapping responsibilities as director-producer-writer-actor for *CITIZEN KANE* and *MAGNIFICENT AMBERSONS,* became bored with essentially only acting. Still, Welles's exotic if somewhat baroque Rochester stands as a beacon to the actor's imperial presence and gravity in his inimitable gallery of memorable performances.

On his relationship with director Stevenson, Welles, in response to PETER BOGDANOVICH's observation that some of the film looks like it had been directed by Welles, said: "Oh, I invented some of the shots—that's part of being that kind of [associate] producer. And I collaborated on it, but I didn't come around behind the camera and direct it. Certainly I did a lot more than a producer ought to, but Stevenson didn't mind that. And I don't want to take credit away from him, all of which he deserves. It was an impossible situation for him, because the basic setup is wrong if an actor is also a producer—it shouldn't happen. In fact, we got along very well, and there was no trouble."

Jane Eyre, initially planned by DAVID O. SELZNICK before passing it on to Twentieth Century–Fox, also featured Margaret O'Brien, Peggy Ann Garner, Sara Allgood, John Sutton, Agnes Moorehead, and Aubrey Mather.

—C.B.

Jazz Story   An unrealized episode in the four-part omnibus film project registered in 1941 under the title IT'S ALL TRUE. *Jazz Story* was planned as a history of American jazz as told through the life of LOUIS ARMSTRONG, with a script by Elliot Paul in collaboration with Armstrong and DUKE ELLINGTON, who was to write and arrange the score. Armstrong was to appear as himself with pianist-singer Hazel Scott as Lil Hardin, Armstrong's first wife.

FRANK BRADY reports that of the four parts of *It's All True,* it was the jazz story that most interested Welles since it would allow him to collaborate with musical heroes Louis Armstrong and Duke Ellington. He also had informally auditioned jazz diva Billie Holiday for a part. Welles had Ellington put on the RKO payroll at $1,000 per week, with promises of more money for salaries for his bandsmen, a role in the film, and ownership of the music. Ellington recalls having written a trumpet solo, promptly losing it, and never hearing much more about the project except for receiving checks adding up to $12,500. Other jazz icons (reportedly, Louis Armstrong and Hazel Scott) were also added to the RKO payroll, eventually swelling the expenditure for the jazz story to $24,750.

Sadly, when RKO succeeded in convincing Welles that the jazz segment lacked commercial viability, the project was dropped. Still, it and other Welles projects reflected his deep love of music in general, and jazz in particular. Today, jazz fans can only imagine what a collaboration between Welles and Armstrong, Ellington and Holiday might have looked, and sounded, like.

—C.B.

Jew Suss   (play, 1931)   A 1925 novel by Lion Feuchtwanger (1884–1958), adapted for the stage in English by Ashley Duke, whose 1931 Dublin debut at the GATE THEATRE featured WELLES in the role of Duke Karl Alexander.

A 16-year-old Welles, as if moved by divine providence, found his way to the fabled Gate Theatre in Dublin, where he presented himself as an 18-year-old New York actor fresh from a season at the Theatre Guild now on holiday. Whether the Gate's founders, actors MICHEÁL MACLIAMMÓIR or HILTON EDWARDS, believed the story will never be known. However, because they had not yet found an actor to essay the role of Duke Karl Alexander for the Dublin premiere of *Jew Suss,* MacLiammóir and Edwards were inclined to give the visitor a close look. Impressed with his imposing height and booming voice, Edwards, after an impromptu audition, signed Welles up for the job.

Blessed with an intrinsic sense of the theatrical and a surplus of self-confidence, the young thespian surpassed everyone's expectations. The Dublin papers raved. Joseph Holloway, dean of the city's theater critics, opined that Welles "looked the uncouth, hard-drinking, loud-voiced brute the author intended him to be and made quite an impression by a clever character study. He was blustering and sensual and repellent," just what the role called for. The most important praise for Welles came from J. J. Hayes, the *New York Time*'s Dublin correspondent, who trumpeted: "This somewhat unpleasant play has been magnificently produced by Hilton Edwards, who also plays the title role. His is a most difficult part because for more than half of the play it is second to that of the Duke Karl Alexander, and when Jew Suss's great moment comes it is too late as the play belongs to the Duke. This is particularly true of the Gate production in which the Duke is played by a young American actor, 18 years old, whose performances is astonishingly fine. This young man is Orson Welles."

Hayes then goes on to reprise Welles's Irish expedition, repeating Welles's false claim that he had appeared at the Theatre Guild in New York and the Goodman Theatre in Chicago. Thus, at the onset of his career as a professional actor, his astonishing triumph at the Gate was inextricably tied to tall tales and outright fabrications. Significantly, the implications of telling lies, creating deceptions, and promulgating falsehoods would become a central theme in the Wellesian oeuvre, a theme that would appear time and again, but with particular frankness in F FOR FAKE. One can only imagine what questions he posed to himself as he took his bows and read the reviews in October 1931. "Was I hired because of a good audition, or because of a good lie? Did they like me for my performance, or because I had draped myself in the mantle of the Theatre Guild and Goodman Theatre?" If he wrestled with such questions, there's no record of them. Indeed, it doesn't seem that he had many second thoughts. In fact, given that one of his duties at the Gate involved feeding stories to the press, one might surmise that he was pleased to have learned at such a tender age how to manipulate the engines of publicity to boost his own fortunes as well as those of his colleagues.

Finally, and most significantly, Welles's triumph at the Gate on October 13, 1931, provided a clarion affirmation of his decision to become a man of the theater. As he told BARBARA LEAMING, "That was the night I had *all* the applause I needed for my life."

German novelist-playwright Lion Feuchtwanger is best known for his historical romances. Born of a Jewish family in Munich, he earned a doctorate in philology and literature. In 1918, he founded the literary paper, *Der Spiegel,* and in 1923, published his first historical novel (*Die hässliche Herzogin Margarete Maultasch* (*The Ugly Duchess Margaret Maultasch*). His finest and most widely known novel, *Jew Suss* (1925; published in English in 1926), is set in 18th-century Germany and reveals a deep psychological awareness, a trait characteristic of his later work. An active pacifist and socialist, Feuchtwanger was forced into exile by the rise of Naziism, moving to France in 1933, and then to the United States in 1940, after some months in a concentration camp, an experience described in the *Devil in France* (1941). His later works include *Proud Destiny* (1947), *This Is the Hour* (1951), and *Jephthah and His Daughter* (1957). Feuchtwanger was a friend of BERTOLT BRECHT and collaborated with him on several plays, including *Leben Eduards II von England.* (1923; *Life of Edward II of England*), an adaptation of *Edward II*

by Marlowe. He died in Los Angeles, in his adopted country, in 1958.

Feuchtwanger's *Jew Suss* tells how a well-to-do and worldly Jew, Suss, assists a minor nobleman, Karl Alexander (the role played by Welles), to rise to power. Eventually taking over the throne, the newly installed Duke Karl Alexander continues to rely on Suss, until he betrays him. Tracking the Jew down to his hiding place, Karl Alexander discovers that Suss has an alluring daughter, whom he tries to rape. In trying to evade him, the daughter falls to her death. At the end of the story, Suss has his revenge by precipitating Karl Alexander's heart attack. Suss is then taken away to his death. In contrast to Feuchtwanger's tragic novel, Ashley Dukes's adaptation tended toward melodrama. As SIMON CALLOW points out, Welles was correct to describe the role of Karl Alexander as "fatter" than that of Jew Suss. As cited by Callow, Welles said that the part of Karl Alexander "runs the gauntlet of fine temper scenes, drunks, daring seductions, rapine, murder, heart attacks and death." In the 1931 Gate Theatre production, Betty Chancellor played the part of Suss's daughter, Naomi, while Hilton Edwards essayed the role of Jew Suss.

References Brady, Frank. *Citizen Welles: A Biography of Orson Welles* (New York: Scribner's, 1989); Callow, Simon. *Orson Welles: The Road to Xanadu* (New York: Penguin, 1995); Leaming, Barbara. *Orson Welles: A Biography* (New York: Penguin Books, 1985).

—C.B.

Journey into Fear

Journey into Fear   Mercury Productions/RKO Radio Pictures, 71 minutes, 1942. **Director:** Norman Foster; **Producer:** Orson Welles; **Executive Producer:** George J. Schaefer; **Screenplay:** Joseph Cotten and Welles (based on *Journey into Fear* by Eric Ambler); **Cinematographer:** Karl Struss; **Editor:** Mark Robson; **Cast:** Joseph Cotten (Howard Graham), Orson Welles (Colonel Haki), Dolores Del Rio (Josette Martel), Ruth Warrick (Stephanie Graham), Agnes Moorehead (Mrs. Mathews), Everett Sloane (Kopeikin), Jack Moss (Banat), Gobo (Jack Durant), Frank Readick (Mathews), Edgar Barrier (Kuvelti), Stefan Schnable (Purser), Hans Conreid (Oo Lang Sang, the Magician), Robert Meltzer (steward), Richard Bennett (ship's captain), Shifra Haran (Mrs. Haklet), Eustace Wyatt (Muller/Prof. Haller), Herbert Drake (steward), Bill Roberts (steward)

Although its direction is credited to NORMAN FOSTER, *Journey into Fear* is generally and properly regarded as an ORSON WELLES film. Made at RKO as part of his initial four-film deal with the studio, Welles was responsible for producing the film. He also co-authored the adaptation of ERIC AMBLER's novel of the same title with JOSEPH COTTEN. And while Cotten played the leading role of Howard Graham, Welles, as an actor, added a memorable turn to his gallery of heavies as the imposing Colonel Haki. Significantly, *Journey into Fear,* along with *THE MAGNIFICENT AMBERSONS* (which Welles was editing during the day while producing the Ambler project at night), can be regarded as the last full-fledged effort of the MERCURY company that Welles co-founded in New York with JOHN HOUSEMAN in 1937.

Although regarded by Welles and his Mercury colleagues as a minor project designed mainly as a diverting means of satisfying the terms of Welles's contract with RKO, *Journey into Fear,* when finally given wide release in 1943, created a favorable impression. The *New York Times* typified the critical reaction: "Out of Eric Ambler's thriller, *Journey into Fear,* Orson Welles and his perennial Mercury Company have made an uneven but generally imaginative and exciting tale of terror. Less ambitious than any of the company's previous productions, the new film at the Palace is nevertheless many notches above the garden variety regularly sent to Broadway ['s first-run picture palaces]. Although Norman Foster has directed it, Mr. Welles, in collaboration with Joseph Cotten, who plays the central role, has written the adaptation, and either directly or indirectly it is Welles's fine flair for melodrama that is stamped on every scene." This 1943 assessment of *Journey into Fear* as a secondary work in the Welles's canon has persisted. Still, for the reasons cited by the anonymous *Times* critic, reasons echoed by virtually all subsequent Welles commentators, *Journey into Fear* deserves consideration.

The convoluted spy story about Turkey's military preparedness centers on the character of Howard Graham (Joseph Cotten), an American arms engineer working with the Turkish navy. The plot is set in motion through a letter from Graham to his wife

Joseph Cotten and Orson Welles in *Journey into Fear* (National Film Society Archive)

(RUTH WARRICK), explaining the couple's mysterious separation in Istanbul. At the start of a trip back to the United States, the Grahams stop in the Turkish capital and are met by Kopeikin (EVERETT SLOANE), a Turkish employee of Graham's company, who under the guise of discussing business, takes Graham to a nightclub. There the intellectually bright but politically naive engineer meets the dancer Josette Martel (DELORES DEL RIO) and her partner Gobo (Jack Durant). When an unsuccessful assassination attempt on Graham results in the death of the nightclub's magician Oo Lang Sang (Hans Conreid), Colonel Haki (Welles), the head of the Turkish secret police, appears. Haki expresses concern for Graham's welfare since the engineer has invaluable knowledge about the armament needs of the Turkish navy; Graham's demise, he points out, would delay Turkey's preparations for its wartime defenses. Sharing a photograph of killer Peter Banat (Jack Moss), who has been hired to terminate Graham by the Nazi agent Muller (Eustace Wyatt), Haki directs Graham to safe passage aboard a tramp steamer headed for Batumi. When Graham protests being separated from his wife, the colonel assures him that the couple will soon be reunited. As Haki offers a dockside farewell, he presents Graham with a pistol, which the flustered Graham eventually stashes under his bed. As Haki puts it, he is "a ballistics expert who has never fired a gun."

Aboard ship, Graham again encounters Josette and Gobo, as well as Kuvelti (Edgar Barrier), a Turkish tobacco salesman; Prof. Haller, ostensibly an archeologist but actually Nazi agent Muller in disguise; and Madame Mathews (AGNES MOOREHEAD) and her socialist husband (Frank Readick). Ill at ease with his perilous circumstances, Graham is reassured by Josette. When the freighter makes its first stop, Graham wires his wife to meet him in Batumi. Setting sail again, Graham discovers a new passenger, the assassin Peter Banat, whom Haki had warned Graham about. Unable to convince the captain to take his situation seriously, Graham is assisted by Josette in trying to stall the assassin's plot. When Graham returns to his cabin, Muller offers to spare his life if the engineer will delay his return to the United States for six weeks, in order to allow the Germans to establish countermeasures against the Turkish navy's defense plans.

When Kuvelti, who turns out to be one of Haki's agents, is found murdered, Graham asks Mathews to deliver a message to the Turkish counsel. In one of the film's bits of comedic irony, Mathews offers Graham a penknife and an umbrella for protection. When the boat docks, Graham is hustled ashore by Banat and Haller into a waiting car. Then, when the car suffers a flat tire, Graham sticks Mathews's little knife into the horn, thus creating a ruckus. In the confusion, Graham takes the wheel, crashes the car into a store window, and flees. Later, in the midst of a storm, Graham finds the hotel where his wife is staying. However, when he enters her room, instead of his wife, he encounters Haller and Banat. After a series of tumultuous events, including Graham's vertiginous escape out a hotel window, Haki suddenly appears on the hotel's ledge and shoots Haller. Banat

returns the fire and wounds Haki. Banat then turns his gun on Graham, but blinded by rain, misses. Graham, forced into being a man of action, struggles with Banat, who falls from the hotel's outer ledge to his death. Safely back in the hotel, Graham finishes the letter to his wife that he had begun on the ship. When the bandaged Haki reappears and tells Graham that his wife is waiting upstairs, the engineer tears up the now completed letter and leaves to join her.

Although Ambler's novel was still selling briskly when the film went into production, Cotten and Welles took a free hand in adapting it. In the Mercury manner, the material was substantially reworked in order to maximize the film medium's dramatic possibilities. For instance, while the novel associates the assassin by olfactory means, in the film, Marat is identified by a scratchy phonograph recording of "C'est mon coeur." The film's exciting conclusion with the struggle atop the rain-swept ledge of the hotel is another Cotten–Welles invention. The most significant change, however, involved Graham's nationality. By making the engineer an essentially apolitical American without strong convictions, Graham is forced by circumstances to come to personal terms with the conflict, and engage the Nazi enemy directly. Like Humphrey Bogart's Rick in *Casablanca* (1942), at the end, Graham emerges both sadder and wiser—and solidly behind America's war effort.

When RKO purchased the film rights to Ambler's novel in early 1941, it was initially slated for adaptation by BEN HECHT. However, RKO boss GEORGE SCHAEFER prevailed on Welles to take on the assignment for Mercury. The studio, interested in grooming Joseph Cotten for stardom, encouraged his casting in the leading role of Graham. When production began in January 1942, Welles, scheduled to leave for Brazil in early February to shoot IT'S ALL TRUE, crammed the shooting of his scenes as Haki into only several days. While hurrying to finish his role of Haki for *Journey into Fear*, Welles was also in the midst of editing the far more complex production of *The Magnificent Ambersons*. To keep everything on schedule and in Welles's hands, Schaefer promised to send editing equipment and editors to Brazil so that Welles could finish both films while also shooting *It's All True*. That, however, would never happen.

One of the great yet little commented on tragedies of film history involves Schaefer's ouster from RKO in June 1942. As a fan of the Boy Wonder, Schaefer had been an effective catalyst in easing Welles's way into feature filmmaking. Indeed, few moguls would have pledged to allow Welles to continue postproduction work on both *The Magnificent Ambersons* and *Journey into Fear* while in Rio de Janeiro, far from the studio's control. Sadly, one of the main reasons for Schaefer's demise at RKO was his perceived coddling of Welles.

CHARLES KOERNER, appointed by RKO's New York–based board of directors to rein in Schaefer's excesses, was a no-nonsense former theater manager who valued "showmanship rather than genius." To italicize the pragmatism of his new regime, Koerner severed the studio's contract with Welles. Thus, both *Ambersons* and *Journey into Fear* were wrested away from Welles and his Mercury staff. Upon Welles's return from Brazil, RKO similarly confiscated the footage for *It's All True*.

In late August 1942, *Journey into Fear* was previewed for the trade. Given that its final assembly had been presided over by workers with no connection to Mercury, it isn't surprising that the film was panned. In an effort to try to salvage the project, Welles agreed as part of his final settlement with RKO to reedit the final reel and shoot more material. He did this without additional compensation. The most important change was Welles's addition of Graham's two voice-over scenes which bookended the film, and helped clarify the plot's complexities. When RKO finally released the film in March 1943, it was done with little fanfare. Nonetheless, as indicated by the favorable March 13, 1943, review in the *New York Times,* the efforts of Welles and Mercury had not gone for naught. While comparing *Journey into Fear* favorably with Hitchcock's spy thrillers, the *Times* also praised the actors: "To select outstanding performances would be to name practically the entire cast. . . . Joseph Cotten gives a deftly suggestive performance as the pursued expert; Agnes Moorehead adds another exacerbating portrait of a shrewish woman; and Jack Moss—also Welles's business manager—nearly steals every scene in which he appears as the pudgy-faced killer. Despite its lapses, *Journey into Fear* is still a terse invitation to heart failure by fright." Along with its attenuated evocations of Wellesian themes dealing with power and corruption, *Journey into Fear* is also notable for its inclusion of the magic show in which the magician is killed during the first attempt on Graham's life. While the setup has no special significance to the story, it is typical of the bits of business added by Welles and Cotten to spice up Ambler's novel. It also is an expression of Welles's lifetime fascination with magic.

In 1976, Daniel Mann directed another version of *Journey into Fear* featuring Sam Waterston, Zero Mostel, and Yvette Mimieux.

—C.B.

Julius Caesar (play, 1937) Following the successful 1937 production of the federally subsidized *DOCTOR FAUSTUS,* WELLES and his producing partner JOHN HOUSEMAN, increasingly apprehensive about the growing political controversies swirling about the FEDERAL THEATRE PROJECT, sought to strike out on their own. Seeking to sustain the momentum of PROJECT 891, the federal theater unit they established in 1936, they organized a new privately owned company that they named MERCURY. The name was inspired by the magazine *American Mercury,* an iconoclastic and liberal journal founded by H. L. Mencken and George Jean Nathan that positioned itself against, as one wag had it, "organized religion, organized politics, and organized anything else." For their first production, they agreed to a modern-dress production of Shakespeare's *Julius Caesar.* It was an auspicious choice.

First, Welles had great affection for the play, having played Cassius and Mark Antony in a Todd School production. Also, *Julius Caesar* was one of the three plays that ROGER HILL and Welles included in their influential promptbook, *EVERYBODY'S SHAKESPEARE.* Although the origins of the spartan, modern-dress concept are unclear, with federal support no longer available, budgetary matters were certainly a factor. Also, given Welles's political liberalism and his concern over the rise of fascism in Europe, it seems certain that the director intended the play as a comment on both Mussolini (and Hitler) and modern dictatorships in general.

Eschewing props and scenery, Welles relied on a series of stark platforms with traps and ramps to suggest through abstract design the brutal harshness of a dictatorial state. The back of the unadorned brick stage with its hatchwork of steampipes was painted a primitive and violent red with a touch of blue. Welles told his young scene designer Sam Leve: "I want to give the audience a *hint* of a scene. No more than that. Give them too much and they won't contribute anything themselves. Give them just a suggestion and you get them working with you. That's what gives the theater meaning: when it becomes a social act." For costumes, Welles found leftover military uniforms from the 1924 production of *What Price Glory?* He had them dyed black and added shiny brass buttons. The conspirators wore contemporary suits and fedoras turned down at the brim in the manner of Hollywood gangsters.

As was his custom, Welles pared the play down to a briskly paced one and a half hours without an intermission. While essentially keeping Shakespeare's original language, he included such modernisms as "Aw, shut up!" and "Let him talk," both of which were uttered to quiet the crowd as Antony begins to deliver his eulogy over Caesar's body. Lines from *Coriolanus* and other Shakespeare plays were added as segues between elisions when something from *Caesar* couldn't be found to bridge the gaps. As with his other theater productions of the period, Welles's rehearsals were arduous. There was the usual grousing among cast and crew. Nonetheless, all participants willingly went along with the ordeal. Welles, after all, was "the boy genius of American theater." And, they were making art. And, also taking a political stand.

On November 11, 1937, just days after the signing of the Anti-Comintern Pact that sealed the military alliance between Germany, Italy, and Japan, the modern-dress *Julius Caesar* opened at the newly christened Mercury Theatre. FRANK BRADY reports that just before the curtain went up, Welles ordered that all the red *EXIT* lights be extinguished. It was, of course, a violation of the New York City fire code. It was also a brilliant theatrical gesture. With the theater in complete darkness, a lone and haunted voice cried out, "Caesar!" With that, the lights came up revealing Caesar, dressed in a fascist uniform, standing alone on the bare stage, exhorting, "Bid every noise be still!" It was an electrifying moment. Later, Welles, as Brutus gave what many consider one of his greatest theatrical performances. He described his Brutus bluntly: "He's the classical picture of the eternal, impotent, ineffectual, fumbling liberal, the reformer who wants to do something about things but doesn't know how, and gets it in the neck in the end. He's dead right all the time—and dead at the final curtain. He's Shakespeare's favorite hero—the fellow who thinks the times are out of joint, but who's really out of joint with his time."

One of the play's most striking scenes is the sinister attack on the poet Gaius Cinna. As played by Norman Lloyd, Cinna is a kind of street poet, a good-hearted pamphleteer who distributes politically subversive verses. When the innocent soul is mistaken for Cornelius Cinna, one of Caesar's assassins, a mob of gangsters, ignoring his plea, "But I am Cinna, the poet," close in on him, tear up his poems, and stab him repeatedly in a death scene paralleling that of Caesar's. The issue of whether or not the bald-pated Caesar played by Joseph Holland was interchangeable with Mussolini was a source of debate. Welles, for his part, initially denied the association. However, three weeks after the show's opening, he told the *New York Post* that the Cinna the Poet scene stood for "the hoodlum element you find in any big city after a war, a mob that is without the stuff that makes them intelligently alive, a lynching mob, the kind of mob that gives you a Hitler or Mussolini."

At a time when the United States was racked by pitched foreign policy debates pitting interventionists versus isolationists, the critics, seemingly not wanting to add fuel to that fire and thus unwittingly cause problems for the production, focused their rave reviews on the show's impressive staging. BROOKS ATKINSON of the *New York Times,* for example, praised the production's stripped down, honest, swift, and vivid nature. When contemporary events were linked to Welles's vision of the play, they were done so obliquely. John Mason Brown of the *New York Post* exclaimed: "Something deathless and dangerous in the world sweeps past you down the darkened aisles at the Mercury and takes possession of the proud, gaunt stage. It is something fearful and turbulent which distends the drama to include the life of nations as well as men. To an extent no other director in our day and country has equaled, Mr. Welles proves in his production that Shakespeare was indeed not of an age but for all time."

For Welles and Houseman, the debut of their Mercury Theatre was a triumph. Brooks Atkinson pronounced plainly: "Move over and make room for the Mercury Theatre." The raves, of course, boosted the box office. The show was also helped by comparisons to a contemporaneous and disastrous mounting of Shakespeare's *Antony and Cleopatra,* which one critic said "died sumptuously on $100,00 worth of Egyptology and a pyramid of adverse criticism." *Julius Caesar* also found favor among schoolchildren, who were bused in from all over the New York area for a dose of culture. The show's brisk pace, clear diction, violence, and 90-minute length were among the assets that helped make it accessible, even to school kids. *Julius Caesar* deserves a footnote in theater history for being the first drama to be commercially recorded in its entirety. The Columbia Records soundtrack album includes everything that was audible in the theater production, the dialogue, MARC BLITZSTEIN's score, the cries of the mob, offstage sounds, and the conversations of secondary characters.

The Mercury production of *Julius Caesar* ran from November 11, 1937, to June 11, 1938, after which it toured Providence, Boston, Hartford, Cleveland, Chicago, Toronto, and Washington, D.C. In addition to Welles (Brutus), Joseph Holland (Julius Caesar), and Norman Lloyd (Cinna the Poet), the play featured soon-to-be Mercury regulars JOSEPH COTTEN (Publicus), GEORGE COULOURIS (Marcus Antonius), MARTIN GABEL (Cassius), and WILLIAM ALLAND (Marullus).

—C.B.

Kael, Pauline (1919–2001) Controversial critic Pauline Kael, who dared to question ORSON WELLES's claims for the authorship of *CITIZEN KANE,* rose to national prominence as the film reviewer for *The New Yorker* until her retirement during the mid-1990s. She began writing film criticism in her mid-30s for the San Francisco quarterly *City Lights,* in 1953; it took her 15 years to get to *The New Yorker,* and once there she had to fight the entrenched stuffiness of that magazine to maintain her conversational style, asserting herself against stylistic demands of editor William Shawn. She came to be admired by the readers of *The New Yorker* and eventually became very influential. She fought pitched battles with *Village Voice* critic Andrew Sarris over the issue of auteur criticism, and she presumed to question the role Orson Welles played in shaping the script of *Citizen Kane,* asserting that more credit should have gone to screenwriter HERMAN J. MANKIEWICZ, who was once a Hearst insider, as Welles was not. If the character CHARLES FOSTER KANE resembled WILLIAM RANDOLPH HEARST, Kael believed it was because of Herman Mankiewicz. She built her thesis in an essay entitled "Raising Kane," first published in *The New Yorker* in 1971, an essay that was reprinted in *The Citizen Kane Book,* published "with illustrations" by the Boston publisher Little, Brown, and Company in 1971, along with "The Shooting Script by Herman J. Mankiewicz and Orson Welles," and "The Cutting Continuity of the Completed

Film." Kael called the film "a *shallow* masterpiece" that created "something aesthetically exciting and durable out of the playfulness of American muckraking satire." She took exception to Welles's claim that "Theatre is a collective experience; cinema is the work of one single person." In "Raising Kane," Kael wrote an extensive biography of Mankiewicz, so famous for his wit and worldliness he was called "the Central Park West Voltaire" by BEN HECHT. She claimed that Mankiewicz "proposed to Welles that they make a 'prismatic' movie about the life of a man seen from several different points of view," and that even before Mankiewicz moved to Hollywood, he was "already caught up in the idea of a movie about Hearst." Moreover, "Orson Welles wasn't around when *Citizen Kane* was written, early in 1940." Welles wanted to take full credit for the film, and when asked years later whether Mankiewicz wrote the scenario, his "set reply" was "Everything concerning Rosebud belongs to him," knowing full well that critics had dismissed the ROSEBUD solution as a mere gimmick. Other critics, such as critic-turned-filmmaker PETER BOGDANOVICH, rose to the challenge of defending Welles against these allegations. In his 1973 edition of *The Cinema of Orson Welles,* PETER COWIE criticized "the continuity published in Pauline Kael's *The Citizen Kane Book,* which deviates in points of detail from the actual film." Kael was a provocative critic of knee-jerk *auteurism,* but her broadside ultimately did little damage to Welles's standing, and, if anything, generated even more serious interest in *Citizen Kane.* Humorist and cartoonist Chuck Jones put the *Kane* controversy into perspective when, according to *Washington Post* critic Tom Shales, he once described Kael's "Raising Kane" essay as "an appauline case of overkael."

Reference Shales, Tom. "Chuck Jones, at the Acme of His Art," *Washington Post,* February 25, 2002 C4.

—J.M.W.

Kafka, Franz (1883–1924) The Prague-born Austro-Czech novelist Franz Kafka is known primarily for his short stories and also for three novels published after his death—*Amerika* (1927), *Das Schloss* (*The Castle,* 1926), and *Der Prozess* (1925). The latter of these was adapted to cinema by ORSON WELLES under the novel's English title, THE TRIAL, in 1963. In this allegory, the central character, "Josef K.," finds himself "arrested one fine morning," but "without having done anything wrong." Welles produced the film in France in 1963, shooting primarily in a French railway station. The film starred ANTHONY PERKINS as Josef K., the victimized protagonist. Welles himself appeared in the role of a lawyer.

Born a Jew in predominantly Catholic Czechoslovakia, Kafka grew up with a mother who was emotionally distant and a father who was dominant and overbearing. Kafka earned a law degree and eventually became an executive for the Workers Accident Insurance Company, but his writing reflects none of the pleasures of material success. Instead, his protagonists, particularly Josef K. in *The Trial* and Gregor Samsa in "The Metamorphosis" (1915), suffer an internal despair and enervation, an inability to fit into a society whose laws and mores seem beyond understanding.

Kafka's work was timely, even prophetic. In his most famous story, Kafka's Gregor Samsa "awoke one morning from uneasy dreams" to find that he had been transformed into a gigantic insect, *Ungeziefer* in German, the same word Hitler would later use to categorize gypsies, Slavs, Jews, and others the Nazis considered social "undesirables." So distinctive was Kafka's style that the word *Kafkaesque* was later coined to describe the alienation, absurdity, terror, and disjunctive grotesqueries of modern life. Kafka

was described by his biographer Frederick Karl as *the* "representative man" of the 20th century, an artist whose allegorical fiction defined the "age of anxiety" during the cold war. Other writers significantly influenced by his work include Samuel Beckett, Harold Pinter, and Gabriel Garcia Marquez.

References Baumer, Franz. *Franz Kafka* (New York: Ungar, 1971); Brod, Max. *Fanz Kafka: A Biography* (New York; Schocken Books, 1960); Sokel, Walter Herbert. *Franz Kafka* (New York: Columbia University Press, 1966).

—R.C.K. and J.M.W.

Karas, Anton (1906–1985) Composed and played the haunting zither theme for CAROL REED's 1949 thriller, THE THIRD MAN, which starred WELLES in the key role of Harry Lime. The story of how an obscure Viennese musician (Karas) came to prominence, is one of pure serendipity. The time: fall 1948. The setting: postwar Vienna. The situation: British director Carol Reed is in town shooting a mysterious thriller based on a story by GRAHAM GREENE called *The Third Man.* Reed, a meticulous planner, had worked out the majority of the production details, except for the music. At that point, all he knew was that he didn't want Strauss waltzes. Then, on an evening stroll through town, Reed stopped outside a tavern, enchanted by the haunting sounds of a zither. Immediately, Reed knew that he had solved his music dilemma. Reed introduced himself to Karas, persuaded him to make a test recording, and, ignoring the protests of those around him who argued for a more conventional score, hired Karas.

For Karas, a family man who for years had played for tips in Vienna taverns, the three-month stay in London to record the score was difficult. Reed, convinced that Karas's zither was going to play an important role in his film, had Karas stay at his home, where Reed's wife, Penelope, translated their German-English conversations. In devising the music for each scene, Karas screened the film hundreds of times. In the end, *The Third Man* wound up with an extensive score with Karas's zither "appearing" in virtually every scene. Just before *The Third Man*'s release, Reed tried to interest Britain's big record companies in a recording tie-in. The response from the music pros was negative—the zither melodies, they said, were too strange, too jangly. When the film debuted in England. in late 1949, with its opening credits superimposed over a closeup of Karas's fingers dancing atop his zither's 30-plus strings, record stores soon began getting requests for the music. Word quickly got back to the record companies, and British Decca (and, later, through its U.S. subsidiary, London Records) rushed a single to the market, which immediately rose to the top of the British pop charts. Decca followed the single with an LP album, whose jacket was graced with a menacing black silhouette of the enigmatic Harry Lime. Even though *The Third Man* didn't open in the United States until 1950, Karas's "Third Man Theme" soon topped the U.S. pop charts, providing a terrific "advance" for the film. During the "Third Man" frenzy, there were at least a dozen "cover" versions of Karas's tune by other performers.

Back in Vienna after scoring the film, Karas returned to the tavern where Reed had first heard him. He was still playing for tips. With the huge success of Reed's film and its score, Karas suddenly found himself lifted from obscurity. Along with the first royalty checks, there was a command performance for the British Royal Family and concert tours throughout the world. Karas recorded several follow-ups to "The Third Man Theme," including "Karol Theme," a tribute to the man who had changed his life. By the early 1950s, Karas, now a rich man after years of toiling in obscurity, was able to buy his own tavern, The Winehouse at the Sign of the Third Man. Thereafter, he only played and recorded for pleasure.

Other zither players who tried to replicate Karas's "Third Man Theme" fell short of the original. In part, that was because Karas had overdubbed several zither parts (in a manner comparable to the overdubbing innovations being made at about the same time in the United States by guitar wizard Les Paul). Additionally, Karas had found that by recording underneath Reed's kitchen table, there was a reverb effect that intensified the aura of the instrument's melancholy nature. In the meantime, Karas had started a zither craze. Later, "The Third Man Theme" was used in the 1951 British radio series, THE ADVENTURES OF HARRY LIME (starring Welles in a more benevolent evocation of the character), and in a late-1950s television series called THE THIRD MAN, featur-

ing Michael Rennie in the title role. Today, Kara's "Third Man Theme" remains an indelible part of our collective conscience.

So powerful was the association between Welles's Harry Lime and Karas's insinuating melody that after *The Third Man*'s 1949 release, whenever Welles entered a restaurant or club that had an orchestra or pianist, the musicians would usually strike up the signature "Third Man Theme." For Welles, who wanted to be recognized primarily for his own work, this reflexive musical association with the Reed-Greene-Karas shaped character became a burden and at times even an irritant.

—C.B.

Kazan, Elia (Elia Kazanjoglou) (1909–)

Elia Kazan appeared in minor roles in ORSON WELLES'S THE SHADOW radio series, which began in spring 1937 for the Mutual Broadcasting System. In his autobiography, *Elia Kazan: A Life* (1988), Kazan discusses seeing Welles appear in the studio after a night of carousing: "Orson had unflagging energy and recuperative powers at that time. . . . Seldom have I been near a man so abundantly talented or one with a greater zest for life." This is in stark contrast to Welles's appearance and fate many years later. Kazan, aware of the wasted potential, comments, "And what about Orson Welles, the most talented and inventive theatre man of my day: What an ass he seemed in the posh restaurants and hotels of Europe's capitals, and how sad later, in financial desperation, making TV commercials."

Elia Kazan, born Elia Kazanjoglou in Istanbul on September 7, 1909, came to America with his parents when he was four years old. He graduated from Williams College, studied drama at Yale University, and in 1932 became an actor and assistant stage manager with the Group Theatre. He directed his first play in 1935 and during the 1940s became well known for directing plays by Tennessee Williams and Arthur Miller. His film-directing career began in 1937 with *The People of Cumberland,* a short documentary about coal miners. He made another documentary, *It's Up to You* (1941), about food rationing, for the U.S. Department of Agriculture. His feature films have often tended to be adaptations of literary works, especially plays: *A Tree Grows in Brooklyn* (1945), *A Streetcar Named Desire* (1951), *East of Eden* (1955), *Splendor in the Grass* (1961), and *The Last Tycoon* (1976), his last film. He has also adapted two of his own novels, *America America* and *The Arrangement,* to film (in 1963 and 1969). Several other Kazan films have tackled controversial subjects: *Pinky* (1949) concerned race; *Gentleman's Agreement* (1947) concerned anti-Semitism; and *On the Waterfront* (1954) concerned union corruption, as well as alluding to the question of "informing," a hot topic since Hollywood was under investigation by the House Un-American Activities Committee. In addition to directing, Kazan also produced many of his films. As a director, he won Oscars for *Gentleman's Agreement* and *On the Waterfront*. He also continued his work in theater, forming the Actors Studio in 1947, directing plays by William Inge and Tennessee Williams on Broadway in the 1950s, and in 1963 becoming co-director of the Repertory Theatre of Lincoln Center for the Performing Arts; but in 1964 he severed his connection with the stage, declaring that "movies is where all the action is." In addition to his autobiography and the two novels adapted to film, Kazan has written three more novels: *The Understudy* (1974), *Act of Love* (1978), and *The Anatolian* (1988).

References Kazan, Elia. *Elia Kazan: A Life* (New York: Da Capo, 1997); ———. *Kazan: The Master Director Discusses His Films* (New York: Newmarket Press, 1999); Michaels, Lloyd. *Elia Kazan: A Guide to References and Resources* (Boston: G.K. Hall, 1985).

—T.L.E.

Kent, Amalia

Amalia Kent, who was a continuity supervisor and a script writer at RKO, helped ORSON WELLES learn the ABC's of script writing. When Welles came to Hollywood, he did not know how shots were described in a screenplay. When he set about writing his film adaptation of Joseph Conrad's *HEART OF DARKNESS* (1939), he was aided by Kent. Welles had compiled a kind of scrapbook that contained passages from the original that he intended to use in the film. According to DAVID THOMSON, Welles "had not known the terminology or the rather stilted discipline of a screenplay, that hybrid of literature and a skeletal plan for making a film." Kent taught him how shots were described. With her help his scrapbook was made into a kind of screenplay. In early 1940, Welles worked with Kent again, this time on *THE SMILER WITH A KNIFE*. Thomson writes, "No one seems disposed to argue that it [*The Smiler with the Knife*] was the work of anyone except Welles and Amalia Kent—though screenwriter Gene Towne apparently gave some useful advice." Kent was also involved in the screenplay for *THE MAGNIFICENT AMBERSONS*. Thomson describes the genesis of the screenplay: "Using King Vidor's yacht, Welles and his script assistant Amalia Kent sailed off to Catalina Island late in July. He fashioned a script—using the radio script as a basis and staying very faithful to the novel. Kent then turned that into a shooting script."

—T.L.E.

King, Henry (1888–1982)

Henry King directed ORSON WELLES in *A PRINCE OF FOXES* (1948). A consummate craftsman and director of great versatility, Henry King's long career spanned almost a half century. Despite a handful of acknowledged masterpieces, however, he still awaits auteur status. Never a maverick, he worked comfortably within the Hollywood studio system. As historian William K. Everson has noted, "For directors of the past to be rediscovered by contemporary critics, they usually have to have been off-beat, ahead of their time, or even abysmally bad but at the same time interesting in a bizarre way. But King fits into none of these categories. Far from being ahead of his time, he was exactly *of* his time." Which, of course, is precisely why he is of great interest.

He was born on June 24, 1886, near Christianburg, Virginia. When he was four years old, the family moved to Lafayette, where he went to high school. His interest in theatrical activities led to a job with the Empire Stock Company, a touring repertory company. His barnstorming days continued with a stint in the Jolly American Tramp Show, with which he traveled across the United States. Engaged by the Lubin West Coast Company, he came to Los Angeles to appear as an actor in the movies. He quickly advanced to an apprenticeship in directing under the supervision of Thomas Ince in 1916 with his first feature, *Little Mary Sunshine*. After a series of purportedly lackluster programmers, he made *Tol'able David* in 1921. This acknowledged classic reveals some of the traits that would distinguish his more mature efforts. The rural story of a young man (Richard Barthelmess) forced by dire circumstances to prove himself a man, is sensitive to landscape and a tribute to the virtues of the family unit. Pudovkin praised its editing strategies in his book, *On Film Technique*. "There was a great deal of me in *Tol'able David*," King recalled. "It was made just eighty miles from where I was born. I knew the people. I knew what the boy's desires were. His experiences were things I had known as a child. Every motion picture that you make has something of yourself in it, something you've learned, something in the back of your mind."

Other notable films in the silent period include a Lillian Gish vehicle, *The White Sister* (1923), the first and still the best version of *Stella Dallas* (1925), and a western that brought Gary Cooper to the screen, *The Winning of Barbara Worth* (1927). The best of his early talkies, *Over the Hill* (1929), returns to the simplicities and virtues of rural family life. This unaffected idealism of the American scene reappears in King's best work of the 1930s and 1940s, when he began to work exclusively for Fox and DARRYL F. ZANUCK in pictures like *State Fair* (1933), starring Will Rogers; *In Old Chicago* (1938), a spectacular re-creation of the Great Chicago Fire; and *Alexander's Ragtime Band* (1938), a thinly disguised biopic of songwriter Irving Berlin; and *Margie* (1943), a loving evocation of a schoolgirl's life in the 1920s. Differing in conception and scope were a Western, *Jesse James* (1939), an overblown political epic, *Wilson* (a dismal failure at the box office in 1944), and several swashbucklers that featured TYRONE POWER (*The Black Swan*, 1942; *Captain from Castile*, 1948). Two psychological thrillers from this period are *Twelve O'Clock High* and *The Gunfighter* (both 1950). Both feature Gregory Peck as a heroic figure beset by the challenges of age, circumstances, and mental turmoil. Action is downplayed in favor of a meditation on a character in crisis.

King's last nine films were shot in the Cinema-Scope wide-screen process. *The Sun Also Rises* (1957) and *The Snows of Kilimanjaro* (1952) were adaptations from Ernest Hemingway; *Carousel* (1956), based on the Rodgers and Hammerstein musical play, and *Love Is a Many-Splendored Thing* (1955) are unabashed romantic essays on love's labors lost, and *I'd Climb the Highest Mountain* (1951) marks a return to King's favorite themes and settings of ordinary country life. Before his death in 1982, King began to enjoy a renewed interest in his work through retrospectives and critical reassessment. He remained active to a ripe old age, passing a pilot's physical and acquiring a flying license at age 94. To the end, he remained matter-of-fact about his work, refusing to indulge in speculations about its "artistic" pretensions. "I just like to tell stories," he said. "Making a motion picture is the greatest fun I've had in my life. You can work yourself completely to death and enjoy every minute of it." To this day, however, as critic Andrew Sarris has noted, King's work is "a subject for further research."

References Coppedge, Walter. *Henry King's America* (Metuchen, N.J.: Scarecrow, 1986); Denton, Clive, et. al. *The Hollywood Professionals: Henry King, Lewis Milestone, Sam Wood* (New York: A.S. Barnes, 1974).

—J.C.T.

King Lear (television, 1953)

Produced for *Omnibus*, CBS's highly touted pioneering Sunday afternoon arts program funded by the Ford Foundation's Television-Radio Workshop, this widely lauded production earned WELLES his best U.S. reviews in years and reunited him with director PETER BROOK, actor MICHEÁL MACLIAMMÓIR (Edgar), and composer VIRGIL THOMSON. The cast also included Alan Badel as the Fool, Beatrice Straight as Goneril, and Natasha Parry, Brook's wife, as Cordelia *King Lear* was produced by Fred Rickey, and hosted by Alistair Cooke.

In 1953, because of tax difficulties with the Internal Revenue Service stemming from the ill-fated 1946 production of *AROUND THE WORLD IN 80 DAYS*, Welles had not set foot in the United States for almost six years. In the interim, an explosion in live televised drama had taken place in the United States. Indeed, when culture commentators refer to "The Golden Age of Television," it is largely because of such live dramatic series such as *Omnibus, Studio One* and *Playhouse 90*. Welles sensed that the New York–based, live television drama scene of the early 1950s was akin to the kind of revolution in live radio drama that he himself had helped lead in New York during the 1930s. Therefore, it was not surprising that he jumped at the invitation to play Lear made by noted British theater director Peter Brook.

Indeed, Welles had longed to play the heroic Lear, which he regarded as the most tragically poignant role in all of English drama. He had had a fling at Lear on radio for the MERCURY THEATRE ON THE AIR. But now, older and wiser, Welles knew that his time for Lear had come. Because *Omnibus* was a 90-minute show, with 17 minutes allocated to commercials, the actual running time had to clock in at exactly 73 minutes. Welles, with Brook's approval, slashed away the subplots. He told a TV critic at the time: "The central story would still be there. That's all people remember anyhow." To preserve as much of the remaining dramatic continuity as possible, the sponsors, in a highly unusual arrangement, agreed to run their ads only before and after the play.

In regard to his running battle with the IRS, Welles was able to work out a deal so that he would be paid in part by check, which the IRS would tax, and in cash, which Welles could pocket. In addition, there was a lavish daily expense account and a posh suite at the Plaza Hotel. Initially, upon seeing his first American television in his room at the Plaza, Welles was appalled by the small and poor quality image, and yet also fascinated by the new medium's possibilities. After two weeks of rehearsals, Welles had become convinced of television's significance largely because of the medium's live, in-the-moment immediacy; the mobility of the cameras; and, in comparison to film, TV's relatively low production costs. However, responding to the outsized claims then being made for TV largely due to its novelty, Welles added a note of skepticism when he told newspaperman Art Buchwald: "Everything you do now in television is considered original. In ten years the critics will kick you in the teeth for doing the same things, and call you arty."

With only a few caveats, the October 18, 1953, live broadcast of *King Lear* was by most accounts a success. As FRANK BRADY points out, over 15 million people saw Welles's and Brook's *King Lear,* more than the number of people who had seen the play since its first appearance at the Globe Theatre in the early 1600s.

TV critic Jack Gould of the *New York Herald Tribune* typified the reactions of the pundits by noting that Welles had "caught the human qualities of the King." There were some complaints about voice-levels, a problem in part exacerbated by the "live drama" format as well as by the poor sound quality of the first generation of television sets. Still, the critical response was overwhelmingly positive. So, too, audience response. In fact, *King Lear* generated more positive mail for *Omnibus* than any of its other presentations.

As a result of the show's success and the publicity heaped on Welles and CBS, Welles met with various CBS executives about other TV ventures. Representatives of the rival NBC and ABC networks entered into negotiations as well. At first, it seemed like the good old days of the late 1930s, when, before signing with RKO, producers were courting him with ardor and dollars. However, the meetings stalled when Welles and his lofty ideas failed to mesh with the increasingly ratings-driven grind then coalescing as the norm for the television industry.

King Lear was a triumph. It was not, however, a cause célèbre comparable to his infamous 1938 radio broadcast of THE WAR OF THE WORLDS. Without a TV deal in hand, and an expense account that had expired, Welles returned to England..

Three years later, Welles returned to New York to star as Lear in a 1956 theatrical production mounted at the City Center. See KING LEAR (play, 1956).

—C.B.

King Lear (play, 1956) In October 1955, Welles returned to the United States from England with hopes of establishing a repertory company in the manner of his hugely successful MERCURY THEATRE of the late 1930s. Working under the aegis of the New York City Center Theatre Company, Welles and Broadway producers MARTIN GABEL and Henry Margolis initially discussed a 1956 winter season that would alternate Ben Jonson's *VOLPONE* (with JACKIE GLEASON as Mosca); Shakespeare's *TWELFTH NIGHT*; *EVERYBODY'S SHAKESPEARE*; *MOBY DICK—REHEARSED*; and *King Lear.* Various problems, especially funding, resulted in a greatly truncated "season." Instead of a two-month repertory season with four plays, only *Lear* would be produced, and then for a mere three-week run.

Welles, returning to the New York stage after a 10-year hiatus following the ruinous AROUND THE WORLD IN 80 DAYS (1946), was understandably nervous. In December 1955, with his dream of reestablishing a Broadway-based repertory company in shambles because of budgetary constraints, Welles also had to confront a chillier climate for producing theater than that which prevailed during the halcyon days of his Mercury and FEDERAL THEATRE project of the late 1930s. Actors Equity, for example, conspired with the U.S. Immigration Service to deny work permits to five British actors that Welles had wanted to use. Later, some of his cast members, knowing that they were second choices, used their union's stringent work rules to thwart Welles's desire for extended rehearsals. "I had a whole English cast which were refused entry," he told biographer Barbara Leaming, "and I had to hurry and find people to take their place. I had a Cordelia who had her coach out there during rehearsals—the Method was in full swing with the actors [then]. And they had all read the small print in the Equity book and quit in the middle of a sentence when the day's work was done! All this was so new to me!"

Welles, who had scored a huge success as Lear in his American television debut in 1953, faced even greater problems. Shortly before the January 12, 1956, debut, Welles fell backstage and broke two bones in his often injured left foot. On opening night, he essayed his Lear with a cast. Given Lear's age and general infirmities, playing the part with a cane really was not that much of a stretch. Still, Welles's performance was savaged by the critics—but not for the cane. The *New York Herald Tribune*'s Walter Kerr complained about Welles's lack of genuine emotion: "He sounds a bass-note at regular intervals, pauses metronomically, varies from shout to whimper on a prearranged schedule. The result is an intelligent automaton at center stage." The *New York Times*'s Brooks Atkinson, a Welles advocate in the 1930s, now took a different tone, concluding that "Welles showed more genius than talent." Although his acting was panned, there was praise for his direction from credible sources such as Eric Bentley of *The New Republic*. Even Atkinson agreed, noting Welles's bold use of space, his audacious omission of an intermission in a three-hour show, and the stirring force of his production. Still, Atkinson kept returning to the subject of acting: "[Welles's] reverberant style of speaking, usually at the top of his voice, has the effect of throwing the lines away; and he also breaks the lines whimsically as though he were not much interested in their meaning."

Welles, in retrospect, seems to have agreed. "I think I may have been very bad opening night," Welles told Leaming. "I was [physically] hurt, but the thing that *really* did it to me was the applause when I [first] appeared. It was so enormous and so long and so sustained that it completely disoriented me. I ceased to be Lear. I just thought, *these people think they've got a great actor come back, and oh Christ, what can I do?* I hate to be applauded except at the end, you know. When they do all that and I look down and see people I know clapping their hands and smiling with happy anticipation, the energy runs right out between my toes. And I think that happened to me to some extent on *Lear*. . . . I think I gave my *worst* performance opening night. Suddenly I felt a very strong sense of not belonging to that audience or to that town, even though they gave me that reception. It's very curious."

Compounding the physical and psychological pains of the nerve-wracking opening night was a completely unforeseen event. Immediately following the performance, Welles stumbled backstage and sprained his right ankle, forcing him to render his Lear from a wheelchair on the second night. Appearing before a full house, Welles, attired in suit and tie, rolled his wheelchair on stage and apologized for seeming more like "the man who came to dinner" than Lear. Knowing that his first responsibility to his backers was "to keep the audience in its seats, at least until the box office closes and the chance for refunds past," he presented what, in essence, was "An Evening with Orson Welles." He read and commented on selections from *Lear*. He fired off quips. "Please don't take pictures," he pleaded with a wry smile. "That clicking noise sounds like the breaking of bones." There were also gentle barbs aimed at the first-night critics as well as at himself.

For the third night and the remainder of the run, Welles soldiered on in costume—and in wheelchair.

To solve the mobility problem, Lear's Fool was delegated the responsibility of getting his master from one spot on stage to the next. As Frank Brady notes, Welles apparently began to enjoy being wheeled about. Still, in what proved to be his last appearance on the New York stage, Welles's experience with this *King Lear* was a personal disaster, a blow to his confidence as an actor, and a finalizing defeat of his dream to install a repertory theater on the Great White Way.

Still, even this storm had a silver lining in that his improvised banter served as a "rehearsal" for his later role as a knowingly self-deprecating television talk show raconteur. On the first night of *Lear*, when he brought up the houselights and apologized, Welles, in the words of David Thomson, "explained the situation as he sought forbearance. He used that favorite ploy that was at the same time self-glorifying and confessional: 'Ladies and gentlemen, this is Orson Welles, and I am in trouble.'" In his 1960s and 1970s television appearances, Welles would perfect a delicate balance between the self-glorifying and the confessional as he won over a new generation of fans who, though they had little knowledge of his films or theater or radio work, nonetheless found something irresistible about this obviously great yet fallen giant who beneath the bluff and bravado palpitated with a compelling sense of the tragic.

Along with Welles in the title role, the cast of the 1956 City Center *King Lear* included Alvin Epstein (Lear's Fool), GERALDINE FITZGERALD (Goneril), VIVECA LINDFORS (Cordelia), Sylvia Short (Regan), and John Colicos (Edmund). The production also reunited Welles with composer MARC BLITZSTEIN, whose nails-on-the-chalkboard harpsichord scoring of Lear's progressive descent into madness was augmented at the play's conclusion by tapes of strident sounds constructed by electronic music pioneer Vladimir Ussachevsky. Supervising affairs for the New York City Center Theatre Company was Jean Dalrymple.

References Brady, Frank. *Citizen Welles: A Biography of Orson Welles* (New York: Scribners, 1989); Higham, Charles. *Orson Welles: The Rise and Fall of an American Genius* (New York: St. Martin's Press, 1985); Leaming, Barbara. *Orson Welles: A Biography* (New York: Viking Press, 1985); Thomson, David. *Rosebud: The Story of Orson Welles* (New York: Knopf, 1996).

—C. B.

King of Kings Metro-Goldwyn-Mayer, 151 minutes, 1961. **Director:** Nicholas Ray; **Producer:** Samuel Bronston; **Screenplay:** Philip Yordan; **Cinematographers:** Frank F. Planer, Milton Krasner, Manuel Berenguer; **Editors:** Harold Kress and Renee Lichtig; **Music:** Miklos Rozsa; **Cast:** Orson Welles (narrator); Jeffrey Hunter (Jesus Christ), Viveca Linfors (Claudia), Hurd Hatfield (Pontius Pilate), Siobhan McKenna (Mary), Rip Torn (Judas), Robert Ryan (John the Baptist), Carmen Seville (Mary Magdalene), Rita Gam (Herodias), George Coulouris

A film directed by Nicholas Ray featuring WELLES as narrator. One of the better Hollywood biblical epics of the period, director Ray's version of the life of Christ is given perspective by a voice-over narrative reportedly written by an uncredited Ray Bradbury and delivered with appropriate gravity by Welles. Events covered are the birth of Jesus in a Bethlehem stable; the prophesies of John the Baptist and his murder; the 40-day ordeal of Jesus in the desert; the selection of the apostles; the betrayal of Jesus by Judas; the Passion; the Crucifixion; the Resurrection; and the Ascension. Produced by Samuel Bronston, and in part inspired by Cecil B. DeMille's 1927 mega-hit of the same title, *King of Kings* featured Jeffrey Hunter (Jesus Christ), Siobban McKenna (Mary, Mother of Jesus), Robert Ryan (John the Baptist), Hurt Hatfield (Pontius Pilate), Ron Randell (Lucius, The Centurion), Viveca Lindfors (Claudia), Rita Gam (Herodias), Carmen Sevilla (Mary Magdalene), Harry Guardino (Barabbas), Rip Torn (Judas), and a veteran of *CITIZEN KANE,* GEORGE COULOURIS, as the Camel Driver.

Shot in Spain, *King of Kings,* like most biblical epics from the first stage of the wide-screen era of the 1950s–60s, earned few raves. Referring to the project, Hollywood insiders had labeled "I Was a Teenage Jesus," British film critic Dilys Powell noted: "I have decided to confer on *King of Kings* both my 1961 Scripture Prizes: (1) Dullest; (2) Most Undenominational." Director Nicholas Ray, in reaction to scribes such as Powell, opined: "They are not hip enough with the times of Christ." Today, the film's pace seems especially tedious. Nonetheless, Welles's grand voice remains impressive throughout.

Reference Kreidl, John Francis. *Nicholas Ray* (Boston: Twayne, 1977).

—C.B.

Kitt, Eartha (1928–) African-American singer, dancer, and sometime actress Eartha Kitt was born on January 26, 1928, in rural South Carolina. By the time she was eight years old, she had moved to Harlem, and she went on to attend the New School of Performing Arts, which opened her career with the Katherine Dunham dance troupe and introduced her to Europe. After touring with Katherine Dunham, she remained in Paris and became a successful chanteuse. When she returned to New York, she became popular at Manhattan supper clubs and ultimately appeared in *New Faces of 1952* on Broadway. That production was later filmed as *New Faces of 1954,* her motion picture debut. On the Broadway stage she starred in the musical *Timbuktu* and the black-cast production of *Kismet.* She continued to appear in films into the 1990s (not all of them distinguished) and was the subject of a 1982 documentary film entitled *All by Myself.*

In 1950, ORSON WELLES, who was having financial problems with his film production of OTHELLO, turned to repertory theater in Paris. With backing from producer Jerry Laven, he staged THE BLESSED AND THE DAMNED, which played at the Théâtre Edouard 7 in Paris. *The Blessed and the Damned* consisted of two short plays: *Time Runs,* a modernized version of Christopher Marlowe's DR. FAUSTUS; and a satire on contemporary Hollywood entitled THE UNTHINKING LOBSTER. According to FRANK BRADY, Welles wanted Eartha Kitt for the part of Helen of Troy in *Time Runs;* Welles himself would play Faust in the second billing. BARBARA LEAMING claims that Kitt had worshipped Welles and had seen CITIZEN KANE five times. During one of the performances, an overly enthusiastic Welles bit Kitt on the lips so hard that she bled. She "suspected it was the conspicuous presence in the front row of an older gentleman friend of hers from the States that triggered Orson's jealous outbursts." *Time Runs* opened on June 19,

1950, to mixed reviews, although Welles's acting, DUKE ELLINGTON's music, and Kitt's singing were all praised. Soon photographs of Welles and Kitt appeared all over Europe with the implication that she was his new love interest. After *The Blessed and the Damned* completed a six-week run in Paris, Welles retitled it, modestly, AN EVENING WITH ORSON WELLES and took it on tour in Germany for a month. German audiences certainly appreciated Welles, but they were even more impressed with Eartha Kitt. Kitt wrote in her autobiography, *Alone with Me* (1976): "Now the papers came out and they said, 'Orson may think it's an evening with Orson Welles, but it's really an evening with Eartha Kitt.' Orson became very jealous. He didn't talk to me for a month." In addition to *Alone with Me,* Kitt wrote other memoirs: *Thursday's Child* (1956), *A Tart Is Not a Sweet* (1976), and *I'm Still Here: Confessions of a Sex Kitten* (1992).

References Kitt, Eartha. *Rejuvenate!: It's Never Too Late* (New York: Scribner's, 2001); ———. *Thursday's Child* (London: Cassell, 1957); ———. *Alone with Me: A New Autobiography* (Chicago: H. Regnery, 1976).

—T.L.E. and J.M.W.

Koch, Howard (1902–1995) John HOUSEMAN hired Howard Koch as a scriptwriter for the MERCURY THEATRE ON THE AIR in 1938. Koch, a graduate of Columbia Law School, had turned to theater after practicing law for five years in Hartsdale, New York. He wrote and produced some plays, one of which Houseman had seen and liked. Koch, responsible for turning out approximately 60 pages of script each week, had done excellent work on *Hell on Ice,* which concerned the DeJong expedition to the North Pole, and *Seventeen,* an adaptation of BOOTH TARKINGTON's popular novel. His third assignment for Mercury was an adaptation of H.G. WELLS's *The War of the Worlds.* Welles wanted the script, which was to be a dramatization of a contemporary occurrence in news bulletin form, to be finished in six days. After it was completed, it was sent for approval to the network, which objected to realistic place names. When the show was aired on October 30, 1938, there was widespread panic as listeners, who either did not hear or ignored the disclaimer at the start of the show, believed that there was indeed an invasion from Mars. Despite the panic, Welles and Mercury were famous. The next week the *Mercury Theatre on the Air* became the CAMPBELL PLAYHOUSE, and three months later, Koch left for a 12-year stint in Hollywood as a screenwriter. He was an immediate success. After writing *The Sea Hawk* (1940) as a vehicle for Errol Flynn, he adapted Somerset Maugham's short story "The Letter" to the screen. Koch, a pacifist, then wrote the acclaimed *Sergeant York* (1941) starring Gary Cooper, and then was co-author of the legendary *Casablanca* (1942). He was then assigned by Jack Warner to write the script for *Mission to Moscow* (1943), a film favorable to the Russians, then our allies. In 1947, after World War II, Jack Warner denounced him as a communist and pointed to his script as evidence. At first he was on the "Gray List," which meant he got some writing assignments; but eventually he was blacklisted. Before he left for Europe, *Letter from an Unknown Woman* (1948) appeared—it was one of his best scripts. In Europe he was exploited by a producer Koch identifies in his autobiography as "Mr. Roman without the *off*," and then went to England, where he and his family socialized with other expatriates. While there he wrote an uncredited script for Joseph Losey, *The Intimate Stranger* (1956). In 1956, he returned to the United States, where he wrote more scripts, most notably *The War Lover* (1962) and an adaptation of D.H. Lawrence's *The Fox* (1967).

Koch's actual contribution to the script for *WAR OF THE WORLDS* is a matter of some dispute. When Hadley Cantril, a sociology professor, wrote *The Invasion from Mars,* an account of the fictional invasion, he referred to Koch as the author of the script. Welles was incensed, declared that other members of the Mercury staff had contributed more to the script than Koch, and demanded that Princeton University, the publisher, add a correction to the book noting that Koch was not the author. Koch, however, held copyright, as part of an agreement with Mercury, for all the scripts that he worked on, including *War of the Worlds.* SIMON CALLOW explains Welles's demands and legal threats as the result of fear: "It had now become essential to him (in his own mind, at any rate) to maintain his position as Renaissance Man. Under constant pressure from a carping, mocking press, he dreaded being found out as less than what he claimed to be."

Reference Koch, Howard. *As Time Goes By: Memoirs of a Writer* (New York: Harcourt Brace Jovanovich, 1979).
—T.L.E.

Kodar, Oja (Oldga Palinkas) (1940?–)

In 1962, when WELLES was filming *THE TRIAL* in Zagreb, he met the woman who was to become his chief creative collaborator for the last 20 years of his life. Oldga Palinkas, whom Welles renamed Oja Kodar, was, according to FRANK BRADY, half Hungarian and half Yugoslavian (more exactly, Croatian). Her father worked on set design for *The Trial.* She acted, wrote screenplays, and sculpted (because of chauvinistic attitudes toward female sculpturors, she exhibited her work under the name of Vladimir Zadrov). According to BARBARA LEAMING, Welles was impressed by a scenario she had written and by her independence of spirit. Leaming quotes producer Dominique Antoine: "He worships her, he really worships her, because she's the first intelligent woman he has had in his life." Although he was still married to PAOLA MORI, his third and last wife, he began an affair with Kodar that lasted until his death. In 1967, he and Kodar were living together in Paris while he was working on *THE IMMORTAL STORY,* and in 1968 when Welles began work on *THE DEEP,* he cast Kodar as the victim of the psychopathic killer who was played by LAURENCE HARVEY. CHARLES HIGHAM reports that there was little love lost between Kodar and JEANNE MOREAU, who also appeared in the film. Kodar also appeared in and received screenwriting credit for Welles's *F FOR FAKE* (1973), a film that begins as a documentary, already shot by François Reichenbach, proceeds to details of Welles's life, in which he admits to being a mountebank, and concludes with a 17-minute segment featuring Kodar, Pablo Picasso, and art forgery. When the segment is completed, Welles admits the Kodar/Picasso story is pure fiction.

Despite the deepening relationship with Kodar, Welles maintained his marriage to Mori, who accepted the sophisticated situation. Brady writes, "Orson had been able to balance these two parts of his personal life for a number of years, keeping both women happy, even though each knew about the other." Welles traveled back and forth between

Sedona, Arizona, and, later, Las Vegas (home and Mori), and Los Angeles (business and Kodar). His Yugoslavian connections, via Kodar, led to roles for himself and for Kodar in *The Secret of Nikola Tesla* (1980). Welles and Kodar also wrote a screenplay for a film version of THE DREAMERS, adapted by ISAK DINESEN from two stories in her *Seven Gothic Tales* (1934). Kodar was to play Pellegrina Leoni, an opera singer, and Welles was to play her close friend. Only a small segment of the movie was shot, but those who have seen it consider it vintage Welles. Another abortive casting endeavor for Kodar involved another film adaptation of *Lear* with Kodar playing Cordelia. When Welles died on October 9, 1985, his will, made three years earlier, provided for not only his three daughters ($10,000 each), but for both Mori (the Las Vegas house) and Kodar (the remainder of the estate). At the November 4, 1985, memorial service for Welles, Kodar spoke out bitterly about the uninvited mourners who did nothing to help Welles while he was alive. Her address, in which she attacked the Hollywood industry and the French government for their treatment of Welles, was greeted with thunderous applause. As part of her inheritance Kodar got the rights to the interviews which director/film critic PETER BOGDANOVICH had conducted with Welles over many years. She asked Bogdanovich to help arrange the material, but he instead recommended that she seek the help of JONATHAN ROSENBAUM, who edited the tapes and manuscripts and published them as *This Is Orson Welles* (1992). In 1988 she and Orson Welles appeared in HENRY JAGLOM's SOMEONE TO LOVE. She was one of the judges at the Venice Film Festival in 1991 and in 1993 was chosen to direct a film entitled *A Time for . . .*, which concerned the conflict between Serbia and Croatia. In 1999 THE BIG BRASS RING, scripted by Welles and Kodar, appeared as a television film directed by George Hickenlooper. The same year Kodar was planning a Welles documentary to be entitled *One Man Band,* based on nearly two tons of recovered and restored Welles footage.

—T.L.E.

Koerner, Charles W. (1897–1946) Charles Koerner, who took over the job of RKO production

head from GEORGE J. SCHAEFER, was responsible for terminating Welles's RKO contract in the summer of 1942. It was a dramatic reversal that no one could have predicted three years earlier when Welles, after Schaefer's two-year courtship, signed the famously liberal July 22, 1939, contract that called for the 24-year "Boy Wonder" to act in, direct, write, and produce films of his own choosing. Schaefer, appointed to his RKO post in 1938, in addition to signing Welles, also helped the studio prosper in the late 1930s. However, with the failure of would-be blockbusters such as John Ford's *Abe Lincoln in Illinois* (1940), the studio's fortunes started to slide. Even with hits by RKO-affiliated producers Sam Goldwyn and Walt Disney, the studio still lost money because of unfavorable profit splits it had negotiated for distributing the product of its independent suppliers.

Schaefer's sinking ship took on more water with the box-office failure of CITIZEN KANE in 1941. With the convoluted fiascos involving Welles's THE MAGNIFICENT AMBERSONS (1942), the aborted IT'S ALL TRUE (shot during 1942), and the star-crossed JOURNEY INTO FEAR (shot in 1942; released in 1943), RKO's New York–based board of directors had seen enough of both Schaefer and Welles. In early 1942, when Wall Street financier Floyd Odlum took over majority interest in RKO, his first act was to fire Schaefer. Odlum replaced Schaefer with Charles Koerner, who had served RKO in New York as general manager of the company's national theater circuit. An astute movie man, Koerner knew the business primarily as an exhibitor. Once arriving in Hollywood to take on the job of head of production, Koerner, acting on behalf of RKO's board, made the dismissal of Welles one of his top priorities.

In mid-1942, with Welles in Brazil shooting *It's All True,* Koerner made his first strike at Mercury Productions by taking over the editing of *The Magnificent Ambersons.* Since Welles's version of the BOOTH TARKINGTON novel had previewed poorly, Koerner, whose motto was "showmanship instead of genius," slashed *Ambersons* so drastically that Welles found it virtually unrecognizable. Even with an hour of the Welles version left on the cutting room floor, and the remainder radically recut for "narrative clarity," Koerner was still not enthusiastic, especially since

Amberson's dark subject matter was deemed out of touch with the wartime vogue for upbeat and uplifting entertainment. Having given up hope of *Ambersons* doing any significant business on its own, Koerner dumped the mutilated version of Welles's opus at the bottom of a double bill headlined by the studio's *Mexican Spitfire Sees a Ghost,* an ersatz comedy starring Lupe Velez and Charles "Buddy" Rogers. When Welles returned to Hollywood on August 22, 1942, with his Mercury colleagues already dismissed, it was clear that his RKO days as a director-producer were numbered. Koerner formally dismissed Welles from RKO in July 1942.

Although Welles commentators and fans almost always cast Koerner as the heavy for having sandbagged the director, the fact that Welles's three RKO releases failed to find audiences should not be forgotten. At the time of Welles's firing, the red ink hemorrhaging from his four failed Mercury projects was approaching $4 million. While Hollywood still sought out Welles as an actor, he was persona non grata as a director-producer. Koerner, without Welles to contend with, earned Odlum's respect by punching up the studio's profits during the remainder of his tenure. As reported by Thomas Schatz in *Boom and Bust: Hollywood in the 1940s,* under Koerner, RKO's profits rose from $600,000 in 1942 to $6.9 million a year later. The trend continued throughout the war. In 1946, when Koerner suddenly died, Dore Schary, an independent producer with an RKO distribution deal, was picked by RKO to succeed the successful showman.

Born in New Orleans, Koerner began his lifelong association with show business as a boy. Shortly after his family moved to Havre, Montana, he found a job as a projectionist. After attending the Shattuck Military Academy at Faribault, Minnesota, Koerner returned to Havre to run a small motion picture theater, which he sold in 1917 when he enlisted for World War I. Following the war, he spent six years working in Butte, Montana, and Portland, Oregon, as a branch manager for Jensen & Von Herberg, who owned a chain of Pacific Northwest movie theaters. In 1925, Koerner joined the George Mann theater circuit of Northern California. When the Mann chain was sold to Hughes-Franklin in 1931, Koerner became Harold B. Franklin's personal representative.

Koerner's career took a significant step forward when Franklin became president of RKO. Indeed, Franklin appointed Koerner to head RKO's theater operations in the Southwest. Koerner subsequently held similar positions in upstate New York, New England, and on the West Coast. In 1941, Koerner was brought to RKO headquarters in New York as general manager of the nationwide RKO theater chain. A year later, in March 1942, with Odlum having wrested control of RKO from Franklin, Odlum named Koerner as acting head of RKO production. On June 25, 1942, the temporary appointment was made permanent. Koerner was now vice president of RKO-Radio Pictures, Inc.

As noted by the *New York Times* in its February 4, 1946, obituary: "Mr. Koerner stepped into Hollywood headlines by asking Orson Welles's Mercury Productions staff to vacate its office in the RKO studio. . . . The break with the Welles organization, which came on July 1, suspended an arrangement by which RKO-Radio Pictures financed and distributed the Welles films. Mr. Koerner declared that 'pending completion of Orson Welles' work in Brazil and his return to Hollywood, there is nothing further to be done at RKO-Radio studios by the representatives of Mr. Welles or Mercury Productions' and cited the urgent need of space by 'those engaged in current productions' at the studio. He also stopped payment of salaries to Mercury employees."

Ironically, for someone having such distaste for Welles, Koerner's name was forever linked to that of his nemesis. The headline of Koerner's obituary in the *Times* read: "Charles W. Koerner of RKO Productions: Theatre Circuit Ex-Manager Dies—Ousted Orson Welles." Although succumbing to leukemia at the age of 49, Koerner's rise from small town projectionist to RKO production head remains an impressive achievement.

—C.B.

Korda, Sir Alexander (Sándor Laszlo Kellner) (1893–1956) FRANK BRADY explains the mutual admiration WELLES and Alexander Korda had for each other in terms of their commonalities: "Both were tall men who shared a passion for hard

work, long cigars, and beautiful women and a hatred of small dogs, noisy children, and southern California." In spite of their respect for each other, they actually were better at planning projects than doing them. In return for Korda's putting up $125,000 for Welles's *Galileo* project, in which he was to direct CHARLES LAUGHTON in the English version of the BERTOLT BRECHT play, Welles agreed to do three films, each for $75,000, for Korda. *SALOME* was to be the first film, but Korda and Welles had different actresses in mind. The film was first postponed until April of 1947, then to August of the same year, and then dropped in favor of a favorite Welles story, that of Cyrano. Korda, however, was short of money and sold the rights to the film. Much the same thing happened to Korda's abortive plans to film *War and Peace* with MERLE OBERON, Korda's wife, and Welles in the lead roles. Korda commented: "My greatest films are those I announced . . . and never made." When CAROL REED, the director Korda picked for *THE THIRD MAN,* wanted Welles to play the relatively small but significant character of Harry Lime, Korda was determined to get the reluctant Welles to do the role. Welles, who needed the money and had already decided to play the part, decided to play hard to get and led Vincent Korda, Alexander's brother, quite a chase all over Europe. Vincent finally caught up with Welles, got him intoxicated, and got him on a plane back to England.. Welles's good-natured prank culminated in his eating just one bite from every piece of fruit in an expensive fruit basket that Korda had provided for him. His Harry Lime was one of Welles's most memorable performances—he enlarged his part by adding dialogue, notably the famous "cuckoo" speech.

Korda was born on September 16, 1893, in Pusztatúrpásztó, Hungary, and after briefly working as a journalist, he began directing Hungarian films in 1916. In 1920, he started directing films in Austria and Germany and then in 1926, went to the United States, where he directed 10 forgettable films before he left in 1930. After a short stay in France, he moved to England, where he founded and headed London Films and made his reputation as a director and producer: His two most important British films were *The Private Life of Henry VIII* (1933) and *Lady Hamilton* (*That Hamilton Woman* in the United States,

1941). In fact, Winston Churchill had requested that Korda make *Lady Hamilton* in the United States. The film contained some speeches that had political implications for England.'s situation in World War II. Churchill's gratitude to Korda resulted in Korda being knighted in 1941—he was the first member of the film industry to be so honored. Korda directed his last film, *An Ideal Husband,* in 1948 and produced his last film, *The Fallen Idol* (based on a GRAHAM GREENE short story "The Basement Room"), also in 1948. From then until his death in 1956, he served as executive producer for over 15 films (one of which was Carol Reed's *The Third Man,* with Welles as Harry Lime) in England..

Although his nephew Michael Korda put a favorable spin on Sir Alexander's career in his book *Charmed Lives: A Family Romance,* Charles Drazin's later study, *Alexander Korda: Britain's Only Movie Mogul,* presents a more balanced treatment. In his [London] *Sunday Times* review of Drazin's book (June 2, 2002), Christopher Silvester described Korda as "adept at persuading others to finance his profligate expenditure. He had insufficient appreciation of the vital element of story in films, but what he did have was an acute understanding of the importance of showmanship, the star system, beauty and spectacle, and also of the need for sleight of hand in business matters." For Korda, "a contract was not so much a legalistic document as a work of art, susceptible to nuances of interpretation." As Korda once remarked to the actor John Loder, "Anyone who gets a raw deal in a film studio is no more deserving of pity than someone who gets beaten up in a whorehouse."

References Drazin, Charles. *Alexander Korda: Britain's Only Movie Mogul* (London: Macmillan, 2002); Korda, Michael. *Charmed Lives: A Family Romance* (New York: Random House, 1979); Kulik, Karol. *Alexander Korda: The Man Who Could Work Miracles* (New Rochelle, N.Y.: Arlington House, 1975).

—T.L.E.

Kremlin Letter, The Twentieth Century–Fox, 166 minutes, 1970. **Director:** John Huston; **Producers:** Carter De Haven and Sam Weisenthal; **Screenplay:** John Huston and Gladys Hill, based on the novel by Noel Behn; **Cinematography:** Ted Haworth; **Editor:** Russell Lloyd;

Music: Robert Drasnin; **Cast:** Orson Welles (Bresnavitch), Bibi Andersson (Erica), Richard Boone (Ward), Nigel Green (Janis), Dean Jagger, Lila Kedrova, Micheál MacLiammóir, Max von Sydow, et al.

A U.S. film directed by JOHN HUSTON starring WELLES as Soviet politician Bresnavitch. John Huston is a great director. Great directors, however, do not always make great films. Such was the case with Huston's *The Kremlin Letter*. Typical of the reviews was that by Nigel Andrews who said: "One of those all-star international spy sagas that trick out an indecipherably tortuous plot with a series of vignettes in which the pleasures of star-spotting are expected to compensate for any narrative longueurs." Welles's vignette as the scheming Soviet big shot Aleksei Bresnavitch belongs to the gallery of treacherous villains that Welles essayed with apparently little effort but with sometimes surprising dramatic effect. While granting Andrews his point as to plot, the pleasures of star-spotting should perhaps not be so quickly written off, especially when that star is Orson Welles. Also featuring Bibi Andersson, Richard Boone, Nigel Green, Dean Jagger, Lila Kedrova, MICHEÁL MACLIAMMÓIR, Patrick O'Neil, Barbara Parkins, George Sanders, Raf Vallone, and Max von Sydow.

Reference Cohen, Allen, and Harry Lawton. *John Huston: A Guide to References and Resources* (New York: G.K. Hall, 1997).

—C.B.

Kubrick, Stanley (1928–1999)

Born in the Bronx, New York City, on July 26, 1928, Stanley Kubrick was influenced by ORSON WELLES. As a director, Kubrick is virtually in a class by himself because he taught himself the various aspects of the filmmaking process and became a director without serving the usual apprenticeship in a film studio, where he would have had to work his way up to the status of director by way of lesser jobs. By the time he began directing films for the major studios, he was able to do so with a degree of independence that few other directors have been able to match. Kubrick oversaw every aspect of production when he made a film: script writing, casting, shooting (often operating the camera himself), editing, and choosing the musical score.

In the early 1950s, Kubrick turned out two documentary shorts for RKO; then he was able to secure financing for two low-budget features that he felt were crucial in helping him to learn his craft. He made both films almost singlehandedly, doing his own camerawork, sound, and editing, besides directing the movies. Then, in 1955, he met James Harris, an aspiring producer; together they made *The Killing,* about a race track robbery. *The Killing* not only turned a modest profit but prompted the now-legendary remark of *Time* magazine that Kubrick "has shown more imagination with dialogue and camera than Hollywood has seen since the obstreperous Orson Welles went riding out of town."

Indeed, Kubrick often employed the fluid tracking shots and extended takes that had become Welles's signature. Although Welles influenced many young directors, says Robert Kolker, only Kubrick had the ability to put into practice the cinematic techniques that Welles had developed in CITIZEN KANE and his subsequent films. Kubrick was as accomplished as Welles in his use of the moving camera, for example. One can compare the backward-moving camera in Welles's THE STRANGER and in Kubrick's *Paths of Glory* (1957).

Stanley Kubrick

Significantly, the fragmented narrative structure of *The Killing* stands alongside *Citizen Kane* in its bold use of flashbacks; for the narrative is carefully pieced together through flashback and voice-over narration. The script, by Kubrick and crime novelist Jim Thompson (*The Grifters*), is based on Lionel White's novel *Clean Break*. The parallel lines of action lead inexorably to the climactic moment when the ringleader, Johnny Clay, gets away with the loot. Kubrick was confident that his method of telling the story by means of fragmented flashbacks would work as well on the screen as it did in the novel. "It was the handling of time that may have made this more than just a good crime film," he told this writer.

In addition, the narrator who conveys to the viewer essential information, voice-over on the sound track, recalls the narrator in the newsreel about CHARLES FOSTER KANE at the beginning of *Citizen Kane,* who gives background information about Kane. Thus, at the beginning of *The Killing,* the narrator contributes to the documentary air of the picture by introducing each member of Johnny Clay's gang and describing how each is implicated in the plot.

In addition, another parallel between Welles and Kubrick is that both made some movies that belong to that class of films known as film noir. This trend in American cinema was already flourishing when Welles made THE LADY FROM SHANGHAI. The pessimistic view of life exhibited in such movies, itself an outgrowth of the disillusionment spawned by World War II, a disillusionment that would continue into the period of uncertainty known as the cold war that was the war's aftermath, is evident in the movie.

Also in keeping with the conventions of film noir is an air of spare, unvarnished realism, typified by the stark, documentary-like quality of the cinematography, especially in the grim scenes that take place at night, often in murkily lit rooms, alleys, and side streets. In essence, the sinister nightmare world of film noir is one of seedy motels, boardinghouses, shabby bars, and cafés. The milieu of film noir is a stark night world of dark angles and elongated shadows, where rain glistens on windows and windshields, and faces are barred with shadows that suggest some imprisonment of body or soul. This dark, brooding atmosphere, coupled with an equally somber view of life, are regular features of film noir, and mark *The Lady from Shanghai* as a superior example of noir.

The Killing is also an accomplished noir film; it is a tough, tightly knit crime thriller about a racetrack robbery carried out by a group of small-time crooks led by Johnny Clay (Sterling Hayden); they hope to pull off one last big job to solve all of their individual financial crises. Some of the strongest dramatic scenes in the movie are those between mousy George Peatty and his sluttish wife, Sherry, who is a femme fatale cut from the same cloth as Elsa Bannister. George is hopelessly in love with Sherry and is constantly afraid that she will two-time him with another man—something she has already done repeatedly. Maddened by her constant condescension, George blurts out that he is involved with a big operation that will make them rich. Sherry shrewdly tries to pry more of the details from him, but George, unaware that he has already said too much, becomes evasive. Later Sherry tells her lover (Vince Edwards) what she has been able to wheedle out of her husband.

George is fatally wounded in a shoot-out with a rival gang. But George Peatty has enough life left in him to struggle into his car and drive home. He is moving with the determination of a man who knows he must accomplish something before he takes his last breath. Once there, he finds Sherry packing to go away with Val, just as he suspected she would. She tries to mollify him with a prefabricated alibi, but for once in his life George is not to be forestalled by his scheming wife. He blasts away with his pistol, the impotent husband finally penetrating his wife with bullets. As George himself falls forward toward the camera, he knocks over a birdcage, symbol of his pitifully narrow existence, which is now at an end.

Both *The Lady from Shanghai* and *The Killing* end with the femme fatale being shot to death by her mortally wounded husband (although Arthur Bannister is killed by his wife, while George Peatty is killed by another crook). JAMES NAREMORE declares that Kubrick had gathered motifs from earlier noir films while making *The Killing*—most particularly from *The Lady from Shanghai;* both films contain a legendary femme fatale. It is clear that the tenets of noir were congenial to both Welles and Kubrick.

Consequently, it is not surprising that both directors would create classic noir films.

Because both Welles and Kubrick began their film careers while still in their 20s, Kubrick was often compared to Welles, America's original enfant terrible. In 1965, Welles told interviewers Juan Cobos, Miguel Rubio, and José Pruneda that, "among those whom I would call the younger generation of directors, Kubrick appears to me to be a giant. . . . What I see in him is a talent not possessed by the great directors of the generation immediately preceding his," such as Nicholas Ray and Robert Aldrich. "Perhaps this is because his temperament is closer to mine."

Kubrick continued to identify and be compared with Welles as an enfant terrible, as Vincent LoBrutto points out in his biography of Kubrick. LoBrutto recounts how Kubrick learned that one of his production assistants, Bob Gaffney, was going to work on a TV commercial in which Welles was appearing. Kubrick dug through his files to find a review of *Citizen Kane* in which Bosley Crowther panned the picture in the *New York Times.* Crowther had complained that the picture was muddled because disconcerting ambiguities in the title character's behavior were left unexplained at the end of the film.

Kubrick said to Gaffney, "Show this to Orson." It seems that Crowther was also appalled by Kubrick's doomsday comedy *Dr. Strangelove,* so his point in sending Crowther's review of *Kane* to Welles was to remind him that some critics do not always know a good film when they see one. Kubrick was working on *2001 A Space Odyssey* at the time—another Kubrick film that, like *Kane,* would prove controversial.

James Howard notes that Kubrick has often been compared to Orson Welles, "who achieved the total creative control which Kubrick enjoyed in perpetuity only once, on his debut feature, *Citizen Kane.*" There is no doubt that, though Kubrick was more successful in maintaining artistic control of his films than Welles was, Welles was an abiding inspiration to Kubrick to make his films his own way.

References Cobos, Juan, Miguel Rubio, and José Pruneda. "Orson Welles," in *Perspectives on Orson Welles,* ed. Morris Beja (New York: G.K. Hall, 1995), 37–62; Cristofer Michael. "Lost Hollywood: Film Noir," *Premiere* 14, no. 7 (March 2001): 58–59; Gifford, Barry. *Out of the Past: Film Noir* (Jackson: University Press of Mississippi, 2000); Howard, James. *Stanley Kubrick Companion* (London: Batsford, 1999); Kael, Pauline. "Lolita," in *For Keeps* (New York: Dutton, 1996) 39–43; Kolker, Robert. *A Cinema of Loneliness* (New York: Oxford University Press, 2000); LoBrutto, Vincent. *Stanley Kubrick: An Autobiography* (New York: Da Capo, 1999); Naremore, James. *More Than Night: Film Noir in Its Contexts* (Los Angeles: University of California Press, 1998); Phillips, Gene. "Stop the World: Stanley Kubrick," in *Stanley Kubrick: Interviews* (Jackson: University Press of Mississippi, 2001), 140–58; "New Pictures: *The Killing,*" *Time,* June 4, 1956, 71.

—G.D.P.

Laage, Barbara (Claire Colombat) (1925–)
Actress Barbara Laage, born Claire Colombat on July
30, 1925, in Menthon–Saint-Bernard, France, had an
affair with ORSON WELLES during 1946–47, when he
attempted to cast the "voluptuous temptress" (CHARLES
HIGHAM's description) in the title role in *SALOME*, a film
he and SIR ALEXANDER KORDA planned to make.
Because she spoke only French, Welles even engaged
an English tutor for her when the two went to Acapulco with Charles Lawton, a cinematographer, and
Welles's current wife, RITA HAYWORTH. The trip was
made to scout locations for Welles's impending *THE
LADY FROM SHANGHAI*. Korda, however, had his own
candidate for the Salome role, Eileen Herlie; Welles dismissed Korda's choice by deliberately mispronouncing
her names as "Helier." The Salome film was subsequently scuttled, and, as Higham puts it, she "drifted
away at the end of 1947."

Laage, who had worked on the stage and in
nightclubs, made her Hollywood debut one year
later in *B. F.'s Daughter* and then became a leading
lady, appearing in European films that were all sexual in nature and content: *La P . . . respectuese/The
Respectful Prostitute* (1952), *Fille d'Amour* (1953), *Un
acte d'Amour/Act of Love* (1954), *Miss Pigalle* (1957).
Arguably her best work came later with *Therese and
Isabelle* (1968), and, FRANÇOIS TRUFFAUT's *Domicile
conjugal/Bed and Board* (1970). She also co-starred
with Gene Kelly in *The Happy Road* (1957).

—T.L.E.

Lady Esther Show, The (radio, 1941–1942)   In
this weekly CBS radio series for the cosmetics firm
of Lady Esther, WELLES and his MERCURY THEATRE
colleagues departed from the Mercury's format of
dramatizing a single literary work in favor of a looser
structure. Although some episodes were devoted to
single stories in the manner of *FIRST PERSON SINGU-
LAR, MERCURY THEATRE ON THE AIR,* and *THE CAMP-
BELL PLAYHOUSE,* most of the Lady Esther sponsored
programs were potpourris featuring multiple stories,
dramatic readings, musical numbers, and humorous
vignettes. DOLORES DEL RÍO, Welles's constant companion at the time, also starred. The initial broadcast
of September 15, 1941, set the pattern. There was a
short playlet, *Srendi Vashtar,* adapted from a story by
Saki; an original radio play about Mexican history
called *Hidalgo;* a reworking of Geoffrey Household's
An Irishman and a Jew; a *Boogie-Woogie* by African-
American jazz piano great Meade Lux Lewis; and a
Welles commentary, the "Almanac," which served as
a preview of his subsequent work as a radio and
newspaper commentator in the mid-1940s. A num-
ber of the shows also featured the Disney character
Jiminy Cricket (voiced by Cliff Edwards) who
turned up to trade quips with Welles. Along with
Mercury regulars such as JOSEPH COTTEN and TIM
HOLT from *THE MAGNIFICENT AMBERSONS,* and RUTH
WARRICK and DOROTHY COMINGORE from *CITIZEN
KANE,* there were guest stars such as Ginger Rogers,

Lucille Ball, Ruth Gordon, ANNE BAXTER, Janet Gaynor, Marsha Hunt, Richard Carlson, and Stu Erwin. The December 29, 1941, show, a Richard Connell tale called *There Are Frenchmen and Frenchmen,* featured RITA HAYWORTH. It was the first meeting between Welles and the dazzling young star destined to become the second Mrs. Orson Welles.

With his departure for Brazil on behalf of the government fast approaching, Welles closed out the *Lady Esther* series on February 1, 1942, with a broadcast of Norman Corwin's *Between Americans,* an apt drama given his impending adventure. At the conclusion of the broadcast, Welles noted that "next week at this same hour, same station, Lady Esther brings you the music of one of your favorites, Freddy Martin and his orchestra." He added: "This is the last time for some while I'll be speaking to you from the United States. Tomorrow night the Mercury Theatre starts for South America. The reason, put more or less officially, is that I've been asked by the Office of the Coordinator of Inter-American Affairs to do a motion picture especially for Americans in all the Americas, a movie which, in its particular way, might strengthen the good relations now binding the continents of the Western Hemisphere. Put much less officially, the Mercury's going down there to get acquainted." That eventually sad and never to be completed motion picture was *IT'S ALL TRUE.*

—C.B.

Lady from Shanghai, The   Columbia Pictures, 86 minutes, 1947. **Director:** Orson Welles; **Associate Producers:** Richard Wilson and William Castle; **Screenplay:** Welles (and, uncredited, Castle, Fletcher Markle, Charles Lederer, and others) (based on *If I Die Before I Wake* by Sherwood King); **Cinematographer:** Charles Lawton, Jr. and Rudolph Maté, Joseph Walker, uncredited; **Editor:** Viola Lawrence; **Cast:** Orson Welles (Michael O'Hara), Rita Hayworth (Elsa Bannister), Everett Sloane (Arthur Bannister), Glenn Anders (George Grigsby), Ted de Corsica (Sidney Broom), Gus Schilling (Goldie), Louis Merrill (Jake), Erskine Sanford (Judge), Carl Frank (District Attorney Galloway), Evelyn Ellis (Bessie), Wong Show Chong (Li), Harry Shannon (horse cab driver), Sam Nelson (captain), Richard Wilson (district attorney's assistant), and players of the Mandarin Theater of San Francisco

The Lady from Shanghai was made because WELLES had needed money for his 1946 stage production of *AROUND THE WORLD IN 80 DAYS* (MICHAEL TODD, who was to finance the Jules Verne adaptation, backed out at the last minute). In desperation, Welles called HARRY COHN, head of Columbia Pictures, and offered to make a film for him free of charge if Cohn would send him the necessary funds. (The amount of money varies with the storyteller.) Welles told PETER BOGDANOVICH that while he was talking with Cohn, he saw some paperback books on display and that he gave Cohn the title of one of them, *Lady from Shanghai.* Actually, the title of the source was Sherwood King's *If I Die Before I Wake,* which was not available in paperback at the time. According to CHARLES HIGHAM in his *The Films of Orson Welles,* "The story of how Welles chose the subject of the movie he was to make for Columbia has been told in half a dozen different versions." Another significant account has Columbia owning the rights and commissioning WILLIAM CASTLE to produce and direct the film. Welles, after talking with Castle and making him the associate producer, took over the film. DAVID THOMSON believes that actor FRANCHOT TONE, to whom Welles was in debt, might have possessed the script. At any rate, Welles initially planned to shoot the film entirely in New York City and to cast BARBARA LAAGE, his current mistress, as the female lead, but Cohn insisted on using RITA HAYWORTH, from whom Welles was being divorced. According to Welles, "It was Harry's idea *and* hers that she play that part, thus making it a big, expensive Hayworth A picture." The rest of the cast was composed mainly of Mercury players (EVERETT SLOANE, GUS SCHILLING, ERSKINE SANFORD) or actors with whom Welles had previously worked. The film had two earlier titles, *Take This Woman* and *Black Irish* (the latter related to Welles's role as Michael O'Hara).

In November of 1946, shooting on the film began in Acapulco, where Welles used Errol Flynn's yacht, *Zaca,* and its crew for the scenes on the *Circe.* According to FRANK BRADY, it was "an extremely arduous shooting," featuring dangerous crocodiles, barracuda, poisonous barnacles, and torrid temperatures, which finally led to Hayworth's collapse from

Welles as Michael O'Hara in *The Lady from Shanghai.*
(Literature/Film Archive)

exhaustion. An assistant cameraman died of a heart attack. When Welles did not shoot any close-ups of Rita Hayworth, editor Viola Lawrence complained to Cohn about the lack of "star" treatment, and at Cohn's insistence, Welles shot some close-ups, which Higham describes as the "most banal and emptily glossy things in the film." When he returned to Hollywood in January, Welles had to reshoot much of the Mexican footage. Welles worked on the noted hall of mirrors set with Lawrence Butler, a special effects expert.

The Lady from Shanghai begins at night in New York's Central Park, where Michael O'Hara, the narrator, first sees Elsa Bannister, who is riding in a horse-drawn cab. Michael, who is attracted to her, tries to engage her in conversation, but is unsuccessful. Since he tells the audience he did not use his head and made a fool of himself, the audience can safely assume that she is the source of his troubles. A

short while later, he hears her scream for help and comes to her rescue by beating some young hoodlums who are accosting her. As he drives her home in the cab, he learns that her parents were White Russians and that she gambled for a living in Macao. In response to his comment that she must be lucky, she says, "You need more than luck in Shanghai." Her comments suggest the disillusionment and callousness of a woman who has been a high-class prostitute. As they near the parking garage, he tells her that he killed a man in Spain, and she offers him a job on the Bannister yacht. Her potentially sinister nature is suggested by the gun she carries in her purse, a gun she inexplicably did not use on the hoodlums. As Michael talks to Elsa, a figure hidden in the shadows is the first of many such voyeurs who spy on each other.

In the next sequence, Arthur Bannister, who can walk only with the aid of two canes, comes to the seamen's hiring hall to recruit Michael, whose work on the typewriter identifies him as a wannabe writer. Because Arthur resembles a crippled spider with twisted limbs, he is in stark contrast to Michael and his mates, who are physically healthy and vital. Michael, who thinks he has the "edge" and is in control of the situation, gets Arthur to buy drinks for him and his mates. When Bannister passes out, Michael takes him home and takes the job on the *Circe,* an appropriately named yacht (the mythical Circe was the goddess who turned men into beasts). As Michael narrates the events, he sees that he, not Arthur, was "unconscious" and that Arthur is as "helpless as a rattlesnake." In true noir fashion, the protagonist who thinks he is in control is actually being duped by others.

Welles introduces the action on the yacht by photographing some swirling water, an eddy that may suggest the maelstrom that Michael will be caught up in. In this sequence Grisby is the voyeur who first watches Elsa, who is wearing a revealing swimsuit, dive off a rock into the water and swim to the yacht. The shot of Elsa on the rocks may also suggest her sirenlike nature. Grisby, who is on a small nearby motorboat, watches Elsa and Mike as they engage in some sexual banter on the yacht. In response to Elsa's "come-on" lines, Michael asks, "Do all rich women play games like this?" Both Michael and Elsa are scared, and Elsa says, "I'm not what you think I am," suggesting that she is not a "golddigger," but her words also relate directly to questions of identity and of appearance and reality. Grisby's parting "So long, kiddies" also suggests that they are relative "babes in the woods." Despite his knowledge that he is a "fathead" for chasing a married woman, Michael cannot resist Elsa, who is seducing him. As she sings, Circlelike (at Cohn's, not Welles's, insistence), above on the deck, Michael, who has been talking with Bessie, the maid, below deck, is drawn up the ladder to her. Later, when Michael is piloting the yacht, Elsa comes up and takes the wheel from him, and then both steer the ship. The "steering" metaphor is particularly apt here, because it involves control and direction, motifs in the film.

At Arthur's ominous beach picnic, Sid Broome, a detective, warns Arthur about a murder plot, but Arthur already is aware of it. Arthur sarcastically and menacingly calls Elsa "darling" and Elsa asks, "Why should anyone want to live around us?" Michael approaches the small group and then tells them an appropriate story about what he saw off the coast of Brazil: sharks eating each other in a feeding frenzy. Although Arthur calls Grisby a shark, it is apparent that there are indeed several sharks in the plot. When they get to Acapulco, Grisby offers Michael $5,000 to pretend to kill him, supposedly so that Grisby can escape a nuclear holocaust (Hiroshima was a current topic) and get away from his wife, who will not give him a divorce, plus collect on an insurance policy—Michael does not stop to think how a "dead" Grisby could collect the money. After Grisby leaves, Elsa joins Michael and tells him she has considered committing suicide by taking an overdose of pills. As they talk, Sid, who has been following them, comes out of the shadows and gets knocked out by Michael. Elsa flees, but Michael catches up with her and asks her to dance. While they dance, Elsa observes that although he is big and strong, Michael cannot take care of himself. The observation is ironic in light of Arthur's apparent weakness but real strength.

When the yacht reaches San Francisco, concluding a journey that has included scenes depicting the results of American capitalism, Michael asks Elsa to go away with him; but she realistically points out their lack of money, a problem that could be solved by Michael's going through with Grisby's apparent plan. Grisby's plan involves Michael and Grisby being seen together, Michael firing shots, presumably at Grisby, signing a confession (worthless, according to Grisby, because the police will never find Grisby's body), and Grisby going off to the "South Seas." When Elsa sees the confession, she tells Michael that she suspects a trap, that Arthur is behind the scheme, and that "there's more to it," a warning that applies to almost everything in the film. This conversation occurs at the aquarium, where she and Michael meet. They talk in front of a water tank, which contains a shark, which continues the shark motif, and an eel, which wriggles past her as she discusses her slippery lawyer husband.

Grisby's plan does not go as Michael thinks it will. When Grisby and Michael arrive at the Bannister beach house, Grisby goes inside and finds Sid, who tells him he knows about the plot to kill Arthur and wants money to keep silent. Grisby shoots Sid, leaves the house, and puts the gun in the glove compartment. After Grisby and Michael leave, Elsa arrives, and Sid tells her that there will not be a fake murder, but a real one, and that the victim will be her husband. She leaves for Arthur's office. Meanwhile, Grisby intentionally steers his car into a truck so that the driver will remember seeing him and Michael together. When they get to the amusement park at the beach, Michael takes the gun from the glove compartment, fires three shots into the ocean, runs on the boardwalk, and then calls the beach house. A dying Sid answers and informs him that he has been framed by Grisby, who intends to kill Arthur. Michael, Elsa, and the police seem to arrive at Arthur's office almost simultaneously and find Grisby's dead body, and the police charge Michael with the murders of Grisby and Sid Broome.

Ironically, Arthur becomes Michael's attorney and takes control of the courtroom at Michael's trial. He jokes with the judge, cross-examines himself, calls his wife as a witness, and seems ready to accomplish his aim of seeing Michael in jail for the rest of his life. David Thomson finds the courtroom scenes marked by "absurdist humor from a different film altogether."

At this point it is Arthur who has the "edge" that Michael discussed earlier in the film. At Elsa's unspoken suggestion (her glance says it all) Michael suddenly takes Arthur's pain-killing pills, and the police take him to the judge's chambers, where they hope to keep him alive. Despite the pills, Michael is able to overcome the police and escape by pretending to be part of another jury. He flees to Chinatown, where he takes refuge in a theater. Elsa, who has seen his escape and who speaks fluent Chinese (as a result of her experiences in China), follows him to the Chinese theater, calls Li, and joins Michael in the audience. PETER COWIE in his *The Cinema of Orson Welles* offers an intriguing explanation for the photographing of the Chinese actors onstage: "The players onstage, with their hieratic gestures and barbaric swordplay, provide a background that evokes the sacrifices and expiatory ceremonies not far removed from the primitive courtroom in which the verdict has only just been given." When the police enter the theater, Michael and Elsa also put on an act: They kiss to avoid being seen, and there is as little emotion in the embrace as there is on the stage. When Michael finds a gun in her purse, he realizes that it is the gun that killed Grisby, but he succumbs to the pills and passes out.

When he comes to, he is in an empty amusement park. This site is a logical venue for a film that has mad characters and a tangled, almost deranged plot. (JAMES NAREMORE describes "the general atmosphere of comic delirium.") Welles visually demonstrates Michael's addled state by using oblique camera angles and superimpositions of swirling bars over his body. Michael now realizes that Elsa and Grisby were working together to kill Arthur, after which she would kill her partner, Grisby. For Michael, the "fun house" is menacing. He slides down a long, zigzag chute between the huge, threatening teeth of a dragon and finds himself in a hall of mirrors, some of which distort images, an appropriate visual metaphor for the many distortions in the film. Elsa shines a flashlight on his face, and he sees multiple reflections of her in the mirrors. Arthur, whose entrance is signaled by the sight of his crippled legs and the two canes, believes that Elsa planned to have him follow her and tells her that he has left an incriminating let-

ter with the district attorney. Gun in hand, Arthur tells her, "Killing you is killing myself" and "I'm tired of both of us." Both begin shooting, shattering one mirrored reflection after another until both are hit. Naremore writes that the "hallucinatory image" reflected in the mirrors "is perfectly expressive of the way the mind can become a hall of mirrors, a distorted, paranoid vision." Michael observes that their behavior is "like the sharks, chewing away at each other." Welles has a close-up of Elsa's face as she lies on the floor; Michael is in the frame, but out of focus in the background, stressing his status as the outsider. As the film ends, he comments again on being a "fool" and trying to forget Elsa as he walks out of the fun house and across the pier to call the police. Arthur's letter to the district attorney will clear Michael of the murders.

In the course of the film there is a great deal of water imagery in addition to the seas that the *Circe* covers. Though it harbors sharks, eels, octopi, and other dangerous predators, it is also redemptive since Michael returns to it at the end of the film. In this most psychologically complex film, water also serves as a metaphor for the unconscious; and the eddy that swirls about surely is intended to suggest the emotional vortex that the characters are caught in.

The Lady from Shanghai contains several Wellesian themes: the evils of unbridled capitalism, the corruption that power inevitably spawns, the emotional isolation of the powerful, the impossibility of knowing the truth about people, and the masks that present appearance as reality. In addition, Welles's own life and his relationships affect the content of the story. It is interesting that when he had to choose a property to film for Columbia, he chose a story with film noir elements, including the femme fatale, the spider woman responsible for the protagonist's plight.

There is much speculation about how the relationship between Welles and Hayworth affected the film. While Welles has denied any intent to make Hayworth seem unattractive, some critics have maintained that cutting her red hair short and dying it blond were part of an effort to photograph her with, in David Thomson's words, "fascinated loathing." Instead of the pert, provocative image she had in *Gilda* (1946), in *The Lady from Shanghai* she appears as an older, grimmer, more severe woman who seems, despite the "glamour girl" shots, as sexless as her husband, Arthur. Although Michael describes his attraction to Elsa, their love scenes lack passion and conviction. Though the film contains leering, sexual innuendo, and voyeurism, there is little love in *The Lady from Shanghai.*

Michael's narration has also been a problem for some critics, for his erudite commentary seems at odds with the image of a virile, hot-tempered sailor who has used his bare hands to kill a man. Yet the film does stress his novelistic ambitions, even though Arthur mocks them. As with most noir narration, the story is narrated in flashback, but in this film the narrator is not explaining what happened; he is attempting to make sense of what happened and seems to fail. In his book *Voices in the Dark,* Jay Telotte examines the use of narration in film noir and finds in Welles's film what he calls a "circular structure," one in which Michael's narration turns back and attempts to find meaning or pattern from his experiences with people who are not what they appear to be. Although he frequently describes himself as a fool, Michael does not seem to have learned very much from those experiences. Telotte points out that Michael's image is also reflected in the mirror sequence that features Arthur and Elsa. Michael, who has accepted as truth everything that Elsa tells him, apparently believes that appearance is reality: Elsa needs his protection; crippled Arthur cannot satisfy Elsa; crazy Grisby simply wants to flee to the South Seas. Telotte comments: "Of course, Michael's swallowing Elsa's story of love for him and fear of her husband is the main example of his being swallowed in a deceptive realm of images, which is in turn symbolized by the mirror maze itself." As Telotte points out, Michael also is wounded in the mirror shootout, and that wound serves to remind him of "his immersion in this consumptive whirl."

When Harry Cohn saw the edited film, he was upset because he could not understand it. He reportedly said, "I'll give $1,000 to anyone who can explain the story to me." Suggestions about revisions were offered, but ultimately Welles and Virginia Van Upp reedited, rescored, and redubbed the film. Preview audiences were not impressed, and Cohn held up the release of the film for a year. Frank Brady speculates that Cohn may have seen that there was a parallel between Michael-Elsa-Arthur and Welles-Hayworth-Cohn and "that such an analogy was too painful for him to accept." The film did not do well at the box office. It cost almost $2 million to make and grossed less than $1.5 million. Welles himself did not like the opening sequence in the park, which he said has no "flavor" and was especially critical of the music, particularly the work of Heinz Roemheld, whom Welles accused of "Disneying," attempting to match physical actions to music. Welles's request that the music be omitted from the gunshot/mirror scene, where it seems not only extraneous, but also distracting, was ignored.

Critical reaction to the film has been mixed. The passage of time may account for Higham's evaluation of it as "even more stimulating, daring, and dazzling" than it was in 1947: "The satirical style, the commentary on riches and corruption, are as intensely Wellesian as ever." While admitting that he could not understand the plot until he had seen the film eight times, JOSEPH MCBRIDE is similarly enthusiastic: "In no other film, not even *Citizen Kane,* do we share with Welles such a spontaneous delight in the exercise of his gifts." On the other hand, Thomson sees the film as disjointed and inconsistent. It is almost as if Welles was content to use the misogyny of film noir but reluctant to make a film that complies with the genre formula for film noir. According to Thomson, Welles "is too superior, or too bored, to make a genre mood consistent and constructive." Despite these misgivings, Thomson believes that the film "has some of the greatest things that Welles would ever do," and there are, indeed, few viewers who can forget the courtroom and mirror sequences.

—T.L.E.

Lady in the Ice, The (ballet, 1953) WELLES'S 1953 ballet entails a simple yet allegorical story line. A young man attending a carnival enters a side show tent to view a hauntingly beautiful woman frozen inside a block of ice. Returning to the carnival grounds late at night after the crowds have dispersed, the young man's love for her melts the ice. Alas, when she kisses him, he turns to ice. "A little parable for our times," Welles said. He further confided to PETER BOGDANOVICH: "It was very successful in London and only moderately so in Paris, where it was very badly lit—as everything always is in Paris." The ballet was intended to illustrate the idea, said Welles, that "two people are never in love with each other to the same degree at the same time." Indeed, the quixotic nature of love, given palpable form in the uncontrollable and ever shifting ice, is a fatalistic force beyond the couple's control. Thematically, the ballet tallies with the doubly articulated issue of disillusionment and defeat, a key motif throughout the Welles canon.

The Lady in the Ice, which opened at London's Stoll Theatre on September 7, 1953, was presented by Roland Petit's Ballet de Paris. Choreographed by Roland Petit and scored by Jean-Michel Demase, the ballet starred Colette Marchand (the lady in the ice), George Reich (the smitten young man), and Joe Milan (the barker). Welles's libretto was further animated by his highly effective décor and costumes. In *Orson Welles: The Rise and Fall of an American Genius,* CHARLES HIGHAM comments on Welles's ragtag collection of fairground loafers and a realistic ticket booth decked out with curtains graced by prehistoric cave drawings. Inside the tent, Welles conjured up an eerie effect in which Mademoiselle Marchand appeared to be actually frozen, a bit of legerdemain derived from Welles's experience in producing his various magic shows.

The Lady in the Ice also reflects Welles's general appreciation for all the performing arts, here, the merging of music and dance in ballet. Working on *The Lady in the Ice* must also have been a pleasant reminder of his days with GEORGE BALANCHINE when Welles partook of the earthy yet ethereal delights of a string of sylphlike ballerinas whose sundry assets had lifted both bodies and souls.

—C.B.

Lafayette (*La Fayette* and *Lafayette* [*Una Spada Per Due Bandiere*]) Copernic-Cosmos/Maco1962, 110 minutes, 1963. **Director:** Jean Dreville; **Producer:** Maurice Jacquin; **Screenplay:** Suzanne Arduini, Jacques Sigurd, Jean-Bernard Luc, François Ponthier, Jean Dreville, Maurice Jacquin; **Cinematographer:** Claude Renoir, Roger Hubert; **Editor:** Rene Le Hanaff;

Cast: Michel Le Royer (Lafayette), Howard St. John (George Washington), Jack Hawkins (Gen. Cornwallis), Wolfgang Preiss (Baron Kalb), Orson Welles (Ben Franklin), Vittorio De Sica (Bancroft), Edmond Purdom (Silas Deane)

A 1962 French/Italian co-production directed by Jean Dreville featuring WELLES in a cameo role as Benjamin Franklin. This mostly French-produced historical drama depicting how French officers helped the American Revolution in 1776 was dismissed by *Halliwell's Film and Video Guide* as having the odor of "the same old indigestible, ill-dubbed, co-produced continental spectaculars which have already turned the stomach in a whole range of lesser screen ratios."

Welles, who had previously played American ambassador to France Franklin in SACHA GUITRY's *ROYAL AFFAIRS IN VERSAILLES* in 1953, told PETER BOGDANOVICH, "I don't know in which I was worse. I was Benjamin Franklin—a part for which no actor in the world is less suited." FRANK BRADY described Welles's Franklin as pasty-looking and *Lafayette* as "disastrously overlong, pedantic, gaudy, and artificial." Although his makeup required four hours to prepare, Welles's cameo was deleted in later versions of the film, perhaps, as Brady suggests, to Welles's advantage. Clearly, this was another instance in which Welles took the money and ran.

The cast included Michel Le Royer (Lafayette), Jack Hawkins (General Cornwallis), Howard St. John (George Washington), Vittoro De Sica (Bancroft), Edmund Purdom (Silas Deane), and Pascale Audret (Madame de Lafayette). Location scenes were shot in Yugoslavia. When it opened in New York in April 1963, *Lafayette*'s original 158-minute running time had been pruned to 110 minutes for the U.S. market.

—C.B.

La Ricotta See *ROGOPAG*

Last Roman, The (*Der Kampf um Rom*) Allied Artists, 94 minutes (U.S.)/ 105 minutes (Part I, Europe), 84 minutes (Part II, Europe), 1968/1975. **Director:** Robert Siodmak; **Producer:** Artur Brauner; **Screenplay:** Ladislas Fodor; **Cinematographer:** Richard Angst;

Music: Riz Ortolani; **Editor:** Alfred Srp; **Cast:** Laurence Harvey (Cethegus), Orson Wells (Justinian), Sylvia Koscina (Theodora), Honor Blackman (Amalswintha), Robert Hoffman (Totila), Harriet Andersson (Mathaswintha), Michael Dunn (Narses), Ingrid Brett (Julia), Lang Jeffries (Belisar)

The 1968 West German-Romanian historic co-production was initially released in Europe in two parts, and running to 189 minutes. Subsequently, it was released in the United States in 1975, in a greatly reduced version of only 94 minutes. Directed by Robert Siodmak, notable for a string of psychological thrillers made for Universal in the mid-1940s which included *The Killers* (1946), *The Last Roman,* according to WELLES, was a mess. When asked by PETER BOGDANOVICH, "What's the name of that one?" Welles jokingly responded, "I don't know— *Erasmus and the Forty Krauts*! A great, huge, cut-rate German spectacle. I play Justinian, and have very little to add to what is going on." When Bogdanovich pointed out that Siodmak used to be good, Welles replied: "You can't blame him for this one. We were all of us bogged down there in Bucharest in the midst of an almost indecipherable plot. As it happens, the period is one in which I'm something of an expert—it being an old dream of mine to make a film about Justinian and Theodora. But they had characters in this one—leading characters—I never heard of. All based, we were told, on heavy German research."

—C.B.

Late Great Planet Earth, The   Amram/RCR, 90 minutes, 1978. **Director:** Robert Amram; **Producer:** Alan Belkin; **Screenplay:** Amram and Hal Lindsey (based on *The Late Great Planet Earth* by Lindsey); **Cinematography:** Michael Werk; **Music:** Dana Kaproff; **Editors:** Victor Costello and Anne Goursaud Epstein; **Cast:** Orson Welles (Narrator), Emile Benoit, Norman Borlaug, Hal Lindsey (Narrator), Timothy Nicely (Leader of the Chase), Aurelio Peccei, Judith Roberts (The Whore of Babylon), George Wald, Howard Whalen (John the Apostle)

The Late Great Planet Earth, a film directed by Robert Amram, is based on Hal Lindsey's apocalyptic books of the same name. In the film, which does not have actors playing roles, Welles appears as an onscreen narrator commenting on how modern phenomena suggest that Old Testament prophecies about the end of the world are in fact being fulfilled. The film, which does not have a conventional plot, is essentially composed of stock footage of horrific events such as tidal waves, earthquakes, and A-bomb explosions. According to Lindsey, two of the three events leading to Armageddon, the creation of Israel and the return of Jerusalem to Israeli control, have already occurred; the third event, the rebuilding of Solomon's Temple on Mt. Moriah, has not happened. Dressed appropriately in black, Welles wanders through the movie asking questions about whether or not these events are coincidental and without cosmic meaning or if Earth is indeed doomed.

—T.L.E.

Laughton, Charles (1899–1962)   Actor Charles Laughton was slated to collaborate with ORSON WELLES on the staging of BERTOLT BRECHT's play *Galileo,* which Laughton and Brecht had been translating into English since December of 1944. Rehearsals were scheduled to begin on August 1, 1946, but Welles, who was still working on the stage version of *AROUND THE WORLD IN 80 DAYS,* kept trying to postpone the production. Producer MIKE TODD, who was to provide the financing for *Around the World,* withdrew his support, which irritated Welles, who had to seek financial backing elsewhere. When Welles learned that Brecht and Laughton, who was to play the title role, had engaged Mike Todd to produce their *Galileo,* Welles was even more upset. He had RICHARD WILSON write to Laughton explaining that Welles would not be able to do the production singlehandedly. Laughton, who was furious, declared that he was not going to tolerate Welles's procrastination. According to DAVID THOMSON, "the *Galileo* faction [Laughton and Brecht] did not comprehend Welles's allegiance to *Around the World.*" At any rate, *Galileo* was finally produced onstage on December 7, 1947, with JOSEPH LOSEY as the director. According to Thomson, "Welles did not much like Brecht, who could be abrasive and what Welles called 'shitty.'" Comparing Welles and Laughton, Thomson declared

Charles Laughton *(National Film Society Archive)*

them "not unalike as actors, larger than life, prodigious but temperamental." While Welles was given to temperamental outbursts, Laughton, according to Thomson, "exercised his power in more devious ways—by delay, indecision, insecurity, and a creeping vulnerability that could turn anyone into his doctor."

Laughton was born in Scarborough, England, on July 1, 1899, and educated at Stonyhurst College before serving his country in World War I. After the war he joined an amateur theater group, then enrolled in the Royal Academy of Dramatic Art. He made his London theatrical debut in 1926, and in 1928 married Elsa Lanchester, an actress with whom he had worked professionally. He made his feature film debut in Britain in 1929, and won an Academy Award in 1933 for his role in *The Private Life of Henry VIII*. By 1935, he played Captain Bligh in *Mutiny on the Bounty* and Javert in *Les Misérables*. He played the artist Rembrandt memorably in 1936, and Quasimodo in *The Hunchback of Notre Dame* in 1939, after being featured by Alfred Hitchcock in *Jamaica Inn* (also 1939). He played Gracchus

in STANLEY KUBRICK's *Spartacus* (1960), and his last feature, *Advise and Consent,* was made in 1962, the year he died. He directed *The Night of the Hunter* (1955), a highly respected film, and might have directed *I Claudius,* had conditions been better in 1937.

References Callow, Simon. *Charles Laughton: A Difficult Actor* (New York: Fromm International Publishers, 1987); Higham, Charles. *Charles Laughton: An Intimate Biography* (Garden City, N.Y.: Doubleday, 1976).

—T.L.E. and J.M.W.

Leaming, Barbara Barbara Leaming, a professor of theater at Hunter College in New York, wrote a well-received biography of WELLES, entitled, simply, *Orson Welles: A Biography,* published by Viking/Penguin in 1985, following her earlier biography of RITA HAYWORTH, *If This Was Happiness,* also published by Viking Press. Her Welles biography, which has been called "definitive," does a thorough job of covering the precocious childhood of the "boy genius," but she stands a bit in awe of the oversized talent Welles developed into and seems to accept everything Welles told her, much of which seems self-serving and some of which is simply inaccurate, especially in its treatment of Welles's father. The book was written with the complete cooperation of the director and apparently shaped by him as well. After the book was published, Leaming and Welles appeared together on *The Merv Griffin Show* to discuss and promote the book. Welles died the night after the show was telecast. Leaming inserts italicized reflections between chapters that reflect upon the nature of writing the biography of an admittedly complicated talent. At the end, reminiscing about THE CRADLE WILL ROCK as if it were a movie, Welles describes himself as a "total stranger," and says, "The way I want to do it is much more interesting than I was." She concludes by wondering how a "mere biographer" can deal with a sorcerer-seducer who is capable of adding "scenes entirely of his own imagining" when remembering his past. The book is certainly readable and packed with information and colorful characters, though the truth is perhaps effected by the subject of this Orson-dominated account. Nonetheless, it is, as the *Boston Herald* described it, an "essential sourcebook for anyone interested in Welles."

—J.M.W. and T.L.E.

Lederer, Charles (1910–1976) Scriptwriter Charles Lederer, the nephew of actress MARION DAVIES, was born on December 31, 1910, in New York City. After a brief career in journalism, he moved to Hollywood in 1931 and became a screenwriter like his friend BEN HECHT. He contributed some dialogue to the critically acclaimed screwball comedy *The Front Page* (1931), which was based on Hecht's play, and wrote or co-scripted many outstanding films, among them *His Girl Friday* (1940), *I Was a Male War Bride* (1949), and *Gentlemen Prefer Blondes* (1953), all directed by Howard Hawks, as well as *Ocean's 11* (1960) and *Mutiny on the Bounty* (1962). He also directed three films: *Fingers at the Window* (1942), *On the Loose* (1951) and *Never Steal Anything Small* (1959). For the stage he co-wrote, with Luther Davis, *Kismet* (1953–54), which he co-adapted to film (1955).

Charles Lederer's relationship to WELLES is closely tied to the making of *CITIZEN KANE* (1941), which had one of its origins in the affair between Marion Davies, his aunt, and WILLIAM RANDOLPH HEARST, who headed a publishing empire, and to the breaking up of Welles's marriage to Virginia Welles, who married Lederer, a good friend of Welles's, in 1941. Before *Citizen Kane* was released, HERMAN MANKIEWICZ asked Lederer to read the script to see if he thought it would offend Marion Davies. He did not think it would and stated that he believed the film was about Robert McCormick, a wealthy publishing magnate, who had divorced his wife to marry GANNA WALSKA, whose opera career he then tried to promote. PAULINE KAEL, on the other hand, maintains that after reading the script, Lederer was concerned, and then the Hearst lawyers were called in. Kael also claims that Lederer gave the script to Davies; Lederer denies this, stating that he gave the script back to Mankiewicz. So, the *Citizen Kane* battle was on.

Lederer's marriage to Virginia, which occurred at Hearst's estate at San Simeon, followed quickly on the heels of Welles's divorce from Virginia, and relations between Welles and Lederer were strained

when Lederer started supporting Christopher, Virginia's daughter, at a time when Welles was financially strapped. CHARLES HIGHAM reports that Lederer was "belligerent and rude" when Welles visited Christopher in 1941. During World War II, Lederer was in India. After his return to the United States and after Welles's second marriage was in serious trouble, Welles moved to a beach house near Marion Davies's estate, where Lederer and his wife, Virginia, were living. This proximity soon led to a reconciliation between the old friends, who became, as BARBARA LEAMING describes it, "great chums." After *MACBETH*, Welles even moved into the Santa Monica home of Lederer, who was now separated from Virginia. Welles contributed a short chase sequence to Howard Hawks's *I Was a Male War Bride* (1949), which Lederer was co-scripting. He was also interested in directing the film adaptation of Edmond Rostand's *Cyrano de Bergerac,* which was originally written by Ben Hecht, but which had been rewritten by Lederer, who brought the script to Welles in Paris. Like so many of Welles's directing projects, including Lederer's scripts for *Portrait of a Murderer* and *Tip for a Dead Jockey,* this was never realized.

Reference Corliss, Richard. *Talking Pictures: Screenwriters in the American Cinema* (New York: Overlook, 1974).

—T.L.E.

Lederer, Virginia Nicholson Welles (1916–) Virginia Nicholson was ORSON WELLES's first wife and the mother of his daughter, Christopher. The daughter of Mr. and Mrs. Leo Nicholson of Wheaton, Illinois, she came from a privileged background. A graduate of Miss Hare's University School for Girls, she met Welles in 1934 at the Todd Summer School Theatre, where she was enrolled as a drama student; for her audition she recited lines from Shakespeare's *Henry IV, Part One.* Her parents paid $250 for her participation in the program, which Welles was directing. She was an understudy for Constance Heron in one of the plays, but did get the chance to play Elizabeth in *Tsar Paul.* During the summer of 1934, she also played the part of an elderly woman in *HEARTS OF AGE,* a short experimental film Welles shot. By the end of the summer she and Welles were involved in a sexual relationship, but her parents were totally opposed to her being involved with an actor.

In the fall of 1934, Welles went to New York City without her, but at ROGER ("Skipper") HILL's urging, Virginia joined Welles there. On November 14, they were married secretly with the Hills as witnesses: but her parents, who had to accept the situation, insisted that they have a "proper" wedding, which took place on December 23, 1934. The ceremony was conducted at the home of Virginia's godmother, Mrs. Herbert Gay, in Llewellyn Park, New Jersey; DR. MAURICE BERNSTEIN, Welles's guardian, was the best man. In the *New York Times* account of the wedding, Virginia, not Welles, got the headline: "Virginia Nicholson Becomes a Bride."

After a short stay in New York, they took, again at Hill's urging, a vacation at Lake Geneva. Upon their return to New York, Welles cast Virginia in the role of Myrtle, Freddie's clueless wife in the stage farce *HORSE EATS HAT.* During the rehearsals there was a considerable amount of tension between the Welleses. SIMON CALLOW reports that when Virginia objected to yet another extended rehearsal and said, "I don't think this is right," Welles responded, "But I do," prompting her to throw a milkshake at him. Callow concludes, "To have a suggestion of his own refused (particularly by his own wife) was unacceptable, smacking of criticism." The problems between the two intensified because Welles was seldom home, often involved in affairs, and generally negligent in his attentions to his wife. According to Callow, Virginia was "still in love with him, but humiliated and lonely, she felt jealous of anyone who shared what appeared to be his real life, the part of it that did not concern her." When Virginia gave birth to Christopher on March 27, 1938, Welles was reportedly involved with two ballerinas, who were his current fixation. Virginia, whose stage name was Anna Stafford, was next cast in Welles's *TOO MUCH JOHNSON,* which included some footage that was later incorporated into the play, which debuted on August 16, 1938. Later that year, she appeared in Welles's stage version of *DANTON'S DEATH* and in the radio versions of *The Count of Monte Cristo, The Man Who Was Thursday, HEART OF DARKNESS* and *A Christmas Carol.* In January of the following year she appeared on two of the Shakespeare recordings Welles

was producing for Columbia Records: *Julius Caesar* and *The Merchant of Venice,* and on June 2nd she appeared with Welles in the CAMPBELL PLAYHOUSE radio version of *Victoria Regina,* which featured HELEN HAYES. This was the last time that Virginia worked with her husband, although later that year he did appear in the radio version of *Mutiny on the Bounty,* which Virginia had co-adapted with JOHN HOUSEMAN and HOWARD KOCH.

When Welles left for Hollywood in 1939, Virginia did not accompany him. The couple had signed a separation agreement on December 16, 1939, and were divorced on February 1, 1940, in Reno, Nevada. Virginia observed that "He had no time for marriage or a family." Callow writes, "Their marriage had irretrievably collapsed under the weight of his obsessive fornication." CHARLES HIGHAM has another explanation: "Perhaps part of the problem was that Virginia was almost Welles's equal in intelligence and she insisted on holding her own in arguments; she was a strong-willed, edgy woman who refused to let her husband run roughshod over her." (Welles did credit Virginia for suggesting that the first production for the NEGRO THEATRE PROJECT should be a *Macbeth* shot in Haiti.)

Soon after the divorce, Virginia married CHARLES LEDERER, a Hollywood scriptwriter and the nephew of MARION DAVIES, WILLIAM RANDOLPH HEARST's movie-star mistress. Relations between Virginia and Welles were strained because he did not make child-support payments on time, and she on more than one occasion had to take him to court. Virginia's marriage to Lederer did not last very long, and when they were divorced, Lederer and Welles became friends. Virginia and daughter Christopher infrequently visited Welles when he was on location or in Europe between projects. Their last visit to him occurred in September of 1951, after which Virginia married Jack Pringle, a businessman who lived in South Africa. After her separation from Welles she appeared in a dozen features between 1945 (*Kiss and Tell*) and 1956 (*Francis in The Haunted House*).

—T.L.E.

Lee, Canada (Leonard Lionel Cornelius Canegate) (1907–1952) African-American

actor Canada Lee appeared in two of ORSON WELLES's theatrical productions, *MACBETH* and *NATIVE SON*. Born in Harlem in 1907, and a childhood friend of Adam Clayton Powell, Jr., Lee was employed in a variety of jobs, including stable boy, jockey, and boxer; his boxing career ended when he lost his sight in one eye. Welles cast him as a cigar-smoking Banquo in the FEDERAL THEATER PROJECT's *Macbeth*, which opened in Harlem on April 14, 1936. CHARLES HIGHAM wrote of the production, "Canada Lee, in particular, was a find, the ghost scene [being] among the most powerful in the production." During the rehearsals for the play the atmosphere was tense because some African Americans thought that the play, which features a black man murdering a young white woman, was an insult to black people. One day when Welles was assaulted by a young black man who was wielding a razor blade, Lee overcame the assailant and may have saved Welles's life. Welles told BARBARA LEAMING, "Canada Lee saved my life." As a result of the experience, "the two became life-long friends," according to FRANK BRADY. After his role in *Macbeth*, Lee had steady employment as an actor and was the operator of the Chicken Coop Club in New York. When Welles directed the stage production of *Native Son*, adapted from RICHARD WRIGHT's novel, he turned again to Lee, whom he cast as Bigger Thomas, the protagonist of the play. In the play, which represented a triumph for Welles and Lee, Leaming wrote, "All the electrifying power and hatred he [Lee] had concentrated in him was unleashed onstage." The critics shared Leaming's enthusiasm. BROOKS ATKINSON, theater critic, called Lee "superb," and Rosamond Gilder, reviewing the play in *Theatre Arts Monthly*, claimed, "Canada Lee has added a figure of heroic dimensions and tremendous implications to the theatre's gallery of great portraits." According to SIMON CALLOW, Lee "for the rest of his short life was thereafter regarded as the finest Black actor of his generation." Before Lee was to depart on a national tour with *Native Son*, there was a problem involving the sale of a car that Lee had not apparently fully paid for. At the trial, Lee was not convicted of a crime, but was warned. A little later, a different District Attorney's Office charged Lee with the same crime, and Welles had to have him bailed

out of jail so he could go on tour with the company. Lee went on to appear in five more films, including Alfred Hitchcock's *Lifeboat* (1944) and Robert Rossen's *Body and Soul* (1949). His last film, the film adaptation of Alan Paton's anti-apartheid novel, *Cry the Beloved Country* (1952), was made in the United Kingdom because Lee's American film career had ended when he was charged with being a communist and was blacklisted for his strong statements in support of the rights of black Americans. He died in 1952, the same year his last film was released.

References Gill, Glenda Eloise. *No Surrender! No Retreat!: African-American Pioneer Performers of the Twentieth-Century American Theater* (New York: St. Martin's Press, 2000).

—T.L.E.

Leigh, Janet (Jeanette Helen Morrison)

(1927–) This attractive American actress will always be remembered for her shower scene in Alfred Hitchcock's *Psycho* (1960), but she was also featured as a victim by ORSON WELLES in *TOUCH OF EVIL* (1958). She was born Jeanette Helen Morrison, in Merced, California, on July 6, 1927, in the San Joaquin Valley, the daughter of Fred Morrison and Helen Lita Westergaard. When Jeanette was two years old, her parents moved to Stockton, California, where she grew up. At the age of 14 she eloped and got married, but the marriage was quietly annulled. After high school she enrolled as a music major at the College of Pacific in Stockton in September 1943. She was noticed by Norma Shearer, the widow of MGM production head Irving Thalberg, approached by MCA, then contracted to MGM. Although she had no real acting experience, she got her first screen role at the age of 20, in *The Romance of Rosy Ridge* (1947), opposite the popular Van Johnson, who suggested her stage name, Janet Leigh.

In *Touch of Evil*, adapted by Welles from the novel *Badge of Evil* by Walt Masterson, Janet Leigh was cast as Susan Vargas, the wife of Mike Vargas (CHARLTON HESTON), innocent newlyweds caught up in the menacing, corrupt world of LOS ROBLES, on the Mexican-American border. In her autobiography, *There Really Was a Hollywood* (Doubleday, 1984), Leigh remembered "Orson" calling upon his friends, such as MARLENE DIETRICH and MERCEDES MCCAMBRIDGE, "to do capsule appearances *not* in the script." She remembered the production heads at Universal as being "leery of his wild reputation" and described the prerehearsals with "Orson, Chuck Heston, Akim Tamiroff, [and] Joseph Calleia." For Welles, she wrote, "rules were made to be broken," but after the director had completed his contractual "first cut," the studio demanded retakes: "They did not understand all of the detours and believed the flow was disjointed." The cast was "compelled to acquiesce because of the Screen Actors Guild code" and provided some "linking, explanatory, dull" shots that hardly improved the picture, which, upon its release, "was disappointing," though it later would be considered a masterpiece.

Janet Leigh and her husband, Tony Curtis, to whom she was married for 10 years, were Hollywood icons during the 1950s. In 1962, she married Bob Brandt. Leigh was nominated for an Oscar in 1960 for *Psycho,* and earned the "Most Popular Star" award in 1961 from the Associated Theater Owners of America. In 1962, she starred with Frank Sinatra in John Frankenheimer's cold war classic film *The Manchurian Candidate.* Before her retirement, she appeared with her daughter, Jamie Lee Curtis, in *The Fog* (1980), assisting her daughter's career that had begun two years earlier with *Halloween.* Janet Leigh's rise to stardom as a Cinderella story was mythic in typical Hollywood fashion.

References Leigh, Janet. *There Really Was a Hollywood* (Garden City, N.Y.: Doubleday, 1984); Saline, Carol, and Sharon J. Wohlmuth. *Mothers and Daughters* (New York: Doubleday, 1997).

—J.M.W.

Leigh, Vivien (Vivian Mary Hartley)

(1913–1967) Vivien Leigh appeared as Jane opposite ORSON WELLES's Rochester in *JANE EYRE,* the last radio production Welles did for THE CAMPBELL PLAYHOUSE. Born in Darjeeling, India, on November 5, 1913, Leigh was educated in England. and on the European continent. Her first film, *Things Are Looking Up,* appeared in 1934, and she made her London stage debut in 1935. Two years later, she starred with SIR LAURENCE OLIVIER in the film *Fire Over England,* and the two married actors began an affair that cul-

minated in divorces from their spouses and their marriage in 1940. (This situation was later ironically reversed when Olivier fell in love with actress Joan Plowright, with whom he was starring in Welles's London stage production of EUGÈNE IONESCO's absurdist drama *RHINOCEROS;* Leigh granted Olivier a divorce, and he married Plowright.) In 1939, she appeared in the film adaptation of Margaret Mitchell's popular novel, *Gone With the Wind,* a story about the South during the Civil War and its aftermath. Her role as Scarlett O'Hara, which she won after fierce competition with other established actresses, brought her her first Academy Award for best actress and the New York Critics' best actress prize. The Scarlett role seems to have typecast her as a beautiful, sexy, vulnerable woman. Her other major films were *That Hamilton Woman* (1941), *Caesar and Cleopatra* (1945), *Anna Karenina* (1948), *A Streetcar Named Desire* (1951, for which she received her second best actress Oscar), *The Roman Spring of Mrs. Stone* (1961), and *Ship of Fools* (1965). Welles was interested in casting her as Lady Macbeth in his *MACBETH* (1948). In response to PETER BOGDANOVICH's "Why?" Welles answered, "I wanted a sexpot . . . and she could speak the lines." Welles had earlier wanted her to play in the first picture he planned to make for RKO, the film adaptation of Edmond Rostand's *Cyrano de Bergerac,* but the deal fell through. She also failed to make appearances in two unrealized Welles-Sir ALEXANDER KORDA planned films: *War and Peace* and OSCAR WILDE's *SALOME.* She suffered from tuberculosis and physical exhaustion and died in 1967, two years after she made her last film, *Ship of Fools.*

References Edwards, Anne. *Vivien Leigh: A Biography* (New York: Simon & Schuster, 1977); Lasky, Jesse L. *Love Scene: The Story of Laurence Olivier and Vivien Leigh* (New York: Crowell, 1978); Vickers, Hugo. *Vivien Leigh* (Boston: Little Brown, 1998).

—T.L.E.

Lillie, Bea (Beatrice Gladys Lillie) (1898–

1989) Bea Lillie, famous stage comedienne (John Mason Brown declared her "a comic law unto herself"), appeared with ORSON WELLES on his *CAMPBELL PLAYHOUSE* radio show on December 16, 1938, in Dodie Smith's *Call It a Day.* Born on May 29,

1898, in Toronto, she was the daughter of a Canadian government official. She left school at the age of 15 to go on the stage and appeared with her sister and mother as a singing trio. In 1914, she made her theatrical debut in London at the Chatham Music Hall and her Broadway debut in *Charlot's Revue of 1924.* She traveled between New York and London to appear on the stage. She became a popular personality on both continents and was friends with such luminaries as CHARLIE CHAPLIN, SHAW, and Churchill. In 1920, she married Sir Robert Peel. She appeared in several plays, most notably NOËL COWARD's *Set to Music* (1939) and, much later, in the stage adaptation of Patrick Dennis's *Auntie Mame* (1958) in the title role. She also appeared in a few films, the best of which were *Around the World in 80 Days* (1956) and *Thoroughly Modern Millie* (1967). Her last stage appearance in New York was in *High Spirits* (1964), a musical version of Coward's *Blithe Spirit. Every Other Inch a Lady,* her autobiography, was published in 1972. She died in 1989.

—T.L.E.

Lindfors, Viveca (Elsa Viveca Torstensdotter Lindfors) (1920–1995)

Lindfors belatedly got the part of Cordelia in Shakespeare's KING LEAR, which WELLES was to adapt, along with Ben Jonson's *Volpone,* for the New York stage in 1955. Welles had originally planned to have five British actors participate in the project, but they were denied entry permits by the Immigration Service, which had responded to pressure by Actors' Equity. Because of financial reasons, *Volpone* was dropped, but Welles hired Lindfors and GERALDINE FITZGERALD, who played Goneril, and went ahead with *King Lear.* Before the premiere, Welles fell and broke two bones in his left foot and had to open in a wheelchair with a cast on his foot In her autobiography, *Viveka-Viveca!* (1981) Lindfors offers a somewhat different account of Welles's accident. She claims that Welles was so distraught at the opening-night reviews of his *King Lear* that he decided to break both his ankles "in his fear of facing his fragility." She writes, "Did he really? The truth only he and his doctor know."

Lindfors, who was born on December 29, 1920, in Stockholm, Sweden, was an excellent choice for

Welles's *Lear* because of her dramatic training at Stockholm's Royal Dramatic Theatre. Although she continued to work in the theater, she did move to films in 1940 and made eight films in Sweden before she moved to the United States in 1946. She signed a contract with Warner Bros. in 1948; her debut film was *To the Victor.* She continued to appear in many films, both in the United States and in Europe, but the films and the roles did not allow her to take advantage of her considerable talent. On the other hand, her stage roles were significant: She appeared in *Anastasia* (1954), *Brecht on Brecht* (1961), and in a one-woman show, *I Am a Woman* (1973). She directed her first film, *Unfinished Business . . . ,* in 1987. She appeared in two films in 1992, *North of Pittsburg* and *The Linguine Incident.* She died three years later on October 25, 1995, in Uppsala in her native Sweden.

Reference Lindfors, Viveca. *Viveka-Viveca!* (New York: Everest House, 1981).

—T.L.E.

Lindsay, Louis

In 1947, Louis Lindsay was ORSON WELLES's editor on his adaptation of SHAKESPEARE's MACBETH. There were problems with the dubbing of the sound track because of some sound experiments Welles tried and because Welles had made free use of Scottish accents, which turned out to be, in some cases, unintelligible. Officials at Republic Studios were concerned. Lindsay took a print with him to Rome, where he worked on the sound track with Welles, who was also busy shooting *Cagliostro,* which later became BLACK MAGIC (1949). Eventually, the Scottish sound track had to be essentially replaced. DAVID THOMSON archly describes the relationship between Welles and Lindsay: "Lou Lindsay, his editor, his friend, his loyalist inquirer after fresh funds, the man who cemented over so many cracks, is owed $30,000 [by Welles]. So new best friends will be in order, fresh saviors."

—T.L.E.

Little Prince, The

In 1943, the children's story by Antoine de Saint Exupéry so enchanted WELLES that he had his lawyer, Jackson Leighter, purchase the book's screen rights. Welles's adaptation of Saint Exupéry's story called for a combination of live action and animation. His efforts to secure Walt Disney's help for the animated sequences were rebuffed. Other Hollywood moguls, wary of Welles because of the lingering controversies spawned by CITIZEN KANE and THE MAGNIFICENT AMBERSONS, were similarly uninterested. Faced with such formidable odds, Welles sold the screen rights to *The Little Prince,* making a handsome profit in the process. Three decades later, in 1974, *The Little Prince* was produced, directed, and brought to the screen by Hollywood veteran Stanley Donen.

—C.B.

Lombard, Carole (Jane Alice Peters)

(1908–1942)   When RKO refused to cast contract actress Lucille Ball in his *The Smiler with a Knife* (an unproduced idea WELLES was considering in 1939), Welles considered Carole Lombard, a close friend of his and the wife of actor Clark Gable. According to Welles, Lombard did not turn down the part; her studio refused to let her do it. At the time she was at the height of her career and popularity. Lombard, who was born on October 6, 1908, in Fort Wayne, Indiana, was brought up in California. Her first film appearance was in *A Perfect Crime* (1921), when she was still in school. After graduating from junior high school, she signed a contract with Fox in 1925 and adopted the stage name of Carol Lombard (in 1930 it became Carole). She acted in a few films, and when her contract was terminated, she signed with Mack Sennett and did two-reel slapstick comedies in 1927–28. She made more feature films, but it was her role in Howard Hawks's *Twentieth Century* (1934) that made her a star comic actor. She made several screwball comedies; her best known films were *My Man Godfrey* (1936) and *To Be or Not to Be* (1942). Her death at the height of her career in 1942, while she was flying back to the West Coast after a bond-selling tour in the Midwest, stunned her fans and her husband, Clark Gable. President ROOSEVELT's heartfelt telegram to Gable commented on her role as star and patriot: "She gave unselfishly of time and talent to serve her country in peace and war. She loved her country. She is and always will be a star, one we shall never forget nor cease to be grateful to." The celebrated relationship between Gable and Lombard, two

Hollywood stars, was rendered on film as *Gable and Lombard* (1976) starring Jill Clayburgh and James Brolin.

References   Ott, Frederick W. *The Films of Carole Lombard* (Secaucus, N.J.: Citadel, 1972); Swindell, Larry. *Screwball: The Life of Carole Lombard* (New York: Morrow, 1975).

—T.L.E.

Long Hot Summer, The

Twentieth Century–Fox, 115 minutes, 1958. **Director:** Martin Ritt; **Producer:** Jerry Wald; **Screenplay:** Irving Ravetch and Harriet Frank, Jr., adapted from William Faulkner's novel *The Hamlet*; **Cinematography:** Joseph La Shelle; **Music:** Alex North; **Cast:** Orson Welles (Will Varner), Paul Newman (Ben Quick), Joanne Woodward (Clara Varner), Anthony Franciosa (Jody Varner), Lee Remick (Eula Varner), Angela Lansbury (Minnie)

WELLES's return to Hollywood in 1956 with wife, Paola, and daughter Beatrice was calculated in large part to help reduce the onerous tax burden still lingering from the debacle of his 1946 Broadway production of AROUND THE WORLD IN 80 DAYS. Helping in this matter was the $150,000 acting fee he received from producer Jerry Wald for his appearance as Will Varner in *The Long Hot Summer.*

Wald, fresh from his hugely successful adaptation of *Peyton Place* (1957), sought to repeat that triumph with another sex-charged, small town, family melodrama. This time, instead of the outwardly prim New England. village of Grace Metalious's Peyton Place, Wald shifted the location to the humid Mississippi delta in an adaption of WILLIAM FAULKNER's *The Hamlet.* With a loosely based but effectively crafted adaptation of the Faulkner novel by Harriet Frank, Jr. and Irving Ravetch, Wald retitled the steamy melodrama *The Long Hot Summer.*

In the film, Welles plays an opinionated plantation owner, the cigar-chomping widower Will Varner, one of whose goals lies in avoiding the matrimonial designs of Minnie Littlejohn, played by Angela Lansbury. Though only 42 at the time of the shooting, Welles turned in a convincing performance as the crusty, 60-something Varner who looks forward to passing on his estates to his grandchildren. With this

Welles with Joanne Woodward in *The Long, Hot Summer* (*Literature/Film Archive*)

desire for grandchildren in mind, Varner taunts his weak-willed son (Anthony Franciosa) for not producing an heir with his baby-doll wife (Lee Remick). Varner's plucky daughter, Clara (JOANNE WOODWARD), older than her brother and unmarried, is considered something of an old maid. However, when a drifter, Ben Quick (PAUL NEWMAN), comes to town, that perception changes as sparks start flying as Clara and Ben begin to take note of each other. Quick, who takes a job as Varner's straw boss, stands his ground against the older man, thus earning Varner's grudging respect. "You're no better than a crook," Varner quips to Quick. "You're no better than a con man," Quick replies. Indeed, Varner soon comes to think that Quick would make an excellent son-in-law, and a man better suited to running an empire than his own son. Clara, initially put off by Quick's blue-collar background, comes to appreciate Quick's honesty and industry. After a melodramatic finale, all ends well for Varner, his daughter Clara, and the roustabout Quick.

The Long Hot Summer was a hit. The pairing of Newman and Woodward, who would soon marry in real life as well as at the end of the film, worked like magic. Welles, too, was effective. Although he often had been accused of overacting, here his performance as the tyrannical Southern landowner was generally praised. Angela Lansbury, who often played characters older than she actually was, won plaudits for her

witty and engaging portrayal of Welles's mistress. Lee Remick, too, was singled out for her sexy and kittenish etching of Eula Varner. Indeed, *The Long Hot Summer* provided significant upgrades in the careers of all concerned.

For Welles, teaming with no-nonsense director Martin Ritt was not easy. As was often the case when the Great Man worked for other directors, there were disputes over camera angles, interpretation of lines, and bits of business. Ritt recalls that "two weeks after we started, you could bet that we wouldn't finish the film." Welles put it a bit more diplomatically: "There was a note of suspicion. I did not know what kind of monkeyshines I would have to put up with, and the cast did not know what kind of caprices they would have to put up with me." Somehow, the two strong-minded men made it through the production.

For Welles, while his acting was again being touted, the trek to Louisiana for *The Long Hot Summer*'s location shoot wound up costing him dearly in terms of his involvement with TOUCH OF EVIL (1958). The moguls at Universal, upset with Welles for having "abandoned" the editing of *Touch of Evil* to take another job, barred the director-actor from the studio after Welles's return to Hollywood from location, thus wresting postproduction control of *Touch of Evil* from him. Welles's decision to appear in *The Long Hot Summer* proved one of the costliest miscalculations of the director's career.

References Miller, Gabriel. *The Films of Martin Ritt* (Jackson: University of Mississippi Press, 2000); Phillips, Gene D. *Fiction, Film, and Faulkner: The Art of Adaptation* (Knoxville: University of Tennessee Press, 1988).

—C.B.

Losey, Joseph (1909–1984)

Losey, Joseph (1909–1984) Stage and film director Joseph Losey worked on the FEDERAL THEATRE PROJECT during the Depression at the same time as ORSON WELLES. Losey was born in La Crosse, Wisconsin, in 1909. After attending Dartmouth and Harvard, he tried a variety of jobs; he was stage manager for several Broadway plays, until he became a stage director himself. His first big break as a director in the professional theater was "The Living Newspaper" in 1936, a project of the Federal Theatre that provided work for some of the thousands of unemployed actors, writers, and technicians during the depression.

Foster Hirsch has written that each Living Newspaper play "was addressed to a particular social problem, usually a grievance of the working class. The politics of the plays were at least incipiently, if not actually and fully, marxist; and the productions were designed to instruct depression audiences and to encourage them to take action. The Living Newspaper dramas were . . . explicitly polemical—newspaper editorials brought vividly to life."

In 1936, Welles, who was also from Wisconsin, directed an all-black production of MACBETH under the aegis of the Federal Theatre. Welles's production was more successful than Losey's production of *Conjure Man Dies,* which also had an all-black cast. David Caute maintains that this incident precipitated "Losey's lifelong sourness towards Welles." Losey told Michel Ciment that he had a higher regard in those days for Welles as a director than as an actor, since he felt Welles too often overacted. He explained to Ciment:

"I knew Welles all the time but never very well. I mean we'd had a kind of nodding distance across rooms, saloons, theatres, and a kind of vaguely hostile telephone or letter correspondence, but we've never been friends and never really trusted each other. I had immense respect for his theatre work, but I never have had any respect for him as an actor." Welles did an adaptation of Labiche's *Italian Straw Hat* (retitled HORSE EATS HAT), produced by JOHN HOUSEMAN, which Losey thought "was imaginative, vigorous and delightful, and I hadn't expected it. I saw Welles once or twice a week. I don't think he liked me and I didn't like him. But anyway, I was so impressed by this production that I went home and sent him a three-page wire which was really a bit extravagant. I thought it was the best theatre production I had ever seen in the United States. After this telegram I never heard from him, and years later I said to John Houseman, 'This is very strange. Do you know anything about it?' He said, 'Yes. Welles showed me the cable. He thought you didn't mean it. He thought you were pulling his leg.'"

After directing several more plays in the legitimate theater, Losey was offered a contract to direct motion

pictures and went to Hollywood briefly in 1938, then went on to make educational shorts in New York before joining the Signal Corps in 1943. When he returned to Hollywood after the war, he made another short, *A Gun in Hand* (1945), which was part of the "Crime Does Not Pay" series, on which FRED ZINNEMANN had spent part of his apprenticeship in the MGM shorts department.

The officials at MGM gave no indication that they intended to elevate Losey to feature production in the foreseeable future. So Losey returned to the theater. German writer BERTOLT BRECHT invited him in 1946 to direct an English-language version of his play *Galileo,* about the controversial 17th-century astronomer. Originally Brecht had sought Welles as director, and Welles was at first enthusiastic about the project because he was much impressed by Brecht's work. He told PETER BOGDANOVICH, "You could tell Brecht was educated by the Jesuits—he had the kind of disciplined brain characterized by Jesuit education. . . . I said to him one day, while we were talking about *Galileo,* that he had written a perfect anti-Communist play." When Brecht asked him what he meant, Welles explained that Brecht was using the pope's antagonism toward Galileo's ground-breaking theories as an implicit parallel to Stalin's ill-treatment of independent thinkers in Russia. "You have made something resolutely anti-Soviet," Welles concluded. But eventually Welles turned down the chance to direct *Galileo* because the production was being backed by MIKE TODD, with whom Welles had had a falling out over Todd's financial backing of his stage production, AROUND THE WORLD IN 80 DAYS.

CHARLES LAUGHTON, who was slated to play the title role, was very disappointed when Welles backed out, as Welles was by far better known than Losey in the mid-1940s. The play was produced by John Houseman, who had worked with Welles in the New York theater, and finally opened on July 30, 1946, at the Coronet Theater in Hollywood. Welles graciously sent Houseman, Laughton, and Brecht congratulatory telegrams on opening night. The production was a success and moved to Broadway on December 7, 1947. By that time, however, Brecht had appeared before the House Un-American Activities Committee (HUAC), which was investigating communist activities in America, and had fled from the United States.

Losey then accepted an offer from RKO to make his first feature, *The Boy with Green Hair* (1948). The film employs the boy's green hair as a symbol of the need for peace, tolerance, and international understanding in the world. His first feature, although untypical of his later films, nevertheless sounded a thematic chord that would reverberate throughout his subsequent films. "I think, basically, if I have one theme," he told this writer, "it is the question of hypocrisy; people who condemn others without looking at themselves."

It was around this time that suspicion that Losey might be a communist began to be asserted. These were the tense cold war years that spawned Senator JOSEPH MCCARTHY's investigations of communists and the House Un-American Activities Committee hearings, which would eventually force Losey to migrate to England when he was blacklisted in Hollywood.

When Losey sought to track down why he had been blacklisted, he found that he was suspect because he had openly supported Adrian Scott, the producer of *The Boy with Green Hair,* when Scott had been blacklisted before him; moreover, Losey's refusal to direct a picture called *I Married a Communist* was also held against him—although he turned the project down because of the inferior script, not because it was anticommunist. Other reasons were Losey's involvement with the Living Newspaper project and because of his association with blacklisted writer Bertolt Brecht, whose play *Galileo* Losey had directed on Broadway in 1947—a play that Losey subsequently filmed in 1975. Finally, Losey was accused by a former friend and colleague of being a former member of the Communist Party.

"Because his acclaimed work for the Living Newspaper had stamped him as a political activist," Foster Hirsch has noted, "Losey was chosen by Brecht to direct the American premiere of *Galileo.*" HUAC considered the production politically suspect, "not only because of Brecht's Communist sympathies, but also because Losey was known to have left-wing associations." As Losey explained to this writer, "They were concerned about my association with

people like Hans Eisler, who wrote the music for Brecht's plays and for my films. He happened to be the brother of Gerhardt Eisler, the head of the German Communist Party at the time, which made them suspect anyone associated with him. I had helped to bring Eisler into this country, and my sponsorship of him was one of the things mentioned in my dossier." (Interestingly enough, in *Guilty by Suspicion,* a 1991 film about the Hollywood blacklist, Losey himself was portrayed as "Joseph Lesser" by film director Martin Scorsese.)

Losey went to England in 1952, where he took whatever work he could find. He was initially hired to direct low-budget features, beginning with *The Sleeping Tiger* (1954). In making this film and his other early British pictures, Losey sought to depart from the established clichés of melodrama, and was willing to battle with his producers in order to improve the scripts he was handed. Losey remembered that his attitude had sometimes caused motion picture distributors to complain, "He made his film; he didn't make ours." To this Losey responded, quite characteristically, "Well, I make my film; and I don't know what their film is."

Losey filmed *The Servant* in 1963, the first of three films he made in collaboration with playwright-screenwriter Harold Pinter. The other two movies Pinter scripted are *Accident* (1967) and *The Go-Between* (1971). All three films explore the moral bankruptcy of society, particularly among those of background and education.

Losey zeroed in on the life of a historical figure in *Galileo* (1975), which he made in England. for the American Film Theater series of filmed plays. "I had done *Galileo* on the stage with Charles Laughton in the title role, and wanted to film it then, but the project fell through," Losey recalled. "The AFT gave me a one million dollar budget, so I had to find ways of simplifying the production," since a historical film could have realistically cost much more. "But this was good discipline for me, and was not at all detrimental to the film"—just as working on a slim budget had definitely not hurt another of his costume dramas, *The Go-Between.*

Galileo relates the life of the 17th-century Italian astronomer Galileo Galilei (Topol), who came under fire from the Vatican over his scientific theories, which at the time were thought to be in conflict with Church doctrine. Long after Galileo's death, his theories were ultimately acknowledged to be in harmony with the tenets of Christian theology; but Losey was interested not so much in portraying a controversy involving science and religion as in delineating the age-old struggle between the individual and authority. *Galileo* is really about "individual responsibility," Losey commented. Perhaps with his own experience with the House Un-American Activities Committee in mind, he added that, in keeping with its literary source, the film implies that "the human race isn't going to survive if people consistently . . . allow themselves to be intimidated. That's the magnificence of that play."

Because the movie's action seldom strays beyond a few basic sets, the film was dismissed by some as a mere photographed stage play. Yet, Losey adroitly brings the play to life on the screen by keeping his camera on the go, as it roves from one character to another, capturing every significant gesture and remark, while Galileo engages in lively debate with the churchmen over his scientific research. In committing to celluloid a play he had wanted to film for more than a quarter of a century, Losey accomplished the fulfillment of a long-cherished wish and created a worthy cinematic transcription of a great modern drama in the bargain.

Although Welles was involved in the Federal Theatre Project as much as Losey and had in fact wanted to direct Brecht's *Galileo,* he was not blacklisted as Losey was. Welles did not, after all, have the number of left-wing associations that Losey had. Welles was even denounced by the Beverly Hills Communist Party in the early 1940s for his views on communism.

The same year that the film of *Galileo* was released, Losey told this writer that Welles had paid dearly for his efforts to achieve artistic freedom as a filmmaker. "Welles has always been one step ahead of the bill collector; he has a long list of unrealized films. He is a magnificent ruin." Although these remarks might seem condescending toward Welles, Losey said that he admired much of Welles's film work. To Ciment, Losey stated:

"I don't think that Welles ever made a single foot of film that was bad. I think you can take almost any sequence out of almost any picture and look at that sequence and say, 'This is work of genius—a man of great power and great talent who has to be respected.' But when these sequences are put together in a picture, they do not make a whole—for me. I don't share the general enthusiasm for *Kane* although I recognize it as a very important breakthrough and that it had an immense influence. The one picture that I feel is practically a perfect work, although I know that Welles says it was inferior, was *Ambersons.*"

Losey had a predilection for THE MAGNIFICENT AMBERSONS since Losey, like Welles, came from a wealthy family in Wisconsin; hence he was aware of how authentically Welles had captured the midwestern milieu of the upper classes at the beginning of the 20th century.

Like Welles, Losey had to face great obstacles in achieving artistic control of his films.

"Working over the years," Losey reflected, "sacrificing the big, juicy jobs for the things I believe in, and doing it with no money and little encouragement, it's been exhausting." Yet, when one ponders the impressive group of films that Losey was able to make with all of the obstacles in his path, one wonders if he would have had it any other way.

References Caute, David. *Joseph Losey: A Biography* (New York: Oxford University Press, 1994); Ciment, Michel. *Conversations with Losey* (New York: Methuen, 1985); Hirsch, Foster. *Joseph Losey* (Boston: Twayne, 1980); Palmer, James, and Michael Riley. *The Films of Joseph Losey* (New York: Cambridge University Press, 1993); Phillips, Gene. *Major Film Directors of the American and British Cinema* (Cranbury, N.J.: Associated University Presses, 1999), 193–208; Welles, Orson, and Peter Bogdanovich. *This Is Orson Welles* (New York: Da Capo, 1998).

—G.D.P.

Los Robles Fictional U.S.-Mexican border town in which the majority of the action of WELLES's magnificent TOUCH OF EVIL (1958) takes place. Designed to evoke the rotting decay of border towns such as Tijuana and Juarez, Welles, at the suggestion of screenwriter Aldous Huxley, evoked the nightmarish world of the fictive Los Robles by shooting on location in Venice, California, which at the turn of the last century, as Venice-by-the-Sea, had been created as a fashionable resort with miles of canals.

—C.B.

Luce, Henry (1898–1967) In response to JOHN HOUSEMAN's plea for funds, Henry and Clare Luce contributed $2,500 so that Houseman and WELLES could stage their production of JULIUS CAESAR at the MERCURY THEATRE in 1937. According to Welles, Henry Luce and his wife both enjoyed the NEWS ON THE MARCH newsreel digest that occurs at the beginning of CITIZEN KANE because it was a stylistic parody of Luce's THE MARCH OF TIME with "its inverted sentences, the taut fact-filled portentous reporting, the standard clichés." In fact, Luce, who was a competitor of WILLIAM RANDOLPH HEARST, became Welles's ally in getting *Citizen Kane* released. *Variety* reported that Luce "has ordered his staff to unleash their guns to get the film released." FRANK BRADY reports that Luce was even rumored to have offered Republic chief GEORGE SCHAEFER $1 million for the film in order to guarantee its release. Welles, however, later became disenchanted with what he considered the reactionary right-wing politics espoused by the Luces and in 1945 warned about the dangers of extreme anti-Russian propaganda.

Henry Luce was born in Tengchow, China, the son of Presbyterian missionaries, on April 3, 1898. He was educated at the Hotchkiss School (1913–16) and at Yale University, where his schooling was interrupted by World War I; he was commissioned as a second lieutenant in the army, but the war ended before he was sent overseas. At Yale he helped to edit the *Daily News,* and after graduation he worked for newspapers in Chicago and Baltimore. With Briton Hadden, a friend at Hotchkiss and Yale, he founded *Time* magazine in 1923; the magazine was immensely popular. After Hadden's death in 1929, Luce, who was now a millionaire, founded *Fortune,* and despite the depression, the journal prospered. In 1932, he bought *Architectural Forum,* and in 1936, began a documentary newsreel series called *The March of Time.*

After his divorce from his first wife in 1935, he married Clare Boothe Brokaw, a playwright who went on to become an ambassador and a member of the U.S. House of Representatives. His next publishing venture was *Life* magazine, which was noted for its splendid photographs. Due to the political stance of his papers and his immense wealth, he became politically influential and was a staunch supporter of the Republican Party and was a close friend of President Eisenhower. An ardent foe of communism, he was blind to the corruption of the Chinese Nationalist Government and was later an avid supporter of the war in Vietnam. To his credit, he was a civil rights advocate and was a major supporter of both the Urban League and the United Negro College Fund. In 1954, he started still another successful magazine, *Sports Illustrated.* Although television may have accounted for *Life*'s declining fortunes, Time, Inc., the major holding company, prospered. Perhaps the most innovative and imaginative journalist of his time, Luce died in Phoenix, Arizona, on February 28, 1967.

References Baughman, James L. *Henry R. Luce and the Rise of the American News Media* (Baltimore: Johns Hopkins, 2001); Herzstein, Robert Edwin. *Henry R. Luce: A Political Portrait of the Man Who Created the American Century* (New York: Scribner's, 1994).

—T.L.E.

Lyons, Bridget Gellert Rutgers University professor of English Bridget Gellert Lyons, as co-editor of the academic journal *Renaissance Quarterly,* was well qualified to edit the "Rutgers Films in Print" series volume CHIMES AT MIDNIGHT (Rutgers University Press, 1988). The book opens with "A Biographical Sketch" and a survey essay entitled "The Shakespearean Camera of Orson Welles" before presenting the film's "Continuity Script," along with "Credits and Cast" information. The script is based essentially upon Shakespeare's *Henry IV, Parts 1 and 2,* but, as Lyons notes, WELLES has also drawn on the other plays in Shakespeare's history tetralogy, *Richard II* and *Henry V,* as well as *The Merry Wives of Windsor* for this FALSTAFF compilation. Only occasionally does Welles interpolate "some language of his own, usually in the form of short neutral phrases that clarify a particular point or simply help to get a character off the screen."

In keeping with the series format, the book offers "Interviews" ("Welles and Falstaff, Juan Cobos and Miguel Rubio," and an interview with KEITH BAXTER, who played Prince Hal), "Reviews" (Bosley Crowther, PAULINE KAEL, John Russell Taylor, Judith Crist, et al.), and "Commentaries" (by C.L. Barber, Dudley Andrew, and MICHAEL ANDEREGG), followed by a "Filmography and Bibliography." *Chimes at Midnight* represented for Welles "the culmination of an involvement with Shakespeare that spanned his entire career as an actor, director, and critic," according to Lyons. In his treatment of Shakespeare's history plays, Welles demonstrated "first his respect for Shakespeare, and then the differences between his own medium and the playwright's." The book makes a useful contribution to Welles scholarship.

—J.M.W.

Macbeth (play, 1936) When JOHN HOUSEMAN was appointed to head the FEDERAL THEATRE PROJECT'S New York-based NEGRO THEATRE PROJECT, an agency under the administration of the WORKS PROGRESS ADMINISTRATION, he turned to 20-year-old ORSON WELLES to put the unit on the map. Virginia Welles, the wunderkind's wife, suggested a radically revised edition of Shakespeare's *Macbeth*. Instead of the traditional Scottish setting, the action would be shifted to Haiti, and based on the life of Henri Christophe, the self-proclaimed king of the island nation who had modeled his wildly extravagant mountain-based court of Sans Souci after that of Louis XVI. As evidenced by the best-selling status of Richard A. Loederer's 1935 book, *Voodoo Fire in Haiti,* Haitian culture was in vogue in mid-1930s America. More significantly, a "voodoo" *Macbeth* would allow Welles and Houseman to credibly use an all-black cast.

The show, which opened on April 14, 1936, at the lavishly refurbished Lafayette Theatre in the middle of Harlem, was set on a nameless Caribbean island in the early 1800s, during the colonization of that then wild territory. The primitive forces at work in the play were signaled at the onset by three voodoo witch doctors, a brilliant transposition of Shakespeare's witches, who utter their ominous prophesy amid the beating of voodoo drums. Here, as elsewhere, Welles sought to underscore Shakespeare's concern with the uncontrollable passions that feed ambition. As Macbeth's vile plan unfolds, the voodoo drums return, reminding us of the destructive nature of blind ambition. In contrast to Welles's protagonist in his film version of MACBETH (1948), here, the "voodoo" Macbeth, driven by the dark side of human nature, is beyond volition.

Nat Karson's sets and Abe Feder's lighting were designed to emphasize a world out of balance. The backdrops, for instance, were dominated by huge abstractions of wildly growing foliage. At other times, to underscore Macbeth's growing paranoia, the stage was plunged into virtual darkness with rumbles of savage tropic storms punctuating the dialogue. For a ballroom scene, Welles, in a clear reference to the ersatz court of Henri Christophe, has his cast togged in European fashions and lilting to a Joseph Lanner waltz. At another point, the assassins who kill Banquo were garbed in black capes and top hats, and used guns instead of the knives called for by Shakespeare.

Since the Negro Theatre Project, like all WPA agencies, was mandated to put as many people to work as possible, Welles and Houseman were obligated to use "actors" of minimal skill and experience. Even with exhaustive rehearsals, Welles felt it necessary to prop up the ends of lines with musical reenforcement. To achieve the aural montages, he had composer VIRGIL THOMSON allude to the sounds of thunder, wind, and lightning with kettledrums, thunder sheets, and a wind machine. Although dubious about the results of his musical pastiche, Thomson's pungent score was widely hailed, thus leading to commissions for forthcoming Shakespearean productions of *Hamlet* (Leslie Howard) and *Antony and Cleopatra* (Tallulah Bankhead).

The story of Welles's work with JACK CARTER (Macbeth) is a saga onto itself. Welles, the youthful white 20-year-old artiste, and Carter, the black ex-boxer, were, indeed, an odd couple. Nonetheless, Welles coaxed a convincing performance from his tough, gangsterlike friend by drinking and whoring as well as rehearsing with him. His other leads, Edna Thomas (Lady Macbeth) and CANADA LEE (Banquo), were seasoned pros who helped greatly in steadying the largely inexperienced cast. In spite of the travails of the unorthodox production, when the "voodoo" *Macbeth* opened on April 14, 1936, it created a sensation.

Interestingly, many black residents of Harlem, initially skeptical of what they feared would be another case of white cultural and financial exploitation, were happily surprised by the all-black cast. It was an event the black community could take pride in. The critics were another story. Although generally awed by Welles's audacious stagecraft, their comments seemed to reflect the period's underlying racism. The restrained yet still pointed reaction of *Fortune*'s critic was typical: "When the U.S. Government produced William Shakespeare's *Macbeth* in Harlem, it stood them up, packed them in, and rolled them in the aisles. The opening was the blackest first night in New York history. The police roped off four city blocks and the sables from downtown and the high yallers from Harlem fought their way to their fifteen to fifty-five cent seats through the biggest crowd ever gathered on upper Seventh Avenue. . . . the play plus the price brought out white intellectuals as well as black enthusiasts."

The *New York World-Telegram*'s Robert Garland was less subtle. Dismissing the play as a Negro minstrel show, Garland stated that *Macbeth* was "colorful, exciting, and a good colored show. It's like *Run Little Chillun* with intervals of familiar quotations." In a scandalous article entitled "Macbeth in Chocolate," critic Robert Littell observed that "whites came in

droves to spread their chilly fingers before the riveting fires of a warmer, happier, simpler race. In watching them, we capture briefly what once we were, long centuries ago before our ancestors suffered the blights of thought, worry, and the printed word."

On the other side of the critical ledger, the *New York Times*'s BROOKS ATKINSON proclaimed that *Macbeth* was "logical and stunning and a triumph of theater art." The public mostly agreed. Despite the mixed critical notices, *Macbeth* played for 12 weeks in New York. It was also a success on the road, packing houses in Bridgeport, Hartford, Dallas, Indianapolis, Chicago, Detroit, Cleveland, and Brooklyn. Significantly, Welles's "voodoo" *Macbeth* offered many blacks—and whites—their first exposure to Shakespeare. Among African-American intellectuals and opinion-makers, the overwhelming consensus was that *Macbeth* had added to the overall worth and self-esteem of the black community.

In the scene of the advance of Birnam Wood, each soldier carried a single palm branch before his face. The camouflage, of course, was purely symbolic. Remarkably, as BRET WOOD notes, there is motion picture documentation. Preserved by the National Archives in Washington, D.C., the brief and highly edited bit of footage captures the forward march of Birnam Wood and Macbeth's death. Though of little use in revealing much about the production's pacing due to its highly edited nature, the brief snippet captured by *Pathé News* nonetheless points out the newsworthiness of the play. Welles's "voodoo" *Macbeth* was one of *the* events of 1936.

—C.B.

Macbeth (play, 1947) In 1947, when WELLES was hired by Republic Pictures to direct and star in a low-budget film adaptation of Shakespeare's *Macbeth*, it was a surprise to all, especially since Republic's claim to fame was as a producer of low-budget westerns. To prove to Hollywood that he could shoot a prestige picture on schedule and within budget, Welles devised a unique plan to prepare for the film. First, he would come up with a tight 94-minute script. Second, he would use the film script as the basis for mounting a stage play version. Third, using the experience of having "rehearsed" for the film via the production of the play, he would shoot the film within a tight three-week schedule. Amazingly, the plan worked. However, the film ran into difficulties during postproduction and was not released until 1948.

To accomplish his "rehearsal" via performance, Welles needed to find a cooperative and convenient venue for the production. Casting about for offers, a deal was struck with the Utah Centennial Festival in Salt Lake City in May 1947. Pleased with having netted a star of Welles's magnitude to headline its festival, the Utah officials agreed to pay for the play's costumes and props, plus allowing Welles use of the costumes for his film. The principal members of the cast were drawn from the MERCURY production troupe, with two notable exceptions, Dan O'Herlihy (MacDuff) and RODDY MCDOWALL (Malcolm). Although JEANNETTE NOLAN (Lady Macbeth) had never before appeared in Mercury's previous theater or movie ventures, she had been a part of the *MERCURY THEATRE ON THE AIR* in New York during the late l930s. She was making her debuts in live theater as well as in film. In the title role was Welles.

Macbeth was one of Welles's favorite plays. He had directed the famous "voodoo" MACBETH for the Negro Division of the FEDERAL THEATRE PROJECT in 1936. Later, when the play toured, Welles was forced to play the title role in black face when his regular Macbeth (JACK CARTER) was indisposed. He had also adapted the play to radio. In his 1947 play-to-film adaptation, which pared the Bard's script down to a brisk 94 minutes, Welles combined several parts into a new character, "A Holy Father." To play that composite character, and in deference to his leading lady, Welles hired Nolan's husband, John McIntire, another veteran of the 1930s' New York radio scene. The simple yet effective stage design, with the apron of the stage extending over the footlights, was patterned after a similar scheme used by Welles in the 1936 "voodoo" *Macbeth.* There were also several sets of stairs leading to the orchestra pit to permit multiple points of entry for the cast. Welles, as usual, scrambled furiously to meet the deadline, rehearsing his cast during the day, while supervising the physical aspects of the production at night. At the end of the troupe's week-long preparations, all was ready.

Giving six performances in four days, May 28–31, 1947, Welles's Utah version of *Macbeth* was richly praised by the local critics. However, it was noted that Nolan, still getting accustomed to performing without a microphone, although a bit weak in the first act, rallied for an impressive reading of the famous "Out damned spot" sleepwalking scene. Welles's Macbeth was reported as particularly convincing because the haunted king looked as if he needed a bath and a good night's sleep. The production's spectacle with its Scottish legions passing down the aisles led by bagpipers and its scary witches in grotesque phosphorescent masks also thrilled audiences.

Significantly, the play clocked in at 94 minutes of nonstop action, a close to ideal running time for a movie. Also of note is the heavy Scottish dialect that Welles used for this version of *Macbeth,* a unique aspect of the production that became a source of controversy with the film. Also, by eliminating the play's usual regal splendor in favor of a harsh almost barbaric décor, Welles was able to focus on the protagonist's inner battle, a struggle between civilized ambition and the naked use of violence to attain the throne.

Listed in the production credits are RICHARD WILSON (Executive Director) and WILLIAM ALLAND (Stage Manager). Additional cast credits include ERSKINE SANFORD (Duncan), Edgar Barrier (Banquo), and Brainerd Duffield (First Witch).

—C.B.

Macbeth Republic Pictures, 107 minutes, 1948. **Director:** Orson Welles; **Producer:** Welles; **Executive Producer:** Charles K. Feldman; **Screenplay:** Welles (based on *Macbeth* by William Shakespeare); **Cinematographer:** John L. Russell; **Editor:** Louis Lindsay; **Cast:** Orson Welles (Macbeth), Jeannette Nolan (Lady Macbeth), Dan O'Herlihy (Macduff), Edgar Barrier (Banquo), Roddy McDowall (Malcolm), Erskine Sanford (Duncan), Alan Napier (a Holy Father), John Dierkes (Ross), Keene Curtis (Lennox), Peggy Webber (Lady Macduff/witch), Lionel Braham (Siward), Archie Heugly (Young Siward), Christopher Welles (Macduff child), Brainerd Duffield (first murderer/witch), William Alland (second murderer), George Chirello (Seyton), Gus Schilling (porter), Jerry Farber

Welles enthroned as Macbeth *(Literature/Film Archive)*

(Fleance), Lurene Tuttle (gentlewoman/witch), Charles Lederer (witch), Robert Alan (third murderer), Morgan Farley (doctor)

By the spring of 1947, ORSON WELLES's marriage to RITA HAYWORTH had effectively ended, and, when *THE LADY FROM SHANGHAI,* his last picture with her, came in three months late and nearly a half million dollars over budget, he lost the financial backing of HARRY COHN and Columbia Pictures. With other projects stalled, Welles considered an offer from the American National Theatre and Academy (ANTA) to direct a Shakespeare play for the 1947 Utah Centennial Festival. At first, he thought about doing KING LEAR and using the stage production as rehearsal for a film deal offered to him by British producer Sidney Bernstein. Finally, however, Welles decided to direct *MACBETH* at Salt Lake City and then film it for Republic Studios, which was famous for low-budget westerns rather than high-culture drama.

A variety of reasons have been suggested for his choices. BARBARA LEAMING writes that Welles decided to do *Macbeth* because the play had been lucky for him in his successful New York directorial debut of the "voodoo" *Macbeth,* set in Haiti and presented at Harlem's Lafayette Theatre in 1936 with an all-black cast. Of his choice of Republic Pictures, Welles himself said, "I went there because I figured it would be cheaper: Everybody would be used to working faster." Many writers have claimed that, to

revive his career, Welles wanted to prove he could make a film within budget and on schedule. DAVID THOMSON disagrees. He believes the film produces too powerful an apocalyptic vision to be dismissed as a mere exercise in fiscal and temporal responsibility and says that the film is the product of Welles's sense of the postatomic, early cold war atmosphere and the "neurotic anguish of film noir." In an interview with PETER BOGDANOVICH, Welles says that the contact with Republic was made by his "chum and partner CHARLIE FELDMAN," who had a deal to make several pictures for Republic Studios head HERBERT YATES. According to Welles, Feldman "simply told him [Yates] that one of them was going to be *Macbeth*." Agreeing to bring in the film for under $800,000, Welles rehearsed his principal actors in Los Angeles and then took them to Utah. Dan O'Herlihy played Macduff, RODDY MCDOWALL was Malcolm, and Lady Macbeth was played by JEANNETTE NOLAN, a young radio actress married to actor John McIntire. Welles filled out the cast with local actors in Utah, rehearsed for two more weeks, and opened at the University Theatre, playing from May 28 to May 31.

Returning to Hollywood, Welles set himself a 23-day shooting schedule and cast the other parts, giving his daughter CHRISTOPHER WELLES the role of young Macduff. MICHAEL ANDEREGG says that Welles's "eccentric casting of minor characters" with "thuglike faces," emphasizes "the banality of the depicted world" in which "evil has quite explicitly become a B movie." Welles began filming on Republic's soundstages on June 23, 1947, met his schedule, and came in under budget, prompting Yates to call *Macbeth* "the greatest individual job of acting, directing, adapting and producing that to my knowledge Hollywood has ever seen." Postproduction problems, however, stretched actual completion out for a year when Welles went to Europe in July and left his assistant, RICHARD WILSON, to supervise the work. Unfavorably compared to OLIVIER's Freudian version of *Hamlet* at the 1948 Venice Film Festival in September, and released to bad reviews the next month, *Macbeth* was reedited, losing about 20 minutes, and redubbed, losing most of the Scottish burr that Welles had used in the stage production and kept in the film. Through the efforts of the UCLA Film Archives and the Folger Shakespeare Library, Welles's original version was made available again in 1979.

The film opens with an amorphous swirl of clouds, and the three witches appear silhouetted on a jagged rock, standing over a cauldron. Images of steam, boiling liquid, fire, and waves dissolve into one another. Anthony Davis comments that this opening sequence "constitutes a clear suggestion that the essence of the film's thematic conflict is to be that of 'form' against 'formlessness.'" As the witches speak, they pull a figure out of the boiling liquid, mimicking a kind of birth, and rough it into a childlike shape with their hands. When they say Macbeth's name, Welles suddenly cuts to the title, in white letters against a black background, "Macbeth by William Shakespeare," and then, "with Orson Welles." After the titles, in a shot reminiscent of many Republic features, two riders on horseback gallop through a stormy landscape and stop short when they see the witches. The clay figure, often described as a voodoo doll, becomes further identified with Macbeth (Orson Welles) when the witches, as they give their prophecy, put a medal around its neck when they pronounce Macbeth Thane of Cawdor and put a crown on its head when they tell him he will be king. Banquo (Edgar Barrier) inquires about his own future, and they tell him he will "get kings, though thou be none" (1.3.67).

As the prophecy concludes, another group of horsemen arrives, and a character Welles added, a Holy Father (Alan Napier), brandishes a cross and chases the witches away, performing, as Robert F. Willson says, "a symbolic function in pursuing the theme of religious good versus pagan evil." In the opening narration Welles gave to the drastically cut version of the film, he says, "The cross itself is newly arrived here. Plotting against Christian law and order are the agents of Chaos, priest of hell and magic—sorcerers and witches." This prologue does not exist in the restored version of the film that is available on video, but several years later in his interview with Peter Bogdanovich, Welles repeats the point, saying, "The main point of that production is the struggle between the old and new religions. I saw the witches as representatives of a Druidical pagan religion suppressed by Christianity—itself a new arrival." Several

critics have commented on this opposition, and visually, the frequent contrast between the cross and the "Y" shaped staffs carried by the witches reinforces it. More recently, however, Anderegg has pointed out that "Christianity is not offered by the film as a positive alternative to the old religion, but rather as an equally oppressive system, itself collaborative with savagery," and he cites the beheading of Cawdor as an example of that savage system. In this early scene, when Macbeth protests that "The Thane of Cawdor lives" (1.3.108), Cawdor appears as a defeated man held standing between two horsemen. As the title is bestowed on Macbeth, Welles shows the medal taken from Cawdor's neck and passed from horseman to horseman until it is handed to Macbeth. Welles divides Macbeth's speech, which begins with "If ill,/Why hath it given me earnest of success,/Commending in a truth. I am Thane of Cawdor" (1.3.131–133), and renders the second more doubting half of it as a voice-over, "If good, why do I yield to that suggestion/Whose horrid image doth unfix my hair . . ." (1.3.134–142), then fills the screen with a close-up of Macbeth's anxious face. After Macbeth and the others ride off, the witches again appear, holding their bent crosses.

Welles follows with a night scene in which Macbeth, Banquo, and the Holy Father sit around a campfire, again recalling Republic westerns, and discuss the prophesies. At the end of the scene, Welles fades from the image of Macbeth summing up his experience to a shot of Lady Macbeth (Jeannette Nolan) lying in bed and continuing the lines from the letter he has sent her (1.5.1–116), leaving out the doubts Shakespeare gave his Lady Macbeth. Lady Macbeth delivers the lines as an interior monologue, breathing anxiously as she lies on a fur-covered bed, then rises and continues staring out a rough window into the moonlight, suggesting perhaps that her appeal to be "unsexed" is directed to the night (1.5.38–54). At the last lines, the screen again fills with the formless clouds, recalling the opening shot of the film.

Here Welles adds an execution scene and cuts between three lines of action to foreshadow the ironic connection between Macbeth and Cawdor. First, Welles shows Macbeth galloping through that same night that Lady Macbeth gazed on as she prayed. Next, he cuts to a scene of men beating huge drums. Third, he shows the Holy Father and the others arriving at the castle with the bound and silent Cawdor in tow. As the drum beat continues, Macbeth rides up to the castle and embraces Lady Macbeth while in the background a body hangs from a gallows. Meanwhile, the chief drummer, photographed from below, continues the ominous rhythm on the drums. At the same time, the Holy Father is presiding over the execution of Cawdor. Then, as Cawdor bends over the chopping block and the executioner raises his axe, Welles cuts again to the drummer, whose last drum stroke parallels the stroke of the executioner's axe and becomes the visual substitute for that image. Welles uses this same shift from the moment of beheading to a substituted and parallel action when Macbeth dies at the end of the film. The technique suggests a comment on the circularity of the story and points to the parallel between the executed traitor and the treacherous Macbeth. Lady Macbeth underscores this connection immediately after the execution of Cawdor, when she says "Great Glamis! worthy Cawdor!/Greater than both . . . I feel now/the future in the instant" (1.5.54–58), lines that Welles moves here from her initial greeting to Macbeth in the play.

As they plot against him, King Duncan (ERSKINE SANFORD) arrives, and Lady Macbeth whispers her plan to Macbeth while everyone kneels to the Holy Father's prayer and Macbeth, in another voice-over, enumerates reasons for not harming Duncan (1.7.12–20). Thomas Pendleton notes that "the inserted prayer develops a strong, if unsubtle, contrast in the Macbeths' plotting to fulfill the witches' prophecy, while their peers pray, 'Protect us from the malice and snares of the Devil.'" Throughout these scenes hanged men remain ominously visible in the background. In another bit of irony, Welles pulls from an earlier scene the conversation in which Malcolm (Roddy McDowall) describes the nobility of Cawdor's death, and, in the film, Duncan looks up at the impaled head of Cawdor and says, "He was a gentleman on whom I built/An absolute trust" (1.4.13–14), then turns to praise Macbeth and Banquo. Duncan's lines could as easily refer to Macbeth

as to Cawdor, and, of course, one of the last shots in the film shows Macbeth's head similarly impaled. As the king and his entourage settle in and Duncan celebrates the hospitality offered him, Welles cuts to Lady Macbeth drugging the wine she will give to Duncan's guards.

Returning to the opening lines of one of Macbeth's speeches, Welles renders the "If it were done" speech (1.7.1–12) as a voice-over, with the camera hovering over Macbeth's head. Then, as Banquo gives Macbeth the diamond Duncan has sent for Lady Macbeth, Welles cuts to Lady Macbeth, dagger in hand, looking at Duncan as he sleeps. Reversing Shakespeare's lines again, Welles first has Macbeth comment on the night, "Now o'er the one half world/Nature seems dead . . ." (2.1.49–56), then picks up the more famous opening lines of the same speech, "Is this a dagger which I see before me . . ." (2.1.33–47). Welles also uses the device of the voodoo doll, introducing the speech with the flash of a dagger before the inanimate doll, which appears briefly. When Lady Macbeth reenters, Welles has Macbeth express his doubts in lines from an earlier section of the play, "We will proceed no further in this business . . ." (1.7.31). She encourages him, and, turning her back to the camera, reveals the anachronistic zipper that has been the focus of many comments. Shortly after, Macbeth comes haltingly down the stairs, and tells her he has done it. Welles places the camera below Macbeth's hands, making them seem huge. When he seems dazed, she takes the bloody daggers from him and puts them back at the murder scene. Yet, shortly after, when Lady Macbeth reenters, she seems very small compared to Macbeth, who fills the foreground. They leave with the sound of the knocking in the background. Focusing mainly on Macbeth, Welles reduces the wonderful Porter's speech to nothing more than "Knock, knock" (2.3.1–21).

Macduff (Dan O'Herlihy) and Lennox (Keene Curtis) enter, with Macduff discovering the murder while Lennox describes the night's ominous signs (3.1.53–61). Rearranging Shakespeare's characters, Welles has Lady Macduff (Peggy Webber) present at the castle to talk with Macduff and has the Holy Father enter Duncan's chambers just as Macbeth has killed the guards. A close-up of the Holy Father's squinting eye clearly indicates his immediate suspicion of Macbeth. When Malcolm enters, it is the Holy Father, rather than Macbeth who tells him "The spring, the head, the fountain of your blood/Is stopp'd, the very source of it is stopp'd" (2.3.97–98). Macbeth's role, in Welles's version of the moments after the killing, is to act very much like a guilty murderer. He walks into the crowd defensively, and, when he asks, "Who could refrain,/That had a heart to love, and in that heart/Courage to make's love known?" (2.3.116–118), Lady Macbeth utters a cry and faints. Both the Holy Father and Macduff, perhaps suggesting civil and religious authority, are accusatory in their questioning. The Holy Father, as opposed to Banquo in the play, says "let us meet/And question this most bloody piece of work" (2.3.127–128). Banquo approaches Macbeth, however, and voices his suspicion, "I fear/Thou play'dst most foully for't" (3.1.2–3). Leaving Banquo, Macbeth goes to Lady Macbeth, who once more tries to get him to go to bed, but he instead discusses his fears about keeping the kingdom. Already, he is able to sum up his killing of Duncan by saying, "We have scorch'd the snake, not kill'd it" (3.2.13–14.). Lady Macbeth explains that they can do nothing about the deed and again urges him to go to bed. Suddenly, Macbeth is startled and says "Methought I heard a voice cry, 'Sleep no more!/Macbeth doth murder sleep'" (2.2.33). Welles, who claimed to admire the second half of the film more, saying that it "is a study of the decay of a tyrant," keeps his focus on Macbeth, who has now become Macbeth the murderer.

Tying the witches more closely to the murder than Shakespeare does, Welles has them appear now with the doll before them, and, as they echo the words that Macbeth will not be able to sleep, the doll begins to sweat profusely, just as Macbeth will in the following scenes of the film. The camera remains on the doll as Welles reinforces the connection between it and Macbeth. Then the scene of the witches putting the crown on the voodoo doll fades to the scene of Lady Macbeth putting the crown on Macbeth's head. As Macbeth stares into a distorting mirror, saying, "To be thus is nothing,/But to be safely thus" (3.1.47–48), he turns from the mirror and stumbles

down the hallway, drinking from a horn. Both Macbeth and Lady Macbeth now wear crowns and heavy dresses, adding mass and apparent discomfort. Macbeth's crown is a square, with spikes at the corners, and, as Welles himself said of the crown he wears in the last scenes of the film, "I looked like the Statue of Liberty in it. But there was no dough for another, and nothing in stock at Western [Costume Company] that would fit me, so I was stuck with it." Keeping his emphasis on Macbeth and Lady Macbeth, Welles has Lady Macbeth talk with Lady Macduff about Macduff's sudden departure. Here Lady Macbeth says the lines Shakespeare gave to Ross (John Dierkes), but with a significant change in effect. When Ross tells Lady Macduff that they do not know whether it was "his wisdom or his fear"(4.2.1–8) that made Macduff flee, Ross is clearly trying to calm her. When Lady Macbeth says it, she is clearly planting seeds of doubt and plotting against Lady Macduff. The speech also provides a link to Macbeth's next lines.

Macbeth is seated on a throne high above everyone else. Welles positions the camera above and behind Macbeth, giving the effect of Macbeth as a foreground silhouette with the dwarfish followers below. Macbeth notes that Macduff and Malcolm have left, "not confessing their cruel murders" (3.1.29–31). When Banquo steps forth, both Lady Macbeth and Macbeth encourage him to return from his ride in time to attend the banquet. Again, ironically, Banquo agrees and leaves with Fleance by his side. As Michael Mullin points out, Welles rearranges events from the play to connect Macduff, Lady Macduff, Malcolm, Banquo, and Fleance in Macbeth's imagination as enemies to his success. Continuing his drinking, Macbeth dismisses the group and speaks, not so much to Lady Macbeth, who remains, as to himself about his fears of Banquo. Welles also pulls from a later scene, to include here remarks on how Duncan "sleeps well" (3.3.24). Then Macbeth calls for the murderers, two extraordinarily rough-looking characters, extras from Republic B movies. Talking later with Lady Macbeth, Macbeth delivers his "Come seeling night" speech (3.2.46–56) as though he were actually conjuring the night as Lady Macbeth, in a similar scene, seemed to do earlier in the film. The image of the bent tree that appears in the background serves as a transition to the next scene where the murderers are perched in a tree. As Banquo and Fleance ride by, the killers jump down and kill Banquo, but Fleance rides off. Immediately after, when they are reporting it, Macbeth and the two murderers seem to be no more than shadows moving through the dark rooms.

Leaving them, Macbeth seems to wander through the tunnels of the castle, hearing Banquo's voice repeating earlier speeches, concluding with his parting words, "I will not fail your feast," a line Welles added. Stopping to wash his face in a run of water flowing down the wall, Macbeth passes huge wine casks, and seems almost accidentally to arrive at the site of the banquet. Here, more than before, the ceiling is low, oppressively hanging over the heads of the guests. Macbeth himself is sweating profusely just as the voodoo doll did earlier. Welles's handling of the ghost scene has attracted commentary. Omitting the line about the full table (3.4.45), Welles clearly places the vision only in Macbeth's mind, showing first the table of guests with the empty chair at the end, then the table with no one at all before him, then the table with only Banquo seated at the end. When Macbeth comments on the "charnel-houses and our graves must send/Those that we bury back," Duncan's ghost appears in Banquo's place. Macbeth overturns the tables, spilling food and drink everywhere. Willson comments that Welles "effectively underscores a central truth of this scene: Macbeth, the usurping king, cannot successfully complete the banquet ceremony that would confirm his place as ruler of Scotland." After the guests and Lady Macbeth leave, Macbeth begins his conjuring of the witches. Welles has omitted the scene of the witches and Hecate (3.5) and moved the speech of the witches (4.1.1–49) to emphasize Macbeth's motivation in calling the witches. The witches here appear only as voices, with Macbeth himself caught in a point of light surrounded by darkness, the camera high above him, as the witches deliver their prophecies. Also omitted is the "show of eight Kings . . . and Banquo last" (4.1.s.d.110).

Macbeth and his men put on their armor while Lady Macbeth seems to wander into the presence of Lady Macduff and her son (Christopher Welles). The implication of this handling of space is that Lady Macduff has remained in the castle. Indeed, the window through the rock, with its bar and knifelike projections, is very similar to the one outside Lady Macbeth's window earlier in the film. While Lady Macduff and her son talk in the foreground, Lady Macbeth stands by the window. When Lady Macbeth leaves, the Holy Father suddenly appears at the window, saying the warning lines delivered by Ross. Macbeth himself comes in to supervise the killing of the children and Lady Macduff. Here Welles reaches back and has Macbeth say the concluding lines of his speech at the end of the banquet scene, "I am in blood/Steep'd in so far that, should I wade no more,/Returning were as tedious as go o'er" (3.4.135–139). Again, its significance is somewhat different placed after the second prophesy of the witches and after the killing of Macduff's family. The killing of Lady Macduff and her children is clearly of a different order than the killing of Duncan and Macbeth and the attempted murder of Fleance. Lady Macbeth's response is also different. In the play, she encourages Macbeth at the end of the banquet scene to get some sleep. In the film, when she has encouraged Macbeth to go to bed, the intent was always clearly sexual. Here, however, she comments instead on their having to "dwell in doubtful joy" (3.2.7). Her dazed manner here serves to introduce her later disturbed state and the sleep-

Welles as Macbeth *(National Film Society Archive)*

walking scene. The implication seems to be that it was the killing of Lady Macduff and the children that was Lady Macbeth's turning point.

The next scene in the film, the scene in England, draws primarily on Act 4, scene 3. Welles seems to use it as a turning point, with the good forces gathering for a counter offensive, yet most critics find this scene to be one of the weakest in the film. Welles omits Malcolm's testing of Macduff and gives several lines to the Holy Father. Here Malcolm simply says that he thinks he could get support in England, and then the Holy Father enters. Again, Welles gives the Holy Father lines originally assigned to Ross, beginning with "Alas, poor country,/Almost afraid to know itself! It cannot/Be call'd our mother, but our grave" (4.3.164–166). He encourages Macduff to return and tells him the news of his family's death. It is worth noting that the entire scene plays with a large stone representation of the cross in the background, and the Holy Father is given Malcolm's closing lines about "the powers above" which "put on their instruments" (4.3.238–239). The next scene shows the troops marching across the scene. The English troops with Malcolm and Macduff at their head all carry long poles topped with a cross. Interestingly, the Holy Father seems to lead the Scottish troops, who instead mostly seem to wear helmets with attached horns.

Macbeth's troops, meanwhile, scurry about through the rock-bound fortress, as Macbeth voices his dependence on the literal truth of the prophecies, "What's the boy Malcolm?/Was he not born of woman?" (5.2.3–4). Again, he towers in the foreground, while his soldiers seem small. Macbeth's voice-over here is not so much a wrestling with temptation, as in Welles's previous use of the device, but an expression of self-doubt, as he says, "my way of life/Is fall'n into the sear" (5.3.22–29). When Seyton (played by Welles's chauffeur, George "Shorty" Chirello) appears at Macbeth's call, his smallness is emphasized by Macbeth's towering figure in the foreground. Macbeth then seems to step only a few feet to the left, making two scenes out of Shakespeare's original one, and he is in the room where Lady Macbeth lies on the fur-covered bed where she first appeared in the film. In the context of Welles's rearrangement of the action, Lady Macbeth's illness is

another indication of his own impending fall. The physician tells Macbeth that Lady Macbeth is "not so sick, my Lord,/As she is troubled with thick-coming fancies/That keep her from her rest" (5.3.37–39). When the doctor leaves, Macbeth stands before the window, armoring himself, and firming his resolve. Elsewhere, Macduff and the followers approach Birnam Wood, and here Macduff, rather than Malcolm, orders cutting the woods for camouflage. Malcolm, in fact, seems ready to take orders, saying "It shall be done" (5.4.7), a line Shakespeare gave to the soldiers.

Welles moves Lady Macbeth's sleepwalking to this point. The Doctor of Physic and the Waiting Gentle Woman see Lady Macbeth approaching in the distance, carrying her candle. Suddenly, shrieking and throwing the candle away, she wrings her hands and speaks in a somewhat slurred manner. Macbeth appears, and, still in a kind of stupor, she tells him to come to bed, recalling her earlier entreaties. He bends over and gives her a long kiss, then suddenly she pulls back and runs away shrieking. Meanwhile, Birnam Wood does begin to march forward as the troops advance toward the castle. In a long shot, Welles silhouettes Macbeth's darkened castle in a way that recalls the first shots of XANADU in *CITIZEN KANE*. Inside, Lady Macbeth wanders through the tunnels, then, finding the edge of the wall, smiles and throws herself off, shrinking into the distance below. The Gentle Woman shrieks, and the next shot is Macbeth, commenting "The time has been, my senses would have cool'd/To hear a night-shriek" (5.4.10–15). He steps out, wearing a crown with more spikes, undoubtedly the "Statue of Liberty" crown, whose shape is echoed in the Stonehenge-like row of colossal stones. At the news of Lady Macbeth's death, Macbeth speaks the "To-morrow, and to-morrow, and to-morrow" speech (5.4.18–28) as a voice-over, with the camera quickly shifting from Macbeth to the flowing clouds, recalling the opening of the film. At the end of the speech, his grieving face fills half the screen. The messenger who comes to tell Macbeth that Birnam Wood is moving toward them is dwarfishly small below the towering Macbeth. As he walks forward, voicing his resolve, the resemblance between the crowned Macbeth and his spiked long spear is noticeable. A quick shot of someone apparently hanging in the bell tower is followed by an overhead shot of Macbeth that flattens him against the black-and-white patterning of the stone floor below him. He calls for Seyton, and discovers that it is Seyton who is hanging from the bell rope, an apparent suicide. Next, shooting up from the area before the castle walls, we see Macbeth appear startled when the soldiers throw down their camouflage. Macduff calls up to Macbeth, who responds defiantly, using lines from earlier in scene five, where Macbeth is really speaking to Seyton. Here Welles turns the speech from a description of the opposing troops to a direct address to them, "Were they [you] not forc'd with those that should be ours/We might have met them [you] dareful, beard to beard,/And beat them [you] backward home" (5.5.5–6). He finishes by throwing his spear into the Holy Man, killing him. When the Holy Man falls, the troops advance, break down the wall, and, carrying torches, storm through the tunnels. Macbeth kills one of his attackers, Young Siward, and shouts out the prophecy that he cannot be killed by anyone of woman born (5.7.11–13). Macduff enters as a giant silhouette with the cross-topped helmet, glowing fire and white smoke behind him. For the first time, Macbeth himself is dwarfed in the long shadow cast by Macduff. When they meet to fight, Macbeth repeats the prophecies, while they fight one-on-one and the troops cheer below. When Macduff answers that he was "from his mother's womb/Untimely ripped," the witches appear in the foreground, repeating the line in their shrill voices. Macbeth turns to run, but, when Macduff taunts him with his future as a prisoner, Macbeth turns to fight, his face hardening in resolve. At the end, Macduff pulls back for a hard swing, Macbeth's face appears in close-up, then the head of the voodoo doll topples off, and the square crown Macbeth wore earlier in the film rolls off—though not from Macbeth's head because he is not wearing one—and lands at the feet of a young man, later revealed to be Fleance, who is pictured holding it. Meanwhile, in a somewhat parallel gesture, Macduff throws Macbeth's head down to the cheering troops. The camera pulls back, and a daylight shot of the silhouetted castle reveals the three witches with their crooked staffs in the foreground. One of them says, "Peace, the charm's

wound up" (1.3.37), a line from their last speech together before Macbeth and Banquo first confronted them in the first act of the play. Their appearance, here, reinforces the sense of fate and of circularity.

Many of the first viewers of Welles's *Macbeth* found the film strange, stilted, and a poor adaptation of Shakespeare's play, and many critics who have written about the play since then seem to be of two minds about it. Anthony Davis, for example, summarizes some of the objections when he notes that the film "reduces . . . dramatic intensity by limiting Macbeth's options," that "As a reflection of Shakespeare's play, the film fails more lamentably," and that "There are seemingly pointless changes in the dramatic action." Nonetheless, he says, it is, "a turning point in the development of Shakespearean cinematic adaptation," because it "asserts for cinema an autonomous artistic claim for a valid expression and presentation of Shakespearean material in terms of a predominant spatial concept." JOSEPH MCBRIDE, who says that "*Macbeth* has highly theatrical, unabashedly non-naturalistic sets, using cardboard rocks for the courtyard of the primitive Scottish castle and Republic's standing set of a salt mine (familiar from countless B-westerns) for parts of the castle's interior," claims that seeing the restored version was a revelation. "What had once appeared 'crude' and 'distracting' in Welles's *Macbeth* to a much younger critic somewhat uncomfortable (like most American critics) with expressionistic, non-naturalistic filmmaking," he says, "no longer seems the product of 'haste and desperation' but a triumphant artistic decision."

Those who admire the film tend to defend it by embracing, as McBride does, exactly those elements that first offended its first viewers, like those at the Venice Film Festival who preferred Olivier's *Hamlet* to Welles's *Macbeth*. JAMES NAREMORE, for example, citing Raymond Durgnat on expressionism, says "*Macbeth* is arguably the purest example of expressionism in the American cinema. It begins with a few highly effective outdoor shots, and then grows progressively less naturalistic as it goes along." Michael Anderegg, however, questions these judgments. According to Anderegg, "In the end all attempts to provide an overarching stylistic or thematic core for Welles's film—whether it be 'expressionistic' or 'surreal' or 'Freudian' or whatever—must necessarily fall short of the film's effect." Instead, he says, "What *Macbeth* exhibits is precisely the tension between an interpretive scheme more or less consistently applied, on the one hand, and on the other, the very real constraints a low budget and a consequently compact shooting schedule—combined with the realities of Welles's production methods, which worked at cross purposes to those constraints—imposed on the project."

References Anderegg, Michael. *Orson Welles, Shakespeare, and Popular Culture* (New York: Columbia University Press, 1999); Buchman, Lorne M. *Still in Movement: Shakespeare on Screen* (New York and Oxford: Oxford University Press, 1991); Davies, Anthony. *Filming Shakespeare's Plays: The Adaptations of Laurence Olivier, Orson Welles, Peter Brook, Akira Kurosawa* (Cambridge, U.K.: Cambridge University Press, 1988); Jorgens, Jack J. *Shakespeare on Film* (Lanham, New York, London: University Press of America, 1991); Leaming, Barbara. *Orson Welles: A Biography* (New York: Penguin Books, 1989); Manvell, Roger. *Shakespeare and the Film* (New York and Washington: Praeger, 1971); McBride, Joseph. *Orson Welles.* rev. ed. (New York: Da Capo Press, 1996); Mullin, Michael. "Orson Welles' *Macbeth*: Script and Screen." *Focus on Orson Welles.* ed. Ronald Gottesman (Englewood Cliffs, N.J.: Prentice Hall, 1976, 136–45); Naremore, James. *The Magic World of Orson Welles.* rev. ed. (Dallas, Tex.: Southern Methodist University Press, 1989); Pearlman, E. "Macbeth on Film: Politics." *Shakespeare and the Moving Image: The Plays on Film and Television.* Anthony Davies and Stanley Wells, eds. (Cambridge, U.K.: Cambridge University Press, 1994), 250–60; Pendleton, Thomas A. "Shakespeare . . . With Additional Dialog" (*Cineaste,* December 15, 1998); Rothwell, Kenneth S. *A History of Shakespeare on Screen: A Century of Film and Television* (Cambridge, U.K.: Cambridge University Press, 1999); Thomson, David. *Rosebud: The Story of Orson Welles* (New York: Alfred A. Knopf, 1996); Welles, Orson, with Peter Bogdanovich, edited by Jonathan Rosenbaum. *This Is Orson Welles* (New York: HarperCollins, 1992); Willson, Robert F. Jr. *Shakespeare in Hollywood, 1929–1956* (Madison and Teaneck, N.J.: Fairleigh Dickinson University Press, 2000).

—R.V.

MacLeish, Archibald (1892–1982)

MacLeish, Archibald (1892–1982)   On March 22, 1935, ORSON WELLES made his debut on national radio by reprising his role of McGafferty in a scene from Archibald MacLeish's experimental play, *Panic,* which had just finished a limited run at New York's Imperial Theatre. In one of the play's pivotal moments, as ticker tapes rattle in the background, McGafferty is asked by his banking colleagues what he plans to do. "Do?" thundered Welles's character. "What do you think I'll do? Pull the blinds on the bank and sail to Bermuda? *This bank will open tomorrow at nine.*" With those lines, the nation's radio audience was introduced to Orson Welles.

The excerpt from *Panic* was produced as a segment for radio's THE MARCH OF TIME, which by subsequently featuring Welles, helped launch the actor's career as one of the medium's foremost creative forces. Welles also appeared in the central role of the radio announcer in MacLeish's *The Fall of the City,* an experimental 1937 radio verse play dramatizing the rise of an American Hitler.

MacLeish, a Pulitzer Prize–winning poet as well as a noted playwright, professor, and public official, whose advocacy of liberal democracy was a recurring motif in his work, was educated at Yale. In 1923, MacLeish, like so many young American artists of the period, went to France to further develop his craft. As an expatriate working in Paris, where he became greatly influenced by Ezra Pound, T. S. Eliot, and the French Symbolists, he published two books of short lyric poems, *The Happy Marriage* (1924) and *Streets in the Moon* (1926), both of which revealed concerns for form and metrics. One of his first dramas, *Nobodaddy* (1926), was a verse play based on the story of Adam and Eve, and Cain and Abel, dealing with the dramatic angst casting human self-consciousness against ßthe backdrop of an indifferent universe. Before returning to the United States in 1928, MacLeish wrote "Ars Poetica" (1926), one of his most frequently anthologized poems.

New Found Land (1930), a work of sublime lyric eloquence, included another of his most popular poems, "You, Andrew Marvell." With the growing menace of fascism, MacLeish turned to what became known as his "public" poems. The first of these narrative works, *Conquistador* (1932), about the exploitation of Mexico, was awarded the Pulitzer Prize. MacLeish's concern over the international collapse of liberal democracy resulted in politically charged works such as *Panic* (1935), about the Great Depression; the radio play *The Fall of the City* (1937), a parable echoing the rise of Hitler; and *Air Raid* (1938), another verse drama written specifically for radio, whose radio commentator, played by the MERCURY's RAY COLLINS, influenced Welles's radio adaptation of THE WAR OF THE WORLDS.

In 1939, MacLeish was appointed Librarian of Congress, a position he held until 1944, when President FRANKLIN ROOSEVELT named him assistant secretary of state, a post he occupied until the conclusion of World War II in 1945. His *Collected Poems 1917–1952,* published in 1952, won another Pulitzer Prize, as did his verse drama, *J.B.,* which was produced on Broadway in 1958. *New and Collected Poems 1917–1976* (1976) anthologizes his remarkably varied output. Although his accomplishments were impressive, today MacLeish is best remembered as a lyric poet. *Reflections,* a series of interviews conducted during his final years, was published in 1986.

References Donaldson, Scott, and R. H. Winnick. *Archibald MacLeish: An American Life* (Boston: Houghton Mifflin, 1992); Ellis, Helen E., Bernard A. Drabeck, and Margaret E.C. Howland. *Archibald MacLeish: A Selectively Annotated Bibliography* (Lanham, Md.: Scarecrow, 1995); Gary, Brett. *The Nervous Liberals: Propaganda Anxieties from World War I to the Cold War* (New York: Columbia University Press, 1999).

—C.B.

MacLiammóir, Micheál (1899–1978)

Irish actor, director, designer, and author, Micheál MacLiammóir played Iago in ORSON WELLES's OTHELLO (1952). He was born in Cork on October 25, 1899, the son of Alfred Anthony and Mary MacLiammóir and educated privately before making his stage debut using the name Alfred Willmore in London in 1911. He studied painting at the Slade School in 1915 and 1916 and later worked in design for the Irish Theatre from 1918 to 1921. In 1928, after seven years abroad painting, MacLiammóir established the Dublin GATE THEATRE with HILTON EDWARDS, and it was at the Gate that he first met the young Orson Welles.

Welles went to Ireland in 1931 at the age of 16 and, stretching the truth, presented himself at the Gate as an experienced actor. MacLiammóir and Edwards, an odd couple, both of them homosexuals who had first met as actors at Anew McMaster's Intimate Shakespeare Company in Dublin, were amused and humored him by offering him a place in the company, after determining that he could, indeed, act. Not only did this give Welles needed experience, but it also enabled him to hone his theatrical skills under the expert guidance of Hilton Edwards. BARBARA LEAMING calls this the "missing link" between Welles's "juvenile productions and what came later." Welles earned accolades playing Duke Karl Alexander in Lion Feuchtwanger's JEW SUSS, which led to other roles at the Gate. After he returned to America, Welles invited MacLiammóir and Edwards to participate in a summer theater festival at the Todd School in Woodstock, Illinois, in 1934, creating something of a scandal, since they were, in the words of Barbara Leaming, "uncloseted homosexuals," quoting Welles, "at the absolute high pitch of their sexuality." MacLiammóir's *Hamlet* was the hit of the summer, however, and the festival was a relative success.

Many years passed before Welles cast MacLiammóir as Iago in his film of *Othello* (1952). In 1950, MacLiammóir joined Welles, playing Mephistopheles for the German tour of AN EVENING WITH ORSON WELLES. They also worked together three years later for the Peter Brook television production of KING LEAR, broadcast from New York in December of 1953, with MacLiammóir in the role of Edgar. Welles was again in contact with the Dubliners in 1960 when working on CHIMES AT MIDNIGHT, but there was a considerable falling out, according to CHARLES HIGHAM, first between Welles and Hilton Edwards, who was to have staged the play adaptation, over money, and then between Welles and MacLiammóir, whom Welles had promised a role in a London production of *The Duchess of Malfi*. When *Malfi* was later canceled, MacLiammóir wrote a letter charging him with "base treachery." MacLiammóir published two memoirs concerning his dealings with Welles: *All for Hecuba* (Methuen, 1946), devoted mainly to his work at the Gate Theatre with Hilton

Edwards, and *Put Money in Thy Purse* (Methuen, 1952), concerning his experiences with Welles and the filmed *Othello*. In 1972, MacLiammóir earned an Equity award for his service to Irish theater (he acted in and designed over 300 productions for Dublin's Gate Theatre), and in 1973 he became a Chevalier de la Légion d'Honneur.

References Fitz-Simon, Christopher. *The Boys: A Double Biography* (London: Heinemann, 1994); Luke, Peter. *Enter Certain Players: Edwards-MacLiammóir and the Gate* (Dublin: Dolmen Press, 1978).

—J.M.W.

Magnificent Ambersons, The RKO/Mercury Production, 88 minutes, 1942. **Director:** Orson Welles; **Producer:** Jack Moss and Welles; **Executive Producer:** George Schaefer; **Screenplay:** Welles (based on *The Magnificent Ambersons* by Booth Tarkington); **Cinematographer:** Stanley Cortez; **Editors:** Robert Wise and Mark Robson; **Music:** Bernard Herrmann (uncredited) with Roy Webb; **Second Unit Directors:** Freddie Fleck and Wise; **Art Direction:** Mark Lee Kirk; **Set Decorations:** A1 Field; **Cast:** Tim Holt (George Minafer), Joseph Cotten (Eugene Morgan), Dolores Costello (Isabel Minafer), Anne Baxter (Lucy Morgan), Agnes Moorehead (Fanny Minafer), Ray Collins (Uncle Jack Amberson), Richard Bennett (Major Amberson), Don Dillaway (Wilber Minafer), Erskine Sanford (Roger Bronson), J. Louis Johnson (Sam), Charles Phipps (Uncle John), Gus Schilling, George Backus; narration by Orson Welles

The Magnificent Ambersons began as a novel written by BOOTH TARKINGTON (1869–1946) as the second part of a trilogy entitled *Growth,* following *The Turmoil* (1915) and preceding *The Midlander* (1923). All three novels dealt with life in the American Midwest, but *Ambersons,* which chronicled three generations of a leading Indiana family, was the most famous novel of the trilogy, earning the Pulitzer Prize in 1918. Tarkington later won a second Pulitzer Prize in 1921 for his novel *Alice Adams*. The dominant character of *The Magnificent Ambersons* is a spoiled and selfish young man, Georgie Amberson Minafer (played by TIM HOLT in the film), who bullies his doting mother, Isabel Amberson Minafer (DOLORES COSTELLO), and prevents her from marrying the industrialist and inventor Eugene Morgan (JOSEPH COTTEN), whom she loves. Eugene had courted Isabel before she married Wilbur Minafer (Don Dillaway), George's wholly undistinguished father, but embarrassed himself and humiliated her as a result of a drunken, youthful prank.

Years later, Eugene, now a widower, returns to "Midland" (which resembles Indianapolis) to establish an automobile production company. After Eugene's return, Wilbur dies. Eugene begins to court Isabel, but the romance is thwarted by Wilbur's sister, George's Aunt Fanny Minafer (AGNES MOOREHEAD), who vainly believes Eugene is interested in her. After George foils his mother's hopes of marrying Eugene, Isabel dies of a broken heart. Eugene is furious with George, and Eugene's daughter, Lucy (ANNE BAXTER), breaks off her romance with George as a consequence. Meanwhile, the Amberson family has been on the decline as the world has changed economically, but George still attempts to maintain his inherited "magnificence." Aunt Fanny loses her inheritance in a failed investment scheme, and since George has squandered his own inheritance, he is forced to take a job in a dynamite factory. Finally, George is hospitalized after being run over by an automobile, but there is a final (if not entirely credible) reconciliation between George and Eugene and his daughter Lucy, after Eugene is moved to forgive George after being touched by Isabel's supernatural solicitation from the spirit world. As a result of his conceit and arrogance, George has lost Lucy Morgan, who loves him, besides ruining his mother's happiness, but the novel gives him a second chance at the end, after his "come-uppance."

ORSON WELLES, who had read *The Magnificent Ambersons,* must have seen material in the book that related to his own life. After all, the book depicted the social context of the American Midwest, where his own family was from. Certainly he was also familiar with the idea of declining family fortunes and with the importance of the automobile. His own father had worked in the automobile business and had not only invested in the industry but had some inventions related to the automobile. In other words, Welles might have seen RICHARD WELLES as the inspiration for the character of Eugene Morgan in

Tim Holt as George Amberson Minafer *(National Film Society Archive)*

Tarkington's novel. It is also possible that Welles might have seen himself as a combination of both Eugene, whose vision and innovation were regarded skeptically, and Georgie, a spoiled young man intent upon having his way, regardless of the cost.

The concept of *The Magnificent Ambersons* in the film is compressed like an accordion, and in the process of being compressed, the accordion plays a rather different tune. In fact, W. Gardner Campbell has claimed in *The Encyclopedia of Novels into Film* (1998) that "Welles's original cut of *The Magnificent Ambersons* enraged RKO precisely because of its striking departures from Tarkington's novel," and the revised "RKO version was actually much more faithful to Tarkington's happy ending than was Welles's version, which was long, frightening, and full of despair." George Amberson Minafer is rendered less despicable as a consequence and is more deserving, perhaps, of the sympathy and forgiveness Eugene finally extends to him. Even the process of Georgie's "come-uppance" is handled differently, less comprehensively, and less effectively. Moreover, the balance between George and Eugene as central characters is disturbed in the film adaptation, which emphasizes George.

Tarkington has been criticized for his bigotry and xenophobia, as seen by the way he celebrates industrial progress and Yankee ingenuity. His attitudes and worldview may now seem dated, but Welles believed him to be an "extraordinary writer." In his two Pulitzer Prize–winning novels, Booth Tarkington displays a rare talent for satire. In *Alice Adams,* Tarkington appears to function as a rather crude but nonetheless effective homespun American equivalent of Jane Austen. In *The Magnificent Ambersons,* however, Tarkington resembles another, later 19th-century British satirist, George Meredith, and his portrait of George Amberson Minafer presents a rough American equivalent of Sir Willoughby Patterne in Meredith's novel, *The Egoist.* Like Sir Willoughby, George is an egotistical scion, unduly proud of his lineage, and an insufferably arrogant snob. Until the end of the novel, George has few redeeming qualities. In Chapter 34 of the novel, Lucy alludes to him as "the worst Indian who ever lived," whose name means "Rides-Down-Everything." Welles apparently intended to give the character a harder edge than he now appears to have in the film. In the second appendix of his book on Welles, CHARLES HIGHAM notes that the scene where George and Isabel discuss Eugene's letter and the question of her remarriage was "recut, rescripted, and reshot" so as to make the tone less angry and so as "to soften the character of the son, evidently on studio orders."

Elsewhere and earlier, scenes in the novel are rendered with astonishing fidelity, a fidelity that is further enhanced by Welles's mise-en-scène. After young George insults Eugene at dinner by rudely suggesting that "automobiles are a useless nuisance," for example, and after Eugene responds by expressing his own doubts about the uncertain "advantages" of progress, then excuses himself, George and Isabel are seated at the table in a two-shot. In the background "Uncle Jack" reenters the room and walks to the fireplace (frame left), as the camera pans left to isolate him and George in another two-shot that removes Isabel from the frame. The uncle's physical distance from George in this shot is as much an index of the uncle's disapproval as Isabel's closeness to her son in the preceding shot was an index of her forgiveness and acquiescence. It also makes sense to have her dropped from the frame as her brother criticizes her son, for she never listens to such criticism. Since she will hear no evil of him, it is as though she were not there.

This kind of meticulous planning is not at all unusual in the film's best sequences. What Welles does most brilliantly is to illustrate the "magnificence" of the Ambersons. He also catches some of the selfishness of Georgie, and he gives a vivid impression of the decline of the family by centering upon the Amberson mansion as an icon and index of the family fortunes. Beyond this, much of what is in the novel had to be compressed, and even Tarkington's richness of detail concerning the decline of the family is considerably abridged. The major in his decline, for example, is compressed in the film to the one long take in close-up that ROBERT WISE directed for the second unit.

The novel succeeds as an extended reflection upon time, progress, and the illusion of permanence in a world of flux; it also succeeds as a heavily sentimental tale of unrequited love between Eugene and Isabel. In the film, as George is thrust into the foreground, Eugene recedes into the background, destroying Tarkington's focus upon the two characters, which balances the perspective of Eugene's stoic maturity against the callowness of George's youth. After George destroys his mother's happiness, his punishment is to bear the responsibility, as head of the family, for looking after his Aunt Fanny, and some of this idea remains in the film. But the conclusion that places Eugene and Fanny arm-in-arm, balancing the older couple against the reconciliation of George and Lucy, is false to Tarkington's scheme. To have Eugene forgive George, finally, for destroying his happiness—that is true to the novel, with its supernatural apparatus for effecting such forgiveness; but to have Eugene then go waltzing off with Fanny is hardly an appropriate conclusion to follow such a noble gesture. But since Eugene has lost his central importance anyway in the film, perhaps it does not matter greatly.

In narrative terms, the story of Welles's film is an abridgment of Tarkington's novel, restructured first by Welles, but ultimately shaped by his colleagues at RKO. Welles had recently negotiated a new contract with RKO, one that did not require him to star in or direct his projects, but one that, more important, took away his right to the final cut. When he failed to return from Brazil, leaving the editing to others, RKO was merely exercising its legal rights.

The first part of the film is admirable in its handling of character and incident, in its sense of décor and mise-en-scène, and in its editing and camera technique. By contrast, the latter part of the film is another matter indeed, but the flawed nature of the film's ending is not, perhaps, entirely the fault of Welles, since it was shaped by other hands than his and not, apparently, according to the director's precise intentions. It is therefore flawed, both as a motion picture and as an adaptation, since it does not faithfully represent its source. Because of its central importance to the career of Orson Welles, *Ambersons* has been discussed by every Welles critic; but the interest is generally in *Ambersons* as "a true *film maudit,* like Stroheim's *Greed,*" as PETER COWIE describes it, and not in Tarkington's 1919 Pulitzer Prize–winning novel.

ANDRÉ BAZIN rhapsodizes about *Ambersons* as the "greater mastery" of the "stylistic inventions" of *CITIZEN KANE* it displays. Clearly, Bazin's interest is in "the technique of the mise-en-scène," the film's "*découpage* in depth" in particular, rather than its value as an adaptation of Tarkington's novel. In *The Magic World of Orson Welles,* JAMES NAREMORE gives a reasonable though brief account of how Welles has transformed his source materials, "giving the film a sharper satiric edge, a greater degree of sexual frustration and madness" that is nonetheless "in keeping with Tarkington's underlying social despair." Like Bazin, Naremore sees the film as a sort of autobiographical exercise: Tim Holt becomes a *Doppelgänger* for the director himself; Joseph Cotten "presumably" resembles Welles's own father; Tarkington's Indianapolis, Indiana, becomes a reflection of Welles's Kenosha, Wisconsin, and so forth.

As a reasonable adaptation, the film is flawed, though what Naremore writes of the director's original design for the ending suggests that the film's ending might have been much closer in spirit to the novel's conclusion, had that design been followed. If the film falters in its conclusion, that is partly the fault of the director, who obviously overextended himself and was not able to see the project through to its conclusion. Not only is there a rift in the directorial styles between those sequences directed by Welles himself and those directed by others (such as

Robert Wise and Freddie Fleck), but there is no reasonable continuity between these dissimilar styles. The photographic style and the scenic style of the first part are in no way approximated by the corresponding styles in the latter part, where even the acting becomes wooden and ineffective (Eugene and Lucy in the garden, for example, and the final business at the hospital). Whether one describes the picture as "baroque" or "classical," it is still seriously flawed, and Welles himself, who decided to pursue another project in South America before seeing the film through its postproduction stages, cannot entirely escape the responsibility for its failures.

According to Charles Higham, something like 53 minutes of footage have been stripped away from the adaptation as Welles originally shot it; and one might generously suppose that, given nearly another hour's worth of screen time, Welles might have provided a much more agreeable handling of his source. In his book *The Films of Orson Welles,* Higham lists the original running time as 148 minutes in the chapter on *Ambersons,* and as 131 minutes in the filmography.

Regardless of the exact count, however, there were obvious and considerable production problems that severely distorted the film's design. The final scene at the hospital (apparently directed by other hands), for example, that concludes with Eugene and Fanny walking off into a state of sentimentally indulgent bliss, arm-in-arm, is embarrassingly awkward, as is the scene in Eugene's study, where father and daughter read about George's accident and Lucy proclaims—without much of an apparent motive—that she intends to visit George in the hospital. Isabel's message from "the other side," and the telepathic communication between father and daughter, painstakingly developed in the novel, are utterly ignored. Obviously the film has been damaged by its hasty and haphazard restructuring at the end.

The disjointed and disruptive style at the end deserves special commentary. While Naremore ridicules Cotten and Agnes Moorehead walking down that "hospital corridor wearing silly, beatific grins," Higham believes that this somehow "echoes, to the tune of a sad, final Herrmann waltz, the precise words of the ending of Tarkington's book." Higham also claims that this scene was directed by

Robert Wise. Naremore, on the other hand, credits Freddie Fleck, not Wise, with the direction, and Roy Webb, rather than BERNARD HERRMANN, with the musical score. (In 1935, Webb was the musical director for George Stevens when he directed his own Tarkington project, *Alice Adams.*)

A letter from Robert Wise to Richard C. Keenan written in 1980 confirms Naremore's credits: "I may have told Charles Higham years ago when I was in Australia that I had directed the hospital scene at the end of the picture," Wise explained: "I did direct retakes and added scenes that are in the final picture, and after thirty years, my memory is a little lax, and I may have presumed I had directed the new ending as well. However, several years ago, Peter Bogdanovich, who was into a book on Welles, told me that he had production reports from the picture that indicated the new ending was directed by Fred Fleck, who had been production manager on the picture."

Wise then goes on to provide a breakdown of the scenes he directed, particularly and most memorably RICHARD BENNETT as Major Amberson "in the fireplace scene," just before the character's death, but that, Wise stipulated, "was during the actual production of the film, while Orson was directing the first unit. In postproduction and in trying to get the film in shape to release, I did direct a couple of new bridging scenes, one involving Dolores Costello and Tim Holt, as I recall, regarding a letter that Joe Cotten had written to her. I think I also directed the scene where Joe wrote that letter." In brief, then, Charles Higham's critical assessment of the film's final scene is no more trustworthy than his sense of the direction.

The film was reedited primarily because it received a mixed response from a preview audience at the Fox Theatre in Pomona, California. One of the review cards read as follows: "The picture was a masterpiece with perfect photography, settings and action. It seemed too deep for the average stupid person. I was disgusted with the way some people received this picture." As a result, the film was shortened by 17 minutes and another preview was held in Pasadena, where the response was more favorable. According to DAVID THOMSON, Welles had every reason for returning to reedit his own film but was reluctant to leave Rio. When JACK MOSS, Welles's new manager, was asked by RKO's Cy Endfield why Welles did not return, Moss showed Endfield footage featuring Brazilian chorus girls and said that Welles, who had shot the footage, told him "I fucked that one . . . and that one . . . and that one." Moss added, "There's no place in the world where he can do what he's doing there." One can only wonder why Welles could have assumed that his intentions could have been intuited or realized by people who did not share his vision of the film.

Even so, the film captured the attention of the Motion Picture Academy. In 1942, Agnes Moorehead was nominated for a best supporting actress Academy Award, Al Fields was nominated for best set decoration, and *The Magnificent Ambersons* was even nominated for best picture, though the Oscar finally went to *Mrs. Miniver.* Moreover, STANLEY CORTEZ was nominated for his camerawork on the picture, even though he had had a falling out with Welles, who thought he was too painstaking and blamed him for the film's running behind schedule and who replaced him with Harry Wild. Ultimately, none of the nominations resulted in Academy Awards.

Had circumstance been kinder or had the director himself been less overconfident and overextended, Orson Welles's second feature film, *The Magnificent Ambersons,* might have outstripped even *Citizen Kane.* Though flawed by its sentimental conclusion, Booth Tarkington's novel was an excellent potential property, the story of the rise and fall of a great and influential family in the American Midwest as the times changed and the industrial revolution reshaped America at the turn of the 20th century. It is the story of a vain and selfish young man who gets a deserved "comeuppance," directed by an overconfident "boy genius" intent upon conquering Hollywood who ultimately would get his own "comeuppance" as the project slipped out of his control and was finally shaped and reduced by a studio intent upon cutting its losses. The film was less a failure than a disappointment. Although it seems fragmented and a bit disjointed, it still reveals flashes of true brilliance. Gardner Campbell rightly described the film as "arguably the greatest 'lost' film of the sound era."

—J.M.W.

***Magnificent Ambersons, The* (television mini–series)** RKO Pictures/Arts & Entertainment Network, 2002. **Director:** Alfonso Arau; **Producers:** Jonas Bauer, Gene Kirkwood, and Norman Stephens; **Executive Producers:** Guido De Angelis and Ted Hartley; **Screenplay:** Welles (based on *The Magnificent Ambersons* by Booth Tarkington); **Music:** Roy Folguera; **Cinematographer:** Kenneth MacMillan; **Editor:** David Martin; **Cast:** Madeleine Stowe (Isabelle Amberson), Bruce Greenwod (Eugene Morgan), Jonathan Rhys-Meyers (George Amberson), Gretchen Mol (Lucy Morgan), Jennifer Tilly (Aunt Fanny), William Hootkins (Uncle George), James Cromwell (Major Amberson)

No doubt this remake was done with the best of intentions, to restore the greatest *film maudit* of WELLES's career to something approximating his original vision, which RKO had cut by more than a third from what Welles had shot, and refigured the ending. The result might have been nominated for four Academy Awards, but the film was a commercial flop that sent the director's career into a tailspin. Regardless, two-thirds of the cursed film was directed by Orson Welles himself and graced by the talents of the MERCURY Players, and talent of that order is difficult to duplicate.

Gretchen Mol is charming enough as Lucy Morgan and could perhaps hold her own against ANNE BAXTER, and Madeleine Stowe comes close to matching DOLORES COSTELLO's Isabelle Amberson, whose consumptive presence is somewhat enlarged in this three-hour remake. Bruce Greenwood makes a valiant attempt at playing the repeatedly disappointed and rebuffed Eugene Morgan, but the memory of JOSEPH COTTEN casts a very large shadow, as does the memory of AGNES MOOREHEAD as Aunt Fanny Minafer. Jennifer Tilly works hard at portraying wacky Aunt Fanny and is given more screen time than Agnes Moorehead had for her gossiping and dithering, but Moorehead accomplished far more in less time. Television critic Tom Shales of the *Washington Post* was impressed by Tilly's "one truly affecting moment" when Fanny is frightened by the reality of poverty, "which was as much of a curse then as it is now." But there are problems with paying too much attention to Aunt Fanny.

James Cromwell provides other grace notes and is quite good as Major Amberson, right down to his "the earth came from the sun" final monologue, but in truth that monologue falls short of the spooky brilliance ailing RICHARD BENNETT brought to that role. As Georgie Amberson Minafer, Jonathan Rhys-Meyers is totally unpleasant, as he is meant to be, with glassy eyes and a cruel twist to his lip as he proclaims those who would thwart him to be riff-raff, but, as Tom Shales noted, the character "dominates too many scenes," and his tirades become tiring: "Huffs and snits are his bread and butter," Shales concluded. Moreover, the remake also works overtime to suggest an Oedipal kink in the relationship between George and his mother. In one scene, George strips down to his underwear while his mother is watching, for example, and in another they kiss longer than a mother and son ought to do. In all instances, of course, the original gave us performances that were directed by Orson Welles, performances that simply are not matched by director Alfonso Arau, best known for *Like Water for Chocolate* (1992), an enjoyable movie, but one not exactly in a league with *CITIZEN KANE*. The remake was broadcast on the A&E (Arts & Entertainment) network on Sunday, January 13, 2002.

The remake locates the action in Indianapolis (no doubt the city Booth Tarkington had in mind, but it is not specified in the novel) and follows the 1942 screenplay Welles wrote without the help of HERMAN MANKIEWICZ, who surely left his mark on *Citizen Kane*. RKO thought the screenplay was overly long and awkward, and the Welles version did not do well with test audiences, so it was whacked down to 88 minutes and provided with a happier and sappier ending than Welles intended. Remaking the film at over twice the original running time may make the story less confusing, but it gives viewers more of George Amberson Minafer than they might wish, without even making TARKINGTON's prediction about the young snob's eventual "comeuppance," as the world changes and neighborhoods change and the Amberson legacy diminishes to the point that the family name is dropped from the social register. That is adequately shown in the remake, so perhaps the point is effectively made dramatically.

In his scornful *Washington Post* review (January 13, 2001, G5), Tom Shales faulted the director for permitting "soap-operatic overacting," perhaps to approximate period acting, though the "histrionics are sometimes laughable." Yes, the A&E version was adapted from the original Welles screenplay, but Welles was clearly more gifted as a director and actor than as a writer. The story begins with the Amberson ball in 1904, then takes viewers back to the summer of 1884, then forward in time "eight years later," then, again, to the summer of 1897, ping-ponging its way to 1904 (again) then to 1906, when, as Shales wrote, "George comes home from his first year at Princeton," where "He is working on a master's in petulance." The worst elements of structural confusion remain, while the rich texture of GREGG TOLAND's black-and-white cinematography is sorely missed, even though the remake "sets a new standard in production for movies on basic cable," which, as Shales noted, "isn't really saying much." Chris Kaltenbach of the *Baltimore Sun* found this "less-than-magnificent" adaptation an "inferior copy of a flawed masterpiece." In the words of Tom Shales, the "finished picture by no means looks like an Orson Welles film," nor does it feel like one. Could anyone 60 years later presume to make the film Welles *might* have made?

—J.M.W.

Man, Beast and Virtue (aka Uomo, la Bestia, e la Virtu)　Rosa Films/Paramount, 87 minutes, 1953.
Director: Steno; **Producers:** Antonio Altaviti and Luigi Di Laurentiis; **Screenplay:** Vitaliano Brancati, Lucio Fulci, Jean Josipovici, Luigi Pirandello, and Steno; **Cinematographer:** Mario Damicelli; **Music:** Angelo Francesco Lavagnino and P.G. Redi; **Editor:** Gisa Radicchi Levi; **Cast:** Toto (Prof. Paolino), Orson Welles (Captain Perella, the Beast), Viviane Romance (Assunta Perella), Mario Castellani (the doctor), Rocco D'Assunta (Zeppo), Carlo Delle Piane (the student)

Based on a story by Luigi Pirandello, the film centers on a romantic triangle involving a husband (ORSON WELLES), a wife (French actress Viviane Romance), and the wife's lover (Italian comic Toto). There is a twist, in that the lover attempts to persuade the wife to reconcile with her husband. The lover's motivation is simple. Because the wife is carrying the lover's baby, the lover wants to avoid the looming responsibilities of paternity. Directed by Stevano Vanziano (under the pseudonym of Steno), the international co-production was shot along the coast of Naples and in nearby Cetora, Italy. Welles, the "Beast" of the title, is a sea captain, a part that called for a full and bushy beard worthy of Neptune. At the film's end, with the lover having attained success and consequently new amatory horizons, the captain finds himself once again together with his wife. Although distributed by Paramount Pictures in the United States, the film was seldom seen, even in Italy.

In his recollections of *L'Uomo, la Bestia e la Virtu* told to PETER BOGDANOVICH, Welles said: "I was 'the beast,' and the 'the man' was a comic called Toto, who claimed to be the direct descendant of someone like Charlemagne and was always addressed as 'Your Highness' because he also claimed to be a prince. Maybe he was. It was very funny: 'Ready for the next scene, Your Highness,' they'd say, and he'd step into the shot and get a custard pie in the face. Viviane Romance was 'the lady.' She spent all of her time trying to hide me from the lens with great, long handkerchiefs. A real old-fashioned movie diva—the kind I'd never been near. I don't know how to describe the picture; it was so odd."

When queried about the director, Welles recalls that "He worked with some writer—they were a team. But Viviane Romance's husband, who was an Egyptian, wrote her dialogue, which bore no relationship to Pirandello, Prince Toto, me, or anything else. And she spoke it in French. The prince and I spoke in Italian, and none of the dialogue made any sense at all. Complete non sequiturs." When asked if he sometimes made fun of those awful films he appeared in, Welles denied the charge: "I've never done that. I really do try—no matter how ashamed I am."

—C.B.

Mancini, Henry (1924–1994) Mancini, the celebrated Hollywood composer best known for having integrated jazz into feature film scoring, received a huge career boost in 1958 due to his evocative jazz-inflected backing for TOUCH OF EVIL, one of WELLES's undisputedly major films.

As a boy, Mancini was encouraged to study music by his father, a steelworker. Learning flute and piano and the rudiments of arranging, Mancini became a student at the Juilliard School of Music in 1942. Although military service during World War II interrupted his formal studies, afterward he received an on-the-job crash course when Tex Beneke hired him as the Glenn Miller Orchestra's pianist and arranger. His first film assignments, providing cues for low-budget Universal films, came when his wife, singer Ginny O'Connor, helped him secure a job scoring a recording date by singer Mel Tormé's Mel-Tones, the trend-setting jazz vocal group with whom O'Connor sang. Mancini's first scoring job was for an Abbott and Costello comedy called *Lost in Alaska* (1952). Later, his big band experience paid off in scores for two major Hollywood biopics, *The Glenn Miller Story* (1954) and *The Benny Goodman Story* (1956). Then in 1958 came his edgy, jazz-drenched atmospherics for Welles's *Touch of Evil*. Accentuating the film's tensions with Latin percussion and jabbing big band blasts, Mancini's score was hailed as a stylistic breakthrough. Mancini brought his jazzy scoring style to an even wider public in the justly lauded scores for the TV detective shows *Peter Gunn* (1959) and *Mr. Lucky* (1960), both created and produced by Blake Edwards. Mancini's productive collaboration with Edwards continued with such big screen successes as *Breakfast at Tiffany's* (1961), whose score included the Oscar-winning song "Moon River." The Mancini-Edwards team achieved another hit with *Days of Wine and Roses* (1962), whose engaging, jazz-flavored theme netted Mancini yet another best song Oscar. Mancini won an Oscar for best original song score for another Edwards film, *Victor/Victoria* (1982). In addition to taking home 20 Grammy Awards, Mancini enjoyed a successful guest conducting career, usually in programs of his own music. In assessing his film scoring legacy, Mancini acknowledged that his greatest contribution was "my use of jazz, and the incorporation of its various idioms into the mainstream of film scoring. If that's a contribution, then it's mine."

Mancini, one of Hollywood's most prolific composers, wrote a number of other fine scores, including *High Time* (1960); *The Great Impostor*

(1960); *The Second Time Around* (1961); *Experiment in Terror* (1962); *Hatari!* (1962); *Charade* (1963); *The Pink Panther* (1964); *A Shot in the Dark* (1964); *The Great Race* (1965); *The Molly Maguires* (1970); *Darlin' Lili* (1970); *The White Dawn* (1974); *W.C. Fields and Me* (1976); *Who Is Killing the Great Chefs of Europe?* (1978); *Mommie Dearest* (1981); *The Man Who Loved Women* (1983); *The Glass Menagerie* (1987); and *Switch* (1991). Just prior to his death from cancer, Mancini was working with lyricist Leslie Bricusse on the score for the stage adaptation of Edwards's *Victor/Victoria,* which successfully returned Julie Andrews (Blake Edward's wife) to Broadway in the role she had created in the 1982 movie.

Mancini's score for *Touch of Evil* became a source of some controversy in the storm raised by Welles's allegation that Universal had taken the film away from him during the editing process and ruined it by chopping it to pieces. In the 1958 prints released by Universal, Welles's bravura tracking shot is underscored with Mancini's pulsating Afro-Latin jazz. In the 1998 "restored" version of the film assembled by Walter Murch from Welles's famous memo to Universal's brass outlining changes Welles unsuccessfully insisted be made before the film's release, Mancini's music is replaced by location music from bars and radios in the long opening shot. Welles also insisted that the credits appearing over the studio's version be dropped, which Murch also did in the "restored" rendition. For today's film fans and scholars, the question is, which opening plays best? Obviously, thanks to Murch, it's useful to have Welles's version to screen and consider. However, many fans prefer the 1958 studio version, finding that it plays more effectively than the Welles/Murch rendition, thanks primarily to the aggressive edginess of Mancini's opening Afro-Latin cue, which effectively foreshadows the film's sense of foreboding and danger; the cue also functions to effectively establish the exotic and wantonly carnal atmospherics of the Mexican-American border town, LOS ROBLES.

References Berg, Chuck. "Jazz in Film and Television," in *The Oxford Companion to Jazz* (New York: Oxford University Press, 2001); Buhler, James, and Caryl Flinn.

Music in the Cinema (Hanover, N.H.: University Presses of New England, 2000); Mancini, Henry, and Gene Lees. *Did They Mention the Music?* (Chicago: Contemporary Books, 1989).

—C.B.

Man for All Seasons, A
Columbia Pictures/Highland, 120 minutes, 1966. **Director:** Fred Zinnemann; **Producers:** Fred Zinnemann and William N. Graf; **Screenplay:** Robert Bolt, adapted from his own play; **Cinematography:** Ted Moore; **Editor:** Ralph Kemplen; **Music:** Georges Delerue; **Cast:** Orson Welles (Cardinal Wolsey), Paul Scofield (Sir Thomas More), Wendy Hiller (Lady Alice), Leo McKern (Cromwell), Robert Shaw (Henry VIII), Susannah York (Margaret), Nigel Davenport (Norfolk), John Hurt (Richard Rich), Corin Redgrave (William Roper), Colin Blakely (Matthew), Vanessa Redgrave (Anne Boleyn)

The British film adaptation of Robert Bolt's hit play of 1960 featured WELLES in the key cameo role of Cardinal Wolsey. In contrast to his act-and-run quickies for mostly mundane movies during the 1960s, Welles scored with the critics and public in his moving portrayal of Cardinal Wolsey opposite Paul Scofield's Sir Thomas More. To enhance the pathos of his performance, Welles convinced director FRED ZINNEMANN to let him use eyedrops to make the pupils of his eyes look bloodshot, thus giving the dying cleric's relentless intensity added impact. Welles, obviously relieved to be among grown-ups, told PETER BOGDANOVICH: "[*A Man for All Seasons*] came right after the *Casino Royale* caper, so you can imagine how grateful I was to be associated with something decent. I enjoyed acting with Scofield. It was a wonderful day—that's all it took."

In its rave review of the film, *Variety* singled out Welles's work: "Orson Welles in five minutes (here an early confrontation, as Cardinal Wolsey, with More), achieves outstanding economy of expression." For Welles, mostly pilloried during the 1960s for what was perceived to be overemoting, such praise was especially welcome. Bosley Crowther in his review of *A Man for All Seasons* in the *New York Times* picked up on the same theme: "Mr. Scofield

Welles as Cardinal Wolsey in Fred Zinnemann's adaptation of Robert Bolt's *A Man for All Seasons* *(Literature/Film Archive)*

is brilliant in his exercise of temperance and restraint, of disciplined wisdom and humor, as he variously confronts his restless King or Cardinal Wolsey, who is played by Orson Welles with subtle, startling glints of poisonous evil that, in this day, are extraordinary for him."

A Man for All Seasons won Oscars for best picture, best actor (Paul Scofield), best director (Fred Zinnemann), best screenplay from another medium (Robert Bolt and Constance Willis), best color cinematography, and best color costume design. In addition, there were Oscar nominations for best supporting actor (Robert Shaw) and best supporting actress (Wendy Hiller). For Welles, it was a reminder to the film world and general public of his forceful and effective acting talent.

References Bogdanovich, Peter, and Orson Welles. *This Is Orson Welles,* ed. Jonathan Rosenbaum (New York: HarperCollins, 1992); Nollerri, Arthur, Jr. *The Films of Fred Zinnemann: Critical Perspectives* (Albany, N.Y.: SUNY Press, 1999); Zinnemann, Fred. *An Autobiography* (London: Bloomsbury, 1992).

—C.B.

Man in the Shadow Universal, 80 minutes, 1957. **Director:** Jack Arnold; **Producer:** Albert Zugsmith; **Screenplay:** Gene L. Coon; **Cinematographer:** Arthur E. Arling; **Editor:** Edward Curtiss; **Cast:** Jeff Chandler (Sheriff Ben Sadler); Orson Welles (Virgil Renchler), Ben Alexander (Ed Begley), Colleen Miller (Skippy Aiken), John Larch (Ed Yates), James Gleason (Hank James), Barbara Lawrence (Helen Sadler), Royal

Dano (Clay Aiken), Paul Fix (Herb Parker), William Schallert (Jim Shaney)

WELLES took the assignment of playing a "heavy" in this low-budget Universal feature because of his desperate need for funds to keep up with his continuing tax problems. Initially, it was to have been a straightforward, two-dimensional good guy (Jeff Chandler) versus bad guy (Welles) affair with a steady drumbeat march toward an inevitable showdown in the last reel. Welles, whom FRANK BRADY speculates might have been embarrassed about acting in a western, rewrote his part without telling anyone. On the first day of shooting, BARBARA LEAMING reports that Welles marched into the studio and announced: "You'll be interested to see the changes for today!" The producer, ALBERT ZUGSMITH, was immediately called. Instead of a confrontation, once Welles's changes were digested, all agreed that they were a distinct improvement. Instead of an out-and-out villain, Welles's despotic rancher became a tortured figure who doesn't want to perpetrate violence but is inadvertently forced to by circumstances. Playing opposite Jeff Chandler's sheriff, Welles's dramatically charged performance as a troubled tyrant with the blood of a Mexican laborer on his hands still plays effectively.

Significantly, Zugsmith and Welles became friends during the production of *Man in the Shadow,* even sharing a bottle of vodka on the last day of the shoot. Soon after, Zugsmith called Welles to act in another Universal picture that he was producing, *Badge of Evil,* later changed to TOUCH OF EVIL, which would become one of Welles's most celebrated films.

—C.B.

Mankiewicz, Herman J. (1897–1953)

Screenwriter Herman Mankiewicz was born in New York City on November 7, 1897, the older brother of Joseph Mankiewicz, who became a film director (*All About Eve*). After attending Columbia University, he became a reporter for the *New York Tribune.* He served in World War I and remained in Europe after the war, for two years as a correspondent for the *Chicago Tribune.* Mankiewicz returned to New York as the first drama critic of *The New Yorker;* he went to Los Ange-

les in 1926 as drama critic for the *Los Angeles Times,* while writing screenplays for silent pictures on the side. Many of his contributions to sound pictures of the 1930s, such as the Marx Brothers' *Duck Soup* (1932) and *The Wizard of Oz* (1939), were uncredited.

ORSON WELLES had engaged Mankiewicz to write scripts for his MERCURY THEATRE radio dramas, and he subsequently asked Mankiewicz to work on CITIZEN KANE. One of the films he wrote, the Edward Arnold vehicle *John Meade's Woman* (1937), contains a scene at the Chicago Opera House and a scene where Meade picks up a young woman on the street—both of which he recycled in the *Kane* script. Otherwise there is little evidence in the more than 40 screenplays he worked on before *Kane* of the superior quality that would distinguish that script.

It seems that Mankiewicz came up with the idea of basing the screenplay on the life of WILLIAM RANDOLPH HEARST, the publishing tycoon. JOHN HOUSEMAN, who had been associated with Welles's Mercury Theatre stage productions, recalls in his autobiography that Welles had asked him over lunch at "21" in New York to come with him to Hollywood to work on a scenario modeled on Hearst and his mistress, the actress MARION DAVIES, and that the premise had been suggested by Mankiewicz. Film historian JONATHAN ROSENBAUM says in *This Is Orson Welles* that Houseman is generally reliable on matters relating to Welles's work.

Because Hearst was a powerful, influential publisher, the nature of the project would have to be veiled in secrecy. So Welles asked Mankiewicz to do a preliminary draft of the screenplay at a secluded ranch at Victorville in the California desert. Mankiewicz was put on the RKO payroll on February 19, 1940, at $1,000 a week, with a bonus of $5,000 when the screenplay was delivered. Houseman agreed to accompany Mankiewicz to the ranch to keep Mankiewicz from going on a binge, since drinking was a decided problem for him.

For his part, Welles had lengthy discussions with Mankiewicz before he departed for Victorville. Welles had planned to introduce the controversial tycoon in the unproduced SMILER WITH A KNIFE with a MARCH OF TIME–style documentary, very much like the newsreel at the beginning of *Kane.* Since the newsreel about Kane's life is in Mankiewicz's script, it is very likely that Welles passed this concept on to Mankiewicz at this point.

Mankiewicz labored until early May on a draft of the script, entitled *American,* 250 pages in length. It unquestionably provided the strong storyline and firm narrative structure that the script for the film needed. *American* presents the life of a publishing magnate narrated in flashback by people who knew him. To present a context for the flashbacks, Mankiewicz—Welles himself acknowledged to PETER BOGDANOVICH—conceived the plot device of the publisher's deathbed utterance, "ROSEBUD," which motivates a journalist to inquire of the tycoon's acquaintances what the word meant to the dying man. *American* concludes with the identification of Rosebud as the sled the publisher cherished as a boy. Actually, Welles had a favorite sled as a lad, but Mankiewicz called it Rosebud in the script after the name of the bicycle he had in his boyhood.

In his introduction to *This Is Orson Welles,* Bogdanovich writes that screenwriter CHARLES LEDERER, who was Marion Davies's nephew (and the new husband of Welles's ex-wife, VIRGINIA NICHOLSON), told him that Mankiewicz requested that he show *American* to Davies; Mankiewicz wanted to know if she thought it was offensive. Although it is generally assumed that Lederer complied with his wish, Lederer did no such thing. He read it himself; "I gave it back to him," because "I knew Marion would never read it." Furthermore, Lederer did not personally feel that the script would offend his aunt: "There were things in it that were based on Hearst and Marion—her jigsaw puzzles, Marion's drinking," but the script was not so much about Hearst and Marion, in his view, as about Harold McCormick and GANNA WALSKA, whom McCormick endeavored unsuccessfully to push into prominence as an opera star, just as Kane tries to make his second wife, Susan, an opera diva. Bogdanovich adds that "Welles always maintained that the story of McCormick," whom Bogdanovich misidentifies as Robert McCormick, "and his untalented wife contributed far more to Kane's personal story than did Hearst's backing of the delightful screen comedienne Marion Davies."

In the years following the release of *Kane,* the myth somehow grew up that Welles was principally responsible for the *Kane* screenplay. "Critics and film historians went along with this," writes Ronald Bower, "until 1971, when PAULINE KAEL exploded the misconception with her controversial article, 'Raising Kane,' wherein she set the record straight as to Mankiewicz being the primary contributor to the screenplay. . . . Mankiewicz's contribution to *Kane* is now the accepted fact." ROBERT CARRINGER emphasizes that, after all, Welles "lacked the patience that original story construction requires"; in fact, all of Welles's other scripts are not originals, but derived from novels or plays. He preferred to contribute to a screenplay, Carringer concludes, by refining and polishing another's work.

Although Richard Barr (formerly Richard Baer), associate producer of *Kane,* declared at the time the film came out that the idea of modeling the script on Hearst was Welles's, Kael rightly endorses Houseman in confirming that the notion originated with Mankiewicz, as indicated above. Since Welles went along with Barr at the time, Kael cites Sara Mankiewicz, Herman's widow, as confirming that her husband supplied this premise for the movie. In addition, Kael quotes Marion Fisher, the babysitter for the Mankiewiczes in those days, who testifies that she took dictation from Mankiewicz on the preliminary draft of a screenplay, framed in flashbacks, in 1925, before Mankiewicz even went to Hollywood. When she observed that the main character resembled William Randolph Hearst, Mankiewicz replied, "Smart girl."

Nevertheless, in Welles's favor it must be emphatically affirmed that he heavily revised Mankiewicz's script draft. Lederer declares that that is beyond question: "Manky was always complaining and sighing about Orson's changes," Lederer said to Bogdanovich. "I read the script of the film, the long one called *American,*" which Welles substantially cut. "I thought it was pretty dull. That was before Orson got to changing it and making it *his* version." Welles, who never hesitated to take his blue pencil to cutting a Shakespeare (SHAKESPEARE BY WELLES) play he planned to film in the years ahead, would not have balked at condensing Mankiewicz's work.

Yet Kael asserts that Welles had a minimal influence on Mankiewicz's draft of the screenplay. She acknowledges that he had preliminary conversations with Mankiewicz before the latter went to the desert ranch, gave him advice by phone and letter while Mankiewicz was there, and made a few revisions on the set. But Welles's contributions went well beyond that, as is evident from a comparison of the rough draft entitled *American,* dated May 9, 1940, and the final shooting script, *Citizen Kane,* dated July 16, 1940, both of which are in the RKO studio files.

One of the major contributions that Welles made to Mankiewicz's *American* draft was to limit the amount of material derived directly from Hearst's life. If the amount of material in *American* about Marion Davies did not give her nephew Charles Lederer pause, it did disturb Welles. Richard Corliss notes that Mankiewicz was a friend of both Hearst and Davies; he had been a guest at San Simeon, where he "kept Marion giggling as they went outside for a swig"— he was aware that Marion often drank on the sly, just as he did. Indeed, Mankiewicz's portrayal of both Hearst and Davies in *American* was considered in some quarters at the studio to be a betrayal of their friendship with him. Welles and Mankiewicz may have shared a private joke that Rosebud was Hearst's pet name for Marion's genitalia, but the plethora of Hearst material in *American* was no laughing matter for Welles. In Welles's opinion, Mankiewicz had included far too much material from Hearst's professional life as a publisher, as well as from his personal life with Davies; it read too much like a fictionalized biography of Hearst rather than the story of a mythical tycoon. As Carringer puts it, a goodly amount of Hearst material survives in the movie; but Welles nevertheless jettisoned a considerable amount from *American* in transforming it into *Citizen Kane.* Consequently, Welles contended in his article, "*Citizen Kane* Is Not About Louella Parson's Boss," published when the film premiered, that the picture was a portrait, not of Hearst, but of "a fictional newspaper tycoon." He undoubtedly had in mind the large chunks of Hearst biography that he had systematically removed from Mankiewicz's script.

Richard Barr, who maintains the doubtful position that Welles conceived the idea of basing Kane on Hearst, is much closer to the truth when he states in *This Is Orson Welles,* "The revisions made by Welles were not limited to mere general suggestions, but included the actual rewriting of dialogue, changing of sequences and characterizations, and also the elimination and addition of certain scenes." Welles scrapped several lengthy expository scenes, chronicling the disintegration of Kane's marriage to his first wife, Emily (RUTH WARRICK); he replaced them with a brisk montage of brief interchanges between Kane and Emily over the breakfast table that crisply shows how they are drifting apart.

After Mankiewicz returned to Hollywood from the Victorville ranch in May, he moved over to MGM to collaborate with CHARLES LEDERER and BEN HECHT on the Clark Gable vehicle *Comrade X* (1940). Carringer declares, "Though he attempted to keep up with the revisions in the following weeks, he ceased to be a guiding hand in the *Citizen Kane* scripting at this point."

In all, Welles had scuttled 75 pages of the script by this time, and on June 18 submitted a tentative script to the front office with the title *Citizen Kane.* The studio brass immediately ordered that the script be condensed still further. With that, Mankiewicz returned to work on the script for another week, until June 27. He took one look at Welles's revisions and fired off a telegram to Houseman, who was in New York, deploring Welles's handiwork. Houseman's answer, recorded in his autobiography, states, "Received your cut version and several new scenes of Orson's. . . . After much careful reading I like all of Orson's scenes" except—surprisingly—the breakfast table montage. For his part, Mankiewicz had reduced the script by another 25 pages, but he was no longer a creative force on the screenplay, as Houseman tactfully makes clear.

Welles's secretary, Katherine Trosper, told Bogdanovich that she seriously questioned Kael's contention that Mankiewicz had little help from Welles on the screenplay: "Orson was always writing and rewriting. I saw scenes written during production," long after Mankiewicz had departed. "Even while he was being made up, Orson was dictating dialogue." In sum, if Kael was right in contending that Mankiewicz deserved more credit for the *Kane* script than he had been accorded prior to her essay, she is wrong in indicating that Welles did not have much of a hand in rewriting the screenplay.

Withal, as Carringer states, "the conclusion seems inescapable that Welles originally intended to take sole credit for the script." To understand his behavior one must recall that, in the days when Welles was doing radio dramatizations of novels and stage plays, the writers who were engaged to collaborate with Welles on radio scripts signed contracts, not with the network, but with Welles's Mercury Theatre Production Company. They assigned any claims of authorship to Welles's company; as a result, Welles was usually credited with the script for a given radio drama, regardless of the actual extent of his contribution to the script.

Similarly, Mankiewicz had signed a contract—not with RKO—but with Welles's independent unit, Mercury Theatre Productions. Hence his draft of the script, *American,* was owned by Welles, and Welles was within his legal rights to list himself as sole author of the script. Rosenbaum points out that Welles's lawyer, ARNOLD WEISSBERGER, brought this matter to Welles's attention and that he, and not Welles, pushed for Welles to be acknowledged sole author of the script. But the lawyer's correspondence with Welles, amply quoted by Carringer, makes it perlucidly clear that Welles knew precisely what Weissberger was up to.

When Mankiewicz got wind of this, he openly claimed in the press that he deserved to have his contribution to the film acknowledged with a co-author screen credit. Furthermore, when Mankiewicz enlisted the Screen Writers Guild to arbitrate the matter, Welles relented. The official screen credit reads: "Original screenplay by Herman J. Mankiewicz and Orson Welles." In a total about-face Welles placed Mankiewicz's name before his.

Welles and Mankiewicz received Academy Awards as co-authors of the script; but neither attended the ceremonies. Mankiewicz later quipped that, had he been present, his acceptance speech would have been, "I am very happy to accept this award in Mr. Welles's absence because the script was written in Mr. Welles's absence"—a typically glib, but hardly fair remark by Mankiewicz.

To be fair to Mankiewicz, he did compose the initial draft of the screenplay at the Victorville ranch "in Welles's absence"; and it was the foundation for all of the revisions that Welles made before and during filming. Mankiewicz's *American* provided the flashback framework, the entire cast of characters, and a significant amount of dialogue; e.g., the flashback to Kane's boyhood, and the reporter's first interview with Susan after Kane's death in the bistro where she sings, are both pretty much as Mankiewicz wrote them.

To be fair to Welles, says Carringer, "Welles added narrative brilliance by editing and tightening Mankiewicz's script; as mentioned, Welles banished a number of expository scenes that weighed down *American* and contributed such stunningly original strokes as the breakfast table sequence." He also made Kane more of a three-dimensional dramatic figure, rather than just a character largely based on Hearst.

Mankiewicz shared an Oscar nomination for *Pride of the Yankees (1942),* the Lou Gehrig story, the following year. But the balance of his career in pictures was troubled by his alcoholism, his compulsive gambling, and his fierce squabbles with the studio bosses, as he moved from one studio to another. He died of uremic poisoning in 1953.

It was in the 1950s that *Citizen Kane* was reissued to great acclaim, and commentators on the film referred more and more to the movie as written and directed by Welles. For one thing, Mankiewicz had already become a footnote in film history. For another, the role of the director was becoming central in film criticism; with the rise of the *auteur* theory, movies were being referred to increasingly as the director's medium. Hence the contribution of writers like Mankiewicz to the films they worked on was being soft-pedaled.

In the wake of Kael's article, which purported to set the record straight, Welles told Bogdanovich that he revised Mankiewicz's script both before and during shooting: "I was the one making the picture. . . . I used what I wanted of Mank's script, and, rightly or wrongly, kept what I liked of my own" in his revised version of the script. In short, *Citizen Kane* was the creative product of both Mankiewicz and Welles, and neither deserves sole credit for the script. Perhaps Welles said it all when he concluded, "Mankiewicz's contribution" to the film "was enormous."

References Bogdanovich, Peter. "Introduction," to *This Is Orson Welles* (New York: Da Capo, 1998), vii–xxxix; Bowers, Ronald. "Herman Mankiewicz" in *International Dictionary of Films and Filmmakers: Writers and Production Artists,* rev. ed., ed. Grace Jeromski (Detroit: St. James Press, 1997), vol. 4, 528–30; Carringer, Robert. *The Making of Citizen Kane* (Los Angeles: University of California Press, 1985); Corliss, Richard. "Praising *Kane*," *Time,* January 29, 1996, 71–74; Houseman, John. *Run-Through: A Memoir* (New York: Simon & Schuster, 1972); Kael, Pauline. "Raising Kane," in *The Citizen Kane Book,* including *Citizen Kane: The Shooting Script* by Herman J. Mankiewicz and Orson Welles (Boston: Little, Brown, 1971); Welles, Orson. "*Citizen Kane* Is Not About Louella Parson's Boss," in *Perspectives on Citizen Kane,* ed. Ronald Gottesman (New York: Da Capo, 1998).

—G.D.P.

Manvell, Roger (1909–1987)

British scholar and critic Roger Manvell's *Film and the Public,* published in Great Britain in 1955, was one of the first books to devote critical attention to the work of ORSON WELLES. In his book, Manvell discusses the films of several "foreign" directors, including Fritz Lang, Sergei Eisenstein, and Vittorio De Sica, but he is particularly impressed by Welles's CITIZEN KANE (1941), which Manvell, described as "one of the richest mines of film technique yet created."

Roger Manvell later wrote two books dealing with film, theater, and Shakespeare. Chapter 5 of Manvell's groundbreaking *Shakespeare & the Film,* published by Praeger in 1971, was entitled "Shakespeare by Orson Welles." After discussing the "much-criticized" adaptations of MACBETH and OTHELLO, Manvell concluded that "*Chimes at Midnight* is one of Orson Welles's finest films, and one of the most successful screen adaptations from Shakespeare so far made." Manvell also discussed the Welles Shakespeare films in *Theater and Film: A Comparative Study of the Two Forms of Dramatic Art, and the Problems of Adaptation of Stage Plays into Films,* published by Fairleigh Dickinson University Press in 1979.

Roger Manvell was a pioneer in cinema studies in Britain. Holding a Ph.D. in English language and literature from London University, he also earned a D.Litt. in film studies from Sussex University, the first senior doctorate in the subject conferred in Britain. He served as head of the Department of Film History at the London Film School and had a visiting fellowship in film studies at Sussex University. He was director of the British Film Academy from 1947 to 1959. In 1973, he came to the United States as Bingham Professor of Humanities at the University of Louisville, and by 1979 was visiting professor of film at Boston University. As an author, Manvell was prolific, writing fiction, biographies of CHARLES CHAPLIN, Ellen Terry, Sarah Siddons, and Annie Besant, and 20 books dealing with film and television. With Heinrich Fraenkel, Manvell also wrote nine books dealing with German history covering Adolf Hitler and other Third Reich figures, such as Rudolf Hess, Hermann Göring, and Heinrich Himmler. Manvell was also editor of the *Journal of the Society of Film and Television Arts* and editor in chief of the *International Encyclopedia of Film* (1972).

—J.M.W.

Man Who Came to Dinner, The (television, 1972)

In November 1972, WELLES appeared on NBC-TV in the *Hallmark Hall of Fame* adaptation of the hit 1939 Broadway play by Moss Hart and George S. Kaufman. As the irascible Sheridan Whiteside, Welles revisited a role that he had considered playing on film in 1940, but which eventually went to Monty Woolley because of Welles's desire to select a serious subject for his first RKO feature, a quest resulting in CITIZEN KANE.

During the 1970s, Welles's principal source of income was television. His justly lauded TV performance as the wheelchair-bound Whiteside was one of the actor's unqualified successes of the decade. Lee Remick, with whom Welles had appeared in THE LONG HOT SUMMER (1958), was also in the cast.

The Moss Hart–George S. Kaufman comedy, a staple of community and dinner theater repertories, opens with literary maven Whiteside (Welles) in a wheelchair. The cantankerous man of letters has slipped on a patch of ice at the front step of the Stanley home and is forced to convalesce therein. Perturbed by the circumstances, Whiteside makes life miserable for the Stanley family and himself. Trying to be polite, a family member asks the literary lion about the state of his health. He replies, "I may vomit." Bored, Whiteside takes pleasure in sowing seeds of distrust and dissatisfaction. In one instance, he succeeds in alienating the Stanley children from their parents. He also turns his nurse so antisocial, that she takes a job in an arms factory with hopes of destroying the human race. When his loyal secretary becomes enamored with a local reporter, Whiteside calls in a glamorous actress to sabotage the romance. He even resorts to blackmail, threatening to disclose that Mr. Stanley's sister was once accused of being an ax murderer. Finally, Whiteside mends and is ready to leave. The family and everyone else utter sighs of relief. Alas, as Whiteside steps out the door, he again slips on the ice. As he is hauled back into the Stanley's home, he bellows threats of initiating another six-week reign of terror.

Hart and Kaufman patterned Whiteside after their friend, author ALEXANDER WOOLLCOTT. The sexy actress Lorraine Sheldon was modeled after Gertrude Lawrence, while the sophisticated Beverly Carlton and madcap Banjo were tips of the hat to NOËL COWARD and Harpo Marx.

Whiteside, though, is the fulcrum around which everything and everybody else whirls. In his review of the 1939 play, the *New York Journal-American's* John Anderson said: "No one so full of the carbolic acid of human kindness; no one with the enthusiasms, the ruthless wit, the wayward taste, disarming prejudice, and relentless sentimentality of the man so carefully undistinguished as the hero" has ever before appeared in the American theater. If Whiteside can be seen as an American incarnation of SHAKESPEARE's FALSTAFF, it was a part that Welles seems destined to have played.

Thanks to NBC-TV and the *Hallmark Hall of Fame,* Welles was able to do just that, projecting himself and his beloved Falstaff into the indelible idiosyncrasies of Sheridan Whiteside.

—C.B.

Man Who Saw Tomorrow, The

Warner Bros., 85 minutes, 1981. **Director:** Robert Guenette; **Producer:** Robert Guenette; **Executive Producer:** David L. Wolper; **Screenplay:** Robert Guenette and Alan Hopgood; **Cinematographers:** Tom Ackerman, Eric Daarstad, and David Haskins; **Editor:** Peter Wood and Scott McLennan; **Cast:** Orson Welles (Narrator), Philip L. Clarke (Voice of Nostradamus)

In the story of Michel de Nostradamus, the 16th-century French physician whose prophecies have been kept alive for centuries, WELLES acted as the narrator, using what one reviewer called his "voice of doom." Ensconced in ample library chairs, he catalogues Nostradamus's prophecies, which are then compared with archive footage, old feature films, newsreels, and dramatizations of events that seem to validate many of his subject's predictions. One of his predictions includes a 1999 Arab nuclear attack on New York City.

—T.L.E.

March of Time, The

(radio, 1931–1951)   This pioneering radio series combining news and drama gave WELLES his first regular employment as a radio performer.

The March of Time began airing in 1931, during the period when network radio was just becoming established. Broadcast by CBS on Friday evenings at 8:30 P.M., the show fused powerful voices, realistic sound effects, and stirring music in an effort to dramatize the week's big news stories. On the occasion of its 1931 debut, the announcer explained: "On a thousand fronts the history of the world moves swiftly forward—Tonight the Editors of *Time,* the weekly newsmagazine, attempt a new kind of reporting of the news—the reenactment as clearly and dramatically as the medium of radio will permit, some memorable scenes from the news of the week—from the march of *Time!*"

At a period when network radio and talking pictures were in their infancies, the networks did not have news departments. Therefore, listeners became familiar with newsmakers like Huey Long, Benito Mussolini, Eleanor Roosevelt, and even President FRANKLIN ROOSEVELT largely through the colorful imitations of the talented *March of Time* cast. In the process, the show became a training ground for a legion of future radio stars, including Orson Welles, and such future Welles associates as AGNES MOOREHEAD, RAY COLLINS, Arlene Francis, and PAUL

STEWART. Welles's first appearance on *The March of Time* was somewhat of a fluke.

On the March 22, 1935, *March of Time* broadcast, Welles made his debut on national radio by reprising his stage role of McGafferty in a scene from Archibald MacLeish's experimental play, PANIC, which had just closed on Broadway after a limited three-day run. As the sound of ticker tapes rattled in the background, McGafferty was asked by his banking colleagues what he planned to do. "Do?" thundered Welles. "What do you think I'll do? Pull the blinds on the bank and sail to Bermuda? *This bank will open tomorrow at nine.*" With those lines, the nation's radio audience was first introduced to Orson Welles.

In the same show, Welles offered another preview of the versatility that would make him America's best-known radio actor of the 1930s. When a baby-effects expert failed to show up for the program's next segment, devoted to Canada's Dionne quintuplets, Welles piped up, "I can do baby voices." After a brief audition, Welles was hired to pinch-hit. Thus, with only the separation of a commercial, Welles was able to impress the radio brass at CBS, first with the imperious bravado of McGafferty, and then with the gurgling coos of Yvonne, Annette, Cecile, Marie, and Emilie Dionne. Thanks to his last-minute heroics in saving the show, Welles was soon added to the cast, thus marking the onset of his productive tenure with *The March of Time*.

Although it never made money for its underwriter, *March of Time* did fulfill its basic intention of promoting and advertising *Time* magazine. Broadcast in various formats, from once to three times a week, and varying in time from 15 to 30 minutes, *The March of Time* aired on either CBS or NBC from 1931 to 1939, and then during the war years, from 1941 to 1945.

The March of Time quickly became a central part of American culture. As media historian Raymond Fielding points out, the authoritative voice of Westbrook Van Voorhis, the show's primary narrator, "was said to be even more familiar than that of President Roosevelt." Significantly, the radio series led to the creation of a motion picture analogue, also titled *The March of Time,* which had an influential tenure in

movie theaters from 1935 to 1951, when it was eclipsed by the rise of television news and the postwar slump of the movie industry.

If parody is among the more significant forms of flattery, then the film version of *March of Time* deserves an additional mention as the model for Welles's 10-minute homage, NEWS ON THE MARCH, which opens *CITIZEN KANE* (1941). Drawing on his experience working on *March of Time* during the mid-1930s, Welles's loving parody is significant not only for its pivotal role in the structuring of *Citizen Kane*'s narrative, but also as the most visible and detailed reminder of the special glories of the *Time*-sponsored newsreel and its radio predecessor.

—C.B.

Marco the Magnificent

Marco the Magnificent IITAC-S.N.C.-Prodi Cinematografica-Avala Film Mounir Rafla-Ital Kaboul-Cinecustodia/MGM, 100 minutes, 1966. **Directors:** Denys de La Patelliere, Noel Howard, Christian-Jaque, and Cliff Lyons; **Producer:** Raoul J. Levy; **Screenplay:** Denys de La Patelliere, Raoul J. Levy, Jacques Remy, and Jean-Paul Rappeneau; **Cinematographer:** Armand Thirard; **Editors:** Jacqueline Thiedot, Noelle Balenci, and Albert Jurgenson; **Cast:** Horst Buchholz (Marco Polo), Anthony Quinn (Kublai Khan), Orson Welles (Ackerman), Omar Sharif (Emir Alaou), Elsa Martinelli (Woman with the Whip)

A 1966 film in which WELLES plays a character-narrator, Ackermann, a Venetian tutor, who in 1271 helps inspire the young Marco Polo to go east. Along with Welles, this Afghanistan/Egypt/France/Italy co-production also starred Horst Buchholz (Marco Polo), Anthony Quinn (Kublai Khan), Omar Sharif (Emir Alaou), Elsa Martinelli (Woman with the Whip), and Akim Tamiroff (Old Man of the Mountain.) In his interview with BOGDANOVICH, Welles reports that producer Raoul Levy had shot a version with Alain Delon that had to be aborted, a disaster that almost ruined the Yugoslav film industry. Later, Levy found new backing and reshot the film with Horst Buchholz, the version finally released as *Marco the Magnificent*. Welles states further that Levy never had a script. "Most of us just made it up as we went along," recalled Welles, which probably helps explain the film's multiple shortcomings. As with *LAFAYETTE,* Welles's cameo is so fleeting that it was eventually cut from the television and later release prints.

—C.B.

Martin, Dean (Dino Paul Crocetti)

(1917–1995) Dean Martin, who started his show business career as second banana to comedian Jerry Lewis, later hosted *The Dean Martin Show* on television years after the Martin and Lewis team had separated. In September of 1967 ORSON WELLES, on the advice of television producer Greg Garrison, made the first of many guest appearances with Martin on the show. Garrison convinced Welles to become involved because Garrison said it would be lucrative and the exposure might rekindle interest in Welles by film producers, as in fact was the case. At this time there was even the possibility that Welles might appear in the title role of FRANCIS FORD COPPOLA's *The Godfather.* "He believed he was physically perfect for the part," according to FRANK BRADY: "He saw himself whispering slowly as his minions and those who sought his favors came to kiss his hand; he envisioned them listening as he dispensed grave advice and wisdom to the 'children' of his family."

Born Dino Paul Crocetti on June 7, 1917, in Steubenville, Ohio, Dean Martin had careers in prizefighting, the steel mills, and card sharking before embarking on the singing career that eventually linked him with Jerry Lewis in 1946 in Atlantic City, New Jersey. The two entertainers quickly formed a very popular and successful show business team performing live, on television, and in films. Ten years later, after the pair had made 16 films together, their partnership broke up. Initially, Lewis's career seemed more promising, but Martin became a star in his own right as a singer, actor, and show business entertainer. He eventually became part of Frank Sinatra's "rat pack," along with Peter Lawford and Sammy Davis, Jr., among others. Martin had a gift not only for comedy but for drama as well. His best-known comedies include *Oceans 11* (1960), *Robin and the Seven Hoods* (1964), and *How to Save a Marriage—And Ruin Your Life* (1968). Other memorable roles were in *The Young Lions* (1958) and *Toys in the Attic* (1963). Perhaps his best film roles, however, were in Vincente

Minnelli's *Some Came Running* (1959), in which he played a happy-go-lucky gambler, hooked up with Frank Sinatra and Shirley MacLaine as a floozy "with a heart of gold," and *Rio Bravo* (1959), a Howard Hawks western made as an angry response to FRED ZINNEMANN's allegorical western, *High Noon* (1952). In *Rio Bravo,* Martin, always one to joke about his drinking, played an alcoholic lawman who reforms himself to save the day. The role in *Some Came Running* was also close to the actor's own temperament. Perhaps Dean Martin succeeded best when playing himself.

References Schnell, William. *Martini Man: The Life of Dean Martin* (Dallas, Tex.: Taylor, 1999); Tosches, Nick. *Dino: Living High in the Dirty Business of Dreams* (New York: Delta, 1992).

—T.L.E. and J.M.W.

Martinelli, Elsa

(1932–   ) The beautiful Italian actress Elsa Martinelli played the role of Hilda, the *Hausfrau* who performs domestic duties outside the courtroom in ORSON WELLES's adaptation of FRANZ KAFKA's *THE TRIAL* (1962). She was born in Gorsseto, Italy, and worked as a barmaid and a model before Kirk Douglas discovered her and featured her in his film, *The Indian Fighter* in 1955. Most of her films were international productions (French and Italian), with a few exceptions: *Hatari!* (1962), *The Pigeon That Took Rome* (1962) and *Rampage* (1963), all American productions. Later work included *Belle Starr* (1979), directed by an uncredited Lina Wertmüller, and *Once Upon a Crime* (1992).

—T.L.E.

Mature, Victor

(1916–1999) Heartthrob actor Victor Mature, who courted RITA HAYWORTH before WELLES captured her heart, acted with Orson Welles in only one film, *THE TARTARS* (1962). Rita Hayworth had co-starred with Victor Mature in *My Gal Sal* (1942). Orson Welles charmed her away from him while Mature was serving in the Coast Guard in 1942. Welles and Mature were not especially close, therefore, when they found themselves cast in Richard Thorpe's film *The Tartars* (1962). Welles told PETER BOGDANOVICH that Mature came to believe Welles had built up his shoes by two inches. Accordingly "he went and got *his* sandals built up three inches high, and he could hardly walk." Welles was amused by this because in all their scenes together, Welles was sitting on a throne. Welles's story has been contested by the production manager, who said that in one scene Welles was supposed to descend the steps from his throne to meet Mature. When Welles saw a Mature wobbling on his high heels, Welles stayed on the last step, keeping one step above Victor Mature. Mature was also irritated that in a particular scene Welles got two close-ups to Mature's one. Director Thorpe agreed to give Mature three close-ups, but the cameraman only pretended to film the extra shots.

Victor Mature was born on January 29, 1916, in Louisville, Kentucky, the son of a Swiss immigrant. After his arrival in Hollywood, he appeared for several years at the Pasadena Playhouse, before being cast

Victor Mature *(National Film Society Archive)*

in his first film, *The Housekeeper's Daughter* (1939). One of his more memorable star turns was playing Doc Holliday in John Ford's classic western, *My Darling Clementine* (1946). He also appeared in many biblical films because of his physique: *Samson and Delilah* (1949), *The Robe* (1953), *Demetrius and the Gladiators* (1954), and even *Androcles and the Lion* (1953), adapted from the play by GEORGE BERNARD SHAW.

—T.L.E. and J.M.W.

Maugham, (William) Somerset (1874–1965)

On December 7, 1931, ORSON WELLES appeared as Lord Porteous in an amateur production of Somerset Maugham's *The Circle* at the Abbey Theatre in Dublin. His performance received mixed reviews. In THREE CASES OF MURDER (1955), an "omnibus" film featuring three separate stories, Welles appeared in "Lord Mountdrago," adapted from Somerset Maugham's short story. In the filmed segment, Welles played a British foreign secretary adept at overwhelming his opponents with his acidic wit. FRANK BRADY observes that Welles seemed perfectly cast since he squared so well with Maugham's description of his character: "He was a brilliant debater and his gift of repartee was celebrated. He had a fine presence: he was a tall, handsome man, rather bald and somewhat too stout, but this gave him solidity and an air of maturity that were of service to him." Brady adds that Welles "gave a performance that was a study in caustic urbanity."

Somerset Maugham, the son of Robert Ormond Maugham, a lawyer who was serving as a legal attaché at the British embassy, was born on January 25, 1874, at the British embassy in Paris. After the death of both his parents, he was sent to live with his uncle, a vicar in Whitstable, England. The French-speaking Maugham, ill at ease in English, soon developed a stammer that he never conquered. Privately educated for the most part, the exception a disastrous year at King's School, Canterbury, he began in 1891 further study in Germany, where he had his first homosexual experience. In 1892, he returned to England to study medicine, and in 1897 he published his first novel, *Liza of Lambeth,* based on his years at Lambeth Hospital. After publishing another novel, a book of short stories, and a travel book, he had his first theatrical success in 1907: *Lady Frederick* ran for over a year at the Royal Court Theatre in London. His service in World War I was followed by the publication of his most famous novel, *Of Human Bondage* (1915), an autobiographical account of his youth. *The Moon and Sixpence,* a novel about the life of Paul Gauguin, was published in 1919, and two years later his play *The Circle* began a long run on the London stage. *Our Betters* (1923) and *The Constant Wife* (1927) were also successful on the stage, and in 1930 he published *Cakes and Ale,* a comedy-of-manners novel. After 1930, he continued to write short stories, novels, criticism and essays, and travel books, but his best work was behind him by then. *The Summing Up,* which he called an "autobiographical sketch," appeared in 1938. When he died on December 16, 1965, he had established a reputation as one of the 20th century's most outstanding and most widely read authors.

References Burt, Forrest D. *W. Somerset Maugham* (Boston: Twayne, 1986); Calder, Robert. *Willie, the Life of W. Somerset Maugham* (New York: St. Martin's Press, 1989); Whitehead, John. *Maugham: A Reappraisal* (Totowa, N.J.: Barnes & Noble, 1987).

—T.L.E.

Mayer, Louis B. (Eliezer [Lazar] Mayer)

(1885–1957) Influential Metro-Goldwyn-Mayer (MGM) chief and staunch Republican, Louis B. Mayer headed the unsuccessful Hollywood effort to prevent the exhibition of ORSON WELLES's *CITIZEN KANE* (1941), a film that depicts a publishing magnate who closely resembles WILLIAM RANDOLPH HEARST, head of Hearst Publishing. After Hollywood columnist LOUELLA PARSONS saw *Citizen Kane,* she warned Hearst, who was her employer, and his lawyers that the film was offensive. At Hearst's prompting, she asked several studio executives, including Mayer, for their help in preventing the distribution and exhibition of the film. She reportedly told them, "If you boys [studio executives] want private lives, I'll give you private lives," a thinly veiled threat that the Hearst newspaper chain would publish details, including their sexual exploits, about their private lives if they did not intervene on Hearst's behalf.

According to FRANK BRADY, Hearst also called Mayer, who was a friend, and, while not threatening the film industry, pointed out that "he would have to do something in retaliation" in order to protect "himself and other publishers from additional attacks from studios." He also reminded Mayer that his newspapers had often helped the studios by suppressing scandalous stories and by providing helpful publicity to certain films. Mayer reportedly "wept in empathy for his old friend" when he saw *Citizen Kane.*

The sympathetic Mayer tried to help Hearst by approaching, through Nicholas Schenck, head of Loew's, MGM's parent company, GEORGE SCHAFER, president of RKO. In his *Hollywood Rajah,* a biography of Mayer, Bosley Crowther wrote that Schenck told Schaefer, "Louis has asked me to speak to you about this picture. He is prepared to pay you what it cost, which he understands is eight hundred thousand dollars, if you will destroy the negative and all the prints." Schaefer, despite the pressure, went ahead with the film, perhaps because he did not want to appease Mayer, who had earlier tried to get him to hire one of his friends to run the RKO studios after Schaefer became president of that studio in 1939. According to Crowther, "Schaefer had no use for Mayer."

Louis B. Mayer, who was born on July 4, 1885, in Minsk, Russia, immigrated to New York with his parents, who subsequently moved to St. John, New Brunswick, Canada. After Mayer finished elementary school, he went to work for his father, who had developed a lucrative scrap metal business. Mayer moved to Boston, where he started his own scrap metal operation and, in 1907, he bought and renovated a decrepit movie theater in Haverhill, Massachusetts, the first theater in what soon became a large theater chain. In 1914, he went into the distribution business and made a small fortune by distributing D. W. Griffith's controversial *The Birth of a Nation* in 1915. Mayer next moved into production with Alco, later to be Metro, which he left in 1917 to form Louis B. Mayer Pictures in Hollywood. When Marcus Loew, head of Metro, gained controlling interests in Mayer's company and in Goldwyn's company, he created MGM, which became, under Mayer's leadership, *the* quality Hollywood film company during the 1930s and 1940s. Mayer's success made him a wealthy man; his salary was the highest in the United States. Politically conservative, he became friends with other wealthy men, including Hearst and Henry Ford. In 1951, Mayer lost control of MGM to Dore Schary, who had worked for him. After his ouster, Mayer worked as an adviser to the Cinerama Company and tried to sway the opinion of Loew's stockholders against the MGM management that succeeded him. He died in 1957.

References Altman, Diana. *Hollywood East: Louis B. Mayer and the Origins of the Studio System* (New York: Carol, 1992); Crowther, Bosley. *Hollywood Rajah: The Life and Times of Louis B. Mayer* (New York: Dell, 1961); Higham, Charles. *Merchant of Dreams: Louis B. Mayer, M.G.M. and the Secret Hollywood* (New York: D.I. Fine, 1993).

—T.L.E.

McBride, Joseph (1947–)

A member of what critic Stanley Kauffmann called the "Film Generation," Joseph McBride was able to interview ORSON WELLES in Los Angeles when the director was "about to start shooting a new film, THE OTHER SIDE OF THE WIND" in August of 1970. At that time, McBride had completed most of the research for his book, *Orson Welles,* published in the "Cinema One" series by Viking Press in 1972. McBride also interviewed writer-director PETER BOGDANOVICH, who was also working with Welles on an interview book entitled *This Is Orson Welles.* Both Bogdanovich and McBride were offered roles in the film Welles was making while they were given the opportunity to observe Welles at work late in his career. The book covers the director's life and career from THE HEARTS OF AGE (1934), which McBride managed to view, to THE IMMORTAL STORY (1968). The book was organized into chapters treating the major films and concludes with "A Catalogue of Orson Welles's Career." Sections of the book had appeared earlier in *Film Quarterly, Sight and Sound,* and *Film Heritage.* After serving as president of the Wisconsin Film Society, McBride worked as a reporter for the *Wisconsin State Journal* and was editor of a small journal, *The Persistence of Vision. Orson Welles* was one of two books he published in 1972, the other being *Focus on*

Howard Hawks, which he edited for Prentice Hall. He later covered the film industry for *Daily Variety* and wrote the iconoclastic, controversial but thoroughly researched *Frank Capra: The Catastrophe of Success,* published by Simon & Schuster in 1992. This was followed by *Steven Spielberg: A Biography,* also published by Simon & Schuster, in 1997.

—J.M.W.

McCambridge, [Carlotta] Mercedes [Agnes] (1918–)

Mercedes McCambridge was especially distinctive as the black-garbed gangleader in ORSON WELLES's TOUCH OF EVIL (1958). She was born on March 17, 1918, in Joliet, Illinois. She started performing on Chicago radio while still a student at Mundelein College and soon became a popular and admired radio actress. Orson Welles, who worked with her on the "Ford Theater" radio series, thought she was "the world's greatest living radio actress." She moved on to New York to assume a role in *Abie's Irish Rose* on radio and made her stage debut in Washington in *Hope for the Best* (1944). Eventually courted by Hollywood, she won a best supporting actress Oscar for her first screen role, in *All the King's Men* (1949). This achievement was followed by *Inside Straight, Lightning Strikes Twice,* and *The Scarf,* all in 1951. She earned another Academy Award nomination in 1956 for her role in George Stevens's *Giant.* However, she is probably best remembered for her strong character roles. In 1954, for example, she appeared in Nicolas Ray's eccentric western *Johnny Guitar,* playing the hateful Emma Small, nemesis of Joan Crawford's character, concluding in one of the strangest western shoot-outs in Hollywood memory. This performance was later matched in intensity in *Touch of Evil* by her rendering of a wicked lesbian gang leader who seductively whispers to the terrified JANET LEIGH: "Do you know what marijuana is?" In her memoir, *There Really Was a Hollywood* (1984), Janet Leigh wrote of McCambridge "In a cameo role as the leader of the gang who attacked me, [she] chilled my bones when she uttered that one line, 'I want to watch!'"

Because of a problem with alcoholism, which she eventually overcame, she made no films between 1961 and 1965 and only a few films thereafter. She preferred using her remarkable voice in radio and off-screen in films. Hers is the effectively terrifying (uncredited) off-screen voice of the devil on the sound track of William Friedkin's *The Exorcist* (1973), for example. Her last screen role was in *Echoes* (1983). She also worked in television: In 1956, she had the lead role in *Wire Service,* and in 1979 she appeared in a miniseries entitled *The Sacketts.* During the 1980s, she performed in national tours of John Pielmeier's *Agnes of God* and Marsha Norman's *'night Mother.* She wrote two autobiographical memoirs, *The Two of Us* (1960) and *The Quality of Mercy* (1981).

References McCambridge, Mercedes. *The Quality of Mercy* (New York: Times Books, 1981); ———, *The Two of Us* (London: P. Davies, 1960).

—J.M.W. and T.L.E.

McCarthy, Joseph (1908–1957) U.S. Republican senator from Wisconsin, 1947–1957 who might have been challenged in his initial race for the Senate in 1946 had WELLES been persuaded to run as a Democrat against him.

Born near Appleton, Wisconsin, in 1908, McCarthy practiced law in Wisconsin and became a circuit judge in 1940. He served with the U.S. Marines in the Pacific during World War II, attaining the rank of captain. In 1946, in a huge upset, McCarthy defeated Senator Robert M. La Follette, Jr., for the Republican senatorial nomination. The Democratic Party, looking to run a strong campaign against the Republican upstart, made a study to assess Welles's chances. They concluded that since McCarthy enjoyed the support of the state's strong dairy interests, Welles's only chance rested with becoming a fully committed campaigner. Welles, who at the behest of PRESIDENT ROOSEVELT had flirted with running for the Senate from California in 1944, decided to bypass the Wisconsin challenge. With Welles out of the picture, Wisconsin Democrats put up a relatively unknown candidate who was handily defeated by McCarthy.

McCarthy's career in the U.S. Senate was obscure until February 1950, when he gained national attention with a speech in Wheeling, West Virginia, charging that the U.S. State Department had been infiltrated by communists. Although a Senate investi-

gating committee had exonerated the State Department and branded the charges a fraud, McCarthy repeated his accusations in a series of inflammatory television and radio appearances. Challenged to produce supporting evidence, McCarthy refused and instead made new allegations. When the Republicans gained control of Congress in 1953, McCarthy, who had been reelected in 1952, was appointed chair of the Senate Government Operations Committee, a powerful post that enabled him to further exploit the public's anxieties about alleged communist infiltration. Through widely publicized hearings amplified by the new medium of television, McCarthy waged an increasingly demagogic campaign to root out subversives through unidentified informers and reckless headline-grabbing accusations. In the process, careers were ruined on the flimsiest evidence, causing his methods to come under increasing attack. In April 1954, McCarthy foolishly accused Secretary of the Army Robert T. Stevens and his aides of concealing evidence of espionage at Fort Monmouth, New Jersey. The army, in turn, accused McCarthy and his chief counsel, Roy Cohn, of seeking by improper means to obtain preferential treatment for a former consultant to the committee, then a private in the army. In 1954, after the widely televised Army-McCarthy hearings, McCarthy and his aides were cleared. Still, the damage was done.

"Exposed" by television, the tide of public opinion started to shift away from the junior senator from Wisconsin. In December 1954, the Senate, acting on a motion of censure, voted to "condemn" McCarthy for contempt of a Senate elections subcommittee that had investigated his financial affairs in 1952, as well as for abuse of fellow senators and insults to the Senate itself during the censure proceedings. After this stern rebuke, McCarthy's influence in the Senate and on the national scene continued to diminish until his death in 1957.

McCarthy's indiscriminate attacks against the wrongly accused gave rise to the term *McCarthyism,* which soon came to refer to similarly groundless assaults abetted by sensationalist tactics, and manipulation of the news media.

Years later, Welles mused on McCarthy for the BBC: "Supposing I did become such a great campaigner and I did defeat him? There would not have been a McCarthy era. I have that on my conscience." He also revealed that he had regarded a Senate seat as a stepping-stone to the presidency. But, he lamented: "I didn't think anybody could get elected president who had been divorced and was an actor." Then, in taking the measure of Ronald Reagan's success, Welles said: "I made a helluva mistake!"

—C.B.

McClintic, Guthrie (1893–1961) Theatrical producer Guthrie McClintic, husband of actress KATHERINE CORNELL, met ORSON WELLES on September 18, 1933. Without asking Welles to read for him, McClintic hired him to play Marchbanks in SHAW's *Candida* and Octavius Moulton Barrett in Rudolph Besier's *The Barretts of Wimpole Street.* McClintic later cast him as Mercutio in *MACBETH.* Welles played the three roles in the Cornell/McClintic repertory company's 36-week national tour 1933–34. With a letter of recommendation from writer THORNTON WILDER, Welles met ALEXANDER WOOLLCOTT, who, in turn, recommended Welles to McClintic as a young man with a familiarity and knowledge of Shakespeare. Although he was impressed by Welles, McClintic disapproved of Welles's "hammy" acting style, which was at odds with the kind of polished consistency that McClintic sought from his actors. McClintic said of Welles's *Candida* role, "His Marchbanks to my way of thinking was never right." Although he was very successful as Mercutio, Welles seemed incapable of pleasing McClintic, who also disapproved of Welles's lifestyle: "He was at all times during this long tour an arresting, stimulating, and at moments exasperating member of the company." When Cornell and McClintic took their *Romeo and Juliet* to Broadway late in 1934, they invited Welles to rejoin the company, but they "demoted" him, asking him to play Tybalt and giving the meatier Mercutio role to Brian Aherne. As a result of his experience with McClintic, Welles rejected conventional methods of staging Shakespeare. Welles's *FIVE KINGS* production was, according to SIMON CALLOW, "the Mercury's definitive claim to creating a new American Shakespearean tradition (Welles's gauntlet flung down, both to the McClin-

tics and to the English upstart, Maurice Evans, who had recently had the audacity to tour the country as Richard II *and* Falstaff)."

Guthrie McClintic, born in Seattle in 1893, moved to New York in 1910 to study acting at the American Academy of Dramatic Art. He began as a stage manager for producer-director Winthrop Ames and got his first directing job in 1918, but the play closed before it got to New York. In 1920, he directed for a stock company in Detroit, doing a play a week for 17 weeks. In 1921, his fortunes improved. He had a Broadway hit, A. A. Milne's *The Dover Road,* and he married actress Katherine Cornell. In the next nine years he produced 26 more plays, among them Michael Arlen's *The Green Hat* (1926), starring Cornell; it was their first collaborative success. By 1930, he had, by repeatedly using the same actors, gathered together a kind of repertory company, one that he was to utilize as he moved from topical, controversial plays to the classics. Rudolph Besier's *The Barretts of Wimpole Street,* one of their first hits (1931), became a staple for the company, and when Welles toured with them in 1933–34 he acted in the play. During the 1930s and 1940s, McClintic produced and directed many plays by Shakespeare, Shaw, Chekhov, and Anouilh, but he stopped directing and producing in 1957. Only George Abbott topped McClintic in the number of Broadway plays staged. As a director, McClintic focused on technique and polish, conducted lengthy readings and rehearsals, and favored working with actors who were articulate and graceful. He was not noted for staging plays that made audiences deal with psychological realism. Skilled at casting, lighting, and stage design, he was a talented director unwilling to take chances, hesitant to experiment, and sure to frustrate the innovative, creative "boy genius," Orson Welles.

Reference McClintic, Guthrie. *Me and Kit* (Boston: Little Brown, 1955).

—T.L.E.

McCormack, Patty (1945–) Patty McCormack appeared with ORSON WELLES in his uncompleted film *DON QUIXOTE,* which was spun off his 30-minute television drama for CBS. When a CBS representative saw some of the unedited footage, which he did not like, CBS refused to grant Welles funds to complete the film. According to FRANK BRADY, Welles was pleased with their decision because he had decided to make a feature film that used the Quixote material, as well as material that would provide Spanish folklore and history. Welles, who narrated the film, had child actress McCormack play a young American tourist whose questions prompt him to narrate the story. At another point in the film McCormack and Welles are shot at the bullring gate. In response to McCormack's "Was Mr. Quixote a bullfighter?" Welles answers, "A bullfighter works for money. Don Quixote was an aficionado." The comment is appropriate since Welles was himself a film aficionado who had to work for money to finance his films. BARBARA LEAMING, who spoke with McCormack about the film, writes, "Where others saw the public persona that Orson calls 'Crazy Welles,' she saw only the 'twinkle in his eye' that gave it all away. She knew he was playing."

Patty McCormack, who was born on August 21, 1945, in Brooklyn, New York, modeled at age four and appeared on television at age seven. She made her film debut in 1951 in *Two Gals and a Guy*, but it was her role as the murderous child in the stage and screen productions of *The Bad Seed* (1954 and 1956) that brought her stardom. In the 1960s, she played rebellious teenagers: *The Explosive Generation* (1961), *The Mini-Skirt Mob,* and *The Young Runaways* (both 1968). McCormack also appeared in television series: *Mama* (1953–57) and *The Poppers* (1979–80). Her film career was effectively over in the late 1960s. When she returned to film in 1988 with *Saturday the 14th Strikes Back,* she was cast as a mother.

—T.L.E.

McDowall, Roddy (Roderick Andrew Anthony Jude McDowall) (1928–1998)

McDowall was cast as Malcolm in WELLES's stage and screen versions of Shakespeare's (see SHAKESPEARE BY WELLES) *MACBETH.* The stage version was the third play performed at the Utah Centennial Festival in Salt Lake City in May 1947. According to FRANK BRADY, "Welles and company were a hit. Salt Lakers were especially dazzled to get a look at former child star Roddy McDowall, as Malcolm." McDowall helped publicize the play by writing a column for Salt Lake City's *Deseret News.* When the film was shot a little later (1948), McDowall was again cast as Malcolm and gave, according to Welles in conversation with PETER BOGDANOVICH, a "very convincing" performance. Born in London on September 17, 1928, McDowall established himself as a child actor and continued in those roles after he was evacuated to the United States in 1940. His best-known films from this period are *How Green Was My Valley* (1941) and *Lassie Come Home* (1942). During the 1950s he worked in television and on the stage. After 1960, he appeared in secondary roles in dozens of films, some distinguished, others not. His best-known films were *The Longest Day* (1962), *Cleopatra* (1963), *The Loved One* (1965), *Inside Daisy Clover* (1966), *The Poseidon Adventure,* and *The Life and Times of Judge Roy Bean* (1972), in addition to the four "Planet of the Apes" films (1968, 1971, 1972, 1973). His last film was *Double Trouble* (1992). He directed Ava Gardner in *Tam Lin / The Devil's Widow* (1971) and was a noted still photographer. His *Double Exposure,* a photography album, was published in 1966. He died in 1998.

—T.L.E.

McGoohan, Patrick (1928–)

In ORSON WELLES's *MOBY DICK—REHEARSED,* which Welles staged in London at the Duke of York's Theatre in 1955, McGoohan was cast as Starbuck, the character who engages Ahab, played by Welles, in endless philosophical debates. According to DAVID THOMSON, "McGoohan cherished Welles, even if he was horrified at the great man's irresponsibility, the drinking and the business folly." Welles, who respected McGoohan's abilities, told PETER BOGDANOVICH that McGoohan would "now be, I think, one of the big actors of his generation if TV hadn't grabbed him."

Patrick McGoohan, although born in Astoria, Queens, New York, on March 19, 1928, became a leading figure on the British stage and then devoted himself primarily to television. He starred in several television action series, such as *Danger Man, The Prisoner, Rafferty,* and *Secret Agent,* playing tough heroes. A guest appearance on the television series *Colombo* won him an Emmy in 1967. He has also directed some of his television shows and a television movie, *Colombo: Agenda for Murder* (1990).

Because of his activity on television, he has appeared in relatively few films, but some of them have been outstanding: *I Am a Camera* (1955), *The Quare Fellow* (1962), *Mary Queen of Scots* (1971), and *Escape from Alcatraz* (1979).

—T.L.E.

Mercury Summer Theatre on the Air   A 1946 half-hour dramatic radio series featuring WELLES.

Within days of the opening of AROUND THE WORLD IN 80 DAYS on Broadway, Welles began a new radio series, the *Mercury Summer Theatre on the Air.* Sponsored by Pabst Blue Ribbon beer, it was devoted to stories that had already been broadcast by the Mercury. For its debut, Welles elected to promote his latest Broadway venture with a musical version of *Around the World in 80 Days* featuring songs from the show by COLE PORTER. "Tonight is one of the first things we ever put on the radio," Welles opened. "And by no coincidence, whatsoever, it is the very latest thing we've put on the stage. You can see it now on Broadway at the Adelphi Theatre, Sunday evenings included—and if you're one of the staunchest friends you'll remember it from among our first Mercury broadcasts." Welles couldn't help but chuckle at the blatant self-promotion, which, along with favorable reviews of the Broadway show, probably didn't hurt the show's initial box-office success.

Broadcast by CBS, the "old wine in new bottles" approach was bestowed on such venerable tales as *The Count of Monte Cristo,* JANE EYRE, and *A PASSENGER TO BALI.* After spiraling costs had forced the cancellation of the disastrous Broadway version of *Around the World in 80 Days,* Welles, his spirits somehow still intact, revamped the format of *Mercury Summer Theatre on the Air.* Instead of dramatizing only past Mercury favorites, Welles opted to finish his contract with several plays that he had never before sent out over the airwaves, including Galsworthy's *The Apple Tree,* Melville's *Moby Dick,* and Shakespeare's KING LEAR (see SHAKESPEARE BY WELLES).

The *Mercury Summer Theatre on the Air* was broadcast nationally by CBS and ran weekly from June 7 to September 13, 1946.

—C.B.

Mercury Theatre   In 1937, WELLES and JOHN HOUSEMAN formed the Mercury Theatre, an offshoot of their successful collaboration in the FEDERAL THEATRE production of THE CRADLE WILL ROCK in the summer of 1937. According to JOHN RUSSELL TAYLOR, the Mercury Theatre published a "Declaration of Principles," similar to the "Declaration of Principles" in CITIZEN KANE: "mixed classics, low prices, no particular political commitment." The theater they used was the Comedy on West 41st Street in New York.

Mercury's first production was the highly successful adaptation (by Welles) of Shakespeare's (see SHAKESPEARE BY WELLES) JULIUS CAESAR. Welles directed, Houseman produced, and MARC BLITZSTEIN wrote the music. In addition to writing and directing, Welles played the part of Brutus. Featured in the cast were two charter members of the Mercury players, JOSEPH COTTEN as Publius and GEORGE COULOURIS as Marc Antony. Others who began long careers with Mercury and continued to work with Welles through the Hollywood years of *Citizen Kane* (1941) and THE MAGNIFICENT AMBERSONS (1942) include AGNES MOOREHEAD, EVERETT SLOANE, and RAY COLLINS. *Julius Caesar* was considered "the definitive Mercury production in its supreme theatricality," according to producer Norman Lloyd. From the start, Welles's theatrical productions were distinctive. John Russell Taylor, who discusses the extent of Welles's contributions to his productions, wrote, "A Welles stage production always looked like a Welles stage production and nothing else, just as a Welles film is always unmistakably a Welles film, in its grandeurs and its follies."

In January 1938, Welles and Houseman directed and produced, respectively, Thomas Dekker's English Renaissance comedy, *The Shoemaker's Holiday.* Both *Caesar* and *Holiday* received unanimous critical acclaim, and played in repertory at the National Theater in Manhattan through the spring of 1938. With the reopening of Marc Blitzstein's *The Cradle Will Rock* (originally produced by Welles and Houseman in the summer of 1937 as a Federal Theatre project) the Mercury Theatre had three productions running simultaneously in New York. The final production of the 1937 season was GEORGE BERNARD SHAW's HEARTBREAK HOUSE, which also received excellent reviews.

In July 1938, Welles expanded the Mercury Theatre operation to include weekly radio dramas adapted, produced, and directed by Welles for CBS. *FIRST PERSON SINGULAR* later became *THE MERCURY THEATRE ON THE AIR,* and later became *THE CAMPBELL PLAYHOUSE.* These radio productions, which aired from July 11, 1938, to June 2, 1939, and from September 10, 1939, to March 31, 1940, were the result of a deal with CBS to produce weekly dramatic programs based on great works of literature that would serve as a summer replacement for Cecil B. DeMille's popular *Lux Radio Theatre.* One major achievement was Welles's ability to persuade many talented and respected professionals to perform in these radio dramas, such as BEA LILLIE, MARY ASTOR, and JOHN BARRYMORE.

The *Mercury Theatre on the Air* gained considerable notoriety with its best-known effort, the October 30th broadcast of H. G. WELLS's *THE WAR OF THE WORLDS.* The program simulated a newscast and convinced close to 2 million people that Martian invaders had landed in New Jersey. In the aftermath Welles was held by some to be a creative genius; others maintained that he was a malicious prankster who deserved to be indicted. He profusely apologized, but the priceless publicity was a positive turning point in his career. The Mercury Players continued to perform on the radio until their final broadcast in 1940; thereafter, they played in repertory along with additional actors, in the theater, on the air, and in the recording studio until 1941.

While these radio dramas were being produced, the Mercury Theatre continued its stage productions in New York. Welles was incredibly busy at the time; his marriage to Virginia Welles was deteriorating, and he was having difficulties with his Mercury partner, John Houseman. After considering several plays, among them *THE IMPORTANCE OF BEING EARNEST* and *TOO MUCH JOHNSON,* the Mercury Company opened its second season with Georg Büchner's *DANTON'S DEATH,* an experimental drama concerning the French Revolution. Even though Welles had received a great deal of publicity about his *War of the Worlds* radio production, reviewers were almost unanimous in their criticism of *Danton's Death.* Despite Welles's innovative expressionistic staging,

reviewers found the play too fragmented. When it closed after 24 performances, it, in effect, marked the end of the Mercury Theatre.

—R.C.K., T.L.E., and J.M.W.

Mercury Theatre on the Air   A 1938 CBS radio series produced by WELLES and his MERCURY THEATRE staff that shocked America with its broadcast of *WAR OF THE WORLDS.*

When CBS opted to renew the 1938 experimental radio drama series, *FIRST PERSON SINGULAR,* it returned to the airwaves the very next week, but under a new name, *Mercury Theatre on the Air.* With Welles directing and JOHN HOUSEMAN presiding over the logistics as executive producer, the new series, now freed from the "first person" narrative format of its predecessor, could pursue a variety of narrative approaches. Emboldened with the success of *First Person Singular,* Welles's first opportunity in radio to wield complete creative control, the 23-year-old whirlwind now chose to exploit his well-known successes with the Mercury Theatre. He also presided over the October 30, 1938, airing of *The War of the Worlds,* radio's single most famous broadcast. The 13 programs broadcast under the banner of *Mercury Theatre on the Air* include:

JULIUS CAESAR (September 11, 1938). Welles's modern dress adaptation of Shakespeare's (see SHAKE-SPEARE BY WELLES) *JULIUS CAESAR* (1937) had been the Mercury Theatre's greatest theatrical triumph. Comparing Caesar's Rome to the contemporary power struggles in Europe, the play had achieved much of its impact through Welles's brilliant mise-en-scène. In adapting the play for radio, Welles's greatest challenge was in finding audio correlatives for the play's spectacular visual effects. The solution was to add a news-style commentary. Because he was playing Brutus, Welles hired H. V. Kaltenborn, dean of radio newscasters, to narrate.

Welles explained his intentions in the broadcast's prologue: "Good evening. *Julius Caesar* was done by the Mercury Theatre without benefit of toga. It was as timely last October as it was sixteen hundred and fifty years after Caesar's murder when Shakespeare wrote it and it is as timely today. A glance at your newspaper headlines and you'll understand why tonight we could wish for the extra dimension of television . . . we have arranged a running commentary on the action of a play. No voice is better known and none could be more suitable than radio's outstanding news commentator, Mr. H. V. Kaltenborn." Kaltenborn's narration was assembled from Roman historian Plutarch's *Lives of the Noble Grecians and Romans,* also Shakespeare's primary historical source and the inspiration for his play. Decades later, Welles would employ the same strategy of using a related historical text, Raphael Holinshed's *Chronicles of England and Scotland,* to elaborate on Shakespeare in his theatrical and film adaptations of CHIMES AT MIDNIGHT. Welles's bold revisionary tactic proved an effective means of bringing out Shakespeare's political subtexts while also achieving narrative continuity.

The cast, reassembled from the 1937 theater production, included MARTIN GABEL as Cassius, GEORGE COULOURIS as Antony, and Joseph Holland as Caesar. MARC BLITZSTEIN's impressive musical score was also used.

Jane Eyre (September 18, 1939). Here, Welles took on the melancholy role of Edward Rochester, a role he would reprise in the 1943 film, *JANE EYRE.* Welles inhabited Rochester a year later in a radio version directed by Cecil B. DeMille for *Lux Radio Theatre* (1944), and, once again, in a broadcast he directed for the MERCURY SUMMER THEATRE (1946). Interestingly, Welles collaborator BERNARD HERRMANN composed the music for Welles's 1938 radio version and also for the 1943 film.

Sherlock Holmes (September 25, 1938). Welles fondly recalled having seen as a child a legendary stage version of Arthur Conan Doyle's Sherlock Holmes tales written by and starring William Gillette, who also wrote TOO MUCH JOHNSON. Since Gillette had died in 1937, Welles, according to FRANK BRADY, used the broadcast as a personal tribute to the memorable actor-playwright. In a number of poignant sequences, Welles effectively deployed sound effects, silences, and minimal dialogue to heighten the aura of danger and suspense.

Oliver Twist (October 2, 1938). An adaptation of Charles Dickens's classic story.

Hell on Ice (October 9, 1938). In a departure from the program's usual fictional format, this edition of *Mercury Theatre on the Air* was given over to an adaptation of the tragic, true-life saga of the De Long expedition chronicled in the book by Edward Ellsberg. Drawing on the captain's log as the basis for the narration, Welles, as the beleaguered explorer, relates the harrowing Arctic tale, which marked a return to the subjective narrative approach so thoroughly exploited by *First Person Singular.*

Seventeen (October 16, 1938). Adapted by HOWARD KOCH at Welles's behest from BOOTH TARKINGTON's short story, this small-town tale finds Welles playing William Sylvanus Baxter, a lovesick and jealous adolescent who falls in love with Lola Pratt and her calflike eyes. Set at the onset of the 20th century, much of the protagonist's behavior would later be elaborated on in Welles's film adaptation of THE MAGNIFICENT AMBERSONS (1942), based on Booth Tarkington's Pulitzer Prize–winning novel. *Seventeen* featured JOSEPH COTTEN and RAY COLLINS, both of whom also appeared in *The Magnificent Ambersons.*

Around the World in 80 Days (October 23, 1938). Welles had long been fascinated with the novels of JULES VERNE and, in particular, *Around the World in 80 Days,* a story he would later turn into a lavish but disastrous theater production called AROUND THE WORLD (1946). Here, working from an adaptation by Howard Koch, the illusion of time passing was cleverly evoked by Bernard Herrmann's metronomic musical segues between scenes. Welles played the role of cold-eyed, globe-trotting adventurer Phineas Fogg.

The War of the Worlds (October 30, 1938). (See THE WAR OF THE WORLDS.)

Heart of Darkness/Life with Father (November 6, 1938). Following the tumult set loose by the sensational broadcast of *The War of the Worlds,* the Mercury company broke with its traditional single-story format to present two different dramatizations. Joseph Conrad's HEART OF DARKNESS, one of Welles's favorite stories, and one which he wanted to make as his first film for RKO, had Welles serving as narrator and playing the evil Kurtz. Special sound effects, including mournfully wailing foghorns and native chants vocalized by Aasta Dafora Horton of "voodoo" MACBETH fame, added to the atmosphere of corrosive degeneration conjured up by Conrad. In

Orson Welles: radio days *(National Film Society Archive)*

the funny and breezily contrasting *Life with Father,* based on *The New Yorker* reminiscences of Clarence Day, Jr., about his prickly upper-class father, Welles took on the roles of the narrator and father.

A Passenger to Bali (November 13, 1938). Based on Ellis St. Joseph's adventures aboard a tramp freighter that first appeared in *Story* magazine, the Welles-adapted drama pits a corrupt Dutch missionary, Rev. Dr. Ralph Walkes (Welles), against the ship's captain. All action takes place on the ship, on the high seas, and in such exotic ports of call as Bangkok and Shanghai. Dramatically, the ship functions as a microcosm in which civilization battles brute force.

The Pickwick Papers (November 20, 1938). Based on the classic novel by Charles Dickens.

Clarence (November 27, 1938). Like *Seventeen* and *The Magnificent Ambersons, Clarence* was another work by midwesterner Booth Tarkington. A hit comedy produced on Broadway (1919), *Clarence* tells the story of a bumbling World War I soldier who helps restore order to the chaotic Wheeler family.

The Bridge at San Luis Rey (December 2, 1938). For the last unsponsored show in the *Mercury Theatre on the Air* series, Welles dramatized the poignant Pulitzer Prize–winning novel, *The Bridge at San Luis Rey,* by THORNTON WILDER. The broadcast was Welles's personal tribute to the famous author who in 1933 had been responsible for helping him get connected to the New York theater scene.

Immediately after the broadcast of *The War of the Worlds,* Welles, at the age of 23, found himself an international celebrity. But what kind of celebrity? At first he feared that CBS might be forced to cancel the *Mercury Theatre on the Air.* Indeed, in his darkest moments, he envisioned being banned from broadcasting. However, Campbell Soups, which had been scouting the program, decided almost immediately to become its sponsor. Although it took weeks for the contractual and logistical details to be worked out, on December 9, 1938, with a broadcast of an adaptation of Daphne duMaurier's *Rebecca,* the *Mercury Theatre on the Air* became THE CAMPBELL PLAYHOUSE.

—C.B.

Mercury Wonder Show, The "I discovered at the age of six," WELLES once recounted, "that almost everything in this world was phony, worked with mirrors. Since then, I've always wanted to be a magician." In 1943, he set about realizing that ambition. Investing over $40,000 of his own money into what was to be called the *The Mercury Wonder Show,* he set up a huge circus tent in the middle of Hollywood at 9000 Cahuenga Boulevard, and after extensive rehearsals, opened the show. Much of the magic was vaudevillian in nature, with cards, lighted cigarettes, bouquets, and rabbits appearing and disappearing to the delight of the mostly sold-out audiences of 2,000 per night. There were also illusions. One of the most spectacular of these involved a substitution. On opening night, JOSEPH COTTEN was tied up in a large sack and stuffed into a trunk. The trunk was then bound with heavy ropes. After concealing the container, Welles uttered "Presto," drew back the curtain, and opened the trunk. Instead of Cotten, up popped the most beautiful girl in the world, the dazzling RITA HAYWORTH. In another popular illusion, Welles sawed the gorgeous pin-up in half.

Welles was in his element. Donning a fez and long black-and-white striped silk robe, he confided to his audience: "Ladies and gentlemen, tonight we are going to reproduce the occult secrets of antiquity, provide original experiments in animal magnetism, and furnish readings on the Magic Crystal, *but* because of the unbelievable strain on the practitioner of this incredible feat, the management must reserve the right to change this position of the program without notice." In the course of the evening, Welles gave psychic readings, ate needles, swallowed fire, hypnotized roosters, and bantered with the audience. The show's pièce de résistance was a bullet-catching illusion. A rifleman fired a live round just to the side of Welles's head that whizzed past harmlessly into an offstage mattress. At the sound of the shot, Welles jerked his head, and slid another bullet hidden in his mouth to his teeth. The audience was stunned. Then, realizing that Welles was safe, and had "caught" the bullet between his teeth, the audience cheered.

Welles did not stint on the show's production. Seeking to establish a carnival atmosphere, he brought in bright red circus wagons, spread sawdust over the floor, hired an assortment of clowns, jugglers, and acrobats, and created a live menagerie that included a lion, tiger, and leopard. Comic hijinks and circus music were other elements that added to the experience. Prevailing on his Hollywood friends, there were dashes of star power as the aforementioned Rita Hayworth, Joseph Cotten, AGNES MOOREHEAD, and MARLENE DIETRICH happily volunteered their services.

The one-month run of *The Mercury Wonder Show* was a huge success. First, it allowed Welles to actualize his dream of being a professional magician. Second, it provided great publicity since Welles allowed servicemen to see the show without charge. Third, after expenses, Welles, who had pledged to donate any profits from ticket sales to charity, wrote out a generous check to the Assistance League, which helped soldiers and sailors in financial difficulties. Fourth, *The Mercury Wonder Show* served as an opportunity to woo the voluptuous Rita Hayworth, who became the second Mrs. Orson Welles on September 7, 1943. Finally, it led to a cameo appearance in his guise as The Great Orson in Universal's *FOLLOW THE BOYS*, a 1943 morale-boosting film produced by CHARLES K. FELDMAN.

The only hitch in the production involved HARRY COHN, head of Columbia Pictures. Cohn, who had invested heavily to help make Hayworth a star, became so angry with the news that his chief "property" was appearing with Welles without compensation that he immediately pulled her from the show on the pretext that it was a violation of her exclusive contract with Columbia. Many have speculated that it was Cohn's ill-fated efforts to separate the couple that intensified the already hot Welles-Hayworth relationship. Filling in for Hayworth was another Welles crony, the exotic Marlene Dietrich.

In an interesting footnote, JOHNNY CARSON reminded Welles, decades later on *The Tonight Show,* that as a struggling young comedian he had participated in a performance of *The Mercury Wonder Show* as a stand-in for the "victim" to be sawed in half by Welles. Carson, like Welles, was an avid amateur magician.

—C.B.

Meredith, Burgess (George Meredith)

(1908–1998)   Actor and director Burgess Meredith was cast as Prince Hal and Henry V to WELLES's FALSTAFF in the five-hour *FIVE KINGS* stage play (1939) that eventually became the film *CHIMES AT MIDNIGHT* (1967). Meredith was excited initially about appearing in the play: "I was fascinated by the talents of Orson Welles, and I joined him in *Five Kings.*" Although his performance was praised, Meredith was not happy with the production and blamed Welles: "We will always remember it as a towering drama that almost came to pass, but that finally turned into a nightmare. It was a brilliant concept of a great man, but the mechanical problems were never solved." Three days before the play opened on February 27, 1939, the overextended Welles appeared with Meredith in the radio version of *State Fair* on THE CAMPBELL PLAYHOUSE. When *Five Kings* opened in Boston, it had never had a real dress rehearsal. Meredith's feelings about the play are revealed in his response to the question about what role he had in *Five Kings:* "I'm Henry V, and it's too bad I didn't perish at Agincourt."

Burgess Meredith, who was born on November 16, 1908, in Cleveland, Ohio, began his theatrical and film career after working as a merchant seaman and businessman. He first appeared on stage in *Winterset* in 1935 and received the critical attention that took him to Hollywood to repeat his *Winterset* role on the screen (1936). He subsequently appeared in many films, either as a lead or in distinctive character roles. His most memorable early role was as George in *Of Mice and Men* (1940), and in 1976 he made his first appearance as the trainer in *Rocky,* for which he received an Oscar nomination for best supporting actor; his other *Rocky* appearances were in *Rocky II* (1979), *Rocky III* (1982), and in *Rocky V* (1990). He won another Oscar nomination for his supporting role in *The Day of the Locust* (1975). He also won an Emmy for his role as lawyer Joseph Welch in "Tale Gunner Joe" (1977), a docudrama about Senator JOSEPH MCCARTHY. Meredith also had many roles on television, the most memorable of which was as the Penguin in the *Batman* series. His autobiography, *So Far, So Good,* was published in 1994.

Reference Meredith, Burgess. *So Far, So Good: A Memoir* (Boston, Little Brown, 1994).

—T.L.E.

Metty, Russell (1906–1978)

Metty, Russell (1906–1978) Cinematographer Russell Metty was born in Los Angeles in 1906. He was employed as a laboratory assistant at Paramount Studios in 1925; in 1929, he went to RKO as an assistant cameraman. In 1935, he was promoted to director of photography. Metty moved from big-budget films like Howard Hawks's *Bringing Up Baby* (1938), with Katharine Hepburn, to low-budget films like *The Falcon's Brother* (1942), an entry in the Falcon detective series, and back again with ease.

Although GREGG TOLAND was the cinematographer on *CITIZEN KANE,* Metty helped ORSON WELLES out during pre-production. He photographed Welles's screen tests of himself, beginning on April 16, 1940, in which Welles tried out the costumes and makeup for Kane at various stages of his life. Since Welles had to age from a youth in his 20s to an elderly man of 75 in the course of the picture, he wanted to be sure from the outset that the aging process would be realistic.

Metty also gave Welles a hand with THE MAGNIFICENT AMBERSONS. Although STANLEY CORTEZ was principal director of photography on the picture, Metty, Harry Wild, and Jack McKenzie shot some scenes, but were uncredited. Cortez was not nearly as experienced as Gregg Toland who had filmed *Kane.* As a result, the young cinematographer was painstakingly slow in lighting a set; and so Welles brought in additional cinematographers like Metty to shoot a few scenes so that the picture did not fall too far behind schedule. Metty already had a reputation for being efficient and fast.

In addition, Metty also figured in an uncompleted Welles project, IT'S ALL TRUE. After Welles finished filming *Ambersons,* the U.S. government commissioned him in 1942 to make a film in Mexico and South America, for which RKO, the studio to which Welles was under contract, had put up the financing. To be precise, the Office of the Coordinator of Inter-American Affairs asked Welles to make a picture that would strengthen the relationship between the Americas during World War II.

It's All True was to be an omnibus film, made up of three parts: an episode highlighting the carnival in Rio (shot in color); an episode with four Brazilian fishermen braving the elements at sea, entitled "Four Men on a Raft"; and "My Name is Bonito," based on a story by the documentarist ROBERT FLAHERTY, about a brave bull that was never killed in the arena and is rewarded by being sent out to pasture. Welles recalls in PETER COWIE's book that the rushes he sent back to Hollywood of the Rio carnival displeased the studio: "No stars, no actors even," as one executive put it; "just a lot of colored people playing their drums and jumping up and down in the streets." The front office decided ultimately that allowing Welles to continue filming was simply throwing good money away after bad; so the picture was shut down.

RKO demanded that Welles surrender the footage for all three episodes. But before he did so, he accepted Russell Metty's offer to arrange the raw footage into a preliminary rough cut, so that Welles could interest potential financial backers in purchasing the footage from the studio and allowing Welles to edit it into a final version as a feature-length film, for which Welles would of course provide a voice-over narration. Welles promised Metty that he would give an explanatory talk prior to the screening for the money men; but he very carelessly forgot to turn up, and the screening was canceled. So Metty's work went for nothing, and the aborted screening spelled the end of the project. The studio brass at RKO was so fed up with Welles that a great deal of the unedited footage was dumped in the Pacific Ocean. But miraculously some of it survived.

In 1985, two-thirds of the rushes for "Four Men on a Raft" were discovered and turned over to the Film Archive at the University of California at Los Angeles. It was turned into a documentary entitled *It's All True: Based on an Unfinished Film by Orson Welles* (1993) by Richard Miller, Myron Meisel, and Bill Krohn (it is available on video cassette).

Metty forgave Welles for the embarrassment that Welles caused him over the screening of *It's All True,* which was canceled, and went on to serve as director of photography on two subsequent Welles pictures. His black-and-white photography on THE STRANGER, with Welles as a Nazi war criminal hiding out in New England, and TOUCH OF EVIL, with Welles as a rogue cop, was outstanding. Metty was physically of Wellesian proportions, even like Welles chewing on a cigar, but, unlike Welles, he could be brusque to the point of rudeness.

Metty was renowned for his complicated crane shots, such as the one that opens *Touch of Evil,* in which the camera, mounted on a 22-foot crane, surveys the entire main street of a town on the Mexican border. Richard Chatten quotes CHARLTON HESTON, who co-starred with Welles in *Touch of Evil,* as saying that many cameramen would ask the director, "Do you want it fast or do you want it good?" Comments Heston, "With Russ, you got both."

Heston described this shot in detail for James Delson:

"Well, for the record, it begins on a close-up" of a man's hand clutching a time bomb, and the camera then "pans just enough to catch the unidentified figure dashing out of the frame." Then Metty's camera "pans down the alley in the direction in which the figure holding the dynamite has fled, on the near side of the building, going in the same direction. You see the figure (and of course now you can't possibly

identify him) dart behind the building. Following with the camera, but still too far away to tell who he is, he lifts the trunk of a car and puts what is obviously a bomb into the car, slams the lid and disappears into the shadows just as the camera, now lifting above the car, picks up the couple coming around the other side of the building and getting in the car. You establish him as a fat political type and she a floozy blond type. And they carry on—there's enough awareness of their dialogue to establish a kind of drunken nonchalance."

The camera zooms up on a Chapman boom as the car drives out of the parking lot and out into the street. The boom sinks down and picks up the car as it passes rundown buildings covered with peeling posters. "The camera then moves ahead of the car; the bomb is ticking all the while, and consequently the filmgoer wonders when it will explode. The car goes through the border station from Mexico into the United States. This extended take (three minutes, 20 seconds in length) comes to a spectacular close as the bomb explodes."

The laying out of this long take was incredibly complicated and was accomplished perfectly by Welles and Metty. In fact, Metty's camerawork serves Welles's intentions throughout the movie. At one point, the mobile camera pushes through the beaded curtains of a smoky Mexican dive, as Vargas (Heston) roughs up an uncooperative suspect, inciting a barroom brawl. Metty's camera is like a whip in this scene, lashing the action into the viewer's face.

Welles insisted that Metty avoid using artificial light for the daytime scenes—an unheard-of technique in Hollywood films of the time; instead, Metty employed natural light in the daytime sequences, which contributed to the stark, newsreellike quality of the cinematography, thereby helping to give the whole movie an air of spare, unvarnished realism. Welles favored Metty's use of natural light sources in the grim scenes that take place at night. This means that there is always an identifiable light source on the set, from which the light would ordinarily come in real life, such as a table lamp. This, too, makes the settings in the film look more like real buildings, and not just movie sets.

FRANK BRADY perceptively declares that Metty was following Welles's very precise instructions during filming and "added little to the conception of the shots." The actual idea of doing the opening scene in a single take, the avoidance of artificial light in the daytime scenes, the camera constantly on the move as it toured the shadowy streets and decaying buildings of the decadent border town—all of this came from Welles.

Metty retired in 1974, leaving behind an impressive track record. In a career that spanned nearly four decades, he served as director of photography for some of the best directors in American cinema, from Orson Welles to STANLEY KUBRICK.

References Brady, Frank. *Citizen Welles: A Biography of Orson Welles* (New York: Scribner's, 1989); Chatten, Richard. "Russell Metty," in *International Dictionary of Films and Filmmakers: Writers and Production Artists,* ed. Grace Jeromski, rev. ed. (Detroit: St. James Press, 1997), vol. 4, 570+; Cowie, Peter. *The Cinema of Orson Welles* (New York: Da Capo, 1989); Curtis, Tony, with Barry Paris. *Tony Curtis: The Autobiography* (New York: William Morrow, 1993); Delson, James. "Heston on Welles," in *Perspectives on Orson Welles,* ed. Morris Beja (New York: G.K. Hall, 1995), 63–72; Higham, Charles. *The Films of Orson Welles* (Los Angeles: University of California Press, 1973); Murch, Walter. "Restoring the Touch of Genius to *Touch of Evil*," *New York Times,* September 6, 1998, sec. 2:1, 16; Stubbs, John. "The Evolution of Welles's *Touch of Evil*," *Cinema Journal* 24, no. 2 (Winter 1985): 19–39; Welles, Orson. "Memo to Universal," in Orson Welles and Peter Bogdanovich, *This Is Orson Welles* (New York: Da Capo, 1998), 491–504.

—G.D.P.

Michael the Brave (Mihai Viteazul) (The Last Crusade)

Romania Film (Buchuresti)/Columbia, 120 minutes, 1973. **Director:** Sergiu Nicolaescu; **Screenplay:** Titus Popovici; **Cinematographer:** George Cornea; **Editor:** Iolanda Mintuleascu; **Cast:** Amza Pellea, Irina Gardescu, Florin Persic, Septimiu Sever, Sergiu Nicolaescu, Aurel Rogalski, Colea Rautu, Orson Welles (not in credits)

According to FRANK BRADY, WELLES appeared in this Romanian epic, which originally (1969) ran for four hours. Cut in half for U.S. and Western European release, it ends with Michael's early victories; his later defeats in his quest to unify Romania were omitted.

—T.L.E.

Miller, Arthur

(1915–) Eminent American playwright and screenwriter who collaborated with WELLES on the 1942–43 radio series, CEILING UNLIMITED.

Fall 1942 proved a difficult period for Welles. Upon returning from a star-crossed trip to South America shooting footage for the eventually aborted *IT'S ALL TRUE,* he had to face the crushing box-office and critical failure of *THE MAGNIFICENT AMBERSONS.* Work, as it had been in the past, proved the best cure for these setbacks. On behalf of the war effort, Welles was asked to produce and star in two new radio programs, *HELLO, AMERICANS* and *Ceiling Unlimited.* The second of these was notable in that it provided a unique opportunity for two 27-year-old veterans of the FEDERAL THEATRE's New York Unit, Welles and future Pulitzer Prize writer Arthur Miller, to collaborate.

Although Miller and Welles had known about each other by reputation, they had never worked together. Miller, one of the main writers assigned to *Ceiling Unlimited,* was surprised and flattered when Welles asked him to come up with a format for the Lockheed-Vega Aircraft Corporation-sponsored aviation show. Miller's response read as follows: " . . . I feel sure about one thing. You don't want any [format]. Your voice is a format. The only two things that must be heard at the beginning of the show every week are your voice and Lockheed-Vega. Those are the two things that must be the same every week but around those two things the variety should be infinite. They alone and by themselves do everything any format can possibly attempt to do. Your voice, if I may say so, portents much." FRANK BRADY, concludes that Miller's prose, "dynamic, almost mythological in tone and cadence, [and] tempered by the patriotic fervor that was part of the day," created a nationally spirited poetry when intoned by Welles.

Miller, who grew up in Brooklyn and was educated at the University of Michigan, soon became one of America's leading playwrights after *Ceiling Unlimited.* His first produced play was *The Man Who*

Had All the Luck (1944), a tale of a man attributing his success to hard work. It ran less than a week. *All My Sons* (1947), a story about a veteran who learns that his father sold defective airplane parts to the government during the war, won the New York Drama Critics Circle Award. Both that award and the Pulitzer Prize went to his most widely known and respected work, *Death of a Salesman* (1949), which deals with the decline and suicide of an aging traveling salesman. His most controversial play, *The Crucible* (1953), a story set during the Salem witch trials, was regarded by many as a thinly disguised attack on JOSEPH MCCARTHY and the senator's demagogic witch-hunts for communists. Miller, himself, soon became a target of the forces of McCarthyism. In 1954, he was called before HUAC (the notorious House Committee on Un-American Activities) and pressed about his alleged communist ties. To his credit, Miller refused to cooperate. Although cited for contempt of Congress, his conviction was overturned on appeal.

Miller's next production was a double bill consisting of *A View from the Bridge,* a story about the murderous jealousy of a longshoreman, and *Memory of Two Mondays,* a slice of workaday life in a Manhattan warehouse. In 1956, Miller was again in the headlines as a result of his marriage to Hollywood sex goddess Marilyn Monroe. In 1961, he wrote his first produced screenplay, *The Misfits* (1961), which was directed by JOHN HUSTON, and starred Monroe and Clark Gable in their last film roles. Miller and Monroe were divorced in 1962. His next full-length play, *After the Fall* (1964), is a semi-autobiographical play based on his marriage to Monroe, while *Incident at Vichy* (also 1964) deals with a group of French citizens arrested by the Nazis. *The Price* (1968), a three-character drama that costarred his sister, the actress Joan Copeland, details the bitter hatred of two brothers. *The Creation of the World and Other Business* (1972), a contemplation of good and evil employing the figures of Adam and Eve, was a failure, as was *The American Clock* (1980), which chronicled the problems of a family set against the background of the depression. Miller enjoyed several successes in television including *Playing for Time* (1980; CBS), a drama about a woman's orchestra formed by concentration

camp prisoners at Auschwitz. In 1985, Dustin Hoffman reprised his stage role of Willy Loman in *Death of a Salesman,* in a much lauded television adaptation by Miller. The playwright similarly adapted his *All My Sons* (1987), *Clara* (1991) and *Broken Glass* (1996) for the small screen. His plays continue to be widely performed and taught.

Miller, a committed liberal, has never hesitated to lace his plays with his progressive philosophy. At the same time, and as attested to by the numerous awards bestowed upon him, Miller, at his best, is a powerful playwright. Among his honors are a Special Tony for Lifetime Achievement (1999), the Dorothy and Lillian Gish Prize (1999), a Special Drama Desk Award for Lifetime Achievement (1998), a Kennedy Center Honors Lifetime Achievement Award (1984), the 1949 Pulitzer Prize in Drama *(Death of a Salesman),* and various Tonys, New Drama Critics Circle Awards, and Emmys for individual plays and television broadcasts.

References Bloom, Harold. *Arthur Miller* (Philadelphia: Chelsea House, 2000); Gussow, Mel. *Conversations with Miller* (London: Nick Hern, 2001); Koorey, Stephanie. *An Annotated and Comprehensive Guide to Arthur Miller's Life and Literature* (Lanham, Md.: Scarecrow, 2001).

—C.B.

Miracle de Sainte Anne, La (film, 1950) As he had done in TOO MUCH JOHNSON (1938) and *AROUND THE WORLD IN 80 DAYS* (1946), WELLES shot part of the story of his one-act play, *THE UNTHINKING LOBSTER,* on film. Since the play was a satire on Hollywood producers of the late 1940s and early 1950s obsessed with producing biblical epics, the use of a film-with-a-play proved an adroit strategy. Of the play, Welles told PETER BOGDANOVICH: "*The Unthinking Lobster* takes place in Hollywood while the town is in the grip of a cycle of religious movies. On one set an Italian neorealist is making the story of a saint like Bernadette who worked miracles and cured the sick. He has just fired the star and replaced her with a secretary from the typists' pool because she seems to have a more spiritual quality. As it turns out, he's only too right. The scene they're shooting has a lot of cripples in it, and the Italian has insisted that, in the interest of believability, on the first day they must be real. So a lot of malformed, miserable people are brought in by the casting department. She blesses them and—behold! They throw away their crutches—they are cured! She *is* a saint. So Hollywood becomes the new Lourdes. People go on their knees through the gates of M-G-M. Little pieces of film are sold as holy amulets. . . . Except for the trade in sacred relics, business is terrible. The industry is only saved by the arrival of an archangel who goes into conference with the studio heads and makes a deal with them: heaven is prepared to suspend any further miracles in Hollywood if, in exchange, Hollywood will stop making religious pictures."

The introductory film featured Juli Gibson in the role of starlet Gloria Granger. Shot in a Parisian park of Butte Chaumont, *La Miracle de Sainte Anne* featured Welles biographer MAURICE BESSY in a small role. "It's got a lot of distinguished Paris celebrities," Welles told Bogdanovich. "It's not supposed to be a very good film—it's just rushes. The play begins in a projection room where they're running rushes."

Like so many other small-scale film projects assembled by Welles, the print of *La Miracle de Sainte Anne* appears to have been lost.

—C.B.

Moby Dick

Moulin/Warner Bros., 116 minutes, 1956. **Director:** John Huston; **Producers:** Huston and Vaughan N. Dean; **Screenplay:** Ray Bradbury and Huston (based on *Moby Dick* by Herman Melville); **Cinematography:** Oswald Morris; **Music:** Philip Sainton; **Editor:** Russell Lloyd; **Cast:** Gregory Peck (Captain Ahab), Richard Basehart (Ishmael), Leo Genn (Starbuck), James Robertson Justice (Captain Boomer), Harry Andrews (Stubb), Bernard Miles (The Manxman), Noel Purcell (Ship's Carpenter), Edric Connor (Daggoo), Mervyn Johns (Peleg), Orson Welles (Father Mapple)

In JOHN HUSTON's film adaptation of Herman Melville's classic American novel, *Moby Dick,* WELLES plays a cameo role as Father Mapple, a fiery preacher who delivers a five-minute sermon from a pulpit shaped like the bow of a ship. Welles's text is from the Old Testament story of Jonah and the whale. The story describes the peril of defying God's will: Jonah attempts to evade God's command that he preach to the people of Nineveh by fleeing on a ship bound for what was then the end of the world. Ahab's quest for the great white whale is seen as analogous to Jonah's futile attempt. As Father Mapple, Welles appears only once, but his thundering sermon is one of the most memorable scenes in the critically acclaimed film. According to Huston, Welles did the scene in one take without making a single mistake. His delivery was enhanced by a generous portion of brandy, which he took just before the cameras rolled. Reaction to his performance was mixed. JAMES NAREMORE found Welles's Father Mapple "hollow and disappointing," and PETER COWIE wrote that "his vignette as Father Mapple in *Moby Dick* is more complementary to his oratory than to his capacity as an actor." FRANK BRADY was more appreciative of Welles's acting efforts.

—T.L.E.

Moby Dick—Rehearsed (The Movie)

Upon the successful completion of the limited run of *MOBY DICK—REHEARSED* at London's Duke of York's Theatre, and recalling his successful 1953 television debut in *KING LEAR* under PETER BROOK's direction, Welles set about making plans for a television movie of his hit play using the London cast. Shooting commenced at the Hackney Empire Theatre in London, and then, briefly, in Turin, Italy, at the Fiat Studio. THOMSON reports that the production came to a rapid halt when the money—whose source and extent no one seemed to know—ran out. PATRICK MCGOOHAN remembers that extensive dialogues between Ahab (Welles) and Starbuck (McGoohan) were shot, which, in the tradition of the philosophical Kane-Leland exchanges in *CITIZEN KANE,* turned out just fine. Although taken aback by Welles's irresponsibility, the drinking, and the lack of business savvy, McGoohan cherished the great man. But in Italy, when the venture came to pieces, McGoohan recalls seeing Welles weeping: "He was a very lonely man."

BARBARA LEAMING, in offering a contrasting version, cites Wolf Mankowitz, who had helped finance the London show: "Orson's attitude is a very pragmatic one. He thinks until you get on the set with the actors and lights and the rest of it, you don't know whether it's going to work or not. And he simply reserves the right as an artist to sort of drop it if it doesn't work. This is always very upsetting to the financiers, who think that they're dealing with a finite and static creature when they're dealing with a creative concept."

In spite of rumors that have periodically surfaced that there is a finished film of Welles's *Moby Dick—Rehearsed* stashed away in some exotic spot, that proposition, according to Leaming, just doesn't hold water. Welles says plainly, echoing Mankowitz above, that he simply gave the project up. "We shot for three days and it was obvious it wasn't going to be any good, so we stopped," he told Leaming. "There was no film made at all. We only did one and a half scenes. I said, let's not go on and waste our money, because it's not going to be any good."

Like so many other events in Welles's career, the truth of the matter probably lies somewhere between money problems and the artistic compromises thus entailed, and the ideal of Welles's pure artistic vision.

—C.B.

Moby Dick—Rehearsed (play, 1955) WELLES

had long been fascinated with Melville's classic novel, which like Shakespeare's (see SHAKESPEARE BY WELLES) *KING LEAR* provided him with yet another dramatic stand-off to the death between men (or beasts) whose overt enmity never quite masks a far more profound and deep-seated mutual respect. As DAVID THOMSON suggests, the comparison of the beleaguered Ahab to the equally beleaguered Welles of the mid-1950s—the self-aware, wounded genius set in rivalry with God—is clear.

In his theatrical adaptation, Welles came up with an ingenious strategy for handling the spectacle of Melville's novel. Instead of trying to realistically re-create the novel's epic events onstage, Welles gave the audience a self-referential play within a play (actually a play within a rehearsal), a backstage meditation involving a troupe of traveling actors in 19th-century New England, who, when the audience first meets them, are in the process of readying a version of *King Lear*. Soon, however, the little company opts to redirect its energies to *Moby Dick*. The 19th-century setting was a particularly astute decision. Indeed, given

his aim of showcasing Melville's lofty sentiments and language, Welles's chest-thumping, Shakespearean style was in perfect tune with the play's 19th-century New England backdrop.

Because what the audience observes is only a rehearsal, the sea, the ship, and the whale are merely "suggested." At several moments, Welles has his actors "aboard" the *Pequod* stand atilt and sway in tandem as if poised on deck in the midst of a roiling tempest. At other times, through strobe and other lighting effects, Welles made the audience seem as if it had plunged to the depths of the sea in a bathysphere. For the London production, which opened for three weeks on June 16, 1955, at the Duke of York's Theatre, Welles assembled a first-rate cast: Joan Plowright (Young Actress/Pip), Gordon Jackson (Young Actor/Ishmael), PATRICK MCGOOHAN (Serious Actor/Starbuck), Kenneth Williams (in a variety of small parts including Very Serious Actor), and Welles as the theater company's Actor-Manager and Captain Ahab. Significantly, Welles also took the role of Father Mapple, the fire-and-brimstone whaling-town preacher, a character Welles had played just two months earlier in JOHN HUSTON's film version of the Melville novel that was released in 1956. Welles's production went smoothly except for Williams, who, as Thomson reports, quickly became disillusioned: "I wish to God I had never *seen* this rotten play, and Orson Welles and the whole filthy tribe of sycophantic bastards connected with this bogus rubbish." Williams, a stickler for staying on script and keeping to blocking patterns worked out in rehearsals, was upset largely because Welles was constantly tinkering with such details as blocking up through and even past opening night. Welles, for his part, was amused, noting, with no small irony, that one of Williams's roles was "Very Serious Actor."

The production also benefited greatly from the contributions of Welles's old colleague from Dublin's GATE THEATRE and the 1934 Todd Summer Festival, HILTON EDWARDS, whose genius for lighting had earned Welles's admiration. Edwards's theatrical panache and peerless technical know-how were among the show's many assets. Another plus was Welles's own brand of Brechtian distancation. He constantly "reminded" the audience that it was watching a play, rather than a naturalistic slice of life, through means such as juxtaposing Ahab's heightened prose against the seamen's slangy exchanges and, of course, the play-within-a-play structure that found the "actors" stepping in and out of and even commenting on their "characters." At the same time, Welles built the maritime atmosphere of the play's sound design with sea chanteys set to Melville's text sung by the actors, and the music of a harmonium.

The London critics were generous in their praise of *Moby Dick—Rehearsed.* "The theatre for Mr. Orson Welles is an adventure; and an adventurer so valiant that our hearts go out even when [he] comes to wreck," opined the *London Times.* "It is outrageous and impossible, but it comes off," said the *News Chronicle.* "As Captain Ahab, Welles has devoured the essence of the living theatre, the lustiness of the Elizabethans and the fearless innocent eye of the barnstorming Victorians." London's *Daily Mail* was similarly ecstatic: "It takes an Orson Welles to conjure a ferocious sea drama out of a background of clothes baskets, packing cases and scraps of irrelevant scenery and to send us away feeling that we, too, have been grappling for our lives with that whale."

Even the prickly KENNETH TYNAN, who had bludgeoned Welles's 1951 London production of OTHELLO, joined the bandwagon: "Mr. Welles has fashioned a peace of pure theatrical megalomania, a sustained assault on the senses which dwarfs anything London has ever seen since, perhaps, the Great Fire. It was exactly fifty years ago last Wednesday evening that Irving made his last appearance in London. I doubt if anyone since then has left his mark more indelibly on every second of a London production than Mr. Welles has on this side of 'Moby Dick.'" Tynan added that if spectators "wish to exert themselves, to have their minds set whirling and their eyes dazzling at sheer theatrical virtuosity, 'Moby Dick' is their opportunity. With it, the theater becomes once more a house of magic." In its limited run, Welles's *Moby Dick—Rehearsed* chalked up 25 performances during its stay at the Duke of York's.

For Welles, and his followers, *Moby Dick—Rehearsed* provided vindication. First, Welles proved that Melville's seemingly "untheatrical" story could indeed be brought to a safe theatrical harbor. Second,

and most significant, he proved anew that the "Boy Wonder" still had the power to make big-time theatrical magic. Simply put, it was his most successful theatrical venture since the glory days of the MERCURY and FEDERAL THEATRE PROJECTS of the late 1930s.

Seven years later, on November 28, 1962, Welles's adaptation opened on Broadway at the Ethel Barrymore Theater, with Rod Steiger taking Welles's roles as Ahab and the Actor-Manager. The New York critics were less generous than their London colleagues. While lauding Welles's theatricality and the stirring readings of Melville's powerful sentiments, they discounted Welles's adaptation as essentially having just skimmed the novel's deep drama. The public seemed to agree. The play ran for only 10 performances.

By that point, it should be pointed out, John Huston's stirring 1956 film adaptation of Melville's masterwork was a still fresh memory, and likely a benchmark against which Welles's New York stage version of *Moby Dick* suffered in comparison, especially given Welles's widely heralded acting turn as Father Mapple.

The script, *Moby Dick—Rehearsed: A Drama in Two Acts,* by Orson Welles, was published by Samuel French, New York, in 1965.

Also see *MOBY DICK—REHEARSED* (The Movie).
—C.B.

Monsieur Verdoux   United Artists, 124 minutes, 1947. **Director:** Charles Chaplin; **Producer:** Chaplin; **Screenplay:** Chaplin (from an idea by Welles); **Cinematographer:** Roland Totheroh and Curt Courant; **Editor:** William Nico; **Music:** Chaplin; **Cast:** Charles Chaplin (Henri Verdoux alias Varnay alias Bonheur alias Floray), Mady Correll (Mona), Allison Roddan (Peter), Robert Lewis (Maurice Bottello), Audrey Betz (Marhta), Martha Raye (Annabella Bonheur), Ada May (Anette), Isobel Elsom (Marie Grosnay)

Chaplin's infamous film about the notorious Landru, the real-life French felon of the 1920s widely known as Bluebeard, was Chaplin's first significant departure from his beloved character of "The Little Tramp." Set during the late 1930s, at the precipice of the war with Germany, Chaplin's Verdoux, although a contented married man and father, is compelled to extreme measures after losing his job as a bank clerk. To keep his little family financially solvent, he woos rich widows and women with savings, murders them, and collects the loot. Although the film was subtitled "A Comedy of Murders," this was black humor in extremis. The film was savagely attacked by the critics, and the public stayed away. Given the grisly subject matter, plus the postwar hounding of Chaplin by the demagogues of the House Un-American Activities Committee, the comedian soon withdrew from the American scene to take up residence in Switzerland, where he lived for the remainder of his life.

WELLES, who regarded Chaplin as a great artist, and who had been introduced to him in the late 1930s by film director King Vidor, claims to have written a script, *The Ladykiller,* which Chaplin later refashioned as *Monsieur Verdoux.* In fact, MERCURY registered several potential titles based on Welles's work. Chaplin, according to Welles, loved the script and agreed to do the project as an RKO-Mercury production with Welles directing. Chaplin soon changed his mind, not wanting to submit to the authority of another director. Later, Welles told PETER BOGDANOVICH that Chaplin's script for *Monsieur Verdoux,* while retaining a lot of Welles's material, had, nonetheless, been "brought up to date. My period was the First World War. . . . [Chaplin] moved it ahead—gave us shots of Hitler and goose-stepping Nazis: you know, social significance."

Welles points out that when *Monsieur Verdoux* opened in New York, there was no acknowledgment of his contribution. Then, when Chaplin was attacked by the New York critics, "the worst lynching by critics you've ever heard," Welles recalled, "the next day—after they'd all said, you know, 'Who gave Chaplin this awful idea?'—up on the screen went my billing: 'Based on an idea suggested by Orson Welles.'" Given the larger-than-life egos of both Chaplin and Welles, their always wary relationship waxed and waned, charting a sinelike wave fluctuating between love and hate, and respect and envy.

—C.B.

Moorehead, Agnes (1906–1974) Born on December 6, 1906, in Clinton, Missouri, Agnes

Moorehead received her master of arts degree at the University of Wisconsin and her Ph.D. in literature at Bradley University. Moorehead graduated to national radio as a member of ORSON WELLES's *MERCURY THEATRE ON THE AIR,* which performed radio dramas. She appeared in *Dracula* (July 11, 1938), *THE WAR OF THE WORLDS* (October 30, 1938), and *Rebecca* (December 9, 1939), among others. She also played opposite Welles in the radio series *THE SHADOW* (1937–38); she was Margot Lane, the Girl Friday of Welles's Lamont Cranston, a mysterious crime fighter.

Welles, who had known Moorehead since his childhood, called her one of the best actresses in the world. Welles inevitably cast her in his first film, *CITIZEN KANE.* In an early scene young Charlie Kane's mother, Mary (Moorehead), negotiates a deal with the banker Mr. Thatcher (GEORGE COULOURIS) in the Kane's boardinghouse in Colorado; with Thatcher as his guardian, young Charlie will be given an education in New York appropriate to a young man who is the heir to a fortune. Mary and Thatcher are seated at a table in the foreground, while Charlie's father Jim (Harry Shannon) paces in the background, uncertain about the agreement: "I don't see why we can't raise our own son just because we came into some money." It seems that a former boarder had left the Kanes stock in a mine that he had wrongly assumed was worthless.

DAVID THOMSON describes the scene:

"It is one of the greatest scenes Welles ever made, on a snowbound Colorado prairie that is done in a studio, with just one isolated log cabin. A gold mine has come into the possession of the Kane parents. In response, the mother signs her boy, Charles, away to the care and guardianship of a Chicago bank and its head, Walter P. Thatcher.

"Why? The question is never answered" in any detailed way. "The father may be a drunk and a bully. But he is nowhere near as strong as the mother (Agnes Moorehead). Is it her love sending the boy away for a better life? Or has she just sold him?

"She goes to the window, raises it and calls out 'Charles' to the boy, who is playing in the snow. Her voice nearly breaks. We hear a mourning wind in the distance. We have Agnes Moorehead's great face—taut in the cold and the crisis. She seems desperate—

at losing the boy? Then she says, quietly, to Thatcher: 'I've got his trunk all packed. I've had it packed for a week now.'"

The scene is entirely dominated by the mother; Moorehead brings Mary Kane to life, comments CHARLES HIGHAM, "so that we see a lifetime of drudgery reflected in the shiny cheekbones, the tight mouth of the hoarder of cash." The scene ends with a close-up of Mary Kane, as she sets her mouth in a hard, tight expression, while holding young Charlie in a last embrace before letting go of him for good. That we remember Agnes Moorehead's performance in the movie, which consists of a single sequence, is high tribute to her talent.

Agnes Moorehead was cast in a still meatier role in THE MAGNIFICENT AMBERSONS, from BOOTH TARKINGTON's novel set at the end of the 19th century in a midwestern town. Welles wanted her to play the neurotic Aunt Fanny, a role he had eliminated from the radio version of *Ambersons* in 1939 because of the time limitations; in fact, he expanded the part in the film well beyond Tarkington's characterization of Aunt Fanny, in order to give full range to Moorehead's acting abilities. Since Welles wrote the role of Fanny with Moorehead in mind, he never considered anyone else for the part, he told PETER BOGDANOVICH: "She'd been all those years with us—it was going to be her great part, and indeed it was,"

Agnes Moorehead with Buddy Swain (young Charles), George Coulouris (Thatcher), and Harry Shannon (James Cain) in *Citizen Kane (Literature/Film Archive)*

particularly in the full version of the film, before it was reedited by the studio.

Ronald Bowers claims the movie charts "the decline and fall of an aristocratic family brought on by the encroaching industrial revolution." After Wilbur Minafer dies, Isobel resides in the Amberson mansion with her aging father, her brother Jack, her sister-in-law Aunt Fanny (Moorehead), and her son George (TIM HOLT). Eugene by now is a widower with a daughter, Lucy, whom George is courting. Still George intervenes when Eugene attempts to court Isobel a second time because George despises Eugene as a social climber, unworthy of his mother. Fanny therefore secretly hopes that maybe Eugene will become interested in her on the rebound, in the wake of losing Isobel for good; but she is doomed to disappointment.

George looks down on his Aunt Fanny as a forlorn old maid, and she resents his condescension: "You're always picking on me—ever since you were a little boy," she whimpers. "It's only poor old Fanny Minafer!" Nevertheless, the childless spinster spoils George as much as his mother does. Fanny watches George gorge himself with her strawberry shortcake, gratified to be useful. The doting Fanny tells George not to eat so fast and inquires if the cake is sweet enough. Still, she is painfully aware that George does not really need her, and that realization leads to her gradually breaking down in the course of the scene; her self-pity floods over into tears. Welles and cinematographer STANLEY CORTEZ shot the present scene in a single take; this extended shot, ANDRÉ BAZIN points out, uninterrupted by cuts to other angles, enables Moorehead to give a sustained performance throughout the scene, and thus build it steadily to a dramatic climax, "with Fanny's final breakdown exploding brutally in the midst of the insignificant dialogue."

JAMES NAREMORE adds that Moorehead skillfully conveys Fanny's torment: her pained, pinched features are matched by "every birdlike gesture of her body," even drawing the viewer's attention when she is not saying a word.

Agnes Moorehead's finest scene comes toward the end, in another sustained take, after George's mother and his grandfather have both passed away and the Amberson fortune has steadily declined by mismanagement. Fanny admits to George that she has no personal funds of her own, and that she is as destitute as he is. As they talk in the mansion's enormous kitchen, it is evident that all of her penny-pinching has not averted her sinking into poverty: "I walked my heels off, looking for a place to live," she moans, for she and George cannot afford to maintain the house and must soon vacate the premises. "I didn't go a single block on a streetcar." She finally collapses on the floor, sobbing helplessly and hopelessly. George forces her to stand up and escorts her down a corridor into the dark drawing room, where the furniture is covered with sheets. The loss of the Amberson family mansion to creditors implicitly represents the passing of the Old Order.

Moorehead reaches a pitch of hysteria in this scene only hinted at in the novel—an indication of how Welles expanded her role in the screenplay. "Agnes Moorehead moves deeply inside the frustration and misery of the character," as Higham describes her performance. "She conveys in high-pitched whines, in querulous outbursts of rage, and in her whole taut, cramped, tightly corseted body and pinched, hawk-like face, in every movement of her hands, in every fit of hysteria, a life wrecked on the rocks of repression."

Welles reshot this scene several times, until Moorehead was actually shedding tears of exhaustion. Some critics have asked whether Welles should have pushed and prodded Moorehead to the extent that he did in shooting this scene for a movie—did the end justify the means? This is not an easy question to answer.

Withal, Agnes Moorehead's best scenes are all in the release version and her superlative performance makes Fanny one of the most memorable characters in the picture. She deserved the Oscar nomination she received, and the best actress award bestowed on her by the New York Film Critics. Moreover, Welles's faith in the film was ultimately justified; although it lost money on its original release, it eventually moved into the black through reissues.

Before leaving Hollywood for South America to shoot IT'S ALL TRUE, Welles produced and starred in

JOURNEY INTO FEAR, which also featured Agnes Moorehead and JOSEPH COTTEN. This World War II thriller about smuggling munitions into Turkey was taken away from him by the studio in the wake of several artistic differences. Welles was replaced by NORMAN FOSTER as director, although he still played Colonel Haki, head of the Turkish Secret Service; he also unofficially supervised the scenes in which he appeared and helped out Foster with some other scenes as well.

Agnes Moorehead continued in films, playing a variety of roles. She appeared with Welles in Robert Stevenson's *JANE EYRE* (1944), in which she attested that Welles privately coached her to play Jane's aunt along the lines of Aunt Fanny in *Ambersons.*

She later played in the remake of *Show Boat* (1951) and John Ford's *How the West Was Won* (1961), to name a couple of significant movies. From 1964 to 1972 she enacted the part of Eudora, a waspish witch, in *Bewitched* on TV, while still making movies until shortly before her death from lung cancer in 1974. Since she had over the years played frustrated, tormented spinsters, most notably in *Ambersons,* it was not surprising, after all, that she wound up as TV's most famous witch. Welles was responsible for launching her career in films, and she never again touched the heights she scaled in *Kane* and *Ambersons.*

References Bazin, André. *Orson Welles: A Critical View,* trans. Jonathan Rosenbaum (New York: Harper & Row, 1978); Bowers, Ronald. *"The Magnificent Ambersons,"* in *International Dictionary of Films and Filmmakers: Films,* ed. Nicolet Elert and Aruna Vasudevan (Detroit: St. James Press, 1997), vol. 1, 403–05; Higham, Charles. *The Films of Orson Welles* (Los Angeles: University of California Press, 1973); Leaming, Barbara. *Orson Welles: A Biography* (New York: Viking, 1985); McBride, Joseph. *Orson Welles* (New York: De Capo, 1996); Naremore, James. *The Magic World of Orson Welles* (Dallas, Tex.: Southern Methodist University Press, 1989); Thomas, François. "Musical Keys to *Kane,*" in *Perspective on Citizen Kane,* ed. Ronald Gottesman (New York: G. K. Hall, 1996), 172–96; Thomson, David. *Rosebud: The Story of Orson Welles* (New York: Vintage, 1997); Welles, Orson, and Peter Bogdanovich. *This Is Orson Welles* (New York: Da Capo, 1998).

—G.D.P.

Moreau, Jeanne (1928–) French actress and sometime femme fatale Jeanne Moreau, made famous by New Wave director FRANÇOIS TRUFFAUT in *Jules and Jim* (1962) played Doll Tearsheet in the ORSON WELLES film *CHIMES AT MIDNIGHT* (1966) and starred with Welles the next year in *THE SAILOR FROM GIBRALTAR* (1967), directed by TONY RICHARDSON. Her first role for Orson Welles was as Miss Burstner in *THE TRIAL* (1963).

Jeanne Moreau was born on January 23, 1928, in Paris and educated at the Lycée Edgar Quinet, then at the Conservatoire National d'Art Dramatique in Paris. By 1948, she was acting with the Comédie Française and with the Théâtre National Populaire. Her first film role came in 1948 in *Dernier amour,* but she really hit her stride working with Louis Malle in *Les Amants* (*The Lovers*) in 1958. She was cast by the most gifted directors of the French New Wave (Godard, Truffaut, Demy, and Louis Malle, in several

Jeanne Moreau

films) and of the international cinema (e.g. Antonioni, Buñuel, RENOIR, Duras, Vadim, LOSEY, Kazan, Fassbinder, and Wenders). She was named best actress at the Cannes Film Festival of 1960 for *Moderato Cantabile,* directed by PETER BROOK, and named Best Foreign Actress by the British Academy for *Viva Maria* (1965), directed by Louis Malle. Honors include the Légion d'honneur and the Ordre Nationale du Mérite et des Arts et Lettres. She also directed films: *Lumière* (1976), *L'Adolescente* (1979), *Lillian Gish* (1984, a documentary made in homage of the great American silent actress), and *Adieu Bonjour* (1994).

Concerning her performance as Doll Tearsheet for Orson Welles, FRANK BRADY opined: "Jeanne Moreau, although brilliant, was often unbelievable as an Elizabethan, sometimes acting as though she had just wandered onto the set of *Chimes at Midnight* in the middle of making a French New Wave film by Jean-Luc Godard." Moreau paid this tribute to Welles at the AFI Life Achievement Award ceremonies: "When he owns the camera, he owns us. Flowing sequences, close-ups, words, camera movements; the eye of Orson Welles's camera, looking, staring, gazing, glaring, creates the magic spell that breaks the bad one. We watch. We know we won't be misled."

References Gray, Marianne. *La Moreau: A Biography of Jeanne Moreau* (London: Warner, 1994); Haskell, Molly. *Holding My Own in No Man's Land: Women and Men, Film and Feminists* (New York: Oxford, 1997).

—J.M.W. and T.L.E.

Mori, Paola (Countess di Girfalco)

(1934–1986) Paola Mori, an Italian actress, was ORSON WELLES's third and last wife and the mother of his third daughter, Beatrice. Her father, the Count di Girfalco, was a colonial administrator for the Italian government. When Mussolini came to power, her father was arrested, brought to Rome, and jailed. Paola, who was born in 1934, a younger sister, and her mother were imprisoned for a while by the British, when they took control of Libya. They were eventually repatriated and lived near Rome. When Mussolini was killed, her father was freed, and the family moved to a luxurious villa in the heart of Rome. Mori's theatrical ambition was opposed by her father but supported by her mother, partly because Italian film production blossomed after the end of World War II. Mori, who was appearing in a bit part in *The Adventures of Don Juan* (1949) starring Errol Flynn, first met Welles at a cast party and then at a party given by Luchino Visconti. The couple spent the evening talking, and Welles was infatuated. Gifts and dinners led to her appearances at different OTHELLO locations and then to her living with him at the Casa Pilozzo, a lavish villa on the outskirts of Rome.

To further Mori's career, Welles cast her in his MR. ARKADIN (1955) as Raina, Arkadin's daughter. DAVID THOMSON sees in the casting a parallel to CITIZEN KANE (1941): "As Kane created an opera house for Susan [Alexander], Welles created a movie for Paolo." Thomson criticizes her acting, finding the love affair between her and the lead unconvincing and questioning Welles's casting decision: "Why should a movie risk its credibility by casting the director's mistress?" In the postproduction editing Mori's speeches had to be dubbed by Billie Whitelaw. Welles and a pregnant Mori were married in London in 1955; PETER BROOK and Natasha Perry served as best man and matron of honor. Thomson writes that after their marriage, "she became nearly invisible in his life." Their daughter, Beatrice, was born in 1955 in New York. During the next few years Welles appeared in several films and often took Mori and Beatrice with him or took them on extensive post-film trips. Welles again cast Mori in another of his films, THE TRIAL (1962), this time in a bit part as a librarian, though her name does not appear in the credits. During the filming of *The Trial,* however, Welles met OJA KODAR, who was to become his lover, companion, and artistic collaborator until his death. After Welles finished shooting some of the unfinished THE DEEP, Mori learned about the relationship between Welles and Kodar, and, according to CHARLES HIGHAM, her response astonished Welles, who "was amazed that the no less remarkable Paola Mori took this new romance in stride without threatening a divorce or creating a scandal." Mori and Welles never divorced, and he divided his time between Mori in Sedona, Arizona, and Kodar in Los Angeles, a one-hour flight away. This situation persisted throughout the 1970s.

According to FRANK BRADY, "Sedona represented home, where Orson could work and think and literally breathe; there he had his wife, Paola, and Beatrice, the youngest of his three daughters." Welles maintained this delicate balance for many years, "keeping both women happy, even though each knew about the other," according to Brady. "Both loved him deeply, and he loved each of them." When Welles died in 1985, however, his will, which called for Kodar to receive the Los Angeles house and the remainder of the estate after the three daughters each received $10,000 and for Mori to get the Las Vegas house (after several years Welles and Mori had moved to Las Vegas from Sedona), was disputed by Mori. She and Kodar were to sign an agreement settling the problem on August 14, 1986; on August 12th Paola was killed in an automobile accident.

—T.L.E.

Moss, Jack

As FRANK BRADY explains, Jack Moss succeeded JOHN HOUSEMAN, who had handled the business end of ORSON WELLES's affairs but who left Hollywood after a blow-up with Welles. Moss, a professional magician, had worked with Welles, who was doing a magic act the summer of 1941 at the California State Fair. Because of his efficiency, diplomacy, and intelligence, he became, as Brady describes him, Welles's business manager and "Mercury's general factotum." When THE MAGNIFICENT AMBERSONS (1942) was being recut and emended in Welles's absence, Moss, the film's acting producer, even directed some of the scenes that were to be added. However, Moss's involvement in revising the film made the film closer to BOOTH TARKINGTON's novel, in just those places where Welles had wanted to depart from it. When GEORGE SCHAEFER at RKO wanted to delete the kitchen scene involving Fanny being teased about her interest in Eugene Morgan, Welles strenuously objected and had Moss personally ask Schaefer about retaining the scene. Moss was successful. DAVID THOMSON notes, however, that many people thought Moss "did a poor job challenging the studio." In JOURNEY INTO FEAR (1942) Welles cast Moss as Petre Banat, the villainous Nazi killer. To get the unwilling Moss to take the role, the only time he ever appeared in a film, Welles had to promise him that he would not have any dialogue. Banat's silence, according to Brady, made him "a more evil and ominous character than he might have been if he had been forced to speak." Later that year, after CHARLES KOERNER, Schaefer's successor at RKO, became irate at the cost overruns on the projected IT'S ALL TRUE, Koerner used problems with editing *Journey into Fear* as his justification for firing the Mercury Players, including Moss. RICHARD WILSON became Moss's successor.

—T.L.E.

Mr. Arkadin (Confidential Report)

Mercury Productions/Filmorsa/Cervantes Films/Sevilla Film Studios, 99 minutes, 1955. **Director:** Orson Welles; **Executive Producer:** Louis Dolivet; **Screenplay:** Welles; **Cinematographer:** Jean Burgoin; **Music:** Paul Misraki; **Editor:** Renzo Luicidi; **Cast:** Orson Welles (Gregory Arkadin), Paola Mori (Raina Arkadin), Robert Arden (Guy Van Stratten), Akim Tamiroff (Jacob Zouk), Michael Redgrave (Burgomil Trebitsch), Patricia Medina (Mily), Mischa Auer (The Professor), Katina Paxinou (Sophie), Jack Watling (Marquis of Rutleigh), Gregoire Aslan (Bracco), Peter Van Eyck (Thaddeus), Suzanne Flon (Baroness Nagel), Tamara Shane (The Blonde), Frederic O'Brady (Oskar), Gordon Heath (pianist)

Like so many other WELLES's projects, *Mr. Arkadin* is a compelling yet compromised work. There were, of course, changes made during the scripting process. There were also changes made during production because of budgetary constraints. However, the most serious and damaging changes took place during postproduction, after the film had been taken away from Welles to be edited by others. In spite of the resulting truncation of Welles's vision, *Mr. Arkadin* remains central to Welles's career largely because of its thematic and narrative connections to his other work, and to his personal life.

As the film opens, a single-engine plane flies above Barcelona on Christmas Day without a pilot. Why? *Mr. Arkadin* proposes to solve the riddle.

On a dark pier in the Naples waterfront, Bracco, who has just been stabbed, whispers the names "Gregory Arkadin" and "Sophie" to Mily, the girlfriend of Guy Van Stratten, a small-time American crook. Taking his last breath, Bracco tells Mily that these names could lead to a fortune. When Mily shares the information with Van Stratten, he investigates and discovers that Arkadin is one of the world's wealthiest men. Arkadin is also a recluse. Therefore, in order to gain access to the old man, he strikes up a relationship with Raina, Arkadin's overly protected daughter who refers to her father as "The Ogre." Invited by Raina to a masquerade party at Arkadin's estate, Van Stratten at last meets the grand man. Expressing concern for his daughter's safety, the mysterious billionaire shows Van Stratten a confidential background report that he has had prepared on the American. Angry at having had his private life probed, Van Stratten says that someone should do a confidential report on Arkadin. Arkadin takes the young man's advice.

Specifically, Arkadin hires Van Stratten to pry into his life before 1927, when Arkadin claims he had lost his memory. Arkadin, it seems, wants to reconstruct and therefore resolve his shadowy past. "The great secret of my life," he tells Van Stratten, "is that I do not know who I am." Setting out with the promise of a handsome commission for successfully uncovering the facts of Arkadin's life as a young man, and perhaps also gaining information that can be used to blackmail Arkadin, Van Stratten encounters a series of eccentrics. In the course of his quest, he meets the proprietor of a flea circus in Copenhagen; a Dutch dealer in stolen goods fronting an antiques store; a Polish baroness; a French secret service agent; Sophie, Arkadin's former partner in a white slave ring, now married to a former general in Mexico; and Zouk, a Munich tailor. One by one, each is murdered. So, too, is Van Stratten's girlfriend, Mily.

Trying to fathom these grisly deeds, Van Stratten finally realizes that Arkadin has set him up as a dupe. After being located by Van Stratten, each person from Arkadin's past has been murdered by the tycoon's thugs. Why? Arkadin's motivation concerns his beloved daughter. Not wanting Raina to discover his unsavory past, Arkadin decides to simply eliminate it, and anyone associated with it. Knowing that he is now in imminent danger of being Arkadin's next victim, Van Stratten contacts Raina, who radios her father. Arkadin, believing that she has now learned the truth from Van Stratten, jumps from his private plane. Thus, the riddle of the opening scene—the puzzle of the abandoned plane flying over the Barcelona Airport—is solved.

The genesis of *Mr. Arkadin* goes back to 1951, when Welles was involved in a radio series produced by the British Broadcasting Corporation based on the famous character he created for director CAROL REED's thriller, *THE THIRD MAN* (1949). The BBC show, which featured Welles in the title role, was called *THE ADVENTURES OF HARRY LIME*. Welles also wrote for the show. For a script of his titled "Greek Meets Greek," Welles's called on actor Frederic O'Brady to play a villain named Gregory Arkadian, which was changed to Arkadin for the film. Welles, taken with the possibility of turning "Greek Meets Greek" into a film, told O'Brady that he saw himself in the role of Arkadin. So as not to discourage his colleague who might have hoped for the same role, Welles promised O'Brady a part in the film, a pledge that he later honored by hiring O'Brady for the part of Oskar.

Working to flesh out the original story, Welles combined "Greek Meets Greek" with another *Lime* story, which opened up on the Marseilles waterfront with a dying man passing on a secret. The resulting

Orson Welles as Gregory Arkadin *(National Film Society Archive)*

screenplay, finished in Rome in March 1953, was called *Masquerade.* Louis Dolivet, Welles's old political friend and publisher of *Free World,* agreed to serve as producer and secured financing from a consortium of Spanish and Swiss bankers. At the time, Welles was also romantically involved with the Countess de Girfalco, whose parents were Italian diplomats serving in Africa. As a backstage Svengali, Welles was determined to cast the exotic young woman, who used the stage name of PAOLA MORI, as Raina, Arkadin's daughter. To that end, he sent Mori off to Dublin for a quick brushing up of her English with friends HILTON EDWARDS and MICHEÁL MACLIAMMÓIR of the GATE THEATRE. For the part of Guy Van Stratten, Welles tapped Robert Arden, a colleague from *The Adventures of Harry Lime.*

Production began in March 1954 in Madrid. At the onset, Welles refashioned the script so that the story would be told through a series of flashbacks, like *CITIZEN KANE.* From Madrid, the company trouped on to Munich, Paris, and then Rome. As Welles continued to revise, rewrite, and shoot, Dolivet made periodic trips to Switzerland to replenish the coffers. After eight months of shooting, Welles tried to finish editing the project for the 1954 Venice Film Festival, then, Europe's most important film market. In the process, he wound up dubbing the voices of O'Brady, the dead man on the dock, and MISCHA AUER, the flea trainer. He's also reputed to have dubbed 15 other parts, as well as the voice of the Munich airport dispatcher. In spite of the Herculean efforts, the Venice deadline was missed. When another deadline at the end of 1954 slid by without Welles having finished, producer Dolivet relieved Welles of his duties. Dolivet assigned the job of finishing the editing to Renzo Lucidi. With pressure from Dolivet to complete the picture, Lucidi dropped the multiple flashback structure.

Although the film undoubtedly suffered from the absence of Welles during the critical last phase of production, the director's hand is everywhere. Thematically, there is the intertwining of power, influence, and will. Like CHARLES FOSTER KANE, Arkadin believes that he can buy and protect both love and position. JOSEPH MCBRIDE describes the phenomenon as it relates to "lucidity." Deceiving themselves as well as those around them, Welles's protagonists wind up self-destructing "at the moment when they can no longer hide their self-deception." Like Hank Quinlin in TOUCH OF EVIL, Arkadin's lies and his efforts to efface them explode in his face. The related theme of corruption, another Wellesian motif, manifests itself not only in Arkadin but also in the selfish and unprincipled Van Stratten, as well as in many of Arkadin's past associates. Ultimately, unable to change, they are monsters.

At one point, Arkadin relates the story of the scorpion and the frog: "A scorpion wanted to cross a river, so he asked the frog to carry him. 'No,' said the frog. 'No, thank you. If I let you on my back you may sting me, and the sting of a scorpion is death.' 'Now where,' asked the scorpion, 'is the logic of that? For scorpions always try to be logical. If I sting you, you will die—I will drown.' So the frog was convinced and allowed the scorpion on his back, but just in the middle of the river he felt a terrible pain and realized that the scorpion *had* stung him after all. 'Logic!,' cried the dying frog, as he started under, bearing the scorpion down with him. 'There is no logic in this!' 'I know,' said the scorpion, 'but I can't help it—it's my character.' Let's drink to character!"

Arkadin is a character who cannot change his nature. He is the powerful scorpion who convinces the gullible frog Van Stratten to swim into the past to find out what he can about Arkadin. With their agreement sealed, Arkadin toasts, "Here's to character." Martin Fitzgerald suggests that "By killing his past, Arkadin is attempting to change his nature. However, the act of killing re-enforces the fact that his nature has not changed."

The film contains a number of memorable characters, including Welles's essaying of the title role. Writing for the *New York Times,* Eugene Archer pointed out that the center of the drama is "precisely focused where it undoubtedly belongs—on Welles himself. As an actor, he is as flamboyant as ever, pouring out metaphors in his mellifluous voice and tilting formidably at the camera every time it swerves in his direction. His Arkadin is less a performance than a presence, and on screen or off, it overwhelms a film, which, for all its strangeness, is seldom less than brilliant." *Variety,* although complaining that *Mr.*

Arkadin's structure didn't live up to that of *Citizen Kane,* nonetheless, found much to enjoy. "Part of Welles's achievement is his delightful employment of senior cinema pros in vividly animated parts. Thus, Katina Paxinou and Michael Redgrave excel as Arkadin's estranged wife and a homosexual antique merchant. Ditto Mischa Auer—with the funniest lines—as maestro of a flea circus, and Akim Tamiroff as the comically forlorn onetime Arkadin associate. Caricatures all, and beautiful." The critics found newcomer Paola Mori, whom Welles married in 1955, promising as well. The only actor to suffer was Robert Arden, who had to endure a barrage of critical slings citing his performance as one-dimensional and without depth.

Today, *Mr. Arkadin* is generally regarded as a fascinating yet minor work in Welles's oeuvre. Still, it should be recalled that in the mid-1950s, the influential French film magazine, *Cahiers du Cinema,* ranked *Mr. Arkadin* as one of the 12 best films ever made. In part, the French critics' support for *Mr. Arkadin* might have been a response to the film's mismanaged promotion, and, therefore, an attempt to secure proper distribution.

The world premiere of the Spanish version of *Mr. Arkadin,* which included Spanish actors in some of the key parts, took place in Madrid on March 15, 1955. The English language version debuted as *Confidential Report* in London on August 11, 1955. The French didn't get to see *Mr. Arkadin* until June 2, 1956. At the same time, producer Dolivet charged Welles with unprofessional behavior in a suit seeking $700,000. The American opening was delayed repeatedly as the court case dragged on for years. Finally, a slightly shortened version of *Mr. Arkadin* opened in New York on October 12, 1962. Years later, Welles described the making of *Mr. Arkadin* as "anguish from beginning to end, two percent movie-making, ninety-eight percent hustling. That's no way to live a life."

—C.B.

Mulvey, Laura (1941–) Feminist filmmaker and critical theorist Laura Mulvey taught cinema at the University of East Anglia in England when she wrote the CITIZEN KANE monograph for the BFI Film Classics Series published by the British Film Institute, London, in 1992. In 1972, she co-edited a book on the cinema of Douglas Sirk and also worked with Claire Johnson and Lynda Myles to organize the "Women's Event" at the Edinburgh Film Festival. In 1974, she co-directed her first film with Peter Wollen, *Penthesilea, Queen of the Amazons,* followed by subsequent collaborations with Wollen: *Riddles of the Sphinx* (1977), *Amy* (1980), *Frida and Tina* (1982), *Crystal Gazing* (1982), and *The Bad Sister* (1983). But Mulvey is perhaps best known for her essay "Visual Pleasure and Narrative Cinema," published in the journal *Screen* (Vol. 16, No. 3, 1975), concerning male fantasies about women and castration, which became a benchmark of feminist film theory.

Writing on the film's 50th anniversary, Mulvey offers "two excuses for his further addition to *Kane* criticism," one being "to bring a European perspective to the film," but, being Laura Mulvey, she is also of course interested in applications of psychoanalytic theory and feminism to the film, not only as one that "depicts women and uses Freud," but also "as a film that challenges conventional relations between screen and spectator and constructs a language of cinema that meshes with the language of the psyche."

—J.M.W.

Muppet Movie, The Henson Associates/Associated Film Distributors, 97 minutes, 1979. **Director:** James Frawley; **Producers:** Jim Henson and David Lazer; **Executive Producer:** Martin Starger; **Screenplay:** Jack Burns and Jerry Juhl; **Cinematographer:** Isidore Mankofsky; **Music:** Kenny Ascher and Paul Williams; **Cast:** Kermit the Frog (himself), Miss Piggy (herself), Orson Welles (himself), Charles Durning, Dom DeLuise, Milton Berle (Mad Man Mooney), Mel Brooks (Professor Max Krassman), James Coburn (El Sleezo Café Owner), Bob Hope (Ice Cream Vendor), Elliot Gould (Beauty Contest Compere), Carol Kane (Myth), Cloris Leachman (Lord's Secretary), Steve Martin (Insolent Waiter), Richard Pryor (Balloon Vendor), Telly Savalas (El Sleezo Tough), Jerry Nelson (voices), Richard Hunt (voices), Dave Goetz (voices)

The first in the successful series of feature films based on Jim Henson's franchise characters first created for Public Television's *Sesame Street, The Muppet Movie* is a good old-fashioned rags-to-riches yarn, tracing the background and rise to stardom of Kermit the Frog. Thanks to agent Dom DeLuise, who is seeking "talent" (specifically, a singing frog) in response to an ad in the show biz paper *Variety,* Kermit leaves the comfortable confines of his swamp to seek his destiny in Hollywood. Since producer Henson's format makes no distinction between his muppets and other forms of life, Kermit (and the audience) meet such stars as Milton Berle, Mel Brooks, James Coburn, Bob Hope, Elliot Gould, Carol Kane, Cloris Leachman, Steve Martin, Richard Pryor, Telly Savalas, ORSON WELLES, and in their last appearance before their deaths, Edgar Bergen and Charlie McCarthy. We also meet Miss Piggy and other characters from the *Sesame Street* children's TV program such as Fozzie Bear, Animal, and Sam. Speaking of the muppets, critic Roger Ebert says, "They turn out, somehow, to have many of the same emotions and motivations that we do. They are vain and hopeful, selfish and generous, complicated and true. They mirror ourselves, except that they're a little nicer."

—C.B.

Muppets Take Manhattan, The   Tri-Star, 94 minutes, 1984. **Director:** Frank Oz; **Producers:** Sidney L. Caplan, Gail March, and Jeffrey M. Sneller; **Screenplay:** Oz and Jim Henson; **Cinematographer:** Bob Paynter; **Music:** Ralph Burns and Jeffrey Moss; **Cast:** Kermit the Frog (himself), Miss Piggy (herself), Orson Welles (himself), Liza Minelli (herself), Dabney Coleman (Martin Price), Joan Rivers (Miss Piggy's co-worker), John Landis (Leonard Winesop), Art Carney (Bernard Crawford), James Coco (Mr. Skeffington), Gregory Hines (rollerskater), Linda Lavin (Kermit's doctor), Brooke Shields

Like THE MUPPET MOVIE, the third installment in the Muppet series, *The Muppets Take Manhattan,* is another venerable show biz yarn. Here, instead of the destination being Hollywood, it's on to the Great White Way—Broadway! In his rise to theatrical stardom, Kermit the Frog has to deal with recalcitrant agents like Dabney Coleman, fight with Liza Minnelli for a bit of respect at Sardi's, and wait tables to support himself at a greasy spoon run by a Greek whose philosophical babblings make little sense in any language. There's even a marriage—Kermit and Miss Piggy! And, as with *The Muppet Movie,* cameos from show biz legends like ORSON WELLES! In the end, however, this is Kermit's movie, whose star power is alluded to by Roger Ebert, who in his 1984 review, in the form of a fan letter to Kermit, concludes: "In the 1940s, you would have been under contract to MGM!"

Napoleon Filmsonor S.A./Francinex/Les Films C.L.M., 190 minutes, 1955. **Director:** Sacha Guitry; **Producer:** Clément Duhour; **Screenplay:** Guitry; **Cinematographer:** Pierre Montazel; **Editor:** Raymond Lamy; **Music:** Jean Françaix; **Cast:** Jean-Pierre Aumont (Régnault de Saint-Jean d'Angély), Jeanne Boitel (Madame de Dino), Pierre Brasseur (Barras), Gianna Maria Canale (Pauline Borghese), Pauline Carton (Une aubergiste), Jean Chevrier (Duroc), Danielle Darrieux (Eléonore Denuelle), Erich von Stroheim (Ludwig van Beethoven), Orson Welles (Sir Hudson Lowe)

Following ROYAL AFFAIRS IN VERSAILLES (1954), GUITRY and WELLES collaborated on the French director's epic production of *Napoleon*. Although the Little General's life had been etched with cinematic élan by Abel Gance in his celebrated silent production of 1927, Guitry deemed that it was time to update the saga, using sound and color and other modern film techniques. Welles elaborated on the project to his French biographer, André Maurois: "There are very few surefire subjects. Napoleon is one of them. You can always write a *Life of Napoleon* and a *Life of Jesus* and find a hundred thousand readers."

Since no studio was large enough to accommodate his lavish sets, Guitry took over the Parc des Expositions in order to re-create the Paris of Napoleonic France. His ensemble of 5,000 extras played the army of Henry IV on one day, and on the next, the revolutionary insurgents. Welles, for his part, essayed Napoleon's jailer, Sir Hudson Lowe, with a glowering snarl. Guitry, an irrepressible ham, emoted the wily Talleyrand, while another legendary director, the famously bald Erich von Stroheim, draped with a wig with a mind of its own, conjured up an apparitionlike Ludwig von Beethoven playing a reduction of the *Eroica* Symphony on piano. Others participating in the antics of Guitry's costume drama were Michele Morgan, Danielle Darrieux, and Maria Schell.

At the star-studded opening night gala in Paris, a tuxedoed and bejeweled crowd that included French president Coty cheered wildly for the three-hour epic. Welles predicted big things for it. So, too, did *Variety,* which said: "The 70-year-old Guitry, who with Cocteau, is France's most versatile theatrical genius has turned the trick again!" These predictions fell short of the mark. For this *Napoleon,* it was the box office that played the part of Waterloo. Nobody seemed to really care. Like Guitry's *Royal Affairs in Versailles,* this slow-moving and bloated *Napoleon* soon dropped from sight.

—C.B.

Naremore, James (1941–) Chancellor's professor of English, Film Studies, and Communication and Culture at Indiana University, James Naremore is the author of several cinema-related books, including, most recently, *Acting in the Cinema* (1998) and *More than Night: Film Noir in Its Contexts* (1998). His most significant early work, however, was *The Magic World of Orson Welles,* published by Oxford University Press in 1978. A "new and revised" updated edition was later published by Southern Methodist University Press in 1989. Upon its original publication in 1978, the book was enthusiastically received by reviewers. Andrew Sarris called it "the most perceptive study of Welles's art," and Stanley Kauffmann, writing for the *Times Literary Supplement,* called it "the best [book] I know about Welles."

The goal of *The Magic World of Orson Welles,* according to George Rehrauer, was "to scrutinize the political and psychological implications" of the films directed by WELLES, and that goal is fully achieved. Naremore provides useful historical and biographical contexts for the films in this well-considered study. The approach is scholarly, yet readable. Individual chapters are devoted to *CITIZEN KANE, THE MAGNIFICENT AMBERSONS, TOUCH OF EVIL, THE TRIAL,* and *CHIMES AT MIDNIGHT,* while lesser films are grouped into other chapters. The revised edition of the book adds an additional chapter entitled "Between Works and Texts." Praising the book for "its wealth of background and close commentary" in *Film Comment,* Tag Gallagher concluded that this "is certainly the best study of Welles."

—J.M.W.

Native Son (play, 1941)   In 1941, with MERCURY THEATRE's disastrous last season still smarting, JOHN HOUSEMAN invited WELLES to direct the Broadway adaptation of RICHARD WRIGHT's sensational 1940 novel. For Houseman, it was an opportunity to try to recoup the losses sustained by *FIVE KINGS* (1939), *DANTON'S DEATH* (1938) and *TOO MUCH JOHNSON* (1938). For Welles, like Houseman, it was a chance to return to Broadway with a triumph, while also reaffirming his liberal pro-black credentials. Also, both men were also acutely aware that with the imminent release of *CITIZEN KANE,* the controversy surrounding Welles's Hollywood debut could only help in boosting the prospects for *Native Son.* Against that backdrop, and putting aside their differences for the moment, Welles accepted Houseman's offer.

Wright's best-selling novel was among the first literary works by a black to receive a broad and generally sympathetic reception by the general public. When theatrical rights for *Native Son* were acquired by Houseman, the producer hired Pulitzer Prize–winning author Paul Green to make the adaptation. Green, a white, agreed on the condition that Wright be included in the process. Although the collaboration between Green and Wright went fairly well, there were problems. For one, Wright's attempts at writing for the stage tended to be novelistic rather than dramatic. There was also local prejudice. Working together in Chapel Hill, where Green taught at the University of North Carolina, Green was informed by university officials that Wright would not be welcome on campus. There was also a near tragic incident in which one of Green's cousins showed up with a gun intent on shooting the black novelist, an act averted by Green's calm reasoning. Upon completion, the script was sent to Welles, who signed on immediately. Interestingly, Welles, who had few compunctions about drastically cutting and reshaping Shakespeare (see SHAKESPEARE BY WELLES), let Green's script stand.

The story of *Native Son* focuses on Bigger Thomas (CANADA LEE), a black man with a long history of trouble. He has grown up both frightened by and hateful of the white society that has ostracized him. Despite that, a rich white man hires him as his chauffeur. When Bigger tries to get his boss's drunk daughter (Anne Burr) safely to bed, he becomes afraid that her incoherent moans will bring the family to the girl's bedroom. Fearing that such a discovery would be misinterpreted, he attempts to quiet the girl by putting a pillow over her face. In the process, he accidentally smothers her. In a state of panic, he burns her body in the basement furnace and flees. He is soon captured, tried, and sentenced to death. While awaiting execution on death row, his fears fade into the conviction that he has played a small but significant role in destroying the security of the white world.

Bigger dies at the end of both the novel and the play, yet instead of mourning his cause as Wright does in the novel, the Green-Welles version celebrates his strength and refusal to bow to white authority.

Rather than seeking easy sympathy, Welles puts Bigger in a Christ-like pose with his arms stretched out to the bars of his cell. Just before the final curtain, Bigger directly confronts the audience by saying: "See what you've done to me . . . you've crucified me."

In another theatrical gesture suggesting the influence of the shock tactics of BERTOLT BRECHT, at the end of a spectacular gunfight between Bigger and the police, Welles had some of the police sweep down the aisles for the onstage capture with guns drawn and ablaze. As the scene closes, Bigger, wielding a huge machine gun, approaches the audience, takes aim, and fires. Like the play's conclusion, Welles's intent of implicating the audience registered loud and clear.

In contrast to most of Welles's other theater work, the sets were realistic. To keep the momentum of the drama building, the play was presented in 10 scenes without intermissions. *Native Son* was, to cite Bred Wood, "an uncompromising look at the hopeless predicament of a man unable to guide his own life. The tragic character is not unlike the *Macbeth* of the [1936] stage version, who was similarly unable to control his destiny. In *Native Son,* however, the curse is not a primitive chant of voodoo priests, but the obstacles posed by our contemporary sociopolitical system."

Amid the seriousness was an inside joke. Mainly for the critics who had previewed the yet unreleased *Citizen Kane,* Welles placed a sled emblazoned with "ROSEBUD" in one scene. Also clever was his decision to withhold programs from the audience until the end of the show, a strategy designed to eliminate the rustling of pages during the play. There were also fascinating uses of sound, including the blast of the furnace's stoker, which served as a leitmotiv for Bigger's crime. *Native Son* reunited Welles with Canada Lee, who had played the cigar-smoking Banquo in the 1936 "voodoo" *MACBETH,* and whom Welles credited with having saved his life from a knife-wielding thug in Harlem. The production also featured in subsidiary roles such Mercury alumni as RAY COLLINS, EVERETT SLOANE, ERSKINE SANFORD, RICHARD WILSON, JACK BERRY, and PAUL STEWART.

The reviews were exultant with particular praise for Canada Lee's moving portrayal as Bigger, and Welles's brilliant direction. The *New York Times,* calling it "a powerful drama," elaborated: "Orson Welles has staged it with imagination and force. These are the first things to be said about the overwhelming play that opened at the St. James last evening, but they hardly convey the excitement of this first performance of a play that represents experience of life and conviction in thought and a production that represents a dynamic use of the stage." One reviewer noted that it provided "a deeply moving, highly exciting evening." Another said that it made Broadway's other offerings seem rather dim and old-fashioned by comparison. Not surprising, in view of the Hearst newspaper chain's all-out assault on *Citizen Kane,* Hearst's *New York Journal-American* trotted out the old anticommunist canard that the play was "propaganda" nearer to Moscow than to Harlem.

Wright was particularly pleased. In an enthusiastic note he said: "I cannot stress too highly my profound respect and admiration for Orson Welles, the director of this play. He is beyond doubt the most courageous, gallant, and talented director on the modern stage in the world today." While the press and liberals gushed, *Native Son* found a relatively limited audience and closed after a run of 114 performances. With the Depression still grinding on and Europe already in flames, one might surmise that in spring 1941 theatergoers were looking for something less lacerating than *Native Son* and its indictment of mainstream society's racism. Still, for Welles and Houseman, it was vindication, and a return to Broadway's winners' circle.

—C.B.

Necromancy

Necromancy Cinerama, 83 minutes, 1973. **Director:** Bert I. Gordon; **Producers:** Sidney L. Caplan, Gail March, and Jeffrey M. Sneller; **Screenplay:** Gordon; **Cinematographer:** Winton C. Hoch; **Music:** Fred Karger; **Cast:** Orson Welles (Mr. Cato), Pamela Franklin (Lori Brandon), Michael Ontkean (Frank Brandon), Lee Purcell (Priscilla), Harvey Jason (Dr. Jay), Lisa James (Georgette), Sue Bernard (Nancy)

In this low-budget horror film, in which two young people become involved in small-town witchcraft, WELLES plays the role of an evil voodoo-doll maker.

Halliwell's Film and Video Guide called it a "Low-key, low-talent thriller overbalanced by its star [Orson Welles]."

—C.B.

Negro Theatre Project (1935–1939)

In the midst of the Great Depression of the 1930s, President FRANKLIN DELANO ROOSEVELT issued a 1935 executive order creating the WORKS PROGRESS ADMINISTRATION (later the Work Projects Administration). It was a vast program designed to put the unemployed back to work. One of the subsidiary agencies created under the Works Progress Administration, popularly known as the WPA, was the FEDERAL THEATRE PROJECT. HALLIE FLANIGAN, a Vassar theater professor and able administrator, headed up the new organization. Under her leadership, the Federal Theatre's New York City branch was organized into five units: The Living Newspaper, a documentarylike experiment designed to tackle the issues of the day; the Popular Price Theatre, for new works by new playwrights; the Experimental Group, for avant-garde productions; the Try-Out Theatre, a kind of farm team for aspiring theater workers; and, the Negro Theatre Project.

For the latter, Flanigan was particularly concerned about appointing individuals sensitive to the volatile issue of race. She chose JOHN HOUSEMAN to head the new venture. Although white, Houseman was an experienced producer and writer. Significantly, he had worked successfully with black performers in the landmark New York production of VIRGIL THOMSON's avant-garde opera, *Four Saints in Three Acts.* And, like all New Dealers, he was a dedicated liberal. Houseman's basic plan was to produce works by black authors, featuring black actors, and classical works whose casts would be chosen without reference to color. To put the project on the map, he asked his young friend ORSON WELLES to helm the unit's first classical production. Welles, fearing that the enterprise would cut into his hectic radio schedule, initially turned the offer down. His wife, Virginia Welles, knowing that her husband ached to return to Shakespeare, pleaded with him to reconsider. He did.

Headquartered at the lovingly refurbished Lafayette Theatre in the middle of Harlem, the Negro Theatre Project achieved its greatest success with Welles's staging of the "voodoo" MACBETH (1936). Transposing the setting from Scotland to Haiti, and employing an all-black cast, and calling on a stirring score by Virgil Thomson punctuated by Haitian drummers, Welles's created a cause célèbre that made the Negro Theatre Project the talk of the town. Heading the cast were the eminent African-American actors Edna Thomas (Lady Macbeth), JACK CARTER (Macbeth), and CANADA LEE (Banquo). In addition to a long run at the Lafayette, Welles's "voodoo" *Macbeth* enjoyed a successful national tour.

In spite of their hit with *Macbeth,* Houseman and Welles petitioned Hallie Flanigan to relieve them of their duties with the Negro Theatre Project, arguing that blacks should have a greater opportunity to direct and produce as well as act. They also were anxious to start their own company. Flanigan listened to their proposal to perform revivals of the great dramatic classics. Approving the request, Flanigan set up the new Welles-Houseman venture at the Maxine Elliott Theatre. Not wanting to scare potential audiences by using the word "classical," they named the new company PROJECT 891, the bureaucratic budget number assigned to them by the government.

In 1939, the Negro Theatre Project was abolished when its parent organization, the Federal Theatre Project, saw its federal funding eliminated by right-wing congressional Republicans.

—C.B.

Newman, Paul (1925–)

Actor and director Paul Newman, who starred with WELLES in THE LONG HOT SUMMER, was born in Cleveland, Ohio, on January 26, 1925; his father was the Jewish proprietor of a sporting goods store and his mother was of Catholic, Hungarian descent. Newman joined the Navy Air Corps during World War II and saw active service as a radio operator in the South Pacific. After he was demobilized, he studied economics at Kenyon College in Ohio, while initiating his acting career by appearing in stock. He finally deserted the business world altogether to enroll in the graduate program at the Yale Drama School; he went to the Actors Studio in New York later on. Newman made his Broadway debut in *Picnic* in 1953; as a result, he was brought to

Hollywood to co-star in *The Silver Chalice* (1955), a second-rate religious epic.

Newman's first important role was that of Rocky Graziano in *Somebody Up There Likes Me* (1956), ROBERT WISE's screen biography of the famous fighter. Newman delineated Rocky's personality as that of a mixed-up adolescent who learned in the ring how to work off the frustrations of his unhappy and underprivileged home life. In so doing, Newman created the definitive screen character he was to play with variations in his best pictures for years to come: the aggressive but sensitive and basically likable young man who could be totally disarmed by unexpected acceptance.

Brick Pollitt in Tennessee Williams's *Cat on a Hot Tin Roof* (1958) clearly still suffers from the lack of affection he experienced as a youngster, even though he is a married man when the story opens. Brick is typical of the very vulnerable Newman protagonist who has withdrawn into his own private world because of the psychic wounds he has sustained from life, a bitter and isolated figure with whom one can easily sympathize. Newman received his first Academy Award nomination for this film.

The same year he starred in *The Long Hot Summer,* which was derived from the novel *The Hamlet* by WILLIAM FAULKNER. Several episodes in the novel constitute self-contained units. Consequently, the screenwriters, Irving Ravetch and Harriet Frank, Jr., simply picked the incidents they judged suitable for the film and jettisoned the rest. They also added some characters and incidents of their own devising. The film's central character is an impecunious fellow named Ben Quick (Newman). Ben falls in love with Clara Varner (JOANNE WOODWARD), a character not in the book; she is the daughter of Will Varner, a wealthy landowner (Welles). This was the first of several films in which the husband-and-wife team of Newman and Woodward would co-star.

"Much of the publicity surrounding the making of the film revolved around the casting of Orson Welles," writes Gabriel Miller. Studio executives were well aware of Welles's reputation as a temperamental and difficult actor; but director Martin Ritt contended that he would be terrific in the part, and the studio acquiesced. "There was a note of suspicion," Welles says in

Miller's book; "I did not know what kind of monkeyshines I would have to put up with," and Paul Newman and the rest of the cast "did not know what kind of caprices they would have to put up with from me." As things turned out, Welles got along much better with the cast than he did with the director.

Will Varner, who is always looking for ways to make a fast buck on a business deal, senses a certain affinity between himself and Ben Quick, whom Will sizes up as both a drifter and a grifter. "You're no better than a crook," Will says to Ben, who replies intrepidly, "You're no better than a con man." Will is impressed by the manner in which the aggressive, attractive young man manages his general store, and he urges Clara to marry him. Ben at first welcomes Will's active support of his campaign for Clara. But he finally tells her that she must be allowed to reach her own decision about whom she wants to marry. Clara, in turn, chooses Ben on her own initiative— and not because her father has sought to pressure her into accepting him.

As for Welles's performance, DAVID THOMSON notes that, "with a face the color of a tobacco leaf, in a straw hat and orange robe, . . . he seems determined to give the impression that he is having a good time." This highly entertaining film was a box office bonanza, with the help of Ritt's spirited direction, the adroit script by Ravetch and Frank, and the appealing performances of Newman and Welles.

Newman turned to directing in 1968 with *Rachel Rachel,* a drama about a lonely spinster, starring his wife, Joanne Woodward. He has directed other films as well, such as Tennessee Williams's *The Glass Menagerie* (1987), once again starring Joanne Woodward. Newman has continued acting well beyond his 70th year in such films as the thrillers *Twilight* (1998), *Where the Money Is* (2000), and *Road to Perdition* (2002), proving his enduring popularity with the mass audience.

References Kael, Pauline. *I Lost it at the Movies* (New York: Boyars, 1994); Kawin, Bruce. *Faulkner and Film* (New York: Ungar, 1977); Kerbel, Michael. *Paul Newman* (New York: Pyramid Books, 1974); Knight, Arthur. "Filming Faulknerland," *Saturday Review,* December 7, 1957, 52; McGilligan, Patrick. "Ritt Large: An Interview with Martin Ritt," *Film Comment* 22, no. 1 (January–February 1986): 38+;

Miller, Gabriel. *The Films of Martin Ritt: Fanfare for the Common Man* (Jackson: University Press of Mississippi, 2000); Quirk, Lawrence. *The Films of Paul Newman* (New York: Citadel, 1976); Thomson, David. *Rosebud: The Story of Orson Welles* (New York: Vintage Books, 1997).

—G.D.P.

News on the March *News on the March,* the 10-minute newsreel segment opening CITIZEN KANE, serves to establish the biographical outlines of CHARLES FOSTER KANE's life and the reporters' quest for the meaning of ROSEBUD. It also is director WELLES's homage to the motion picture edition of *The March of Time* (1935–51), and its radio predecessor, also THE MARCH OF TIME (1931–39; 1941–45). In fact, it was a 1935 appearance on a *March of Time* broadcast that launched Welles's high-profile radio career and national celebrity, and, in turn, the opportunity to direct *Citizen Kane.*

For audiences in 1941, the impact of *News on the March* was not only narrative. It was also a resonant parody of one of the period's most important sources of news. In 1941, both film and radio versions of the *March of Time* were interlocked icons of American popular culture. As media historian Raymond Fielding points out, the authoritative voice of the show's narrator, Westbrook Van Voorhis, "was said to be even more familiar than that of President Roosevelt." In *News on the March,* Van Voorhis is effectively emulated by WILLIAM ALLAND, who also plays the part of reporter Jerry Thompson.

The sequence's brisk cutting, effective voice-over narration, and stirring music are direct reflections of Welles's mid-1930s' experience with *March of Time.* The parody is also a testimony to Welles's affection for the show's and newsreel's adroit combining of news and drama, a powerful combination that Welles himself had already exploited in the notorious 1938 broadcast of WAR OF THE WORLDS.

Ironically, with the original film and radio versions *March of Time* now largely distant memories, today, the *News on the March* sequence has added cultural significance as the most visible and poignantly detailed reminder of the special glories of a radio show and newsreel that both informed and entertained.

—C.B.

Nichols, Mike (Michael Igor Peschkowsky)
(1931–) ORSON WELLES had a supporting role as General Dreedle in Mike Nichols's film adaptation of Joseph Heller's internationally acclaimed novel, *CATCH-22* (1970). Welles, who wanted to direct the film adaptation, believed that an adaptation of the novel could have been "the movie of the century," "a ground-breaking movie," as he described it to BARBARA LEAMING. As directed by Nichols, however, Welles thought the film was "really dreadful." CHARLES HIGHAM concurs: "Mike Nichols utterly ruined the novel." Higham adds, "Making *Catch-22* was a punishment [for Welles] . . . because Welles tried to direct his own scenes and instead had to endure the rock-hard temperament of Mike Nichols." Welles's efforts to direct were described in a *Newsweek* article written by Raymond Sokolov (March 1969), who was on location for the filming. When PETER BOGDANOVICH mentioned the matter to Welles, Welles minimized his directorial efforts and cited the article as a source of rumors about the difficulty of working with him.

Mike Nichols was born on November 6, 1931, in Berlin and immigrated to the United States with his Jewish family when he was seven years old. He attended the University of Chicago, where he became interested in acting. He moved to New York City and studied under Lee Strasberg, but returned to Chicago when he could not find any acting jobs in New York. With Elaine May, Alan Arkin, Barbara Harris, and Paul Sills, he formed an improvisational troupe, which performed at the Compass. Nichols and May then forged a partnership and toured nationally, honing the improvisational skills that led to the successful *An Evening with Mike Nichols and Elaine May,* which played on Broadway (1960). In 1963, he turned to directing on Broadway with *Barefoot in the Park.* Before he made his film directing debut in 1966, with *Who's Afraid of Virginia Woolf?,* he had also directed several successful Broadway plays, including *Luv* and *The Odd Couple.* Nichols's *The Graduate* (1967), his second film, won an Oscar for best director. Since *Catch-22,* Nichols has made several significant films, including *Carnal Knowledge* (1971), *Silkwood* (1983), *Working Girl* (1988), *Postcards from the Edge* (1990), and *Primary Colors* (1998). Both *Silkwood* and *Working Girl* earned Nichols Oscar

Mike Nichols

nominations for best director. Nichols resides in New York, where he has continued to direct for the stage. In addition to his Academy Award recognition, he has won at least a half dozen Tony Awards.

Reference Schuth, H. Wayne. *Mike Nichols* (Boston: Twayne, 1978).

—T.L.E. and J.M.W.

Noble, Peter (1917–1997) British critic Peter Noble, the editor of *The British Film Yearbook* series and the author of books on British theater and film, and film personalities such as Erich von Stroheim and Bette Davis, wrote *The Fabulous Orson Welles,* published by Hutchinson & Co., Ltd. (London), in 1956. This profusely illustrated study focuses upon ORSON WELLES's theatrical career, including his work with the FEDERAL THEATRE PROJECT and MERCURY THEATRE, his radio broadcasts, and five films: CITIZEN KANE, THE MAGNIFICENT AMBERSONS, THE STRANGER, MACBETH, and OTHELLO. Noble also includes chapters on Welles's involvement with THE THIRD MAN and the stage play of MOBY DICK. The book tends to be anecdotal rather than scholarly and quotes copiously from interviews with Welles's colleagues and associates. The book has a general index, but the index is not inclusive. Still, this was one of the first book-length treatments of Welles and his career.

—T.L.E. and J.M.W.

Nolan, Jeannette (1911–1998) WELLES and Nolan first met in New York during the mid-1930s when both were regulars in the ensemble cast of the radio version of THE MARCH OF TIME. In the late 1930s, Nolan was also a member of Welles's MERCURY THEATRE ON THE AIR. In 1947, when Welles was signed by Republic Pictures to direct and star in a film adaptation of Shakespeare's MACBETH, one of his first tasks was to find a big-name actress for the pivotal role of Lady Macbeth. The part was offered, but turned down due to various problems, to Tallulah Bankhead, MERCEDES MCCAMBRIDGE, ANNE BAXTER, and AGNES MOOREHEAD. Finally, Welles selected former New York radio colleague, Jeannette Nolan, as his leading lady. Although Nolan had never before appeared onstage or onscreen, Welles was confident that she was up to the job, largely on the basis of the many radio broadcasts that they had done together. It must have been reassuring to Nolan to know that many of the other production members were also Mercury radio alumni.

Welles's plan of attack was unique. Working from a highly abridged 94-minute version of Shakespeare's script, Welles first mounted *Macbeth* in a six-performance theatrical run in Salt Lake City. Thus, having "rehearsed" for the film via a live production of the play, Welles was ready to set his *Macbeth* before the cameras. Playing opposite Welles in the title role, Nolan was praised for her portrayal of Lady Macbeth in both stage and film versions. Her "Out damned spot" sleepwalking scene was particularly noted. BRADY points out that Nolan had a particular appreciation for Welles's tiring and often exasperating search for perfection. Even when pushed to the limit in a five-and-a-half hour shoot devoted to recording one 16-line speech, Nolan kept working until Welles was finally satisfied. Partly in appreciation of Nolan's support, Welles found a role for John McIntire, her husband, by combining several small roles into a new character, "A Holy Father," who functioned as a kind of expositional chorus. The stage version of *Macbeth* was produced in Salt Lake City in May 1947. The film version was shot in June and July 1947, but not released until 1948 because of postproduction difficulties.

In the 50 years following her screen debut as Lady Macbeth, Nolan appeared in a number of films, usually in supporting roles. She was the mother of Lorenz Hart (Mickey Rooney) in *Words and Music* (1948), and teamed with husband John McIntire in *No Sad Songs for Me* (1950). She gave a powerful dramatic performance as the widow of a suicidal cop in Fritz Lang's *The Big Heat* (1953). Nolan also appeared in a number of westerns, most notably *Two Rode Together* (1961) and *The Man Who Shot Liberty Valance* (1962, both directed by John Ford). Her voice was heard in two Disney animated features, as Ellie Mae in *The Rescuers* (1977), and as Widow Tweed in *The Fox and the Hound* (1981).

On television, Nolan won continuing roles in *The Virginian* (1958–59), *Hotel de Pare* (1959–60), and *The Richard Boone Show* (1963–64), for which she won an Emmy for the lead role in the episode "Vote No on 11!" She also appeared in such series as *The Golden Girls* (as the mother of Betty White's Rose; 1985), *St. Elsewhere* (along with her husband as elderly patients; 1986), and *Cagney & Lacey* (as a woman accused of witchcraft; 1987).

Her final feature film appearance was a cameo as Robert Redford's elderly mother in *The Horse Whisperer* (1998).

—C.B.

Oberon, Merle (Estelle Merle O'Brien Thompson)

Oberon, Merle (Estelle Merle O'Brien Thompson) (1911–1979)   Famous for her beauty, star actress Merle Oberon was supposed to have played Natasha to ORSON WELLES's Pierre Bezukov in a film adaptation of Leo Tolstoy's *War and Peace,* that SIR ALEXANDER KORDA intended to produce, with Welles as director. Unfortunately, this was destined to become one of the director's many failed projects. Born Estelle Merle O'Brien Thompson in Tasmania (according to most sources), she was the daughter of a British railway engineer and Ceylonese mother. She was educated in India and arrived in England at the age of 17. Using the name Queenie O'Brien, she found work as a movie extra and was "discovered" by Alexander Korda, who promptly cast her as Anne Boleyn in his historical spectacles, *The Private Life of Henry VIII* (1933) and *The Private Life of Don Juan* (1934). She was married to Korda from 1939 until 1945, when she settled in Hollywood with her second husband, cinematographer Lucien Ballard, whom she married in 1945. Oberon played Cathy Linton to LAURENCE OLIVIER's Heathcliff in *Wuthering Heights* (1939), George Sand in *A Song to Remember* (1945), and Empress Josephine to Marlon Brando's Napoleon in *Desiree* (1954). Her last film was *Interval* (1973), which she also produced. Thereafter, she lived comfortably in retirement until her death in 1979.

References   Higham, Charles. *Princess Merle: The Romantic Life of Merle Oberon* (New York: Pocket Books, 1985); ———. *Merle: A Biography of Merle Oberon* (Sevenoaks [Kent]: New English Library, 1984).

—T.L.E. and J.M.W.

O'Brien, Edmond

O'Brien, Edmond (1915–1985)   Edmond O'Brien joined ORSON WELLES's MERCURY THEATRE in 1937 and appeared in both radio and stage productions. His most notable performance with the Mercury Theatre was as Marc Antony in Shakespeare's (see SHAKESPEARE BY WELLES) *JULIUS CAESAR,* which was on a five-week tour beginning January 20, 1938. The production, which played in Providence, Boston, Hartford, Washington, D.C., Cleveland, Chicago, and Toronto, received excellent reviews but had only modest audiences. Much later in his career O'Brien rejoined Welles, who cast him in *THE OTHER SIDE OF THE WIND,* which was never completed.

O'Brien, who was born on September 10, 1915, in New York City, appeared in amateur stage productions while still in his teens. He attended Fordham University but withdrew when he got a scholarship to the Neighborhood Playhouse School of the Theatre. He joined the Mercury Theatre after a season in summer stock and some small roles on the Broadway stage. In Hollywood, O'Brien was frequently cast in crime films and prison films because of his apparent toughness, films such as *Prison Break* (1938), *The Killers* (1946), *White Heat* (1949, with

Jimmy Cagney), and *D.O.A.* (1950), in which he perhaps played his most memorable role, as a dying man seeking the identity of his killer. Other memorable films in which O'Brien starred include *Pete Kelly's Blues* (1955), *The Great Imposter* (1961), *The Man Who Shot Liberty Valance, Birdman of Alcatraz,* and *The Longest Day* (all in 1962), and *The Wild Bunch* (1969), another classic western. He also worked extensively in television, starring in three series: *Johnny Midnight* (1960), *Sam Benedict* (1962–63), and *The Long, Hot Summer* (1965). Moreover, he became a television director and then made two feature films for television: *Shield for Murder* (1954, with HOWARD W. KOCH), and *Mantrap* (1961). O'Brien won an Oscar as best supporting actor for his role in *The Barefoot Contessa* (1954). Ten years later, he was again nominated for an Oscar for *Seven Days in May* (1964). O'Brien died of Alzheimer's disease in 1985.

—T.L.E.

Oedipus the King Universal Pictures/Rank/ Crossroads, 97 minutes, 1968. **Director:** Philip Saville; **Producer:** Michael Luke; **Screenplay:** Michael Luke and Philip Saville; **Cinematography:** Walter Lassally; **Editor:** Paul Davies; **Music:** Janni Christou; **Cast:** Orson Welles (Tiresias), Christopher Plummer (Oedipus), Richard Johnson (Creon), Donald Sutherland (Chorus Leader), Lilli Palmer (Jocasta), Cyril Cusack (Messenger), Roger Livesey (Shepherd)

A British film directed by Philip Saville featuring WELLES as Tiresias. Like so many of his acting jobs during the 1960s, Welles's involvement in the filming of the screen version of Sophocles's classic Greek tragedy was limited. When PETER BOGDANOVICH asked about the film, Welles responded: "How do I know? I was only on it one day. Had that one speech—you know what those Greek tragedies are like. It was rather an odd idea, it seemed to me, to film *Oedipus* in a ruined Greek theatre, but costumed in the period in which the story is supposed to have originally happened. Bewildering." *Variety,* however, praised Welles's work as well as Saville's adaptation: "Lilli Palmer, as the ill-fated Jocasta, does not fully bring out the tragic personality until the final bitter scene, and Orson Welles is unusually subdued, but all

the more effective, as Tiresias, the blind prophet of doom."

Oedipus the King also featured Christopher Plummer in the title role, Richard Johnson as Creon, and Donald Sutherland as the Chorus Leader.

—C.B.

Olivier, [Lord] Laurence (1907–1989) It was inevitable that Laurence Olivier, the most celebrated and respected Shakespearean actor-director in the English-speaking world during the 20th century, would cross paths with ORSON WELLES, and, in fact, the two giants clashed when put together onstage. The creative dispute came when Welles mounted a production of the absurdist play RHINOCEROS by the Romanian-born avant-garde French playwright EUGÈNE IONESCO, an allegory of totalitarian conformity, which Welles adapted for the Royal Court Theatre in April of 1960. The production, directed and designed by Welles, featured Joan Plowright and Laurence Olivier, but the actor and director did not get along. Welles told BARBARA LEAMING that Olivier sabotaged the production, claiming that "he behaved terribly" and deviously. Although Olivier took Welles's directions without arguing directly with the director, "he took every actor aside and told them that I was misdirecting them," Welles complained. "Instead of making it hard for me to direct *him,* he made it almost impossible for me to direct the *cast.*" Welles was so humiliated that he stopped attending rehearsals because he felt the production "had been wrested away from him." Consequently, this was the last play production Welles would undertake.

Laurence Olivier was born the son of the Reverend Gerard Kerr Oliver, an Anglican minister, on May 22, 1907, in the London suburb of Dorking, in Surrey. He was educated at All Saints Choir School, Marylebone, before entering the Central School of Speech Training and Dramatic Art to study with Elsie Fogarty, who also trained Peggy Ashcroft and Ralph Richardson. His acting career began with the Birmingham Repertory Company in 1927. By 1928, he was performing in London's Royal Court Theatre. He made his film acting debut in 1930 in *Too Many Crooks,* produced and directed by George King.

Sir Laurence Olivier *(National Film Society Archive)*

Olivier developed into an actor's actor, famous for his many renderings of Shakespeare's greatest roles, but among his favorite non-Shakespearean roles was Archie Rice, the lead character of John Osborne's *The Entertainer,* directed by TONY RICHARDSON, and later adapted by Richardson to the screen. Olivier directed several memorable films—*Henry V* (1945), *Hamlet* (1948), *Richard III* (1955), *The Prince and the Showgirl* (1957, adapted by Terrence Rattigan from his play, *The Sleeping Prince*), and *Three Sisters* (adapted from Chekhov's play for the American Film Theatre in 1970). But acting was Olivier's main avocation, primarily onstage, but also occasionally onscreen, particularly in his later years, since cinema acting was less strenuous. In 1963, Olivier was appointed director of the Royal National Theatre, a position he held for 10 years until 1973.

Among his many honors, Olivier was knighted in 1947, then later elevated to baron in 1970, taking the title Lord Olivier of Brighton, where he kept a town house. His benchmark screen adaptation of Shake-

speare's *Hamlet* won multiple Academy Awards for best director, best actor, and best picture in 1948. In 1979, the Motion Picture Academy awarded him an honorary Oscar for his lifetime contributions to the art of film. In addition to this honor, Olivier was granted the gold medallion of the Swedish Academy of Literature, the Order of the Yugoslav Flag, and the French Legion of Honor. Perhaps the most fitting tribute came, however, when the largest theater of the Royal National Theatre complex on the South Bank in London was named in his honor.

References   Burns, Richard. *Vivien Leigh and Laurence Olivier* (New York: Stein and Day, 1975); Gourlay, Logan. *Olivier* (New York: Stein and Day, 1975); Spoto, Donald. *Laurence Olivier: A Biography* (New York: Cooper Square Press, 2001).

—J.M.W.

Operation Cinderella (1953)

Operation Cinderella was an unrealized project WELLES described to PETER BOGDANOVICH as "The best comedy script I ever wrote," intended as a Hollywood satire about the "occupation" of a small town in Italy by a movie crew. The town is divided "between the collaborators—those who play along with the movie company—and the underground who tries to get rid of them." Welles wrote what he considered a great part for Anna Magnani as the Cinderella figure, "a local girl they've picked up," who leaves the town and her fiancé at the end with the movie company on a bus that will take her to Hollywood and stardom.

—J.M.W.

Orson Welles' Almanac (newspaper column, 1945)

Although not a political ideologue, WELLES was a man of the world, with liberal political views. He had championed the downtrodden, opposed fascism, spoke out on behalf of racial equality, and in 1944, campaigned vigorously for FRANKLIN DELANO ROOSEVELT. He had also grown weary of Hollywood and radio. Therefore, in 1945, when Welles was approached by Robert Hall of the *New York Post* to write a column for the paper, he didn't have to think twice. Given carte blanche to expound on politics, the arts, entertainment, and whatever else might appeal to him, Welles signed on immediately.

Everyone had high hopes. Although Welles was to be paid $200 for each column, Hall thought that with syndication fees from around the country, the weekly feature would soon net $80,000 a year. Writing under the banner *Orson Welles' Almanac* with a photo placed strategically in the logo, the column commenced in January 1945. In an interview about his new career, Welles said: "The column is so important that I plan to devote all my time to it as soon as I can. I've given up all my Hollywood work except to act in one picture each year." Thanks to the clout of the *New York Post,* the column was carried at the outset by such respected papers as the *St. Louis Post-Dispatch* and *Detroit News.*

The first editions of the *Orson Welles' Almanac* covered a variety of items. There was a prescient look at the looming cold war. On a personal level, there was a broadside aimed at Westbrook Pegler, WILLIAM RANDOLPH HEARST's favorite columnist, who in print had recently insulted Frank Sinatra, a Welles friend. There were also excerpts from the *Farmer's Almanac,* items of gossip, astrological tidbits, and, for good measure, cooking tips. Some columns were devoted to celebrities such as French film director SACHA GUITRY, then being tried as a Nazi collaborator. There were discussions of the acting styles of Henry Irving and JOHN BARRYMORE, and a roasting of the National Academy of Arts and Sciences for its awards, which Welles described as foolish and snobbish. He also took up the cause for particular artists such as the painter Ignacio Zuloaga.

The columns became increasingly political. His liberal sentiments resonated in ringing endorsements of various New Deal programs. When President Roosevelt died on April 12, 1945, a devastated Welles changed the name of the column to *Orson Welles Today* to signify what he intended to be his column's heightened relevance. His political views took on even greater vigor. Welles, in spite of his pledge to focus his energies on writing, was still highly involved with movies and radio. As a result, he found it increasingly difficult to meet deadlines. Robert Hall, in exasperation, took to sending berating telegrams in hopes of prodding him. At the same time, although the column had a following in big cities, it never caught on in more conservative sec-

tions of the country. Welles's liberal views just didn't play in the heartland. In an effort to right the ship, Hall tried to get Welles to write more about show business. Welles, however, was adamant about freely espousing his political views.

Six months after its inception, the *Orson Welles' Almanac/Orson Welles Today* column was dropped by the *New York Post.* There just weren't enough syndication sales. Making no attempt to sell it elsewhere, Welles, too, dropped the column, thus bringing his journalistic career to a permanent close.

—C.B.

Orson Welles's Almanac (radio, 1944) After successfully hosting THE JACK BENNY SHOW during the comedian's illness in 1943, WELLES accepted an offer from Mobil Oil to preside over his own radio variety show. Borrowing from Benny's format, Welles surrounded himself with a comedic entourage that included Miss Grimace, a recalcitrant secretary, and Prudence Pratt, who supplied questionable household hints. While Benny was kidded for his cheapness, a similarly put-upon Welles was taunted about his weight. Like Benny's show, and virtually all other radio variety programs, *Orson Welles's Almanac* had a live studio audience whose responsive outbursts and applause became part of the overall performance. There were also guest celebrities. During the show's six-month run in early 1944, Welles traded quips with such stars as Groucho Marx, Lionel Barrymore, Lucille Ball, CHARLES LAUGHTON, and even Hedda Hopper, an old nemesis who with Louella Parsons had led the charge against CITIZEN KANE. Also on hand was Lud Gluskin's big band to provide popular tunes of the day.

Welles, intrigued with the comedy-variety format, conceived of himself in the Fred Allen mode, someone who wasn't a comedian per se, but someone who was funny because of his split-second reactions and timing. There was much ad-libbed banter with guests, anticipating the free and easy exchanges that characterized his later television appearances with DEAN MARTIN, JOHNNY CARSON, MERV GRIFFIN, and DICK CAVETT. There was also a segment in which Welles would list famous dates, celebrity anniversaries and birthdays, and miscellaneous items such as the fact that soda water contains no soda. At the end of each program, and in stark contrast to the typical variety show of the period, Welles gave a dramatic reading of something serious such as a soliloquy from *Hamlet* or an excerpt from the writings of Thomas Paine.

Welles, a lifelong jazz fan, replaced Lud Gluskin's big band with a group of seasoned Dixieland pros, which included clarinetist Jimmie Noone and drummer Zutty Singleton, two African Americans who helped pioneer the New Orleans sound. He regarded the musicians as friends and had them rehearse at his home prior to each week's broadcast. For the April 20 program, Welles had promised Noone that the band would be given a slot to perform the clarinetist's haunting "The Jimmie Noone Blues." Sadly, Noone died of a heart attack the night before the broadcast. The next night, the band played Noone's composition with Wade Barkley sitting in on clarinet. After the poignant lament, Welles went to the microphone and very quietly recited the Twenty-third Psalm. The audience sat stunned. Welles retreated from the stage. It was one of radio broadcasting's most touching and eloquent moments.

Originating in Los Angeles, *Orson Welles's Almanac* was broadcast regionally. In the end, the program's attempt to balance comedic antics with serious material failed to impress network executives as having the broad-based appeal deemed essential for national distribution. Still, the program provided Welles a unique opportunity to experiment with comedy and the kind of casual jocularity that later became a hallmark of television talk shows. It would also serve as useful background for his two forays into television in 1955, THE ORSON WELLES SKETCHBOOK and *AROUND THE WORLD WITH ORSON WELLES*.

—C.B.

Orson Welles's Great Mysteries

(television, 1973–1974) This British-made television series of 26 episodes capitalized on WELLES's popularity in England. Although his name appeared in the title, his participation in each 30-minute show was limited to providing an introduction written by the show's staff. Nonetheless, the syndicated series proved popular in Britain and abroad.

—C.B.

Orson Welles Sketchbook, The

(television, 1955) Harkening back to the informal monologue format of ORSON WELLES'S ALMANAC (1941–42), the six programs in the British Broadcasting Company (BBC) series were essentially 15-minute "essays" on various topics appealing to WELLES. For the initial program broadcast on April 24, 1955, Welles talked about his early days as an actor at Dublin's GATE THEATRE. In this and the subsequent programs, the "talking head" format was enlivened by shots of Welles actually drawing, ergo the "Sketchbook" of the title. Other topics covered during the next five weeks included the challenges of police work, a recollection of a childhood meeting with the magician Houdini, a reminiscence on the broadcast of THE WAR OF THE WORLDS, and reflections on JOHN BARRYMORE and bullfighting. The British public and critics loved the show. In fact, on the basis of its success, Welles was offered another TV series, *AROUND THE WORLD WITH ORSON WELLES*.

The Orson Welles Sketchbook was produced in London by Huw Wheldon for the BBC-TV Drama Department, and ran from April 24 to May 28, 1955.

—C.B.

Orson Welles Story, The

(television, 1980) The British Broadcasting "Arena" production by Alan Yentob and Leslie Megahey (who narrated) was taped in Las Vegas and featured WELLES, PETER BOGDANOVICH, JOHN HUSTON, ANTHONY PERKINS, ROBERT WISE, et al. Bogdanovich later considered it the longest (at 210 minutes) "and (in many respects) best" of all of Welles's television interviews. Ten years later, it was shortened by about an hour and released for American audiences on the TNT cable network under the title *With Orson Welles: Stories from a Life in Film*.

—J.M.W.

Othello

(play, 1951) This powerhouse theatrical production of *Othello*, which opened on October 18, 1951, for a six-week run at the St. James Theatre in London, was produced by LAURENCE OLIVIER in association with S. A. Gorlinsky and the Mercury Arts Society, Ltd. Starring WELLES in the title role of

Othello, Welles's adaptation, based on his screenplay rather than a fresh reworking of the original script, also featured Peter Finch (Iago), Gudrun Ure (Desdemona), and Maxine Audley (Emilia), plus John Van Eyssen, Basil Lord, Keith Pyott, Edward Mulhare, Michael Ware, Diane Foster, and Aubrey Richards.

Though initiated by Olivier, who had never seen Welles in a legitimate stage performance, the project dovetailed perfectly with Welles's efforts to help promote his then ongoing cinematic rendering of OTHELLO, which was eventually released in 1952. Welles was also inspired by the challenge of making his debut on the London stage as both a star and director and international celebrity in a full-blown Shakespearean production mounted in its birthplace, under the aegis of no less a personage than the first man of English theater, Laurence Olivier.

Welles's approach was unorthodox. First, in order to shape the players according to his own designs, he insisted on hiring actors who previously had never played Shakespeare onstage. Much to the chagrin of MICHEÁL MACLIAMMÓIR, who had essayed Iago in Welles's screen version, the role of Iago went to a young Peter Finch, principally a film actor and, significantly, a protégé of Olivier. For Desdemona, he cast Gudrun Ure, who had dubbed SUZANNE CLOUTIER's voice for Welles's film adaptation of *Othello.*

To keep rehearsals and performances fresh, Welles constantly changed his own entrances. He would suddenly appear from stage left, then stage right, from the back curtains, or from down stairways, without any advance notice to his colleagues. Caught up in his directing chores, and reflecting his antipathy for learning his own lines, Welles often forgot his cues and dialogue. On opening night at the St. James, he made a dramatic entrance, took several steps, suddenly stopped, and uttered "Fuck!," a line not scripted by the Bard of Avon. This bit of improvisation was inspired by his realization that he had made his entrance too early. Loud enough to be heard by those in the front rows, a startled first-nighter uttered a whispered rejoinder, "Did he really say what I thought he said?"

Other stories from the production that became legend include his towering physical stature. As FRANK BRADY tells it, Welles, although inches taller than virtually everyone else in the cast, wore four-inch lifts to appear even more enormous. Dwarfing his colleagues with a device that his English cohorts felt unnecessary and pretentious, Welles—"looking ten feet tall and appearing to weigh some three or four hundreds pounds," to cite Brady—registered a heightened impact.

John Griffin, London correspondent for the *New York Herald Tribune,* called the production a "star vehicle for a star actor" and commented favorably on Welles's ability to bring to life "the methodical, ingenious mind of the Moorish general." In the *New Statesman,* T. C. Worsley wrote: "The great lumbering dazed bull which Mr. Welles gives us for Othello may have its shortcomings in detail; but the fact remains that it imposes itself on us so powerfully and terrifyingly that we hardly notice them. This huge, goaded figure rolls onto the stage with a dreadful fog of menace and horror, thickening, wave after wave, with each successive entrance. The very deliberation of his movements, of his great lifted head and rolling bloodshot eyes, and the deep slow notes rumbling from his massive chest, pile up the sense of inevitability almost to the point of the unbearable. In the end we long (and isn't this the point of tragedy?) for the tension to burst."

One of the few sour notes came from KENNETH TYNAN, the young English critic just then starting to make a name for himself. In spite of a genuine affection for Welles, Tynan wrote: "No doubt about it, Orson Welles has the courage of his restrictions." Welles responded with diplomatic tact and remained on friendly terms with Tynan, an indication of his largeness of spirit.

Olivier, for his part, was delighted by the experience. Indeed, the two titanic talents agreed to build on the collaboration, something they achieved in 1960, with the English language debut in London of EUGÈNE IONESCO's absurdist classic, *RHINOCEROS.*

Winston Churchill was among the celebrities who had been attracted to the St. James to take the measure of Welles's genius—and celebrity. After the show, Churchill went backstage to Welles's dressing room, where instead of just saying "hello," instead, proclaimed: "Most potent, grave and reverent signiors, my most approved good masters. . . ." Churchill dazzled the American star by reciting several of Othello's speeches including one that Welles's had deleted from the production.

Welles's celebrity, freshly fluffed by the raves for *Othello,* led to a midnight divertissement at the London Coliseum, where Welles performed his magic act for Princess Elizabeth (today, Queen Elizabeth), and the Duke of Edinburgh. Playing the role of gracious and deferential guest, Welles prefaced his turn by saying, "I have just come from the St. James Theatre, where I have been murdering Desdemona—or Shakespeare, according to which newspaper you read!" The royals were charmed. Indeed, soon after, Princess Margaret twice took in Welles's limning of Othello, going backstage on each occasion to congratulate him. Once again, Welles was in his glory, an eminent man of the theater, and, indeed, an eminent man of the world.

Significantly, the London *Othello* enabled Welles to reclaim some of the respect that had eroded at home in the wake of the disastrous AROUND THE WORLD IN 80 DAYS (1946). And because many of his recent European ventures had been largely unreported in the United States, the favorable reviews of *Othello* in papers like the *New York Times* and *New York Herald Tribune* helped remind American sophisticates and tastemakers that the "Wonder Boy" was still alive and well and, indeed, kicking. Thanks largely to *Othello,* Welles was soon invited to return to the United States to make his American television debut in KING LEAR (1953), for CBS's *Omnibus* in a production directed by PETER BROOK.

—C.B.

Othello (The Tragedy of Othello: The Moor of Venice)

United Artists, 90 minutes, 1952. **Director:** Orson Welles; **Producer:** Welles; **Screenplay:** Welles adapted from *Othello* by William Shakespeare; **Cinematographers:** Anchise Brizzi, G.R. Aldo, George Fanto, Obadan Troiani, and Alberto Fusi; **Editors:** Jean Sacha, John Shepridge, Renzo Lucidi, and William Morton; **Cast:** Orson Welles (Othello), Micheál MacLiammóir (Iago), Suzanne Cloutier (Desdemona), Robert Coote (Roderigo), Michael Laurence (Cassio), Hilton Edwards (Brabantio), Fay Compton (Emilia), Nicholas Bruce (Lodovico), Jean Davis (Montano), Doris Dowling (Bianca), Joseph Cotten (senator), Joan Fontaine (page), Abdullah Ben Mohamet (Desdemona's page)

WELLES'S *Othello* is famous for the time it took to make the film, a story chronicled by MICHEÁL MACLIAMMÓIR in his charming diary, *Put Money in Thy Purse,* and again by Welles in his seldom seen 1978 documentary, FILMING OTHELLO, which he shot for a West German television station. In July of 1947, after his 23-day filming of MACBETH, Welles went to Europe to act in Gregory Ratoff's BLACK MAGIC. There he became involved in negotiations with ALEXANDER KORDA to film Edmond Rostand's play *Cyrano de Bergerac,* but the offer fell through when Korda sold the story rights to raise money, and Welles turned to developing ideas to film Shakespeare's (see SHAKESPEARE BY WELLES) *Othello.* With his designer, ALEXANDER TRAUNER, Welles drew on the work of the Venetian Renaissance painter Vittore Carpaccio for the costumes and for many of the images in the film. They intended to "build the island of Cyprus on the Côte d'Azur," and, as Welles explains it, to create an artificial Venice as well, because "If for three-fourth of our film we were to inhabit an invented world rather than a series of real locations, then our version of reality would have been merely mocked by those famous and familiar old stones of Venice." A series of financial setbacks forced Welles to drop this plan, and instead he decided to use less expensive real locations in Morocco, the country Shakespeare's Moor would likely have called home.

According to BARBARA LEAMING, Welles had received reports from the producer of *Black Magic* that American backers for *Othello* were likely to be put off by "conflicting reports about the job he had done in *Macbeth*" and by the notion that having "a black central character" might be "a box-office liability." Welles financed much of the film himself, raising some of the money by acting in other projects, as he had earlier done with the unfinished film IT'S ALL TRUE. DARYLL ZANUCK helped him get the role of Cesare Borgia in HENRY KING's PRINCE OF FOXES. Alexander Korda got him the role of Harry Lime in CAROL REED's THE THIRD MAN, and Welles played a Mongol chieftain in HENRY HATHAWAY's THE BLACK

ROSE. Initially, Welles had struck a deal with Italian producer Montatori Scalera, who had first suggested the project to Welles and offered to finance *Othello,* but, in June of 1949, when Scalera Studios went broke, Welles, his actors, and his Italian filming crew, who had just landed in the Moroccan coastal city of Mogador, found themselves stranded without money and without costumes.

Welles's inspired solution was to turn a local fish market into a Turkish bath and the scene of Roderigo's murder. Most of the characters wore bath towels, eliminating the need for costumes, and meanwhile, according to Welles, "Jewish tailors were hired and pictures of Carpaccio gentlemen and ladies were shown to them, and pretty soon the costumes slowly began to be made." The process of filming and of raising money to continue filming stretched over three years, from the summer of 1949 to the premiere at Cannes in 1952. Welles shot parts of *Othello* in Venice, Rome, and Morocco, among other places, contributing to what several writers have referred to as a "fractured" effect in the final product. In *Filming Othello,* Welles says, "Pieces were separated not just by place trips, but by breaks in time. Nothing was in continuity. I had no script girl. There was no way for the jigsaw picture to be put together, except in my mind. Over a span of sometimes months, I had to keep all the details in memory. Not just from sequence to sequence, but from cut to cut." The fragmentation of the process was such, Welles explains, that "Iago steps from the portico of a church in Torcello, an island in the Venetian lagoon, into a Portuguese cistern off the coast of Africa. . . . Roderigo kicks Cassio in Massaga and gets punched back in Orgete, a thousand miles away." In spite of the filming conditions, Welles's *Othello* received high praise and shared the Palme d'Or at Cannes in 1952, with *Two Cents Worth of Hope,* by Renato Castellani, the director who two years later filmed his own adaptation of *Romeo and Juliet.*

Welles opens his *Othello* with a small, darkened image of a face upside down, eyes shut. Slowly, the camera reveals more until it is apparent that a man is on a bier being carried by monks in a procession, their dark robes silhouetted against the sky. In a more fragmented manner, Welles adds a parallel procession of white-robed monks carrying the bier of a woman dressed in white but covered by a dark veil. Moving in the opposite direction, a man is being pulled by a chain attached to a collar around his neck. This character, Iago (Micheál MacLiammóir), is thrown into a metal cage that is slowly hauled up the wall of a castle, and the dark-eyed figure inside stares down at the passing images. The camera slides down to a darkened screen, and the titles appear, "The Tragedy of Othello," then "A Motion Picture Adaptation of the play by William Shakespeare." Several writers have pointed out the influence of Sergei Eisenstein in this opening montage, and Kathy Howlett argues that the framework draws on "the narrative sequence of Carpaccio's paintings . . . which begins and ends with *The Martyrdom of the Pilgrims and Funeral of St. Ursula.*" Welles had, of course, used a circular structure by opening with the ending in previous films, such as CITIZEN KANE and would use it again in his next film, MR. ARKADIN. The effect, according to MICHAEL ANDEREGG, makes Welles's *Othello* "a mystery story," whose flashback structure will "emphasize the pattern of inevitability inherent in the story." Welles moves the opening narrative along very quickly by reading the opening lines from Shakespeare's source, the *Hecatommithi* by Venetian Renaissance author Giraldi Cinthio, and by compacting most of the first act into little more than a prelude to Othello's appearance before the assembled Venetian senators, where Desdemona's father, Brabantio (HILTON EDWARDS), has brought his complaint that Othello (Orson Welles) used magic to seduce Desdemona (SUZANNE CLOUTIER). Even the dramatic confrontation between Othello and Brabantio in the second scene of Shakespeare's play is reduced to a brief almost throwaway line as Othello stands on a balcony and calmly tells the men in gondolas, "Keep up your bright swords, for the dew will rust them" (1.2.59).

Welles also rearranges Iago's lines in this opening section in a way that seems characteristic of his treatment throughout the film. The very first lines in the film are Iago's: "I have told thee often, and I retell thee again and again, I hate the Moor," taken from the last scene of the first act (1.3.364–366), as is most of the opening dialogue between Roderigo and

Iago. Welles then takes the waking of Brabantio from the first scene, leaving out the racial epithets and using only a few lines from the second scene. The narrative voice provides the information that the Venetians are giving Othello command of the forces to protect them from the Turks. The camera then cuts to Othello as he listens to the charges, and it stays with him in close-up as he explains how he won Desdemona. Later, after Brabantio has issued his warning that Desdemona might someday deceive Othello, and Othello has asked Iago to care for Desdemona, Welles inserts the lines from the first scene in which Iago explains his anger at Othello's having chosen Cassio as his lieutenant.

Throughout this compression of Shakespeare's first act, Welles makes Othello the real focus, with Roderigo and Iago orbiting his sphere of influence, reacting to what Othello does. He presents Roderigo's despair first because it seems tied to the visual image of the marriage, which is told rather than shown in Shakespeare's play. The issue of Iago's hatred and deception, though announced in his opening line, is developed only after Othello entrusts Desdemona to Iago, underscoring Iago's deceptiveness and Othello's complete trust. These shifts, in other words, clarify and reinforce the motivation of the characters as Welles reshapes Shakespeare's play. At the same time, Welles omits those lines in which Iago explains himself or his philosophy. MacLiammóir explains that Welles believed Iago "was in his opinion impotent; this secret malady was, in fact to be the keystone of the actor's approach. . . . 'Impotent,' he roared . . . 'that's why he hates life so much—they always do.'" According to MacLiammóir, he and Welles also agreed on a characterization in which, "no single trace of the Mephistophelean Iago is to be used: no conscious villainy; a common man, clever as a wagonload of monkeys, his thought never on the present moment but always on the move after the move after next"; they saw Iago as "a business man dealing in destruction with neatness, method, and a proper pleasure in destruction with neatness, method, and a proper pleasure in his work." Another instructive change that demonstrates Welles's method is his alteration of a brief comment Othello makes to Desdemona as they leave the senate. Welles takes the last three lines of Othello's speech in which he asks Iago to look after Desdemona and makes them into a new scene, so that Othello's lines "Come, Desdemona, I have but an hour/Of love, of worldly matter and direction,/To spend with thee. We must obey the time" (1.3.298–300) are spoken in a bedroom where the newlyweds consummate their marriage. Welles then fades from a scene of the lovers embracing to a scene of a stormy coast with cannon, walls, and soldiers braced against the waves.

Several writers have commented on the profound difference between the filmed worlds of Venice and Cyprus. Jack Jorgens, in particular, develops the notion of an "Othello style" and an "Iago style" in Welles's method of shooting, "If the film's grandeur, hyperbole, and simplicity are the Moor's, its dizzying perspectives and camera movements, tortured compositions, grotesque shadows, and insane distortions are Iago's, for he is the agent of chaos." In Venice, according to Jorgens, Iago "is but a shadow on a canal, a whisper echoing in the cathedral," but in Cyprus, "Armaments and the fortress represent a cruder, and in the end hopelessly inadequate, way of dealing with the 'Turk' in man," and "We move inside the labyrinthine bowels of the fortress, into vaulted halls, long staircases, sewers where the deceptively placid water mirrors endless arches, and the Turkish bath were the sweat and steam lead to a crescendo of rushing water at Roderigo's death."

Here, as in the beginning of the film, a brief comment from Iago sets the action in motion. Welles cuts most of Shakespeare's landing scene and focuses on Iago's comment as he watches Cassio greet Desdemona: "He takes her by the palm; ay well said, whisper. With as little a web as this will I ensnare as great a fly as Cassio" (2.1.167–169). When the newly arrived Othello tells Cassio "look you to the guard to-night" (2.3.1), Welles cuts briefly to a reaction shot from Iago, who is clearly weaving his plot. Reorganizing the logic of the action, Welles then has the Herald read Othello's proclamation, calling for "each man to what sport and revels his [addiction] leads him" (2.2.5–6). This section of the film concentrates on how Iago gets Roderigo to help him in the plot to remove Cassio. When Roderigo at one point protests that he cannot think ill of Desdemona,

Welles conveys Iago's attitude by having a braying ass punctuate the brief silence as Iago stares at Roderigo. Welles shows Iago playing Roderigo and Cassio against each other by having Roderigo leave the lower corner of the frame just as Cassio enters the diagonally opposite upper corner to greet Iago, who remains in place as the pivot of the action. Just as he has quickly converted Roderigo to his purposes, Iago soon convinces the weak-stomached Cassio to take a first drink. Balancing the characters, Welles first has Cassio look to the lit window in the darkened tower where Othello and Desdemona reunite, then, in another shot, he has Roderigo look at the same image. Inside the bedroom, Welles uses only shadows to portray the newlyweds. He keeps the focus of the film on Iago's machinations and shows an intensifying montage of scenes of the party as Cassio gets drunk. As Jorgens describes it, these scenes are more and more shaped by the Iago style, with partial views, shadowed scenes, and tilted frames and a latticework of shadows obscuring the vision, images of the web that the spidery Iago weaves.

Welles moves the action here into an underground cistern full of arches where Roderigo runs through the shallow water as Cassio and Montano struggle. The visual impact of the scene suggests some parallels to the sewer scenes in Carol Reed's *The Third Man,* which Welles made during this time. Welles also seems to emphasize the contrast between Othello's high tower and Iago's subterranean plot. Shakespeare has his Othello step into the fight as it is broken up, but Welles instead has his Othello send someone below to bring the brawlers up into the light, where he waits for them. Another element of contrast develops as Othello walks out from the castle and stands in the darkened foreground of the frame, and Desdemona, in a white gown, remains in the well-lit area above him. As Lorne Buchman notes, "Early in the film the director shoots Othello in clear light, but as the film progresses we see him increasingly in shadow." Othello's face is mostly in shadow in this scene, and, after he has removed Cassio from office and stands next to Desdemona, the darkness of his robed and shadowed figure contrasts with the shimmering whiteness of Desdemona, recalling, by way of contrast, how similar to each other they looked when they declared their love before the Venetian senate. Welles, it should be noted, probably made his Othello North African rather than black, not simply, as Peter Donaldson says, because "Othello's blackness does not count for much in Welles," but also because the ambiguity, as in this scene, allows him more dramatic options.

Welles again divides one of Shakespeare's scenes, punctuating the time shift with a rooster's crow. He moves Iago's conversation with the disgraced Cassio from immediately after Othello and Desdemona leave (2.3.258) to a new morning, giving Cassio time to have sobered up and become receptive to Iago's suggestion to have Desdemona intervene with Othello. Welles juxtaposes this scene with one in which he turns one of Iago's soliloquies into a speech and has Iago explain his plan to Roderigo, closing again with the image of "the net/That will enmesh them all" (2.3.353–362). As Iago leaves, laughing, Welles uses a long shot to include the iron cage, hanging prophetically against the tower and over Iago's diminished image. Shortly after, as the plan begins to work, Desdemona stands on the wall and waves to Othello below, then turns to Cassio, who is behind her asking for her help. Just as Cassio turns to leave, Iago and Othello appear in the foreground, with Iago noticing Cassio in the distance walking away from Desdemona. Othello, as Welles plays him, is in good humor when his new bride asks to speak about Cassio's case. He puts her off, and he and Iago begin one of the more noted scenes in the film, the long walk along the wall as Iago plants the seeds of doubt in Othello's imagination.

Anderegg comments, "In sharp contrast to *Macbeth,* there are few long takes in *Othello,*" but in this shot, "The tracking camera, which parallels the movement of Othello and Iago as they walk along the battlements, binds the two men together, reinforcing and locking into place what the dialog tentatively but inexorably works for." The scene is also, as Anthony Davis writes, "the point at which Othello relinquishes the view of the great harmony of the world he once believed in beyond doubt." Visually, the scene is remarkable for being perhaps the most open picture of castle, sea, and sky, which are held together in this single shot as the two men match steps until Iago's line, "Why then I think Cassio is an honest man" (3.3.129), at which point Iago walks out of the frame and Othello remains, suddenly stopped by his first real doubt. When the two men leave the wall and enter a darkened room where Iago helps Othello out of his armor, Welles reinforces the contrast between the former day and the interior night by the use of shadows and mirrors. Iago first helps Othello out of his armor, an image that PETER BOG-DANOVICH suggests shows what Iago has been "doing to him emotionally at the time." There in the darkened room, Othello demonstrates the effects of his transformation when he stares into a mirror. As Samuel Crowl says, Welles uses the "mirror to capture both Othello's loss of assured identity and the powerful masculine vanity that identity was based upon." In one shot, Welles has Iago in the background talking to an Othello in the foreground who is visible only as a mirror image. By the time Desdemona enters, at the end of this sequence, she is clearly unaware of the impossible gulf between them as Othello furtively pulls her to him, then pushes her away, and throws open the curtains to their bedroom, and stares at their bed.

Emilia (Fay Compton) has her first real moment in the film when she appears, dwarfed by the high-walled room, and finds the handkerchief that Desdemona dropped and Othello stepped on as he angrily left the room. Focusing primarily on Othello, Welles minimizes the relationship between Desdemona and Emilia. Emilia seems important in this film more to convey the handkerchief to Iago and, later, to reveal the truth to Othello just before Iago kills her than she is as the friend of Desdemona. Welles cuts Emilia's line from the arrival in Cyprus scene and omits her from the scene in which Desdemona talks with Cassio; her scene with Iago, as she gives him the handkerchief, is brief.

When Othello comes back into the light, he leaves Desdemona and goes back to the wall overlooking the sea, where Iago joins him again. Now, however, the camera is positioned somewhat below as it outlines Iago or Othello separately against the sky or against a raging surf below. The frequently tilted frame distorts the relative height of the two men, and, when he asks Iago to kill Cassio, Othello

becomes a small figure in the background while Iago dominates the frame. While Iago descends into the narrow crowded alleys of the city to plant the handkerchief in Cassio's quarters, Desdemona passes through the labyrinthine interior to meet Othello. Welles keeps husband and wife in separate frames, except for showing their hands touching, and Othello withdraws his hand when Desdemona cannot produce the handkerchief. Here again, Welles reinforces the contrast between Othello's growing darkness and her nearly luminous whiteness. Shortly after, Othello's darkness is again emphasized when he wears a white hooded robe and meets with Iago, then watches in the shadows, peering through a narrow crevice, while Iago engages Cassio in a conversation that Othello takes to be about Desdemona (4.1.93–169). Welles takes the lines of Othello's admiration—"she might lie by an emperor's side and command him tasks" (4.1.184–185)—from one scene and his rage—"I will chop her into messes. Cuckold me!" (5.1.200)—from another scene. At this last line, he introduces cannon fire that announces the impending arrival of Lodovico from Venice.

The cannon fire frames a series of actions that leads up to the killings, unifying the intensifying actions that occur between the cannon fire and Othello's meeting with the Venetians. Welles moves Iago's taunting images about being "naked with her friend in bed" (4.1.3–4) and lying "With her? On her; what your will" (45.1.35) from the opening of Shakespeare's fourth act, and renders Othello's trance (4.1.43) with a sudden shift from the cross-hatched shadows covering Othello and Iago to the sudden expanse of sky as Othello stares openmouthed at the circling gulls overhead and at the inverted image of the crowds watching him. This subjective vision contrasts with the images of the approaching ships, the scurrying soldiers, and the preparations for the visitors. In the midst of it, Welles has Othello, dark against the empty sky, say lines from much earlier, "Farewell the tranquil mind. . . . Farewell! Othello's occupation's gone" (3.3.348–357). The effect of putting these lines here, as the ship docks and lowers sail, is to reinforce Othello's understanding of his loss as he sees himself withdraw from the world represented by Venice and, here specifically, by its emissaries.

From this stance, Lodovico's news that Venice calls Othello back and will put Cassio in his place, seems to make Othello's lines prophetic. In this scene, the Venetians, Lodovico, Desdemona, Cassio, and even Iago, appear separated and distant from Othello, especially after Othello strikes Desdemona.

The following scene between Othello and Desdemona shows the couple in an immense and somewhat smoky room. The massive space reinforces the distance between the couple, and, when Desdemona protests she is falsely accused, and Othello says, "I cry you mercy then./I took you for that cunning whore of Venice/That married with Othello" (4.2.88–89), Desdemona seems to shrink into the architecture, recalling the use of massive shapes in the scenes between Susan and Kane in the XANADU scenes of *Citizen Kane*. After a pair of brief scenes in which Othello first meets with Iago to set plans in motion and then returns to order Desdemona to bed, Welles begins two threads of actions that spin out from these plans.

The first of these is the famous bathhouse scene in which Welles draws lines from Iago's enlisting Roderigo to kill Cassio (4.2.172–245) and from two scenes later when the attack actually occurs (5.1.1–65). In doing so, Welles creates an intensity that he underscores by having it take place in a world of steam and slats, where the obscured images recall the earlier examples of the Iago style. This effect is further intensified by the sound of the mandolins, here perhaps recalling the use of zither music in *The Third Man,* whose title theme became an internationally popular hit. In the sequence as filmed, Iago first calms the exasperated Roderigo, then manages to enlist him in the plot to kill Cassio. In this scene, Roderigo's small white dog, which has appeared in earlier scenes and been passed between Roderigo and Iago here takes on a greater importance. According to Welles, he used a breed called the tenerife because "All the dandies in Carpaccio fondle exactly that dog." In this scene the dog follows Roderigo, tottering precariously on the slats, accidentally alerting Cassio when it barks, and innocently witnessing Iago's plot unravel. When his attack on Cassio fails, Roderigo hides under the flooring and calls out to Iago when he hears him pass. Welles again uses the

bands of vertical lines across the screen, this time the slats from Roderigo's view as Iago runs his sword through them to kill him.

The second line of action is the parallel killing of Desdemona. As a transition between the two sequences, Welles uses another shot of the lighted window in the tower where Othello and Desdemona spent their first night in Cyprus, and of the cage silhouetted again the night sky. Of the important scene between Desdemona and Emilia, Welles omits Desdemona's story of her mother's maid Barbary and the "Willow" song that she sang, perhaps removing some of the poignancy of Shakespeare's original scene. In the opening of this sequence, Welles positions the camera low, catching the somewhat oppressive line of the ceiling in the shot. Desdemona goes through a doorway and sits in a barred window, talking to Emilia as though through a confessional. Welles keeps Emilia's assertion that women can do as men do (4.3.84–103), but ends Desdemona's response with "Good night, good night," and omits her prayer, "Not to pick bad from bad, but by bad mend" (4.3.104–105). Explaining Desdemona's diminished role, Virginia Mason Vaughan describes a "Desdemona style," parallel to the styles identified with Othello and Iago, which, she says, is "not so much expressed by disjunctive editing, rapid changes in scale, and manipulations of space, as by moments of light and stillness." expressive of what Vaughan calls "her *to-be-looked-at-ness,*" because "Desdemona's role is to be the object of masculine exchange."

Othello appears first as a shadow, perhaps intended to recall the first bedroom scene in Cyprus. His voice, saying "It is the cause . . ." (5.2.1–6), is heard before Othello himself appears in the frame, divided by shadows and darkened throughout the sequence. By contrast, Desdemona is again a white image in the dim light of the room. When Othello directly accuses her of giving the handkerchief to Cassio, she rises from the bed, losing her will only after he tells her Cassio confessed to using her. Othello obscures her face by holding a sheet over her face and begins to strangle her. Welles cuts to the exterior view again, with the iron cage still swinging next to the tower. Cutting back to the room, Welles again uses the almost disembodied voice of Othello before his image enters the frame. Emilia rushes in, hears Desdemona's last words, and comes back to Othello, who calls Desdemona a liar and a whore, and says Iago told him so. Othello disappears back into the bedroom and shuts the door behind him, just as Lodovico, Iago, and the others enter. Emilia protests the accusation and tells the truth about the handkerchief, at which point Iago stabs her. As she lies dying, and the others pursue Iago, the camera shows Othello behind an almost impossibly high gate, perhaps five times his height. Emilia dies on the floor, her last words only two phrases from the speech Shakespeare gives her, "she was chaste; she lov'd thee" (5.2.249). Here Welles cuts to Othello's surprised reaction, then to the tilted frame of the pursuit and capture of Iago. Welles keeps only a few of Othello's lines here. He tells them he has a weapon (5.2.267), asks why Iago did what he did (5.2.301–302), and says his famous last speech (5.2.340–351), ending with the word "this" and omitting the closing lines about slaying the Turk (5.2.352–355). Welles uses swirling disorienting subjective shots as Othello, having stabbed himself, makes his way back to the bed. As Othello lifts Desdemona's body, an oval hatch above him opens and Lodovico and the others stare down at him. For his dying speech, Othello's face is surrounded by darkness, a shaft of light on his face. When he dies, he falls to the bed, with Desdemona still in his arms, and Welles cuts back to the procession that began the film, again allowing the camera to slip down the wall to a darkened frame and the titles.

In spite of winning the Palme d'Or, Welles's *Othello,* as Kenneth Rothwell summarizes it, "opened to a hostile reception" both in England and in America, and "the ultimate insult came with the movie's 1955 release in the United States when box-office receipts amounted to a pathetic $40,000." Critical reception since then has been much kinder. Jack J. Jorgens, for example, says, "Welles's *Othello* is one of the few Shakespeare films in which the images on the screen generate enough beauty, variety, and graphic power to stand comparison with Shakespeare's poetic images." Anthony Davies writes, "For the first time in this examination of specific Shakespearean films, we are faced with a film which aims at reconciling theatrical drama with the realism of non-theatrical spatial elements." JAMES NAREMORE praises the film, saying it "seems almost classically proportioned. The story is lucid, the acting naturalistic, the visual compositions relatively simple and pleasing to the eye." Nearly all critics admire Welles's *Othello* far more than his *Macbeth.* Michael Anderegg, in his excellent book on Welles, says, "*Othello* is, in a sense, *Macbeth* turned inside out, the internal becoming external, the implosion becoming explosion, the act of pulling all toward a central point becoming a moving out and away from the center." Echoing Jorgens, Anderegg observes, "While dispensing with so much of Shakespeare's verbal poetry, Welles creates a visual poetry of his own, a poetry inspired rather than dictated by Shakespeare."

There are, however, some exceptions. JOSEPH MCBRIDE argues that "*Othello* as a story stubbornly resists much of Welles's moral framework, and his style, never more floridly expressionistic, is for the most part unsuited for a character conflict that depends so much on psychologically subtle, introspective development." Welles's *Macbeth,* he says, "succeeds in its stylization largely because of *Macbeth*'s comparatively simpler, more elemental conflict—Lady Macbeth's evil is relatively single-minded and direct, compared to the devious treachery of Iago." Stanley Kauffmann, in his review of the 1992 release of the film, makes a similar point when he says, "Welles spends a good deal of this time finding ways to evade acting rather than acting." For him, Welles's "second Shakespeare film lacks the integration and tensions of the earlier one, lacks too a sense of having melded theatre and film"; he concludes that "without the performance he could have given, what is the point of all the rest, no matter how lusciously shot?"

References Anderegg, Michael. *Orson Welles, Shakespeare, and Popular Culture* (New York: Columbia University Press, 1999); Buchman, Lorne M. *Still in Moment: Shakespeare on Screen* (New York and Oxford: Oxford University Press, 1991); Corliss, Richard. "Superbly in Synch with Shakespeare," *Time,* March 20, 1992; Crowdus, Gary. "Othello" (*Cineaste.* December 1995); Crowl, Samuel. *Shakespeare Observed: Studies in Performance on Stage and Screen* (Athens: Ohio University Press, 1992); Davies, Anthony. *Filming Shakespeare's Plays: The Adaptations of*

Laurence Olivier, Orson Welles, Peter Brook, Akira Kurosawa (Cambridge, U.K.: Cambridge University Press, 1988); Donaldson, Peter S. "Mirrors and M/Others: The Welles *Othello." Shakespearean Films / Shakespearean Directors* (Boston: Unwin Hyman, 1990, 93–126); Howlett, Kathy M. *Framing Shakespeare on Film* (Athens: Ohio University Press, 2000); Jorgens, Jack J. *Shakespeare on Film* (Lanham, Md.: New York, London: University Press of America, 1991); Kauffmann, Stanley. "Restoring Welles." *New Republic,* March 9, 1992; Leaming, Barbara. *Orson Welles: A Biography* (New York: Penguin Books, 1989); MacLiammóir, Micheál. *Put Money in Thy Purse: The Filming of Orson Welles's* Othello, (London: Columbus Books, 1988); McBride, Joseph. *Orson Welles,* rev. ed. (New York: Da Capo Press, 1996); Naremore, James. *The Magic World of Orson Welles.* rev. ed. (Dallas, Tex.: Southern Methodist University Press, 1989); Pendleton, Thomas. "Shakespeare . . . with additional dialog." *Cineaste,* December 15, 1998; Rothwell, Kenneth S. *A History of Shakespeare on Screen: A Century of Film and Television* (Cambridge, U.K.: Cambridge University Press, 1999); Thomson, David. *Rosebud: The Story of Orson Welles* (New York: Alfred A. Knopf, 1996); Vaughan, Virginia Mason. *Othello: A Contextual History* (Cambridge, U.K.: Cambridge University Press, 1994); Welles, Orson. *Filming Othello: A Complete Transcription* (http://www.film.tierranet.com/directors/o.welle/fothello.html); Welles, Orson, with Peter Bogdanovich, edited by Jonathan Rosenbaum. *This Is Orson Welles* (New York: HarperCollins, 1992).

—R.V.

Other Side of the Wind, The

SACI (Teheran, Iran)/Les Film de l'Astrophore (Paris), 1970–1976. **Director:** Orson Welles; **Producer:** Dominique Antoine; **Screenplay:** Welles, Oja Kodar **Production Managers:** Frank Marshall, Larry Jackson; **Production Associate:** Neil Canton; **Cinematographer:** Gary Graver; **Production Designer:** Polly Platt; **Locations:** Los Angeles; Flagstaff, and Carefree, Arizona; Paris and Orvilliers, France; **Cast:** John Huston (Jake Hannaford), Bob Random (John Dale), Joseph McBride (Mr. Pister), Susan Strasberg (Juliette Rich), Peter Bogdanovich (Brooks Otterlake), Tonio Sellwart (The Baron), Lilli Palmer (Zarah Valeska), Howard Grossman (Mr. Higgam), With: Cathy Lucas, Norman Foster, Edmond O'Brien, Cameron Mitchell, Mercedes McCambridge, Gary Graver, Richard Wilson, Dennis Hopper, Curtis Harrington, John Carroll, Paul Mazursky, Henry Jaglom, Claude Chabrol, Stephane Audran, Benny Rubin

The melancholy saga behind *The Other Side of the Wind* goes back to an unproduced 1963 script for a film that was to be called THE SACRED BEASTS, which WELLES hoped to make in the mid-1960s. Drawing on his love of bullfighting and his misgivings about Hollywood, the plot of *The Sacred Beasts* concerned an old American director who had retired to Spain to indulge his preoccupations with bullfights and café society. The project was abandoned when *The Moment of Truth* (1964; *Il Momento della Verità*), director Francesco Rosi's Italian-Spanish production about bullfighting, failed at the box office in spite of positive reviews.

In 1970, Welles resurrected *The Sacred Beasts.* Working with his companion OJA KODAR, Welles called the new project *The Other Side of the Wind,* a title that he never explained. In revising the script, the bullfighting was dropped and the action shifted to Los Angeles. Due largely to Kodar's influence, the film became a self-conscious meditation on masculinity. It also was an insider's knowing broadside aimed at the fatuous social-cultural dynamics of 1970s' Hollywood. Finally, and in spite of Welles's denials, it was also a semi-autobiographical rumination of an old film man looking back at the ambiguities of his own life and career.

The six-year production process that led to a 1976 rough cut was anything but organized. Exercising his penchant for improvisation as never before, Welles constantly fiddled with the script, a single copy he jealously guarded. The story changed according to whim, happenings on the set, the availability of resources, the sudden appearance of fresh ideas, and other flashes of inspiration. As a result, continuity became problematic. Cast members grew older, as well as fatter or leaner. Some even had the temerity to die. Still, just about everyone in cast and crew stuck with the project.

The continuity issue was further exacerbated by the project's shaky finances. When Welles got a fresh infusion of funds, he reassembled his troupe, and shot until the money ran out again. Welles biographer

JOSEPH MCBRIDE recalls that on four separate occasions, he had to shave off a beard in order to get back into his character of Mr. Pister. Amazingly, JOHN HUSTON, who played the central character of film director Jake Hannaford, didn't join the project until the third year of production. During that period, Welles had focused on filming secondary scenes and the film-within-a-film, also called *The Other Side of the Wind,* which Huston's character is directing as his last hurrah.

The film's centerpiece is a gala 75th birthday party given for aging Hollywood director Jake Hannaford. Drawing heavily from the figure of Ernest Hemingway, Welles's Hannaford is a swaggering macho man well known for his sexual bravado and political radicalism. However, Welles adds an unsettling undercurrent by suggesting that Hannaford is a closeted homosexual. Here and elsewhere, Welles seems to have used *The Other Side of the Wind* to settle old scores. The suggestion of Hannaford's/Hemingway's homesexuality is, in large part, a payback for a 1937 incident in which Hemingway fired Welles from a job narrating THE SPANISH EARTH because Hemingway thought Welles's voice sounded "faggoty." Hemingway wasn't the only noted figure to weather Welles's lingering wrath.

Critic PAULINE KAEL, whose *Citizen Kane Book* had enraged Welles by suggesting that he had stolen a screenwriting credit from HERMAN J. MANKIEWICZ, is pilloried through the character of the supercilious Juliette Rich, played by Susan Strasberg. Similarly, Welles biographer CHARLES HIGHAM is sent up as Higgam, a haughty journalist played with a British accent by PETER BOGDANOVICH, another Welles biographer. Bogdanovich, serving double duty, also plays Brooks Otterlake, a successful young director given to expensive cashmere sweaters and such, much like Bogdanovich himself. Along with these specific references, Hollywood takes it on the chin in a more general way via the swarm of partygoers composed of nattering journalists, critics, academics, assorted dilettantes, and camera crews who in aggregate further underscore the shallowness of Tinseltown.

At age 75, Hannaford ultimately emerges as a complex and demi-tragic character. We learn, for example, that his last film, a largely improvised work shot on a shoestring budget, has been rejected by the Hollywood moguls who once sang his praises. He is also torn by his simultaneous attractions to the handsome lead actor in his uncompleted film and a sexy young actress. As his sycophants' drug- and alcohol-fueled encomiums become increasingly inflated, he finds himself at once flattered and nauseated. And when footage of his new "commercial" work-in-progress is screened for the crowd, he is forced to confront his darker side and his own cupidity. Worn down by the evening, Hannaford excuses himself, and drives away in a sports car he had planned to give the young actor. Later, we learn that he has been killed in an auto accident.

In spite of the film's heavy thematics, the location shoots were often like reunions. For instance, directors influenced by CITIZEN KANE such as Curtis Harrington, Paul Mazursky, Claude Chabrol, Dennis Hopper, and Henry Jaglom dropped by for cameos. So, too, did Mercury alumni and trusted friends such as NORMAN FOSTER, RICHARD WILSON, MERCEDES MCCAMBRIDGE, EDMOND O'BRIEN, Cameron Mitchell, and cameraman Gary Graver. His beloved Oja Kodar had her cameo as well. And John Huston? Given that Welles had appeared in three films presided over by Huston—MOBY DICK (1956), THE ROOTS OF HEAVEN (1958), and THE KREMLIN LETTER (1970)—both men enjoyed reversing roles. Friends not able to directly participate but who nonetheless were alluded to include MARLENE DIETRICH, who was evoked in the role of hostess Zarah Valeska, played winningly by Lilli Palmer. The financing of the film was as convoluted as its production. At various points, Welles and Kodar invested their own money, a sum totaling close to a quarter million dollars. There also were investments by Astrophore Films, a Parisian-based Iranian company headed by Medhi Mouscheri, the brother-in-law of the Shah of Iran. Other funds came from Spain. Through the six-year production period, Mouscheri's Astrophore Films contributed over a million dollars.

An already muddled funding picture grew even darker when money was embezzled from the project by one of the non-Iranian investors. Then, when the Shah was forced to flee Iran in the wake of that country's fundamentalist revolution, the Paris-based Astrophore Films fell into legal limbo. Although Welles estimated that the film was nearly 90 percent complete, the negative and workprints were locked away in a laboratory in Paris by agents of the Ayatollah Khomeini. Thus, Welles was never able to complete the project. To this day, *The Other Side of the Wind* remains entombed in a film lab in Paris.

Interestingly, when Welles was presented with the American Film Institute's third Life Achievement Award in 1975, he insisted that two clips from *The Other Side of the Wind* be included in the televised presentation. Thanks to these excerpts, and sequences shown at the Screen Directors' Guild in Hollywood during the same period, we have at least a hint of what promises to become, once it is liberated, an indispensable part of the Welles canon.

—C.B.

Out of Darkness (television, 1956) In the 1950s, the major U.S. television networks devoted a good deal of prime time to hard-hitting documentary probes of pressing contemporary issues. *Out of Darkness,* one of the period's most trenchant examinations of mental illness, was made in 1956 by veteran documentarian Albert Wasserman for Irving Gitlin's documentary unit at CBS News. Edited from material shot over many months, *Out of Darkness* followed a psychiatrist's work with a catatonic youngster who had not spoken for months. The film's dramatic high point occurs when the girl reenters the world of speech. Touching the doctor's cuff link, she exclaims: "That's pretty. Is it a real pearl?" A much-lauded commentary delivered by Welles added continuity and dramatic emphasis to the story of the struggle and eventual triumph of the determined doctor-patient team.

Later, *Out of Darkness* became the subject of an experiment that helped change the course of documentary. Robert Drew, a pioneer of the cinema vérité movement who admired the film, thought that the film's real power resided in its images and actual location sounds, rather than in Welles's commentary. To test his hypothesis, Drew took a print of the film and deleted the narration. Audiences, when shown this version without Welles's voice-over "guidance," were forced to make sense of the footage for themselves. To Drew, as broadcast historian Erik Barnouw points out, "the experience seemed more powerful—difficult, demanding, but in the end, more meaningful." Thus, cinema vérité's elimination of the omniscient narrator's voice arose in part because of the attention drawn to that convention by Welles's commanding "voice of authority" in *Out of Darkness.*

Reference Rosenthal, Alan. *The Documentary Conscience* (Berkeley: University of California Press, 1980).

—C.B.

Pampered Youth Vitagraph, 7 reels (65 minutes), 1925. **Director and Producer:** David Smith; **Screenplay:** Jay Pilcher; **Cinematography:** David Smith; **Cast:** Cullen Landis (George Minafer), Ben Alexander (young George); Allan Forrest (Eugene Morgan), Alice Calhoun (Isabel Minafer), Emmitt King (Major Amberson), Charlotte Merriam (Lucy Morgan)

Pampered Youth, adapted by Jay Pilcher and directed by David Smith in 1924 (though not released until 1925), was the first Hollywood version of BOOTH TARKINGTON's novel, *The Magnificent Ambersons,* later adapted and directed by ORSON WELLES. This silent film generally followed the plot of Tarkington's novel, but gave it a "Hollywood" ending, described by the *AFI Catalogue* as follows: "When Major Amberson dies, George is forced to go to work. George is reconciled to Eugene when Eugene rescues Mrs. Minafer from a fire in the Amberson mansion." The box-office failure of *Pampered Youth* was attributed in part to the way it changed the novel's ending with the reconciliation between George Minafer (Cullen Landis) and Eugene Morgan (Allan Forrest) and George's giving Eugene his permission to marry his mother. Tarkington's story was forgotten until 1927, when, in the wake of Warners sound-on-film success, *The Jazz Singer,* Warners sought the sound film rights to *The Magnificent Ambersons,* a deal concluded in 1929. The adaptation was assigned to veteran screenwriter Julien Josephson. The project was shelved until 1938, however, when a second adaptation was penned by Charles Linton Tedford. Again, Warners was pessimistic about its prospects. Thus, when RKO began negotiations on behalf of Welles to acquire the film rights for *The Magnificent Ambersons.* Warners was pleased to sell it for a small amount, along with the Josephson and Tedford scripts, which Welles used for background. Whether or not the earlier Vitagraph version of Tarkington's story influenced Orson Welles is open to dispute.

References Munden, Kenneth W., ed. *American Film Institute Catalogue: Feature Films, 1921–1930.* (New York and London: R.R. Bowker, 1971); Slide, Anthony. *The Big V: A History of the Vitagraph Company* (Metuchen, N.J.: Scarecrow, 1987)

—C.B. and J.M.W.

Panic (play, 1935) A play by ARCHIBALD MACLEISH, starring WELLES as McGafferty. In March 1935, the Phoenix Theatre production of Archibald MacLeish's verse play, *Panic,* opened on Broadway for a limited three-night run at the Imperial Theatre. Heading the cast was Welles, who played McGafferty, a bold, larger-than-life financier who in mid-February 1933, attempts to halt the nation's banking crisis. When a group of unemployed workers storms into a financial summit headed by McGafferty, the worker's leader, a blind prophet, casts a spell on McGafferty, sending the tycoon into a downward psychological spiral and, with him, any hope of stabilizing the nation's crumbling banking system.

MacLeish, a Pulitzer Prize–winning poet, was also a respected economist armed with a Yale law degree. In his review of the play, the *New York Times*'s BROOKS ATKINSON noted that since "Mr. MacLeish is also one of the editors of *Fortune* and is reputed to have a brilliant mind for the economy, it is assumed that his knowledge of his subject is worth respecting." Here, the poet-economist is perhaps best viewed as an apologist for the nation's faulty fiscal leadership since *Panic* asserts that the banking collapse of 1933 was a matter of supernatural rather than rational forces.

Atkinson praised the boldness of MacLeish's experiment, while expressing reservations about the difficulty of comprehending the verse dialogue. "*Panic,* which is difficult to read in book form," noted the *Times* critic, "is, to this attentive listener, nebulous on the stage." Atkinson was not alone. Most of the other New York critics were similarly baffled. Another problem stemmed from the play's pessimism. In 1935, after six years of the Depression, audiences were looking for plays and movies that were upbeat, that offered hope, and if not that, at least several hours of diversion. Nonetheless, *Panic* occupies a special place in American theater history and in the career of Welles.

Whatever reservations critics and audiences had about the play, its poetic form, its subject matter, or its pessimistic theme, there was unanimity about the star turn by the precocious 19-year-old Welles playing a late-50s plutocrat. The influential Atkinson, for one, singled out the young actor for praise calling his McGafferty "excellent." Whitney Bolton of the *New York Telegraph* gushed that "Orson Welles was the triumph of the hour—he is bluff, defiant, bullocklike and brutal." The *New York American* called Welles "one of the most promising artists of our day." The play also provided Welles with an entree into big time radio when a scene was broadcast the following week as a segment on CBS's THE MARCH OF TIME.

Panic, although a three-day experimental foray, was an event not to be missed. There was MacLeish,

of course. There were also luminaries from the New York stage such as director James Light, designer Jo Mielziner, choreographer Martha Graham, and composer VIRGIL THOMPSON. The producer was JOHN HOUSEMAN. Indeed, *Panic* was the first of many Welles-Houseman collaborations. In such company, and with such publicity, the young actor finally had a chance to shine. Welles's star potential was suddenly the talk of the town. Welles's wife, Virginia, played one of the women of the Chorus and served as assistant stage manager.

Significantly, echoes of McGafferty would resonate just six years later in Welles's greatest role, CHARLES FOSTER KANE, the central character of his greatest creation, *CITIZEN KANE*.

—C.B.

Panic (radio, 1935) On March 22, 1935, Orson Welles made his debut on national radio by reprising his stage role of McGafferty in a scene from ARCHIBALD MACLEISH's experimental play *PANIC,* which had just finished an exclusive three-night run during the previous week at New York's Imperial Theatre. As the sound of ticker tapes rattle in the background, McGafferty is asked by his banking colleagues what he plans to do. "Do?" thundered Welles. "What do you think I'll do? Pull the blinds on the bank and sail to Bermuda? *This bank will open tomorrow at Nine.*" With those lines, the nation's radio audience was first introduced to Orson Welles.

The scene from *Panic* was produced as a segment for *THE MARCH OF TIME,* which was first broadcast in 1931 as a companion to the weekly *Time* magazine and its motion picture analogue, *The March of Time* newsreel. In the same show, Welles offered a preview of the versatility that would make him America's best-known radio actor of the 1930s. When a baby-effects expert was not available for the next segment of the show devoted to Canada's Dionne quintuplets, Welles piped up, "I can do baby voices." After a brief audition, Welles was hired to pinch-hit. Thus, with only the separation of a commercial, Welles was able to impress the radio brass at CBS, first with the imperious bravado of McGafferty, and then with the gurgling coos of Yvonne, Annette, Cecile, Marie, and Emilie Dionne. The broadcast of March 22, 1935, also marked the onset on Welles's long and productive tenure with *The March of Time.*

—C.B.

Parsons, Louella (Louella Oettinger)

(1893–1972) A famous Hollywood gossip columnist syndicated in the Hearst newspaper chain, Louella Parsons played an important role in the furor over the links between WILLIAM RANDOLPH HEARST, her employer, and Kane, the newspaper tycoon in WELLES's *CITIZEN KANE* (1941). Parsons, whose *Hollywood Hotel* radio show was replaced on the air by Welles's *CAMPBELL PLAYHOUSE,* was initially an avid Welles supporter and, despite not having seen the film, provided it with favorable advance publicity. Hearst had an advance copy of *Friday,* a journal that published a fabricated story in which Welles was quoted as having said, "Wait until the woman [Parsons] finds out the picture's about her boss." Hearst called Parsons, informed her about the article, and ordered her to screen the film, which she did the next day, accompanied by two Hearst lawyers. After the screening, Parsons and the lawyers left hurriedly without saying a word to Welles. She sent a telegram to Hearst, informing him that it was worse than they had expected and would be detrimental to his reputation. She was ordered to stop *Citizen Kane.* She subsequently called GEORGE SCHAEFER at RKO and told his secretary that it was a "matter of life and death for RKO" and threatened a lawsuit. After talking with Welles, Schaefer called Parsons and told her that the film was not about Hearst and that it would be released on schedule on February 14. FRANK BRADY quotes Parsons as threatening. "If you boys want private lives, he'll [Hearst] give you private lives," intimating that studio heads would have their private lives exposed to the public. She also called LOUIS B. MAYER at MGM and other studio heads and threatened Hearst repercussions to the entire Hollywood movie industry. All were concerned about what Hearst attacks might do to the industry, and Mayer offered his help to Parsons/Hearst. Parsons was relentless. She called every member of the RKO board and threatened to have their private lives exposed in the Hearst newspapers. Other calls went to David Sarnoff, president of RCA, which had an interest in RKO, W. G. Van Schmus, manager of Radio City Music Hall, a possible screening venue, Harry M. Warner, who controlled what was shown at his theaters, and, reportedly, NELSON ROCKEFELLER, who owned a lot of RKO stock. She even went to Will Hayes of the Motion Picture Association, but Hayes, while offering sympathy, did nothing to prevent the release of the picture. Parsons, who believed that Welles had deliberately misled her about the film, continued her animus against Welles after the film was released. She advised RITA HAYWORTH, soon to become the second Mrs. Welles, not to marry him; and then in her syndicated column predicted that the marriage would not last. According to CHARLES HIGHAM, she disparagingly termed Welles "the Brain who married Rita Hayworth." Higham also claims that Parsons "kept most people in Hollywood from hiring Welles." Parsons's power was rivaled only by her competitor, Hedda Hopper.

Parsons was born on August 6, 1893, in Freeport, Illinois, but had her career in Hollywood. In addition to writing her Hollywood gossip column, she wrote two volumes of her memoirs, *The Gay Illiterate* (1944), an allusion to her malapropisms and use of the English language, and *Tell It to Louella* (1961). Perhaps because of her influence, she also appeared in some films, among them *Hollywood Hotel* (1937), *Without Reservations* (1946), and *Starlift* (1951). She hosted *Hollywood Hotel* on the radio. The program featured Hollywood celebrities who, in exchange for some choice gossip, would have their next films publicized. John Durning described the show as "a mutual backscratching vehicle, publicizing the stars' movies, promoting their names, and keeping Miss Parsons at the top of radio row." Parsons died in 1972.

Reference Eels, George. *Hedda and Louella* (New York: Warner, 1973).

—T.L.E.

Passenger to Bali, A (radio, 1938) Directed by

WELLES and produced by the MERCURY THEATRE ON THE AIR, *A Passenger to Bali* was adapted by Welles from a short story by Ellis St. Joseph that first appeared in *Story* magazine. Based on St. Joseph's adventures on a tramp freighter in the Pacific, the story pitted a corrupt Dutch missionary, Rev. Dr. Ralph Walkes (Welles), against the ship's master, Captain English. All action took place on the ship, on the high seas, and in such exotic ports of call as Bangkok and Shanghai. Dramatically, the ship functions as a microcosm in which civilization battles brute force. Broadcast by CBS in 1938.

—C.B.

Perkins, Anthony (1932–1992) Famous for his remarkable portrayal of the psychopathic killer Norman Bates in Alfred Hitchcock's *Psycho* (1960), actor Anthony Perkins also played Josef K. in the ORSON WELLES screen adaptation of FRANZ KAFKA's *THE TRIAL* (1962). Born on April 4, 1932, in New York City, the son of actor Osgood Perkins (1892–1937), Perkins was educated first at Rollins College in Winter Park, Florida, then at Columbia University. His stage debut was in 1946 in summer stock theater in Brattleboro, Vermont. At age 21 he made his film debut, playing opposite Jean Simmons in *The Actress* (1953), directed by George Cukor. In 1956, he was nominated for an Academy Award for best supporting actor in *Friendly Persuasion,* directed by William Wyler.

Upon the release of *The Trial* in Paris, Welles was criticized for having cast Perkins as Josef K., but the director defended his choice to BARBARA LEAMING: "I think everybody has an idea of K as some kind of little Woody Allen. That's who they think K is. But it's very clearly stated in the book that he is a young executive on his way up." In effect, Welles cast Perkins because of the aggressiveness he saw in Perkins. Perkins has commented on Welles's ability to finish films despite casting problems and financial limitations: "He's a wonderful manipulator—and I mean that in the best sense—of people and their soft spots and the ways to get them behind his vision of things."

Psycho made Perkins a star actor and assured him of roles for other top directors, such as Jules Dassin (*Phaedra,* 1961), René Clément (*Is Paris Burning?,* 1965), Claude Chabrol (*Le Scandale,* 1967, and *La Decade prodigieuse,* 1971), MIKE NICHOLS (*Catch-22,* 1970), JOHN HUSTON (*The Life and Times of Judge Roy Bean,* 1972), Alan Rudolph (*Remember My Name,*

(1979), and Ken Russell (*Crimes of Passion,* 1984), for example. But his talent for sensitive and vulnerable roles was, in an odd way, undercut by *Psycho,* which initially propelled him to stardom. Toward the end of his career he was still doing Norman Bates in such sequels as *Psycho II* (1983), *Psycho III* (which he also directed in 1986), and *Psycho IV* (1990). As long as he lived, could a *Psycho* sequel be made without him? As Hitchcock critic Robin Wood has written, "The ghost of Norman Bates could not be exorcised." Perkins died of AIDS in 1992.

References Bergan, Ronald. *Anthony Perkins: A Haunted Life* (London: Warner, 1996); Mackay, Michael and Ketti Frings. *Tony Perkins: Shooting Star* (Dayton, Ohio: Weekly Publications, 1958); Winecoff, Charles. *Split Image: The Life of Anthony Perkins* (New York: Plume, 1997).

—J.M.W.

Perkins, V.I. (1936–) British critic V.I. Perkins, a lecturer at Warwick University since 1978, wrote the "Film Classics" monograph on *THE MAGNIFICENT AMBERSONS,* published by the British Film Institute in 1999. Born in Devon in 1936, Perkins was educated at the Alphington Primary School, Hele's School, Exeter, and Exeter College, Oxford, where he studied modern history. He lectured at Hornsey College of Art and for the Extra-Mural Department of London University before becoming a teacher-adviser for the British Film Institute's Education Department. Before taking his post at Warwick University, Perkins headed Film Studies at the Berkshire College of Education. Perkins was a founder-member of the editorial board for the journal *Movie,* and went on to write *Film as Film: Understanding and Judging Movies,* published by Penguin Books in 1972, a book that helped to revolutionize film study in Britain.

Perkins considers the ruination of *The Magnificent Ambersons* as "one of the greatest tragedies of movie history" and praises the film "as one of cinema's glories—an incisive, moving, generous and thrillingly accomplished work." Although WELLES tried "to protect the overall design of the film—the movement from the remembered hope of springtime into a world of regret and decay," finally Welles "could do nothing to protect the film from improvement because its fate was bound up with the fate of the studio boss," GEORGE SCHAEFER at RKO, whose "managerial record was, more and more clearly, disastrous." Welles's editor, ROBERT WISE, "sought to excuse the job done on the film by conceding that as a work of art, it was 'a better picture in its original-length version: as an accomplishment. But we were faced with the reality of not art, but business, and what to do with something that wouldn't play.'" The "Tarkington Problem" of adapting the film to cinema was based on BOOTH TARKINGTON's unsuccessful attempt to contrive "the semblance of a happy ending, for a story whose logic would not go that way." At the end, fidelity was impossible. The challenge of adapting the film was to "invent a finale that would be actable and powerful, plausible but not flatly depressing." The book traces the film's production history and offers a careful analysis of the attempted solutions.

—J.M.W.

Pettey, Tom   Tom Pettey, the RKO publicist in Rio de Janeiro, worked with ORSON WELLES on publicity while Welles was shooting IT'S ALL TRUE in Brazil. While the bickering continued over the reediting of Welles's THE MAGNIFICENT AMBERSONS (1942), Welles had Pettey issue a press release to the effect that he would "shoot the conquest of Peru," a statement that CHARLES HIGHAM termed a "classic case of whistling in the dark." About the Carnival footage that Welles shot, Pettey wrote to HERBERT DRAKE, Welles's press agent, "As for the film story, only God and Orson know; Orson doesn't remember." According to Pettey, when things were going well, Welles would "pick up a gal and vanish in his car for hours" or pick a fight with someone on the set, and nothing would get done. According to DAVID THOMSON, Pettey had begun the Rio adventure as an admirer of Welles, but "then the bullshit factor set in."

—T.L.E.

Pirandello, Luigi (1867–1936)   In 1934, WELLES adapted LUIGI PIRANDELLO's *Tonight We Improvise* for THE MARCH OF TIME radio series. The broadcast was designed to honor Pirandello's having won the Nobel Prize for literature. In 1953, Welles appeared in *L'Uomo, la Bestia e la Virtù* (*Man, Beast and Virtue*), an Italian epic film adapted from Pirandello. Welles told PETER BOGDANOVICH, "I was 'the beast' and 'the man' was a comic named Toto."

Luigi Pirandello, who was born on June 28, 1867, in Agrigento, Sicily, was educated in schools in Agrigento and Palermo before studying law at the University of Rome (1887–89) and philosophy at the University of Bonn (1889–91), where he received his doctorate. He taught and was co-editor of *Ariel* (1898) before he produced his first play, *L'epilogo* (staged as *La Morsa*), in 1910. He toured and directed his own company Teatro d'Arte from 1925 to 1928. During 1928–33 he lived outside Italy, mostly in Berlin and Paris. A prolific writer, he wrote more than 50 plays, many of which were translated into English, almost 30 works of fiction, many translated, six volumes of poetry, three screenplays, and three books of essays. His most famous play is *Sei personaggi in cerca d'autore* (1921, *Six Characters in Search of an Author*), the first of three plays in the "theater in the theater" trilogy. He won the Nobel Prize for literature in 1934 and was a member of the Italian Academy and the Légion d'Honneur (France).

References   Bassanesse, Fiora A. *Understanding Luigi Pirandello* (Columbia: University of South Carolina Press, 1997); Bassnett, Susan. *Luigi Pirandello* (New York: Grove, 1983); Mattaei, Renate. *Luigi Pirandello* (New York: F. Ungar, 1973).

—T.L.E.

Porter, Cole (1892–1964)   In 1946, WELLES and Porter, the legendary Broadway and Hollywood tunesmith, collaborated on AROUND THE WORLD IN 80 DAYS, Welles's musical extravaganza, which ran for 75 performances at New York's Adelphi Theatre.

Welles had been enamored of JULES VERNE's well-known 1873 adventure novel since the late 1920s, when he had seen a ragtag yet memorable stage adaptation as a child. Later, at the height of his career as a broadcast dramatist, Welles presided over radio adaptations of Verne's picaresque story in 1938, 1939, and 1945.

Significantly, Welles had also envisioned *Around the World in 80 Days* as a film. However, his 1940 scenario was rejected by RKO head GEORGE SCHAEFER because of its projected high cost. In early 1946, casting about for a vehicle that would return him to Broadway, Welles dug out the rejected screenplay, quickly reworked it as a musical spectacular, engaged the legendary Cole Porter to write the songs, and searched for backers. "Orson Welles and Cole Porter, together, on Broadway!" It seemed like a can't-miss proposition.

Welles's concept for musicalizing *Around the World in 80 Days* was big, brassy, and bold, a fireworks display of disparate elements drawn from music, drama, dance, film, and even the circus. In the end, the juxtapositions proved too jarring. The *New York Times's* Lewis Nichols, for one, opined, "There are too many styles fighting among themselves. Mr. Welles, as Knark Fix, plays the part with vast burlesque and is, himself, very funny at it. He has given Arthur Margetson some amusing lines as Fogg, which that actor plays suavely. The rest of the show wanders off from the comedy, however." There were other problems.

Perhaps the biggest disappointment was the surprisingly prosaic Porter score. Prior to hiring Porter, Welles had been told by Broadway insiders that the great composer's creative juices had run dry. However, if Welles had any thoughts about scuttling Porter, they were trumped by the director's excitement in working with one of Broadway's greatest living musical legends. Also, any such plans would have been scotched by Broadway impresario MIKE TODD, one of *Around the World*'s principal backers. After all, it was Porter who had been largely responsible for one of Todd's greatest hits, the 1943 Broadway musical smash, *Something for the Boys.*

Around the World in 80 Days proved another matter. Significantly, not one of Porter's tunes made it to the hit parade. Likewise, not one of the show's tunes enjoyed later success as a standard. Taking pity on Welles's precarious financial investment in *Around the World in 80 Days,* and perhaps feeling bad that his contribution had not been up to par, Porter, who had negotiated an extravagant contract, proved a gentleman and friend by agreeing to forgo his lucrative royalty agreement until the show started turning profits. Given the show's tepid reviews and huge production expenses and payroll, that never happened.

Porter, born in Peru, Indiana, on June 9, 1891, was wealthy from birth. His family, although

indulging his early interest in song, warned the young man against pursuing a career in music. Heeding that advice to the extent of keeping his musical passions extracurricular, Porter, in 1913, graduated from Yale, and then moved to Harvard to study law. The siren song of music eventually overwhelmed him, and Porter transferred to Harvard's School of Music. At both Yale and Harvard, Porter had penned songs for college shows. At Harvard, he wrote a musical comedy, *See America First* (1916), that featured a young Clifton Webb. In 1919, while continuing his studies in Paris, he wrote "An Old Fashioned Garden," his first hit. The song was picked up for Raymond Hitchcock's Broadway revue, *Hitchy-Koo of 1919,* for which Porter also wrote the score. The show enjoyed a two-year run, permitting Porter to establish himself as a composer independent of the family fortune from which he had now been disowned. He soon returned to France, where he and his new wife led a lavish society life.

Thanks to his own income and his wife's private fortune, Porter was able to compose largely for his own amusement and that of his cosmopolitan friends in New York and Paris. He was also sought out by Broadway showmen who prevailed upon him to contribute to revues such as *Hitchy-Koo of 1922* and *Greenwich Village Follies of 1924.* In 1928, E. Ray Goetz persuaded him to write songs for an entire show, *Paris* (1928), one of which, "Let's Do It," became a huge hit. Finally, Porter began to take his talent seriously.

Porter's Broadway shows, for which he generally wrote both the music and lyrics, include *Fifty Million Frenchmen* (1929), *Wake Up and Dream* (1929), *The New Yorkers* (1930), *Gay Divorce* (1932), *Anything Goes* (1934), *Jubilee* (1935), *Red, Hot and Blue* (1936), *You Never Know* (1938), *Leave It to Me!* (1938), *DuBarry Was a Lady* (1939), *Panama Hattie* (1940), *Let's Face It* (1941), *Something for the Boys* (1943), and *Seven Lively Arts* (1944). After the letdown of *Around the World in 80 Days* (1946), Porter returned to form with *Kiss Me, Kate* (1948), *Can-Can* (1950), and *Silk Stockings* (1955).

While Porter's shows occupy a special place in the history of the Broadway musical, his indelible tunes have had an even greater impact by providing a good part of the "sound track" that has accompanied the sophisticated side of American popular culture from the 1920s to the present. Indeed, Porter's songs have become standards, beloved by successive generations of crooners, thrushes, jazzers, lounge lizards, and their respective fans. Evergreens from the Porter songbook include "You Do Something to Me," "What Is This Thing Called Love?," "Love for Sale," "Night and Day," "Anything Goes," "I Get a Kick Out of You," "You're the Top," "Begin the Beguine," "Just One of Those Things," "My Heart Belongs to Daddy," "Friendship," "I Love You," "Everytime We Say Goodbye," "I Love Paris," "It's All Right With Me," and "All of You." Porter's clever novelty song, "Brush Up Your Shakespeare" from *Kiss Me, Kate,* became a standard part of Welles's cabaret and television acts.

A number of Porter's Broadway shows were adapted to the screen, including *Fifty Million Frenchmen* (1931), *The Gay Divorcé* (1934; based on *Gay Divorce*), *Anything Goes* (1936), *Panama Hattie* (1942), *Dubarry Was a Lady* (1943), *Kiss Me Kate* (1953), a remake of *Anything Goes* (1956), *Silk Stockings* (1957) and *Can-Can* (1959). Porter songs were featured in other films such as *Born to Dance* (1936), *Rosalie* (1937), *Broadway Melody of 1940* (1940), *Let's Face It* (1943), *Something to Shout About* (1943), *Hollywood Canteen* (1944), *The Pirate* (1948), *Stage Fright* (1950), *High Society* (1956), *Les Girls* (1957), and *At Long Last Love* (1975), which revived many of his songs including "Miss Otis Regrets." *Night and Day* (1946), a largely "fictive" film-biography of Porter, starred Cary Grant as the composer.

The sophisticated songwriter injured his leg in a riding accident in 1937. After many corrective surgeries, in 1956, he was forced to have the leg amputated. In spite of the constant physical pain, Porter composed some of the most brilliant and lasting tunes in the repertory of what musicologist Alec Wilder calls "the American popular song." Porter died on a Santa Monica operating table in 1964 in the midst of surgery for a kidney stone.

References Kimball, Robert, and Brendan Gill. *Cole* (Woodstock, N.Y.: Overlook, 2001); McBrien, William. *Cole Porter: A Biography* (New York: Vintage, 2000).

—C.B.

Power, Tyrone (1914–1958)   Actor Tyrone Edmund Power III, described as "the last idol" by biographer Fred Lawrence Guiles, was born on May 5, 1914, in Cincinnati, Ohio, to a theatrical family. His great-grandfather, Tyrone the Elder, was born in County Waterford, Ireland, in 1795, and first appeared on stage in Monmouth, Wales, playing Duke Orlando in *As You Like It*. This began a successful career that took him first to London, then to New York, Philadelphia, and other American cities. The star's father also built a successful acting career in America during the first two decades of the 20th century. Distinguished acting was a family tradition. Onstage, Power played Tybalt to ORSON WELLES's Mercutio in the Maurice Evans revival of *Romeo and Juliet* that toured 77 cities in 39 weeks. On this tour, Power was noticed by a talent scout for Universal; though he was advised by KATHERINE CORNELL to turn down the seven-year contract that was eventually offered in 1935, he signed later that year with Twentieth Century–Fox. In various genre roles, he played characters as diverse as Jesse James, Brigham Young, and the swashbuckling Zorro in the sound remake of *The Mark of Zorro* (1940). More "serious" literary roles included Larry Darrell in *The Razor's Edge* (1946) and Jake Barnes in *The Sun Also Rises* (1957).

Power starred with Orson Welles in two films. In *PRINCE OF FOXES* (1949), directed by HENRY KING and adapted to cinema by Milton Krims from the novel by Samuel Shellabarger, Power played the Italian Renaissance adventurer Andrea Orsini attempting to thwart the ruthless quest for power of Cesare Borgia (Orson Welles). According to FRANK BRADY, Power stood in awe of Welles and "seemed more of a disciple than an equal." Without director Henry King's knowledge, Welles even suggested "subtle changes and nuances" that Power could use in his role. In *THE BLACK ROSE* (1950), adapted by Talbot Jennings from Thomas B. Costain's novel, directed by HENRY HATHAWAY, he played the 13th-century Saxon adventurer Walter of Gurnie, who flees to England with a price on his head, travels to China, returns to England with remarkable inventions, and is finally knighted by King Edward. On his way to China, he encounters a fierce Mongol warlord, Bayan of the

Thousand Eyes, "played to the hilt by Orson Welles," in the words of the *Herald Tribune* reviewer.

Power's successful Hollywood career ended when the actor died in Madrid, Spain, on November 15, 1958, after having collapsed during the filming of *Solomon and Sheba,* directed by King Vidor, and co-starring Gina Lollobrigida and George Sanders. The film was reshot, with Yul Brynner recast in the role Power was to have played.

References Arce, Hector. *The Secret Life of Tyrone Power* (New York: Bantam Books, 1980); Belafonte, Dennis, and Alvin H. Marill. *The Films of Tyrone Power* (Secaucus, N.J.: Citadel, 1979); Guiles, Fred Lawrence. *Tyrone Power: The Last Idol* (San Francisco: Mercury House, 1990).

—J.M.W.

Prince of Foxes Twentieth Century–Fox, 107 minutes, 1949. **Director:** Henry King; **Producers:** Darryl F. Zanuck and Sol C. Siegel; **Screenplay:** Milton Krims, adapted from the novel by Samuel Shellabarger; **Cinematography:** Leon Shamroy; **Editor:** Barbara McLean; **Music:** Alfred Newman; **Cast:** Orson Welles (Cesare Borgia), Tyrone Power (Orsini), Wanda Hendrix (Camilla), Felix Aylmer (Verano), Everett Sloane (Belli), et al.

A U.S. film directed by HENRY KING starring WELLES in the role of Cesare Borgia. Shot mostly in Italy, this DARRYL F. ZANUCK production featured Welles and good pal TYRONE POWER (as Andrea Orsini) in a deliberately paced 16th-century costume drama about which Richard Mallett of *Punch* said: "This pretentious chapter of pseudo-history never rises above the merely spectacular, hovers mostly around the conventionally banal, and descends once to the unpardonably crude." Hedda Hopper offered another view: "It's a little too early to predict the Oscar-winning player for the best supporting actor next year, but Henry King has picked him—Orson Welles as Borgia in *Prince of Foxes.* Henry said that everybody told him he would have trouble with Welles; that he'd never be on time; and some days wouldn't even show. 'I've never worked with anyone as cooperative,' says King." In fact, Welles was not nominated for best supporting actor; rather, the category was won by Dean Jagger for his sensitive performance in *Twelve O'Clock High*. Still, Hopper's high praise was noted.

Indeed, most critics gave Welles an enthusiastic thumbs-up. *Variety* gushed that Welles had "tastefully etched his finest screen portrait to date." Even LOUELLA PARSONS, HEARST's attack dog who had savaged *CITIZEN KANE* on behalf of her boss William Randolph Hearst, relented: "Although Orson Welles is never my favorite actor, I must admit he doesn't overact too much as Borgia. This is the awesome Orson at his best." *Prince of Foxes* pulled in audiences around the world except for Germany. As FRANK BRADY points out, Welles's insatiable appetite for publicity had led him to write in a Paris newspaper: "I don't find many anti-Nazis in Germany today." Germans, understandably, were outraged and boycotted the film, costing Fox an estimated $250,000.

For Welles, the picture was an opportunity to observe veteran director Henry King, enjoy Italian hospitality, carouse with Tyrone Power, and raise $100,000 (his salary) to help keep his *OTHELLO* on track. Based on the 1947 novel of the same title by

Welles as Cesare Borgia in *Prince of Foxes* (*National Film Society Archive*)

Samuel Shellabarger, the Twentieth Century–Fox historical drama was produced by Darryl F. Zanuck and featured, in addition to Powers and Welles, Wanda Hendrix, Marina Berti, Everett Sloane, and Katrina Paxinou.

Reference Thomas, Tony, Clive Denton, and Kingsley Canham. *The Hollywood Professionals: Henry King, Lewis Milestone, Sam Wood* (New York: A.S. Barnes, 1974).

—C.B.

Project 891 The administrative number of the "classical" unit of the FEDERAL THEATRE PROJECT taken as the group's name.

Following the success of the "voodoo" MACBETH, a 1936 production of the NEGRO THEATRE PROJECT, a division of the Federal Theatre Project, JOHN HOUSEMAN and WELLES convinced HALLIE FLANAGAN, the FTP's executive director, that it was time for them to move on to another federally funded project. They argued that African Americans should have an opportunity to produce and direct on their own. As FRANK BRADY points out, they also aspired to create a theater—with the federal government serving as "angel"—whose primary mission would be to perform revivals of great dramatic classics, a kind of theater analogue to Mortimer Adler's "Great Books" program at the University of Chicago. A formal request was made to establish a classical unit under the FTP's aegis, and that it be permitted to move into the Maxine Elliott Theatre in midtown Manhattan, which the government had just leased from the Shubert organization. Flanagan agreed with the aim of giving greater opportunities to blacks. She also wanted to keep the dynamic duo of Welles and Houseman busy under the banner of the FTP, and promptly agreed to their request. Offices at the theater were set up immediately to coordinate the group's schedule and logistics. The unit's first production, HORSE EATS HAT, a reworking of the 1851 farce by Eugene Labiche and Marc Michel, opened at the Maxine Elliott Theatre on September 26, 1936.

Wanting to avoid the word *classical* in publicizing itself for fear that its fare might be considered too highbrow, Houseman and Welles simply appropriated the administrative number given the unit by the government, thus naming their group "Project 891." The venture proved to be short-lived. In 1939, as a result of Congress refusing to provide further funding for what its conservative members regarded as "left-wing, pro-Roosevelt propaganda," the Federal Theatre Project and its various units, including Project 891, ceased to exist.

—C.B.

Rathbone, [Philip St. John] Basil

(1892–1967) Although he is best known as Sir Arthur Conan Doyle's Sherlock Holmes and as a formidable screen villain, Basil Rathbone had a distinguished stage career and appeared in dozens of films on both sides of the Atlantic. He was born on June 13, 1892, in Johannesburg, South Africa, to British parents. He was educated in England, where he made his stage debut in 1911. During the 1920s, his stage persona was that of a romantic lead, and onstage he appeared in many classical dramas, mostly in Shakespearean productions. His Shakespeare background earned him a position in the touring company that KATHERINE CORNELL and her husband, GUTHRIE MCCLINTIC, organized in 1933 through 1935, a company that also included ORSON WELLES. As Robert Browning in *The Barretts of Wimpole Street,* Rathbone received favorable reviews. One reviewer wrote: "The character [Robert Browning] is expertly conceived as a foil for Elizabeth, creating a fine light and shade, and Rathbone plays it with every regard for its nuances." Rathbone temporarily left the company and played Mr. Murdstone in George Cukor's screen version of Charles Dickens's *David Copperfield* (1935). Before the picture's release, Rathbone had rejoined the Cornell Company in a production of *Romeo and Juliet* at the Martin Beck Theatre. Rathbone went on to play Tybalt in the Cukor film adaptation of *Romeo and Juliet* (1936).

In his autobiography, *Basil Rathbone: In and Out of Character* (1962), Rathbone had few comments about Welles. He did discuss Welles's 1933 performance as Marchbanks in SHAW's *Candida:* "Marchbanks was played by Orson Welles, whose performance was so fatuously unpleasant that Morrell became, by contrast, a deeply sympathetic character, which most certainly was not Mr. Shaw's intention." After the Cornell tour, Rathbone's career propelled him into scores of films. He appeared in 14 Sherlock Holmes films, for example, and often appeared as a villain in swashbucklers such as *Captain Blood* (1935) and *The Adventures of Robin Hood* (1938), and in thrillers, such as *Tales of Terror* (1962) and *The Comedy of Terrors* (1963). One of his more forgettable horror films was *The Ghost in the Invisible Bikini* (1966). He died in 1967, the same year that his *Hillbillys in a Haunted House* was released.

References Druxman, Michael B. *Basil Rathbone: His Life and His Films* (South Brunswick, N.J.: A.S. Barnes, 1976); Rathbone, Basil. *Basil Rathbone: In and Out of Character* (New York: Limelight, 1962).

—T.L.E.

Reed, Carol

(1906–1976) The British director Carol Reed, who directed ORSON WELLES in *THE THIRD MAN,* was born in London in 1906 and came to films from the theater. Reed felt that his background in the theater gave him a penchant for filming thrillers. "As a young man in the theater," he recalled, "I became an assistant to Edgar Wallace, who wrote and produced so many melodramas. It helped me to see the appealing values of thrillers." When he moved on to a career in films, he at first was assigned to be a dialogue director by British producers. In this capacity, he quickly demonstrated his talent for coaching actors. He was shortly advanced to directing low-budget films, and once he had proved his competence and dependability at this level of production, he was promoted in the ranks of studio directors and given a greater degree of freedom in the choice and handling of the subjects he filmed. Reed's early films, such as *The Stars Look Down* (1941), are not remarkable. But he went on to direct films that—although still modestly made by Hollywood standards—demonstrated incontestably the artistry of which British filmmakers like himself were capable.

Reed went on to work on some of the best documentaries to come out of World War II, such as the Academy Award–winning *The True Glory* (1945). He also directed the documentarylike theatrical film *The Way Ahead* (1944), an uncompromising portrayal of army life during wartime. The experience that Reed gained in making wartime documentaries also was reflected in his postwar films, enabling him to develop further in films such as *Odd Man Out* (1947) the strong sense of realism that had first appeared in *The Stars Look Down*. The documentary approach that Reed employed to tell the story of *Odd Man Out* (which deals with a group of anti-British insurgents in Northern Ireland, whose leader is relentlessly pursued by the British) found a responsive audience.

In depicting in this and other movies a hunted, lonely hero caught in the middle of a crisis usually not of his own devising, Reed suggests that one can achieve maturity and self-mastery only by accepting the challenges that life puts in one's way and by struggling with them as best one can. *The Fallen Idol* (1948) clearly exemplifies this theme; it is also the first of a trio of masterpieces that Reed made in collaboration with novelist-screenwriter GRAHAM GREENE, one of the most significant creative associations between a writer and a director in cinema history. The team followed *The Fallen Idol* with *The*

Sir Carol Reed, director *(National Film Society Archive)*

Third Man (1949), a brilliant thriller that focused on the black market in postwar Vienna. The hero of *The Third Man* is Holley Martins (JOSEPH COTTEN), an American who has come to Vienna at the invitation of an old school chum, Harry Lime (Orson Welles). Martins learns that Lime was involved in the most sordid of postwar rackets: trafficking in black-market penicillin of such inferior quality that it has caused widespread sickness and death. Shaken and disillusioned, Martins agrees to help the police capture Lime, and the film reaches its climax in an exciting chase through the shadowy sewers of Vienna. There is a memorable shot near the end of the sequence taken from street level, showing Lime's fingers desperately reaching through a sewer grating in a vain attempt to escape to the street through a manhole by dislodging its cover. With that, Harry Lime walked straight into cinema history on the strength of a hand clutching at a sewer grating. *The Third Man* won the Grand Prize at the Cannes Film Festival.

Reed attributed the phenomenal success of the picture to its being one of the first British films to be shot almost entirely on location. This enabled him to give an authentic documentary look to the film right from the opening tour of the city, in which a narrator tells the audience that Vienna is no longer the glamorous prewar city of Strauss waltzes, but a ravaged, decadent postwar city. It is just this corrupt atmosphere that Reed, with the help of Robert Krasker's Academy Award–winning cinematography, captures in the film.

Another great contribution to the movie's atmosphere was made by the haunting musical score composed by ANTON KARAS and played by him on the zither.

Reed's selection of Orson Welles to play Harry Lime was another stroke of genius. Initially, Welles had turned down the part, but Reed persuaded him to try playing a scene. The day that Welles arrived on location in Vienna, Reed was preparing to shoot the chase through the sewers, and Welles complained that the bad air in the sewer passages would give him pneumonia. "Finally I persuaded him to shoot the scene," Reed told me. "Then Orson conferred with the cameraman, made some suggestions; and we did the chase again. Of course he was sold on finishing the picture by then, and he gave a superlative performance."

Lime's corrupt charm is perfectly epitomized in a line Greene credits Welles with adding to his dialogue. Harry tells Holley not to be troubled by the decadence of Vienna, since out of the Italy of the Middle Ages, which was just as decadent, came the Renaissance, while a respectable country like Switzerland only managed to produce the cuckoo clock.

Although *The Third Man* was an enormous critical and popular success, a decade was to go by before Reed and Greene worked together again, this time on *Our Man in Havana* (1959), a spy thriller based on Greene's own novel, centering on a diffident British vacuum cleaner salesman living in Havana, who gets enmeshed in a web of international espionage. Because most of Reed's films in the next decade, such as *The Agony and the Ecstasy* (1965), were not comparable to the earlier films mentioned, it was thought that he had passed his peak for good. *Oliver!* (1968), however, proved that Reed was back in top form, for it won him the Academy Award as best director and was itself named the best picture of the year. Reed received other important awards throughout his professional life. He won British Academy Awards for *Odd Man Out, The Fallen Idol,* and *The Third Man,* which also garnered the Grand Prize at the Cannes International Film Festival. In addition, he was knighted in 1952. A genuinely self-effacing man, Reed was never impressed by the honors he received. He told this writer that his recipe as a filmmaker was "to give the public what I like, and hope they will like it too."

References Cowie, Peter. *Seventy Years of Cinema* (New York: A.S. Barnes, 1969); Gribble, Jim. "*The Third Man:* Greene and Reed," *Literature/Film Quarterly* 26, no. 3 (Summer 1998): 235–39; Houston, Penelope. *Contemporary Cinema* (Baltimore: Penguin Books, 1969), 38; Kael, Pauline. *Kiss Kiss Bang Bang* (New York: Columbia University Press, 1987); Phillips, Gene. "Carol Reed: The Disenchanted," in *Major Film Directors of the American and British Cinema,* rev. ed. (Cranbury, N.J.: Associated University Presses, 1999), 163–76; Schwab, Ulrike. "Authority and Ethics in *The Third Man,*" *Literature/Film Quarterly* 28, no. 1 (Winter 2000): 2–6; Sragow, Michael. "Truer to the Main Man of *The Third Man,*" *New York Times,* May 9, 1999, sec. 2: 19, 28; Wapshott, Nicholas. *Carol Reed: A Biography* (New York: Knopf, 1994).

—G.D.P.

Return to Glenascaul Dublin Gate Theatre, 23 minutes, 1951. **Director:** Hilton Edwards; **Producer:** Edwards and Micheál MacLiammóir; **Screenplay:** Edwards; **Cinematographer:** George Fleischmann; **Editor:** Joseph Sterling; **Music:** Hans Gunther Stumpf; **Cast:** Michael Laurence (Sean Merriam), Shelah Richards (Mrs. Campbell), Helena Hughes (Lucy Campbell), John Dunne (Daly), Isobel Clouser (the Short Woman), Ann Clery (the Tall Woman), Orson Welles (Himself)

HILTON EDWARDS, who with MICHEÁL MACLIAMMÓIR had been responsible for the 16-year-old WELLES's professional acting debut at Dublin's GATE THEATRE in 1931, had become bitten by the cinema bug as a result of appearing in Welles's first European film, OTHELLO, although the troubled production would eventually take Welles four years, 1948–52, to complete.

For his first effort as a film director, Edwards called on Welles to narrate a short tale that combined mystery and humor. Shot in Dublin, the 22-minute *Return to Glenascaul* opens with Welles relating a ghost story told to him by a man who had given him a lift in the Irish countryside on a dark, foggy night. At one point, there's an inside joke. When the man explains that his car's engine is not operating properly, Welles retorts that "I've had trouble with my distributor, too." It was a not too subtle reference to Welles's problem of getting his films properly promoted and booked, a situation that had applied to virtually all his films up to that point, from CITIZEN KANE to his then ongoing production of *Othello.*

PETER COWIE and others believe that *Return to Glenascaul* reflected a good deal of Wellesian finesse. "One has the feeling that the hand of the master may have chosen a camera angle here, or set an extra shadow there," opined Cowie. Ironically, given Welles's own strained relationship with the Hollywood establishment, *Return to Glenascaul* earned an Academy Award nomination for best short picture in 1952.

—C.B.

Reynolds, Burt (1936–)

Reynolds, Burt (1936–) Although actor Burt Reynolds did not appear in any of WELLES's films, the two became friends, and they lunched together at Ma Maison, Welles's favorite Los Angeles restaurant, the day before Welles died. At that luncheon the two men discussed a Welles project, THE MAGIC SHOW, which contained some footage of Welles performing magic tricks and interviews with several people, including Reynolds. Reynolds asked Welles to direct an upcoming episode of *Amazing Stories,* a television series he was starring in. He also told Welles that he would be happy to appear in any film that Welles would direct and gave Welles permission to use his name in order to secure financial backing for the project. Reynolds's offer to appear in a Welles picture is a bit odd since he was one of six Hollywood actors who had turned down $2 million to play the leading role in THE BIG BRASS RING, one of Welles's last film deals gone sour. According to DAVID THOMSON in *Rosebud,* the script was not that good and the part was not appealing: "Pellarin [the leading role] is not much more than a gay wet dream." Thomson also casts a shadow on the Reynolds/Welles friendship. BARBARA LEAMING

mentions an exchange between Reynolds and Welles on a television show. After Welles chides Reynolds about having a Florida theater named after him, Reynolds responds with a "fat" joke that hurts the immense Welles, who is no longer able to laugh at his weight. Thomson writes of this occasion: "He had to laugh at Reynolds's mean joke, and he had to smile on that insecure actor so that Burt would not give up on him. Reynolds was then 'big,' and even a meal ticket for Welles . . . is this hell?"

Burt Reynolds was born on February 11, 1936, in Waycross, Georgia, but he and his family moved to Palm Beach, Florida, where he grew up. He won a football scholarship at Florida State University and had a promising professional career, which was derailed by a knee injury and a car accident. He left school in 1955, went to New York, and eventually got a break when he appeared in a revival of *Mr. Roberts* and secured some television roles in series such as *Gunsmoke, Hawk,* and *Dan August.* He began his film career as a stuntman in the early 1960s, but did not achieve stardom until the 1970s. But then his star soared: For five consecutive years he was the number-one male box-office attraction. His glib put-downs and charming manner on television and his centerfold appearance in *Cosmopolitan* (April 1972) led to better screen roles. His role in *Deliverance* (1972), in which he played a macho suburban male adrift on a river in the South, established him as a serious actor, but he is best known for his work in comedies, where he plays a "good ole boy" with a "heart of gold." His "cracker" image is consistent with his roles in films having to do with fast cars, such as the *Smokey and the Bandit* movies with Jackie Gleason and the *Cannonball Run* series. Drawing on his football expertise, he also appeared in *The Longest Yard* (1974) and *Semi-Tough* (1977). He continued to work in film, but could not sustain his standing as a leading man in the 1990s. He did create a stir among both fans and critics in 1997, however, as a strong member of the ensemble cast in *Boogie Nights,* directed by Paul Thomas Anderson.

—T.L.E. and J.M.W.

Rhinoceros (play, 1960)

Rhinoceros (play, 1960) A French absurdist play by EUGÈNE IONESCO, whose 1960 English language premiere in London was directed by ORSON WELLES. Earlier in the year amid the deepening disaster of the theatrical rendition of Welles's CHIMES AT MIDNIGHT playing in Dublin, came an opportunity for redemption in the form of an invitation from Ionesco to direct *Rhinoceros* for the London stage. Welles, drawn to the play's themes of freedom and conformity and also to the element of absurdity in life and art, accepted. In this paradigmatic exemplar of the Theater of the Absurd, everyone turns into a rhinoceros except for Berenger, an Everyman, who resists.

The English language version of *Rhinoceros* staged by Welles at the Royal Court Theatre was a hit for several reasons. First, there was the cachet of the then fashionable absurdism of Ionesco (and also Samuel Beckett). Second, the key role of Berenger was played by the charismatic LAURENCE OLIVIER, England's first man of theater. Third, many curiosity-seekers flocked to the theater in order to witness the theatrical coupling of Olivier and leading lady Joan Plowright, then in the midst of a highly publicized affair (which would culminate in Olivier's divorce from VIVIEN LEIGH and eventual marriage to Plowright). Fourth, there were many Welles's admirers (and detractors) who wanted to see for themselves whether or not the once Boy Wonder would succeed (or fall flat on his face).

For Welles, directing *Rhinoceros* put him back in the public and theatrical spotlight. The production, however, was not without problems. Olivier, in turmoil because of his tumultuous personal life, was particularly testy about taking direction from Welles. At one point shortly before the opening, Olivier had Welles barred from the theater. Welles, significantly, became increasingly disenchanted with the play. His solution to what he saw as its emptiness was to cram in as much Wellesian business as possible. Thus, there was a TV monitor showing rhinoceroses running wild down streets, simulated rhinoceros stampedes through an English pub (a change of setting from the original play's Parisian street scene), and an array of staging, lighting, and sound/music effects all designed to whip up the action and fill the stage.

In spite—or perhaps because—of the turmoil, the five-week run of *Rhinoceros* at the Royal Court was a success. Among the raves, the *New York Times* said simply that "Orson Welles has directed the play with vigor." Welles, himself, was a bit more reserved. "We made a lot of money out of that production, and the critics liked it," he mentioned to PETER BOGDANOVICH. "I didn't like the play. I agreed to it because I thought the gimmick was good enough so that you could invent an evening in the theatre about it. And it worked. . . . But throughout rehearsals, every day, it seemed to me that I liked Ionesco less as a playwright." Still, *Rhinoceros* was an unqualified triumph, a poignant reminder of Welles's glory years as a powerful theatrical force, and a harbinger of yet more exciting projects to come.

—C.B.

Richardson, Sir Ralph (1902–1983)   Sir Ralph Richardson appeared as Dr. Watson in "The Final Problem," the last in a series of Sherlock Holmes episodes that were produced by Harry Alan Towers for the British Broadcasting Corporation in 1951. In the last episode, JOHN GIELGUD played Holmes, and WELLES played the villainous Professor Moriarty. Richardson and SIR LAURENCE OLIVIER, the two famous Shakespearean interpreters, were often mentioned as possibly working with Welles, but there were few collaborations involving the trio. Welles, who was impressed by both of them, praised Richardson's performance as FALSTAFF in the 1945 London productions of *Henry IV, Parts I and II*. According to Garry O'Connor in *Ralph Richardson: An Actor's Life* (1982), Welles came backstage after one of the performances and told Richardson, he "thought I'd done all right as Falstaff [in the 1939 *FIVE KINGS*] but the thing I must say, Ralph, I never matched you at the end." When Welles produced *CHIMES AT MIDNIGHT* (1966), he had Richardson as the narrator tying together loose ends.

Sir Ralph Richardson (knighted in 1947, when his friend and rival Laurence Olivier was passed over for the honor) was born on December 19, 1902, in Cheltenham, England. After a brief stint as an office boy he turned to the stage in 1920 and became a leading figure specializing in Shakespeare at the Old Vic in the 1930s and 1940s. Although he appeared in many films—his first was *The Ghoul* (1933)—he had a more successful career on the stage. His most outstanding films include *Four Feathers* (1939), *Anna Karenina* and *The Fallen Idol* (1948), *Outcast of the Islands* (1951), *Richard III* (1955), *Exodus* (1960), *Long Day's Journey into Night* (1962), *Doctor Zhivago* (1965), *David Copperfield* (1970), *A Doll's House* and *O Lucky Man!* (1973), and *Chariots of Fire* (1981). Ralph Richardson died in 1983.

References Clough, Valerie. *Sir Ralph Richardson: A Life in the Theatre* (Worthing: Churchman, 1989); Miller, John. *Ralph Richardson: The Authorized Biography* (North Pomfret, Vt.: Pan Books, 1996); O'Connor, Garry. *Ralph Richardson: An Actor's Life* (New York: Applause, 1982).

—T.L.E.

Richardson, Tony (Cecil Antonio Richardson) (1928–1992)

British director Tony Richardson cast ORSON WELLES as Louis of Mozambique in his film adaptation of THE SAILOR FROM GIBRALTAR (1967), a novel by Marguerite Duras. The script was by Christopher Isherwood, and the cast included JEANNE MOREAU, Vanessa Redgrave, John Hurt, and Hugh Griffith. It was not one of Welles's best roles: CHARLES HIGHAM wrote that Welles "appeared to virtually no effect" in the film, and DAVID THOMSON was more critical and snide: "He [Welles] was fatuous in a disaster, *The Sailor from Gibraltar,* an adaptation from Marguerite Duras which Tony Richardson was making out of love for Jeanne Moreau." Since Vanessa Redgrave, Richardson's wife, was in the cast, the situation must have been awkward. In fact, Redgrave divorced him for adultery in 1967, naming Moreau as correspondent.

Tony Richardson, who was born on June 5, 1928, in Saltaire, Shipley, Yorkshire, was educated at Wadham College, Oxford, where he was president of both the Oxford University Experimental Theatre Club and the Oxford University Dramatic Society. In the early 1950s, he became a theater director and television producer for the British Broadcasting Corporation. He was both active and influential in the Royal Court Theatre, where he, along with George Devine, revolutionized British theater, by mounting John Osborne's play *Look Back in Anger,* which he later also directed as a film for Woodfall, the production company he formed with John Osborne. Along with Lindsay Anderson and Karel Reisz, Richardson

helped to initiate the "Free Cinema" movement in Britain, while also writing film articles first for *Sequence,* then for *Sight and Sound,* Britain's most influential film journal. During the 1960s Richardson made several innovative features in Britain that reflected the goals of the "Angry Young Men," notably *A Taste of Honey* (1962) and *The Loneliness of the Long-Distance Runner* (1962). These were followed by his Academy Award–winning adaptation of Henry Fielding's massive satiric novel, *Tom Jones* (1963). After making two prosaic French features starring Jeanne Moreau, he returned to form with *The Charge of the Light Brigade* (1968), *Ned Kelly* (1970), *Joseph Andrews* (his second Fielding adaptation, 1977), *Hotel New Hampshire* (1984), and *Blue Skies,* completed in 1991 but not released until 1994. Richardson died from AIDS-related complications in 1992.

References Richardson, Tony. *The Long-Distance Runner: An Autobiography* (New York: Morrow, 1993); Welsh, James M., and John Tibbets, eds. *The Cinema of Tony Richardson: Essays and Interviews* (Albany: State University of New York Press, 1999).

—T.L.E. and J.M.W.

RKO Radio Pictures, Inc.

ORSON WELLES released three feature films through the RKO studio, CITIZEN KANE (1941), THE MAGNIFICENT AMBERSONS (1942), and THE STRANGER (1946). One of Hollywood's "Big Five" film companies, RKO was the only major studio born directly out of the talking picture revolution. Its roots were in the Film Booking Office of America (FBO), a small production/distribution company whose chief star was Strongheart the Dog. In 1926, Joseph P. Kennedy acquired FBO and joined forces a year later with David Sarnoff, the president of Radio Corporation of America (RCA). Sarnoff needed a showcase for his new optical sound system, trademarked "Photophone," a rival to Warner's Vitaphone and Fox's Movietone. Theaters controlled by the vaudeville circuit of Keith-Albee-Orpheum were added to the conglomerate in 1928. The giant $300 million corporation was named the Radio-Keith-Orpheum Corporation and the famous radio tower was adopted as its image. *Rio Rita,* an adaptation of the Broadway smash musical, was RKO's first release in 1929.

In 1931, DAVID O. SELZNICK became production chief. After a series of notable releases—including *What Price Hollywood?* (1932), *A Bill of Divorcement* (1932), and *King Kong* (1933)—he was replaced by Merian C. Cooper in 1933. Less stable than its competitors, RKO remained in a perpetual state of chaos the rest of its corporate life. A succession of studio heads came and went, including B.B. Kahane, Samuel Briskin, Pandro S. Berman, and tycoon HOWARD HUGHES. The Hughes years sowed the seeds of the studio's downfall with aborted projects and disastrous releases such as *The Conqueror* (1956). Hughes sold the studio to General Teleradio, Inc. (a subsidiary of General Tire and Rubber Company) in 1955, the first time a major film company became the property of a broadcast entity. Its film library of 700 titles was then sold to a television syndicator, the C&C Television Corporation for $15.2 million—the first major studio to release its pre-1948 film package (along with a few post-1948 titles) to the new medium. In 1957, Desilu Productions bought the RKO lot for its television production.

Despite its checkered history, RKO is remembered for its splendidly diverse output. In addition to the aforementioned Welles films, some of the highlights include the Astaire-Rogers musicals, from *Flying Down to Rio* (1932) to *The Story of Vernon and Irene Castle* (1939). During the World War II years, a remarkable series of horror films emerged from the Val Lewton unit, including *The Cat People* (1943) and *The Body Snatchers* (1944). The immediate postwar years saw several notable films under the short-lived tutelage of production chief Dore Schary—*Crossfire* (1947), *They Live by Night* (1947), and *Out of the Past* (1947). A number of important stars and filmmakers built their reputations at the studio—Orson Welles, George Cukor, Katharine Hepburn, composer Max Steiner, Edward Dmytryk, and Robert Mitchum.

RKO remains in existence as a corporate entity of General Tire, RKO General, Inc. It has abandoned the motion picture field in favor of broadcasting and cable television.

—J.C.T

RKO 281 HBO/Time Warner Entertainment/ BBC Films, 83 minutes, 1999. **Director:** Benjamin Ross;

Producer: Sue Armstrong; **Executive Producers:** Ridley Scott and Tony Scott; **Screenplay:** John Logan; **Cinematographer:** Mike Southon, B.S.C.; **Editor:** Alex Mackie; **Production Design:** Maria Djurkovic; **Art Director:** Lucinda Thomas; **Music:** John Altman; **Cast:** Liev Schreiber (Orson Welles), James Cromwell (William Randolph Hearst), Melanie Griffith (Marion Davies), John Malkovich (Herman J. Mankiewicz), Liam Cunningham (Gregg Toland), Roy Scheider (George Schaefer), Kerry Shale (Bernard Herrmann), Brenda Blethyn (Louella Parsons), Fiona Shaw (Hedda Hopper), Anastasia Hille (Carole Lombard), David Suchet (L.B. Mayer), Roger Allam (Walt Disney), Simeon Andrews (John Houseman), Jay Benedict (Darryl Zanuck), Ron Berglas (David O. Selznick), Joseph Long (Harry Cohn), Olivier Pierre (Sam Goldwyn), Angus Wright (Joseph Cotten), Aaron Keeling (young Orson).

This WELLES biopic was "based in part" on the television documentary *The Battle Over Citizen Kane,* aired on the "American Experience" series. Like *CITIZEN KANE,* it begins with a *faux* newsreel, following a sequence of young Orson on his ninth birthday. His bedridden mother tells him to make a wish, and as he blows out the candles on his birthday cake, the black-and-white newsreel footage commences, tracing the career of the "boy genius" who is about to conquer Hollywood. The newsreel is being screened by Louis B. Mayer (David Suchet), who predicts that Welles will fail at RKO and that then he will be able to hire him on the cheap.

The action then cuts to San Simeon, the Hearst mansion, where Welles (Liev Schreiber) and HERMAN MANKIEWICZ (John Malkovich) are getting tuxed up for a formal dinner. Welles is doing card tricks and says, of movies, "You know what it's all about, Mank? Magic." They discuss possible subjects for his first film: "OK, Mank, what are we gonna write?" After Welles impresses the guests with a magic trick over dinner, he expresses interest in making a film about the great Spanish matador Manolete, but WILLIAM RANDOLPH HEARST (James Cromwell) expresses distaste over the topic of bullfighting. Welles then makes an insulting comment about the Hearst "zoo" on an estate that is half the size of Rhode Island. The two men do not get along. Later, Welles walks through the mansion and notices an uncompleted jigsaw puzzle on the floor.

Back in Hollywood, Mankiewicz shows Welles notes he has started for a novel about Hearst, and Welles is interested, even though Mankiewicz warns him about Hearst's power and influence. It's about "Love on his own terms," Mankiewicz explains. Welles responds, "Love on your own terms, because those are the only terms anyone has ever known. There's your tragedy." Mankiewicz agrees: "Orson, I'm in. I'll write it." Welles then promises to get JOHN HOUSEMAN on the project.

When Hearst gossip columnist LOUELLA PARSONS (Brenda Blethyn) gets wind of the project, she has lunch with Welles and asks: "The story's about a publisher. You're not doing Hearst, are you?" Welles assures "I'm not doing Hearst," but of course he is. Mankiewicz completes a script that Welles considers "too long," but adds: "It's a brilliant script. It needs some shaping, that's all." The working title is *The American*. Producer GEORGE SCHAEFER (Roy Scheider), who really wanted Welles to film *THE WAR OF THE WORLDS,* but has indulged the "boy genius" by agreeing to the "American" project, suggests another title, *Citizen Kane*. Welles gives himself a crash course in filmmaking by watching John Ford's *Stagecoach* (1939).

A dispute develops with Mankiewicz when Welles takes the writer's name off the script, because the director claims he took 350 pages of "drunken drivel" and turned it into a script himself. The relationship between Welles and Mankiewicz seems consciously to parallel the relationship between CHARLES FOSTER KANE and Jed Leland in *Kane,* when scenes of *Kane* with Leland, who has crawled into a bottle when faced with the prospect of reviewing Susan Alexander Kane's opera performance in Chicago, are intercut with shots of Mankiewicz drinking at home. Eventually, Welles invites Mankiewicz back and shows him the shooting script, which has the writer's name on it. Mankiewicz returns to the set and makes more script suggestions.

Miffed because she was not invited to a private screening of the rough cut of the film, Hedda Hopper (Fiona Shaw) bulls her way into the screening room and slaps Welles to show her displeasure. After seeing the rough-cut, Hopper calls Hearst and asks why Louella had not told him about what Welles was doing. Hearst then confronts Louella and puts her job on the line. "How do you feel when you are lied to?" he asks her. "I want blood," she says. Hearst encourages her by saying "Good. Retain that feeling." Hearst is especially upset by the way the film uses the name "ROSEBUD," his pet name for his mistress's private parts.

Meanwhile, the Hearst empire is not doing well. "How does one get $125 million in debt," MARION DAVIES (Melanie Griffith) asks her benefactor. "One buys things," he answers, with a line that might have come out of *Citizen Kane*. Davies taunts Hearst about the film the same way Susan Alexander taunts Kane over Leland's negative review (which, in fact, Kane wrote himself): "They nailed us, didn't they? A crazy old man and his whore! But at least he married her," she says, crying. So Hearst conspires with Louella to destroy the picture. Louella takes some nasty sex photos to L.B. Mayer and threatens to blackmail his operation if he does not promise to "kill *Citizen Kane*."

In a meeting with all the major studio heads, Mayer suggests that they offer GEORGE SCHAEFER $800,000 to buy *Citizen Kane,* with the understanding that they will then destroy the prints. Schaefer takes the offer to Welles, just as the director is pontificating, morally, "What does it profit a man to gain the whole world if he loses his soul?" Welles is enraged and calls Schaefer a "treacherous little shit," then calms down and begs him to let the director talk to the stockholders. At that meeting, Welles argues on the analogy with Hitler, appealing to their idealism: "No one can tell us what to say and what to do. Today you have the chance to let the dream triumph." Afterward, Schaefer tells him, "We open May 1st."

Hearst has other pressing problems. He is going bankrupt. Davies remains loyal to Hearst and pawns a million dollars worth of jewelry to help Hearst financially. "We'll be liquidating twelve papers," Hearst's accountant says, again echoing *Citizen Kane*. The film imagines a chance dramatic exchange between Welles and Hearst in an elevator, with Hearst predicting the later problems Welles will face. The film ends on opening night, when George Schaefer tells Welles, "I got the axe this morning."

Liev Schreiber does a reasonably good job of portraying Welles as the petulant, self-indulgent "boy genius," and John Malkovich is consistently convincing as Mankiewicz, as is James Cromwell as Hearst, even though Cromwell is rather too thin for the part. Roy Scheider is excellent as George Schaefer, and David Suchet is chilling as L.B. Mayer. Angus Wright is not at all convincing as JOSEPH COTTEN, however, and Melanie Griffith, no doubt on instructions, misfires by playing Marion Davies as a drunken ditz. Commentators have claimed that Hearst was most upset by the portrayal of Susan Alexander Kane as an untalented slut. Davies was talented, and the dramatization does her a disservice. The "docudrama" works too hard at pushing the parallels between Hearst and Kane, and between Davies and Susan Alexander, but in general it popularizes the crisis of *Citizen Kane* reasonably well and is far more entertaining than one might have expected.

—J.M.W.

Robinson, Edward G. (1893–1973)

Edward G. Robinson, who acted in THE STRANGER, was born in Bucharest, Romania, on December 12, 1893, and named Emmanuel Goldenberg. In 1903, his family moved to the United States, where he grew up on New York's Lower East Side. He studied acting at New York's City College (not Columbia University, as some sources say) and won a scholarship to the American Academy of Dramatic Art, at which point he changed his name to Edward G(oldenberg) Robinson. He played on Broadway between 1915 and 1930. With the advent of sound pictures, he began acting in movies, scoring a triumph as the racketeer Rico Bandello in Mervyn LeRoy's *Little Caesar* (1931). After being typecast in gangster roles, he made a point of playing characters at times who were on the right side of the law, such as the insurance investigator who breaks open a case of fraud and murder in Billy Wilder's *Double Indemnity* (1944). Robinson achieved tragic stature in Fritz Lang's *Scarlet Street* (1945) as a hapless bookkeeper involved with a scarlet woman. The following year he appeared in *The Stranger*, which co-starred and was directed by ORSON WELLES.

In *The Stranger* Welles plays Franz Kindler, a former Nazi who escaped from Europe during World War II, and is now teaching at a New England prep school under the name of Charles Rankin. He hopes to hide there indefinitely from Wilson, the government agent who hopes to bring him to justice (Edward G. Robinson). Mary, Rankin's wife (LORETTA YOUNG), initially has no knowledge of her husband's sordid past. The peaceful atmosphere of the village belies the presence of a monstrous war criminal lurking there.

As it happened, Robinson was not Welles's first choice for Wilson; he wanted AGNES MOOREHEAD, who had been with Welles from his radio days, to play the part. "I thought it would be much more interesting to have a spinster lady on the heels of this Nazi," he explained to PETER BOGDANOVICH. But producer SAM SPIEGEL, who later clashed with director David Lean on *Lawrence of Arabia,* would not hear of it.

Spiegel (who called himself S. P. Eagle at that point) asked Welles to direct *The Stranger* on the stipulation that he could modify the script as much as he wished prior to filming; but he was under no circumstances to revise any scenes during shooting. Welles agreed to do Spiegel's bidding because he wanted to show Hollywood that he could tackle a job on order and for hire and to do it well. (His previous directorial assignment, JOURNEY INTO FEAR, had been taken away from him by the studio, though he acted in the film.) Welles did rework some scenes with scriptwriter ANTHONY VEILLIER, after screenwriter-director JOHN HUSTON (uncredited) had made some revisions. Also Edward Nims, the film's editor, who later edited TOUCH OF EVIL, deleted several pages from the screenplay, with Welles's approval, before the film went into production, in order to save time and money.

Yet Welles admitted to Peter Bogdanovich that he cheated on his promise to Spiegel to the extent that he added some comic relief, much to Robinson's dismay, in the scenes set in the local drugstore, by way of the checker-playing pharmacist Mr. Potter (Billy House), a bona fide New England eccentric. Welles wrote on the set some interchanges with a satiric touch between Potter and his customers, ranging from dotty matrons to shrill teens. (Welles even posted notices, scrawled in his own hand, around the

Edward G. Robinson as Wilson, the detective in *The Stranger*, with Loretta Young and Orson Welles *(Literature/Film Archive)*

drugstore; e.g., the note "No Slugs" is next to the pay phone.)

Robinson was already in a sour mood because he was not Welles's first choice for Wilson. Welles thought casting Robinson was obvious casting; putting Agnes Moorehead in the part was not obvious casting. Moreover, Robinson, who was aware that Welles was still being touted as a Hollywood *wunderkind,* told friends that he did not see anything special in Welles as a director. So when Robinson observed Welles beefing up Billy House's part on the set, that was the last straw. He complained to the front office, "I'm the star; who is this Billy House?" Billy House had been a burlesque comic, and Welles thought it good to allow House to provide a modicum of comic relief occasionally and lighten the grim proceedings. House actually stole a scene or two from Robinson when they appeared together;

so, as Welles later remarked, "Maybe Eddie was right" to complain.

Robinson showed that he could be temperamental more than once during shooting. FRANK BRADY records that when Robinson objected to being photographed on his "bad side," Loretta Young graciously volunteered, "Okay, shoot me on my bad side and keep him happy." Welles commented, "The director has to carry on a continual courtship with the people he sticks in front of the lens." But he was willing to mollify Robinson if it meant avoiding quarrels that would cause delays which entailed falling behind schedule.

Withal, Robinson turns in a restrained performance as the shrewd war crimes investigator, portraying Wilson as a dogged searcher for truth and justice. Welles helps him along with some intriguing cinematic touches. In one scene, Wilson shows Rankin's wife some newsreels that illustrate some of the atrocities Rankin committed during the war. The flickering light of the movie projector is the only light in the room. This suggests that Wilson is shedding some partial light on Rankin's dark past for her.

The Stranger is a crisp and effective film noir that looks forward to Welles's LADY FROM SHANGHAI. James Agee thought it a "tidy, engaging thriller about a Nazi arch-criminal that was right out of Hitchcock's top drawer." Indeed, the monstrous villain hiding out in a sleepy small town recalls Hitchcock's *Shadow of a Doubt* (1943). Agee found *The Stranger* less "pretentious and arty" than Welles's earlier films. "In quite a modest way the picture is, merely, much more graceful, intelligent, and enjoyable than most other movies."

CHARLES HIGHAM commends Robinson's portrayal of Wilson: "Here is a man dedicated to bringing to earth a dangerous and elusive quarry and to shattering the illusions of the man's wife. . . . Wilson's is a process of exposing nerves in a cozy world that knows nothing of brutality," and in the end he triumphs. Accordingly, the title of the film does not refer chiefly to Rankin, who is a well-known member of the community when *The Stranger* begins; it refers to Wilson, who is the real stranger in town. He's an outsider who meddles in other people's affairs—at least so he initially appears.

Despite their differences while making the picture, Welles assured Bogdanovich, "I think Robinson is one of the best movie actors of all time." Although neither Welles nor Robinson remembered the film with enthusiasm, *The Stranger* remains the only film Welles ever directed that turned a profit on first release. The picture cost a little over $1 million, and it tripled that amount in revenues during its initial run.

Robinson supported patriotic causes during World War II; for example, he made innumerable propaganda broadcasts to occupied Europe (he spoke eight languages). Yet he was accused of being involved in communist front organizations after the war. This was the period in which the House Un-American Activities Committee (HUAC) was searching out communists in the film industry and elsewhere during the cold war years that followed

World War II. Robinson testified before HUAC and was exonerated of all charges.

Robinson continued acting for the remainder of his life, scoring in John Huston's *Key Largo* (1948) as a gangster who recalled his role in *Little Caesar.* Other highlights of his career include Cecil B. DeMille's *Ten Commandments* (1956) and *The Cincinnati Kid* (1965). He was awarded a posthumous Academy Award after his death from cancer in 1973, in recognition for his entire screen career.

References Agee, James. *Agee on Film: Essays and Reviews* (New York: Grosset and Dunlap, 1958); Brady, Frank. *Citizen Welles: A Biography of Orson Welles* (New York: Scribner's, 1989); Cowie, Peter. *The Cinema of Orson Welles* (New York: Da Capo, 1989); Higham, Charles. *The Films of Orson Welles* (Los Angeles: University of California Press, 1973); Welles, Orson, and Peter Bogdanovich. *This Is Orson Welles* (New York: Da Capo, 1998).

—G.D.P.

Robson, Mark (1913–1978) Director Mark Robson served as assistant editor on ORSON WELLES's CITIZEN KANE (1941) and THE MAGNIFICENT AMBERSONS (1942), and was the editor for JOURNEY INTO FEAR (1943). When ROBERT WISE replaced George Crone as editor on *Citizen Kane,* he brought Robson with him. In order to make the newsreel NEWS ON THE MARCH sequence more realistic, Wise and Robson, according to SIMON CALLOW, "shocked their colleagues by dragging the completed sequence across the floor and trampling on it, in order to create the authentically grainy and battered effect. The result of all this was the single most impressive, most spoken-of element in the movie." Robson also commented on the XANADU set: "He had a huge set of Xanadu built on Stage 9 at RKO and then didn't know what to do with it. He feigned sickness and stayed home until he figured out how to use the set. What he finally decided was brilliant." When Welles was in Brazil, and *The Magnificent Ambersons* required final editing and postproduction work, it was done by Wise and Robson, among others. Robson alone edited *Journey into Fear.*

Mark Robson was born in Montreal on December 4, 1913, and studied political science and economics at UCLA before going to law school at

Pacific Coast University. His film career began in 1932 at Fox Studios, where he was in the art department. He moved to RKO in 1935, where as Robert Wise's assistant, he began working with Welles. After editing Val Lewton's *Cat People* (1942), he became a director specializing in horror films. His first few films include *The Ghost Ship* (1943) and *Isle of the Dead* (1945). In the boxing-film genre, he directed two outstanding movies: *Champion* (1949) and *The Harder They Fall* (1956). Other outstanding films were *Home of the Brave* (1949), *The Bridges at Toko-Ri* (1955), *The Inn of the Sixth Happiness* (1958), *Von Ryan's Express* (1965), and *Happy Birthday Wanda June* (1971). Popular but trashy films include *Peyton Place* (1957) and *Valley of the Dolls* (1967). While working on location in Italy on *Avalanche Express* (1979), he had a heart attack and died in London in 1978.

Reference Higham, Charles, and Joel Greenberg. *The Celluloid Muse: Hollywood Directors Speak* (New York: New American Library, 1972).

—T.L.E.

Rockefeller, Nelson (1908–1979)

During World War II, Nelson Rockefeller worked for the U.S. Department of State as coordinator of Inter-American affairs, a post he held from 1940 to 1944. The work of this branch of the State Department was of particular importance to the war effort of the United States, which desperately needed to maintain a cultural and political alliance (or at the very least, neutrality) with the countries of Central and South America. As a part of this extended "good neighbor" policy, Rockefeller and his associate John Hay ("Jock") Whitney, with the full compliance of RKO president GEORGE SCHAEFER, persuaded ORSON WELLES to boost the war effort by taking an RKO film crew to Brazil to make a documentary on the *Carnaval* celebration in Rio de Janeiro. The film, entitled *IT'S ALL TRUE,* was never completed, and the entire project became a fiasco of budget overruns and poor communication between Welles and RKO executives. The South American venture was, according to Welles, the "the key disaster" of his entire career.

Nelson Rockefeller was the second of five sons of noted philanthropist John D. Rockefeller Jr., and the grandson of John D. Sr., founder of Standard Oil.

Following his graduation from Dartmouth in 1930, Nelson served a brief apprenticeship in banking, working in New York, Paris, and London. In the early 1930s, he became the leasing and rental agent for Rockefeller Center, and gradually moved up to become chairman of the board. Art was one of his varied interests, and for many years he was a trustee of the Museum of Modern Art. In 1954, he founded the Museum of Primitive Art in New York City.

Nelson Rockefeller was elected governor of New York in 1958, and briefly considered campaigning for the presidency on the Republican ticket in 1960. In 1962, he was reelected governor and campaigned actively for the Republican nomination for the presidency in 1964. He lost by a narrow margin to Senator Barry Goldwater. Rockefeller was reelected governor for a third term in 1966, and in 1968 made a late and unsuccessful bid for the presidential nomination, losing to Richard Nixon on the first ballot. In 1970, Rockefeller was elected to a fourth term as governor of New York, but resigned in 1973 to accept the vice presidency offered by then president Gerald R. Ford, who had become president following the Nixon resignation. When his term expired in 1977, Rockefeller sought no further political office. He was, perhaps, the most influential liberal Republican of his era.

References Lockwood, John E. *Century Memorials: Nelson Aldrich Rockefeller, 1908–1979* (New York: The Century Association, 1982); Reich, Cary. *The Life of Nelson Rockefeller* (New York: Doubleday, 1996).

—R.C.K.

RoGoPaG (*La Ricotta* episode)

Cineriz, 122 minutes total (35 minutes for *La Ricotta*), 1963. **Directors:** Pier Paolo Pasolini, Roberto Rossellini, Jean-Luc Godard, and Ugo Gregoretti; **Producer:** Alfredo Bini; **Screenplay:** Pasolini, et al.; **Cinematography:** Tonino Delli Colli, et al.; **Editor:** Nino Baragli, et al.; **Music:** Carlo Rustichelli; **Cast:** Orson Welles (the film director), Mario Cipriani (Stracci), Laura Betti (the "star"), Vittorio La Paglia (the journalist), Maria Bernardini, Ettore Garofalo, Tomas Milian, Franca Pasut, et al.

An Italian omnibus film featuring WELLES in the sequence *La Ricotta,* directed by Pier Paolo Pasolini.

As in THE V.I.P.S., Welles plays a film director. Welles's director in *La Ricotta,* in contrast to the pompously vacuous Max Buda of Anthony Asquith's *The V.I.P.s,* is Pasolini's pawn, a caricature of bloated Hollywood arrogance designed to serve as a satiric whipping boy for the Italian director's Marxist inflected, anticapitalist screed. As a crucifixion is being staged, Welles's director reads from Pasolini's book *Mamma Roma:* "Italy has the most illiterate masses and the most ignorant bourgeoisie in Europe. The average man is a dangerous criminal, a monster. He is a racist, a colonialist, a defender of slavery, a mediocrity."

Upon release, Pasolini's film was deemed so blasphemous that the director was tried and found guilty of insulting the state religion of Italy. Although an appeals court later reversed the decision, Pasolini's troubled film had only a limited release, putting the director's career temporarily on hold. *La Ricotta,* as might be surmised, certainly did nothing for Welles either, especially among Italians.

Interestingly, Welles had planned his own version of the Christ story in the early 1940s, a version that was to be set in the contemporary American Midwest. *La Ricotta,* much to Welles's dismay, was the closest he ever got to directing anything from the Bible.

The film's title, *RoGoPaG,* derives from the initials of the four directors involved: Roberto Rossellini, Jean-Luc Godard, Pier Paolo Pasolini, and Ugo Gregoretti. After surviving its legal difficulties because of Pasolini's episode, *RoGoPaG* was given a limited re-release under the title *Laviamoci il cervello (Let's Wash Out Our Brains).*

Reference Rohdie, Sam. *The Passion of Pier Paolo Pasolini* (London: BFI, 1995).

—C.B.

Roosevelt, Franklin Delano (1882–1945)

While serving as president of the United States, Franklin Delano Roosevelt created his distinctive New Deal approach to overcome the Depression. In his second New Deal program, Roosevelt, who became one of WELLES's heroes, established the FEDERAL THEATRE PROJECT, which in turn developed the NEGRO THEATRE PROJECT, which was run by JOHN HOUSEMAN, who brought in Orson Welles to stage the legendary "voodoo" MACBETH in 1936. In 1942, Welles left the unfinished MAGNIFICENT AMBERSONS (1942) and went to Brazil to make IT'S ALL TRUE, a film designed to improve U.S.–Latin American relations. The project was, according to Welles, instigated by the U. S. government; and Welles claims that "[President] Roosevelt himself helped to persuade me that I really had no other choice [than to make the Brazilian film]." Welles, who campaigned vigorously for Roosevelt when he ran for reelection as president in 1944, became a close friend of the president. According to DAVID THOMSON, they occasionally traveled together on the train and "got on: FDR said they were the two best, or most chronic, actors in America." Welles, who became a dollar-a-year man for the Democratic administration, worked as a consultant in the Secretary of War's Finance Division for the duration of the war. In addition to opening the fifth war Loan Drive with a symposium on American democracy, he put together "The Texarkana Program," a broadcast that featured Hollywood personalities JOSEPH COTTEN, Danny Kaye, and AGNES MOOREHEAD. In recognition for these events and other campaign appearances and speeches (he even stood in for Roosevelt in a debate with Thomas Dewey at the Astor Hotel), Roosevelt cabled him the following: "I deeply appreciate everything you have done and are doing. . . . The most important thing is for you to get well and be around for the last days of the campaign." After he won reelection, Roosevelt again expressed his thanks for Welles's work on his behalf: "It was a great show in which you played a great part." When Roosevelt died, Welles participated in the radio tribute to the dead president: "Our last president was a member of my family. He lived in our home as I know he lived in yours. My home seems empty now as yours does."

Franklin Delano Roosevelt was born on January 30, 1882, on his wealthy family's estate in Dutchess County, New York. Educated by Swiss tutors, both at home and abroad, until he was 14, he then attended Groton, a prestigious and academically challenging private school in Massachusetts. He entered Harvard University in 1900, married his distant cousin Eleanor Roosevelt in 1905, then entered Columbia Law School. Although he did not finish law school, he did pass the bar exam and began to practice law. He got into politics in 1910, when he won a seat in the New York State Senate; he was reelected in 1912, but went to Washington to serve as assistant secretary of the navy. He remained active in New York politics, however, and in 1920 he was the unsuccessful candidate for vice president on the national Democratic ticket. In August of 1921, he contracted polio and never recovered the use of his legs. Despite the physical handicap, which he succeeded in hiding from the country, he stayed in politics, backing Al Smith, the Democratic nominee for president in 1924 and 1928. He ran for governor of New York in 1928 and was elected, giving him visibility and credibility and enabling him to get the Democratic nomination for president in 1932. Campaigning with the promise of a "new deal," a term that came to be associated with him, he defeated Herbert Hoover, who had come to be associated with the Depression that plagued the country. Roosevelt instituted several programs (Social Security Act, National Labor Relations Act, and the WORKS PROGRESS ADMINISTRATION [WPA]) during his first term and was reelected. In his second term, many parts of the New Deal were enacted to help the poor, labor unions, and the farmers. By the end of his second term, he was more involved in foreign policy, including efforts to improve relations with South America through his "Good Neighbor" policy and efforts to support the Allies in their fight against German aggression. During his third term, America declared war on Japan and Germany, and in 1944 he won his fourth term. After the Yalta Conference, where the Allies divided up postwar Europe, but before the atomic bomb was dropped on Hiroshima, Roosevelt died on April 12, 1945.

References Burgan, Michael. *Franklin D. Roosevelt* (Minneapolis: Compass Point Books, 2002); Burns, James MacGregor. *The Three Roosevelts: A Biography of a Family That Transformed America* (London: Atlantic, 2001); Uschan, Michael, V. *Franklin D. Roosevelt* (San Diego: Lucent Books, 2002).

—T.L.E.

Roots of Heaven, The
Twentieth Century–Fox, 131 minutes, 1958. **Director:** John Huston; **Producer:** Darryl F. Zanuck; **Screenplay:** Romain Gary and Patrick Leigh-Fermor, adapted from the novel by Romain Gary; **Cinematography:** Oswald Morris; **Editor:** Russell Lloyd; **Music:** Malcolm Arnold; **Cast:** Orson Welles (Cy Sedgwick), Errol Flynn (Forsythe), Juliette Greco (Minna), Trevor Howard (More), Eddie Albert (Abe Fields), Paul Lukas (Saint Denis), Herbert Lom (Orsini), et al.

In the early 1950s, WELLES had borrowed a considerable sum from producer DARRYL ZANUCK to help finish *OTHELLO* (1952). Six years later, Welles agreed to appear in Zanuck's *The Roots of Heaven* without a fee in order to reduce the debt. *The Roots of Heaven* was also an opportunity for Welles to act with pal Errol Flynn and renew his friendship with JOHN HUSTON, who had directed Welles in *MOBY DICK* (1955). Based on a novel by Romain Gary, and shot mostly on location in French Equatorial Africa, the film centered on a conservationist (Trevor Howard) crusading to stop the senseless killing of elephants. Welles played Cy Sedgwick, a puffed-up television commentator who eventually comes to support the conservationist's cause. While most agreed with the sentiment of the film's conservationist message, the scenario for *The Roots of Heaven,* co-authored by novelist Gary and Patrick Leigh-Fermor, failed to click. Typical of the brickbats hurled at the writing were the comments of distinguished critic Stanley Kauffmann: "The Huston who did *Sierra Madre* would have lighted his cigar with this script." Still, for Welles, it was an opportunity to lighten his debt to Zanuck by $15,000.

The Roots of Heaven, shot in CinemaScope, also featured Juliette Greco, Eddie Albert, Paul Lukas, Herbert Lom, Gregoire Aslan, Friedrich Ledebur, and Edric Connor.

—C.B.

"Rosebud"
"Rosebud" was the last word spoken by CHARLES FOSTER KANE in ORSON WELLES's *CITIZEN KANE* (1941). A reporter is assigned to discover what "Rosebud" meant to Kane, providing the rationale for the multilayered plot, tracing Kane's life that follows. At the end of the film, the reporter doesn't have a clue about the exact meaning, nor does the audience, until, in an inspired tour de force of dramatic irony, the camera sweeps over the rubble of

Kane's possessions to reveal a sled being consumed by flames. The film's final shot therefore reveals *what* "Rosebud" was, but what it meant to Kane remains a matter of speculation. Kane was on his way to visit his warehouse where the sled was kept the night he met Susan Alexander with a toothache, the night that changed his life and was destined to ruin both his first marriage and his political ambitions. Earlier in the Colorado sequence of the film, young Charlie Kane is seen playing with the sled in the snow the day that Walter Parks Thatcher takes him away from his parents to boarding school, but the name of the sled is not revealed at that point, since the sled is seen covered with snow.

"Rosebud" is not merely a sled, however. It is a mystery, the mystery that propels the plot of the film; it is certainly a symbol, perhaps of an innocent young boy's need for love; but the most that can be said is that "Rosebud" is what Alfred Hitchcock would have called a "McGuffin," a plot device that appears to have great significance, more significance than is in fact involved. As Thompson, the reporter, correctly remarks at the end of the film, "I don't think any word can explain a man's life." As DAVID THOMSON, the critic, has noted, "no one in the film hears the word 'Rosebud,'" only the film viewer, so how could the world have known about it?" Likewise, only the film audience sees the name on the sled after it has been pitched into the furnace, having been led merely to what Thomson calls "a painful enigma."

The "Rosebud" gimmick was especially infuriating to WILLIAM RANDOLPH HEARST because, it has been suggested, "Rosebud" was his pet name for the clitoris of his mistress, the actress MARION DAVIES. Hearst took exception to the film because it paralleled his life to an extent, but especially in the way it portrayed Susan Alexander Kane, Kane's mistress, the Marion Davies figure, as an untalented singer. If there were parallels between Davies, an accomplished actress, and Susan, then the comparison would have been false and unfair, but, of course, the film was far more than simply a biographical account of a newspaper tycoon.

"Rosebud" was also the title of David Thomson's book, *Rosebud: The Story of Orson Welles,* published by Alfred A. Knopf in 1996, which attempts to probe the larger mystery of Orson Welles. Thomson describes the whole film as "a metaphor about extraordinary talent, charm and power that have no faith in themselves." In this context, "Rosebud" is a metaphor within a metaphor. He concludes that Welles "had been so deeply admired since birth, so praised, so spoiled, that he had never been able to muster faith in love," and that "Rosebud" refers "to the possibility that there never was real love [and] that solitude is the only reliable condition." He then quotes Kane's chilling toast to his friend Jed Leland "to love on my terms. Those are the only terms anybody ever knows, his own."

—J.M.W.

Rosenbaum, Jonathan (1943–) Film critic for the *Chicago Reader* and author of *Moving Places* and *Placing Movies* (both 1995), *Movies as Politics* (1997), and *Movie Wars* (2000), Jonathan Rosenbaum performed a small miracle when asked to edit, organize, and give shape to the book that was to become *This Is Orson Welles,* finally published by HarperCollins in 1992, years after its inception. WELLES and PETER BOGDANOVICH had collaborated on a book that Bogdanovich could not complete on his own because of personal and professional complications. The manuscript was lost for five years after contracts with two publishers had lapsed. The Yugoslav actress and sculptor, OJA KODAR, who had been Welles's companion and collaborator, approached Rosenbaum about editing the material after Welles died on October 10, 1985. Rosenbaum first met Kodar when he attended the tribute to Welles held at the Directors Guild in Hollywood. Rosenbaum invited both Bogdanovich and Kodar to speak at another Welles tribute he was organizing for the Rotterdam Film Festival, which Kodar attended, though Bogdanovich did not. By 1987, it was clear that Bogdanovich would not have time to complete and update the material on his own, and at that point Kodar asked Rosenbaum to edit the material, amounting to over 1,300 pages of the final draft of the unfinished manuscript, transcribed from reel-to-reel tape, and revised by Welles. A year later, Rosenbaum received most of the original tapes, which Bogdanovich had found in 1987; earlier drafts surfaced in 1991. In his *Times Literary Supplement* review of

May 7, 1993, Michael Church credited Rosenbaum for having turned "the mountain of transcripts into a book," significant for "its detailed chronology and notes," and, especially, "its publication of the lost section of *The Magnificent Ambersons*," which gave the work "major film-historical importance." In brief, then, Rosenbaum preserved this primary source material and made it coherent, adding nearly 30 pages of notes to qualify "the veracity of the text" and explain facts that may have been "blatantly falsified." Through his efforts, an important record was preserved.

Rosenbaum later offered an evaluation of the career of Orson Welles in Chapter 10 of his polemic *Movie Wars: How Hollywood and the Media Conspire to Limit What Films We Can See* (A Cappella Books, 2000), praising the director for his "compulsion to keep moving creatively" and "his refusal to repeat himself." Unlike PAULINE KAEL and ROBERT CARRINGER, Rosenbaum is in agreement with film historian Douglas Gomery, who regards Welles as an independent filmmaker who was able to exploit the Hollywood system to his advantage, rather than having been exploited by it. Rosenbaum sides with Carringer in rejecting Kael's conclusions about the authorship of *CITIZEN KANE,* but he parts company with both Gomery and Carringer because of their conclusion that "RKO was commercially justified in tampering with *Ambersons,* despite the fact that the resulting hybrid still lost the studio an enormous amount of money." Rosenbaum contends that Welles had final cut on other films besides *Citizen Kane*— both versions of *MACBETH,* for example, and the first two versions of *OTHELLO.* He defends Welles as a director who "loved to work," maligned by critics (naming CHARLES HIGHAM, DAVID THOMSON, and SIMON CALLOW) who never met him, as an obese and slothful hedonist. Fifteen years after the director's death, Rosenbaum claims, "we are still years away from being able to grasp the breadth of Welles's film work, much less evaluate it."

—J.M.W.

Royal Affairs in Versailles (Si Versailles m'était conté) C.L.M.-Cocinor/Times Film Corporation, 165 minutes, 1953. **Director, Producer, Screenplay:** Sacha Guitry; **Cinematography:** Louis

Née; **Music:** Jean Françaix; **Cast:** Orson Welles (Benjamin Franklin), Jean-Louis Barrault (Fénelon), Claudette Colbert (Mme de Montespan), Sacha Guitry (Louis XIV), Brigitte Bardot (Mme de Rosille), et al.

Produced, directed, and written by SACHA GUITRY, then one of the grand old men in French cinema, *Royal Affairs in Versailles* is a chronicle about the famous French palace from its initial construction in 1661 to the present. Magnificently photographed in Eastman color in the actual chateau of Versailles, a concession begrudgingly made by the French Ministry of Beaux Arts, the film proved long on pomp and short on dramatic appeal. When WELLES's Franklin appears, it is to request financial aid for the United States from the scandalous Louis XIV, played by Guitry. The film opened in New York in 1957. Reactions to Welles ranged from the *New York Times*'s Bosley Crowther's "conspicuous" to *The New Yorker*'s barb that "Benjamin Franklin, played by Orson Welles, looks like a botched embalming job, and his mortuary croaking contributes nothing in the way of wisdom to the affair." In spite of a huge budget for production and promotion, the film was quickly withdrawn from theaters around the world.

Welles, for his part, had fond memories of Guitry. When asked by PETER BOGDANOVICH about *Royal Affairs in Versailles* and *NAPOLEON,* Welles said: "Dear God in heaven, they were lousy; but Sacha was superb. A truly great type, you know—from another happier, hammier world, and hugely endowed for success in it." In addition to Welles and Guitry, *Royal Affairs in Versailles* featured CLAUDETTE COLBERT, Jean-Pierre Aumont, Edith Piaf, Jean Marais, and Lana Marconi. Released in France in 1954 under the title *Si Versailles m'était conté (If I Were Told about Versailles).*

Reference Knapp, Bettina. *Sacha Guitry* (Boston: Twayne, 1981).

—C.B.

Rutherford, Dame Margaret (1892–1972)
Dame Margaret Rutherford was cast as Mistress Quickly in ORSON WELLES's *CHIMES AT MIDNIGHT* (1966), Welles's filmic compilation of the FALSTAFF

material from several plays of Shakespeare. She also appeared with Welles in THE V.I.P.S (1963), directed by Anthony Asquith, in which she played the duchess of Brighton, earning an Academy Award for her role. Rutherford, a talented British character actress of stage and screen, was born on May 11, 1892, in London. First educated at Wimbledon Hill School, she initially taught speech and piano, then went on to study theater at the Old Vic, making her stage debut in 1925 playing Miss Prism in *The Importance of Being Earnest;* years later she reprised this role in Asquith's 1953 film adaptation of OSCAR WILDE's play. In 1957, she also played Lady Bracknell in the same Wilde play. Her first film role, however, was in *Dusty Ermine* in 1936, but she is best known for her role as the bicycle-riding clairvoyant, Madame Arcati, in *Blithe Spirit,* which she first played on stage in 1940 and then played in David Lean's film adaptation of 1945. Before she appeared in *Chimes at Midnight,* Rutherford had appeared in many films, including *I'm All Right Jack* (1959) and *Murder, She Said* (1961). Rutherford appeared as the indomitable Miss Marple in three more Agatha Christie mystery films of the 1960s. In *Chimes at Midnight,* there was a clash in acting styles between SIR JOHN GIELGUD's classical method of interpreting Shakespeare and the more realistic, earthy style of Rutherford and KEITH BAXTER, who played Prince Hal. There were also problems with the sound track of the film, and Rutherford's speech about the death of Falstaff was marred by the "persistent hum of the generator," according to BARBARA LEAMING. Leaming adds, that while audiences can hear the generator in the background, "the eloquence of her performance is such that you barely notice it." Named Dame Commander, O.B.E. (Order of the British Empire) in 1967, Margaret Rutherford died on May 22, 1972.

References   Johns, Eric. *Dames of the Theater* (New Rochelle, N.Y.: Arlington House, 1975); Keown, Eric. *Margaret Rutherford: An Illustrated Study of Her Work for Stage and Screen, with a List of Her Appearances* (London: Rockliff, 1956); Rutherford, Margaret, and Gwen Robyns. *Margaret Rutherford: An Autobiography* (London: W.H. Allen, 1972); Simmons, Dawn Langley. *Margaret Rutherford: A Blithe Spirit* (London: A. Baker, 1984).

—T.L.E and J.M.W.

Sacred Beasts, The This was an unproduced script by WELLES based on his love and appreciation of bullfighting. In its original version, the plot of *The Sacred Beasts* concerned an old Hollywood filmmaker who had given himself over to bullfights and café society. Based on his youthful experiences in Spain, Welles hoped to produce the script in the mid-1960s. However, the project was abandoned when *The Moment of Truth* (1964, *Il Momento della Verità*), an Italian–Spanish co-production directed by Francesco Rosi failed at the box office in spite of positive reviews.

Eventually, in collaboration with OJA KODAR, Welles reworked the script for *The Sacred Beasts*. The new version, transported from Spain to Hollywood, would be called THE OTHER SIDE OF THE WIND. Although Welles and Kodar invested over a quarter of a million dollars in the project, it was fated to be yet another star-crossed project. In intermittent production for seven spotty and sporadic years, 1970–76, the uncompleted *The Other Side of the Wind* featured Welles crony and colleague JOHN HUSTON as Hollywood film director Jake Hannaford.

—C.B.

Safe Place, A BBS/Columbia, 92 minutes (U.S.), 1971. **Director:** Henry Jaglom; **Producer:** Bert Schneider; **Screenplay:** Henry Jaglom; **Cinematographer:** Dick Kratina; **Editor:** Peiter Berema; **Cast:** Tuesday Weld, Orson Welles, Jack Nicholson, Philip Proctor

FRANK BRADY, in noting that not all of WELLES's acting appearances of the 1970s were bad, points to Jaglom's *A Safe Place*, "in which he plays a thoroughly lovable, Jewish, chess-playing magician who offers such mystical lines as: 'Last night in my sleep I dreamed that I was sleeping, and dreaming in that sleep that I had awakened, I fell asleep.'"

A Safe Place, Jaglom's first feature film, might best be described as a nonnarrative fantasy dealing with the emotional insecurities of a young woman (Tuesday Weld). Her relationship with a magician of dubious powers (Welles) dovetails with her quest to reclaim the innocence of her past. Intercut with the Weld-Welles footage is a dreamlike fantasy involving two men (Jack Nicholson and Philip Proctor) who serve but cannot fulfill the woman's needs. Although inviting psychological interpretations, *A Safe Place* is perhaps better understood as a reflection of Jaglom's nostalgia for the magic of Hollywood's Golden Age. The presence of Welles as a magician underscores this reading. The sentimentality of the vintage songs selected for the sound track also adds to the sense of "pastness." However, at the end, thanks in large part to Jaglom's free-flowing transitions between fantasy and reality, it's clear that the heroine (or any of us) cannot go back, that, indeed, the past is forever sealed away, entombed in an icy void of a galaxy far, far away. Jaglom, like so many first-time directors of the period, owed his opportunity to helm a studio film to the youth cycle spawned by *The Graduate* (1967) and *Easy Rider* (1969). Appealing to mostly middle-class, college-educated young people, *A Safe Place* was noted for Tuesday Weld's emotionally moving performance. But, as critic Chris Petit reminds us, "With Welles as presiding spirit, it's also funnier than you might expect."

Jaglom, an acolyte of Welles during the 1970s, who made repeated efforts to secure a film deal for his mentor, appeared in the maestro's still unreleased feature THE OTHER SIDE OF THE WIND, a project produced during the period 1970–76, but locked away in a Paris film lab because of legal snarls.

—C.B.

Sailor of Gibraltar, The   United Artists, 89 minutes, 1967. **Director:** Tony Richardson; **Producer:** Neil Hartley and Oscar Lewenstein; **Screenplay:** Christopher Isherwood, Don Magner, and Richardson (based on the novel by Marguerite Duras); **Cinematographer:** Raoul Coutard; **Editor:** Anthony Gibbs; **Music:** Antoine Duhamel; **Cast:** Jeanne Moreau (Anna), Ian Bannen (Alan), Orson Welles (Louis de Mozambique), Vanessa Redgrave (Sheila), Zia Moyheddin (Noori), Hugh Griffith (Llewellyn), Eleanor Bron (Carla), and John Hurt (John)

Adapted from a 1952 novel by Marguerite Duras, *Le marin de Gibraltar,* Christopher Isherwood fashioned a scenario around Anna (JEANNE MOREAU), who in the midst of an around-the-Mediterranean quest for the enigmatic mariner of the title, sails into Alexandria for a visit with Louis of Mozambique, played by a flamboyant WELLES. Louis, a gregarious peddler of information, offers Anna yet another worthless clue. However, in keeping with the picaresque tradition of this maritime variation of the road film, Welles's character serves to add exoticism, here, of the North African variety. As for the plot, Louis's information, though a dead end, nonetheless propels Anna, and us, into the film's next sequence. Considering the considerable talents involved, including noted French cinematographer Raoul Coutard, the film was a disappointment. *Variety,* in what was at best a tepid review, complained that "Orson Welles is wasted on a brief bit as an information peddler." Distributed by Lopert Pictures.

—C.B.

Salkind, Alexander (1915–1997)   A noted Russian-born film producer, Salkind, and his father, Michael, sought out WELLES to direct and star in a film based on the Gogol story "Taras Bulba." Welles accepted on the condition that he also be allowed to write the adaptation. When Welles asked about the budget, Alexander Salkind replied that they had no money. Welles replied with gales of laughter. He immediately decided that they were kindred spirits with whom he could collaborate. Alas, just as Welles was finishing his script, news came that a big budget Hollywood version of *Taras Bulba* with Yul Brynner, Tony Curtis, and Christine Kaufman was being planned, a production that was eventually released in 1962.

In spite of the setback, the Salkinds, who were determined to collaborate with Welles, suggested a number of books, mostly out-of-copyright Russian novels, from which he could choose another picture. Although Welles pleaded for an opportunity to develop an original project, the Salkinds insisted on an adaptation. Eventually, Welles and the Salkinds settled on FRANZ KAFKA's *The Trial,* the celebrated novel posthumously published in 1925 as *Der Prozess.* In part, based on a 1962 British Film Institute poll of international film critics that had named CITIZEN KANE as the top film of all time, the Salkinds were able to raise the money necessary to get the project under way. The resulting film directed and scripted and starring Welles, and also titled THE TRIAL, was released in 1962, with Alexander and Michael Salkind credited as executive producers. The warm if sometimes prickly relationship between Alexander Salkind and Welles began in 1959, when Welles appeared in his production of AUSTERLITZ (1960).

Born in Gdansk, Poland (at the time, Danzig, Germany), in 1915, of Russian-Jewish descent, Alexander Salkind was raised in Berlin, where his father, Michael, produced films. Accompanying his father to Cuba on various production ventures, Salkind remained in Latin America for a number of years. In the late 1950s, however, he returned to Europe, where he later produced high-budget international co-productions, often in collaboration with his son, Ilya, who was born in Mexico City in 1948.

Among Salkind's films are *Austerlitz* (*The Battle of Austerlitz;* 1960); *The Trial* (1962); *Ballad in Blue* (*Blues for Lovers,* 1965); *Cervantes* (*Young Rebel;* 1967); *The Light at the Edge of the World* (1971); *Kill!* (*Kill Kill Kill, Bluebeard;* 1972); *The Three Musketeers* (1974); *The Four Musketeers* (1975); *The Prince and the Pauper* (*Crossed Swords;* 1977); *Superman* (1978); *Superman II* (1981); *Superman III* (1983); *Supergirl* (1984); and, *Santa Claus: The Movie* (1985).

—C.B.

Salome   This unproduced project commissioned by British producer ALEXANDER KORDA in 1946, and based on the 1893 historical tragedy by OSCAR WILDE, would have starred WELLES in a double role as Herod and, in a contemporary framing story, as playwright Wilde. The adaptation of Wilde's Bible-based play by Fletcher Markle and Welles opens and closes on Wilde seated in a French café, discussing Salome over an absinthe.

In spite of Korda's and Welles's enthusiasm, the project soon ran into difficulties. For one, Welles and Korda could not agree on a leading lady to play the title role. Also, the script raised the eyebrows of Joseph Breen, head of the infamous Production Code Administration, the industry watchdog charged by Hollywood's major studios to make sure that movies did not offend. On October 6, 1946, Breen pointed out to Korda and Welles, that, among other things, Herod's lust for Salome, his stepdaughter and niece, was perverse and therefore unacceptable. Finally, there was geography. With Welles in Hollywood working on THE LADY FROM SHANGHAI and Korda busy in London, the long-distance negotiations via cable regarding *Salome* broke down. Years later, and ever philosophical, Welles told PETER BOGDANOVICH that "we [Korda and Welles] hated disagreeing, so we were both relieved, I think, when he got bored with it."

—C.B.

Sanford, Erskine (1880–1950)   Erskine Sanford was an established radio actor before he joined ORSON WELLES's MERCURY THEATRE ON THE AIR in 1938, when he was almost 60 years old. He also appeared in Welles's stage productions and films. In 1938, he played the part of Mazzini Dunn in Welles's stage adaptation of GEORGE BERNARD SHAW's HEARTBREAK HOUSE, and later he was cast in the ill-fated DANTON'S DEATH, but in an onstage accident involving a defective elevator, he broke his leg. In 1939, he acted in another Welles failure, FIVE KINGS. He appeared as the president in the radio adaptation of Charles Dickens's *A Tale of Two Cities,* and when Welles moved to Hollywood, Sanford and many Mercury regulars went with him and were signed to RKO contracts. He was originally slated to act in Welles's proposed film adaptation of Joseph Conrad's HEART OF DARKNESS, but the project was scuttled. However, when Welles cast his CITIZEN KANE (1941), Sanford appeared as the elderly, inefficient, comical *Inquirer* editor, whom Welles dismisses. According to FRANK BRADY, "Erskine Sanford's drift toward befuddlement colored the revisions in the character of Carter, the bewildered, imminently departing editor." Sanford also appeared in Welles's radio production of "His Honor, the Mayor," which was broadcast on April 6, 1941, and in Welles's stage adaptation of RICHARD WRIGHT's NATIVE SON, which opened in New York on March 24, 1941. In Welles's THE MAGNIFICENT AMBERSONS (1942), Sanford took on the role of Benson, George Minafer's bumbling, officious law-firm boss. His stock role as a comic character served him well in THE LADY FROM SHANGHAI (1947), in which he played the judge in Michael's almost surreal murder trial. In Welles's MACBETH, Sanford played Duncan, the king. Sanford appeared in only one film that was not directed by Welles, *Ministry of Fear* (1944), which was directed by Fritz Lang. Sanford died in 1950, only three years after playing his last film role.

—T.L.E.

Schaefer, George (1889–1982)   After working as sales chief for United Artists and also at Paramount, George Schaefer became president of RKO STUDIOS from 1938 to 1942 and hired young ORSON WELLES (at age 24) to act, direct, write, and produce four movies. Schaefer had entered the film industry in 1914 as secretary to Lewis J. Selznick. At the time of his appointment as chief executive by RKO owner Floyd Odlum, the highly respected and talented Pandro S. Berman was vice president in charge of production. Berman and Schaefer strongly disagreed over Schaefer's policy of bringing in outside production units to operate at the studio in place of in-house projects. Berman subsequently resigned, leaving Schaefer free to assume all production responsibilities. One of the outside production units that Schaefer brought under contract was Orson Welles's Mercury Players. Under the terms of an unprecedented contract, Welles was hired to produce, direct, and act in two films that were guaranteed to be released by RKO. The first of these, CITIZEN KANE (1941), aroused the ire of WILLIAM RANDOLPH HEARST when it was determined that the film was a thinly disguised biography of the powerful newspaper magnate. LOUELLA PARSONS, the Hearst movie critic, threatened Schaefer with "one of the most beautiful lawsuits in history" if *Kane* was released. To his credit, Schaefer resisted extraordinary pressure from powerful Hollywood and New York interests allied with Hearst to withhold the picture from release and to destroy the negative, perhaps because Welles had threatened a lawsuit in the event that RKO might fail to release the film. *Kane* was released under a boycott by Hearst newspapers and the established theater chains. Although critically acclaimed by the relatively few discerning reviewers who saw it, the boycott and the lack of publicity virtually destroyed any chance of a financial success for RKO.

Despite the controversy and the disappointing financial return from *Citizen Kane,* Schaefer rationalized that the clearly evident artistic quality of the picture would bring considerable prestige to RKO. He approved Welles's second project, a film of BOOTH TARKINGTON's novel THE MAGNIFICENT AMBERSONS (1942). *Ambersons* also received its share of critical acclaim, but was ultimately a box-office failure. Schaefer had pressed Welles to have the picture ready for release by Easter, but Welles, under a mandate by the State Department's Office of Inter-American Affairs, had to leave for Brazil in February 1942 to film a documentary on the Rio Carnival season. He was unable to supervise the final editing.

ROBERT WISE followed Welles's directions to the best of his ability and assembled a cut for preview. After a preview for a group of executives sent by RKO's owner, Floyd Odlum, Schaefer ordered Wise to make cuts to reduce running time. Schaefer had done his best to respect the integrity of Welles's film and to consult with Welles, despite the difficulty of civilian communication during wartime; but Schaefer was now in a difficult position. Two sneak previews in the spring of 1942, one in Pomona and the other in Pasadena, brought audience reactions that were extremely disappointing. By this time Odlum had lost confidence in Schaefer, and replaced him as president with N. Peter Rathvon. Rathvon brought in CHARLES KOERNER, head of RKO distribution, as production chief. Koerner ordered that *Ambersons,* without further attempts at consultation with Welles, be reduced by 45 minutes prior to its theatrical release. During his tenure at RKO, Schaefer had promoted large-budget projects with an emphasis on "artistic" quality. Koerner was believed to be an executive who knew what the public would pay to see, and in a reversal of Schaefer's policies, proclaimed RKO the studio of "showmanship instead of genius."

In recognition of his contributions to the war effort, both distributing films to armed forces abroad and producing training films for the army during World War II, Schaefer received the Motion Picture Associations first award for civic and patriotic service.

Reference Rohauer, Raymond. *George Schaefer: A Tribute* (New York: NYCC, 1969).

—R.C.K.

Schilling, Gus (August E. Schilling)

(1908–1957) Native New Yorker Gus Schilling began his career as a burlesque and musical comedy comedian. His specialty was earnest, gullible, nervous types. He broke into films through his association with WELLES's Mercury Players in New York, performing in stage and radio plays. Schilling was among the actors who did tests, along with Robert Coote and EVERETT SLOANE, for Welles's initial project, a film based on Joseph Conrad's HEART OF DARKNESS. This project, however, was never realized. Schilling was also cast as Bardolph in Welles's FIVE KINGS project, which also failed to materialize. Welles subsequently cast Schilling as the waiter in CITIZEN KANE (1941) who introduces Thompson, the reporter (WILLIAM ALLAND), to the now dissipated Susan Alexander Kane (DOROTHY

COMINGORE) in an Atlantic City night club. Schilling also had small roles in Welles's THE MAGNIFICENT AMBERSONS (1942), THE LADY FROM SHANGHAI, and MACBETH (1948), in which he had the comic role of the Porter. Other films in his career include *Mexican Spitfire Out West* (1940); *Ice Capades, It Started with Eve, Appointment for Love* (1941); *Broadway, You Were Never Lovelier* (1942); *Chatterbox, Hers to Hold* (1943); *It's a Pleasure, a Thousand and One Nights* (1945); *Calendar Girl* (1947); *Our Very Own* (1950); *On Dangerous Ground* (1952); *Run for Cover* (1955); and *Bigger Than Life* (1956), his last film. He died shortly thereafter in 1957.

—R.C.K.

Schneider, Albert

Albert Schneider was ORSON WELLES's first manager. He began as Welles's booking agent for his radio shows and then became his manager. His first major achievement was creating a deal for Welles to do the radio show FIRST PERSON SINGULAR, which required that Welles write, direct, perform, and produce nine weekly programs for the Columbia Broadcasting System. The shows were to be adaptations of well-known literary works. His second coup, the one that made Welles the envy of Hollywood veterans, was the 1939 RKO deal that paid Welles $150,000 a film and gave him control of the films he wanted to produce. According to SIMON CALLOW, Schneider "was playing a brilliant game of brinksmanship." This entailed rejecting the offers of RKO head GEORGE SCHAEFER, who was pressing Welles for a positive response. Since Welles was preoccupied with getting financial backing for his FIVE KINGS project, Schneider could let Schaefer think that Welles would have to postpone his filmmaking ambitions. Callow's account pays tribute to Schneider's negotiating expertise: "Like any suitor, Schaefer became more ardent with every rejection, until finally, backed by ARNOLD WEISSBERGER's legal brilliance, the masterly Schneider secured a contract for his client (in the form of Mercury Productions) the likes of which no one in Hollywood has ever had before or since." After the abortive HEART OF DARKNESS project, Welles was financially strapped but refused to take any responsibility for the situation. Instead, he accused Schneider of "passing it [the money] away." It was Schneider

again who helped Welles financially, this time by arranging a lecture tour for Welles, who was without funds prior to the shooting of CITIZEN KANE. The tour, a financial success, also helped establish Welles as an entertainer, a role he would exploit on talk shows near the end of his life.

—T.L.E.

Schneider, Romy (Rosemarie Albach-Retty)

(1938–1982) Actress Romy Schneider appeared in ORSON WELLES's film adaptation of FRANZ KAFKA's THE TRIAL (1962) as Leni, described by JAMES NAREMORE as "a vixenish woman with a 'physical defect,'" who "deceives and manipulates K., at one point trying to seduce both him and the client Bloch at the same time." Despite the "physical defect," a webbed hand, Leni, like Hilda (ELSA MARTINELLI), is too beautiful, Naremore believes, to suggest the "truly Kafkaesque imagery of sexual unhealthiness" of the novel. Regardless of her appropriateness, Schneider was physically appealing in the role, which led to roles in American productions.

Romy Schneider, who was born on September 23, 1938, in Vienna, was the daughter of film actors. As a teenager, she starred in several "Sissi" films (concerning the Hapsburg royal family) during the 1950s; the material from her earlier films was eventually shaped into a feature film, *Forever My Love* (1962), and released in the United States. In 1962, her appearance in *The Trial* and in Luchino Visconti's *Boccaccio '70* made her an international film star. She made three American films (*The Cardinal,* 1963; *Good Neighbor Sam,* 1964; and *Bloodline,* 1979) as well as such international co-productions as *What's New Pussycat?* (1965), *My Lover My Son* (1970), and *10:30 P.M. Summer* (1966). After 1970, she no longer made films in the United States, though she continued to appear regularly, at least once a year, in French and German films. Her last film, *La Passante du Sans-Souci/La Passante* (a French and German production, 1982), appeared the year of her death of a heart attack in 1982.

—T.L.E.

Second Hurricane, The

(opera, 1937) *The Second Hurricane,* an opera for children by AARON

COPLAND, one of America's leading 20th-century composers, was unique in calling for a cast of children. The libretto by Edwin Denby, in support of various Depression programs designed to make productive use of schoolboys, deals with an aviator who calls on the help of high school volunteers to help flood victims. With four boys and two girls aboard for the mission, the aviator takes off, only to be forced down by poor weather. At first, the members of the group fight as individuals for food and other advantages. But as the hurricane looms, the young people are forced to cooperate, thus learning the value of teamwork and comradeship.

Denby strategized that a theatrical work about young people should be brought to the stage by America's youngest actor-director, who also happened to be enjoying his celebrity as America's "Boy Wonder." Copland made the pitch to WELLES, playing him portions of the score, which was simple in style to match the opera's youthful theme and cast. Welles was taken with Copland's music and Denby's story and immediately signed on. The press loved the story, and high school actors-singers flooded in for auditions. Welles, who must have been reminded of his glory days at the Todd School, enjoyed the process and cast the majority of the roles from the Professional Children's School. The adult role, the aviator, was played by JOSEPH COTTEN at a salary of $10 per performance.

Financial support for the venture came from Copland's backer, Mary Lescze, who obtained additional underwriting from such prominent members of the New York arts community as Mrs. Leopold Stokowski, Carl Van Vechten, and Lincoln Kirstein. Welles, a rehearsal taskmaster, proved considerate of his young charges. However, as his energies became overtaxed with preparations for THE CRADLE WILL ROCK and his multiple radio commitments, he turned over much of the last-minute direction to Hiram Sherman. *The Second Hurricane* opened in May 1937 at the Playhouse on Grand Street for three well-received experimental performances, and a radio broadcast arranged by Welles. A year later, with sponsorship from the leftist magazine *New Masses,* excerpts from the work were presented on radio with commentary by Welles.

—C.B.

Secret of Nikola Tesla, The (Tajna Nikole Tesle)
Zagreb Film-Kinematografi, 120 minutes, 1980. **Director:** Krsto Papic; **Screenplay:** Ivo Bresan, Ivan Kusan, and Krsto Papic; **Cinematographer:** Ivica Rajkovic; **Cast:** Orson Welles (J.P. Morgan), Strother Martin (George Westinghouse), Dennis Patrick (Thomas Edison), Petar Bozovic (Nikola Tesla), Oja Kodar

In the film about the Yogoslavian Tesla, an electrical genius who did his creative work at the turn of the last century, WELLES played Morgan as a shrewd investor who initially helped fund Tesla's efforts, but who finally withdrew his support when he saw that he could not reap big profits from Tesla's work.

—T.L.E.

Seiderman, Maurice
(1907–1989) Maurice Seiderman, whom WELLES believed was "one of the two or three great makeup men of our time," designed and developed the makeup process that enabled Welles, in the title role of CITIZEN KANE (1941), to age from his 20s to his 70s. Seiderman was a Russian immigrant whose father had worked as a makeup artist for the Moscow Art Theatre. Seiderman had studied at the Art Students' League in New York City and also worked extensively in the theater during the 1920s, most notably on Max Reinhardt's stage production of *The Miracle* (1924). During the 1930s, Seiderman moved to Hollywood, where he began working for RKO, even though he was not a union member. He did the makeup for all the principal actors in *Winterset* (1936), as well as the makeup for Katharine Hepburn in *Mary of Scotland* (1936) and Ginger Rogers in *Shall We Dance* (1937). He had also done the makeup for *Swiss Family Robinson* (1940).

In the summer of 1940, Welles met Seiderman at RKO. In a small corner work area in the makeup studio, Seiderman had done some modeling in clay, which especially impressed Welles. Seiderman subsequently convinced him that he could do the aging process for all of the actors in *Citizen Kane* in such a way that normal face movements would not be hampered and constricted as they usually were with the conventional process used to simulate aging, a process that generally produced stiffness and a lack of normal facial mobility in the subject. Another problem was that the Mercury Players were not recognizable to American filmgoers. Accordingly, Seiderman transformed them into familiar genre types. For example, the young Charley Kane was modeled, according to Norman Gambill, after the strong, heroic cowboy type. There are obvious physical resemblances to both Spencer Tracy and Clark Gable. In middle age Kane resembles the typical middle-aged tycoon embodied in Edward Arnold. The elder Kane, appropriately enough, was modeled after WILLIAM RANDOLPH HEARST and Samuel Insull. According to another source, the inspiration for the large domed head of Kane at the height of his powers was inspired by the image of Fantazius Mallare, a character in *The Kingdom of Evil,* a novel by BEN HECHT. Because he was not a union member, Seiderman could not receive credit for makeup on the film; in fact, Mel Berns, then head of makeup at RKO, wanted to receive the credit. Welles refused, and no one received official credit for makeup. Welles, however, did run full-page ads in the Hollywood trade papers, extolling Seiderman as "the best make-up man in the world." Later, when Welles was speaking to Frances Perkins, ROOSEVELT's secretary of labor, he mentioned the credit situation to her; the following day, Seiderman got his union card. In an interview with Gambill, Seiderman had nothing but praise for Welles, who gave him artistic freedom: "This is why I loved Orson Welles, and still do. It is also why I quit pictures even after becoming head of RKO's makeup department; there were no other people like Welles to work with."

Following *Citizen Kane,* Seiderman continued his association with Welles. He designed all the makeup for THE MAGNIFICENT AMBERSONS (1942), JOURNEY INTO FEAR (1943), MACBETH (1948), OTHELLO (1952), and TOUCH OF EVIL (1958), as well as Welles's makeup for JANE EYRE (1944), *The Secret Life of Joseph Stalin* (1952), THE LONG HOT SUMMER (1957), COMPULSION (1959), and FERRY TO HONG KONG (1959). In addition to the Welles films, Seiderman was responsible for the makeup on many RKO films while serving as the head of the makeup department from 1944 to 1947. After 1960, Seiderman's work for film was virtually over. He turned his attention to painting and sculp-

ture in the 1960s and to scientific endeavors: the Waring Blender, synthetic skin, and soft contact lenses. In addition, he is the co-inventor of the artificial cornea. The work with the lenses probably grew out of his work with colored contact lenses that he made for actors in several films. He left Hollywood for Montana, and died of heart disease in Port Angeles, Washington, on July 20, 1989.

—T.L.E. and R.C.K.

Selznick, David O. (1902–1965)   David O. Selznick first met ORSON WELLES on May 18, 1937, after having seen him perform in DOCTOR FAUSTUS the night before. According to DAVID THOMSON in *Showman,* a biography of Selznick, "They got on very well: David had no doubt about Welles's talent, and they were two equally spoiled boys." Selznick even offered Welles a job in charge of his story department at Selznick International. Welles turned down the offer and suggested JOHN HOUSEMAN, his partner at Mercury, for the position. (Houseman was hired as Selznick's "associate" in 1941.) In December of 1938 Selznick, who was impressed by Welles's use of the first-person narration in the radio broadcast of REBECCA, recommended its use to Alfred Hitchcock, who was about to adapt the Du Maurier novel to film, and in June of 1939 he again wrote to Hitchcock, expressing his shock and disappointment at the screenplay he received from him and reiterating his intent to follow the Welles treatment: "If we do in motion pictures as faithful a job as Welles did on the radio, we will likely have the same success that the book had and the same success that Welles had." In 1942, when Selznick wrote to WILLIAM GOETZ at Twentieth Century–Fox about JANE EYRE, Selznick's "deserted child," he suggested that Goetz invite Welles to a casting meeting for the film: "I know few people in the history of the business who have shown such a talent for exact casting, and for digging up new people."

However, when Selznick heard that Welles was to receive producer or associate producer credit on *Jane Eyre,* he cautioned Goetz against that course of action, even though Welles's contract gave him associate producer status, because it would damage the reputation of ROBERT STEVENSON, the producer: "Orson is such a personality that if he is credited as a producer, Stevenson's credit is likely to degenerate into something of a stooge status." When he co-financed and co-produced THE THIRD MAN (1949), Selznick again expressed some concern about Welles, this time as Harry Lime (Selznick had wanted Robert Mitchum for the part) and also as scriptwriter. He wanted co-producer ALEXANDER KORDA to know that "Cotten and Welles are both frustrated writers" who "are both experts at ridicule so will disparage any lines written by other than outstanding Americans and compete with each other in tearing dialogue apart with what could be resultant mess." Welles, in turn, told PETER BOGDANOVICH that Selznick was guilty of taking credit where none or little was due on *Jane Eyre*. According to Welles, Selznick only loaned Korda a few actors for the film, but when the film was released in the United States, Selznick got most of the credit. Welles claims that two years after the film opened and Korda knew about Selznick's taking undeserved credit, Korda told Selznick that he hoped he didn't die before Selznick because he feared that Selznick would be "sneaking out to the graveyard at night and scratching my name off the tombstone."

David O. Selznick was born into the film business on May 10, 1902, in Pittsburgh: Lewis J. Selznick, his father, was a film executive concerned with the production and distribution of films; Myron Selznick, his brother, became a talent scout and producer. Selznick began working for his father, made several documentaries in 1923, and went to Hollywood in 1926, where he was first employed by LOUIS B. MAYER, who had been a partner of his father's and was now in charge of MGM. A short time later, he left MGM, where he was dissatisfied with his position as associate producer of the studio's "B" films, and moved first to Paramount and then to RKO, where he was vice president in charge of production. Mayer, who was his father-in-law, rehired him as vice president and producer in 1933. After he produced several quality films for MGM, the ambitious Selznick formed Selznick International in 1936 and in 1939 produced (in addition to doing some casting, directing, and writing) the incredibly successful *Gone With the Wind*. *Rebecca* (1940), directed by Alfred Hitchcock, whom Selznick had brought from England, was his

next critical and financial success. He made several big-budget films in the 1940s, turned to co-producing films (such as *The Third Man*) in Europe in the 1950s, and made *A Farewell to Arms,* a film adaptation of Ernest Hemingway's novel and Selznick's last film, in 1957. Selznick, who broke ground as one of the first independent producers during the declining years of the studio system, was the alleged inspiration for the protagonist/producer, played by Kirk Douglas, in *The Bad and the Beautiful* (1952). Selznick died in 1965.

References Leff, Leonard. *Hitchcock and Selznick: The Rich and Strange Collaboration of Alfred Hitchcock and David O. Selznick in Hollywood* (Berkeley: University of California Press, 1999); Thomson, David. *Showman: The Life of David O. Selznick* (New York: Knopf, 1992).

—T.L.E.

Shadow, The (radio, 1937–1938)   In the 1930s, radio was a purveyor of American popular culture every bit as influential as the movies. *The Shadow,* an exemplar of the medium's earliest and most popular crime dramas, was one of the Mutual Broadcasting Company's more successful ventures. However, as ratings began to falter, Mutual sought to revamp the show's format. When the show was relaunched in 1937, the Shadow, instead of merely being the narrator, was now the show's central character, a modern-day Sherlock Holmes who solved crimes too difficult for the police to unravel. Another innovation was a supernatural gift, a power picked up in the Orient enabling the Shadow to cloud men's minds, thus making himself invisible. Finally, the character was given a double identity: By day, he was Lamont Cranston, "a wealthy young man–about–town"; by night, as the Shadow he fought an unceasing war on crime by "using sophisticated methods that may shortly be available to regular law-enforcement agencies." As SIMON CALLOW points out, the character became a prototype for subsequently bifurcated superheroes such as Batman, Superman, and Captain Marvel. To play Mutual's new larger-than-life figure, the network selected Broadway's and radio's Boy Wonder, ORSON WELLES. Although the fourth Shadow in the show's history, Welles was the first Lamont Cranston.

The new format catapulted the program far beyond its previous heights. On Sunday evenings from 5:00 to 5:30 P.M., it seemed that all of America stopped to tune in Welles's evocation of Lamont Cranston and his crime-fighting alter-ego. Indeed, *The Shadow* became the most popular mystery-crime show on the air. "Shadow" clubs were formed. There were blizzards of fan mail. There were also special promotions at which Welles would turn up donning a black hat, cape, and mask. Welles added mystery to his role by using a microphone filter to give his lines an even icier, more ominous edge. Curiously, the program's trademark opening—the eerie strains of Saint-Saens's *Omphale's Spinning Wheel;* the Shadow's curling, bass-register laugh; and the lines: "Who knows what evil lurks in the heart of man? The Shadow knows . . . the weed of crime bears bitter fruit. Crime does not pay! The Shadow knows!"— did not involve Welles. Mutual, judging Welles's laugh too adolescent, preferred the show's old introduction. Of course, no one knew. In fact, the show's sonic signature, which would become as closely associated with Welles as the Harry Lime theme from THE THIRD MAN 12 years later, was actually delivered by Frank Readick, Jr., Welles's predecessor as the Shadow.

Callow notes wittily that Welles played Cranston with a casual charm "in the more or less English accent still synonymous with a private income" with its suggestions of silk dressing gowns and cigarette holders, and a brocaded manner worthy of NOËL COWARD. As the invisible Shadow, Welles shifted into an ominous mode of omniscience and mysterious foreboding. Also memorable was AGNES MOOREHEAD, a colleague of Welles from THE MARCH OF TIME, as the Shadow's loyal assistant, Margo Lane. Other *March of Time* regulars hired for *The Shadow's* makeover were EVERETT SLOANE and Ted de Corsia. Initially, Welles's identity as the actor playing the Shadow was to have remained secret. But, as Callow points out, nothing pertaining to Welles could remain a secret for long.

In fact, the role of the Shadow added immensely to Welles's fame beyond Broadway. Such was the power of radio. It was a point made by *Time* magazine in its May 9, 1938, cover story on Welles, which,

while saluting his theater accomplishments, stated that radio was his "mainstay," mentioning in support *The Shadow* and *The March of Time.*

—C.B.

Shakespeare by Welles The documented facts of William Shakespeare's life have often served as little more than the premise for the stories told about him. John Manningham, for example, in his 1602 diary recorded the humorous story, known as the "William the Conqueror and Richard III anecdote," about a bawdy encounter between Shakespeare, Richard Burbage, and an amorous playgoer. More recently, writers Tom Stoppard and Marc Norman account for Shakespeare's early years in London by giving a slightly sitcom demeanor to the struggling young writer of *Shakespeare in Love* (1998). At the same time, the notion that Edward de Vere, the 17th earl of Oxford, is a more likely author of the plays than "the Stratford man" has found a home in popular discussions of the authorship question. The legal documents provide a simple outline for Shakespeare's life, recording his birth on April 26, 1564, his marriage to Anne Hathaway on November 27, 1582, the christening of a daughter, Susanna, on May 26, 1583, and twins, Hamnet and Judith, on February 2, 1585, as well as the burial of Hamnet on August 11, 1596. Shakespeare's will is dated March 25, 1616, and his burial is recorded a month later on April 25, 1616. To these may be added various documents regarding his parents, siblings, and children, as well as the records of Shakespeare's purchases of New Place in Stratford-upon-Avon in 1597 and land in Old Stratford in 1602, and the records of Shakespeare's association with the Lord Chamberlain's Men in 1595, the King's Men in 1603, and his purchase of the Blackfriars Gatehouse in 1613.

Several contemporary allusions by people who apparently knew Shakespeare fill in these outlines. Robert Green, in *A Groat's Worth of Wit* (1592), refers to Shakespeare as "an upstart crow." Ben Jonson in *Sejanus* (1603) lists Shakespeare as one of the "principal tragedians," and John Heminges and Henry Condell in the 1623 First Folio, include Jonson's famous poem, which claims that the "Sweet Swan of Avon" had "small Latin and less Greek," along with

William Shakespeare

remarkable point in history, the transition from the Middle Ages to the Renaissance, the bridging of the old world and the new one. In his precocious essay, "On Staging Shakespeare and on Shakespeare's Stage," written when he was still a teenager and published in *EVERYBODY'S SHAKESPEARE* (1934), Welles says, "it is wise to remember, if we would really appreciate him, that he doesn't properly belong to us but to another world that smelled assertively of columbine and gun powder and printer's ink and was vigorously dominated by Elizabeth." Some decades later, Welles makes the point more specifically, explaining to PETER BOGDANOVICH that:

> Shakespeare . . . was very close to the origins of his own culture: the language he wrote had just been formed; the old England, the old Europe of the Middle Ages, still lived in the memory of the people of Stratford. He was very close, you understand, to quite another epoch, and yet he stood in the doorway of our "modern" world. His lyricism, his comic zest, his humanity came from these ties with the past. The pessimism, of course, is closer to our modern condition. . . . He was a country boy, the son of a butcher, who'd made it into court. He spent years getting himself a coat of arms. He wrote mostly about kings.

Leonard Digges's somewhat awkward lines identifying the playwright with the Stratford man:

> Shakespeare, at length thy pious fellows give
> The world thy works: thy works, by which, out live
> Thy tomb, thy name must, when that stone is rent,
> And Time dissolves thy Stratford Monument,
> Here we alive shall view thee still.

In 1661, more than 40 years after Shakespeare's death, John Aubrey began writing the gossipy stories he gathered from the families of people who knew Shakespeare and was able to report that Shakespeare was the son of a butcher, visited his family in Warwickshire once a year, and knew Latin because he had once been a schoolmaster.

ORSON WELLES's story of Shakespeare's significance emphasizes the dramatist's position at a

This view that Shakespeare was strategically placed at a time of divided values perhaps underlies Welles's heightened contrast of values in the "old and new religions" in his *MACBETH* (1948), of Othello and Iago in his *OTHELLO* (1952), and of King Henry IV and FALSTAFF in *CHIMES AT MIDNIGHT* (1966). Certainly it explains his characterization of Falstaff as "one of the only great characters in all dramatic literature who is essentially *good*." According to Welles, "Every country has its 'Merrie England,' a season of innocence, a dew-bright morning of the world, and Falstaff—that pot-ridden old rogue—is its perfect embodiment. All the rogery and the tavern wit and the liar and bluff is simply a turn of his—it's a little song he sings for his supper. It isn't what he's about."

Welles's relationship with Shakespeare's plays began in his infancy and lasted until his death. Explaining why he disliked *A Midsummer Night's*

Dream, Welles told Bogdanovich that the play has been his "reading primer. You'll have to try it—just read the first scene of *Midsummer Night's Dream* and imagine it's the first thing you ever had to spell out." SIMON CALLOW writes that "from early manhood Welles never passed a day of his life without thinking of Shakespeare and planning projects based on the plays." Only a few days before he died in 1985, Welles lined up the shots for the modern version of *JULIUS CAESAR* that he had planned and put off several times over his life. His first connection with *Julius Caesar* was in 1929 when, as a 14-year-old schoolboy, he adapted the play and took the roles of Marc Antony and Cassius. Later, he was immensely successful with the famous 1937 modern-dress fascist version of the play, called *Caesar,* and in 1953 Welles had interested Egyptian king Farouk to finance a film with Richard Burton as Caesar and himself as Brutus but aborted his plans when he heard about the Joseph L. Mankiewicz version then in production. Ten years later, in 1963, he planned to shoot it for Italian television, and in 1978 he scripted an abridged version, without Brutus, for *Orson Welles Solo.* When he died seven years later, he had just begun filming it.

Indeed, many of Welles's Shakespeare projects surfaced then submerged only to surface again in a different form, a pattern easily demonstrated by his four completed Shakespeare film adaptations. His famous "voodoo" *MACBETH,* presented in 1936 at the Lafayette Theatre in Harlem, New York, influenced his filmed *Macbeth,* which he prepared for by presenting the play at the Utah Centennial days before he began filming in Hollywood with substantially the same cast. His filmed *Othello* differs only in the sequence of his obsession. He began his interrupted and extended filming of the play in 1949, a process well documented by MICHEÁL MACLIAMMÓIR's book, *Put Money in Thy Purse* (1952), then, while he was editing the film, Welles staged the play in 1951, this time using Peter Finch, rather than MacLiammóir, as Iago, and finally returned to it once more in the documentary *FILMING OTHELLO* (1978). His 1966 film, *Chimes at Midnight* began as the conflation of *Henry VI* and *Richard III,* sometimes known as *Winter of Our Discontent* (1930), that was his project at the Todd School for Boys when Welles was only 15. In 1939,

he tried the same material on Broadway as *FIVE KINGS,* and then reworked it and presented it at the Dublin's GATE THEATRE in 1960, hoping to take it to London. That effort failed, but Welles eventually found money to begin filming it in Spain in 1964. His 40-minute filmed adaptation of *The Merchant of Venice,* completed in 1969, is, as JONATHAN ROSENBAUM says, "probably the least known of Welles's completed films, and the last of his realized Shakespeare adaptations" because "the sound track of two of the three reels was stolen in Rome." *The Merchant of Venice* was one of the three plays prepared by Welles and his former headmaster, ROGER HILL, as *Everybody's Shakespeare,* a volume that also included *Twelfth Night* and *Julius Caesar,* and was revised in 1939 as *The Mercury Shakespeare.*

Welles formed his concept of how to approach Shakespeare's plays in his early days at the Todd School, where, as RICHARD FRANCE notes, Roger Hill had his "Todd Troupers" specialize in "truncated versions of Shakespeare" and "imbued his students with the notion that Shakespeare was meant neither to be studied nor dissected, but rather to be enjoyed and, above all, acted." While working on his senior production, according to BARBARA LEAMING, "Orson's technique of adaptation consisted of using a crayon to excise and rearrange passages in a huge one-volume Shakespeare that he seemed to carry about with him at all times." That same spirit is apparent in *Everybody's Shakespeare,* where Welles's sketches and the additions of stage directions make the book less a reading text than an acting version, a text from which to produce the plays.

No doubt his own unusual opportunity to develop his interest in Shakespeare led Welles to complain about the way the dramatist was being taught elsewhere, saying "It's terrible what's done to Shakespeare in the schools. You know, it's amazing that people do still go to him after what they've been through in the classroom," and he specifically protests the influence of academics, who "befuddle and bemuse." The view that the plays should be approached primarily in terms of Shakespeare the dramatist, rather than using them to teach philology or morals, was, however, hardly new. Although Laurence Levine documents how by the turn of the last century, "Shakespeare remained readily and easily accessible but less and less as a living playwright and more and more as a literary classic," works such as Richard G. Moulton's *Shakespeare as Dramatic Artist* (1885) and Arthur Quiller-Couch's *Shakespeare's Workmanship* (1918) emphasized Shakespeare's stagecraft. Perhaps the most significant work in this vein was that of Harley Granville-Barker, who produced the first three volumes of *The Players' Shakespeare* in 1923, and wrote in his "Introduction" to the *Prefaces to Shakespeare* (1927), "what is all the criticism finally for, if not to keep Shakespeare alive? And he must always be most alive—even if roughly and rudely alive—in the theatre." At least some of Welles's efforts in promoting Shakespeare should be seen as a part of this wider effort to emphasize performance in teaching Shakespeare. *Everybody's Shakespeare* clearly has a pedagogical aim. In the late 1930s, Welles recorded his Mercury Players productions of *Twelfth Night, The Merchant of Venice, Julius Caesar,* and *Macbeth* for Columbia Records, and, without mentioning those recordings, then in progress, Welles and Roger Hill in a 1938 article in *English Journal* argue that the teaching of Shakespeare could be enlivened and made successful by using recordings, since teachers are often "incapable of reading Shakespeare aloud or instructing their charges in adequately reading Shakespeare aloud."

Over his long career, Welles acted in several of Shakespeare's plays and read scenes and speeches from them in many settings, including such unlikely venues as the *I Love Lucy* show, *The Dean Martin Show,* and a Las Vegas nightclub show in which he did a magic act and read from *Julius Caesar,* KING LEAR, and *The Merchant of Venice.* His major contributions in shaping, or reshaping, Shakespeare's plays, however, are the three plays he directed before going to Hollywood and his three completed Shakespeare films. In all six of these major efforts, Welles showed his flexibility in responding to his financial circumstances, his sense of what an adaptation for a modern audience should do, and his concern for the demands of the specific medium. MICHAEL ANDEREGG explains that Welles was influenced by the two tendencies of the "new stagecraft," which "championed highly decorative or concept-oriented work," as well as

encouraging attempts "to recreate, insofar as possible, the simplicity, speed, and intimacy of Elizabethan staging." Perhaps as a result, Welles gave the impression, as Richard France says in his discussion of Welles's theater, that he "was possessed of an imagination and sense of originality altogether unbounded by any theoretical restraints."

When he came to do the "voodoo" *Macbeth,* Welles had the financial backing of the W.P.A.'s NEGRO THEATRE PROJECT, then headed by JOHN HOUSEMAN, who was committed to presenting an Elizabethan play. Houseman writes that Virginia, Welles's first wife, came up with the idea of setting *Macbeth* in Haiti. According to Welles, "We were very anxious to do one of Shakespeare's dramas in the Negro Theatre, and *Macbeth* seemed, in all respects, the most adaptable. The stormy career of Christophe, who became 'The Negro King of Haiti' and ended by killing himself when his cruelty led to a revolt, forms a striking parallel to the history of Macbeth." By most reports, the resulting production was an overpoweringly successful theatrical experience, even if some of the critics complained there was not enough Shakespeare in the resulting play. Pictures of the sets and costumes give only a partial sense of its effect. According to Richard France, "Welles sought a totality of sensual experience through the use of sight and sound, employing rhetorical content as a structural device, inextricable from that construction of which it was a part." One way that Welles achieved a unified effect was to simplify the story and change its emphasis. In Welles's version, Shakespeare's three witches are supplemented by Hecate and 60 witch doctors, and the overwhelming impression is that Macbeth becomes simply the instrument of the abiding evil they represent.

His strategy in the filmed version of the play aimed at some of the same effects. JAMES NAREMORE makes the point that "Every time Welles adapted *Macbeth,* his basic strategy was much the same: he gave it a primitive, exotic setting, and tried to eradicate its Renaissance manners." The fact that his financial circumstances were diminished when he made the film is often offered as a way of explaining what many see as the film's failure. Welles himself noted that he went to Republic Studios to make the picture because he "figured it would be cheaper." Welles added the character of a Holy Father who is somewhat ambiguously contrasted with the witches. Another addition is the voodoo doll, which often functions as a visual parallel to Macbeth, appearing, for example, both crowned and later beheaded only shortly before Macbeth himself does. Filmed in black-and-white, with strangely angled shots that sometimes overwhelm the characters and distort spatial relationships, and burdened with sound problems, this *Macbeth* has few apologists. Seen another way, however, Welles's use of Republic's B movie sets, awkward costumes, and expressionistic techniques, as JOSEPH MCBRIDE says in the revised edition of his book on Welles, "no longer seems the product of 'haste and desperation' but a triumphant artistic decision."

If his "voodoo" *Macbeth* demonstrated the expressionistic and extravagant impulse in Welles, his *Caesar* seemed to represent a more restrained one. Michael Anderegg says, "Without the generous government support that had made an elaborate *Macbeth* possible, Welles fell back on an idea he had absorbed at the [Dublin] Gate. *Caesar* depended for its effects on lighting and the conceptual clarity that made such a dependence possible." He used a small cast, a relatively bare stage, and focused the play on the first three acts of Shakespeare's play, reducing the last two acts to the quarrel between Brutus and Cassius, an offstage suicide by Brutus, and Marc Antony's closing speech, omitting the battles, Octavius, and Caesar's ghost. John Houseman says, "The decision to use modern dress was not an economic one and it was not conceived as a stunt. It was an essential element of Orson's conception of *Julius Caesar* as a political melodrama with clear contemporary parallels." To further underscore the relevance of the play, Welles subtitled it "The Death of a Dictator" and distributed handbills announcing the play as if it were part of the daily news.

Something of the same ability to make the best use of available resources drives his *Othello*. Here, however, the artistic vision and control of the medium seem, to many critics, more unified than in his earlier Shakespeare film. Certainly Welles was forced by the circumstances of the process to be more inventive. With his *Macbeth,* Welles had the advantage of a unified, rapid shooting schedule, completing the film in less than a month, not counting the year in disastrous postproduction work. *Othello,* however, took more than three years and was shot in such a fragmented manner that characters walk out of a room in one country and, some years later, step into a room in another country, with only Welles's memory, vision, and editing skills putting the events together. Using a circular structure that begins the film with the funeral procession of Othello and Desdemona as a caged Iago watches, Welles emphasizes the connection between the two men and subordinates the roles of Desdemona, Emilia, and Roderigo. Visually, the killing of Roderigo in the bathhouse and the long walk that Othello and Iago take along the seawall are extraordinary constructions, the one made up of elliptical action pieced together out of several short bits of film, the other caught in a long take as Iago gains control of Othello. Especially in the interior scenes, the use of light and shadow recalls similar effects in CITIZEN KANE, and the use of mirrors, perhaps borrowed from Renaissance iconography but also in *Citizen Kane* and THE LADY FROM SHANGHAI, conveys the dissolution of Othello's character.

Of his three Shakespeare adaptations for the stage, *Five Kings* is the only one that Welles chose to present in period. He transported *Macbeth* to 19th-century Haiti and *Julius Caesar* to a 20th-century fascist state. His chain-mail and armor-suited production of *Five Kings,* by all reports, failed because, as Anderegg puts it, "Welles reach seems to have exceeded his grasp." John Houseman perhaps uses a more telling image when he says that "To tell the story of *Five Kings* is like trying to record the terminal stages of a complicated and fatal disease." Putting aside Houseman's argument that the combination of previous successes and Welles's dissipation caused the play's failure and the demise of the MERCURY THEATRE, the play itself, in process over most of Welles's life, was perhaps not yet at a point that it could succeed. For this incarnation of the story, Welles developed a version that included, as Robert Hapgood describes it, "the whole career of Harry Monmouth from Prince Hal cavorting with Falstaff in the tavern to King Henry V wooing Katherine after his victory at Agincourt." Welles himself later admitted it was too much for one night. In addition to its narrative unwieldiness, *Five Kings,* as Welles developed it for the stage, required a huge revolving platform that allowed actors to move from one location to another as the scenery changed behind them. Although Houseman calls it "a dynamic theatrical concept," it was also impractical and did not work.

With *Chimes at Midnight,* Welles finally seems to have gained some measure of control over the sprawling material that took Shakespeare five plays to cover and Welles a lifetime to rewrite. Recognizing that the story as he had tried to tell it lacked a clear focus, Welles seems to emphasize Prince Hal's choice between the values represented by his father, Henry IV, and those represented by Falstaff. Further, he managed to localize these values in the contrast between the tavern and the castle. Falstaff, however, becomes the real focus, because more than being about the Prince's choice, the film becomes the story of Falstaff's being rejected. Anderegg argues that "to shift the thematic emphasis away from Hal toward Falstaff . . . moves away from history and toward satire." What Welles does here, perhaps more drastically than in his previous revisions of Shakespeare, is to use Shakespeare as raw material for the new work that is *Chimes at Midnight,* a play less about how a young king gains the crown than about how he loses the world that Falstaff, in Welles's view, represents. Critics, such as David Thomson, who disagree with this view of Falstaff tend to dislike the film, and some of the same people see Welles himself as a type of Falstaff, the man who wastes his gifts. The film is notable for its use of close-ups, often motivated as much by a skimpy budget as by other criteria, and for its influential and skillfully edited battle scene montage.

Kenneth Rothwell perhaps gives the safest summary when he says that Welles's work "is Dionysian and passionate, rough-hewn and unpredictable, and uncommodified." In his adaptations, Welles cannot be said to have been concerned with treating the plays as historic documents or in simply transmitting the Shakespeare that exists in textbooks. In any strict sense, Welles's adaptations of *Macbeth* and *Julius Caesar* and his film *Chimes at Midnight* would have to be described as merely based on Shakespeare. Although money was often a problem, a comparison of the stage and film versions of *Macbeth* shows that financial restrictions may have dictated the means but not the overall aim of his adaptations. Often, regardless of the monetary resources for his films, Welles tended toward an expressionistic use of architecture to convey the sense of characters overwhelmed by circumstances—the walls of Macbeth's cavernous castle, Othello's massive rooms and cisterns, the contrast between King Henry's castle and Falstaff's tavern, as well as Kane's XANADU. In this regard, Welles's use of sound is instructive. On the one hand, his use of drums in the "voodoo" *Macbeth,* like his use of bells in *Chimes at Midnight,* indicates an interest in providing a device to underscore and unify the visual spectacle. Additionally, even in his stage productions, Welles tended to use sound to link scenes, but it would be inaccurate to say that Welles as a former radio personality emphasized the aural over the visual. For example, as Russell Jackson points out, Welles differs from other directors of Shakespeare films in "the degree in which Welles is content to allow speech to be overheard, slurred, and generally subordinated to other priorities of staging and filming." The spoken word might be subordinated to the visual, but sound may be used to unify the whole. Welles varied his practice to achieve a final effect rather than to privilege any particular element.

References Anderegg, Michael. *Orson Welles, Shakespeare, and Popular Culture* (New York: Columbia University Press, 1999); Callow, Simon. *Orson Welles: The Road to Xanadu* (London: Jonathan Cape, 1995); Chambers, E. K. *William Shakespeare: A Study of Facts and Problems,* 2 vols. (Oxford: Clarendon Press, 1930); Davis, Anthony. *Filming Shakespeare's Plays* (Cambridge, U.K.: Cambridge University Press, 1988); Denning, Michael. *The Cultural Front* (London and New York: Verso, 1996); Eastman, Arthur M. *A Short History of Shakespearean Criticism* (New York: W. W. Norton and Company, Inc. 1968); France, Richard, ed. *Orson Welles on Shakespeare,* 1990 (New York, London: Routledge, 2001); ———. *The Theatre of Orson Welles* (Lewisburg, Penn.: Bucknell University Press, 1977); Hapgood, Robert. "*Chimes at Midnight* from Stage to Screen: The Art of Adaptation" (*Shakespeare Survey 39*) 30–52; Honan, Park. *Shakespeare: A Life* (Oxford, U.K.: Oxford University Press, 1999); Houseman, John. *Run-Through*

(New York: Simon & Schuster, 1972); Jackson, Russell. "Shakespeare and the Cinema," in *The Cambridge Companion to Shakespeare,* Margreta de Grazia and Stanley Wells, eds. (Cambridge, U.K.: Cambridge University Press, 2001), 217–33; Leaming, Barbara. *Orson Welles: A Biography* (New York: Penguin, 1989); Levine, Lawrence W. *Highbrow/Lowbrow* (Cambridge, Mass.: Harvard University Press, 1988); Lyons, Bridget Gellert. ed. *Chimes at Midnight* (New Brunswick, N.J. and London: Rutgers University Press, 1988); MacLiammóir, Micheál. *Put Money in Thy Purse,* 1952 (London: Columbus, 1976); McBride, Joseph. *Orson Welles,* rev. ed. (New York: Da Capo Press, 1996); Marder, Louis. *His Exits and His Entrances* (London: John Murray, 1963); Mason, Pamela. "Orson Welles and Filmed Shakespeare" in *The Cambridge Companion to Shakespeare on Film* (Cambridge, U.K.: Cambridge University Press, 2000) 183–98; Naremore, James. *The Magic World of Orson Welles,* rev. ed. (Dallas, Tex.: Southern Methodist University Press, 1989); Rothwell, Kenneth S. *A History of Shakespeare on Screen* (Cambridge, U.K.: Cambridge University Press, 1999); Styan, J. L. *The Shakespeare Revolution: Criticism and Performance in the Twentieth Century* (London: Cambridge University Press, 1977); Taylor, Gary. *Reinventing Shakespeare* (New York: Oxford, U.K.: Oxford University Press, 1989); Thompson, David. *Rosebud: The Story of Orson Welles* (New York: Alfred A. Knopf, 1966); Welles, Orson, and Peter Bogdanovich. *This Is Orson Welles,* Jonathan Rosenbaum, ed. (New York: HarperCollins, 1992); ———, and Roger Hill, eds. *The Mercury Shakespeare* (New York: Harper, 1939); ———, and Roger Hill, "On the Teaching of Shakespeare and Other Great Literature" (*English Journal,* 1938), 464–68.

—R.V.

Shaw, George Bernard (1856–1950)

ORSON WELLES's life-long interest in the works of George Bernard Shaw dates back to at least 1929, when Welles and his young Todd Players staged Shaw's *Androcles and the Lion* for the Woodstock Women's Club. While acting in Dublin at the GATE THEATRE in 1932, he appeared in several of the repertory company's productions, including Shaw's *Man and Superman.* That same year, while he was in England and only 17 years old, Welles claimed that he, aided by letters of introduction, actually met Shaw, who listened to him expound about the theater.

SIMON CALLOW, however, is dubious, wondering what kind of letters would have been necessary for Welles to gain access to Shaw. After being hired by KATHERINE CORNELL and GUTHRIE MCCLINTIC, who were about to begin their national tour with a repertory company, one of Welles's first assignments was to play the role of the romantic young poet Marchbanks in Shaw's *Candida.* In 1937, Welles and JOHN HOUSEMAN formed the MERCURY THEATRE, a repertory company, and one of their first productions was Shaw's *HEARTBREAK HOUSE,* which was staged in April 1938. In the production, Welles cast himself in the role of the 90-year-old Shotover. Wearing his Shotover makeup, Welles appeared on the May 9th cover of *Time* magazine, over the caption "From Shadow to Shakespeare, Shoemaker to Shaw," allusions to Welles's radio role as the Shadow, his productions of Shakespeare, and Thomas Dekker's *Shoemaker's Holiday,*

George Bernard Shaw

which the Mercury Theatre was also staging. As a result of Welles's negotiations with Shaw, the play was to be produced as it was written, which reined in Welles's creative ambitions for the play, which ran for six weeks and received mostly favorable reviews. Shaw's royalty demands were, in FRANK BRADY's words, "stiff: based on weekly receipts, Shaw was to receive 15 percent for everything over $1,500; 10 percent from $500 to $1,500; 7 1/2 percent from $250 to $500; and 5 percent for under $250." As a result, the play lost money for the Mercury Theatre.

George Bernard Shaw, who was born in Dublin on July 26, 1856, was educated in Dublin schools and worked as an office boy and cashier before moving to London in 1876. There he became a journalist who wrote music, art, and drama criticism for the *Pall Mall Gazette* and the *Dramatic Review.* His first produced play was *Widowers' Houses: A Didactic Realistic Play* (1992), which was followed by a string of well-known successes: *Arms and the Man* (1894), *Candida* (1897), *The Devil's Disciple* (1897). Many of his plays were adapted to film; he even wrote the screenplays for *Arms and the Man, Major Barbara, Caesar and Cleopatra,* and *Pygmalion* (for which he won an Oscar—the play later became the musical *My Fair Lady* and finally the award-winning film *My Fair Lady*). *The Devil's Disciple, Saint Joan,* and *Androcles and the Lion* also were adapted to film. In addition to the 55 plays that he wrote, Shaw published some screenplays, eight novels, and 60 miscellaneous collections of essays, debates, and critical works. A prolific correspondent, Shaw had some 14 volumes of his letters published. Besides writing, Shaw was active in politics. After joining the Fabian Society in 1884, a socialist organization, he helped found the Labour Party; with fellow Fabians Sidney and Beatrice Webb, he also helped establish the London School of Economics (1895) and later the *New Statesman* (1913). He was also a lifelong advocate of spelling reform and a phonetic alphabet, an interest that appears in his *Pygmalion* and its various offshoots. He received the Nobel Prize for literature in 1926.

—T.L.E.

Sherlock Holmes (radio, 1952)

In the wake of the success of WELLES's two previous BBC radio series, THE ADVENTURES OF HARRY LIME and THE BLACK MUSEUM, Welles was asked to star as the lead in a new show, *Sherlock Holmes,* based on the exploits of Sir Arthur Conan Doyle's beloved detective. Welles, consumed with putting the final postproduction touches on OTHELLO, his own 1952 film, declined. In his place, BBC producer Harry Alan Towers (who had worked with Welles as producer of *Harry Lime* and *The Black Museum*) hired JOHN GIELGUD for the role. Welles, however, took time to appear in the program's concluding broadcast as Professor Moriarty, enabling him to add yet another arch-villain to his ever growing gallery of dramatic rogues and mountebanks. In "The Final Problem," the show's last installment, the evil mathematician Moriarty confronts Holmes atop the Alps in a death-clash struggle overlooking the abyss at Reichenbach Falls. Later, two sets of footprints are discovered in the snow at the precipice's edge. The bodies, however, are never found. The BBC series also featured RALPH RICHARDSON as Holmes's loyal companion, Dr. Watson.

—C.B.

Shoemaker's Holiday, The (play, 1938)

Flush with the critical and box office success of JULIUS CAESAR (1937), the fledgling MERCURY THEATRE sought a comic change of pace for its next theatrical venture. Although there had been two marginal 20th-century revivals in 1911 and 1913, it was Welles's 1938 resuscitation of Thomas Dekker's 1600 farce that rescued *The Shoemaker's Holiday* from the footnotes of theatrical history. As he had done with *Julius Caesar,* Welles began by excising half of the original script, in this instance to accentuate the antic comings-and-goings of the shoemaker's tale. Departing from his usual routine of both acting and directing, Welles, because of his heavy daytime radio schedule and his evening commitment to playing Brutus in the ongoing *Julius Caesar,* worked only as director. Producer JOHN HOUSEMAN handled the logistics.

Welles was attracted to Dekker's comedy because of its Elizabethan ribaldry, dash, and extravagance. Indeed, *The Shoemaker's Holiday* was first performed on New Year's Day in 1600 for an audience that included Queen Elizabeth. Set during the reign of

King Henry V, the story concerns the love of aristo-crat Roland Lacy for Rose, a commoner, the daugh-ter of the Lord Mayor of London. Lacy's uncle, the Earl of Lincoln, seeking to thwart the affair because of Rose's diminished pedigree, sends Lacy off to the war in France. The lovesick Lacy deserts and returns to London where, in the guise of a shoemaker in service to the Lord Mayor's shoe supplier, soon finds himself back in Rose's arms. When Lacy is brought up on charges of desertion, a genial monarch pardons him and he immediately weds his beloved Rose.

Welles's *The Shoemaker's Holiday* proved a huge critical and box office hit. Like the cinematic screw-ball comedies of the period such as Frank Capra's *It Happened One Night* (1934), the show's madcap qual-ity tapped into the reassuring fantasies that love con-quers all and that social class is but a trifle. Simon Callow describes the play as "brimful of uncontrol-lable life, interweaving the classes, with a plot loosely revolving around the advancement of Simon Eyre, the legendary Lord Mayor of London, [which] is so human, so rich and so universally appealing, that it can be taken in many different ways." One critic cited by Callow, Rosamond Gilder, saw parallels to contemporary life: "Simon Eyre is the prototype of all the lads who make good; the industrious appren-tice who becomes Lord Mayor of London or Presi-dent of the United States; the poor boy who earns a fortune but never forgets his friends." Eleanor Flexner, writing in the leftist journal *New Masses,* had another take: "The play is laden with sentiments for the times: a passionate democracy of the spirit, a hatred of wars which tear families asunder, reverence for the men who toil with their hands, and an abhor-rence for the fetishes of wealth and position." Welles biographer Charles Higham says that the play skill-fully conveys "the essentially democratic nature of the British people, each knowing his place in society, the humblest working man on joyous terms with royalty, and each sensing himself part of a larger organism structured in terms of class yet definably English, making every individual a part of a special club."

Welles, a lover of all things Elizabethan, focused much of his attention on revving up the basics of farce, the madcap complications, the mistaken iden-

tities, the jibing of cuckolded husbands, and the spec-tacle of lusty women being lusty women. Frank Brady adds: "For Welles as well as Dekker, it was a tribute to the common working man and the exu-berant life of sixteenth-century London. Such life is not without is naughtier aspects, but only a few play-goers objected to the bawdy language and anal sounds. It's also likely that some of the double enten-dres went over the heads of the audience as did the similarity of the name of the character 'Firk' to another four-letter word, and Welles's unexpurgated script caused just the slightest flurry of protest in the New York papers."

The play's prologue called on Dekker's original preamble: "Take all in good worth that is well inten-tioned, for nothing is purposed but mirth. Mirth lengtheneth long life, which with all other blessings I heartily wish you." It was a perfectly concocted bro-mide for depression-weary audiences. Welles was again hailed by the New York critics as a genius. *Commonweal* proclaimed that "by increasing [the play's] tempo and pointing up the characters, Mr. Welles has increased its value both as a human docu-ment and as a study of Elizabethan London." Writing in the *New York Times*, Brooks Atkinson said: "If there was any doubt after *Julius Caesar* that the Mercury Theatre is the liveliest drama household in town, *The Shoemaker's Holiday* should dispel it, for the Dekker comedy is the funniest jib of the season and the new year has begun with a burst of theatrical hilarity." Significantly, by confining his role to directing, Welles received the best notices of his career. Would Welles have scaled even greater heights had he focused his multiple talents in his own work on either directing or acting? It is a question worth pondering. Callow comments: "Perhaps partly because he wasn't in it, *The Shoemaker's Holiday* was altogether more achieved than *Caesar*; a unified conception executed with great skill."

The Mercury Theatre production of *The Shoe-maker's Holiday* opened on January 1, 1938, and ran in repertory with *Julius Caesar* for 64 performances, until April 1, 1938. The cast included Whitford Kane (Simon Eyre, the Lord Mayor of London), JOSEPH COTTEN (Roland Lacy), Ruth Ford (Jane), Chubby Sherman (Firk), Alice Frost (Rose), Edith Barrett

(Sybil), GEORGE COULOURIS (King), Vincent Price (Master Hammond), Norman Lloyd, Frederic Tozere (Sir Hugh Lacy), and RICHARD WILSON. The score, which had to employ the same trumpet/horn/keyboard/percussion ensemble called for by MARC BLITZSTEIN's musical backdrop for *Julius Caesar*, was by Lehman Engel.

References Brady, Frank. *Citizen Welles: A Biography of Orson Welles* (New York: Scribners, 1989); Callow, Simon. *Orson Welles: The Road to Xanadu* (New York: Viking Press, 1995); Higham, Charles. *Orson Welles: The Rise and Fall of An American Genius* (New York: St. Martin's Press, 1985); Thomson, David. *Rosebud: The Story of Orson Welles* (New York: Knopf, 1996).

—C.B.

Shores, Lynn

Lynn Shores, the RKO unit production manager for the *IT'S ALL TRUE* film shot in Brazil, was an outspoken critic of ORSON WELLES and the adversary of RICHARD WILSON, Welles's right-hand man. When the RKO people arrived in Rio de Janeiro in January of 1942, they lacked lights; Shores negotiated with the Brazilian army to use their anti-aircraft lights As the shooting progressed, Shores became increasingly critical of Welles's methods. At the same time that Welles, Wilson, and the CIAA Brazilian office were expressing their approval of the project, Shores was dispatching his own vitriolic messages to the RKO office. According to FRANK BRADY, within a month Shores described the "venture as a 'horrible nightmare for me personally.'" When the inventive Welles created an episode involving four fishermen and attempted to insert it into the film, Shores advised GEORGE SCHAEFER at RKO, and the episode was turned down. There were budget problems, morale among the crew was low, and Welles was often absent. When Welles decided to spend $6,000 to rent a plane to inspect locations in Fortaleza, Shores was really upset but signed the contract for the plane. When RKO officials saw the Carnival footage that Welles had shot, they were not impressed, and they were terribly concerned about the cost overruns. Welles was ignoring RKO telegrams and not doing much shooting. In late March, Shores reported: "Welles has been concentrating entirely on his radio program . . . and has left

the picture high and dry." Schaefer, who was concerned about losing his job, sent Phil Reisman to Brazil to monitor the situation. After a distraught Schaefer tendered his resignation, N. Peter Rathvon and CHARLES KOERNER took over at RKO. Koerner, who was intent on getting rid of Welles, asked Shores to compile negative information about Welles so RKO could shift the onus in possible lawsuits from RKO to Welles. Welles understandably saw Shores as sabotaging him for the RKO boss. Just before Welles returned to the United States, Welles learned that RKO, through Shores, had placed notices in the Rio papers to the effect that RKO would not be responsible for any debts incurred by Welles while in Brazil. The film was never finished.

—T.L.E.

Sloane, Everett (1909–1965)

Noted character actor who upon losing his job as a Wall Street runner following the 1929 financial crash, turned to acting onstage and in radio. In radio, Sloane regularly appeared in *The Goldbergs, The Crime Doctor,* and, for eight years, THE SHADOW, which marked his initial collaboration with Welles. He made his Broadway debut in 1935 (*Boy Meets Girl*), then in 1938 joined Welles's MERCURY THEATRE, acting in both its radio and theatrical productions. He went with Welles to Hollywood and made an impressive debut in CITIZEN KANE (1941) as Bernstein. He also played key roles in two more Welles films, as Kopeikin in JOURNEY INTO FEAR (1943), and as Arthur Bannister in THE LADY FROM SHANGHAI (1948).

BARBARA LEAMING points out that the diminutive Sloane was tormented by what he perceived as his own physical unattractiveness, a situation that made his relationship with the dashing Welles problematic. Although Welles had directed Sloane in his greatest roles, Sloane bitterly resented not being cast in the handsome leading man roles that Welles handled so easily. It's a shame, then, that Sloane dropped out of the Welles production of OTHELLO where his intrinsic resentment of the director might have made his Iago and Welles's Othello a particularly memorable match.

In recalling Sloane, Welles told PETER BOGDANOVICH that "Everett Sloane was basically a radio actor; he'd never really learned to *move*. He was like a marionette. That was OK for Bernstein in *Kane*. But it didn't seem to me that a marionette would be a great criminal lawyer [i.e., the character of Banister in *The Lady from Shanghai*]. So I made him an elaborate sort of cripple. And, of course, he loved it. All actors like to play cripples."

Welles, in discussing *Kane* with Bogdanovich, recalls that "Everett Sloane, who aged with me [in the film], never wore any makeup at all! We just shaved his head and put the white around it. And he couldn't have been more than twenty-one. It had a profound effect on him. Because he thought, 'How can I represent a seventy-five-year-old man without makeup? It must be that my nose is too big.' And he began bobbing it. He must have had twenty operations before he killed himself. He must have thought, 'If I could ever bob my nose right, then I'll be a leading man.'"

In addition to his work for Welles, Sloane appeared as a character actor in a number of other films including PRINCE OF FOXES (1949; with Welles); *The Men* (1950); *The Desert Fox* (1951); *The Big Knife* (1955); *Somebody Up There Likes Me* (1956); *Patterns* (1956); *Lust for Life* (1956); *Marjorie Morningstar* (1958); *Home from the Hill* (1960); and *The Patsy* (1964). In 1965, Sloane took his own life with an overdose of sleeping pills.

—C.B.

Small, Edward (1891–1977)

Produced BLACK MAGIC (1949), starring ORSON WELLES. Small, a successful independent American film producer, was a New York born and bred stage actor who set up a talent agency in Hollywood in the early 1920s. After establishing himself as a motion picture producer in the mid-1920s, and following the introduction of talkies, Small co-founded Reliance Pictures in 1932, whose product was distributed through United Artists. In 1938, he organized Edward Small Productions, presiding over many commercially successful films including *Black Magic* (1947), for which he persuaded Welles to play the evil magician Cagliostro under the direction of Welles's friend, Gregory Ratoff. Like other producers, Small sought out Welles in order to enhance his own prestige. Unlike other producers, Small got along well with his famous colleague, although during their association Welles was functioning as an actor rather than as a director. During the shooting of *Black Magic* in Rome, Small and Welles talked excitedly about the possibility of working together on Welles-directed versions of MOBY DICK and OTHELLO. Alas, *Black Magic* was destined to be their only collaboration.

Over the course of a career spanning almost a half century, Small produced a large number of successful films, including *I Cover the Waterfront* (1933); *The Count of Monte Cristo* (1934); *The Last of the Mohicans* (1936); *The Man in the Iron Mask* (1939); *The Corsican Brothers* (1941); *The Fuller Brush Man* (1948); *Kansas City Confidential* (1952); *Witness for the Prosecution* (1958); *Solomon and Sheba* (1959); *Boy! Did I Get a Wrong Number* (1966); and *The Christine Jorgensen Story* (1970).

—C.B.

Smiler with a Knife, The

WELLES's first feature film screenplay, *The Smiler with a Knife*, was adapted from a novel by Nicholas Blake, a pseudonym under which British poet C. Day-Lewis wrote detective stories. Blake's original story concerned a sinister fascist plot to set up a dictatorship in England.

Welles's script was written in 1939, shortly after he had been signed by RKO to make his first film. Although Welles had had his heart set on an adaptation of Joseph Conrad's HEART OF DARKNESS for his Hollywood debut, when that project encountered resistance from RKO's brass and the film industry's censorship board, he turned to Blake's novel as a backup.

Transposing Blake's setting from England to the United States, Welles added a dash of satire and sophisticated humor to the story of a newlywed couple who accidentally happen onto a plot to take over America. He envisioned the protagonist Chilton, whom he would play, as a kind of debonair antihero in the manner of Nick Charles of the *Thin Man* series. For his leading lady, he first wanted CAROLE LOMBARD (whose studio refused the offer), then Lucille Ball (who was nixed by RKO), and finally Rosalind Russell (who was reluctant to appear under the direction of a newcomer such as Welles). Anticipating the NEWS ON THE MARCH sequence, which opens CITIZEN KANE, Welles planned an introductory newsreel styled after THE MARCH OF TIME that would chronicle the deteriorating political and economic conditions making possible the rise of an American dictator.

Although Welles turned Blake's story into a comedy-thriller in the manner of Hitchcock's *The Thirty-Nine Steps* (1939), at center was Welles's concern with the growing threat of fascism, a theme he had treated so effectively in his landmark theatrical version of Shakespeare's JULIUS CAESAR (1937). The plot to establish an American fascist state discovered by the young newlyweds echoed the headline story of the Christian Front's attempted coup d'état against President ROOSEVELT earlier in 1939. It also tapped into general anxieties among many Americans of a right-wing plot to take over the country led by someone such as Charles Lindbergh, one of Hitler's most persuasive American supporters.

Finally, RKO, concerned about its declining share of the world market because of the rise of fascism and therefore nervous about pictures that might ruffle feathers of totalitarian states still importing American films, nixed Welles's adaptation of *The Smiler with the Knife*. Welles, for his part, wasn't terribly troubled. Although he had put a major effort into and learned much from the exercise of writing his first screenplay, he grew increasingly anxious about wanting to make his film debut a singular and monumental work rather than a routine thriller. After more thrashing about for ideas, Welles met screenwriter HERMAN J. MANKIEWICZ. It was the collaboration of Welles and Mankiewicz that ultimately provided the blueprint for what turned out to be the greatest American film of all time, *Citizen Kane*.

—C.B.

Smith, Dame Maggie (1934–) Maggie

Smith appeared in EUGÈNE IONESCO's *RHINOCEROS*, a play directed by WELLES in London in 1960, and later appeared with Welles in THE *V.I.P.S* (1963). She was born on December 28, 1934, in Ilford, England. After training at the Oxford Playhouse School, she made her London stage debut in 1952 and her New York stage debut in *New Faces* (1956). She was not originally cast in *Rhinoceros*, but when Joan

Plowright, who was playing Daisy, left the show because her affair with LAURENCE OLIVIER became known, Smith replaced her. (Olivier was married to VIVIEN LEIGH at the time and was playing the part of Berenger opposite Plowright in the play.) Smith played Daisy for six weeks beginning June 8, 1960, and received, for the most part, excellent reviews. Michael Coveney reports that she had little rehearsal time with Welles, who had real problems on the set with Olivier, who, Welles told BARBARA LEAMING, was undermining his direction of the play. Smith was described by the *News Chronicle* as "cool, crisp and wonderfully matter-of-fact as Daisy," and *The Stage* maintained that she was "gradually developing into an actress of distinction." Before *Rhinoceros,* she had been seen as only an extremely talented comic actress. Three years later, she and Welles were cast in *The V.I.P.s,* Smith as Miss Mead and Welles, in a case of inspired casting, as a film producer anxious to leave the country for tax reasons. Also in the cast were Elizabeth Taylor and Richard Burton. In one segment with Burton, Smith stole the scene. In Burton's words, she "committed grand larceny," and Burton never worked with her again. After *The V.I.P.s,* Smith went on to good roles in several excellent films, receiving Oscars or Oscar nominations, including *The Pumpkin Eater* (1964), *Othello* (1965, Oscar nomination for her role as Desdemona), *The Prime of Miss Jean Brodie* (1969, a best actress Oscar), *Travels with My Aunt* (1972, a best actress Oscar nomination), *California Suite* (1978, a best supporting actress Oscar), and *A Room with a View* (1986, a best supporting actress Oscar nomination). She has won British Film Academy Awards as best actress for her roles in *A Private Function* (1984) and *The Lonely Passion of Judith Hearne* (1987). She also received a Tony in 1990 for her role in *Lettice and Lovage* and an Emmy nomination for her role in the PBS version of *Suddenly Last Summer* (1993). Her most recent role was that of an aristocratic doyenne in Robert Altman's *Gosford Park* (2001), a whodunit set at an English country manor but also, surprisingly, a solid work of social criticism.

Reference Coveney, Michael. *Maggie Smith: A Bright Particular Star* (London: Victor Gollancz, 1992).

—T.L.E.

Someone to Love ICA/International Rainbow/
Jagfilm, 105 minutes, 1987. **Director:** Harry Jaglom; **Pro-
ducers:** M.H. Simonson; **Screenplay:** Jaglom; **Cine-
matographer:** Hanania Baer; **Cast:** Orson Welles
(Himself), Jaglom (Danny Sapir), Andrea Marcovicci
(Helen Eugene), Michael Emil (Mickey Sapir), Sally
Kellerman (Edith Helm), Oja Kodar (Yolena), Stephen
Bishop (Blue), David Frishberg (Harry)

On Valentine's Day, a film director throws a party for
his single and divorced friends and, ironically, has
them questioned on-camera about their attitudes
dealing with loneliness, love, and relationships. Essentially a succession of turns before the camera by various actors and actress, but intermittently interesting
and notable for WELLES's final appearance on film,
Someone to Love concludes with Welles's finalizing
command of "Cut"!

Originally titled *Is It You?,* and then changed to
Someone to Love, Welles accepted minimum-scale
wages to act in Harry Jaglom's low-budget film. In
the film, as in life, Welles played the part of an older
director who mentors Jaglom, the younger director
staging the party. Welles, in response to a query on
loneliness, scripted his own response: "We're born
alone, we live alone, we die alone. Only through our
love and friendship can we create the illusion for the
moment that we're not alone." Three months later,
Welles would die of a heart attack.

Released two years after Welles's death on October 10, 1985, Jaglom prefaced the film, "Dedicated
with Love to Orson Welles."

—C.B.

Song of Myself (radio, 1953) FRANK BRADY
reports that WELLES was enormously successful with
a reading of Walt Whitman's "Song of Myself" for the
British Broadcasting Company. The poem of 52 sections and some 1,300 lines was published without
title in the 1855 Whitman anthology, *Leaves of Grass.*
The expansive work was given the title "Song of
Myself" in 1881. Considered by Whitman devotees
as his most important work, and also his best known,
the poem revolutionized American verse by departing from traditional standards of rhyme, meter, and
form. It also introduced frank sexual themes and

imagery. Among its notable features are repetition,
exclamation, and an incantatory voice. Many sections, driven by Whitman's unrelentingly compelling
rhythms, are catalogs of individuals, locations, and
actions that had moved the poet. As Brady notes,
Welles seemed to perfectly capture the lament over
"the sickness and desperate revolt at the close of a life
without elevation or naivete," as Whitman had
described the work.

Welles's bravura performance with its nuanced
variations of pace, tone, and inflection captivated the
BBC audience and the critics. For one, the radio
commentator for the *Times Educational Supplement*
waxed that "no other known voice could have so sat-
isfyingly brought out the vigor, weight and sweep of
Whitman's lines." The *London Sunday Times* called it
"A virtuoso performance which added up to perfect
radio. . . . It is not easy to believe that any listener
even mildly susceptible to fine acting could fail to
feel a communicated surge of life and hope and optimism while Mr. Welles was speaking."

Welle's recitation with its highly effective "dialect-
less and somewhat wearied intonation," as Brady put
it, has been re-released in various audio formats since
its 1953 BBC broadcast.

—C.B.

Southern Star, The EuroFrance-Capitole-Colum-
bia, 104 minutes, 1969. **Director:** Sidney Hayers; **Pro-
ducer:** Roger Duchet; **Screenplay:** David Pursall, Jack
Seddon, Jean Giono, based on a novel by Jules Verne; **Cin-
ematographer:** Raoul Coutard; **Editor:** Tristam Cones;
Cast: George Segal (Dan Rockland), Ursula Andress
(Erica Kramer), Orson Welles (Plankett), Ian Hendry
(Capt. Karl Ludwig), Harry Andrews (Kramer), Johnny
Sekka (Matakit)

Promoted with the publicity tag, "Africa explodes
into a thousand surprises!," *The Southern Star* was an
adventure comedy whose plot revolved around the
finding, losing, and eventual recovery of the largest
diamond in the world, "The Southern Cross" of the
title. Based on Jules Verne's 1884 novel, *L'étoile du sud,
le pays des diamants,* there's a romantic subplot to
occupy leads George Segal and Ursula Andress.
WELLES, as was so often the case during this phase of

his career, was cast as a villain, here the sinister Plankett. "I did it as a comic gay Cockney," Welles told PETER BOGDANOVICH, who asked, "Funny?," to which Welles replied, "Not too bad, maybe. But nobody noticed it. The picture bombed." Again, one can imagine Welles, bored with the project, resorting to his inimitable brand of campy gamesmanship, a diversion also designed to distract himself and his colleagues from the sweltering heat of the location shoot in Senegal.

—C.B.

Spanish Earth, The
Contemporary Historians, Inc., 52 minutes, 1938. **Director:** Joris Ivens; **Producer:** Herman Shumlin; **Writers:** John Dos Passos, Lillian Hellman, Ernest Hemingway, and Archibald MacLeish; **Cinematographer:** John Ferno; **Editor:** Hela van Dongen; **Narrators:** Ernest Hemingway, Jean Renoir, Orson Welles

Joris Ivens, the celebrated Dutch documentarian, was brought to the United States by a group of prominent writers and artists (including Lillian Hellman and Dorothy Parker), who commissioned him to make a film about the Spanish Civil War. Filming in war-torn Spain, at great risk to his crew, which included Ernest Hemingway, who had been charged with writing the narration, Ivens brought back a shocking collection of images that he edited in New York. The result was a hard-hitting film that paid tribute to the cause of the Spanish Loyalists in their fight against the Nazi-backed Franco government. While many winced at the violence recorded by Ivens, others deemed it a classic. *Time,* for example, said: "Not since the silent French film, *The Passion of Joan of Arc,* has such dramatic use been made of the human face. As face after face looks out from the screen the picture becomes a sort of portfolio of portraits of the human soul in the presence of disaster and distress. These are the earnest faces of speakers at meetings and in the villages talking war, exhorting the defense."

The film's sound track initially featured *WELLES* reading Hemingway's narration, and snippets of Spanish folk tunes assembled by VIRGIL THOMSON and MARK BLITZSTEIN. However, when Hemingway heard the narration, he thought that Welles's voice sounded "faggoty." He immediately fired Welles, choosing to narrate the film himself. As a result of the incident, Welles maintained an intense dislike of Hemingway for the rest of his life.

Decades later, in the mid-1970s, Welles exacted a bit of a payback through the character of Jake Hannaberry (JOHN HUSTON), an ostensibly macho Hemingway-esque figure, who in *THE OTHER SIDE OF THE WIND* wrestles with a closeted homosexual urge. However, since *The Other Side of the Wind* remains locked up in a Paris film lab, Welles's bit of revenge is known only to his most ardent fans.

—C.B.

Spiegel, Sam
(1903–1985) Producer Sam Spiegel, who used the pseudonym "S. P. Eagle" for a short time (early 1940s until 1954) during his film career, produced *THE STRANGER* (1946), which was directed by ORSON WELLES. Spiegel, whom DAVID THOMSON described as "part hustler, part man of the world, bon vivant, talker," bought the film rights to Victor Trivas's story and approached Welles, whom he wanted to cast in the role of the Nazi hiding his past in a Connecticut town. After Welles accepted the part, Spiegel approached WILLIAM GOETZ of International Pictures about providing the financing for the picture. The contract called for Welles, who would also direct the film, to receive $2,000 per week with a $100,000 bonus if he completed the film on schedule and within budget. (Actually, he did complete it on time and under budget!) There is considerable disagreement about how and why Welles came to direct the film. CHARLES HIGHAM and Thomson believe that Spiegel originally did not want Welles to direct; he wanted JOHN HUSTON as the director. Welles, however, would not appear in the film unless he also directed it. According to Higham, "He [Spiegel] understood the risk involved and knew that he would be criticized by everyone in Hollywood for taking it, but he decided to go ahead." Welles has a slightly different account, one that accuses Goetz of being the one reluctant to have Welles direct and one that makes Welles responsible for Spiegel's Hollywood success: "Spiegel was only allowed in because Goetz wanted the picture as a package and I was part of it—very much against

Goetz's wishes. That's what got Spiegel's foot in the door as a producer."

In what many critics believe is Welles's least Wellesian film, Welles followed the ANTHONY VEILLIER script closely, although Spiegel had understood that John Huston would do some "doctoring" on the Veillier screenplay. Spiegel's job involved keeping a close eye on Welles in terms of time and money. According to FRANK BRADY, Welles was held closely in check: "There was only one way: the Spiegel way." As a result, the 20 minutes of South American footage Welles shot, ostensibly as background for his Nazi character's South American adventures, was cut from the film because it was seen as irrelevant and the producers wanted Welles to "stick with the script." Welles, on the other hand, who may have planned to use the footage for his unfinished IT'S ALL TRUE, told PETER BOGDANOVICH that the footage "was much the best thing in the picture—or at least the stuff I liked the best, probably because I wrote it."

Spiegel, whom Frank Brady refers to as Welles's "friend from *The Stranger* days," later reportedly offered Welles the opportunity to direct the film adaptation of Pierre Boulle's novel *The Bridge on the River Kwai*. Welles, who believed that he had a deal with Spiegel, cancelled other commitments and waited for four months, only to hear that the film, directed by David Lean, was being shot in Ceylon, now Sri Lanka.

Spiegel, born on November 11, 1903, in Jaroslau, Austria (now Jaroslaw, Poland), was educated at the University of Vienna. In 1927, he came to Hollywood, where he worked briefly as a translator before he went to Berlin, where he produced German and French versions of international films. When the Nazis came into power in 1933, the Jewish Spiegel left Germany to make films elsewhere in Europe before he immigrated to the United States in 1935. Before he produced *The Stranger,* he had coproduced *Tales of Manhattan* (1942); but *The Stranger* firmly established him as an effective and efficient Hollywood producer. Spiegel, who went on to be one of the finest independent Hollywood producers, produced three films that won Oscars for best picture and were both critically and financially very successful: *On the Waterfront* (1954), *The Bridge on the River Kwai* (1957), and *Lawrence of Arabia* (1962). In recog-

nition of his stature and success, he was the recipient of the Irving Thalberg Memorial Award at the 1963 Academy Award ceremonies. He went on to produce *Nicholas and Alexandra* (1971) in England, and his last film was, appropriately, *The Last Tycoon* (1976).

References Fraser, Natasha. *The Life and Times of Sam Spiegel* (Boston: Little, Brown, 2000); Sinclair, Andrew. *Spiegel: The Man behind the Pictures* (Boston: Little, Brown, 1987).

—T.L.E.

Spielberg, Steven (1947–)

Director Steven Spielberg was born in Cincinnati in 1947, but was raised in Arizona, near Los Angeles. When his family moved from Cincinnati to Arcadia, Arizona, in 1957, Spielberg was uprooted from the familiar life he had known in the Midwest to settle in unfamiliar territory. Douglas Brode comments that Spielberg did not discover CITIZEN KANE until years later; "when he did, he would—like most movie lovers—consider it the greatest film ever made. For Spielberg, though, the intense reaction must have been personal and emotional": He could identify with young Charlie Kane, suddenly swept away from familiar surroundings to live in a different milieu. "Little Charlie Kane tries to hang on to this Rosebud sled, representing the simplicity and innocence he is being torn away from. Today that bit of movie memorabilia is owned by Steve Spielberg," as we shall shortly see. He began making short films as a teenager in Phoenix, Arizona; and he made five student films while he was earning a degree in English at California State College. *Amblin'* (1969) marked his debut as a professional filmmaker, as it was shown at the Atlanta Film Festival, and earned him a contract with Universal to make films for TV.

Spielberg was first employed as a TV director at Universal Studios in 1969, at the age of 23. He was aware that some people in the TV industry wanted him to fail. "He appeared to be a precocious innocent in a world of hardened veterans, as he encountered all the prejudices that a previous *wunderkind,* Orson Welles, had experienced thirty years earlier," as Philip Taylor has written. He was young and in a hurry, and some of the technicians he worked with resented him.

Spielberg was hired to do an episode of the TV series *Columbo,* starring Peter Falk as the rumpled, shrewd detective. The segment was entitled "Murder by the Book" (1971), and the cinematographer was RUSSELL METTY, who had shot *THE STRANGER* and *TOUCH OF EVIL* for ORSON WELLES.

Spielberg's first theatrical feature was *The Sugarland Express* (1974), and the director of photography this time was Vilmos Zsigmond, who had just shot *The Long Goodbye* (1973) for Robert Altman. Unlike Metty, Zsigmond was impressed with the intrepid young director. Taylor cites Zsigmond as saying at the time, "He's only twenty-seven years old, but the way he directs a film makes you think that he must have many features behind him, and it's really unbelievable. I can only compare him to Orson Welles, who was a very talented director when he was very young."

Filmmakers of Spielberg's generation "worshipped Welles," says DAVID THOMSON; "they took it for granted that he had forged their path, and made the status of the movie director something to be honored." For Welles maintained that film directors were artists, even if that sometimes meant that they would not get along with the studio brass.

Sugarland Express, a film about a pair of fugitives on the run from the law, was followed by Spielberg's first blockbuster, *Jaws* (1975), a suspenser about a monstrous shark, a film that was also welcomed by the critics.

Close Encounters of the Third Kind (1977) was another critical and popular success, a science-fiction picture that reflects the sort of inquisitive awe for the unknown that recalls STANLEY KUBRICK's *2001.* (In fact, Spielberg screened *2001* several times while he was making *Close Encounters,* because he regards it as a model sci-fi film.) He went on to make *Raiders of the Lost Ark* (1981) an exciting adventure tale, which spawned two sequels. *E. T. The Extraterrestrial* (1982), which concerns the friendship of a boy and an alien, was the most successful movie of all time, until Spielberg made *Jurassic Park,* about dinosaurs running amok in a contemporary amusement park; this film surpassed *E. T.* as the all-time box office champion, when it was released in 1993.

The chance for Spielberg to own the fabled ROSE-BUD sled came in 1982, when it was auctioned at the

Director Steven Spielberg *(Literature/Film Quarterly Archive)*

Sotheby-Parke Gallery in New York. The Rosebud sled was made of balsa wood painted red and stenciled with a white flower with green leaves. In actual fact, three Rosebud sleds were made for *Citizen Kane;* one was burned in the furnace at film's end, when much of the deceased Kane's memorabilia are consigned to the flames. One was owned by Tom Mankiewicz, the son of HERMAN MANKIEWICZ, who co-authored the screenplay with Welles; and the third one belonged to John Hall, the archivist at RKO studios. Hall had purchased it from a studio watchman, who had discovered it in a heap of discarded props. It was Hall who put the sled up for auction on June 9, 1982, at the gallery in New York, where the opening bid was $15,000. Spielberg bid for the sled by phone from California. The bids rose to $50,000, and Spielberg finally outbid the competition by raising his final bid another $5,000.

Spielberg explains in BRADY's Welles biography that he acquired the Rosebud sled because it is "a symbolic medallion of quality in movies. When you look at Rosebud, you don't think of fast dollars, fast sequels and remakes. This to me says that the movies of my generation had better be good." Welles mischievously quipped to the press at the time that "the sled he bought is a fake." Spielberg understandably was not amused.

Spielberg prizes the sled as an authentic artifact of film history that reflects his esteem for Welles as a director. Indeed, Spielberg paid tribute to Welles at the end of *Raiders of the Lost Ark* (1981) by recalling a shot from the end of *Kane:* The camera pulls back to show a long shot of the great hall of Kane's castle, XANADU. Kane's collection of paintings and statues, scattered pell-mell all over the place, are surrounded by large packing cases. What disposition will be made of them in the wake of Kane's death is anybody's guess. Among the bric-a-brac is the old sled Rosebud, which Kane had cherished from his childhood; it lies among the discarded items that have been consigned to a blazing furnace, where the flames devour it.

In the parallel scene in *Raiders,* Indiana Jones (Harrison Ford) searches for the legendary Ark of the Covenant, which dates from the time of Moses. It is reported to confer supernatural powers on its owner. Indiana recovers it from the hands of the Nazis, who had wished to use its preternatural powers for their own nefarious purposes. Indiana Jones turns it over to the American government, which has it crated up and dispatched to a top-secret warehouse for eventual scientific analysis. Brode observes: "As the camera slowly pulls back," the way Orson Welles's camera retreats from the Rosebud sled at the end of *Kane,* "we see the enormity of the cavernous building and sense without the need of words . . . that ages will have passed before anyone gets past all the other crates to open this one." Spielberg confirmed that this scene was a deliberate reference to the similar scene in *Kane.*

Steven Spielberg has yet another link to Welles, which involves Welles's unproduced film derived from THE CRADLE WILL ROCK, a play which he had directed on the New York stage in 1937. In those days, Welles was involved with the FEDERAL THEATRE PROJECT during the Depression, along with JOSEPH LOSEY and other young directors who would eventually go to Hollywood. During the Depression, the

U.S. government had set the Federal Theatre Project in motion to put unemployed actors, writers, and technicians back to work.

In 1984, producer Michael Fitzgerald commissioned screenwriter Ring Lardner, Jr. (*M*A*S*H*) to write a script for *The Cradle Will Rock* that would encompass the backstage drama of the opening night performance. Welles agreed to direct the picture and revised the script. Rupert Everett was to play the young Welles and Amy Irving was cast as Virginia Nicholson, Welles's first wife. But three weeks before shooting was to commence, the financing began to fall through.

It so happened that Amy Irving was married to Steven Spielberg at the time; and Welles invited them to a lunch at Hollywood's Ma Maison to discuss the film. In the course of the luncheon conversation, Spielberg primarily questioned Welles about the specifics of making *Kane.* When Welles got around to hazarding that he could use some help in financing *Cradle,* Spielberg was completely unresponsive. Afterward, Welles wondered how a man who had purchased the Rosebud sled for $55,000 just a few months earlier would pass up the chance to back a Welles film. Perhaps, after all, Spielberg had never forgiven Welles for saying that the sled that Spielberg cherished was a fake. (It was an ill-advised joke for Welles to make in any case.) Soon after the fateful luncheon, Fitzgerald told Welles that he would have to abandon *The Cradle Will Rock* for lack of funds. To be fair to Spielberg, although he was a Welles aficionado, he was also a canny businessman; and the Welles project did not seem promising at a time when other backers were pulling out.

Welles died a year later, but Spielberg's career continued to flourish. Spielberg formed Amblin Entertainment in 1984 (named for his first commercial short subject), as an independent production company; in 1994, he joined forces with two multimedia moguls, David Geffen and Jeffrey Katzenberg, to found Dreamworks, one of Hollywood's largest and most influential independent production companies. Spielberg's preoccupation with the business side of moviemaking, as evidenced by his involvement in Amblin and Dreamworks, indicates his determination to have total creative control of the films he directs. And like Welles, Spielberg aims to make movies that express his own personal vision.

Spielberg received the Irving Thalberg Award for his body of work from the Motion Picture Academy at the Oscar ceremonies in 1986. He received his first Academy Award as best director for *Schindler's List* (1993), a drama of the Holocaust, and his second best director Oscar for *Saving Private Ryan* (1998), a World War II epic in which he told the story from the point of view of the common soldier.

Stanley Kubrick announced in 1995 that he was planning to make *A.I.,* a science-fiction film. But Kubrick's death in March 1999, only days after finishing the final cut of *Eyes Wide Shut,* ended all hopes that he would make *A.I.* Accordingly, Steven Spielberg stepped into the breach and announced that he would make *A.I.,* working from a revised version of Kubrick's prose treatment and turning it into a full-scale screenplay, dealing with an android boy who wants to be human.

In 2000, Spielberg received the Britannia Award from the British Academy of Film and Television— Los Angeles. That year the Britannia Award was renamed the Stanley Kubrick Award. *A.I.* (2001) is considered by Spielberg to be the creative product of himself and Stanley Kubrick.

In one sense, Welles got his own back concerning the film of *The Cradle Will Rock,* which Spielberg declined to back. Tim Robbins wrote and directed his own version of *The Cradle Will Rock* (1999), built around the events of the historic opening night, featuring Angus Macfadyen in a bravura performance as the young Welles and Cary Elwes as JOHN HOUSEMAN. Robbins's film was applauded as a rousing and astonishing tribute to Welles and to the power of theater.

Despite the contretemps over Welles's script for *Cradle,* Spielberg never lost his admiration for Welles as a great director. Steven Schiff writes that Spielberg was aware that he had learned from Welles "how to stage a shot, how to shift the viewer's eyes from foreground to background, and how to shuttle characters in and out of the frame at precisely the right moment."

References Brode, Douglas. *The Films of Steven Spielberg* (New York: Carol, 1995); Daly, Steve. "Humanoid Nature: *A.I.,*" *Entertainment Weekly,* July 13, 2001, 24–30; Higham, Charles. *The Films of Orson Welles* (Los Angeles: University of California Press, 1973); McBride, Joseph. *Steven Spielberg: A Biography* (New York: Simon & Schuster, 1997); Schiff, Stephen. "Seriously Spielberg," in *Steven Spielberg: Interviews* (Jackson: University Press of Mississippi, 2000), 171–92; Taylor, Philip. *Steven Spielberg* (New York: Continuum, 1992); Thomson, David. *Rosebud: The Story of Orson Welles* (New York: Vintage Books, 1997).

—G.D.P.

Start the Revolution Without Me Norbud/Warner Bros., 91 minutes, 1979. **Director:** Bud Yorkin; **Producer:** Bud Yorkin; **Screenplay:** Lawrence J. Cohen; **Cinematographer:** Jean Tournier; **Editor:** Ferris Webster; **Cast:** Gene Wilder (Claude Coup/Philippe DeSisi), Donald Sutherland (Charles Coup/Pierre DeSisi), Hugh Griffith (King Louis XVI), Orson Welles (Narrator), Jack MacGowan (Jacques Cabriolet), Billie Whitelaw (Queen Marie Antoinette), Victor Spinetti (Duke d'Escargot), Denise Coffey (Anna Duvall), Ewa Aulin (Christina)

This venture into feature filmmaking by Bud Yorkin and Norman Lear, famous for producing TV's *All in the Family,* is set in 18th-century France and involves the madcap consequences of a mix-up of two sets of twins at birth. Recalling the zany antics of comic opera, the fast-paced comings-and-goings are held together by a narration delivered with appropriate theatrical panache by WELLES. At the end of the film, Welles suddenly appears on screen in a 20th-century setting and tries to wrap up the story by narrating from a history book. Without warning, two young men, who look like descendants of the characters we've met in the 18th century, enter and shoot Welles, thus inscribing their own places in history.

—C.B.

Stevens, Ashton (1872–1951) Chicago's most influential theater critic from 1910 to 1951, who predicted great things for the adolescent WELLES.

In 1931, in the pages of WILLIAM RANDOLPH HEARST's *Chicago Herald American,* Stevens wrote: "Given as good an education as will adhere to him at a good college, young and not ill-looking Orson Welles is as likely as not to become my favorite actor. True, it will be four or five years before he has attained his majority and a degree and I have yet to see him act. But I like the way he handles a difficult situation and to lay my plans long ahead, I am going to put a clipping of this paragraph in my betting book. If Orson is not at least a leading man by the time it has yellowed, I'll never make another." Although Stevens had not yet seen the boy act, he nonetheless knew of him and his "genius" through having vetted pieces of music criticism that Welles had written for the local *Highland Park News.* Stevens had become aware of the boy's precocity through friendships with Welles's father, RICHARD WELLES, and mentor, DR. MAURICE BERNSTEIN.

Significantly, after Welles and Stevens had met and struck up a friendship, the courtly critic regaled the young man with extravagant tales about his boss, newspaper magnate William Randolph Hearst, upon whom the character of CHARLES FOSTER KANE in *CITIZEN KANE* was largely shaped. The veteran reporter also served as the model for *Citizen Kane's* Jedediah Leland, another of that film's indelible roles.

—C.B.

Stevenson, Robert (1905–1986)

Robert Stevenson, who had earlier been picked by RKO to direct *JOURNEY INTO FEAR* (1943) but had not received the assignment, directed *JANE EYRE* (1944), in which ORSON WELLES played Rochester, ironically at the suggestion of then enemy JOHN HOUSEMAN. Welles, who was unhappy at not being in charge of the film, demonstrated his feelings by showing up late and then, according to DAVID THOMSON, by "ordering a reading of the script, preparatory to giving notes and instructions." Thomson adds, "The very courteous Stevenson (two years on the project by then) had to swallow the insult." Welles has said that he merely produced the picture, but he also claimed that he rewrote the script and "invented some of the shots." FRANK BRADY explains why Stevenson was the logical choice to direct *Jane Eyre:* "He was a member of a professional group known as the Brontë Society and had spent years studying the history and traditions that provide the background for Charlotte Brontë's novel and the film." Despite Welles's contributions, Brady believes that Stevenson did have ten-

uous control of the film: "Although ten years Welles's senior and having over a dozen films to his credit, Stevenson felt rather intimidated by the giant actor with the colossal reputation." CHARLES HIGHAM does not agree that the film is Stevenson's: "Although the director, Robert Stevenson . . . insists that Welles had nothing whatsoever to do with the direction, the physical evidence is quite to the contrary," Higham points out that "the whole first half of the film is Wellesian to a degree."

Director Robert Stevenson, who was born in London in 1905, studied science at Cambridge, but his graduate psychology courses there made him interested in film. In 1930, he started as a screenwriter and began directing two years later. With *King Solomon's Mines* (1937), he became a major director, and from 1939 to 1949 was under contract with DAVID O. SELZNICK, who had brought him to the United States and who loaned him out to direct for other studios. He worked at RKO from 1949 to 1956, when he joined Walt Disney Studios. There he made the films he is remembered for: *Old Yeller* (1957), *The Absent-Minded Professor* (1961), *Son of Flubber* (1963), *Mary Poppins* (1964), *The Love Bug* (1969), *Bedknobs and Broomsticks* (1971), and *The Shaggy D. A.* (1976).

—T.L.E.

Stewart, James G.

James G. Stewart, who was in charge of postproduction sound at RKO, worked with ORSON WELLES on Welles's *CITIZEN KANE* (1941). According to DAVID THOMSON, Stewart, who had been trained in radio, knew that Welles had used innovative techniques with sound in his radio broadcasts and looked forward to working with him: "He [Welles] wanted to meet Stewart, to be able to trust him, to assure him. Stewart was delighted, and he quickly felt blessed to be learning so much." Stewart told ROBERT CARRINGER that much of "what he knows aesthetically about sound came from Welles." Despite what he regarded as a lack of warmth and camaraderie in Welles, Stewart described his work on *Kane* and *THE MAGNIFICENT AMBERSONS* (1942) as "one of the most significant experiences of his working life."

—T.L.E.

Stewart, Paul (1908–1986) Paul Stewart, who joined the MERCURY THEATRE in 1938, was born on March 13, 1908, in New York City. While he was in high school and at Columbia University, he was appearing onstage, and after graduation he moved into radio broadcasting. In his role as producer, he hired WELLES to appear on the *School of the Air of the Americas.* When Welles formed the *MERCURY THEATRE ON THE AIR,* he, in turn, hired Stewart, who did much of the producing for the series. According to Stewart, "At first Orson tried to produce the *Mercury Theatre on the Air* on his own, but he was incapable of doing so, being a very poorly organised man, and Houseman, at least in the beginning, knew nothing about radio." SIMON CALLOW regards Stewart as the "indispensable linchpin" of the Mercury Theatre. It was Stewart who supervised the recording of each show on shellac discs, which would then be played for Welles's revisions, usually the next day when the show was to be aired. Welles described Stewart to PETER BOGDANOVICH as "one of the main pillars of our Mercury broadcasts. He can't be given too much credit." When Welles was busy working on the *FIVE KINGS* production, Stewart, according to Callow, "ran the programmes very efficiently, and Houseman produced them with skill and taste" in Welles's almost complete absence. When the flap over script credit for *THE WAR OF THE WORLDS* broadcast occurred, Welles was determined that HOWARD KOCH should not get the writing credit. Welles said that Paul Stewart "did a great deal of writing on 'War of the Worlds.'" Stewart also appeared in *HIS HONOR, THE MAYOR,* which Welles wrote and narrated for radio April 6, 1941. *CEILING UNLIMITED,* a radio program Welles did for Lockheed-Vega, aircraft manufacturers during World War II, also featured Paul Stewart. When Welles made *CITIZEN KANE,* his first film, he cast several Mercury regulars, including Stewart, in key roles. As Raymond, the smooth, somewhat sinister butler, Stewart was very effective. In fact, it was, according to FRANK BRADY, Stewart's own "ability to produce a sinister persona that influenced the rewriting of his part of Raymond the butler."

After his work with Welles, Stewart went on to appear in many films, usually as a cold-blooded, sinister villain in westerns and gangster films. Among his best films are *Champion* (1949), *Twelve O'Clock High* (1950), *The Bad and the Beautiful* (1952), *The Greatest Story Ever Told* (1965), *In Cold Blood* (1967), and *The Day of the Locusts* (1975). In addition to his film roles, Stewart also directed and acted in television. His last film role before his death in 1986 was for Paul Mazursky in *Tempest* (1982).

—T.L.E.

Stockwell, Dean (1936–) Dean Stockwell appeared with WELLES and BRADFORD DILLMAN in RICHARD FLEISCHER's *COMPULSION* (1959), a film that parallels the Leopold-Loeb murder of Bobby Franks in 1924. In the film, he played the part of the submissive friend who plots with the Dillman character to commit a perfect murder. Welles played their lawyer. The three actors shared the best actor award in Cannes in 1959 for their roles in the film. Stockwell was a child star whose film career started in 1945 and ended in 1951—during that period he appeared in at least 15 films, some of them quite good: *The Green Years* (1946), *The Boy with Green Hair* (1948), *The Secret Garden* (1949), and *Kim* (in the title role, 1950). Shortly after he resumed his acting career in 1957, he was cast in *Compulsion.* Of the many films he made between 1959 and 1982 only *Sons and*

Actor Dean Stockwell *(National Film Society Archive)*

Lovers (1960) and *Long Day's Journey into Night* (1962) are memorable. Stockwell's career had a resurgence in 1983 when he appeared in *Paris, Texas,* which won the grand prize at Cannes in 1984. In 1984, he played the fiendish Dr. Yueh in *Dune* and was cast as the pansexual weirdo in David Lynch's *Blue Velvet* in 1986. In *Gardens of Stone* (1987) and *The Player* (1992) Stockwell had serious roles, but in *Married to the Mob* (1988) he displayed his comic talents as Tony "The Tiger" Russo. During the 1990s he has appeared in several films, the last of which was *Air Force One* (1997).

—T.L.E.

Stranger, The
RKO, 95 minutes, 1946. **Director:** Orson Welles; **Producer:** S. P. Eagle [Sam Spiegel]; **Executive Producer:** William Goetz; **Screenplay:** Anthony Veiller with John Huston and Welles (uncredited) based on an original story by Victor Trivas; **Cinematographer:** Russell Metty; **Editor:** Earnest Nims; **Cast:** Orson Welles (Franz Kindler/Charles Rankin), Loretta Young (Mary Longstreet), Philip Merivale (Judge Longstreet), Edward G. Robinson (Wilson), Bryon Keith (Dr. Lawrence), Richard Long (Noah Longstreet), Billy House (Potter), Martha Wentworth (Sarah), Konstantin Shayne (Konrad Meinike), Theodore Gottlieb (Farbright), Pietro Sosso (Mr. Peabody)

CHARLES HIGHAM reasonably considered "Date with Destiny," the screenplay of *The Stranger* "a triumph of dramatic construction and irony." The action is set in small-town New England, but the tranquil surface of Harper, Connecticut, is deceptive. It recalls Hitchcock's Santa Rosa, California, in *Shadow of a Doubt* (1943), where serial killer Charles Oakley (JOSEPH COTTEN) goes to spend time with his unsuspecting sister and her family to escape from the law, hiding out in wholesome America. In *The Stranger,* Charles Rankin (ORSON WELLES) is another evil outsider who has infiltrated an American idyllic town to escape his past, but he represents a different order of evil.

Charles Oakley was the notorious "Merry Widow murderer" in *Shadow of a Doubt.* Charles Rankin, a Nazi war criminal on the run in *The Stranger,* has assumed the identity of a history professor at the Harper School for Boys and is about to wed Mary (LORETTA YOUNG), the daughter of Judge Longstreet (Philip Merivale), a Supreme Court justice. Rankin is in fact the notorious Franz Kindler, pursued by Inspector Wilson (EDWARD G. ROBINSON) of the Allied War Crimes Commission. Wilson describes Kindler as the man "who conceived the theory of genocide, [the] mass killing of the populations of conquered countries." Whereas Charles Oakley was simply a serial killer, Franz Kindler was a mass murderer.

Wilson has baited a trap to find Kindler. As he explains, he has released Konrad Meinike (Konstantin Shayne, brother-in-law of AKIM TAMIROFF), a "one-time executive officer for Franz Kindler" who is awaiting execution in a prison camp in Czechoslovakia, "on the chance that he might lead me to Kindler." Wilson is obsessed by his mission. After giving instructions in Europe to "Leave the cell door open," so that Meinike can escape, Wilson says of Kindler, "This obscenity must be destroyed!" Claiming to be Polish, the escaped Meinike travels by ship to Latin America, where he contacts an ex-Nazi photographer, who tells him that Kindler is living in Connecticut under the assumed name of Rankin.

With Wilson tailing him, Meinike arrives in Harper and goes to the Harper School. Aware that he is being followed, Meinike gets the drop on Wilson and knocks him unconscious, then goes to Rankin's home on the very day Rankin is to marry Mary Longstreet. Mary tells him that Charles is not at home, but he soon meets Rankin on the street thereafter. Rankin arranges to meet Meinike later in the woods, where he strangles him to protect his cover. "They freed you so you'd lead them to me," Rankin says before killing Meinike, who urges Rankin to proclaim his guilt and confess his sins. Rankin later buries Meinike in the woods while the wedding reception is in progress. Later on, Mary's dog, Red, keeps trying to dig up Meinike's body, which seems to suggest that it takes a Red to sniff out a Nazi. Rankin poisons the dog.

Meinike has left his suitcase with Soloman Potter (Billy House), owner of a local drugstore. Potter is visited by Wilson, who has assumed the identity of an antique dealer especially interested in clocks. Potter tells Wilson about the Rankin-Longstreet marriage and Wilson later finds out from Mary's brother, Noah (Richard Long), that Rankin, like Kindler, is also an authority on clocks, and that he plans to repair the Strasbourg clock in the Harper church tower. That clock is a dominant symbol in the film. It is first seen behind the film's titles, and as it chimes, a mechanical avenging angel pursues Satan in a circular movement beneath the clock face. The Harper clock symbolizes time running out as well as Wilson's pursuit of Kindler.

Wilson gets invited to a dinner party and meets Rankin. Wilson has decided that Rankin is "above suspicion" until the dinner conversation turns to politics. Mary is caught off guard by what her husband has said about Germany: "Why Charles, I'm surprised at you for advocating a Carthaginian peace." Rankin responds, "As an historian, let me remind you that the world hasn't had much trouble with Carthage for the last 2,000 years." Rankin then remarks to Wilson, "The German sees himself as the innocent victim of world envy and hatred, conspired against, set upon by inferior peoples, inferior nations. He cannot admit to error, much less to wrongdoing—not the German." Rankin does not believe "that people can be reformed, except from within. The basic principles of equality and freedom never have [and] never will take root in Germany." When Noah then mentions Marx, Rankin responds: "But Marx wasn't a German. Marx was a Jew."

After this remark, Wilson changes his mind about leaving Harper: "Who but a Nazi would deny that Karl Marx was a German because he was a Jew? I think I'll stick around for a while," he concludes. From that point forward, the net begins to close around Rankin. Wilson goes fishing with Noah and confides his suspicions to Mary's brother. He tells Noah that Mary suspects nothing and knows "nothing at all, except that [Rankin] didn't want her to admit having seen someone she did see," Meinike, in other words. Rankin, meanwhile, fabricates a story to explain that Meinike was the brother of a girl who was drowned in a boating accident in Switzerland. "He knew I hadn't murdered her, but he told me he'd be willing to call it an accident," in return for "compensation." But then, he tells Mary, Meinike appeared again "on our wedding day" to blackmail

Rankin. He first tells her he gave the brother "all the money I had in the world, and he went away again," but later admits to her that he killed the man and the dog as well because this "little man" was also threatening to blackmail Judge Longstreet. Mary becomes a willing accessory because, she says, "I'm already a part of it, because I'm a part of you."

The Stranger has been seriously underrated in the Welles canon. In theme and technique it is Hitchcockian in the way an innocent person, misguided by love, is drawn into a web of guilt and complicity and in the way suspense is built at the end. Mary continues to protect her husband even after she hears Inspector Wilson's lecture on Nazi atrocities and even after Charles himself confesses Meinike's murder to her. At the end, however, horrified by Wilson's disclosures and in a state of shock, Mary decides to kill the now fugitive Charles. She knows he is hiding in the clock tower. Her ghostly walk to the tower is effectively filmed by cinematographer RUSSELL METTY in low-angle shots as she walks, slowly, dressed

Orson Welles as Franz Kindler in *The Stranger* (Literature/ Film Archive)

in a coat over her nightgown through the snow-covered cemetery toward the tower. The extreme low angle shots and the distorted music enforce the idea of her psychological disturbance. She goes up the ladder as if in a trance, carrying the empty box she will use as a pretense to have Charles lift her up over the broken rung at the top, the rung that was to have caused her death earlier.

Mary's brother Noah then arrives at the scene with Inspector Wilson. Shots are fired, and one of them inadvertently hits the mechanism of the clock, causing it to run out of control at an insane pace. The hands spin crazily and the allegorical figures race around its base: The times are out of joint. Charles, hit, falls out of the tower window, lands on the ledge, and is then impaled by the allegorical figure of St. Michael holding an extended sword. Satan is destroyed and cast down, symbolically. The conclusion of this film is recalled by the carousel spinning out of control at the end of Hitchcock's *Strangers on a Train* (1951), suggesting a cross-fertilization of imagery and technique between Welles and Hitchcock. Just as Charlie was used as bait in *Shadow of a Doubt* to catch the killer, Mary is used as bait in *The Stranger.* The moral implications are also similar for both characters in their involvement with and assent to evil. Charlie is willing to let her Uncle Charlie escape by train at the end of *Shadow of a Doubt* and puts her own life in jeopardy when Uncle Charlie, at the end, decides to push her off the moving train. Likewise, Mary at first refuses to betray her husband, even after he admits to having committed a murder and is then herself put in jeopardy. The facile expectation that good will triumph over evil is rendered somewhat less comfortable by the presence of an intelligent, capable, and convincing villain played by Welles himself.

According to DAVID THOMSON, who thinks Rankin is an "Ivy League professor," Welles considered *The Stranger* "his worst film," even though it was "the only movie Welles ever made that showed a profit on first release." Thomson agrees with JOSEPH MCBRIDE that Robinson would have been better suited for the role of Kindler, but that is surely questionable, considering how effectively Welles was later to play the corrupt Harry Lime in THE THIRD MAN

(1949), which has a scene that parallels *The Stranger,* when Lime remarks to Holley Martins (Joseph Cotten) from the top of an oversized Ferris wheel about how insignificant the people below seem—"like dots." From the clock tower in *The Stranger* Welles likens the people below to "ants." He tells Mary, "They searched the woods. I watched them. Like God, looking at little ants." Like Harry Lime, Franz Kindler casts a long and menacing shadow. Charles Higham thought the portrayal of Kindler was "one of the American cinema's few convincing portraits of a fascist."

This melodrama is a bit over the top, but it is effectively suspenseful and menacing, well photographed and well directed. The performances are on target and Edward G. Robinson is especially good as the obsessed Nazi-hunter. Welles originally wanted AGNES MOOREHEAD to play the role. "TONY VEILLER liked the idea," Welles told PETER BOGDANOVICH, but SAM SPIEGEL and BILL GOETZ disagreed. Although Welles considered Robinson "one of the best movie actors of all time," he thought the casting was "too obvious," with Robinson as Wilson. Welles was disappointed because the front office "removed at least two reels of material," involving the chase through South America, material that would have made the picture "more interesting visually," in the director's opinion. The conclusion is both ironic—Kindler impaled by the clockwork he himself set in motion—and arguably tragic, as Kindler falls, literally, from his godlike perch, a fallen angel of death.

References Higham, Charles. *The Films of Orson Welles* (Berkeley: University of California Press, 1970); Thomson, David. *Rosebud: The Story of Orson Welles* (New York: Knopf, 1996); Welles, Orson, and Peter Bogdanovich. *This Is Orson Welles,* ed. Jonathan Rosenbaum (New York: HarperCollins, 1992).

—J.M.W.

Sullavan, Margaret (Margaret Brooke)

(1909–1960) Margaret Brooke Sullavan was born in Norfolk, Virginia, on May 16, 1909, to wealthy parents. During her career (1933–50) she appeared in 16 films, and while she never received any acting awards, she was highly regarded as an actress. Her best performance was in *Back Street* (1941), in which she played an outsider, the "other woman." She won the New York Film Critics' best actress award for her role in *Three Comrades* (1938). Filmgoers will also recall her role in *The Shop Around the Corner* (1940), which was later remade as *You've Got Mail* (1998). After 1943, she made only one more film, *No Sad Songs for Me* (1950). She did continue to appear onstage, despite some problems with deafness, until she died in 1960, when she committed suicide by an overdose of barbiturates.

In 1939, she appeared with WELLES in his radio adaptation of Daphne Du Maurier's *Rebecca* on Welles's THE CAMPBELL PLAYHOUSE, which was the successor to his MERCURY THEATRE ON THE AIR. Welles played De Winter and she played the second Mrs. De Winter and narrated the story. SIMON CALLOW described her performance as "fresh and true," and DAVID O. SELZNICK, who was about to produce *Rebecca* as a film, was so taken by the radio production ("one of the greatest successes the radio has ever known") that he sent a transcript of the program to Alfred Hitchcock, who was to direct the film adaptation. After the radio performance, Welles and Sullavan engaged in some flirtatious conversation, and then Welles spoke to author Du Maurier and used for the first time, according to FRANK BRADY, the expression "obediently yours."

Reference Lawrence J. Quirk. *Margaret Sullavan: Child of Fate* (New York: St. Martin's Press, 1986).

—T.L.E.

Sutherland, Edward (1895–1974) In 1944,
CHARLES K. FELDMAN organized some of the Hollywood actors who under the auspices of the Hollywood Victory Committee had entertained American servicemen. The Hollywood actors appeared in *FOLLOW THE BOYS,* produced by Universal Pictures and directed by Edward Sutherland. ORSON WELLES, who had performed magic acts for the troops, was in the film with MARLENE DIETRICH (who was the person Welles sawed in half), Sophie Tucker, Jeannette MacDonald, Dinah Shore, Slapsie Maxie Rosenbloom, and Donald O'Connor, as well as singing groups such as the Andrews Sisters.

Sutherland was born of American parents who were living in London. Starting out as a child actor

and vaudevillian, Sutherland broke into films as a stuntman in 1914. After playing in some Keystone comedies and being the juvenile lead in some films, he moved to the other side of the camera in 1923, when he was appointed CHARLIE CHAPLIN's assistant director on *A Woman of Paris.* He became a director the following year and continued to direct films until the late 1940s, though he did direct *Bermuda Affair* in 1957. He specialized in comedy and made some films with W. C. Fields (*International House,* 1933, for example) and also made some films about World War II. *Abie's Irish Rose* (1946), which he also produced, was probably his best-known film. After World War II, he turned to directing and producing for television.

—T.L.E.

Swiss Family Robinson RKO Radio Pictures,
Inc., 94 minutes, 1940. **Director:** Edward Ludwig; **Producers:** Gene Towne and Graham Barker; **Associate Producer:** Donald J. Ehlers; **Assistant Director:** Sam Ruman; **Screenplay:** Walter Ferris, Gene Towne, and Graham Barker (based on the 1899 novel *Swiss Family Robinson* by Johann David Wyss); **Cinematographer:** Nicholas Musuraca; **Editor:** George Crone; **Special Effects:** Vernon L. Walker; **Art Director:** Van Nest Polglase; **Music:** Anthony Collins (and Franz Schubert's Quartette in A Minor, op. 28); **Cast:** Thomas Mitchell (William Robinson), Edna Best (Elizabeth Robinson), Freddie Bartholomew (Jack Robinson), Terry Kilburn (Ernest Robinson), Tim Holt (Fritz Robinson), Baby Bobby Quillan (Francis Robinson), Christian Rub (Thoren), John Wray (Ramsey), Herbert Rawlinson (Captain), (uncredited, Orson Welles, narrator)

WELLES, who had just signed a lavish contract with RKO to direct his first feature film (which had yet to be determined), was asked by the studio to narrate *Swiss Family Robinson.* Although providing such a service was a violation of his contract, which stipulated that Welles work only on his own films, the legalities of the situation were ignored by all parties. Because RKO was paying him what the studio deemed a fortune, Welles did the narration as a "favor" to his new employer at the rate of $25 per day, the wage rate for extras.

Although Welles's electrifying appearance as CHARLES FOSTER KANE in *CITIZEN KANE* is understandably listed by virtually all Welles commentators as his Hollywood acting debut, in fact, it was in *Swiss Family Robinson* that Welles, the now professional film actor, albeit at $25 a day, first met the general public in the hushed darkness of Hollywood's opulent picture palaces and more modest Bijou Dreams.

Based on the 1827 novel by Johann Rudolf Wyss, RKO's adaptation of *Swiss Family Robinson* depicts the classic story of a family marooned on an uninhabited island who find a peaceful existence far from the tumult of the "civilized" world. The film features Thomas Mitchell, Edna Best, Freddie Bartholomew, TIM HOLT, and Terry Kilburn.

—C.B.

Tamiroff, Akim (1900–1972)   In WELLES's films his friend Akim Tamiroff specialized in playing disreputable, repellent characters. In *MR. ARKADIN* (1962) he played Jakob Zouk, whose mumbling and filthy appearance is juxtaposed with the articulate, well-dressed Van Stratten. FRANK BRADY believes that Welles got "one of the best performances out of Akim Tamiroff since his role in *For Whom the Bell Tolls.*" In *TOUCH OF EVIL* he was Uncle Joe Grandi, a Mexican buffoon and gangster, whose bloated face fills the screen after he is strangled by Quinlan. Welles described Tamiroff's character as a "comic heavy" acting in a melodrama. In response to PETER BOGDANOVICH's comment about the strangulation scene being "vaguely sexual," Welles agreed: "Tamiroff was great in it [the scene]: when he looked at that gun, it was every cock in the world." In *DON QUIXOTE,* which was never finished or released, he is Sancho Panza, Don Quixote's comical sidekick. In *THE TRIAL* (1963) he worked for a fraction of his regular salary in the role of Bloch, Hastler's pathetic, obsequious client who is humiliated by Hastler (Welles). Tamiroff and Welles also were assigned roles in *MARCO THE MAGNIFICENT* (1964).

Born in Baku, Azerbaijan, on the Caspian Sea, where his father was an oil worker, Akim Tamiroff grew up in Moscow, where he attended the prestigious Moscow Art Theater. He subsequently became part of the Theater's touring repertory company, and when he came to the United States in 1923, he stayed. He then joined Balieff's Chauve Souris troupe, performed with his wife, Tamara Shayne, in nightclubs, and finally appeared on Broadway with Al Jolson in *Wunderbar.* He and his wife left for Hollywood after he had another Broadway role, this time in *Miracle at Verdun.* He made his Hollywood film debut in 1934 in *Sadie McKee.* Never a lead, he was a character actor who appeared in over 75 films. Often his heavy Russian accent was indispensable for his roles, and when he offered to take English lessons, the studios reportedly advised him not to. For his role as a shady Russian baker in Paris in *Anastasia* (1956), Bosley Crowther praised him as being in "fascinating form." He was twice nominated for Academy Awards, first as the Chinese general in *The General Died at Dawn* (1936), and then as Pablo, the guerrilla leader in *For Whom the Bell Tolls* (1943). Other memorable films include *The Lives of a Bengal Lancer* (1935), *Union Pacific* (1939), *Tortilla Flat* (1942), *The Bridge of San Luis Rey* (1944), *Romanoff and Juliet* (1961), *Topkapi* (1964), and *Lord Jim* (1965). His last film was *A Rose for Everyone* (1967). In 1959, he again appeared on Broadway, this time as the lead in *Rashomon.* He died in Palm Springs, California, on September 17, 1972.

—T.L.E.

Tarkington, (Newton) Booth (1869–1946) This Hoosier novelist and playwright wrote the

Pulitzer Prize–winning novel *The Magnificent Ambersons* in 1918 that was to be the source of ORSON WELLES's second feature film. Tarkington was born in Indianapolis, Indiana, on July 29, 1869, and educated first at the Phillips Exeter Academy in New Hampshire, then at Purdue University in Lafayette, Indiana, and at Princeton University. The "gentleman from Indiana" who wrote *The Gentleman from Indiana,* a popular novel published in 1899, served as Republican delegate in the Indiana legislature from 1902 to 1903, but his true forte was letters rather than politics. He became a significant interpreter of small-town middle-American family life, satirical at his best, sentimental when not at his best, but acutely aware of the world changing around him. Among his most successful early novels were *Monsieur Beaucaire* (1900), a romance he later adapted for the stage and screen, and two nostalgic and popular adolescent novels, *Penrod* (1914) and *Seventeen* (1916). His most critically successful novels, however, were *The Magnificent Ambersons,* which won the Pulitzer Prize for fiction in 1919, and *Alice Adams* (1921), which won another Pulitzer Prize in 1922. Throughout this period, Tarkington also wrote plays in collaboration with Harry Leon Wilson, notably *The Man from Home* (1906), about Hoosiers abroad, and later building to his four-act dramatization of *Seventeen* that ran for 225 performances in New York at the Booth Theatre in 1916, *Mister Antonio* (1916), and *Up from Nowhere* (1919). Between 1931 and 1946, 10 motion pictures were made from Tarkington materials, including *Penrod* (Warners, 1937), *Seventeen* (Paramount, 1940), *Monsieur Beaucaire* (Paramount, 1946), *Gentle Julia* (Fox, 1936), *Clarence* (Paramount, 1937), *Little Orvie* (RKO, 1940), *Alice Adams* (1935), and, of course THE MAGNIFICENT AMBERSONS (RKO, 1942). The best of these have been unjustly neglected, notably *Alice Adams,* with George Stevens directing a young Katharine Hepburn at the top of her form in the lead, and *Ambersons,* described by PETER COWIE as a "true *film maudit,* like Stroheim's *Greed,"* which like *Ambersons,* was shaped by the studio rather than the director. Though expressing regrets that the work of this "extraordinary writer" had become "hopelessly dated," Welles told PETER BOGDANOVICH, "I can't pay enough tribute to Tarkington." Booth Tarkington died in Indianapolis on May 19, 1946.

References Fennimore, Keith J. *Booth Tarkington* (New York: Twayne, 1974); Woodress, James Leslie. *Booth Tarkington: Gentleman from Indiana* (Philadelphia: Lippincott, 1955).

—J.M.W.

Tartars, The Lux Film-Dubrava Film/MGM, 83 minutes, 1961. **Directors:** Richard Thorpe, Ferdinando Baldi; **Producer:** Riccardo Gualino; **Screenplay:** Sabatino Ciuffni, Ambrogio Molteni, Gaio Fratini, Oreste Palella, Emmimmo Salvi, and Julian Vroome de Kassel; **Cinematographers:** Amerigo Gengarelli, Elios Vercelloni; **Editor:** Maurizio Lucidi; **Cast:** Victor Mature (Oleg), Orson Welles (Burandai), Folco Lulli (Togrul), Liana Orfei (Helga), Bella Cortez (Samia), Luciano Marin (Eric), Arnoldo Foa (Chu-lung)

This cumbersome yet financially successful costume drama takes place in the early Middle Ages on the Russian steppes. WELLES is the villainous Tartar chieftain, Burandai, who opposes the Viking leader, Oleg (VICTOR MATURE). Although one critic described Welles's Tartar chief as "looking like a walking house," the overstuffed production did allow Welles to best Victor Mature, his old rival for the hand of RITA HAYWORTH, by stealing scenes. The rivalry, as Welles shared with PETER BOGDANOVICH, also extended to footwear: "Victor Mature had been told—incorrectly—that I had built up my shoes by two inches to make myself look taller. So he went and got his sandals built three inches high and he could hardly walk. Very funny sandals, too—he looked like a brassiered carioca girl in a carnival. And he could barely get across the stage in those things," a situation that gave Welles "style points" in his climactic sword fight with Mature's understandably wobbly Oleg.

More significantly, it was on the set of *The Tartars* that Welles met the father-son editing team of Renzo and Maurizio Lucidi. The Lucidis would later collaborate with the director on DON QUIXOTE, the tortuously protracted project that was finally assembled for release in 1992, long after Welles's 1985 death.

—C.B.

Taylor, John Russell (1935–) The author of *The Angry Theatre* (1962), British journalist and critic John Russell Taylor was born in Dover in 1935 and educated at Cambridge University. After becoming film critic for the London *Times* in 1961 and a regular contributor to *Sight and Sound,* he wrote several books treating cinema, starting with *Cinema Eye, Cinema Ear: Some Key Film-Makers of the Sixties* (1964), and followed by *Directors and Directions: Cinema for the Seventies* (1975), and *Hitch: The Life and Times of Alfred Hitchcock* (1978), among other titles. Taylor left his position as film reviewer for the London *Times* in 1973 to become a professor of cinema studies at the University of Southern California, although he continued to serve as American cultural correspondent for the London newspaper. In 1999, he published *Orson Welles: A Celebration* in the Applause Legend Series. The WELLES book runs to only 150 pages, less than half the length of his authorized biography of Hitchcock. The approach is breezy, readable, and journalistic. It is an adequate and personalized introduction that "celebrates" the life and career of the director, but it pales in comparison to the work of other Welles biographers.

—J.M.W.

Ten Days Wonder (La Decade Prodigieuse)

Les Films La Boetie/Levitt-Pickman, 101 minutes, 1972. **Director:** Claude Chabrol; **Producer:** Andre Genoves; **Screenplay:** Paul Gardner, Paul Gegauff, based on the mystery novel by Ellery Queen; **Cinematographer:** Jean Rabier; **Editor:** Jacques Gaillard; **Cast:** Orson Welles (Theo Van Horn), Anthony Perkins (Charles Van Horn), Marlene Jobert (Helene Van Horn), Michel Piccoli (Paul Regis), Guido Alberti (Ludovic)

Chabrol, one of the leading lights of the vaunted French New Wave, hired WELLES to portray an old, reclusive rich man who lives in a house that he has deliberately preserved in the manner of the 1920s in order to create the illusion that he has not aged. Michel Piccoli plays an outsider who invades the mansion to expose the millionaire's hermetically sealed existence. "Unfortunately," as CHARLES HIGHAM points out, "the movie was too much of a *roman à clef* to work independently of Welles's personality." Higham also confirms the critical consensus regarding Chabrol's rather pedestrian direction.

Still, for Welles, the paycheck helped finance his ongoing production of *THE OTHER SIDE OF THE WIND.*

—C.B.

Ten Million Ghosts (play, 1936)

In the midst of his PROJECT 891 production of *HORSE EATS HAT* (1936), and his numerous commitments to radio, WELLES, driven by his compulsion to be everywhere at once, agreed to take a leading role in playwright Sidney Kingsley's *Ten Million Ghosts.* Like Kingsley's successful *Dead End,* set in the hoodlum-producing slums of New York City's lower east side, *Ten Million Ghosts* was a social problem drama. Kingsley took aim at the coterie of powerful arms merchants that many liberals of the period regarded as warmongers. Part of Welles's motivation for considering *Ten Million Ghosts* was his awareness that the film rights for *Dead End* had been picked up by Samuel Goldwyn for the then unprecedented amount of $165,000. Welles figured that if *Ten Million Ghosts* enjoyed a comparable success, his association with the play might be his ticket to Hollywood.

Kingsley's drama, a scathing attack on the international arms trade, also played to Welles's fascination with munitions magnate SIR BASIL ZAHAROFF, whom Welles had portrayed for an episode of radio's *MARCH OF TIME* in 1936. Although Welles was directing *Horse Eats Hat* and playing the character of Mugglethorp for the FEDERAL THEATRE's Project 891 at the same time that he was rehearsing his role as Andre Pequot for *Ten Million Ghosts,* he planned to reconcile this impossible schedule by resigning his part as Mugglethorp once the Kingsley play began its run.

Ten Million Ghosts opened at the St. James Theater on October 23, 1936. In spite of the huge success of *Dead End,* Kingsley's new play, which he also produced and staged, folded after only one performance. Its failure, according to FRANK BRADY, can be explained by the preference of cash-strapped depression theatergoers for escapist fare. *Ten Million Ghost's* condemnation of shadowy arms merchants thus found itself at odds with audiences looking for glamour, glitz, and girls—in short, entertainment.

Although Welles would have to wait for the sensational broadcast of *THE WAR OF THE WORLDS* (1938) before gaining a Hollywood contract, *Ten Million*

Ghosts did presage his eventual entry into film. In a variation of the Shakespearean device of a play within a play, Welles helped Kingsley concoct a scene in which the arms barons watch a film of soldiers being butchered in battle. Welles, to heighten the impact of the World War I newsreel footage, suggested using an actual onstage projector. When the news footage reveals the seemingly senseless slaughter, the arms merchants are forced to defend themselves against accusations of warmongering made by a newspaper reporter and an idealistic young airman, the character of Andre Pequot played by Welles. Silhouetted against the flickering screen—a foreshadowing of the conclusion of NEWS ON THE MARCH sequence from CITIZEN KANE—the arms makers become a virtual "screen" on which the images of dying soldiers are projected. Although *Ten Million Ghosts* was generally panned, Welles's inspired and ironic use of the combat news footage was unanimously praised. Hollywood was getting closer.

—C.B.

Third Man, The   British Lion Film/London Film, 93 minutes, 1949. **Director:** Carol Reed; **Producers:** Alexander Korda, Reed, and David O. Selznick; **Screenplay:** Graham Greene; **Cinematographer:** Robert Krasker, **Music:** Anton Karas; **Cast:** Orson Welles (Harry Lime), Joseph Cotten (Holley Martins), Alida Valli (Anna Schmidt), Trevor Howard (Major Calloway), Paul Horbiger (Porter), Ernst Deutsch (Baron Kurtz), Erich Ponto (Dr. Winkel), Siegfried Breuer (Popescu)

ORSON WELLES starred in this film. GRAHAM GREENE, an English novelist and screenwriter, collaborated on three masterful films with director CAROL REED: *The Fallen Idol* (1948) was based on Greene's short story, "The Basement Room," and focuses on a youngster who suspects the family butler of murdering his wife; *The Third Man* (1949), for which Greene wrote an original screenplay dealing with the black market in postwar Vienna; and *Our Man in Havana* (1959), a spy spoof about a British undercover agent working in pre-Castro Cuba. This trio of films represents one of the most significant creative associations between a writer and director in the history of film. *The Third Man* is the peak of their collaboration.

The hero of the film is Holley Martins (JOSEPH COTTEN), an American writer of pulp westerns, who has come to Vienna at the invitation of an old school chum, Harry Lime (Orson Welles). Upon his arrival, Martins is shocked to learn that Lime is being buried that day, having been the victim of a traffic accident. At the cemetery, Martins meets Anna, Lime's mistress (Alida Valli), and Major Calloway (Trevor Howard), the British army officer in charge of investigating Lime's death. Martins learns that Lime was involved in the most sordid of postwar rackets: trafficking in black market penicillin of such inferior quality that it has caused widespread sickness and death.

In a pivotal episode, Martins goes to see Anna to tell her what he has discovered about Harry. As they talk, Martins pets the cat that is roaming about Anna's flat. The cat recoils from him and Anna explains, "He only liked Harry." The camera follows the cat over to the window, where it jumps over the sill and climbs down to the street below. Then it goes over to a dark doorway where a man's feet can be seen protruding. The cat licks one of the shoes.

By this time, Martins has left Anna's apartment and is walking along the street. He suspects that there is someone in the same doorway and that he is being followed. Martins challenges the man to come out into the open. In a window above him, someone draws back a curtain to look out and see what the commotion is about. For only a second, a shaft of

Joseph Cotten as Holley Martins and Orson Welles as Harry Lime in *The Third Man* (Literature/Film Archive)

light falls across the doorway and reveals to Martins what the audience already suspects: It is Harry Lime.

When Calloway hears what has happened, he exhumes the body buried in Harry Lime's grave. It is that of Joseph Harbin, who had been working as a double agent for Calloway as a member of Lime's gang until he was found out. Lime's fake death, therefore, served not only to make the police think he was out of the way, but also to provide an inconspicuous way of disposing of Harbin.

Martins arranges through Kurtz to meet Harry in an amusement park. The two take a ride on the Ferris wheel, which has closed compartments, so that they can talk in private. Martins tries to stir Harry's sense of humanity by asking him if he has any guilty feelings about his victims, and Harry replies by pointing through the window of the car to the crowd below. He asks Martins how much pity he would feel if one of those dots moving about far below stopped moving forever: "If I said you can have £20,000 for every dot that stops, would you really, old man, tell me to keep my money—or would you calculate how many dots you could afford to spare?"

As they part, Harry says to Martins, "When you make up your mind, send me a message—I'll meet you any place, any time, and when we do meet, old man, it's you I want to see, not the police. . . . And don't be so gloomy. . . . After all, it's not that awful— you know what the fellow said: In Italy for thirty years under the Borgias they had warfare, terror, murder, bloodshed—and they produced Michelangelo, Leonardo da Vinci, and the Renaissance. In Switzerland they had brotherly love, five hundred years of democracy and peace, and what did that produce? The cuckoo clock. So long, Holley."

"The popular line of dialogue concerning Swiss cuckoo clocks," Graham Greene told this writer, "was written into the script by Mr. Orson Welles." Because Greene has given Welles credit for that bit, the myth somehow has grown up that Welles wrote his whole part; e.g., PETER COWIE baldly gives the story as fact in *Seventy Years of Cinema* in the course of his treatment of the film. But the only dialogue for which Welles is surely responsible is the line for which Greene has given him credit. That Welles did not write his own part, however, in no way detracts from the superb way in which he plays it. Welles radiates a clever charm and sinister fascination that makes us readily understand how he has been able to manipulate Holley Martins for his own advantage, from the time that they were at school together.

Calloway has made every effort to get Martins over his immature illusions about Lime. In order to convince him that he should act as a decoy for Lime's capture, Calloway takes Martins on a tour of a hospital where he can see the victims of Lime's penicillin racket. PAULINE KAEL dislikes the hospital scene because in her view it underlines more than it should the social message of the film. "The ghastly hospital scene (which is based on facts) seems a little unfair," she writes in *Kiss Kiss Bang Bang*. "We've been enjoying all this decadence and stylish acting and these people living on their nerves, and then we're forced to take evil seriously."

On the contrary, Reed asks his audience to take evil seriously throughout the film and not just in the hospital scene. *The Third Man* is not a spy spoof in which the moral implications of the characters' behavior can be disregarded. Reed rather develops his story in terms of a moral dilemma. Holley Martins must decide if a man whom he has admired since childhood is in reality a criminal who should be turned over to the authorities. The search into Lime's past in which Martins engages becomes then a moral investigation on Holley's part to determine whether or not he should assist in Lime's capture.

On the other hand, although the story of the penicillin racket in which Harry Lime was implicated was based on truth, Greene points out that he used this reality only as a background for a fictional tale. In general, he says, he and Reed did not want to make a film that might be thought propagandist: "We had no desire to move people's political emotions; we wanted to entertain them, to frighten them a little, to make them laugh." Hence, neither the hospital scene nor any other sequence in the film is designed in such a soberingly realistic way that it takes the edge off the film's value as entertainment.

After what Martins has seen in the hospital, he agrees to lure Harry to a café where Calloway can arrest him. Anna comes to the café because she knows that Harry is going to meet Martins there. Anna guesses that the rendezvous is a trap. As Harry enters the café, it is she who cannot bear to see him captured, so she shouts to him to escape and he disappears.

The climax of the film is the pursuit of Lime through the sewers of Vienna. It is the perfect setting for the action: sinister shadows thrown by flashlights on the tunnel walls; the rushing waters and the footsteps echoing through the passages. Lime is wounded, but manages to pull himself up an iron stairway in order to try to escape to the street through a manhole. But he is too weak to dislodge the cover, and there is a memorable shot taken from the street level showing Lime's fingers reaching vainly through the sewer grating.

Martins finds Harry struggling with the grille. Harry, who has lost his gun, stares painfully at Martins, who still has one. Calloway and his men hear a

Welles as Harry Lime in *The Third Man* (*National Film Society Archive*)

shot echo through the darkness, and they turn a searchlight in that direction. Martins emerges into its beam, sadly hanging his head. In the end, in spite of all of the reasons that Martins had to despise Harry, he has done him one last favor.

ANTON KARAS made a great contribution to the movie's atmosphere with the haunting musical score composed and played by him on the zither. Reed discovered Karas playing in a Viennese café while he was scouting locations for the film, and brought him back to London to record the score.

Greene attributes the extraordinary success of *The Third Man* at the box office in some part to the popularity of "The Third Man Theme," which Karas composed for the film. Greene says, "I indicated in the script that there should be a tune associated with Harry Lime," but of course neither Greene nor anyone else could have imagined that the music would become so popular in its own right. For his part, Reed explains the success of the film by saying that it was one of the first British films to be shot almost entirely on location instead of in the insulated atmosphere of a studio. In this way, Reed was able to capture, with the help of Robert Krasker's Academy Award–winning photography, the brooding, corrupt atmosphere of a ruined postwar city. As Pauline Kael puts it in *Kiss Kiss Bang Bang,* the film showed us how war had changed the survivors, made them "tired, ravaged opportunists." The city took on a strong presence of its own in the foreground of the film, and the simple American who stumbled into it was like a tourist in hell, while all the time "the melancholy twang of the zither brought evil seductively close."

Reed's selection of Orson Welles to play Harry Lime was another stroke of genius. Initially, Welles had turned down the part, but Reed persuaded him to try playing a scene. The day that Welles arrived on location in Vienna, Reed was preparing to shoot the chase through the sewers, and Welles complained that the bad air in the sewer passages would give him pneumonia. "Finally I persuaded him to shoot the scene," Reed told this writer. "Then Orson conferred with the cameraman, made some suggestions; and we did the chase again. Of course he was sold on finishing the picture, and he gave a superlative performance."

Welles, with his suave and evil charm, so dominates the few scenes in which he appears that one seems to remember him as having had a larger part than he actually did. Brought to life by Welles, Harry Lime walked straight into cinema's mythology, Penelope Houston has written, "on the strength of a line of dialogue about Switzerland and cuckoo clocks and a shot of a hand clutching at a sewer grating."

On the film's 50th anniversary in 1999, Reed's original director's cut of *The Third Man* was released to theaters in the United States and shortly after on videocassette. It contains 11 minutes of footage that DAVID O. SELZNICK, the American distributor of the movie, had trimmed from the American release prints of the picture. (The director's cut was released in Britain and throughout Europe.)

Selznick also removed the director Carol Reed's narration of the opening prologue and substituted one by Joseph Cotten in his role as Holley Martins. It seems that ALEXANDER KORDA, who was releasing the film in Europe, asked Reed to add the prologue in order to explain the political climate of postwar Vienna; Korda feared that international audiences would not otherwise grasp the situation.

"That little prologue was added three months after principal photography was completed," Reed recalled. "So I had to dub the voice-over narration myself, since Cotten was long gone from the picture by then." But when David Selznick released the film in the United States, he had Cotten redub the narration for the American prints. In the director's cut, then, Reed's narration has been restored—quite appropriately, since it is right that the director of the film, who is, after all, telling the story to the audience, should introduce the film in the prologue.

References Cowie, Peter. *Seventy Years of Cinema* (New York: Barnes, 1969); Gribble, Jim. "*The Third Man:* Greene and Reed," *Literature/Film Quarterly* 26, no. 3 (Summer 1998): 235–39; Houston, Penelope. *Contemporary Cinema* (Baltimore: Penguin Books, 1969), 38; Kael, Pauline. *Kiss Kiss Bang Bang* (New York: Bantam Books, 1969), 13; Moss, Robert. *The Films of Carol Reed* (New York: Columbia University Press, 1987); Phillips, Gene. "Carol Reed: The Disenchanted," in *Major Film Directors of the American and British Cinema,* rev. ed. (Cranbury, N.J.: Associated University Presses, 1999), 163–76; Sragow,

Harry Lime's attempted escape through the sewers of Vienna in *The Third Man* *(Literature/Film Archive)*

Michael. "Truer to the Main Man of *The Third Man,*" *New York Times,* May 9, 1999, sec. 2: 19, 28; Schwab, Ulrike. "Authority and Ethics in *The Third Man,*" *Literature/Film Quarterly* 28, no. 1 (Winter 2000): 2–6; Wapshott, Nicholas. *Carol Reed: A Biography* (New York: Knopf, 1994).

—G.D.P.

This Is My Best (radio, 1945) Sponsored by Cresta Blanca and aired nationally by CBS, *This Is My Best* was a half-hour dramatic radio series presided over by WELLES. For its first broadcast, Welles turned to Joseph Conrad's HEART OF DARKNESS, a story he had adapted to radio in 1938 for MERCURY THEATRE ON THE AIR. Here, however, Welles based his retelling of Conrad's tale on the 1939 film script that he had hoped would become his first project for RKO. Because he had devoted so much thought to Conrad's 1902 novella, Welles's 1945 radio version made effective use of sound, whose effects included the rattling of the slaves' chains and the suffering cries of a madman. While greatly pared down because of the program's 30-minute time slot, the *Heart of Darkness* broadcast probably comes closest to suggesting what Welles's proposed film might have been like. In addition to producing and directing, Welles played the roles of Marlow and Kurtz. In part, the selection of *Heart of Darkness* was motivated by Welles's desire to find backing for the film.

The other broadcasts in the *This Is My Best* series were *Miss Dilly Says No,* a satirical glimpse into a major film studio with Ann Sothern and Francis X. Bushman; *Snow White,* a dramatization of the Walt Disney film with Jane Powell; an adaptation of F. SCOTT FITZGERALD's short story, "The Diamond as Big as the Ritz"; a retelling of Robert Lewis Stevenson's *The Master of Ballantrae* with RAY COLLINS and AGNES MOOREHEAD; *I'll Not Go Back,* by Milton Geiger, and, *Anything Can Happen,* by George and Helen Papashvily. In retrospect, the title of the last show *Anything Can Happen,* proved prophetic. After its airing, Welles and *This Is My Best* were immediately terminated by the program's advertising agency, which regarded an upcoming episode, *Don't Catch Me,* as a conflict of interest; specifically, Welles was accused of selecting the story to promote its sale as a film rather than because it was "good radio." While the promotional angle was undoubtedly true, it should be recalled that this kind of cross-media promotion was more the rule than the exception, then, as well as now. Throughout *This Is My Best*'s brief run of six installments, Welles again proved that when it came to radio drama, he had few peers.

—C.B.

Thomson, David (1941–) Thomson, the author of the cantankerous *Biographical Dictionary of Film* (Morrow, 1976; revised and expanded in the Knopf edition of 1994), wrote an eccentric book entitled *Rosebud: The Story of Orson Welles,* published by Knopf in 1996. Born and educated in London, Thomson wrote for the *Independent on Sunday* (London) and at least two reputable American journals, *Film Comment* and *The New Republic,* besides the less serious *Movieline.* After teaching film studies at Dartmouth College, he later moved to California and settled in San Francisco. Thomson claims to have edited the *Journal of Gastronomy* and was screenwriter for the award-winning documentary *The Making of a Legend: Gone with the Wind.* Another eccentric book was *Warren Beatty and Desert Eyes* (1987), an innovative but sometimes mean-spirited meditation on biography and on Hollywood power, the biography of

Warren Beatty balanced by a parallel narrative concerning a handsome, mysterious, reclusive and powerful matinee idol known as "Eyes." This was followed by a far more conventional book, *Showman: The Life of David O. Selznick,* which won the Michael Powell Film Book of the Year Award in 1992.

The style of *Rosebud* is more than a little indulgent. The approach is decidedly postmodern, which means creative, provocative, and readable for those who may approve. Those who do not will be more skeptical of undocumented innuendoes presented as being potentially factual. There is a danger here of pretentious prevarication disguised as entertaining episodes where the author debates with himself (and his imaginary publisher) and speculates for his own amusement. According to Michiko Kakutani in the *New York Times* (June 7, 1996), Thomson "eschews the effort to give us another comprehensive biography" of the director and instead chooses "to write a quirky, highly subjective book" that speculates about "our imagined Welles" and offers "digressions about the author's own experiences." The result is "a kind of prose equivalent to *Citizen Kane,* with Welles, instead of Kane, as the subject of a detective-like inquiry into the past." Kakutani objected to Thomson's "self-important and gratuitous asides" from his own life and found the book flawed for its "irresponsible speculation." Janet Maslin was rather more tolerant in her *New York Times Book Review* evaluation (June 30, 1996). According to Maslin, the "book's real strength is in analyzing the chaos and self-destructiveness of the post-Kane years." Thomson finds PAULINE KAEL's argument over the authorship of CITIZEN KANE "misguided," and argues the merits of Welles's later literary adaptations, such as THE TRIAL, CHIMES AT MIDNIGHT, and THE IMMORTAL STORY. Maslin found Thomson "arrogant, sometimes galling, [but] often uncannily right," and "never dull."

—J.M.W.

Thomson, Virgil (1896–1989) Composer Virgil Thomson wrote scores for several of WELLES's most important theatrical productions, including the famed "voodoo" staging of MACBETH (1936) for the NEGRO THEATRE PROJECT, and *HORSE EATS HAT*

(1936), which initiated PROJECT 891, the unit of the FEDERAL THEATRE PROJECT charged with producing "classical" dramas.

The multifaceted Thomson was raised in Kansas City, Missouri, where he began his musical training at the age of five. By the time he was 12, he was performing professionally on both piano and organ. At Harvard, he continued his musical studies while taking advantage of the college's broad liberal arts curriculum. In the mid-1920s, he moved to Paris to study with noted composition pedagogue Nadia Boulanger. He also became part of the city's thriving avant-garde scene, becoming friends with Jean Cocteau, Igor Stravinsky, Erik Satie, the composers of Les Six, and Gertrude Stein, the expatriate American author who would write the librettos for two of Thomson's most important works, the operas *Four Saints in Three Acts* (1928) and *The Mother of Us All* (1947), the latter a musical limning of the life of suffragist Susan B. Anthony.

Thomson returned to the United States in the early 1930s and settled in New York, where he became a central figure in the city's vibrant arts scene. In 1934, he enjoyed a well-publicized mounting of *Four Saints in Three Acts* with an all-black cast directed by JOHN HOUSEMAN, an excerpt of which was broadcast on THE MARCH OF TIME. In 1935, the orbs of Welles, Houseman, and Thomson crossed in a production of ARCHIBALD MACLEISH's experimental verse play, *PANIC,* in which the three participated as actor (Welles played the part of the industrialist McGafferty), director, and composer, respectively. Thomson, whose style had shifted in the mid-1920s from dissonant complexity to melodic simplicity, produced scores whose transparency and folklike melodies complemented rather than clashed with the drama. However, in his pastiche for *MacBeth,* Thomson, at Welles's urging, added voodoo drummers, orchestrations of Joseph Lanner waltzes, melodies in a turn-of-the-last-century manner akin to "Hearts and Flowers," and several original trumpet fanfares. Welles also had Thomson meld musical sound effects such as thunder, wind, and lightning to finesse prominent lines of dialogue. Although Thomson had dismissed prospects for adding anything of significance to Shakespeare, his pungent score struck a res-

onant chord with theater people, which led to commissions to score a forthcoming Leslie Howard production of *Hamlet* and a Tallulah Bankhead staging of *Antony and Cleopatra.*

Pleased with Thomson's work on *Macbeth,* Welles invited the composer to score HORSE EATS HAT, a reworking of a French farce by Eugene Labiche and Marc Michel called *The Italian Straw Hat.* As the debut offering of Project 891, the classical wing of the Federal Theatre Project, Welles and producer Houseman wanted something that was bold and catchy. To accompany the play's racy dialogue, and such madcap antics as collapsing props and slapstick chases up and down the aisles, Welles encouraged Thomson to use a light, zany musical touch. Thomson responded with a lively musical patch-work quilt that included gypsy waltzes, turkey trots, bugle calls, piano rags, and a surrealistic mosaic of gestures à la Satie and Offenbach written by Thomson protégé PAUL BOWLES, but orchestrated by Thomson.

The ability to seamlessly weave musical materials from disparate sources into flowing unified wholes served Thomson well in his celebrated Americanesque scores for the prize-winning documentary films, *The River* (1937), *The Plow That Broke the Plains* (1938), and *Louisiana Story* (1948), for which he won a Pulitzer Prize. Thomson was also an incisive music journalist who served as the *New York Herald-Tribune's* music critic from 1940 to 1954. His criticism, much of it culled from his newspaper reviews, was anthologized in *The Musical Scene* (1945) and *The Art of Judging Music* (1948).

Welles and Thomson enjoyed one final collaboration in 1953, when the actor made his American television debut playing the title role in KING LEAR in a 73-minute production directed by PETER BROOK for the prestigious CBS Sunday afternoon arts show, *Omnibus.* It should be noted that Thomson also helped pave the way for THE CRADLE WILL ROCK by persuading Welles to let the then unknown MARC BLITZSTEIN audition the social musical for him in 1936.

References Tommasini, Anthony. *Virgil Thomson: Composer on the Aisle* (New York: Norton, 1998); ———. *Conversation Piece: Virgil Thomson* (New York: Bravo, 1961).
—C.B.

Three Cases of Murder
Wessex Associated Artists, 99 minutes, 1955. **Directors:** Wendy Toye, David Eady, and George More; **Producers:** Ian Dalrymple, Alexander Paal, and Hugh Perceval; **Screenplay:** Donald Wilson, Sidney Carroll, Ian Dalrymple, based on stories by Roderick Wilkinson, Brett Halliday, and W. Somerset Maugham; **Cinematographer:** Harry Fischbeck; **Editor:** Edward Dmytryk; **Cast:** Alan Badel (Mr. X), John Gregson (Edgar Curtain), Orson Welles (Lord Mountdrago), Elizabeth Sellars (Elizabeth Grange), Jack Lambert (Inspector Acheson)

In postwar Europe, the vogue for omnibus films included the box-office hits *Quartet* (1948) and *Trio* (1950). Curiously, *Three Cases of Murder,* produced in Britain by Ian Dalrymple for Associated Artists first opened in the United States because British distributors did not deem the trio of thrillers a strong draw. However, when U.S. response proved strong, the distributor, Warner Bros., opened the film in London.

Although the critics generally yawned in response to the anthology's first two episodes, the third, "Lord Mountdrago," created a buzz. Directed by George More O'Farrell, and based on a story by Somerset Maugham, the film features WELLES as a bombastic British foreign secretary who flays his enemies with a razor-sharp wit. One of his opponents is a young MP (Member of Parliament) from a Welsh mining town who pledges revenge. In describing the character, Maugham wrote: "He was a brilliant debater and his gift of repartee was celebrated. He had a fine presence: he was a tall, handsome man, rather bald and somewhat too stout, but this gave him solidity and an air of maturity that were of service to him." It was a part seemingly tailor-made for Welles.

The story takes a psychological turn when Mountdrago starts having nightmarish dreams in which he is humiliated by the young MP. On days following such dreams, the Welsh MP ridicules him in Parliament in a way suggesting that he knows exactly what Mountdrago has dreamt the night before. Thrown into a panic, Mountdrago wonders if he is going mad, or if he is suffering the pangs of a troubled conscience. Convinced that the young man is trying to drive him insane, Mountdrago plots to murder him. FRANK BRADY's assessment of Welles's

performance as "a study in caustic urbanity" tallied with the critics who repeatedly singled out Welles for praise.

In addition to Welles, the cast for the "Lord Mountdrago" episode of *Three Cases of Murder* included Helen Cherry, Alan Badel, Andre Morell, and Peter Burton.

—C.B.

Time Runs
(play, 1950) In 1950, WELLES accepted an invitation to produce an evening of theatrical divertissements for the Théâtre Edouard VII in Paris. For the second part af his omnibus program, which would be called THE BLESSED AND THE DAMNED, Welles hit upon the idea of modernizing the legend of Dr. Faustus by teasing out such hellish implications of the postwar period as the specter of the atomic bomb. While shrouding his stage in black velvet and suggesting a sense of claustrophobic paranoia italicized with an allusion to high prisonlike gates, Welles's design also offered a ray of hope—and, perhaps, heaven—via a patch of blue sky.

Welles used Christopher Marlowe's 1604 DOCTOR FAUSTUS as his basic template. He also pulled dialogue from Milton and Dante. Significantly, given his antipathy for most things German, and in particular that country's recent Nazi past, Welles completely shunned Goethe's take on the Faustian legend. To accent the 20th-century ambience, Welles called on jazz great DUKE ELLINGTON to provide original music. For a dash of exoticism, he hired a young unknown he had spotted singing up a storm in a Paris nitery, star-to-be EARTHA KITT. Welles assigned the alluring African-American diva the leading role of Faustus's beloved, Helen of Troy. HILTON EDWARDS, who had given Welles his first professional acting job at Dublin's GATE THEATRE in 1931, was cast as Mephistopheles, while Welles cast himself in the pivotal role of Dr. John Faustus.

Time Runs opened on Kitt, dressed as a student in sweater and slacks, who cautiously but curiously approaches a statue of Faustus (Welles). Slowly, the statue begins to move. Beckoning her to fully restore him to life with a kiss, she complies. In the ensuing psychological battle, the play's contemporary yet timeless concerns are punctuated by torch songs limned by Ellington and sung by Kitt. *Time Runs,* while reflecting Welles's preoccupation with the Faust story that first found theatrical form in PROJECT 891's production of *Doctor Faustus* in 1937, provided a lighter, livelier, up-to-the-minute contemporary take on the legend. In *Time Runs,* the struggle facing Dr. Faustus, essentially external rather than internal, is directed against the cataclysmic terrors of modernity.

When the six-week run in Paris expired, Welles extensively revised the show to tour Germany. Of the revisions, the most significant was the substitution of a condensed version of the first act of OSCAR WILDE's *THE IMPORTANCE OF BEING EARNEST* in place of the Welles satire on Hollywood called *THE UNTHINKING LOBSTER.* Significantly, *Time Runs* was retained. However, in the part of Mephistopheles, Hilton Edwards was replaced by his partner from the Gate Theatre, MICHEÁL MACLIAMMÓIR.

Presented in English, the two set-pieces of *The Blessed and the Damned* (i.e., *The Unthinking Lobster* and *Time Runs*) were synopsized bilingually in the program. The accompanying notes by Welles indicated that "The two plays were written to be performed together. They deal, respectively, with a lost soul and with an inspired one, and are intended to develop, in contrasting styles, contrasting ideas regarding the state of Grace and the state of damnation."

The production, which garnered raves, was lauded by *Le Monde* as "a stage masterpiece." Still, most Parisians faced difficulties with the often rapidly paced English dialogue, which along with the summer doldrums caused a drop-off at the box office. Still, Welles had created a splash. Further publicity came when news photos of Welles and Kitt snapped at trendy bistros such as Bricktop's began appearing in papers across Europe. In the words of FRANK BRADY, there was "the implication that the enticing Miss Kitt was not only his Trilby but also the new love of his life." In her autobiography, *Alone with Me,* Kitt waxed ecstatic about Welles: "Orson Welles really introduced me to a marvelous gourmet type of living. Him and Rubirosa. I tell you, I was absolutely spoiled by the best kind of men!"

—C.B.

Todd, Michael ("Mike") (Avram Goldenbogen) (1907–1958)

In 1945, when WELLES resurrected his script for a stage production of *AROUND THE WORLD IN 80 DAYS,* he approached Mike Todd to produce it on Broadway. Welles told PETER BOGDANOVICH that COLE PORTER had persuaded him to have Todd direct, because he was "such an inspired hustler." In fact, Todd, who was born on June 22, 1907, in Minneapolis, had become a successful Broadway producer after trying his hand at several different businesses. In 1937, he produced *Call Me Ziggy,* which closed after three performances, followed it with *The Man from Cairo,* which lasted 22 performances, and finally made it with *The Hot Mikado,* derived from the Gilbert and Sullivan operetta. After a few more shows, Todd produced *Star and Garter,* starring Gypsy Rose Lee, who also provided financing for the show, and *Something for the Boys,* which featured Ethel Merman singing Cole Porter songs. At the end of World War II, Todd had four plays running on Broadway, among them a highly praised *Hamlet,* which would have a run of 131 performances, and *The Would-Be Gentleman,* adapted from Molière. Because of his success he was a logical choice to produce Welles's *Around the World in 80 Days,* and he and Welles were also slated to produce BERTOLT BRECHT's *The Life of Galileo,* which had not been staged. Todd agreed to put up $40,000 for *Around the World in 80 Days,* but when the play went into rehearsals in Boston, he was impressed and appalled by the scale and cost of the production Welles was planning. Todd withdrew from the play as producer, but there is some disagreement about what happened. According to Todd, Welles's last-minute idea for including a spouting oil well on the stage indicated that Welles was "still ad-libbing the script," and Todd was unwilling to back a play without an established script. Welles stated that "when it became apparent that, among other things, he [Todd] was in no position to provide finances, I was forced to take over the responsibility of this myself." Brecht and CHARLES LAUGHTON, who was to play the title role in *The Life of Galileo,* still wanted Welles to work on the project, but Welles did not want to work with Todd, who was to be the producer. After some time had passed, Laughton wrote Welles an angry letter,

charging him with "procrastination." BARBARA
LEAMING, Welles's "official biographer," claims that
Laughton's charge is "unjust," considering the financial and personal sacrifices Welles made to free himself to do the project. Welles also told Bogdanovich
that ALEXANDER KORDA had sold the film rights to
Around the World in 80 Days to Mike Todd and
implied that some of the ideas for Todd's film were
taken from Welles's screenplay. Welles, who probably
resented the money that Todd made on the film,
quoted Toots Shor, one of Todd's friends, on Todd:
"Well, I don't know about Mike when he crashed,
but when he got *into* the plane, he was a son-of-a-
bitch."

Todd entered the film business in 1945, establishing Michael Todd Productions, but he went through
bankruptcy in 1949. In 1951, he and Lowell Thomas
formed Thomas–Todd Productions and got into the
wide-screen film business. He was a founder of Cinerama, but sold his shares to join with Joseph M.
Schenck and utilize Todd-AO, a 65mm wide-screen
process. *Oklahoma!* (1955), which Todd adapted from
the stage play, was a financial bonanza, surpassed only
by his *Around the World in 80 Days,* which made even
more money. In 1957, he married Elizabeth Taylor,
and a short year later died in the crash of his private
plane, which was ironically named "The Lucky Liz"
in her honor. He had been on his way to New York
to accept the "Showman of the Year" from the
National Association of Theater Managers.

Reference Cohn, Art. *The Nine Lives of Mike Todd*
(London: Hutchinson, 1958).

—T.L.E.

Toland, Gregg (1904–1948) The cinematographer who photographed CITIZEN KANE, Gregg
Toland, was born on May 29, 1904, in Charleston,
Illinois. He left school and went to Hollywood,
where he worked as an office boy at Twentieth Century–Fox at age 15. In 1920, he became an assistant
cameraman, serving his apprenticeship with the distinguished cameraman George Barnes on the films
that Barnes photographed for independent producer
Samuel Goldwyn. In 1929 and 1930, he rose to co-
cinematographer with Barnes on some early sound
films, such as *One Heavenly Night* (1930), directed by

George Fitzmaurice, who was noted for his visual
flare in directing pictures. Under Barnes's tutelage,
Toland learned fluid camera movement and impec-
cable lighting techniques.

When Barnes moved on to work at Warners and
other studios in 1931 (later earning an Academy
Award for Hitchcock's *Rebecca,* 1940), Toland was
promoted by Goldwyn to the post of full-fledged
director of photography; he remained under contract
to Goldwyn for the balance of his career. In 1931,
Toland photographed two more movies for Fitzmaurice, *The Devil to Pay* and *The Unholy Game.*

From the beginning of his career as a cinematographer, Toland was alert to the technical advances
introduced by other cameramen such as James Wong
Howe. For example, Howe was the cinematographer
on William K. Howard's *Transatlantic* (1931), in which
Edmund Lowe played a con man traveling on an
ocean liner. Howe created the claustrophobic feeling
of life aboard ship by insisting that the set designer
put muslin ceilings on the sets. Since motion pictures
were usually shot with all the big lights needed to
illuminate the set placed overhead, Howe had to
redesign the lighting on the sets to accommodate the
ceilings, placing the large lamps in front of the set
near the camera. Nearly a decade later, Toland and
WELLES implemented this technique on *Citizen Kane.*

Toland thrived while working for Goldwyn since
the independent producer encouraged Toland's penchant for technical innovation, which would not
have been the case if Toland had been employed by a
big studio such as Metro-Goldwyn-Mayer. He had
designed his own camera lenses and had a permanent
handpicked camera crew.

Toland worked on a wide variety of films, including the Eddie Cantor vehicle *The Kid from Spain*
(1932; his apprentice cameramen on that film was
FRED ZINNEMANN, who would one day direct Orson
Welles in *A MAN FOR ALL SEASONS*). In 1936, he photographed *The Road to Glory* for Howard Hawks; the
film was one of the better movies made about World
War I, with Warner Baxter playing a heroic French
officer blinded in battle. Both the direction and the
cinematography were lauded in reviews.

Toland made six films with William Wyler—one
of the most significant creative associations between

Welles with cinematographer Gregg Toland on the set of *Citizen Kane* *(National Film Society Archive)*

a director and a cameraman in cinema history. Their first collaboration was *These Three* (1936), an adaptation of the Lillian Hellman play *The Children's Hour* (1936). This was followed by *Dead End* (1937), based on the Sidney Kingsley play about juvenile delinquents growing up in the New York slums. Toland's expert cinematography is on view right from the start. Film historian Mike Cormack writes that Wyler and Toland would always discuss in detail each scene in a film, in order to determine how it could best be photographed, before going on the studio floor to shoot it. "When photographing a scene, Toland wanted to catch the mood," Wyler explained. "He and I would discuss a picture from beginning to end. The style of photography would vary" from one film to the next. Thus, in *Dead End* they often employed flat, harsh lighting: "We didn't try to make anybody look pretty." Furthermore, the action of the story takes place within the span of a single day. Hence the early scenes in the movie, which take place in day-

time, are photographed with bright lighting, while the later scenes, which take place in the evening, are photographed in a shadowy style. So, as Mike Cormack says, "As the plot darkens, so does the lighting. The darkest scenes are the narrative's most extreme and dangerous conflicts."

Toland made expert use of camera movement in *Dead End*. Since the film was derived from a play, Wyler told this writer in conversation, "I employed several long takes in the film, in order to allow the camera to move around and thus keep the film from looking static and stagey." The film's opening shot is an extraordinary example of a long take in which there is a great deal of adroit camera movement.

Toland's next film with Wyler was *Wuthering Heights* (1939), starring LAURENCE OLIVIER as Heathcliff and MERLE OBERON as Cathy, two doomed lovers. Toland establishes the movie's bleak, brooding atmosphere with the prologue that opens the film: It is a stormy winter night, and a lone traveler named Lockwood seeks refuge at a forbidding mansion known as Wuthering Heights (*wuthering* is an archaic term for stormy weather). There he meets Heathcliff, now an elderly man, and the rest of the inhabitants of the gloomy mansion, including Ellen Dean (Flora Robson), the aging housekeeper. The atmosphere of Wuthering Heights is dark and shadowy, a reflection of the brooding passions associated with the fierce love of Heathcliff and Cathy, which was spawned there. It is no surprise that Toland won an Oscar for his work on the film.

Toland actually volunteered to work on *Citizen Kane*. He explained to Welles that he had seen some of the productions Welles had directed for the FEDERAL THEATRE PROJECT in New York and was impressed by the fresh and imaginative way that Welles had staged the action. Accordingly, Welles arranged with Goldwyn to borrow Toland, his personal camera equipment, and his four-man camera crew, who had been working with him for 15 years, to shoot *Kane*. Welles told PETER BOGDANOVICH that Toland was the greatest gift that an inexperienced director could have: "I was calling for things only a beginner would have been ignorant enough to think anybody could ever do; and there he was, *doing* them." Toland wrote in *Popular Photography,* "Welles's use of the cinematographer as a real aid to him in telling the story, and his appreciation of the camera's story-telling potentialities helped me immeasurably. He was willing—and this is very rare in Hollywood—that I take weeks to achieve a desired photographic effect. The photographic approach to *Citizen Kane* was planned and considered long before the first camera turned." Altogether, Toland was on the film for six months, including pre-production and actual shooting. While preparing to photograph *Kane,* Toland compared notes about lighting the sets with cinematographer RUSSELL METTY, who would later photograph THE STRANGER and TOUCH OF EVIL for Welles. "Welles wanted to avoid the established Hollywood conventions, most of which are accepted by audiences because of their frequent use. And this frequent use of conventions is dictated by pressure of time and reluctance to deviate from the accepted."

In *Citizen Kane,* Toland, at Welles's instigation, perfected several inventive techniques, some of which he had experimented with before, to tell the story of newspaper publisher CHARLES FOSTER KANE. Welles did not want the studio administration to know that he and Toland were experimenting with unconventional techniques. So he reported that he was going to spend a few days shooting tests, starting on July 22, 1940. These "tests" continued until July 29, when the front office finally found out that actual shooting had commenced, prior to the official starting date of July 30; he was simply told to carry on.

On the first day of shooting that was done under the guise of tests, Welles and Toland began with a scene involving source lighting. This means that there is always an identifiable light source of the set, from which the light would ordinarily come in real life; e.g., a window in the daytime, a lamp at night. This makes the settings look more like real buildings, and not just movie sets.

The first scene Welles and Toland shot used source lighting to good advantage. The scene in question is set in a projection room where some reporters watch a newsreel about Kane in order to come to some understanding of the man and his life. After the film is over, the room is dimly lit by a ray of light coming from the projection booth, leaving the room in semi-darkness. This indicates that those present are still pretty much in the dark about what Kane was really like.

Kane's life is gradually depicted in the course of the film by a series of expertly edited flashbacks. Jerry, the intrepid reporter (WILLIAM ALLAND), interviews various people who knew Kane; and their recollections are presented in flashback. Hence Jerry must piece together the facts as they come to light. The newsreel at the beginning of the film, already mentioned, gives a brief summary of Kane's whole life to the viewer. Its purpose is to help the viewer situate the various flashbacks that occur throughout the film within the framework of Kane's entire life, as each of them occurs.

Another example of source lighting occurs in one of the flashbacks: In the scene in which Kane's second wife, Susan (DOROTHY COMINGORE), makes her operatic debut, Welles gives the filmgoer a sense of what a theatrical performance is like from the point of view of the performer. He photographs the footlights and spotlights from the point of view of Susan, who is onstage. This gives the viewer a sense of Susan's stage fright, as the stage lights mercilessly expose her as the mediocre opera singer she really is.

In the past, cinematographers had avoided shooting directly at light sources because it produced a glare that eclipsed the image photographed. Toland took advantage of a new technical advance whereby he coated the camera lens with a thin layer of magnesium fluoride, minimizing the glare of the lights shining onto it. "Our coated lens," writes Toland in *Popular Photography,* "permitted us to shoot directly into lights without anything like the dire results usually encountered."

Toland employed in *Kane* the kind of long takes that he had used in *Dead End.* "We arranged our action," he explains, "so as to avoid direct cuts, to permit panning or dollying from one angle to another whenever that type of camera action fitted the continuity."

In an early scene, young Charley Kane's mother, Mary (AGNES MOOREHEAD), negotiates a deal with the banker Mr. Thatcher (GEORGE COULOURIS) in the Kane's boardinghouse in Colorado: With Thatcher as his guardian, young Charlie will be given an education in New York appropriate to a young man who is the heir to a fortune. Mary and Thatcher are seated at a table in the foreground, while Charlie's father, Jim (Harry Shannon), paces in the background, uncertain about the agreement: "I don't see why we can't raise our own son just because we came into some money."

In the course of this extended take, Toland cleverly works his camera around the actors as it unobtrusively glides about the set, so that the pace of the action never falters. Toland employs the procedure known as "precutting the film inside the camera" by closing in at times for a close shot to emphasize a key gesture or to capture a significant facial expression, and then falling back for a medium shot as the action continues. Because Welles rarely opted to interrupt these unbroken takes by the insertion of other shots when the footage was finally cut together, he virtually eliminated the need for any editing in these particular scenes.

Welles and Toland utilized fluid camera movement throughout the film. There is, for example, the way that they photographed the NO TRESPASSING sign on the gate of Kane's estate, which appears both at the beginning and the end of the film. At the beginning, the camera climbs over the gate to which the sign is attached. The camera moves forward through a series of lap dissolves toward the forbidding castle at the top of the hill. This implies that we are going to be taken beyond the protective wall of privacy that Kane has built around himself, so that we can find out what he was really like. But this opening shot is reversed at the end of the film, so that we wind up outside the gate once more, looking at the same sign.

"We are back to square one," LAURA MULVEY comments. This signifies that we never did come to a deep understanding of the man, at least to the extent that we thought we would. In short, Welles implies that we never do get to know anyone the way that they know themselves.

Welles encouraged Toland to use deep-focus photography in a number of scenes. The deep-focus lens makes all the objects on the screen, both in the foreground and in the background, in sharp focus at all times. This gives a greater illusion of depth to the scene. As Toland points out, "By way of example, scenes which conventionally would require a shift from close-up to full shot were planned so that the action would take place simultaneously in extreme foreground and extreme background."

When Jerry interviews Susan Alexander Kane, she is a faded chanteuse singing torch songs in a shabby cabaret. This scene opens with an extraordinary example of deep-focus photography. The camera takes in a neon sign, EL RANCHO, on the roof of the squalid building. Then it photographs Susan from above, through a cracked skylight, as she sits at a table in a cheap café, drinking alone. This implies that we are looking down on her as someone who at this point in her life has sunk to a low state of drunken dissipation. Thus, shooting downward at characters from above diminishes them in stature.

In the course of her interview with Jerry, Susan recalls an episode, shown in flashback, in which the deep-focus lens is again used significantly. When Susan is taking a singing lesson, Kane enters the room from the background in center screen, and walks toward her in the foreground, thereby dominating the screen all the while. This signifies how he likewise dominates Susan.

As mentioned, Welles and Toland decided to have muslin ceilings on most of the sets. As Toland explained in *Popular Photography*:

"*Citizen Kane* sets have ceilings because we wanted reality, and we felt that it would be easier to believe a room was a room if its ceiling could be seen in the picture. Furthermore, lighting effects in unceilinged rooms generally are not realistic because the illumination comes from unnatural angles. We planned most of our camera setups to take advantage of the ceilings, in some cases even building the sets so as to permit shooting upward from floor level."

Toland often photographed Kane with low-angle shots—which would necessarily take in the ceiling. The purpose of the low-angle shots of Kane was that shooting upward at a character from below increases their stature, i.e., it makes the person look more imposing. Because Kane, who is a wealthy, influential man, is such an imposing figure, he is often photographed from a low angle, with the camera shooting upward at him. This means that we are looking up to him, as a person of wealth and prestige, as we see him towering over his associates.

The final innovative cinematic technique Toland used is the wide-angle lens, which he put to good purpose in the movie. The wide-angle lens can encompass a hugh setting in a single composition. Thus Welles and Toland often employ the wide-angle lens in the scenes set in Kane's cavernous mansion, since it can compress the entire expanse of a huge room in the mansion in a single shot. This helps to underscore the atmosphere of emptiness and loneliness that characterizes Kane's marriage to his second wife, Susan. "At Xanadu," JAMES NAREMORE comments, "rooms become so large that people shrink," as they are "terrifyingly dwarfed by their possessions."

Toland's brilliant achievements on *Citizen Kane* placed him at the head of his profession. Since he remained under contract to Samuel Goldwyn, he returned to the Goldwyn Studios after finishing *Kane* and made another film with William Wyler, *The Little Foxes* (1941), from the Lillian Hellman play. In *The Little Foxes,* Wyler and Toland employed the deep-focus photography he had perfected on *Kane.*

During World War II, Toland served as a lieutenant in the navy's photography unit and co-directed *December 7,* a war documentary (1943), with director John Ford, for whom Toland had photographed *The Grapes of Wrath* (1940) and *The Long Voyage Home* (1940). After the war, Toland was director of photography for the last time on a Wyler film, *The Best Years of Our Lives* (1946).

Toland made only three more films. *A Song Is Born* (1948) was one of his last pictures. It was a remake of *Ball of Fire* (1941), and was once again directed by Howard Hawks. Toland had also been the cameraman of *Ball of Fire,* as well as another Hawks movie, *The Road to Glory.* He died of a heart attack on September 28, 1948, at the age of 44. He once reflected, late in his career, that he felt miserable about the run-of-the-mill movies he had to photograph on assignment over the years. At such times, he says in PAULINE KAEL's *Citizen Kane Book,* he "felt like a whore"—because he was doing it for the money. But his professional association with Orson Welles was one of the legendary alliances of director and cinematographer in film history. "Photographing *Citizen Kane* was the most exciting pro-

fessional adventure of my career," he said with justly earned pride.

References Affron, Charles. *"The Best Years of Our Lives,"* in *International Dictionary of Films and Filmmakers: Films,* ed. Nicolet Elert and Aruna Vasudevan (Detroit: St. James Press, 1996), vol. 1, 104; Cormack, Mike. *Ideology and Cinematography in Hollywood, 1930–39; Dead End and Other Films* (New York: St. Martin's Press, 1994); Kael, Pauline. "Raising Kane," in *The Citizen Kane Book* (Boston: Little, Brown, 1971), 3–84; Mulvey, Laura. *Citizen Kane* (London: British Film Institute, 1992); Naremore, James. *The Magic World of Orson Welles* (Dallas, Tex.: Southern Methodist University Press, 1989); Phillips, Gene. "William Wyler," in *Exiles in Hollywood: Major European Film Directors in America* (Cranbury, N.J.: Associated University Presses, 1998), 59–100; Toland, Gregg. "How I Broke the Rules in *Citizen Kane,"* in *Perspectives on Citizen Kane,* ed. Ronald Gottesman (New York: G.K. Hall, 1996), 569–72; ———. "Realism for *Citizen Kane,"* *American Cinematographer* 22, no. 2 (February 1941): 54–55; Welles, Orson, and Peter Bogdanovich, *This Is Orson Welles* (New York: Da Capo, 1998).

—G.D.P.

Tomorrow Is Forever International Pictures, 105 minutes, 1946. **Director:** Irving Pichel; **Producer:** David Lewis; **Screenplay:** Lenore J. Coffee (from the novel by Gwen Bristow); **Cinematographer:** Joseph Valentine; **Editor:** Ernest Nims; **Music:** Max Steiner; **Cast:** Orson Welles (John A. McDonald/Erich Kessler), Claudette Colbert (Elizabeth Hamilton), George Brent (Lawrence Hamilton), Lucille Watson (Aunt Jessica), Richard Long (John Andrew Hamilton), and Natalie Wood (Margaret Ludwig)

In this adaptation of the 1943 novel by Gwen Bristow, WELLES plays a disfigured and crippled chemist presumed to have been killed in World War II. Twenty years later, Welles's protagonist returns home with a surgically altered face to find his wife (CLAUDETTE COLBERT) remarried. Bored during production since he was not directing and because of a lachrymose script that he dismissed as a "weepie," Welles resorted to pranks to help pass the time. Not surprisingly, his performance, according to most critics, was perfunctory. So, too, was the slow-moving film. Still, *Tomorrow Is Forever* found a sympathetic female audience as a "woman's picture." For Welles, the film served to keep him in front of the public. Also, Welles's impressive salary of $100,000 allowed him to perpetuate his lavish lifestyle and pursue personal projects.

—C.B.

Tone, Franchot (Stanislas Pascal Franchot Tone) (1905–1968)   Actor Franchot Tone, erstwhile friend of ORSON WELLES, sued him, apparently for unpaid wages for his appearance in *Mexican Melodrama,* another unrealized film project, which was begun in 1940 and reactivated in 1941 and 1942. Initially, Welles was to produce, direct, and co-star with DOLORES DEL RIO, but a year later Welles turned the directing over to NORMAN FOSTER. The contract, which was allegedly drawn up on December 26, 1941, presumably called for Tone to appear in the film for $75,000. However, according to CHARLES HIGHAM, by late 1945 only $10,000 had been paid. The suit was still pending in 1947, but within a year it was settled out of court. DAVID THOMSON has another theory about the suit, contending that it stemmed from rights that Tone might have had to Sherwood King's *If I Die Before I Wake,* the source for *THE LADY FROM SHANGHAI* (1948).

Born on February 27, 1905, the son of a wealthy industrialist, Franchot Tone first became interested in acting at Cornell University, where he was president of the Dramatic Club. After his stage debut in stock in 1927, he moved to the Broadway stage and then to films in the early 1930s. His first screen role was in *The Wiser Sex* (1932). He made seven films in 1933, including *Gabriel Over the White House.* Under contract to MGM, he made several films during the 1930s, three of which are noteworthy: *Mutiny on the Bounty* (Oscar nomination as best actor, 1935), *The Lives of a Bengal Lancer* (1935), *Three Comrades* (1938). He continued to make films during the 1940s, but tended to concentrate on the stage. In 1956, he was featured in Arthur Penn's *Mickey One,* and in 1965–66 he appeared in the *Ben Casey* television series. He died of cancer in 1968.

—T.L.E.

Too Much Johnson (film, 1938)   Although *CITIZEN KANE* would not appear until 1941, by the mid-1930s, WELLES's attention had increasingly been drawn to the movies. For example, in his 1936 FEDERAL THEATRE PROJECT production of *HORSE EATS HAT,* the influence of RENÉ CLAIR's exuberant silent film comedy *The Italian Straw Hat* (1927) was clear. Two years later, in the summer of 1938, in the midst of planning his theatrical adaptation of the 1894 W. S. Gillette comedy, *TOO MUCH JOHNSON,* Welles decided to add "filmmaker" to his list of impressive credentials. Indeed, his unique plan called for a multimedia production in which stage and screen segments would be seamlessly integrated to add spice to Gillette's venerable turn-of-the-last-century farce. Stylistically, Welles drew inspiration from the frenzied slapstick of Mack Sennett's Keystone Kops. There would be madcap chases, speeding cars, pratfalls, and acts of comic derring-do. In ballyhooing what was planned as the opening production of the MERCURY THEATRE's second season, Welles told the press: "The first [1894] production of *Too Much Johnson,* at the turn of the century, revolutionized American comedy because of its fast-paced performance, its irreverence, and its absolutely delightful zaniness." Welles, in turn, wanted to create his own revolution by blending film and theater into one organic whole.

The initial plan called for three film segments. The first film, about 20 minutes in length, would open the show, establish the characters, and set up the comic double-romance. Additional 10-minute film prologues would introduce the second and third acts. The screen-to-stage segues were designed to carry the narrative forward without a "break" in the action. The first film sequence, for example, was to end with one of the characters jumping onto a departing boat; then, without pause, the character, now "live," would be thrust onto the stage to begin the first theatrical scene. It was a bold vision requiring meticulous planning, an expanded budget for the cost of the film, and adequate rehearsal to ensure the smooth integration of the screen and stage elements. Unfortunately, *Too Much Johnson* was saddled with financial problems, lack of organization, and an overburdened Welles, whose already crammed schedule of radio and theatrical commitments was pushed beyond the pale by his involved, hands-on discovery of the magic of the movies.

Indeed, Welles's greatest problem in overseeing *Too Much Johnson* was that the production of the film took on a life of its own. In preparing for his new role as film director, Welles screened the Sennett classics *Love, Honor and Behave* and *The Lion and the Girl*. He also studied CHAPLIN's *The Kid* and *The Rink*. Harold Lloyd's *Professor Beware,* which had just opened in New York, was another touchstone, as was Lloyd's influential *Safety Last*. As a tyro film director, Welles adapted his own approach, patiently acting out bits of business in rehearsal, and then bellowing out further instructions as the camera rolled. His cast, drawn from the versatile Mercury Theatre company, included his wife, Virginia Welles, JOSEPH COTTEN, Arlene Francis, ERSKINE SANFORD, and RICHARD WILSON. There were also small parts for composer MARC BLITZSTEIN, producer JOHN HOUSEMAN, *New York Herald Tribune* drama critic HERBERT DRAKE, and a pert teenage actress, Judith Tuvim, who would later make her name as Judy Holliday. Welles himself stepped in for a brief scene as one of the Kops.

Welles hired Paul Dunbar, a young Pathe newsreel cameraman, as his cinematographer. Although Dunbar wanted to shoot in 35mm, the standard professional film format, Welles insisted that he use the amateur 16mm gauge to reduce the cost of raw or unexposed footage. To give the film the speeded-up jerkiness associated with silent film comedy, Welles had Dunbar "under-crank" to accelerate the action. Other silent era special effects included the use of an obvious miniature of the SS *Munificence,* which conveys the characters from New York to Havana. Not concerned with verisimilitude, Welles carted in potted palms to simulate the Cuban jungle. As a new student of Soviet director Vsevelod Pudovkin via his book *Film Acting,* which had just been published in English in 1937, Welles employed a bit of what Pudovkin called "creative anatomy." Simply put, when he needed a more ample bosom for a tight close-up of Arlene Francis's character hiding a photo of her lover in her cleavage, he had his secretary, AUGUSTA WEISSBERGER, and her generous natural endowment, stand in for Francis.

With opening night just a week away, and after 10 days of largely improvised shooting, Welles had a Moviola installed in his suite at the St. Regis Hotel, where he began the task of editing. Tied up by the editing process and rehearsals and broadcasts of FIRST PERSON SINGULAR, Welles made only occasional trips to the Stony Creek Summer Theatre in Connecticut to rehearse his cast. Another complication involved Paramount Studios, which informed Welles that it owned the screen rights to *Too Much Johnson,* and that if the play-film production reached Broadway, there might be substantial royalties to pay. The Mercury was also behind in its salary payments to many of its actors. Welles had also attempted to trim expenses by treating the shoot as a rehearsal for the play; Actors Equity intervened and declared that a film is a performance even if it is a component of the play. The upshot was that Mercury owed the cast and crew full union wages. Yet another hurdle involved the film laboratory, which wouldn't release some of the footage until all previous bills had been paid. The cost for explanatory intertitles between scenes was another unanticipated expense. As for music, Marc Blitzstein offered to improvise "live" behind the film in order to save the expense of adding a synchronized music track.

The final blow came when a 16mm projector was taken to the Stony Creek Summer Theatre. In a test run with some of the completed footage, it was discovered that the auditorium with its low ceiling would not accommodate the throw of the projector's image. At this point, with much of the film still far from completion, instead of moving to another theater, the film was dropped altogether. Thus, on opening night, Welles's grand multimedia design had been totally decimated. Welles, thoroughly embarrassed by the mess, stayed away from the opening. The play *sans* film version of *Too Much Johnson* ran a mercifully brief two weeks, August 16–29, 1938. It never opened on Broadway.

In spite of the failure, the film produced for *Too Much Johnson* is important for its contribution to the notion of "expanded theater." Most significantly, *Too Much Johnson* signals a discernible shift of Welles's focus from theater and radio to film—and to Hollywood. Indeed, *Too Much Johnson* is today best seen as a giant step in the education of Welles, an education that just two and a half years later would help give the world CITIZEN KANE.

As FRANK BRADY reports, the last known print of *Too Much Johnson* was accidentally burned in a fire in Welles's Spanish villa in the 1970s.

—C.B.

Too Much Johnson (play, 1938) To follow up the MERCURY THEATRE's smash 1937 debut season, Welles decided to open the troupe's second season with a unique mixed-media production of W. S. Gillette's 1894 comedy *Too Much Johnson*. A romp in the grand manner of comic operas and theatrical farces, the double love-story involved a rapid-fire series of romantic intrigues, mistaken identities, the switching of documents, and ever shifting alliances. One of the love stories featured JOSEPH COTTEN and Arlene Francis as passionate but adulterous lovers. The second story dealt with a sad young girl played by Virginia Welles, whose heartless father sends her to Cuba as a mail-order bride. The settings ranged from New York City to Cuba, from the hustle-bustle of big city life to the tropical exoticism of a Cuban sugar plantation.

Reducing the script to about an hour of stage time, Welles planned to supplement the live action with elaborate film segments in the manner of the manic chases of Mack Sennett's Keystone Kops. The first segment would open the show by introducing the central characters and establishing the nature of the serio-comic conflicts; the other segments would serve as prologues to the second and third acts. The three films were intended to seamlessly, and entertainingly, bridge the line of action from stage to screen. In the first film, intended to run about 20 minutes, the screen reveals a dashing Joseph Cotten on his way to an assignation with the young and lovely Arlene Francis. Suddenly, Francis's husband (Edgar Barrier) appears, and a chase ensues over New York rooftops and streets. Finally, to escape, Cotten jumps aboard a boat departing for Cuba. As the husband lunges after Cotten onscreen, he lands "live" onto the stage of the theater, thus starting the play.

No longer supported by the FEDERAL THEATRE PROJECT, Welles and his increasingly estranged business partner, producer JOHN HOUSEMAN, had difficulty raising funds. During the rehearsals for *Too Much Johnson* and the shooting of the accompanying film, Welles was distracted by directing and performing in a new half-hour radio dramatic series for CBS, FIRST PERSON SINGULAR, a summer replacement for the *Lux Radio Theatre*. Welles also became happily absorbed with his firsthand discovery of the magic of film, which distressed Houseman due to the show's limited budget. Indeed, Welles wound up spending the bulk of the limited production funds on the film. Given his increasing involvement with shooting and editing the film, which had taken on a life of its own, and his various radio commitments, Welles had little time to adequately rehearse the theatrical part of the show. To keep the project afloat, Welles, as he often did during the late 1930s, plowed a substantial part of his radio earnings into the production. Still, there were labor problems with Actors Equity, and other economic woes due largely to the escalating costs of the film. Finally, time and money ran out. When the play went into rehearsal at the Stony Creek Summer Theatre in Connecticut, it was discovered that the still roughly edited film segments could not be properly projected due to the theater's cramped dimensions. Thus, *Too Much Johnson* opened on August 16, 1938, as a strictly theatrical proposition. The theater's small size also limited some of the theatrical special effects that Welles had planned to use.

Given the last-minute gutting of the filmed segments, the pared-down nature of Welles's adaptation, and the overall lack of production polish, it isn't surprising that *Too Much Johnson* closed meekly after its two-week trial run on August 29, 1938. Houseman, who had not been involved in the play's rehearsals, judged the performance as "trivial, tedious and underrehearsed." The critics and audiences agreed. As for the director's reaction, FRANK BRADY reports that on opening night Welles sequestered himself in his hotel room, "despondent, filled with guilt and self-recrimination." *Too Much Johnson* never reached Broadway.

Still, *Too Much Johnson* remains an important landmark in Welles's career. Given a bit more time and money, the experimental multimedia *Too Much Johnson* might have turned out to be a widely influential theatrical innovation. In spite of its failure, *Too Much Johnson* still exerted an influence on those theater practitioners who like Welles sought a new and bold "expanded theatre."

Welles's absorption with the filmic aspects of *Too Much Johnson* is also significant in that it signals a shift in Welles's thinking beyond radio and theater to film—and to Hollywood. In retrospect, *Too Much Johnson* can be seen as an important phase of the gestational period that three years later would see the birth of Orson Welles—filmmaker extraordinaire.

—C.B.

Touch of Evil Universal-International. 93 minutes, 1958. **Director:** Orson Welles; **Producer:** Albert Zugsmith; **Assistant Directors:** Phil Bowles and Terry Nelson; **Screenplay:** Welles (from a previous script by Paul Monash; based on the novel, *Badge of Evil,* by Whit Masterson); **Cinematographer:** Russell Metty; **Art Directors:** Alexander Golitzen and Robert Clatworthy; **Music:** Henry Mancini; **Editors:** Virgil Vogel, Aaron Stell, and Edward Curtiss; **Cast:** Orson Welles (Hank Quinlan), Charlton Heston (Ramon Miguel "Mike" Vargas), Janet Leigh (Susan Vargas), Joseph Calleia (Pete Menzies), Akim Tamiroff ("Uncle Joe" Grandi), Valentin De Vargas (Pancho), Ray Collins (District Attorney Adair), Dennis Weaver (Motel Clerk), Joanna Moore (Marcia Linnekar), Mort Mills (Schwartz), Marlene Dietrich (Tanya), Victor Milan (Manolo Sanchez), Lalo Rios (Risto), Michael Sargent (Pretty Boy), Mercedes McCambridge (Gang Leader, the "Brunette"), Joseph Cotten (Coroner), Zsa Zsa Gabor (Madame of Strip Joint), Phil Harvey (Blaine), Joi Lansing (Zita), Harry Shannon (Police Chief Gould), Rusty Wescoatt (Casey), Gus Schilling (Eddie Farnham), Wayne Taylor (Gang Member), Ken Miller (Gang Member), Raymond Rodriguez (Gang Member), Arlene McQuade (Ginnie), Dominick Delgarde (Lackey), Joe Basulto (Delinquent), Jennie Dias (Jackie), Yolanda Bojorquez (Bobbie), Eleanor Dorado (Lia), John Dierkes (Plainclothes Cop)

Touch of Evil is now regarded by most film commentators as being, along with CITIZEN KANE, one of WELLES's transcendent masterpieces. This was not initially the case. Indeed, the film was released by Universal at the bottom end of a double bill in May 1958, because the studio was worried about how the public would respond to what Universal executives regarded as its fragmented and unconventional style. For Welles, who hadn't made a film in Hollywood for 10 years,

the utter lack of studio support was depressing. *Time* and *Newsweek,* the country's top national news weeklies, didn't even bother to review it. When it was covered, opinions varied. *Variety,* catty as ever, said: "Smacks of brilliance and ultimately flounders in it." *Films in Review* was absolutely severe: "Sums up all the negative characteristics which appeal to Welles. . . . He must return to the moral values of America if he is ever to be the artist he could be." On the plus side were writers such as Paul Beckley of the *New York Herald Tribune:* "A personal tour-de-force—Rembrandtesque." Still, denied any substantive promotional support from Universal, *Touch of Evil* received little press coverage. It wasn't a surprise, then, that the film flopped at the American box office.

In contrast, when *Touch of Evil* was released in Europe, it was hailed as a work of art. Helping heal the disappointment of the film's disastrous American showing, the European release was an auspicious moment for Welles. In large part, the enthusiastic European reception given *Touch of Evil* was a result of the then emerging *politique des auteur,* or auteur theory, which proposed the director as a film's central creative and organizing force. In late 1958, with the gathering force of *auteur* criticism about to spill out everywhere, and with Welles positioned by European critics as the "neglected" American director most in need of critical resuscitation, *Touch of Evil* became a cause célèbre. Although initially booked for a two-week run in Paris, due largely to the influence of the *auteur* critics of *Cahiers du Cinéma* and other influential film magazines, *Touch of Evil* played for an entire winter. *Touch of Evil* also won two top prizes at the Brussels Film Festival, for best film and best performance by an actor, both of which were awarded to Welles. With Welles's critical stock rising throughout Europe, *Touch of Evil* eventually acquired a cult following in the United States. When a longer 108-minute version of the film was released by Universal in 1978, the critical revision of *Touch of Evil* as an "official" screen classic was once again affirmed. Final certification of the film's masterwork status came with Walter Murch's much-heralded "director's cut" version of the Welles's classic of 1998.

With thematic and stylistic roots in the classic film noir of the 1940s, and based on the novel *Badge of*

Welles, Janet Leigh, and Akim Tamiroff in *Touch of Evil* (*National Film Society Archive*)

Evil by Whit Masterson, *Touch of Evil* is, in many ways, a dark and suspenseful pulp-fiction yarn. Significantly, its conventional melodramatic elements are transformed by Welles's narrative and cinematic flair into a singular work reflecting the director's thematic concerns with power, corruption, and betrayal. The story opens with film history's most famous tracking shot, which introduces us to Mexican narcotics agent Mike Vargas (CHARLTON HESTON), his new American wife, Susan (JANET LEIGH), a bomb-planting hoodlum working for Mexican druglord Uncle Joe Grandi, the seedy Mexican border town of LOS ROBLES, the ominous "touches of evil" that immediately establish the film's noirish atmospherics, and the shocking car bomb explosion that sets the film's action in motion.

At the center of the story is the obese, hulking, dissipated figure of Detective Hank Quinlan (Welles), who like the actor-director's CHARLES FOSTER KANE, is a demi-tragic, larger-than-life authority figure corrupted by power. Because the dynamiting assassination of the middle-aged American businessman Linnekar and his young blond girlfriend Zita took place on the American side of the U.S.–Mexican border, Quinlan and his trusted colleague Pete Menzies (Joseph Calleia) head up the investigation.

Although a motive for the murders hasn't been established, Vargas, fearing that Mexicans might be blamed (a credible assumption given the racial-nationalist tensions along the border), offers to help Quinlan. Vargas sends Susan to their Mexican hotel to wait. On her way back, she is cornered by a handsome young Mexican whom she calls Pedro (Valentin de Vargas), who takes her to meet Grandi (Akim Tamiroff). The local crime boss warns Susan that she had best persuade her husband to drop a drug case against one of Grandi's relatives in Mexico City. Not sensing the gravity of her situation, she laughs off the threat, suggesting that Grandi has seen too many gangster movies.

At the same time, Quinlan, Menzies, and Vargas begin their investigation at the strip club where Linnekar picked up Zita. Vargas, searching outside the club, is attacked with acid. Having missed his target, the hoodlum is chased by Vargas. Meanwhile, hearing the honky-tonk tinklings of a distant player piano, Quinlan follows the music to a run-down bordello, where he meets Tanya (MARLENE DIETRICH), an old flame. At first she doesn't recognize him. Welles, perhaps playing with Freud's notion of orality, has Quinlan munching on a candy bar, and Tanya puffing on a cigar. Finally recognizing the grotesque figure as Quinlan, she says: "You're a mess, honey."

Susan, now presumably safe in her hotel, undresses. Suddenly, a flashlight from a room in the building across the alley shines. Blinded and annoyed, Susan unscrews a light bulb and throws it defiantly at the voyeur, one of Grandi's thugs. When Vargas returns, Susan informs him that she is returning home until he finishes the investigation. Then, when a photo of Susan and Pancho is delivered by another of Grandi's minions, she vows to stay to support her husband. However, she insists on moving to a motel on the American side.

The action and suspense tighten as Welles cuts between Susan in her room at the Mirador Motel, and the apartment of Sanchez, a shoe clerk living with Marcia Linnekar (the daughter of the murdered man), whom Quinlan suspects of the bombing. As Quinlan bullies the hapless Sanchez trying to force a confession, Vargas's unease over the detective's investigative methods heightens. Vargas, excusing himself from the interrogation to wash his hands, knocks over a shoebox, sees that it is empty, and returns it to its original resting place. Wanting to check up on Susan, Vargas departs for a minute to call the motel. When he returns, Vargas learns that Menzies has found several sticks of dynamite in the shoebox that Vargas had seen empty just minutes previously. Vargas intimates that he knows that Quinlan and Menzies have framed Sanchez. Quinlan, clearly agitated at being "caught," blusters out of the apartment with Grandi in tow. In turn, Vargas leaves with Schwartz, a U.S. lawman sympathetic to the Mexican drug enforcer, to start building a case against Quinlan.

In the meantime, the conniving Grandi persuades Quinlan to set Vargas up by making it appear that his wife is a drug addict. Grandi's plot is activated by his gang of youthful thugs who terrorize Susan at the deserted Minador Motel, drug her, and leave her half naked in a run-down Mexican hotel, hoping that when she revives, she will think the worse. Grandi believes that the public embarrassment of Susan's addiction will cause Vargas to resign, thereby causing the dismissal of the Mexico City drug case against Grandi's relative.

Quinlan, although still projecting his tough guy persona, is beginning to fall apart with the realization that his reputation as a cop who always gets his man is on the verge of being destroyed by Vargas and Schwartz. Having fallen off the wagon, the now drunk Quinlan is found by the faithful Menzies. As they talk, Quinlan recalls his wife's murder by strangulation, and that he never caught the murderer. This exchange adds pathos to the compellingly detestable Quinlan. It also helps rationalize Quinlan's corrupt framing of suspects; in the 30 years since the unsolved mystery of his wife's murder, Quinlan has never allowed a case to go unsolved.

Vargas, unaware of Susan's plight, proves to his colleagues that Quinlan set up Sanchez with dynamite that the detective himself had bought. Without warning, a boozy Quinlan breaks into the meeting, accusing Vargas of using his position to procure drugs for his wife. Vargas, now in a panic over Susan, rushes to the Mirador, finds her missing, and races to town to find Grandi, whom he now realizes is in league with Quinlan. In the dingy hotel room where Susan lies drugged, Quinlan, now aware that Grandi might betray him, dons gloves and strangles the petty criminal. Later, when Susan awakes, her gaze fixes on the inert bulging eyes of the dead Grandi slumped over the bed frame just above her. As Vargas's car speeds down the street past her hotel, Susan's screams out the window go unheard.

Vargas, his anxiety now at fever pitch, bursts into Grandi's bar, tells the gang members that he's now a husband and not a cop, and demands to know of Susan's whereabouts. Upon learning that she's been arrested for Grandi's murder as well as for drug use, Vargas dashes to the jail to console her. Menzies, who now understands that he's been Quinlan's dupe, shows Vargas a cane that was found in Susan's hotel room. The cane belongs to Quinlan, who, years earlier, had been compelled to use it after being hobbled by having taken a bullet meant for Menzies. This poignant incident—the betrayal of one who has saved your life—typifies the Wellesian penchant for irony found throughout the film. Menzies, now utterly disgusted with himself and with Quinlan, offers to help Vargas trap Quinlan into a confession by wearing a wire connected to a tape recorder operated by Vargas. Fleshing Quinlan out of Tanya's brothel, Menzies sets up the confession as the partners walk through a nighttime maze of oil derricks towering above a polluted river. In one of the film's most gripping moments, when Quinlan discovers Menzies's betrayal, he opens fire on his old friend. Quinlan next prepares to gun down Vargas. However, in a final act of heroic atonement, the wounded Menzies shoots Quinlan. "That's the second bullet I've taken for you," Quinlan wheezes. The carcass of the corrupt cop then falls dead into the muck and slime of the sewage-clogged river.

When Welles was invited to consider directing *Touch of Evil,* it had been 10 years since he had last directed in Hollywood (see MACBETH, 1947). Initially, Welles was approached by producer ALBERT ZUGSMITH to portray Hank Quinlan. When Zugsmith told Charlton Heston, who had already signed to play Mike Vargas that Welles had also been hired, Heston, assuming that Welles would be directing as well as acting, expressed his delight. Although Zugsmith had not thought about using Welles as the film's director, the producer, anxious to keep his young leading man happy, offered Welles $125,000 to act and direct, and, if he choose, to also write the script.

Although Paul Monach had penned an adaptation of Whit Masterson's hard-boiled novel, Welles, who claimed never to have read *Badge of Evil,* came up with a highly revamped script and shooting style, which like LADY FROM SHANGHAI, was a radical departure from Hollywood's usual way of handling pulp material. As revealed in the now famous 1957 memo that Welles wrote to Universal's top brass pleading for restoration of his elaborate editing scheme, the same memo used by Walter Murch in his 1998 "restoration" of Welles's original version of the film, Welles envisioned *Touch of Evil* as a thematically and technically innovative work rather than a conventional "B" picture.

There are significant changes from the novel. For example, Welles switched the ethnicity of Vargas's wife from Mexican to high society Philadelphian, thus enabling him to explore racial tensions within the contexts of marriage as well as work. He also invented characters. He wrote Tanya, in part, for his friend Marlene Dietrich. Although appearing in only a few scenes, Tanya serves a Greek chorus–like function with her dry, detached observations. For example, when the drunk Quinlan implores, "Read my future," she responds, "You haven't got any." "Huh?" Quinlan asks, to which Tanya replies, "Your future's all used up. Why don't you go home?" In addition to foreshadowing Quinlan's fate, the intimacy between the former lovers suggests a once promising future that was ultimately wasted. The theme of unfulfilled promise is alluded to again at the end of the film when Tanya wistfully concludes: "He was some kind of man."

Welles created the part of the motel night clerk specifically for DENNIS WEAVER. An ardent fan of Weaver's Chester for the then top-rated *Gunsmoke* television show, Welles closed down the set for three days to focus exclusively on Weaver's scenes. In addition to Weaver's high-strung and creepy character's suggestion of sexual repression, Welles and Weaver forged a role that Alfred Hitchcock later expanded in the character of ANTHONY PERKINS's Norman Bates for *Psycho* (1960); for the same film, Hitchcock "borrowed" heavily from *Touch of Evil*'s sexually provocative Susan in fleshing out the pivotal role of Marion Crane. Significantly, the representations of sexual violation and perversion in the scene in which Susan is beset by the gang broke new ground in 1958 Hol-

Marlene Dietrich in *Touch of Evil* (*National Film Society Archive*)

lywood. Tom Conley, commenting on the same scene, notes: "Supine, heaving, self-fetishizing in the bondage of her corset, Suzy's pose epitomizes Hollywood's confabulation of desire, before the camera tears it to shreds through daring innuendo in the editing and framing. She is seen sliced up (across Venetian blinds), and is then subjected to a simulated gang-rape." In *Psycho,* Janet Leigh is again sliced and diced.

In one of his most memorable performances, a gargantuan 270-pound Welles added another 40 pounds of padding and makeup to accentuate the porcine dimensions of the corrupt Quinlan. Using a wide-angle lens to further italicize the grotesque parameters of his distended body, Welles brings a Shakespearean dimension to the star-crossed Quinlan recalling the decadence of the disgusting FALSTAFF of the second part of *Henry the Fourth.* Set against the obscene appearance of Quinlan is the virile and handsome Heston as Mike Vargas, the quintessence of the "good" which balances Quinlan's "evil." Playing with stereotypes, Welles had Heston darken his skin to a swarthy shade, thus reversing the convention of the white Anglo-Saxon Hollywood hero. Leigh, too, is effective in providing Susan with appropriate dramatic gravity. Most of the other characters, major and

minor, form, in the words of Howard H. Prouty, "a gallery of grotesques, quite unusual for an American film at that time, ranging from the merely eccentric to downright bizarre." Along with Dietrich and Weaver, the most prominent of these are Tamiroff's fumbling gangsterisms as Grandi, and Calleia's canine faithful and tick-nervous Menzies.

Welles took great care with the construction of the film's sound track. Individual voices and sounds are choreographed for maximum dramatic and atmospheric effect. The haunting sound of Henry Mancini's pianola theme signifying a nostalgic past where Tanya and Quinlan were lovers is especially poignant. The cacophonous din of the rock and roll piped into Susan's lonely room at the Mirador Motel is another telling musical-aural effect; it also serves to foreshadow the gang's onslaught. Welles pumps up important lines of dialogue in similar fashion. When Tanya offers her offhand and impromptu eulogy over Quinlan, her words—"Too bad. He was a great detective but a lousy cop"—sting like an icy stiletto. The most famous example of Welles's virtuosic handling of sound occurs at the end of the film, where the conversation between Quinlan and Menzies undergoes continuous permutation. There is the talk of the two men set against the percussive thumping of the motors of the oil wells. The sounds of the voices amplified by Vargas's recorder add to the mix. The texture thickens again when the voices transmitted by the recorder's speaker echo off the bridge. Indeed, it is the echo that alerts Quinlan to his betrayal by Menzies and Vargas's complicity. A few minutes later, when the tape is replayed, we hear Quinlan's admission of guilt as we see him taking his last breath.

Welles, hoping to reestablish himself in Hollywood with *Touch of Evil,* sailed through the scripting and shooting phases of the project. Indeed, the Universal brass were pleased with the rushes. Like all those who have championed the film, they were impressed with RUSSELL METTY's brilliant black-and-white cinematography, and the bravura uninterrupted opening boom shot that begins with a close-up of a bomb being placed in the trunk of a car, continues with the progress of the car from Mexico to the United States and the introduction of

Mike and Susan Vargas walking along the main street of Los Robles, and concludes with the concussive explosion that galvanizes the action.

As with most of his other films, problems started to arise with the onset of postproduction. Universal, thinking that it was getting a conventional albeit stylish thriller, was stunned by Welles's rough cut. Instead of a smooth, linear story, Welles had created a highly fragmented tale whose complex patterns of intercutting had been determined as much by the pulse of the visual rhythms as by the forward momentum of the narrative. His goal had been to construct an eerie and nightmarish atmosphere. In the midst of trying to negotiate the studio's demands for greater clarity, Welles departed for New York to guest on *The Steve Allen Show*. With Welles out of town, the studio took control of the film, bringing back Heston and Leigh to shoot pick-ups with another director to help clarify the continuity. Welles, heartbroken at what he deemed the undoing of his vision, wrote a 58-page memo specifying a long list of changes to the studio's version of the film. About 20 percent of these were heeded. For instance, a longer scene with Vargas and Weaver's night clerk was reinserted. Still, Welles was prevented from finishing the film on his own terms.

Part of the problem for Welles and the studio involved Universal's precarious financial position. Having lost faith in *Touch of Evil*'s earning potential, Universal was not in a position to allow Welles to protract the editing process. Furthermore, as Martin Fitzgerald suggests, "far from butchering *Touch of Evil,* Universal was probably more concerned with getting some money back from its investment." When the film was released in 1958, it was Welles's "short" 93-minute version. Ironically, when a "long" version was released some two decades later, it was mistakenly thought to be Welles's long-lost "uncut" rendition; actually, it was the studio's previously unreleased 1958 preview cut, the same print that had inspired Welles's 58-page memo.

Today, many Welles fans point to Walter Murch's 1998 "restored" version as the definite version of *Touch of Evil*. There is merit to the claim. In the most significant alteration conforming to Welles's memo, Murch was able to delete the opening credits from the virtuosic three-minute and 40-second boom shot

(Welles had wanted the credits placed at the film's end). Murch, again following Welles's memo, also changed the opening shot's musical underscoring. Instead of Henry Mancini's throbbing Latin jazz, we now hear various musical sources fade in and fade out as if we were walking past Los Robles's bars and honky-tonks along with Mike and Susan Vargas.

When released in 1958, *Touch of Evil* had an immediate impact on Jean-Luc Godard and FRANÇOIS TRUFFAUT, who would soon lead the French New Wave to international prominence. In turn, the work of Godard and Truffaut (and Welles) would directly influence the new wave of 1960s' film students whom critic Stanley Kauffmann aptly described as "The Film Generation." Walter Murch sums up the enduring legacy of Welles's 1958 incomplete and flawed and yet still vital masterpiece: "The impact, direct and indirect, of *Touch of Evil* continues: its fertile stylistic innovations and its themes of corruption and the crossing of actual and metaphoric borders, are reinterpreted every five years or so—the most recent examples being Curtis Hanson's *L.A. Confidential* and John Sayles's *Lone Star.*"

Simply put, *Touch of Evil* is a film classic.

References Conley, Tom. "Touch of Evil," *The International Dictionary of Films and Filmmakers: Volume I,* ed. Christopher Lyon (Chicago: St. James Press, 1984); Fitzgerald, Martin. *The Pocket Essential Orson Welles* (Harpenden, Herts, Eng.: Pocket Essentials, 2000); Murch, Walter. "Restoring the Touch of Genius to a Classic," *New York Times,* September 6, 1998; Prouty, Howard H. "Touch of Evil," *Magill's Survey of the Cinema,* Frank N. Magill, ed. (Englewood Cliffs, N.J.: Salem Press, 1980).

—C.B.

Towers, Harry Alan (1920–) During World War II, Harry Alan Towers, who was working for the British Broadcasting Corporation (BBC), was the producer of three radio series that featured ORSON WELLES: *THE BLACK MUSEUM, SHERLOCK HOLMES,* and *THE ADVENTURES OF HARRY LIME.* Towers, who hoped to capitalize on the enormous success of CAROL REED's *THE THIRD MAN* (1949), which featured Orson Welles as Harry Lime, got Welles in March 1951 to assume the role of Harry Lime and to write some of the 39 scripts for the show, which was later syndicated in the United States as *The Third Man: The Lives of Harry Lime*. Welles did the narration for *The Black Museum*, which consisted of cases taken from the files of Scotland Yard. For *Sherlock Holmes*, Welles appeared only in the final episode as Professor Moriarity. Welles participated in the three series to get money to finance his film OTHELLO. Towers also produced the 1972 film version of *Treasure Island* which starred Welles as Long John Silver.

Harry Alan Towers, who worked for the BBC during World War II, successfully negotiated a radio contract in 1947 between the BBC and NOËL COWARD, who had been decidedly cool to the idea of appearing on the radio. Towers was also the author, with Leslie Mitchell, of *The March of the Movies* (1947), and in 1949 published *Show Business: Stars of the World of Show Business*. After moving to the United States, he appeared in several films, among them *The Secret of Dorian Grey* (1970), *The Call of the Wild* (1972), and *Treasure Island* (1994). With Gregory Harrison, he made *Running Wild* (2001), a video-recording.

—T.L.E.

Trauner, Alexander (Alexandre) (1906–1994)

Alexander Trauner worked as art director of ORSON WELLES's *Cyrano*, one of his unrealized film projects, and on his OTHELLO (1952). Despite his financial problems on *Othello*, which frequently caused Welles to leave to get more money, Welles and Trauner planned to re-create the island of Cyprus on the Côte d'Azur. Trauner, however, was also able to improvise economically. According to CHARLES HIGHAM, Trauner, on location in Morocco and lacking the costumes due to arrive from Florence, "had other costumes made by obscure Jewish tailors working out of tiny shops in the Moroccan cities." Trauner also used a lavatory chain from a hotel to serve as the chain for Desdemona's ornate purse. Despite the problems, Trauner was impressed by Welles's artistic vision but concerned about what he regarded as his self-destructiveness: "When all goes well, he will find an excuse which will immediately throw everything he has done into question." Welles was also impressed with Trauner, whom he described to PETER BOGDANOVICH as a "man of great brilliance and acuity," a "wonderful art director and an

extraordinary fellow." In Paris, Welles and Trauner mapped out the production of *Cyrano,* which was to be done for ALEXANDER KORDA, but was finally scrapped. Trauner also prepared some production details for *The Thousand and One Nights* and *The Merchant of Venice,* also unrealized Welles film projects.

Alexander Trauner was born on August 3, 1906, in Budapest, but moved to Paris, where his paintings could be exhibited. He subsequently became the assistant to Lazare Meerosn, a critically acclaimed art director. After serving as an assistant art director during 1933–34, he became an art director for *Drôle de Drame/Bizarre Bizarre* (1937). When the Germans occupied France during World War II, the Jewish Trauner went into hiding, but he continued to work as an uncredited art director on such films as *Les Visiteurs du Soir/The Devil's Envoys* (1942) and *Les Enfants du Paradis/Children of Paradise* (1945). After the war, he served as art director for many American films, especially those with foreign settings. Some of his most well-known films are *Land of the Pharaohs* (1955), *Witness for the Prosecution* (1958), *The Apartment* (1960), *Irma la Douce* (1963), and *The Man Who Would Be King* (1975). There is a kind of ironic déjà vu in his last film, *Reunion* (1988), which is about a Jewish-American businessman who returns to Germany to find an Aryan friend from his boyhood; the film uses extensive flashbacks to show how anti-Semitism affects the friends.

—T.L.E.

Treasure Island (*La Isla Del Tesoro*)

Mass-films-Eguiluz-F.D.L.-CCC, 131 minutes, 1972. **Director:** John Hough; **Producer:** Harry Alan Towers; **Screenplay:** Wolf Mankowitz and O.W. Jeeves (Orson Welles), based on a novel by Robert Louis Stevenson; **Cinematographers:** Cecilio Paniagua and Ginger Gemell; **Editor:** Nicholas Wentworth; **Cast:** Orson Welles (Long John Silver), Kim Burfield (Jim Hawkins), Lionel Stander (Billy Bones), Walter Slezak (Squire Trelawney), Jean Lefebvre (Benn Gunn)

Treasure Island, Robert Louis Stevenson's classic 1883 adventure novel, is a boys' coming-of-age story relating the adventures of young Jim Hawkins and a group of pirates led by Long John Silver who are trying to locate an abandoned treasure trove. A peren-

Welles as Long John Silver and Kim Burfield as Jim
Hawkins in *Treasure Island (National Film Society Archive)*

nial favorite, the novel had been successfully adapted
to film in 1934 and 1950. Unfortunately, the 1972
British/French/German/Spanish version fell flat.
Halliwell's Film and Video Guide dismisses it as a "spir-
itless and characterless international remake with
poor acting, production, and dubbing." CHARLES
HIGHAM reports that Welles was shot only from the
waist up because "his leg was too fat to be bent double to allow for the attachment of a wooden leg."
Ironically, the film used a script worked up by Wolf
Mankowitz from a scenario written by Welles in the
mid-1960s, for what was to have been Welles's version of the Stevenson novel; in recognition of that
fact, the 1972 *Treasure Island* lists as co-screenwriter
one "O.W. Jeeves" (the great man himself, presumably seeking a degree of anonymity).

—C.B.

Trent's Last Case

Wilcox-Neagle/BL, 90 minutes,
1952. **Director:** Herbert Wilcox; **Producer:** Herbert
Wilcox; **Screenplay:** Pamela Wilcox Bower, based on the
novel by E.C. Bentley; **Cinematographer:** Max Greene;
Editor: Bill Lewthwaite; **Cast:** Margaret Lockwood
(Margaret Manderson), Michael Wilding (Philip Trent),
Orson Welles (Sigsbee Manderson), John McCallum (John
Marlowe), Miles Malleson (Burton Cupples)

Due largely to his early 1950s successes in two
prominent BBC radio dramas, THE ADVENTURES OF

HARRY LIME and THE BLACK MUSEUM, WELLES was
sought out for starring roles in three mid-1950s
British films, *Trent's Last Case,* THREE CASES OF
MURDER, and TROUBLE IN THE GLEN. The first of
these, *Trent's Last Case,* was based on the celebrated
1913 detective novel of the same title by E. C. Bentley. Bentley, weary of infallible sleuths like SHERLOCK
HOLMES, created in the figure of Philip Trent
(painter, crime reporter, and amateur detective), a
hero at once less reliable and therefore more believ-
able. The result was a new kind of detective fiction
strong on character development and style and, as
FRANK BRADY observes, tremendously appealing to
filmmakers. Agatha Christie judged Bentley's novel as
"one of the three best detective stories ever written."

The film centers on Sigsbee Manderson (Welles),
an industrial tycoon who is found dead at his country estate. It appears that he has committed suicide.
Trent (Michael Wilding), however, is suspicious,
believing that Manderson has been murdered. In the
course of his investigation, Trent meets the dead
man's secretary, whom he suspects of the crime, and
Manderson's seductive and poised widow with
whom he falls in love. The unexpected denouement
and plot twists were of the sort that had made British
films of the period so popular in the United States.

Because *Trent's Last Case* commences with the
death of Manderson, a plot turn reminiscent of CITI-
ZEN KANE, Welles appears only in flashbacks as the
different characters drudge up their recollections of
what happened during the night of the shooting.
Despite its deliberate pacing, audiences on both sides
of the Atlantic liked the film. So, too, did many of the
critics. The *New York Times* said: "Orson Welles makes
the best of his belated appearance. In new makeup—
aquiline nose, black homburg, graying hair—he is a
tough broody schemer, a composite of Machiavelli
and a Wall Street tycoon." *Variety* echoed the *Times,*
noting that "Orson Welles is every bit the villainous
and almost insane millionaire."

CHARLES HIGHAM points out that *Trent's Last Case*
also includes a private joke. In one of the film's flashbacks, Welles's treacherous millionaire speaks of having seen Welles's 1951 production of OTHELLO at the
St. James Theatre in London: "Ah, *Othello* . . . didn't
like the leading actor much but got a big kick out of

the play. Yessir, that Shakespeare knew something about human nature, didn't he?" The "leading actor," by the way, was Welles himself.

—C.B.

Trial, The (*Le Procès*) RKO, 118 minutes, 1963. **Director:** Orson Welles; **Producer:** Alexander and Michael Salkind; **Screenplay:** Welles (based on *The Trial* by Franz Kafka; **Cinematographer:** Edmond Richmond; **Editor:** Yvonne Martin; **Cast:** Jeanne Moreau (Miss Burstner), Akim Tamiroff (Bloch), Elsa Martinelli (Hilda), Romy Schneider (Leni), Anthony Perkins (Josef K), Orson Welles (Albert Hastler, Advocate), Arnold Foa (Inspector A), Suzanne Flon (Miss Pitt), Madeleine Robinson (Mrs. Grubach), William Kearns (Assistant Inspector 1), Jess Hahn (Assistant Inspector 2), Wolfgang Reichmann (Courtroom Guard), Maydra Shore (Irmie), Max Haufler (Uncle Max), William Chappell (Titorelli), Thomas Holtzmann (Bert, Law Student), Fernand Ledoux (Chief Clerk), Maurice Teynac (Deputy Manager), Michael Lonsdale (Priest), Max Buchsbaum (Examining Magistrate), Jean-Claude Remoulex (First Policeman), Raul Delfosse (Second Policeman), Karl Studer (Man in Leather)

ALEXANDER and Michael SALKIND, who had produced Abel Gance's THE BATTLE OF AUSTERLITZ (1960), in which WELLES had appeared, offered to finance a film for Welles. From the list of possible projects they offered him, Welles selected FRANZ KAFKA's *The Trial* as the most promising. Because of financial problems, the Salkinds could not get the film under way until 1962, when shooting began in Yugoslavia. When money problems resurfaced, the Salkinds wanted to halt production, but Welles kept the film moving by shifting the location from Yugoslavia to Paris, where he used the Gare d'Orsay, an empty train station. PETER COWIE believes the choice of Gare d'Orsay was "a stroke of genius. The monstrous perspectives, dwarfing the characters, the vistas of imprisoned glass, the iron stairways, and myriad corridors combine to form a symbolic background to the film that is an equivalent to the labyrinthine ways and mournful buildings of Prague." The set suggests the kind of totalitarian world that Kafka described in his novel. Because of the financial problems, Welles was forced to pay his actors and crew out of his own pocket.

Welles's film adaptation of Franz Kafka's *The Trial* begins with Welles's narration of a story that is depicted through the use of pin-screen pictures. In the story, which serves as prologue to the film, a man approaches a door, but is refused admission by a guard. Eventually, the man gives up all his possessions and grows childish in his old age. When he finally asks the guard why no one else has come to the door seeking admission, he is told that the door is intended only for him. Then the door is shut forever.

This prologue is followed by a close-up of a man's face as he lies in bed. The man, known only as "Josef K" (ANTHONY PERKINS), is surprised to see a man in his room since he maintains that the door was locked from the inside. The first of many such inexplicable events, the action suggests, in light of the dreamlike prologue and K's somnolent state, that what follows may be not only a nightmarish experience but also a real nightmare. Another man enters, and K identifies

Welles in *The Trial* (*National Film Society Archive*)

the two intruders as police. They tell K that he is under arrest and then proceed to try to extort K's shirts and belongings. Inexplicably, three men from K's office are now in K's room. K asks, "Who accuses me?" There is no answer, nor is his crime identified. As the police query K and search his room, they twist his answers and engage in a bizarre exchange about circular and oval shapes; he logically explains holes in the floor as the holes made when the former tenant, a dentist, installed a dental chair in the room. Logic, however, is not valued in this nightmare. K's innocent slip of the tongue (or perhaps his Freudian slip) when he refers to photography as pornography further implicates him to the police, who ask, "You're not going to be a troublemaker?" and "You're not claiming innocence?" The growing assumption is that K is indeed guilty until proven innocent, but proving oneself innocent is impossible, as K discovers. After telling K that he can go about his job, even though he is under arrest, the police leave.

After a brief talk with his landlady, Mrs. Grubach (Madelaine Robinson), about the morals of Miss Burstner (JEANNE MOREAU), K encounters Miss Burstner, who says she has had a "long, hard night." In response to his awkward advances she asks, "You're not getting any funny ideas, are you?" Of course he is, and he kisses her. After telling her about the police visit (they have also, again inexplicably, searched her room), he assures her of his innocence. She suggests that it is an elaborate prank, but the conversation soon involves philosophical questions about the nature of innocence and guilt. He admits that he has a history of feeling guilty and asks if anyone can be 100 percent innocent. Miss Burstner, who now appears to be concerned about becoming involved in his arrest, asks, "What's your problem?" She does not mean his arrest; she implies that he has some kind of character fault. She hopes "it's not political."

When K goes to work, the setting is reminiscent of Fritz Lang's *M,* a very expressionistic set of countless robotlike employees at their desks; its resemblance to a bureaucratic prison rather than an office suggests that the entire society is a prison. Soon after his arrival, his boss tells him that a young woman is there to see him. She is his cousin Irmie (Maydra Shore), but the suspicious boss implies that she is sex-

ually involved with him, and K guiltily sends her away. When he returns to his lodgings, he finds Miss Pittl (Suzanne Flon) pulling a heavy trunk that belongs to Miss Burstner. In response to his questions and offers of help, the woman asks, "Do you pretend to have nothing to do with it?" K, who has been unwilling to accept Miss Burstner's ouster and perhaps realizes that he was responsible for it, asks, "Why am I always in the wrong?" The answer is, "Examine your conscience."

K next appears at the opera, where he is told that he is to be questioned outside working hours and is given a map so that he can find the interrogation site. The two men who are to eventually kill K lurk in the shadows as K receives his instructions. While he wanders through a mazelike area, he encounters a large number of people who are wearing numbers—he cannot comprehend that they are just like him. Finally, he enters an almost empty room, where Hilda (ELSA MARTINELLI) directs him to an enormous courtroom that seems more like an auditorium. At this point, the long takes are replaced by quick cuts, which are maintained through the remainder of the film. K is reproached for being an hour late and asked if he is a house painter. His negative response is greeted with sarcastic laughter that suggests that none of his comments will be taken seriously. Furious and frustrated at his lack of control, K launches into a futile verbal attack on the system and suggests that the "Establishment" is behind his accusation. When his denunciation receives ambiguous applause, K leaves the room, dwarfed by a huge door. He then meets the two policemen who are now being savagely beaten by unidentified people because of their extortion of K. K does not want them punished, but his interference is futile, and so he is again responsible for others' misfortunes. Somehow, for surely the interrogation courtroom and K's office are not connected, K arrives at his office, where his Uncle Max (Max Haufler) confronts him about the arrest and worries about how the family will be affected. At the end of this brief conversation, hundreds of employees rise together to go home at the end of the day. (Obviously, the interrogations are not conducted outside working hours, or, in fact, time and space are so blurred that attempting to logically determine place and hour is impossible.) Max wants to help, but his efforts are futile and comic. At Max's suggestion, they try to get a computer to find out the nature of the charge, but the attempt fails—access is denied just as it was in the prologue. The second attempt involves getting the help of the Advocate (Orson Welles), who is not easily accessible because of the maze that his clients must negotiate in order to reach him and because he feigns illness or sleep when they arrive. Because the first plea is not read, the Advocate urges K to go directly to the third plea (what happened to the second one?). K leaves but not before he and Leni (ROMY SCHNEIDER), the Advocate's mistress, engage in sex on a floor strewn with books. Interrupted by the Advocate's call, K glimpses Bloch (AKIM TAMIROFF), who is what K will become. K then enters the empty interrogation courtroom, connected physically and metaphorically to the Advocate's rooms. When he looks at the books of the Examining Magistrate (Max Buchsbaum), he finds pornographic pictures instead of judicial material. K then encounters other accused people with blank, hopeless faces; but he still does not understand his kinship with them. Lost and confused, he wanders around a huge room until he gets directions to outside. There, dwarfed by enormous statues, he meets his young relative, who asks ironically, "Is everything under control?"

K next appears at the Advocate's, where he sees Lenie with Bloch, who is "one of the Advocate's best clients." Bloch, a pathetic figure, tells a secret to K: He has other advocates. Bloch further suggests K will be found guilty because of the "set of his lips," even though K's case is still at the "hopeful stage." K tells Bloch a secret in return: He is dismissing the Advocate. When he informs the Advocate of his decision, he is told that he is "like many others." To demonstrate K's sorry situation, he has Bloch brought to him. The Advocate proceeds to humiliate Bloch, who is forced to kiss the Advocate's hand. In disgust, K leaves.

Lenie then suggests K visit Titorelli (William Chappell), a painter who is supposedly influential with the judges he paints. Titorelli's "studio" is a kind of chicken coop with slats through which young girls, children of the court, stare. Titorelli asks which kind of acquittal K seeks: ostensible or indefinite (neither a real acquittal); a definite acquittal is not possible. A terrified K is pressured into buying pictures he does not want in order to escape from the painter and the girls. K's escape route takes him directly to a huge cathedral, where he sees other accused people. In the cathedral where he has taken refuge, a priest (Michael Lonsdale) tells him that his case is going badly (there is no trial) and that he "expects too much from women." The Advocate appears and tells him the story that is dramatized in the prologue, but this time K is superimposed on the illustration. When the Advocate repeats the words of the guard in the illustration ("And now I'm going to close it [the door]," the Advocate and the guard become one. As he flees, K meets the priest, who calls him his "son." The defiant K responds, "I am not your son."

K walks, but is quickly accosted by two burly men who escort him to what appears to be an abandoned rock quarry. K takes off his shirt, which is placed under his head as he reclines upon the rocks. When he is given a knife, he refuses to kill himself and tells them they will have to kill him. They climb up the side of the quarry and throw some dynamite into the quarry. K picks up the dynamite, and the next shot is of a mushroom-shaped cloud caused by the explosion. Some critics have interpreted the cloud as a reference to the atomic bomb dropped on Hiroshima, but Welles has denied that he intended to make the connection. Cowie comments on the end of the film: "The main impression is one of complete finality, catastrophe, waste, physical death."

Visually, the world of *The Trial* is like a nightmare with spatial dislocations and synthetic geography. One sequence involves K leaving the Gare D'Orsay in Paris, then walking on the steps of the Palazzo di Giustizia, filmed in Rome, to meet the waiting Irmie, walking together to a factory entrance that was filmed in Milan, and then returning alone to his apartment, which was shot in Zagreb. Like an expressionistic film, *The Trial* contains sets with painted shadows, claustrophobic rooms, huge statues that dwarf characters, strobe lighting, and an amazing collection of close-ups and shots taken from oblique angles.

The K in Kafka's novel may or, more probably, may not have been innocent. The K of Welles's film is never legally convicted of a crime, but there is much to imply that he is not "innocent." He enjoys exercising control at work, but, more important, he is obsessive about women. He confuses photography with pornography, takes a voyeuristic interest in Miss Burstner, and willingly yields to the blandishments of several women in the film. As the priest points out, "he expects too much from women." As appealing as the women may be, three women in the film are physically deformed: Irmie limps, Miss Pittl has a club foot, and the beautiful Leni has weblike fingers. All is not as it appears, and eroticism is mingled with physical decay that mirrors the emotional decay of the Nazi-like state. K himself admits feeling guilty, even as a child; and in the course of the film he is implicated in several events that adversely affect other people.

The film was well received in Europe and had its admirers. Cowie regards it as "Welles's finest film since *Kane*"; but, for the most part, British and American audiences and critics have been harsh in their judgments of *The Trial*, which in many ways is like CITIZEN KANE, TOUCH OF EVIL, and CHIMES AT MIDNIGHT in being almost pure Welles, without outside interference. CHARLES HIGHAM calls it "the stylistic antithesis of Kafka's great creation" and "the least successful of his directed films." Some of the criticism had to do with the casting of Anthony Perkins as K. BARBARA LEAMING quotes Welles on the subject: "I think everybody has an idea of K, as some kind of little *Woody Allen. That's* who they think K is. But it's very clearly stated in the book that he is a young executive on his way up." It was Perkins's aggressiveness that appealed to Welles, whose K does not meekly submit to his persecutors, but who defies them.

—T.L.E.

Trilby (play, 1934) In July 1934, a 19-year-old WELLES made his debut as a theater director of note thanks to a production of *Trilby*, an adaptation of the popular 1894 novel by George Du Maurier, produced for the WOODSTOCK DRAMA FESTIVAL, in Illinois. The novel focuses on Trilby O'Ferrall, a Parisian artist's model, who is loved by three English arts students. When her engagement to one of them, William Bagot, nicknamed Little Billee, is broken off, Trilby falls under the spell of the sinister Svengali, a Hungarian musician who trains her voice through hypnosis and catapults her to stardom as a singer. The pair travel across Europe on acclaimed concert tours, Trilby as La Svengali, the celebrated singer, and Svengali, as the orchestra conductor who commands the details of each performance. When the domineering Svengali falls ill and dies of heart failure, his spell over Trilby is broken, and she loses her voice. Trilby then becomes sick and soon dies. Du Maurier's story of Trilby's mesmeric domination by Svengali soon became the stuff of popular mythology and language. Indeed, dictionaries now routinely include "Svengali" as a term indicating a person who completely dominates another, usually with selfish or evil motives, after the manipulative hypnotist of the same name in the novel *Trilby.*

Although he had directed student plays at the Todd School, Welles's direction of *Trilby* for the Woodstock Drama Festival is indicative of his own Svengali-like ambition to control and expand the parameters of his theatrical career. Welles, while using Todd students for extras and crew, now had seasoned professionals at his command. For the title role of Trilby, Welles, who had assumed the role of Woodstock's casting director, hired Louise Prussing, a Chicagoan with four years experience on the London stage, and a featured role opposite Paul Muni in the recent Broadway hit *Counselor at Law.* MICHEÁL MACLIAMMÓIR and HILTON EDWARDS, his former employers from Dublin's GATE THEATRE, whom he had convinced to come to Woodstock, were respectively cast as Little Billee and Taffy. For the part of Angele, he selected a bright 18-year-old blond beauty, Virginia Nicholson, who would soon become the first Mrs. Orson Welles. In the pivotal role of Svengali, Welles, aware that many famous actors had first made their names in the part, cast himself. Modeling his performance after that of JOHN BARRYMORE in the 1931 Hollywood film adaptation, Welles added Dracula-esque fangs and a pallid complexion to intensify the aura of evil. He also bulked up his nose, as he did in virtually all his theater and film portrayals of older, powerful men. As FRANK BRADY explains: "Orson felt that his short, somewhat puglike nose was attractive enough to be acceptable for his off-the-stage appearance, but for the theater he thought his nose was far too undramatic and immature. Since the nose is the most prominent feature of the face, the ideal theatrical proboscis, in his opinion, was one that could be seen, in perfect outline, from the last seat in the balcony, a John Barrymore nose that compelled notice, produced admiration, perhaps even awe, and might on occasion even strike terror in the hearts of the audience." In his Welles biography, ANDRÉ BAZIN put it this way: "For Welles to act without a fake nose was a little like acting naked in front of the footlights."

Welles's direction, given his inexperience, was surprisingly subtle. Sensitive to the challenges of his actors, the pros as well as the amateurs, he not only directed the action but also helped his players understand the motivations of their characters. When *Trilby* opened on July 12, 1934, to a supportive crowd of Woodstock locals, relatives, and friends of the cast, and prominent Chicago patrons, the press was, though at times perplexed, nonetheless enthusiastic. Charles Collins of the *Chicago Tribune* noted Welles's "lank, oily whiskers and Semitic nose" but concluded that Welles was a youth "with a strong promise of a brilliant future." Lloyd Lewis of the *Chicago Daily News* thought that Welles's Svengali looked like "a composite photograph of a hoot owl, Abe Lincoln, Ben Hecht and John Brown of Osawatomie" but was so powerful that one could only "quail and shiver." In general, it seems that, aside from the disparaging reminiscences of MacLiammóir voiced years later, *Trilby* was a happy show whose cast and crew had genuinely enjoyed working with the tyro director. For Welles, given the positive responses by audiences and critics, *Trilby* provided positive affirmation of his acting as well as directing talents. Indeed, after the first reviews, a trip to the Woodstock Drama Festival became a vogue for theater and arts lovers from Chicago and the surrounding area. In just two years, Welles—the director—would take New York by storm with his audacious direction of the infamous "voodoo" *MACBETH.*

—C.B.

Trouble in the Glen Wilcox-Neagle/Republic, 91 minutes, 1954. **Director:** Herbert Wilcox; **Producers:** Herbert J. Yates and Herbert Wilcox; **Screenplay:** Frank S. Nugent, based on a story by Maurice Walsh; **Cinematographer:** Max Greene; **Editor:** Reginald Beck; **Cast:** Orson Welles (Sanin Cejadory), Victor McLaglen (Parlan), Forrest Tucker (Maj. Lance Lansing), Margaret Lockwood (Marissa Mengues)

In 1954, WELLES, again strapped for cash, agreed to reunite with producer-director Herbert Wilcox and actress Margaret Lockwood with whom he had worked in 1952 on *TRENT'S LAST CASE.* The new project, situated in the Scottish Highlands and shot in color, was adapted by screenwriter Frank S. Nugent from a novel by Maurice Walsh, who had teamed in similar fashion for *The Quiet Man,* the classic 1952 romantic comedy directed by John Ford. Here, the comedic plot centered on an Argentinean millionaire (Welles) who returns to the Scottish estate of his grandfather to take up residence in the ancestral castle with his spirited daughter (Lockwood). When the new laird dismisses one of his servants for having insulted him on a fishing trip, a feud with the townspeople erupts, a tiff exacerbated when the tycoon closes off the main road running across his land. Into the fray enters an American ex-paratrooper (Forrest Tucker), who is in Scotland to visit his 11-year-old daughter, a victim of polio who has been adopted by a local couple. In the meantime, the ex-soldier and the millionaire's daughter, after an initial spat, fall in love. In a concluding party scene celebrating the couple's engagement and community solidarity, everyone beams, even the laird, a sunny denouement standing in stark contrast to the grisly demises usually meted out to Welles's bullying movie plutocrats.

FRANK BRADY, in his assessment of the heavy-handed Celtic comedy, concludes: "Not even Orson, despite a ludicrously tartaned appearance—smoking a cigar, dressed in a pleated kilt, with a white fur sporran dangling in front of his crotch, his elephantine legs swathed in plaid stockings—could engender any critical hilarity." Still, his performance was judged "eloquent" by the *Los Angeles Examiner,* "effective" by the *New York Herald Tribune,* and "one of the best things in the picture" by *Variety.*

Trouble in the Glen also featured Victor McLaglen, John McCallum, Eddie Byren, Archie Duncan, and Ann Gudrun.

—C.B.

Truffaut, François (1932–1984) The pioneering French New Wave director François Truffaut was an early advocate of the cinema of ORSON WELLES and wrote a lengthy tribute to Welles that was published as the "Foreword" of ANDRÉ BAZIN's study, *Orson Welles: A Critical View,* published by Les Editions du Cerf in 1972. Truffaut's own book, *The Films of My Life,* published in English by Simon & Schuster in 1978, includes a section on Welles that features Truffaut's enthusiastic treatments of CITIZEN KANE, MR. ARKADIN, and TOUCH OF EVIL.

Truffaut was born in Paris on February 6, 1932, to Janine de Monferrand, an unwed mother, and legally adopted by Roland Truffaut the following October. He was an only child, and, as biographers Antoine de Becque and Serge Toubiana have observed, an unwanted one, taken, at the age of three, to the home of his maternal grandparents, with whom he lived until his grandmother's death, at which time he returned to live with his parents. After attending the Lycée Rollin, he organized a film club, the Cercle Cinémane (the Movie Mania Circle) in the late 1940s. The critic André Bazin hired Truffaut as his personal secretary, a job that enabled him to live independently of his parents. In October 1950, Truffaut enlisted in the army, but deserted on the eve of his pending departure to French Indochina. As a consequence, he was incarcerated and imprisoned. Released from the service in February 1952, he was taken in by the Bazin family and began writing articles for Bazin's journal, *Cahiers du cinéma,* founded in April 1951.

By 1957, Truffaut had made two short films, *Une Visite* (1955) and *Les Mistons* (1957) but his "breakthrough" year was 1959, when he directed his first feature film, *Les Quatre Cents Coups* (*The 400 Blows*), an astonishingly inventive picture that helped to launch the French New Wave, which was soon followed by two more films that quickly consolidated his growing international reputation—*Tirez sur le pianiste* (*Shoot the Piano Player,* 1960) and *Jules et Jim*

(*Jules and Jim,* 1961), the latter adapted from the novel by Henri-Pierre Roché. Though he enjoyed a productive and distinguished career, Truffaut died young at the age of 52 of an incurable brain tumor in Paris on October 21, 1984. His many awards include best director at the Cannes Film Festival for *The 400 Blows,* the Prix Louis Delluc, and an Academy Award for best foreign language film for *La Nuit américaine* (*Day for Night,* 1973).

—J.M.W. and J.C.T.

Tsar Paul (play, 1934) The production of *Tsar Paul* by Russian author Dmitri Mereshkovsky (1865–1941) was included in the 1934 summer repertory of the WOODSTOCK DRAMA FESTIVAL as a star vehicle for HILTON EDWARDS, who along with MICHEÁL MACLIAMMÓIR, had journeyed from Dublin's GATE THEATRE to the American heartland to work with their young protégé, WELLES. It also marked the American premiere of the historic drama by Merezhkovsky, a White Russian who had fled the Soviet Union in 1920. Directed by Edwards and showcasing him in the lead role as the mad Russian despot, the production also featured MacLiammóir as Tsarevich, Welles as Count Pahlen, and Virginia Nicholson as Elizabeth. The performance earned good notices all the way around. However, while the critics had been kind to Welles's idiosyncratic Svengali in *TRILBY* and Claudius in *HAMLET,* the two other plays in the festival's basic repertory, they especially praised his Lord Pahlen.

Charles Collins of the *Chicago Tribune* was among those waxing ecstatic: "The surprise of the performance is Orson Welles as Pahlen. Mr. Welles hides his 19-year-old face behind make-up that is a cross between the Saracen Saladin and General Pershing, a swarthy, weather-tanned face of sixty, military, stern, zealously patriotic. Restrained within the monosyllabic nature of a soldier, Mr. Welles is an exceedingly good actor. The overboyish exuberance which made him caricature Svengali and the Danish king, is withheld here by Pahlen's self-discipline. Mr. Welles has, for the moment at least, quit trying to scare his audience to death, and is the artist, making Pahlen come alive by thinking and moving as Pahlen would think and move. Welles catches the chained fervor of

Pahlen so perfectly." Part of the credit should also have gone to the director, Hilton Edwards.

The critical raves underscore a fascinating point made by MacLiammóir. It was the Irish actor's contention that if early on Welles had submitted himself to strong directors like Edwards, he might have turned out to be a more nuanced actor. Combining acting and directing in the same production was not something MacLiammóir believed healthy for Welles's artistic development. However, as SIMON CALLOW points out, cutting back to just acting was a proposition that the ambitious Welles could never accept. Still, it seems clear, given the evidence of the Woodstock Drama Festival, that some of his best early acting work took place under the direction of others. "His Pahlen," in Callow's words, "is a glimpse of the different sort of actor that he might have been."

—C.B.

Twelfth Night (film, 1933) *Twelfth Night* was shot with a motion picture camera loaned to WELLES by ROGER HILL, head of the Todd School and Welles's lifelong friend. The little film, shot in the amateur 16mm film gauge, was made to document a highly edited Todd School production of the play codirected by a teenaged Welles and Hill for presentation at the Chicago Drama Festival. Its importance is that it marks Welles's first attempt to conjure up a dramatic experience through the medium of the motion picture. It also provides a record of Welles's imaginative approach to the play, which featured a twelve-foot-high book with pages that turned as each new scene was introduced. Welles's goal was to help his audience understand that drama springs to life from the printed word, and that the two media, literature and theater, are therefore inextricably bound. It was a ploy that had the added benefit of promoting the forthcoming publication of a lavishly illustrated prompt book for *Twelfth Night* by Welles and Hill under the banner, *EVERYBODY'S SHAKESPEARE.*

FRANK BRADY, on the basis of a screening of the film provided by Roger Hill, describes *Twelfth Night* as "perfectly preserved with rich color and quite professionally focused but without any camera movement, or pronounced flourishes or angles. It was

simply shot from one point of view, perhaps from the middle of the tenth row of the theatre: an amateur recording of the play on film rather than a piece of cinema."

In 1933, when *Twelfth Night* was screened for audiences, it was accompanied by a phonograph record with a narration that has been especially prepared by Welles.

—C.B.

Twentieth Century (television, 1955) Closely following the classic 1932 BEN HECHT–Charles MacArthur backstage comedy, the 1955 adaptation of *Twentieth Century* centers on the flamboyant theater producer Oscar Jaffe (WELLES), who is desperately seeking a hit to recoup his fortune and reputation. Ensconced in a suite aboard the crack cross-country passenger train, the Twentieth Century Limited, Jaffe is hoping to sign fading screen star Lily Garland (Betty Grable) to play Mary Magdalene for a new production of *The Passion Play*. Jaffe is also trying to elude his creditors. In the process, the Hecht-MacArthur escapade treats us to an ongoing battle-of-the-sexes played against a nonstop argument dealing with the relative merits of theater (defended by Jaffe) versus the movies (defended by Lily). In 1932, the smash Broadway hit was made into a 1934 movie blockbuster, also *Twentieth Century,* which starred Welles's old friend JOHN BARRYMORE as Jaffe, and CAROLE LOMBARD as Lily. The spirited 1955 Welles-Grable television adaptation was broadcast by CBS Television in 1955.

—C.B.

Tynan, Kenneth (Peacock) (1927–1980) Called by *New York Times* theater critic Benedict Nightingale "the *enfant terrible* of London literary journalism," Kenneth Tynan began his journalistic career with *The Spectator* in 1951, then became "the bravura theatre critic" of *The Evening Standard* and, finally, of *The Observer.* In 1950 ORSON WELLES met the young Kenneth Tynan while touring Britain and generously wrote an introduction for *He That Plays the King,* Tynan's first book of collected criticism. Tynan returned the favor in 1951 by describing Welles's OTHELLO as "Citizen Coon" in *The Evening*

Standard, stating that Welles had "the courage of his restrictions." When Tynan later interviewed Welles for *Playboy* and *Show* magazine, however, Welles got his revenge by telling lies that Tynan failed to check against the facts. CHARLES HIGHAM summarized the inaccuracies: "Welles told Tynan that he was from unmixed English colonial stock, when in fact his family had both Welsh and French elements; that his father was born in Virginia and moved to Wisconsin because he owned two factories there, when in fact he was the son of an obscure Missouri railroad clerk." Moreover, Welles claimed that "he owed his name to a Chicago businessman, when in fact he owed it to his district attorney great-grandfather, Orson Sherman Head" and inaccurately claimed to be related to Under Secretary of State Sumner Welles and to Adlai Stevenson. But Tynan was extravagant in his praise of *MOBY DICK,* which he claimed was "a sustained assault on the senses which dwarfs anything London has seen since, perhaps, the Great Fire." *The Times* reviewer was more subdued about this "madly impossible stage representation."

Born in 1927, Kenneth Peacock Tynan was the illegitimate son of Rose Tynan of Birmingham and Sir Peter Peacock, a businessman who had a proper family in Warrington, where he served six terms as mayor, according to *The Life of Kenneth Tynan* (1988), written by his widow, Kathleen Tynan. "In any real sense of the word," Tynan once remarked, "I was born at Oxford," where he reinvented himself as a notorious dandy, given to wearing velvet collars. Tynan's room at Magdalen College was above the room where OSCAR WILDE had once lived, appropriate, perhaps, since Tynan attempted to top Wilde with his own flamboyance. "Have a care with that trunk, my man," he once told his Oxford college porter. "It is freighted with gold shirts." The shirts were outrageously coordinated with his purple doeskin suit. By the time John Osborne, George Devine, and TONY RICHARDSON revolutionized postwar British theater at the Royal Court, Tynan was on the cultural scene, though Richardson claimed that Tynan "had no effect whatsoever on the fortunes of *Look Back in Anger,*" Osborne's defining play. But Tynan had called Osborne's *Anger* "the best young play of its decade," and his influence was undeniable, as he was later to become literary manager of Britain's National Theatre, a position he held from 1963 until 1973. And his wit was remarkable: "What, when drunk, one sees in other women," Tynan once quipped, "one sees in [Greta] Garbo sober." He entitled his profile of Roman Polanski "Magnetic Pole." Tynan once described himself as a "literary sprinter."

Tynan was the author of three plays, the most notorious being the farcical sex review *Oh! Calcutta,* and of eight books, notably *Tynan Right & Left: Plays, Films, People, Places & Events* (1967), *The Sound of Two Hands Clapping* (1975), and *Show People: Profiles in Entertainment* (1979), a collection of pieces originally published in *The New Yorker.* Julian Barnes of *The Observer* described Tynan as "a glittering profiler," as well as a "consistently serious libertarian." Tynan died of pulmonary emphysema at the age of 53 on July 26, 1980, in Santa Monica, California. For the BBC2 tribute *Reputations* (1982), playwright Tom Stoppard paid Tynan the highest compliment when asked what Tynan had contributed to British theater by answering "He made it worthwhile trying to be good."

References Lahr, John. *The Diaries of Kenneth Tynan* (New York: Bloomsbury, 2001); Tynan, Kathleen. *The Life of Kenneth Tynan* (London: Phoenix, 1987).

—J.M.W.

Una su tredici (a.k.a. *12 + 1,* or *Twelve + One Chairs*) COFCICEF, 95 minutes, 1970. **Director:** Nicholas Gessner; **Producer:** Claude Giroux; **Screenplay:** Mino Guirrini, Marino Onorati, Marc Beham (and, uncredited, Orson Welles, who wrote his own scene); **Cinematographer:** Giuseppi Ruzzolini; **Cast:** Orson Welles (Markan), Vittorio Gassmann, Sharon Tate, Terry Thomas, Mylene Demongeot

According to BOGDANOVICH and ROSENBAUM, ORSON WELLES makes a brief appearance in this film to perform some magic. The script was adapted from a Russian folktale about a wealthy matron who claims on her deathbed that she has hidden jewels in the upholstery of one of 12 chairs that are no longer in her possession. The fable was the same source that Mel Brooks used in his *The Twelve Chairs,* also released in 1970. Gessner's film featured Sharon Tate's last role, shot so as to disguise her pregnancy, and released after her death in 1969.

—T.L.E. and J.M.W.

Unthinking Lobster, The (play, 1950) This unusually titled one-act play was written by WELLES to be included in the evening of theatrical divertissements called *THE BLESSED AND THE DAMNED,* which was staged at the Théâtre Edouard VII in Paris, in July 1950. Like his radio play, *I Lost My Girlish Laughter,* produced in 1939 as an episode for THE CAMPBELL PLAYHOUSE, Welles took on a familiar target, Hollywood moguls. Here, however, Welles's lampoon had the advantage of incorporating the author's own stormy experiences with Hollywood's hierarchy. There's also a topical element in that *The Unthinking Lobster* specifically spoofs blockbusters like Cecil B. DeMille's *Samson and Delilah* (1949) and other overstuffed biblical epics then playing to packed cinemas around the world.

Welles, who must have been aware that he was likely pouring gasoline on his already incendiary ties to Hollywood, carried on, perhaps convinced that word of a one-act play produced in Paris would never be picked up by the philistines of the movie colony on the other side of the world. Therefore, his satiric comedy of manners pulled no punches in its skewering of crass movie moguls, modeled in large part on those producers who had made his life so difficult in recent years. Further potshots were aimed at communists, gossip columnists, Vassar College, and Romanoff-esque restaurants, also familiar Wellesian targets. There was even a barb directed at JOSEPH MCCARTHY, the junior Republican U.S. senator from Wisconsin, whom Welles might have bested at the polls had he accepted the entreaties of his home state Democrats who had urged him to run in the 1946 election.

The plot of *The Unthinking Lobster* centers on a movie starlet who, playing the role of the saint Anne de Beaumont, discovers to her astonishment that the "miracles" created by her character are taking place in real life. As a result, the production is brought to a standstill as cripples and other malformed souls interrupt the filming to be healed. In the role of producer Jack Behoovian, Welles plays a loud, cigar-chomping mogul devoid of any artistic pretenses. For Behoovian, there is only one goal—to produce a hit.

As he had done in TOO MUCH JOHNSON (1938) and AROUND THE WORLD IN 80 DAYS (1946), Welles shot some of the play's story on film and incorporated it into the performance. In this case, given its subject of filmmaking, the use of a movie sequence proved an adroit choice. The play opens, like CITIZEN KANE, in a projection room where rushes are being previewed by the brass. The lights dim for what Welles called, La Miracle de Sainte Anne, a "cinematic overture" in which a group of cripples, extras in the biblical epic, are cured by a young actress. As the live action resumes, the studio has been transformed into a Lourdes-like shrine. It is a scene of chaos. Cripples beg to be healed. Curiosity-seekers purchase little pieces of film touted as holy amulets. To the consternation of the producer, all production has ceased. Heaven is not pleased. Finally, an angel is sent to broker the impasse—if Hollywood will stop making religious movies, then Heaven, in exchange, will bring a halt to the disruptive miracles. The responsible parties agree, and, as the curtain descends, all is well.

Presented in English, *The Unthinking Lobster* and its companion piece, TIME RUNS, received rave reviews, with *Le Monde* calling *The Blessed and the Damned* "a stage masterpiece."

Significantly, Welles viewed his hastily assembled one-act play as a pilot, a test run, so to speak, for a full-blown feature film. However tantalizing the idea, it was, sadly, not to be.

In addition to Welles, the cast featured SUZANNE CLOUTIER in the leading role of Miss Pratt, and longstanding Welles friend HILTON EDWARDS in the supporting role of L'Archeveque, both of whom were involved in Welles's ongoing film adaptation of OTHELLO.

—C.B.

Upon This Rock   Marstan/American Continental, 90 minutes, 1970. **Director:** Harry Rasky; **Producer:** Stanley Abrams; **Screenplay:** Harry Rasky; **Cinematography:** Aldo Ponti; **Cast:** Orson Welles (Michelangelo), Ralph Richardson (guide), Dirk Bogarde, and Edith Evans

This documentary was originally planned as a television special about Michelangelo's artistic involvement with St. Peter's Basilica, the seat of the Vatican in Rome.

—T.L.E. and J.M.W.

Vallee, Rudy (Hubert Prior Vallee)
(1901–1986)   During the 1940s actor and singer
Rudy Vallee hosted *The Rudy Vallee Show,* sponsored
by Sealtest, on the radio. Among the guests that made
the show so popular were ORSON WELLES and JOHN
BARRYMORE, the "Great Profile." Vallee, born on July
28, 1901, in Island Point, Vermont, intended to
become a pharmacist like his father, but soon switched
to a musical career, playing the saxophone and singing.
At the University of Maine (later immortalized in
Vallee's Maine "Stein Song") he formed in own band,
and he continued to perform professionally even after
he transferred to Yale University. After graduation from
Yale, he formed the Connecticut Yankees and became
a popular "crooner" on the radio, in nightclubs, and in
the theater. The title of *The Vagabond Lover* (1929), his
first film, was taken from one of his most popular
songs and also became one of his nicknames. Most of
his early films were light romantic comedies, the best
of which were directed by Preston Sturges, *The Palm
Beach Story* (1942) and Harold Lloyd's *Mad Wednesday*
(1947).

   In addition to his films, Rudy Vallee hosted radio
shows that featured famous actors and actresses. Vallee
credits John Barrymore for much of his radio success
and writes, "The shows on which he [Barrymore]
and Orson Welles traded insults between each other
or when the two Barrymore brothers slugged it out
verbally with Welles were classics." One of the insults
involved Barrymore dismissing Welles with "Why,
he's another John Barrymore." Vallee continued to
make films well into the 1970s, but in many of them
he was cast as an eccentric, prissy millionaire. Only a
few of his later films will be familiar to current
moviegoers: *How to Succeed in Business Without Really
Trying* (1967), for example, and *The Night They Raided
Minsky's* (1968, in which he was only the narrator).
He was the author of two autobiographical works:
My Time Is Your Time (1962) and *Let the Chips Fall . . .*
(1975).

   References   Marks, Edward Bennett. *They All Sang:
From Tony Pastor to Rudy Vallee* (New York: Viking, 1934);
Vallee, Rudy. *My Time Is Your Time* (New York: I. Oblensky,
1962).

—T.L.E.

Van Sant, Gus (1952–)   A pioneer of the
new "Queer" cinema of the 1980s, Gus Van Sant was
the first openly gay director to become a mainstream
Hollywood filmmaker during the 1990s as a result of
two "art-house" features, *Drugstore Cowboy* (1989)
and *My Own Private Idaho* (1991). The latter film,
inspired by ORSON WELLES's *CHIMES AT MIDNIGHT,*
restructured and updated the action of Welles's
Shakespeare compilation of the "Henriad" (primarily
the plays *King Henry IV, Parts I and II*) to contemporary Portland, Oregon, where Van Sant lives and
works. Just as *My Own Private Idaho* was a homage to

Welles, later in the decade Van Sant paid tribute to Alfred Hitchcock in his 1998 remake of *Psycho* (1960). As Tom Poe has written, Van Sant "approached the task as if he had been given the opportunity to restore rather than to re-make the classic film, which he chose to film in color, "with new actors" who brought "a more contemporary feel to the story of Marion Crane (Anne Heche) and Norman Bates (Vince Vaughn). Otherwise, however, Van Sant's *Psycho* was "a remarkably faithful, even reverential reconstruction of the original film, largely employing Hitchcock's storyboards and an only slightly augmented version of the original BERNARD HERRMANN score."

In his tribute to Orson Welles, Van Sant took far more liberties with the text of Shakespeare and with *Chimes at Midnight*. Welles had cited writing credits for Holinshead and Shakespeare, but Van Sant credited himself as the writer of *My Own Private Idaho,* though he also cited "additional dialogue by William Shakespeare." After the critical success of *Drugstore Cowboy* in 1989, Van Sant turned to two screenplays he had already written, combining a story of street hustlers in Portland, Oregon, with his updated adaptation of *Henry IV,* and focusing, as Welles had done, on the story of Shakespeare's FALSTAFF. The result has been called "Van Sanitized" Shakespeare, but, as Hugh Davis has written, Van Sant's "greatest inspiration is clearly and admittedly Welles's film, to which he is paying homage as much as he is reviving Shakespeare."

The characters in Van Sant's film are remote equivalents of the characters to be found in Shakespeare and Welles, as Davis explains: "Prince Hal becomes Scott Favor, [the] young son of Portland's mayor (King Henry IV), who is currently in disfavor with his father, for he spends his time with hustlers and drug addicts. The older Bob Pigeon, Scott's former lover, mentor, and "true father" (or so Scott proclaims), steps into the role of Falstaff. . . . Budd and company represent Shallow and company, who frequent the Boar's Head tavern (in the plays and *Chimes*). Jane Lightfoot, who owns the old hotel where the characters spend their time (the film's equivalent to the Boar's Head), takes the part held by Mistress Quickly, although her name also alludes to

Jane Nightwork, an old friend whom Shallow mentions to Falstaff in *2 Henry IV* (III.ii.204), and in the beginning of *Chimes,* as the two recall how old they have become. Another character, Mike Waters, becomes "a second avatar of Falstaff in this restructured Henriad." Bob Pigeon is the traditional Falstaff, "recognizable by his girth, his age, and his wit, but Mike also takes the role of the knight" in Van Sant's retelling of Shakespeare by way of Welles. But Waters is more a boon-companion brother than the father figure of Falstaff in the "Henriad."

Gus Van Sant was born in Louisville, Kentucky, on July 24, 1952. His family later moved to Connecticut, and, eventually, to Portland, Oregon. According to Tom Poe, "Van Sant became interested in filmmaking at an early age and began making short Super-8 films at the age of twelve. He continued making films as an art student at the Rhode Island School of Design and, following graduation, worked as a sound engineer for Roger Corman." Thereafter, Van Sant's black-and-white film *Mala Noche* (1985), adapted from the autobiographical novel by Walt Curtis, became a hit at gay and lesbian film festivals. *Drugstore Cowboy* (1989), praised for its hard-edged realism, was the first Van Sant film to gain wide theatrical distribution.

After the success of *My Own Private Idaho,* Van Sant's career faltered with his adaptation of the Tom Robbins cult novel *Even Cowgirls Get the Blues* (1994), but rebounded the next year with *To Die For* (1995), adapted by Buck Henry from Joyce Maynard's novel about a vapid housewife (Nicole Kidman), who yearns to become a media celebrity. Even more successful was *Good Will Hunting* (1997), scripted by actors Matt Damon and Ben Affleck. Van Sant's *Psycho* that followed in 1998 was regarded as something of an oddity, but Van Sant again recovered mainstream success with *Finding Forrester* (2000), concerning the relationship between an African-American teenager and a reclusive writer played by Sean Connery.

As Tom Poe has noted, Van Sant, "the first openly and politically engaged gay filmmaker" to achieve mainstream acceptance in Hollywood, effectively challenged homophobia in the film industry, though some gay critics have criticized him for being a "sell-out, not unlike the characters in his two most compelling mainstream films, working-class Will Hunting and the marginalized African-American high school student in *Finding Forrester,* who struggle to find their own way within establishment culture."

References Davis, Hugh H. "*My Own Private Idaho* and Shakespeare in the Streets," *Literature/Film Quarterly,* 29 (2001), 116–21; Poe, Tom. "Gus Van Sant," in *The Encyclopedia of Filmmakers,* ed. John C. Tibbetts and James M. Welsh (New York: Facts On File, 2002).

—J.M.W.

Veiller,   Anthony (1903–1965)   Writer-producer Anthony Veiller wrote the screenplay for *THE STRANGER,* directed by ORSON WELLES in 1946. According to DAVID THOMSON, SAM SPIEGEL persuaded International Pictures to finance the project with the understanding that JOHN HUSTON would be involved in rewrites. Welles "claimed to have been involved in rewrites, but in most respects he was under close orders to deliver the picture without frills or changes." BARBARA LEAMING, on the other hand, claims "uncredited assistance from John Huston and Orson Welles" on the screenplay.

Born in New York City, the son of producer-director Bayard Veiller on June 23, 1903, Veiller was educated at Antioch College and Union College in New York and worked as theater manager and publicist before turning to a distinguished career as a screenwriter. Among his later films were *Moulin Rouge* (1953), *The List of Adrian Messenger* (1963), and *The Night of the Iguana* (1964), all of which were directed by John Huston.

—T.L.E. and J.M.W.

Verne, Jules (Jules-Gabriel Verne) (1828–1905)   In the late 1920s, Orson Welles saw a stage adaptation of Jules Verne's popular novel, *Around the World in Eighty Days,* which he first adapted to radio in 1938 as one of his MERCURY THEATRE broadcasts. He played Phileas Fogg, the protagonist. After HOWARD HUGHES flew around the world in three days, Welles used the occasion to present the work again, this time on his CAMPBELL PLAYHOUSE radio series. Six years later, in 1945, he presented it again, this time on his THIS IS MY BEST radio series. Welles

was so intrigued by the novel that he adapted it to film in a screenplay that he tried unsuccessfully to sell to RKO. In 1946, he revised the screenplay, adapting it to the stage and sought financial backing, which was to come from producer MIKE TODD. After seeing the musical in rehearsal and realizing that Welles had no firm script, Todd withdrew his financing (Welles claimed that Todd simply lacked the funding). Welles managed to get the play, which was a hit on Broadway, produced; but he did not get the opportunity to adapt it for the screen. In 1965, Welles appeared in *THE SOUTHERN STAR,* a film adapted from another Jules Verne novel.

Jules Verne was born on February 8, 1828, in Nantes, France. His father, Pierre, was a well-respected lawyer who saw that his son, Jules, received a good education. Verne first attended a school conducted by Mme. Sambin, and later, when he was nine, he entered the junior seminary of St. Donatian in Nantes, then the seminary, and then the Lycée Royal. In 1846, he began his law studies at home, but he moved to Paris, where he took his first-year law examinations and completed *Alexandre VI,* a five-act tragedy. In Paris, he met Alexandre Dumas *père,* which increased his interest in the theater. In the period between 1850 and 1860 Verne wrote several comedies, six libretti, and one serious drama; only two of the plays were staged. His efforts at fiction were more successful: *The Mutineers,* a novel, was first published in 1851. Influenced by Edgar Allan Poe, Verne wrote "Un Voyage en Ballon" (1851), which derived from two Poe stories: "The Balloon Hoax" and "The Unparalleled Adventure of One, Hans Pfaal." The first time Verne used science in his writing was in *Maître Zacharius ou l'horloger qui a perdu son âme* (*The Clockmaker Who Lost His Soul,* 1854). *Cinq Semaines en Ballon* (1863, *Five Weeks in a Balloon*) and *Voyage au Centre de la Terre* (1863, *Journey to the Center of the Earth*) followed. In 1869, Verne published, in serial form, both *Twenty Thousand Leagues Under the Sea* and the second part of *From the Earth to the Moon. Le Tour du monde en quatre-vingt jours* (*Around the World in Eighty Days*), his most famous novel and the subject of musical and film adaptations, appeared in 1873. He continued to write, but his best and most-remembered novels were behind him. He is best known as one of the most important figures in the creation of science fiction.

References   Avrane, Patrick. *Jules Verne* (Paris: Stock, 1997); Lottman, Herbert R. *Jules Verne: An Exploratory Biography* (New York: St Martin's Press, 1996); Lynch, Laurence W. *Jules Verne* (New York: Twayne, 1992).

—T.L.E.

Viertel, Peter (1920–   )

Novelist and screenwriter Peter Viertel worked first with JOHN HUSTON and later with ORSON WELLES. He was the son of Bertold Viertel (1885–1953), the Austrian-born poet, novelist, playwright, actor, and director of stage and screen, and the Polish-born actress Salka Steuermann Viertel (1889–1978) who wrote screenplays for Greta Garbo (notably, *Queen Christina* and *Anna Karenina*) and whose Santa Monica salon during the war years was a magnet for European émigré intellectuals, writers, and composers such as Bertrand Russell, Igor Stravinsky, BERTOLT BRECHT, Thomas Mann, and Aldous Huxley, which, as John Huston wrote in his biography *An Open Book* (1980), "earned her a place on the blacklist."

At ease, therefore, with celebrities, Viertel befriended Ernest Hemingway in Cuba and wrote the screenplays for *The Sun Also Rises* and *The Old Man and the Sea*. He also worked with Huston and ANTHONY VEILLER on *Beat the Devil* and scripted the final scenes for Huston on *The African Queen,* since James Agee's health would not allow the writer to travel to Africa. In her memoir on *The Making of The African Queen* (1987), Katharine Hepburn remembered Viertel as "a damned good writer" and "an absolute angel" who "saved my sanity."

In his biography *John Huston* (1978), Axel Madsen wrote: "The humiliations of writing the final version of *The African Queen* drove Peter Viertel to publish a novel starring a thinly disguised Huston as a macho director who becomes a crazed big-game hunter and wrecks the preparations for a picture in Africa." According to *Time* magazine, Huston objected to Viertel's "malicious" portrait of him in the novel *White Hunter, Black Heart* (1953). Working with James Bridges and Burt Kennedy in 1990, Viertel later adapted his novel for the motion picture directed by Clint Eastwood, who played John Wilson, the Huston

figure, a considerable departure from his usual screen persona. Viertel's character, Peter Verrill, was played by Jeff Fahey. In 1992, Viertel published *Dangerous Friends: At Large with Huston and Hemingway in the Fifties*.

During the mid-1960s, Peter Viertel worked with Welles in Spain on a screenplay adapted from *The Survivors,* a play Viertel had written with Irwin Shaw; but this turned into a failed project when financing for the production was not forthcoming. Welles also discussed with Viertel an idea he had for another film "about an old man's obsessive admiration for a young torero; the protagonist of this story was an aging movie director intent on recapturing the magic of his youth by following a young bullfighter around Spain," as described by DAVID THOMSON in his book, *Rosebud*. When Viertel asked if the protagonist would be based on himself or Hemingway, Welles answered that it would be "About both of us."

References   Hepburn, Katharine. *The Making of The African Queen* (New York: Knopf, 1987); Huston, John. *An Open Book* (New York: Knopf, 1980); Madsen, Axel. *John Huston: A Biography* (Garden City, N.Y.: Doubleday, 1978).

—J.M.W.

Vikings, The

Brynaprod S.A., 114 minutes, 1958. **Director:** Richard Fleischer; **Producer:** Jerry Bressler; **Screenplay:** Dale Wasserman and Calder Willingham (from the novel by Edison Marshall); **Cinematographer:** Jack Cardiff; **Editor:** Hugo Williams; **Music:** Mario Nascimbene; **Cast:** Kirk Douglas (Einar), Tony Curtis (Eric), Ernest Borgnine (Ragnar), Janet Leigh (Morgana), James Donald (Egbert) and Orson Welles (Narrator)

This large-scale epic of Viking warriors on the prowl was adapted by screenwriter Calder Willingham from the novel *The Vikings* by Edison Marshall. A rousing, big-budget spectacle shot on location in Norway, the story centers on a struggle between two half brothers for the throne of Northumbria. With top production values, stirring action sequences, a dramatic musical score by Mario Nascimbene, and an effective publicity campaign that included a voyage of a Viking longboat from Oslo to New York, *The Vikings* was a big moneymaker. The film also got a lift from a strong cast that included Kirk Douglas (Einar) and Tony Curtis (Eric) as the half brothers, Ernest

Borgnine (King Ragnar) as their father, JANET LEIGH (Princess Morgana) as the object of the brothers' romantic attentions, and James Donald (Lord Egbert) as the effete English noble whose downfall the audience cheers. WELLES's narration, which for one viewer resonated like Thor's horn, functioned to provide the historical frame in which the story unfolds.

—C.B.

V.I.P. (novel, 1953) *V.I.P.,* based on WELLES's radio script "Buzzo Gospel" for the 1951–52 BBC radio series, *THE ADVENTURES OF HARRY LIME,* was initially worked up by Welles for ALEXANDER KORDA as a treatment for a satirical film. When asked by PETER BOGDANOVICH if Korda bought the idea, Welles responded: "He didn't go that far. He gave me all the cigars I wanted and he died soon afterward, so I didn't get to *not* make that one, either." The last phrase is a reference to the litany of Welles ideas suggested to but ultimately quashed by Korda.

The treatment, which was eventually fleshed out to the point of becoming a slim book, was translated into French and adapted to the form of a novel by MAURICE BESSY, who became one of the director's first important biographers (see *Orson Welles,* published in French, in 1963; Bessy's study, translated by Ciba Vaughan and subtitled "An Investigation in His Films and Philosophy," was subsequently published in English in 1971). *V.I.P.,* published by Gallimard (Paris) in 1953 as *Une Grosse Legume* (*A Big Shot* or *Big Wheel*), also included a glowing preface by Bessy.

Bessy's foreword, as FRANK BRADY points out, follows the French tradition initiated by Baudelaire's adulatory introduction to Edgar Allan Poe in attempting to understand the misunderstood, or allegedly misunderstood, nature of an American genius. Bessy's main point is that in the early 1950s, Welles was largely underappreciated, a lonely and restless creator always in motion, traveling from place to place in pursuit of his work, who, as a result of that nomadic lifestyle, became a citizen of the world. For Bessy, the droll *V.I.P* (or *Une Grosse Legume*) was a small yet nonetheless brilliant spark cast off by the colussus that was Welles.

Set on Malinha, a tiny island in the middle of the Mediterranean on the brink of revolution at the height of the cold war, the story centers on the misadventures of an American soft-drink salesman (Joe Boone-Cutler) who is mistaken for an undercover agent by a comically inept dictator (the Mussolini-like Admiral Cuccibamba). Brady calls it "a slapstick comedy of errors employing the standard farcical devices of mistaken identity and broadly sketched character types." Welles said: "It's about the Coca-Cola and Pepsi-Cola empires—a farce about capitalist imperialism, the communist menace, and all that. It's set in one of those mythical kingdoms, someplace about the size of Luxembourg but in the Mediterranean—the last place on earth without either a Pepsi or a Coca-Cola concession. It's about competing imperialism and the cold war. They [i.e., the natives of Malinha] have been living off American aid ever since the [Second World] war in order to keep off the communist menace. The truth is, they have no communists—but that's their own well-kept secret."

Like the delightful yet politically savvy *The Mouse That Roared* (Jack Arnold; 1959) and *One, Two, Three* (Billy Wilder; 1961), *V.I.P* is a breezy satire sending up American naivete, international capitalism, and cold war politics. Reading more like a fleshed-out treatment for a film comedy rather than a novel, *V.I.P.* garnered cautiously respectful reviews, largely because of Bessy's warm testimonial and the French public's understandable curiosity about the enigma that was Orson Welles.

—C.B.

V.I.P.s, The Metro-Goldwyn-Mayer, 119 minutes, 1963. **Director:** Anthony Asquith; **Producer:** Anatole de Grunwald; **Screenplay:** Terrance Rattigan; **Cinematographer:** Jack Hildyard; **Editor:** Frank Clarke; **Music:** Miklos Rosza; **Cast:** Elizabeth Taylor (Frances Andros), Richard Burton (Paul Andros), Louis Jourdan (Marc Champselle), Maggie Smith (Miss Mead), Rod Taylor (Les Mangrum), Elsa Martinelli (Gloria Gritti), Linda Christian (Miriam Marshall), Dennis Price (Commander Millbank), Robert Coote (John Coburn), Margaret Rutherford (the duchess of Brighton) and Orson Welles (Max Buda)

Although *The V.I.P.s* was designed as a vehicle to exploit the then front-page romantic exploits of Richard Burton and Elizabeth Taylor, WELLES's turn as film director Max Buda stands out as an interesting parody of both himself and Hungarian-born British film producer ALEXANDER KORDA, an intimate Welles associate from the 1950s. Just as Welles was haunted in real life by tax agents everywhere, so, too, is Buda. TV personality David Frost, playing a reporter, greets Buda at Heathrow Airport. "Aren't you rather overweight?" he asks Buda. "Overweight, *me*?" retorts Buda, who then realizes the reporter is referring to his luggage.

Later, Buda, bundled in a luxurious fur-collared coat topped with a Tyrolean hat, waxes philosophical about filmmaking. "It is not the purpose of the modern cinema to entertain," he opines with a heavy Hungarian accent. "*Never*. No, we use our cameras to search. To use as a scalpel." Here, as elsewhere during the last decades of his life, Welles was willing to hoist himself aloft as a figure for satiric reflection. Buda, to cite DAVID THOMSON, is at once grandiloquent, flagrantly bogus, and sincerely bogus. For most commentators, Buda was Korda-esque and Wellesian. Welles, however, claimed that he didn't recognize anyone in particular in Buda. An admirer of director Asquith, Welles cautioned PETER BOGDANOVICH that "You couldn't judge Asquith on *The V.I.P.s:* the picture was made by the Burtons and written for them by Terry Rattigan—an old-fashioned Metro potboiler, sort of junior *Grand Hotel*."

In spite of any possible indignities resulting from his portrayal of Buda, for Welles, the last laugh following such acting-for-hire engagements was the paycheck at the end of the shoot used to leverage backing for his own projects, in this case, DON QUIXOTE.

—C.B.

Voyage of the Damned Associated General Films/Incorporated Television Company/AVCO Embassy Pictures, 155 minutes, 1976. **Director:** Stuart Rosenberg; **Producer:** Robert Fryer; **Screenplay:** David Butler and Steve Shagan (from the book *The Voyage of the Damned* by Gordon Thomas and Max Morgan Witts; **Cinematography:** Billy Williams; **Music:** Lalo Schifrin; **Editors:** Tom Priestly and Desmond Saunders; **Cast:** Faye Dunaway (Denise Kreisler), Oskar Werner (Dr. Kreisler), Lee Grant (Lillian Rosen), Sam Wanamaker (Carl Rosen), Lynn Frederick (Anna Rosen), David de Keyser (Joseph Joseph), Della McDermott (Julia Strauss), Genevievi West (Sarah Strauss), Max von Sydow (Captain Schroeder), Malcolm MacDowell (Max Gunter) Denholm Elliott (Admiral Canaris), James Mason (Remos), Wendy Hiller (Rebecca Weiler), José Ferrer (Manuel Benitez), Julie Harris (Alice Fienchild), Katharine Ross (Mira Hauser), Janet Suzman (Leni Strauss), and Orson Welles (Estedes)

Set in 1939 and based on a true story, *Voyage of the Damned,* directed by Stuart Rosenberg, chronicles the ill-fated attempt of German-Jewish refugees to seek sanctuary in Havana, Cuba, after crossing from Hamburg, Germany, on the SS *St. Louis.* When the ship docks in Havana, however, none of the 937 passengers were given permission to land because the German government had managed to subvert their efforts to gain asylum, and the ship is routed back to Nazi Germany and almost certain death for the refugees. The voyage of the *St. Louis* became an international controversy, as the governments of Britain, France, Belgium, and Holland agreed to accept some of the passengers, but, by 1945, only 240 of the refugees had survived. Playing Raoul Estedes, WELLES was part of an all-star cast that included Faye Dunaway, Max von Sydow, Oskar Werner, Malcolm McDowell, James Mason, Wendy Hiller, José Ferrar, Julie Harris, Lee Grant, Katherine Ross, and Janet Suzman. Although reviews were mixed, the film earned Academy Award nominations for Lalo Schifrin's musical score, for the adapted screenplay by Steve Shagan and David Butler, and for Lee Grant as best supporting actress, and Golden Globe nominations for Oskar Werner as best supporting actor and for best film drama, an award won that year by *Rocky*.

—J.M.W.

Walska, Ganna (Hanna Puacz) (1887–1984)
Opera singer Ganna Walska is one of the probable
models for would-be opera singer Susan Alexander,
second wife of Kane in CITIZEN KANE (1941). DAVID
THOMSON comments on the ties between the two
singers: "It is in Chicago that Kane builds an opera
house for Susan Alexander to attempt *Salammbô*. But
the real opera house in Chicago was run by the agri-
cultural machinery tycoon Harold McCormick. He
was married to Edith Rockefeller, but in 1920 he
intended to present his Polish mistress, Ganna Walska,
there, in [the opera] *Zaza*." Welles, who had spent a
great deal of his life in Chicago, would have known
this story well. FRANK BRADY offers as proof of the
connection a telegram that BERNARD HERRMANN sent
to Welles on July 23, 1940, part of which reads: "Feel
that Suzie should have a small but rather good voice.
This is the ticklish part of it. Even 'G.W.' had something of a voice." McCormick later divorced Rockefeller and married Walska.

She was born in Poland in 1887 and changed her
given name of Hanna Puacz to Madame Ganna Walska, a name she retained through six marriages. She
left her third husband, the very wealthy Alexander
Smith Cochran, to marry Harold McCormick, heir
to the International Harvester fortune. During the
nine-year marriage, McCormick bought her the
Théâtre des Champs Elysées in Paris and insured full
houses for her American operatic tours by giving
away free tickets. After divorcing McCormick, she
was married to Harry Grindell-Matthews, then
divorced him three years later and married Theos
Bernard, who encouraged her to buy Lotusland, a
40-acre garden near Santa Barbara, California.

References Crawford, Sharon. *Ganna Walska
Lotusland: The Garden and Its Creators* (Santa Barbara, Calif.:
Companion Press, 1996); Walska, Ganna. *Always Room at
the Top* (New York: R.R. Smith, 1943).

—T.L.E.

War of the Worlds, The (radio, 1938) Aired by
CBS on October 30, 1938, the notorious 60-minute
adaptation of English novelist H.G. WELLS's popular
science-fiction novel created a panic among thousands of listeners who thought they were listening to
an "earwitness" account of an actual invasion from
Mars. How did the show create such an immediate
and extraordinary sensation? Was the show that daring, that original? And, finally, what impact did the
program have on ORSON WELLES's career?

At first, the project of adapting H.G. Wells's novel
to radio seemed unpromising. After all, Welles's
MERCURY THEATRE ON THE AIR had been specializing
in literary classics of timeless appeal such as *Julius
Caesar, Jane Eyre,* and *Oliver Twist*. In fact, *The War of
the Worlds* had at one point been dropped from the
Mercury schedule in favor of an adaptation of R. D.
Blackmore's *Lorna Doone*. However, when Welles

started worrying that the 19th-century novel might be too dated and staid, the Wells novel was hastily put back into the lineup. The first critical change made by Welles, producer JOHN HOUSEMAN, and scriptwriter HOWARD KOCH was to update the novel's time and place, moving the story from turn-of-the-last-century England to the contemporary East Coast of the United States. The second crucial alteration was to tell the story within the format of a live radio news broadcast, a technique that had been successfully used in *The Fall of the City* (1937), in which Welles had appeared, and in the MERCURY THEATRE's modern dress theatrical adaptation of Shakespeare's *JULIUS CAESAR* (1937), and its subsequent radio adaptation just weeks earlier on September 11, 1938, where it had served as the debut program for the *Mercury Theatre on the Air*. CBS, concerned that the program might seem too real, ordered a number of script changes underscoring the program's dramatic, rather than news, status. For Welles and company, the basic fear was that the story might appear too absurd.

With the changes in place, the broadcast went out over CBS on Sunday evening, October 30, 1938. The first several minutes of program were intentionally prosaic, indeed, routine. The first words came from announcer Dan Seymour who said: "The Columbia Broadcasting System and its affiliated stations present Orson Welles and the Mercury Theatre on the Air in *The War of the Worlds* by H.G. Wells. Ladies and gentlemen: the director of the Mercury Theatre and the star of these broadcasts, Orson Welles." With that, as with the other *Mercury on the Air* broadcasts, Welles provided the evening's setup. "We know now that in the early years of the twentieth century this world was being watched closely by intelligences greater than man's and yet as mortal as his own. We know now that as human beings busied themselves with their various concerns they were scrutinized and studied, perhaps almost as narrowly as a man with a microscope might scrutinize the transient creatures that swarm and multiply in a drop of water. Across an immense ethereal gulf, minds that are to our minds, as ours are to the beasts of the jungles, intellects vast, cool, and unsympathetic, regarded this earth with envious eyes and slowly and surely drew their plans against us."

After Welles's prologue came a weather bulletin, and then a cut to a fashionable New York hotel ballroom and the society music of Ramon Raquello and his orchestra. After a minute of music, there is a news flash reporting that Professor Pierson (Welles) of the Princeton Observatory has seen explosions of gas occurring at regular intervals on the planet Mars. The music, Hoagy Carmichael's "Star Dust," returns. As the broadcast proceeds, Raquello's music suffers more frequent and longer interruptions until it is made clear that earth is being invaded. One of the program's eeriest moments, a remote pick-up from Grovers Mill, New Jersey, reports a creature emerging from an alien craft and sending out rays that instantly ignite everything in its path. In mid-sentence, the voice of the "eye witness" falls silent except for ominous crackles of static.

In the studio, the CBS switchboard started receiving calls. Newspapers across the country did, too. The *New York Times,* for one, reported 875 calls. Priests were called to deliver last rites. Police stations were swamped as well. A half hour into the program, panic had seized thousands of people who were in flight, speeding along highways to try to distance themselves from the Martian menace.

Even though there was an announcement at the "intermission" that indeed what people were listening do was a dramatization of H.G. Wells's *The War of the Worlds,* the panic, exacerbated by the program's clever narrative and production strategies, continued to snowball. It didn't help that the brief intermission was late, not coming until 40 minutes after the broadcast's start. Although Welles had been forced to alter some details at the behest of CBS—the Museum of Natural History was changed to "National History Museum"; the National Guard to "Militia"; the U.S. Weather Bureau to "Government Weather Bureau"—other actual facts and names left no doubt for many that they were ear-witnesses to a disaster of unprecedented scale. At the end of the drama, an announcer, now atop the Broadcasting Building (Welles wasn't allowed to use "CBS"), describes the Martians' march on Manhattan. "This is the end now . . . Smoke comes out . . . black smoke, drifting over the city. People in the streets see it now. They're running toward the East River . . . thousands of them, dropping like rats. Now the smoke's spreading faster. It's reached Times Square. People are trying to run away but it's no use. They're falling like flies. Now the smoke's crossing Sixth Avenue . . . Fifth Avenue . . . a . . . a hundred years away . . . it's fifty feet . . ." There is a long pause, then the thump of the announcer's falling body, and then the haunting last gasps of the city. Then, silence. Suddenly, a ham operator is heard searching for someone to respond. And, then, again, silence. Finally, after an epiloguelike conclusion in which Prof. Pierson meditates on war and violence, Welles as Welles, the evening's host, returns: "This Is Orson Welles, ladies and gentlemen, out of character to assure you that *The War of the Worlds* has no further significance than as the holiday offering it was intended to be . . . the Mercury Theatre's own radio version of dressing up in a sheet and jumping out of a bush and saying "Boo!" Starting now, we couldn't soap all your windows and steal all your garden gates by tomorrow night . . . so we did the next best thing. We annihilated the world before your very ears and utterly destroyed CBS." As the brilliantly produced broadcast concluded, police were at the studio door trying to shut the program down.

In the wake of the panic there were postmortems from pundits, politicians, and the Federal Communications Commission, whose task it was to regulate broadcasting "in the public interest." One immediate policy change was the banning of fictional news bulletins in radio dramas. As for the panic, some thought that because of war fears, many in the public were receptive to the possibility of catastrophe. Others praised the program for providing a de facto case study probing the kind of mass hysteria that made phenomena like the rise of Hitler and anti-Semitism possible. Princeton psychologist HADLEY CANTRIL, in the scholarly *The Invasion from Mars* (1940), suggested that factors such as low educational attainment had proved to correlate positively with a propensity to panic.

For Welles, the extraordinary reactions to *The War of the Worlds* accelerated his rise to international prominence. Yes, there had been his recent appearance on the May 9, 1938, cover of *Time* magazine. But, now, everyone knew of his exploits—"Orson Welles" was a household name.

In the stormy days following the broadcast, many in the Mercury company, including Welles, worried that CBS would be forced to cancel the program. Instead, the Campbell Soup Company thought that Welles, now "The Man from Mars," could help sell soup. On December 9, 1938, with the broadcast of an adaptation of Daphne deMaurier's *Rebecca,* the *Mercury Theatre on the Air* became THE CAMPBELL PLAYHOUSE.

Along with Welles, the cast for *The War of the Worlds* included Frank Readick, WILLIAM ALLAND, RAY COLLINS, Kenneth Delmar, PAUL STEWART, RICHARD WILSON, Carl Frank, William Herz, Stefan Schnabel, and Howard Smith. The musical score was composed by BERNARD HERRMANN.

—C.B.

Warrick, Ruth (1915–) Ruth Warrick, actress, was born in St. Louis, Missouri, on June 29, 1915, and graduated from the University of Missouri. She started her professional career as a singer on radio and as an actress off-Broadway. Her first screen appearance was as Kane's first wife, Emily, in *CITIZEN KANE.* ORSON WELLES had noticed her picture while perusing a stack of glossy photos submitted to him by Central Casting, and he remembered her from a radio appearance that they had made on the same show in the late 1930s. "I'm not looking for an actress that can *play* a lady," Welles states in CALLOW's book; "I want an actress who *is* a lady." Ruth Warrick filled the bill: The well-modulated voice she cultivated on radio and on the stage gave her the refined and cultured tone needed for the patrician Emily Norton, the president's niece.

Her screen test with Welles marked the first time either of them had appeared on camera in Hollywood; and several of the studio officials and staff assembled to watch. Welles was to recite a line of dialogue, to which Warrick was to answer, "That is typical of you, Mr. Kane." Self-conscious because of the crowd gathered to see what he could do as a screen actor, Welles fluffed his line, not once but eight times. On the ninth try, he finally got it right; and Warrick, perhaps herself flustered at all the retakes of such a simple interchange, responded, "That is typical of you, Mr. Welles"—thus ruining the ninth take. It was

Ruth Warrick as Emily Holmes Norton Kane and the "love nest" with Dorothy Commingore, Welles, and Ray Collins in *Citizen Kane* *(Literature/Film Archive)*

evident that Ruth Warrick should play Kane's first wife, Emily.

In order to shave the budget and the shooting schedule, Welles scrapped several expository scenes centering on the erosion of Kane's first marriage as they were written in HERMAN MANKIEWICZ's original draft of the script. Instead, he substituted a brisk montage to cover the action. ROBERT CARRINGER notes that Welles wrote in the revised script at this point: "The following scenes cover a period of nine years—and are played on the same set with only changes in lighting, special effects outside the window, and wardrobe."

The breakup of his first marriage is spanned in flashback in a most inventive way: Kane is seen in a series of shots sitting across the breakfast table from his first wife. Each succeeding flashback shows the distance between them growing, as the table between them literally gets longer, from the first flashback to the last. This is a subtle way of symbolizing the increasing estrangement between the couple. Indeed, the series of flashbacks is climaxed by a shot of Kane's first wife reading a newspaper that is a rival to the one that Kane himself publishes.

ROBERT WISE, who later became a director himself, edited *Citizen Kane*. He remembers that he worked with Welles very closely on the breakfast

table scene. It had been carefully designed in the script, he explains, but "we played with that a long time, and it was in the cutting room where . . . that whole marvelous sequence was really worked out the way it got in the picture."

Leigh Woods observes very perceptively that Ruth Warrick's "refined tone and mid-Atlantic dialect" in her role as Emily perfectly fit Welles's "authoritative and cultured way of speaking" as Kane. By contrast, DOROTHY COMINGORE's "thin, squeaky speaking voice" as Kane's second wife, Susan, "leaves her conspicuously mismatched with Kane's orotund tendencies"—thereby prefiguring the unhappy outcome that results "when Kane leaves the former debutante Emily Norton for the plain-spoken Susan Alexander and her chorus girl voice."

Ruth Warrick published her autobiography, *The Confessions of Phoebe Tyler,* in 1980, the title referring to the character she played on the soap opera *All My Children.* She gave Welles a copy of her book after taping a segment of a TV talk show with him about the making of *Kane.* According to BARBARA LEAMING, Welles was initially chagrined to find that she alluded in her book to an amorous encounter she had had with him in what Welles now thought of as the "prehistoric past" when *Kane* was made. On second thought, he decided that turning up in a former ladyfriend's memoirs was inevitable.

By the time Welles was casting his next film after *Kane,* THE MAGNIFICENT AMBERSONS, Warrick had become a mother and could not consider playing in the movie. She did appear in *JOURNEY INTO FEAR* as the wife of JOSEPH COTTEN. Welles began directing this film, about smuggling munitions into Turkey during World War II, but the studio soon replaced him with NORMAN FOSTER, as his relationship with RKO continued to deteriorate. He did retain his role as Colonel Hakim, the head of the Turkish Secret Service, however. But he never acted with Ruth Warrick again.

Warrick remained in films throughout the 1940s; after a long absence from the screen, she returned to Hollywood in the late 1960s, but appeared onscreen only sporadically, while making her mark in *All My Children* on TV in the 1970s. Her last movie was the little-seen *Returning* in 1990.

References Callow, Simon. *Orson Welles: The Road to Xanadu* (New York: Penguin, 1997); Carringer, Robert. *The Making of Citizen Kane* (Los Angeles: University of California Press, 1985); Leaming, Barbara. *Orson Welles: A Biography* (New York: Viking, 1985); Wise, Robert. "As the Editor, You're the Audience," *Film Comment,* Special Welles issue, 12 (March–April 1977), 21; Woods, Leigh. "The Acting in *Citizen Kane,*" in *Perspectives on Citizen Kane,* ed. Ronald Gottesman (New York: G. K. Hall, 1996), 213–28.

—G.D.P.

Waterloo Columbia Pictures, 132 minutes, 1970. **Director:** Sergei Bondarchuk; **Producer:** Thomas Carlisle; **Executive Producer:** Dino De Laurentiis; **Screenplay:** Bondarchuk, Vittorio Bonicelli, and H.A.L. Craig; **Cinematographer:** Armando Nanuzzi; *Editors:* Said Menyalshchikov, Yelena Mikhajlova, and Semyon Valyushok; **Music:** Nino Rota; **Cast:** Rod Steiger (Napoleon), Christopher Plummer (Wellington), Orson Welles (Louis XVIII), Jack Hawkins (General Piction), Virginia McKenna (duchess of Richmond), Dan O'Herlihy (Marshal Ney), Rupert Davies (Gordon), Phillipe Forquet (La Bedoyere), Ian Ogilvy (De Lancey), Peter Davies (Lord Hay), and Michael Wilding (Ponsonby)

The epic Italian-Soviet-British co-production lensed by noted Soviet actor-director Sergei Bondarchuk was a visually spectacular but plot-impoverished attempt to chronicle the career of Napoleon, tracing his return to power from his exile in Elba to his crushing 1815 defeat at Waterloo. Although failing to fully develop Napoleon's character, *Waterloo* was praised for its convincing hour-long staging of the historic battle of the title.

Speaking to PETER BOGDANOVICH about the Napoleon movies he had worked on, WELLES in response to a question about AUSTERLITZ, wryly recalled: "In that one I invented the steamboat [as inventor Robert Fulton]. It was nice to be with old Abel Gance [who directed *Austerlitz*]. He invented an awful lot of things in movies that are coming back in style now. . . . They call me in for all the Napoleon movies, though. *Waterloo* is the latest—the big one by Bondarchuk."

—C.B.

Weaver, Dennis (1924–) Character actor Dennis Weaver brilliantly improvised his role as the night motel clerk in TOUCH OF EVIL (1958) under WELLES's close supervision. Weaver was born on the Fourth of July, 1924, in Joplin, Missouri, and educated at the University of Oklahoma. He served as a navy pilot in World War II and played his first Hollywood role in the Budd Boetticher Western, *Horizons West* in 1952. *Touch of Evil* probably marked the pinnacle of Weaver's movie career, though wider recognition came through his television acting. Indeed, it was his portrayal as gimpy sidekick Chester in the popular television Western series, *Gunsmoke* that led to his casting in *Touch of Evil*. His television career extended to *Kentucky Jones, Gentle Ben,* and *McCloud,* in the last of which he starred as a folksy detective from the Old West dealing with urban crime.

Welles told PETER BOGDANOVICH that he thought "that Dennis Weaver in *Gunsmoke* was one of the greatest actors around," and added that he "wrote a part for him." According to CHARLES HIGHAM, Dennis Weaver's part "as a stammering hotel clerk, echoed the character of Welles's brother Richard, who was wandering around the northwest of America, from one job to another." BARBARA LEAMING claims that Weaver's role was "largely built up out of the actor's inspired improvisation." She writes that Welles encouraged Weaver to depart from the script in order to develop "the unexpectedly complex minor character, who so clearly anticipates the hysterical look that Anthony Perkins portrays in *Psycho.*" According to FRANK BRADY, "Dennis Weaver gave one of the most memorable performances of his career, perhaps the most stylized and effective in the film."

Reference Weaver, Dennis. *All the World's a Stage* (Charlottesville, Va.: Walsch Books, 2001).

—T.L.E. and J.M.W.

Weissberger, Arnold (1907–1981) Harvard-educated Arnold Weissberger was ORSON WELLES's attorney and legal adviser and the brother of AUGUSTA WEISSBERGER, who acted as secretary to Welles and JOHN HOUSEMAN. Arnold and Augusta helped Houseman and actress Rose MacLendon, co-heads of the NEGRO THEATRE PROJECT, plan its program in 1936. After Augusta introduced him to Welles, Arnold, who was with the Wall Street film of Liederman, Hess, Strauser, and Schwartz, became Welles's attorney. His first task was to review Welles's contract with CBS, who was producing Welles's radio show FIRST PERSON SINGULAR. When he discovered that Welles was legally responsible, for plagiarism, libel, and any trouble ensuing from a broadcast, he succeeded in getting CBS to drop the last responsibility and make it the responsibility of CBS. Weissberger's acumen was responsible for relieving Welles of responsibility for any damages, other than for libel or plagiarism, caused by the 1938 WAR OF THE WORLDS radio broadcast. In 1939, as Welles's agent and with the help of Albert Schneider, he obtained the 63-page RKO contract that gave Welles the right of final cut over the films he made for the studio. Because Welles was still involved with THE CAMPBELL PLAYHOUSE back in New York, the Ward Wheelock Agency there pressured Welles to give up the RKO deal and return to New York. Weissberger represented Welles and on August 1, 1939, apparently resolved the differences between Welles and Wheelock, but some sniping continued.

The following year, when Welles was having financial problems, he had Weissberger handle his money; and when it appeared certain that he would be drafted, Welles enlisted Weissberger to help him get a deferment, using his dependent child Christopher or his position at RKO, where his being drafted would leave many people unemployed. About his role as Welles's business manager, Weissberger wrote, "As you know, most large money earners in Hollywood, who have persons like myself in charge of their affairs, are kept on fairly stringent budgets and are told what they may and may not spend. Orson does not like to conduct his affairs that way." According to DAVID THOMSON, Weissberger, who stayed in New York, and Richard Baer, Welles's West Coast financial watchdog, had tried to put Welles on an allowance so that money could be saved for taxes and alimony/child support payments to Virginia, whom he had just divorced. Other legal problems involved the possibility of WILLIAM RANDOLPH HEARST suing Welles and/or RKO if CITIZEN KANE was released. Weissberger believed that Hearst had no case, but

convinced Welles to publicly state that he did not base Kane's character on Hearst's.

Welles was also having trouble with HERMAN MANKIEWICZ concerning credit for the script of Citizen Kane. Weissberger, who feared possible negative publicity, advised him not to let the matter go to the Screen Writers' Guild. So that Welles would be in compliance with the RKO contract that called upon him to write, direct, produce, and star in his films, Weissberger had included in Mankiewicz's contract a clause that all his work would, in effect, be the property of Mercury (Welles). When PAULINE KAEL's The Citizen Kane Book (1971) appeared, with her claim that Mankiewicz should have full credit for the screenplay, the problem resurfaced. An incensed Welles asked Weissberger about possibly suing Kael and her publishers for libel, but Weissberger wisely advised Welles to drop the idea. Weissberger believed that because malice could not be proven and Kael's ideas were only her opinions, that the libel suit would be unsuccessful. He also pointed out that since Bantam Books, Kael's publisher, had paid Welles reprint fees to include the script of Citizen Kane in the Kael book, it would be both unwise and inappropriate to sue them. After Weissberger's death in February 1981, the L. Arnold Weissberger Award recognizing outstanding theatrical achievement was created in his honor. The first recipient of the award was Joseph Papp. Also an agent and celebrity photographer, Weissberger published two volumes of photographs, Close-Up and Famous People. Beside Welles, his clients included Igor Stravinsky, Helen Hayes, Laurence Olivier, Otto Preminger, Martha Graham, and Plácido Domingo. Orson Welles delivered the eulogy at his funeral.

—T.L.E.

Weissberger, Augusta (1910–2000)

In 1935, ORSON WELLES hired Augusta Weissberger as his secretary and, later, business manager. When Welles needed a contract for his up-coming FIRST PERSON SINGULAR radio show with CBS, he needed legal help; and she recommended her brother, Arnold, who became Welles's attorney. During the rehearsals of his "voodoo" MACBETH (1936) Weissberger recorded Welles's comments about the acting. When the MERCURY THEATRE was established in 1937, JOHN HOUSEMAN was president; Welles was vice president; and Weissberger was secretary. When the company started receiving funds, she was made business manager. Although her work was primarily clerical, she did on one occasion appear in a Welles film. When Welles was shooting the film clip that was to be included in the staged farce TOO MUCH JOHNSON (1938), she was called upon to substitute for actress Arlene Francis, whose bosom Welles considered not large and matronly enough for the character she was playing. FRANK BRADY comments, "Although she was scarcely older than Arlene Francis and actually a rather small woman, the somewhat rounder, more abundant top half of her body fit the specific needs of the scene. Weissberger cheerfully complied and, amidst the catcalls of the cast and crew, gained her once-in-a-lifetime opportunity to be, at least in part, in a motion picture." When Welles was preparing to air his radio broadcast of THE WAR OF THE WORLDS, Weissberger, along with ROGER HILL, advised him that the script was not really credible. In 1939, Weissberger stayed in New York to handle Mercury business when Welles received the RKO contract and went to Hollywood. She later followed him to Hollywood, and when he left the unfinished MAGNIFICENT AMBERSONS (1942) to go to Brazil to begin filming IT'S ALL TRUE; she went along as his personal assistant. The widow of Stefan Schenker, she died on May 19, 2000, in New York City.

—T.L.E.

Welles, Beatrice Ives (1882–1924) Beatrice

Ives was born in 1882 to parents who had enough money initially to provide her with many advantages. Her father, Benjamin, had made his money, enough to be what WELLES would later describe as "comfortable," through coal mining; but when there was a slump in the coal industry in the late 1880s, he lost his coal mines to creditors. Despite the declining family fortunes (at one point they were reduced to taking in boarders), the Ives survived in Springfield, Ohio, partly because of the music lessons that Mrs. Ives and Beatrice gave to piano students. Beatrice herself was an accomplished pianist and possessed a

fine singing voice, and it was she who was responsible for Orson's musical talents. She was also a champion of women's rights and a literary intellectual, someone who would seem to be a strange choice for DICKIE WELLES, whose own musical tastes were more of the popular variety and who was known to be more comfortable with chorus girls. The fundamental differences between the two seemed obvious, but they were not the reason that the impending marriage was opposed by Dickie's mother, who believed that Beatrice was interested in Dickie's money. Despite her opposition, the marriage took place in Chicago on November 21, 1903, at the Church of Our Savior, an Episcopalian church. Beatrice, who had studied to be a "stenographer" in order to have a "real" job, did not work after her marriage to Dickie. Instead, she threw herself into her cultural and political activities. In Kenosha, where the couple lived, she was active in the Women's Club, gave piano recitals, and ran the Choral Society's concerts. Despite the fears of the male members of the Kenosha Board of Education, she became the head of that organization, as well as heading the local censorship board. These activities reflect what CHARLES HIGHAM regards as her outstanding characteristics: severity, puritanism, and sternness. Her commanding voice and impressive appearance were intimidating, and Orson Welles was intent on earning her respect. She doted on Orson, whom she favored over Dick, his older brother, and often took Orson with her to musical events and intellectual soirees. She also performed original compositions, melding piano and voice, at the Milwaukee Art Institute. When the problems between Dickie and her persisted, they separated; Orson was six at the time. He went to live with his mother, but spent vacations with his father. After the separation, which was also prompted by her affair (which may have been platonic) with DR. MAURICE BERNSTEIN, family friend and physician, all parties moved to Chicago. According to BARBARA LEAMING, Beatrice, also known as "Trixie," "flourished in Chicago," where she soon belonged to the socially elite, established a salon, where she entertained leading musicians and intellectuals, and became a popular hostess. In 1922, she became frail, and her health deteriorated. Two days after Orson's ninth birthday she was taken to

Chicago's Memorial Hospital, where the doctors diagnosed her problem as hepatitis, or yellow jaundice. She died two days later, May 10, 1924.

Although Orson was only nine years old at the time of her death, she had a profound influence upon him. He also possessed a distinctive voice, one that made him a popular narrator in films, and a love for music, though he did stop playing the piano in public after her death. He seems to have been driven in part by a desire to achieve, to please a demanding, if absent, mother. Higham finds her influence in the portrait of George Minafer's mother in THE MAGNIFICENT AMBERSONS, and PETER BOGDANOVICH sees ties between her and Mrs. Kane in CITIZEN KANE. Welles, however, has denied that he modeled young Kane's mother after his own mother.

—T.L.E.

Welles–Smith, Beatrice Judith (1955–)

Beatrice Welles was born on November 13, 1955, the youngest of ORSON WELLES's three daughters. Her mother was Welles's third wife, PAOLA MORI (Countess di Girfalco), who had starred with Welles in his MR. ARKADIN (1955). Since Beatrice was born while Welles was preparing his OTHELLO, BARBARA LEAMING aptly described her as "his Cordelia, the beloved youngest of three daughters." FRANK BRADY wrote that Welles's closest relationship with his daughters was with Beatrice, with whom "he truly acted as a father." In part, Welles was close to Beatrice because he stayed married, despite many affairs, including a long one with OJA KODAR, to PAOLA MORI. The three traveled together throughout Europe, spending some time after THE TRIAL (1962) at the Villa Mori, Paola's family home at Frenese; and when Welles returned to the United States, his home address, according to Leaming, was "wherever Paola and Beatrice were." In retrospect, his casting Beatrice as the boy page who mourns for the dying FALSTAFF (Welles) in CHIMES AT MIDNIGHT (1966) foreshadows Beatrice, almost 20 years later, carrying her father's ashes to Ronda, Spain, where they were placed in a blue urn in a small brick wall on the country estate of bullfighter Antonio Ordonez, who had been his friend.

Beatrice toured with several musical groups including the Osmonds and the Rolling Stones, wrote reviews and features for the London *Times,* and according to Frank Brady, influenced her father's musical tastes. An excellent student, she did some modeling and was employed at a local radio station in Sidona, Arizona, where she, Paola, and Welles (when he was not in Los Angeles with Kodar) lived. In 1975, when he received his award from the American Film Institute, she, described by Leaming as his "towering blonde look-alike daughter," and Paola sat beside Welles. Although he had not been very close to his two other daughters, he was close to Beatrice. Brady wrote, "Only Beatrice, the most attractive of the three women [daughters], a tall and Junoesque beauty with fair hair and a voluptuous figure, has been close to Welles in recent years."

—T.L.E.

Welles, Christopher (1938–)

Christopher Welles, the daughter of WELLES and his first wife, Virginia, was born on March 27, 1938, at the Presbyterian Hospital in New York. Welles sent telegrams to friends announcing, "Christopher, she is born." FRANK BRADY maintains that the seemingly strange choice of names was motivated only by Welles's sense of "Christopher" having an attractive sound: "It had no further significance to him beyond its melody." SIMON CALLOW notes Welles's "cavalier" approach to naming the child and describes a photograph of the young mother, father, and child: "Virginia looks strongly and almost defiantly at the camera while Welles stares down somewhat theatrically at the bundle of flesh in her mother's arms. There is nothing remotely spontaneous about the pose." BARBARA LEAMING reports that Welles was even flirting with a nurse in the maternity ward because she moved like a ballerina, and at the time Welles was sexually involved with ballerinas. Three months after Christopher's birth, Welles was, according to Callow, "juggling numerous paramours." Welles saw little of Christopher during his lifetime, other than occasional visits, and after his second marriage (the one to RITA HAYWORTH) ended, he saw her mostly on holidays. Five years after their marriage, Virginia and Welles were legally separated. Christopher was left behind with a domestic helper while Welles was in California and her mother was in Ireland. Welles and

Virginia agreed to terms that called for Welles to pay child support of $1,600 a year until Christopher was 10 years old and then $2,400 a year until she was 21. Because of Welles's financial problems, he was worried about making the payments and had an adjustment made that limited his liability in the event of severe financial losses. After the divorce, Virginia requested a lump sum settlement before her impending marriage to CHARLES LEDERER, MARION DAVIES's nephew. Welles's refusal, according to Barbara Leaming, "showed an abandonment of responsibility to his former wife and his child; he gave no inkling of enthusiasm for paying for Christopher's upbringing." After their marriage when Virginia and Charles took Christopher to San Simeon, WILLIAM RANDOLPH HEARST's estate, where Hearst and Davies, his long-standing mistress, entertained, Christopher was told to stay out of Hearst's sight since Hearst associated her with Welles and CITIZEN KANE, Welles's thinly veiled film account of Hearst's life. Virginia and Welles continued to squabble over support payments, and Welles faced court appearances regarding his failure to make child-support payments. Welles regularly sent Christopher gifts at Christmas and on her birthdays, but he rarely saw her. When Christopher was staying at Marion Davies's Santa Monica estate, it was awkward for Welles to pick her up at the home of the woman he had portrayed as an alcoholic in *Citizen Kane.* Christopher did visit Welles in Acapulco when he was shooting *THE LADY FROM SHANGHAI,* but with Rita on the set, he had little time for her. Barbara Leaming recounts an interesting episode on the set when the neglected Christopher threw a tantrum and demanded to be included in the movie. An exasperated Welles told her that she was to play the part of a brat eating an ice cream and instructed the cameraman to pretend to be filming her. Christopher's acting ambitions were realized a few years later when she was paid $150 a week to play the part of Macduff's son in Welles's film adaptation of *MACBETH.* Brady puts an interesting spin on this casting, "which put him, as Macbeth, in the curious position of engineering the murder of one of his own children on the screen. Christopher had some acting talent, and she delighted Welles with her imitations of various personalities, including her father, when she and Vir-

ginia visited him on the set of his *OTHELLO* September 15, 1949. According to CHARLES HIGHAM, he did not see either Christopher or Virginia for years. He later expressed his disappointment at her not pursuing an acting career. Christopher spent a year as the only girl at the Todd School, which Welles and his brother Dickie had attended, and also spent two years at a private school in Switzerland. Following her graduation, she went to work at the Chicago offices of the Container Corporation, where she met Norman R. De Haan, whom she married in 1957. Welles flew to Chicago to attend the wedding. After her divorce from De Haan, Christopher married Irwin Fodor and moved to New York, where she wrote poetry and designed educational materials. She told Brady a few years before Welles's death that she had had little or no contact with her father and added that she had no idea how to get in touch with him. When Welles died in 1985, Christopher inherited $10,000 from her father.

—T.L.E.

Welles, Orson (1915–1985)

By the age of 26, Orson Welles achieved extraordinary success as the most dynamic showman of the New York FEDERAL THEATRE PROJECT; the co-founder and director of the most critically acclaimed repertory company in America, the MERCURY THEATRE; creator of the most sensational radio broadcast in history, *THE WAR OF THE WORLDS;* and co-writer producer, director, and star in what is still regarded as the most important American movie since the birth of the talkies, *CITIZEN KANE.* He also was a novelist, painter, ballet scenarist, public orator, magician, columnist, and bullfighter. He was as overwhelming as his enormous girth.

Welles was born on May 6, 1915, in Kenosha, Wisconsin, to RICHARD HEAD WELLES, a prosperous wagon manufacturer and inventor, and BEATRICE IVES WELLES, a gifted concert pianist, who divorced when he was six. She died in 1924; and Welles, considered by TRUFFAUT the most musical of directors, did nothing with music thereafter. His father died in 1930, and Welles became the ward of DR. MAURICE BERNSTEIN, a Chicago physician and family friend. Welles made his stage debut in 1918 as a walk-on in *Samson and Delilah* at the Chicago Opera and continued to adapt, direct, design, and/or act in plays, especially Shakespeare (see SHAKESPEARE BY WELLES) at the Todd School for Boys in Woodstock, Illinois. Notable was *Bright Lucifer,* embodying his major themes of midwestern pastoral, grotesque terror, and family drama. Sent by his guardian to Ireland rather than Harvard to pursue painting, Welles instead finagled his first professional role at the Dublin GATE THEATRE. Following success in character roles he moved on to the Abbey Theatre. Unable to secure a work permit in London, he returned home.

Through THORNTON WILDER Welles met critic ALEXANDER WOOLLCOTT, who introduced him to director GUTHRIE MCCLINTIC and actress KATHARINE CORNELL. They cast Welles as Octavius Moulton-Barrett for their 36-week tour of *The Barretts of*

Young Orson Welles *(National Film Society Archive)*

Wimpole Street and as Marchbanks in *Candida*. With his Todd School mentor ROGER HILL he produced EVERYBODY'S SHAKESPEARE, a series of textbooks, and a summer theater festival. There Welles made his first film, HEARTS OF AGE, a silent, black-and-white one-reeler in which his first wife, Virginia Nicholson, appeared. He subsequently rejoined the Cornell tour as Tybalt in *Romeo and Juliet.*

JOHN HOUSEMAN, the Romanian-born producer, saw him and began their collaboration for the WORKS PROGRESS ADMINISTRATION and their own MERCURY THEATRE in 1937. The first thing that impressed Houseman about Welles was the "surprising vibration" of his voice. His signature voice and its intimate quality gained Welles success on radio as well as onstage. His radio work involved THE MARCH OF TIME, in which he played such diverse characters as FRANKLIN D. ROOSEVELT, Hirohito, and all five Dionne quintuplets. He also played the title role in THE SHADOW. Within a year of his 1935 debut, he commanded a salary second only to the highest-paid movie stars. In 1938, he had his own radio show, FIRST PERSON SINGULAR. Welles helped Houseman write the *Dracula* and *Julius Caesar* scripts, two of the first 10. Soon renamed THE MERCURY THEATRE ON THE AIR, the show moved to CBS prime time Sunday (8–9 P.M.). The most notorious of the broadcasts was THE WAR OF THE WORLDS, the realistic dramatization of H.G. WELLS's novella that frightened approximately 1,750,000 of the estimated 9 million listeners. Welles's use in radio of voice-over narration and complex narratives influenced his films. His radio experimentation also marked his simultaneous theater productions, all New Deal expressionism. "voodoo" MACBETH, set in Haiti with a black cast (suggested by Virginia Welles), creatively used sound techniques from radio and horror movies to shock audiences and dismay critics.

Welles and Houseman then started their own classical PROJECT 891 with the WPA. In *HORSE EATS HAT,* Welles translated French farce into surrealist slapstick; in *The Tragic History of Doctor Faustus,* he strove for magical effects through arty lighting and sound; and in THE CRADLE WILL ROCK, he defied WPA and union edicts and presented an impromptu version of MARK BLITZSTEIN's radical pro-labor opera in an unscheduled venue to rave reaction. For his and Houseman's first and best Mercury Theatre presentation, Welles staged *JULIUS CAESAR* in modern dress with contemporary political allusions. It later rotated with an oratorio version of *Cradle*.

Welles continued his Mercury Theatre onstage until he took its actors to Hollywood. Welles's first feature film, *Citizen Kane* (1941), for RKO, became a discourse on method because of his encyclopedic technical range, especially deep focus with revolutionary cameraman GREGG TOLAND. Besides deep focus, *Kane*'s simultaneous dialogue, reflections and chiaroscuro, moving camera, and sound from outside the frame increased the expressionistic effect. For all its qualities that established Welles as a major talent, *Kane*'s resemblance to WILLIAM RANDOLPH HEARST's life caused problems in distribution and in Welles's future in film. *Kane* still draws controversy. PAULINE KAEL argued the film was a shallow masterpiece and

Orson Welles

the script was the sole work of HERMAN J. MANKIEWICZ. JAMES NAREMORE disagreed, calling it the product of an individual artist (and a company of his associates) working at a particular movie studio at a particular historical moment. Problems with RKO over *Kane* continued with studio changes in THE *MAGNIFICENT AMBERSONS* (1942) when Welles left to film the unfinished *IT'S ALL TRUE* (1942) in Brazil. Although *Ambersons* resonates with Welles's life story and his reverence for the preindustrial past, it is the only film he directed and didn't act in. To fit a double feature, it was drastically cut, although STANLEY CORTEZ's fluent camera movement remains one of its strengths.

Welles strove to make his next three films on time and under budget for various studios, but *THE LADY FROM SHANGHAI* (1948) with his second wife, RITA HAYWORTH, angered Columbia boss HARRY COHN with its bizarre visual dissonances, camera work, and imagery about greed and lust; and *THE STRANGER* (1946), and the pessimistic, moralistic *Macbeth* (1948) the first of Welles's Shakespeare trilogy about the destructive effect of power, all flopped at the box office. Considered in Hollywood as unreliable, extravagant, and unbankable with his outrageous and idiosyncratic films, Welles did not make another Hollywood film for a decade. He continued to act in films, which at the end of his career totaled 61.

JANE EYRE (1943) established his stardom, and he moved to Europe in 1947 to act in such films as *THE THIRD MAN* (1949), as a means to produce his own films. In Europe, and filming on location with few resources, he made the visually poetic *OTHELLO* (1952), the burlesque thriller *MR. ARKADIN* (*Confidential Report,* 1955), the KAFKA terror *THE TRIAL* (1961), and the Shakespeare-based *CHIMES AT MIDNIGHT* (*Falstaff,* 1966).

Welles returned to the United States to star in PETER BROOK's TV *KING LEAR* to critical acclaim, the first of many TV roles, and to Hollywood for *TOUCH OF EVIL* (1958), a film of visual fascination and moral ironies. Brutally recut, it gained a critical reputation in Europe and was recently restored. Ironically, *FILMING OTHELLO* was his last work, a documentary about his *Othello* that had won the 1952 Grand Prix in Cannes. He left 37 films, scripts, and outlines, from

Charles Foster Kane (Welles) shows his "Declaration of Principles" to Jed Leland (Joseph Cotten) and Mr. Bernstein (Everett Sloane) *(Literature/Film Archive)*

HEART OF DARKNESS in 1939 to *THE CRADLE WILL ROCK* in 1984. Welles died at 70. His ashes were interred two years afterward in Spain in an unmarked grave.

—J.C.T.

Welles, Rebecca (1944–)

Rebecca Welles, ORSON WELLES's second daughter, was born on December 17, 1944; her mother was actress RITA HAYWORTH, Welles's second wife. Although she looked like her father, he did not seem very interested in her. According to Shifra Haran, "I don't think Mr. Welles ever paid any attention to her—just not in the cards. Now, on the contrary, Prince Aly [Rita's next husband] played with her, talked to her. He was *crazy* about her. Mr. Welles never did that. FRANK BRADY observed that Rebecca, named for the heroine in Sir Walter Scott's *Ivanhoe,* was not "one of his [Welles's] favored children," perhaps because Aly Khan had replaced him in her affections. After his divorce from Hayworth was finalized, Welles saw little of Rebecca, though he often sent her gifts, but just as often reneged on her financial support. In 1956, Hayworth sued him for $22,450 in back child-support payments. According to Brady, in the late 1970s, when Rebecca would have been in her mid-30s, she wrote to him from the state of Washington "to see if I could supply her with certain information

about her parents." She also stated in interviews that she and her sculptor husband were living in poverty in Tacoma, Washington, in the 1970s. Welles then asked her about appearing with him in a commercial, but, according to CHARLES HIGHAM, "apart from scattered correspondence they were not in touch again." She later divorced the sculptor, but continued to live in Tacoma. When Welles died in 1985, she, like her sisters, Christopher and Beatrice, received $10,000 from his estate.

—T.L.E.

Welles, Richard Head (Richard Hodgdon Wells) (1872–1930)

Richard Welles, ORSON WELLES's father, was the son of a relatively wealthy wagon manufacturer. At the age of 25 he assumed a responsible position with the Badger Brass Company, which was incorporated in 1897. According to Orson Welles, his father invented the acetylene gas heater, which eventually replaced traditional kerosene lamps, and a collapsible picnic outfit that was adapted and sold to the American government for use as a mess kit during World War I. He also worked on inventing the automobile, but thinking the vehicle was impractical never sought patents for his ideas. There is an obvious parallel between Welles and Eugene Morgan, the automobile manufacturer in BOOTH TARKINGTON's *THE MAGNIFICENT AMBERSONS,* which Orson Welles adapted to the screen. (Welles did know Tarkington, as well as WILLIAM RANDOLPH HEARST, whose career Orson mirrored in the title character of *CITIZEN KANE.*) The creative and talented investor and businessman met Beatrice Ives when he was 31 years old, and they were married in Chicago on November 21, 1903. Because of his excessive drinking, womanizing, and lavish spending, his marriage was in trouble almost from the start. By the time Orson Welles was six, his parents had separated. His mother met DR. MAURICE BERNSTEIN, who competed with Orson's father for his affection and who played a significant role in Orson Welles's life. When he was nine, his mother died, and he went to Chicago to live in with his father and Bernstein, his two "fathers." Orson's father retired from an active business life to have more time for Orson, though he had written off Orson's older brother, Dickie, who was a terrible disappointment to his father. After a short time in the public schools, Orson was enrolled at the age of 10 in the private Todd School, where the headmaster was Skipper Hill, who liked Orson and became still another father figure for him. During the five years that Orson spent at Todd, he spent short vacations with Bernstein and longer holidays with his father, who frequently took him on trips, including ones to Jamaica and the Far East. FRANK BRADY notes that because of his father's drinking, other passengers might have wondered who was taking care of whom. Orson also spent time with his father at the Sheffield Hotel in Grand Detour, Illinois, which his father owned until it burned down in 1928. Fearing Welles's father's negative influence on Orson, Bernstein and Hill collaborated to keep Orson away from his father as much as possible. Welles's father died on December 28, 1930. The official causes of death were chronic myocarditis and nephritis; but there were also rumors about his drinking himself to death, and JOHN HOUSEMAN, who had been Orson's close friend and collaborator in the 1930s, said that he had "died by his own hand." His will granted six-sevenths of his estate to Orson and one-seventh to Dickie.

—T.L.E.

Welles, Richard Ives, Jr. (1905–1975)

Richard Welles, Jr., ORSON WELLES's older brother, was born in 1905, and from the beginning, according to SIMON CALLOW, "he failed to please." His stammer suggested that he lacked intelligence, and he was shy, insecure, and sullen. Soon after Orson was born, "Dickie," as he was known, was sent to the Todd School, which Callow describes as "having a reputation for dealing with problem cases." BARBARA LEAMING quotes a Todd alumnus as saying that the school was "an island for lost boys." Dickie was expelled from the school, but the reason for his dismissal is unknown. After his expulsion, his father banished him from the family. Leaming writes that his father's dislike for Dickie was so intense that when he heard that Dickie might be the corpse that had been found on the banks of the Mississippi he said, "That's good, at least the family is rid of him." Dickie roamed the country, working at odd jobs, much to his father's fury and embarrassment.

Callow writes, "No praise for him, no laughter; no plans and no hopes." Orson was the favored son. When Dickie was 25 years old, his father and DR. MAURICE BERNSTEIN plotted to have Dickie certified insane (dementia simplex) and committed to the Kanakee institution for the insane. During his 10-year confinement there, he was not once visited by anyone in his immediate family; Irene Lefkow, a cousin who was appointed as his guardian, was the only "family" visitor. When his father died in 1930, he was not allowed to attend the funeral. According to the terms of his father's will, he was to get one-seventh of his father's estate (approximately $6,500); Orson was to get the rest (about $37,000).

Orson was fairly successful at getting some of the money from Dr. Bernstein, who was in charge of the money; Dickie was less fortunate and lived in plain circumstances at Kanakee. After Dickie finally won, through writs of habeas corpus, his freedom, he embarrassed Orson by claiming that he had written THE WAR OF THE WORLDS and coming to the MERCURY THEATRE office with his wife, Mildred, whom he had met at a midnight mission for derelicts. While Orson did send Dickie some money every month, clearly Orson did not want his older brother about. Between 1938 and his brother's death in 1975, the brothers met only once. At one of Orson's MERCURY WONDER SHOWS, Dickie appeared and volunteered to saw MARLENE DIETRICH in two. Orson asked the volunteer who he was; Dickie responded, "Don't you know your own brother?" After that meeting, Orson continued supporting Dickie, but the support was meager. In 1942, Dickie worked as a night janitor at the NEGRO THEATRE PROJECT headquarters. When not working at similar jobs, he was in and out of mental institutions. He was briefly in a monastery and for a time worked as a social worker at the Hull House in Chicago. According to Orson, "He got fired from Hull House because he took a prostitute upstairs and locked himself in with her, and they couldn't get him down for days." When he died in 1975, Orson, who had continued with some financial support, arranged to have the funeral paid for, but ARNOLD WEISSBERGER, who was supposed to take care of the matter, did not pay for the funeral. Instead, Dickie's meager estate was attached by the public administrator to pay for it.

Despite the lack of interaction between the two brothers, Dickie had quite an impact on Orson's life. First, Orson feared, according to CHARLES HIGHAM, that he might be susceptible to the same mental problems that Dickie had. Leaming writes that for Orson, Dickie was a nuisance because he was "a loathsome and distorted image of his own strangeness." Second, Dickie found his way into Welles's work. *Marching Song,* a play that Welles wrote with ROGER HILL, concerns the American abolitionist John Brown, and the freeing of American slaves. In the play, the character of John Brown's son closely parallels Dickie. Higham writes, "John Brown's son is an echo of Richard Ives Welles at Kanakee; he is portrayed as crazed, deeply disturbed, an idiot 'with a loose, wet mouth and saucer eyes.'" Welles seemed to be unable to rid himself of the "nuisance."

—T.L.E.

Welles, Virginia See LEDERER, VIRGINIA NICHOLSON WELLES.

Wells, H[erbert] G[eorge] (1866–1946)
The author of THE WAR OF THE WORLDS, from which ORSON WELLES's celebrated MERCURY THEATRE radio production was drawn, was born the third son of a middle-class shopkeeper in Bromley, Kent, in 1866. After serving an apprenticeship with a draper and teaching at Midhurst Grammar School, he received a scholarship to the Normal School of Science in London, where he studied biology under T.H. Huxley. Following the publication in 1893 of two textbooks, he began writing scientific romances, most notably *The Time Machine* (1895), *The Island of Dr. Moreau* (1896), *The War of the Worlds* (1897), *When the Sleeper Wakes* (1899), and *First Men in the Moon* (1901). "In many of these stories," writes science-fiction writer and historian Brian Aldiss, "Wells proved himself the great originator of science fictional ideas. They were new with him, and have been reworked endlessly since." Ever seeking to fuse his scientific and progressive social interests, he joined the Fabian Society in 1903, the League of Nations movement after World War I, and sought to align American and Soviet interests in his fight against fascism and in his attempts to envision a world utopia (see *The Work,*

Wealth, and Happiness of Mankind, 1931, and *The Shape of Things to Come,* 1933). Wells's *Experiment in Autobiography* appeared in 1933. After a long illness, Wells died of cancer in 1946.

Wells's long and sometimes contentious involvement with the film medium began in 1895 with his association with British film pioneer Robert W. Paul. They applied for a patent for a film projection device that would simulate a journey through time (arguably inspired by Wells's description of the eponymous device in *The Time Machine*). Thereafter, references to the "cinematograph" appear frequently in his stories; and in the 1930s he wrote the screenplays for *Things to Come* (subsequently revised by Lajos Biro) and *The Man Who Could Work Miracles* (1937). Among the many other films adapted from his stories are James Whale's *The Invisible Man* (1933), *The Island of Lost Souls* (1933), George Pal's *The War of the Worlds* (1953), and Pal's *The Time Machine* (1960).

The radio adaptation by Orson Welles and HOWARD KOCH of *The War of the Worlds* for a Mercury broadcast on Halloween, 1938, updated the novel and shifted the location from England to New Jersey, presenting it in terms of a breaking news story. That version, along with the Pal 1960 version (likewise updated), have tended to obscure the merits of Wells's original narrative, in which an unnamed Narrator relates the tale of his travails following a Martian invasion six years earlier outside London. "No one would have believed in the last years of the nineteenth century," he begins, "that this world was being watched keenly and closely by intelligences greater than man's. . . ." His narrative continues with the arrival of a Martian cylinder in the rural district of Woking. An emerging Martian, described as a "grayish rounded bulk" with "Gorgon groups of tentacles" around the V-shaped mouth, vaporizes onlookers with a "Heat-Ray." More cylinders arrive, decimating the British soldiers who stand in their way. With their colossal walking tripods and poisonous Black Smoke, the Martians lay waste to the area and force the evacuation of London. Eventually, however, the Martians fall prey to bacterial infection, "slain, after all man's devices failed, by the humblest things that God, in his wisdom, has put on this earth." The Narrator returns home to find his wife alive and well. However, after coming back to London, he is disillusioned by the spectacle of survivors roaming the streets like ghosts of the past, "phantasms in a dead city, the mockery of life in a galvanized body."

The War of the Worlds, like all of Wells's best work, is a canny blend of scientific extrapolation, social commentary, evolutionary theory, and gothic horror. It speculates on the possibilities of space travel: "Before the cylinder fell there was a general persuasion that through all the deep of space no life existed beyond the petty surface of our minute sphere. Now we see further. If the Martians can reach Venus, there is no reason to suppose that the thing is impossible for men. . . ." It serves as a cautionary fable about the British colonialists' appropriation of "primitive" peoples in the building of Empire. In the very first page, the Narrator notes: "Minds that are to our minds as ours are to those of the beasts that perish, intellects vast and cool and unsympathetic, regarded this earth with envious eyes, and slowly and surely drew their plans against us." Regarding Wells's pet theme of the possibilities of human evolution, commentator Thomas M. Renzi points out that the appearance of the Martians resembles descriptions in an early essay, "The Man of the Year Million," regarding what man may become if evolution should proceed in a certain direction: "The Martians bear out this speculation, coming from an older planet and being further along the evolutionary scale." As a tale of pure terror, *The War of the Worlds* takes on the aspects of a vampire story: The Martians' motive for invading the Earth is self-preservation—they have left their dying planet seeking not only sanctuary, but a fresh food supply.

In spite of its many adaptations in various media, and in spite of the flimsy "invaders from Mars" imitations that have sprung up in its wake in pulp magazines and on the screen, the original novel, *The War of the Worlds,* still stands on its own, commanding attention as a chilling, yet thought-provoking achievement. In its time, it elicited a critic from the *Daily News* to remark that it caused "insufferable distress to the feelings." Let *that* stand as its enduring testament.

References Aldiss, Brian. *Billion Year Spree: The True History of Science Fiction* (Garden City, N.Y.: Doubleday & Company, Inc., 1973); Renzi, Thomas C. *H.G. Wells: Six Scientific Romances Adapted for Film* (Metuchen, N.J.: Scarecrow, 1992); West, Anthony. *H.G. Wells: Aspects of a Life* (New York: Random House, 1984).

—J.C.T.

Where Is Parsifal?   Terence Young, 84 minutes, 1984. **Director:** Henri Helman; **Producer:** Daniel Carrillo; **Screenplay:** Berta Dominquez; **Cinematographer:** Norman Langley; **Editors:** Russell Lloyd and Peter Hollywood; **Cast:** Tony Curtis (Parsifal Katzenellenbogen), Cassandra Domenica (Elba), Erik Estrada (Henry Board II), Peter Lawford (Montague Chippendale), Donald Pleasence (Mackintosh), Orson Welles (Klingslor)

In this remake of *You Can't Take It with You,* ORSON WELLES played the part of a rich gypsy who attempts to buy a laser typewriter from the Curtis character. Despite the presence of some major film actors, the frenetic comedy failed and did not receive much critical attention, nor was it widely distributed.

—T.L.E.

Whitney, John Hay (Jock Whitney) (1904–1982) Government official Jock Whitney helped to instigate ORSON WELLES's *IT'S ALL TRUE,* a projected four-part documentary to be shot in Brazil, which was originally scheduled as *Pan-American,* a film about life in North and South America. It was purportedly the idea of Ourival Fontes, minister of propaganda and popular culture in Brazil. CHARLES HIGHAM believes that Fontes "proposed a multifaceted picture of Brazilian life to John Hay Whitney and Walt Disney during their South American tour in October 1941," and President Vargas of Brazil supported the plan, which also had State Department backing. According to FRANK BRADY, "Nelson Rockefeller, a large RKO stockholder and Coordinator of Inter-American Affairs (CIAA) and admirer of Orson Welles, became involved in the rethinking of the movie." As a result of negotiations between RKO and the CIAA, John Hay Whitney, who headed the CIAA film division, informed Welles that the film would be "an extension of President Roosevelt's Good Neighbor [policy]." The American government promised up to $300,000 to offset a pos-

sible box-office loss for RKO. In a letter to PETER BOGDANOVICH, Orson Welles wrote, "I went [to Rio de Janeiro, Brazil] because it was put to me in the very strongest terms by Jock [John Hay Whitney] and Nelson [Rockefeller] that this would represent a sorely needed contribution to inter-American affairs. I was told that the value of this project would not lie in the film itself but *in the fact of making it.*" DAVID THOMSON has a quite different story. He speculates that Welles, guilty because of his successful effort to avoid the draft, was "moved by the state of the war and wanted to do something." Thomson maintains that Rockefeller and Whitney originally had in mind "a few broadcasts, and perhaps a lecture tour in South America. It was Welles who blew up the balloon." Welles, on the other hand, declared that he "loathed the idea of carnival." Thomson not only insists that Welles wanted to go, but he also claims that the U.S. government "put no money into the venture." If Thomson is correct, Welles's decision to go and his later decision not to return are Welles's fault, not the fault of the government that pushed Welles into making the ill-fated *It's All True.*

Businessman and philanthropist John Hay Whitney was born in Ellsworth, Maine, on August 17, 1904. He graduated from Yale University in 1926 and then studied a year at Oxford, but he had to leave when his father died. When he took over his father's business in 1927, it was worth $179 million. Whitney had a lifelong interest in theater and film. He backed more than 40 plays on Broadway, owned Pioneer Pictures (1933), which introduced Technicolor, and was in charge of the New York operations for Selznick International. In addition to his work with the CIAA, he served in the army, rising to the rank of colonel before he was captured and escaped from the Germans in France. In 1946, he established the John Hay Whitney Foundation, a philanthropical organization, and the J.H. Whitney Corporation, which invested in several businesses, including Minute Maid orange juice. Concerned about the *New York Herald Tribune,* he formed a company that bought the *Tribune* and other papers. Ultimately, the *Tribune* was lost, but the *International Herald Tribune* survives to this day. In recognition for his support of the Republican Party he was named ambassador to

the Court of St. James, 1957–60. He continued to serve the government in a variety of posts and died in 1982.

Reference   Kahn, Ely Jacques. *Jock: The Life and Times of John Hay Whitney* (Garden City, N.Y.: Doubleday, 1981).

—T.L.E.

Wilde, Oscar (Fingal O'Flahertie Wills)

(1854–1900)   ORSON WELLES had a lifetime fascination with the works of playwright Oscar Wilde, whom he was fond of quoting as a youth. When Welles began adapting classical works for his radio shows, he turned to Wilde's plays, and he later planned to adapt them to the screen. In 1938, Welles planned to have his Mercury Players stage Wilde's THE IMPORTANCE OF BEING EARNEST, but had to abandon the plans when Hiram Sherman, a Mercury actor Welles intended to cast in the male lead, suddenly left the Mercury troupe. In 1946, Welles and singer Bing Crosby made an album that featured an adaptation of Wilde's *The Happy Prince.* Welles also planned to adapt Wilde's SALOME to the screen and with Fletcher Markle wrote a screenplay for the film, which was to be produced by ALEXANDER KORDA. The script, however, ran into problems with Joseph Breen, the film "censor," who objected to Herod's lust for his stepdaughter and niece, Salome, and Salome's kissing the severed head of John the Baptist. Welles was also arguing with Korda about who should play the part of Salome—Welles wanted to cast BARBARA LAAGE, his current mistress. The film was never made, though the screenplay was published in French critic MAURICE BESSY's book on Welles. When Welles went to Germany in 1950, he included a condensed version of Wilde's *The Importance of Being Earnest* in his show, which was entitled "AN EVENING WITH ORSON WELLES." While in Germany, Welles shot some scenes of the Wilde play, but the footage has been lost.

Oscar Wilde was born on October 16, 1854, in Dublin, Ireland, the son of Sir William Wilde, a famous surgeon and oculist. After attending the Portora Royal School in Enniskillen, he enrolled at Trinity College, Dublin, and then entered Magdalen College, Oxford, in 1974. After graduation he went to London, where he moved among the social and intellectual elite. For the next few years he lectured abroad, edited *The Woman's World,* and published short stories. In 1890, his novel *The Picture of Dorian Gray,* which was adapted to film in 1945 and 1974, appeared; it was followed by *Lady Windermere's Fan* (1892), the first of his society comedies and a play that was adapted to film in 1926. That same year *Salome* was banned by the Lord Chamberlain, but it was published in France in 1894. *The Importance of Being Earnest,* Wilde's most popular play, appeared in 1895; it was adapted to film in 1952. At the time of his artistic triumph, Wilde experienced profound personal humiliation. He sued the Marquis of Queensbury for criminal libel (the Marquis, incensed at Wilde's relationship with Lord Alfred Douglas, his son, had accused him of being a sodomite), but the Marquis was acquitted, and Wilde was convicted and sentenced to two years' hard labor, which he spent at Reading, where he wrote *De Profundis* (1897). After his release, he left England for good, adopted the name Sebastian Melmoth, and toured Europe. He wrote *The Ballad of Reading Gaol,* which appeared in 1898. He died in the spring of 1900 in Paris.

References Smidgall, Gary. *The Stranger Wilde: Interpreting Oscar* (New York: Dutton, 1994); Stokes, John. *Oscar Wilde: Myths, Miracles, and Imitations* (New York: Cambridge, 1996).

—T.L.E.

Wilder, Thornton (1897–1975) Writer Thornton Wilder first met ORSON WELLES at a party after Welles had returned from Ireland, where he had his first real acting experience. Wilder, who was then a professor of English at the University of Chicago and the author of plays and a few novels, including the acclaimed *The Bridge of San Luis Rey,* gave Welles a letter of introduction to ALEXANDER WOOLLCOTT, who in turn introduced him to KATHERINE CORNELL and GUTHRIE MCCLINTIC, the husband-and-wife theater team who were planning an extensive United States tour. McClintic and Cornell hired Welles to play some supporting roles in their repertory company. An appreciative Welles wrote to Wilder: "You have given me a whole ring of keys to this city." Another debt to Wilder, according to PETER BOG-DANOVICH, was the much-praised breakfast sequence

involving CHARLES FOSTER KANE and his first wife, Emily Norton, from CITIZEN KANE (1941), which Welles admitted to having "stolen" from a scene in Wilder's one-act play, *The Long Christmas Dinner.*

In 1934, when Welles was at the Woodstock Summer Theatre, he met Wilder again, and the two had frequent conversations. The last production of Welles's MERCURY THEATRE ON THE AIR (December 4, 1938) was an adaptation of Wilder's *The Bridge of San Luis Rey,* which had won the Pulitzer Prize; and when Welles was planning his FIVE KINGS stage production, he offered the role of Holinshed, the Chorus of the play, to Wilder, who had earlier played the role of the Stage Manager in his own play, *Our Town.* Wilder was not available. After the *Mercury Theatre on the Air* was succeeded by Welles's CAMPBELL PLAYHOUSE, Welles adapted Wilder's *Our Town,* which had won a Pulitzer Prize for 1937–38, for his new show.

Thornton Wilder, who was born on April 17, 1897, in Madison, Wisconsin, received an excellent education. After attending the Thatcher School in Ojai, California, he attended Berkeley High School; upon graduation in 1915, he enrolled at Oberlin College (1915–17) and then at Yale University, where he received his A. B. degree in 1920. He studied at the American Academy in Rome and then at Princeton University, where he received his master's degree in 1926. He then taught at the prestigious Lawrenceville Academy and became a part-time lecturer in comparative literature at the University of Chicago (1930–36). By the time he met Welles, Wilder had written several plays, most of which were produced at Yale; but his *The Trumpet Shall Sound* (1926) was produced at the American Laboratory Theatre in New York, and his *Pullman Car Hiawatha* was staged at the Circle in the Square Theatre in New York in 1932. *Our Town* (1938), with its bare sets and its ability to manipulate time and space, was his first major financial and critical success and won the Pulitzer Prize for drama. (With Frank Craven and Harry Chandlee, Wilder also wrote the screenplay for *Our Town* [1940].) *The Skin of Our Teeth* (1942) won him a second Pulitzer Prize for drama. His *The Merchant of Yonkers* (1939) was adapted from a play by Johann Nestroy, who had, in turn, adapted his play from John Oxenford's *A Well-Spent Day* (1938). Wilder's comedy was then revised as *The Matchmaker* (itself adapted to film in 1958 and 1997), which was the basis for the extremely successful Broadway musical *Hello, Dolly!*, later adapted to film with Barbra Streisand and Walter Matthau in 1969. Wilder wrote six more novels, several more plays, and collections of essays before his death in 1975. He was awarded many honorary degrees and won several awards including the Pulitzers, the Presidential Medal of Freedom (1963), and the National Book Award (1968). He was a member of the Order of the British Empire (1945), the Légion d'Honneur (France, 1951), and the Orders of Merit in Peru and Germany (1957).

References Blank, Martin, ed. *Critical Essays on Thornton Wilder* (New York: G.K. Hall, 1996); Castronova, David. *Thornton Wilder* (New York: Ungar, 1986); Lifton, Paul. *Vast Encyclopedia: The Theatre of Thornton Wilder* (Westport, Conn.: Greenwood, 1995).

—T.L.E.

Wilson, Richard (1915–1991) Born in McKeesport, Pennsylvania, on December 25, 1915, and educated at the University of Denver, Wilson first intersected with the Wellesian orbit in 1937, when he joined the MERCURY THEATRE. Participating in Mercury's various stage, radio, and film undertakings through 1951, Wilson was one of WELLES's closest and most trusted lieutenants. During his tenure with Welles, Wilson played small parts as a reporter in *CITIZEN KANE* (1941) and as the district attorney's assistant in *THE LADY FROM SHANGHAI* (1948). Significantly, Wilson served as associate producer for *The Lady from Shanghai* as well as for *MACBETH* (1948). After Mercury Enterprises eventually collapsed, Wilson produced B pictures such as *The Golden Blade* (1953) and *Ma and Pa Kettle at Home* (1954). He soon turned to directing. Among his films, many of them western and gangster titles, are *Man with the Gun* (1955), *Raw Wind in Eden* (1957), *Al Capone* (1959), and *Invitation to a Gunfighter* (1964).

Wilson, like JOHN HOUSEMAN before him, tried to keep Welles tethered to the financial and logistical realities of production. In contrast to the famously despised Houseman, however, Welles esteemed and trusted Wilson to the end. In a letter to PETER BOGDANOVICH, for example, Welles says: "I think you've already met Dick Wilson. If you spend time with him, as I hope you will, you're going to find that he's invaluable [as a source on Welles]. He was not only my right hand during those years but in South America [a reference to IT'S ALL TRUE] and deserves the title of executive producer. You'll find him very fair-minded, the very opposite of a yes-man."

Wilson had a long history of helping serious Welles scholars and commentators. The second edition of Professor ROBERT L. CARRINGER's authoritative study, *The Making of Citizen Kane* (1996), for example, carries the foreword, "In Memoriam, Richard Wilson, 1915–1991," a tip-of-the-hat to Wilson for having helped make key materials in the Mercury Theatre archives available to Carringer. Wilson, often left alone in the Mercury office to tend to the vexatious problems of paying bills and bringing projects to closure while the Great Man was off acting to replenish the coffers, seems to have possessed a stable yet nimble soul that was one part banker, one part entrepreneur, and one part mind reader able to "imagine" how Welles wanted things done. BARBARA LEAMING suggests that toward the end of the Wilson-Welles relationship in the late 1940s, with Welles often overseas, Wilson was, in effect, running a shadow organization as the American head of Mercury Enterprises. Against all odds, and with a bank balance often in the red, Wilson made a valiant effort to keep Mercury afloat. When the good ship Mercury was finally scuttled in the early 1950s, the loyal Wilson was forced to move on.

—C.B.

Wise, Robert (1914–) Arriving in Hollywood from rural Indiana during the Great Depression, Robert Wise first established himself as a talented film editor at RKO, where he helped ORSON WELLES assemble both *CITIZEN KANE* (1941) and *THE MAGNIFICENT AMBERSONS* (1942). He soon found employment thereafter as a journeyman director for Val Lewton and ultimately established himself as a genre master, destined to make some of the most popular and memorable films of the 1950s and

1960s. Wise was born in Winchester, Indiana, on September 10, 1914, and educated in the Hoosier state. Forced by economic constraints to drop out of Franklin College near Indianapolis, Wise migrated to Hollywood. Only eight years after his arrival, Wise was nominated for an Academy Award for his editing of *Citizen Kane* in 1941, although 20 years were to pass before he would win a second Oscar for directing *West Side Story* (sharing the credit and the honors with co-director and choreographer Jerome Robbins), a film that was honored as the best picture of 1961. Further recognition came in 1965 when *The Sound of Music* also won Academy Awards for best directing and best picture. In 1966, moreover, the Motion Picture Academy granted Wise the Irving G. Thalberg Memorial Award, its highest accolade.

In 1933, his father's business was failing, and, as Wise told the National Film Society in 1978, "there was no money to go back" for his second year of college. "I couldn't get a job in my hometown," Wise explained, but his older brother, David, "had come out to California five years before and managed to get a job at RKO," working in the accounting office. When the younger Wise arrived in Hollywood in July of 1933, his brother got him "a couple of

appointments with department heads at RKO." The second of these was with Jimmy Wilkerson, "who headed up the editorial department—the film editing department—at RKO, and he happened to need a kid in the film-shooting room to check the prints and run the projector." This modest assignment launched Wise on a very successful Hollywood career.

Before long Wise had become a film editor, serving such talents as George Stevens on *Alice Adams* (1935) and Orson Welles on that director's earliest and potentially greatest features. His first assignment as director came when he was working for the Val Lewton production unit in 1943. Gunther Van Fritsch, who had begun a film entitled *Curse of the Cat People,* had committed the unforgivable "sin" of falling behind schedule in a low-budget operation where time was of the essence. Given the opportunity to complete this picture, Wise demonstrated a remarkable ability to create an effective supernatural ambience while working on a very low budget with limited resources. Later supernatural films would follow, most notably *The Haunting* (1963), with Julie Harris and Claire Bloom, based on Shirley Jackson's *The Haunting of Hill House,* and *Audrey Rose* (1977), adapted by Frank DeFellita from his novel and starring Anthony Hopkins and Marsha Mason.

Wise proved adaptable to other genre pictures as well. *The Body Snatcher* (1945) has been recognized as a classic of the horror genre, for example, and *The Set-Up* (1949), with Robert Ryan as an over-the-hill boxer who refuses to "fix" a fight although pressured by mobsters, won the Jury Prize at the Cannes Film Festival. A second fight film followed in 1956, *Somebody Up There Likes Me,* which starred PAUL NEWMAN as the boxer Rocky Graziano, a biopic scripted by Ernest Lehman that also won an Oscar for its cinematography. *I Want to Live!* (1956), another biopic, told the story of Barbara Graham, convicted and executed in 1955 for her alleged participation in the murder of Mabel Monohan in Burbank, California, in 1953. Wise was nominated for an Academy Award for best director, and Susan Hayward won an Oscar as best actress for her portrayal of Barbara Graham. An immense critical success, the film was sin-

Robert Wise

gled out by the *New York Times* as one of the "Ten Best Films of 1958."

Wise's most popular genre pictures, however, were musicals and science fiction. *The Day the Earth Stood Still* (1951), a "friendly" alien message film encouraging peace and cooperation among nations during the height of the arms race and the cold war, has since become a cult classic. This was followed by *The Andromeda Strain* (1971), adapted from Michael Crichton's novel concerning the threat posed to humankind by a deadly alien virus, and *Star Trek-The Motion Picture* (1979), adapted from Gene Roddenberry's long-running cult television space opera that ran on NBC television from 1966 to 1969. Nominated for Academy Awards for art direction, visual effects, and musical score, the picture later generated six sequels.

Wise had his most astonishing popular success with musicals, however, starting with *West Side Story* (1961), adapted from the play by Arthur Laurents, with music by Leonard Bernstein and lyrics by Stephen Sondheim, originally directed and choreographed for the stage by Jerome Robbins. The play was a musical adaptation and updating of Shakespeare's *Romeo and Juliet*. "Everything about *West Side Story*," critic PAULINE KAEL wrote, "is supposed to stun you with its newness, its size, the wonders of its photography, editing, cinematography, [and] music. It's nothing so simple as a musical, it's a piece of cinematic technology." Though Kael was probably damning with faint praise, the craftsmanship was quite remarkable and audiences were dazzled. A 1977 American Film Institute poll proclaimed it to be one of the 50 "Greatest American Films of all Time."

West Side Story was then followed in 1965 by *The Sound of Music,* adapted by Ernest Lehman from the play by Howard Lindsay and Russel Crouse, with lyrics by Oscar Hammerstein II and music by Richard Rodgers. The musical had in turn been adapted from *The Story of the Trapp Family Singers,* by Maria von Trapp, an account of the von Trapp family under pressure in Austria during the Third Reich. This film was graced by the presence of Christopher Plummer as Captain von Trapp, and, especially, by Julie Andrews as Maria, whose singing talent helped to propel the film to the AFI list of the 50 "Greatest

American Films." Besides winning five Academy Awards, the film generated Golden Globe awards (best motion picture and best actress for musical/comedy), the Writers Guild Award for Best-Written American Musical for Ernest Lehman, the Directors Guild Award for Wise's direction, and the Producers Guild David O. Selznick Award for Wise. Always a perennial favorite, *The Sound of Music* enjoyed a popular revival in London in 2000, when a cult craze saw spectators dressing up as nuns and Nazis and coming in droves to sing along with the music and interact with the screen story, following the example of *The Rocky Horror Picture Show.*

In 1966, Wise directed *The Sand Pebbles,* starring Steve McQueen as a sailor on a gunboat, the USS *San Pedro,* on the Yangtze River in China in 1926, the first American film made in Taiwan, and one with subtle echoes of America's involvement in Southeast Asia at the time the picture was filmed. *The Sand Pebbles* garnered seven Academy Award nominations and led to the Thalberg Award for Wise, a capstone for his career. The last film Wise directed, *Rooftops,* in 1989, was a musical, but was also intended as a tough urban drama, but the film fell far short of being successful. Critic Frank Thompson notes that "although Wise did not develop a particular style that can be read throughout each of his motion pictures," he was "a master craftsman [and] a superb entertainer," who belongs, commercially, "in the pantheon of movie makers." Before the tremendous later successes of George Lucas and Steven Spielberg, Robert Wise "was among the most profitable filmmakers in history."

Among his other accomplishments, Wise served as president of the Motion Picture Academy of Arts and Sciences from 1985 to 1987. He chaired the Directors Guild Special Projects Committee for 20 years beyond his appointment in 1976 and was elected as trustee of the American Film Institute in 1982. In 1988, he received the D.W. Griffith Award for outstanding achievement and a lifetime contribution to film from the Directors Guild of America. In 1992, he received the National Medal of the Arts from President George Bush. He was well regarded in Hollywood for his kindness and cooperation as well as his quiet competence and his abilities to create blockbuster hits.

Other Films *Mademoiselle Fifi* (1944), *Blood on the Moon* (1948), *The House on Telegraph Hill* (1951), *The Desert Rats* (1953), *So Big* (1953), *Executive Suite* (1954), *Run Silent, Run Deep* (1958), *Odds Against Tomorrow* (1959), *Two for the Seesaw* (1962), *Star!* (1968), *The Hindenberg* (1975).

References Thompson, Frank. *Robert Wise: A Bio-Bibliography* (Westport, Conn.: Greenwood, 1995); Welsh, Jim. "A Tribute to Robert Wise," *American Classic Screen*, V:5 (1980); Wise, Robert. "Dialogue on Film," *American Film* (November 1975).

—J.M.W.

Wonder Show, The (radio, 1936–1937) By 1937, network radio had become firmly established as one of the basic forms of leisure entertainment in America. It was also a period of tremendous productivity for the 22-year-old WELLES. On radio, in addition to his anonymous impersonations of newsmakers for THE MARCH OF TIME, he was also thrilling national audiences as the ethereal incarnation of THE SHADOW. He was also bringing poetry to life over the air and guesting in various roles in the Federal Theatre Radio Division's series of classical plays. There were guest shots on *Roses and Drums,* an NBC weekly series about the Civil War. And for those who might be under the impression that Welles resorted to commercials only in his later years, it is well to recall that during this period he also served as the voice of My-T-Fine chocolate pudding. In the evenings, he was appearing in the FEDERAL THEATRE production of *DOCTOR FAUSTUS,* a play he also directed.

As if the above activities were not enough, on weekends Welles flew to Chicago to appear on *The Wonder Show* for the Mutual Broadcasting System. In addition to narrating the series, Welles portrayed the showman, The Great McCoy. Appealing to his love of turn-of-the-century popular theater, each episode was based around the production of an old-fashioned melodrama. Among the warhorses resurrected for the series were *Bertha the Sewing Machine Girl; The Relief of Lucknow;* and *Sweeney Todd,* based on George Dibdin Pitt's 1847 melodrama, *The String of Pearls,* long a favorite at New York's Bowery Theatre.

—C.B.

Wood, Bret Bret Wood, a representative for the independent film distribution company Kino International, is the author of *Orson Welles: A Bio-Bibliography,* published by Greenwood Press in 1990. The book begins with a biographical sketch, followed by a "Welles Chronology," a "Discography," and separate listings for theater, radio, and film credits. A standard feature of books in this series is an annotated bibliography of books and monographs about the subjects as well as an annotated listing of periodical literature. There is also, of course, a listing of books written and edited by ORSON WELLES. The book attempts to be comprehensive and contains much valuable information.

—J.M.W.

Wood, Natalie (Natasha Virapaeff) (1938–1981) As a child actress Natalie Wood played Margaret, a psychologically scarred child from war-torn Europe in *Tomorrow Is Forever* (1946), directed by her mentor, Irving Pichel. In the film, Margaret is adopted by John McDoland, an American chemist, played by ORSON WELLES. Welles was impressed by her performance, which required some emotional depth, and by her mastery of a Germanic accent. About the accent this role required, Wood remarked: "I didn't know what that particular accent was, but when they explained it, it was no trouble to do. . . . I really think acting is a natural thing for kids to do anyway," she later said, modestly. "She was professional when I first saw her," Welles said. "I guess she was just born professional."

Natalie Wood was born in San Francisco, California, on July 20, 1938, the daughter of an architect of Russian origins and a ballerina of French descent. She attended studio schools and public schools and made her film debut in a bit part at the age of five in *Happy Land* (1943), which was directed by Irving Pichel, who also cast her in *Tomorrow Is Forever.* Pichel was also instrumental in the decision to Anglicize Natasha to Natalie; she was named "Wood" as a tribute to the Hollywood director Sam Wood. As a child actress she also appeared as the little girl, Susan Walker, who is persuaded to believe in Santa Claus in the very popular *Miracle on 34th Street* (1947).

Actress Natalie Wood *(National Film Society Archive)*

Thereafter, Wood continued to play children's roles until 1955, when she reinvented herself as an ingénue, as a troubled teenager, Judy, in Nicholas Ray's *Rebel Without a Cause,* resulting in Academy Award attention. The following year she was again nominated for an Academy Award for her portrayal of Debbie, the "lost" orphan captured by the renegade Comanche in John Ford's classic western, *The Searchers* (1956). In 1961, she played the Juliet-like Maria in Robert Wise's *West Side Story* and as Wilma Dean Loomis in Elia Kazan's *Splendor in the Grass.* Other significant roles include the title role in *Gypsy* (1962), the Oscar-nominated role in *Love with a Proper Stranger* (1963), the title role in Robert Mulligan's *Inside Daisy Clover* (1966), and as Carol Sanders in Paul Mazursky's *Bob and Carol and Ted and Alice* (1969). Twice married to actor Robert Wagner, she died in a drowning accident while on vacation with her husband off Santa Catalina Island, November 29, 1981.

Reference Nickens, Christopher. *Natalie Wood: A Biography in Photographs* (Garden City, N.Y.: Doubleday/Dolphin, 1986).

—T.L.E. and J.M.W.

Woodstock Drama Festival In spring 1934, an 18-year-old WELLES embarked on an ambitious plan to produce a summer drama festival at his alma mater, the Todd School, in Woodstock, Illinois. The repertory season, while featuring the Todd Players, would star Welles's former employers from Dublin's GATE THEATRE, MICHEÁL MACLIAMMÓIR and HILTON EDWARDS. Welles also persuaded Louise Prussing, a well-known Chicagoan with impressive Broadway and London credentials to join the troupe. With the backing of ROGER "SKIPPER" HILL, his mentor and the head of the Todd School, Hill and Welles secured financial support from Woodstock's city fathers and from fund-raising dinners held in Chicago. Significant revenue also was generated by the $500 tuition fees paid by the families of students registered for a hands-on course in drama administered through the Todd School, whereby the youngsters gained experience as extras and members of the production crew. For its venue, the festival hired the venerable Woodstock Opera House, a turn-of-the-century horseshoe theater on whose stage had appeared such luminaries as Jane Addams and Count Leo Tolstoy.

The repertory consisted of productions of *HAMLET,* for MacLiammóir, *TSAR PAUL,* for Edwards; and *TRILBY,* which Welles would direct and star in as Svengali. It was a bold plan, but one which succeeded. Welles, using his considerable promotional talents, invited Chicago's top drama critics, all of whom raved about the shows and the "Boy Wonder." Audiences, too, enjoyed the pre-performance dinners and Woodstock's provincial charms. They also enjoyed the plays and the performances of the precocious Welles, the two flamboyant Irishmen, the lovely Prussing, and the bright youngsters enrolled in Todd's summer drama course. On the heels of the first reviews, a trip to Woodstock soon became a must-do for the artistic elite of Chicago and the surrounding communities. Toward the end of the season, there was an impromptu production of *THE*

DRUNKARD, a sober morality tale from 1844, which had been turned on its head and given a new lease on life as a comedy by a small Los Angeles theater in 1933.

The season was a rousing success for all concerned. For MacLiammóir and Edwards, it was an opportunity to visit America for the first time. For Welles, it was an opportunity to broaden his compass. In addition to acting, Welles proved with *Trilby* that he had the right stuff for directing. He also demonstrated a remarkable flair as an entrepreneur. Indeed, the Woodstock Drama Festival had been his idea. And while receiving substantial support from Roger Hill and various patrons, it was Welles who converted that dream into a living, breathing, thriving reality.

The Woodstock Drama Festival was also significant for having given Welles his first opportunity to creatively work in film through the satiric HEARTS OF AGE, co-directed with William Vance. It was also at Woodstock that Welles met and fell in love with a beautiful 18-year-old student enrolled in the drama course. Her name was Virginia Nicholson. In the midst of the summer season, Welles proposed, and shortly thereafter, the young Miss Nicholson became the first Mrs. Orson Welles.

—C.B.

Woodward, Joanne (1930–) Actress Joanne Woodward played Clara Varner, daughter of Will Varner, played by ORSON WELLES, in Martin Ritt's THE LONG HOT SUMMER (1958), a loose film adaptation of WILLIAM FAULKNER's *The Hamlet* combined with some of his short stories. In the film, DAVID THOMSON finds one scene that approaches what he terms "emotional truth"; it is the reconciliation scene between father (Welles) and daughter (Woodward). Welles told PETER BOGDANOVICH, "I enjoyed very much working with Joanne Woodward."

Joanne Woodward was born on February 27, 1930, in Thomasville, Georgia. She acted in high school plays and at Louisiana State University, worked in the Greenville, South Carolina, community theater, and then enrolled in New York's Neighborhood Playhouse. She did some work on television and on the stage before making her screen debut in *Count Three and Pray* (1955). For her role as a young

woman with multiple personalities in *The Three Faces of Eve* (1957) she won a best actress Oscar. Married to actor PAUL NEWMAN, who has co-starred with her in some films and directed her in others, she has starred in many fine films and television movies. Directed by Newman, she won an Oscar nomination for her title role in *Rachel, Rachel,* as a frumpy woman attempting to cope with "singleness" and the best actress award at the Cannes Film Festival for her role in *The Effect of Gamma Rays on Man-in-the-Moon Marigolds* (1972). Other fine performances were in *Mr. and Mrs. Bridge* (1990), co-starring with Newman, and *Philadelphia* (1993).

References Harris, Roy. *Eight Women of the American Stage; Talking about Acting* (Portsmouth, N.H.: Heinemann, 1997); Morella, Joe. *Paul and Joanne: A Biography of Paul Newman and Joanne Woodward* (New York: Dell, 1988).

—T.L.E.

Woollcott, Alexander Humphreys (1887–1943) Alexander Woollcott, who has been called America's first radio superstar, was famous for his caustic wit and impeccable taste. He was immortalized as the irascible Sheridan Whiteside in the classic Kaufman and Hart comedy *The Man Who Came to Dinner,* a role that Woollcott himself played onstage. FRANK BRADY described Woollcott as ORSON WELLES's friend and mentor, who introduced Welles to GUTHRIE MCCLINTIC and KATHERINE CORNELL, with whom Welles later toured. According to Brady, Woollcott was also instrumental in getting the Theatre Guild to collaborate with the Mercury Players on Welles's FIVE KINGS project. As a raconteur of the airways, Woollcott was a model for Welles. According to Howard Teichmann in his book *Smart Aleck: The Wit, World and Life of Alexander Woollcott* (1976), Woollcott sent the following telegram to Welles after THE WAR OF THE WORLDS broadcast of 1938: "DEAR ORSON—THIS ONLY GOES TO PROVE MY CONTENTION THAT ALL INTELLIGENT PEOPLE LISTEN TO CHARLIE MCCARTHY." Woollcott once said that Orson Welles was "the greatest voice on the airwaves," a high compliment, given the source.

Alexander Woollcott was born in Phalanx, New Jersey, on January 19, 1887. He was educated at

Central High School in Philadelphia and at Hamilton College near Clinton, New York. In 1909, he became a reporter for the *New York Times,* advancing to the position of drama critic in 1914, a position to which he returned after service in World War I. In 1922, he became the drama critic for the New York *Herald.* By 1929, Woollcott was writing his weekly column, "Shouts and Murmurs," for *The New Yorker* and presiding over the daily luncheons of the "Algonquin Wits" (with Franklin P. Adams, Heywood Broun, George S. Kaufman, Deems Taylor, Robert Benchley, Dorothy Parker, Donald Ogden Stewart, Ring Lardner, Harold Ross, et al.) at the famous Round Table of the Algonquin Hotel. He became a radio personality and celebrity as a result of his long-running radio show, "The Town Crier" (1930–42). He suffered a fatal heart attack while participating in "The People's Forum" radio program on January 23, 1943.

Reference Teichmann, Howard. *Smart Aleck: The Wit, World and Life of Alexander Woollcott* (New York: W.M. Morrow, 1976).

—J.M.W.

Work Projects Administration/Works Progress Administration (1935–1943)

This notable U.S. government agency was created in the midst of the Great Depression through an executive order issued by President FRANKLIN DELANO ROOSEVELT in 1935. At first called the Works Progress Administration, the WPA was renamed the Work Projects Administration when it was moved into the Federal Works Agency in 1939. For WELLES and JOHN HOUSEMAN, Welles's business partner of the mid-1930s through the early 1940s, the WPA was significant for having included the FEDERAL THEATRE PROJECT, which supported some of Welles's boldest theater productions under the subsidiary banners of the NEGRO THEATRE PROJECT and PROJECT 891.

Established at a moment when unemployment was the nation's greatest scourge, the WPA was initially headed by Harry L. Hopkins, one of Roosevelt's closest lieutenants. In outline form, the combination economic relief-and-stimulus plan was simple. The federal government would create jobs for persons on welfare, thus increasing their purchasing power, which in turn would spur the nation's economy. At the same time, in utilitarian projects such as the construction of airports, roads, bridges, and buildings, the nation's infrastructure would be substantially strengthened. Indeed, during its tenure, WPA projects resulted in the creation of 116,000 buildings, 78,000 bridges, 651,000 miles of roads, and the improvement of over 800 airports.

Other parts of the WPA's comprehensive back-to-work plan included the Federal Art Project, the Federal Writers' Project, and the aforementioned Federal Theatre Project. Nearly 10,000 drawings, paintings, and pieces of sculpture were produced under the aegis of the WPA. Many public buildings, especially post offices, were adorned with richly expressive murals, again, thanks to the WPA. The WPA also sponsored thousands of musical compositions and performances, as well as a series of guidebooks to various parts of the country. At its peak, the WPA had more than 3 1/2 million workers on its roster; altogether, the WPA employed more than 8 million workers during its eight-year run.

The WPA, in spite of the multitude of good works produced under its sponsorship, was nonetheless assailed by right-wing Republicans, who viewed the vast agency as little more than a vote-getting scheme concocted by Roosevelt and his fellow New Dealers. The criticism hit a fever pitch in a 1939 Senate committee charged with WPA oversight. As a result, WPA funding was slashed, which led to the 1939 abolishment of the Federal Theatre Project and its various subsidiaries, including the Negro Theatre Project. Political conservatives, who had railed against the Federal Theatre Project's perceived and real left-wing slant, were particularly glad to see the demise of government supported theater. When news of the dramatic budgetary curtailment of WPA funding was made public, a strike was organized by WPA workers to protest cuts in wages and projects. It failed.

As war clouds gathered over Europe, and American factories tooled up to provide munitions to its European allies, employment began to steadily increase, which led to further cuts in the WPA's budget. With America's entry into World War II on December 8, 1941, the rationale for the WPA dissolved as men by the millions joined the military, and men and women by an even greater number went to work in arms factories running 24 hours a day. In June 1943, with the nation at war, the WPA officially went out of business.

—C.B.

Wright, Richard (1908–1960) Wright was a critically acclaimed African-American writer who wrote three important novels from the perspective of what it is like to be black in a predominantly white America: *Native Son* (1940), *Black Boy* (1945), and *The Outsider* (1953). After the publication of *Native Son,* the story of a black man who murders a white woman in a particularly brutal fashion, Wright was interested in having dramatist Paul Green adapt the novel to the stage. Green, who was shocked by the novel's brutality, turned down Wright's literary agent, Paul Reynolds. Green also declined producer Cheryl Crawford's offer to adapt the novel. However, when JOHN HOUSEMAN approached Green, he accepted the offer contingent upon Wright's traveling from Mexico to work with him on the script and being allowed to make the communist elements comic, as well as changing the character of Bigger Thomas to seem less a victim and more responsible for his behavior. Despite Wright's leftist leanings, he agreed to Green's terms. Wright and Green worked together at Chapel Hill, North Carolina, during July and August of 1940. Wright's efforts at dramatic adaptation were generally unsuccessful because he was more of a novelist than a dramatist. The script was completed in November and, despite some misgivings, ORSON WELLES decided to go ahead with the project. According to CHARLES HIGHAM, Welles's decision was based on an effort to restore his association with Houseman, an opportunity to express his feelings about black oppression in America, and to produce a theatrical triumph equal to the success he thought CITIZEN KANE would have on the screen.

After seven weeks in rehearsal, the play opened in New York at the St. James Theatre on March 24, 1941. Welles presented the play without programs or an intermission. It received excellent critical notices and ran for 114 performances. The *Time* reviewer called it "by all odds the strongest drama of the season," for example. Of Welles's direction, BROOKS ATKINSON wrote in the *New York Times* "when he [Welles] applies to theatricalism of his personal nature to a stage problem, something exciting comes into existence." However, the Hearst newspapers, understandably biased against Welles because of the *Citizen Kane* scandal, were critical of the play and of Welles. In light of the widespread knowledge that Wright was a communist, the *Journal American's* accusation that the play was "Communistic" was no doubt part of a wider Hearst campaign to discredit Welles. The production was especially notable because it marked the end of Welles's association with John Houseman.

Born in abject poverty near Natchez, Mississippi, Wright left home at 15 and gradually drifted north, working as an itinerant laborer. He arrived in Chicago in 1934, at the height of the Depression, and became interested in the labor movement. He joined the Communist Party in 1936, and remained a party member until he became disillusioned by the party's failure to address adequately racial issues in America. His novel *The Outsider* was a depiction of an African American's experience as a member of the Communist Party. In 1938, Wright won a prize offered by *Story* magazine for his "Uncle Tom's Children." The following year he won a Guggenheim Fellowship, enabling him to write *Native Son,* his most popular novel. The novel was produced as a motion picture in Argentina (1951), with Wright in the lead role as Bigger Thomas. In 1986, Jerrold Freedman directed a second diluted film adaptation of *Native Son* starring Oprah Winfrey, Geraldine Page, Carroll Baker, Matt Dillon, with Akosua Busia as Bigger Thomas.

Reference Phillips, Elizabeth C. *Richard Wright's "Native Son"* (New York: Barnes and Noble, 1998).

—R.C.K., T.L.E., and J.M.W.

Xanadu In *CITIZEN KANE,* Xanadu is CHARLES FOSTER KANE's palatial estate in Florida, modeled after WILLIAM RANDOLPH HEARST's San Simeon estate in California.

Xanadu is the fictional province in China mentioned by Samuel Taylor Coleridge in that author's laudanum-induced poetic vision called *Kubla Khan*. Specifically, in Coleridge's poem, Xanadu was the site of the "stately pleasure dome" that Kubla Khan decreed.

Storyboard drawing of Xanadu *(National Film Society Archive)*

Kubla Khan (1216–94), grandson of Genghis Khan, was the Mongol emperor of China who in 1264 established his court at what is now Peking. His Yuan dynasty brought great advances in commerce and culture, vividly described by Marco Polo, whose account inspired Coleridge's *Kubla Khan*. The unfinished 1797 poem was written, according to its author, in an opium-induced sleep. When he arose, Coleridge began transcribing his vision. In the course of an interruption by a visitor, the remainder of Coleridge's poetic vision vanished.

In 1941, "Xanadu" was borrowed from Coleridge by Welles and co-screenwriter HERMAN J. MANKIEWICZ for the "stately pleasure dome" constructed by Charles Foster Kane for his second wife, Susan Alexander Kane, in the script for *Citizen Kane.* While drawing on Khan's Edenic garden as sketched by Coleridge, the Welles-Mankiewicz' Xanadu for *Citizen Kane* also makes sly and ironic reference to William Randolph Hearst's Xanadu-esque "pleasure dome," the gargantuan San Simeon estate Hearst erected in California.

Today, largely because of the iconic stature of *Citizen Kane* in contemporary popular culture, "Xanadu" stands as a synonym for any huge and ostentatious mansion that while functioning as a residence, more significantly, serves as a symbolic monument to an unbridled capitalistic ego.

—C.B.

Yates, Herbert J. (1880–1966) ORSON WELLES's friend and partner CHARLES K. FELDMAN had a deal with Herbert J. Yates, president of Republic Pictures, to make some films for him. According to Welles, Feldman "simply told him [Yates] that one of them was going to be *MACBETH*." Yates, who reportedly was ready for Republic to offer a few departures from the B pictures that were the studio norm, signed Welles to produce *Macbeth*. The budget was set for $700,000, with $100,000 going to Welles, who would act, direct, and produce the film; Welles was responsible for covering costs in excess of the budget. Welles told BOGDANOVICH, "Yates didn't know who or what *Macbeth* was." However, BARBARA LEAMING writes that Yates was enthusiastic about the final product, which "demonstrated beyond a doubt" that a "superior product" could be made cheaply and well. Yates told Welles that *Macbeth* was "the greatest individual job of acting, directing, adapting and producing that to my knowledge Hollywood has ever seen."

Herbert J. Yates was born on August 24, 1880, in Brooklyn. Educated at Columbia University, he went into the tobacco business when he was 19 and became a sales executive. In 1910, he got into the film business by providing financial support for films featuring Roscoe "Fatty" Arbuckle. Two years later, he formed a processing lab that grew through acquisitions and mergers into Republic Pictures Corporation, which he headed. Like other Hollywood moguls who married their stars or made their loves into stars, Yates married actress Vera Ralston in 1952; she had been Republic's "star" since the 1940s. Yates retired from Republic in 1959 and died in 1966.

—T.L.E.

Young, Loretta (Gretchen Michaela Young) (1913–2000) Loretta Young was very striking as the innocent Mary Rankin, married to the Nazi in disguise Charles Rankin, played by ORSON WELLES in *THE STRANGER* (1946). She was born on January 6, 1913, in Salt Lake City, Utah. When her parents separated, Young, who was only three years old, moved with her mother and sisters to Hollywood. She and her sisters soon began working as child extras in movies. Young's first screen appearance came when she was 14 years old in *Naughty But Nice* (1927). At the age of 16, she played a circus performer opposite Lon Chaney in *Laugh Clown Laugh* (1928). Young moved on to ingenue roles and then to mature ones. In 1933, she left First National and signed with Twentieth Century–Fox as a contract player, using her considerable beauty rather than her native acting ability.

Young did serviceable work for Orson Welles in *The Stranger* (1946), which BRADY calls an atypical Wellesian production, a film that came in under budget and on time. During the shooting of the film, Welles did have to make a few concessions, particularly for devoutly Roman Catholic Young, who objected to being photographed cutting church and who objected to cast members and crew swearing on the set. Seeing that nothing could be done about the latter, she set up a "swear box" for swearers to contribute a quarter for their indiscretions, according to BARBARA LEAMING. CHARLES HIGHAM writes that Young "may not have agreed with Welles's politics, but she certainly admired his talent."

When cast in *The Farmer's Daughter* (1947), Loretta Young proved that she could act by earning an Academy Award. She later received an Oscar nomination for her role in *Come to the Stable* (1949). Having made nearly 100 films, she abandoned her movie career in 1953 and easily moved to television, where she starred in *The Loretta Young Show,* which ran for eight years, and then acted in a television drama series called *The New Loretta Young Show* (1962–63). As a television actress and personality she won three Emmy Awards. Her autobiography entitled *The Things I've Learned* appeared in 1961. An astute businesswoman capable of protecting her interests, Young sued NBC in 1972 for the unlawful exhibition of her television shows abroad. She won $600,000. Her last professional appearance was in *Christmas Eve* (1986), a television drama.

References Anderson, Joan Wester. *Forever Young: The Life, Loves and Enduring Faith of a Hollywood Legend; The Authorized Biography of Loretta Young* (Allen, Tex.: Thomas More, 2000); Morella, Joe, and Edward Z. Epstein. *Loretta Young: An Extraordinary Life* (Santa Barbara, Calif.: Landmark Books, 1987).

—T.L.E. and J.M.W.

Young, Stark (1881–1963)

Drama critic Stark Young of the *New Republic* reviewed many of ORSON WELLES's New York theatrical productions. Young was impressed by the lighting, which he called "cosmic chiaroscuro" in Welles's stage version of MACBETH (1936), but he dismissed the madcap HORSE EATS HAT (1936) as "not so much vigorous as unnecessary." Young, however, had high praise for DR. FAUSTUS (1937), particularly for Welles's acting: "Marlowe's play is spoken above the average by Mr. Orson Welles, who has a beautiful even voice, perfectly placed, and has, too, a remarkable sense of timing." While he did not like the lack of textual fidelity in Welles's JULIUS CAE-SAR (1938), Young did admire "its energy, lively attack,

sincerity, and bold theatrical intelligence" and described Welles's Brutus as "the prototype of a bewildered liberal, a great man with all the faults and virtues of liberalism." Young believed that Welles had failed to understand Shakespeare's (see SHAKESPEARE BY WELLES) ideas about aristocracy. Of Welles's stage adaptation of RICHARD WRIGHT's *NATIVE SON* (1941), the usually critical Young praised the acting of CANADA LEE (as Bigger Thomas) and the acting and directing of Welles: "It may at times be quite ham, but this is not too dreadful a fault in these soft days."

Stark Young, who was born on October 11, 1881, in Como, Mississippi, was educated at the University of Mississippi and Columbia University. He started teaching in 1904 at the University of Mississippi, and later taught at the University of Texas and at Amherst College. After publishing two volumes of poetry in 1906, he turned his attention to drama. In 1912, he published *Addio, Madretto and Other Plays,* and in 1917 published articles in the *New Republic,* where he began to write drama reviews in 1922. He left the *New Republic* in 1924 to review plays for the *New York Times,* but returned to the *New Republic* a year later. He resigned from the *New Republic* in 1947 but continued to paint, which he had begun in 1942, and to exhibit his paintings. A prolific writer, he wrote several books about the theater, five novels, and several plays, as well as translations of Chekhov and Machiavelli and an autobiography, *The Pavilion* (1951). Two volumes of his correspondence were published in 1975. He died in 1963.

References Pilkington, John. *Stark Young* (Boston: Twayne, 1985); Pilkington, John, ed. *Stark Young: A Life in the Arts* (Baton Rouge: Louisiana State University Press, 1975).

—T.L.E.

Yule, George

George Yule, uncle to RICHARD WELLES, Orson's father, was the superintendent of the Bain Wagon Works, a company that controlled most of the transportation in Kenosha, Wisconsin. Richard Welles worked at the Bain Wagon Works, where he advanced rapidly. Eventually, he, his uncle, and Charles N. Frost, an industrialist, formed the Badger Brass Company in 1897, and it was there that Richard, who served as secretary-treasurer, created the inventions that made him a wealthy man.

—T.L.E.

Zaharoff, Sir Basil (Basileois Zacharias)
(1850–1936)   Born in Anatolia, Turkey, probably of Greek-Russian parents and educated in England, Zaharoff is best known as having headed the Vickers-Armstrong munitions firm, for which he served as both director and chairman. For his provision of arms to the Allies during World War I, Zaharoff was knighted by King George V, and also decorated by the French government. However, he was regarded by many as a shadowy and unsavory figure, thus giving rise to the sobriquet "the mystery man of Europe." Indeed, Zaharoff was charged with having used his connections with Europe's top political leaders to promote international tensions in order to boost his vast and far-flung arms empire. There were also accusations that, in spite of his British citizenship and his presumed loyalty to the Crown, he had financial holdings in Germany's Krupp and Czechoslovakia's Skoda munitions firms.

Welles first studied "the mystery man of Europe" when he was asked to portray Zaharoff for a segment of radio's THE MARCH OF TIME on the occasion of the arms merchant's death in 1936. Later, in fleshing out the character of CHARLES FOSTER KANE for CITIZEN KANE, Welles drew on his knowledge of Zaharoff, as well as the figures of newspaper tycoon WILLIAM RANDOLPH HEARST, industrialist HOWARD HUGHES, and McGafferty, the powerful banker created by ARCHIBALD MACLEISH for the 1935 play, PANIC.

Welles returned to Sir Basil Zaharoff, as well as Charles Foster Kane, in crafting the leading character for the novel and script of MR. ARKADIN. Here, and in Citizen Kane and TOUCH OF EVIL, as well as in his various film and theater adaptations of Shakespeare (see SHAKESPEARE BY WELLES), what fascinated Welles was the corrupting influences of power. In Zaharoff, and these other larger-than-life figures, Welles also undoubtedly saw aspects of himself and his own quest for power and control.

References   Allfrey, Anthony. *The Life and Legend of Sir Basil Zaharoff* (London: Weidenfeld and Nicolson, 1988); McCormick, Donald. *Pedlar of Death: The Life of Sir Basil Zaharoff* (London: Macdonald, 1965).

—C.B.

Zanuck, Darryl F.   (1902–1979)   In charge of production at Twentieth Century–Fox in 1942, Darryl Zanuck assigned ORSON WELLES the role of Edward Rochester in JANE EYRE (1944), opposite Joan Fontaine in the title role. According to CHARLES HIGHAM, Welles wrangled with Zanuck and insisted that he have top billing over Joan Fontaine. Years later in 1958, Zanuck encouraged Welles to act as the renowned lawyer Clarence Darrow in COMPULSION (1959). In this instance, Welles shared best actor honors at the Cannes Film Festival with his co-stars BRAD DILLMAN and DEAN STOCKWELL.

Zanuck also helped Welles in other ways. While Welles was filming his OTHELLO, for example, he ran out of money and turned to Zanuck, who, according to Charles Higham, gave him $75,000 (BARBARA LEAMING maintains it was $85,000) in exchange for Twentieth Century–Fox's 60 percent ownership of the film. During this period, Zanuck also helped Welles obtain movie roles so that the director could raise additional money for his *Othello* project. Unfortunately, years later, Zanuck apparently forgot the financial problems that Welles had had with *Othello* and said that Welles "keeps making a picture and stopping because he gets bored with it and goes away," according to Leaming.

Born in Wahoo, Nebraska, on September 5, 1902, Darryl Zanuck had ambitions of being a writer after several of his letters home from the front in World War I were published in *Stars and Stripes.* By 1923, he was working as a screenwriter at Warner Bros. Zanuck managed the studio as Jack Warner's assistant from 1928 until 1933, when he left Warners to form Twentieth Century Pictures with Joseph Schenck, which then merged to become Twentieth Century–Fox in 1934. As head of production until 1956, Zanuck turned the studio into a major power in Hollywood. He remained C.E.O. of Twentieth Century–Fox until 1971. Despite Zanuck's unwillingness to finance Welles's later projects, Welles told PETER BOGDANOVICH, "I'm very fond of Darryl. He was by all odds the best and brightest of the big studio bosses."

References Custen, George Frederick. *Twentieth Century's Fox: Darryl F. Zanuck and the Culture of Hollywood* (New York: Basic Books, 1999); Gussow, Mel. *Don't Say Yes Until I Finish Talking: A Biography of Darryl F. Zanuck* (Garden City, N.Y.: Doubleday, 1971); Mosley, Leonard. *Zanuck: The Rise and Fall of Hollywood's Last Tycoon* (Santa Barbara, Calif.: Landmark Books, 1987).

—T.L.E. and J.M.W.

Zinnemann, Fred (1907–1997) Director

Fred Zinnemann directed ORSON WELLES in *A MAN FOR ALL SEASONS.* Born in Vienna on April 29, 1907, Fred Zinnemann first turned to law as a career. "When I received my master's degree in law in 1927, I felt that I would be bored stiff working in law the rest of my life," Zinnemann told this writer. "So I decided to try a career that would be more adventurous, and decided to attend the Technical School for Cinematography in Paris." When Zinnemann finished his work at the film school, he went to Germany and became an assistant cameraman. In 1929, he worked on a film called *Menschen am Sontag* (*People on Sunday*), a semi-documentary about four young people spending a weekend in the country. The film was directed by Robert Siodmak and written by Billy Wilder, both of whom, like Zinnemann, would later migrate to Hollywood and become directors there.

After Zinnemann arrived in Hollywood in 1929, he met ROBERT FLAHERTY, the distinguished pioneer of documentary filmmaking, whose realistic techniques would influence Zinnemann's own films. Zinnemann was able to utilize the experience gained in his association with Flaherty on his first directorial assignment, a semi-documentary entitled *The Wave* (1935), about the life of the fishermen in the Gulf of Vera Cruz, where he spent a year filming in the jungle. On the strength of *The Wave,* Zinnemann was hired by the Short Subject Department at Metro-Goldwyn-Mayer in 1937. After making a variety of short subjects, he was at last promoted in 1941 to making features at MGM. His first notable film was *The Seventh Cross* (1944), which starred Spencer Tracy as an anti-Nazi who tries to flee Germany in 1936, after escaping from a concentration camp. Impressed by *The Seventh Cross,* a European producer asked Zinnemann to make a film in Europe about displaced European children after World War II. The thematic note found repeatedly in his films is initially sounded in the very title of this, his first major success, *The Search* (1948). In that film the search is aimed at establishing the identity of a lad who has lost touch with his family through the cruelly impersonal events of war. This search by an individual for his self-image is the principal motif in all of Zinnemann's subsequent films. The individual achieves self-awareness by meeting a crisis; and once he or she has genuinely come to know themselves, they are capable of establishing a place for themselves in society.

Thus in *High Noon* the hero is a brave marshal (Gary Cooper) standing alone against a vengeful

Director Fred Zinnemann *(National Film Society Archive)*

gunman and his gang. The movie set a precedent in western films by showing a hero who is in no way superhuman, but who is instead quite capable of feeling fear while he is executing his duty. Cooper won an Oscar for playing an individual who achieves self-awareness by overcoming his fear and facing a challenge with courage. Zinnemann often develops this theme in his films by focusing on an individual who wants to achieve his self-identity while trying to function within a large institution such as the army. Hence, this theme was picked up in *From Here to Eternity* (1953), in which Montgomery Clift played an army private who refuses to knuckle under to his tyrannical commanding officer. *From Here to Eternity* was showered with Academy Awards, including honors for best picture and best director. The film deserved to be honored, for Zinnemann produced a ruggedly realistic, tightly constructed version of James Jones's sprawling novel, set in an American base in Hawaii in 1941. It is indicative of the sense of realism Zinnemann brought to the film that the news-

reel footage of the Japanese bombing of Pearl Harbor that he worked into the picture at the movie's climax meshed perfectly with the material he had shot himself for the same sequence.

Another critical and popular success was *A Man for All Seasons* (1966), Zinnemann's screen version of Robert Bolt's play about Thomas More (Paul Scofield). Thomas More had been the teacher and friend of King Henry VIII, and became chancellor of the realm after the fall of Cardinal Wolsey. Henry's first wife, Catherine of Aragon, had not given him a male heir, and the pope would not annul his marriage in order to allow Henry to marry his mistress, Anne Boleyn. Henry accordingly broke with the Church of Rome and appointed himself head of the Church of England. Thomas More experienced a crisis of conscience over accepting Henry VIII as head of the Church of England, as well as his king, and refused to sanction the king's actions. And so More was in due course executed for treason.

The film, like the play before it, is not really about Roman Catholicism, but about selfhood; that is, the movie portrays an individual's efforts to remain true to himself by steadfastly refusing to compromise his moral principles. Referring to the film's theme, Zinnemann reflected, "I have always been concerned with the problem of the individual who struggles to preserve his personal integrity and self-respect"; clearly, the trial and execution of Thomas More represents such a struggle.

Robert Bolt wrote a disciplined script that, like his original play, is literate without being literary. Moreover, the movie is shot through with applications for our own day. More tells Cardinal Wolsey (Orson Welles) at one point, "When statesmen forswear their own consciences for the sake of their public duties, they are leading their country into chaos."

When Zinnemann was setting up the production, he phoned screenwriter PETER VIERTEL, who had recently worked with Welles on an unproduced screenplay. Zinnemann asked Viertel if he should offer Welles the part of Cardinal Wolsey in *A Man for All Seasons*. According to DAVID THOMSON, Viertel replied that Welles would be difficult to work with, "but it will be one of the highlights of your picture."

Zinnemann recalls in his autobiography that "Welles had been quite difficult to track down. When I finally met him, in an apartment in Curzon Street in London, he was sitting behind a magnum of champagne, complaining of liver trouble." He was reluctant to play the part at first. "He arrived on the set only superficially acquainted with his lines." (Martin Ritt registered a similar complaint about Welles when he was directing him in THE LONG HOT SUMMER.) "Fortunately," Zinnemann continued, "his personality and his genius were so immense (and Paul Scofield's patience so enormous) that he succeeded in creating the illusion of absolute self-confidence."

Welles played Wolsey swathed in the scarlet robes of a cardinal; production designer John Box painted the walls of Wolsey's chambers in the same shade of scarlet as the cardinal's robes. Zinnemann adds that Box got the brilliant idea of "putting this huge man in a tiny, cramped office; Welles filled it with his presence." This was the scene in which Wolsey had a meeting with Thomas More; for his part, Welles told PETER BOGDANOVICH, he enjoyed acting with Scofield and remembered working on the movie as a wonderful experience.

While shooting the scene in which the Duke of Norfolk (Nigel Davenport) comes to collect the chancellor's golden chain from Wolsey, the cardinal is dying. Welles persuaded Zinnemann to allow him to use eyedrops that made his pupils bloodshot, which added to the haggard appearance of the dying man. Zinnemann remembered that Welles demonstrated his "marvelous, endearing sense of humor": After Davenport as Norfolk played the scene with Welles as Wolsey, he inquired, as he was about to take his leave, "Have you any message for the King?" Welles responded that he should tell the King that the take was no good, because the noise of a plane could be heard passing overhead.

Film critic Philip Hartung confessed that he had initially feared that Zinnemann would turn "Bolt's thoughtful stageplay into an elaborate pageant about sixteenth-century England. I was wrong, of course; and I should have realized that Zinnemann was a man of high purpose and integrity, and was more interested in the drama of people than in easy though handsome spectacle."

Welles's performance was generally well received; indeed, Joel Super observes that Welles's presence "added authority to the film without overpowering it." *A Man for All Seasons* won Academy Awards for best picture, best actor (Paul Scofield), and once again for Zinnemann as best director.

Zinnemann made *The Day of the Jackal* (1973), about an attempted assassination of Charles de Gaulle. The movie marked a return to the spare semi-documentary style of such earlier films as *The Search* and *From Here to Eternity*. He employed a similar approach in filming *Julia* (1977). This picture derived from Lillian Hellman's memoir of her friend Julia (Vanessa Redgrave, in an Oscar-winning performance). Julia becomes a political activist in Europe in the turbulent years preceding World War II, and involves Lillian (Jane Fonda) in the resistance movement against the Nazis. *Julia* was lauded as a gripping, provocative drama.

Besides the Oscars bestowed on Zinnemann's work, he received his most prestigious prize in 1970, when the Directors Guild of America conferred on him its highest honor, the Life Achievement Award, for his entire body of work. Surveying his long career, Zinnemann mused, "The director has much more freedom today in making a film than he had during the anonymous days in Hollywood, when films were made on an assembly line." Nevertheless, he was quick to point out that some of his best pictures were made under the studio system. "I will always think of myself as a Hollywood director," he added, "not only because I grew up in the American film industry, but also because I believe in making films that will please a mass audience, and not just in making films that will express my own personality or ideas. I have always tried to offer an audience something positive in a film, and to entertain them as well; and if I have managed to do that, I am satisfied."

References Hartung, Philip. *"A Man for All Seasons,"* in *American Film Directors,* ed. Stanley Hochman (New York: Ungar, 1974), 529; Phillips, Gene. "Fred Zinnemann: The Vanishing Hero," in *Exiles in Hollywood: Major European Film Directors in America* (Cranbury, N.J.: Associated University Presses, 1998), 139–76; Super, Joel. "Fred Zinnemann, *A Man for All Seasons,"* in *The Films of Fred Zinnemann: Critical Perspectives,* ed. Arthur Nolletti, Jr.

(Albany: State University of New York Press, 1999), 157–78; Thomson, David. *Rosebud: The Story of Orson Welles* (New York: Vintage Books, 1997); Welles, Orson, and Peter Bogdanovich. *This Is Orson Welles* (New York: Da Capo, 1998); Zinnemann, Fred. *A Life in the Movies: An Autobiography* (New York: Scribner's, 1992).

—G.D.P.

Zugsmith, Albert (1910–1993)

Produced WELLES's critically esteemed 1958 film, TOUCH OF EVIL. Albert Zugsmith, proclaimed by Hollywood insiders as "King of the B's," was one of movie industry's most active producers of low- and medium-budget films. After attending the University of Virginia, Zugsmith began a career in journalism, which eventually took him to Atlantic City, where he served as publisher-editor of the *Atlantic City Daily News;* he was also a broadcasting executive. In the early 1950s, he jumped to the film business as a producer at Universal.

Welles and Zugsmith first met at Universal in 1957 on the set of MAN IN THE SHADOW, a low-budget western starring Welles and produced by Zugsmith. By the end of the shoot, the actor and producer had become friends. At the same time, Zugsmith, in the midst of trying to develop a Whit Masterson novel (*Badge of Evil*) for production, sought out CHARLTON HESTON for the lead. Heston, initially reluctant to take on what seemed yet another prosaic police story, warmed to the project once Zugsmith told him that Welles had been hired to play the "heavy." Heston, a Welles admirer, recalls having then asked Zugsmith to hire Welles to also direct, realizing, as BARBARA LEAMING has suggested, that being directed by Welles could only enhance his own development as an artist. Zugsmith, however, has a different memory, recalling that Welles, on the last day of shooting *Man in the Shadow,* had suggested that he direct a picture for the producer. In turn, Zugsmith handed him a copy of *Badge of Evil* to see if Welles could come up with a suitable script. Welles, for his part, says that Zugsmith deceived Heston in order to get him to agree to doing the picture, claiming that Welles had been hired to direct when he hadn't. Heston is reported to have responded by saying, "Any picture that Orson Welles is directing, I'll be glad to be in." Before Heston could talk to his idol, Zugsmith immediately called Welles with an offer to direct. Welles's response? "Yes, if I can write the script and pay no attention to the book it comes from. I had two and a half weeks before it started. And I invented a whole new story that was *Touch of Evil.*" As several commentators have pointed out, it could be that Zugsmith, Heston, and Welles are telling the truth as they recall it.

It is important to underscore Zugsmith's key role in helping return Welles to a Hollywood director's chair after a decade-long exile spawned by the still swirling clouds of controversy stirred by his previous two studio films, THE LADY FROM SHANGHAI (1948) and MACBETH (1948).

With *Touch of Evil,* like most of his other films, Welles ran into problems during postproduction. Zugsmith and Universal, exasperated with Welles's procrastination in the editing suite, eventually relieved him of further responsibilities. Later, Welles claimed that Universal had taken *Touch of Evil* away from him. Zugsmith, however, insisted that the film expressed Welles's creativity and talent, and that any "tampering" done by the studio was actually more like copyediting designed to sharpen his grammar and dot his "i's" and cross his "t's."

Today, in spite of that controversy, after CITIZEN KANE, *Touch of Evil* (whether in its original studio release or its later "reconstructed director's cut" version), stands as one of Welles's enduring and unimpeachable accomplishments.

Although Zugsmith produced serious films for Universal such as *Man in the Shadow, Touch of Evil,* and Douglas Sirk's *Written on the Wind* (1956), he is best remembered for producing cheap exploitation films and harrowing melodramas such as *The Incredible Shrinking Man* (1957), *High School Confidential* (1958), and *The Beat Generation* (1959). As a producer-director, Zugsmith was responsible for such lurid fare as *Sex Kittens Go to College* (1960), *Confessions of an Opium Eater* (1962), and *The Incredible Sex Revolution* (1965).

—C.B.

CONTRIBUTORS

▫ ▫ ▫

C.B. Chuck Berg is a professor of theater and film at the University of Kansas where he heads the film-video program; Chuck is also a jazz musician and critic and a long-standing member of the Society for Cinema Studies and University Film and Video Association. Author of *An Investigation of the Motives for and Realization of Music to Accompany the American Silent Film* (1976), he also contributed to both *The Encyclopedia of Novels into Film* (Facts On File, 1998) and *The Encyclopedia of Stage Plays into Film* (Facts On File, 2001).

G.D.P. The Rev. Gene D. Phillips, S.J., teaches English and film at Loyola University of Chicago and is a contributing editor for *Literature/Film Quarterly*. He was the coauthor of *The Encyclopedia of Stanley Kubrick* (Facts On File, 2002) and has also contributed to *The Encyclopedia of Novels into Film* (Facts On File, 1998) and *The Encyclopedia of Stage Plays into Film* (Facts On File, 2001). A prolific writer and critic, Father Phillips is the author of several books treating film directors—Ken Russell (1979), John Schlesinger (1981), George Cukor (1982), and Alfred Hitchcock (1984)—and other books treating Graham Greene, Joseph Conrad, F. Scott Fitzgerald, William Faulkner, and Tennessee Williams.

J.C.T. Series editor John C. Tibbetts, associate professor of theater and film at the University of Kansas, was coeditor (with Jim Welsh) of *The Encyclopedia of*

Novels into Film (Facts On File, 1998), *The Cinema of Tony Richardson: Essays and Interviews* (1999), *The Encyclopedia of Stage Plays into Film* (Facts On File, 2001), and *The Encyclopedia of Filmmakers* (2002). He also edited *Dvořák in America, 1892–1895* (1993) and is currently writing a book on composers on film for Yale University Press. He is well known as a film and music critic and as a broadcaster in Kansas City, where he lives.

J.M.W. Series editor James M. Welsh, professor of English at Salisbury University (Maryland), is editor-in-chief of *Literature/Film Quarterly,* and the founding president of the Literature/Film Association. The author of earlier books on French director Abel Gance (1978) and British directors Peter Watkins (1986) and Tony Richardson (1999), he was coeditor (with John Tibbetts) of *The Encyclopedia of Novels into Film* (Facts On File, 1998), *The Encyclopedia of Stage Plays into Film* (Facts On File, 2001), *The Encyclopedia of Filmmakers* (2002), and (with Richard Vela) of *Shakespeare into Film* (Facts On File, 2002).

R.C.K. Richard C. Keenan is chair of the English Department at the University of Maryland, Eastern Shore, in Princess Anne, Maryland. He has served as a contributing editor of *Literature/Film Quarterly* and was also a contributor to *The Encyclopedia of Novels into Film* (Facts On File, 1998).

R.V. Richard Vela, professor of English and theater at the University of North Carolina at Pembroke, is a contributing editor of *Literature/Film Quarterly* and also coeditor (with Jim Welsh) of *Shakespeare into Film* (Facts On File, 2002). A specialist both in Hispanic studies and Shakespeare adaptations, he has published in *PostScript, Film and Philosophy,* and other journals, and also contributed to *The Mestizo Anthology of Chicano Literature.*

R.W. Ron Wilson recently completed his Ph.D. in cinema studies at the University of Kansas and is currently researching a book on the Interstate Theatre Circuit in Wichita Falls, Texas. He wrote entries both for *The Encyclopedia of Stage Plays into Film* (Facts On File, 2001) and *The Encyclopedia of Filmmakers* (Facts On File, 2002).

T.L.E. Thomas L. Erskine, professor of English and former English chair and academic dean at Salisbury University in Maryland, was the founding editor of *Literature/Film Quarterly.* He most recently served with Connie L. Richards as series editor of the Rutgers University Press "Women Writers Text and Contexts" series and was co-editor of *Video Versions: Film Adaptations of Plays on Video* (2000).

ORSON WELLES:
A SELECTED BIBLIOGRAPHY

Anderegg, Michael. *Orson Welles, Shakespeare, and Popular Culture.* New York: Columbia University Press, 1999.

Bazin, André. *Orson Welles: A Critical View.* Trans. Jonathan Rosenbaum. Foreword by François Truffaut. Preface by Jean Cocteau. Paris: Editions Chavane, 1950; New York: Harper & Row, 1998.

Beja, Morris. *Perspectives on Orson Welles.* New York: G.K. Hall & Co., 1995.

Bessy, Maurice. *Orson Welles. Cinema d'Aujourd'hui* Series No.6. Paris: Editions Seghers, 1963, 1970.

———. *Orson Welles.* Trans. Ciba Vaughan. New York: Crown Publishers, 1963.

Bogdanovich, Peter. *The Cinema of Orson Welles.* New York: Museum of Modern Art, 1961.

Bogdanovich, Peter, and Orson Welles. *This Is Orson Welles.* Ed. Jonathan Rosenbaum. New York: HarperCollins, 1992.

Brady, Frank. *Citizen Welles: A Biography of Orson Welles.* New York: Scribners, 1989.

Callow, Simon. *Orson Welles: The Road to Xanadu.* New York: Viking Press, 1995.

Carringer, Robert L. *The Making of Citizen Kane.* Berkeley: University of California Press, 1985.

Comito, Terry, ed. *Touch of Evil.* New Brunswick, N.J.: Rutgers University Press, 1985.

Cowie, Peter. *The Cinema of Orson Welles.* New York: Da Capo Press, 1973.

———. *A Ribbon of Dreams: The Cinema of Orson Welles.* Cranbury, N.J.: A.S. Barnes & Co., 1965.

Davies, Marion. *The Times We Had: Life with William Randolph Hearst.* Indianapolis: Bobbs-Merrill, 1975. [Foreword by Orson Welles]

Fowler, Roy Alexander. *Orson Welles: A First Biography.* London: Pendulum Publications, 1946.

France, Richard. *The Theatre of Orson Welles.* Lewisburg, Pa.: Bucknell University Press, 1977.

France, Richard, ed. *Orson Welles on Shakespeare: The W.P.A. and Mercury Theatre Playscripts.* Westport, Conn.: Greenwood Press, 1990.

Gottesman, Ronald, ed. *Focus on Citizen Kane.* Englewood Cliffs, N.J.: Prentice Hall, 1971.

———. *Focus on Orson Welles.* Englewood Cliffs, N.J.: Prentice Hall, 1976.

Higham, Charles. *The Films of Orson Welles.* Berkeley: University of California Press, 1970.

———. *Orson Welles: The Rise and Fall of an American Genius.* New York: St. Martin's Press, 1985.

Hill, Roger, and Orson Welles. *Mercury Shakespeare.* New York: Harper, 1939.

Houseman, John. *Entertainers and the Entertained: Essays on Theatre, Film, and Television.* New York: Simon & Schuster, 1986.

———. *Final Dress.* New York: Simon & Schuster, 1983.

———. *Front and Center.* New York: Simon & Schuster, 1979.

———. *Run-Through: A Memoir.* New York: Simon & Schuster, 1972.

Howard, James. *The Complete Films of Orson Welles.* New York: Citadel, 1991.

Ishaghpour, Youssef. *Orson Welles Cinéaste: Une Caméra Visible.* 3 vols. Paris: Éditions de la Différence, 2001.

Kael, Pauline. *The Citizen Kane Book.* Boston: Little, Brown, and Co., 1971.

Koch, Howard. *The Panic Broadcast.* New York: Avon Books, 1971.

Kodar, Oja, and Orson Welles. *The Big Brass Ring.* Santa Barbara, Calif.: Santa Teresa Press, 1987.

Leaming, Barbara. *Orson Welles: A Biography.* New York: Viking Press, 1985.

Lyons, Bridget Gellert, ed. *Chimes at Midnight.* New Brunswick, N.J.: Rutgers University Press, 1988.

McBride, Joseph. *Orson Welles.* Rev. ed. New York: Da Capo Press, 1996.

———. *Orson Welles, Actor and Director.* New York: Jove Publications (Harcourt Brace Jovanovich), 1977.

MacLiammóir, Micheál. *All for Hecuba.* London: Methuen, 1946.

———. *Put Money in Thy Purse: The Diary of the Film of Othello.* Introduction by Orson Welles. London: Methuen, 1952.

Maland, Charles J. *American Visions: The Films of Chaplin, Ford, Capra, and Welles.* New York: Arno Press, 1977.

Meryman, Richard. *Mank: The Wit, World and Life of Herman Mankiewicz.* New York: William Morrow, 1978.

Mulvey, Laura. *Citizen Kane.* London: BFI, 1992.

Naremore, James. *The Magic World of Orson Welles.* New York: Oxford University Press, 1978. Rev. edn. Dallas, Tex.: Southern Methodist University Press, 1989.

Noble, Peter. *The Fabulous Orson Welles.* London: Hutchinson, 1956.

Perkins, V.I. *The Magnificent Ambersons.* London: BFI, 2000.

Rosenbaum, Jonathan. *Movie Wars: How Hollywood and the Media Conspire to Limit What Films We Can See.* Chicago: Acappella Books, 2000.

Sokol, Robert A. *The Failure of Andre Bazin's Realist Film Theory to Address the Perceptual Realism of Painted Sets, Matts and Backgrounds in Orson Welles's* Citizen Kane. Masters Thesis, University of Kansas, 1999.

Taylor, John Russell. *Orson Welles: A Celebration.* Boston: Little Brown, 1986.

———. *Orson Welles: A Celebration.* New York: Applause Books, 1998.

Thomson, David. *Rosebud: The Story of Orson Welles.* New York: Knopf, 1996.

Tynan, Kenneth. *He That Plays the King.* London and Toronto: Longmans, 1950.

Welles, Orson, and Peter Bogdanovich. *This Is Orson Welles.* Ed. Jonathan Rosenbaum. New York: HarperCollins, 1992.

Wood, Bret. *Orson Welles: A Bio-Bibliography.* Westport, Conn.: Greenwood Press, 1990.

INDEX

■ ▢ ▢

Note: **Boldface** page numbers denote main entries. Page numbers followed by *f* indicate figures.

A

Academy Awards and nominations
    for Astor, Mary 7–8
    for Auer, Mischa 9
    for *The Battle of Neretva* 12
    for *The Battle Over Citizen Kane* 13
    for Baxter, Anne 13
    for Bogart, Humphrey 166
    for *Citizen Kane* 49–50, 118, 247
    for Colbert, Claudette 59
    for Copland, Aaron 66
    for Cortez, Stanley 239
    for Coward, Noël 77
    for Fields, Al 239
    for Fitzgerald, Geraldine 112
    for Garland, Judy 121
    for Gielgud, John 124
    for Gleason, Jackie 124
    for Grant, Lee 405
    for Hayes, Helen 136–137
    for Hayward, Susan 424
    for Hecht, Ben 145
    for *From Here to Eternity* 436*f*
    for Herrmann, Bernard 50, 150, 151
    for Houseman, John 163
    for Huston, John 165–166
    for Huston, Walter 167
    for Johnson, Ben 23
    for Kahn, Madeline 23
    for Krasker, Robert 368
    for Laughton, Charles 210
    for Leachman, Cloris 23
    for Lehman, Edward 424
    for Leigh, Janet 214
    for Leigh, Vivien 214
    for "The Look of Love" 34
    for *The Magnificent Ambersons* 239
    for *A Man for All Seasons* 243, 437
    for Mancini, Henry 241
    for Mankiewicz, Henry 247
    for McCambridge, Mercedes 254
    for Mellors, William 65
    for Moorehead, Agnes 239, 272
    for Nichols, Mike 285–286
    for O'Brien, Edmond 289
    for Olivier, Laurence 290
    for O'Neal, Tatum 23
    for *Paper Moon* 23
    for Redgrave, Vanessa 437
    for Reed, Carol 314–315
    for Richardson, Tony 318
    for Robinson, Edward G. 323
    for Rutherford, Margaret 329
    for Shaw, George Bernard 345
    for Smith, Maggie 349
    for Spiegel, Sam 352
    for Spielberg, Steven 355
    for Tamiroff, Akim 363
    for Toland, Gregg 374, 375
    for Tone, Franchot 379
    for Truffaut 395
    for *Voyage of the Damned* 405
    for Wayne, John 135
    for Welles 247
    for Wise, Robert 424
    for Wood, Natalie 427
    for Woodward, Joanne 428
    for Young, Loretta 433
    for Zinneman, Fred 436*f*
"Admiral of the Sea" 1
The Adventures of Harry Lime **1–3**, 19, 188, 276, 387, 404
"AFI's 100 Years . . . 100 Passions" 23
Alexander, Susan *See* Susan Alexander

Alexander Korda: Britain's Only Movie Mogul (Drazin) 198
Alice Adams (Tarkington) 235, 236, 364, 424
Alland, William **3**
    in *The Battle Over Citizen Kane* 13
    in *Citizen Kane* 3, 376
    on Hearst 12
    in *Heart of Darkness* 3
    in *Julius Caesar* 3, 185
    Macbeth and 225
    in Mercury Theatre 3
    in *Orson Welles: The Rise and Fall of an American Genius* (Higham) 155
    in *Treasure Island* 109
    in *The War of the Worlds* 408
Ambler, Eric **3–4**, 181–182
American 245–247 *See also Citizen Kane*
The American Cinema (Hathaway) 136
"The American Experience" 12–13
American Film Institute Lifetime Achievement Award 17, 33, 166, 274, 303
American Film Institute "Working with Welles" seminar 85, 156
American Shakespeare Festival 21, 163
Amerika (Kafka) 187
Anastasia 136, 215, 363
Anderegg, Michael A. **4**
    on *Chimes at Midnight* 42, 43, 48, 222, 343
    on *Five Kings* 342
    on *Julius Caesar* 342
    on *Macbeth* 226, 227, 232–233
    on *Othello* 295, 297, 300
    on Shakespeare, adaptation of 341
Anderson, Lindsay 22
Andrews, Nigel 199
Anna Karenina 214, 403
Anouilh, Jean 171
Antoinette Perry Awards *See* Tony Awards and nominations

Apocalypse Now 66, 69–70
Arau, Alfonso 240
Archer, Eugene 82–83, 277
Arden, Robert 277
Arena, the Story of the Federal Theatre Project (Flanagan) 114
Arkin, Alan 36*f*, 285
Armstrong, Louis **4–5,** 21, 97, 179
Around the World in 80 Days **5–7**
    basis for 402
    film rights to 374
    financing of 18, 27, 58, 125
    Garrison, Greg, and 84
    Goetz, William, and 125
    King Lear (play) and 192
    King Lear (television) and 190–191
    The Lady from Shanghai and 203
    Lillie, Bea, in 215
    Mercury Summer Theatre on the Air and 258
    on *Mercury Theatre on the Air* 260
    music for 5–6, 258, 308–309
    tax burden from 216
Around the World with Orson Welles 7
"Ars Poetica" (MacLeish) 233
Artists' Front to Win the War 37–38
A. S. Barnes 78
Ashby, Hal 93
Ashley, Ted 122
Astin, John 122
Astor, Mary **7–8,** 7*f*, 259
Atkinson, J. Brooks **8**
    on Carter, Jack 33
    on Cornell, Katherine 71
    on *Danton's Death* 81
    on *Doctor Faustus* 90
    on *Julius Caesar* 184–185
    on *King Lear* 192
    on Lee, Canada 213
    on *Macbeth* 224
    on *Native Son* 430
    on *Panic* 305
    on *The Shoemaker's Holiday* 346
Aubry, Cecile 20, 56–57
Audley, Maxine 293
Auer, Jane 25
Auer, Mischa **8–9,** 277–278
Austerlitz **9,** 331
auteur theory 14
Avery, Tex 28
Azaria, Hank 80

B

Bacharach, Burt 34
The Bad and the Beautiful 163, 337, 357
Baichwal, Jennifer 25
Baird, Bill 89, 160
Baird, Cora 89
Balanchine, George **10,** 25, 208
Baldi, Ferdinando 82
Ball, Lucille
    on *The Campbell Playhouse* 30
    Fountain of Youth and 117

on *The Lady Esther Show* 203
on *Orson Welles's Almanac* 291
    The Smiler with a Knife and 216, 348
Ballard, Lucien 288
Balsam, Martin 36*f*
Barnes, Julian 397
Barnum's American Museum 94
Baroncelli, Jacques de 56
The Barretts of Wimpole Street 14, 71, 256, 313, 415
Barr, Richard 245–246
Barrier, Edgar 143, 182, 225, 227, 381
Barrymore, John **10–12,** 11*f*
    on *Campbell Playhouse* 259
    Costello, Dolores, and 72–73
    in *The Green Goddess* 128
    Julius Caesar and 11
    nose of 177
    in *Orson Welles's Almanac* 291
    Orson Welles Sketchbook and 292
    on *The Rudy Vallee Show* 11, 400
    in *Trilby* 11, 393
    in *Twentieth Century* 396
Barrymore, Lionel 94, 291
Barthelmess, Richard 190
"The Basement Room" (Greene) 129, 366
The Battle of Austerlitz **9,** 331
The Battle of Neretva **12,** 85
The Battle Over Citizen Kane **12–13,** 319
Baxter, Anne **13–14,** 158, 203, 235
Baxter, John 22
Baxter, Keith **14,** 40, 42, 123, 222
Bazin, André **14**
    on fake noses 394
    in *Focus on Citizen Kane* (Gottesman) 126
    and French New Wave 17
    interview with, on Shakespeare 48
    on *The Magnificent Ambersons* 237, 272
Beatty, Warren 17, 177, 370
Beckley, Paul 382
Beery, Noah 30
The Beggar's Opera 27 *See also The Three-penny Opera*
Belasco, David 74
Belmondo, Jean-Paul 34, 172
Benamou, Catherine 175
Bennett, Richard **14–15,** 238
Benny, Jack 127–128, 176
Bentley, Eric 192
Berg, Gertrude 30
Bergman, Andrew 124
Bergman, Ingrid 32
Berlin Film Festival 108
Bernstein, Dr. Maurice **15–16**
    Gate Theatre and 121–122
    guardianship of 155, 414, 418
    Welles, Beatrice (mother), and 412, 417
    at Welles's wedding 212
Berry, John **16–17,** 282
Bessy, Maurice **17,** 40, 155, 267, 404
The Big Brass Ring **17–18,** 107, 177, 196, 316

Black Irish See The Lady from Shanghai
blacklist 16, 63, 195, 213, 219–220
Black Magic **18–19,** 215, 348
Blackmer, Sidney 94
The Black Museum **19,** 387–388
The Black Rose **19–20,** 134, 135, 294–295, 310–311
The Black Swan 104, 190
Blades, Reuben 80
Blair, Betsy 57
The Blessed and the Damned **20,** 97, 194, 372–373, 398 *See also An Evening with Orson Welles*
Blethyn, Brenda 320
Blitzstein, Marc **20–21**
    Communist loyalty of 81
    and *Cradle Will Rock* 79, 80
    in *It's All True* (play) 172–173
    Julius Caesar score by 21, 185, 258, 260
    King Lear score by 193
    The Shoemaker's Holiday and 347
    The Spanish Earth and 351
    Thomson, Virgil, and 371
    Too Much Johnson and 25, 380
Bogdanovich interviews
    on *Austerlitz* 410
    on *The Battle of Neretva* 12
    on Bennett, Richard 14
    on Brecht 218
    on *Casino Royale* 104
    on *Catch-22* 285
    on *Chimes at Midnight* 43, 45
    on *Citizen Kane* 148, 247
    on Comingore 62–63
    on *Compulsion* 64
    on Costello, Dolores 72
    on Dietrich 87
    on Dinesen, Isak 88
    on *Don Quixote* 91
    on *Ferry to Hong Kong* 105
    on Gielgud 124
    on Gleason 124
    on Guitry 328
    on *Heart of Darkness* 68, 142
    on *Hello Americans* 146
    on *Henry V* 45
    on Holt, Tim 158
    on Houseman 162
    on *It's All True* 421
    on *Jane Eyre* 178–179
    on *Journey Into Fear* adaptation 3–4
    on Korda, Alexander 332
    on *The Lady in the Ice* 208
    on *The Lady from Shanghai* 138, 203
    on *The Last Roman* 209
    on Leigh, Vivien 214
    on *The Long Hot Summer* 102
    on *Macbeth* 227
    on *Man, Beast and Virtue* 241, 308
    on *A Man for All Seasons* 242, 437
    on *Marco the Magnificent* 250–251
    on Mature, Victor 251–252, 364
    on McDowall, Roddy 257

on McGoohan, Patrick 257
on *Monsieur Verdoux* 38, 270
on Moorehead, Agnes 271–272
on *Oedipus the King* 289
on *Operation Cinderella* 290
on Republic Studios 226
on *The Rhinoceros* 317
rights to 196
on Robinson, Edward G. 321, 323
on "Rosebud" 245
on Selznick 337
on Shakespeare 339–340
on Sloane, Everett 347
on *The Southern Star* 351
on Stewart, Paul 357
on *The Stranger* 321, 352, 360
on Susan Alexander bedroom scene 3
on Tamiroff, Akim 363
on Tarkington, Booth 364
on Todd, Michael 373
on Toland, Gregg 375–376
on *Touch of Evil* 153
on Trauner, Alexander 388
on *The Unthinking Lobster* 266–267
on *The V.I.P.s* 404
on *Waterloo* 410
on Weaver, Dennis 410
on Wilder, Thornton 422
on Woodward, Joanne 428
on Zanuck 435
Bogdanovich, Peter **21–23**
in *The Battle Over Citizen Kane* 13
Callow, Simon, compared to 29
on *Citizen Kane* authorship 186
Directed by John Ford and 88
in *F for Fake* 23
in *Focus on Orson Welles* (Gottesman) 126
on *Hearts of Age* 143
on *The Immortal Story* 170
McBride interview with 254
on *The Orson Welles Story* 292
on *Othello* 298
in *The Other Side of the Wind* 23, 302
This Is Orson Welles and 23, 146, 148, 327–328
on *Una su tredici* 398
on Welles, Beatrice (mother) 413
Bolt, Robert 436
Bolton, Whitney 305
Bonanova, Fortunio 53
"Bonito, the Bull" 113, 116
Borneman, Ernest 2
Boulanger, Nadia 20, 66
Bourbon, Diana **24,** 30
Bower, Ronald 245
Bowles, Paul **24–25,** 89, 160
Boyer, Charles 34, 172
Bradbury, Ray 193
Brady, Frank **25–26**
on *The Adventures of Harry Lime* 2
on *Austerlitz* 9
on Baxter, Keith 14
on Bessy, Maurice 404

on *Butterfly* 28
Callow, Simon, compared to 29
on *Cavalcade* 76
on *Citizen Kane* 144, 147
on Cloutier, Suzanne 57
on Comingore 61
on *Compulsion* 64
on *The Count of Monte Cristo* 110
on *Crack in the Mirror* 78
on deal with Cohn, Harry 58
on *Doctor Faustus* score 25
on *The Dreamers* 93
on Edwards, Hilton 96
on German tour of *An Evening with Orson Welles* 97
on Gleason 124
on *The Godfather* 251
on Hayworth 58, 137
on Hearst 139–140
on Houseman estrangement 163
on Huston, Walter 167
on *The Importance of Being Earnest* 170
on *It's All True* 420
on *Jazz Story* 5, 179
on *Journey into Fear* 144
on *Julius Caesar* 184
on Katherine Cornell's stage company 71
on *King Lear* 191, 193
on Kodar, Oja 195–196
on Korda, Alexander 197–198
on *The Lady from Shanghai* 203, 207
on *Lafayette* 208
on Lee, Canada 213
on *The Long Hot Summer,* production of 102
on Mayer, Louis B. 253
on McDowall, Roddy 257
on Metty, Russell 265
on *Michael the Brave* 265
on Moreau, Jeanne 274
on Mori, Paola 195–196, 275
on Moss, Jack 275
on Nolan, Jeannette 286–287
on *Othello* 293
on Parsons, Louella 306
on Philip Trent 389
on Power, Tyrone 310
on *Prince of Foxes* 104, 311
on Project 891 312
on *A Safe Place* 330
on Sanford, Erskine 332
on Shaw 345
on *Sherlock Holmes* 260
on *The Shoemaker's Holiday* 346
on *Song of Myself* 350
on Stevenson, Robert 356
on Stewart, Paul 357
on *The Stranger* 352, 432
on Susan Alexander, basis for 406
on Tamiroff, Akim 363
on *Ten Million Ghosts* 365
on *Three Cases of Murder* 252, 372

on *Too Much Johnson* 381
on *Trilby* 11, 394
on *Trouble in the Glen* 394
on *Twelfth Night* 396
on *The War of the Worlds* authorship 31
on Weaver, Dennis 410
on Welles, Beatrice (daughter) 413
on Welles, Christopher 413
on Welles, Rebecca 417
on Welles, Richard (father) 418
on Woollcott, Alexander 428
Brandt, Joe 59
"Break of Hearts" 138
Brecht, Bertolt **26**
in *Cradle Will Rock* 80
The Cradle Will Rock and 79
Feuchtwanger and 180
Horse Eats Hat and 160
Ionesco on 171
The Life of Galileo by 26, 198
Losey, Joseph, and 218–219
Native Son and 282
Breslin, Jimmy 13
The Bridge at San Luis Rey 261, 363, 422
Bright Lucifer 11, 16, 156, 415
British Academy of Film and Television Arts awards and nominations 151, 315, 349
Brittania Award 355
Brook, Peter **26–27,** 190, 274
Brooks, Mel 157, 279
Brown, John Mason 71, 184–185, 214
Brownlow, Kevin 32
"Brush Up Your Shakespeare" 84, 310
Brussels Film Festival 382
Brynner, Yul 12
Buchman, Lorne 297
Büchner, Georg 81
Buchsbaum, Max 363
Bugs Bunny Superstar **27–28**
Buñuel, Luis 57, 143
Burfield, Kim 389, 389f
Burr, Anne 281
Burroughs, William 25
Burton, Richard 349, 404
Busch, Niven 94
Butler, Lawrence 204
Butterfly **28**

C

Calleia, Joseph 383, 386
Calley, John 122
Callow, Simon **29**
on Alland, William 3
on audience perception of Shakespeare 98
on Bernstein, Maurice 16
on Bourbon, Diana 24
on *Citizen Kane* 149
on Cotten, Joseph 74
on Coulouris, George 75
on Coward, Noël, and Welles 76
on Drake, Herbert 92
on *Five Kings* 42, 256

on *Hamlet* 133–134
on *Heart of Darkness* 68
on *Hearts of Age* 144
on Herrmann, Bernard 146
on Houseman, relationship with
    161–162
on *Jew Suss* 180
on *Journey into Fear* 117
on *Julius Caesar* score 21
on Lederer, Virginia 212
on Lee, Canada 213
on "Nickel under Foot" 21
on Robson, Mark 323
on Schneider, Albert 334
on *The Shadow* 337–338
on Shaw and Welles 344
on *The Shoemaker's Holiday* 346
on Stewart, Paul 357
on Sullavan, Margaret 361
on *Tsar Paul* 396
on *War of the Worlds* authorship 195
on Welles, Christopher 413
on Welles, Richard (brother) 418
Campbell, Gardner 239
The Campbell Playhouse **29–31** *See also Mercury Theatre on the Air*
    Around the World in 80 Days on 5, 402
    Astor, Mary, on 7, 259
    Bourgon, Diana, and 24
    Cotten, Joseph, in 73
    Coward, Noël, mentioned in 77
    Goddard, Paulette, on 124
    Hayes, Helen, on 30, 136
    in Hollywood 24, 30
    Houseman on 162
    Huston, Walter, on 167
    The Lady Esther Show and 202
    Leigh, Vivien, on 24, 30–31, 214
    Lillie, Bea, on 214, 259
    Mercury Theatre and 259
    Our Town on 422
    RKO and 411
    State Fair on 262
    War of the Worlds and 408
Candida 71, 256, 313, 344–345, 415
Canfield, Mark 78
Cannes Film Festival
    awards of
        for *Compulsion* 65, 87, 115, 434
        for *The 400 Blows* 395
        for Moreau, Jeanne 274
        for *Othello* 295
        for *Paris, Texas* 358
        for *The Third Man* 129, 314
        for Woodward, Joanne 428
    Chimes at Midnight at 172
    Cocteau and 58
    Don Quixote at 92
    Maria Candelario at 86
Cantril, Albert Hadley **31,** 408
"The Captain's Chair," in *It's All True* 113
*Captured on Film: The True Story of Marion
    Davies* **31–32**

Carpenter, John 80
Carringer, Robert L. **32–33,** 68, 245, 247,
    409
Carson, Johnny 33, 36, 262
Carter, Jack **33–34,** 89, 143, 224, 225
Casino Royale **34–35,** 104, 145
Castle, William **35,** 59, 203
Catch-22 **36,** 36*f,* 285, 307
The Cat's Meow 23
Cavalcade 76
Cavalcade of America, "Admiral of the Sea"
    on 1
Cavett, Dick **36**
C.B.C. Film Company 59
CBS
    Ceiling Unlimited on 36
    Don Quixote and 91, 259
    Mercury Theatre on the Air and 24, 29,
        407–408
Ceiling Unlimited **36–37,** 146, 265, 357
censorship 64
Center for International Creation 27
Central School of Speech Training and Dra-
    matic Art 74
"C'est mon coeur" 182
Chandler, Jeff 244
Chaplin, Charles **37–39** *See also Monsieur
    Verdoux*
    Comingore and 37, 60
    on *The Drunkard, or, The Fallen Saved* 94
    Goddard, Paulette, and 124
    legacy of xii
    Lillie, Bea, and 215
    Sutherland, Edward, and 361
    Too Much Johnson and 380
    Welles compared to 14
Chappell, William 392
Charles Foster Kane (character) **39–40,** 49*f,*
    52*f,* 75*f See also Citizen Kane*
    Don Quixote and 91
    Gatsby and 126
    Hearst and 40, 50, 55, 139–140
        and Drake, Herbert 92
    idea for 244, 245
    Kael on 186
    and Parsons, Louella 306
    mystery of 51, 54
    newspaper empire of 52–53
    physical movements of 3
    Rosebud and 326–327
    score motif for 147–148, 149
Charmed Lives: A Family Romance (Korda,
    M.) 198
Chicago Drama Festival 396
Chimes at Midnight (film) xii, **40–48,** 41*f,*
    45*f,* 100*f,* 416
    adaptation of 343
    Don Quixote and 91
    Edwards, Hilton, and 96
    Everybody's Shakespeare and 98
    evolution of 340
    Falstaff in 100
    financing of 42

Five Kings and 112
    Gielgud in 42–43, 123–124
    Is Paris Burning? and 172
    It's All True and 175
    Moreau, Jeanne, in 42, 44, 45*f,* 273
    My Own Private Idaho and 400–401
    narration of 42–43
    ownership of 55
    preservation of 55
    Rutherford, Margaret, in 42–43,
        328–329
    shooting of 42
    success of 84
    values in 339
    Welles, Beatrice (daughter), in 46, 413
Chimes at Midnight (Lyons) 221–222
Chimes at Midnight (play) 14, **40,** 42, 234
Chirello, George "Shorty" 231
Chomette, Henri 56
Christians, Mady 141
Chronicles of England, Scotland, and Ireland
    (Holinshed) 98
Church, Michael 23
Ciment, Michael 218
cinéma commenté 132
Cinéma d'Hier, Cinéma d'Aujourd'hui 56
The Cinema of Orson Welles (Bogdanovich)
    22
The Cinema of Orson Welles (Cowie) *See A
    Ribbon of Dreams: The Cinema of Orson
    Welles* (Cowie)
Citizen Kane **48–55,** 49*f,* 52*f,* 416 *See also
    Charles Foster Kane* (character)
    acting in 49, 55
    Alland, William, in 3, 376
    authorship of 49 (*See also The Citizen
        Kane Book* (Kael); "Raising Kane"
        (Kael))
            Carringer, Robert, on 32
            and Drake, Herbert 92
            and Hecht, Ben 144
            and Houseman 162
            and Mankiewicz 244–247
            and revisions 245–246
            Rosenbaum, Jonathan, on 328
            Thomson, David, on 370
            and Weissberger, Arnold 411
    in *The Battle Over Citizen Kane* 12–13
    cinéma commenté in 132
    cinematography for viii, 32, 49–50,
        374–378, 375*f,* 416
    Collins, Ray, in 60, 60*f*
    Comingore in 51, 55, 60–63, 61*f,* 376,
        409*f*
    controversy over 50, 55
        and Drake, Herbert 92
        Fowler, Roy, on 118
        and *His Honor, the Mayor* 156
    Cotten, Joseph, in 73, 75*f*
    Coulouris, George, in 51, 74, 76*f,* 271*f,*
        376–377
    Davies, Marion, and 31–32, 61–62,
        83–84

death in xii
directing of 50
DVD release of 13
editing of 328, 423–424
The Godfather trilogy and 69
Heart of Darkness and 69
Hearts of Age and 143
The Immortal Story compared to 170
importance of xv, 78
It's All True and 175
The Killing and 200
Lederer, Charles, and 211, 245
makeup for 335–336
Metty, Russell, and 263, 376
Moorehead, Agnes, in 51, 55, 270–273, 271*f*, 376–377
mystery in 51, 54
premiere of 14, 118, 156
release of, attempt to block 140, 221, 253, 306
reputation of 49
at RKO 49, 318
Robson, Mark, and 323
Rosebud in 326–327
Sanford, Erskine, in 332
Schaefer, George, and 196, 333
Schilling, Gus, in 333–334
score for 147–149
screen testing for viii–ix, 62, 263, 376
script for 49
Shannon, Harry, in 51, 377
Sloane, Everett, in 51, 55, 75*f*, 76*f*, 347–348
sound for 356
Stevens, Ashton, and 356
Stewart, Paul, in 51, 357
story of 49
suicide scene in 53, 55
technique in 50, 54–55
Toland, Gregg, and viii, 32, 49–50, 374–378, 375*f*, 416
Warrick, Ruth, in vii–ix, 408–409, 409*f*
Welles, Beatrice (mother), and 413
Welles's youth and 50
Wilson, Richard, in 423
Wise, Robert, and 423–424
Zaharoff, Basil, and 434
The Citizen Kane Book (Kael) 55, 186–187
Citizen Welles: A Biography of Orson Welles (Brady) 25–26
Citizen Welles, Inc. **55**
Clair, René **56**
Clay, Jean 29
Cloutier, Suzanne **56–57,** 295, 399
Cocteau, Jean 14, **57–58,** 143, 164
Coggio, Roger 169
Cohn, Harry **58–59,** 416
Around the World in 80 Days financing and 6, 203
Hayworth and 137, 262
If I Should Die before I Wake and 35
The Lady from Shanghai and 203–207, 226

Colbert, Claudette **59–60,** 125, 378–379
Coleridge, Samuel Taylor 431*f*
The Colgate-Palmolive Theatre 118
Collins, Charles 133, 395
Collins, Ray **60**
Air Raid and 234
on *The Campbell Playhouse* 24, 30
on *Ceiling Unlimited* 37
in *Citizen Kane* 50, 53, 60, 60*f*, 61*f*, 409*f*
in *Dracula* 109
Heart of Darkness and 143
on *Hello Americans* 145
in *His Honor, the Mayor* 156
in *The Magnificent Ambersons* 60
on *March of Time* 249
in *Native Son* 60, 282
in *Seventeen* 260
on *This Is My Best* 370
in *Touch of Evil* 60
in *The War of the Worlds* 408
Collins, Richard 63, 144
Colonial Theater 112
Columbia Studios 58, 116, 125, 138–139
Comingore, Dorothy **60–63**
Chaplin and 37, 60
in *Citizen Kane* 51, 55, 60–63, 61*f*, 376, 409*f*
on *The Lady Esther Show* 202
Committee for the First Amendment 166
communism *See also* House Un-American Activities Committee
Berry, John, and 16
Danton's Death and 81–82
His Honor, the Mayor and 157
McCarthy, Joseph, and 255–256
Robinson, Edward G., and 321
Welles investigated for 140
The Complete Films of Orson Welles (Howard) 164
Compton, Fay 298
Compulsion **63–65**
Dillman, Brad, in 87, 115, 357
Fleischer, Richard, and 115
makeup for 336
redubbing of 65
Stockwell, Dean, in 63–65, 87, 115, 357
success of 78
Zanuck and 434
Comrade X 246
Confidential Report See Mr. Arkadin
Conrad, Joseph 142, 142*f*
Conreid, Hans 181
Cooper, Merian C. 114
Coote, Robert 143
Copland, Aaron **65–66**
Bowles, Paul, and 25
Five Kings score by 112–113
The Second Hurricane and 25, 66, 334–335
Todd, Michael, and 373
Copley Theatre 74
Coppola, Francis Ford 22, **66–70,** 67*f*, 172
Corliss, Richard 246

Cormack, Mike 375
Corman, Roger 22, 401
Cornell, Katherine **71**
acting company of 71, 156, 415
in *Antony and Cleopatra* 152
McClintic, Guthrie, and 71, 256
Power, Tyrone, and 310
Rathbone, Basil, and 313
Woollcott and 422, 428
Cortese, Valentina 19
Cortez, Stanley **71–72,** 154–155, 416
Cosmopolitan Pictures 62, 83
Costain, Thomas 19
Costello, Dolores **72–73,** 72*f*, 158*f*, 235
Cotten, Joseph **73–74,** 74*f*
on *The Campbell Playhouse* 24, 30
on *Ceiling Unlimited* 37
in *Citizen Kane* 50, 51, 55, 73, 75*f*
in *Danton's Death* 81
in *Doctor Faustus* 90
in *Duel in the Sun* 94
in *F for Fake* 74
Hayworth and 137
on *Hello Americans* 145
in *Horse Eats Hat* 73, 160, 161
in *Journey into Fear* 73–74, 116–117, 144, 181–183, 181*f*, 273
in *Julius Caesar* 185, 258
on *The Lady Esther Show* 202
in *The Magnificent Ambersons* 73, 158*f*, 235, 238
in Mercury Theatre 73
in *The Mercury Wonder Show* 74, 261
in *Orson Welles: The Rise and Fall of an American Genius* (Higham) 155
in *Othello* 74
in *RKO 281* 321
in *The Second Hurricane* 73, 335
in *Seventeen* 260
in *Shadow of a Doubt* 358
in *The Shoemaker's Holiday* 346
in "The Texarkana Program" 74, 325
in *The Third Man* 74, 130, 314, 366, 366*f*
in *Too Much Johnson* 73, 380, 381
in *Touch of Evil* 74, 152
Coulouris, George **75–76**
on *The Campbell Playhouse* 24, 30
in *Citizen Kane* 51, 74, 76*f*, 271*f*, 376–377
in *Dracula* 109
in *Heartbreak House* 141
Heart of Darkness and 143
in *Henry V* 74
in *Julius Caesar* 74–75, 185, 258, 260
in *King of Kings* 193
in Mercury Theatre 74–75
in *The Shoemaker's Holiday* 347
The Count of Monte Cristo 110, 212, 258
"A Country Tale" (Dinesen) 168
Coward, Noël **76–77,** 77*f*
Cowie, Peter **78**
on *Citizen Kane* 78
on *The Citizen Kane Book* (Kael) 186

on Coppola and Welles 69
on *Don Quixote* 91
on *It's All True* 263
on *The Lady from Shanghai* 206
on *The Magnificent Ambersons* 13, 237, 364
on *Moby Dick* 267
on *Return to Glenascaul* 316
on *The Third Man* 367
on *The Trial* 126, 390, 392, 393
Crack in the Mirror **78–79,** 87, 115
Cradle Will Rock x, **79–80,** 355
The Cradle Will Rock **79,** 415–416
commissioning of 21
Copland and 65–66
dedication of 26
under Federal Theatre Project 103
Houseman and 79, 162
in *It's All True* (play) 172
Mercury Theatre and 258
screenplay for 417
The Second Hurricane and 335
Spielberg and 354
in *The Theatre of Orson Welles* (France) 119
Thomson, Virgil, and 371
Crist, Judith 34–35, 172, 222
Crittenden, Jordan 122
Cromwell, James 240, 319, 321
Crowl, Samuel 298
Crowther, Bosley 201
Chimes at Midnight reviewed by 222
on *Citizen Kane* suppression 253
on *A Man for All Seasons* 242–243
on *Royal Affairs in Versailles* 328
Currie, Finlay 20
Curtis, Keene 228
Curtis, Tony 214, 403
Cusack, John 80
Cyrano de Bergerac 18, 211, 214, 294, 388

D

Da Capo See *The Dreamers*
Dali, Salvador 25, 57, 143
Dalrymple, Ian 372
Danton's Death **81–82**
Gabel, Martin, in 120
Lederer, Virginia, in 212
by Mercury Theatre 162, 259
Native Son and 281
Sanford, Erskine, in 332
score for 21
in *The Theatre of Orson Welles* (France) 119
Darnton, Nina 32
da Silva, Howard 79, 172–173
Dassin, Jules 78
Davenport, Nigel 437
David and Goliath **82–83,** 91–92
Davies, Anthony 43, 232, 297, 300
Davies, Marion **83–84,** 83*f*
in *Captured on Film: The True Story of Marion Davies* 31–32

in *Cradle Will Rock* 80
Hearst and 140
Lederer, Charles, and 211, 245
Mankiewicz and 246
portrayal of, in *Citizen Kane* 13, 50, 61–62
in *RKO 281* 320–321
Rosebud and 320, 327
Davis, Bette 7, 74
Davis, Hugh 401
Dawson, Michael 55
The Day of the Locust 35, 263, 357
Dead Calm See *The Deep*
Dead Reckoning See *The Deep*
The Dean Martin Comedy Show **84,** 251, 341
La Decade Prodigieuse See *Ten Days Wonder*
The Deep 12, **84–86,** 134, 195
de Hory, Elmyr 105–107, 164
Del Río, Dolores 86
affair with 30
at *Citizen Kane* premiere 118
in *Journey into Fear* 86, 181
on *The Lady Esther Show* 202
Mexican Melodrama and 379
in *Orson Welles: The Rise and Fall of an American Genius* (Higham) 155
Denby, Edward 25, 66, 160, 335
De Niro, Robert 122
DePalma, Brian 122
Der Prozess (Kafka) See *The Trial*
Desilu Productions 117–118, 319 See also Ball, Lucille
de Vargas, Valentin 384
"The Diamond as Big as the Ritz" (Fitzgerald) 111, 370
The Dick Cavett Show 36
Dierkes, John 229
Dietrich, Marlene **86–87,** 87*f*
in *Follow the Boys* 86, 104, 116, 262, 361
in *The Mercury Wonder Show* 86, 261
Mr. Arkadin and 87
The Other Side of the Wind and 87, 302
in *Touch of Evil* 86–87, 152, 214, 384, 385, 386*f*
Dietz, John, *The War of the Worlds* authorship and 31
Dillaway, Don 235
Dillman, Bradford 63–65, 78, **87,** 115, 357
Dinesen, Isak **87–88,** 93, 168
Directed by John Ford 22, **88**
The Directors Company 22
Dmytryk, Edward 16
Doctor Faustus **89–90,** 415 See also *Time Runs*
Brook, Peter, and 27
Carter, Jack, in 33
Houseman and 89, 162
in *It's All True* (play) 172
lighting in 81, 117
score for 25
in *The Theatre of Orson Welles* (France) 119
Young, Stark, on 433

Documentary on St. Peter's Basilica **89**
Dolivet, Louis 277
Donald, James 404
Donaldson, Peter 297
Donen, Stanley 216
Don Quixote **90–92**
Auer, Mischa, in 8
Lucidi, Renzo, and 364
McCormack, Patty, in 91–92, 256–257
Tamiroff, Akim, in 92, 363
Douglas, Kirk 403
Dracula 109, 146, 270, 415
Drake, Herbert **92,** 143, 308, 380
The Dreamers 88, **92–93,** 177, 196
"The Dreamers" (Dinesen) 88
Drew, Robert 303
Dr. Strangelove 201
The Drunkard, or, The Fallen Saved **93–94,** 96, 427–428
Duel in the Sun **94–95,** 167
Duffield, Brainerd 225
Dunbar, Paul 380
Dunham, Katherine 194
Dunne, Irene 24
Dunst, Kirsten 23
Durant, Jack 181
Durning, John 306

E

Eastwood, Clint 17, 177
Ebert, Roger 157, 279
"Echoes" (Dinesen) 88
Edwards, Hilton **96**
in *The Blessed and the Damned* 20
Chimes at Midnight and 40, 234
in *The Drunkard, or, The Fallen Saved* 94
in *An Evening with Orson Welles* 97
in *Filming Othello* 108
at Gate Theatre 121–122
Hamlet and 133–134
Jew Suss and 179
MacLiammóir and 96, 234
Moby Dick–Rehearsed and 268
Mori, Paola, and 277
in *Othello* 295
Return to Glenascaul directed by 315–316
in *Time Runs* 97, 372
in *Trilby* 393
in *Tsar Paul* 395
in *The Unthinking Lobster* 399
at Woodstock Summer Theatre Festival 96, 234, 427–428
Edwards, Vince 200
Eisenstein, Sergei 14
Elley, Derek 23
Ellington, Duke 5, 20, **96–97,** 179, 372
Ellis, Jack C. 114
Elwes, Cary 23, 80
Emery, John 143
Emmy awards and nominations 287, 433
endorsements xii
Epstein, Michael 12
Eshley, Norman 169–170

Esquire magazine 21, 111
Essanay Studios 37
Evans, Maurice 256
An Evening with Orson Welles **97** *See also*
  The Blessed and the Damned
    The Importance of Being Earnest in 20,
    41, 97, 170, 373, 421
    King Lear and 192
    MacLiammóir in 234
Everson, William K. 189
Everybody's Shakespeare (Hill and Welles) xv,
  98–99, 155–156, 183, 339, 415

F

The Fabulous Orson Welles (Noble) 286
Fairbanks, Douglas, Jr. 7, 13
The Fallen Idol 129, 198, 314, 366
The Fall of the City 233–234, 407
false noses 18, 394
Falstaff See Chimes at Midnight (film)
Falstaff, Sir John 40, 41*f*, **100–101**
  in battle scenes 45
  in *Chimes at Midnight* 40–48, 100, 101*f*
  Don Quixote and 91
  in *Five Kings* 112
  Richardson, Ralph, as 317
  Touch of Evil and 386
Famous Artists 104
Famous Players–Lasky 7
A Farewell to Arms 136, 145, 337
Faulkner, William **101–103,** 216
Feder, Abe 89, 223
Federal Theatre Project **103–104** *See also*
  Negro Theatre Project; Project 891
    Cotten, Joseph, with 73
    The Cradle Will Rock and 21, 79
    Flanagan, Hallie, with 103, 114
    Horse Eats Hat and 159–161
    Julius Caesar under 183
    Losey, Joseph, with 217
    Macbeth and 33, 159
    Mercury Theatre and 258
    in *Orson Welles on Shakespeare: The
      W.P.A. and Mercury Theatre Playscripts*
      (France) 119
    Roosevelt and 325
    Welles with 415
    under Works Progress Administration
      429
Feldman, Charles K. 34, **104,** 115, 226, 262,
  361, 432
Ferguson, Perry 32
Ferry to Hong Kong **104–105,** 336
Feuchtwanger, Lion 179–180
F for Fake **105–107,** 106*f*
  Bogdanovich in 23
  cinematography for 28
  Cotten, Joseph, in 74
  Hughes, Howard, and 164
  It's All True and 175
  Kodar, Oja, in 106–107, 106*f*, 195
  magician in xi
  sexuality in 107

F for Fake trailer **107**
Fields, W.C. 116, 361
film, collaborative nature of 55
Film and the Public (Manvell) 248
*Film as Film: Understanding and Judging
  Movies* (Perkins, V.I.) 307
Filming Othello 107, **108,** 294, 340, 416
film in plays
  in *Around the World in 80 Days* 6–7
  in *The Green Goddess* 128
  in *Ten Million Ghosts* 366
  in *Too Much Johnson* 6, 73, 379–381
  in *The Unthinking Lobster* 399
The Films of Orson Welles (Higham) 154,
  238
"The Final Problem" 317, 345
financing
  for *Around the World in 80 Days* 6, 18,
    27, 58, 125, 373, 402
      The Lady from Shanghai and 203
  for *Chimes at Midnight* 42
  for *The Deep* 85
  for *Doctor Faustus* 90
  for *Don Quixote* 91–92
  for *The Dreamers* 93
  for *Filming Othello* 108
  for *Five Kings* 112–113, 128
  for *Julius Caesar* 221
  for *The Life of Galileo* 198, 209
  for *Macbeth* 18, 104, 224–226, 341–342,
    432
  for *Othello* 20, 294–295, 311, 326, 388,
    435
  for *The Other Side of the Wind* 302–303,
    365
  for *The Stranger* 351
  for *The Trial* 331
Finch, Peter 293
First National Studios 37
First Person Singular **108–110,** 415
  contract for 411
  Gabel, Martin, on 120
  The Lady Esther Show and 202
  Mercury Theatre and 259
  Schneider, Albert, and 334
  Too Much Johnson and 380
Fitzgerald, Ella 21
Fitzgerald, F. Scott **111**
Fitzgerald, Geraldine **111–112,** 141, 193,
  215
Fitzgerald, Martin 277, 387
Five Kings **112–113**
  adaptation of 342
  Chimes at Midnight and 40
  Copland and 66
  Don Quixote and 91
  evolution of 340
  financing of 112–113, 128
  Houseman and 162
  McClintic, Guthrie, and 256
  by Mercury Theatre 42, 162
  Meredith, Burgess, in 42, 112–113, 262
  Native Son and 281

  in *Orson Welles on Shakespeare: The
    W.P.A. and Mercury Theatre Playscripts*
    (France) 119
  Sanford, Erskine, in 332
  Schilling, Gus, in 333
  in *The Theatre of Orson Welles* (France)
    119
  Wilder, Thornton, and 422
  Woollcott and 428
Flaherty, Robert Joseph **113–114,** 263, 435
Flanagan, Hallie **114**
  and *The Cradle Will Rock* 79, 80
  with Federal Theatre Project 103
  Horse Eats Hat and 159
  Negro Theatre Project and 283
  Project 891 and 312
Fleck, Freddie 238
Fleischer, Richard 63–64, 78, **114–115**
"Flicker Flashbacks" 115
Flon, Suzanne 391
Focus on Citizen Kane (Gottesman) 78, 126
  The Films of Orson Welles (Higham) and
    154
Focus on Howard Hawks (McBride) 254
Focus on Orson Welles (Gottesman) 126
Fogerty, Elsie 74
Follow the Boys **115–116**
  Dietrich in 86, 262, 361
  Feldman, Charles K., and 104
  magic in xi, 262
  Sutherland, Edward, and 361
Fontaine, Joan 125, 178*f*
Ford, John
  AFI Life Award for 33
  Bogdanovich book on 22
  Directed by John Ford and 88
  westerns of, *Chimes at Midnight* com-
    pared to 45
Forrest, Allan 304
For Whom the Bell Tolls 76, 363
Foster, Norman **116–117**
  It's All True and 174, 175
  Journey into Fear directed by 116–117,
    151, 181
  Mexican Melodrama and 379
  in *The Other Side of the Wind* 302
Fountain of Youth **117–118**
"Four Men on a Raft" **173–174,** 264
Four Saints in Three Acts 163, 283, 371
Fowler, Roy A. **118**
Fox Studios 138, 190, 324
France, Richard **118–119,** 340, 341
Franciosa, Anthony 217
Francis, Arlene
  in *Danton's Death* 81
  Gabel, Martin, and 120
  in *Horse Eats Hat* 161
  on *March of Time* 249
  in *Too Much Johnson* 380, 381
Frank, Harriet, Jr. 102
"Free Cinema" 318
The Free Company 156–157
Freleng, Friz 28

G

Friedkin, William 22
Frischauer, Willi 119
The Front Page 145, 165, 211
Frost, David **119,** 405
Fulton Theatre 137

Gabel, Martin **120**
    in *Danton's Death* 81, 120
    in *Dracula* 109
    in *Julius Caesar* 120, 185, 260
    King Lear and 120, 191
Gaffney, Bob 201
Gaiety Theatre 40, 96
Galileo 219–220 *See also The Life of Galileo*
Gance, Abel 9
Garland, Judy **120–121**
Garland, Robert 224
Garrison, Greg 84, 251
Gate Theatre **121–122**
    Chimes at Midnight at 40
    The Drunkard, or, The Fallen Saved at 94
    Edwards, Hilton, at 96, 234
    Fitzgerald, Geraldine, in 111
    Jew Suss at 121–122, 179
    MacLiammóir at 96, 234
    Return to Glenascaul and 315–316
    Shaw, George Bernard, and 344
    Welles at 76, 106
Geer, Will 79
Germany
    An Evening with Orson Welles and 97
    Filming Othello and 108
    Kitt, Eartha, in 194
    Prince of Foxes in 311
    Welles and 20, 97
Get to Know Your Rabbit **122–123**
Gielgud, Sir John **123–124,** 123*f*
    in *Chimes at Midnight* 42–43
    Rutherford, Margaret, and 329
    on *Sherlock Holmes* 317, 345
Gilbert, Lewis 104–105
Gilder, Rosamond 213
Gillette, William 260, 379, 381
Gillmor, Dan 92
Ginsberg, Allen 25
Gish, Lillian 7, 94, 190
Gleason, Jackie **124,** 316
Gluskin, Lud 292
Godard, Jean-Luc 22, 387
Goddard, Paulette **124–125**
The Godfather trilogy 69, 251
Goetz, William **125,** 336, 351–352
Goldmark, Rubin 66
Goldner, Charles 19
Goldwyn Company 83, 165, 374 *See also* Metro-Goldwyn-Mayer
Gone With the Wind 124–125, 145, 214, 337, 370
"Good Neighbor" policy *See It's All True*
Goodnow, Edward 74
Gottesman, Ronald 78, 118, **126**
Gottfredsen, Frederick J. 127

Gottfredsen, Mary Blanche Head Wells **126–127,** 144
Gould, Jack 3, 191
Grable, Betty 396
Graham, Martha 305
Graham, Sheilah 111
Grahame, Margot 19
Grammy awards 241
Grand Médaille d'Or de la Société des Auteurs 132
Granville-Barker, Harvey 341
Graver, Gary 28, 93, 107, 302
Greco, Juliette 78
Greene, Graham 1–2, **128–131,** 129*f,* 314, 366
The Green Goddess 6, 11, **127–128**
Green, Paul 281, 430
Greenwood, Bruce 239
Greenwood Press 118
Grierson, John 113
Griffin, John 293
Griffin, Merv 36, **131–132**
Griffith, D.W. xii, 7, 14
Griffith, Melanie 320–321
Guild, Nancy 18–19
Guiles, Lawrence 83
Guillerman, John 164
Guitry, Sacha **132,** 280, 291, 328

H

Haedrich, Marcel 78
Hall, John 353
Halliwell's Film and Video Guide 28, 157, 208, 389
Hamlet **133–134,** 162, 290, 427
The Hamlet (Faulkner) 101–103, 283
Hampton, Howard 70
Hapgood, Robert 42, 45, 342–343
Haran, Shifra 120
Hardwicke, Sir Cedric **134**
Harper and Row 98–99
Harris, James 199
Harry Lime (character) *See The Adventures of Harry Lime; The Third Man*
Hartung, Philip 437
Harvey, Laurence 85, **134–135,** 134*f,* 195
Hathaway, Henry 19–20, **135–136**
Haufler, Max 391
Hawkins, Jack 20
Hawks, Howard 22, 23, 374, 378
Hayden, Sterling 200
Hayes, Helen 30, **136–137**
Hayes, J.J. 179–180
Hayes, Will 306
Haymes, Dick 139
Hayton, Lennie 159
Hayworth, Rita 18, **137–139,** 416
    at Columbia Studios 58
    Cotten, Joseph, and 74
    Del Río, Dolores, and 86
    Follow the Boys and 116
    Garland, Judy, and 120
    Horne, Lena, and 159

    in *The Lady from Shanghai* 35, 137–138, 203
    lawsuit by 417
    Mature, Victor, and 137, 251
    in *The Mercury Wonder Show* 58, 137, 261
    Parsons, Louella, and 137, 306
    in "There Are Frenchmen and French-men" 137, 203
    The Vikings and 364
    Welles, Christopher, and 413
Headley, J. 90
Hearst, William Randolph **139–140,** 140*f*
    in *The Battle Over Citizen Kane* 12
    in *Captured on Film: The True Story of Marion Davies* 31–32
    in *Cradle Will Rock* 80
    Davies, Marion, and 83–84
    His Honor, the Mayor and 156–157
    Kane and 40, 50, 55, 139–140
        and Drake, Herbert 92
        idea for 244, 245
        Kael on 186
        and Parsons, Louella 306
    Lederer, Charles, and 211
    Luce, Henry, and 221
    in *RKO 281* 319–320
    Rosebud and 320, 327
    Schaefer, Charles, and 333
Heartbreak House **141–142**
    Coulouris, George, in 75
    Fitzgerald, Geraldine, in 111–112
    by Mercury Theatre 162, 258, 344
    Sanford, Erskine, in 141, 332
Heart of Darkness **142–143,** 417
    adaptation of 67–69, 189
    Alland, William, in 3
    Apocalypse Now and 66, 67–70
    battle over 30
    Carter, Jack, and 33–34
    Houseman and 162
    Lederer, Virginia, in 212
    on *Mercury Theatre on the Air* 260–261
    Schilling, Gus, and 333
    Stanley and Livingstone and 134
    story of 67
    on *This Is My Best* 369–370
The Hearts of Age
    Cocteau and 57–58
    Death in xii
    Gottfredsen, Mary, and 127
    Lederer, Virginia, in 143, 211
    at Woodstock Drama Festival 428
Hecht, Ben **144–145**
    Casino Royale and 34, 145
    on Cohn, Harry 59
    Journey into Fear and 144, 182
    Lederer, Charles, and 211
    on Mankiewicz 186
    Twentieth Century and 396
Helen Hayes Theatre 137
Heller, Joseph 34, 36
Hello Americans 37, **145–146**

Hemingway, Ernest 66, 88, 166, 302, 351, 403
Henry, Buck 36
Henry IV, Part I 40, 42, 100, 112
Henry IV, Part II 40, 42, 100, 112
Henry Street Settlement 66
Henry V 40, 42, 74, 112, 123, 135
Hepburn, Katharine 30, 364
Herrmann, Bernard **146–151,** 146f
   Academy Award nomination for 50
   Around the World in 80 Days score by 260
   on *The Campbell Playhouse* 24
   on *Ceiling Unlimited* 37
   Citizen Kane and 49–50
   Dracula score by 109
   in *Focus on Citizen Kane* (Gottesman) 126
   on *Hello Americans* 145
   Jane Eyre score by 260
   The Magnificent Ambersons score and 238
   Psycho score by 401
   on Susan Alexander 62, 406
   The War of the Worlds and 31, 408
Herrmann, Edward 23
Herr, Michael 69
Heston, Charlton **152–154**
   in *The Complete Films of Orson Welles* (Howard) 164
   in *Focus on Orson Welles* (Gottesman) 126
   on Metty, Russell 264
   in *Touch of Evil* 152–154, 213, 383–387, 438
   on Welles's reputation 63
Higham, Charles **154–155**
   on Baxter, Keith 14
   on Bernstein, Maurice 15
   on *Bright Lucifer* (play) 11
   Callow, Simon, compared to 29
   on Carter, Jack 33
   on *Catch-22* 285
   Citizen Welles and 25–26
   on *The Deep* 85
   on *The Dreamers* 93
   on Edith Moson 16
   on Fitzgerald, Geraldine 112
   on Fleischer, Richard 115
   on Frost, David 119
   on Gielgud 123
   on Gottfredsen, Mary 127
   on Harvey, Laurence 134
   on Hayworth 58, 137
   on *Hearts of Age* 144
   on Holt, Tim 158
   on Houseman, reunion with 131
   on *The Immortal Story* 168
   on *It's All True* 420
   on *Journey into Fear* 144
   on Kodar, Oja 195
   on Laage, Barbara 202
   on *The Lady from Shanghai* 203, 204
   on *The Lady in the Ice* 208

on Lederer, Charles 211
on Lederer, Virginia 212
on Lee, Canada 213
on *The Long Hot Summer* 102
on MacLiammóir, Micheál 234
on *The Magnificent Ambersons* 150, 236, 238
on *Mexican Melodrama* 379
on Moorehead, Agnes 271, 272
on Mori, Paola 274
on *Native Son* 430
The Other Side of the Wind and 154, 302
on Parsons, Louella 306
on Pettey, Tom 308
on Robinson, Edward G. 323
on *The Sailor from Gibraltar* 318
on *The Shoemaker's Holiday* 346
on Stevenson, Robert 356
on *The Stranger* 351, 358, 360
on Susan Alexander 62
on *Ten Days Wonder* 365
on *Tomorrow Is Forever* 59
on Trauner, Alexander 388
on *Trent's Last Case* 389
on Tynan, Kenneth 397
on Weaver, Dennis 410
on Welles, background of 155
on Welles, Beatrice (mother) 412
on Welles, Christopher 414
on Welles, Rebecca 417
on Welles, Richard (brother) 419
on Young, Loretta 433
on Zanuck 434
Hill, Roger ("Skipper") **155–156**
   The Deep and 85
   Everybody's Shakespeare by 98, 415
   Falstaff and 48
   Lederer, Virginia, and 212
   on *Richard III* 41
   Twelfth Night and 396
   Woodstock Summer Theatre Festival and 427
His Honor, the Mayor 140, **156–157,** 332, 357
Une Histoire Immortelle   See The Immortal Story
History of the World: Part I **157**
Hitchcock, Alfred xii, 22, 23
Hoax   See F for Fake
Holiday, Billie 179
Holinshed, Raphael 98
Holland, Joseph 184
Holloway, Joseph 179
Hollywood Cameramen (Higham) 154–155
Hollywood Victory Committee 115
Holt, Tim 13, **157–159,** 158f, 202, 235, 236f, 272, 362
homosexuality 17, 64
Hopper, Hedda
   Citizen Kane and 92, 118, 139
   on *Orson Welles's Almanac* 291
   Parsons, Louella, and 306
   on *Prince of Foxes* 311
   in *RKO 281* 320

Horne, Lena **159,** 177
Horse Eats Hat **159–161,** 415
   basis for 56
   Cotten, Joseph, in 73
   Flanagan, Hallie, and 114
   Houseman and 161
   Lederer, Virginia, in 161, 212
   Losey, Joseph, on 161, 218
   Project 891 and 312
   score for 25, 160, 370–371
   success of 89
   Young, Stark, on 433
Horton, Aasta Dafora 260
House, Billy 322, 358
House of Cards **164**
Houseman, John **161–164,** 162f
   on *The Campbell Playhouse* 162
   Citizen Kane and 32, 148–149, 244, 246
   in *Cradle Will Rock* 80
   The Cradle Will Rock and 79, 162
   Doctor Faustus and 89, 162
   Dracula and 109
   estrangement from 112, 162–163
   with Federal Theatre Project 103, 325
   on *Five Kings* 342
   on Flanagan, Hallie 114
   Four Saints in Three Acts and 163, 371
   on *Hamlet* performance 161
   Heartbreak House and 111–112, 141
   Heart of Darkness and 162
   Horse Eats Hat and 160, 161
   in *It's All True* (play) 172–173
   Jane Eyre and 356
   Julius Caesar and 163, 183–185, 342
   on Kane and Hearst 244
   The Life of Galileo and 26, 218
   Macbeth and 159, 161, 223
   in Mercury Theatre 162, 258–259
   with *Mercury Theatre on the Air* 24, 29–30, 162, 259
   on *The Merv Griffin Show* 131
   Moss, Jack, and 275
   Native Son and 60, 281, 430
   with Negro Theatre Project 103–104, 283, 325
   Panic and 161, 305
   Project 891 and 312
   in *RKO 281* 320
   Selznick and 163, 336
   The Shoemaker's Holiday and 345
   Too Much Johnson and 380, 381
   The War of the Worlds authorship and 31, 407
   Weissburger, Arnold, and 410–411
   Welles and 71, 161–163, 415
   on Welles, Richard (father) 418
House Un-American Activities Committee
   Blitzstein, Marc, before 21
   Brecht before 26, 218–219
   Chaplin and 270
   Comingore and 63
   Huston, John, and 166
   Kazan, Elia, and 189

Miller, Arthur, before 266
Robinson, Edward G., and 321
Houston, Penelope 130, 369
Howard, James **164**
Howard, Trevor 366
Howlett, Kathy 295
Hughes, Howard 40, 55, 105, 106,
164–165, 319
Hughes, Ken 34
Huston, John **165–167**, 267
Casino Royale and 34
in *The Complete Films of Orson Welles*
(Howard) 164
Journey into Fear and 321
The Kremlin Letter and 199
on *The Orson Welles Story* 292
in *The Other Side of the Wind* 302, 330
The Roots of Heaven and 326
The Stranger and 402
Huston, Walter 94, **167**

I

If I Die Before I Wake 35, 203 *See also The*
Lady from Shanghai
I'll Never Forget What's 'is Name **168**
I Love Lucy xi, 341
The Immortal Story 84, 87, 93, 107, **168–170**
The Importance of Being Earnest **170**, 421
in *An Evening with Orson Welles* 20, 41,
97, 170, 373, 421
by Mercury Theatre 259
Institut des Hautes Études Ciné-
matographiques 14
Intermission Productions 55
Internal Revenue Service (IRS) 27, 105,
190–191, 216
International Center of Theater Research
27
International Pictures 125
Intimate Shakespeare Company 96, 234
The Invasion from Mars (Cantril) 31, 195,
408
Ionesco, Eugène **171,** 316–317
Irving, Clifford 105–107, 164
Ishaghpour, Youssef **171–172**
La Isla Del Tesoro See Treasure Island
Is Paris Burning? **172**
The Italian Straw Hat (Labiche) 25, 56,
159–160 *See also Horse Eats Hat*
It's All True **173–174**, 416
Armstrong, Louis, and 4–5
Around the World in 80 Days financing
and 6
Ellington, Duke, and 96–97
Flaherty, Robert, and 113–114
Foster, Norman, and 116
Goetz, William, and 125
Hello Americans and 145
Journey into Fear and 174, 182–183
Koerner, Charles, and 174, 175, 183,
196
The Lady Esther Show and 203
The Magnificent Ambersons and 237

Metty, Russell, and 263–264
Pettey, Tom, and 308
Rockefeller and 324
Roosevelt and 325
Schaefer, George, and 196
Shores, Lynn, and 347
Weissberger, Augusta, and 412
Whitney, Jock, and 420
It's All True (play) **172–173**
It's All True: Based on an Unfinished Film by
Orson Welles **174–175,** 264
Izzard, Eddie 23

J

The Jack Benny Show **176,** 291
Jackson, Gordon 268
Jackson, Larry 28
Jackson, Russell 343
Jaglom, Henry **176–177**
The Big Brass Ring and 17
in *The Complete Films of Orson Welles*
(Howard) 164
The Dreamers financing and 93
in *The Other Side of the Wind* 176, 302,
331
A Safe Place directed by 330
in *Someone to Love* 177, 350
Jane Eyre **177–179,** 178*f,* 416
on *The Campbell Playhouse* 24, 30–31
It's All True and 174
Leigh, Vivien, in 24, 30–31, 214
on *Mercury Summer Theatre on the Air*
258, 260
on *Mercury Theatre on the Air* 259–260
Moorehead, Agnes, in 273
Selznick and 125, 336–337
Stevenson, Robert, and 356
Zanuck and 434
Jarman, Reginald 40
Jason, Rick 117
Jazz Story 4–5, 96–97, **179**
Jew Suss 121–122, **179–180**
Johnson, Martin and Osa 114
Johnson, Samuel 100
Jones, Cherry 80
Jones, Chuck 28
Jones, Jennifer 94
Jorgens, Jack
on *Chimes at Midnight* 47
in *Focus on Orson Welles* (Gottesman)
126
on *Othello* 296–297, 300
Josephson, Julien 304
Journey into Fear **180–183,** 181*f*
authorship of 144
basis for 3–4, 181–182
Bennett, Richard, in 14–15
Cotten, Joseph, in 73–74, 116–117,
144, 181–183, 181*f,* 273
Del Río, Dolores, in 86, 181
directing of 116–117, 181, 321
Drake, Herbert, in 92
editing of 174

Hecht, Ben, and 144, 182
It's All True and 174, 182–183
The Magnificent Ambersons and 182
makeup for 336
Mercury Theatre and 181
Moorehead, Agnes, in 182–183, 272
Moss, Jack, in 181–183, 275
Robson, Mark, and 323
Schaefer, George, and 196
score for 151
Sloane, Everett, in 181, 347
Stevenson, Robert, and 356
Warrick, Ruth, in ix–x, 181, 409
Joyce, James 66
Judson, Edward 138
Julius Caesar **183–185**
adaptation of 342
Alland, William, in 3, 185
Barrymore, John, and Welles in 11
Cotten, Joseph, in 185, 258
Coulouris, George, in 74–75, 185, 258
Danton's Death compared to 81
in *An Evening with Orson Welles* 97
in *Everybody's Shakespeare* 98, 183
Gabel, Martin, in 120, 185
Houseman and 163, 183–185
Lederer, Virginia, in 212
Luce, Henry, and 221
by Mercury Theatre 162, 258, 288, 415,
416
on *Mercury Theatre on the Air* 259–260
in *Orson Welles on Shakespeare: The*
W.P.A. and Mercury Theatre Playscripts
(France) 119
procrastination on 340
score for 21, 185
set design for 184
The Smiler with a Knife and 349
in *The Theatre of Orson Welles* (France)
119
at Todd School 155, 183
Young, Stark, on 433
Julliard School of the Performing Arts 163,
241
Jurgens, Curt 12, 105

K

Kael, Pauline **186–187** *See also* "Raising
Kane" (Kael)
Chimes at Midnight reviewed by 222
on Comingore 60
on Lederer, Charles, and *Citizen Kane*
211
The Other Side of the Wind and 302
on *The Third Man* 367
on *West Side Story* 424
Kafka, Franz **187,** 390
Kaminsky, Stuart 154
Der Kampf um Rom See The Last Roman
Kane, Charles Foster *See* Charles Foster
Kane
Karas, Anton 1–2, **187–188,** 315, 368
Karl, Frederick 187

Karno, Fred 37
"Karol Theme" (Karas) 188
Karson, Nat 160, 223
Kauffmann, Stanley 79, 80, 107, 300, 326
Kazan, Elia 25, 188, **188–189**
Keller, Harry 153
Kennedy Center Life Achievement Award 137, 266
Kent, Amalia **189**
Kerr, Walter 192
Keystone Studios 37, 92
Khan, Aly 59, 139, 417
Kidman, Nicole 86, 401
King, Henry 104, **189–190**, 311
King, Sherwood 35
King Lear (play) **191–193**
    Atkinson, Brooks, review of 8
    Fitzgerald, Geraldine, in 111, 193, 215
    Gabel, Martin, and 120, 191
    Lindfors, Viveca, in 193, 215
    score for 193
King Lear (radio) 258
King Lear (television) **190–191**, 371, 416
    Brook, Peter, and 26–27, 190
    MacLiammóir in 190, 234
    Othello and 294
    score for 190
King of Kings **193–194**
Kingsley, Sidney 365
Kitt, Eartha 20, 57, 97, **194**, 372–373
Knox, Alexander 79
Koch, Howard **194–195**
    Around the World in 80 Days adapted by 260
    O'Brien, Edmond, and 289
    Rebecca adapted by 30
    Seventeen adapted by 194, 260
    The War of the Worlds authorship and 31, 194–195, 407, 419
Kodar, Oja **195–196**
    The Big Brass Ring and 18, 196
    in *The Deep* 85
    The Dreamers and 88, 92–93, 196
    in *F for Fake* 106–107, 106f, 195
    and "The Heroine" (Dinesen) 168
    Moreau, Jeanne, and 85, 195
    Mori, Paola, and 85, 195–196, 274–275
    The Other Side of the Wind and 301
    The Sacred Beasts and 330
    This Is Orson Welles (Bogdanovich) and 23, 196, 327–328
Koerner, Charles W. **196–197**
    Drake, Herbert, and 92
    It's All True and 174, 175, 183, 196
    The Magnificent Ambersons and, editing of 196–197
    at RKO studio 72, 333
    Shores, Lynn, and 347
Kolker, Robert 199
Korda, Sir Alexander **197–198**
    Around the World in 80 Days financing and 6, 374
    Cyrano de Bergerac and 18

Paris by Night and 88
Salome and 332
The Third Man and 1–2, 198, 369
The V.I.P.s and 405
War and Peace and 198, 288
Koscina, Sylva 12
Krasker, Robert 368
The Kremlin Letter **198–199**, 302
Krohn, Bill 175
Krüger, Hardy 12
Kruger, Otto 94
Kubrick, Stanley **199–201**, 199f, 355
Kurant, Willy 85, 169

L

Laage, Barbara 138, **202**, 203, 421
Lacy, Catherine 79
The Lady Esther Show **202–203**
The Lady in Ice **207–208**
The Ladykiller See *Monsieur Verdoux*
The Lady from Shanghai **203–207**, 204f, 416
    Alland, William, on 3
    Around the World in 80 Days and 6
    authorship of 35
    Castle, William, and 35
    Cohn, Harry, and 226
    in film noir genre 200
    in *Focus on Orson Welles* (Gottesman) 126
    Hayworth in 35, 137–138, 203–207
    location scouting for 202
    Macao in 169, 204
    Mexican Melodrama and 379
    narration in 207
    payment for 58–59
    Sanford, Erskine, in 203, 332
    Schilling, Gus, in 203, 334
    Sloane, Everett, in 203, 347–348
    story of 204–206
    The Stranger and 323
    Welles, Christopher, and 414
    Wilson, Richard, in 423
Laemmle, Carl 59
Lafayette **208**
Lafayette Theatre 33, 104, 223, 283
Landru, Henri 38
Lang, Fritz 22, 23, 26, 332
Lansbury, Angela 102, 216
The Last Crusade See *Michael the Brave*
The Last Roman **208–209**
The Late Great Planet Earth **209**
Latimore, Frank 19
Laughton, Charles **209–210**, 210f
    Cortez, Stanley, and 72
    in *The Green Goddess* 128
    in *The Life of Galileo* 26, 198, 218, 373–374
    on *Orson Welles's Almanac* 291
    Welles compared to 133
Lawrence, Viola 204
Leachman, Cloris 22–23, 279
Leaming, Barbara **210–211**, 289
    on Bernstein, Maurice 16

on *The Black Rose* 20
Callow, Simon, compared to 29
on Carter, Jack 33
on *Casino Royale* 104
on *Catch-22* 285
on *Chimes at Midnight* 47–48
Citizen Welles and 25–26
on Cotten, Joseph 74
on deal with Cohn, Harry 58
on *The Deep* 85
on *The Dreamers* 88
fabrications told to, by Welles 210
on *F for Fake* 105
Fleischer, Richard, interview with 64
on Garland, Judy 120
on Gate Theatre 234
on German tour of *An Evening with Orson Welles* 97
on Gottfredsen, Mary 127
on Hill, Roger 155
on *Is Paris Burning?* 172
on *The Jack Benny Show* 176
on *Jane Eyre* 178
on *Jew Suss* 180
on Kitt, Eartha 194
on Kodar, Oja 195
on Lederer, Charles 211
on Lee, Canada 213
on *The Life of Galileo* 374
on *Macbeth* 226
on *Man in the Shadows* 244
on McCormack, Patty 257
on *The Merv Griffin Show* 131, 210
on *Moby Dick–Rehearsed* 267–268
on *Monsieur Verdoux* 38
on *Othello* 294
on Reynolds, Burt 316
on *Richard III* 41
on Rutherford, Margaret 329
on Shakespeare, adapting 340
on Sloane, Everett 347
on *The Stranger* 402
on *Touch of Evil* 438
on Warrick, Ruth 409
on Weaver, Dennis 410
on Welles, Beatrice (daughter) 413
on Welles, Beatrice (mother) 412
on Welles, Christopher 413
on Welles, Richard (brother) 418
on Wilder, Thornton 423
on Yates, Herbert 432
on Young, Loretta 433
Lear, Norman 355
Lederer, Charles 83, **211**, 212, 245, 414
Lederer, Virginia Nicholson Welles **211–212**, 415
    in *Danton's Death* 81
    on *Hearts of Age* 143
    in *Horse Eats Hat* 161
    in *It's All True* (play) 172–173
    lawsuit by 138, 414
    Macbeth and 212, 223, 283, 415
    in *Panic* 305

in *Too Much Johnson* 212, 380, 381
in *Trilby* 393
in *Tsar Paul* 395
Lee, Canada **212–213,** 224, 281–282, 433
Légion d'Honneur
    for Gielgud 124
    for Guitry, Sacha 132
    for MacLiammóir 234–235
    for Moreau, Jeanne 274
    for Olivier 290
    for Pirandello 308
    for Wilder, Thornton 423
Leigh, Janet 154, **213–214,** 383, 383*f,* 386, 387, 404
Leigh, Vivien 24, 30–31, **214,** 317
Lejeune, C.A. 19
Lennon, Thomas 12
Leve, Sam 184
Levine, Laurence 340–341
Levy, Raoul 250
Lewis, Jerry 36, 84, 251
Lewis, John L. 79
Lewis, Lloyd 394
The Life of Galileo
    Brecht and 26
    financing for 198, 209, 373
    Laughton, Charles, and 26, 209, 218, 373–374
    Losey, Joseph, and 218
    review of 8
Life with Father 120, 260–261
Light, James 305
Lighten, Louis D. 20
Lillie, Bea **214–215,** 259
Lime, Harry *See The Adventures of Harry Lime; The Third Man*
Lindfors, Viveca 193, **215**
Lindsay, Louis **215**
Lindsey, Hal 209
Littell, Robert 224
Little, Brown, and Company 186
The Little Prince **215–216**
The Lives of a Bengal Lancer 9, 135, 363, 379
Living Newspaper plays 103, 217–218, 219, 283
Lloyd, Norman 143, 184, 258
Lockheed-Vega Aircraft 36
Lockwood, Margaret 394
Lom, Herbert 20
Lombard, Carole **216,** 348, 396
Long, Richard 359
Long Day's Journey into Night 87, 112, 358
The Long Hot Summer **216–217,** 217*f*
    basis for 101–103, 216
    line memorization for 65
    makeup for 336
    Newman, Paul, in 217, 283–284
    Woodward, Joanne, in 102, 217, 217*f,* 283, 428
Lonsdale, Michael 392
"The Look of Love" 34
Losey, Joseph 26, 63, 161, **217–220,** 218
Los Robles **220–221,** 383

Lucas, William 79
Luce, Henry **221**
Lucidi, Renzo 277, 364
Lumet, Sidney 23
Lunt, Alfred 128
Lupino, Ida 30
Lyons, Bridget Gellert 46, **221–222**

M

Macbeth (film) **225–233,** 226*f,* 230*f,* 416
    Alland, William, in 3
    editing of 18, 215, 328
    Everybody's Shakespeare and 98
    evolution of 340
    Feldman, Charles and 226, 432
    financing for 104, 341–342
    makeup for 336
    McDowall, Roddy, in 226, 228, 257
    Nolan, Jeannette, in 225, 226–227, 286–287
    Sanford, Erskine, in 225, 228, 332
    Schilling, Gus, in 334
    score for 146, 223–224
    values in 339
    Welles, Christopher, in 226, 230, 414
    Wilson, Richard, in 423
    Yates, Herbert, and 104, 226, 432
Macbeth (play, 1936) **223–224,** 415
    adaptability of 341
    in *The Battle Over Citizen Kane* 12
    Carter, Jack, in 33, 224, 225
    Cocteau at 58
    Everybody's Shakespeare and 98
    evolution of 340
    Flanagan, Hallie, and 114
    Houseman and 159, 161
    Lederer, Virginia, and 212, 283, 415
    Lee, Canada, in 213, 224
    under Negro Theatre Project 103–104, 283, 325
    in *Orson Welles on Shakespeare: The W.P.A. and Mercury Theatre Playscripts* (France) 118–119
    Project 891 and 312
    score for 283, 370–371
    success of 159
    in *The Theatre of Orson Welles* (France) 119
    Young, Stark, on 433
Macbeth (play, 1947) 214, **224–225,** 257, 340
MacDonald, Jeanette 115–116, 361
"Mack the Knife" 21
MacLeish, Archibald 156, 161, **233–234,** 304–305
MacLiammóir, Micheál **234–235**
    in *The Blessed and the Damned* 20
    Chimes at Midnight and 40, 234
    in *The Drunkard, or, The Fallen Saved* 94
    Edwards, Hilton, and 96, 234
    in *An Evening with Orson Welles* 97
    in *Filming Othello* 108
    at Gate Theatre 121–122

    in *Hamlet* 133
    in *The Importance of Being Earnest* 170
    Jew Suss and 179
    in *King Lear* 27, 190, 234
    in *The Kremlin Letter* 199
    Mori, Paola, and 277
    in *Othello* 234, 295–296
    in *Time Runs* 97, 373
    in *Trilby* 393
    in *Tsar Paul* 395–396
    at Woodstock Summer Theatre Festival 96, 234, 427–428
magic
    in *An Evening with Orson Welles* 20
    in *Follow the Boys* 115
    in *The Mercury Wonder Show* 261–262, 426
    Welles fascination with xi
The Magic World of Orson Welles (Naremore) 281
Magnani, Anna 290
The Magnificent Ambersons **235–239,** 416
    See also Pampered Youth
    basis for 364
    Baxter, Anne, in 13, 235
    Bennett, Richard, in 14–15, 238
    on *The Campbell Playhouse* 167
    Chimes at Midnight compared to 100
    Collins, Ray, in 60
    Comingore and 62
    Cortez, Stanley, and 71–72, 154–155
    Costello, Dolores, in 72–73, 235
    Cotten, Joseph, in 73, 235, 238
    editing of 32–33, 174, 238
        Cotten, Joseph, and 73–74
        It's All True and 237
        Journey into Fear and 182
        Koerner, Charles, and 196–197
        and Moss, Jack 275
        Rosenbaum, Jonathan, on 328
        and Schaefer, Charles 333
        and Wise, Robert 423–424
    Gottfredsen, Mary, and 127
    Holt, Tim, in 13, 157–158, 235, 236*f,* 272
    irising in 81
    It's All True and 174, 175
    Kent, Amalia, for 189
    Losey, Joseph, on 220
    makeup for 336
    Mercury Theatre and 181
    Metty, Russell, and 263
    Moorehead, Agnes, in 235, 238, 271–272
    at RKO 32–33, 236, 237, 318
    Robson, Mark, and 323
    Sanford, Erskine, in 332
    Schaefer, George, and 196, 307–308, 333
    Schilling, Gus, in 334
    score for 147, 150–151, 238
    screenplay for 236, 237, 240
    sound for 356

Toland, Gregg, and 240
updating of 85
Warrick, Ruth, and 409
Welles, Beatrice (mother), and 413
Welles, Richard (father), and 235–236, 417
Wise, Robert, and 423–424
The Magnificent Ambersons (mini-series) **239–240**
The Magnificent Ambersons: A Reconstruction (Carringer) 32–33
The Making of Citizen Kane (Carringer) 32
The Making of a Legend: Gone With the Wind (Thomson) 370
Malkovich, John 319, 321
Mallett, Richard 311
The Maltese Falcon 7–8, 165, 167
Man, Beast and Virtue **240–241,** 308
A Man for All Seasons 65, **242–243,** 243*f*, 435–437
Mancini, Henry **241–242**
Mankiewicz, Herman J. **244–247**
   in *The Battle Over Citizen Kane* 13
   Citizen Kane authorship and 21, 32, 49, 55, 83–84, 416
      and Hecht, Ben 144
      and Houseman 162
      Kael, Pauline, in (*See The Citizen Kane Book* [Kael]; "Raising Kane" [Kael])
      and revisions 245–246, 409
      Weissberger, Arnold, and 411
   on Comingore 60
   His Honor, the Mayor, and 156
   in *RKO 281* 319–320
Mankiewicz, Tom 353
Mann, Daniel 183
Man in the Shadow **243–244,** 438
Manvell, Roger **248**
"The Man Who Broke the Bank at Monte Carlo" 72
The Man Who Came to Dinner **248–249,** 428
The Man Who Saw Tomorrow **249**
Marching Song 156, 419
The March of Time **249–250,** 415
   Citizen Kane and 285
   Four Saints in Three Acts on 371
   Luce, Henry, and 221
   narration of 3
   Nolan, Jeannette, on 286
   Panic on 233, 305–306
   Tonight We Improvise on 308
   Zaharoff, Basil, and 365, 434
Margaret, Princess 34
Marco the Magnificent **250–251,** 363
Margetson, Arthur 309
Margolis, Henry 120
Marich, Marie S. 25–26
Marion Davies Children's Clinic 32
Markle, Fletcher 35
Marlowe, Christopher 89
Marshall, Herbert 94, 128

Martin, Dean 84, **251**
Martin, Tony 138
Martinelli, Elsa **251,** 334, 391
Mature, Victor 136, 137, **251–252,** 252*f*, 364
Maugham, W. Somerset **252–253,** 372
Maxine Elliott Theater
   The Cradle Will Rock and 21, 79, 172
   Doctor Faustus at 33
   Horse Eats Hat at 56, 160
   Project 891 at 283, 312
Mayer, Louis B. **253–254**
   birthday party for 164
   in *Citizen Kane* controversy 140, 306
   Garland, Judy, and 121
   Goetz, William, and 125
   Hearst and 83
   Horne, Lena, and 159
   in *RKO 281* 319
   Selznick and 337
McBride, Joseph **254**
   on *Chimes at Midnight* 45, 48
   on *F for Fake* trailer 107
   in *Focus on Orson Welles* (Gottesman) 126
   on *Hearts of Age* 143
   on *The Lady from Shanghai* 207
   on *Macbeth* 232, 342
   on *Mr. Arkadin* 277
   on *Othello* 300
   on *The Other Side of the Wind* 302
   on *The Stranger* 360
McCambridge, Mercedes **254–255**
   in *The Other Side of the Wind* 302
   in *Touch of Evil* 214, 254
McCarthy, Joseph **255–256**
   The Crucible and 266
   The Unthinking Lobster and 398
McClintic, Guthrie **256,** 415
   acting company of 156
   Cornell, Katherine, and 71
   Rathbone, Basil, and 313
   Woollcott and 422, 428
McCormack, Patty 91–92, **256–257**
McCormick, Harold 40, 62, 211, 245, 406
McCormick, Robert *See* McCormick, Harold
McDowall, Roddy 225, 226, 228, **257**
Mcfayden, Angus 80
McGoohan, Patrick **257–258,** 267, 268
McGrath, Joseph 34
McGraw-Hill 99
McIntire, John 225, 287
Medal of Freedom 86
Meisel, Myron 175
Mellors, William 65
The Merchant of Venice 388
   The Dean Martin Comedy Show and 84
   Edwards, Hilton, and 96
   in *Everybody's Shakespeare* 98
   evolution of 340
   Lederer, Virginia, in 212

The Mercury Shakespeare See Everybody's Shakespeare (Hill and Welles)
Mercury Summer Theatre on the Air **258**
Mercury Theatre **258–259**
   Alland, William, in 3
   Berry, John, in 16
   Citizen Kane and 49, 55
   Collins, Ray, with 60
   Cotten, Joseph, in 73
   Coulouris, George, in 74–75
   Danton's Death by 81–82, 162
   vs. *First Person Singular* 108–109
   Fitzgerald, Geraldine, with 111–112
   Five Kings by 42
   founding of 183, 415
   Gabel, Martin, in 120
   Heartbreak House by 141–142, 344
   Heart of Darkness by 143
   Houseman in 162
   Journey into Fear and 181
   Julius Caesar at 221
   O'Brien, Edmond, in 288
   in *Orson Welles on Shakespeare: The W.P.A. and Mercury Theatre Playscripts* (France) 119
   The Shoemaker's Holiday by 162, 258, 344, 345
   Sloan, Everett, in 347
   Stewart, Paul, at 357
   Too Much Johnson by 259, 379–381
   Weissberger, Augusta, and 412
   Wilson, Richard, with 423
Mercury Theatre on the Air **259–261,** 415 *See also The Campbell Playhouse*
   Alland, William, on 3
   Around the World in 80 Days on 5
   First Person Singular and 110
   Foster, Norman, and 116
   Herrmann, Bernard, and 146
   Houseman with 162
   King Lear on 191
   Koch, Howard, with 194–195
   The Lady Esther Show and 202
   Mankiewicz and 244
   Mercury Theatre and 259
   Moorehead, Agnes, with 270
   Nolan, Jeannette, on 225, 286
   A Passenger to Bali on 261, 306–307
   Sanford, Erskine, on 332
   script authorship and 247
   Stewart, Paul, and 357
   The War of the Worlds and 259, 406–408, 419
The Mercury Wonder Show **261–262**
   Cotten, Joseph, in 74, 261
   Dietrich in 86, 261
   Follow the Boys and 115
   Hayworth and 58, 137
   magic in xi
   Moorehead, Agnes, in 261
   Welles, Richard (brother), at 418
Meredith, Burgess 42, 112–113, 125, **262–263**

Mereshkovsky, Dmitri 395
Merivale, Philip 358
The Merry Wives of Windsor 40, 46, 112
The Merv Griffin Show 119, 131, 210
"The Metamorphosis" (Kafka) 187
Metro-Goldwyn-Mayer
    Astor, Mary, at 8
    Cosmopolitan Pictures and 83
    Garland, Judy, at 121
    Mayer, Louis B., at 253–254
    Selznick at 337
    Zinneman, Fred, at 435
Metty, Russell **263–265**
    Citizen Kane and 263, 376
    Spielberg and 353
    The Stranger and 359–360
    Touch of Evil and 153, 386
Mexican Melodrama 379
MGM *See* Metro-Goldwyn-Mayer
Michael the Brave **265**
Mielziner, Jo 305
Milius, John 69
Miller, Arthur 37, 72, 171, **265–266**
Miller, Gabriel 102, 284
Minnelli, Liza 121, 279
Minnelli, Vincent 121
La Miracle de Sainte Anne **266–267,** 399
Moby Dick 18, 165, 258, **267,** 302, 397
Moby Dick—Rehearsed (film) 257, **267–268**
Moby Dick—Rehearsed (play) 191, **268–269**
Mohr, Hal 72
Mol, Gretchen 80, 239
The Moment of Truth 85, 301, 330
Monsieur Verdoux 38–39, **269–270**
Moore, Hazel 16
Moorehead, Agnes **270–273**
    on *The Campbell Playhouse* 24, 30
    in *Citizen Kane* 51, 55, 270–273, 271*f*, 376–377
    in *Dracula* 109
    in *His Honor, the Mayor* 156
    in *Jane Eyre* 273
    in *Journey into Fear* 182–183, 272
    in *The Magnificent Ambersons* 235, 238, 271–272
    on *March of Time* 249
    in *The Mercury Wonder Show* 261
    in *Rebecca* 270
    on *The Shadow* 270, 338
    The Stranger and 321–322, 360
    in "The Texarkana Program" 325
    on *This Is My Best* 370
    in *The War of the Worlds* 270
Moreau, Jeanne **273–274,** 273*f*
    in *Chimes at Midnight* 42, 44, 45*f*, 273
    in *The Deep* 85
    in *The Immortal Story* 87, 168–170
    Kodar, Oja, and 85, 195
    Richardson, Tony, and 318
    in *The Sailor from Gibraltar* 273, 318, 331
    in *The Trial* 273, 391
Mori, Paola 85, 195–196, **274–275,** 277, 413

Moss, Jack 181–183, 239, **275**
Moulton, Richard G. 341
Movie Wars (Rosenbaum) 4, 32, 327–328
Mr. Arkadin xii, **275–278,** 276*f,* 416
    The Adventures of Harry Lime and 2, 276
    Auer, Mischa, in 8, 277–278
    Dietrich and 87
    location scouting for 27
    Mori, Paola, in 274, 277, 413
    Tamiroff, Akim, in 363
    Zaharoff, Basil, and 434
Muhl, Edward 153–154
Muir, Florabel 138
Mulvey, Laura 62, **278,** 377
The Muppet Movie **278–279**
The Muppets Take Manhattan **279**
Murray, Bill 80
Mutiny on the Bounty 73, 210, 211, 212, 379
Mutual Studios 37
"My Favorite Duck" 28
"My Friend Bonito" 116–117, **173–174,** 263
My Own Private Idaho 400–401

N

Napier, Alan 227
Napoleon 132, **280**
Naremore, James **280–281**
    on *Chimes at Midnight* 45
    on *Citizen Kane* cinematography 378
    on Costello, Dolores 72
    in *Focus on Orson Welles* (Gottesman) 126
    on *The Immortal Story* 169
    on *The Killing* 200–201
    on *The Lady from Shanghai* 206
    on *Macbeth* 232, 341
    on *The Magnificent Ambersons* 237
        credits for 238
        Moorehead, Agnes, in 272
        score for 150, 238
    on *Othello* 300
    on Schneider, Romy 334
    on Shakespeare and Welles 48
narration
    for *Bugs Bunny Superstar* 27–28
    for *Chimes at Midnight* 42–43
    for *The Crucifixion* 88
    for *History of the World: Part I* 157
    for *It's All True* 263–264
    for *To Kill a Stranger* 88
    for *The Lady from Shanghai* 207
    for *The Last of the Wild Mustangs* 88
    for *The Late Great Planet Earth* 209
    for *Out of Darkness* 303
    for *Salvador Dali par Jean-Christophe Averty* 88
    for *The Spanish Earth* 302, 351
    for *Swiss Family Robinson* 361–362
    for *The Vikings* 63, 404
National Medal of Arts 137
National Public Radio 36

Native Son **281–282,** 430
    Berry, John, in 16, 282
    Collins, Ray, in 60, 282
    Houseman and 60, 163
    Lee, Canada, in 213, 281–282
    Sanford, Erskine, in 282, 332
    Sloane, Everett, in 282
    Stewart, Paul, in 282
    Welles in, review of 8
    Wilson, Richard, in 282
    Young, Stark, on 433
Necromancy **282–283**
Negro Theatre Project **283**
    under Federal Theatre Project 103–104
    Houseman and 161
    Macbeth under 159, 212, 223–224, 341
    Roosevelt and 325
    Weissburger, Arnold, and 410–411
    Welles, Richard (brother), at 418
    under Works Progress Administration 429
Neill, Sam 86
Nero, Franco 12
Newman, Paul 17, 217, **283–284,** 424
News on the March **285**
    basis for 250
    in *Citizen Kane* opening 51
    Kane in 39
    Luce, Henry, and 221
    Robson, Mark, and 323
Nichols, Lewis 6, 309
Nichols, Mike 36, **285–286**
Nicholson, Jack 17, 177, 330
"Nickel under Foot" 21, 26, 79
Nieto, José 43
Nims, Edward 153–154, 321
Niven, David 34
Nobel Prize 101, 308, 345
Noble, Peter 57, **286**
Nolan, Jeannette 225, 226–227, **286–287**
Noone, Jimmie 292
North Star Productions 88, 93
noses, false 18, 394
Nostradamus 249
Nugent, Frank S. 394

O

Oberon, Merle 198, **288**
O'Brady, Frederic 276
O'Brien, Edmond **288–289,** 302
O'Connor, Donald 116, 361
O'Connor, Gary 317
Oedipus the King **289**
O'Herlihy, Dan 225, 226, 228
Oldcastle, Sir John *See* Falstaff, Sir John
Olivier, Laurence **289–290,** 290*f*
    on *The Campbell Playhouse* 30
    Henry V of 45, 290
    Leigh, Vivien, and 214
    Othello produced by 292–293
    Plowright, Joan, and 349
    in *Rhinoceros* 40, 77, 171, 214, 289, 317
Olympia Theatre 96

Omnibus 27, 190–191
O'Neal, Tatum 23
Operation Cinderella **290**
Order of Merit 128
Organisation Radio-Télèvision Français (ORTF) 168
Orson Welles (McBride) 254
Orson Welles: A Bio-Bibliography (Wood) 426
Orson Welles: A Biography (Leaming) 210
Orson Welles: A Celebration (Taylor) 365
Orson Welles: A Critical View (Bazin) 14, 395
Orson Welles: A First Biography (Fowler) 118
Orson Welles: An Investigation into His Films and Philosophy (Bessy) 17
Orson Welles: The One-Man Band, The Deep in 86
Orson Welles: The Rise and Fall of an American Genius (Higham) 85, 154, 155
Orson Welles: The Road to Xanadu (Callow) 29
Orson Welles, Shakespeare, and Popular Culture (Anderegg) 4
Orson Welles Cinéaste: Une Caméra Visible (Ishaghpour) 171–172
Orson Welles's Almanac 7, 202, **291–292**
Orson Welles's Great Mysteries **292**
Orson Welles on Shakespeare: The W.P.A. and Mercury Theatre Playscripts (France) 118–119
The Orson Welles Show 137
The Orson Welles Sketchbook 7, **292**
The Orson Welles Story **292**
Oscar, Henry 20
Othello (film) **294–300,** 416 *See also Filming Othello*
　adaptation of 342
　The Adventures of Harry Lime and 3
　art direction for 388
　The Black Rose and 20
　Cloutier, Suzanne, in 56–57, 295
　Cotten, Joseph, in 74
　Don Quixote compared to 91
　editing of 328
　Edwards, Hilton, in 295
　Everybody's Shakespeare and 98
　evolution of 340
　financing for 20, 294–295, 311, 326, 388, 435
　Hill, Roger, and 156
　location scouting for 274
　MacLiammóir in 234, 295–296
　makeup for 336
　restoration of 4, 55
　Sloane, Everett, and 347
　Small, Edward, and 18
　Tynan, Kenneth, on 293, 396–397
　values in 339
Othello (play) 97, **292–294,** 389
The Other Side of the Wind **301–303**
　Bogdanovich and 23
　cinematography for 28
　Dietrich and 87, 302
　financing for 302–303, 365
　Hemingway in 302, 351
　Higham, Charles, and 154, 302
　Jaglom in 176, 331
　McBride interview and 254
　O'Brien, Edmond, in 288
　The Sacred Beasts and 330
　sexuality in 107, 302
O'Toole, Peter 34, 168
Out of Darkness **303**

P

Paar, Jack 33, 36
Padovani, Lea 18, 56–57
Palace Theatre 128
Palmer, Lilli 87, 302
Pampered Youth **304**
Panic (play) 161, 233–234, 250, **304–305,** 371
Panic (radio) **305–306**
Paramount Studios
　Cortez, Stanley, at 72
　Cosmopolitan Pictures and 83
　Dietrich at 86
　Goddard, Paulette, at 125
　Hecht, Ben, at 145
　It's All True and 175
　Metty, Russell, at 263
　Selznick at 337
Parker, Dorothy 83
Parlo, Dita 143
Parrish, Robert 34
Parsons, Louella **306**
　in *Citizen Kane* controversy 118, 253, 333
　Hayworth and 137, 306
　on *Prince of Foxes* 311
　in *RKO 281* 320
A Passenger to Bali 258, 261, **306–307**
Pathé Exchange 113
Pathé News 71–72, 224
"Pat Hobby and Orson Welles" (Fitzgerald) 111
Paul, Edgerton 143–144
Paul, Elliot 179
Paxinou, Katina 278
Peabody Awards 118
Peck, Gregory 94, 190
Pegler, Westbrook 291
Perkins, Anthony 187, 292, **307,** 390
Perkins, Frances 336
Perkins, V.I. **307–308**
Perry, Natasha 274
Petit, Chris 331
Pettet, Joanna 34
Pettey, Tom **308**
Peyton, Charles 90
Phoenix Theatre 304
Pilcher, Jay 304
Pioneer Pictures 421
Pirandello, Luigi **308**
Platt, Polly 22–23
Plowright, Joan
　in *Moby Dick–Rehearsed* 268
　in *Rhinoceros* 77, 171, 214, 289, 317, 349

Poe, Tom 401
Polacco, Giorgio 16
politique des auteurs 14
Pollock, Arthur 81
Porter, Cole 5–6, 258, **308–310**
Pottier, Richard 82
Pound, Ezra 66
Powell, Dilys 193–194
Powell, Michael 164
Power, Tyrone 19–20, 135, 190, **310–311**
Preminger, Otto 23
Price, Vincent 141
Prince of Foxes **311–312,** 311f
　Feldman, Charles K., and 104
　in Germany 20
　King, Henry, and 189
　Othello and 294
　Power, Tyrone, in 310, 311
　Sloane, Everett, in 348
Pringle, Jack 212
The Private Life of Henry VIII 198, 210, 288
Le Procès See The Trial
Proctor, Philip 330
Project 891 **312,** 415
　Doctor Faustus and 89
　Horse Eats Hat and 56
　Julius Caesar and 183
　origin of 283
　under Works Progress Administration 429
Proud Destiny (Feuchtwanger) 180
Prussing, Louise 133, 393
Psycho 213, 307, 385, 401
Pudovkin 190
Pulitzer Prize
　for Atkinson, J. Brooks 8
　for MacLeish, Archibald 233–234
　for Miller, Arthur 265–266
　for Tarkington, Booth 235, 363–364
　for Thomson, Virgil 371
　for Wilder, Thornton 422
Purcell, Noel 105
Put Money in Thy Purse (MacLiammóir) 234–235, 294, 340

Q

Quiller-Couch, Arthur 341

R

Rachel Rachel 112, 284, 428
racism, *It's All True* and 175
Raft, George 34, 115–116
"Raising Kane" (Kael) 186–187
　Bogdanovich and 21
　Bower, Ronald, on 245
　F for Fake and 106
　Hecht, Ben, and 144
　Rosenbaum, Jonathan, on 32
Rajkovic, Ivica 85
Rank Organization 105
Rathbone, Basil **313**
Ratoff, Gregory 18, 348
Ravetch, Irving 102

Ray, Nicholas 193–194
Readick, Frank 143, 182, 338, 408
Rebecca
    on *Campbell Playhouse* 30, 261
    Moorehead, Agnes, in 270
    score for 147
    Selznick and 30, 336, 361
    Sullavan, Margaret, in 361
Redford, Robert 17, 88, 177
Redgrave, Michael 278
Redgrave, Vanessa 80, 318, 437
Reed, Carol **313–315**
    Greene, Graham, and 129, 314, 366
    Karas, Anton, and 187–188
    The Third Man directed by 130,
        187–188, 366–367
Reed, Oliver 168
Reichenbach, François 105, 107, 164
Reiguera, Francisco 92
Reinhardt, Max 81, 86
Remick, Lee 217, 248
Rennie, Michael 20, 188
Renoir, Jean 14, 26
Republic Pictures 18, 215, 224–226,
    341–342, 432
Return to Glenascaul **315–316**
Rey, Fernando 43
Reynolds, Burt 17, 124, 177, **316**
Rhinoceros 171, **316–317**
    Chimes at Midnight and 40
    Coward, Noël, on 77
    Olivier in 40, 77, 171, 214, 289
    Plowright, Joan, in 77, 171, 214, 289
    Smith, Maggie, in 349
Rhys-Meyers, Jonathan 240
Rhythm Boys 116
A Ribbon of Dreams: The Cinema of Orson
    Welles (Cowie) 78
Rice, Elmer 103
Richard II 40, 44
Richard III 41, 134
Richardson, Sir Ralph 42, 123, **317–318,**
    345
Richardson, Tony **318**
    The Chairs and 171
    critical background of 22
    Gielgud and 123
    Olivier and 290
    on Tynan, Kenneth 397
La Ricotta See *RoGoPaG*
Riley, Brooks 69
Ritt, Martin 65, 101–102, 217, 437
Rivera, Diega 80
RKO Radio Pictures, Inc. **318–319**
    The Campbell Playhouse and 24
    Citizen Kane at 49, 318
    contract with viii, 30, 334, 411
    Cortez, Stanley, at 72
    Fleischer, Richard, at 115
    Heart of Darkness at 67, 69, 142, 369
    Hughes, Howard, and 165
    It's All True and 97, 174, 175
    Jazz Story and 179

Journey into Fear at 181
Kent, Amalia, at 189
Koerner, Charles, at 72, 92, 174, 175,
    183, 196–197
Kubrick, Stanley, at 199
    The Magnificent Ambersons editing and
        32–33, 236, 237
Metty, Russell, at 263
Robson, Mark, at 324
Schaefer, George, at 72, 332–333
Seiderman, Maurice, at 335–336
Selznick at 319, 337
Shores, Lynn, at 347
The Smiler with a Knife and 216, 348
Stevenson, Robert, at 356
Stewart, James G., at 356
The Stranger at 318
Swiss Family Robinson and 361–362
Wise, Robert, at 424
RKO 281 **319–321**
Robbins, Tim 21, 80, 355
Robeson, Paul 159
Robinson, Edward G. **321–323,** 322f, 358,
    360
Robinson, Madelaine 391
Robson, Mark 13, **323–324**
Rockefeller, Edith 62, 406
Rockefeller, Nelson 306, 324
    Citizen Kane and 324
    in *Cradle Will Rock* 80
    It's All True and 173–174, 324, 420
Rodway, Norman 43
Roe, Tig 19
RoGoPaG **324–325**
Romance, Viviane 240
Romeo and Juliet 8, 71, 256, 310, 313
Rooney, Mickey 121
Roosevelt, Franklin Delano 174, **325–326**
    campaign for 290
    It's All True and 325
    on Lombard, Carole 216
    March of Time and 249
    Works Projects Administration and
        429
The Roots of Heaven 302, **326**
"Rosebud" **326–327**
    Kane and 39, 54
    in *Native Son* 282
    origin of 186, 245, 320
    purchase of 49, 352–353
    score motif for 147, 149
Rosebud: The Story of Orson Welles (Thomson)
    17, 327, 370
Rose, David 121
Rosenbaum, Jonathan **327–328**
    on *The Deluge at Nordenay* 168
    on *The Dreamers* 93
    on *Heart of Darkness* 67
    on Houseman 244
    on *The Lady from Shanghai* authorship
        35
    on *The Merchant of Venice* 340
    on "Raising Kane" 32

This Is Orson Welles (Bogdanovich) and
    23, 196
    on *Una su tredici* 398
Rosenberg, Stuart 405
Rosenbloom, Slapsie Maxie 116, 361
Rosenthal, Jean 81, 172
Rosher, Charles 72
Ross, Katharine 122
Rothwell, Kenneth 300, 343
Royal Academy of Dramatic Arts
    Baxter, Keith, at 14
    Gielgud at 123
    Hardwicke, Cedric, at 134
    Harvey, Laurence, at 135
Royal Affairs in Versailles 59, 132, 208, **328**
Royal Court Theatre 171, 317
Ruby, Thelma 40
Rudolphsheim 127
The Rudy Vallee Show, Barrymore, John, and
    Welles on 11, 400
Russell, Rosalind 348
Rutherford, Dame Margaret 42–43, **328–329**

S

The Sacred Beasts 84–85, 301, **330**
A Safe Place xii, 176–177, **330–331**
The Sailor from Gibraltar 273, 318, **331**
Salammbo (Reyer) 148–149
Salkind, Alexander **331–332**
Salome **332**
    basis for 421–422
    Brook, Peter, and 27
    Hayworth in 139
    Laage, Barbara, and 202, 421
    Leigh, Vivien, and 214
    publication of 17
Salvador Dali par Jean-Christophe Averty, nar-
    ration for 88
Sanford, Erskine **332**
    in *Heartbreak House* 141, 332
    Heart of Darkness and 143
    in *His Honor, the Mayor* 156
    in *The Lady from Shanghai* 203, 332
    in *Macbeth* 225, 228, 332
    in *The Magnificent Ambersons* 332
    on *Mercury Theatre on the Air* 332
    in *Native Son* 282, 332
    in *A Tale of Two Cities* 109
    in *Too Much Johnson* 380
San Simeon 83, 140, 211, 414, 431
Sarandon, Susan 80
Sargent, Alvin 23
Sarnoff, David 306
Sarris, Andrew 107, 126, 186, 190
Savage, Bernard, in *Doctor Faustus* 90
Saville, Philip 289
Sayers, Michael 34
Schaefer, George **332–333**
    and *Around the World in 80 Days* 5
    Citizen Kane release and 221, 306
    firing of 174, 183, 196, 333
    Heart of Darkness and 143
    It's All True and 174

Journey into Fear and 182–183, 196
The Magnificent Ambersons and 275, 307–308, 333
Parsons, Louella, and 306, 333
in *RKO 281* 320
at RKO studio 72, 332–333
Welles signed by viii, 334
Scharock, Roger 128–129
Scheider, Roy 320, 321
Schenck, Nicholas 253
Schilling, Gus 203, **333–334**
Schneider, Albert **334**
Schneider, Romy **334,** 392
Schoenberg, Arnold 20
Schreiber, Liev 319, 321
Scofield, Paul 436–437
Scott, Hazel 5
The Second Hurricane 25, 66, 73, **334–335,** 335
The Secret of Nikola Tesla 196, **335**
Segal, George 350
Seiderman, Maurice **335–336**
Sellers, Peter 34, 104
Selznick, David O. **336–337**
    Duel in the Sun and 94
    Houseman and 163, 336
    It's All True and 125
    Jane Eyre and 125, 336–337
    Mayer, Louis B., and 337
    Rebecca and 30, 336, 361
    at RKO 319, 337
    Showman: The Life of David O. Selznick (Thomson) 370
    Stevenson, Robert, and 356
    The Third Man and 77, 130, 337, 369
Sennett, Mack
    Chaplin and 37
    shooting style of 91
    Too Much Johnson and 379–380, 381
Seven Arts 125
Seven Gothic Tales (Dinesen) 88
Seventeen 194, 260, 364
sexuality 17, 64, 385–386
Seymour, Dan 109, 407
The Shadow **337–338**
    The Adventures of Harry Lime and 3
    Coward, Noël, and 76
    Gabel, Martin, on 120
    Kazan, Elia, on 188
    Moorehead, Agnes, on 270
    Sloane, Everett, on 338, 347
    Welles on xii, 415
Shakespeare, William **338–343,** 339f, 340–341
Shakespeare & the Film (Manvell) 248
Shakespeare—Hit or Miss? (Gielgud) 124
Shales, Tom 13, 239–240
Shannon, Harry 51, 377
Shaw, Fiona 320
Shaw, George Bernard 141–142, 215, **344–345,** 344f
Shayne, Konstantin 358
Shearer, Norma 83

Sheehan, Winfield 138
Sheen, Martin 69
Shepherd, Cybill 22–23
Sherlock Holmes 19, 260, **345,** 387
Sherman, Hiram 335, 421
Shilling, Gus 143
Shoedsack, Ernest B. 114
The Shoemaker's Holiday **346–347**
    Balanchine, George, and 10
    Cotten, Joseph, in 73, 346
    Coulouris, George, in 347
    by Mercury Theatre 162, 258, 344, 345
    music for 347
    in *The Theatre of Orson Welles* (France) 119
    Wilson, Richard, in 347
Shore, Dinah 116, 361
Shores, Lynn 347
Shurlock, Geoffrey 64
Singleton, Zutty 292
Siodmak, Robert 209, 435
Si Versailles m'était conté 59, 132, 208, **328**
Skybell, Steven 80
Sleepy Lagoon Defense Committee 63
Sloane, Everett **347–348**
    on *The Campbell Playhouse* 24, 30
    on *Ceiling Unlimited* 37
    in *Citizen Kane* 51, 55, 75f, 76f, 347–348
    on *Hello Americans* 145
    in *His Honor, the Mayor* 156
    in *Journey into Fear* 347
    in *Journey into Fear* 181
    in *The Lady from Shanghai* 203, 347–348
    in Mercury Theatre 347
    in *Native Son* 282
    Othello and 347
    on *The Shadow* 338, 347
Small, Edward 18, **348**
The Smiler with a Knife 165, 189, 216, 244, **348–349**
Smith, David 304
Smith, Dame Maggie **349**
Smothers, Tommy 122
Sokoloff, Vladimir 81–82, 143
Someone to Love 177, 196, **350**
"Something About Joe" 159
Song of Myself **350**
Southern, Terry 34
The Southern Star **350–351,** 402
Una Spada Per Due Bandiere See *Lafayette*
The Spanish Earth 302, **351**
Spenser, Jeremy 105
Spiegel, Sam 321, **351–352**
Spielberg, Steven 49, **352–355,** 353f
Stalling, Carl W. 28
Stanley Kubrick Award 355
Stanley Theater 128
Stanton, Olive 172–173
Start the Revolution Without Me **355**
Steichen, Edward 71
Steiner, Ralph 66

Stein, Gertrude 25
Stella Adler's Theatre Studio 21
Stevens, Ashton **355–356**
Stevenson, Robert 125, 177, 336, **356**
Stewart, James G. **356**
Stewart, Paul **357**
    on *Ceiling Unlimited* 37
    in *Citizen Kane* 51, 357
    on *Hello Americans* 145
    in *His Honor, the Mayor* 156
    on *March of Time* 249–250
    at Mercury Theatre 357
    in *Native Son* 282
    in *The War of the Worlds* 408
    The War of the Worlds authorship and 31, 357
St. John, Ellis, *Journey into Fear* and 144
Stockwell, Dean 63–65, 87, 115, **357–358,** 357f
Stoney Creek Theatre 35
"The Story of Samba" See *It's All True*
Stowe, Madeleine 239
The Stranger 322f, **358–360,** 359f, 416
    death in xii
    financing for 351
    Goetz, William, and 125
    Hayworth and 138
    Metty, Russell, and 153, 264
    Paths of Glory and 199
    preservation of 55
    at RKO 318
    Robinson, Edward G., in 321
    screenplay for 402
    Spiegel, Sam, and 302, 321, 351–352
    Young, Loretta, in 321–322, 322f, 358, 432–433
Strasberg, Susan 302
Streep, Meryl 88
Stroheim, Erich von 14
Struss, Karl 72
subjective point of view 68, 142
Suchet, David 319, 321
Sullavan, Margaret **360–361**
Sundance Film Festival 13
Sunderland, Nan 167
Super, Joel 437
Susan Alexander (character) 53–54
    basis for 62–63, 211, 245, 406
    cinematography for 377–378
    Davies, Marion, and 31–32, 61–62, 83–84
    musical score and 148–149
    suicide scene of 53, 55
Sutherland, Edward 361
Una su tredici 398
Swan, Buddy 51, 271f
Swiss Family Robinson **361–362**
Syms, Sylvia 105

T

Tachella, Jean-Claude 14
Tajna Nikole Tesle See *The Secret of Nikola Tesla*

Take This Woman See The Lady from Shanghai
"Tale Gunner Joe" 263
Tamiroff, Akim **363**
  in *Black Magic* 19
  in *Don Quixote* 92, 363
  in *Touch of Evil* 383*f,* 384, 386
  in *The Trial* 363, 392
Tantivy Press 78
Tarkington, Booth **363–364**
The Tartars 251, **364**
Tasca, Alessandro 42
Taylor, Elizabeth 177, 349, 374, 404
Taylor, John Russell 34, 222, 258, **364–365**
Taylor, Philip 352
Tedford, Charles Linton 304
Ten Days Wonder **365**
Ten Million Ghosts 162, **365–366**
Termite Terrace 28
"The Texarkana Program" 74, 325
Thalberg, Irving 83
Théâtre Edouard VII 20, 97
Theatre Guild 112
The Theatre of Orson Welles (France) 118–119
"There Are Frenchmen and Frenchmen" 137, 203
The Third Man **366–369,** 367*f,* 369*f,* 416
  The Adventures of Harry Lime and 1
  Cotten, Joseph, in 74, 130, 314, 366, 366*f*
  Coward, Noël, and 77
  death in xii
  Korda, Alexander, and 1–2, 198
  music for 187–188, 315, 368
  Othello and 297, 299
  performance in 65
  Reed, Carol, and 130, 187–188, 313–315, 366
  screenplay for 129–130
  Selznick and 77, 130, 337
The Third Man: The Lives of Harry Lime See The Adventures of Harry Lime
"This Is America" 115
This Is My Best 5, **369–370,** 402
This Is Orson Welles (Bogdanovich) 23, 146, 148, 327–328
Thomas, Bob 58
Thomas, Edna 224
Thompson, Howard 104–105
Thompson, Jim 200
Thomson, David **370**
  on *The Adventures of Harry Lime* 3
  on *The Big Brass Ring* 17, 316
  on *Chimes at Midnight* 42, 343
  on Dinesen, Isak 87–88
  on *Doctor Faustus* 33
  on *Duel in the Sun* 94
  on Falstaff 48
  on *The Fountain of Youth* 117–118
  on Frost, David 119
  on *Heart of Darkness* screenplay 189
  on Horne, Lena 159
  on *Horse Eats Hat* 25

  on Houseman estrangement 163
  on Hughes, Howard 165
  on *It's All True* 421
  on *Jane Eyre* 356
  on *King Lear* 193
  on *The Lady from Shanghai* 138, 203, 205, 206
  on Laughton, Charles 209–210
  on *The Life of Galileo* 209
  on Lindsay, Louis 215
  on *The Long Hot Summer* 103, 284
  on *Macbeth* 104, 226
  on *The Magnificent Ambersons,* editing of 238–239
  on McGoohan, Patrick 257
  on *Moby Dick–Rehearsed* 267
  on Moorehead, Agnes, in *Citizen Kane* 270–271
  on Mori, Paola 274
  on Moss, Jack 275
  on *The Other Side of the Wind* 403
  on Pettey, Tom 308
  on Roosevelt, and Welles 325
  on Rosebud 327
  on *The Sailor from Gibraltar* 318
  on Selznick 336
  on Spiegel, Sam 351
  on Spielberg 353
  on *The Stranger* 360, 402
  on *The Third Man* 74
  on Todd School 155
  on *The V.I.P.s* 405
  on Weissberger, Arnold 411
  on Woodward, Joanne 428
Thomson, Virgil **370–371**
  Five Kings and 112
  Horse Eats Hat and 25, 56, 159, 370–371
  King Lear and 27, 190, 371
  at *Macbeth* 58
  Macbeth score by 223–224, 283, 370–371
  Panic score by 305, 371
  The Spanish Earth and 351
Three Cases of Murder 252, **372**
The Threepenny Opera 21, 26, 79
Tichachek, Stephen J. 81
Tilly, Jennifer 239
Time Runs 194, **372–373**
  basis for 372
  in *The Blessed and the Damned* 20, 373
  Cloutier, Suzanne, in 57
  in *An Evening with Orson Welles* 97, 373
  Kitt, Eartha, in 194, 372–373
  MacLiammóir, Micheál, in 97, 373
  The Unthinking Lobster and 399
'*Tis Pity She's a Whore* 156, 161
Titania Palast 97
Tobin, Dan 117
Todd, Michael **373–374**
  Around the World in 80 Days financing and 5–6, 309, 373, 402
  The Life of Galileo and 26, 373

Todd Press 98
Todd School for Boys *See also* Woodstock Drama Festival
  Everybody's Shakespeare and 98–99
  Hill, Roger, at 155
  Julius Caesar at 155, 183
  Lederer, Virginia, and 211
  Shakespeare and 340
  Welles at 41, 415, 418
  Welles, Christopher, at 414
  Welles, Richard (brother), at 418
Toland, Gregg **374–378**
  Academy Award nomination for 50
  Citizen Kane and viii, 32, 49–50, 374–378, 375*f,* 416
  in *Focus on Citizen Kane* (Gottesman) 126
  The Magnificent Ambersons and 240
Tomorrow Is Forever 59, 125, **378–379,** 426
Tone, Franchot 203, **379**
The Tonight Show xi, xii, 33, 36, 131
Tony Awards and nominations 8, 124, 159, 266
Too Much Johnson (film) 25, 73, 92, **379–381**
Too Much Johnson (play) **381–382**
  Cotten, Joseph, in 381
  Danton's Death and 81
  film in 6, 73
  Francis, Arlene, in 381
  and Houseman 381
  Lederer, Virginia, in 212, 381
  by Mercury Theatre 259, 381–382
  Native Son and 281
  score for 25
  Weissberger, Augusta, and 380, 412
Toto 240
Touch of Evil **382–387,** 416
  basis for 382–383
  Collins, Ray, in 60
  Cotten, Joseph, in 74
  Dietrich in 86–87, 152, 214, 384, 385, 386*f*
  editing of 321, 387
  The Godfather trilogy and 69
  Heston, Charlton, in 152–154, 213, 383, 385, 387
  Leigh, Janet, in 154, 213, 383, 383*f,* 387
  The Long Hot Summer and 217
  Los Robles in 220–221
  makeup for 336
  McCambridge, Mercedes, in 214, 254
  Metty, Russell, and 264, 386
  post-production of 153–154
  restoration of 387
  score for 241–242
  success of 63
  Tamiroff, Akim, in 363, 383*f,* 384, 386
  Weaver, Dennis, in 385, 410
  Zugsmith, Albert, and 385, 438

Towers, Harry Alan 1, 345, **387–388**
  The Adventures of Harry Lime and 387
  The Black Museum and 19
  Sherlock Holmes and 387
The Tragedy of Othello: The Moor of Venice See
  Othello
The Tramp 37
Trauner, Alexander 294, **388**
Treasure Island 109, 388, **388–389**, 389*f*
The Treasure of the Sierra Madre 158–159,
  166, 167
Trent's Last Case **389–390**
The Trial **390–393**, 390*f*, 416
  basis for 187
  Chaplin on 39
  financing for 331
  Gielgud and 123
  Gleason and 124
  Kodar, Oja, and 85, 195
  Martinelli, Elsa, in 251, 334, 391
  Moreau, Jeanne, in 273
  Mori, Paola, in 274
  Perkins, Anthony, in 187, 307, 390
  preservation of 55
  Salkind, Alexander, and 331
  Schneider, Romy, in 334, 392
  Tamiroff, Akim, in 363, 392
Trilby 11, **393–394**, 427–428
Trosper, Katherine 246
Trouble in the Glen **394–395**
Truffaut, François **395**
  Callow, Simon, compared to 29
  on *Citizen Kane* 49
  critical background of 22
  in *Focus on Citizen Kane* (Gottesman)
    126
  in *Orson Welles: A Critical View* (Bazin)
    14
  Touch of Evil and 387
Truth and Lies See *F for Fake*
Tsar Paul 211, **395–396**, 427
Tucker, Forrest 394
Tucker, Sophie 116, 361
Turturro, John 80
Twelfth Night 98, 134, 137, 155, 191, **396**
12 + 1 **398**
Twentieth Century 145, 216, **396**
Twentieth-Century Fox 125, 310, 434
"The Tycoon Who Tried to Raze 'Kane'"
  (Shales) 13
Tynan, Kenneth **396–397**
  fabrications told to, by Welles 155
  in *Focus on Orson Welles* (Gottesman)
    126
  Ionesco and 171
  on *Moby Dick* 397
  on *Moby Dick–Rehearsed* 269
  on *Othello* 293, 396–397

U

Uccello 45
United Service Organization (USO) 115
Universal International 125

Universal Studios 165
University of California at Los Angeles film
  school 66
The Unthinking Lobster 194, **398–399**
  in *The Blessed and the Damned* 20,
    97
  Cloutier, Suzanne, in 57
  La Miracle de Sainte Anne in 266–267
Uomo, la Bestia, e la Virtu **240–241**, 308
Upon This Rock 399
Ure, Gudrun 57, 293
Ustinov, Peter 57

V

Vallee, Rudy **400**
Valli, Alida 366
Vance, William 57, 143–144
Van Dyke, Willard 66
Van Horne, Harriet 118
Van Sant, Gus **400–402**
Van Schmus, W.G. 306
Vassar Experimental Theatre 103, 114
vaudeville 127–128, 160
Vaughan, Ciba 17
Vaughan, Vince 401
Vaughan, Virginia Mason 299
Veiller, Anthony 125, 321, 352, **402**
Venice Film Festival
  awards of, for Cotten, Joseph 74
  Cloutier, Suzanne, at 57
  It's All True at 175
  Kodar, Oja, at 196
  Macbeth at 226
Venice Theater 21, 79, 80
Vérité et mensonges See *F for Fake*
Verne, Jules 5–7, **402–403**
Vidal, Gore 17, 172
Vidor, King 94
Viertel, Peter **403**, 436
The Vikings 63, 114, **403–404**, 404
V.I.P. 404
The V.I.P.s 119, 325, 329, 349, **404–405**
Volpone 124, 191, 215
von Sternberg, Josef 86
"voodoo" *Macbeth* See *Macbeth* (play, 1936)
Voyage of the Damned 405

W

Wald, Jerry 101–102, 216
Walsh, Maurice 394
Walska, Ganna 62, 211, 245, **406**
Ward Wheelock Advertising Agency 24, 30,
  411
Warner, Harry M. 306
Warner Bros.
  Costello, Dolores, at 73
  DePalma, Brian, at 122
  Huston, John, at 165
  Lindfors, Viveca, at 215
  The Magnificent Ambersons and 304
  Three Cases of Murder and 372
  Zanuck at 435
War and Peace 198, 614, 288

Warrick, Ruth vii–x, viii*f*, **408–409**
  in *The Battle Over Citizen Kane* 13
  in *Citizen Kane* vii–ix, 51, 52*f*,
    408–409, 409*f*
  Comingore and 60–61
  in *Journey into Fear* ix–x, 181, 409
  on *The Lady Esther Show* 202
  The Magnificent Ambersons and 409
The War of the Worlds xii, **406–408**, 415
  Air Raid and 234
  authorship of 31, 194–195, 357
  basis for 419
  in *The Battle Over Citizen Kane* 12
  cast of 408
  CBS contract and 411
  Danton's Death and 82
  deception of 106
  importance of xv
  The Invasion from Mars (Cantril) and
    31
  Mercury Theatre on the Air and 259
  Moorehead, Agnes, in 270
  publicity from 24, 29
  RKO and viii
  score for 147
  Weissberger, Augusta, and 412
  Woollcott on 428
Washington Square Players 71
Waterloo **410**
Watson, Emily 80
Watts, Richard, Jr. 82
Weaver, Dennis 385, **410**
Webb, Alan 42
Webber, Peggy 228
Webb, Roy 151, 238
Weill, Kurt 20
Weine, Robert 143
Weissberger, Arnold 247, **410–411**
Weissberger, Augusta 380, **411–412**
Weld, Tuesday 330–331
Welles, Beatrice Ives (mother) 15, 127,
  412–413, 414, 417
Welles, Christopher 211, 212, 226, 230,
  413–414
Welles, Orson **414–417**, 415*f*, 416*f* See also
  Bogdanovich interviews
  biographical, difficulty in xv, xvii
  in *Catch-22* 36*f*
  celebrity of xii
  Compulsion redubbing and 65
  death of 196
  as Falstaff 41*f*, 45*f*
  on Kane 54
  naming of 127
  reinvention of xi–xii
  religion of 131
Welles, Rebecca 138, **417**
Welles, Richard Head (father) 48, 126–127,
  235–236, 414, **417–418**
Welles, Richard Ives, Jr. (brother) 127,
  418–419
Welles-Smith, Beatrice Judith (daughter)
  46, 413, **413**

Welles, Virginia *See* Lederer, Virginia Nicholson Welles
Wells, H.G. 406, **419–420**
Wells, Richard Hodgdon *See* Welles, Richard Head
Wells, Richard Jones 126–127
West Side Story 424–425, 427
Wheldon, Huw 7
When Are You Going to Finish Don Quixote? 92
Where Is Parsifal? **420**
Whipple, Sidney B. 81–82
Whitcomb, Ian 28
Whitelaw, Billie 274
White, Lionel 200
Whitman, Walt 350
Whitney, John Hay **420–421**
Widmark, Richard 136, 159
Wilcox, Herbert 394
Wilde, Oscar 170, **421–422**
Wilder, Billy 34, 435
Wilder, Thornton 71, **422–423**
"A Wild Hare" 28
Wilding, Michael 389
William Goetz Productions 125
Williams, Charles 84
Williams, Kenneth 268
Williams, Tennessee 25, 32
Willingham, Calder 403
Willson, Millicent 140
Wilson, J. Dover 100
Wilson, Richard **423**
  in *Citizen Kane* 423
  in *His Honor, the Mayor* 156
  It's All True and 175
  in *The Lady from Shanghai* 423
  The Life of Galileo and 209
  in *Macbeth* 423
  Macbeth and 104, 225, 226
  Moss, Jack, and 275
  in *Native Son* 282
  in *The Other Side of the Wind* 302
  in *The Shoemaker's Holiday* 347
  Shores, Lynn, and 347
  in *Too Much Johnson* 380
  in *The War of the Worlds* 408

Windsor Theatre 79
Winner, Michael 168
Winterset 263, 335
Wise, Robert **423–425,** 424*f*
  Academy Award nomination for 50
  in *The Battle Over Citizen Kane* 13
  Citizen Kane and viii, 50, 409
  The Magnificent Ambersons and
    and Cotten, Joseph 73–74
    editing of 13, 308
    and Herrmann, Bernard 150–151
    second-unit work of 237
  in *Orson Welles: The Rise and Fall of an American Genius* (Higham) 155
  on *The Orson Welles Story* 292
  at RKO 424
  Robson, Mark, and 323–324
With Orson Welles: Stories from a Life in Film 292
The Wizard of Oz 121, 244
Wolfsohn, Leopold 66
Wollen, Peter 278
The Wonder Show **426**
Wood, Bret 90, 224, 282, **426**
Wood, Natalie **426–427,** 427*f*
Wood, Robin 307
Woods, Leigh 62, 409
Woodstock Drama Festival **427–428**
  The Drunkard, or, The Fallen Saved at 93–94
  Edwards, Hilton, at 96, 234
  Hamlet in 133
  Hearts of Age at 143
  Hill, Roger, and 156
  MacLiammóir at 96, 234
  Trilby at 393, 427–428
  Tsar Paul at 395, 427
Woodward, Joanne 72, 102, 217, 217*f*, 283, 428, **428**
Woollcott, Alexander Humphreys 71, 249, 415, 422, **429**
Woolley, Monty 248
Working with Orson Welles 85, 108
"Working with Welles" seminar 85
  Hill, Roger, at 156

Works Projects Administration 172, **429–430** *See also* Federal Theatre Project
Worsley, T.C. 293
Wottiz, Walter 169
WPA *See* Works Projects Administration
Wright, Angus 321
Wright, Richard 281–282, **430**
Wuthering Heights 112, 145, 288, 375
Wuthering Heights (opera) 151
Wyatt, Eustace 141, 182
Wyler, William 374–375

X

Xanadu 50, 54, **431,** 431*f*
  cinematography for 377
  Robson, Mark, on 323
  Susan Alexander in 62

Y

Yates, Herbert J. 104, 226, 432, **432**
"You, Andrew Marvell" (MacLeish) 233
Young, Loretta 321–322, 322*f*, 358, 432–433, **432–433**
Young, Stark 81–82, **433**
"Youth from Vienna" (Collier) 117
Yule, George **433**

Z

Zadora, Pia 28
Zaharoff, Sir Basil 40, 55, 365, **434**
Zandt, Philip Van 51
Zane, Billy 86
Zanuck, Darryl F. **434–435**
  Compulsion and 434
  Crack in the Mirror and 78, 87
  Goetz, William, and 125
  Hathaway, Henry, and 136
  Jane Eyre and 434
  King, Henry, and 190
  Othello financed by 326, 435
  Ratoff, Gregory, and 18
Zanuck, Richard 78, 115
Zinnemann, Fred 65, 374, **435–437,** 436*f*
Zorina, Vera 10
Zsigmond, Vilmos 353
Zugsmith, Albert 244, 385, **438**